and Results!

Real People, Real World, Real Life

Max
Age 18

Pheonix

MILESTONES

McGraw-Hill Education's Milestones is a powerful video-based learning tool that allows students to experience life as it unfolds. A limited number of Milestones videos are now available in McGraw-Hill Connect® for Santrock's *Adolescence* 16e.

McGraw Hill Education connect®

Genevieve
Age 17

ADOLESCENCE

Sixteenth Edition

JOHN W. SANTROCK
University of Texas at Dallas

Mc
Graw
Hill
Education

ADOLESCENCE, SIXTEENTH EDITION

Published by McGraw-Hill Education, 2 Penn Plaza, New York, NY 10121. Copyright © 2016 by McGraw-Hill Education. All rights reserved. Printed in the United States of America. Previous editions © 2014, 2012, and 2010. No part of this publication may be reproduced or distributed in any form or by any means, or stored in a database or retrieval system, without the prior written consent of McGraw-Hill Education, including, but not limited to, in any network or other electronic storage or transmission, or broadcast for distance learning.

Some ancillaries, including electronic and print components, may not be available to customers outside the United States.

This book is printed on acid-free paper.

2 3 4 5 6 7 8 9 0 RMN 21 20 19 18 17 16

ISBN 978-0-07-811718-3
MHID 0-07-811718-6

Senior Vice President, Products & Markets: *Kurt L. Strand*
Vice President, General Manager, Products & Markets: *Michael Ryan*
Vice President, Content Design & Delivery: *Kimberly Meriwether David*
Managing Director: *William Glass*
Executive Director: *Krista Bettino*
Director, Product Development: *Meghan Campbell*
Lead Product Developer: *Dawn Groundwater*
Senior Product Developer: *Judith Kromm*
Product Developer: *Vicki Malinee, Van Brien & Associates*
Marketing Manager: *Christina Yu*
Director, Content Design & Delivery: *Terri Schiesl*
Program Manager: *Debra Hash*
Content Project Managers: *Sheila M. Frank, Jodi Banowetz*
Buyer: *Sandy Ludovissy*
Design: *Matt Backhaus*
Content Licensing Specialists: *Carrie Burger, Ann Marie Jannette*
Cover Image: © *Hero Images/Getty Images*
Compositor: *Aptara®, Inc.*
Printer: *R. R. Donnelley*

All credits appearing on page are considered to be an extension of the copyright page.

Library of Congress Cataloging-in-Publication Data

Santrock, John W.
    Adolescence / John W. Santrock. — Sixteenth Edition.
        pages cm
    ISBN 978-0-07-811718-3 (alk. paper) — ISBN 0-07-811718-6 (alk. paper)
1. Adolescence. 2. Adolescent psychology. I. Title.
    HQ796.S26 2015
    305.235—dc23

                                                                2015023423

brief contents

contents

CHAPTER 12   CULTURE   401

© Rolf Bruderer/Blend Images/Corbis RF

CHAPTER 13   PROBLEMS IN ADOLESCENCE AND EMERGING ADULTHOOD   433

© BananaStock/PunchStock RF

about the **author**

John W. Santrock

John Santrock received his Ph.D. from the University of Minnesota in 1973. He taught at the University of Charleston and the University of Georgia before joining the program in Psychology in the School of Behavioral and Brain Sciences at the University of Texas at Dallas, where he currently teaches a number of undergraduate courses. He has taught the undergraduate course in adolescence once or twice a year for more than three decades.

John Santrock (back row middle) with the 2015 recipients of the Santrock Travel Scholarship Award in developmental psychology. Created by Dr. Santrock, this annual award (now in its sixth year) provides undergraduate students with the opportunity to attend a professional meeting. A number of the students shown here attended the Society for Research in Child Development meeting in 2015.
Courtesy of Jessica Serna

John has been a member of the editorial boards of *Child Development* and *Developmental Psychology*. His research has focused on children and adolescents in divorced families, and his father custody research is widely cited and used in expert witness testimony to promote flexibility and alternative considerations in custody disputes. He also has conducted research on social cognition, especially the influence of affectively-toned cognition on self-regulation. John also has authored these exceptional McGraw-Hill texts: *Psychology* (7th edition), *Children* (13th edition), *Life-Span Development* (15th edition), *A Topical Approach to Life-Span Development* (8th edition), and *Educational Psychology* (5th edition).

For many years, John was involved in tennis as a player, teaching professional, and coach of professional tennis players. At the University of Miami (FL), the tennis team on which he played still holds the NCAA Division I record for most consecutive wins (137) in any sport. His wife, Mary Jo, has a master's degree in special education and has worked as a teacher and a Realtor. She created the first middle school behavioral disorders special education program in Clarke County, Georgia. He has two daughters—Tracy and Jennifer—both of whom are now Realtors. In 2015, Jennifer was inducted into the SMU Athletic Hall of Fame. He has one granddaughter, Jordan, age 23, who just completed the MBA program at Southern Methodist University and is now working at Ernst & Young in Dallas. He also has two grandsons, Alex, age 10, and Luke, age 9. In the last decade, John also has spent time painting expressionist art.

Dedication:

To my daughters, Tracy and Jennifer, who, as they matured, helped me to appreciate the marvels of adolescent development.

expert consultants

Adolescent development has become an enormous, complex field, and no single author, or even several authors, can possibly keep up with all of the rapidly changing content in the many periods and different areas in this field. To solve this problem, author John Santrock has sought the input of leading experts about content in a number of areas of adolescent development. These experts have provided detailed evaluations and recommendations in their area(s) of expertise.

The following individuals were among those who served as expert consultants for one or more of the previous editions of this text:

Susan Harter	Gerald Patterson	James Rest
Valerie Reyna	Nancy Galambos	Daniel Lapsley
John Schulenberg	Peter Benson	Luc Goosens
Charles Irwin	Catherine Cooper	Seth Schwartz
Ruth Chao	L. Monique Ward	Brad Brown
Wyndol Furman	Bonnie Leadbetter	Candice Feiring
Elizabeth Susman	Reed Larson	Daniel Offer
Shirley Feldman	Lisa Crockett	Harold Grotevant
Lisa Diamond	Allan Wigfield	James Byrnes
James Marcia	Lawrence Walker	Duane Buhrmester
Kathryn Wentzel	Pamela King	Lorah Dorn
Moin Syed	Daniel Keating	Jerome Dusek
Bonnie Halpern-Felsher	Diane Halpern	Elizabeth Trejos-Castillo
Joseph Allen	Jane Kroger	Robert Roeser
Nancy Guerra	John Gibbs	Darcia Narváez

Following are the expert consultants for the sixteenth edition, who (like those of previous editions) literally represent a *Who's Who* in the field of adolescent development.

Su Yeong Kim Dr. Kim is a leading expert on cultural, ethnic, and family dimensions of adolescent development. She obtained her undergraduate degree at Arizona State University and her Ph.D. at the University of California—Davis. She currently is a professor in the Department of Human Development and Family Sciences at the University of Texas—Austin. The main focus of Dr. Kim's research is the intersection of family and cultural contexts in the development of adolescents of immigrants to the United States. Among her research interests are acculturation, tiger parenting, and language brokering in immigrant families (especially Chinese American and Mexican American). Dr. Kim is a Fellow in Division 45 (Society for the Psychological Study of Culture, Ethnicity, and Race) of the American Psychological Association and also a Fellow in the Association for Psychological Science. She also has been a recipient of the Young Scientist Award from the International Society for the Study of Behavioral Development. Dr. Kim is on the editorial board of a number of research journals, including *Journal of Family Psychology* and *Journal of Youth and Adolescence.*

"I recommend this Adolescence *textbook by John Santrock to all of my colleagues. The Connections theme, where he connects topical processes in development to the real world, truly makes the . . . research material come alive for students. The use of developmental connections is particularly effective in tying concepts across chapters of the book. The coverage of the latest research on the topics is truly impressive, showing John Santrock's command of the burgeoning and fast-paced research on adolescence. The addition of over 1,000 new citations published in the last several years makes this updated text truly* on pace with the current pulse of the field of adolescence." —**Su Yeong Kim** *University of Texas—Austin*

James A. Graham Dr. Graham is a leading expert on the community aspects of ethnicity, culture, and development. He obtained his undergraduate degree from Miami University and received masters and doctoral degrees in developmental psychology from the University of Memphis. Dr. Graham's current position is Professor of Psychology, The College of New Jersey (TCNJ). His research addresses the social-cognitive aspects of relationships between group and dyadic levels across developmental periods in community-based settings. Three interdependent dimensions of his research program examine (1) populations that are typically understudied, conceptually limited, and methodologically constrained; (2) development of empathy and prosocial behavior with peer groups and friends; and (3) developmental science in the context of community-engaged research partnerships. Currently, he is Coordinator of the Developmental Specialization in Psychology at TCNJ. For a decade, Dr. Graham taught graduate courses in psychology and education in Johannesburg, South Africa, through TCNJ's Graduate Summer Global Program. He is the co-author of *The African American Child: Development and Challenges* (2nd ed.). Dr. Graham has presented his work at a variety of international and national conferences and has published articles in a wide range of journals, including *Social Development, Child Study Journal, Behavior Modification, Journal of Multicultural Counseling and Development,* and *American Journal of Evaluation.*

Valerie Reyna Dr. Reyna is one of the world's leading experts on the development of the adolescent's brain and cognitive development. She obtained her Ph.D. from Rockefeller University. Currently, she is a faculty member in human development, psychology, cognitive science, and neuroscience (IMAGINE program) at Cornell University. Dr. Reyna also currently is co-director of the Cornell University Magnetic Resonance Imaging Facility and of the Center for Behavioral Economics and Decision Research. She created fuzzy-trace theory, a model of memory and decision-making that is widely applied in law, medicine, and public health. Her recent work has focused on the neuroscience of risky decision making and its implications for health and well-being, especially in adolescents; applications of cognitive models and artificial intelligence to improving understanding of genetics (in breast cancer, for example); and medical and legal decision making (about jury awards, medication decisions, and adolescent culpability). Past President of the Society for Judgment and Decision Making, she is a Fellow of numerous scientific societies and has served on the scientific panels of the National Science Foundation, National Institutes of Health, and National Academy of Sciences. Dr. Reyna is the incoming Editor of *Psychological Science in the Public Interest* and also has been an associate editor for *Psychological Science* and *Developmental Review*. Reyna has received many years of research support from private foundations and U.S. government agencies, and currently serves as principal investigator of several grants and awards (such as from the National Institutes of Health). Her service has included leadership positions in organizations dedicated to equal opportunity for minorities and women, and on national executive and advisory boards of centers and grants with similar goals, such as the Arizona Hispanic Center of Excellence, National Center of Excellence in Women's Health, and Women in Cognitive Science (supported by a National Science Foundation ADVANCE leadership award).

Allan Wigfield Dr. Wigfield is one of the world's leading experts on the roles of motivation, achievement, and schools in adolescent development. He obtained his Ph.D. from the University of Illinois and a post-doctoral degree from the University of Michigan. Dr. Wigfield currently is Professor in the Department of Human Development, Distinguished Scholar-Teacher, and University Honors Faculty Fellow at the University of Maryland.

His research focuses on the development of motivation across the school years in different areas. In recent years his research has focused on motivation for reading and classroom interventions to improve reading motivation, engagement, and comprehension. Dr. Wigfield's research has been supported by grants from a number of agencies and organizations, including the National Science Foundation. He has authored more than 125 peer-reviewed journal articles and book chapters on the development of motivation and other topics, and has edited four books and six special issues of journals on the development of motivation, and the development of reading comprehension and motivation. Dr. Wigfield has been Associate Editor of both the *Journal of Educational Psychology* and *Child Development.* He is a Fellow of Division 15 (Educational Psychology) of the American Psychological Association, the Association for Psychological Science, and the American Educational Research Association. He has won national awards for his research and teaching. Recently, he was the lead author on the achievement motivation chapter for *Handbook of Child Psychology and Developmental Science* (7th ed.) (2015).

Kate C. McLean Dr. McLean is a leading expert on adolescent and emerging adult identity development. She obtained her Ph.D. from the University of California—Santa Cruz and currently is a professor of Psychology at Western Washington University, having previously been on the faculty at the University of Toronto. Her research focuses on how individuals develop a storied understanding of self, or a narrative identity. She is especially interested in individual differences in narrative identity and how they are linked to adjustment and well-being, as well as the social contexts of identity development. Her current projects include the intersection between personal and cultural master narratives, and the role of family stories in identity development. Dr. McLean serves on the board of the Association for Research in Personality and is the newsletter editor for APA's Division 7 (Developmental Psychology). She is also an Associate Editor for the *Journal of Adolescent Research, Journal of Research in Personality,* and *Memory.* Dr. McLean is the co-editor of the *Oxford Handbook of Identity Development* (2015) and the author of the forthcoming book (from Oxford University Press), *The Co-authored Self: Family Stories and the Construction of Personal Identity.*

Jennifer Connolly Dr. Connolly is one of the world's leading experts on the socioemotional aspects of adolescent development, especially peer and romantic relationships. She obtained her doctoral degree in Clinical Psychology from Concordia University and is currently a Professor of Clinical-Developmental Psychology and the Director of the Undergraduate Psychology Program at York University in Toronto. Dr. Connolly's research focuses on peer and romantic relationships and their emergence during adolescence and emerging adulthood. Normative developmental pathways, relationship problems including bullying and dating violence, and vulnerable youths' relationships are topics she is currently studying. Dr. Connolly has published extensively in such journals as *Journal of Research on Adolescence*, *Child Development*, and *Journal of Adolescence*.

"I think the chapter (Peers, Romantic Relationships, and Lifestyles) is excellent. . . . This chapter provides extensive coverage of current theory and research on peer relations, including excellent coverage of romantic relationships in the emerging adult years. The literature cited is up-to-date. The narrative reporting of the evidence is accurate and unbiased. The writing is clear and the ideas are easy to follow. . . . I would add that the chapter is written in an engaging manner which I think students will respond to favorably. The integration of pauses for personal reflection will be well received by students and course instructors alike. . . . This will be especially true for the sections on emerging adulthood and hence it is good to provide structure for these reflections." —**Jennifer Connolly** *York University*

Eva S. Lefkowitz Dr. Lefkowitz is one of the world's leading experts on sexual health in adolescence and the transition to adulthood. She obtained her Ph.D. from the University of California—Los Angeles in Developmental Psychology and is currently a professor in Human Development at Pennsylvania State University. She uses a developmental perspective to examine sexual behaviors and attitudes during adolescence and the transition to adulthood. Dr. Lefkowitz emphasizes the importance of recognizing the multidimensional aspects of sexual health, considering physical, cognitive, emotional, and relational aspects of health and well-being. She has been a principal investigator, co-investigator, or faculty mentor on projects funded by numerous agencies and organizations, including the National Institute of Child Health and Development. Dr. Lefkowitz has published more than 50 peer-reviewed articles and 7 book chapters, as well as a recent edited volume of *New Directions in Child and Adolescent Development*. She held leadership roles in the Society for Research on Adolescence (SRA) and the Society for the Study of Emerging Adulthood (SSEA), including chairing the SRA membership committee and consensus committee, and serving on the Founding Board of the SSEA. Dr. Lefkowitz has served as Associate Editor for *Developmental Psychology*, on the editorial board for *Emerging Adulthood*, and as a reviewer for 25 other journals.

"Yes, the perspective seems balanced, and the chapter overall covers the most important/prominent topics in the area of adolescent sexuality. . . . I appreciate the sex positive framing. Great that there are some recent citations on sex and the Internet. The chapter is overall very readable and summarizes past research quite well. Thanks for the opportunity to read it. I enjoyed it, and it pointed me toward some references I wasn't familiar with. —**Eva Lefkowitz** *Pennsylvania State University*

Sam Hardy Dr. Hardy is a leading expert on moral development and identity development. He received his Ph.D. in developmental psychology from the University of Nebraska-Lincoln, and completed a post-doctoral degree in lifespan development and longitudinal data analysis at the University of Virginia. He is currently a psychology professor at Brigham Young University. Dr. Hardy works at the intersection of developmental and personality psychology, with expertise in adolescent social and personality development. His research focuses on investigating the ways in which morality, identity, and religiosity develop, interrelate, and predict positive and negative behaviors in adolescents and young adults. Dr. Hardy has published widely on these topics in scientific journals. He also is currently on the editorial boards for *Developmental Psychology*, *Journal of Research on Adolescence*, *Journal of Youth and Adolescence*, and *Journal of Moral Education*.

"A key strength of this text that makes it stand out from all other texts is its coverage of positive topics such as moral development, values, and religion/spirituality. These are increasingly hot topics in the field that receive almost no attention in other books. There is a whole chapter on them in John Santrock's book. Another strength is his process of revising the text, where he solicits feedback from leaders in the field to make sure he is accurate and current." —**Sam Hardy** *Brigham Young University*

Santrock—connecting *research* and *results!*

As a master teacher, John Santrock connects current research with real-world application, helping students see how adolescent psychology plays a role in their own lives and future careers. Through an integrated, personalized digital learning program, students gain the insight they need to study smarter, stay focused, and improve their performance.

Personalized Study, Better Data, Improved Results

Now available for *Adolescence!*

McGraw-Hill Education's SmartBook® is an adaptive learning program designed to help students stay focused and maximize their study time. Based on metacognition, and powered by McGraw-Hill LearnSmart®, SmartBook's adaptive capabilities provide students with a personalized reading and learning experience that helps them identify the concepts they know, and more importantly, the concepts they *don't* know.

Make It Effective.

Unlike other eBooks, SmartBook is adaptive. SmartBook creates a personalized reading experience by highlighting the most impactful concepts a student needs to learn at that moment in time. This ensures that every minute spent with SmartBook is returned to the student as the most value-added minute possible.

Make It Informed.

SmartBook continuously adapts, highlighting content based on what the student knows and doesn't know. Real-time reports quickly identify the concepts that require more attention from individual students—or the entire class. Because SmartBook is personalized, it detects the content individual students are most likely to forget and refreshes them, helping improve retention.

Real People, Real World, Real Life

McGraw-Hill Education's Milestones is a powerful video-based learning tool that allows students to experience life as it unfolds, from infancy through emerging adulthood. A limited number of Milestones videos are now available for viewing within the McGraw-Hill Connect Media Bank for Santrock's, *Adolescence,* 16e.

MILESTONES

Max
Age 18

Pheonix

Genevieve
Age 17

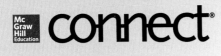

connect®

Current Research, Guided by Experts

With more than 1200 research citations and reviewed by experts in the field, Adolescence provides the most thorough and up-to-date information on issues related to today's adolescents and emerging adults.

connecting with adolescents

Are Social Media an Amplification Tool for Adolescent Egocentrism?

Are teens drawn to social media to express their imaginary audience and personal fable's sense of uniqueness? One analysis concluded that amassing a large number of friends (audience) may help to validate adolescents' perception that their life is a stage and everyone is watching them (Psychster Inc., 2010). Also, a recent study found that Facebook use does indeed increase self-interest (Chiou, Chen, & Liao, 2014).

A look at a teen's home Twitter comments may suggest to many adults that what teens are reporting is often rather mundane and uninteresting. Typical tweets might include updates like the following: "Studying heavy. Not happy tonight." or "At Starbucks with Jesse. Lattes are great." Possibly for adolescents, though, such tweets are not trivial but rather an expression of the personal fable's sense of uniqueness.

Might social media, such as Facebook, increase adolescent egocentrism?
© David J. Green-lifestyle themes/Alamy

What do you think? Are social media, such as Facebook and Twitter, amplifying the expression of adolescents' imaginary audience and their personal fable's sense of uniqueness? (Source: Psychster Inc., 2010)

preface

Making Connections . . . From My Classroom to *Adolescence* to You

When I wrote the Preface for the first edition of *Adolescence* in 1980, I never envisioned I would be sitting here today in 2015 writing the Preface for the book's sixteenth edition. It is extremely gratifying that more undergraduate students in the world continue to learn from this text than any other.

As with adolescent development, there have been major changes and transitions across the 16 editions. Over the course of these many editions, the field has become transformed from one in which there were only a handful of scholars (mainly in the United States) studying adolescent development to the thousands of researchers around the world today who are making enormous strides in our understanding of adolescence and emerging adulthood. When I wrote early editions of *Adolescence*, there were no discussions of such topics as adolescents' brain development, decision making, self-regulation, attachment, self-efficacy, religious and spiritual development, and immigration because research on those topics in the adolescent years had not yet been conducted.

Across the last three and a half decades, I have seen not only a dramatic increase in the quantity of research studies on adolescence and emerging adulthood but also an equally impressive increase in the quality of research. For example, today there are far more high-quality longitudinal studies that provide important information about developmental changes from childhood through emerging adulthood than there were several editions ago. In addition, there is increasing concern about improving the quality of life for adolescents, resulting in more applied research and intervention efforts.

Having taught an undergraduate class on adolescent development two to four times every year for three decades, I'm always looking for ways to improve my course and text. Just as McGraw-Hill looks to those who teach the adolescence course for input, each year I ask the 50 to 70 students in my adolescent development course to tell me what they like about the course and the text, and what they think could be improved. What have my students told me lately about my course, this text, and themselves?

More than ever before, one word highlights what students have been talking about in the last several years when I ask them about their lives and observe them: **Connecting.** Connecting and communicating have always been important themes of adolescents' lives, but the more I've talked with students recently, the more the word *connecting* comes up in conversations with them.

In further conversations with my students, I explored how they thought I could improve the course and the text by using *connecting* as a theme. Following is an outgrowth of those conversations focused on a *connections* theme and how I have incorporated it into the main goals of the sixteenth edition:

1. **Connecting with today's students** To help students learn about adolescent development more effectively.

2. **Connecting research to what we know about development** To provide students with the best and most recent *theory and research* in the world today about adolescence and emerging adulthood.

3. **Connecting topical processes in development** To guide students in making *topical connections* across different aspects of adolescent development.

4. **Connecting development to the real world** To help students understand ways to *apply* content about adolescence and emerging adulthood to the real world and improve the lives of youth; and to motivate them to think deeply about *their own personal journeys of youth* and better understand who they were, are, and will be.

Connecting with Today's Students

In *Adolescence,* I recognize that today's students are as different in some ways from the learners of the last generation as today's discipline of life-span development is different from the field 30 years ago. Students now learn in multiple modalities; rather than sitting down and reading traditional printed chapters in linear fashion from beginning to end, their work preferences tend to be more visual and more interactive, and their reading and study often occur in short bursts. For many students, a traditionally formatted printed textbook is no longer enough when they have instant, 24/7 access to news and information from around the globe. Two features that specifically support today's students are the adaptive ebook, Smartbook (see page xvi), and the learning goals system.

The Learning Goals System

My students often report that the adolescent development course is challenging because of the amount of material covered. To help today's students focus on the key ideas, the Learning Goals System I developed for *Adolescence* provides extensive learning connections throughout the chapters. The learning system connects the chapter opening outline, learning goals for the chapter, mini-chapter maps that open each main section of the chapter, *Review, Connect, Reflect* questions at the end of each main section, and the chapter summary at the end of each chapter.

The learning system keeps the key ideas in front of the student from the beginning to the end of the chapter. The main headings of each chapter correspond to the learning goals that are presented in the chapter-opening spread. Mini-chapter maps that link up with the learning goals are presented at the beginning of each major section in the chapter.

Then, at the end of each main section of a chapter, the learning goal is repeated in *Review, Connect, Reflect,* which prompts students to review the key topics in the section, connect to existing knowledge, and relate what they learned to their own personal journey through life. *Reach Your Learning Goals,* at the end of the chapter, guides students through the bulleted chapter review, connecting with the chapter outline/learning goals at the beginning of the chapter and the *Review, Connect, Reflect* questions at the end of major chapter sections.

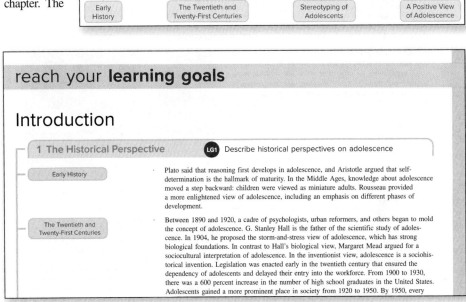

Connecting Research to What We Know about Development

Over the years, it has been important for me to include the most up-to-date research available. The tradition of obtaining detailed, extensive input from a number of leading experts in different areas of life-span development continues in this edition. Biographies and photographs of the leading experts in the field of adolescent development appear on pages xii–xiv, and the extensive list of chapter-by-chapter highlights of new research content are listed on pages xxii–xxxiii. Finally, the research discussions have been updated in every area and topic. I expended every effort to make this edition of *Adolescence* as contemporary and up-to-date as possible. To that end, there are more than 1,200 citations from 2013, 2014, 2015, and 2016.

Connecting Developmental Processes

Too often we forget or fail to notice the many connections from one point or topic in development to another.

developmental **connection**

Brain Development

Might there be a link between changes in the adolescent's brain and risk taking and sensation seeking? Connect to "The Brain and Cognitive Development."

Developmental Connections, which appear multiple times in each chapter, point readers to where the topic is discussed in a previous or subsequent chapter. *Developmental Connections* highlight links across topics and age periods of development *and* connections between biological, cognitive, and socioemotional processes. These key developmental processes are typically discussed in isolation from each other, and students often fail to see their connections. Included in the *Developmental Connections* is a brief description of the backward or forward connection.

Also, a *Connect* question appears in the section self-reviews—*Review, Connect, Reflect*—so students can practice making connections between topics. For example, students are asked to connect the discussion of autonomy and attachment to what they have already read about emotional development.

Connecting Development to the Real World

In addition to helping students make research and developmental connections, *Adolescence* shows the important connections between the concepts discussed and the real world. In recent years, students in my adolescence course have increasingly told me that they want more of this type of information. In this edition, real-life connections are explicitly made through the chapter opening vignette, *Connecting with Health and Well-Being, Connecting with Adolescents, Connecting with Emerging Adults,* and *Connecting with Careers.*

Each chapter begins with a story designed to increase students' interest and motivation to read the chapter. For example, the chapter on moral development introduces you to Jewel Cash, an emerging adult who was raised by a single mother in a Boston housing project and has become a vocal and active participant in improving her community.

Connecting with Health and Well-Being describes the influence of development in a real-world context on topics including increasing adolescents' self-esteem, effective sex education, parenting moral children and adolescents, strategies for emerging adults and their parents, effective and ineffective strategies for making friends, and coping strategies in adolescence and emerging adulthood.

Connecting with Adolescents and ***Connecting with Emerging Adults*** share personal experiences from real adolescents and emerging adults. *Connecting with Resources for Improving the Lives of Adolescents* at the end of each chapter describes numerous resources such as books, websites, and organizations that provide valuable information for improving the lives of adolescents in many different areas.

Connecting with Careers profiles careers ranging from an educational psychologist to a family and consumer science educator, a marriage and family therapist, and a career counselor.

connecting with health and well-being

How Can We Raise Moral Children and Adolescents?

Parental discipline contributes to children's moral development, but other aspects of parenting also play an important role, including providing opportunities for perspective taking and modeling moral behavior and thinking. Nancy Eisenberg and her colleagues (Eisenberg, Spinrad, & Knafo, 2015; Eisenberg, Spinrad, & Morris, 2014; Eisenberg & Valiente, 2002) suggest that when parents adopt the following strategies they are more likely to have children and adolescents who behave morally:

- Are warm and supportive, use inductive reasoning, and engage in authoritative parenting
- Are not punitive and do not use love withdrawal as a disciplinary strategy
- Use inductive discipline
- Provide opportunities for the children and youth to learn about others' perspectives and feelings
- Involve children and youth in family decision making and in the process of thinking about moral decisions
- Model moral behaviors and thinking themselves, and provide opportunities for their children and youth to do so
- Provide information about what behaviors are expected and why
- Foster an internal rather than an external sense of morality
- Help children and youth to understand and regulate negative emotion rather than becoming overaroused

Parents who show this configuration of behaviors likely foster concern and caring about others in their children and youth, and create a positive parent-child relationship. A recent study found that adolescents' moral motivation was positively linked to the quality of

What are some parenting characteristics and practices that are linked with children's and adolescents' moral development?
© Digital Vision/Getty Images RF

study, securely attached children's willing, cooperative stance was linked to positive future socialization outcomes such as a lower incidence of externalizing problems (high levels of aggression, for example) (Kochanska & others, 2010b).

Recently, an interest has developed in determining which parenting strategies work best when children and adolescents are confronted with situations in which they are exposed to values outside the home that conflict with parental values (Grusec, 2006). Two strategies that parents often use in this regard are cocooning and prearming (Bugental & Goodnow, 2006). Cocooning occurs when parents

connecting with adolescents

Rochelle Ballantyne, Chess Star

Rochelle Ballantyne, a Stanford University student who grew up in Brooklyn, New York, is close to becoming the first female African American to reach the level of chess master (Kastenbaum, 2012). Born in 1995, she grew up in a single-parent family in a lower-income context. Her grandmother taught her to play chess because she didn't want Rochelle's impoverished background to prevent her from reaching her full potential. Rochelle was fortunate to attend I.S. 318, an inner-city public middle school where the chess team is one of the best in the United States. Rochelle has won several national chess championships and she is a rising star in the world of chess. Rochelle's motivation and confidence are reflected in her comment: "When I push myself, then nothing can stop me."

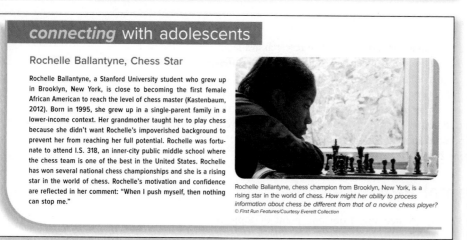

Rochelle Ballantyne, chess champion from Brooklyn, New York, is a rising star in the world of chess. *How might her ability to process information about chess be different from that of a novice chess player?*
© First Run Features/Courtesy Everett Collection

The careers highlighted extend from the Careers Appendix that provides a comprehensive overview of careers in adolescent development to show students where knowledge of adolescent development could lead them.

Part of applying development to the real world is understanding its impact on oneself. An important goal I have established for my adolescence course and *Adolescence* is to motivate students to think deeply about their own journey of life. To further encourage students to make personal connections to content in this edition, *Reflect: Your Own Personal Journey of Life* appears in the end-of-section reviews in each chapter. This feature involves a question that asks students to reflect on some aspect of the discussion in the section they have just read and connect it to their own life. For example, students are asked:

connecting with careers

Grace Leaf, College/Career Counselor and College Administrator

Grace Leaf is a counselor at Spokane Community College in Washington. She has a master's degree in educational leadership and is working toward a doctoral degree in educational leadership at Gonzaga University in Washington. Her college counseling job has involved teaching, orientation for international students, conducting individual and group advising, and doing individual and group career planning. Leaf tries to connect students with their own goals and values and helps them design an educational program that fits their needs and visions. Following a long career as a college counselor, she is now vice-president of instruction at Lower Columbia College in Washington.

For more information about what career counselors do, see the Careers in Adolescent Development appendix.

Grace Leaf counsels college students at Spokane Community College about careers.
Courtesy of Grace Leaf

- *What are some examples of circumstances in which you think you were stereotyped as an adolescent?*
- *How was your adolescence likely similar to, or different from, the adolescence of your parents and grandparents?*

In addition, students are asked a number of personal connections questions in the photograph captions.

Content Revisions

A significant reason why *Adolescence* has been successfully used by instructors for fifteen editions now is the painstaking effort and review that goes into making sure the text provides the latest research on all topic areas discussed in the classroom. This new edition is no exception, with more than 1,200 citations from 2013, 2014, 2015, and 2016.

New research highlights include very recent studies linking attachment styles to relationship issues in adolescence and emerging adulthood; more precise discoveries about the adolescent's changing brain; expanded and updated information about the importance of families in children's and adolescents' moral development; and links between parenting styles and adolescent academic achievement.

Below is a sample of the many chapter-by-chapter changes that were made in this new edition of *Adolescence*.

Chapter 1: Introduction

- New coverage of Laurence Steinberg's (2014) view, as discussed in his recent book, *Age of Opportunity*, that while the majority of adolescents are making the journey through adolescence to adulthood in a positive manner, too many are not; in support of his view, he describes such problems as the much lower achievement of U.S. adolescents compared with their counterparts in many other countries, a drop in U.S. college graduation rates, high levels of alcohol abuse, too many adolescent girls becoming pregnant by age 20, and the tripling of adolescent obesity rates in recent decades.

- Updated statistics on the percentage of U.S. children and adolescents under 18 years of age living in poverty, including data reported separately for African American and Latino families (De Navas-Walt & Proctor, 2014).

- Inclusion of information from a recent national survey that found 45 percent of U.S. 18- to 29-year-olds considered themselves between adolescence and full-fledged adulthood, but through their twenties they steadily increased their description of themselves as full-fledged adults (Arnett, 2012).

- Two new additions to the end-of-chapter section, Resources for Improving the Lives of Adolescents: (1) Laurence Steinberg's (2014) *Age of Opportunity: Lessons from the New Science of Adolescent Development,* and (2) Jeffrey Arnett's (2014a) *Emerging Adulthood* (2nd ed.).

Chapter 2: Puberty, Health, and Biological Foundations

- Includes some content changes based on feedback from leading expert Elizabeth Susman.

- Description of a recent study of 9- to 17-year-old boys that found testosterone levels peaked at 17 years of age (Khairullah & others, 2014).

- Coverage of a recent study in which DHEA concentrations increased 24 months before breast development in girls (Biro & others, 2014).

- Inclusion of recent research that documented the growth of the pituitary gland during adolescence and found that its volume was linked to circulating blood levels of estradiol and testosterone (Wong & others, 2014).

- New section that evaluates the potential roles of leptin and kisspeptins in pubertal onset and change (Roa & Tena-Sempere, 2014; Skorupskaite, George, & Anderson, 2014).

- Inclusion of a recent study of United Kingdom undergraduates that found 35 percent of females but only 8 percent of males expressed moderate or marked concern with their body image (El Ansari, Dibba, & Stock, 2014).

- Description of a recent research review that concluded there is insufficient quality research to confirm that changing testosterone levels in puberty are linked to adolescent males' moods and behavior (Duke, Balzer, & Steinbeck, 2014).

- Discussion of recent research that found early-maturing girls engaged in sexual intercourse earlier than late-maturing girls and had more unstable sexual relationships (Moore, Harden, & Mendle, 2014).

- Coverage of a recent study that found late-maturing boys had a more negative body image in the early high school years than early-maturing boys (de Guzman & Nishina, 2014).

- Inclusion of a recent analysis of the health status and health outcomes of U.S. adolescents and young adults across the last decade that found few indicators changing in this time frame, although there were improvements for adolescents and young adults in rates of unintentional injury, assault, and tobacco use, and for adolescents in levels of sexual/reproductive health (Park & others, 2014).

- Updated information about the continuing drop in vegetable and fruit consumption by U.S. adolescents through 2013 (Kann & others, 2014).

- Coverage of a recent analysis that found family dinners in France were more likely to emphasize fruits and vegetables than were family dinners in the United States (Kremer-Sadlik & others, 2015).

- Description of a 10-year longitudinal study that revealed the more frequently adolescents ate family meals the less likely they were to be overweight or obese in early adulthood (Berge & others, 2015).

- New national data on the percentage of adolescents who eat breakfast every day of the week (Kann & others, 2014).

- Inclusion of recent research in which increased screen time was linked to increased consumption of food and beverages with low nutritional quality and decreased consumption of fruits and vegetables (Falbe & others, 2014).

- Updated data on gender and ethnic variations in adolescent exercise rates for U.S. adolescents, including updated Figure 9 (Kann & others, 2014).

- Updated national data on the percentage of U.S. adolescents who participated on at least one sports team, including gender and ethnic variations (Kann & others, 2014).

- Description of recent research that found highly physically fit adolescents had better connectivity between brain regions than did less physically fit adolescents (Herting & others, 2014).

· Coverage of a recent meta-analysis that concluded fathers play a more important role in the physical activity levels of their adolescent sons than in those of their adolescent daughters (Yao & Rhodes, 2015).

· Updated data on the percentage of adolescents who participate in a physical education class daily (Kann & others, 2014).

· Discussion of recent research indicating that adolescents who get less than 7.7 hours of sleep per night have more emotional and peer-related problems, higher levels of anxiety, and higher levels of suicidal ideation (Sarchiapone & others, 2014).

· Inclusion of a longitudinal study of more than 1.1 million Swedish males that found 18-year-olds who had lower levels of cardiovascular fitness had increased risk of developing early-onset dementia and mild cognitive impairment 42 years later (Nyberg & others, 2014).

· New commentary noting that recent research indicates that exercise can be effective in reducing ADHD symptoms (Kamp, Sperlich, & Holmberg, 2014).

· Coverage of a recent study in which daughters' participation in sports was related to both parents' exercise habits while sons' participation was linked only to fathers' exercise habits (Sukys & others, 2014).

· Coverage of a study that found high school girls' participation in sports increased from 1971 to 2012 (Bassett & others, 2015).

· Inclusion of recent research indicating that triad risk factors were prevalent among female high school athletes but that knowledge of the female athlete triad was low among athletes and their coaches (Brown, Wengreen, & Beals, 2014).

· Discussion of recent research that found a lack of information about the female athlete triad among college coaches as well (Frideres, Mottinger, & Palao, 2015).

· Inclusion of recent national data on the percentage of U.S. ninth- to twelfth-graders who got 8 hours or more of sleep on school nights (Kann & others, 2014).

· Coverage of a national study that confirmed adolescents get less sleep as they get older, that adolescent sleep generally declined from 1991 to 2012, that girls were less likely to get 7 or more hours of sleep per night than boys, as were ethnic minority, urban, and low-SES adolescents (Keyes & others, 2015).

· Inclusion of recent research in which sleep problems in adolescence were associated with a lower level of working memory and in turn this lower level of working memory was linked to greater risk taking (Thomas & others, 2014).

· New discussion suggesting that adolescents' sleep debt is linked to their electronic media use, caffeine intake, changes in the brain, and early school starting times (Owens, 2014).

· Description of a recent study connecting early school starting times to a higher vehicle crash rate among adolescent drivers (Vorona & others, 2014).

· Inclusion of the recent recommendation by the American Academy of Pediatrics that schools institute start times from 8:30 to 9:30 a.m. to improve students' academic performance and quality of life (Adolescent Sleep Working Group, AAP, 2014).

· Updated content on the number of genes that humans have and a recent prediction that humans likely have fewer than 20,000 genes (Abyzov & others, 2013; Ezkurdia & others, 2014).

· New description of recent research on how exercise and nutrition can modify the behavior of genes (Lindholm & others, 2014; Ma & others, 2015).

· New content on how sleep deprivation can influence gene expression in negative ways such as increased inflammation, expression of stress-related genes, and impairment of protein functioning (Da Costa Souza & Ribeiro, 2015).

· Coverage of a recent research review that concluded the young scientific area of gene x environment (G x E) interaction is plagued by difficulties in replicating results, inflated claims, and other weaknesses (Manuck & McCaffery, 2014).

· New entry in Resources for Improving the Lives of Adolescents: David Moore's (2015) recent book, *The Developing Genome*, which provides valuable information about the epigenetic view and suggests that genetic explanations of development too often have been overblown.

Chapter 3: The Brain and Cognitive Development

· New discussion of increased focal activity in a brain region and increasing connectedness across regions as adolescents develop (Markant & Thomas, 2013).

· New content on the view of neuroscientist Mark Johnson and his colleagues (Johnson, Jones, & Gliga, 2015) that development of the prefrontal cortex likely orchestrates the functions of many other brain regions during development.

· Coverage of a recent study in which working memory deficits at age 15 were linked to a higher level of risk-taking behavior at age 18 (Thomas & others, 2015).

· Discussion of Robert Sternberg's (2014b) recent definition of intelligence as the ability to adapt to, shape, and select environments.

· Updated descriptions of the most recent versions of the Wechsler scales of intelligence (Syeda & Climie, 2014).

· Discussion of a recent study in which emotional intelligence abilities were linked to academic achievement above and beyond cognitive and personality factors (Lanciano & Curci, 2014).

· New section entitled "The Neuroscience of Intelligence."

· Inclusion of recent research indicating that a distributed neural network involving the frontal and parietal lobes is linked to higher intelligence (Vahktin & others, 2014).

· New Figure 17 indicating the areas of the brain associated with higher intelligence.

· Inclusion of information from a recent meta-analysis of processing speed that confirmed processing speed increases through the childhood and adolescent years (Verhaeghen, 2013).

- New research indicating that children with learning disabilities in reading and math have working memory deficits (Peng & Fuchs, 2015).

- Inclusion of Robert Sternberg's (2014b) commentary about how research on the brain's role in intelligence has been more productive in producing answers to some questions than to others.

- Description of a recent meta-analysis of 53 studies conducted since 1972 that found IQ scores have been rising about 3 points per decade since that year and that the rate of increase in IQ scores does not seem to be diminishing (Trahan & others, 2014).

- Description of a recent analysis that concluded the underrepresentation of African Americans in STEM subjects and careers is linked to practitioners' expectations that they have less innate talent than non-Latino Whites (Leslie & others, 2015).

- Expanded content on whether social media might serve as an amplification tool for adolescent egocentrism and coverage of a recent study that found Facebook use increases self-interest (Chiou, Chen, & Liao, 2014).

- New entry in Resources for Improving the Lives of Adolescents: *The Neuroscience of Decision Making* (2014) edited by Valerie Reyna and Vivian Zayas, which describes many research and social implications of adolescents' risky decision making.

Chapter 4: The Self, Identity, Emotion, and Personality

- Some changes made based on recommendations from leading expert Kate McLean.

- Inclusion of recent research involving Hong Kong secondary school students in which the main content of hoped-for selves focused on school and career (Zhu & others, 2014). In this study, girls had more strategies for attaining positive possible selves than did boys.

- Description of a recent study that found low and decreasing self-esteem during adolescence was linked with adult depression two decades later (Steiger & others, 2014).

- New content on how most studies of self-esteem are correlational in nature and discussion of a recent longitudinal study of adolescents in which self-esteem predicted subsequent changes in social support but not the reverse (Marshall & others, 2014).

- Coverage of recent research indicating that inflated praise, although well intended, may cause children with low self-esteem to avoid important learning experiences, such as tackling challenging tasks (Brummelman & others, 2014).

- New section on self-regulation in adolescence with special emphasis on its important role in achievement and health (Casey, 2015; Wigfield & others, 2015).

- New discussion of effortful control as a key aspect of self-regulation and a recent study that found effortful control at 17 years of age predicted academic persistence and educational attainment at 23 to 25 years of age (Veronneau & others, 2014).

- Coverage of some factors that might help adolescents develop better self-regulation and some factors that might inhibit their development of self-regulation (McClelland & others, 2015).

- New description of child and adolescent precursors to adult health and longevity, including the view of Nancy Eisenberg and her colleagues (2014) that early development of self-regulation fosters conscientiousness later in life, both directly and through its link to academic motivation/success and internalized compliance with norms.

- Updated and expanded discussion of the narrative approach to identity (McAdams & McLean, 2013; Pasupathi, 2015; Singer & Kasmark, 2015).

- Coverage of a recent study that examined identity domains using both identity status and narrative approaches with the interpersonal domain (especially dating and friendship aspects) frequently mentioned (McLean & others, 2015). In the narrative approach, family stories were common.

- Inclusion of recent research in which planfulness was a consistent predictor of engagement in identity exploration and commitment (Luyckx & Robitschek, 2014).

- Expanded description of why college often produces some key changes in an individual's identity (Arnett, 2014; Arnett & Fishel, 2013).

- Extensive revision, updating, and organization of the discussion of the Big Five factors of personality, including a separate description of each factor.

- Description of recent research that found individuals high in openness to experience are more likely to engage in identity exploration (Luyckx & others, 2014) and have superior cognitive functioning across the life span (Briley, Domiteaux, & Tucker-Drob, 2014).

- Inclusion of research in which individuals high in conscientiousness were less stressed and had better health (Gartland & others, 2014).

- Coverage of recent research indicating that individuals high in extraversion had fewer sleep problems (Hintsanen & others, 2014) and a more positive sense of well-being (Soto & others, 2015).

- Discussion of research in which adolescents who were high in agreeableness and conscientiousness engaged in fewer counterproductive workplace behaviors (absenteeism, substance abuse on the job, and theft, for example) 18 years later (Le & others, 2014).

- Description of recent research linking high levels of neuroticism to a variety of negative outcomes, including higher rates of drug dependence (Valero & others, 2014) and lower levels of well-being 40 years later (Gale & others, 2013).

- New entry in Resources for Improving the Lives of Adolescents: *Oxford Handbook of Identity Development* edited by Kate McLean and Moin Syed (2015), in which most of the leading experts in adolescent and emerging adult identity development provide contemporary reviews of research and theory.

Chapter 5: Gender

- Updated research on the lack of benefits when students attend same-sex schools (Bigler, Hayes, & Liben, 2014; Leaper & Brown, 2015; Pahlke, Hyde, & Allison, 2014).
- Description of the most recent National Assessment of Educational Progress report (2014) in which girls continue to have higher reading achievement scores than boys do.
- Updated data on the gender difference in dropping out of school (National Center for Education Statistics, 2014).
- Coverage of a recent national U.S. survey indicating that females' rate of college attendance has exceeded that of males since 1996 (Pew Research Center, 2014).
- New discussion of the lack of research on effects of social media on girls' and boys' body image concerns, and a recent review that argued a special research interest should be the effects of social media on adolescent girls' body images and eating disorders (Perloff, 2014).
- Inclusion of recent research in which parents were provided content about the value of encouraging their adolescents to take math and sciences for improving future career opportunities (Harackiewicz & others, 2012). Adolescents whose parents were given these materials took more math and science courses in high school, especially daughters of college-educated mothers.
- Coverage of a longitudinal study in which preschool relational aggression predicted adolescent relational aggression for girls but not for boys (Nelson & others, 2014).
- New description of a gender difference involving empathy in which girls show more empathy in childhood and adolescence than do boys (Christov-Moore & others, 2014).
- Inclusion of information from a meta-analysis in which females are better than males at recognizing nonverbal displays of emotion (Thompson & Voyer, 2014).
- Two new entries in Resources for Improving the Lives of Adolescents: "Gender Similarities and Differences" by Janet Shibley Hyde (2014) and "Analysis and Evaluation of the Rationales for Single-Sex Schooling" by Rebecca Bigler, Amy Hayes, and Lynn Liben.

Chapter 6: Sexuality

- Discussion of a recent study in which adolescents' music video consumption was linked to asking for and having received sexting messages (Van Ouytsel, Ponnet, & Walrave, 2014).
- New content on the special concern about sexting, including a recent national study of the percentage of adolescents who send and receive sexual pictures (Ybarra & Mitchell, 2014).
- Inclusion of recent research indicating the presence of sexual scripts in heterosexual emerging adults for sex drive, physical and emotional sex, sexual performance, initiation and gateway scripts, and sexual evaluation (Sakaluk & others, 2014).
- New coverage of a recent study of young adult men that found two main sexual scripts: (1) a traditional masculine "player" script, and (2) a script that emphasized mutual sexual pleasure (Morrison & others, 2015).

- Updated national data on the percent of adolescents at different age levels who have engaged in sexual intercourse, including gender and ethnic variations, with updates in Figures 1 and 2 (Kann & others, 2014).
- Description of a recent Swedish study of more than 3,000 adolescents indicating that sexual intercourse prior to age 14 was linked to a number of risky sexual behaviors at age 18 (Kastbom & others, 2015).
- Coverage of recent research in which Spanish-speaking immigrant youth engaged in more sexual risk behaviors than English-speaking immigrant Latino youth, native Latino youth, and non-Latino White youth (Haderxhanaj & others, 2014).
- Inclusion of a recent study that found difficulties and disagreements between Latino adolescents and their parents were linked to the adolescents' early sexual initiation (Cordova & others, 2014).
- Discussion of a recent study that revealed adolescent females who skipped school or failed a test were more likely to have frequent sexual intercourse and less likely to use contraceptives (Hensel & Sorge, 2014).
- Description of a recent meta-analysis in which the link between impulsivity and risky sexual behavior in adolescence was more characteristic of females than males (Dir, Coskunpinar, & Cyders, 2014).
- New research indicating that adolescent males who play sports engage in more risky sexual behavior while adolescent females who play sports engage in less risky sexual behavior (Lipowski & others, 2015).
- Coverage of recent research indicating that 40 percent of 22-year-olds reported recently having had a casual sex partner (Lyons & others, 2015).
- Inclusion of recent research of more than 3,900 18- to 25-year-olds that found having casual sex was negatively linked to well-being and positively related to psychological distress (Bersamin & others, 2014).
- New discussion of a recent study of almost 8,000 emerging adults that found males had more permissive sexual attitudes, especially regarding casual sexual encounters, than did females (Sprecher, Treger, & Sakaluk, 2013).
- Description of recent research in which frequent viewing of pornography by college students was associated with a higher incidence of hooking up and a higher number of different hookup partners (Braithwaite & others, 2015).
- Inclusion of a recent study that revealed 20 percent of first-year college women students engaged in hooking up at least once during the school year and that certain characteristics were linked with a likelihood of hooking up (Fielder & others, 2013).
- New commentary about "friends with benefits" and the high level of casual sex that is now common among emerging adults (Owen, Fincham, & Manthos, 2013).
- New discussion of possible sexual health risks for sexual minority youth (Morgan, 2014).
- New coverage of a recent study of 15- to 20-year-olds in which bisexual and lesbian youth had an earlier sexual

debut and had more male and female sexual partners than their heterosexual counterparts (Tornello, Riskind, & Patterson, 2014). In this study, bisexual women reported more sexual risk behavior than lesbian or heterosexual women.

· Updated and expanded description of physical and mental health risks of sexual minority youth (Rosario & others, 2014).

· Inclusion of recent research that found a higher rate of substance use and suicidal ideation and attempts in sexual minority youth, especially when they lacked connections with adults at their school (Seil, Desai, & Smith, 2014).

· Coverage of a recent research review of more than 300 studies that concluded bisexual youth have higher rates of suicidal ideation and attempts than their gay, lesbian, and heterosexual counterparts (Pompili & others, 2014).

· Discussion of a recent study of more than 72,000 youth (more than 6,200 of them sexual minority youth) in which the sexual minority youth had a higher incidence of suicidal ideation, planning, and attempts than the heterosexual youth (Bostwick & others, 2014).

· Description of a recent study that revealed family support was linked to a decreased risk of suicide attempts in sexual minority youth (Reisner & others, 2014).

· Updated data on the percentage of adolescents who use contraceptives (Kann & others, 2014).

· Updated statistics on the continuing decline in overall adolescent pregnancy rates in the United States and the decline in all ethnic groups, including updates in Figures 4 and 5 (Martin & others, 2015).

· Inclusion of a recent cross-cultural study of adolescent pregnancy rates in 21 countries (Sedgh & others, 2015).

· New coverage of recent research on the negative interactions of adolescent mothers with their infants and an intervention program that improved mothers' behaviors and children's outcomes (Guttentag & others, 2014; Riva Crugnola & others, 2014).

· Description of recent research that indicated higher levels of maternal education were linked to children's reading and math achievement through the eighth grade but the achievement of adolescent mothers' children never reached the levels of non-adolescent mothers' children (Tang & others, 2015).

· Coverage of a recent study of long-term life outcomes in a number of areas for African American teen versus nonteen mothers and fathers (Assini-Meytin & Green, 2015).

· Inclusion of recent research that found a substantial decrease in the percentage of abortions obtained by U.S. adolescents from 2002 to 2011 (Pazol & others, 2014).

· Discussion of a recent research review of 150 intervention studies conducted from 2001 to 2013 identifying three elements of intervention programs that were the most successful at reducing HIV in adolescents: (1) an enabling environment, (2) information and service provision, and (3) social support (Hardee & others, 2014).

· New description of the U.S. government's Teen Pregnancy Prevention (TPP) program directed by the recently created Office of Adolescent Health (Koh, 2014).

· Inclusion of a recent meta-analysis that revealed 60 percent of rape victims do not acknowledge their rape, with an especially high percentage not acknowledging rape in the college years (Wilson & Miller, 2015).

· Coverage of a recent national study of involvement in various types of adolescent relationship abuse, such as psychological abuse, sexual abuse, and sexual harassment (including online sexual harassment) (Taylor & Mumford, 2015).

· Description of an effective intervention program, "Shifting Boundaries," that reduced the frequency of dating violence victimization in young adolescents (Taylor, Mumford, & Stein, 2015).

· New entry in Resources for Improving the Lives of Adolescents: "Positive and Negative Outcomes of Sexual Behaviors," edited by Eva Lefkowitz and Sara Vasilenko (2014), which provides a contemporary look at a wide range of adolescent sexuality topics.

Chapter 7: Moral Development, Values, and Religion

· Some changes made to chapter based on feedback from leading expert Sam Hardy.

· New section on Jonathan Haidt's (2013) criticism of Kohlberg's view of moral reasoning as always conscious and deliberate, noting Kohlberg's lack of attention to the automatic, intuitive precursors of moral reasoning.

· New section on the criticism that Kohlberg's moral development theory ignores the importance of emotion in moral thinking.

· Expanded and updated discussion of the importance of families in children's and adolescents' moral development (Dunn, 2014; Eisenberg, Spinrad, & Knafo, 2015; Thompson, 2014).

· Discussion of a recent study that found empathy increased from 12 to 16 years of age (Allemand, Steiger, & Fend, 2015). Also in this study, adolescent girls showed more empathy than did their male counterparts, and adolescent empathy predicted a number of social competencies (adult empathy, communication skills, and relationship satisfaction, for example) two decades later.

· New coverage of the role empathy can play in prosocial behavior (Eisenberg, Spinrad, & Morris, 2014).

· Inclusion of recent research in which sympathy in childhood predicted increases in moral reasoning and social justice values in early adolescence (Daniel & others, 2014).

· Expanded discussion of contemporary views of conscience to include its roots in close relationships, construction from advances in self-understanding and understanding of others, and links to affective feelings (Thompson, 2014).

· Expanded and updated discussion of the view of Sam Hardy and his colleagues (Hardy & others, 2014a, b) regarding the role of morality in identity formation.

· Inclusion of recent research with college students in which moral identity predicted all five health outcomes assessed (anxiety, depression, hazardous alcohol use, sexual risk taking, and self-esteem) (Hardy & others, 2014b).

- Description of a recent study in which a higher level of moral identity was found to possibly reduce the negative effects of moral disengagement and low self-regulation (Hardy, Bean, & Olsen, 2015).
- Added commentary noting that the point of conducting research on moral exemplars is to study the ideal endpoint of moral development.
- Expanded description of social domain theory based on the views of Judith Smetana (2013) and Eliot Turiel (2014, 2015).
- New content involving Darcia Narváez's (2010, 2014) recommendation that moral education in schools give more attention to sustaining climates that include a positive learning environment and caring contexts.
- Coverage of a recent study on how extensively children and adolescents cheat and factors involved in whether they cheat (Ding & others, 2014).
- Updated information about the goals of first-year college students in relation to the relative importance they place on developing a meaningful philosophy of life versus becoming very well-off financially (Eagan & others, 2014).
- Coverage of a recent national poll that found 30 percent of U.S. individuals younger than 30 years of age have no religious affiliation, the highest percentage since the Pew Research Center (2012) began polling this topic in 2007.
- Inclusion of recent research that found youth generally thought about spirituality in positive ways (James, Fine, & Turner, 2012). In this study, 10- to 18-year-olds' self-ratings of spirituality were linked to the 5 Cs of Positive Youth Development.
- Description of a recent study that found when youth attend religious services with their parents, this activity increases the positive influence of parenting on their psychological well-being (Petts, 2014).
- Inclusion of two new entries in Resources for Improving the Lives of Adolescents: "Prosocial Development" by Nancy Eisenberg, Tracy Spinrad, and Ariel Knafo (2015); and "The Nature and Functions of Religious and Spiritual Development in Childhood and Adolescence" by Pamela King and Chris Boyatzis (2015).

Chapter 8: Families

- Some changes made based on feedback from leading expert Su Yeong Kim.
- Coverage of a recent study that revealed a low level of parental monitoring was linked to sexual risk taking in Iranian high school students (Ahmadi & others, 2013).
- Description of a recent study that revealed low parental monitoring was associated with adolescent depression (Yap & others, 2014).
- Inclusion of recent research indicating that low parental monitoring was a key factor in predicting a developmental trajectory of delinquency and substance use in adolescence (Wang & others, 2014).
- New research on 10- to 18-year-olds in which lower disclosure to parents was linked to antisocial behavior (Criss & others, 2015).

- New discussion of fathers' and mothers' roles in adolescent development, including recent research on adolescents in two-parent non-Latino White and African American families, with special attention given to the important contribution fathers can make to adolescents' development (Lam, McHale, & Crouter, 2012; Stanik, Riina, & McHale, 2013).
- Description of a recent research review that concluded the negative effects of father absence are especially found for these outcomes: lower rates of high school graduation, problems in socioemotional development in children and adolescents, and adult mental health problems (McLanahan, Tach, & Schneider, 2013).
- Coverage of a recent study in which high levels of parent-adolescent conflict were associated with lower levels of adolescent empathy throughout the six years of the study (Van Lissa & others, 2015).
- Inclusion of recent research in which a higher level of parent-adolescent conflict was associated with higher levels of anxiety, depression, and aggression, and lower self-esteem (Smokowski & others, 2015).
- Description of a recent study of homeless youth in Chicago and San Francisco that found they had high rates of psychological disorders (especially mood disorders, antisocial personality disorder, and substance-related disorder) (Quimby & others, 2012).
- Revised definition of secure attachment that includes different age periods rather than focusing only on infancy.
- Coverage of a recent study of adolescents and emerging adults from 15 to 20 years of age that found insecure attachment to mothers was linked to becoming depressed and remaining depressed (Agerup & others, 2015).
- Inclusion of recent research that found avoidant attachment predicted suicidal behavior in adolescents (Sheftall, Schoppe-Sullivan, & Bridge, 2014).
- Description of a recent study in which insecure attachment with mothers and fathers was linked to a lower level of parents' knowledge about adolescents' whereabouts (Jones & Cassidy, 2014).
- Discussion of a recent meta-analysis that found a lower percentage of U.S. college students are securely attached and a higher percentage are insecurely attached than in the past (Konrath & others, 2014).
- Inclusion of recent research in which secure attachment in adults was linked to fewer sleep disruptions than insecure avoidant or anxious attachment (Adams & McWilliams, 2015).
- Description of a recent study that found newlywed spouses were more likely to engage in infidelity when either they or their partner had an anxious attachment style (Russell, Baker, & McNulty, 2013).
- Discussion of a recent study in which individuals who had experienced their parents' divorce were more at risk for engaging in a suicide attempt during their lifetime (Alonzo & others, 2014).
- Inclusion of recent research that revealed children were more likely to have behavior problems if the post-divorce family environment was less supportive and less stimulating, their

mother was less sensitive and more depressed, and if their household income was lower (Weaver & Schofield, 2015).

· Coverage of a recent study that found middle-aged adults positively supported family responsibility to emerging adult children but were more ambivalent about providing care for aging parents, viewing it as both a joy and a burden (Igarashi & others, 2013).

· Inclusion of recent research that found U.S. divorce rates increased from 1990 to 2008, with the increase due to a doubling of the divorce rate in individuals over 35 years of age, while the divorce rate remained stable or declined in the youngest couples (Kennedy & Ruggles, 2014).

· Description of a 7 percent increase in the divorce rate from 1997 to 2009 in Norway (Reiter & others, 2013).

· Discussion of a recent study of 14- to 17-year-olds in Spain in which those living in non-divorced intact families who perceived the presence of a high degree of marital conflict between their parents engaged in more and higher-risk sexual activity than their counterparts living in divorced families (Orgiles, Carratala, & Espada, 2015).

· New research indicating that parental divorce during childhood was linked to worse cohabiting/marital relationships from 16 to 30 years of age, but that these associations were influenced by a variety of factors, including childhood sexual abuse and lower SES status of the child at birth (Fergusson, McLeod, & Horwood, 2014).

· Description of recent research on almost 3,000 adolescents that revealed a negative association of the father's, but not the mother's, unemployment on the adolescents' health (Bacikova-Sleskova, Benka, & Orosova, 2014).

· New content indicating that an increasing number of adoptions in the next decade will come from the child welfare system (Grotevant & McDermott, 2014).

· Coverage of a recent research review that concluded children who are adopted are more likely than those growing up with biological parents to have problems in three areas: externalized, internalized, and attentional (Grotevant & McDermott, 2014).

· New coverage of a longitudinal study on the positive outcomes of contact for birth mothers, adoptive parents, and birth children (Grotevant & others, 2013).

· Discussion of a recent longitudinal study that revealed when adopted children reached adulthood, adoptive parents described open adoption positively and saw it as serving the child's best interests (Siegel, 2013).

· Inclusion of recent research that found more positive parenting in adoptive gay father families and fewer child externalizing problems in these families than in heterosexual families (Golombok & others, 2014).

· Description of recent research in which both self-reports and observations indicated that lesbian and gay couples shared child care more than heterosexual couples, with lesbian couples being the most supportive (Farr & Patterson, 2013).

· Coverage of recent research on Mexican American adolescents in which having family obligation values was linked to lower substance use, which was due in part to less association with deviant peers and a higher level of adolescent disclosure to parents (Telzer, Gonzales, & Fuligni, 2014).

· New entry in Resources for Improving the Lives of Adolescences: *Getting to 30: A Parent's Guide to the 20-Something Years* by Jeffrey Arnett and Elizabeth Fishel (2014).

Chapter 9: Peers, Romantic Relationships, and Lifestyles

· Some changes made based on feedback from leading expert Jennifer Connolly.

· Description of a recent study that compared the effects of parent, teacher, and peer events and found that negative peer events (fighting or arguing with a peer, for example) were most likely to account for maintaining depressive symptoms across a two-year period in early adolescence (Herres & Kobak, 2015).

· Discussion of a longitudinal study from 13 to 23 years of age in which adolescents' autonomy from peer influences predicted long-term success in avoiding problematic behavior but also more difficulty in establishing strong friendships in emerging adulthood (Allen, Chango, & Szwedo, 2014).

· Coverage of a recent study in which having friends who engage in delinquency is associated with early onset and more persistent delinquency (Evans, Simons, & Simons, 2015).

· Inclusion of recent research in which college students with risky social networks (friends who drink, for example) were ten times more likely to engage in alcohol abuse (Mason, Zaharakis, & Benotsch, 2014).

· Expanded discussion of how parents influence their adolescents' peer relations (Pallini & others, 2014).

· Discussion of a recent study in which adolescents' dating popularity was associated with their peer popularity (Houser, Mayeux, & Cross, 2015).

· Coverage of a recent study that indicated low peer status in childhood was linked to an increased probability of being unemployed and having mental health problems in adulthood (Almquist & Brannstrom, 2014).

· Description of a recent study of 13- to 23-year-olds that revealed early adolescent pseudomature behavior was associated with a desire to be popular with peers (Allen & others, 2014). In this study, pseudomature behavior was linked to long-term problems in close relationships, substance abuse, and a higher level of criminal behavior.

· Discussion of a recent study of young adolescents in which anger displays and depression were linked to being unpopular with peers (Martinez & others, 2014).

· New developmental connections between increased concern about bullying in adolescence and increased dating violence and acquaintance rape in adolescence and emerging adulthood.

· Inclusion of recent research involving Malaysian adolescents that found those who felt lonely were more likely to show symptoms of depression (Kaur & others, 2014).

· Inclusion of recent research supporting a normative three-stage sequence of the development of romantic relationship and two off-time sequences (early starters and late bloomers) (Connolly & others, 2013). In this study, the early starters had more externalizing symptoms while the on-time and late bloomers did not show any indications of maladjustment.

- Discussion of recent research indicating that an increasing number of children are growing up in homes in which their parents never got married and that this is far more likely to occur when the mother has a low level of education (Gibson-Davis & Rackin, 2014; Pew Research Center, 2015).
- Updated statistics on the number of U.S. adults who are cohabiting, which increased to 7.8 million in 2012 (Vespa, Lewis, & Kreider, 2013).
- New research that found the risk of marital dissolution between cohabitors and those who married without previously cohabiting was much smaller when they cohabited in their mid-twenties or later (Kuperberg, 2014).
- Updating of marriage statistics in the United States (U.S. Census Bureau, 2013).
- Updating of the dramatic increase in online matchmaking, with more than 41 million people in the United States having tried online matchmaking in 2014, up from about 6 million in 2006 (statisticbrain, 2014).
- Coverage of a recent study that explored what U.S. never-married men and women are looking for in a potential spouse (Wang, 2014).
- Discussion of recent research that found newlyweds who had a high level of general dispositional optimism had higher marital satisfaction across the first year of the marriage while newlyweds who had a higher level of specific relationship optimism had more marital problems across this time frame (Neff & Geers, 2013).
- New discussion of recent research in which individuals who had higher numbers of relationships prior to marriage were less likely to have a high-quality marriage (Rhoades & Stanley, 2014).
- Coverage of a recent study that found couples who participated in premarital education had higher marital quality (Rhoades & Stanley, 2014).
- New commentary about Russia having the highest divorce rate in the world (UNSTAT, 2011).
- Discussion of a recent study that revealed a heightened state of romantic love in young adults was linked to stronger depression and anxiety symptoms but better sleep quality (Bajoghli & others, 2014).
- New discussion of a recent national study of more than 19,000 individuals that found more than one-third of marriages now begin with online contact and that these marriages are slightly less likely to break up and are characterized by slightly higher marital satisfaction than marriages that begin in offline contexts (Cacioppo & others, 2013).
- Inclusion of content from a recent Pew Research Center (2015) poll of 40- to 50-year-old U.S. women that found those with a master's degree or higher educational attainment first became mothers at age 30 but their counterparts with a low level of education first became mothers at age 24.
- Coverage of a recent study in which low levels of agreeableness and conscientiousness, and high levels of neuroticism and openness to experience, were linked to daily experiences over time that negatively impacted relationship quality and eventually led to a marital breakup (Solomon & Jackson, 2014).
- Description of a recent study in Finland that found divorce rates peak approximately 5 to 7 years into a marriage and then the rate gradually declines (Kulu, 2014).
- New entry in Resources for Improving the Lives of Adolescents: "Friendships, Romantic Relationships, and Other Dyadic Peer Relationships in Childhood and Adolescence: A Unified Relational Perspective" by Wyndol Furman and Amanda Rose (2015).

Chapter 10: Schools

- New coverage of the recently developed Common Core Standards Initiative to provide more detailed guidelines and milestones for students to achieve at each level, and a discussion of the controversy the Standards have generated (Common Core State Standards Initiative, 2014).
- Discussion of a recent study of more than 19,000 individuals from 18 to 25 years of age that found those who dropped out of high school were more likely than high school graduates to smoke cigarettes daily, report having attempted suicide in the previous year, and be arrested for larceny, assault, and drug possession or sales (Maynard, Salas-Wright, & Vaughn, 2015).
- Updated data on school dropouts showing a continuing decline in rates for various ethnic groups (Child Trends, 2014; National Center for Education Statistics, 2014).
- Updated content on how overwhelmed U.S. college students are with all they have to do (Eagan & others, 2014).
- Updated and expanded coverage of how much more money college graduates earn than high school graduates per year and in a lifetime (Daly & Bengali, 2014).
- Updated description of countries that had the highest percentages of adults with a college education and the highest percentages of young people who were expected to graduate from college in a recent year, and the reasons why the United States has a lower standing in these percentages than in the past (OECD, 2014).
- Description of recent research that found a decline in U.S. but not Chinese young adolescents' sense of responsibility to parents across the seventh and eighth grades was linked to how much the young adolescents valued school and engaged in academic achievement (Qu & Pomerantz, 2015).
- New coverage of Eva Pomerantz' (2014) parenting recommendations related to students' motivation in school.
- Inclusion of recent research indicating that having supportive friends was linked to a lower level of bullying and victimization (Kendrick, Jutengren, & Stattin, 2012).
- Coverage of a recent meta-analysis in which positive parenting behavior was related to a reduced likelihood that an adolescent would become either a bully/victim or a victim at school (Lereya, Samara, & Wolke, 2013).
- Discussion of recent research revealing higher rates of depression and suicide in children who are the victims of bullying (Undheim, 2013; Yen & others, 2014).

- Description of a recent study that found peer victimization in the fifth grade was linked to worse physical and mental health in the tenth grade (Bogart & others, 2014).
- Inclusion of information from a recent meta-analysis that found both negative and positive parenting practices were linked to bullying and victimization (Lereya, Samara, & Wolke, 2013).
- Discussion of a recent analysis that concluded bullying can have long-term effects, including difficulty in establishing long-term relationships and difficulties at work (Wolke & Lereya, 2015).
- New research review that found interventions that focused on the whole school, such as Olweus', were more effective in reducing bullying than interventions involving classroom curricula or social skills training (Cantone & others, 2015).
- Expanded and updated discussion of the costs and benefits of bullying in the context of the peer group, including a longitudinal study that revealed short-term benefits for bullies in the peer group (Reijntjes & others, 2013).
- Description of a recent study that indicated peer victimization during the elementary school years was a leading indicator of internalizing problems in adolescence (Schwartz & others, 2015).
- Discussion of a recent meta-analysis that revealed being the victim of cyberbullying was linked to stress and suicidal ideation (Kowalski & others, 2014).
- Inclusion of information from a recent meta-analysis in which traditional bullying occurred twice as much as cyberbullying and that those who engaged in cyberbullying were often likely to have also engaged in traditional bullying (Modecki & others, 2014).
- Coverage of recent research that found cyberbullying was more strongly associated with suicidal ideation than traditional bullying (van Geel, Vedder, & Tanilon, 2014).
- Inclusion of recent research in which cyberbullying contributed to depression and suicidal ideation above and beyond the contribution of traditional types of bullying (Bonanno & Hymel, 2013).
- Coverage of a longitudinal study in which adolescents experiencing social and emotional difficulties were more likely to be both cyberbullied and traditionally bullied than to be traditionally bullied only (Cross, Lester, & Barnes, 2015).
- Coverage of a recent study that found immigrant adolescents who participated in extracurricular activities improved their academic achievement and increased their school engagement (Camacho & Fuligni, 2015).
- Discussion of a recent Australian study that found extracurricular participation in the eighth grade was linked to a lower likelihood of binge drinking through the eleventh grade (Modecki, Barber, & Eccles, 2014).
- Updated data from the 2011–2012 school year on the percentage of students who receive special education services and the areas in which they receive those services, including updated Figure 2 (Condition of Education, 2014).
- New coverage of the recent research interest focused on the possibility that neurofeedback might reduce the level of ADHD symptoms in children (Gevensleben & others, 2014; Steiner & others, 2014a, b).
- New information about how neurofeedback works, including links between EEG patterns and the main brain region involved in using neurofeedback with children with ADHD.
- Description of a recent experimental study that found biofeedback was effective in reducing ADHD symptoms and also improved children's academic performance (Meisel & others, 2013).
- New coverage of the possibility that exercise might improve the functioning of children with ADHD, including recent research indicating that a single 20-minute bout of moderately intense aerobic exercise improved the neurocognitive functioning and inhibitory control of children with ADHD (Pontifex & others, 2013).
- New description of reasons why aerobic exercise might reduce negative symptoms in children with ADHD (Chang & others, 2012).
- Updated data on the percentage of time students with disabilities spend in the general classroom, which revealed that the percentage reached the highest level (61 percent) since it was first assessed (Condition of Education, 2014).
- New entry in Resources for Improving the Lives of Adolescents: "Children at School" by Robert Crosnoe and Aprile Benner (2015), which provides a contemporary perspective on the importance of the social aspects of schools and notes that current social policy focuses mainly on the academic aspects.

Chapter 11: Achievement, Work, and Careers

- Discussion of two recent studies that documented the importance of autonomy support, self-determination, and intrinsic motivation in increasing adolescents' exercise (Christiana & others, 2014; Gourlan, Sant, & Boiche, 2014).
- New discussion of recent research in which underachieving high school students who read online modules about how the brain changes when people learn and study improved their grade point averages (Paunesku & others, 2015).
- Description of a longitudinal study of university students in which a nonlimited theory of mind predicted better self-regulation and higher grades (Job & others, 2015).
- New section on delay of gratification that describes Walter Mischel and colleagues' classic research using the marshmallow task (Mischel & Moore, 1973) and longitudinal studies that link delay of gratification in young children to a number of academic, achievement, and health outcomes in adolescence, emerging adulthood, and adulthood (Mischel, 2014; Moffitt, 2012; Zayas, Mischel, & Pandey, 2014).
- Discussion of recent research on how parents' and adolescents' achievement expectations are linked to achievement outcomes (Wang & Benner, 2014).
- Inclusion of recent research in which positive expectations of 10th-grade students, their parents, and their English and math teachers predicted their educational attainment four years later (Gregory & Huang, 2013).

- New description of the lower academic expectations parents and teachers have for African American adolescent boys than for African American adolescent girls (Rowley & others, 2014).
- Coverage of a recent study in which older adolescents who spent a larger part of their life in poverty showed less persistence on a challenging task (Fuller-Roswell & others, 2015).
- Inclusion of recent research indicating that the superior academic performance of Asian American children was due to their greater effort and not to advantages in tested cognitive abilities or sociodemographic factors (Hsin & Xie, 2014).
- New discussion of recent research on some negative outcomes of authoritarian parenting on Chinese-American immigrant children (Zhou & others, 2012).
- New coverage of recent research by Su Yeong Kim and her colleagues (2013) that found supportive parenting was a more common style than tiger parenting with Chinese American adolescents and that supportive parenting was more likely to be associated with positive developmental outcomes than was tiger parenting.
- New coverage of two recent books on the strong disciplinary orientation of Chinese parents: *Battle Hymn of the Tiger Mom* (Chua, 2011) and *Tiger Babies Strike Back* (Keltner, 2013).
- Inclusion of recent research in which parents' perfectionism was linked to their children's and adolescents' higher anxiety level (Affrunti & Woodruff-Borden, 2014).
- Description of a recent study that found high school students with paid part-time jobs were more likely to drink alcohol, binge drink, and use marijuana (Leeman & others, 2014).
- Updated data on the percentage of full-time and part-time college students who work while attending college (National Center for Education Statistics, 2013).
- New coverage of the unemployment rate of recent college graduates and the high percentage who have to take jobs that do not require a college degree (Center for Economic and Policy Research, 2014; Gabor, 2014).
- Coverage of a national survey in which 50 percent of U.S. high schools had student-to-counselor ratios of more than 250 to 1 (Radford & Ifill, 2009).
- Updated information about the types of jobs that will be the fastest growing through 2022 in the United States (Occupational Outlook Handbook, 2014/2015) and inclusion of this handbook as a new entry in Resources for Improving the Lives of Adolescents.
- New entry in Resources for Improving the Lives of Adolescents: "Development of Achievement Motivation and Engagement" by Allan Wigfield and others (2015) that provides information about many aspects of theories, research, and applications focused on adolescent achievement.
- New entry in Resources for Improving the Lives of Adolescents: *The Marshmallow Text: Mastering Self-Control* by Walter Mischel (2014). A leading psychologist describes many aspects of self-control and delay of gratification in the lives of children, adolescents, and adults, including many strategies for improving these cognitive skills.

Chapter 12: Culture

- Some changes made in this chapter based on expert consultant Su Yeong Kim's comments.
- Discussion of a recent study that found from 1990 to 2007, 18- to 65-year-old Chinese increasingly included individualistic characteristics in their descriptions of what constitutes happiness and subjective well-being (Steele & Lynch, 2013).
- Coverage of a longitudinal study from 1970 to 2008 which found that although China is still characterized by collectivistic values, the frequency of words used in China that index individualistic values has increased (Zeng & Greenfield, 2015).
- Updated statistics on poverty levels in U.S. families with children and adolescents, including data for ethnic groups and single-mother-headed households (De Navas-Walt & Proctor, 2014).
- Description of recent research that found youth in upwardly mobile, upper-middle-SES families are more likely to engage in drug use and have more internalized and externalized problems (Luthar, Barkin, & Crossman, 2013).
- Inclusion of recent research with youth that revealed living in neighborhoods where poverty increased from the time they were 11 to 19 years of age was associated with an increase allostatic load, except when the youth experienced high emotional support (Brody & others, 2014).
- Coverage of a recent intervention program (the Positive Action program) that was used with third- to eighth-graders in 14 schools in low-income areas of Chicago (Lewis & others, 2013). Compared with a control group, students in the intervention program engaged in lower rates of violence-related behavior and received fewer disciplinary referrals and school suspensions.
- Discussion of a recent study of more than 500 high school students living in low-income areas of Los Angeles who were selected through a random admissions lottery to attend high-performing charter schools, which resulted in the students doing better on standardized tests of math and English and being less likely to drop out of school (Wong & others, 2014).
- Updated biography of Carolyn Suárez-Orozco in *Connecting with Careers.*
- Description of a recent study of Chinese American and Korean American adolescents in which the adolescents often served as language brokers for their immigrant parents and this brokering was associated with other aspects of parent-adolescent relationships and adolescent outcomes (Shen & others, 2014).
- Inclusion of recent research by Su Yeong Kim and her colleagues (2015) that found Chinese American adolescents with a Chinese-oriented father have a faster decline over time in their grade point average, as well as associations of other aspects of acculturation with student outcomes.
- Coverage of a recent study of Chinese American adolescents in which a discrepancy in parent-adolescent American orientation was linked to parents' use of unsupportive parent techniques, which in turn was related to an increased sense of parent-adolescent alienation, which was further

associated with lower academic success and a higher level of depression in adolescents (Kim & others, 2013).

- Description of a recent research review that concluded mental health outcomes (depression and anxiety, for example) were the most commonly reported associations with racial discrimination (Priest & others, 2013).

- Discussion of a recent study of Dominican American, Chinese American, and African American sixth- to eighth-graders in which Chinese Americans and boys perceived that they experienced more racial discrimination than did African Americans and girls (Niwa, Way, & Hughes, 2014).

- Coverage of a recent study of more than 2,300 18- to 30-year-old African American and Latino college students that revealed perceived ethnic group discrimination was linked to depressive symptoms in both ethnic groups; however, having a positive ethnic identity lowered the depressive symptoms for Latino but not African American students (Brittian & others, 2015).

- New information from a research review with details about the complexities of why media multitasking can interfere with learning and driving (Courage & others, 2015).

- Inclusion of a recent study of more than 10,000 9- to 16-year-olds that found each hour-per-day increase in use of television, electronic games, and DVDs/videos was linked with increased consumption of foods with low nutritional quality (Falbe & others, 2014).

- Inclusion of recent research with 9- to 11-year-olds that revealed a higher number of screens in the child's bedroom was associated with a higher likelihood of obesity (Chaput & others, 2014).

- Coverage of a recent research review that concluded more extensive screen time was linked to negative sleep outcomes, especially for computer use, video games, and mobile devices (Hale & Guan, 2015).

- Discussion of a recent study in which playing violent video games was associated with a higher degree of desensitization to violence (Brockmyer, 2015).

- Coverage of a recent study in which playing action video games improved attentional control (Chisholm & Kingstone, 2015).

- Discussion of a recent study that found video game consumption was linked to rape myth acceptance through connections with interpersonal aggression and hostile sexism (Fox & Potocki, 2015).

- Description of a recent research review that found when children's and adolescents' screen time exceeded two hours a day, they were more likely to be overweight or obese (Atkin & others, 2014).

- Inclusion of recent research in which duration of screen time was linked to depression and anxiety (Maras & others, 2015).

- Description of recent research that revealed excessive Internet use by adolescents was linked to not getting adequate sleep (Suris & others, 2014) and to elevated blood pressure (Cassidy-Bushrow & others, 2015).

- Inclusion of recent research in which a higher degree of parental monitoring of media use was linked to a number of

positive outcomes (more sleep, better school performance, less aggressive behavior, and more prosocial behavior) (Gentile & others, 2014b).

- New entry in Resources for Improving the Lives of Adolescents: "Children and Socioeconomic Status" by Greg Duncan, Kathryn Magnuson, and Elizabeth Votruba-Drzal in R.M. Lerner (Ed.), *Handbook of Child Psychology and Developmental Science* (7th ed.).

- New entry in Resources for Improving the Lives of Adolescents: *The African American Child* (2nd ed.) by Yvette Harris and James Graham (2014) that covers many aspects of the lives of African American children and adolescents.

- New entry in Resources for Improving the Lives of Adolescents: *Media and the Well-Being of Children and Adolescents* by Amy Jordan and Daniel Romer (Eds.) (2014).

Chapter 13: Problems in Adolescence and Emerging Adulthood

- Coverage of a recent study in which parental psychiatric status, offspring personality at 11 years of age, and offspring internalizing and externalizing symptoms predicted the subsequent development of major depressive disorder (Wilson & others, 2014).

- Description of a recent study in which externalizing problems increased during adolescence and then declined in emerging adulthood (Petersen & others, 2015).

- Discussion of recent research in 21 countries that revealed adolescents' stress levels were highest with parents and at school while their lowest stress levels occurred with peers and romantic partners (Persike & Seiffge-Krenke, 2012, 2014).

- Inclusion of recent research in which having a positive outlook was the most important cognitive factor associated with a decrease in adolescents' depression severity during the 36 weeks after they began taking antidepressant medication (Jacobs & others, 2014).

- Updated data from the Monitoring the Future study on national trends in the use of various drugs by eighth, tenth, and twelfth graders (Johnston & others, 2015).

- Description of recent research on adolescents indicating that neighborhood disadvantage was linked to a higher level of alcohol use two years later, mainly through a pathway that included exposure to delinquent peers (Trucco & others, 2014).

- Coverage of a recent study in which low parental knowledge of adolescents' peer relations and behavior, and friends' delinquency predicted adolescent substance abuse (McAdams & others, 2014).

- Discussion of a recent study that found early onset of drinking and a quick progression to drinking to intoxication were linked to drinking problems in high school (Morean & others, 2014).

- New coverage of adolescents' use of E-cigarettes, including a description of their characteristics and their inclusion in the University of Michigan Monitoring the Future study for the first time in 2014 (Johnston & others, 2015). In this study, E-cigarette use surpassed tobacco cigarette use by U.S. adolescents.

- New content on synthetic marijuana, including a description of its characteristics and its declining use by U.S. adolescents from 2011 to 2014 (from 11 to 6 percent annual use) (Johnston & others, 2015).

- New research that revealed early- and rapid-onset trajectories of alcohol, marijuana, and substance use were associated with substance use in early adulthood (Nelson, Van Ryzin, & Dishion, 2015).

- Inclusion of research on a recent intervention study that found a combination of a parent program and a teacher development program led to a reduction in the incidence of conduct disorder in African American boys from low-income backgrounds (Dawson-McClure & others, 2015).

- Discussion of a recent study in which youth with conduct disorder that began in childhood had more cognitive impairment, psychiatric problems, and serious violent offenses than youth with conduct disorder characterized by the onset of antisocial behavior in adolescence (Johnson & others, 2015).

- Description of a recent study in which parental monitoring and youth disclosure in the fall of grade 6 were linked to a lower level of delinquency in grade 8 (Lippold & others, 2014).

- Inclusion of recent research in which mothers' reports of their sons' impulsiveness at 15 years of age predicted the sons' arrest record up to 6 years later (Bechtold & others, 2014).

- Discussion of a recent research review indicating that prevention programs focused on the family context were more effective in reducing persistent delinquency than were individual and group-focused programs (de Vries & others, 2015).

- Recent research that found mild to moderate levels of early adolescent depressive behaviors were associated with negative developmental outcomes in emerging adulthood (Allen & others, 2014).

- New information from a research review that concluded SSRIs show clinical benefits for adolescents at risk for moderate and severe depression (Cousins & Goodyer, 2015).

- Updated data on trends in suicidal behavior in U.S. adolescents (Kann & others, 2014).

- Inclusion of recent research in which both depression and hopelessness were predictors of whether adolescents would repeat a suicide attempt across a six-month period (Consoli & others, 2015).

- Description of a recent study in which adolescents with an insecure avoidant attachment style had a higher incidence of suicide attempts (Sheftall, Schoppe-Sullivan, & Bridge, 2014).

- Coverage of recent research that found peer victimization was linked to suicidal ideation and suicide attempts, with cyberbullying more strongly associated with suicidal ideation than traditional bullying (van Geel, Vedder, & Tanilon, 2014).

- Inclusion of recent research indicating that authoritative parenting was linked to fewer adolescent suicide attempts, while rejecting/neglecting parenting was associated with a greater likelihood of adolescent suicide attempts (Donath & others, 2014).

- Description of a recent study that revealed playing sports predicted lower suicidal ideation in boys and that venting by talking to others was associated with lower suicidal ideation in girls (Kim & others, 2014).

- New discussion of the lack of a national study of suicide rates in sexual minority adolescents and inclusion of recent research in Boston indicating that suicidal ideation and attempts were higher in adolescents living in neighborhoods with a higher rate of crimes against gay, lesbian, and bisexual adolescents (Duncan & Hatzenbuehler, 2014).

- Description of a recent study in which more recent and frequent substance use among young adolescents increased the likelihood of suicidal ideation and attempts in African American youth (Tomek & others, 2015).

- Updated data on the increasing percentage of U.S. adolescents who are obese (Ogden & others, 2014) and developmental changes in obesity from kindergarten to early adolescence (Cunningham, Kramer, & Narayan, 2014).

- Inclusion of a recent international study of adolescents in 56 countries that found fast food consumption was linked to higher body mass index (Braithwaite & others, 2014).

- Description of a recent study in which adolescents who ate meals with family members were less likely to be overweight or obese as adults (Berge & others, 2015).

- New discussion of the likely brain changes in adolescents who are anorexic (Fuglset & others, 2015).

- Inclusion of recent research indicating that anorexic adolescents have an elevated level of perfectionism (Lloyd & others, 2014).

- Discussion of a recent study that indicated family therapy was effective in helping anorexic adolescent girls to gain weight over the course of one year (Gabel & others, 2014).

- Coverage of a recent study that found bulimics have difficulty controlling their emotions (Lavender & others, 2014).

- Description of a recent study that revealed being overweight or obese increased from 25.6 percent for college freshman to 32 percent for college seniors (Nicoteri & Miskovsky, 2014).

- Inclusion of recent results from the Fast Track early intervention study, which found that the early intervention was effective in reducing rates of violent and drug crimes at age 25 and increasing well-being at age 25 (Dodge & others, 2015).

- Update on the Add Health study that now includes interview data with individuals into the adulthood years and is called the National Longitudinal Study of Adolescent to Adult Health (2015).

- New entry in Resources for Improving the Lives of Adolescents: *Ordinary Magic* by leading expert Ann Masten (2014a), which describes multiple pathways that children and adolescents can follow to become resilient in the face of numerous adversities, such as homelessness, wars, and disasters.

- New entry in Resources for Improving the Lives of Adolescents: *Help Your Teenager Beat an Eating Disorder* (2nd ed.) by leading experts James Lock and Daniel Le Grange (2015).

- New entry in Resources for Improving the Lives of Adolescents: National Longitudinal Study of Adolescent to Adult Health (2015). The website for this study provides access to many studies involving the adolescent problems discussed in this chapter.

Online Instructor Resources

The resources listed here accompany *Adolescence,* 16th edition. Please contact your McGraw-Hill representative for details concerning the availability of these and other valuable materials that can help you design and enhance your course.

Instructor's Manual Broken down by chapter, these include chapter outlines, suggested lecture topics, classroom activities and demonstrations, suggested student research projects, essay questions, and critical thinking questions.

Test Bank and Computerized Test Bank This comprehensive Test Bank includes multiple-choice and essay questions. Organized by chapter, the questions are designed to test factual, applied, and conceptual understanding. All test questions are compatible with EZ Test, McGraw-Hill's Computerized Test Bank program.

PowerPoint Slides These presentations cover the key points of each chapter and include charts and graphs from the text. They can be used as is, or you may modify them to meet your specific needs.

Acknowledgments

I very much appreciate the support and guidance provided to me by many people at McGraw-Hill. Krista Bettino, Executive Director, Products and Markets, has provided excellent guidance, vision, and direction for this book. Vicki Malinee provided considerable expertise in coordinating many aspects of the editorial process. Janet Tilden again did an outstanding job as the book's copy editor. Sheila Frank did a terrific job in coordinating the book's production. Jennifer Blankenship provided me with excellent choices of new photographs for this edition. Dawn Groundwater, Lead Product Developer, did excellent work on various aspects of the book's development, technology, and learning systems. Thanks also to Ann Helgerson and A.J. Laferrera for their outstanding work marketing *Adolescence*.

I also want to thank my wife, Mary Jo, our children, Tracy and Jennifer, and our grandchildren, Jordan, Alex, and Luke, for their wonderful contributions to my life and for helping me to better understand the marvels and mysteries of children, adolescence, and emerging adulthood.

EXPERT CONSULTANTS

As I develop a new edition, I consult with leading experts in their respective areas of adolescent development. Their invaluable feedback ensures that the latest research, knowledge, and perspectives are presented throughout the text. Their willingness to devote their time and expertise to this endeavor is greatly appreciated. The Expert Consultants who contributed to this edition, along with their biographies and commentary, can be found on pages xii–xiv.

REVIEWERS

I owe a special debt of gratitude to the reviewers who have provided detailed feedback on *Adolescence* over the years.

Alice Alexander, *Old Dominion University;* **Sandy Arntz,** *Northern Illinois University;* **Frank Ascione,** *Utah State University;* **Carole Beale,** *University of Massachusetts;* **Luciane A. Berg,** *Southern Utah University;* **David K. Bernhardt,** *Carleton University;* **Fredda Blanchard-Fields,** *Louisiana State University;* **Kristi Blankenship,** *University of Tennessee;* **Belinda Blevins-Knabe,** *University of Arkansas;* **Robert Bornstein,** *Miami University;* **Ioakim Boutakidis,** *Fullerton State University;* **Geraldine Brookins,** *University of Minnesota;* **Jane Brower,** *University of Tennessee—Chattanooga;* **Deborah Brown,** *Friends University;* **Janine Buckner,** *Seton Hall University;* **Nancy Busch-Rossnagel,** *Fordham University;* **James I. Byrd,** *University of Wisconsin—Stout;* **Cheryl A. Camenzuli,** *Hofstra University;* **Elaine Cassel,** *Marymount University;* **Mark Chapell,** *Rowan University;* **Stephanie M. Clancy,** *Southern Illinois University—Carbondale;* **Ronald K. Craig,** *Cincinnati State College;* **Gary Creasey,** *Illinois State University;* **Laura Crosetti,** *Monroe Community College;* **Rita Curl,** *Minot State University;* **Peggy A. DeCooke,** *Northern Illinois University;* **Nancy Defates-Densch,** *Northern Illinois University;* **Gypsy Denzine,** *Northern Arizona University;* **Imma Destefanis,** *Boston College;* **R. Daniel DiSalvi,** *Kean College;* **James A. Doyle,** *Roane State Community College;* **Mark W. Durm,** *Athens State University;* **Laura Duvall,** *Heartland Community College;* **Kimberly DuVall-Early,** *James Madison University;* **Celina Echols,** *Southern Louisiana State University;* **Richard M. Ehlenz,** *Lakewood Community College;* **Gene Elliot,** *Glassboro State University;* **Steve Ellyson,** *Youngstown State University;* **Robert Enright,** *University of Wisconsin—Madison;* **Jennifer Fager,** *Western Michigan University;* **Lisa Farkas,** *Rowan University;* **Douglas Fife,** *Plymouth State College;* **Urminda Firlan,** *Michigan State University;* **Leslie Fisher,** *Cleveland State University;* **Martin E. Ford,** *Stanford University;* **Gregory T. Fouts,** *University of Calgary;* **Mary Fraser,** *San Jose State University;* **Rick Froman,** *John Brown University;* **Charles Fry,** *University of Virginia;* **Anne R. Gayles-Felton,** *Florida A&M University;* **Margaret J. Gill,** *Kutztown University;* **Sam Givham,** *Mississippi State University;* **William Gnagey,** *Illinois State University;* **Page Goodwin,** *Western Illinois University;* **Nicole Graves,** *South Dakota State University;* **B. Jo Hailey,** *University of Southern Mississippi;* **Dick E. Hammond,** *Southwest Texas State University;* **Sam Hardy,** *Brigham Young University;* **Frances Harnick,** *University of New Mexico, Indian Children's Program, and Lovelace-Bataan Pediatric Clinic;* **Dan Houlihan,** *Minnesota State University;* **Kim Hyatt,** *Weber State University;* **June V. Irving,** *Ball State University;* **Beverly Jennings,** *University of*

Colorado at Denver; **Joline Jones,** *Worcester State College;* **Linda Juang,** *San Francisco State University;* **Alfred L. Karlson,** *University of Massachusetts—Amherst;* **Lynn F. Katz,** *University of Pittsburgh;* **Carolyn Kaufman,** *Columbus State Community College;* **Michelle Kelley,** *Old Dominion University;* **Marguerite D. Kermis,** *Canisius College;* **Roger Kobak,** *University of Delaware;* **Tara Kuther,** *Western Connecticut State University;* **Emmett C. Lampkin,** *Scott Community College;* **Royal Louis Lange,** *Ellsworth Community Center;* **Philip Langer,** *University of Colorado;* **Heidi Legg-Burross,** *University of Arizona;* **Tanya Letourneau,** *Delaware County College;* **Neal E. Lipsitz,** *Boston College;* **Nancy Lobb,** *Alvin Community College;* **Daniel Lynch,** *University of Wisconsin—Oshkosh;* **Joseph G. Marrone,** *Siena College;* **Ann McCabe,** *University of Windsor;* **Susan McCammon,** *East Carolina University;* **Sherri McCarthy-Tucker,** *Northern Arizona University;* **E. L. McGarry,** *California State University—Fullerton;* **D. Rush McQueen,** *Auburn University;* **Sean Meegan,** *Western Illinois University;* **Jessica Miller,** *Mesa State College;* **John J. Mirich,** *Metropolitan State College;* **John J. Mitchell,** *University of Alberta;* **Suzanne F. Morrow,** *Old Dominion University;* **Lloyd D. Noppe,** *University of Wisconsin—Green Bay;* **Delores Vantrice Oates,** *Texas Southern University;* **Daniel Offer,** *University of Michigan;* **Shana Pack,** *Western Kentucky University;* **Michelle Paludi,** *Michelle Paludi & Associates;* **Joycelyn G. Parish,** *Kansas State University;* **Ian Payton,** *Bethune-Cookman College;* **Andrew Peiser,** *Mercy College;* **Peggy G. Perkins,** *University of Nevada;* **Richard Pisacreta,** *Ferris State University;* **Gayle Reed,** *University of Wisconsin—Madison;* **James D. Reid,** *Washington University;* **Vicki Ritts,** *St. Louis Community College;* **Anne Robertson,** *University of Wisconsin—Milwaukee;* **Melinda Russell-Stamp,** *Weber State University;* **Traci Sachteleben,** *Southwestern Illinois College;* **Tonie E. Santmire,** *University of Nebraska;* **Douglas Sawin,** *University of Texas;* **Mary Schumann,** *George Mason University;* **Paul Schwartz,** *Mount St. Mary College;* **Jane Sheldon,** *University of Michigan—Dearborn;* **Kim Shifren,** *Towson University;* **Susan Shonk,** *State University of New York;* **Ken Springer,** *Southern Methodist University;* **Ruby Takanishi,** *Foundation for Child Development;* **Patti Tolar,** *University of Houston;* **Vern Tyler,** *Western Washington University;* **Rhoda Unger,** *Montclair State College;* **Angela Vaughn,** *Wesley College;* **Elizabeth Vozzola,** *Saint Joseph's College;* **Barry Wagner,** *Catholic University of America;* **Rob Weisskrich,** *California State University—Fullerton;* **Deborah Welsh,** *University of Tennessee;* **Andrea Wesley,** *University of Southern Mississippi;* **Wanda Willard,** *State University of New York—Oswego;* **Carolyn L. Williams,** *University of Minnesota;* **Shelli Wynants,** *California State University.*

chapter 1

INTRODUCTION

chapter outline

1 The Historical Perspective

Learning Goal 1 Describe historical perspectives on adolescence

Early History

The Twentieth and Twenty-First Centuries

Stereotyping of Adolescents

A Positive View of Adolescence

2 Today's Adolescents in the United States and Around the World

Learning Goal 2 Discuss the experiences of adolescents in the United States and around the world

Adolescents in the United States

The Global Perspective

3 The Nature of Development

Learning Goal 3 Summarize the developmental processes, periods, transitions, and issues related to adolescence

Processes and Periods

Developmental Transitions

Developmental Issues

4 The Science of Adolescent Development

Learning Goal 4 Characterize the science of adolescent development

Science and the Scientific Method

Theories of Adolescent Development

Research in Adolescent Development

© Image Source/Getty Images RF

Jeffrey Dahmer's senior portrait in high school.
© AP Images

Jeffrey Dahmer had a troubled childhood and adolescence. His parents constantly bickered before they divorced. His mother had emotional problems and doted on his younger brother. He felt that his father neglected him, and he had been sexually abused by another boy when he was 8 years old. But the vast majority of people who suffered through a painful childhood and adolescence do not become serial killers as Dahmer did. Dahmer murdered his first victim in 1978 with a barbell and went on to kill 16 other individuals before being caught and sentenced to 15 life terms in prison.

A decade before Dahmer's first murder, Alice Walker, who would later win a Pulitzer Prize for her book *The Color Purple,* spent her days battling racism in Mississippi. Born the eighth child of Georgia sharecroppers, Walker knew the brutal effects of poverty. Despite the counts against her, she went on to become an award-winning novelist. Walker writes about people who, as she puts it, "make it, who come out of nothing. People who triumph."

Alice Walker.
© Noah Berger/AP Images

Consider also the changing life of Michael Maddaus (Broderick, 2003; Masten, Obradovic, & Burt, 2006). During his childhood and adolescence in Minneapolis, his mother drank heavily and his stepfather abused him. He coped by spending increasing time on the streets, being arrested more than 20 times for his delinquency, frequently being placed in detention centers, and rarely going to school. At 17, he joined the Navy and the experience helped him to gain self-discipline and hope. After his brief stint in the Navy, he completed a GED and began taking community college classes. However, he continued to have some setbacks with drugs and alcohol. A defining moment as an emerging adult came when he delivered furniture to a surgeon's home. The surgeon became interested in helping Michael, and his mentorship led Michael to volunteer at a rehabilitation center and then to get a job with a neurosurgeon. Eventually, he obtained his undergraduate degree, went to medical school, got married, and started a family. Today, Michael Maddaus is a successful surgeon. One of his most gratifying volunteer activities is telling his story to troubled youth.

Dr. Michael Maddaus, counseling a troubled youth.
Courtesy of Dr. Michael Maddaus

What leads one adolescent like Jeffrey Dahmer, so full of promise, to commit brutal acts of violence and another, like Alice Walker, to turn poverty and trauma into a rich literary harvest? How can we attempt to explain how someone like Michael Maddaus can turn a childhood and adolescence shattered by abuse and delinquency into a career as a successful surgeon while another person seems to come unhinged by life's minor hassles? Why is it that some adolescents are whirlwinds—successful in school, involved in a network of friends, and full of energy—whereas others hang out on the sidelines, mere spectators of life? If you have ever wondered what makes adolescents tick, you have asked yourself the central question we explore in this book.

preview

This edition of *Adolescence* is a window into the nature of adolescent development—your own and that of every other adolescent. In this first chapter, you will read about the history of the field of adolescent development, the characteristics of today's adolescents in the United States and the rest of the world, and the ways in which adolescents develop.

1 The Historical Perspective (LG1) Describe historical perspectives on adolescence

| Early History | The Twentieth and Twenty-First Centuries | Stereotyping of Adolescents | A Positive View of Adolescence |

What have the portraits of adolescence been like at different points in history? When did the scientific study of adolescence begin?

> In no order of things is adolescence the simple time of life.
>
> —JEAN ERSKINE STEWART
> *American writer, 20th century*

EARLY HISTORY

In early Greece, the philosophers Plato and Aristotle both commented about the nature of youth. According to Plato (fourth century B.C.), reasoning doesn't belong to childhood but rather first appears in adolescence. Plato thought that children should spend their time in sports and music, whereas adolescents should study science and mathematics.

Aristotle (fourth century B.C.) argued that the most important aspect of adolescence is the ability to choose, and that self-determination is a hallmark of maturity. Aristotle's emphasis on the development of self-determination is not unlike some contemporary views that see independence, identity, and career choice as the key themes of adolescence. Aristotle also recognized adolescents' egocentrism, commenting once that adolescents think they know everything and are quite sure about it.

In the Middle Ages, children and adolescents were viewed as miniature adults and were subjected to harsh discipline. In the eighteenth century, French philosopher Jean-Jacques Rousseau offered a more enlightened view of adolescence, restoring the belief that being a child or an adolescent is not the same as being an adult. Like Plato, Rousseau thought that reasoning develops in adolescence. He said that curiosity should especially be encouraged in the education of 12- to 15-year-olds. Rousseau argued that, from 15 to 20 years of age, individuals mature emotionally, and their selfishness is replaced by an interest in others. Thus, Rousseau concluded that development has distinct phases. But his ideas were speculative; not until the beginning of the twentieth century did the scientific exploration of adolescence begin.

THE TWENTIETH AND TWENTY-FIRST CENTURIES

The end of the nineteenth century and the early part of the twentieth century saw the invention of the concept we now call adolescence. Between 1890 and 1920, a number of psychologists, urban reformers, educators, youth workers, and counselors began to develop the concept. At this time, young people, especially boys, were increasingly viewed as passive and vulnerable—qualities previously associated only with adolescent females. When G. Stanley Hall's book on adolescence was published in 1904 (see the next section), it played a major role in restructuring thinking about adolescence.

G. Stanley Hall's Storm-and-Stress View
G. Stanley Hall (1844–1924) pioneered the scientific study of adolescence. In 1904, Hall published his ideas in a two-volume set: *Adolescence*. Hall was strongly influenced by Charles Darwin, the famous evolutionary

G. Stanley Hall, father of the scientific study of adolescence.
© Mary Evans/Sigmund Freud Copyrights/The Image Works

Anthropologist Margaret Mead in the Samoan Islands. *How does Mead's view of adolescence differ from G. Stanley Hall's?*
© AP Images

theorist. Applying Darwin's view to the study of adolescent development, Hall proposed that development is controlled primarily by biological factors.

The **storm-and-stress view** is Hall's concept that adolescence is a turbulent time charged with conflict and mood swings. In his view, adolescents' thoughts, feelings, and actions oscillate between conceit and humility, good intentions and temptation, happiness and sadness. An adolescent might be nasty to a peer one moment and kind the next moment; in need of privacy one moment but seconds later want companionship.

Hall was a giant in the field of adolescence. He began the theorizing, systematizing, and questioning that went beyond mere speculation and philosophizing. Indeed, we owe the beginnings of the scientific study of adolescence to Hall.

Margaret Mead's Sociocultural View of Adolescence

Anthropologist Margaret Mead (1928) studied adolescents on the South Sea island of Samoa. She concluded that the basic nature of adolescence is not biological, as Hall envisioned, but rather sociocultural. In cultures that provide a smooth, gradual transition from childhood to adulthood, which is the way adolescence is handled in Samoa, she found little storm and stress associated with the period. Mead's observations of Samoan adolescents revealed instead that their lives were relatively free of turmoil. Mead concluded that cultures that allow adolescents to observe sexual relations, see babies born, regard death as natural, do important work, engage in sex play, and know clearly what their adult roles will be tend to promote a relatively stress-free adolescence. However, in cultures like the United States, in which children are considered very different from adults and adolescents are restricted from full participation in society, the period is more likely to be stressful.

More than half a century after Mead's Samoan findings were published, her work was criticized as biased and error-prone (Freeman, 1983). Current criticism states that Samoan adolescence is more stressful than Mead suggested and that delinquency appears among Samoan adolescents just as it does among Western adolescents. Despite the controversy over Mead's findings, some researchers have defended Mead's work (Holmes, 1987).

The Inventionist View

Although adolescence has a biological base, as G. Stanley Hall argued, it also has a sociocultural base, as Margaret Mead maintained. Indeed, sociohistorical conditions contributed to the emergence of the concept of adolescence. According to the **inventionist view,** adolescence is a sociohistorical creation. Especially important in this view of adolescence are the sociohistorical circumstances at the beginning of the twentieth century, a time when legislation was enacted that ensured the dependency of youth and made their move into the economic sphere more manageable. These sociohistorical circumstances included a decline in apprenticeship; increased mechanization during the Industrial Revolution, which raised the level of skill required of laborers and necessitated a specialized division of labor; the separation of work and home; age-graded schools; urbanization; the appearance of youth groups such as the YMCA and the Boy Scouts; and the writings of G. Stanley Hall.

Schools, work, and economics are important dimensions of the inventionist view of adolescence. Some scholars argue that the concept of adolescence was invented mainly as a by-product of the movement to create a system of compulsory public education. In this view, the function of secondary schools is to transmit intellectual skills to youth. However, other scholars argue that the primary purpose of secondary schools is to deploy youth within the economic sphere. In this view, American society conferred the status of adolescence on youth through child-saving legislation (Lapsley, Enright, & Serlin, 1985).

Historians now call the period between 1890 and 1920 the "age of adolescence." In this period, lawmakers enacted a great deal of compulsory legislation aimed at youth. In virtually every state, they passed laws that excluded youth from most employment and required them to attend secondary school. Much of this legislation included extensive enforcement provisions. Two clear changes resulted from this legislation: decreased employment and increased school attendance among youth. From 1910 to 1930, the number of 10- to 15-year-olds who were gainfully employed dropped about 75 percent. In addition, between 1900 and 1930 the number of high school graduates increased substantially. Approximately 600 percent more individuals graduated from high school in 1930 than in 1900. Let's take a closer look at how conceptions of adolescence and experiences of adolescents changed with the changing times of the twentieth century and beyond.

storm-and-stress view G. Stanley Hall's concept that adolescence is a turbulent time charged with conflict and mood swings.

inventionist view The view that adolescence is a sociohistorical creation. Especially important in this view are the sociohistorical circumstances at the beginning of the twentieth century, a time when legislation was enacted that ensured the dependency of youth and made their move into the economic sphere more manageable.

Further Changes in the Twentieth Century and the Twenty-First Century

Discussing historical changes in the way individuals have experienced adolescence involves focusing on changes in generations. A *cohort* is a group of people who are born at a similar point in history and share similar experiences as a result. For example, individuals who experienced the Great Depression as teenagers are likely to differ from their counterparts who were teenagers in the 1950s during the optimistic aftermath of World War II. In discussing and conducting research on such historical variations, the term **cohort effects** is used, which refers to influences attributed to a person's year of birth, era, or generation, but not to actual chronological age (Schaie, 2012). Let's now explore potential cohort effects on the development of adolescents and emerging adults in the last half of the twentieth century and the early part of the twenty-first century.

1950s to 1970s   By 1950, the developmental period referred to as adolescence had come of age. It encompassed not only physical and social identities but a legal identity as well, for every state had developed special laws for youth between the ages of 16 and 20. Getting a college degree—the key to a good job—was on the minds of many adolescents during the 1950s, as was getting married, starting a family, and settling down to the life of luxury depicted in television commercials.

Although adolescents' pursuit of higher education continued into the 1960s, many African American adolescents not only were denied a college education but received an inferior secondary education as well. Ethnic conflicts in the form of riots and sit-ins became pervasive, and college-age adolescents were among the most vocal participants.

Political protests reached a peak in the late 1960s and early 1970s when millions of adolescents reacted violently to what they saw as the United States' immoral participation in the Vietnam War. By the mid-1970s, the radical protests of adolescents began to abate along with U.S. involvement in Vietnam. Political activism was largely replaced by increased concern for upward mobility through achievement in high school, college, or vocational training. Material interests began to dominate adolescents' motives again, while ideological challenges to social institutions began to recede.

During the 1970s the feminist movement changed both the description and the study of adolescence. In earlier years, descriptions of adolescence had pertained more to males than to females. The dual family and career objectives that female adolescents have today were largely unknown to female adolescents of the 1890s and early 1900s.

Millennials   In recent years, generations have been given labels by the popular culture. The most recent label is **Millennials,** which applies to the generation born after 1980—the first to come of age and enter emerging adulthood in the new millennium. Two characteristics of Millennials stand out: (1) their ethnic diversity, and (2) their connection to technology. A recent analysis also described Millennials as "confident, self-expressive, liberal, upbeat, and open to change" (Pew Research Center, 2010, p. 1).

Because their ethnic diversity is greater than that of prior generations, many Millennial adolescents and emerging adults are more tolerant and open-minded than their counterparts in previous generations. One survey indicated that 60 percent of today's adolescents say their friends include people from diverse ethnic groups (Teenage Research Unlimited, 2004). Another survey found that 60 percent of U.S. 18- to 29-year-olds had dated someone from a different ethnic group (Jones, 2005).

Another major change that characterizes Millennials is their dramatically increased use of media and technology (Calvert, 2015; Lever-Duffy & McDonald, 2015; Smaldino & others, 2015). According to one analysis,

> They are history's first "always connected" generation. Steeped in digital technology and social media, they treat their multi-tasking hand-held gadgets almost like a body part—for better or worse. More than 8-in-10 say they sleep with a cell phone glowing by the bed, poised to disgorge texts, phone calls, e-mails, songs, news, videos, games, and wake-up jingles. But sometimes convenience yields to temptation. Nearly two-thirds admit to texting while driving (Pew Research Center, 2010, p. 1).

As just indicated, there likely are both positive and negative aspects to how the technology revolution is affecting youth. Technology can provide an expansive, rich set of knowledge that, if used in a constructive way, can enhance adolescents' education (Taylor

© Stanca Sanda/Alamy

- - - - - - - - - - - ➤
developmental **connection**
Technology
When media multitasking is taken into account, 11- to 14-year-olds spend an average of almost 12 hours exposed to media per day. Connect to "Culture."

cohort effects Characteristics related to a person's year of birth, era, or generation rather than to his or her actual chronological age.

Millennials The generation born after 1980, the first to come of age and enter emerging adulthood in the new millennium. Two characteristics of Millennials stand out: (1) their ethnic diversity, and (2) their connection to technology.

& Fratto, 2012). However, the possible downside of technology was captured in a recent book, *The Dumbest Generation: How the Digital Age Stupefies Young Americans and Jeopardizes Our Future (Or, Don't Trust Anyone Under 30)*, written by Emory University English professor Mark Bauerlein (2008). Among the book's themes are that many of today's youth are more interested in information retrieval than information formation, don't read books and aren't motivated to read them, can't spell without spellcheck, and have become encapsulated in a world of iPhones, text messaging, Facebook, YouTube, MySpace, *Grand Theft Auto* (the video's introduction in 2008 had first-week sales of $500 million, dwarfing other movie and video sales), and other technology contexts. In terms of adolescents' retention of general information and historical facts, Bauerlein may be correct. And, in terms of some skills, such as adolescents' reading and writing, there is considerable concern—as evidenced by U.S. employers spending $1.3 billion a year to teach writing skills to employees (Begley & Interlandi, 2008). However, in terms of cognitive skills such as thinking and reasoning, he likely is wrong, given that IQ scores have been rising significantly since the 1930s (Flynn, 2013). Further, there is no research evidence that being immersed in a technological world of iPhones, Facebook, and YouTube impairs thinking skills (Begley & Interlandi, 2008). We will have much more to discuss about intelligence in the chapter on "The Brain and Cognitive Development" and about technology in the chapter on "Culture."

Another concern about the current generation of adolescents was voiced in *The Path to Purpose* by leading expert on adolescence William Damon (2008). Damon argues that many American adults have become effective at finding short-term solutions to various tasks and problems to get through their lives, and they are instilling the same desire for immediate gratification and shortsighted thinking in their children and adolescents. In Damon's view, although these short-term solutions (such as getting homework done, getting a good grade on a test tomorrow, and making a team) are often necessary adaptations to a situation, they can distract adolescents from thinking about their life purpose by exploring questions such as "What kind of person do I want to be?" "What do I want to do with my life?" "Why should I try to be successful?" Damon further emphasizes that parents can help to remedy this problem by presenting their adolescent sons and daughters with options and guiding them through choices, as well as talking with them about paths, themes, and issues in their own lives that they find meaningful and communicating how they have coped with setbacks and dilemmas. A recent study of Asian American ninth- and tenth-graders revealed that engagement in purpose on a daily basis was linked to daily family assistance (doing simple chores such as helping to make dinner), social role fulfillment (feeling like a good son or daughter), and participating in extracurricular activities (Kiang, 2012). Adolescent leisure time was negatively related to purpose in this study.

We will expand on Damon's concept of the path to purpose later in this edition in our discussions of identity exploration; moral development, values, and religion; and achievement and careers.

Although a majority of adolescents are making the journey of life from childhood to adulthood through adolescence in a competent manner, far too many are not. Laurence Steinberg (2014), in a book titled *Age of Opportunity*, called attention to some of the problems today's American adolescents are experiencing: U.S. adolescents' achievement in a number of academic areas, such as math and science, is far lower than their counterparts in many countries, especially Asian countries; the United States no longer has the highest college graduation rate and recently was not even in the top ten; approximately 20 percent of U.S. high school seniors engage in alcohol abuse; almost one-third of U.S. adolescent girls become pregnant by the age of 20; and adolescent obesity has increased threefold in recent decades. As we discuss adolescent development in other chapters, we will address problems such as these in much greater detail.

So far in this chapter we have considered the important sociohistorical circumstances surrounding the development of the concept of adolescence, evaluated how society has viewed adolescents at different points in history, and examined several major changes that characterize the current generation of adolescents. Next we will explore why we need to exercise caution in generalizing about the adolescents of any era. As you read about the stereotyping of adolescents, think about how the book we just described—*The Dumbest Generation* (Bauerlein, 2008)—might reflect this stereotyping.

---

developmental **connection**

Identity

Damon argues that too many youths today are indecisive and aren't making adequate progress toward identity resolution. Connect to "The Self, Identity, Emotion, and Personality."

STEREOTYPING OF ADOLESCENTS

A **stereotype** is a generalization that reflects our impressions and beliefs about a broad category of people. All stereotypes carry an image of what the typical member of a specific group is like. Once we assign a stereotype, it is difficult to abandon it, even in the face of contradictory evidence.

Stereotypes of adolescents are plentiful: "They say they want a job, but when they get one, they don't want to work." "They are all lazy." "All they think about is sex." "They are all into drugs, every last one of them." "Kids today don't have the moral fiber of my generation." "The problem with adolescents today is that they all have it too easy." "They are so self-centered." Indeed, during most of the twentieth century and the beginning of the twenty-first century, adolescents have been portrayed as abnormal and deviant rather than normal and nondeviant. Consider Hall's image of storm and stress. Consider, too, media portrayals of adolescents as rebellious, conflicted, faddish, delinquent, and self-centered. Especially distressing is that, when given evidence of youths' positive accomplishments—that a majority of adolescents participate in community service, for example—many adults either deny the facts or say that they must be exceptions (Youniss & Ruth, 2002).

Stereotyping of adolescents is so widespread that adolescence researcher Joseph Adelson (1979) coined the term **adolescent generalization gap,** which refers to generalizations that are based on information about a limited, often highly visible group of adolescents. Some adolescents develop confidence in their abilities despite negative stereotypes about them. And some individuals (like Alice Walker and Michael Maddaus, discussed at the beginning of this chapter), triumph over poverty, abuse, and other adversities.

A POSITIVE VIEW OF ADOLESCENCE

The negative stereotyping of adolescents is overdrawn (Lerner & others, 2013). In a cross-cultural study, Daniel Offer and his colleagues (1988) found no support for such a negative view. The researchers assessed the self-images of adolescents around the world—in the United States, Australia, Bangladesh, Hungary, Israel, Italy, Japan, Taiwan, Turkey, and West Germany—and discovered that at least 73 percent of the adolescents had a positive self-image. The adolescents were self-confident and optimistic about their future. Although there were some

Have adolescents been stereotyped too negatively? Explain.
© Tom Grill/Corbis RF

stereotype A generalization that reflects our impressions and beliefs about a broad group of people. All stereotypes refer to an image of what the typical member of a specific group is like.

adolescent generalization gap Adelson's concept of generalizations being made about adolescents based on information regarding a limited, often highly visible group of adolescents.

exceptions, as a group the adolescents were happy most of the time, enjoyed life, perceived themselves as capable of exercising self-control, valued work and school, expressed confidence in their sexuality, showed positive feelings toward their families, and felt they had the capacity to cope with life's stresses—not exactly a storm-and-stress portrayal of adolescence.

Old Centuries and New Centuries For much of the last century in the United States and other Western cultures, adolescence was perceived as a problematic period of the human life span in line with G. Stanley Hall's (1904) storm-and-stress portrayal. But as the research study just described indicates, a large majority of adolescents are not nearly as disturbed and troubled as the popular stereotype suggests.

The end of an old century and the beginning of the next has a way of stimulating reflection on what was, as well as visions of what could and should be. In the field of psychology in general, as in its subfield of adolescent development, psychologists have looked back at a century in which the discipline became too negative (Seligman & Csikszentmihalyi, 2000). Psychology had become an overly grim science in which people were too often characterized as being passive victims. Psychologists are now calling for a focus on the positive side of human experience and greater emphasis on hope, optimism, positive individual traits, creativity, and positive group and civic values, such as responsibility, nurturance, civility, and tolerance (King, 2013, 2014, 2016).

Generational Perceptions and Misperceptions Adults' perceptions of adolescents emerge from a combination of personal experience and media portrayals, neither of which produces an objective picture of how typical adolescents develop (Feldman & Elliott, 1990). Some of the readiness to assume the worst about adolescents likely involves the short memories of adults. Adults often portray today's adolescents as more troubled, less respectful, more self-centered, more assertive, and more adventurous than they were.

However, in matters of taste and manners, the youth of every generation have seemed radical, unnerving, and different from adults—different in how they look, how they behave, the music they enjoy, their hairstyles, and the clothing they choose. It is an enormous error to confuse adolescents' enthusiasm for trying on new identities and indulging in occasional episodes of outrageous behavior with hostility toward parental and societal standards. Acting out and boundary testing are time-honored ways in which adolescents move toward accepting, rather than rejecting, parental values.

Positive Youth Development What has been called positive youth development (PYD) in adolescence reflects the positive psychology approach. Positive youth development emphasizes the strengths of youth and the positive qualities and developmental trajectories that are desired for youth (Benson & Scales, 2011; Bowers & others, 2014). Positive youth development has especially been promoted by Jacqueline Lerner, Richard Lerner, and their colleagues (2009, 2013, 2015), who have recently described the "Five Cs" of PYD:

- *Competence*, which involves having a positive perception of one's actions in domain-specific areas—social, academic, physical, career, and so on
- *Confidence*, which consists of an overall positive sense of self-worth and self-efficacy (a sense that one can master a situation and produce positive outcomes)
- *Connection*, which is characterized by positive relationships with others, including family, peers, teachers, and individuals in the community
- *Character*, which comprises respect for societal rules, an understanding of right and wrong, and integrity
- *Caring/compassion*, which encompasses showing emotional concern for others, especially those in distress

Lerner and her colleagues (2009, 2013, 2015) conclude that to develop these five positive characteristics, youth need access to positive social contexts—such as youth development programs and organized youth activities—and competent people—such as caring teachers, community leaders, and mentors. We will further explore youth development programs in the chapter on "Peers, Romantic Relationships, and Lifestyles." In the chapter on "Problems in Adolescence and Emerging Adulthood," we will examine Peter Benson's emphasis on the importance of developmental assets in improving youth development, which reflects the positive youth development approach.

Wanting to Be Treated as an Asset

"Many times teenagers are thought of as a problem that no one really wants to deal with. People are sometimes intimidated and become hostile when teenagers are willing to challenge their authority. It is looked at as being disrespectful. Teenagers are, many times, not treated like an asset and as innovative thinkers who will be the leaders of tomorrow. Adults have the power to teach the younger generation about the world and allow them to feel they have a voice in it."

—Zula, age 16
Brooklyn, New York

Which perspective on adolescent development does this comment appear to take?

Review *Connect* Reflect

 LG1 Describe historical perspectives on adolescence

Review

- What was the early history of interest in adolescence?
- What characterized adolescence in the twentieth century, and how are adolescents changing in the twenty-first century?
- How extensively are adolescents stereotyped?
- What are the benefits of a positive view of adolescence?

Connect

- How have the social changes of the twentieth century, as described in this section, influenced society's views of adolescence?

Reflect *Your Own Personal Journey of Life*

- You likely experienced some instances of stereotyping as an adolescent. What are some examples of circumstances in which you think you were stereotyped as an adolescent?

---

2 Today's Adolescents in the United States and Around the World

 LG2 Discuss the experiences of adolescents in the United States and around the world

Adolescents in the United States

The Global Perspective

You should now have a good sense of the historical aspects of adolescence, the stereotyping of adolescents, and the importance of considering the positive aspects of many adolescents' development. Now let's further explore the current status of adolescents.

ADOLESCENTS IN THE UNITED STATES

Growing up has never been easy. In many ways, the developmental tasks today's adolescents face are no different from those of adolescents 50 years ago. For a large majority of youth, adolescence is not a time of rebellion, crisis, pathology, and deviance. Rather, it is a time of evaluation, decision making, commitment, and finding a place in the world.

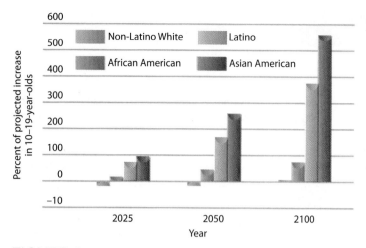

FIGURE 1

PROJECTED PERCENTAGE INCREASE IN ADOLESCENTS AGED 10–19, 2025–2100. An actual decrease in the percentage of non-Latino White adolescents 10 to 19 years of age is projected through 2050. By contrast, dramatic percentage increases are projected for Asian American (233% by 2050 and 530% by 2100) and Latino (175% by 2050 and 371% by 2100) adolescents.

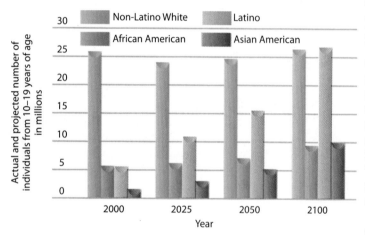

FIGURE 2

ACTUAL AND PROJECTED NUMBER OF U.S. ADOLESCENTS AGED 10–19, 2000–2100. In 2000, there were more than 25 million non-Latino White adolescents 10–19 years of age in the United States, while the numbers for ethnic minority groups were substantially lower. However, projections for 2025 through 2100 reveal dramatic increases in the number of Latino and Asian American adolescents to the point at which in 2100 it is projected that there will be more Latino than non-Latino White adolescents in the United States and more Asian American than African American adolescents.

contexts The settings in which development occurs. These settings are influenced by historical, economic, social, and cultural factors.

social policy A national government's course of action designed to influence the welfare of its citizens.

However, adolescents are not a homogeneous group. Most adolescents successfully negotiate the lengthy path to adult maturity, but a substantial minority do not (Duncan, Magnuson, & Votruba-Drzal, 2015; McLoyd, Purtell, & Hardaway, 2015). Socioeconomic, ethnic, cultural, gender, age, and lifestyle differences influence the developmental trajectory of every adolescent.

Social Contexts   Of special interest to researchers is how social contexts influence adolescent development (Leventhal, Dupere, & Shuey, 2015; Murry & others, 2015). **Contexts** are the settings in which development occurs; they are influenced by historical, economic, social, and cultural factors. To understand how important contexts are in adolescent development, consider the task of a researcher who wants to discover whether today's adolescents are more racially tolerant than those of a decade or two ago. Without reference to the historical, economic, social, and cultural aspects of race relations, adolescents' racial tolerance cannot be fully evaluated. Each adolescent's development occurs against a cultural backdrop of contexts that includes family, peers, school, religion, neighborhood, community, region, and nation, each with its cultural legacies (Crosnoe & Benner, 2015; King & Boyatzis, 2015; Rubin, Bukowski, & Bowker, 2015).

The cultural context for U.S. adolescents is changing with the dramatic increase in adolescents who have immigrated from Latino and Asian countries (Fuligni & Tsai, 2015; Murry & others, 2015). Figure 1 shows the projected percentage increases for non-Latino White, Latino, African American, and Asian American adolescents through 2100. Notice that Asian Americans are expected to be the fastest-growing ethnic group of adolescents, with a growth rate of more than 500 percent by 2100. Latino adolescents are projected to increase almost 400 percent by 2100. Figure 2 shows the actual numbers of adolescents in different ethnic groups in the year 2000, as well as the projected numbers through 2100. Notice that by 2100 Latino adolescents are expected to outnumber non-Latino White adolescents. Recent research indicates that a strong sense of family obligations may help immigrants achieve a positive pattern of adaptation (Telzer & others, 2013).

In recent years, there has been a growing realization that research on adolescent development needs to include more children from diverse ethnic groups (Schaefer, 2015). A special concern is the discrimination and prejudice experienced by ethnic minority children (Banks, 2014; Cushner, McClelland, & Safford, 2015; Marks & others, 2015; Renzetti & Kennedy-Bergen, 2015).

These changing social contexts receive special attention in this edition with separate chapters on families, peers, schools, work, and culture. As we see next, some experts argue that the social policy of the United States should place stronger emphasis on improving the contexts in which adolescents live.

Social Policy and Adolescents' Development   **Social policy** is the course of action designed by the national government to influence the welfare of its citizens. Currently, many researchers in adolescent development are attempting to design studies whose results will guide wise and effective social policy decision making (Fisher & others, 2013; Granger, Tseng, & Wilcox, 2014; Lerner & others, 2013, 2015).

Peter Benson and his colleagues (Benson, 2010; Benson & Scales, 2009, 2011; Benson & others, 2006) have argued that the United States has a fragmented social policy for youth that too often has focused only on the negative developmental deficits of adolescents, especially health-compromising behaviors such as drug use and delinquency, and not enough on

Peter Benson, President, Search Institute

Peter Benson (1946–2011) was the president of the Search Institute in Minneapolis from 1985 until his death in 2011. The Search Institute is an independent, nonprofit organization whose mission is to advance the well-being of children and adolescents. The Institute conducts applied scientific research, provides information about many aspects of improving adolescents' lives, gives support to communities, and trains people to work with youth.

Benson obtained his undergraduate degree in psychology from Augustana College, a master's degree in the psychology of religion from Yale University, and a Ph.D. in social psychology from the University of Denver. He directed a staff of 80 individuals at the Search Institute, lectured widely about youth, and consulted with a number of communities and organizations on adolescent issues.

Under Benson's direction, the Search Institute determined through research that a number of assets (such as family support and

Peter Benson talks with adolescents.
Photo courtesy of Search Institute®

good schools) serve as a buffer to prevent adolescents from developing problems and increase the likelihood that adolescents will competently make the transition from adolescence to adulthood.

positive strength-based approaches. According to Benson and his colleagues (2004, p. 783), a strength-based approach to social policy for youth

> adopts more of a wellness perspective, places particular emphasis on the existence of healthy conditions, and expands the concept of health to include the skills and competencies needed to succeed in employment, education, and life. It moves beyond the eradication of risk and deliberately argues for the promotion of well-being.

In their view, what the United States needs is a *developmentally attentive* youth policy, which would emphasize "the family, neighborhood, school, youth organization, places of work, and congregations as policy intervention points. Transforming schools into more developmentally rich settings, building linkages across multiple socializing institutions, launching community-wide initiatives organized around a shared vision of strength building, and expanding funding for quality out-of-school programs" would reflect this policy (Benson & others, 2004, p. 798). In a recent survey, only 20 percent of U.S. 15-year-olds reported having meaningful relationships outside of their family that are helping them to succeed in life (Search Institute, 2010).

Research indicates that youth benefit enormously when they have caring adults in their lives in addition to parents or guardians. Caring adults—such as coaches, neighbors, teachers, mentors, and after-school leaders—can serve as role models, confidantes, advocates, and resources. Caring-adult relationships are powerful when youth know they are respected, that they matter to the adult, and that the adult wants to be a resource in their lives (Benson, 2010). To read about Peter Benson's career and work, see the *Connecting with Careers* profile.

Children and adolescents who grow up in poverty represent a special concern (Duncan, Magnuson, & Votruba-Drzal, 2015; McLoyd, Purtell, & Hardaway, 2015). In 2013, 19.9 percent of U.S. children and adolescents lived in families with incomes below the poverty line, and African American (27.2 percent) and Latino (23.5 percent) families with children and adolescents had especially high rates of poverty (De Navas-Walt & Proctor, 2014). The U.S. poverty rate for children and adolescents was an increase from 2001 (16.2 percent) but down from a peak of 22.7 percent in 1993 and also down from 21.8 percent in 2012. One study revealed that the more years 7- to 13-year-olds spent living in poverty, the higher their physiological indices of stress were elevated (Evans & Kim, 2007).

developmental connection

Socioeconomic Status

Adolescents growing up in poverty experience widespread environmental inequalities. Connect to "Culture."

Doly Akter, Improving the Lives of Adolescent Girls in the Slums of Bangladesh

Doly Akter, age 17, lives in a slum in Dhaka, Bangladesh, where sewers overflow, garbage rots in the streets, and children are undernourished. Nearly two-thirds of young women in Bangladesh get married before they are 18. Doly organized a club supported by UNICEF in which girls go door-to-door to monitor the hygiene habits of households in their neighborhoods. The monitoring has led to improved hygiene and health in the families. Doly's group has also managed to stop several child marriages by meeting with parents and convincing them that the marriages are not in their daughters' best interests. When talking with parents in their neighborhoods, the girls in the club emphasize how important it is for their daughters to stay in school and how doing so will improve their future. Doly says the girls in her UNICEF group are far more aware of their rights than their mothers ever were (UNICEF, 2007).

Doly Akter, a 17-year-old from Bangladesh, is highly motivated to improve the lives of youth in her country.
Naser Siddique/UNICEF Bangladesh

What insights might U.S. adolescents draw from Doly's very different experience of growing up?

The U.S. figure of 19.9 percent of children and adolescents living in poverty is much higher than figures from other industrialized nations. For example, Canada has a child poverty rate of 9 percent and Sweden has a rate of 2 percent.

The well-being of adolescents should be one of America's foremost concerns (Lerner & others, 2015; Wigfield & others, 2015). The future of our youth is the future of our society. Adolescents who do not reach their full potential, who make fewer contributions to society than it needs, and who do not take their place in society as productive adults diminish our society's future.

THE GLOBAL PERSPECTIVE

developmental **connection**

Culture

Cross-cultural studies compare a culture with one or more other cultures. Connect to "Culture."

The way adolescence is presented in this text is based largely on the writing and research of scholars in the Western world, especially Europe and North America. In fact, some experts argue that adolescence is typically thought of in a "Eurocentric" way (Nsamenang, 2002). Others note that advances in transportation and telecommunication are spawning a global youth culture in which adolescents everywhere wear the same type of clothing and have similar hairstyles, listen to the same music, and use similar slang expressions (Larson, Wilson, & Rickman, 2009). A recent study of more than 11,000 adolescents from 18 countries living mainly in middle- and upper-income families found that in all of these countries adolescents were experiencing considerable stress about their future (Seiffge-Krenke, 2012). Most adolescents gave a high stress rating (1 or 2) to their fear of not being able to pursue the vocational training or academic studies they desired; the majority of adolescents assigned a medium stress rating (3 or 4) to their fear of becoming unemployed; and the majority of adolescents gave a low stress rating (7 or 8) to the potential difficulty they might have in combining their education or employment with marriage and family.

However, cultural differences among adolescents have by no means disappeared (Mistry & Dutta, 2015). Consider some of the following variations of adolescence around the world (Brown & Larson, 2002):

- Two-thirds of Asian Indian adolescents accept their parents' choice of a marital partner for them.

- In the Philippines, many female adolescents sacrifice their own futures by migrating to the city to earn money that they can send home to their families.

- Street youth in Kenya and other parts of the world learn to survive under highly stressful circumstances. In some cases abandoned by their parents, they may engage in delinquency or prostitution to provide for their economic needs.

- In the Middle East, many adolescents are not allowed to interact with the other sex, even in school.

- Youth in Russia are marrying earlier to legitimize sexual activity.

Thus, depending on the culture being observed, adolescence may involve many different experiences.

Rapid global change is altering the experience of adolescence, presenting new opportunities and challenges to young people's health and well-being. Around the world, adolescents' experiences may differ depending on their gender, families, schools, peers, and religion. However, some adolescent traditions remain the same in various cultures. Brad Brown and Reed Larson (2002) summarized some of these changes and traditions in the lives of the world's youth:

Boys-only Muslim school in the Middle East.
© Marwan Naamani/AFP/Getty Images

- *Health and well-being.* Adolescent health and well-being have improved in some areas but not in others. Overall, fewer adolescents around the world die from infectious diseases and malnutrition now than in the past (UNICEF, 2015). However, a number of adolescent health-compromising behaviors (especially illicit drug use and unprotected sex) continue to be at levels that place adolescents at risk for serious developmental problems. Extensive increases in the rates of HIV in adolescents have occurred in many sub-Saharan countries (UNICEF, 2014, 2015). Almost two-thirds of the adolescent deaths in the world occur in just two regions, sub-Saharan Africa and southeast Asia, yet only 42 percent of the world's adolescents live in those regions (Fatusi & Hindin, 2010).

- *Gender.* Around the world, the experiences of male and female adolescents continue to be quite different (UNICEF, 2014, 2015). Except in a few areas, such as Japan and Western countries, males have far greater access to educational opportunities than females do. In many countries, adolescent females have less freedom to pursue a variety of careers and to engage in various leisure activities than males do. Gender differences in sexual expression are widespread, especially in India, Southeast Asia, Latin America, and Arab countries, where there are far more restrictions on the sexual activity of adolescent females than on that of males. These gender differences do appear to be narrowing over time. In some countries, educational and career opportunities for women are expanding, and in some parts of the world control over adolescent girls' romantic and sexual relationships is decreasing.

- *Family.* One study revealed that in 12 countries around the world (located in Africa, Asia, Australia, Europe, the Middle East, and the Americas), adolescents validated the importance of parental support in their lives (McNeely & Barber, 2010). However, variations in families across countries also characterize adolescent development. In some countries, adolescents grow up in closely knit families with extended kin networks that provide a web of connections and reflect a traditional way of life. For example, in Arab countries, "adolescents are taught strict codes of conduct and loyalty" (Brown & Larson, 2002, p. 6). However, in Western countries such as the United States, many adolescents grow up in divorced families and stepfamilies. Parenting in many families in Western countries is less authoritarian than in the past. Other trends that are occurring in many countries around the world "include greater family mobility, migration to urban areas, family members working in distant cities or countries, smaller families, fewer extended-family households, and increases in mothers' employment" (Brown & Larson, 2002, p. 7). Unfortunately, many of these changes may reduce the ability of families to provide time and resources for adolescents.

Asian Indian adolescents in a marriage ceremony.
© Dan Gair/Photolibrary/Getty Images

Street youth in Rio de Janeiro.
© Ricardo Mazalan/AP Images

School. In general, the number of adolescents enrolled in school in developing countries is increasing. However, schools in many parts of the world—especially Africa, South Asia, and Latin America—still do not provide education to all adolescents (UNICEF, 2014, 2015). Indeed, there has been a decline in recent years in the percentage of Latin American adolescents who have access to secondary and higher education (Welti, 2002). Further, many schools do not provide students with the skills they need to be successful in adult work.

Peers. Some cultures give peers a stronger role in adolescence than other cultures do. In most Western nations, peers figure prominently in adolescents' lives, in some cases taking on responsibilities that are otherwise assumed by parents. Among street youth in South America, the peer network serves as a surrogate family that supports survival in dangerous and stressful settings. In other regions of the world, such as in Arab countries, peers have a very limited role, especially for girls.

In sum, adolescents' lives are characterized by a combination of change and tradition. Researchers have found both similarities and differences in the experiences of adolescents in different countries (Goodnow & Lawrence, 2015; Zhang & Sternberg, 2012), which we will discuss in more detail in other chapters.

Review Connect Reflect

LG2 Discuss the experiences of adolescents in the United States and around the world

Review
- What is the current status of today's adolescents? What is social policy? What are some important social policy issues concerning today's adolescents?
- How is adolescence changing for youth around the globe?

Connect
- Do you think adolescents in other countries experience stereotyping, as described earlier in the chapter? If so, why or how?

Reflect *Your Own Personal Journey of Life*
- How was your adolescence likely similar to, or different from, the adolescence of your parents and grandparents?

3 The Nature of Development

LG3 Summarize the developmental processes, periods, transitions, and issues related to adolescence

Processes and Periods

Developmental Transitions

Developmental Issues

In certain ways, each of us develops like all other individuals; in other ways, each of us is unique. Most of the time, our attention focuses on our individual uniqueness, but researchers who study development are drawn to our shared as well as our unique characteristics. As humans, we travel some common paths. Each of us—Leonardo da Vinci, Joan of Arc, George Washington, Martin Luther King, Jr., you, and I—walked at about the age of 1, talked at about the age of 2, engaged in fantasy play as a young child, and became more independent as a youth.

What do we mean when we speak of an individual's development? **Development** is the pattern of change that begins at conception and continues through the life span. Most development involves growth, although it also includes decay (as in death and dying). The pattern is complex because it is the product of several processes.

development The pattern of change that begins at conception and continues through the life span. Most development involves growth, although it also includes decay (as in death and dying).

PROCESSES AND PERIODS

Human development is determined by biological, cognitive, and socioemotional processes. It is often described in terms of periods.

Biological, Cognitive, and Socioemotional Processes **Biological processes** involve physical changes in an individual's body. Genes inherited from parents, the development of the brain, height and weight gains, advances in motor skills, and the hormonal changes of puberty all reflect biological processes. We discuss these biological processes extensively in the chapter on "Puberty, Health, and Biological Foundations."

Cognitive processes involve changes in an individual's thinking and intelligence. Memorizing a poem, solving a math problem, and imagining what being a movie star would be like all reflect cognitive processes. The chapter on "The Brain and Cognitive Development" discusses cognitive processes in detail.

Socioemotional processes involve changes in an individual's emotions, personality, relationships with others, and social contexts. Talking back to parents, aggression toward peers, assertiveness, enjoyment of social events such as an adolescent's senior prom, and gender-role orientation all reflect the role of socioemotional processes. Nine chapters focus on socioemotional processes in adolescent development.

Biological, cognitive, and socioemotional processes are intricately interwoven. Socioemotional processes shape cognitive processes, cognitive processes advance or restrict socioemotional processes, and biological processes influence cognitive processes. Although you will read about these processes in separate chapters of this edition, keep in mind that you are studying about the development of an integrated human being who has only one interdependent mind and body (see Figure 3).

Nowhere is the connection across biological, cognitive, and socioemotional processes more obvious than in two rapidly emerging fields:

· *Developmental cognitive neuroscience*, which explores links between development, cognitive processes, and the brain (Casey, 2015)
· *Developmental social neuroscience*, which examines connections between socioemotional processes, development, and the brain (Blakemore & Mills, 2014; Steinberg, 2015a, b)

Periods of Development Human development is commonly described in terms of periods. We consider developmental periods that occur in childhood, adolescence, and adulthood. Approximate age ranges are given for the periods to provide a general idea of when they begin and end.

Childhood Childhood includes the prenatal period, infancy, early childhood, and middle and late childhood.

The **prenatal period** is the time from conception to birth—approximately 9 months. It is a time of tremendous growth—from a single cell to an organism complete with a brain and behavioral capabilities.

Infancy is the developmental period that extends from birth to 18 or 24 months of age. Infancy is a time of extreme dependency on adults. Many psychological activities—for example, language, symbolic thought, sensorimotor coordination, social learning, and parent-child relationships—begin in this period.

Early childhood is the developmental period that extends from the end of infancy to about 5 or 6 years of age, sometimes called the preschool years. During this time, young children learn to become more self-sufficient and to care for themselves. They develop school readiness (following instructions, identifying letters) and spend many hours in play and with peers. First grade typically marks the end of early childhood.

Middle and late childhood is the developmental period that extends from the age of about 6 to 10 or 11 years of age. In this period, sometimes called the elementary school years, children master the fundamental skills of reading, writing, and arithmetic, and they are formally exposed to the larger world and its culture. Achievement becomes a central theme of the child's development, and self-control increases.

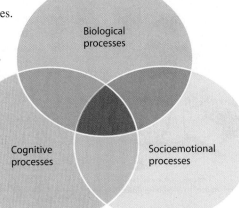

FIGURE 3

DEVELOPMENTAL CHANGES ARE THE RESULT OF BIOLOGICAL, COGNITIVE, AND SOCIOEMOTIONAL PROCESSES. These processes interact as individuals develop.

developmental connection

Brain Development

Might there be a link between changes in the adolescent's brain and risk taking and sensation seeking? Connect to "The Brain and Cognitive Development."

biological processes Physical changes in an individual's body.

cognitive processes Changes in an individual's thinking and intelligence.

socioemotional processes Changes in an individual's personality, emotions, relationships with other people, and social contexts.

prenatal period The time from conception to birth.

infancy The developmental period that extends from birth to 18 or 24 months of age.

early childhood The developmental period extending from the end of infancy to about 5 or 6 years of age; sometimes called the preschool years.

middle and late childhood The developmental period extending from about 6 to about 10 or 11 years of age; sometimes called the elementary school years.

"This is the path to adulthood. You're here."
© Robert Weber/The New Yorker Collection/cartoonbank.com.

One's children's children's children. Look back to us as we look to you; we are related by our imaginations. If we are able to touch, it is because we have imagined each other's existence, our dreams running back and forth along a cable from age to age.

—ROGER ROSENBLATT

Contemporary American writer

adolescence The developmental period of transition from childhood to adulthood; it involves biological, cognitive, and socioemotional changes. Adolescence begins at approximately 10 to 13 years of age and ends in the late teens.

early adolescence The developmental period that corresponds roughly to the middle school or junior high school years and includes most pubertal change.

late adolescence The developmental period that corresponds approximately to the latter half of the second decade of life. Career interests, dating, and identity exploration are often more pronounced in late adolescence than in early adolescence.

early adulthood The developmental period beginning in the late teens or early twenties and lasting through the thirties.

middle adulthood The developmental period that is entered at about 35 to 45 years of age and exited at about 55 to 65 years of age.

late adulthood The developmental period that lasts from about 60 to 70 years of age until death.

Adolescence As our developmental timetable suggests, considerable development and experience have occurred before an individual reaches adolescence. No girl or boy enters adolescence as a blank slate, with only a genetic code to determine thoughts, feelings, and behaviors. Rather, the combination of heredity, childhood experiences, and adolescent experiences determines the course of adolescent development. As you read this chapter and others, keep in mind the continuity of development between childhood and adolescence.

Defining adolescence requires a consideration not only of age but also of sociohistorical influences: recall our discussion of the inventionist view of adolescence. With the sociohistorical context in mind, we define **adolescence** as the period of transition between childhood and adulthood that involves biological, cognitive, and socioemotional changes. A key task of adolescence is preparation for adulthood. Indeed, the future of any culture hinges on how effective this preparation is.

Although the age range of adolescence can vary with cultural and historical circumstances, in the United States and most other cultures today adolescence begins at approximately 10 to 13 years of age and ends in the late teens. The biological, cognitive, and socioemotional changes of adolescence range from the development of sexual functions to abstract thinking processes to independence.

Increasingly, developmentalists describe adolescence in terms of early and late periods. **Early adolescence** corresponds roughly to the middle school or junior high school years and includes most pubertal change. **Late adolescence** refers approximately to the latter half of the second decade of life. Career interests, dating, and identity exploration are often more pronounced in late adolescence than in early adolescence. Researchers often specify whether their results generalize to all of adolescence or are specific to early or late adolescence.

The old view of adolescence was that it is a singular, uniform period of transition resulting in entry to the adult world. Current approaches emphasize a variety of transitions and events that define the period, as well as their timing and sequence. For instance, puberty and school events are key transitions that signal entry into adolescence; completing school and taking one's first full-time job are key transitional events that signal an exit from adolescence and entry into adulthood.

Today, developmentalists do not believe that change ends with adolescence (Park & others, 2014). Remember that development is defined as a lifelong process. Adolescence is part of the life course and as such is not an isolated period of development. Though it has some unique characteristics, what takes place during adolescence is connected with development and experiences in both childhood and adulthood (Cicchetti & Toth, 2015).

Adulthood Like childhood and adolescence, adulthood is not a homogeneous period of development. Developmentalists often describe three periods of adult development: early adulthood, middle adulthood, and late adulthood.

Early adulthood usually begins in the late teens or early twenties and lasts through the thirties. It is a time of establishing personal and economic independence, and career development intensifies.

Middle adulthood begins at approximately 35 to 45 years of age and ends at some point between approximately 55 and 65 years of age. This period is especially important in the lives of adolescents whose parents are either in, or about to enter, this adult period. Middle adulthood is a time of increasing interest in transmitting values to the next generation, deeper reflection about the meaning of life, and enhanced concern about a decline in physical functioning and health. In the "Families" chapter, we see how the maturation of both adolescents and parents contributes to the parent-adolescent relationship.

Eventually, the rhythm and meaning of the human life span wend their way to **late adulthood,** the developmental period that lasts from approximately 60 or 70 years of age until death. This is a time of adjustment to decreasing strength and health and to retirement and reduced income. Reviewing one's life and adapting to changing social roles also characterize late adulthood, as do lessened responsibility and increased freedom. Figure 4 summarizes the developmental periods in the human life span and their approximate age ranges.

DEVELOPMENTAL TRANSITIONS

Developmental transitions are often important junctures in people's lives. Such transitions include moving from the prenatal period to birth and infancy, from infancy to early childhood,

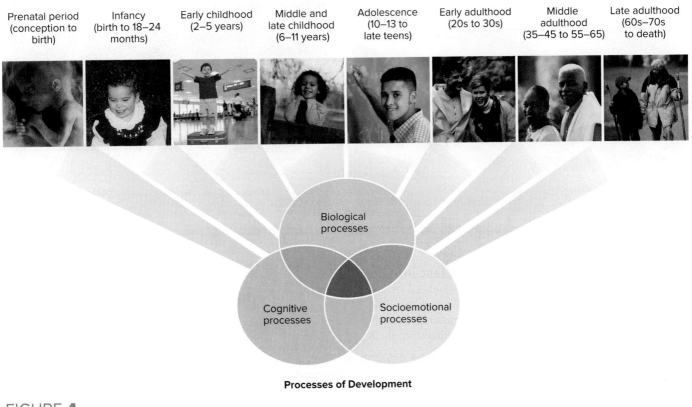

Periods of Development

| Prenatal period (conception to birth) | Infancy (birth to 18–24 months) | Early childhood (2–5 years) | Middle and late childhood (6–11 years) | Adolescence (10–13 to late teens) | Early adulthood (20s to 30s) | Middle adulthood (35–45 to 55–65) | Late adulthood (60s–70s to death) |

Biological processes

Cognitive processes

Socioemotional processes

Processes of Development

FIGURE 4

PROCESSES AND PERIODS OF DEVELOPMENT. The unfolding of life's periods of development is influenced by the interaction of biological, cognitive, and socioemotional processes.

(left to right) © Brand X Pictures/PunchStock RF; Courtesy of Dr. John Santrock; © Digital Vision/Alamy RF; © Corbis RF; © Comstock/PictureQuest RF; © Corbis RF; © Corbis RF; © Corbis RF

and from early childhood to middle and late childhood. For our purposes, two important transitions are from childhood to adolescence and from adolescence to adulthood. Let's explore these transitions.

Childhood to Adolescence The transition from childhood to adolescence involves a number of biological, cognitive, and socioemotional changes. Among the biological changes are the growth spurt, hormonal changes, and sexual maturation that come with puberty. In early adolescence, changes take place in the brain that allow for more advanced thinking. Also at this time, adolescents begin to stay up later at night and sleep later in the morning.

Among the cognitive changes that occur during the transition from childhood to adolescence are thinking more abstractly, idealistically, and logically. In response to these changes, parents place more responsibility for decision making on the young adolescent's shoulders, although too often adolescents make decisions that are filled with risk, especially when they are with their peers. Compared with children, adolescents process information faster, can sustain their attention longer, and engage in more effective executive function, which includes monitoring and managing their cognitive resources, exercising cognitive control, and delaying gratification.

Among the socioemotional changes adolescents undergo are a quest for independence, conflict with parents, and a desire to spend more time with peers. Conversations with friends become more intimate and include more self-disclosure. As children enter adolescence, they attend schools that are larger and more impersonal than their neighborhood elementary schools. Achievement becomes more serious business, and academic challenges increase. Also at this time, increased sexual maturation produces a much greater interest in romantic relationships. Young adolescents also experience more dramatic mood swings than they did when they were children.

In sum, the transition from childhood to adolescence is complex and multidimensional, involving change in many different aspects of an individual's life. Negotiating this transition successfully requires considerable adaptation and thoughtful, sensitive support from caring adults.

developmental **connection**

Schools

The transition to middle or junior high school can be difficult and stressful for many students. Connect to "Schools."

Developmental transitions from childhood to adolescence involve biological, cognitive, and socioemotional changes. *What are some of these changes?*
© Ariel Skelley/Blend Images LLC/Getty Images RF

Adolescence to Adulthood Another important transition occurs from adolescence to adulthood (Arnett, 2012, 2014a). It has been said that adolescence begins in biology and ends in culture. That is, the transition from childhood to adolescence begins with the onset of pubertal maturation, whereas the transition from adolescence to adulthood is determined by cultural standards and experiences.

Emerging Adulthood Recently, the transition from adolescence to adulthood has been referred to as **emerging adulthood,** which takes place from approximately 18 to 25 years of age. Experimentation and exploration characterize the emerging adult. At this point in their development, many individuals are still exploring which career path they want to follow, what they want their identity to be, and which lifestyle they want to adopt (for example, single, cohabiting, or married).

Jeffrey Arnett (2006, 2014a, b) described five key features that characterize emerging adulthood:

· *Identity exploration*, especially in love and work. Emerging adulthood is the time during which key changes in identity take place for many individuals (Schwartz & others, 2012).
· *Instability*. Residential changes peak during emerging adulthood, a time during which there also is often instability in love, work, and education.
· *Self-focused*. According to Arnett (2006, p. 10), emerging adults "are self-focused in the sense that they have little in the way of social obligations, little in the way of duties and commitments to others, which leaves them with a great deal of autonomy in running their own lives."

emerging adulthood The developmental period occurring from approximately 18 to 25 years of age; this transitional period between adolescence and adulthood is characterized by experimentation and exploration.

connecting with emerging adults

Chris Barnard

Emerging adult Chris Barnard is a single 24-year-old. Two years ago he moved back in with his parents, worked as a temp, and thought about his next step in life. One of the temp jobs became permanent. Chris now works with a trade association in Washington, D.C. With the exception of technology, he says that his life is similar to what his parents' lives must have been like as they made the transition to adulthood.

Chris' living arrangements reflect the "instability" characteristic of emerging adulthood. While in college, he changed dorms each

year; then as a senior he moved to an off-campus apartment. Following college, Chris moved back home, then moved to another apartment, and now is in yet another apartment. In Chris' words, "This is going to be the longest stay I've had since I went to college. . . . I've sort of settled in" (Jayson, 2006, p. 2D).

Would you characterize Chris' life experiences since college as continuous or discontinuous?

Do Health and Well-Being Change in Emerging Adulthood?

What characterizes the health and well-being of emerging adults as compared with adolescents? John Schulenberg and his colleagues (Johnston, O'Malley, & Bachman, 2004; Schulenberg & Zarrett, 2006) have examined this question. For the most part, life does get better for most emerging adults. For example, Figure 5 shows a steady increase in self-reported well-being from 18 through 26 years of age. Figure 6 indicates that risk taking decreases during the same time frame.

Why does the health and well-being of emerging adults improve over their adolescent levels? One possible answer is the increasing choices individuals have in their daily living and life decisions during emerging adulthood. This increase can lead to more opportunities for individuals to exercise self-control in their lives. Also, as we discussed earlier, emerging adulthood provides an opportunity for individuals who engaged in problem behavior during adolescence to get their lives together. However, the lack of structure and support that often characterizes emerging adulthood can produce a downturn in health and well-being for some individuals (Schulenberg & Zarrett, 2006).

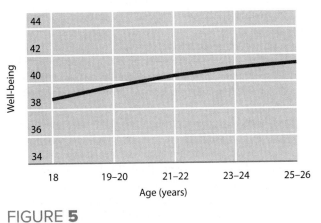

FIGURE 5

WELL-BEING THROUGH EMERGING ADULTHOOD. *Note:* Scores are based on a combination of self-esteem (8 items), self-efficacy (5 items), and social support (6 items); possible responses range from disagree (1) to agree (5).

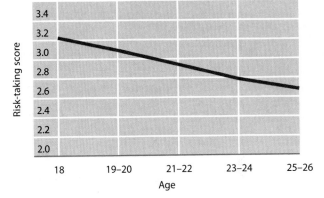

FIGURE 6

RISK TAKING THROUGH EMERGING ADULTHOOD. *Note:* The two Risk-Taking Scale items ranged from 1 (disagree) to 5 (agree). The risk-taking score was the average of the two items that assessed whether the emerging adult got a kick out of doing things that are a little dangerous and enjoyed doing something a little risky.

What factors can emerging adults control that might influence whether their health and well-being improve over their adolescent levels?

· *Feeling in-between.* Many emerging adults don't consider themselves adolescents or full-fledged adults. In a recent national survey, 45 percent of U.S. 18- to 29-year-olds reported that they considered themselves in-between but in the course of their twenties they steadily increased their self-perception of being a full-fledged adult (Arnett, 2012).

· *The age of possibilities, a time when individuals have an opportunity to transform their lives.* Arnett (2006) describes two ways in which emerging adulthood is the age of possibilities: (1) many emerging adults are optimistic about their future; and (2) for emerging adults who have experienced difficult times while growing up, emerging adulthood presents an opportunity to reorient their lives in a more positive direction.

Recent research indicates that these five aspects characterize not only individuals in the United States as they make the transition from adolescence to early adulthood, but also their counterparts in European countries and Australia (Sirsch & others, 2009). Although emerging adulthood does not characterize development in all cultures, it does appear to occur in those in which assuming adult roles and responsibilities is postponed (Kins & Beyers, 2010).

Does life get better for individuals when they become emerging adults? To explore this question, see the *Connecting with Health and Well-Being* interlude.

Becoming an Adult   Determining just when an individual becomes an adult is difficult. In the United States, the most widely recognized marker of entry into adulthood is holding a more or less permanent, full-time job, which usually happens when an individual finishes school—high school for some, college for others, graduate or professional school for still others. However, other criteria are far from clear. Economic independence is one marker of adult status, but achieving it is often a long process. College graduates are increasingly returning to live with their parents as they attempt to establish themselves economically. A longitudinal study found that at age 25 only slightly more than half of the participants were fully financially independent of their family of origin (Cohen & others, 2003). The most dramatic findings in this study, though, involved the extensive variability in the individual trajectories of adult roles across ten years from 17 to 27 years of age; many of the participants moved back and forth between increasing and decreasing economic dependency. One study revealed that continued co-residence with parents during emerging adulthood slowed down the process of becoming a self-sufficient and independent adult (Kins & Beyers, 2010).

Other studies show that taking responsibility for oneself is likely an important marker of adult status for many individuals (Arnett, 2012, 2013; Lowe & others, 2012). In one study, more than 70 percent of college students said that being an adult means accepting responsibility for the consequences of one's actions, deciding on one's own beliefs and values, and establishing a relationship with parents as an equal adult (Arnett, 1995). In another study, both parents and college students agreed that taking responsibility for one's actions and developing emotional control are important aspects of becoming an adult (Nelson & others, 2007). However, parents and college students didn't always agree on other aspects of what it takes to become an adult. For example, parents were more likely than college students to emphasize that driving safely and not getting drunk are important aspects of becoming an adult.

At some point in the late teens through the early twenties, then, individuals reach adulthood. In becoming an adult, they accept responsibility for themselves, become capable of making independent decisions, and gain financial independence from their parents (Arnett, 2006, 2014a). The new freedoms and responsibilities of emerging adulthood represent major changes in individuals' lives. Keep in mind, though, that considerable continuity still glues adolescence and adulthood together. For example, a longitudinal study found that religious views and behaviors of emerging adults were especially stable and that their attitudes toward drugs were stable to a lesser degree (Bachman & others, 2002).

What we have said so far about the determinants of adult status mainly addresses individuals in industrialized societies, especially the United States. In developing countries, marriage is often a more significant marker for entry into adulthood than in the United States, and it usually occurs much earlier than in the United States (Arnett, 2007, 2014a; Eccles, Brown, & Templeton, 2008). Thus, some developmentalists argue that the term "emerging adulthood" applies more to Western countries such as the United States and European countries, and to some Asian countries such as Japan, than to developing countries (Arnett, 2007). In a recent study, the majority of 18- to 26-year-olds in India felt that they had achieved adulthood (Seiter & Nelson, 2011).

Contextual variations in emerging adulthood also may occur in cultures and sub-populations within a country (Arnett & Brody, 2008). For example, in the United States, "Mormons marry early and begin having children . . . so they have a briefer period of emerging adulthood before taking on adult roles" (Arnett, 2004, p. 22). Also, a recent study revealed that at-risk youth entered emerging adulthood slightly earlier than the general population of youth (Lisha & others, 2012). Further, in some countries, such as China and India, emerging adulthood is more likely to occur in urban areas than in rural areas because young people in the urban areas of these countries "marry later, have children later, obtain more education, and have a greater range of occupational and recreational opportunities" (Arnett, 2004, p. 23).

What determines an individual's well-being in the transition to adulthood? In the view of Jacquelynne Eccles and her colleagues (Eccles, Brown, & Templeton, 2008; Eccles & Gootman, 2002), three types of assets are especially important in making a competent transition through adolescence and emerging adulthood: intellectual development, psychological/emotional development, and social development. Figure 7 provides examples of these three types of assets.

Intellectual development

Knowledge of essential life and vocational skills

Rational habits of mind—critical thinking and reasoning skills

Good decision-making skills

In-depth knowledge of more than one culture

Knowledge of skills necessary to navigate through multiple cultures

School success

Psychological and emotional development

Good mental health including positive self-regard

Good emotional self-regulation and coping skills

Good conflict resolution skills

Mastery motivation and positive achievement motivation

Confidence in one's personal efficacy

Planfulness

Sense of personal autonomy/responsibility for self

Optimism coupled with realism

Coherent and positive personal and social identity

Prosocial and culturally sensitive values

Spirituality and/or a sense of purpose in life

Strong moral character

Social development

Connectedness—perceived good relationships and trust with parents, peers, and some other adults

Sense of social place/integration—being connected and valued by larger social networks

Attachment to prosocial/conventional institutions such as school, church, out-of-school youth development centers

Ability to navigate in multiple cultural contexts

Commitment to civic engagement

FIGURE **7**

PERSONAL ASSETS THAT FACILITATE POSITIVE YOUTH DEVELOPMENT.

Resilience At the beginning of the chapter, you read the captivating story of Michael Maddaus, who got his life together as an emerging adult following a troubled childhood and adolescence. Michael Maddaus was resilient. What do we mean by the term *resilience?* **Resilience** refers to adapting positively and achieving successful outcomes in the face of significant risks and adverse circumstances. In Project Competence, Ann Masten and her colleagues (Masten, 2009, 2011, 2013, 2014a, b, c; Masten, Obradovic, & Burt, 2006; Masten & Tellegen, 2012; Masten & others, 2015) examined the resilience of individuals from childhood through adulthood. They found that adults who experienced considerable adversity while growing up but became competent young adults were characterized by certain individual and contextual factors. Competence was assessed in areas such as achievement, conduct, and social relationships. In emerging adulthood (assessed at 17 to 23 years of age), individuals who became competent after experiencing difficulties while growing up were more intelligent, experienced higher parenting quality, and were less likely to have grown up in poverty or low-income circumstances than their counterparts who did not become competent as emerging adults.

What characterizes emerging adulthood? Even when emerging adults have experienced a troubled childhood and adolescence, what are some factors that can help them become competent?
© Juice Images/Getty Images RF

A further analysis focused on individuals who were still showing maladaptive patterns in emerging adulthood but had gotten their lives together by the time they were in the late twenties and early thirties. The three characteristics shared by these "late-bloomers" were support by adults, being planful, and showing positive aspects of autonomy. In other longitudinal research, "military service, marriage and romantic relationships, higher education, religious affiliations, and work opportunities may provide turning-point opportunities for changing the life course during emerging adulthood" (Masten, Obradovic, & Burt, 2006, p. 179).

A recent review and analysis of research on resilience in the transition to adulthood concluded that the increased freedom that is available to emerging adults in Western society places a premium on the capacity to plan ahead, delay gratification, and make positive choices (Burt & Paysnick, 2012). Also emphasized in resilient adaptation during emerging adulthood was the importance of forming positive close relationships—to some degree with parents, but more often with supportive romantic partners, close friends, and mentors.

Is Adolescence Taking Too Long? Joseph and Claudia Allen (2009) titled their book *Escaping the Endless Adolescence: How We Can Help Our Teenagers Grow Up Before They Grow Old*, and opened the book with a chapter titled, "Is Twenty-five the New Fifteen?" They argue that in recent decades adolescents have experienced a world that places more challenges on maturing into a competent adult. In their words (p. 17):

> Generations ago, fourteen-year-olds used to drive, seventeen-year-olds led armies, and even average teens contributed labor and income that helped keep their families afloat. While facing other problems, those teens displayed adultlike maturity far more quickly than today's, who are remarkably well kept, but cut off from most of the responsibility, challenge, and growth-producing feedback of the adult world. Parents of twenty-somethings used to lament, "They grow up so fast." But that seems to be replaced with, "Well, . . . Mary's living at home a bit while she sorts things out."

The Allens conclude that what is happening to the current generation of adolescents is that after adolescence, they are experiencing "more adolescence" instead of adequately being launched into the adult years. Even many adolescents who have gotten good grades and then as emerging adults continued to achieve academic success in college later find themselves in their mid-twenties not having a clue about how to find a meaningful job, manage their finances, or live independently.

The Allens offer the following suggestions for helping adolescents become more mature on their way to adulthood:

· *Provide them with opportunities to be contributors.* Help them move away from being consumers by creating more effective work experiences (quality work apprenticeships, for example), or service learning opportunities that allow adolescents to make meaningful contributions.

developmental **connection**

Community

Service learning is linked to many positive outcomes for adolescents. Connect to "Moral Development, Values, and Religion."

resilience Adapting positively and achieving successful outcomes in the face of significant risks and adverse circumstances.

What are some strategies parents can use to help their adolescents become more competent and mature as they move toward adulthood?
© Jupiterimages/Getty Images

- *Give candid, quality feedback to adolescents.* Don't just shower praise and material things on them, but let them see how the real world works. Don't protect them from criticism, constructive or negative. Protecting them in this way only leaves them ill-equipped to deal with the ups and downs of the real world of adulthood.
- *Create positive adult connections with adolescents.* Many adolescents deny that they need parental support or attachment to parents, but to help them develop maturity on the way to adulthood, they do. Exploring a wider social world than in childhood, adolescents need to be connected to parents and other adults in positive ways to be able to handle autonomy maturely.
- *Challenge adolescents to become more competent.* Adults need to do fewer things for adolescents that they can accomplish for themselves. Providing adolescents with opportunities to engage in tasks that are just beyond their current level of ability stretches their minds and helps them to make progress along the road to maturity.

DEVELOPMENTAL ISSUES

Is development due more to nature (heredity) or to nurture (environment)? Is it more continuous and smooth or discontinuous and stage-like? Is it due more to early experience or to later experience? These are three important issues raised in the study of adolescent development.

Nature and Nurture   The **nature-nurture issue** involves the debate about whether development is primarily influenced by nature or nurture. Nature refers to an organism's biological inheritance, nurture to its environmental experiences. "Nature" proponents claim that the most important influence on development is biological inheritance. "Nurture" proponents claim that environmental experiences are the most important influence.

According to the nature advocates, just as a sunflower grows in an orderly way—unless flattened by an unfriendly environment—so does the human grow in an orderly way. The range of environments can be vast, but the nature approach argues that evolutionary and genetic processes produce commonalities in growth and development (Brooker, 2015; Mader & Windelspecht, 2016). We walk before we talk, speak one word before two words, grow rapidly in infancy and less so in early childhood, experience a rush of sexual hormones in puberty, reach the peak of our physical strength in late adolescence and early adulthood, and then physically decline. The nature proponents acknowledge that extreme environments—those that are psychologically barren or hostile—can depress development. However, they believe that basic growth tendencies are genetically wired into humans (Brooker, 2016; Cowan, 2015).

By contrast, other psychologists emphasize the importance of nurture, or environmental experiences, in development (Thompson, 2015). Experiences run the gamut from the individual's biological environment—nutrition, medical care, drugs, and physical accidents—to the social environment—family, peers, schools, community, media, and culture.

Some adolescent development researchers maintain that, historically, too much emphasis has been placed on the biological changes of puberty as determinants of adolescent psychological development. They recognize that biological change is an important dimension of the transition from childhood to adolescence, one that is found in all primate species and in all cultures throughout the world. However, they argue that social contexts (nurture) play important roles in adolescent psychological development as well, roles that until recently have not been given adequate attention (McLoyd, Purtell, & Hardaway, 2015).

Continuity and Discontinuity   Think for a moment about your development. Was your growth into the person you are today gradual, like the slow, cumulative growth of a seedling into a giant oak? Or did you experience sudden, distinct changes during your growth, like the remarkable transformation from a caterpillar into a butterfly (see Figure 8)? The **continuity-discontinuity issue** focuses on the extent to which development involves gradual,

- - - - - - - - - ➤

developmental **connection**

Nature and Nurture

The epigenetic view emphasizes the ongoing, bidirectional interchange between heredity and environment. Connect to "Puberty, Health, and Biological Foundations."

nature-nurture issue Issue involving the debate about whether development is primarily influenced by an organism's biological inheritance (nature) or by its environmental experiences (nurture).

continuity-discontinuity issue Issue regarding whether development involves gradual, cumulative change (continuity) or distinct stages (discontinuity).

early-later experience issue Issue focusing on the degree to which early experiences (especially early in childhood) or later experiences are the key determinants of development.

cumulative change (continuity) or distinct stages (discontinuity). For the most part, developmentalists who emphasize experience have described development as a gradual, continuous process; those who emphasize nature have described development as a series of distinct stages.

In terms of continuity, a child's first word, while seemingly an abrupt, discontinuous event, is actually the result of weeks and months of growth and practice. Similarly, puberty, while also appearing to be abrupt and discontinuous, is actually a gradual process that occurs over several years.

In terms of discontinuity, each person is described as passing through a sequence of stages in which change is qualitatively, rather than quantitatively, different. As the oak moves from seedling to giant tree, it becomes more oak—its development is continuous. As a caterpillar changes into a butterfly, it does not become more caterpillar; it becomes a different kind of organism—its development is discontinuous. For example, at some point a child moves from not being able to think abstractly about the world to being able to. This is a qualitative, discontinuous change in development, not a quantitative, continuous change.

Early and Later Experience   Another important debate is the **early-later experience issue,** which focuses on the degree to which early experiences (especially those that take place early in childhood) or later experiences are the key determinants of development (Ellwardt & others, 2015; Thompson, 2015). That is, if infants or young children experience negative, stressful circumstances in their lives, can the impact of those experiences be outweighed by later, more positive experiences in adolescence? Or are the early experiences so critical, possibly because they are the infant's first, prototypical experiences, that they cannot be overridden by a later, more enriched environment in childhood or adolescence?

The early-later experience issue has a long history, and developmentalists continue to debate it. Some emphasize that unless infants experience warm, nurturant caregiving in the first year or so of life, their development will never be optimal (Cassidy & others, 2011; Moutsiana & others, 2015). Plato was sure that infants who were rocked frequently became better athletes. Nineteenth-century New England ministers told parents in Sunday sermons that the way they handled their infants would determine their children's future character. The emphasis on the importance of early experience rests on the belief that each life is an unbroken trail on which a psychological quality can be traced back to its origin.

Continuity

Discontinuity

FIGURE 8

CONTINUITY AND DISCONTINUITY IN DEVELOPMENT. *Is human development like a seedling gradually growing into a giant oak? Or is it more like a caterpillar suddenly becoming a butterfly?*

To what extent is an adolescent's development due to early or later experiences?
(left) © Stockbyte/Getty Images RF; (right) © Photodisc/Getty Images RF

developmental **connection**

Families

Secure attachment to parents increases the likelihood that adolescents will be socially competent. Connect to "Families."

The early-experience doctrine contrasts with the later-experience view that, rather than achieving statue-like permanence after change in infancy, our development resembles the ebb and flow of a river. The later-experience advocates argue that children and adolescents are malleable throughout development and that later sensitive caregiving is just as important as earlier sensitive caregiving (Antonucci, Ajrouch, & Birditt, 2014; Hsu & others, 2015). A number of life-span developmentalists, who focus on the entire life span rather than only on child development, stress that too little attention has been given to the influence of later experiences on development (Luo & Waite, 2014; Machielse, 2015). They accept that early experiences are important contributors to development but assert that they are no more important than later experiences. Jerome Kagan (1992, 2000, 2010, 2013) points out that even children who show the qualities of an inhibited temperament, which is linked to heredity, have the capacity to change their behavior.

Evaluating the Developmental Issues   As we consider further these three salient developmental issues—nature and nurture, continuity and discontinuity, and early and later experience—it is important to realize that most developmentalists consider it unwise to take an extreme position on these issues. Development is not all nature or all nurture, not all continuity or all discontinuity, and not all early experience or all later experience. Nature and nurture, continuity and discontinuity, and early and later experience all affect our development throughout the life span. For example, in considering the nature-nurture issue, the key to development is the interaction of nature and nurture rather than the influence of either factor alone (Moore, 2013, 2015). An individual's cognitive development, for instance, reflects heredity-environment interaction, not heredity or environment alone. Much more about the role of heredity-environment interaction appears in the chapter on "Puberty, Health, and Biological Foundations."

Although most developmentalists do not take extreme positions on the developmental issues we have discussed, this consensus has not meant the absence of spirited debate about how strongly development is determined by these factors (Kagan, 2013; Luong, Rauers, & Fingerman, 2015; Park & others, 2014; Starr & others, 2016). Consider adolescents who, as children, experienced poverty, parental neglect, and poor schooling. Could enriched experiences in adolescence overcome the "deficits" they encountered earlier in development? The answers developmentalists give to such questions reflect their stance on the issues of nature and nurture, continuity and discontinuity, and early and later experiences. The answers also influence public policy about adolescents and how each of us lives throughout the human life span.

Review *Connect* Reflect

LG3 Summarize the developmental processes, periods, transitions, and issues related to adolescence

Review

- What are the key processes involved in adolescent development? What are the main childhood, adolescent, and adult periods of development?
- What is the transition from childhood to adolescence like? What is the transition from adolescence to adulthood like?
- What are three important developmental issues?

Connect

- Describe how nature and nurture might each contribute to an individual's degree of resilience.

Reflect *Your Own Personal Journey of Life*

- As you go through this course, reflect on how you experienced various aspects of adolescence. Be curious. Ask your friends and classmates about their experiences in adolescence and compare them with yours. For example, ask them how they experienced the transition from childhood to adolescence. Also ask them how they experienced, or are experiencing, the transition from adolescence to adulthood.

Science and the Scientific Method	Theories of Adolescent Development	Research in Adolescent Development

How can we answer questions about the roles of nature and nurture, stability and change, and continuity and discontinuity in development? How can we determine, for example, whether an adolescent's achievement in school changes or stays the same from childhood through adolescence, and how can we find out whether positive experiences in adolescence can repair the harm done by neglectful or abusive parenting in childhood? To effectively answer such questions, we need to turn to science.

SCIENCE AND THE SCIENTIFIC METHOD

Some individuals have difficulty thinking of adolescent development as being a science in the same way that physics, chemistry, and biology are sciences. Can a discipline that studies pubertal change, parent-adolescent relationships, or adolescent thinking be equated with disciplines that investigate how gravity works and the molecular structure of compounds? The answer is *yes*, because science is not defined by what it investigates but by how it investigates. Whether you are studying photosynthesis, Saturn's moons, or adolescent development, it is the way you study the subject that matters.

There is nothing quite so practical as a good theory.

—KURT LEWIN
American social psychologist, 20th century

In taking a scientific path to study adolescent development, it is important to follow the *scientific method* (Smith & Davis, 2013). This method is essentially a four-step process: (1) conceptualize a process or problem to be studied, (2) collect research information (data), (3) analyze data, and (4) draw conclusions.

In step 1, when researchers are formulating a problem to study, they often draw on theories and develop hypotheses. A **theory** is an interrelated, coherent set of ideas that helps to explain phenomena and make predictions. It may suggest **hypotheses,** which are specific assertions and predictions that can be tested. For example, a theory on mentoring might state that sustained support and guidance from an adult make a difference in the lives of children from impoverished backgrounds because the mentor gives the children opportunities to observe and imitate the behavior and strategies of the mentor.

THEORIES OF ADOLESCENT DEVELOPMENT

This section discusses key aspects of four theoretical orientations to development: psychoanalytic, cognitive, behavioral and social cognitive, and ecological. Each contributes an important piece to the adolescent development puzzle. Although the theories disagree about certain aspects of development, many of their ideas are complementary rather than contradictory. Together they let us see the total landscape of adolescent development in all its richness.

Sigmund Freud, the pioneering architect of psychoanalytic theory. *What are some characteristics of Freud's theory?*
© Bettmann/Corbis

Psychoanalytic Theories   **Psychoanalytic theories** describe development as primarily unconscious (beyond awareness) and heavily colored by emotion. Psychoanalytic theorists emphasize that behavior is merely a surface characteristic and that a true understanding of development requires analyzing the symbolic meanings of behavior and the deep inner workings of the mind. Psychoanalytic theorists also stress that early experiences with parents extensively shape development. These characteristics are highlighted in the main psychoanalytic theory, that of Sigmund Freud (1856–1939).

Freud's Theory   As Freud listened to, probed, and analyzed his patients, he became convinced that their problems were the result of experiences early in life. He thought that as children grow up, their focus of pleasure and sexual impulses shifts from the mouth to the anus and eventually to the genitals. As a result, according to Freud's theory, we go through five stages of psychosexual development: oral, anal, phallic, latency, and genital (see

theory An interrelated, coherent set of ideas that helps explain phenomena and make predictions.

hypotheses Specific assertions and predictions that can be tested.

psychoanalytic theories Theories that describe development as primarily unconscious and heavily colored by emotion. Behavior is merely a surface characteristic, and the symbolic workings of the mind have to be analyzed to understand behavior. Early experiences with parents are emphasized.

Oral stage	Anal stage	Phallic stage	Latency stage	Genital stage
Infant's pleasure centers on the mouth.	Child's pleasure focuses on the anus.	Child's pleasure focuses on the genitals.	Child represses sexual interest and develops social and intellectual skills.	A time of sexual reawakening; source of sexual pleasure becomes someone outside the family.
Birth to 1½ Years	1½ to 3 Years	3 to 6 Years	6 Years to Puberty	Puberty Onward

FIGURE 9
FREUDIAN STAGES

Figure 9). Our adult personality, Freud (1917) claimed, is determined by the way we resolve conflicts between sources of pleasure at each stage and the demands of reality.

Freud stressed that adolescents' lives are filled with tension and conflict. To reduce the tension, he thought adolescents bury their conflicts in their unconscious mind. Freud said that even trivial behaviors can become significant when the unconscious forces behind them are revealed. A twitch, a doodle, a joke, a smile—each might betray unconscious conflict. For example, 17-year-old Barbara, while kissing and hugging Tom, exclaims, "Oh, *Jeff*, I love you so much." Repelled, Tom explodes: "Why did you call me Jeff? I thought you didn't think about him anymore. We need to have a talk!" You probably can remember times when such a "Freudian slip" revealed your own unconscious motives.

Freud (1917) divided personality into three structures: the id, the ego, and the superego. The id consists of instincts, which are an individual's reservoir of psychic energy. In Freud's view, the id is totally unconscious; it has no contact with reality. As children experience the demands and constraints of reality, a new structure of personality emerges—the ego, which deals with the demands of reality. The ego is called the "executive branch" of personality because it makes rational decisions.

The id and the ego have no morality—they do not take into account whether something is right or wrong. The superego is the moral branch of personality. The superego takes into account whether something is right or wrong. Think of the superego as what we often refer to as our "conscience." You probably are beginning to sense that both the id and the superego make life rough for the ego. Your ego might say, "I will have sex only occasionally and be sure to take the proper precautions because I don't want a child to interfere with the development of my career." However, your id is saying, "I want to be satisfied; sex is pleasurable." Your superego is at work, too: "I feel guilty about having sex outside of marriage."

Freud considered personality to be like an iceberg. Most of personality exists below our level of awareness, just as the massive part of an iceberg is beneath the water's surface. The ego resolves conflict between its reality demands, the id's wishes, and the superego's constraints through *defense mechanisms*. These are unconscious methods of distorting reality that the ego uses to protect itself from the anxiety produced by the conflicting demands of the three personality structures. When the ego senses that the id's demands may cause harm, anxiety develops, alerting the ego to resolve the conflict by means of defense mechanisms.

According to Freud, *repression* is the most powerful and pervasive defense mechanism. It pushes unacceptable id impulses out of awareness and back into the unconscious mind. Repression is the foundation on which all other defense mechanisms rest, since the goal of every defense mechanism is to repress, or to push threatening impulses out of awareness. Freud thought that early childhood experiences, many of which he believed are sexually laden, are too threatening and stressful for people to deal with consciously, so they repress them.

However, Peter Blos (1989), a British psychoanalyst, and Anna Freud (1966), Sigmund Freud's daughter, argued that defense mechanisms provide considerable insight into adolescent development. Blos stated that regression (in psychoanalytic theory, a defense mechanism in which an individual seeks to return to an earlier developmental period when faced with stress) during adolescence is actually not defensive at all, but rather an integral, normal, inevitable, and universal aspect of puberty. The nature of regression may vary from one adolescent to the next. It may involve compliance, and cleanliness, or it may involve a sudden return to the passiveness that characterized the adolescent's behavior during childhood.

Anna Freud (1966) developed the idea that defense mechanisms are the key to understanding adolescent adjustment. She maintained that the problems of adolescence are not

Anna Freud, Sigmund Freud's daughter. *How did her view differ from her father's?*
© Barton Silverman/The New York Times/Redux Pictures

rooted in the id, or instinctual forces, but in the "love objects" in the adolescent's past. Attachment to these love objects, usually parents, is carried forward from the infant years and merely toned down or inhibited during the childhood years, she argued. During adolescence, these urges might be reawakened, or, worse, newly acquired urges might combine with them.

Bear in mind that defense mechanisms are unconscious; adolescents are not aware they are using them to protect their egos and reduce anxiety. When used temporarily and in moderation, defense mechanisms are not necessarily unhealthy. However, defense mechanisms should not be allowed to dominate an individual's behavior and prevent a person from facing reality. Sigmund Freud's theory has been significantly revised by a number of other psychoanalytic theorists as well. Many contemporary psychoanalytic theorists stress that he overemphasized sexual instincts; they place more emphasis on cultural experiences as determinants of an individual's development. Unconscious thought remains a central theme, but most contemporary psychoanalysts argue that conscious thought plays a greater role than Freud envisioned. An important revisionist of Freud's ideas was Erik Erikson, whose theory is discussed next.

Erikson's Psychosocial Theory   Erik Erikson recognized Freud's contributions but argued that Freud misjudged some important dimensions of human development. For one thing, Erikson (1950, 1968) said we develop in *psychosocial* stages, rather than in *psychosexual* stages, as Freud maintained. According to Freud, the primary motivation for human behavior is sexual in nature; according to Erikson, it is social and reflects a desire to affiliate with other people. According to Freud, our basic personality is shaped in the first five years of life; according to Erikson, developmental change occurs throughout the life span. Thus, in terms of the early- versus later-experience issue we discussed earlier in the chapter, Freud argued that early experience is far more important than later experiences, whereas Erikson emphasized the importance of both early and later experiences.

In **Erikson's theory,** eight stages of development unfold as we go through life (see Figure 10). At each stage, a unique developmental task confronts individuals with a crisis that must be resolved. According to Erikson, this crisis is not a catastrophe but a turning point marked by both increased vulnerability and enhanced potential. The more successfully an individual resolves the crises, the healthier development will be.

Trust versus mistrust is Erikson's first psychosocial stage, which is experienced in the first year of life. Trust in infancy sets the stage for a lifelong expectation that the world will be a good and pleasant place to live.

Autonomy versus shame and doubt is Erikson's second stage, occurring in late infancy and toddlerhood. After gaining trust, infants begin to discover that their behavior is their own, and they start to assert their independence.

Initiative versus guilt, Erikson's third stage of development, occurs during the preschool years. As preschool children encounter a widening social world, they face new challenges that require active, purposeful, responsible behavior. Feelings of guilt may arise, though, if the child is irresponsible and is made to feel too anxious.

Erik Erikson with his wife, Joan, an artist. Erikson generated one of the most important developmental theories of the twentieth century. *Which stage of Erikson's theory are you in? Does Erikson's description of this stage characterize you?*
© Jon Erikson/The Image Works

Industry versus inferiority is Erikson's fourth developmental stage, occurring approximately in the elementary school years. Children now need to direct their energy toward mastering knowledge and intellectual skills. The negative outcome is that the child can develop a sense of inferiority—feeling incompetent and unproductive.

During the adolescent years, individuals explore who they are, what they are all about, and where they are going in life. This is Erikson's fifth developmental stage, *identity versus identity confusion*. If adolescents explore roles in a healthy manner and arrive at a positive path to follow in life, they achieve a positive identity; if not, identity confusion reigns.

Erikson's Stages	Developmental Period
Integrity versus despair	Late adulthood (60s onward)
Generativity versus stagnation	Middle adulthood (40s, 50s)
Intimacy versus isolation	Early adulthood (20s, 30s)
Identity versus identity confusion	Adolescence (10 to 20 years)
Industry versus inferiority	Middle and late childhood (elementary school years, 6 years to puberty)
Initiative versus guilt	Early childhood (preschool years, 3 to 5 years)
Autonomy versus shame and doubt	Infancy (1 to 3 years)
Trust versus mistrust	Infancy (first year)

FIGURE **10**
ERIKSON'S EIGHT LIFE-SPAN STAGES

- - - - - - - - - ⇒

developmental **connections**

Identity

Adolescents and emerging adults can be classified as having one of four identity statuses: diffusion, foreclosure, moratorium, or achievement. Connect to "The Self, Identity, Emotion, and Personality."

Erikson's theory Theory that includes eight stages of human development. Each stage consists of a unique developmental task that confronts individuals with a crisis that must be faced.

Jean Piaget, the famous Swiss developmental psychologist, changed the way we think about the development of children's minds. *What are some key ideas in Piaget's theory?*
© Yves de Braine/Black Star/Stock Photo

Intimacy versus isolation is Erikson's sixth developmental stage, which individuals experience during early adulthood. At this time, individuals face the developmental task of forming intimate relationships. If young adults form healthy friendships and create an intimate relationship with another individual, intimacy will be achieved; if not, isolation will result.

Generativity versus stagnation, Erikson's seventh developmental stage, occurs during middle adulthood. By generativity Erikson means primarily a concern for helping the younger generation to develop and lead useful lives. The feeling of having done nothing to help the next generation is stagnation.

Integrity versus despair is Erikson's eighth and final stage of development, which individuals experience in late adulthood. During this stage, a person reflects on the past. If the person's life review reveals a life well spent, integrity will be achieved; if not, the retrospective glances likely will yield doubt or gloom—the despair Erikson described.

Evaluating Psychoanalytic Theories   Contributions of psychoanalytic theories include an emphasis on a developmental framework, family relationships, and unconscious aspects of the mind. Criticisms include a lack of scientific support, too much emphasis on sexual underpinnings, and an image of people that is too negative.

Cognitive Theories   Whereas psychoanalytic theories stress the importance of the unconscious, cognitive theories emphasize conscious thoughts. Three important cognitive theories are Piaget's cognitive developmental theory, Vygotsky's sociocultural cognitive theory, and information-processing theory.

Piaget's Cognitive Developmental Theory   **Piaget's theory** states that individuals actively construct their understanding of the world and go through four stages of cognitive development. Two processes underlie this cognitive construction of the world: organization and adaptation. To make sense of their world, adolescents organize their experiences. For example, they separate important ideas from less important ideas and connect one idea to another. In addition to organizing their observations and experiences, they adapt, adjusting to new environmental demands (Miller, 2011).

Piaget (1954) also maintained that people go through four stages in understanding the world (see Figure 11). Each stage is age-related and consists of a distinct way of thinking, a different way of understanding the world. Thus, according to Piaget, cognition is qualitatively different in one stage compared with another. What are Piaget's four stages of cognitive development like?

The *sensorimotor stage*, which lasts from birth to about 2 years of age, is the first Piagetian stage. In this stage, infants construct an understanding of the world by coordinating sensory experiences (such as seeing and hearing) with physical, motoric actions—hence the term *sensorimotor*.

Piaget's theory A theory stating that children actively construct their understanding of the world and go through four stages of cognitive development.

The *preoperational stage*, which lasts from approximately 2 to 7 years of age, is Piaget's second stage. In this stage, children begin to go beyond simply connecting sensory information

Sensorimotor stage	Preoperational stage	Concrete operational stage	Formal operational stage
The infant constructs an understanding of the world by coordinating sensory experiences with physical actions. An infant progresses from reflexive, instinctual action at birth to the beginning of symbolic thought toward the end of the stage.	The child begins to represent the world with words and images. These words and images reflect increased symbolic thinking and go beyond the connection of sensory information and physical action.	The child can now reason logically about concrete events and classify objects into different sets.	The adolescent reasons in more abstract, idealistic, and logical ways.
Birth to 2 Years of Age	**2 to 7 Years of Age**	**7 to 11 Years of Age**	**11 Years of Age Through Adulthood**

FIGURE **11**

PIAGET'S FOUR STAGES OF COGNITIVE DEVELOPMENT

with physical action and represent the world with words, images, and drawings. However, according to Piaget, preschool children still lack the ability to perform what he calls *operations*, which are internalized mental actions that allow children to do mentally what they previously could only do physically. For example, if you imagine putting two sticks together to see whether they would be as long as another stick without actually moving the sticks, you are performing a concrete operation.

The *concrete operational stage*, which lasts from approximately 7 to 11 years of age, is the third Piagetian stage. In this stage, children can perform operations that involve objects, and they can reason logically as long as they can apply reasoning to specific or concrete examples. For instance, concrete operational thinkers cannot imagine the steps necessary to complete an algebraic equation, which is too abstract for thinking at this stage of development.

The *formal operational stage*, which appears between the ages of 11 and 15 and continues through adulthood, is Piaget's fourth and final stage. In this stage, individuals move beyond concrete experiences and think in abstract and more logical terms. As part of thinking more abstractly, adolescents develop images of ideal circumstances. They might think about what an ideal parent is like and compare their parents to this ideal standard. They begin to entertain possibilities for the future and are fascinated with what they can be. In solving problems, they become more systematic, developing hypotheses about why something is happening the way it is and then testing these hypotheses. We examine Piaget's cognitive developmental theory further in the chapter on "The Brain and Cognitive Development."

There is considerable interest today in Lev Vygotsky's sociocultural cognitive theory of child development. *What were Vygotsky's basic claims about children's development?*
A.R. Lauria / Dr. Michael Cole, Laboratory of Human Cognition, University of California, San Diego

Vygotsky's Sociocultural Cognitive Theory

Like Piaget, the Russian developmentalist Lev Vygotsky (1896–1934) emphasized that individuals actively construct their knowledge. However, Vygotsky (1962) gave social interaction and culture far more important roles in cognitive development than Piaget did. **Vygotsky's theory** is a sociocultural cognitive theory that emphasizes how culture and social interaction guide cognitive development.

Vygotsky portrayed development as inseparable from social and cultural activities (Gauvain & Perez, 2015). He stressed that cognitive development involves learning to use the inventions of society, such as language, mathematical systems, and memory strategies. Thus, in one culture, individuals might learn to count with the help of a computer; in another, they might learn by using beads. According to Vygotsky, children's and adolescents' social interaction with more-skilled adults and peers is indispensable to their cognitive development (Mahn & John-Steiner, 2013). Through this interaction, they learn to use the tools that will help them adapt and be successful in their culture. Later we will examine ideas about learning and teaching that are based on Vygotsky's theory.

Information-Processing Theory

Information-processing theory emphasizes that individuals manipulate information, monitor it, and strategize about it. Unlike Piaget's theory, but like Vygotsky's theory, information-processing theory does not describe development as stage-like. Instead, according to this theory, individuals develop a gradually increasing capacity for processing information, which allows them to acquire increasingly complex knowledge and skills (Kuhn, 2013).

Robert Siegler (2006, 2013), a leading expert on children's information processing, states that thinking is information processing. In other words, when adolescents perceive, encode, represent, store, and retrieve information, they are thinking. Siegler emphasizes that an important aspect of development is learning good strategies for processing information (Ramani & Siegler, 2014; Siegler & Lorte-Forgues, 2015; Siegler & Thompson, 2014; Siegler & others, 2015). For example, becoming a better reader might involve learning to monitor the key themes of the material being read.

© Frankie Angel/Alamy

Evaluating Cognitive Theories

Contributions of cognitive theories include a positive view of development and an emphasis on the active construction of understanding. Criticisms include skepticism about the pureness of Piaget's stages and too little attention to individual variations.

Behavioral and Social Cognitive Theories *Behaviorism* essentially holds that we can study scientifically only what we can directly observe and measure. Out of the behavioral tradition grew the belief that development is observable behavior that can be learned through experience with the environment (Chance, 2014). In terms of the continuity-discontinuity issue we discussed earlier in this chapter, the behavioral and social cognitive theories

Vygotsky's theory A sociocultural cognitive theory that emphasizes how culture and social interaction guide cognitive development.

information-processing theory A theory emphasizing that individuals manipulate information, monitor it, and strategize about it. Central to this approach are the processes of memory and thinking.

Albert Bandura developed social cognitive theory.

Courtesy of Dr. Albert Bandura

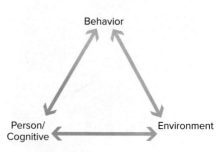

FIGURE **12**

BANDURA'S SOCIAL COGNITIVE THEORY.
Bandura's social cognitive theory emphasizes reciprocal influences of behavior, environment, and person/cognitive factors.

social cognitive theory The view that behavior, environment, and person/cognition are the key factors in development.

Bronfenbrenner's ecological theory A theory focusing on the influence of five environmental systems: microsystem, mesosystem, exosystem, macrosystem, and chronosystem.

emphasize continuity in development and argue that development does not occur in stage-like fashion. Let's explore two versions of behaviorism: Skinner's operant conditioning and Bandura's social cognitive theory.

Skinner's Operant Conditioning   According to B. F. Skinner (1904–1990), through *operant conditioning* the consequences of a behavior produce changes in the probability of the behavior's occurrence. A behavior followed by a rewarding stimulus is more likely to recur, whereas a behavior followed by a punishing stimulus is less likely to recur. For example, when an adult smiles at an adolescent after the adolescent has done something, the adolescent is more likely to engage in the activity again than if the adult gives the adolescent a nasty look.

In Skinner's (1938) view, such rewards and punishments shape development. For example, Skinner's approach argues that shy people learn to be shy as a result of experiences they have while growing up. It follows that modifications in an environment can help a shy adolescent become more socially oriented. Also, for Skinner the key aspect of development is behavior, not thoughts and feelings. He emphasized that development consists of the pattern of behavioral changes that are brought about by rewards and punishments.

Bandura's Social Cognitive Theory   Some psychologists agree with the behaviorists' notion that development is learned and is influenced strongly by environmental interactions. However, unlike Skinner, they argue that cognition is also important in understanding development. **Social cognitive theory** holds that behavior, environment, and person/cognition are the key factors in development.

American psychologist Albert Bandura (1925–) is the leading architect of social cognitive theory. Bandura (1986, 2001, 2004, 2009, 2010a, b, 2012) emphasizes that cognitive processes have important links with the environment and behavior. His early research program focused heavily on *observational learning* (also called *imitation*, or *modeling*), which is learning that occurs through observing what others do. For example, a young boy might observe his father yelling in anger and treating other people with hostility; with his peers, the young boy later acts very aggressively, showing the same characteristics as his father's behavior. Social cognitive theorists stress that people acquire a wide range of behaviors, thoughts, and feelings through observing others' behavior and that these observations play an important part in adolescent development.

What is *cognitive* about observational learning in Bandura's view? He proposes that people cognitively represent the behavior of others and then sometimes adopt this behavior themselves.

Bandura's (2009, 2010a, b, 2012) most recent model of learning and development includes three elements: behavior, the person/cognition, and the environment. An individual's confidence that he or she can control his or her success is an example of a person factor; strategies are an example of a cognitive factor. As shown in Figure 12, behavior, person/cognitive, and environmental factors operate interactively.

Evaluating Behavioral and Social Cognitive Theories   Contributions of the behavioral and social cognitive theories include an emphasis on scientific research and environmental determinants of behavior. Criticisms include too little emphasis on cognition in Skinner's views and inadequate attention given to developmental changes.

Ecological Theory   One ecological theory that has important implications for understanding adolescent development was created by Urie Bronfenbrenner (1917–2005). **Bronfenbrenner's ecological theory** (1986, 2004; Bronfenbrenner & Morris, 1998, 2006) holds that development reflects the influence of five environmental systems: microsystem, mesosystem, exosystem, macrosystem, and chronosystem (see Figure 13).

The *microsystem* is the setting in which the adolescent lives. These contexts include the adolescent's family, peers, school, and neighborhood. It is in the microsystem that the most direct interactions with social agents take place—with parents, peers, and teachers, for example. The adolescent is not a passive recipient of experiences in these settings but someone who helps to construct the settings.

The *mesosystem* involves relations between microsystems or connections between contexts. Examples are the relation of family experiences to school experiences, school experiences to religious experiences, and family experiences to peer experiences. For example, adolescents whose parents have rejected them may have difficulty developing positive relations with teachers.

The *exosystem* consists of links between a social setting in which the adolescent does not have an active role and the individual's immediate context. For example, a husband's or an adolescent's experience at home may be influenced by a mother's experiences at work. The mother might receive a promotion that requires more travel, which might increase conflict with the husband and change patterns of interaction with the adolescent.

The *macrosystem* involves the culture in which adolescents live. *Culture* refers to the behavior patterns, beliefs, and all other products of a group of people that are passed on from generation to generation.

The *chronosystem* consists of the patterning of environmental events and transitions over the life course, as well as sociohistorical circumstances. For example, divorce is one transition. Researchers have found that the negative effects of divorce on children often peak in the first year after the divorce (Hetherington, 2006). By two years after the divorce, family interaction is less chaotic and more stable. As an example of sociohistorical circumstances, consider how the opportunities for adolescent girls to pursue a career have increased during the last fifty years.

Bronfenbrenner (2004; Bronfenbrenner & Morris, 2006) has added biological influences to his theory and describes the newer version as a bioecological theory. Nonetheless, ecological, environmental contexts still predominate in Bronfenbrenner's theory.

Contributions of the theory include a systematic examination of macro and micro dimensions of environmental systems, and attention to connections between environmental systems. Criticisms include inadequate attention to biological factors, as well as too little emphasis on cognitive factors.

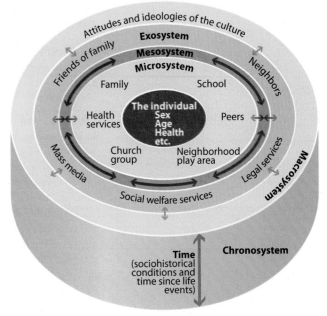

FIGURE **13**

BRONFENBRENNER'S ECOLOGICAL THEORY OF DEVELOPMENT. Bronfenbrenner's ecological theory consists of five environmental systems: microsystem, mesosystem, exosystem, macrosystem, and chronosystem.

An Eclectic Theoretical Orientation   No single theory described in this chapter can explain entirely the rich complexity of adolescent development, but each has contributed to our understanding of development. Psychoanalytic theory best explains the unconscious mind. Erikson's theory best describes the changes that occur in adult development. Piaget's, Vygotsky's, and the information-processing views provide the most complete description of cognitive development. The behavioral and social cognitive and ecological theories have been the most adept at examining the environmental determinants of development.

In short, although theories are helpful guides, relying on a single theory to explain adolescent development probably would be a mistake. This book instead takes an **eclectic theoretical orientation,** which does not follow any one theoretical approach but rather selects from each theory whatever is considered its best features. In this way, you can view the study of adolescent development as it actually exists—with different theorists making different assumptions, stressing different empirical problems, and using different strategies to discover information.

RESEARCH IN ADOLESCENT DEVELOPMENT

If scholars and researchers follow an eclectic orientation, how do they determine that one feature of a theory is somehow better than another? The scientific method discussed earlier provides the guide. Through scientific research, the features of theories can be tested and refined (Rosnow & Rosenthal, 2013; Trochim, Donnelly, & Arora, 2016).

Generally, research in adolescent development is designed to test hypotheses, which in some cases are derived from the theories just described. Through research, theories are modified to reflect new data and occasionally new theories arise.

In the twenty-first century, research on adolescent and emerging adult development has expanded a great deal (Schwartz, 2015a, b; Susman & Dorn, 2013). Also, research on adolescent development has increasingly examined applications to the real worlds of adolescents (Lerner & others, 2015; Masten, 2014a, b; Masten & others, 2015). This research trend involves a search for ways to improve the health and well-being of adolescents. The increased application emphasis in research on adolescent development is described in all of the chapters

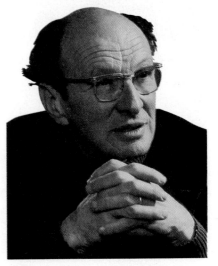

Urie Bronfenbrenner developed ecological theory, a perspective that is receiving increased attention. *What is the nature of ecological theory?*
Cornell University Photography

Truth is arrived at by the painstaking process of eliminating the untrue.

—**Sir Arthur Conan Doyle**
British physician and detective-story writer, 20th century

eclectic theoretical orientation An orientation that does not follow any one theoretical approach but rather selects from each theory whatever is considered the best in it.

in this text. Let's now turn our attention to how data on adolescent development are collected and to research designs that are used to study adolescent development.

Methods for Collecting Data Whether we are interested in studying pubertal change, cognitive skills, parent-adolescent conflict, or juvenile delinquency, we can choose from several ways of collecting data. Here we consider the measures most often used, beginning with observation.

Observation Scientific observation requires an important set of skills. For observations to be effective, they have to be systematic (Jackson, 2016). We need to have some idea of what we are looking for. We have to know whom we are observing, when and where we will observe, how we will make the observations, and how we will record them.

Where should we make our observations? We have two choices: the laboratory and the everyday world.

When we observe scientifically, we often need to control certain factors that determine behavior but are not the focus of our inquiry (Stangor, 2015). For this reason, some adolescent development research is conducted in a **laboratory,** a controlled setting with many of the complex factors of the "real world" removed. Laboratory research does have some drawbacks, however. First, it is almost impossible to conduct laboratory research without the participants' knowing they are being studied. Second, the laboratory setting is unnatural and therefore can cause the participants to behave unnaturally. Third, people who are willing to come to a university laboratory may not fairly represent groups from diverse cultural backgrounds. In addition, people who are unfamiliar with university settings and with the idea of "helping science" may be intimidated by the laboratory setting.

Naturalistic observation provides insights that sometimes cannot be achieved in the laboratory (Jackson, 2016). **Naturalistic observation** means observing behavior in real-world settings, making no effort to manipulate or control the situation. Life-span researchers conduct naturalistic observations in neighborhoods, at schools, sporting events, work settings, and malls, and in other places adolescents frequent.

Survey and Interview Sometimes the best and quickest way to get information about adolescents is to ask them for it. One technique is to interview them directly. A related method is the survey (sometimes referred to as a questionnaire), which is especially useful when information from many people is needed (Madill, 2012). A standard set of questions is used to obtain people's self-reported attitudes or beliefs about a specific topic. In a good survey, the questions are clear and unbiased, allowing respondents to answer unambiguously.

When conducting surveys or interviews with adolescents, what are some strategies that researchers need to exercise?
© Burger/phanie/Phanie Sarl/Corbis

laboratory A controlled setting in which many of the complex factors of the "real world" are removed.

naturalistic observation Observation of behavior in real-world settings.

standardized test A test with uniform procedures for administration and scoring. Many standardized tests allow a person's performance to be compared with the performance of other individuals.

Surveys and interviews can be used to study a wide range of topics from religious beliefs to sexual habits to attitudes about gun control to beliefs about how to improve schools. Surveys and interviews today are conducted in person, over the telephone, and on the Internet.

One problem with surveys and interviews is the tendency of participants to answer questions in a way that they think is socially acceptable or desirable rather than telling what they truly think or feel. For example, on a survey or in an interview, some adolescents might say that they do not take drugs even though they do.

Standardized Test A **standardized test** has uniform procedures for administration and scoring. Many standardized tests allow a person's performance to be compared with the performance of other individuals; thus they provide information about individual differences

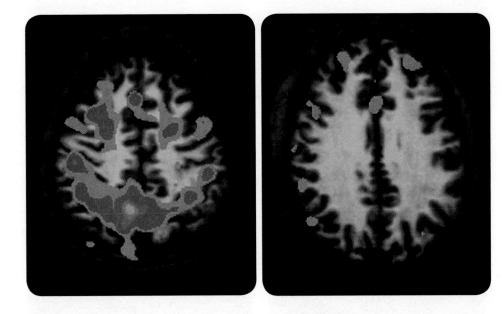

FIGURE **14**

BRAIN IMAGING OF 15-YEAR-OLD ADOLESCENTS. The two brain images indicate how alcohol can influence the functioning of an adolescent's brain. Notice the pink and red coloring (which indicates effective brain functioning involving memory) in the brain of the 15-year-old non-drinker while engaging in a memory task, and the lack of those colors in the brain of the 15-year-old under the influence of alcohol.
Dr. Susan Tapert, University of California, San Diego

among people (Watson, 2012). One example is the Stanford-Binet intelligence test. Your score on the Stanford-Binet test tells you how your performance compares with that of thousands of other people who have taken the test.

One criticism of standardized tests is that they assume a person's behavior is consistent and stable, yet personality and intelligence—two primary targets of standardized testing—can vary with the situation. For example, adolescents may perform poorly on a standardized intelligence test in an office setting but score much higher at home, where they are less anxious.

Physiological Measures   Researchers are increasingly using physiological measures when they study development at different points in the life span (de Haan, 2015; Kennedy & others, 2015). Hormone levels are increasingly used in developmental research. Cortisol is a hormone produced by the adrenal gland that is linked to the body's stress level and has been used in studies of temperament, emotional reactivity, and peer relations (Gunnar, Doom, & Esposito, 2015). Also, as puberty unfolds, the blood levels of certain hormones increase. To determine the nature of these hormonal changes, researchers analyze blood samples from adolescent volunteers (Susman & Dorn, 2013). The body composition of adolescents also is a focus of physiological assessment. There is a special interest in the increase in fat content in the body during pubertal development.

Until recently, little research had focused on the brain activity of adolescents. However, the development of neuroimaging techniques has led to a flurry of research studies. One technique that is being used in a number of them is *magnetic resonance imaging (MRI)*, in which radio waves are used to construct images of a person's brain tissue and biochemical activity (Casey, 2015). Figure 14 compares the brain images of two adolescents—one a non-drinker, the other a heavy drinker—while engaged in a memory task.

Experience Sampling   In the **experience sampling method (ESM),** participants in a study are given electronic pagers. Then, researchers "beep" them at random times. When they are beeped, the participants report on various aspects of their immediate situation, including where they are, what they are doing, whom they are with, and how they are feeling.

The ESM has been used in a number of studies to determine the settings in which adolescents are most likely to spend their time, the extent to which they spend time with parents and peers, and the nature of their emotions. Using this method, Reed Larson and Maryse Richards (1994) found that across the thousands of times they reported their feelings, adolescents experienced emotions that were more extreme and more fleeting than those of their parents. For example, adolescents were five times more likely than their parents to report being "very happy" when they were beeped, and three times more likely to feel "very unhappy" (see Figure 15).

Case Study   A **case study** is an in-depth look at a single individual. Case studies are performed mainly by mental health professionals, when for practical or ethical reasons the

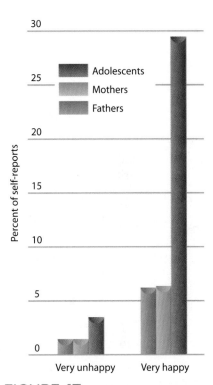

FIGURE **15**

SELF-REPORTED EXTREMES OF EMOTION BY ADOLESCENTS, MOTHERS, AND FATHERS USING THE EXPERIENCE SAMPLING METHOD. In the study by Reed Larson and Maryse Richards (1994), adolescents and their mothers and fathers were beeped at random times by researchers using the experience sampling method. The researchers found that adolescents were more likely to report emotional extremes than their parents were.

experience sampling method (ESM) Research method that involves providing participants with electronic pagers and then beeping them at random times, at which point they are asked to report on various aspects of their lives.

case study An in-depth look at a single individual.

FIGURE 16

PLASTICITY IN THE BRAIN'S HEMISPHERES. (*a*) Michael Rehbein at 14 years of age. (*b*) Michael's right hemisphere (*left*) has reorganized to take over the language functions normally carried out by corresponding areas in the left hemisphere of an intact brain (*right*). However, the right hemisphere is not as efficient in processing speech as the left, and more areas of the brain are recruited to process speech.
Courtesy of The Rehbein Family

(a)

(b)

unique aspects of an individual's life cannot be duplicated and tested in other individuals. A case study provides information about one person's fears, hopes, fantasies, traumatic experiences, upbringing, family relationships, health, or anything else that helps the psychologist to understand the person's mind and behavior (Yin, 2012).

Consider the case study of Michael Rehbein, which illustrates the flexibility and resilience of the developing brain. At age 7, Michael began to experience uncontrollable seizures—as many as 400 a day. Doctors said that the only solution was to remove the left hemisphere of his brain where the seizures were occurring. Though Michael's recovery was slow, eventually his right hemisphere began to reorganize and take over functions that normally reside in the brain's left hemisphere, such as speech. The neuroimage in Figure 16 shows this reorganization of Michael's brain vividly.

Although case histories provide dramatic, in-depth portrayals of people's lives, we must be cautious in generalizing from them. The subject of a case study is unique, with a genetic makeup and personal history that no one else shares. In addition, case studies involve judgments of unknown reliability. Psychologists who conduct case studies rarely check to see whether other psychologists agree with their observations.

In conducting research on adolescent development, in addition to a method for collecting data you also need a research design. There are three main types of research design: descriptive, correlational, and experimental.

Descriptive Research   All of the data-collection methods that we have discussed can be used in **descriptive research,** which aims to observe and record behavior. For example, a researcher might observe the extent to which adolescents are altruistic or aggressive toward each other. By itself, descriptive research cannot prove what causes specific phenomena, but it can reveal important information about people's behavior (Leedy & Ormrod, 2016).

Correlational Research   In contrast with descriptive research, correlational research goes beyond describing phenomena to provide information that will help us to predict how people will behave (Heiman, 2014; Levin, Fox, & Forde, 2014). In **correlational research,** the goal is to describe the strength of the relationship between two or more events or characteristics. The more strongly the two events are correlated (or related or associated), the more effectively we can predict one event from the other.

For example, to study whether adolescents of permissive parents have less self-control than other adolescents, you would need to carefully record observations of parents' permissiveness and their children's self-control. You could then analyze the data statistically to yield

descriptive research Research that aims to observe and record behavior.

correlational research Research whose goal is to describe the strength of the relationship between two or more events or characteristics.

Observed Correlation: As permissive parenting increases, adolescents' self-control decreases.

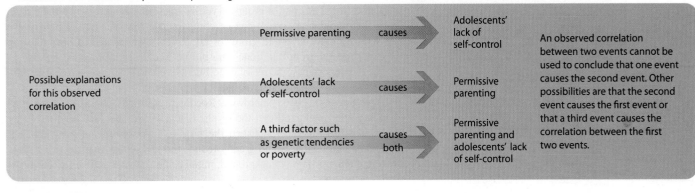

FIGURE 17
POSSIBLE EXPLANATIONS OF CORRELATIONAL DATA

a numerical measure, called a **correlation coefficient,** a number based on a statistical analysis that is used to describe the degree of association between two variables. The correlation coefficient ranges from -1.00 to $+1.00$. A negative number means an inverse relation. For example, researchers often find a negative correlation between permissive parenting and adolescents' self-control. By contrast, they often find a positive correlation between parental monitoring of children and adolescents' self-control.

The higher the correlation coefficient (whether positive or negative), the stronger the association between the two variables. A correlation of 0 means that there is no association between the variables. A correlation of $-.40$ is stronger than a correlation of $+.20$ because we disregard whether the correlation is positive or negative in determining the strength of the correlation.

A caution is in order, however (Heiman, 2015; Howell, 2014). Correlation does not equal causation. The correlational finding just mentioned does not mean that permissive parenting necessarily causes low self-control in adolescents. It could have that meaning, but it also could mean that an adolescent's lack of self-control caused the parents to simply throw up their arms in despair and give up trying to control the adolescent. It also could mean that other factors, such as heredity or poverty, caused the correlation between permissive parenting and low self-control in adolescents. Figure 17 illustrates these possible interpretations of correlational data.

Experimental Research   To study causality, researchers turn to **experimental research.** An experiment is a carefully regulated procedure in which one or more factors believed to influence a specific behavior are manipulated while all other factors are held constant. If the behavior under study changes when a factor is manipulated, researchers say that the manipulated factor has caused the behavior to change (Christensen, Johnson, & Turner, 2015). In other words, the experiment has demonstrated cause and effect. The cause is the factor that was manipulated. The effect is the behavior that changed because of the manipulation. Nonexperimental research methods (descriptive and correlational research) cannot establish cause and effect because they do not involve manipulating factors in a controlled way (Stangor, 2015).

All experiments involve at least one independent variable and one dependent variable. The **independent variable** is the factor that is manipulated. The term *independent* indicates that this variable can be manipulated independently of all other factors. For example, suppose we want to design an experiment to establish the effects of peer tutoring on adolescents' achievement. In this example, the amount and type of peer tutoring could be the independent variable.

The **dependent variable** is the factor that is measured; it can change as the independent variable is manipulated. The term *dependent* indicates that this variable depends on what happens as the independent variable is manipulated. In the peer tutoring study, adolescents' achievement would be the dependent variable. It might be assessed in a number of ways, perhaps by scores on a nationally standardized achievement test.

In an experiment, researchers manipulate the independent variable by giving different experiences to one or more experimental groups and one or more control groups. An *experimental group* is a group whose experience is manipulated. A *control group* is a group that

correlation coefficient A number based on a statistical analysis that is used to describe the degree of association between two variables.

experimental research Research that involves an experiment, a carefully regulated procedure in which one or more of the factors believed to influence the behavior being studied are manipulated while all other factors are held constant.

independent variable The factor that is manipulated in experimental research.

dependent variable The factor that is measured in experimental research.

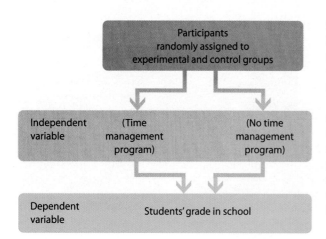

FIGURE **18**
RANDOM ASSIGNMENT AND EXPERIMENTAL DESIGN

is treated like the experimental group in every way except for the manipulated factor. The control group serves as a baseline against which the effects on the manipulated group can be compared. In the peer tutoring study, we would need to have one group of adolescents who received peer tutoring (experimental group) and one who did not (control group).

An important principle of experimental research is *random assignment*—assigning participants to experimental and control groups by chance (Gravetter & Forzano, 2016; Kantowitz, Roediger, & Elmes, 2015). This practice reduces the likelihood that the results of the experiment will be affected by preexisting differences between the groups. In our study of peer tutoring, random assignment would greatly reduce the probability that the two groups differed in age, family background, initial achievement, intelligence, personality, or health.

To summarize, in our study of peer tutoring and adolescent achievement, we would assign participants randomly to two groups. One (the experimental group) would be given peer tutoring and the other (the control group) would not. The different experiences that the experimental and control groups receive would be the independent variable. After the peer tutoring had been completed, the adolescents would be given a nationally standardized achievement test (the dependent variable). Figure 18 applies the experimental research method to a different problem: whether a time management program can improve adolescents' grades.

Time Span of Research   A special concern of developmentalists is the time span of a research investigation (Cicchetti & Toth, 2015; Kadlecova & others, 2015). Studies that focus on the relation of age to some other variable are common. Researchers have two options: They can study different individuals of varying ages and compare them, or they can study the same individuals as they age over time.

Cross-Sectional Research   **Cross-sectional research** involves studying people all at one time. For example, a researcher might study the self-esteem of 10-, 15-, and 20-year-olds. In a cross-sectional study, all participants' self-esteem would be assessed at one time.

The main advantage of a cross-sectional study is that researchers do not have to wait for the individuals to grow older. Despite its time efficiency, however, the cross-sectional approach has its drawbacks. It gives no information about how individuals change or about the stability of their characteristics. The increases and decreases of development—the hills and valleys of growth and development—can become obscured in the cross-sectional approach. For example, in a cross-sectional study of self-esteem, average increases and decreases might be revealed. But the study would not show how the life satisfaction of individual children waxed and waned over the years. It also would not tell us whether younger children who had high or low self-esteem as young adults continued to have high or low self-esteem, respectively, when they became older.

Longitudinal Research   **Longitudinal research** involves studying the same individuals over a period of time, usually several years or more. In a longitudinal study of self-esteem, the researcher might examine the self-esteem of a group of 10-year-olds, then assess their self-esteem again when they are 15, and then again when they are 20.

Longitudinal studies provide a wealth of information about such important issues as stability and change in development and the importance of early experience for later development. However, they are not without their problems (Reznick, 2013). They are expensive and time consuming. The longer the study lasts, the more participants drop out—they move, get sick, lose interest, and so forth. Changes in the participant group can bias the outcome of a study, because those who remain may be dissimilar to those who drop out. Those individuals who remain in a longitudinal study over a number of years may be more compulsive and conformity-oriented, for example, or they might lead more stable lives.

Where Is Research on Adolescence Published?   Regardless of whether you pursue a career in adolescent development, psychology, or some related scientific field, you can benefit by learning about the journal process. As a student you might be required to look up original research in journals. As a parent, teacher, clinician, youth worker, or mentor you might want to consult journals to obtain information that will help you understand

cross-sectional research A research strategy that involves studying different people of varying ages all at one time.

longitudinal research A research strategy in which the same individuals are studied over a period of time, usually several years or more.

and work more effectively with adolescents. And as an inquiring person, you might look up information in journals after you have heard or read something about adolescence that piqued your curiosity.

A journal publishes scholarly and academic information, usually in a specific domain such as physics, math, sociology, or our current interest, adolescent development. Scholars in these fields publish most of their research in journals, which are the source of core information in virtually every academic discipline.

An increasing number of journals publish information about adolescent development. Among the leading journals in adolescent development are the *Journal of Research on Adolescence, Journal of Youth and Adolescence, Journal of Early Adolescence, Journal of Adolescence, Journal of Adolescent Research,* and *Journal of Adolescent Health.* You also can read about research on adolescents in other journals on human development, such as *Child Development, Developmental Psychology, Journal of Applied Developmental Psychology, Social Development, Cognitive Development,* and *Development and Psychopathology.* Further, a number of journals that do not focus solely on human development publish articles on various aspects of human development, including adolescence. These journals include the *Journal of Educational Psychology, Sex Roles, Journal of Cross-Cultural Research, Journal of Marriage and the Family, Exceptional Children,* and *Journal of Consulting and Clinical Psychology.*

Every journal has a board of experts who evaluate articles submitted for publication. Each submitted paper is accepted or rejected on the basis of factors such as its contribution to the field, methodological excellence, and clarity of writing. Some of the most prestigious journals reject as many as 80 to 90 percent of the articles submitted.

Journal articles are usually written for other professionals in the specialized field of the journal's focus; therefore, they often contain technical language and terms specific to the discipline that are difficult for nonprofessionals to understand. They usually consist of the following elements: abstract, introduction, method, results, discussion, and references.

The *abstract* is a brief summary that appears at the beginning of the article. The abstract lets readers quickly determine whether the article is relevant to their interests. The *introduction* introduces the problem or issue that is being studied. It includes a concise review of research relevant to the topic, theoretical ties, and one or more hypotheses to be tested. The *method* section consists of a clear description of the participants evaluated in the study, the

© McGraw-Hill Companies, Mark Dierker, photographer

measures used, and the procedures that were followed. The method section should be sufficiently clear and detailed so that reading it allows another researcher to repeat or replicate the study. The *results* section reports the analysis of the data collected. In most cases, the results section includes statistical analyses that are difficult for nonprofessionals to understand. The *discussion* section describes the author's conclusions, inferences, and interpretation of what was found. Statements are usually made about whether the hypotheses presented in the introduction were supported, limitations of the study, and suggestions for future research. The last part of the journal article, called *references*, includes bibliographic information for each source cited in the article. The references section is often a good resource for finding other articles relevant to a topic that interests you.

Where do you find journals such as those we have described? Your college or university library likely has some of them, and some public libraries also carry journals. Online resources such as PsycINFO and PubMed can facilitate the search for journal articles.

The research published in the journals mentioned above shapes our lives. It not only informs the work of other adolescent development researchers, but it also informs the practices of law and policy makers, clinicians, educators, parents, and many others. In fact, much of what you will find that is new in this edition comes directly from research that can be found in the journals mentioned above.

Conducting Ethical Research

Ethics in research may affect you personally if you ever serve as a participant in a study. In that event, you need to know your rights as a participant and the responsibilities of researchers to assure that these rights are safeguarded.

If you ever become a researcher in life-span development yourself, you will need an even deeper understanding of ethics. Even if you carry out experimental projects only in psychology courses, you must consider the rights of the participants in those projects. A student might think, "I volunteer in a home for individuals with an intellectual disability several hours per week. I can use the residents of the home in my study to see if a specific treatment helps improve their memory for everyday tasks." But, without proper permissions, the most well-meaning, kind, and considerate studies still violate the rights of the participants.

Today, proposed research at colleges and universities must pass the scrutiny of a research ethics committee before the research can be initiated. In addition, the American Psychological Association (APA) has developed ethics guidelines for its members. The code of ethics instructs psychologists to protect their participants from mental and physical harm. The participants' best interests need to be kept foremost in the researcher's mind (Jackson, 2016). APA's guidelines address four important issues. First, *informed consent*—all participants must know what their research participation will involve and what risks might develop. Even after informed consent is given, participants must retain the right to withdraw from the study at any time and for any reason. Second, *confidentiality*—researchers are responsible for keeping all of the data they gather on individuals completely confidential and, when possible, completely anonymous. Third, *debriefing*—after the study has been completed, participants should be informed of its purpose and the methods that were used. In most cases, the experimenter also can inform participants in a general manner beforehand about the purpose of the research without leading participants to behave in a way they think that the experimenter is expecting. Fourth, *deception*—in some circumstances, telling the participants beforehand what the research study is about substantially alters the participants' behavior and invalidates the researcher's data. In all cases of deception, however, the psychologist must ensure that the deception will not harm the participants and that the participants will be told the complete nature of the study (will be debriefed) as soon as possible after the study is completed.

Minimizing Bias

Studies of adolescent development are most useful when they are conducted without bias or prejudice toward any particular group of people. Of special concern is bias based on gender and bias based on culture or ethnicity.

Gender Bias   Society continues to have a **gender bias,** a preconceived notion about the abilities of females and males that prevents individuals from pursuing their own interests and achieving their potential. But gender bias also has had a less obvious effect within the field of adolescent development. For example, too often researchers have drawn conclusions about

- - - - - - - - ➤

developmental **connection**

Gender

Research continues to find that gender stereotyping is pervasive. Connect to "Gender."

gender bias A preconceived notion about the abilities of females and males that prevents individuals from pursuing their own interests and achieving their potential.

females' attitudes and behaviors from research conducted with males as the only participants (Hyde & Else-Quest, 2013).

When gender differences are found, they sometimes are unduly magnified (Hyde, 2014). For example, a researcher might report in a study that 74 percent of the boys had high achievement expectations versus only 67 percent of the girls and go on to talk about the differences in some detail. In reality, this might be a rather small difference. It also might disappear if the study were repeated, or the study might have methodological problems that don't allow such strong interpretations.

Cultural and Ethnic Bias   At the same time that researchers have been struggling with gender bias, there is an increasing awareness that research needs to include more people from diverse ethnic groups (Schaefer, 2015; Spencer, Swanson, & Harpalani, 2015). Historically, members of ethnic minority groups (African American, Latino, Asian American, and Native American) have been discounted from most research in the United States and simply thought of as variations from the norm or average. Because their scores don't always fit neatly into measures of central tendency (such as a mean score to reflect the average performance of a group of participants), minority individuals have been viewed as confounds or "noise" in data. Consequently, researchers have deliberately excluded them from the samples they have selected. Given the fact that individuals from diverse ethnic groups were excluded from research on adolescent development for so long, we might reasonably conclude that adolescents' real lives are perhaps more varied than research data have indicated in the past.

Researchers also have tended to overgeneralize about ethnic groups. **Ethnic gloss** is using an ethnic label such as African American or Latino in a superficial way that portrays an ethnic group as being more homogeneous than it really is. For example, a researcher might describe a research sample like this: "The participants were 20 Latinos and 20 Anglo-Americans." A more complete description of the Latino group might be something like this: "The 20 Latino participants were Mexican Americans from low-income neighborhoods in the southwestern area of Los Angeles. Twelve were from homes in which Spanish is the dominant language spoken, 8 from homes in which English is the main language spoken. Ten were born in the United States, 10 in Mexico. Ten described themselves as Mexican American, 4 as Mexican, 3 as American, 2 as Chicano, and 1 as Latino." Ethnic gloss can cause researchers to obtain samples of ethnic groups that are not representative of the group's diversity, which can lead to overgeneralization and stereotyping.

Research on ethnic minority children and their families has not been given adequate attention, especially in light of their significant rate of growth within the overall population. Until recently, ethnic minority families were combined in the category "minority,"

developmental **connection**

Diversity

Too often differences between ethnic minority groups and the non-Latino White majority group have been characterized as deficits on the part of ethnic minority groups. Connect to "Culture."

ethnic gloss Use of an ethnic label such as African American or Latino in a superficial way that portrays an ethnic group as being more homogeneous than it really is.

Look at the two photographs, one of all non-Latino White males (*left*) and one of a diverse group of females and males from different ethnic groups, including some non-Latino White individuals (*right*). Consider a topic in adolescent development, such as parenting, identity, or cultural values. *If you were conducting research on this topic, might the results be different depending on whether the participants in your study were the individuals in the left photograph or the individuals in the right photograph?*
(left) © PA/Topham/The Image Works; (right) © Thomas Craig/Photolibrary/Getty Images

Pam Reid, Educational and Developmental Psychologist

When she was a child, Pam Reid liked to play with chemistry sets. Reid majored in chemistry during college and wanted to become a doctor. However, when some of her friends signed up for a psychology class as an elective, she also decided to take the course. She was intrigued by learning about how people think, behave, and develop—so much so that she changed her major to psychology. Reid went on to obtain her Ph.D. in psychology (American Psychological Association, 2003, p. 16).

For a number of years, Reid was a professor of education and psychology at the University of Michigan, where she also was a research scientist at the Institute for Research on Women and Gender. Her main focus has been on how children and adolescents develop social skills, with a special interest in the development of African American girls (Reid & Zalk, 2001). In 2004, Reid became provost and executive vice-president at Roosevelt University in Chicago, and in 2007 she became president of Saint Joseph College in Hartford, Connecticut.

Pam Reid (center) with some of the graduate students she mentored at the University of Michigan.
Courtesy of Dr. Pam Reid

For more information about the work that educational psychologists do, see the "Careers in Adolescent Development" appendix.

which masks important differences among ethnic groups as well as diversity within an ethnic group. At present and in the foreseeable future, the growth of minority families in the United States will be mainly due to the immigration of Latino and Asian families. Researchers need to take into account their acculturation level and the generational status of both parents and adolescents (Gauvain & Perez, 2015). More attention needs to be given to biculturalism because many immigrant children and adolescents identify with two or more ethnic groups (Fuligni & Tsai, 2015; Schwartz & others, 2015a, b, c; Updegraff & Umana-Taylor, 2015).

Pam Reid is a leading researcher who studies gender and ethnic bias in development. To read about her interests, see the *Connecting with Careers* profile.

Review Connect Reflect

LG4 Characterize the science of adolescent development

Review

- What is the nature of the scientific study of adolescent development? What is meant by the concept of theory?
- What are four main theories of adolescent development?
- What are the main methods used to collect data on adolescent development? What are the main research designs? What are some concerns about potential bias in research on adolescents?

Connect

- Which research method do you think would best address the question of whether adolescents around the world experience stereotyping?

Reflect *Your Own Personal Journey of Life*

- Which of the theories of adolescent development do you think best explains your own adolescent development?

Introduction

1 The Historical Perspective

LG1 Describe historical perspectives on adolescence

Early History

- Plato said that reasoning first develops in adolescence, and Aristotle argued that self-determination is the hallmark of maturity. In the Middle Ages, knowledge about adolescence moved a step backward: children were viewed as miniature adults. Rousseau provided a more enlightened view of adolescence, including an emphasis on different phases of development.

The Twentieth and Twenty-First Centuries

- Between 1890 and 1920, a cadre of psychologists, urban reformers, and others began to mold the concept of adolescence. G. Stanley Hall is the father of the scientific study of adolescence. In 1904, he proposed the storm-and-stress view of adolescence, which has strong biological foundations. In contrast to Hall's biological view, Margaret Mead argued for a sociocultural interpretation of adolescence. In the inventionist view, adolescence is a sociohistorical invention. Legislation was enacted early in the twentieth century that ensured the dependency of adolescents and delayed their entry into the workforce. From 1900 to 1930, there was a 600 percent increase in the number of high school graduates in the United States. Adolescents gained a more prominent place in society from 1920 to 1950. By 1950, every state had developed special laws for adolescents. Two changes in the current generation of adolescents and emerging adults—called Millennials—involve their increasing ethnic diversity and their connection to technology. Cohort effects refer to characteristics attributed to a person's year of birth, era, or generation rather than to his or her actual chronological age.

Stereotyping of Adolescents

- Negative stereotyping of adolescents in any historical era has been common. Joseph Adelson described the concept of the "adolescent generalization gap," which states that generalizations are often based on the behavior of a limited set of highly visible adolescents.

A Positive View of Adolescence

- For too long, adolescents have been viewed in negative ways. Research shows that a considerable majority of adolescents around the world have positive self-esteem. The majority of adolescents are not highly conflicted but rather are searching for an identity.

2 Today's Adolescents in the United States and Around the World

LG2 Discuss the experiences of adolescents in the United States and around the world

Adolescents in the United States

- Adolescents are heterogeneous. Although a majority of adolescents successfully make the transition from childhood to adulthood, too large a percentage do not and are not provided with adequate opportunities and support. Different portraits of adolescents emerge depending on the particular set of adolescents being described. Contexts, the settings in which development occurs, play important roles in adolescent development. These contexts include families, peers, schools, and culture. Social policy is a national government's course of action designed to influence the welfare of its citizens. The U.S. social policy on adolescents needs revision to provide more services for youth. Benson and his colleagues argue that U.S. youth social policy has focused too much on developmental deficits and not enough on strengths.

The Global Perspective

- There are both similarities and differences in adolescents across different countries. Much of what has been written and researched about adolescence comes from American and European scholars. With technological advances, a youth culture with similar characteristics may be emerging. However, there still are many variations in adolescents across cultures. In some countries, traditions are being continued in the socialization of adolescence, whereas in others, substantial changes in the experiences of adolescents are taking place. These traditions and changes involve health and well-being, gender, families, schools, and peers.

3 The Nature of Development

 Summarize the developmental processes, periods, transitions, and issues related to adolescence

Processes and Periods

Development is the pattern of movement or change that occurs throughout the life span. Biological processes involve physical changes in the individual's body. Cognitive processes consist of changes in thinking and intelligence. Socioemotional processes focus on changes in relationships with people, in emotion, in personality, and in social contexts. Development is commonly divided into these periods: prenatal, infancy, early childhood, middle and late childhood, adolescence, early adulthood, middle adulthood, and late adulthood. Adolescence is the developmental period of transition between childhood and adulthood that involves biological, cognitive, and socioemotional changes. In most cultures, adolescence begins at approximately 10 to 13 years of age and ends in the late teens. Developmentalists increasingly distinguish between early adolescence and late adolescence.

Developmental Transitions

Two important transitions in development are from childhood to adolescence and from adolescence to adulthood. In the transition from childhood to adolescence, pubertal change is prominent, although cognitive and socioemotional changes occur as well. It sometimes has been said that adolescence begins in biology and ends in culture. The concept of emerging adulthood has been proposed to describe the transition from adolescence to adulthood. Five key characteristics of emerging adulthood are identity exploration (especially in love and work), instability, being self-focused, feeling in-between, and experiencing possibilities to transform one's life. Competent individuals in emerging adulthood who experienced difficulties while growing up often turned their lives in a positive direction through relationships with supportive adults, intelligence, and planfulness. Among the criteria for determining adulthood are self-responsibility, independent decision making, and economic independence. A recent proposal argues that adolescence is taking too long and that adolescents aren't being provided with adequate opportunities to mature.

Developmental Issues

Three important issues in development are (1) the nature-nurture issue (is development mainly due to heredity [nature] or environment [nurture]?), (2) the continuity-discontinuity issue (is development more gradual and cumulative [continuity] or more abrupt and sequential [discontinuity]?), and (3) the early-later experience issue (is development due more to early experiences, especially in infancy and early childhood, or to later experiences?). Most developmentalists do not take extreme positions on these issues, although these topics are debated extensively.

4 The Science of Adolescent Development

 Characterize the science of adolescent development

Science and the Scientific Method

To answer questions about adolescent development, researchers often turn to science. They usually follow the scientific method, which involves four main steps: (1) conceptualize a problem, (2) collect data, (3) analyze data, and (4) draw conclusions. Theory is often involved in conceptualizing a problem. A theory is a coherent set of interrelated ideas that helps to explain phenomena and to make predictions. Hypotheses are specific assertions and predictions, often derived from theory, that can be tested.

Theories of Adolescent Development

According to psychoanalytic theories, development primarily depends on the unconscious mind and is heavily couched in emotion. Two main psychoanalytic theories were proposed by Freud and Erikson. Freud theorized that individuals go through five psychosexual stages. Erikson's theory emphasizes eight psychosocial stages of development. Cognitive theories emphasize thinking, reasoning, language, and other cognitive processes. Three main cognitive theories are Piaget's, Vygotsky's, and information processing. Piaget's cognitive developmental theory proposes four stages of cognitive development with entry into the formal operational stage taking place between 11 and 15 years of age. Vygotsky's sociocultural cognitive theory emphasizes how culture and social interaction guide human development. The information-processing approach stresses that individuals manipulate information, monitor it, and strategize about it. Two main behavioral and social cognitive theories are Skinner's operant conditioning and social cognitive theory. In Skinner's operant conditioning, the consequences of a behavior produce changes in the probability of the behavior's occurrence. In social cognitive theory, observational learning is a key aspect of life-span development.

Bandura emphasizes reciprocal interactions among person/cognitive, behavioral, and environmental factors. Ecological theory is Bronfenbrenner's environmental systems view of development. It proposes five environmental systems. An eclectic orientation does not follow any one theoretical approach but rather selects from each theory whatever is considered the best in it.

Research in Adolescent Development

The main methods for collecting data about life-span development are observation (in a laboratory or a naturalistic setting), survey (questionnaire) or interview, standardized test, physiological measures, experience sampling method, and case study. Three main research designs are descriptive, correlational, and experimental. Descriptive research aims to observe and record behavior. In correlational research, the goal is to describe the strength of the relationship between two or more events or characteristics. Experimental research involves conducting an experiment, which can determine cause and effect. To examine the effects of time and age, researchers can conduct cross-sectional or longitudinal studies. Scientific research about adolescents is published in a wide range of research journals. Researchers' ethical responsibilities include obtaining participants' informed consent, ensuring confidentiality, debriefing them about the purpose of the study and potential personal consequences of participating, and avoiding unnecessary deception of participants. Researchers need to guard against gender, cultural, and ethnic bias in research.

key **terms**

adolescence
adolescent generalization gap
biological processes
Bronfenbrenner's ecological
  theory
case study
cognitive processes
cohort effects
contexts
continuity-discontinuity issue
correlation coefficient
correlational research
cross-sectional research
dependent variable

descriptive research
development
early adolescence
early adulthood
early childhood
early-later experience issue
eclectic theoretical orientation
emerging adulthood
Erikson's theory
ethnic gloss
experience sampling method
  (ESM)
experimental research
gender bias

hypotheses
independent variable
infancy
information-processing theory
inventionist view
laboratory
late adolescence
late adulthood
longitudinal research
middle adulthood
middle and late childhood
Millennials
naturalistic observation

nature-nurture issue
Piaget's theory
prenatal period
psychoanalytic theories
resilience
social cognitive theory
social policy
socioemotional processes
standardized test
stereotype
storm-and-stress view
theory
Vygotsky's theory

key **people**

Joseph Adelson
Claudia Allen
Joseph Allen
Jeffrey Arnett
Albert Bandura
Peter Benson
Peter Blos

Urie Bronfenbrenner
Brad Brown
William Damon
Jacquelynne Eccles
Erik Erikson
Anna Freud
Sigmund Freud

G. Stanley Hall
Reed Larson
Jacqueline Lerner
Richard Lerner
Ann Masten
Margaret Mead
Daniel Offer

Jean Piaget
Maryse Richards
Robert Siegler
B. F. Skinner
Laurence Steinberg
Lev Vygotsky

resources for **improving the lives of adolescents**

Encyclopedia of Adolescence

B. Bradford Brown and Mitch Prinstein (Eds.) (2011)

New York: Elsevier

> A three-volume set with more than 140 articles written by leading experts in the field of adolescent development. Topics covered in this very contemporary overview include various biological, cognitive, and socioemotional processes.

Escaping the Endless Adolescence

Joe Allen and Claudia Allen (2009)

New York: Ballantine

> A superb, well-written book on the lives of emerging adults, including extensive recommendations for parents on how to effectively guide their children through the transition from adolescence to adulthood.

Age of Opportunity: Lessons from the New Science of Adolescence

Laurence Steinberg (2014)

Boston: Houghton Mifflin

> Leading researcher Laurence Steinberg writes about recent discoveries in the field of adolescent development that can help parents and educators better understand teens. Steinberg especially highlights recent research on the development of the adolescent's brain.

The Search Institute (www.search-institute.org)

> The Search Institute conducts large, comprehensive research projects to help define the pathways to healthy development for 12- to 25-year-olds. The Institute develops practical resources based on this research to foster reform, parent education, effective after-school programs, and community mobilization. Many resources are available for downloading from the Institute's website.

Emerging Adulthood (2nd ed.)

Jeffrey Arnett (2014a)

New York: Oxford University Press

> Jeffrey Arnett, who coined the term "emerging adulthood," provides an update of research on emerging adulthood that includes recent polls that he has taken of 18- to 29-year-olds.

appendix

Careers in Adolescent Development

Some of you may be quite sure about what you plan to make your life's work. Others may not have decided on a major yet and are uncertain about which career path you want to follow. Each of us wants to find a rewarding career and enjoy the work we do. The field of adolescent development offers an amazing breadth of career options that can provide extremely satisfying work.

If you decide to pursue a career in adolescent development, what career options are available to you? There are many. College and university professors teach courses in adolescent development, education, family development, and medicine. Middle school and high school teachers impart knowledge, understanding, and skills to adolescents. Counselors, clinical psychologists, and physicians help adolescents to cope more effectively with the unique challenges of adolescence. And various professionals work with families of adolescents to improve the adolescent's development.

By choosing one of these career options, you can guide youth in improving their lives, help others to understand them better, or even advance the state of knowledge in the field. You can have an enjoyable time while you are doing these things. Although an advanced degree is not absolutely necessary in some areas of adolescent development, you usually can expand your opportunities (and income) considerably by obtaining a graduate degree. Many careers in adolescent development pay reasonably well. For example, psychologists earn well above the median salary in the United States.

If you are considering a career in adolescent development, as you go through this term, try to spend some time with adolescents of different ages. Observe their behavior; talk with them about their lives. Think about whether you would like to work with youth in your life's work.

Another worthwhile activity is to talk with people who work with adolescents. For example, if you have some interest in becoming a school counselor, call a school, ask to speak with a counselor, and set up an appointment to discuss the counselor's career path and work. Be prepared with a list of questions to ask, and take notes if you wish.

Working in one or more jobs related to your career interests while you are in college can also benefit you. Many colleges and universities offer internships or work experiences for students who major in fields such as development. In some instances, these opportunities are for course credit or pay; in others, they are strictly on a volunteer basis. Take advantage of these opportunities. They can provide you with valuable experiences to help you decide whether this is the right career area for you, and they can help you get into graduate school, if you decide you want to go.

In the following sections, we profile careers in three areas: education/research; clinical/counseling/medical; and families/relationships. These are not the only career options in the field of adolescent development, but they should provide you with an idea of the range of opportunities available and information about some of the main career avenues you might pursue. In profiling these careers, we address the amount of education required, the nature of the training, and a description of the work.

Education/Research

Education and research offer a wide range of career opportunities to work with adolescents. These range from being a college professor to secondary school teacher to school psychologist.

College/University Professor

Courses in adolescent development are taught in different programs and schools in colleges and universities, including psychology, education, child and family studies, social work, and medicine. They are taught at research universities that offer one or more master's or Ph.D. programs in development; at four-year colleges with no graduate programs; or at community colleges. The work college professors do includes teaching courses either at the undergraduate or graduate level (or both); conducting research in a specific area; advising students and/or directing their research; and serving on college or university committees. Some college instructors do not conduct research but instead focus mainly on teaching. Research is most likely to be part of the job description at universities with master's and Ph.D. programs.

A Ph.D. or master's degree almost always is required to teach in some area of adolescent development in a college or university. Obtaining a doctoral degree usually takes four to six years of graduate work. A master's degree requires approximately two years of graduate work. The training involves taking graduate courses, learning to conduct research, and attending and presenting papers at professional meetings. Many graduate students work as teaching or research assistants to professors, an apprenticeship relationship that helps them to develop their teaching and research skills.

If you are interested in becoming a college or university professor, you might want to make an appointment with your instructor to learn more about the profession and what his or her career/work is like. **You can also read a profile of a counseling psychologist and university professor in the "Gender" chapter.**

Researcher

In most instances, individuals who work in research positions will have either a master's degree or Ph.D. in some area of adolescent development. They might work at a university, perhaps in a research program; in government at agencies such as the National Institute of Mental Health; or in private industry. Those who have full-time research positions generate innovative research ideas, plan studies, and carry out research by collecting data, analyzing the data, and then interpreting it. Some spend much of their time in a laboratory; others work outside the lab in schools, hospitals, and other settings. Researchers usually attempt to publish their research in a scientific journal. They often work in collaboration with other researchers and may present their work at scientific meetings, where they learn about other research.

Secondary School Teacher

Secondary school teachers teach one or more subjects, prepare the curriculum, give tests, assign grades, monitor students' progress, conduct parent-teacher conferences, and attend in-service workshops. At minimum, becoming a secondary school teacher requires an undergraduate degree. The training involves taking a wide range of courses, with a major or concentration in education, as well as completion of a supervised practice-teaching internship. **Read profiles of secondary school teachers in the chapters on "The Brain and Cognitive Development" and "Achievement, Work, and Careers."**

Exceptional Children (Special Education) Teacher

Teachers of exceptional children concentrate their efforts on individual children who either have a disability or are gifted. Among the children they might work with are children with learning disabilities, ADHD (attention deficit hyperactivity disorder), intellectual disability, or a physical disability such as cerebral palsy. Some of their work is done outside of the regular classroom, some of it in the regular classroom. The exceptional children teacher works closely with both the regular classroom teacher and parents to create the best educational program for each student. Becoming a teacher of exceptional children requires a minimum of an undergraduate degree. The training consists of taking a wide range of courses in education with a concentration of courses in educating children with disabilities or children who are gifted. Teachers of exceptional children often continue their education after obtaining their undergraduate degree, and many attain a master's degree in special education.

Family and Consumer Science Educator

Family and consumer science educators may specialize in early childhood education or instruct middle and high school students about matters such as nutrition, interpersonal relationships, human sexuality, parenting, and human development. Hundreds of colleges and universities throughout the United States offer two- and four-year degree programs in family and consumer science. These programs usually include an internship requirement. Additional education courses may be needed to obtain a teaching certificate. Some family and consumer science educators go on to graduate school for further training, which provides preparation for jobs in college teaching or research. **Read a profile of a family and consumer science educator in the "Sexuality" chapter.**

Educational Psychologist

Most educational psychologists teach in a college or university setting and conduct research on learning, motivation, classroom management, or assessment. These professors help to train students to enter the fields of educational psychology, school psychology, and teaching. Many educational psychologists have a doctorate in education, which requires four to six years of graduate work. **Read a profile of an educational psychologist in the "Introduction" chapter.**

School Psychologist

School psychologists focus on improving the psychological and intellectual well-being of elementary and secondary school students. They may work in a school district's centralized office or in one or more schools where they give psychological tests, interview students and their parents, consult with teachers, and provide counseling to students and their families. School psychologists usually have a master's or doctoral degree in school psychology. In graduate school, they take courses in counseling, assessment, learning, and other areas of education and psychology.

Clinical/Counseling/Medical

A wide variety of clinical, counseling, and medical professionals work with adolescents, from clinical psychologists to adolescent drug counselors and adolescent medicine specialists.

Clinical Psychologist

Clinical psychologists seek to help people with their psychological problems. They work in a variety of settings, including colleges and universities, clinics, medical schools, and private practice. Most clinical psychologists conduct psychotherapy; some perform psychological assessment as well; and some do research.

Clinical psychologists must obtain either a Ph.D. that involves clinical and research training or a Psy.D. degree, which involves only clinical training. This graduate training, which usually takes five to seven years, includes courses in clinical psychology and a one-year supervised internship in an accredited setting. In most cases, candidates for these degrees must pass a test to become licensed to practice and to call themselves clinical psychologists. **Read a profile of a clinical psychologist in the "Problems in Adolescence and Emerging Adulthood" chapter.**

Psychiatrist

Like clinical psychologists, psychiatrists might specialize in working with adolescents. They might work in medical schools, both as teachers and researchers, in medical clinics, and in private practice. Unlike psychologists, however, psychiatrists can administer psychiatric drugs to clients. Psychiatrists must first obtain a medical degree and then do a residency in psychiatry. Medical school takes approximately four years to complete and the psychiatric residency another three to four years.

Psychiatric Nurse

Psychiatric nurses work closely with psychiatrists to improve adolescents' mental health. This career path requires two to five years of education in a certified nursing program. Psychiatric nursing students take courses in the biological sciences, nursing care, and psychology and receive supervised clinical training in a psychiatric setting. Designation as a clinical specialist in adolescent nursing requires a master's degree or higher in nursing.

Counseling Psychologist

Counseling psychologists go through much the same training as clinical psychologists and work in the same settings. They may do psychotherapy, teach, or conduct research, but they normally do not treat individuals with severe mental disorders, such as schizophrenia. Counseling psychologists must have either a master's degree or a doctoral degree, as well as a license to practice their profession. One type of master's degree in counseling leads to the designation of licensed professional counselor. **Read a profile of a counseling psychologist in the "Gender" chapter.**

School Counselor

School counselors help students to identify their abilities and interests, and then guide them in developing academic plans and exploring career options. High school counselors advise students on choosing a major, meeting the admissions requirements for college, taking entrance exams, applying for financial aid, and obtaining vocational and technical training. School counselors may also help students to cope with adjustment problems, working with them individually, in small groups, or even in the classroom. They often consult with parents, teachers, and school administrators when trying to help students with their problems. School counselors usually have a master's degree in counseling. **Read a profile of a high school counselor in the "Achievement, Work, and Careers" chapter.**

Career Counselor

Career counselors help individuals to identify their career options and guide them in applying for jobs. They may work in private industry or at a college or university, where they usually interview individuals to identify careers that fit their interests and abilities. Sometimes career counselors help individuals to create professional résumés, or they conduct mock interviews to help them prepare for a job interview. They may also create and promote job fairs or other recruiting events to help individuals obtain jobs. **Read a profile of a career counselor in the "Achievement, Work, and Careers" chapter.**

Social Worker

Social workers are often involved in helping people with their social or economic problems. They may investigate, evaluate, and attempt to rectify reported cases of abuse, neglect, endangerment, or domestic disputes. They can intervene in families if necessary and provide counseling and referral services to individuals and families. They often work for publicly funded agencies at the city, state, or national level, although increasingly they work in the private sector in areas such as drug rehabilitation and family counseling. In some cases, social workers specialize in certain types of work. For example, family-care social workers often work with families in which a child, adolescent, or older adult needs support services. Social workers must have at least an undergraduate degree from a school of social work, including course work in various areas of sociology and psychology. Some social workers also have a master's or doctoral degree.

Drug Counselor

Drug counselors provide counseling to individuals with drug-abuse problems, either on an individual basis or in group therapy sessions. They may work in private practice, with a state or federal agency, for a company, or in a hospital setting. Some specialize in working with adolescents. At a minimum, drug counselors must have an associate degree or certificate. Many have an undergraduate degree in substance-abuse counseling, and some have master's and doctoral degrees. In most states, drug counselors must fulfill a certification procedure to obtain a license to practice.

Health Psychologist

Health psychologists work with many different health-care professionals, including physicians, nurses, clinical psychologists, psychiatrists, and social workers, in an effort to improve the health of adolescents. They may conduct research, perform clinical assessments, or give treatment. Many health psychologists focus on prevention through research and clinical interventions designed to foster health and reduce the risk of disease. More than half of all health psychologists provide clinical services. Among the settings in which health psychologists work are primary care programs, inpatient medical units, and specialized care programs in areas such as women's health, drug treatment, and smoking cessation.

Health psychologists typically have a doctoral degree (Ph.D. or Psy.D.) in psychology. Some receive training in clinical psychology as part of their graduate work. Others have obtained their doctoral degree in some area other than health psychology and then pursue a postdoctoral degree in health psychology. A postdoctoral degree usually takes about two additional years of graduate study. Many doctoral programs in clinical, counseling, social, and experimental psychology have specialized tracks in health psychology.

Adolescent Medicine Specialist

Adolescent medicine specialists evaluate the medical and behavioral problems that are common among adolescents, including growth disorders (such as delayed puberty), acne, eating disorders, substance abuse, depression, anxiety, sexually transmitted infections, contraception and pregnancy, and sexual identity concerns. They may work in private practice, in a medical clinic, in a hospital, or in a medical school. As a medical doctor, they can administer drugs and may counsel parents and adolescents on ways to improve the adolescent's health. Many adolescent medicine specialists on the faculty of medical schools also teach and conduct research on adolescents' health and diseases.

Adolescent medicine specialists must complete medical school and then obtain further training in their specialty, which usually involves at least three more years of schooling. They must become board certified in either pediatrics or internal medicine.

Families/Relationships

Adolescents sometimes benefit from help that is provided to the entire family. One career that involves working with adolescents and their families is marriage and family therapy.

Marriage and Family Therapist

Many individuals who have psychological problems benefit when psychotherapy is provided within the context of a marital or family relationship. Marriage and family therapists may provide marital therapy, couple therapy to individuals who are not married, and family therapy to two or more members of a family.

Marriage and family therapists must have a master's or doctoral degree. Their training is similar to that of a clinical psychologist but with a focus on marital and family relationships. In most states, professionals must go through a licensing procedure to practice marital and family therapy. **Read a profile of a marriage and family therapist in the "Families" chapter.**

chapter 2

PUBERTY, HEALTH, AND BIOLOGICAL FOUNDATIONS

chapter outline

© Jupiterimages/Getty Images RF

I **am pretty confused. I wonder whether I am weird or normal.** My body is starting to change, but I sure don't look like a lot of my friends. I still look like a kid for the most part. My best friend is only 13, but he looks like he is 16 or 17. I get nervous in the locker room during PE class because when I go to take a shower, I'm afraid somebody is going to make fun of me since I'm not as physically developed as some of the others.

—ROBERT, AGE 12

I don't like my breasts. They are too small, and they look funny. I'm afraid guys won't like me if they don't get bigger.

—ANGIE, AGE 13

I can't stand the way I look. I have zits all over my face. My hair is dull and stringy. It never stays in place. My nose is too big. My lips are too small. My legs are too short. I have four warts on my left hand, and people get grossed out by them. So do I. My body is a disaster!

—ANN, AGE 14

I'm short and I can't stand it. My father is six feet tall, and here I am only five foot four. I'm 14 already. I look like a kid, and I get teased a lot, especially by other guys. I'm always the last one picked for sides in basketball because I'm so short. Girls don't seem to be interested in me either because most of them are taller than I am.

—JIM, AGE 14

The comments of these four adolescents in the midst of pubertal change under-score the dramatic upheaval in their bodies following the calm, consistent growth of middle and late childhood. Young adolescents develop an acute concern about their bodies.

preview

Puberty's changes are perplexing to adolescents. Although these changes bring forth doubts, fears, and anxieties, most adolescents move through adolescence in a healthy manner. We will explore many aspects of pubertal change in this chapter, ranging from growth spurts and sexual maturation to the psychological aspects of puberty. We will also examine other topics related to adolescent physical development, including health and the roles of evolution, heredity, and environment in adolescent development.

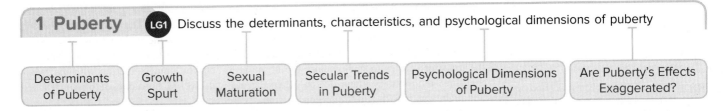

| 1 Puberty | **LG1** Discuss the determinants, characteristics, and psychological dimensions of puberty |

| Determinants of Puberty | Growth Spurt | Sexual Maturation | Secular Trends in Puberty | Psychological Dimensions of Puberty | Are Puberty's Effects Exaggerated? |

Puberty can be distinguished from adolescence. For virtually everyone, puberty ends long before adolescence is exited. Puberty is often thought of as the most important marker for the beginning of adolescence. **Puberty** is a brain-neuroendocrine process occurring primarily in early adolescence that provides stimulation for the rapid physical changes that take place during this period of development (Susman & Dorn, 2013).

puberty A brain-neuroendocrine process occurring primarily in early adolescence that provides stimulation for the rapid physical changes that accompany this period of development.

In youth, we clothe ourselves with rainbows and go brave as the zodiac.

—Ralph Waldo Emerson
American poet and essayist, 19th century

DETERMINANTS OF PUBERTY

Although we do not know precisely what initiates puberty, a number of complex factors are involved (Berenbaum, Beltz, & Corley, 2015; Hoyt & Falconi, 2015; Susman & Dorn, 2013). Puberty is accompanied by changes in the endocrine system, weight, and body fat, but we don't know if these are a cause or a consequence of puberty (Dorn & Biro, 2011). Also, there is increased interest in the role that birth weight, rapid weight gain in infancy, obesity, and sociocultural factors might play in pubertal onset and characteristics. As discussed next, heredity is an important factor in puberty.

Heredity   Puberty is not an environmental accident. Programmed into the genes of every human being is the timing for the emergence of puberty (Tu & others, 2014). Puberty does not take place at 2 or 3 years of age and it does not occur in the twenties. Recently, scientists have begun to conduct molecular genetic studies in an attempt to identify specific genes that are linked to the onset and progression of puberty (Amstalden & others, 2014). Nonetheless, as you will see later, puberty takes place between about 9 and 16 years of age for most individuals. Environmental factors can also influence its onset and duration (Susman & Dorn, 2013).

Hormones   Behind the first whisker in boys and the widening of hips in girls is a flood of **hormones,** powerful chemical substances secreted by the endocrine glands and carried throughout the body by the bloodstream. Two classes of hormones have significantly different concentrations in males and females: **androgens,** the main class of male sex hormones, and **estrogens,** the main class of female hormones. Note that although these hormones function more strongly in one sex or the other, they are produced by both males and females.

Testosterone is an androgen that plays an important role in male pubertal development (Werner & Holterhus, 2014). Testosterone is primarily secreted from testes in boys. Throughout puberty, rising testosterone levels are associated with a number of physical changes in boys, including the development of external genitals, an increase in height, and voice changes (Goji & others, 2009). Testosterone level in adolescent boys is also linked to sexual desire and activity (Cameron, 2004). *Estradiol* is an estrogen that plays an important role in female pubertal development. Estradiol is primarily secreted from ovaries in girls. As estradiol levels rise, breast development, uterine development, and skeletal changes occur. The identity of hormones that contribute to sexual desire and activity in adolescents is less clear for girls than it is for boys (Cameron, 2004). Boys and girls experience an increase in both testosterone and estradiol during puberty. However, in one study, testosterone levels increased 18-fold in boys but only 2-fold in girls during puberty; estradiol levels increased 8-fold in girls but only 2-fold in boys during puberty (Nottelmann & others, 1987) (see Figure 1). Also, a recent study of 9- to 17-year-old boys found that testosterone level peaked at 17 years of age (Khairullah & others, 2014).

The Endocrine System   Puberty is not a specific event but rather a process that unfolds through a series of coordinated neuroendocrine changes (Berenbaum & others, 2015; Hoyt & Falconi, 2015; Susman & Dorn, 2013). Puberty onset involves the activation of the hypothalamic-pituitary-gonadal (HPG) axis (see Figure 2). The *hypothalamus* is a structure in the higher portion of the brain that monitors eating, drinking, and sex. The *pituitary gland* is the endocrine gland that controls growth and regulates other glands. The *gonads* are the sex glands—the testes in males, the ovaries in females. How does the endocrine system work? The pituitary gland sends a signal via gonadotropins (hormones that stimulate sex glands) to the testes or ovaries to manufacture the hormone. Then, through interaction with the hypothalamus, the pituitary gland detects when the optimal level of hormones has been reached and maintains it with additional gonadotropin secretions.

Levels of sex hormones are regulated by two hormones secreted by the pituitary gland: *FSH (follicle-stimulating hormone)* and *LH (luteinizing hormone)*. FSH stimulates follicle development in females and sperm production in males. LH regulates estrogen secretion and ovum development in females and testosterone production in males (Addo & others, 2014). In addition, the hypothalamus secretes a substance called *GnRH (gonadotropin-releasing hormone)*, which is linked to pubertal timing (Lomniczi, Wright, & Ojeda, 2014).

hormones Powerful chemicals secreted by the endocrine glands and carried through the body by the bloodstream.

androgens The main class of male sex hormones.

estrogens The main class of female sex hormones.

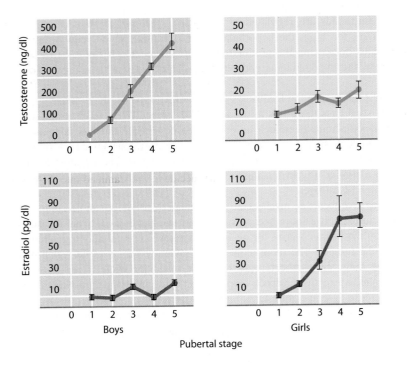

FIGURE 1

HORMONE LEVELS BY SEX AND PUBERTAL STAGE FOR TESTOSTERONE AND ESTRADIOL. The five stages range from the early beginning of puberty (stage 1) to the most advanced stage of puberty (stage 5). Notice the significant increase in testosterone in boys and the significant increase in estradiol in girls.

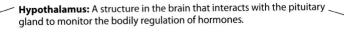

Hypothalamus: A structure in the brain that interacts with the pituitary gland to monitor the bodily regulation of hormones.

Pituitary: This master gland produces hormones that stimulate other glands. It also influences growth by producing growth hormones; it sends gonadotropins to the testes and ovaries and a thyroid-stimulating hormone to the thyroid gland. It sends a hormone to the adrenal gland as well.

Thyroid gland: It interacts with the pituitary gland to influence growth.

Adrenal gland: It interacts with the pituitary gland and likely plays a role in pubertal development, but less is known about its function than about sex glands. Recent research, however, suggests it may be involved in adolescent behavior, particularly for boys.

The gonads, or sex glands: These consist of the testes in males and the ovaries in females. The sex glands are strongly involved in the appearance of secondary sex characteristics, such as facial hair in males and breast development in females. The general class of hormones called estrogens is dominant in females, while androgens are dominant in males. More specifically, testosterone in males and estradiol in females are key hormones in pubertal development.

FIGURE 2
THE MAJOR ENDOCRINE GLANDS INVOLVED IN PUBERTAL CHANGE

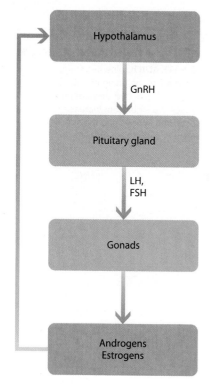

FIGURE 3

THE FEEDBACK SYSTEM OF SEX HORMONES

adrenarche Puberty phase involving hormonal changes in the adrenal glands, which are located just above the kidneys. These changes occur from about 6 to 9 years of age in girls and about one year later in boys, before what is generally considered the beginning of puberty.

gonadarche Puberty phase involving the maturation of primary sexual characteristics (ovaries in females, testes in males) and secondary sexual characteristics (pubic hair, breast and genital development). This period follows adrenarche by about two years and is what most people think of as puberty.

menarche A girl's first menstrual period.

spermarche A boy's first ejaculation of semen.

These hormones are regulated by a *negative feedback system*. If the level of sex hormones rises too high, the hypothalamus and pituitary gland reduce their stimulation of the gonads, decreasing the production of sex hormones. If the level of sex hormones falls too low, the hypothalamus and pituitary gland increase their production of the sex hormones.

Figure 3 shows how the feedback system works. In males, the pituitary gland's production of LH stimulates the testes to produce testosterone. When testosterone levels rise too high, the hypothalamus decreases its production of GnRH, and this decrease reduces the pituitary's production of LH. When the level of testosterone falls as a result, the hypothalamus produces more GnRH and the cycle starts again. The negative feedback system operates in a similar way in females, except that LH and GnRH regulate the ovaries and the production of estrogen.

This negative feedback mechanism in the endocrine system can be compared to a thermostat and furnace. If a room becomes cold, the thermostat signals the furnace to turn on. The action of the furnace warms the air in the room, which eventually triggers the thermostat to turn off the furnace. The room temperature gradually begins to fall again until the thermostat once again signals the furnace to turn on, and the cycle is repeated. This type of system is called a *negative* feedback loop because a *rise* in temperature turns *off* the furnace, while a *decrease* in temperature turns *on* the furnace.

The level of sex hormones is low in childhood but increases in puberty (Mouritsen & others, 2014). It is as if the thermostat is set at 50 degrees F in childhood and then becomes set at 80 degrees F in puberty. At the higher setting, the gonads have to produce more sex hormones, and they do so during puberty.

Growth Hormones   We know that the pituitary gland releases gonadotropins that stimulate the testes and ovaries. For example, a recent study documented that the pituitary gland grows in adolescence and that its volume is linked to circulating blood levels of estradiol and testosterone (Wong & others, 2014). In addition, through interaction with the hypothalamus, the pituitary gland also secretes hormones that lead to growth and skeletal maturation either directly or through interaction with the *thyroid gland*, located in the neck region (see Figure 2).

At the beginning of puberty, growth hormone is secreted at night. Later in puberty, it also is secreted during the day, although daytime levels are usually very low (Susman, Dorn, & Schiefelbein, 2003). Cortisol, a hormone that is secreted by the adrenal cortex, also influences growth, as do testosterone and estrogen (Kang & others, 2014; Stroud & others, 2011).

Adrenarche and Gonadarche   Two phases of puberty are linked with hormonal changes: adrenarche and gonadarche (Berenbaum & others, 2015; Dorn & Biro, 2011). **Adrenarche** involves hormonal changes in the adrenal glands, located just above the kidneys. These changes occur surprisingly early, from about 6 to 9 years of age in girls and about one year later in boys, before what is generally considered the beginning of puberty (Dorn & others, 2006). During adrenarche and continuing through puberty, the adrenal glands secrete adrenal androgens, such as dehydroepiandrosterone (DHEA). A recent study revealed that DHEA concentrations increased 24 months prior to breast development in girls (Biro & others, 2014). However, adrenarche is not well understood (Dorn & Biro, 2011).

Gonadarche, which follows adrenarche by about two years, is the period most people think of as puberty. Gonadarche involves the maturation of primary sexual characteristics (ovaries in females, testes in males) and secondary sexual characteristics (pubic hair, breast, and genital development) (Dorn & others, 2006). "The hallmark of gonadarche is reactivation of the hypothalamic-pituitary-gonadal axis (HPG). . . . The initial activation of the HPG axis was during the fetal and neonatal period" (Dorn & others, 2006, p. 35).

In the United States, the gonadarche period begins at approximately 9 to 10 years of age in non-Latino White girls and 8 to 9 years in African American girls (Herman-Giddens, Kaplowitz, & Wasserman, 2004). In boys, gonadarche begins at about 10 to 11 years of age. **Menarche,** the first menstrual period, occurs in mid- to late gonadarche in girls. In boys, **spermarche,** a boy's first ejaculation of semen, occurs in early to mid-gonadarche. Robert, Angie, Ann, and Jim, the adolescents who were quoted at the beginning of this chapter, are in various phases of adrenarche and gonadarche.

Weight and Body Fat Some researchers argue that a child must reach a critical body mass before puberty, especially menarche, emerges (Ackerman & others, 2006). A number of studies have found that higher weight, especially obesity, is linked to earlier pubertal development (Addo & others, 2014; Kaplowitz, 2009). For example, a recent study of more than 46,000 children and adolescents in 34 countries found that obesity was linked to earlier onset of menarche (Currie & others, 2012). Another recent study revealed that puberty began earlier in overweight boys and later in underweight boys (Tomova, Robeva, & Kumanov, 2015).

Other scientists have hypothesized that the onset of menarche is influenced by the percentage of body fat in relation to total body weight, although a precise percentage has not been consistently verified. However, both anorexic adolescents whose weight drops dramatically and females who participate in certain sports (such as gymnastics and swimming) may not menstruate. In boys, undernutrition may delay puberty (Susman, Dorn, & Schiefelbein, 2003).

What are some of the factors that likely determine the onset of puberty?
© Corbis RF

Leptin and Kisspeptins Reproduction is an energy-demanding function and thus puberty is said to be "metabolically gated" as a way to prevent fertility when energy conditions are very low (Roa & Tena-Sempere, 2014; Sanchez-Garrido & Tena-Sempere, 2013). Also, as we just indicated, obesity is linked to earlier menarche. The metabolic control of puberty, ranging from energy deficit to extreme overweight, results from the action of hormones and sends information to the GnRH neurons (Chehab, 2014).

The hormone *leptin*, which is secreted by fat cells and in abundance stimulates the brain to increase metabolism and reduce hunger, has been proposed to play an important role in regulating puberty, especially in females (Akhter & others, 2014; Faroogi & O'Rahilly, 2014). Some researchers argue that leptin deficiency inhibits food intake and reduces body fat, thus delaying pubertal onset or interrupting pubertal advances, and that leptin treatment can restore puberty (Bellefontaine & others, 2014). Further, recently *kisspeptins*, which are products of the Kiss 1 gene, have been reported to regulate GnRH neurons and thus play a role in pubertal onset and change (Skorupskaite, George, & Anderson, 2014). Interestingly, the Kiss 1 gene was discovered by researchers in Hershey, Pennsylvania, and named in recognition of Hershey chocolate kisses!

Are leptin and kisspeptins key factors in the onset of puberty and pubertal change? At this point, researchers aren't sure whether leptin and kisspeptins precede puberty and have a causative role in pubertal onset or are the consequence of other pubertal changes (Condorelli & others, 2014; Cravo & others, 2013).

Weight at Birth and in Infancy Might puberty's onset and characteristics be influenced by birth weight and weight gain during infancy? There is increasing research evidence for this link (Ibanez & others, 2011). Low-birth-weight girls experience menarche approximately 5 to 10 months earlier than normal-birth-weight girls, and low-birth-weight boys are at risk for small testicular volume during adolescence (Ibanez & de Zegher, 2006). A recent study confirmed that rapid weight gain in infancy was associated with earlier menarche (Salgin & others, 2015). A recent research review concluded that early growth acceleration soon after birth that reaches a peak in the first 2 to 4 years of life predicts very early pubertal onset for girls (Papadimitriou & others, 2010). This review also noted that this early growth acceleration is present in children who become overweight or obese later in childhood and adolescence.

How might birth weight and weight gain in infancy be linked to pubertal onset?
© DPD ImageStock/Alamy

Sociocultural and Environmental Factors Might sociocultural and environmental factors be linked to pubertal timing? Recent research indicates that cultural variations and early experiences may be related to earlier pubertal onset. Adolescents in developed countries and large urban areas reach puberty earlier than their counterparts in less-developed countries and rural areas (Graham, 2005). For example, a recent study of more than 15,000 girls in China revealed that menarche occurred much earlier in urban than rural girls (Sun & others, 2012). Children who have been adopted from developing countries to developed countries often enter puberty earlier than their counterparts who continue to live in developing countries

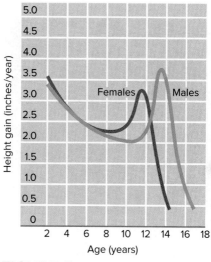

FIGURE 4

PUBERTAL GROWTH SPURT. On average, the peak of the growth spurt that characterizes pubertal changes occurs two years earlier for girls (11½) than for boys (13½).

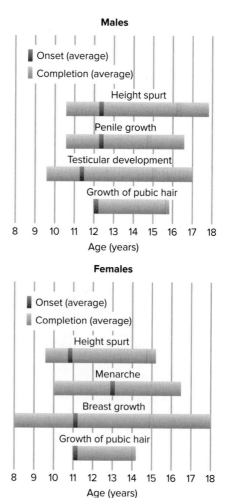

FIGURE 5

NORMAL RANGE AND AVERAGE DEVELOPMENT OF SEXUAL CHARACTERISTICS IN MALES AND FEMALES

(Teilmann & others, 2002). African American females enter puberty earlier than Latina and non-Latina females, and African American males enter puberty earlier than non-Latino males (Talpade, 2008).

Early experiences that are linked to earlier pubertal onset include adoption, father absence, low socioeconomic status, family conflict, maternal harshness, child maltreatment, and early substance use (Arim & others, 2011; Deardorff & others, 2011; Ellis & others, 2011). In many cases, puberty comes months earlier in these situations, and this earlier onset of puberty is likely explained by high rates of conflict and stress in these social contexts (Behie & O'Donnell, 2015). One study revealed that maternal harshness in early childhood was linked to early maturation as well as sexual risk taking in adolescence (Belsky & others, 2010). Another study found that early onset of menarche was associated with severe child sexual abuse (Boynton-Jarrett & others, 2013).

GROWTH SPURT

Growth slows throughout childhood, and then puberty brings forth the most rapid increases in growth since infancy. Figure 4 shows that the growth spurt associated with puberty occurs approximately two years earlier for girls than for boys. For girls, the mean beginning of the growth spurt is 9 years of age; for boys, it is 11 years of age. The peak of pubertal change occurs at 11½ years for girls and 13½ years for boys. During their growth spurt, girls increase in height about 3½ inches per year; boys, about 4 inches.

An individual's ultimate height is often a midpoint between the biological mother's and the biological father's height, adjusted a few inches down for a female and a few inches up for a male. The growth spurt typically begins before menarche and ends earlier for girls. The growth spurt for boys, as indicated earlier, begins later and ends later than it does for girls.

Boys and girls who are shorter or taller than their peers before adolescence are likely to remain so during adolescence. At the beginning of adolescence, girls tend to be as tall as or taller than boys of their age, but by the end of the middle school years most boys have caught up with them, or in many cases even surpassed them in height. Though height in elementary school is a good predictor of height later in adolescence, as much as 30 percent of an individual's height in late adolescence is unexplained by the child's height in elementary school.

The rate at which adolescents gain weight follows approximately the same developmental timetable as the rate at which they gain height. Marked weight gains coincide with the onset of puberty (Marceau & others, 2011). Fifty percent of adult body weight is gained during adolescence (Rogol, Roemmich, & Clark, 1998). At the peak of this weight gain, girls gain an average of 18 pounds in one year at roughly 12 years of age (approximately six months after their peak height increase). Boys' peak weight gain per year (20 pounds) occurs about the same time as their peak increase in height, about 13 to 14 years of age. During early adolescence, girls tend to outweigh boys, but—just as with height—by about 14 years of age, boys begin to surpass girls in weight.

In addition to increases in height and weight, puberty brings changes in hip and shoulder width. Girls experience a spurt in hip width, whereas boys undergo an increase in shoulder width. In girls, increased hip width is linked with an increase in estrogen. In boys, increased shoulder width is associated with an increase in testosterone (Susman & Dorn, 2009).

Finally, the later growth spurt of boys produces a greater leg length in boys than in girls. In many cases, boys' facial structure becomes more angular during puberty, whereas girls' facial structure becomes rounder and softer.

SEXUAL MATURATION

Think back to the onset of your puberty. Of the striking changes that were taking place in your body, what was the first that occurred? Researchers have found that male pubertal characteristics develop in this order: increased penis and testicle size; appearance of straight pubic hair; minor voice change; first ejaculation (spermarche—this usually occurs through masturbation or a wet dream); appearance of kinky pubic hair; onset of maximum growth; growth of hair in armpits; more detectable voice changes; and growth of facial hair. Three of the most noticeable signs of sexual maturation in boys are penis elongation, testes development, and growth of facial hair. The normal range and average age of development for these sexual characteristics, along with height spurt, are shown in Figure 5.

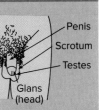

Penis
Scrotum
Testes
Glans
(head)

1.
No pubic hair. The testes, scrotum, and penis are about the same size and shape as those of a child.

2.
A little soft, long, lightly colored hair, mostly at the base of the penis. This hair may be straight or a little curly. The testes and scrotum have enlarged, and the skin of the scrotum has changed. The scrotum, the sack holding the testes, has lowered a bit. The penis has grown only a little.

3.
The hair is darker, coarser, and more curled. It has spread to thinly cover a somewhat larger area. The penis has grown mainly in length. The testes and scrotum have grown and dropped lower than in stage 2.

4.
The hair is now as dark, curly, and coarse as that of an adult male. However, the area that the hair covers is not as large as that of an adult male; it has not spread to the thighs. The penis has grown even larger and wider. The glans (the head of the penis) is bigger. The scrotum is darker and bigger because the testes have gotten bigger.

5.
The hair has spread to the thighs and is now like that of an adult male. The penis, scrotum, and testes are the size and shape of those of an adult male.

FEMALE SEXUAL DEVELOPMENT

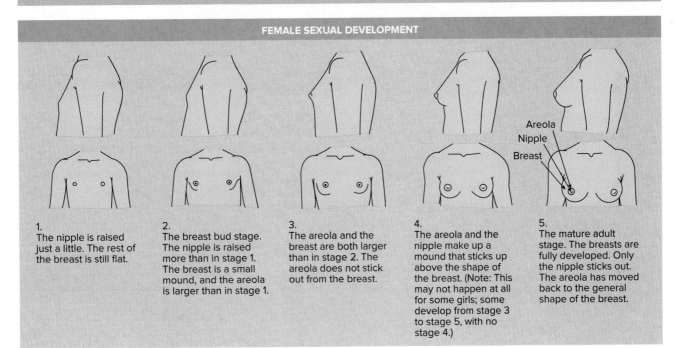

Areola
Nipple
Breast

1.
The nipple is raised just a little. The rest of the breast is still flat.

2.
The breast bud stage. The nipple is raised more than in stage 1. The breast is a small mound, and the areola is larger than in stage 1.

3.
The areola and the breast are both larger than in stage 2. The areola does not stick out from the breast.

4.
The areola and the nipple make up a mound that sticks up above the shape of the breast. (Note: This may not happen at all for some girls; some develop from stage 3 to stage 5, with no stage 4.)

5.
The mature adult stage. The breasts are fully developed. Only the nipple sticks out. The areola has moved back to the general shape of the breast.

FIGURE 6

THE FIVE PUBERTAL STAGES OF MALE AND FEMALE SEXUAL DEVELOPMENT

Figure 6 illustrates the typical course of male and female sexual development during puberty. The five numbers in Figure 6 reflect the five stages of secondary sexual characteristics known as the Tanner stages (Tanner, 1962). A recent longitudinal study revealed that on average, boys' genital development preceded their pubic hair development by about 4 months (Susman & others, 2010). In this study, African American boys and girls began puberty almost one year earlier than non-Latino White boys and girls.

What is the order of appearance of physical changes in females? On average, breast development occurs first, followed by the appearance of pubic hair. Later, hair appears in the armpits. As these changes occur, the female grows in height, and her hips become wider than her shoulders. Her first menstruation (menarche) occurs rather late in the pubertal cycle.

Attractive Blonde Females and Tall Muscular Males

When columnist Bob Greene (1988) called Connections in Chicago, a chat line for teenagers, to find out what young adolescents were saying to each other, he learned that the first things the boys and girls asked about—after first names—were physical descriptions. The idealism of the callers was apparent. Most of the girls described themselves as having long blonde hair, being 5 feet 5 inches tall, and weighing 110 pounds. Most of the boys said that they had brown hair, lifted weights, were 6 feet tall, and weighed 170 pounds.

Would current research on gender differences likely predict these responses? Why or why not?

Initially, her menstrual cycles may be highly irregular, and for the first several years she might not ovulate every cycle. In some instances, a female does not become fertile until two years after her period begins. No voice changes occur that are comparable to those in pubertal males. By the end of puberty, the female's breasts have become more fully rounded. Two of the most noticeable aspects of female pubertal change are pubic hair and breast development. Figure 5 shows the normal range and average development for two of these female sexual characteristics and provides information about menarche and height spurt. Figure 6 illustrates the typical course of female sexual development during puberty. A longitudinal study revealed that on average, girls' breast development preceded their pubic hair development by about two months (Susman & others, 2010).

Note that there may be wide individual variations in the onset and progression of puberty. For boys, the pubertal sequence may begin as early as 10 years of age or as late as 13½. It may end as early as 13 years or as late as 17. The normal range is wide enough that given two boys of the same chronological age, one might complete the pubertal sequence before the other one has begun it. For girls, the normal age range for menarche is even wider, between 9 and 15 years of age.

Precocious puberty is the term used to describe the very early onset and rapid progression of puberty. Judith Blakemore and her colleagues (2009) described the following characteristics of precocious puberty. Precocious puberty is usually diagnosed when pubertal onset occurs before 8 years of age in girls and before 9 years of age in boys. Precocious puberty occurs approximately 10 times more often in girls than in boys. When precocious puberty occurs, it usually is treated by medically suppressing gonadotropic secretions, which temporarily stops pubertal change (Alikasifoglu & others, 2015; Neely & Crossen, 2014). The reason for this treatment is that children who experience precocious puberty are ultimately likely to have short stature, early sexual capability, and the potential for engaging in age-inappropriate behavior (Blakemore, Berenbaum, & Liben, 2009).

SECULAR TRENDS IN PUBERTY

Imagine a toddler displaying all the features of puberty—a 3-year-old girl with fully developed breasts, or a slightly older boy with a deep male voice. One proposal was that this is what we would likely see by the year 2250 if the age at which puberty arrives continued to drop at the rate at which it was falling for much of the twentieth century (Petersen, 1987). However, we are unlikely to ever see pubescent toddlers because of genetic limits on how early puberty can occur (Elks & Ong, 2011). The earlier arrival of pubertal onset historically is believed to be due to improved health and nutrition.

The term **secular trends** refers to patterns of pubertal onset over historical time, especially across generations. For example, in Norway, menarche now occurs at just over 13 years of age, compared with 17 years of age in the 1840s (Ong, Ahmed, & Dunger,

precocious puberty The very early onset and rapid progression of puberty.

secular trends Patterns of the onset of puberty over historical time, especially across generations.

2006). In the United States, where children mature physically up to a year earlier than in European countries, menarche now occurs at about 12½ years of age compared with over 14 years of age a century ago (see Figure 7). An increasing number of U.S. girls are beginning puberty at 8 and 9 years of age, with African American girls developing earlier than non-Latino White girls (Herman-Giddens, 2007). A recent research review concluded that age at menarche has not fallen as much as the onset of puberty (Dorn & Biro, 2011). Further, a recent study concluded that boys also are entering puberty earlier (Herman-Giddens & others, 2012). In this study, non-Latino White boys entered puberty on average at 10 years of age, a year earlier than had been documented previously. However, this study has been criticized for aspects that could have skewed the results toward earlier pubertal onset. For example, the sample was obtained by having physicians volunteer to participate, meaning that earlier maturing boys may have been overrepresented as parents brought their sons to the physicians because of health concerns.

More specific conclusions about changes in pubertal onset have recently been proposed. For example, a recent research review concluded that early puberty does seem to be occurring only in overweight girls but that obesity delays pubertal onset in boys (Walvoord, 2010). In this review, it was concluded that earlier puberty in girls is directly linked to the increase in overweight and obesity.

So far, we have been concerned mainly with the physical dimensions of puberty. As we see next, the psychological dimensions of puberty are also important.

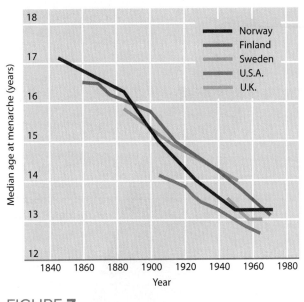

FIGURE 7

MEDIAN AGES AT MENARCHE IN SELECTED NORTHERN EUROPEAN COUNTRIES AND THE UNITED STATES FROM 1845 TO 1969. Notice the steep decline in the age at which girls experienced menarche in five different countries. Recently the rate of decrease in the age at which girls experience menarche has been slowing.

PSYCHOLOGICAL DIMENSIONS OF PUBERTY

A host of psychological changes accompanies an adolescent's pubertal development (Berenbaum & others, 2015). Try to remember when you were entering puberty. Not only did you think of yourself differently, but your parents and peers also began treating you differently. Maybe you were proud of your changing body, even though it perplexed you. Perhaps you or your parents felt they could no longer sit in bed and watch television with you or even kiss you good night.

Far less research has been conducted on the psychosocial aspects of male pubertal transitions than on female pubertal transitions, possibly because of the difficulty o detecting when the male transitions occur. Wet dreams are one marker, yet there has been little research on the topic. Not only are the effects of puberty easier to study in girls, they also are more likely to have a strong effect on girls because they are more obvious than the pubertal changes in boys. For example, female breast enlargement is much easier to see in most societies than male genital growth.

Body Image   One psychological aspect of puberty is certain for both boys and girls: Adolescents are preoccupied with their bodies (Leone & others, 2014). Perhaps you looked in the mirror on a daily, or sometimes even hourly, basis as a young teenager to see whether you could detect anything different about your changing body. Preoccupation with one's body image is strong throughout adolescence, but it is especially acute during puberty, a time when adolescents are more dissatisfied with their bodies than in late adolescence.

Gender Differences   Gender differences characterize adolescents' perceptions of their bodies (de Guzman & Nishina, 2014). In general, throughout puberty girls are less happy with their bodies and have more negative body images than do boys, which to some extent

Adolescents show a strong preoccupation with their changing bodies and develop mental images of what their bodies are like. *Why might adolescent males have more positive body images than adolescent females?*
© age fotostock/SuperStock

© Ingram Publishing/Alamy RF

may be due to media portrayals of the attractiveness of being thin and the increase in body fat in girls during puberty (Benowitz-Fredericks & others, 2012). A recent study of undergraduate students in the United Kingdom found that 35 percent of females but only 8 percent of males reported being moderately or markedly concerned with their body image (El Ansari, Dibba, & Stock, 2014).

As pubertal change proceeds, girls often become more dissatisfied with their bodies, probably because their body fat increases (Yuan, 2010). In contrast, boys become more satisfied as they move through puberty, probably because their muscle mass increases. However, when the entirety of adolescence was considered, rather than just puberty, a recent study found that both boys' and girls' body images became more positive as they moved from the beginning to the end of adolescence (Holsen, Carlson Jones, & Skogbrott Birkeland, 2012).

The following studies shed further light on gender differences in body image during adolescence:

· Adolescent girls placed a higher aesthetic value on body image but had a lower aesthetic satisfaction with their bodies than did adolescent boys (Abbott & Barber, 2010).

· The profile of adolescents with the most positive body images was characterized by health-enhancing behaviors, especially regular exercise (Frisen & Holmqvist, 2010).

· Among non-Latino White, Latino, African American, and Asian American adolescents, the psychological well-being (self-esteem and depression, for example) of non-Latino White girls was the most influenced and that of non-Latino White boys the least influenced by body perceptions (Yuan, 2010).

· The negative aspects of puberty for girls appeared in a study that explored 400 middle school boys' and girls' perceptions of the best and worst aspects of being a boy or a girl (Zittleman, 2006). In the views of the middle school girls, at the top of the list of the worst things about being a girl was the biology of being female, which included such matters as childbirth, PMS, periods, and breast cancer. The middle school boys said certain aspects of discipline—getting into trouble, being disciplined, and being blamed more than girls even when they were not at fault—were the worst things about being a boy. However, another aspect of physical development was at the top of the girls' list of the best things about being a girl—appearance (which included choosing clothes, hairstyles, and beauty treatments). Boys said the best thing about being a boy was playing sports.

Body Art An increasing number of adolescents and college students are obtaining tattoos and getting parts of their bodies pierced (Mayers & Chiffriller, 2008). Many of these youth engage in such body modifications to be different, to stamp their identity as unique. In one study of adolescents, 60 percent of the students with tattoos had academic grades of A's and B's (Armstrong, 1995). In this study, the average age at which the adolescents got their first tattoo was 14 years of age. Some studies indicate that tattoos and body piercings are markers for risk taking in adolescence (Deschesnes, Fines, & Demers, 2006). One study revealed that having multiple body piercings is especially a marker for risk-taking behavior (Suris & others, 2007). However, other researchers argue that body art is increasingly used to express individuality and self-expression rather than rebellion (Armstrong & others, 2004).

Use of body art, such as tattoos and body piercing, is increasing in adolescence and emerging adulthood. *Why do youth engage in such body modification?*
© Corbis RF

Hormones and Behavior Are concentrations of hormones linked to adolescent behavior? Hormonal factors are thought to account for at least part of the increase in negative and variable emotions that characterize adolescents (Vermeersch & others, 2008). In boys higher levels of androgens are associated with violence and acting-out problems (Van Goozen & others, 1998). However, a recent research review concluded that there is insufficient quality research to confirm that changing testosterone levels during puberty are linked to mood and behavior in adolescent males (Duke, Balzer, & Steinbeck, 2014).

There is also some indication that increased estrogen levels are linked to depression in adolescent girls (Blakemore, Berenbaum, & Liben, 2009). Further, high levels of adrenal androgens are associated with negative emotions in girls (Susman & Dorn, 2009). One study found that early-maturing girls with high levels of adrenal androgens had higher emotional arousal and depression than did other girls (Graber, Brooks-Gunn, & Warren, 2006).

However, hormonal factors alone are not responsible for adolescent behavior (DeRose & Brooks-Gunn, 2008). For example, one study found that social factors accounted for two to four times as much variance as hormonal factors in young adolescent girls' depression and anger (Brooks-Gunn & Warren, 1989). Another study found little direct connection between adolescent males' and females' testosterone levels and risk-taking behavior or depression (Booth & others, 2003). In contrast, a link with risk-taking behavior depended on the quality of parent-adolescent relations. When relationship quality decreased, testosterone-linked risk-taking behavior and symptoms of depression increased. And, in a recent study, negative life events mediated links between hormones (estradiol and an adrenal hormone) and aggression in 10- to 14-year-old girls (Graber, Brooks-Gunn, & Warren, 2006). Thus, hormones do not function independently; hormonal activity is influenced by many environmental factors, including parent-adolescent relationships. Stress, eating patterns, sexual activity, and depression can also activate or suppress various aspects of the hormone system (DeRose & Brooks-Gunn, 2008).

developmental **connection**

Nature of Development

Biological, cognitive, and socioemotional processes interact in development. Connect to "Introduction."

Early and Late Maturation   Did you enter puberty early, late, or on time? When adolescents mature earlier or later than their peers, they often perceive themselves differently (Bralic & others, 2012; de Rose & others, 2011; Negriff, Susman, & Trickett, 2011). In the Berkeley Longitudinal Study conducted many years ago, early-maturing boys perceived themselves more positively and had more successful peer relations than did late-maturing boys (Jones, 1965). The findings for early-maturing girls were similar but not as strong as for boys. Also, a recent study found that in the early high school years, late-maturing boys had a more negative body image than early-maturing boys (de Guzman & Nishina, 2014).

In the Berkeley Longitudinal Study, when the late-maturing boys were in their thirties, however, they had developed a more positive identity than the early-maturing boys had (Peskin, 1967). Perhaps the late-maturing boys had had more time to explore life's options, or perhaps the early-maturing boys continued to focus on their physical status instead of paying attention to career development and achievement.

An increasing number of researchers have found that early maturation increases girls' vulnerability to a number of problems (Blumenthal & others, 2011; Hamilton & others, 2014; Sontag-Padilla & others, 2012). Early-maturing girls are more likely to smoke, drink, be depressed, have an eating disorder, engage in delinquency, struggle for earlier independence from their parents, and have older friends; and their bodies are likely to elicit responses from males that lead to earlier dating and earlier sexual experiences (Copeland & others, 2010; Negriff, Susman, & Trickett, 2011; Verhoef & others, 2014). For example, a recent study confirmed that early maturation was linked to depression in young adolescent girls (Rudolph & others, 2014). Further, recent research has found that early-maturing girls tend to have sexual intercourse earlier and have more unstable sexual relationships (Moore, Harden, & Mendle, 2014). And early-maturing girls are less likely to graduate from high school and more likely to cohabit and marry earlier (Cavanagh, 2009). Apparently the combination of their social and cognitive immaturity and early physical development result in early-maturing girls being more easily lured into problem behaviors, not recognizing the possible long-term effects of these on their development.

When does early or late maturation become a health issue? To read further about early and late maturation, see the *Connecting with Health and Well-Being* interlude.

What are some risk factors associated with early maturation in girls?
© Britt Erlanson/Getty Images RF

How Can Early and Late Maturers at Risk for Health Problems Be Identified?

Adolescents whose development is extremely early or late are likely to come to the attention of a physician. Children who experience precocious puberty, which we discussed earlier in this chapter, and boys who have not had a growth spurt by age 16 or girls who have not menstruated by age 15 are likely to come to the attention of a physician. Girls and boys who are early or late maturers but are still well within the normal range are less likely to be seen by a physician. Nonetheless, these boys and girls may have fears about being abnormal that they will not raise unless a physician, counselor, or other health-care provider introduces the topic. A brief discussion of the usual sequence and timing of events, and the large individual variations in them, may be all that is required to reassure many adolescents who are maturing very early or late.

Health-care providers may want to discuss an adolescent's early or late development with parents as well. Information about peer pressures can be helpful, especially the peer pressures on early-maturing girls to date and to engage in adult-like behavior. For girls and boys who are in the midst of puberty, the transition to middle school, junior high school, or high school may be more stressful than for those who are not yet in puberty or have already completed it (Wigfield & others, 2006, 2015).

If pubertal development is extremely late, a physician may recommend hormonal treatment (Fenichel, 2012). This approach may or may not be helpful (Soliman & Sanctis, 2012). In one study of extended pubertal delay in boys, hormonal treatment helped to increase height, dating interest, and peer relations in several boys but brought little or no improvement in other boys (Lewis, Money, & Bobrow, 1977).

In sum, most early- and late-maturing individuals manage to weather puberty's challenges and stresses successfully. For those who do not, discussions with sensitive and knowledgeable health-care providers and parents can improve the adolescent's coping abilities.

How might a sensitive health-care provider address the concerns of an adolescent boy or girl regarding early or late pubertal development?

ARE PUBERTY'S EFFECTS EXAGGERATED?

Some researchers question whether puberty's effects are as strong as was once believed. Have the effects of puberty been exaggerated? Puberty affects some adolescents more strongly than others and influences some behaviors more strongly than others. Body image, interest in dating, and sexual behavior are quite clearly affected by pubertal change. In one study, early-maturing boys and girls reported more sexual activity and delinquency than late maturers (Flannery, Rowe, & Gulley, 1993). Yet, if we look at overall development and adjustment over the human life span, puberty and its variations have less dramatic effects than is commonly thought for most individuals. For some young adolescents, the path through puberty is stormy, but for most it is not. Each period of the human life span has its stresses, and puberty is no different. Although puberty poses new challenges, the vast majority of adolescents cope with the stresses effectively. Besides the biological influences on adolescent development, cognitive and social or environmental influences also shape who we become (DeRose & Brooks-Gunn, 2008; Sontag & others, 2008). Singling out biological changes as the dominant influence during adolescence may not be wise.

Although extremely early and late maturation may be risk factors in development, we have seen that the overall effects of early or late maturation often are not great. Not all early maturers will date, smoke, and drink, and not all late maturers will have difficulty with peer relations. In some instances, the effects of an adolescent's grade level in school are stronger than maturational timing (Petersen & Crockett, 1985). Because the adolescent's social world is organized by grade level rather than physical development, this finding is not surprising. However, it does not mean that age of maturation has no influence on development. Rather, we need to evaluate puberty's effects within the larger framework of interacting biological, cognitive, and socioemotional contexts.

Anne Petersen has made numerous contributions to our understanding of puberty and adolescent development. To read about her work and career, see the *Connecting with Careers* profile.

Anne Petersen, Researcher and Administrator

Anne Petersen has had a distinguished career as a researcher and administrator with a main focus on adolescent development. Petersen obtained three degrees (B.A., M.A., and Ph.D.) from the University of Chicago in math and statistics. Her first job after she obtained her Ph.D. was as a research associate/professor involving statistical consultation, and it was on this job that she was introduced to the field of adolescent development, which became the focus of her subsequent work.

Petersen moved from the University of Chicago to Pennsylvania State University, where she became a leading researcher in adolescent development. Her research included a focus on puberty and gender. Petersen also has held numerous administrative positions. In the mid-1990s Petersen became deputy director of the National Science Foundation and from 1996 to 2005 was senior vice-president for programs at the W. K. Kellogg Foundation. In 2006, she became the deputy director of the Center for Advanced Study in the Behavioral Sciences at Stanford University and also assumed the position of professor of psychology at Stanford. Subsequently, Petersen started her own foundation—Global Philanthropy Alliance—that develops young social entrepreneurs in Africa to acquire skills that will help them contribute to the social health of their families and communities. She also is a member of the faculty at the Center for Growth and Human Development at the University of Michigan.

Anne Petersen, interacting with adolescents.
Courtesy of Anne Petersen, W.K. Kellogg Foundation

Petersen says that what inspired her to enter the field of adolescent development and take positions at various universities and foundations was her desire to make a difference for people, especially youth. Her goal is to make a difference for youth in the United States and around the world. She believes that too often adolescents have been neglected.

Review Connect Reflect

LG1 Discuss the determinants, characteristics, and psychological dimensions of puberty

Review
- What are puberty's main determinants?
- What characterizes the growth spurt in puberty?
- How does sexual maturation develop in puberty?
- What are some secular trends in puberty?
- What are some important psychological dimensions of puberty?
- Are puberty's effects exaggerated?

Connect
- How do nature and nurture affect pubertal timing?

Reflect *Your Own Personal Journey of Life*
- Think back to when you entered puberty. How strong was your curiosity about the pubertal changes that were taking place? What misconceptions did you have about those changes?

2 Health   **LG2** Summarize the nature of adolescents' and emerging adults' health

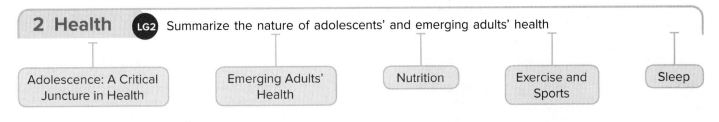

| Adolescence: A Critical Juncture in Health | Emerging Adults' Health | Nutrition | Exercise and Sports | Sleep |

Why might adolescence be a critical juncture in health? What characterizes emerging adults' health? What are some concerns about adolescents' eating habits? How much do adolescents exercise, and what role do sports play in their lives? Do adolescents get enough sleep? These are among the questions we explore in this section.

ADOLESCENCE: A CRITICAL JUNCTURE IN HEALTH

Adolescence is a critical juncture in the adoption of behaviors that are relevant to health (Kadivar & others, 2014; Latt & others, 2015; Quinlan-Davidson & others, 2014). Many of the behaviors that are linked to poor health habits and early death in adults begin during adolescence (Feinstein, Richter, & Foster, 2012). Conversely, the early formation of healthy behavior patterns, such as regular exercise and a preference for foods low in fat and cholesterol, not only has immediate health benefits but helps in adulthood to delay or prevent disability and mortality from heart disease, stroke, diabetes, and cancer (Schiff, 2015).

Unfortunately, even though the United States has become a health-conscious nation, many adolescents (and adults) still smoke, have poor nutritional habits, and spend too much of their lives as "couch potatoes." Why might many adolescents develop poor health habits? In adolescence, many individuals reach a level of health, strength, and energy that they will never match during the remainder of their lives. Given this high level of physical strength, good health, and energy, it is not surprising that many adolescents develop poor health habits.

Many health experts conclude that improving adolescents' health involves far more than taking them to the doctor's office when they are sick. Increasingly, experts recognize that whether or not adolescents develop health problems depends primarily on their behavior (Teague, MacKenzie, & Rosenthal, 2015). These experts' goals are (1) to reduce adolescents' *health-compromising behaviors*, such as drug abuse, violence, unprotected sexual intercourse, and dangerous driving; and (2) to increase adolescents' *health-enhancing behaviors*, such as exercising, eating nutritious foods, wearing seat belts, and getting adequate sleep.

One study found that the following activities, resources, and relationships were effective in promoting adolescents' health-enhancing behaviors (Youngblade & others, 2006): (1) participation in school-related organized activities, such as sports; (2) availability of positive community resources, such as Boys & Girls Clubs, and volunteering; and (3) secure attachment to parents. In this study, health-enhancing behavior was assessed by asking adolescents the extent to which they engaged in behaviors such as wearing a seat belt and participating in physical activities in and out of school.

developmental **connection**

Social Cognition

The social context plays an important role in adolescent decision making. Connect to "The Brain and Cognitive Development."

Risk-Taking Behavior   One type of health-compromising behavior that increases in adolescence is risk taking (Heneghan & others, 2015; Steinberg, 2015a; Telzer, Ichien, & Qu, 2015). One study revealed that sensation seeking increased from 10 to 15 years of age and then declined or remained stable through the remainder of adolescence and into early adulthood (Steinberg & others, 2008). However, even 18-year-olds are "more impulsive, less future-oriented, and more susceptible to peer influence" than adults in their mid- to late twenties (Steinberg, 2008).

One study of adolescents concluded that increased risk of having a motor vehicle crash was linked to a general tendency to take risks (Dunlop & Romer, 2010). Of course, not all adolescents are high risk takers and sensation seekers. Another study classified young adolescents as stable high, moderately increasing, and stable low sensation seekers (Lynne-Landsman & others, 2010). In this study, the stable low sensation-seeking young adolescents engaged in low levels of substance use, delinquency, and aggression.

Ron Dahl (2004, p. 6) provided the following vivid description of adolescent risk-taking:

What are some characteristics of adolescents' risk-taking behavior?
© Chris Garrett/Getty Images

> Beginning in early adolescence, many individuals seek experiences that create high intensity feelings. . . . Adolescents like intensity, excitement, and arousal. They are drawn to music videos that shock and bombard the senses. Teenagers flock to horror and slasher movies. They dominate queues waiting to ride the high-adrenaline rides at amusement parks. Adolescence is a time when sex, drugs, very loud music, and other high-stimulation experiences take on great appeal. It is a developmental period when an appetite for adventure, a predilection for risks, and a desire for novelty and thrills seem to reach naturally high levels. While these patterns of emotional changes are evident to some degree in most adolescents, it is important to acknowledge the wide range of individual differences during this period of development.

Researchers also have found that the more resources there are in the community, such as youth activities and adults as role models, the less likely adolescents are to engage in risky behavior (Yancey & others, 2011). One study found that a higher level of what was labeled *social capital* (in this study, number of schools, number of churches/temples/synagogues, and number of high school diplomas) was linked with lower levels of adolescent risky behavior (in this study, gunshot wounds, pregnancy, alcohol and drug treatment, and sexually transmitted infections) (Youngblade & Curry, 2006). Another study revealed that "hanging out" with peers in unstructured contexts was linked with an increase in adolescents' risk-taking behavior (Youngblade & Curry, 2006). Further, adolescents who had better grades were less likely to engage in risk taking than their counterparts with lower grades. And parental monitoring and communication skills are linked to a lower level of adolescent risk taking (Chen & others, 2008). A recent study revealed that perceiving parents as strong monitors and rule setters was linked to less risky driving by adolescents (Mirman & others, 2012).

Recently, neurobiological explanations of adolescent risk taking have been proposed (Casey, 2015; Steinberg, 2015a, b). The *prefrontal cortex*, the brain's highest level that is involved in reasoning, decision making, and self-control, matures much later (continuing to develop in late adolescence and emerging adulthood) than the *amygdala*, which is the main structure involved in emotion in the brain. The later development of the prefrontal cortex combined with the earlier maturity of the amygdala may explain the difficulty younger adolescents have in putting the brakes on their risk-taking adventures. These developmental changes in the brain provide one explanation of why risk taking declines as adolescents get older (Steinberg, 2015a, b). We will consider much more about these developmental changes in the adolescent brain in the chapter on "The Brain and Cognitive Development."

developmental **connection**

Brain Development

Although the prefrontal cortex shows considerable development in childhood, it is still not fully mature in adolescence. Connect to "The Brain and Cognitive Development."

What can be done to help adolescents satisfy their motivation for risk taking without compromising their health? One strategy is to increase the social capital of a community, as was recommended in the study previously described (Youngblade & others, 2006). As Laurence Steinberg (2004, p. 58) argues, another strategy is to limit

> opportunities for immature judgment to have harmful consequences. . . . Thus, strategies such as raising the price of cigarettes, more vigilantly enforcing laws governing the sale of alcohol, expanding access to mental health and contraceptive services, and raising the driving age would likely be more effective in limiting adolescent smoking, substance abuse, suicide, pregnancy, and automobile fatalities than strategies aimed at making adolescents wiser, less impulsive, and less short-sighted.

It also is important for parents, teachers, mentors, and other responsible adults to effectively monitor adolescents' behavior (Williams, Burton, & Warzinski, 2014). In many cases, adults decrease their monitoring of adolescents too early, leaving them to cope with tempting situations alone or with friends and peers (Masten, 2004). When adolescents are in tempting and dangerous situations with minimal adult supervision, their inclination to engage in risk-taking behavior combined with their lack of self-regulatory skills can make them vulnerable to a host of negative outcomes.

Health Services   Adolescents underutilize health-care systems (Hoover & others, 2010). Health services are especially unlikely to meet the needs of younger adolescents, ethnic minority adolescents, and adolescents living in poverty (Yeung & others, 2014; Tebb & others, 2015). There is a need for specialized training of adolescent health-care personnel that takes into account the numerous emotional and social changes adolescents experience and the implications of those changes for their behavior and health. However, not all of the blame should be placed on health-care providers. Many adolescents don't believe that health-care providers can help them. And some health-care providers may want to provide better health care for adolescents but lack adequate training and/or time during their visit.

Professional guidelines for adolescents recommend annual preventive visits with screening and guidance for health-related behaviors. However, a recent large-scale survey revealed that only 38 percent of adolescents had experienced a

© Thomas Barwick/Getty Images

What is the pattern of adolescents' use of health services?
© Spencer Grant/PhotoEdit

preventive visit in the previous 12 months, and few were given guidance for health-related behaviors (Irwin & others, 2009). Of special concern is the low use of health services by older adolescent males (Hoover & others, 2010). A U.S. study found that 16- to 20-year-old males have significantly less contact with health-care services than 11- to 15-year-old males (Marcell & others, 2002). In contrast, 16- to 20-year-old females have more contact with health-care services than do younger females. And one study found that adolescents were much more likely to seek health care for problems related to disease than problems related to mental health, tobacco use, or sexual behavior (Marcell & Halpern-Felsher, 2007).

Among the chief barriers to better health care for adolescents are cost, poor organization and availability of health services, lack of confidentiality, and reluctance on the part of health-care providers to communicate with adolescents about sensitive health issues (Hoover & others, 2010; Tebb & others, 2015). Few health-care providers receive any special training in working with adolescents. Many say they feel unprepared to provide services such as contraceptive counseling or to evaluate what constitutes abnormal behavior in adolescents. Health-care providers may transmit to their patients their discomfort in discussing topics such as sexuality and drugs, causing adolescents to avoid discussing sensitive issues with them (Marcell & Millstein, 2001).

A recent study examined the delivery of preventive health-care services to emerging adults 18 to 26 years of age (Lau & others, 2013). In this study, rates of preventive services to emerging adults were generally low. Females were more likely to receive health-care services than males.

Leading Causes of Death   Medical improvements have increased the life expectancy of today's adolescents and emerging adults compared with their counterparts in the early twentieth century. Still, life-threatening factors do exist in adolescents' and emerging adults' lives (Park & others, 2014; Teplin & others, 2014).

The three leading causes of death in adolescence and emerging adulthood are accidents, homicide, and suicide (National Center for Health Statistics, 2014). Almost half of all deaths from 15 to 24 years of age are due to unintentional injuries, approximately three-fourths of them involving motor vehicle accidents. Risky driving habits, such as speeding, tailgating, and driving under the influence of alcohol or other drugs, may be more important contributors to these accidents than lack of driving experience. In about 50 percent of motor vehicle fatalities involving adolescents, the driver has a blood alcohol level of 0.10 percent—twice the level designated as "under the influence" in some states. A high rate of intoxication is also found in adolescents who die as pedestrians or while using recreational vehicles.

- - - - - - - - ➤

developmental **connection**

Problems and Disorders

Both early and later experiences may be involved in suicide attempts. Connect to "Problems in Adolescence and Emerging Adulthood."

The Society for Adolescent Health and Medicine (SAHM) published a position paper on adolescents and driving (D'Angelo, Halpern-Felsher, & Anisha, 2010). SAHM recommends a three-stage process to begin after the sixteenth birthday with each stage requiring a minimum of 6 months to finish. One recommended course for this three-stage approach is learner's permit, restricted provisional license, and full license. Also recommended is an increase in the number of hours the adolescent is observed driving before moving to the next stage. Further information about graduated driver licensing (GDL) programs for adolescents appears in the chapter on "The Brain and Cognitive Development" in the context of adolescent decision making (Keating & Halpern-Felsher, 2008).

Homicide also is another leading cause of death in adolescents and emerging adults, especially among African American males, who are three times more likely to be killed by guns than to die of natural causes. Suicide is the third leading cause of death in adolescence and emerging adulthood. Since the 1950s, the adolescent and emerging adult suicide rate has tripled, although it has declined in recent years.

Students comfort each other in Canisteo, New York, at a memorial on the bridge where four adolescents from Jasper, New York, were killed in a car crash in 2007.
© Evening Tribune, Lynn Brennan/AP Images

EMERGING ADULTS' HEALTH

Emerging adults have more than twice the mortality rate of adolescents (Park & others, 2008). As indicated in Figure 8, males are mainly responsible for the higher mortality rate of emerging adults.

Also, compared with adolescents, emerging adults engage in more health-compromising behaviors, have more chronic health problems, are more likely to be obese, and are more likely to have a mental health disorder (Irwin, 2010). In a recent analysis, most health and health care indicators changed little across the last decade for adolescents and young adults (Park & others, 2014). In this analysis, improvements for adolescents and young adults occurred in rates of unintentional injury, assault, and tobacco use, and also adolescents improved in sexual/reproductive health. Also in this analysis, young adults continued to engage in greater health risks and have worse health outcomes than did adolescents.

Although emerging adults may know what it takes to be healthy, they often don't apply this information to their own behavior (Furstenberg, 2006). In many cases, emerging adults are not as healthy as they seem. Few emerging adults stop to think about how their personal lifestyles will affect their health later in their adult lives (Sakamaki & others, 2005). As emerging adults, many of us develop a pattern of not eating breakfast, not eating regular meals, and relying on snacks as our main food source during the day; eating excessively to the point where we exceed the normal weight for our height; smoking moderately or excessively; drinking moderately or excessively; failing to exercise; and getting by with only a few hours of sleep at night (Cheng & others, 2012; Monahan & others, 2012). These lifestyles are associated with poor health (Insel & Roth, 2012). In the Berkeley Longitudinal Study—in which individuals were evaluated over a period of 40 years—physical health at age 30 predicted life satisfaction at age 70, more so for men than for women (Mussen, Honzik, & Eichorn, 1982).

There are some hidden dangers in the peaks of performance and health in early adulthood. Young adults can draw on physical resources for a great deal of pleasure, often bouncing back easily from physical stress and abuse. However, this behavior can lead them to push their bodies too far. The negative effects of abusing one's body might not show up in emerging adulthood, but they probably will surface during early adulthood or middle adulthood (Rathunde & Csikszentmihalyi, 2006).

NUTRITION

Nutrition is an important aspect of health-compromising and health-enhancing behaviors (Schiff, 2015). The eating habits of many adolescents are health-compromising, and an increasing number of adolescents have an eating disorder (Donatelle, 2015; Finistrella & others, 2015; Langsford & others, 2015). A comparison of adolescents in 28 countries found that U.S. and British adolescents were more likely to eat fried food and less likely to eat fruits and vegetables than adolescents in most other countries that were studied (World Health Organization, 2000). A recent national survey found that only 37 percent of U.S. adolescents ate breakfast every day during the week before they took the survey (Kann & others, 2014).

Concern is often expressed over adolescents' tendency to eat between meals. However, their choice of foods is much more important than the time or place of eating. Fresh vegetables and fruits as well as whole-grain products are needed to complement the foods adolescents commonly choose, which tend to be high in protein and energy value. A recent analysis found that family dinners in France were more likely to emphasize fruits and vegetables than were family dinners in the United States (Kremer-Sadlik & others, 2015). In recent decades U.S. adolescents have been decreasing their intake of fruits and vegetables. The National Youth Risk Survey found that U.S. high school students showed a linear decrease in their intake of fruits and vegetables from 1999 through 2013 (Kann & others, 2014). A research review found that two family factors were linked to increased fruit and vegetable consumption by adolescents: availability of fruits and vegetables in the home and consumption of fruits and vegetables by parents (Pearson, Biddle, & Gorely, 2009). And one study revealed that eating regular family meals during early adolescence was linked to healthy eating habits five years later (Burgess-Champoux & others, 2009). Thus, parents play an important role in adolescents' nutrition through the food choices they make available to adolescents, by serving as models for healthy or unhealthy nutrition, and by including adolescents in regular

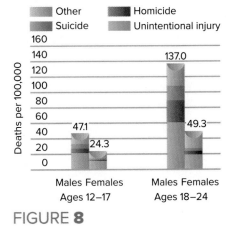

FIGURE 8
MORTALITY RATES OF U.S. ADOLESCENTS AND EMERGING ADULTS

© Image Source/PunchStock RF

family meals. Also, a recent study found that increased screen time (TV, electronic games, DVDs) was linked to increased consumption of foods and beverages with low nutritional quality and decreased consumption of fruits and vegetables (Falbe & others, 2014).

More frequent family meals are linked to a number of positive outcomes for adolescents, including better dietary intake, lower substance use, and better academic success (Eisenberg & others, 2004; Harrison & others, 2015; National Center on Addiction and Substance Abuse, 2011; Woodruff & others, 2010). A 10-year longitudinal study revealed that the more often adolescents ate family meals the less likely they were to be overweight or obese in early adulthood (Berge & others, 2015). One study found that family meal frequency for adolescents remained relatively constant from 1999 to 2010, but decreases occurred for these subgroups: girls, middle school students, Asian Americans, and youth from low-SES backgrounds (Neumark-Sztainer & others, 2013). Another study found that adolescent girls whose families functioned effectively (getting along well together, confiding in each other, and effective planning of family activities, for example) were more likely to eat meals with other family members, to consume more fruits and vegetables, and to eat breakfast (Berge & others, 2013). In the same study, adolescent boys who had better family functioning also had more frequent family meals, ate breakfast more often, and consumed less fast food.

Schools also can play an important role in adolescents' eating patterns. One study revealed that a comprehensive school intervention in the fourth and fifth grades resulted in increased vegetable consumption two years later (Wang & others, 2010). And a recent study found that promoting positive nutritional practices in a low-income middle school increased students' intake of fruit and fiber while decreasing their cholesterol levels (Alaimo & others, 2015).

A special concern in American culture is the amount of fat in our diet. Many of today's adolescents virtually live on fast-food meals, which contribute to the high fat levels in their diet (Blake, 2013, 2015). A longitudinal study revealed that frequent intake of fast food (three or more times a week) was reported by 24 percent of 15-year-old males and 21 percent of 15-year-old females (Larson & others, 2008). At 20 years of age, the percent increased to 33 percent for males but remained at 21 percent for the females.

Another special concern in adolescents' diets is the recent increase in consumption of energy drinks that tend to have high caffeine levels. A recent research review found that such energy drink consumption was linked to increased substance abuse and risk-taking behavior (Ali & others, 2015).

We will have much more to discuss about nutrition in the chapter on "Problems in Adolescence and Emerging Adulthood." There we also examine three eating disorders: obesity, anorexia nervosa, and bulimia nervosa.

developmental **connection**

Problems and Disorders

The percentage of overweight and obese adolescents has increased dramatically in recent years. Connect to "Problems in Adolescence and Emerging Adulthood."

EXERCISE AND SPORTS

Do American adolescents get enough exercise? How extensive is the role of sports in adolescent development? The answers to these questions influence adolescents' health and well-being.

Exercise   In the fourth century B.C., Aristotle commented that the quality of life is determined by its activities. Today, we know that exercise is one of the principal activities that improve the quality of life, both in adolescence and adulthood (Donatelle, 2016; Wuest & Fisette, 2015).

Developmental Changes   Researchers have found that individuals become less active as they reach and progress through adolescence (Pate & others, 2009). A national study of U.S. 9- to 15-year-olds revealed that almost all 9- and 11-year-olds met the federal government's moderate to vigorous exercise recommendations per day (a minimum of 60 minutes a day), but only 31 percent of 15-year-olds met the recommendations on weekdays and only 17 percent met the recommendations on weekends (Nader & others, 2008). Also, a longitudinal study found that total physical activity (in school and out of school) was stable from 5 to 8 years of age but fell progressively from 9 to 15 years of age (Metcalf & others, 2015). And a recent national study found that adolescent boys were much more likely to engage in 60 minutes or more of vigorous exercise per day than were girls (Kann & others, 2014). Yet another national study of U.S. adolescents revealed that physical activity increased until 13 years of age in boys and girls but then declined through 18 years of age (Kahn & others, 2008). In this study, adolescents were more likely to engage in regular exercise when they wanted to present a positive body image to their friends and when exercise was important to their parents.

Ethnic differences in exercise participation rates of U.S. adolescents also occur, and these rates vary by gender. As indicated in Figure 9, the National Youth Risk Survey found that non-Latino White boys exercised the most and African American girls the least (Kann & others, 2014). Do U.S. adolescents exercise less than their counterparts in other countries? A comparison of adolescents in 28 countries found that U.S. adolescents exercised less and ate more junk food than did adolescents in most of the other countries (World Health Organization, 2000). Just two-thirds of U.S. adolescents exercised at least twice a week compared with 80 percent or more of adolescents in Ireland, Austria, Germany, and the Slovak Republic. U.S. adolescents were more likely to eat fried food and less likely to eat fruits and vegetables than were adolescents in most other countries studied. U.S. adolescents' eating choices were similar to those of adolescents in England.

Positive Benefits of Exercise in Adolescence Exercise is linked with a number of positive outcomes in adolescence (Hoare & others, 2014; Peykari & others, 2015). One study revealed that physical fitness in adolescence was linked to physical fitness in adulthood (Mikkelsson & others, 2006). Regular exercise has a positive effect on adolescents' weight status (Ten Hoor & others, 2014). One study revealed that regular exercise from 9 to 16 years of age especially was associated with normal weight in girls (McMurray & others, 2008). Other positive outcomes of exercise in adolescence are reduced triglyceride levels, lower blood pressure, and a lower incidence of type 2 diabetes (Anyaegbu & Dharnidharka, 2014; Koozehcian & others, 2014). One study found that adolescents in the lowest 20 percent of cardiorespiratory fitness were at risk for cardiovascular disease (Lobelo & others, 2010). Other recently reported research indicated that eighth-, tenth-, and twelfth-grade students who engaged in higher levels of exercise had lower levels of alcohol, cigarette, and marijuana use (Terry-McElrath,

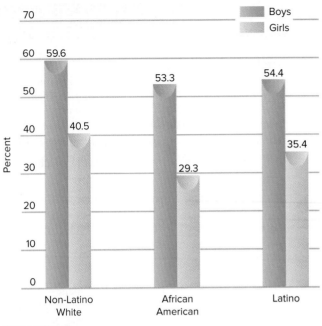

FIGURE 9

EXERCISE RATES OF U.S. HIGH SCHOOL STUDENTS IN 2013: GENDER AND ETHNICITY. *Note:* Data are for high school students who were physically active doing any kind of physical activity that increased their heart rate and made them breathe hard some of the time for a total of at least 60 minutes per day on five or more of the seven days preceding the survey. (*Source:* After Kann & others, 2014, Table 95.)

In 2007, Texas became the first state to test students' physical fitness. The student shown here is performing the trunk lift. Other assessments include aerobic exercise, muscle strength, and body fat. Assessments will be done annually.
© *Dallas Morning News, Vernon Bryant Photographer*

In Pitiful Shape

A lot of kids in my class are in pitiful physical shape. They never exercise, except in gym class, and even then they hardly break a sweat. During lunch hour, I see some of the same loafers hanging out and smoking a bunch of cigarettes. Don't they know what they are doing to their bodies? All I can say is that I'm glad I'm not like them.

I'm on the basketball team, and during the season, the coach runs us until we are exhausted. In the summer, I still play basketball and swim often. I don't know what I would do without exercise. I couldn't stand to be out of shape.

—Brian, age 14

What are some of the lifelong benefits of the positive health habits cited in this passage?

O'Malley, & Johnston, 2011). Also, a recent study revealed that a daily morning running program for three weeks improved the sleep quality, mood, and concentration of adolescents (Kalak & others, 2012).

Research studies also underscore other positive benefits of exercise for adolescents. A recent study found that adolescents with high levels of physical fitness had better connectivity between brain regions adolescents who were less fit (Herting & others, 2014). Another study revealed that adolescents who were more physically fit had electrophysiological brain profiles indicative of a higher level of task preparation and response inhibition (which benefit learning and academic achievement) than their less physically fit counterparts (Stroth & others, 2009). Further, a longitudinal study of more than 1.1 million Swedish males found that 18-year-olds who had lower cardiovascular fitness had an increased risk of early-onset dementia and mild cognitive impairment 42 years later (Nyberg & others, 2014).

An exciting possibility is that physical exercise might act as a buffer against the stress adolescents experience and improve their mental health and life satisfaction (Wood & others, 2012). Consider the following support for this possibility:

· A recent study of depressed adolescents with low levels of exercise revealed that a 12-week exercise intervention lowered their rates of depression (Dopp & others, 2012).
· Higher levels of physical activity at 9 and 11 years of age predicted higher self-esteem at 11 and 13 years of age (Schmalz & others, 2007).
· A nine-month physical activity intervention with sedentary adolescent girls improved their self-image (Schneider, Dunton, & Cooper, 2008).
· High school seniors who exercised frequently had higher grade-point averages, used drugs less frequently, were less depressed, and got along better with their parents than those who rarely exercised (Field, Diego, & Sanders, 2001).

A recent research review concluded that aerobic exercise also increasingly is linked to children's and adolescents' cognitive skills (Best, 2011). Researchers have found that aerobic exercise has benefits for children's and adolescents' attention, memory, effortful and goal-directed thinking and behavior, and creativity (Best, 2011; Budde & others, 2008; Davis & others, 2007, 2011; Hillman & others, 2009; Hinkle, Tuckman, & Sampson, 1993; Monti, Hillman, & Cohen, 2012; Pesce & others, 2009). And two recent studies of young adolescents found that regular exercise was associated with higher academic achievement (Chen & others, 2013; Hashim, Freddy, & Rosmatunisah, 2012). Further, researchers recently have revealed that exercise reduces the symptoms of attention deficit hyperactivity disorder (ADHD) (Kamp, Sperlich, & Holmberg, 2014).

Roles of Families, Peers, Schools, and Screen-Based Activity in Adolescent Exercise What contextual factors influence whether adolescents engage in regular exercise? Four influences are families, peers, schools, and screen-based activity.

Families   Parents have an important influence on adolescents' exercise patterns. Children and adolescents benefit when parents engage in regular exercise and are physically fit. Children whose parents got them involved in regular exercise and sports during the elementary school years are likely to continue engaging in exercise on a regular basis as adolescents. One study revealed that 9- to 13-year-olds were more likely to engage in physical activity during their free time if they felt safe, had a number of places to be active, and had parents who participated in physical activities with them (Heitzler & others, 2006). Also, a recent study found that daughters' participation in sports was related to both parents' exercise habits while sons' participation was linked only to fathers' exercise habits (Sukys & others, 2014). And a recent meta-analysis also found that fathers had more influence on the physical activity of their adolescent sons than on that of their adolescent daughters (Yao & Rhodes, 2015).

Peers   Peers often influence adolescents' physical activity (Lu & others, 2014; Spencer & others, 2014). A recent study revealed that female adolescents' physical activity was linked to their male and female friends' physical activity while male adolescents' physical activity was associated with their female friends' physical activity (Sirard & others, 2013). In a recent research review, peer/friend support of exercise, presence of peers and friends, peer norms, friendship quality and acceptance, peer crowds, and peer victimization were linked to adolescents' physical activity (Fitzgerald, Fitzgerald, & Aherne, 2012). Consider these studies described in the review:

How do peers influence adolescents' exercise?
© Jacek Chabraszewski/Getty Images

· **Peer/friend support.** Friend support for physical activity was a stronger predictor of adolescent physical activity than support from parents or siblings (Duncan & others, 2007).

· **Presence of peers and friends.** Adolescent boys at risk for being overweight were less active than thin boys when alone but as active as thin boys when a peer was present (Rittenhouse, Salvy, & Barkley, 2011).

· **Friendship quality and acceptance.** Higher levels of friendship quality and acceptance were linked to youths' continued participation in youth soccer (Ulrich-French & Smith, 2009).

· **Peer crowd affiliation.** Adolescents who affiliated with "jocks" and "populars" exercised considerably more than their counterparts who affiliated with other crowds (MacKey & La Greca, 2007).

· **Peer victimization.** Being victimized by peers predicted less willingness to engage in physical activity in overweight youth (Gray & others, 2008).

Schools   Some of the blame for the poor physical condition of U.S. children and adolescents falls on U.S. schools, many of which fail to provide physical education classes on a daily basis (Fung & others, 2012). A recent national survey revealed that in 2013 only 29 percent of U.S. ninth- through twelfth-graders participated in physical education classes all five days in an average school week (Kann & others, 2014). Males (35 percent) were more likely to participate at this level than females (24 percent). Ninth-graders were most likely to regularly take a PE class (42 percent); the least likely were twelfth-graders (20 percent).

Does pushing children and adolescents to exercise more vigorously in school make a difference? In one study, sedentary adolescent females were assigned to one of two groups: (1) a special physical education class that met five times a week with about 40 minutes of activity daily (aerobic dance, basketball, swimming, or Tae Bo) for four of the five days and a lecture/discussion on the importance of physical activity and ways to become more physically active on the fifth day; or (2) a control group that did not take a physical education class (Jamner & others, 2004). After four months, the participants in the physical education class had improved their cardiovascular fitness and

How might screen time be linked to adolescents' lower exercise levels?
© Hero Images/Corbis

developmental **connection**

Technology

When media multitasking is taken into account, U.S. 11- to 14-year-olds use media an average of nearly 12 hours a day. Connect to "Culture."

© Photodisc/Getty Images RF

developmental **connection**

Schools

Adolescents who participate in extracurricular activities, such as sports, have higher grades, are more engaged in school, and are less likely to drop out of school. Connect to "Schools."

lifestyle activity (such as walking instead of driving short distances). Other research studies have found positive benefits for programs designed to improve the physical fitness of students (Rosenkranz & others, 2012).

Screen-Based Activity *Screen-based activity* (watching television, using computers, talking on the phone, texting, and instant messaging for long hours) is associated with lower levels of physical fitness in adolescence (Bassett & others, 2015; Mitchell, Pate, & Blair, 2012). One study revealed that children and adolescents who engaged in the highest amounts of daily screen-based activity (TV/video/video game use in this study) were less likely to exercise daily (Sisson & others, 2010). In this study, children and adolescents who engaged in low physical activity and high screen-based activity were almost twice as likely to be overweight as their more active, less sedentary counterparts (Sisson & others, 2010).

A recent research review concluded that screen-based activity is linked to a number of adolescent health problems (Costigan & others, 2013). In this review, a higher level of screen-based sedentary behavior was associated with being overweight, having sleep problems, being depressed, and having lower levels of physical activity/fitness and psychological well-being (higher stress levels, for example).

Sports Sports play an important role in the lives of many adolescents. A recent national study revealed that in 2013, 54 percent of ninth- through twelfth-grade U.S. students played on at least one sports team at school or in the community (Kann & others, 2014). The 54 percent figure represents a 4 percent drop from 2011. In the 2013 assessment, boys (60 percent) were more likely to play on a sports team than girls (48.5 percent). African American boys had the highest participation rate (66 percent) and Latino females the lowest participation rate (45 percent) (Kann & others, 2014). In another recent assessment, high school girls' participation increased between 1971 and 2012 (Bassett & others, 2015).

Sports can have both positive and negative influences on adolescent development (Echlin & others, 2014). Many sports activities can improve adolescents' physical health and well-being, self-confidence, motivation to excel, and ability to work with others (Gaudreau, Amiot, & Vallerand, 2009). Adolescents who spend considerable time in sports are less likely than others to engage in risk-taking behaviors such as using drugs. The following recent studies confirmed the positive benefits of organized sports for adolescents:

· Among a wide range of activities (other physical activity, physical education, screen time, and diet quality, for example), team sports participation was the strongest predictor of lower risk for being overweight or obese (Drake & others, 2012).

· Adolescents who participated in sports were less likely to engage in risk-taking activities such as truancy, cigarette smoking, sexual intercourse, and delinquency than nonparticipants in sports (Nelson & Gordon-Larsen, 2006).

· Adolescents who participated in sports plus other activities had more positive outcomes (competence, self-concept, and connectedness, for example) than adolescents who participated in sports alone, school groups alone, or religious groups alone, or who engaged in no group activities (Linver, Roth, & Brooks-Gunn, 2009). However, participating in sports had more positive outcomes than no involvement in activities.

· Young adolescents who participated both in sports programs and youth development programs were characterized by positive development (academic competence, confidence, character, caring, and social connection, for example) (Zarrett & others, 2009).

Sports also can have negative outcomes for adolescents: the pressure to achieve and win, physical injuries, distraction from academic work, and unrealistic expectations for success as an athlete (Smucny, Parikh, & Pandya, 2015). One downside of the extensive participation in sports by American adolescents is pressure by parents and coaches to win at all costs. Researchers have found that adolescents' participation in competitive sports is linked with competition anxiety and self-centeredness (Smith & Smoll, 1997). Furthermore, some adolescents spend so much time in sports that their academic performance suffers.

Injuries are common when adolescents play sports (Clausen & others, 2014; Lee, Hardy, & Zetterberg, 2015; Rossler & others, 2014). A national study of ninth- through twelfth-graders revealed that of the 80 percent of adolescents who exercised or played sports during the 30 previous days, 22 percent had seen a doctor or nurse for an exercise- or sports-related injury (Eaton & others, 2008). Ninth-graders were most likely to incur exercise- or sports-related injuries, twelfth-graders the least likely.

Increasingly, adolescents are pushing their bodies beyond their capabilities, stretching the duration, intensity, and frequency of their training to the point that they cause overuse injuries (Patel & Baker, 2006). Another problem that has surfaced is the use of performance-enhancing drugs, such as steroids, by adolescent athletes (Elliot & others, 2007).

What are some positive and negative aspects of sports participation in adolescence?
© Lisa Peardon/Getty Images

Coaches play an important role in youth sports (Bosselut & others, 2012; Cushion, Ford, & Williams, 2012). Too often youth coaches create a performance-oriented motivational climate that is focused on winning, receiving public recognition, and performing better than other participants. But other coaches place more emphasis on mastery motivation that focuses adolescents' attention on developing their skills and meeting self-determined standards of success. Researchers have found that athletes who have a mastery focus are more likely than others to see the benefits of practice, to persist in the face of difficulty, and to show significant skill development over the course of a season (Roberts, Treasure, & Kavussanu, 1997).

A final topic involving sports that needs to be examined is the **female athlete triad,** which involves a combination of disordered eating (weight loss), amenorrhea (absent or irregular menstrual periods), and osteoporosis (thinning and weakening of bones) (Deimel & Dunlap, 2012; Nazem & Ackerman, 2012; Rauh, Barrack, & Nichols, 2014). Once menstrual periods have become somewhat regular in adolescent girls, not having a menstrual period for more than three or four months can reduce bone strength. Fatigue and stress fractures may develop. The female athlete triad often goes unnoticed. A recent study found that triad risk factors were prevalent among female high school athletes but that knowledge of the female athlete triad was low among the athletes and their coaches (Brown, Wengreen, & Beals, 2014). Another recent study revealed a lack of information about the female athlete triad among college coaches as well (Frideres, Mottinger, & Palao, 2015). Recent research studies suggest that the incidence of the female athlete triad is low, but that a significant number of female adolescents and college students have one of the characteristics of the disorder, such as disordered eating, menstrual irregularity, or osteoporosis (Thein-Nissenbaum & others, 2012).

SLEEP

Might changes in sleep patterns between childhood and adolescence contribute to adolescents' health-compromising behaviors? There has been a surge of interest in adolescent sleep patterns (Carskadon & Tarokh, 2014; Louca & Short, 2015; Mendelson & others, 2015; Owens, 2014; Perkinson-Gloor, Lemola, & Grob, 2013; Tarokh, Carskadon, & Ackerman, 2014; Telzer & others, 2013).

In a recent national survey of youth, only 32 percent of U.S. adolescents got eight or more hours of sleep on an average school night (Kann & others, 2014). In this study, the

developmental **connection**

Achievement

Carol Dweck argues that a mastery orientation (focusing on the task and process of learning) produces more positive achievement outcomes than a performance orientation in which the outcome—winning—is the most important aspect of achieving. Connect to "Achievement, Work, and Careers."

female athlete triad A combination of disordered eating, amenorrhea, and osteoporosis that may develop in female adolescents and college students.

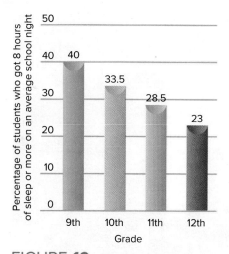

FIGURE **10**

DEVELOPMENTAL CHANGES IN U.S. ADOLESCENTS' SLEEP PATTERNS ON AN AVERAGE SCHOOL NIGHT

How might caffeine intake be associated with inadequate sleep during adolescence?
© Burger/Phanie/Alamy

percentage of adolescents getting this much sleep on an average school night decreased as they got older (see Figure 10).

Another study also found that adolescents are not getting adequate sleep. The National Sleep Foundation (2006) conducted a U.S. survey of 1,602 caregivers and their 11- to 17-year-olds. Forty-five percent of the adolescents got inadequate sleep on school nights (less than 8 hours). Older adolescents (ninth- to twelfth-graders) got markedly less sleep on school nights than younger adolescents (sixth- to eighth-graders)—62 percent of the older adolescents got inadequate sleep compared with 21 percent of the younger adolescents. Adolescents who got inadequate sleep (8 hours or less) on school nights were more likely to feel tired or sleepy, to be cranky and irritable, to fall asleep in school, to be in a depressed mood, and to drink caffeinated beverages than their counterparts who got optimal sleep (9 or more hours). Also, a national study confirmed that adolescents get less sleep as they get older (Keyes & others, 2015). In this study, adolescent sleep generally declined from 1991 to 2012. Further, girls were less likely than boys to report that they got 7 or more hours of sleep per night, as were adolescents from ethnic minority, urban, and low-SES families in comparison with adolescents from other groups.

Studies also confirm that adolescents in other countries are not getting adequate sleep (Leger & others, 2012). A recent research review found that Asian adolescents' bedtimes were even later than those of their peers in North America and Europe, which results in less total sleep on school nights and more daytime sleepiness for the Asian adolescents (Gradisar, Gardner, & Dohnt, 2011).

The following recent studies document the link between getting too little sleep and having problems during adolescence:

· Adolescents who got less than 7.7 hours of sleep per night on average had more emotional and peer-related problems, high anxiety, and a higher level of suicidal ideation (Sarchiapone & others, 2014).

· Adolescents who slept 7 hours or less per night engaged in more delinquent acts than their counterparts who slept 8 to 10 hours per night (Clinkinbeard & others, 2011).

· Sleep disturbances (insomnia, for example) at 16 years of age predicted sleep disturbances at 23, 33, and 42 years of age (Dregan & Armstrong, 2010).

· In a recent experimental study, 16 adolescents underwent a sleep manipulation that included five consecutive nights of sleep deprivation (6½ hours in bed) and five nights of healthy sleep duration (10 hours in bed) (Beebe, Rose, & Amin, 2010). The two types of sleep were counterbalanced by administering them in varied sequences. At the end of each session, the participants watched educational films and took related quizzes in a simulated classroom. The adolescents who had experienced the unhealthy sleep condition had lower quiz scores and were less attentive to the films.

· A longitudinal study in which adolescents completed daily diaries every 14 days in ninth, tenth, and twelfth grades found that regardless of how much students studied each day, when the students sacrificed sleep time to study more than usual, they had difficulty understanding what was taught in class and were more likely to struggle with class assignments the next day (Gillen-O'Neel, Huynh, & Fuligni, 2013).

· Sleep problems during adolescence were associated with a lower level of working memory and in turn this lower level of working memory was linked to greater risk taking (Thomas & others, 2014).

Why are adolescents getting too little sleep? Among the reasons given are those involving electronic media, caffeine, and changes in the brain coupled with early school start times (Owens, 2014). In one study, adolescents averaged engaging in four electronic activities (in some case simultaneous use of different devices, after 9 p.m.) (Calamaro, Mason, & Ratcliffe, 2009). Engaging in these electronic activities in the evening can replace sleep time, and such media use may increase sleep-disrupting arousal (Cain & Gradisar, 2010; Wu & others, 2015).

Caffeine intake also likely is related to adolescents not getting adequate sleep (Owens, 2014). Greater caffeine intake as early as 12 years of age is linked to later sleep onset, shorter sleep duration, and increased daytime sleepiness (Bryant Luddin &

Wolfson, 2010; Orbeta & others, 2006). The association of caffeine consumption and daytime sleepiness is also related to lower academic achievement (James, Kristjansson, & Sigfusdottir, 2011). Further, researchers have yet to study how adolescent sleep patterns might be influenced by very high levels of caffeine intake involving high-energy drinks.

Many adolescents, especially older adolescents, stay up later at night and sleep longer in the morning than they did when they were children. These findings have implications for the hours during which adolescents learn most effectively in school (Colrain & Baker, 2011).

Mary Carskadon and her colleagues (Carskadon, 2002, 2004, 2006, 2011; Carskadon & Tarokh, 2014; Crowley & Carskadon, 2010; Jenni & Carskadon, 2007; Kurth & others, 2010; Tarokh & Carskadon, 2008, 2010; Tarokh, Carskadon, & Achermann, 2014) have conducted a number of research studies on adolescent sleep patterns. They found that when given the opportunity adolescents will sleep an average of 9 hours and 25 minutes a night. Most get considerably less than 9 hours of sleep, especially during the week. This short-

What are some developmental changes in sleep patterns during adolescence?
© Gareth Brown/Corbis

fall creates a sleep deficit, which adolescents often attempt to make up on the weekend. The researchers also found that older adolescents tend to be sleepier during the day than younger adolescents. They theorized that this sleepiness was not due to academic work or social pressures. Rather, their research suggests that adolescents' biological clocks undergo a shift as they get older, delaying their period of wakefulness by about one hour. A delay in the nightly release of the sleep-inducing hormone melatonin, which is produced in the brain's pineal gland, seems to underlie this shift (Eckerberg & others, 2012). Melatonin is secreted at about 9:30 p.m. in younger adolescents and approximately an hour later in older adolescents.

Carskadon has suggested that early school starting times may cause grogginess, inattention in class, and poor performance on tests. Based on her research, some schools are now starting classes later (Cassoff & others, 2013). For example, school officials in Edina, Minnesota, decided to start classes at 8:30 a.m. rather than the usual 7:25 a.m. With the new starting time there have been fewer referrals for discipline problems and fewer students who report being ill or depressed. The school system reports that test scores have improved for high school students but not for middle school students. This finding supports Carskadon's suspicion that early start times are likely to be more stressful for older than for younger adolescents. Also, a recent study found that just a 30-minute delay in school start time was linked to improvements in adolescents' sleep, alertness, mood, and health (Owens, Belon, & Moss, 2010). Further, a recent study revealed that early high school start times were linked to higher rates of vehicle crashes among adolescent drivers (Vorona & others, 2014). Based on such research, the American Academy of Pediatrics recently advocated that schools institute start times from 8:30 to 9:30 a.m. to improve students' academic performance and quality of life (Adolescent Sleep Working Group, AAP, 2014).

Do sleep patterns change in emerging adulthood? Research indicates that they do (Galambos, Howard, & Maggs, 2011; Kloss & others, 2011, 2014; Wolfson, 2010). In a recent study which revealed that more than 60 percent of college students were categorized as poor-quality sleepers, it appears that the weekday bedtimes and rise times of first-year college students are approximately 1 hour and 15 minutes later than those of seniors in high school (Lund & others, 2010). However, the first-year college students had later bedtimes and rise times than third- and fourth-year college students, indicating that at about 20 to 22 years of age, a reverse in the timing of bedtimes and rise times occurs. In this study, poor-quality sleep was linked to worse physical and mental health, and the students reported that emotional and academic stress negatively affected their sleep.

In Mary Carskadon's sleep laboratory at Brown University, an adolescent girl's brain activity is being monitored. Carskadon (2005) says that in the morning, sleep-deprived adolescents' "brains are telling them it's night time . . . and the rest of the world is saying it's time to go to school" (p. 19).
© Courtesy of Jim LoScalzo

Review

- Why is adolescence a critical juncture in health? How extensive is risk taking in adolescence? How good are adolescents at using health services? What are the leading causes of death in adolescence?
- What characterizes emerging adults' health?
- What are some concerns about adolescents' eating habits?
- What roles do exercise and sports play in adolescents' lives?
- What are some concerns about adolescent sleep patterns?

Connect

- Compare adolescents' health issues with those of emerging adults.

Reflect *Your Own Personal Journey of Life*

- What were your health habits like from the time you entered puberty to the time you completed high school? Describe your health-compromising and health-enhancing behaviors during this time. After graduating from high school, have you reduced your health-compromising behaviors? Explain.

---

3 Evolution, Heredity, and Environment

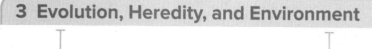

LG3 Explain the contributions of evolution, heredity, and environment to adolescent development

The Evolutionary Perspective   The Genetic Process   Heredity-Environment Interaction

There are one hundred and ninety-three living species of monkeys and apes. One hundred and ninety-two of them are covered with hair. The exception is the naked ape, self-named *Homo sapiens*.

—Desmond Morris
British zoologist, 20th century

The size and complexity of the adolescent's brain emerged over the long course of evolution. Let's explore the evolutionary perspective on adolescent development and then examine how heredity and environment interact to influence adolescent development.

THE EVOLUTIONARY PERSPECTIVE

In terms of evolutionary time, humans are relative newcomers to the Earth. If we think of the broad expanse of time as a calendar year, then humans arrived on Earth in the last moments of December (Sagan, 1977). As our earliest ancestors left the forest to feed on the savannahs and finally to form hunting societies on the open plains, their minds and behaviors changed. How did this evolution come about?

Natural Selection and Adaptive Behavior   *Natural selection* is the evolutionary process that favors those individuals of a species who are best adapted to survive and reproduce. To understand natural selection, let's return to the middle of the nineteenth century, when the British naturalist Charles Darwin (1809–1882) was traveling the world, observing many different species of animals in their natural habitats. In his groundbreaking book, *On the Origin of Species* (1859), Darwin noted that most species reproduce at rates that would cause enormous increases in their population and yet populations remained nearly constant. He reasoned that an intense struggle for food, water, and resources must occur among the many young born in each generation, because many of them do not survive. Darwin believed that those who do survive to reproduce and pass on their genes to the next generation are probably superior to others in a number of ways. In other words, the survivors are better adapted to their world than the nonsurvivors (Raven & others, 2014). Over the course of many generations, Darwin reasoned, organisms with the characteristics needed for survival would compose a larger and larger percentage of the population, producing a gradual modification of the species. If environmental conditions changed, however, other characteristics might be favored by natural selection, moving the evolutionary process in a different direction.

To understand the role of evolution in behavior, we need to understand the concept of adaptive behavior (Starr, Evers, & Starr, 2015, 2016). In evolutionary conceptions of psychology, **adaptive behavior** is a modification of behavior that promotes an organism's survival in the natural habitat. All organisms must adapt to specific places, climates, food sources, and ways of life in order to survive (Hoefnagels, 2015; Johnson, 2015). In humans, attachment ensures an infant's closeness to the caregiver for feeding and protection from danger. This behavioral characteristic promotes survival just as an eagle's claw, which facilitates predation, ensures the eagle's survival.

Evolutionary Psychology Although Darwin introduced the theory of evolution by natural selection in 1859, his ideas only recently have been used to explain behavior. The field of **evolutionary psychology** emphasizes the importance of adaptation, reproduction, and "survival of the fittest" in explaining behavior. Because evolution favors organisms that are best adapted to survive and reproduce in a specific environment, evolutionary psychology focuses on the conditions that allow individuals to survive or perish. In this view, the process of natural selection favors those behaviors that increase organisms' reproductive success and their ability to pass their genes on to the next generation (Durrant & Ellis, 2013).

David Buss' (2000, 2008, 2012, 2015) ideas on evolutionary psychology have produced a wave of interest in how evolution can explain human behavior. Buss argues that just as evolution shapes our physical features such as our body shape and height, it also influences our decision making, our aggressive behavior, our fears, and our mating patterns.

© Tom Brakefield/Getty Images RF

Evolutionary Developmental Psychology There is growing interest in using the concepts of evolutionary psychology to understand human development (Anderson & Finlay, 2014; Bjorklund, 2012; Brune & others, 2012; Bugental, Corpuz, & Beaulieu, 2015). Following are some ideas proposed by evolutionary developmental psychologists (Bjorklund & Pellegrini, 2002).

One important concept is that an extended childhood period evolved because humans require time to develop a large brain and learn the complexity of human societies. Humans take longer to become reproductively mature than any other mammal (see Figure 11). During this extended childhood period, they develop a large brain and acquire the experiences needed to become competent adults in a complex society.

Another key idea is that many evolved psychological mechanisms are *domain-specific*. That is, the mechanisms apply only to a specific aspect of a person's makeup. According to evolutionary psychology, information processing is one example. In this view, the mind is not a general-purpose device that can be applied equally to a vast array of problems. Instead, as our ancestors dealt with certain recurring problems such as hunting and finding shelter, specialized modules evolved that process information related to those problems: for example, a module for physical knowledge for tracking animals, a module for mathematical knowledge for trading, and a module for language.

Evolved mechanisms are not always adaptive in contemporary society. Some behaviors that were adaptive for our prehistoric ancestors may not serve us well today. For example, the food-scarce environment of our ancestors likely led to humans' propensity to gorge when food is available and to crave high-caloric foods, a trait that that might lead to an epidemic of obesity when food is plentiful.

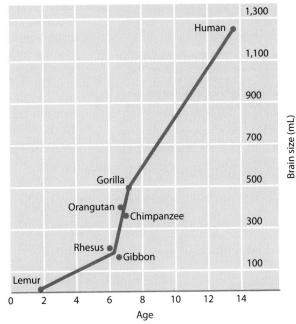

FIGURE 11

THE BRAIN SIZES OF VARIOUS PRIMATES AND HUMANS IN RELATION TO THE LENGTH OF THE JUVENILE PERIOD

Evaluating Evolutionary Psychology Albert Bandura (1998), the author of social cognitive theory, has criticized the "biologizing" of psychology. Bandura acknowledges the influence of evolution on human adaptation and change. However, he rejects what he calls "one-sided evolutionism," in which social behavior is seen as the product of evolved biology. Bandura stresses that evolutionary pressures favored biological adaptations that encouraged the use of tools, allowing humans to manipulate, alter, and construct new environmental conditions. In time, humans' increasingly complex environmental innovations produced new pressures that favored the evolution of specialized brain systems to support consciousness, thought, and language.

adaptive behavior A modification of behavior that promotes an organism's survival in the natural habitat.

evolutionary psychology An approach that emphasizes the importance of adaptation, reproduction, and "survival of the fittest" in explaining behavior.

developmental **connection**

Social Cognitive Theory

Bandura's social cognitive theory emphasizes reciprocal connections between behavior, environment, and person (cognitive) factors. Connect to "Introduction."

In other words, evolution gave humans body structures and biological potentialities, not behavioral dictates. Having evolved our advanced biological capacities, we can use them to produce diverse cultures—aggressive or pacific, egalitarian or autocratic. As American scientist Stephen Jay Gould (1981) concluded, in most domains, human biology allows a broad range of cultural possibilities. The sheer pace of social change, Bandura (1998) notes, underscores the range of possibilities biology permits.

The "big picture" idea of natural selection leading to the development of human traits and behaviors is difficult to refute or test because it is on a time scale that does not lend itself to empirical study. Thus, studying specific genes in humans and other species—and their links to traits and behaviors—may be the best approach for testing ideas coming out of the evolutionary psychology perspective.

THE GENETIC PROCESS

Genetic influences on behavior evolved over time and across many species. The many traits and characteristics that are genetically influenced have a long evolutionary history that is retained in our DNA. In other words, our DNA is not just inherited from our parents; it's also what we've inherited as a species from the species that came before us. Let's take a closer look at DNA and its role in human development.

How are characteristics that suit a species for survival transmitted from one generation to the next? Darwin did not know because genes and the principles of genetics had not yet been discovered. Each of us carries a "genetic code" that we inherited from our parents. Because a fertilized egg carries this human code, a fertilized human egg cannot grow into an egret, eagle, or elephant.

DNA and the Collaborative Gene Each of us began life as a single cell weighing about one twenty-millionth of an ounce! This tiny piece of matter housed our entire genetic code—instructions that orchestrated growth from that single cell to a person made of trillions of cells, each containing a perfect replica of the original genetic code. That code is carried by our genes. What are they and what do they do?

chromosomes Threadlike structures that contain deoxyribonucleic acid, or DNA.

DNA A complex molecule that contains genetic information.

genes The units of hereditary information, which are short segments composed of DNA.

The nucleus of each human cell contains **chromosomes,** which are thread-like structures that contain the remarkable substance deoxyribonucleic acid, or DNA. **DNA** is a complex molecule that contains genetic information. It has a double helix shape, like a spiral staircase. **Genes,** the units of hereditary information, are short segments composed of DNA, as you can see in Figure 12. They direct cells to reproduce themselves and to assemble proteins. Proteins,

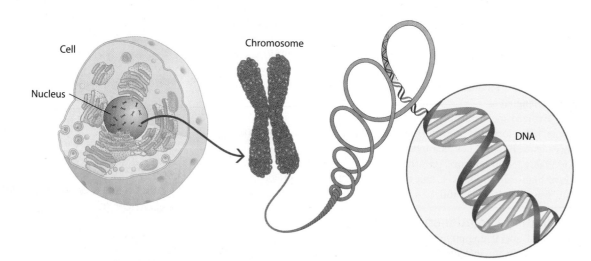

Cell

Nucleus

Chromosome

DNA

FIGURE **12**

CELLS, CHROMOSOMES, GENES, AND DNA. (*Left*) The body contains trillions of cells, which are the basic structural units of life. Each cell contains a central structure, the nucleus. (*Middle*) Chromosomes and genes are located in the nucleus of the cell. Chromosomes are made up of threadlike structures composed of DNA molecules. (*Right*) A gene, a segment of DNA that contains the hereditary code. The structure of DNA is a spiraled double chain.

in turn, serve as the building blocks of cells as well as the regulators that direct the body's processes (Brooker, 2016; Cowan, 2015; Starr & others, 2016).

Each gene has its own function, and each gene has its own location, its own designated place on a specific chromosome. Today, there is a great deal of enthusiasm about efforts to discover the specific locations of genes that are linked to certain functions (Brooker, 2015, 2016; Mason & others, 2015). An important step in this direction was accomplished when the Human Genome Project and the Celera Corporation completed a preliminary map of the human *genome*—the complete set of instructions for making a human organism.

One of the big surprises of the Human Genome Project was a report indicating that humans have only about 30,000 genes (U.S. Department of Energy, 2001). More recently, the number of human genes has been revised downward again to approximately 21,500 (Ensembl Human, 2008). Further, recent analysis proposes that humans may actually have fewer than 20,000 protein-producing genes (Abyzov & others, 2014; Ezkurdia & others, 2014). Scientists had thought that humans had as many as 100,000 or more genes. They had also believed that each gene programmed just one protein. In fact, humans appear to have far more proteins than they have genes, so there cannot be a one-to-one correspondence between them (Commoner, 2002; Moore, 2015). Each segment of DNA is not translated, in automaton-like fashion, into one and only one protein. It does not act independently, as developmental psychologist David Moore (2001) emphasized by titling his book *The Dependent Gene*.

Rather than being an independent source of developmental information, DNA collaborates with other sources of information to specify our characteristics (Moore, 2013, 2015). The collaboration operates at many points. Small pieces of DNA are mixed, matched, and linked by the cellular machinery. That machinery is sensitive to its context—that is, it is influenced by what is going on around it. Whether a gene is turned "on," working to assemble proteins, is also a matter of collaboration. The activity of genes (genetic *expression*) is affected by their environment (Kahn & Fraga, 2009; Lickliter & Honeycutt, 2015; Moore, 2015). For example, hormones that circulate in the blood make their way into the cell, where they can turn genes "on" and "off." And the flow of hormones can be affected by environmental conditions such as light, day length, nutrition, and behavior. Numerous studies have shown that external events outside the cell and the person, and internal events inside the cell, can excite or inhibit gene expression (Craft & others, 2014; Dedon & Begley, 2014).

Recent research has documented that factors such as stress, exercise, nutrition, respiration, radiation, temperature, and sleep can influence gene expression (Craft & others, 2014; Dedon & Begley, 2014; Donnelly & Storchova, 2015; McInnis & others, 2015). For example, one study revealed that an increase in the concentration of stress hormones such as cortisol produced a fivefold increase in DNA damage (Flint & others, 2007). Another study found that exposure to radiation changed the rate of DNA synthesis in cells (Lee & others, 2011). And recent research indicates that sleep deprivation can affect gene expression in negative ways such as increased inflammation, expression of stress-related genes, and impairment of protein functioning (da Costa Souza & Ribeiro, 2015).

Scientists have found that certain genes become turned on or off as a result of exercise mainly through a process called *methylation*, in which tiny atoms attach themselves to the outside of a gene (Lindholm & others, 2014). This process makes the gene more or less

THE WIZARD OF ID

By permission of John L. Hart FLP, and Creators Syndicate, Inc.

capable of receiving and responding to biochemical signals from the body (Reynolds, 2014). In this way the behavior of the gene, but not its structure, is changed. Researchers also have found that diet may affect gene behavior through the process of methylation (Ma & others, 2015; Taylor, Jones, & Henagan, 2014).

In short, a single gene is rarely the source of a protein's genetic information, much less of an inherited trait (Gottlieb, 2007; Moore, 2015). Rather than being a group of independent genes, the human genome consists of many collaborative genes.

The term *gene-gene interaction* is increasingly used to describe studies that focus on the interdependence of two or more genes in influencing characteristics, behavior, diseases, and development (Hu, Wang, & Wang, 2014; Sarlos & others, 2014). For example, recent studies have documented gene-gene interaction in immune system functioning during childhood (Reijmerink & others, 2011), asthma (Lee & others, 2014), alcoholism (Yokoyama & others, 2013), cancer (Jin & Lee, 2015; Mandal, Abebe, & Chaudhary, 2014), and cardiovascular disease (Kumar & others, 2014; Musameh & others, 2015).

Genotype and Phenotype   No one possesses all the characteristics that his or her genetic structure makes possible. A person's genetic heritage—the actual genetic material—is called a **genotype.** Not all of this genetic material is apparent in our observed and measurable characteristics. The way an individual's genotype is expressed in observed and measurable characteristics is called a **phenotype.** Phenotypes include physical traits, such as height, weight, eye color, and skin pigmentation, as well as psychological characteristics, such as intelligence, creativity, personality, and social tendencies.

For each genotype, a range of phenotypes can be expressed (Johnson, 2015; Simon, 2015). Imagine that we could identify all the genes that would make an adolescent introverted or extraverted. Could we predict introversion or extraversion in a specific person from our knowledge of those genes? The answer is no, because even if our genetic model was adequate, introversion and extraversion are characteristics that are shaped by experience throughout life. For example, a parent might push an introverted child into social situations, encouraging the child to become more gregarious. Or the parent might support the child's preference for solitary play.

Twin studies compare identical twins with fraternal twins. Identical twins develop from a single fertilized egg that splits into two genetically identical organisms. Fraternal twins develop from separate eggs, making them genetically no more similar than nontwin siblings. *What is the nature of the twin study method?*
© Jack Hollingsworth/Getty Images RF

HEREDITY-ENVIRONMENT INTERACTION

So far, we have discussed genes and how they work, and one theme is apparent: Heredity and environment interact to produce development. Whether we are studying how genes produce proteins or how they influence a person's height, we end up discussing heredity-environment interactions. Is it possible, though, to untangle the influence of heredity from that of environment and discover the role of each in producing individual differences in development? When heredity and environment interact, how does heredity influence the environment and vice versa?

Behavior Genetics   **Behavior genetics** is the field that seeks to discover the influence of heredity and environment on individual differences in human traits and development (Krushkal & others, 2014; Lickliter & Honeycutt, 2015). If you think about all of the people you know, for example, you have probably realized that they differ in terms of their levels of introversion/extraversion. Behavior geneticists try to figure out what is responsible for such differences—that is, to what extent do people differ because of differences in genes, environment, or a combination of these?

To study the influence of heredity on behavior, behavior geneticists often use either twin or adoption situations (Jansen & others, 2015; Tan & others, 2015). In the most common **twin study,** the behavioral similarity of identical twins is compared with the behavioral similarity of fraternal twins. *Identical twins* (called monozygotic twins) develop from a single fertilized egg that splits into two genetically identical replicas, each of which becomes a person. *Fraternal twins* (called dizygotic twins) develop from separate eggs and separate sperm. Although fraternal twins share the same womb, they are no more alike genetically than are nontwin brothers and sisters, and they may be of different sexes.

By comparing groups of identical and fraternal twins, behavior geneticists capitalize on the basic knowledge that identical twins are more similar genetically than are fraternal twins

genotype A person's genetic heritage; the actual genetic material.

phenotype The way an individual's genotype is expressed in observed and measurable characteristics.

behavior genetics The field that seeks to discover the influence of heredity and environment on individual differences in human traits and development.

twin study A study in which the behavioral similarity of identical twins is compared with the behavioral similarity of fraternal twins.

Am I an "I" or "We"?

College freshman Colin Kunzweiler (2007) wrote about his thoughts and experiences related to being an identical twin:

As a monozygotic individual, I am used to certain things. "Which one are you?" happens to be the most popular question I'm asked, which is almost always followed by "You're Colin. No, wait, you're Andy!" I have two names: one was given to me at birth, the other thrust on me in random, haphazard way. . . . My twin brother and I are as different from each other as caramel sauce is from gravy. We have different personalities, we enjoy different kinds of music, and I am even taller than he is (by a quarter of an inch). We are different; separate; individual. I have always been taught that I should maintain my own individuality; that I should be my own person. But if people keep constantly mistaking me for my twin, how can I be my own person with my own identity?

"Am I an 'I' or 'We'?" was the title of an article written by Lynn Perlman (2008) about the struggle twins have in developing a sense of being an individual. Of course, triplets have the same issue, possibly even more strongly so. One set of triplets entered a beauty contest as one person and won the contest!

Perlman, an identical twin herself, is a psychologist who works with twins (her identical twin also is a psychologist). She says that how twins move from a sense of "we" to "I" is a critical task for them as children and sometimes even as adults. For nontwins, separating oneself from a primary caregiver—mother and/or father—is an important developmental task in childhood, adolescence, and emerging adulthood. When a child has a twin, the separation process is likely to be more difficult because of the constant comparison with a twin. Since they are virtually identical in their physical appearance, identical twins are likely to have more problems in distinguishing themselves from their twin than are fraternal twins.

The twin separation process often accelerates in adolescence when one twin is likely to mature earlier than the other (Pearlman, 2013). However, for some twins it may not occur until emerging adulthood when they may go to different colleges and/or live apart for the first time. And for some twins, even as adults their separation can be emotionally painful. One 28-year-old identical twin female got a new boyfriend but found that the relationship caused a great deal of stress and conflict with her twin sister (Friedman, 2013).

In Lynn Perlman's (2008) view, helping twins develop their own identities needs to be done on a child-by-child basis, taking into account their preferences and what is in their best interests. She commented that most of the twins she has counseled consider having a twin a positive experience, and while they also are usually strongly attached to each other they are intensely motivated to be considered unique persons.

(Carlson, Mendle, & Harden, 2014; Fearon & others, 2014). For example, one study found that conduct problems were more prevalent in identical twins than fraternal twins; the researchers concluded that the study demonstrated an important role for heredity in conduct problems (Scourfield & others, 2004).

However, several issues complicate interpretation of twin studies (Mandelman & Grigorenko, 2011). For example, perhaps the environments of identical twins are more similar than the environments of fraternal twins. Adults might stress the similarities of identical twins more than those of fraternal twins, and identical twins might perceive themselves as a "set" and play together more than fraternal twins do. If so, observed similarities in identical twins could be more strongly influenced by the environment than the results suggested.

In an **adoption study,** investigators seek to discover whether the behavior and psychological characteristics of adopted children are more like those of their adoptive parents, who have provided a home environment, or more like those of their biological parents, who have contributed their heredity (Cvijetic & others, 2014; Kendler & others, 2012). Another form of the adoption study involves comparing adopted and biological siblings.

Heredity-Environment Correlations   The difficulties that researchers encounter when they interpret the results of twin studies and adoption studies reflect the complexities of heredity-environment interaction. Some of these interactions are heredity-environment correlations—that is, there is a potential for individuals' genes to influence the types of environments to which they are exposed. In a sense, individuals "inherit" environments that are related or linked to genetic propensities (Klahr & Burt, 2014; Plomin & others, 2014). Behavior geneticist Sandra Scarr (1993) described three ways that heredity and environment are correlated (see Figure 13):

·   **Passive genotype-environment correlations** occur because biological parents, who are genetically related to the child, provide a rearing environment for the child. For example, the parents might have a genetic predisposition to be intelligent and read skillfully.

adoption study A study in which investigators seek to discover whether the behavior and psychological characteristics of adopted children are more like their adoptive parents, who have provided a home environment, or more like those of their biological parents, who have contributed their heredity. Another form of adoption study involves comparing adopted and biological siblings.

passive genotype-environment correlations Correlations that occur because biological parents, who are genetically related to the child, provide a rearing environment for the child.

Heredity-Environment Correlation	Description	Examples
Passive	Children inherit genetic tendencies from their parents, and parents also provide an environment that matches their own genetic tendencies.	Musically inclined parents usually have musically inclined children and they are likely to provide an environment rich in music for their children.
Evocative	The child's genetic tendencies elicit stimulation from the environment that supports a particular trait. Thus genes evoke environmental support.	A happy, outgoing child elicits smiles and friendly responses from others.
Active (niche-picking)	Children actively seek out "niches" in their environment that reflect their own interests and talents and are thus in accord with their genotype.	Libraries, sports fields, and a store with musical instruments are examples of environmental niches children might seek out if they have intellectual interests in books, talent in sports, or musical talents, respectively.

FIGURE 13

EXPLORING HEREDITY-ENVIRONMENT CORRELATIONS

evocative genotype-environment correlations Correlations that occur because an adolescent's genetically shaped characteristics elicit certain types of physical and social environments.

active (niche-picking) genotype-environment correlations Correlations that occur when children seek out environments that they find compatible and stimulating.

shared environmental experiences Siblings' common experiences such as their parents' personalities and intellectual orientation, the family's socioeconomic status, and the neighborhood in which they live.

nonshared environmental experiences The adolescent's own unique experiences, both within a family and outside the family, that are not shared by a sibling.

Because they read well and enjoy reading, they provide their children with books to read. The likely outcome is that their children, given their own inherited predispositions from their parents, will become skilled readers.

- **Evocative genotype-environment correlations** occur because an adolescent's genetically shaped characteristics elicit certain types of physical and social environments. For example, active, smiling children receive more social stimulation than passive, quiet children do. Cooperative, attentive adolescents evoke more pleasant and instructional responses from the adults around them than uncooperative, distractible adolescents do. Athletically inclined youth tend to elicit encouragement to engage in school sports. As a consequence, these adolescents tend to be the ones who try out for sports teams and go on to participate in athletically oriented activities.

- **Active (niche-picking) genotype-environment correlations** occur when children seek out environments that they find compatible and stimulating. *Niche-picking* refers to finding a setting that is suited to one's abilities. Adolescents select from their surrounding environment some aspect that they respond to, learn about, or ignore. Their active selections of environments are related to their specific genotype. For example, attractive adolescents tend to seek out attractive peers. Adolescents who are musically inclined are likely to select musical environments in which they can successfully perform their skills.

Scarr concludes that the relative importance of the three genotype-environment correlations changes as children develop from infancy through adolescence. In infancy, much of the environment that children experience is provided by adults. Thus, passive genotype-environment correlations are more common in the lives of infants and young children than they are for older children and adolescents, who can extend their experiences beyond the family's influence and create their environments to a greater degree.

Critics argue that the concept of heredity-environment correlation gives heredity too much influence in determining development (Gottlieb, 2007; Moore, 2013, 2015). Heredity-environment correlation stresses that heredity determines the types of environments children experience. Next, we examine a view that emphasizes the importance of the nonshared environment of siblings and their heredity as important influences on their development.

Shared and Nonshared Environmental Experiences Behavior geneticists emphasize that another way of analyzing the environment's role in heredity-environment interaction is to consider experiences that adolescents share in common with other adolescents living in the same home, as well as experiences that are not shared (Burt, 2014; Waszczuk & others, 2015; White & others, 2014).

Shared environmental experiences are siblings' common experiences, such as their parents' personalities or intellectual orientation, the family's socioeconomic status, and the neighborhood in which they live. By contrast, **nonshared environmental experiences** are an adolescent's unique experiences, both within the family and outside the family; these are not shared with a sibling. Even experiences occurring within the family can be part of the "nonshared environment." For example, parents often interact differently with each sibling, and siblings interact differently with parents. Siblings often have different peer groups, different friends, and different teachers at school.

Behavior geneticist Robert Plomin (2004) has found that common rearing, or shared environment, accounts for little of the variation in adolescents' personality or interests. In other words, even though two adolescents live under the same roof with the same parents, their personalities are often very different. Further, behavior geneticists argue that heredity influences the nonshared environments of siblings in the manner we described earlier when discussing the concept of heredity-environment correlations (Plomin, 2011). For example, an adolescent who has inherited a genetic tendency to be athletic is likely to spend more time in environments related to sports, whereas an adolescent who has inherited a tendency to be musically inclined is more likely to spend time in environments related to music.

The Epigenetic View The heredity-environment correlation view emphasizes how heredity directs the kind of environmental experiences individuals have. However, earlier we discussed how DNA is collaborative, not determining an individual's traits in an independent manner but rather in an interactive manner with the environment (Moore, 2013, 2015). In line with the concept of a collaborative gene, the **epigenetic view** emphasizes that development is the result of an ongoing, bidirectional interchange between heredity and the environment (Gottlieb, 2007; Lickliter & Honeycutt, 2015; Moore, 2015). Figure 14 compares the heredity-environment correlation and epigenetic views of development.

Tennis stars Venus and Serena Williams. *What might be some shared and nonshared environmental experiences they had while they were growing up that contributed to their tennis stardom?*
© Greg Wood/AFP/Getty Images

An increasing number of studies are exploring how the interaction between heredity and environment influences development, including interactions that involve specific DNA sequences (Manuck & McCaffery, 2014). The epigenetic mechanisms involve the actual molecular modification of the DNA strand as a result of environmental inputs in ways that alter gene functioning (Davies & Cicchetti, 2014).

One study found that individuals who have a short version of a gene labeled 5-HTTLPR (a gene involving the neurotransmitter serotonin) have an elevated risk of developing depression only if they *also* lead stressful lives (Caspi & others, 2003). Thus, the specific gene did not directly cause the development of depression; rather the gene interacted with a stressful environment in a way that allowed the researchers to predict whether individuals would develop depression. A recent meta-analysis indicated that the short version of 5-HTTLPR was linked with higher cortisol stress reactivity (Miller & others, 2013). Recent studies also have found support for the interaction between the 5-HTTLPR gene and stress levels in predicting depression in adolescents and older adults (Petersen & others, 2012; Zannas & others, 2012).

In other research, adolescents who experienced negative life events drank heavily only when they had a particular variation of the CRHR1 gene (Blomeyer & others, 2008). And a recent study found that an interaction of a higher genetic plasticity index based on five gene variations and supportive parenting was linked to a higher level of adolescent self-regulation (Belsky & Beaver, 2011). The type of research just described is referred to as **gene × environment (G × E) interaction**—the interaction of a specific measured variation in DNA and a specific measured aspect of the environment (Oppenheimer & others, 2013). Although there is considerable enthusiasm about the concept of gene × environment interaction, a recent research review concluded that the area is plagued by difficulties in replicating results, inflated claims, and other weaknesses (Manuck & McCaffery, 2014). The science of G × E interaction is very young, and in the next several decades it will likely produce more precise findings.

Conclusions About Heredity-Environment Interaction Heredity and environment operate together—or cooperate—to produce a person's intelligence, temperament, height, weight, ability to pitch a baseball, ability to read, and so on. If an attractive, popular, intelligent girl is elected president of her senior class in high school, is her success due to heredity or to environment? Of course, the answer is both.

The relative contributions of heredity and environment are not additive. That is, we can't say that such-and-such a percentage of nature and such-and-such a percentage of experience make us who we are. Nor is it accurate to say that full genetic expression happens once, around conception

Heredity-Environment Correlation View

Heredity ⟶ Environment

Epigenetic View

Heredity ⟷ Environment

FIGURE 14

COMPARISON OF THE HEREDITY-ENVIRONMENT CORRELATION AND EPIGENETIC VIEWS

epigenetic view Belief that development is the result of an ongoing bidirectional interchange between heredity and environment.

gene × environment (G × E) interaction The interaction of a specific measured variation in DNA and a specific measured aspect of the environment.

developmental **connection**

Nature and Nurture

The nature and nurture debate is one of the main issues in the study of adolescent development. Connect to "Introduction."

or birth, after which we carry our genetic legacy into the world to see how far it takes us. Genes produce proteins throughout the life span, in many different environments. Or they don't produce these proteins, depending in part on how harsh or nourishing those environments are.

The emerging view is that many complex behaviors likely have some genetic loading that gives people a propensity for a specific developmental trajectory (Plomin & others, 2014). However, the actual development requires more: an environment. And that environment is complex, just like the mixture of genes we inherit (Cicchetti & Toth, 2015; Thompson, 2015). Environmental influences range from the things we lump together under "nurture" (such as parenting, family dynamics, schooling, and neighborhood quality) to biological encounters (such as viruses, birth complications, and even biological events in cells).

In developmental psychologist David Moore's (2013, 2015) view, the biological systems that generate behaviors are extremely complex, but too often these systems have been described in overly simplified ways that can be misleading. Thus, although genetic factors clearly contribute to behavior and psychological processes, they don't determine these phenotypes independently from the contexts in which they develop. From Moore's (2013, 2015) perspective, it is misleading to talk about "genes for" eye color, intelligence, personality, or other characteristics. Moore commented that in retrospect we should not have expected to be able to make the giant leap from DNA's molecules to a complete understanding of human behavior any more than we should anticipate being able to easily link air molecules in a concert hall with a full-blown appreciation of a symphony's wondrous experience.

Imagine for a moment that a cluster of genes is somehow associated with youth violence (this example is hypothetical because we don't know of any such combination). The adolescent who carries this genetic mixture might experience a world of loving parents, regular nutritious meals, lots of books, and a series of masterful teachers. Or the adolescent's world might include parental neglect, a neighborhood in which gunshots and crime are everyday occurrences, and inadequate schooling. In which of these environments are the adolescent's genes likely to manufacture the biological underpinnings of criminality?

If heredity and environment interact to determine the course of development, is that all there is to answering the question of what causes development? Are adolescents completely at the mercy of their genes and environment as they develop? Genetic heritage and environmental experiences are pervasive influences on adolescents' development. But in thinking about what causes development, adolescents not only are the outcomes of their heredity and the environment they experience, but they also can author a unique developmental path by changing the environment. As one psychologist recently concluded:

> In reality, we are both the creatures and creators of our worlds. We are . . . the products of our genes and environments. Nevertheless, . . . the stream of causation that shapes the future runs through our present choices. . . . Mind matters. . . . Our hopes, goals, and expectations influence our future (Myers, 2010, p. 168).

Review Connect Reflect

LG3 Explain the contributions of evolution, heredity, and environment to adolescent development

Review

- What role has evolution played in adolescent development? How do the fields of evolutionary psychology and evolutionary developmental psychology describe evolution's contribution to understanding adolescence?
- What is the genetic process?
- What is the nature of heredity-environment interaction?

Connect

- Which side of the nature and nurture issue does evolutionary developmental psychology take? Explain.

Reflect *Your Own Personal Journey of Life*

- A friend tells you that she has analyzed your genetic background and environmental experiences and reached the conclusion that the environment definitely has had little influence on your intelligence. What would you say to this person about her ability to make this diagnosis?

Puberty, Health, and Biological Foundations

1 Puberty

- Determinants of Puberty

- Growth Spurt

- Sexual Maturation

- Secular Trends in Puberty

- Psychological Dimensions of Puberty

- Are Puberty's Effects Exaggerated?

LG1 Discuss the determinants, characteristics, and psychological dimensions of puberty

· Puberty is a brain-neuroendocrine process occurring primarily in early adolescence that provides stimulation for the rapid physical change involved in this period of development. Puberty's determinants include heredity, hormones, weight, and percentage of body fat. Two classes of hormones that are involved in pubertal change and have significantly different concentrations in males and females are androgens and estrogens. The endocrine system's role in puberty involves the interaction of the hypothalamus, pituitary gland, and gonads. FSH and LH, which are secreted by the pituitary gland, are important aspects of this system. So is GnRH, which is produced by the hypothalamus. The sex hormone system is a negative feedback system. Leptin and kisspeptins have been proposed as pubertal initiators but research has not consistently supported this role. Growth hormone also contributes to pubertal change. Low birth weight and rapid weight gain in infancy are linked to earlier pubertal onset. Puberty has two phases: adrenarche and gonadarche. The culmination of gonadarche in boys is spermarche; in girls, it is menarche.

· The onset of pubertal growth occurs on the average at 9 years of age for girls and 11 years for boys. The peak of pubertal change for girls is 11½ years; for boys it is 13½ years. Girls grow an average of 3½ inches per year during puberty; boys grow an average of 4 inches.

· Sexual maturation is a key feature of pubertal change. Individual variation in puberty is extensive and is considered to be normal within a wide age range.

· Secular trends in puberty took place in the twentieth century, with puberty coming earlier. Recently, there are indications that earlier puberty is occurring only for overweight girls.

· Adolescents show heightened interest in their bodies and body images. Younger adolescents are more preoccupied with these images than are older adolescents. Adolescent girls often have a more negative body image than adolescent boys do. Adolescents and college students increasingly have tattoos and body piercings (body art). Some scholars conclude that body art is a sign of rebellion and is linked to risk taking, whereas others argue that increasingly body art is used to express uniqueness and self-expression rather than rebellion. Researchers have found connections between hormonal change during puberty and behavior, but environmental influences need to be taken into account. Early maturation often favors boys, at least during early adolescence, but as adults late-maturing boys have a more positive identity than early-maturing boys. Early-maturing girls are at risk for a number of developmental problems. Some scholars doubt that puberty's effects on development are as strong as was once envisioned. Most early- and late-maturing adolescents weather the challenges of puberty successfully. For those who do not adapt well to pubertal changes, discussions with knowledgeable health-care providers and parents can improve the coping abilities of early- or late-maturing adolescents.

· Puberty has important influences on development, but the significance of these influences needs to be considered in terms of the entire life span. Some scholars argue that too much emphasis has been given to the biological changes of puberty.

2 Health

- Adolescence: A Critical Juncture in Health

LG2 Summarize the nature of adolescents' and emerging adults' health

· Many of the behaviors that are linked to poor health habits and early death in adults begin during adolescence. Engaging in healthy behavior patterns in adolescence, such as regular exercise, helps to delay disease in adulthood. Important goals are to reduce adolescents' health-compromising behaviors and to increase their health-enhancing behaviors. Risk-taking behavior increases during adolescence and combined with a delay in developing self-regulation makes adolescents vulnerable to a number of problems. Developmental changes in the brain have recently been proposed as an explanation for adolescent risk-taking behavior. Among the strategies for preventing increased motivation for risk taking from compromising adolescents' health are to limit their opportunities for harm and to monitor their behavior. Adolescents underutilize health services. The three leading causes of death in adolescence are accidents, homicide, and suicide.

Emerging Adults' Health

- Although emerging adults have a higher death rate than adolescents, emerging adults have few chronic health problems. However, many emerging adults don't stop to think about how their personal lifestyles will affect their health later in their lives.

Nutrition

- Special nutrition concerns in adolescence are eating between meals, the amount of fat in adolescents' diets, and increased reliance on fast-food meals.

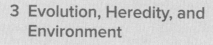
Exercise and Sports

- A majority of adolescents are not getting adequate exercise. At approximately 13 years of age, their rate of exercise often begins to decline. American girls especially have a low rate of exercise. Regular exercise has many positive outcomes for adolescents, including a lower risk of being overweight and higher self-esteem. Family, peers, schools, and screen-based activity influence adolescents' exercise patterns. Sports play an important role in the lives of many adolescents. Sports can have positive outcomes (improved physical health and well-being, confidence, ability to work with others) or negative outcomes (intense pressure by parents and coaches to win at all costs, injuries). Recently, the female athlete triad has become a concern.

Sleep

- Adolescents like to go to bed later and get up later than children do. This pattern may be linked to developmental changes in the brain. A special concern is the extent to which these changes in sleep patterns in adolescents affect academic behavior and achievement. Developmental changes in sleep continue to occur in emerging adulthood.

3 Evolution, Heredity, and Environment

LG3 Explain the contributions of evolution, heredity, and environment to adolescent development

The Evolutionary Perspective

- Natural selection—the process that favors the individuals of a species that are best adapted to survive and reproduce—is a key aspect of the evolutionary perspective. Evolutionary psychology is the view that adaptation, reproduction, and "survival of the fittest" are important influences on behavior. Evolutionary developmental psychology has promoted a number of ideas, including the view that an extended "juvenile" period is needed to develop a large brain and learn the complexity of human social communities. Critics argue that the evolutionary perspective does not give adequate attention to experience or the role of humans as a culture-making species.

The Genetic Process

- The nucleus of each human cell contains chromosomes, which contain DNA. Genes are short segments of DNA that direct cells to reproduce and manufacture proteins that maintain life. DNA does not act independently to produce a trait or behavior. Rather, it acts collaboratively. Genotype refers to the unique configuration of genes, whereas phenotype involves observed and measurable characteristics.

Heredity-Environment Interaction

- Behavior genetics is the field concerned with the degree and nature of behavior's hereditary basis. Methods used by behavior geneticists include twin studies and adoption studies. In Scarr's view of heredity-environment correlations, heredity directs the types of environments that children experience. Scarr describes three genotype-environment correlations: passive, evocative, and active (niche-picking). Scarr argues that the relative importance of these three genotype-environment correlations changes as children develop. Shared environmental experiences refer to siblings' common experiences, such as their parents' personalities and intellectual orientation, the family's socioeconomic status, and the neighborhood in which they live. Nonshared environmental experiences involve the adolescent's unique experiences, both within a family and outside a family, that are not shared with a sibling. Many behavior geneticists argue that differences in the development of siblings are due to nonshared environmental experiences (and heredity) rather than to shared environmental experiences. The epigenetic view emphasizes that development is the result of an ongoing, bidirectional interchange between heredity and environment. Many complex behaviors have some genetic loading that gives people a propensity for a specific developmental trajectory. However, actual development also requires an environment, and that environment is complex. The interaction of heredity and environment is extensive. Much remains to be discovered about the specific ways that heredity and environment interact to influence development.

key terms

active (niche-picking) genotype-environment correlations
adaptive behavior
adoption study
adrenarche
androgens
behavior genetics
chromosomes
DNA
epigenetic view
estrogens
evocative genotype-environment correlations
evolutionary psychology
female athlete triad
gene × environment (G × E) interaction
genes
genotype
gonadarche
hormones
menarche
nonshared environmental experiences
passive genotype-environment correlations
phenotype
precocious puberty
puberty
secular trends
shared environmental experiences
spermarche
twin study

key people

Albert Bandura
David Buss
Mary Carskadon
David Moore
Robert Plomin
Sandra Scarr

resources for improving the lives of adolescents

The Society for Adolescent Health and Medicine
(www.adolescenthealth.com)
This organization is a valuable source of information about competent physicians who specialize in treating adolescents. It maintains a list of recommended adolescent specialists across the United States. The society also publishes the *Journal of Adolescent Health*, which contains articles on a wide range of health-related and medical issues involving adolescents.

National Adolescent Health Information Center (NAHIC)
(http://nahic.ucsf.edu/)
This organization, associated with the University of California–San Francisco, has an excellent Web site that includes adolescent health data; recommendations for research, policy, and programs; health-care resources; and information about a national initiative to improve adolescent health.

Journal of School Health (www.blackwellpublishing.com)
This journal publishes articles that pertain to the school-related aspects of children's and adolescents' health, including a number of health education programs.

The Developing Genome
David Moore (2015)
New York: Oxford University Press
David Moore provides valuable information about the epigenetic view of development and describes how genetic explanations often have been overblown.

chapter 3

THE BRAIN AND COGNITIVE DEVELOPMENT

chapter outline

1 The Brain

Learning Goal 1 Describe the developmental changes in the brain during adolescence

The Neuroconstructivist View

Neurons

Brain Structure, Cognition, and Emotion

Experience and Plasticity

2 The Cognitive Developmental View

Learning Goal 2 Discuss the cognitive developmental view of adolescence

Piaget's Theory

Vygotsky's Theory

3 The Information-Processing View

Learning Goal 3 Characterize the information-processing view of adolescence

Cognitive Resources

Attention and Memory

Executive Function

4 The Psychometric/ Intelligence View

Learning Goal 4 Summarize the psychometric/ intelligence view of adolescence

Intelligence Tests

Multiple Intelligences

The Neuroscience of Intelligence

Heredity and Environment

5 Social Cognition

Learning Goal 5 Explain how social cognition is involved in adolescent development

Adolescent Egocentrism

Social Cognition in the Remainder of This Edition

One of my most vivid memories of my oldest daughter, Tracy, involves something that happened when she was 12 years of age. I had accompanied her and her younger sister, Jennifer (10 at the time), to a tennis tournament. As we walked into a restaurant to have lunch, Tracy bolted for the restroom. Jennifer and I looked at each other, wondering what was wrong. Five minutes later Tracy emerged, looking calmer. I asked her what had happened. Her response: "This one hair was out of place and every person in here was looking at me!"

Consider another adolescent—Margaret. During a conversation with her girlfriend, 16-year-old Margaret said, "Did you hear about Catherine? She's pregnant. Do you think I would ever let that happen to me? Never."

Also think about 13-year-old Adam as he describes himself: "No one understands me, especially my parents. They have no idea of what I am feeling. They have never experienced the pain I'm going through."

Comments like Tracy's, Margaret's, and Adam's reflect the emergence of egocentric thought during adolescence. When we think about thinking, we usually consider it in terms of school subjects like math and English, or solutions to intellectual problems. But people's thoughts about social circumstances also are important. Later in the chapter we will further explore adolescents' social thoughts.

preview

When we think about adolescence, we often focus on the biological changes of puberty or socioemotional changes, such as the motivation for independence, relations with parents and peers, and problems such as drug abuse and delinquency. Further, when developmentalists have studied cognitive processes, their main focus has been on infants and young children, not on adolescents. However, you will see in this chapter that adolescents also display some impressive cognitive changes and that increasingly researchers are finding that these changes are linked to the development of the brain. Indeed, to begin this chapter, you will read about the explosion of interest in the changing adolescent brain, and then you will study three different views of cognitive development: cognitive developmental, information processing, and psychometric. At the chapter's close you will study social cognition, including the emergence of adolescent egocentrism.

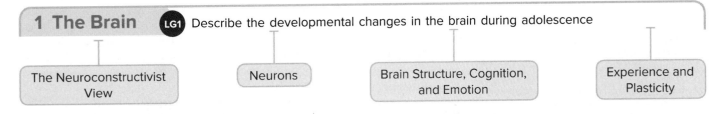

1 The Brain   **LG1** Describe the developmental changes in the brain during adolescence

| The Neuroconstructivist View | Neurons | Brain Structure, Cognition, and Emotion | Experience and Plasticity |

Until recently, little research had been conducted on developmental changes in the brain during adolescence. Although research in this area is still in its infancy, an increasing number of studies are under way (Ernst & others, 2015; Raznahan & others, 2014; Reyna & Zayas, 2014). Scientists now note that the adolescent's brain differs from the child's brain and that the brain continues to develop during adolescence (Blakemore & Mills, 2014; Casey, 2015; Steinberg, 2015a, b).

The thoughts of youth are long, long thoughts.

—HENRY WADSWORTH LONGFELLOW
American poet, 19th century

FIGURE 1

THE NEURON. (a) The dendrites of the cell body receive information from other neurons, muscles, or glands. (b) An axon transmits information away from the cell body. (c) A myelin sheath covers most axons and speeds information transmission. (d) As the axon ends, it branches out into terminal buttons.

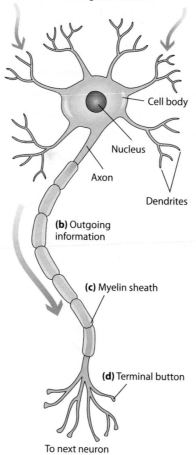

(a) Incoming information

Cell body

Nucleus

Axon

Dendrites

(b) Outgoing information

(c) Myelin sheath

(d) Terminal button

To next neuron

neuroconstructivist view Developmental perspective in which biological processes and environmental conditions influence the brain's development; the brain has plasticity and is context dependent; and cognitive development is closely linked with brain development.

neurons Nerve cells, which are the nervous system's basic units.

myelination The process by which the axon portion of the neuron becomes covered and insulated with a layer of fat cells, which increases the speed and efficiency of information processing in the nervous system.

synapses Gaps between neurons, where connections between the axon and dendrites occur.

corpus callosum A large bundle of axon fibers that connect the brain's left and right hemispheres.

prefrontal cortex The highest level of the brain's frontal lobes that is involved in reasoning, decision making, and self-control.

limbic system A lower, subcortical system in the brain that is the seat of emotions and experience of rewards.

amygdala A portion of the brain's limbic system that is the seat of emotions such as anger.

The dogma of the unchanging brain has been discarded, and researchers are focusing primarily on context-induced plasticity of the brain over time (Zelazo, 2013). The development of the brain mainly changes in a bottom-up, top-down sequence with sensory, appetitive (eating, drinking), sexual, sensation-seeking, and risk-taking brain linkages maturing first and higher-level brain linkages such as self-control, planning, and reasoning maturing later (Zelazo, 2013). This extensive plasticity is further explored in the next section, which describes the neuroconstructivist view of brain development.

THE NEUROCONSTRUCTIVIST VIEW

Not long ago, scientists thought that our genes primarily determine how our brains are "wired" and that the cells in the brain responsible for processing information just develop on their own with little or no input from environmental experiences. According to that view, whatever brain your genes have provided to you, you are essentially stuck with it. That view of the brain, however, turned out to be wrong. Instead, it is clear that the brain has plasticity and its development depends on context (Casey, 2015).

The brain depends on experiences to determine how connections are made (Monahan & others, 2015; Stiles & others, 2015; Zelazo, 2013). Before birth, it appears that genes mainly direct basic wiring patterns in the formation of the brain. Neurons grow and travel to distant places awaiting further instructions. After birth, the inflowing stream of sights, sounds, smells, touches, language, and eye contact helps to shape the brain's neural connections. Throughout the human life span, experiences continue to influence the functioning of the brain (Park & others, 2014).

In the increasingly popular **neuroconstructivist view,** (a) biological processes (genes, for example) and environmental experiences (enriched or impoverished, for example) influence the brain's development; (b) the brain has plasticity and is context dependent; and (c) development of the brain is linked closely with cognitive development. These factors constrain or advance the construction of cognitive skills (Monahan & others, 2015; Westermann, Thomas, & Karmiloff-Smith, 2011). The neuroconstructivist view emphasizes the importance of interactions between experiences and gene expression in the brain's development, much as the epigenetic view proposes (Dennis & others, 2014; Holman & de Villers-Sidani, 2014).

NEURONS

Neurons, or nerve cells, are the nervous system's basic units. A neuron has three basic parts: the cell body, dendrites, and axon (see Figure 1). The dendrite is the receiving part of the neuron, and the axon carries information away from the cell body to other cells. Through a process called **myelination,** the axon portion of a neuron becomes covered and insulated with a layer of fat cells (called the myelin sheath), increasing the speed and efficiency of information processing in the nervous system (Buttermore, Thaxton, & Bhat, 2013). Myelination continues during adolescence and emerging adulthood (Steinberg, 2015a, b).

In the language of neuroscience, the term *white matter* is used to describe the whitish color of myelinated axons, and the term *gray matter* refers primarily to dendrites and the cell body of the neuron (see Figure 2). A significant developmental change in adolescence is the increase in white matter and the decrease in gray matter in the prefrontal cortex (Christakou, 2014; Giedd, 2012; Markant & Thomas, 2013). Most accounts emphasize that the increase in white matter across adolescence is due to increased myelination, although a recent analysis proposed that the white matter increase also might be due to an increase in the diameter of axons (Paus, 2010).

In addition to the encasement of axons through myelination, another important aspect of the brain's development is the dramatic increase in connections between neurons, a process that is called synaptogenesis (Emes & Grant, 2013). **Synapses** are gaps between neurons, where connections between the axon and dendrites take place. Synaptogenesis begins in infancy and continues through adolescence.

Researchers have discovered that nearly twice as many synaptic connections are made as will ever be used (Huttenlocher & Dabholkar, 1997). The connections that are used are strengthened and survive, while the unused ones are replaced by other pathways or disappear altogether (Campbell & others, 2012). That is, in the language of neuroscience, these connections will be "pruned." What results from this pruning is that by the end of adolescence individuals have "fewer, more selective, more effective neuronal connections than they did as children" (Kuhn, 2009, p. 153). And this pruning indicates that the activities adolescents choose to engage in and not to engage in influence which neural connections will be strengthened and which will disappear.

With the onset of puberty, the levels of *neurotransmitters*—chemicals that carry information across the synaptic gap between one neuron and the next—change (McEwen, 2013). For example, an increase in the neurotransmitter dopamine occurs in both the prefrontal cortex and the limbic system during adolescence (Ernst & Spear, 2009). Increases in dopamine have been linked to increased risk taking and the use of addictive drugs (Hou & others, 2014). Researchers have found that dopamine plays an important role in reward seeking (Steinberg, 2014).

BRAIN STRUCTURE, COGNITION, AND EMOTION

Neurons do not simply float in the brain. Connected in precise ways, they form the various structures in the brain. The brain is hierarchically organized and mainly develops from the bottom up, with sensory areas reaching full maturity before the higher-level association areas of the prefrontal cortex.

Using functional magnetic resonance imaging (fMRI) to scan the brain, scientists have recently discovered that adolescents' brains undergo significant structural changes (Blakemore & Mills, 2014; Casey, 2015; Giedd & others, 2012; Mills & others, 2014; Monahan & others, 2015; Pokhrel & others, 2013). An fMRI creates a magnetic field around a person's body and bombards the brain with radio waves. The result is a computerized image of the brain's tissues and biochemical activities.

Among the most important structural changes in the brain during adolescence are those involving the corpus callosum, the prefrontal cortex, the limbic system, and the amygdala. The **corpus callosum**, a large bundle of axon fibers that connects the brain's left and right hemispheres, thickens in adolescence, and this thickening improves adolescents' ability to process information (Giedd, 2008). Advances in the development of the **prefrontal cortex**—the highest level of the frontal lobes that is involved in reasoning, decision making, and self-control—continue through the emerging adult years, approximately 18 to 25 years of age (Blakemore & Mills, 2014). However, at a lower, subcortical level, the **limbic system,** which is the seat of emotions and where rewards are experienced, matures much earlier than the prefrontal cortex and is almost completely developed by early adolescence (Blakemore & Mills, 2014). The limbic system structure that is especially involved in emotion is the **amygdala.** Figure 3 shows the locations of the corpus callosum, prefrontal cortex, the limbic system, and the amygdala.

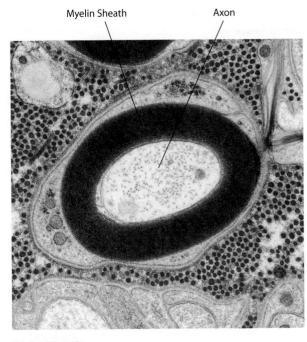

Myelin Sheath   Axon

FIGURE 2

A MYELINATED NERVE FIBER. The myelin sheath, shown in brown, encases the axon (white). This image was produced by an electron microscope that magnified the nerve fiber 12,000 times. *What role does myelination play in the brain's development?*
© Steve Gschmeissner/Science Source

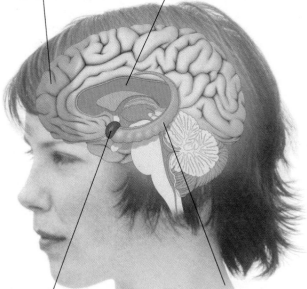

Prefrontal cortex
This "judgment" region reins in intense emotions but doesn't finish developing until at least emerging adulthood.

Corpus callosum
These nerve fibers connect the brain's two hemispheres; they thicken in adolescence to process information more effectively.

Amygdala
Limbic system structure especially involved in emotion.

Limbic system
A lower, subcortical system in the brain that is the seat of emotions and experience of rewards. This system is almost completely developed by early adolescence.

FIGURE 3

THE PREFRONTAL CORTEX, LIMBIC SYSTEM, AMYGDALA, AND CORPUS CALLOSUM

developmental **connection**

Brain Development

Developmental social neuroscience is a recently developed field that focuses on connections between development, socioemotional factors, and neuroscience. Connect to "Introduction."

In late adolescence and emerging adulthood, the increase in myelination allows greater connectivity and integration of brain regions (Giedd & others, 2012). For example, the important connections between the prefrontal cortex and limbic system strengthen in late adolescence and emerging adulthood (Casey, 2015; Steinberg, 2015a, b). This strengthening is especially important for emotional control (Mills & others, 2014).

Leading researcher Charles Nelson (2003) points out that although adolescents are capable of very strong emotions, their prefrontal cortex hasn't adequately developed to the point at which they can control these passions. It is as if the prefrontal cortex doesn't yet have the brakes to slow down the limbic system's emotional intensity and reward focus. Another researcher describes adolescence as a period that combines "early activation of strong 'turbocharged' feelings with a relatively un-skilled set of 'driving skills' or cognitive abilities to modulate strong emotions and motivations" (Dahl, 2004, p. 18).

Recall from the earlier discussion of neurotransmitters that dopamine production increases in early adolescence, which is linked to increased reward seeking and risk taking. Dopamine activity is greater in the limbic system pathways in early adolescence than at any other point in development (Steinberg, 2015a, b). In recent research conducted by Laurence Steinberg (Albert & Steinberg, 2011a, b; Steinberg, 2011, 2015a, b), preference for immediate rewards (assessed in such contexts as a gambling task and a video driving game) increased from 14 to 16 years of age and then declined. Also, in Steinberg's (2011, 2015a, b) research, adolescents' belief that the benefits of risk taking override its potential negative outcomes peaks at about 14 to 16 years of age. By contrast, impulse control increases in a linear fashion from preadolescence to emerging adulthood.

The increase in risk taking in adolescence is usually thought to result in negative outcomes. However, there are some aspects of risk taking that benefit adolescents. Being open to new experiences and challenges, even risky ones, can help adolescents to stretch themselves to learn about aspects of the world they would not have encountered if they had shied away from such exploration (Allen & Allen, 2009). Later in the chapter, we will revisit the issue of risk taking in the context of adolescents' sense of invulnerability and recent research that distinguishes between different types of vulnerability (Lapsley & Hill, 2010; Lapsley & Stey, 2012).

In middle and late childhood, there is increased focal activation within a specific brain region, such as the prefrontal cortex, but only limited connections across distant brain regions. By the time individuals reach emerging adulthood, there is an increase in connections across brain areas (Markant & Thomas, 2013). The increased connectedness (referred to as brain networks) is especially prevalent across more distant brain regions (Markant & Thomas, 2013). Thus, as adolescents develop, greater efficiency and focal activation occurs in local area of the brain, and simultaneously there is an increase in brain networks across different brain regions (Dwyer & others, 2014; Markant & Thomas, 2013).

Developmental neuroscientist Mark Johnson and his colleagues (Johnson, Grossmann, & Cohen-Kadosh, 2009; Johnson, Jones, & Gliga, 2015) have proposed that the prefrontal cortex likely orchestrates the functions of many other brain regions during development. As part of this neural leadership and organizational role, the prefrontal cortex may provide an advantage to neural connections and networks that include the prefrontal cortex. In their view, the prefrontal cortex likely coordinates the best neural connections for solving a problem.

A topic of some controversy involves which comes first—biological changes in the brain or experiences that stimulate these changes (Lerner, Boyd, & Du, 2008). Consider a study in which the prefrontal cortex thickened and more brain connections formed when adolescents resisted peer pressure (Paus & others, 2007). A recent study also found that adolescents from Mexican backgrounds with greater family obligation values showed decreased activation in the brain's regions (ventral striatum) involving reward sensitivity, which was linked to less real-life risk-taking behavior, and increased activation in the brain's regions (prefrontal cortex) involving cognitive control, which was associated with better decision-making skills (Telzer & others, 2014).

Scientists have yet to determine whether the brain changes come first or whether the brain changes are caused by experiences with peers, parents, and others. Once again, we encounter the nature-nurture issue that is so prominent in examining development through the life span. Nonetheless, there is adequate evidence that environmental experiences make important contributions to the brain's development (Monahan & others, 2015; Zelazo, 2013).

According to leading expert Jay Giedd (2007, pp. 1–2D), "Biology doesn't make teens rebellious or have purple hair or take drugs. It does not mean you are going to do drugs, but it gives you more of a chance to do that."

Does our increased understanding of changes in the adolescent brain have implications for the legal system? For example, can the recent brain research we have just discussed be used to argue that because the adolescent's brain, especially the higher-level prefrontal cortex, is still developing, adolescents are less mature than adults and therefore should not receive the death penalty for acts of violence? Leading expert Elizabeth Sowell (2004) points out that scientists can't do brain scans on adolescents to determine whether they should be tried as adults. In 2005, giving the death penalty to adolescents (under the age of 18) was prohibited by the U.S. Supreme Court, but the topic continues to be debated (Cauffman & others, 2015; Steinberg, 2015a, b).

EXPERIENCE AND PLASTICITY

Scientists are especially interested in the extent to which environmental experiences influence the brain's development. They also want to know how much plasticity the brain retains as individuals progress through childhood, adolescence, and adulthood (Casey, 2015; Nudo & McNeal, 2013). One analysis indicated that early adolescence is a time of considerable plasticity in the brain (Gogtay & Thompson, 2010). Let's examine three questions involving the roles of experience and plasticity in the development of the brain in adolescence:

Lee Malvo was 17 years old when he and John Muhammad, an adult, went on a sniper spree in 2002, terrorizing the Washington, D.C., area and killing 10 people. A 2005 U.S. Supreme Court ruling stated that individuals who are 18 years of age and under, like Malvo, cannot be given the death penalty. *Are there implications regarding what scientists are learning about the adolescent's brain for legal decisions, such as the death penalty?*
© Davis Turner-Pool/Getty Images

· *Can new brain cells be generated in adolescence?* Until close to the end of the twentieth century, scientists argued that the brain generated no new cells (neurons) after the early childhood years. However, it is now accepted that neurogenesis can occur in humans (Peretto & Bonafanti, 2014), although researchers have documented neurogenesis only in two brain regions: the hippocampus, which is involved in memory, and the olfactory bulb, which is involved in smell (Pallotto & Deprez, 2014; Seib & Martin-Villalba, 2015). It also is not known what functions these new brain cells perform, and at this point researchers have documented that they last only a few weeks (Nelson, 2006). Researchers currently are studying factors that might inhibit and promote neurogenesis, including various drugs, stress, and exercise (Gregoire & others, 2014). They also are examining how the grafting of neural stem cells to various regions of the brain, such as the hippocampus, might increase neurogenesis (Farioli-Vecchioli & others, 2014).

· *Can the adolescent's brain recover from injury?* In childhood and adolescence, the brain has a remarkable ability to repair itself (Nelson, 2013). We previously discussed Michael Rehbein, whose left hemisphere was removed because of brain seizures. The plasticity of the human brain was apparent as his right hemisphere reorganized itself to take over functions that normally take place in the left hemisphere, such as speech. The brain retains considerable plasticity in adolescence, and the earlier a brain injury occurs, the higher the likelihood of a successful recovery (Yen & Wong, 2007).

· *What do we know about applying information about brain development to adolescents' education?* Unfortunately, too often statements about the implications of brain science for secondary education are speculative and far removed from what neuroscientists know about the brain (Blakemore & Mills, 2014; Bradshaw & others, 2012; Fischer & Immordino-Yang, 2008). We don't have to look any further than the hype about "left-brained" individuals being more logical and "right-brained" individuals being more creative to see that links between neuroscience and brain education are incorrectly made.

Another commonly promoted link between neuroscience and brain education is the assertion that most of the key changes in the brain occur prior to adolescence (Fischer & Immordino-Yang, 2008). However, recent research on the plasticity of the adolescent's brain and the continuing development of the prefrontal cortex through adolescence support the view that education can benefit adolescents considerably (Blakemore & Mills, 2014; Giedd, 2012). In this regard, higher-level cognitive functioning, especially in managing one's thoughts, engaging in goal-directed behavior, and controlling emotions, as discussed later in this chapter, are especially important potential areas of change in adolescence (Bradshaw & others, 2012).

What do we know about applying information about brain development to adolescents' education?
© Fuse/Getty Images RF

In closing this section on the development of the brain in adolescence, a caution is in order. Much of the research on neuroscience and the development of the brain in adolescence is correlational in nature, and thus causal statements need to be scrutinized.

Review Connect Reflect

LG1 Describe the developmental changes in the brain during adolescence

Review
- What characterizes the neuroconstructivist view?
- What are neurons? How do the brain's neurons change in adolescence?
- What changes involving brain structure, cognition, and emotion occur in adolescence?
- How much plasticity does the brain have in adolescence?

Connect
- Relate the structural changes in the brain that occur during adolescence to psychological dimensions of puberty.

Reflect *Your Own Personal Journey of Life*
- Evaluate your lifestyle in terms of factors such as your exercise, eating habits, whether you get adequate sleep, and how much you challenge yourself to learn and achieve. Considering what you have learned about the brain's plasticity, what are some implications for your lifestyle's influence on the development of your brain in adolescence and emerging adulthood?

2 The Cognitive Developmental View

LG2 Discuss the cognitive developmental view of adolescence

Piaget's Theory

Vygotsky's Theory

The process of brain development that we have just discussed provides a biological foundation for the cognitive changes that characterize adolescence. Reflect for a moment about your thinking skills as a young adolescent. Were your thinking skills as good then as they are now? Could you solve difficult abstract problems and reason logically about complex topics? Or did those skills improve during your high school years? Can you describe any ways in which your thinking skills are better now than they were in high school?

We have briefly examined Jean Piaget's theory of cognitive development. Piaget was intrigued by the changes in thinking that take place during childhood and adolescence. In this section, we further explore his ideas about adolescent cognition, as well as the increasingly popular sociocultural cognitive theory of Lev Vygotsky.

PIAGET'S THEORY

We begin our coverage of Piaget's theory by describing the main processes he viewed as responsible for cognitive changes throughout the life span. Then we examine each of his cognitive stages, giving special attention to concrete operational and formal operational thought.

Cognitive Processes Piaget's theory is the best-known, most widely discussed theory of adolescent cognitive development. According to his theory, adolescents are motivated to understand their world because doing so is biologically adaptive. Adolescents actively construct their own cognitive worlds; information doesn't just pour into their minds from the environment. To make sense of the world, adolescents organize their experiences, separating important ideas from less important ones and connecting one idea to another. They also adapt their thinking to include new ideas because the additional information furthers their understanding.

Jean Piaget, the main architect of the field of cognitive development, at age 27.
© Camera Press/R.Crane/Redux

We are born capable of learning.

—JEAN-JACQUES ROUSSEAU
Swiss-born French philosopher, 18th century

In actively constructing their world, adolescents use schemas. A **schema** is a mental concept or framework that is useful in organizing and interpreting information. Piaget was especially interested in how children and adolescents use schemas to organize and make sense out of their current experiences.

Piaget (1952) found that children and adolescents use and adapt their schemas through two processes: assimilation and accommodation. **Assimilation** is the incorporation of new information into existing knowledge. In assimilation, the schema does not change. **Accommodation** is the adjustment of a schema in response to new information. In accommodation, the schema changes.

Suppose, for example, that a 13-year-old girl wants to learn how to use a new smartphone her parents have given her for her birthday. Although she has never had the opportunity to use one, from her experience and observation she realizes that she needs to press a button to turn on the phone. This behavior fit into an existing conceptual framework (assimilation). Once the phone is activated, she presses an icon on the screen but it doesn't take her to the screen she wants. She also wants to add an application but can't figure out how to do that. Soon she realizes that she needs help in learning how to use the smartphone—either by studying the instructions further or getting help from a friend who has experience using this type of phone. This adjustment in her approach shows her awareness of the need to alter her conceptual framework (accommodation).

Equilibration, another process Piaget identified, is a shift in thought from one state to another. At times adolescents experience cognitive conflict or a sense of disequilibrium in their attempt to understand the world. Eventually they resolve the conflict and reach a balance, or equilibrium, of thought. Piaget maintained that individuals move back and forth between states of cognitive equilibrium and disequilibrium.

Stages of Cognitive Development Piaget theorized that individuals develop through four cognitive stages: sensorimotor, preoperational, concrete operational, and formal operational (see Figure 4). Each of these age-related stages consists of distinct ways of thinking.

schema A mental concept or framework that is useful in organizing and interpreting information.

assimilation The incorporation of new information into existing knowledge.

accommodation An adjustment of a schema in response to new information.

equilibration A mechanism in Piaget's theory that explains how individuals shift from one state of thought to the next. The shift occurs as individuals experience cognitive conflict or a disequilibrium in trying to understand the world. Eventually, the individual resolves the conflict and reaches a balance, or equilibrium, of thought.

Sensorimotor Stage

Infants gain knowledge of the world from the physical actions they perform on it. Infants coordinate sensory experiences with these physical actions. An infant progresses from reflexive, instinctual action at birth to the beginning of symbolic thought toward the end of the stage.

Birth to 2 Years of Age

Preoperational Stage

The child begins to use mental representations to understand the world. Symbolic thinking, reflected in the use of words and images, is used in this mental representation, which goes beyond the connection of sensory information with physical action. However, there are some constraints on the child's thinking at this stage, such as egocentrism and centration.

2 to 7 Years of Age

Concrete Operational Stage

The child can now reason logically about concrete events, understands the concept of conservation, organizes objects into hierarchical classes (classification), and places objects in ordered series (seriation).

7 to 11 Years of Age

Formal Operational Stage

The adolescent reasons in more abstract, idealistic, and logical (hypothetical-deductive) ways.

11 Years of Age Through Adulthood

FIGURE **4**

PIAGET'S FOUR STAGES OF COGNITIVE DEVELOPMENT
(Left to right): © Stockbyte/Getty Images RF; © BananaStock/PunchStock/Getty Images RF; © image100/Corbis RF; © Jose Pelaez/Corbis RF

This *different* way of understanding the world is what makes one stage more advanced than another; simply knowing more information does not make an adolescent's thinking more advanced. Thus, in Piaget's theory, a person's cognition is *qualitatively* different in one stage compared with another.

Sensorimotor and Preoperational Thought   The **sensorimotor stage,** which lasts from birth to about 2 years of age, is the first Piagetian stage. In this stage, infants construct an understanding of the world by coordinating sensory experiences (such as seeing and hearing) with physical, motoric actions—hence the term *sensorimotor.*

The **preoperational stage,** which lasts approximately from 2 to 7 years of age, is the second Piagetian stage. In this stage, children begin to represent the world with words, images, and drawings. Symbolic thought goes beyond simple connections of information and action.

Concrete Operational Thought   The **concrete operational stage,** which lasts approximately from 7 to 11 years of age, is the third Piagetian stage. Logical reasoning replaces intuitive thought as long as the reasoning can be applied to specific or concrete examples. According to Piaget, concrete operational thought involves operations—mental actions that allow individuals to do mentally what earlier they did physically.

Piaget used the term *conservation* to refer to an individual's ability to recognize that the length, number, mass, quantity, area, weight, and volume of objects and substances does not change through transformations that alter their appearance. Concrete operational thinkers have conservation skills; preoperational thinkers don't.

Another characteristic of concrete operational thought is *classification*, or class inclusion reasoning. Children who engage in classification can systematically organize objects into hierarchies of classes and subclasses.

Although concrete operational thought is more advanced than preoperational thought, it has limitations. Logical reasoning replaces intuitive thought as long as the principles can be applied to specific, *concrete* examples. For example, the concrete operational child cannot imagine the steps necessary to complete an algebraic equation, an abstract statement with no connection to the concrete world.

Formal Operational Thought   The **formal operational stage** is Piaget's fourth and final stage of cognitive development. Piaget argued that this stage emerges at 11 to 15 years of age. Adolescents' developing power of thought opens up new cognitive and social horizons. What are the characteristics of formal operational thought? Most significantly, formal operational thought is more abstract than concrete operational thought. Adolescents are no longer limited to actual, concrete experiences as anchors for thought. They can conjure up make-believe situations—events that are purely hypothetical possibilities or strictly abstract propositions—and try to reason logically about them.

The abstract quality of the adolescent's thought at the formal operational level is evident in the adolescent's verbal problem-solving ability. Whereas the concrete operational thinker would need to see the concrete elements A, B, and C to be able to make the logical inference that if A = B and B = C, then A = C, the formal operational thinker can solve this problem merely through verbal representation.

Another indication of the abstract quality of adolescents' thought is their increased tendency to think about thought itself. As one adolescent commented, "I began thinking about why I was thinking what I was. Then I began thinking about why I was thinking about why I was thinking about what I was." If this statement sounds abstract, it is, and it characterizes the adolescent's enhanced focus on thought and its abstract qualities. Later in this chapter, we return to the topic of thinking about thinking, which is called *metacognition*.

Besides being abstract, formal operational thought is full of idealism and possibilities. Whereas children frequently think in concrete ways about what is real and limited, adolescents begin to engage in extended speculation about ideal characteristics—qualities they desire in themselves and others. Such thoughts often lead adolescents to compare themselves and others in regard to such ideal standards. And, during adolescence, the thoughts of individuals are often fantasy flights into future possibilities. It is not unusual for adolescents to become impatient with these newfound ideal standards and perplexed over which of many ideals to adopt.

At the same time that adolescents think more abstractly and idealistically, they also think more logically. Adolescents begin to reason more as a scientist does, devising ways to solve

"Ben is in his first year of high school and he's questioning all the right things."
© Edward Koren/The New Yorker Collection/
www.cartoonbank.com.

sensorimotor stage Piaget's first stage of development, lasting from birth to about 2 years of age. In this stage, infants construct an understanding of the world by coordinating sensory experiences with physical, motoric actions.

preoperational stage Piaget's second stage, which lasts approximately from 2 to 7 years of age. In this stage, children begin to represent their world with words, images, and drawings.

concrete operational stage Piaget's third stage, which lasts approximately from 7 to 11 years of age. In this stage, children can perform operations. Logical reasoning replaces intuitive thought as long as the reasoning can be applied to specific or concrete examples.

formal operational stage Piaget's fourth and final stage of cognitive development, which he argued emerges at 11 to 15 years of age. It is characterized by abstract, idealistic, and logical thought.

problems and test solutions systematically. Piaget gave this type of problem solving an imposing name, **hypothetical-deductive reasoning**—that is, the ability to develop hypotheses, or best guesses, about how to solve problems, such as algebraic equations. Having developed a hypothesis, the formal operational thinker then systematically deduces, or concludes, the best path to follow in solving the problem. In contrast, children are more likely to solve problems by trial and error.

Piaget maintained that formal operational thought is the best description of how adolescents think. Formal operational thought is not a homogeneous stage of development, however. Not all adolescents are full-fledged formal operational thinkers. Instead, some developmentalists argue that the stage of formal operational thought consists of two subperiods (Broughton, 1983):

· *Early formal operational thought.* Adolescents' newfound ability to think in hypothetical ways produces unconstrained thoughts with unlimited possibilities. In this early period, flights of fantasy may submerge reality and the world is perceived subjectively and idealistically. Assimilation is the dominant process in this subperiod.

· *Late formal operational thought.* As adolescents test their reasoning against experience, intellectual balance is restored. Through accommodation, adolescents begin to adjust to the upheaval they have experienced. Late formal thought may appear in the middle adolescent years.

Might adolescents' ability to reason hypothetically and to evaluate what is ideal versus what is real lead them to engage in demonstrations like this one in support of public education? What other causes might be attractive to adolescents' newfound cognitive abilities of hypothetical-deductive reasoning and idealistic thinking?
© Jim West/Alamy

In this two-subperiod view, assimilation characterizes early formal operational thought; accommodation characterizes late formal operational thought (Lapsley, 1990).

In his early writings, Piaget (1952) indicated that both the onset and consolidation of formal operational thought are completed during early adolescence, from about 11 to 15 years of age. Later, Piaget (1972) revised his view and concluded that formal operational thought is not completely achieved until later in adolescence, between approximately 15 and 20 years of age.

Still, his theory does not adequately account for the individual differences that characterize the cognitive development of adolescents, which have been documented in a number of investigations (Kuhn, 2009). Some young adolescents are formal operational thinkers; others are not. For instance, a review of investigations about formal operational thought revealed that only about one of every three eighth-grade students is a formal operational thinker (Strahan, 1983). Some investigators have found that formal operational thought increased with age in adolescence; others have not found this result. In fact, many college students and adults do not think in formal operational ways. Investigators have found that from 17 to 67 percent of college students think on the formal operational level (Elkind, 1961; Tomlinson-Keasey, 1972).

At the same time that many young adolescents are just beginning to think in a formal operational manner, others are at the point of consolidating their concrete operational thought, using it more consistently than they did in childhood. By late adolescence, many youth are beginning to consolidate their formal operational thought, using it more consistently. And there often is variation across the content areas of formal operational thought, just as there is in concrete operational thought in childhood. A 14-year-old adolescent might reason at the formal operational level when analyzing algebraic equations but not when solving verbal problems or when reasoning about interpersonal relations.

Evaluating Piaget's Theory   What were Piaget's main contributions? Has his theory withstood the test of time? In this section, we examine both Piaget's contributions and the criticisms of his work.

Contributions   Piaget has been a giant in the field of developmental psychology. We owe to him the present field of cognitive development as well as a long list of masterful concepts of enduring power and fascination, including assimilation, accommodation, conservation, and

hypothetical-deductive reasoning Piaget's term for adolescents' ability, in the formal operational stage, to develop hypotheses, or best guesses, about ways to solve problems; they then systematically deduce, or conclude, the best path to follow in solving the problem.

An outstanding teacher and education in the logic of science and mathematics are important cultural experiences that promote the development of operational thought. *Might Piaget have underestimated the roles of culture and schooling in children's cognitive development?*
© Wendy Stone/Corbis

hypothetical-deductive reasoning, among others. We also owe to Piaget the current vision of children as active, constructive thinkers (Miller, 2011).

Piaget was a genius when it came to observing children. His careful observations documented inventive new ways to discover how children act on and adapt to their world. Piaget showed us some important things to look for in cognitive development, such as the shift from preoperational to concrete operational thinking. He also pointed out that children need to make their experiences fit their schemas, or cognitive frameworks, yet they can simultaneously adapt their schemas based on information gained through experience. He also revealed that cognitive change is likely to occur if the context is structured to allow gradual movement to the next higher level. We owe to Piaget the current belief that a concept does not emerge suddenly, full blown, but develops instead through a series of partial accomplishments that lead to an increasingly comprehensive understanding.

Criticisms   Piaget's theory has not gone unchallenged (Miller, 2011). Questions are raised about the timing and nature of his stage view of cognitive development, whether he failed to adequately study in detail key cognitive processes, and the effects of culture on cognitive development. Let's consider each of these criticisms in turn.

In terms of timing and stages, some cognitive abilities have been found to emerge earlier than Piaget had thought (Johnson & Hannon, 2015; Stiles & others, 2015). For example, conservation of number (which Piaget said emerged at approximately 7 years of age in the concrete operational stage) has been demonstrated as early as age 3 (which instead is early in Piaget's preoperational stage). Other cognitive abilities often emerge later than Piaget indicated (Casey, 2015). Many adolescents still think in concrete operational ways or are just beginning to master formal operations. Even as adults, many individuals are not formal operational thinkers. The evidence does not support Piaget's view that prior to age 11 children don't engage in abstract thinking and that from 11 years onward they do (Kuhn, 2009). Thus, adolescents' cognitive development is not as stage-like as Piaget envisioned (Muller & Kerns, 2015; Ricco, 2015).

One group of cognitive developmentalists, the **neo-Piagetians,** conclude that Piaget's theory does not adequately focus on attention, memory, and cognitive strategies that adolescents use to process information, and that Piaget's explanations of cognitive changes are too general. They especially maintain that a more accurate vision of children's and adolescents' thinking requires more knowledge of the strategies they use, how rapidly and automatically they process information, the particular cognitive tasks involved in processing information, and the division of cognitive problems into smaller, more precise steps.

The leading proponent of the neo-Piagetian view has been Canadian developmental psychologist Robbie Case (1992, 2000). Case accepts Piaget's four stages of cognitive development but emphasizes that a more precise description of changes within each stage is needed. He notes that children's and adolescents' growing ability to process information efficiently is linked to their brain growth and memory development. In particular, Case cites the increasing ability to hold information in working memory (a workbench for memory similar to short-term memory) and to manipulate it more effectively as critical to understanding cognitive development.

neo-Piagetians Theorists who argue that Piaget got some things right but that his theory needs considerable revision. In their revision, they give more emphasis to information processing that involves attention, memory, and strategies; they also seek to provide more precise explanations of cognitive changes.

Finally, culture and education exert stronger influences on development than Piaget envisioned (Gauvain & Perez, 2015). For example, the age at which individuals acquire conservation skills is associated to some extent with the degree to which their culture provides relevant educational practice (Cole, 2006). In many developing countries, educational opportunities are limited and formal operational thought is rare. You will read shortly about Lev Vygotsky's theory of cognitive development, in which culture is given a more prominent role than in Piaget's theory.

Cognitive Changes in Adulthood As we discussed earlier, according to Piaget adults and adolescents use the same type of reasoning. Adolescents and adults think in qualitatively the same way. Piaget did acknowledge that adults can be quantitatively more advanced in their knowledge. What are some ways that adults might be more advanced in their thinking than adolescents?

Realistic and Pragmatic Thinking Some developmentalists have proposed that as young adults move into the world of work, their way of thinking does change. One idea is that as they face the constraints of reality, which work promotes, their idealism decreases (Labouvie-Vief, 1986).

Reflective and Relativistic Thinking William Perry (1970, 1999) also described changes in cognition that take place in early adulthood. He said that adolescents often view the world in terms of polarities—right/wrong, we/they, or good/bad. As youth age into adulthood, they gradually move away from this type of absolutist thinking as they become aware of the diverse opinions and multiple perspectives of others. Thus, in Perry's view, the absolutist, dualistic thinking of adolescence gives way to the reflective, relativistic thinking of adulthood.

Expanding on Perry's view, Gisela Labouvie-Vief (2006) proposed that the increasing complexity of cultures in the past century has generated a greater need for more reflective, complex thinking that takes into account the changing nature of knowledge and challenges. She also emphasizes that the key aspects of cognitive development in emerging adulthood include deciding on a specific worldview, recognizing that the worldview is subjective, and understanding that diverse worldviews should be acknowledged. In her perspective, considerable individual variation characterizes the thinking of emerging adults, with the highest level of thinking attained only by some. She argues that the level of education emerging adults achieve especially influences how likely they are to maximize their cognitive potential.

developmental **connection**

Emotion

Emotional fluctuations in early adolescence may be linked to hormone levels. As adolescents move into adulthood, their emotions become less extreme. Connect to "Puberty, Health, and Biological Foundations" and "The Self, Identity, Emotion, and Personality."

Cognition and Emotion Labouvie-Vief and her colleagues (Labouvie-Vief, 2009; Labouvie-Vief, Gruhn, & Studer, 2010) also argue that to understand cognitive changes in adulthood it is necessary to consider how emotional maturity might affect cognitive development. They conclude that although emerging and young adults become more aware that emotions influence their thinking, at this point thinking is often swayed too strongly by negative emotions that can produce distorted and self-serving perspectives. In this research, a subset of emerging adults who are high in empathy, flexibility, and autonomy are more likely to engage in complex, integrated cognitive-emotional thinking. Labouvie-Vief and her colleagues have found that the ability to think in this cognitively and emotionally balanced, advanced manner increases in middle adulthood. Further, they emphasize that in middle age, individuals become more inwardly reflective and less context-dependent in their thinking than they were as young adults. In the work of Labouvie-Vief and her colleagues, we see the effort to discover connections between cognitive and socioemotional development, which is an increasing trend in the field of life-span development.

Is There a Fifth, Postformal Stage? Some theorists have pieced together these descriptions of adult thinking and have proposed that young adults move into a new qualitative stage of cognitive development, postformal thought (Sinnott, 2003). **Postformal thought** has the following characteristics:

· *Reflective, relativistic, and contextual.* As young adults engage in solving problems, they might think deeply about many aspects of work, politics, relationships, and other areas of life (Labouvie-Vief, 1986). They find that what might be the best solution to a problem at work (with a boss or co-worker) might not be the best solution at home (with a romantic partner). Thus, postformal thought holds that the correct answer to a problem requires reflective thinking and may vary from one situation to another. Some psychologists argue that reflective thinking continues to increase and becomes more internal and less contextual in middle age (Labouvie-Vief, Gruhn, & Studer, 2010; Mascalo & Fischer, 2010).

What are some characteristics that have been proposed for a fifth stage of cognitive development called postformal thought?
© Yuri Arcurs/Alamy RF

postformal thought Thought that is reflective, relativistic, and contextual; provisional; realistic; and open to emotions and subjective.

What are some characteristics of wisdom?
© Image Source/Corbis RF

· *Provisional.* Many young adults also become more skeptical about the truth and seem unwilling to accept an answer as final. Thus, they come to see the search for truth as an ongoing and perhaps never-ending process.

· *Realistic.* Young adults understand that thinking can't always be abstract. In many instances, it must be realistic and pragmatic.

· *Recognized as being influenced by emotion.* Emerging and young adults are more likely than adolescents to understand that their thinking is influenced by emotions. However, too often negative emotions produce thinking that is distorted and self-serving at this point in development.

One effort to assess postformal thinking is the 10-item Complex Postformal Thought Questionnaire (Sinnott & Johnson, 1997). The questionnaire gives you an opportunity to evaluate the extent to which your thinking has reached the postformal level. A recent study found that the questionnaire items reflect three main categories of postformal thinking: (1) taking into account multiple aspects of a problem or situation; (2) making a subjective choice in a particular problem situation; and (3) perceiving underlying complexities in a situation (Cartwright & others, 2009).

One study using the Complex Postformal Thought Questionnaire revealed that college students who had more cross-category friends (based on categories of gender, age, ethnicity, socioeconomic status, and sexual orientation) scored higher on the postformal thought measure than did their counterparts who had fewer cross-category friends (Galupo, Cartwright, & Savage, 2010). Cross-category friendships likely stimulate individuals to move beyond either/or thinking, critically evaluate stereotypical thinking, and consider alternative explanations.

How strong is the evidence for a fifth, postformal stage of cognitive development? Researchers have found that young adults are more likely to engage in postformal thinking than adolescents are (Commons & Richards, 2003). But critics argue that research has yet to document that postformal thought is a qualitatively more advanced stage than formal operational thought.

Wisdom Paul Baltes and his colleagues (2006) define **wisdom** as expert knowledge about the practical aspects of life that permits excellent judgment about important matters. This practical knowledge involves exceptional insight about human development and life matters, good judgment, and an understanding of how to cope with difficult life problems. Thus, wisdom, more than standard conceptions of intelligence, focuses on life's pragmatic concerns and the human condition.

In regard to wisdom, research by Baltes and his colleagues (Baltes & Kunzmann, 2007; Baltes, Lindenberger, & Staudinger, 2006; Baltes & Smith, 2008) has led to the following conclusions:

· *High levels of wisdom are rare.* Few people, including older adults, attain a high level of wisdom. That only a small percentage of adults show wisdom supports the contention that it requires experience, practice, or complex skills.

· *The time frame of late adolescence and early adulthood is the main age window for wisdom to emerge.* No further advances in wisdom have been found for middle-aged and older adults beyond the level they attained as young adults, but this may have been because the problems studied were not sufficiently relevant to older adults' lives.

· *Factors other than age are critical for wisdom to develop to a high level.* For example, certain life experiences, such as being trained and working in a field concerned with difficult life problems and having wisdom-enhancing mentors, contribute to higher levels of wisdom. Also, people higher in wisdom have values that are more likely to consider the welfare of others rather than their own happiness.

wisdom Expert knowledge about the practical aspects of life that permits excellent judgment about important matters.

- *Personality-related factors, such as openness to experience and creativity, are better predictors of wisdom than cognitive factors such as intelligence.*

A recent study compared college students and older adults on a wisdom scale that consisted of three dimensions: cognitive, reflective, and affective (Ardelt, 2010, p. 199):

- *Cognitive* scale items measured the absence of cognitive wisdom and included items about not having the ability or being unwilling to understand something thoroughly ("ignorance is bliss," for example), and tending to perceive the world as either/or instead of more complex ("People are either good or bad," for example), and being unaware of ambiguity and uncertainty in life ("There is only one right way to do anything," for example).
- *Reflective* scale items evaluated having the ability and being willing to examine circumstances and issues from different perspectives ("I always try to look at all sides of a problem," for example) and the lack of self-examination and self-insight ("Things often go wrong for me through no fault of my own," for example).
- *Affective* scale items assessed positive and caring emotions ("Sometimes I feel a real compassion for everyone," for example) and the lack of those characteristics ("It's not really my problem if others are in trouble and need help," for example).

On the overall wisdom scale, which included an assessment of all three dimensions combined, no differences were found between the two age groups. However, older adults who were college educated scored higher on the reflective and affective, but not the cognitive, dimensions of wisdom than did the college students.

Robert J. Sternberg (2013), whose theory of intelligence we will consider later in the chapter, argues that wisdom is linked to both practical and academic intelligence. In his view, academic intelligence is a necessary but in many cases insufficient requirement for wisdom. Practical knowledge about the realities of life also is needed for wisdom. For Sternberg, balance between self-interest, the interests of others, and contexts produces a common good. Thus, wise individuals don't just look out for themselves—they also need to consider others' needs and perspectives as well as the specific context involved. Sternberg assesses wisdom by presenting problems to individuals that require solutions highlighting various intrapersonal, interpersonal, and contextual interests. He also emphasizes that such aspects of wisdom should be taught in schools (Sternberg, 2013). It is Sternberg's emphasis on using knowledge for the common good in a manner that addresses competing interests that mainly differentiates it from the view of wisdom developed by Baltes and his colleagues.

VYGOTSKY'S THEORY

Lev Vygotsky's (1962) theory has stimulated considerable interest in the view that knowledge is *situated* and *collaborative* (Mahn & John-Steiner, 2013). That is, knowledge is distributed among people and their environments, which include objects, artifacts, tools, books, and the communities in which people live. This distribution suggests that knowing can best be advanced through interaction with others in cooperative activities.

One of Vygotsky's most important concepts is the **zone of proximal development (ZPD),** which refers to the range of tasks that are too difficult for an individual to master alone, but that can be mastered with the guidance and assistance of adults or more-skilled peers. Thus, the lower level of the ZPD is the level of problem solving reached by an adolescent working independently. The upper limit is the level of thinking the adolescent can accept with the assistance of an able instructor (see Figure 5). Vygotsky's emphasis on the ZPD underscored his belief in the importance of social influences on cognitive development (Daniels, 2011).

In Vygotsky's approach, formal schooling is but one of the cultural agents that determine an adolescent's growth. Parents, peers, the community, and the culture's technological orientation also influence adolescents' thinking (Gauvain & Perez, 2015). For example, parents' and peers' attitudes toward intellectual competence affect adolescents' motivation to acquire knowledge. So do the attitudes of teachers and other adults in the community.

Upper limit

Level of additional responsibility child can accept with assistance of an able instructor

Zone of proximal development (ZPD)

Lower limit

Level of problem solving reached on these tasks by child working alone

FIGURE 5

VYGOTSKY'S ZONE OF PROXIMAL DEVELOPMENT (ZPD). Vygotsky's zone of proximal development has a lower limit and an upper limit. Tasks in the ZPD are too difficult for the child or adolescent to perform alone. They require assistance from an adult or a more-skilled youth. As children and adolescents experience the verbal instruction or demonstration, they organize the information in their existing mental structures so they can eventually perform the skill or task alone.
© Jose Luis Pelaez, Inc./Blend Images/Getty Images RF

zone of proximal development (ZPD) Vygotsky's concept that refers to the range of tasks that are too difficult for an individual to master alone, but that can be mastered with the guidance or assistance of adults or more-skilled peers.

	Vygotsky		Piaget
Sociocultural Context	Strong emphasis		Little emphasis
Constructivism	Social constructivist		Cognitive constructivist
Stages	No general stages of development proposed		Strong emphasis on stages (sensorimotor, preoperational, concrete operational, and formal operational)
Key Processes	Zone of proximal development, language, dialogue, tools of the culture		Schema, assimilation, accommodation, operations, conservation, classification
Role of Language	A major role; language plays a powerful role in shaping thought		Language has a minimal role; cognition primarily directs language
View on Education	Education plays a central role, helping children learn the tools of the culture		Education merely refines the child's cognitive skills that have already emerged
Teaching Implications	Teacher is a facilitator and guide, not a director; establish many opportunities for children to learn with the teacher and more-skilled peers		Also views teacher as a facilitator and guide, not a director; provide support for children to explore their world and discover knowledge

FIGURE 6

COMPARISON OF VYGOTSKY'S AND PIAGET'S THEORIES

(Vygotsky): A.R. Lauria / Dr. Michael Cole, Laboratory of Human Cognition, University of California, San Diego; (Piaget): © Bettmann/Corbis

Even though their theories were proposed at about the same time, most of the world learned about Vygotsky's theory later than they learned about Piaget's theory, so Vygotsky's theory has not yet been evaluated as thoroughly. Vygotsky's view of the importance of sociocultural influences on children's development fits with the current belief that it is important to evaluate the contextual factors in learning (Crosnoe & Benner, 2015; Murry & others, 2015).

Although both theories are constructivist, Vygotsky's is a **social constructivist approach,** which emphasizes the social contexts of learning and the construction of knowledge through social interaction. In moving from Piaget to Vygotsky, the conceptual shift is from the individual to collaboration, social interaction, and sociocultural activity (Gauvain & Perez, 2015). The end point of cognitive development for Piaget is formal operational thought. For Vygotsky, the end point can differ, depending on which skills are considered to be the most important in a particular culture. For Piaget, children construct knowledge by transforming, organizing, and reorganizing previous knowledge. For Vygotsky, children and adolescents construct knowledge through social interaction (Mahn & John-Steiner, 2013). The implication of Piaget's theory for teaching is that children need support to explore their world and discover knowledge. The main implication of Vygotsky's theory for teaching is that students need many opportunities to learn with the teacher and more-skilled peers. In both Piaget's and Vygotsky's theories, teachers serve as facilitators and guides, rather than as directors and molders of learning. Figure 6 compares Vygotsky's and Piaget's theories.

Criticisms of Vygotsky's theory also have surfaced. Some critics point out that Vygotsky was not specific enough about age-related changes (Gauvain, 2013). Another criticism focuses on Vygotsky not adequately describing how changes in socioemotional capabilities contribute to cognitive development. Yet another criticism is that he overemphasized the role of language in thinking. Also, his emphasis on collaboration and guidance has potential pitfalls. Might facilitators be too helpful in some cases, as when a parent becomes too overbearing and controlling? Further, some adolescents might become lazy and expect help when they might have done something on their own.

social constructivist approach Approach that emphasizes the social contexts of learning and the construction of knowledge through social interaction.

Review *Connect* Reflect

 LG2 Discuss the cognitive developmental view of adolescence

Review

- What is Piaget's view of adolescence? What are some contributions and criticisms of Piaget's theory? What are some possible cognitive changes in adulthood?
- What is Vygotsky's view of adolescence?

Connect

- Compare the concepts of postformal thought and wisdom.

Reflect *Your Own Personal Journey of Life*

- Think back to when you were 8 years old and 16 years old. Imagine that you are watching a political convention on television at these two different ages. In terms of Piaget's stages of cognitive development, how would your perceptions of the proceedings likely have differed when you were at these two different ages? What would you have "seen" and comprehended as an 8-year-old? What would you have "seen" and comprehended as a 16-year-old? What Piagetian concepts would these differences in your cognition reflect?

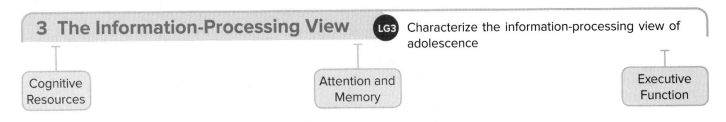

3 The Information-Processing View

LG3 Characterize the information-processing view of adolescence

Cognitive Resources

Attention and Memory

Executive Function

We have briefly discussed the information-processing view. We saw that information processing includes how information gets into adolescents' minds, how it is stored, and how adolescents retrieve information to think about and solve problems.

Information processing is both a framework for thinking about adolescent development and a facet of that development. As a framework, the information-processing view includes certain ideas about how adolescents' minds work and how best to study those workings (Kuhn, 2013; Siegler, 2012, 2013, 2015; Siegler & Lortie-Forgues, 2015; Siegler & others, 2015). As a facet of development, information processing changes as children make the transition from adolescence to adulthood. Changes in attention and memory, for example, are essentially changes in the way individuals process information.

Deanna Kuhn (2009) has discussed some important characteristics of adolescents' information processing and thinking. In her view, in the later years of childhood, and continuing in adolescence, individuals approach cognitive levels that may or may not be achieved, in contrast with the largely universal cognitive levels that young children attain. By adolescence, considerable variation in cognitive functioning is present across individuals. This variability supports the argument that adolescents are producers of their own development to a greater extent than are children.

In our exploration of information processing, we will discuss developmental changes in attention, memory, and a number of higher-order cognitive processes involved in executive function. But first let's examine the importance of cognitive resources in processing information.

COGNITIVE RESOURCES

Information processing is influenced by both the capacity and the speed of processing. These two characteristics are often referred to as *cognitive resources*, and adolescents—especially older adolescents—are better than children at managing and deploying these resources in controlled and purposeful ways (Kuhn & Franklin, 2006).

Most information-processing psychologists argue that an increase in capacity improves processing of information (Halford & Andrews, 2011). For example, as adolescents' information-processing capacity increases, they likely can hold in mind several dimensions of a topic or problem simultaneously, whereas younger children are more prone to focus on only one dimension.

What is the role of processing speed? Generally, fast processing is linked with good performance on cognitive tasks (Tam & others, 2015). However, some compensation for slower processing speed can be achieved through effective strategies.

There is abundant evidence that the speed with which cognitive tasks are completed improves dramatically across the childhood and adolescent years (Hommel, Li, & Li, 2004; Kail, 2007; Kuhn, 2009). In one study, 10-year-olds were approximately 1.8 times slower in processing information than young adults on tasks involving reaction time and abstract matching (Hale, 1990). Twelve-year-olds were approximately 1.5 times slower than young adults, but 15-year-olds processed information on the tasks as fast as the young adults. Also, a recent study of 8- to 13-year-old children revealed that processing speed increased with age, and also that the developmental change in processing speed preceded an increase in working memory capacity (Kail, 2007). Further, a recent study of 9- to 14-year-olds found that faster processing speed was linked to a higher level of oral reading fluency (Jacobson & others, 2011). A recent meta-analysis (use of statistical techniques to combine the results of studies) confirmed that processing speed improved from childhood through adolescence (Verhaeghen, 2013). In this meta-analysis, the processing speed began to slow down in the latter part of early adulthood and continued to decline thereafter through the remainder of the life span.

ATTENTION AND MEMORY

When adolescents process information quickly, they have to focus their attention on the information. And, if they need to use the information later, they will have to remember it. Attention and memory are key aspects of adolescents' information processing.

attention Concentration and focusing of mental resources.

selective attention Focusing on a specific aspect of experience that is relevant while ignoring others that are irrelevant.

divided attention Concentrating on more than one activity at the same time.

sustained attention The ability to maintain attention to a selected stimulus for a prolonged period of time.

executive attention Type of attention that involves planning actions, allocating attention to goals, detecting and compensating for errors, monitoring progress on tasks, and dealing with novel or difficult circumstances.

memory The retention of information over time.

Attention   **Attention** is the concentration and focusing of mental effort. Individuals can allocate their attention in different ways (Ellison & others, 2014; Ristic & Enns, 2015). Psychologists have labeled these types of allocation as selective attention, divided attention, sustained attention, and executive attention.

- **Selective attention** is focusing on a specific aspect of experience that is relevant while ignoring others that are irrelevant. Focusing on one voice among many in a crowded room is an example of selective attention.
- **Divided attention** involves concentrating on more than one activity at the same time. An example of divided attention is text messaging while listening to an instructor's lecture.
- **Sustained attention** is the ability to maintain attention to a selected stimulus for a prolonged period of time. Staying focused on reading this chapter from start to finish without interruption is an example of sustained attention.

What are some changes in attention during childhood and adolescence?
© John Henley/Corbis

Executive attention involves planning actions, allocating attention to goals, detecting and compensating for errors, monitoring progress on tasks, and dealing with novel or difficult circumstances. An example of executive attention is effectively deploying attention to engage in the aforementioned cognitive tasks while writing a 10-page paper for a history course.

Let's further explore divided, sustained, and executive attention. In one investigation, 12-year-olds were markedly better than 8-year-olds, and slightly worse than 20-year-olds, at dividing their attention between two tasks (Manis, Keating, & Morrison, 1980). Adolescents may have more resources available to them than children (through increased processing speed, capacity, and automaticity), or they may be more skilled at directing the resources.

One trend involving divided attention is adolescents' multitasking, which in some cases involves dividing attention not just between two activities but between three or even more (Bauerlein, 2008). A major influence on the increase in multitasking is the availability of multiple electronic media. If a key task is at all complex and challenging, such as trying to figure out how to solve a homework problem, multitasking considerably reduces attention to the key task (Myers, 2008).

Sustained and executive attention also are very important aspects of adolescent cognitive development. As adolescents are required to engage in larger, increasingly complex tasks that require longer time frames to complete, their ability to sustain attention is critical for succeeding on the tasks. An increase in executive attention supports the rapid increase in effortful control required to effectively engage in these complex academic tasks (Rothbart, 2011).

As with any cognitive process, there are wide individual differences in how effectively adolescents use these different types of attention in their everyday lives. For example, individuals with attention deficit hyperactivity disorder (ADHD) have severe problems in effectively allocating attention.

Memory   There are few moments when adolescents' lives are not steeped in memory. Memory is at work with each step adolescents take, each thought they think, and each word they utter. **Memory** is the retention of information over time. It is central to mental life and to information processing (Howe, 2015). To successfully learn and reason, adolescents need to hold on to information and retrieve it when necessary. Three important memory systems—short-term memory, working memory, and long-term memory—are involved in adolescents' learning.

- - - - - - - ➤
developmental **connection**
Media
One study revealed that when media multitasking is taken into account, 11- to 14-year-olds use media nearly 12 hours a day (Rideout, Foehr, & Roberts, 2010). Connect to "Culture."

Is multitasking beneficial or distracting for adolescents?
© Image Source/Getty Images RF

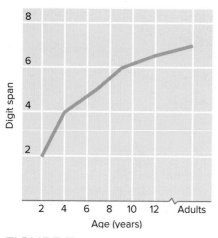

FIGURE 7

DEVELOPMENTAL CHANGES IN MEMORY SPAN. In one study, memory span increased about three digits from 2 years of age to five digits at 7 years of age (Dempster, 1981). By 12 years of age, memory span had increased on average another 1½ digits.

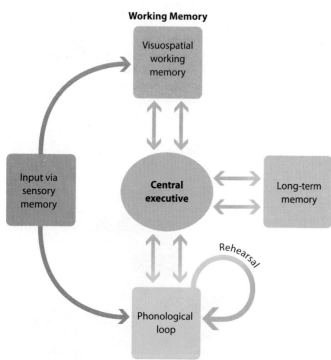

FIGURE 8

WORKING MEMORY. In Baddeley's working memory model, working memory is like a mental workbench where a great deal of information processing is carried out. Working memory consists of three main components: the phonological loop and visuospatial working memory serve as assistants, helping the central executive do its work. Input from sensory memory goes to the phonological loop, where information about speech is stored and rehearsal takes place, and to visuospatial working memory, where visual and spatial information, including imagery, is stored. Working memory is a limited-capacity system, and information is stored there for only a brief time. Working memory interacts with long-term memory, using information from long-term memory in its work and transmitting information to long-term memory for longer storage.

Short-Term Memory   *Short-term memory* is a limited-capacity memory system in which information is retained for as long as 30 seconds, unless the information is rehearsed (repeated), in which case it can be retained longer. A common way to assess short-term memory is to present a list of items to remember, which is often referred to as a memory span task. If you have taken an IQ test, you probably were asked to remember a string of numbers or words. You simply hear a short list of stimuli—usually digits—presented at a rapid pace (one per second, for example). Then you are asked to repeat the digits back. Using the memory span task, researchers have found that short-term memory increases extensively in early childhood and continues to increase in older children and adolescents, but at a slower pace. For example, in one investigation, memory span increased by 1½ digits between the ages of 7 and 12 (Dempster, 1981) (see Figure 7). Keep in mind, though, that individuals have widely varying memory spans, as reflected in their scores on IQ assessments and various aptitude tests.

Working Memory   Short-term memory is like a passive storehouse with shelves to store information until it is moved to long-term memory. *Working memory* is a kind of mental "workbench" where individuals manipulate and assemble information when they make decisions, solve problems, and comprehend written and spoken language (Baddeley, 2008, 2010a, b, 2012, 2013) (see Figure 8). Many psychologists prefer the term *working memory* over *short-term memory* to describe how memory works. Working memory is described as more active and powerful in modifying information than is short-term memory.

In one study, the performances of individuals from 6 to 57 years of age were examined on both verbal and visuospatial working memory tasks (Swanson, 1999). As shown in Figure 9, working memory increased substantially from 8 through 24 years of age no matter what the task. Thus, the adolescent years are likely to be an important developmental period for improvement in working memory. Note that working memory continues to improve through the transition to adulthood and beyond.

Working memory is linked to many aspects of children's and adolescents' development (Cowan, 2014; Reznick, 2014). One study revealed that working memory capacity at 9 to 10 years of age predicted foreign language comprehension two years later, at 11 to 12 years of age (Andersson, 2010). Another study found that the prefrontal cortex plays a more important role in working memory in late adolescence than in early adolescence (Finn & others, 2010). And a recent research review concluded that children with learning difficulties in reading and math have working memory deficits (Peng & Fuchs, 2015).

A recent study found that working memory deficits at age 15 were associated with risk taking behavior at age 18 (Thomas & others, 2015). Working memory serves as a cognitive filter that allows individuals to hold information in their mind to consider the potential consequences of their actions. Thus, when individuals have working memory deficits, it may contribute to risky decision making (Thomas & others, 2015).

Long-Term Memory   *Long-term memory* is a relatively permanent memory system that holds huge amounts of information for a long period of time. Long-term memory increases substantially in the middle and late childhood years and improvement likely continues during adolescence, although this has not been well documented by researchers. If anything at all is known about long-term memory, it is that it depends on the learning activities engaged in when an individual is acquiring and remembering information (Pressley & Hilden, 2006). Most learning activities fit under the category of *strategies*, activities under the learner's conscious control. There are many such activities, but one of the most important is organization, the tendency to group or arrange items into categories. We will have more to discuss about strategies shortly.

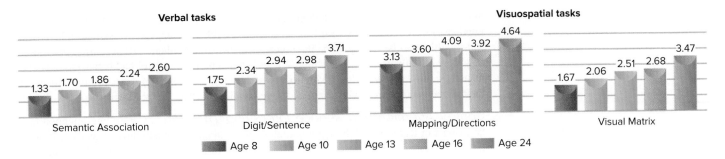

Verbal tasks

Semantic Association: 1.33, 1.70, 1.86, 2.24, 2.60

Digit/Sentence: 1.75, 2.34, 2.94, 2.98, 3.71

Visuospatial tasks

Mapping/Directions: 3.13, 3.60, 4.09, 3.92, 4.64

Visual Matrix: 1.67, 2.06, 2.51, 2.68, 3.47

Age 8   Age 10   Age 13   Age 16   Age 24

FIGURE 9

DEVELOPMENTAL CHANGES IN WORKING MEMORY. *Note:* The scores shown here are the means for each age group, and the age also represents a mean age. Higher scores reflect superior working memory performance.

EXECUTIVE FUNCTION

Attention and memory are important dimensions of information processing, but other dimensions also are important. Especially important in adolescent cognition are higher-order, complex cognitive processes that involve an umbrella-like concept called **executive function.** These cognitive processes are linked to the development of the brain's prefrontal cortex and involve managing one's thoughts to engage in goal-directed behavior and exercise self-control (Carlson, Claxton, & Moses, 2015; Fuhs & Others, 2014; Muller & Kerns, 2015; Peng & Fuchs, 2014). Executive function is hard at work when adolescents are making decisions, thinking critically, and engaged in thinking about thinking.

Executive function becomes increasingly strong during adolescence (Kuhn, 2009; Kuhn & Franklin, 2006). This executive function

assumes a role of monitoring and managing the deployment of cognitive resources as a function of task demands. As a result, cognitive development and learning itself become more effective. . . . Emergence and strengthening of this executive (function) is arguably the single most important and consequential intellectual development to occur in the second decade of life (Kuhn & Franklin, 2006, p. 987).

Cognitive Control   **Cognitive control** involves effective control and flexible thinking in a number of areas, including controlling attention, reducing interfering thoughts, and being cognitively flexible. Cognitive control also has been referred to as *inhibitory control* or *effortful control* to emphasize the ability to resist a strong inclination to do one thing but instead to do what is most effective (Fino & others, 2014).

Across childhood and adolescence, cognitive control increases with age (Casey, 2015). The increase in cognitive control is thought to be due to the maturation of brain pathways and circuitry we considered earlier in the chapter. For example, one study found less diffusion and more focal activation in the prefrontal cortex from 7 to 30 years of age (Durston & others, 2006). The activation change was accompanied by increased efficiency in cognitive performance, especially in *cognitive control.*

Think about all the times adolescents and emerging adults need to engage in cognitive control, such as the following activities (Galinsky, 2010):

- making a real effort to stick with a task, avoiding interfering thoughts or environmental events, and instead doing what is most effective;
- stopping and thinking before acting to avoid blurting out something that they might later wish they hadn't said;
- continuing to work on something that is important but boring when there is something a lot more fun to do, but inhibiting their behavior and doing the boring but important task, saying to themselves, "I have to show the self-discipline to finish this."

A longitudinal study of an important dimension of executive function—inhibitory control—found that 3- to 11-year-old children who early in development showed better

What characterizes executive function?
© ColorBlind Images/Getty Images

developmental **connection**

Cognitive Development

Researchers recently have found that sleep deficits during adolescence are related to lower working memory. Connect to "Puberty, Health, and Biological Foundations."

executive function An umbrella-like concept that involves higher-order, complex cognitive processes that include exercising cognitive control, making decisions, reasoning, thinking critically, thinking creatively, and metacognition.

cognitive control The capacity to control attention, reduce interfering thoughts, and be cognitively flexible.

inhibitory control (able to wait their turn, not easily distracted, more persistent, and less impulsive) were more likely to still be in school, less likely to engage in risk-taking behavior, and less likely to be taking drugs in adolescence (Moffitt & others, 2011). Thirty years after they were initially assessed, the children with better inhibitory control had better physical and mental health (they were less likely to be overweight, for example), earned more money in their career, were more law-abiding, and were happier (Moffitt, 2012; Moffitt & others, 2011).

Control Attention and Reduce Interfering Thoughts   Controlling attention is a key aspect of learning and thinking in adolescence and emerging adulthood (Rueda & Posner, 2013). Distractions that can interfere with attention in adolescence and emerging adulthood come from the external environment (other students talking while the student is trying to listen to a lecture, or the student turning on a laptop during a lecture and looking at a new friend request on Facebook, for example) or intrusive distractions from competing thoughts in the individual's mind. Self-oriented thoughts, such as worrying, self-doubt, and intense emotionally laden thoughts may especially interfere with focusing attention on thinking tasks (Walsh, 2011).

Be Cognitively Flexible   *Cognitive flexibility* involves being aware that options and alternatives are available and adapting to the situation. Before adolescents and emerging adults adapt their behavior in a situation, they need to become aware that they ought to change their way of thinking and be motivated to do so. Having confidence in their ability to adapt their thinking to a particular situation, an aspect of *self-efficacy,* also is important in being cognitively flexible (Bandura, 2012).

Some critics argue that not much benefit is derived from placing various cognitive processes under the broader concept of executive function. Although we have described a number of components of executive function here—cognitive inhibition, cognitive flexibility, and so on—a consensus has not been reached on what the components are, how they are connected, and how they develop. That said, the concept of executive function is not likely to go away any time soon, and further research, especially meta-analyses, should provide a clearer picture of executive function and how it develops through the life span (Luszcz, 2011).

Decision Making   Adolescence is a time of increased decision making—which friends to choose; which person to date; whether to have sex, buy a car, go to college; and so on (Christakou, 2014). How competent are adolescents at making decisions? In some reviews, older adolescents are described as more competent than younger adolescents, who in turn are more competent than children (Keating, 1990). Compared with children, young adolescents are more likely to generate different options, examine a situation from a variety of perspectives, anticipate the consequences of decisions, and consider the credibility of sources.

One study documents that older adolescents are better at decision making than younger adolescents are (Lewis, 1981). Eighth-, tenth-, and twelfth-grade students were presented with dilemmas involving the choice of a medical procedure. The oldest students were most likely to spontaneously mention a variety of risks, to recommend consultation with an outside specialist, and to anticipate future consequences. For example, when asked a question about whether to have cosmetic surgery, a twelfth-grader said that different aspects of the situation need to be examined along with its effects on the individual's future, especially relationships with other people. In contrast, an eighth-grader presented a more limited view, commenting on the surgery's effects on getting turned down for a date, the money involved, and being teased by peers.

In sum, older adolescents often make better decisions than do younger adolescents, who in turn, make better decisions than do children. The ability to regulate one's emotions during decision making, to remember prior decisions and their consequences, and to adapt subsequent decision making on the basis of those consequences appears to improve with age at least through early adulthood (Klaczynski, Byrnes, & Jacobs, 2001).

What are some of the decisions adolescents have to make? What characterizes their decision making?
© Big Cheese Photo/SuperStock RF

However, older adolescents' decision-making skills are far from perfect, but of course, we also are not perfect decision makers as adults (Kuhn, 2009). Adolescents and adults who are impulsive and seek sensation are often not very effective decision makers, for example (Galvan & others, 2007).

Being able to make competent decisions does not guarantee that individuals will make them in everyday life, where breadth of experience often comes into play. As an example, driver-training courses improve adolescents' cognitive and motor skills to levels equal to, or sometimes superior to, those of adults. However, driver training has not been effective in reducing adolescents' high rate of traffic accidents, although recently researchers have found that implementing a graduated driver licensing (GDL) program can reduce crash and fatality rates for adolescent drivers (Keating, 2007). GDL components include a learner's holding period, practice-driving certification, night-driving restriction, and passenger restriction. In addition to GDL, parental monitoring and expectations can reduce adolescents' driving accidents (Keating & Halpern-Felsher, 2008). For example, parents can restrict and monitor the presence of adolescents' peers in the vehicle.

Most people make better decisions when they are calm rather than emotionally aroused, which may especially be true for adolescents (Rivers, Reyna, & Mills, 2008; Steinberg & others, 2009). Recall from our discussion of brain development earlier in the chapter that adolescents have a tendency to be emotionally intense. Thus, the same adolescent who makes a wise decision when calm may make an unwise decision when emotionally aroused (Giedd, 2012). In the heat of the moment, then, adolescents' emotions are especially likely to overwhelm their decision-making ability.

The social context plays a key role in adolescent decision making (Monahan & others, 2015; Steinberg, 2015a, b). For example, adolescents' willingness to make risky decisions is more likely to occur in contexts where substances and other temptations are readily available (Gerrard & others, 2008; Reyna & Rivers, 2008). Recent research reveals that the presence of peers in risk-taking situations increases the likelihood that adolescents will make risky decisions (Albert & Steinberg, 2011a, b). In one study of risk taking involving a simulated driving task, the presence of peers increased an adolescent's decision to engage in risky driving by 50 percent but had no effect on adults (Gardner & Steinberg, 2005). One view is that the presence of peers activates the brain's reward system, especially dopamine pathways (Steinberg, 2015a, b).

It also is important to consider how the stress level of situations and individual differences in risk taking can influence adolescents' decisions. Few research studies have examined how trait-like tendencies might influence the decisions adolescents make in stressful and risky situations. A recent study found that adolescents took more risks in stressful than

How do emotions and social contexts influence adolescents' decision making?
© Scott Houston/Corbis

nonstressful situations (Johnson, Dariotis, & Wang, 2012). However, risk taking in the stressful conditions was associated with the type of risk taker the adolescent was. In the stressful condition, impulsive risk takers were less accurate and planful; calculated risk takers took fewer risks; and conservative risk takers engaged in low risk taking in both the nonstressful and stressful conditions.

Adolescents need more opportunities to practice and discuss realistic decision making. Many real-world decisions on matters such as sex, drugs, and daredevil driving occur in an atmosphere of stress that includes time constraints and emotional involvement. One strategy for improving adolescent decision making in such circumstances is to provide more opportunities for them to engage in role-playing and group problem solving. Another strategy is for parents to involve adolescents in appropriate decision-making activities.

To better understand adolescent decision making, Valerie Reyna and her colleagues (Reyna & Brainerd, 2011; Reyna & Farley, 2006; Reyna & others, 2010, 2011) have proposed the **fuzzy-trace theory dual-process model,** which states that decision making is influenced by two cognitive systems—"verbatim" analytical thinking (literal and precise) and gist-based intuition (simple, bottom-line meaning)—which operate in parallel. According to this theory, it is gist-based intuition that benefits adolescents' decision making most. In this view, adolescents don't benefit from engaging in reflective, detailed, higher-level cognitive analysis about a decision, especially in high-risk, real-world contexts where analysis would cause them to get bogged down in trivial detail. In such contexts, adolescents need to rely on the simple, bottom-line reality that some circumstances are so dangerous that they must be avoided at all costs.

In risky situations it is important for an adolescent to quickly get the *gist,* or meaning, of what is happening and glean that the situation is a dangerous context, which can cue personal values that will protect the adolescent from making a risky decision (Reyna & others, 2011). A recent experiment showed that encouraging gist-based thinking about risks (in addition to providing factual information) reduced self-reported risk-taking up to one year after exposure to the curriculum (Reyna & Mills, 2014). Further, adolescents who have a higher level of trait inhibition (self-control that helps them to manage their impulses effectively) and find themselves in risky contexts are less likely to engage in risk-taking behavior than their adolescent counterparts who have a lower level of trait inhibition (Chick & Reyna, 2012). However, some experts on adolescent cognition argue that in many cases adolescents benefit from both analytical and experiential systems (Kuhn, 2009).

How might mindfulness training improve adolescents' development?
© Chris Clinton/Taxi/Getty Images

fuzzy-trace theory dual-process model
States that decision making is influenced by two systems—"verbatim" analytical thinking (literal and precise) and gist-based intuition (simple, bottom-line meaning), which operate in parallel; in this model, it is the gist-based system that benefits adolescents' decision making most.

critical thinking Thinking reflectively and productively and evaluating the evidence.

Critical Thinking   **Critical thinking** is thinking reflectively and productively and evaluating evidence (Galinsky, 2010; Sternberg & Sternberg, 2013). In this book, the third part of the Review *Connect* Reflect sections challenges you to think critically about a topic or an issue related to the discussion. Thinking critically includes asking not only what happened, but how and why; examining supposed "facts" to determine whether there is evidence to support them; evaluating what other people say rather than immediately accepting it as the truth; and asking questions and speculating beyond what is known to create new ideas and new information.

Mindfulness   According to Ellen Langer (2005), *mindfulness*—being alert, mentally present, and cognitively flexible while going through life's everyday activities and tasks—is an important aspect of thinking critically. Mindful adolescents maintain an active awareness of the circumstances in their life and are motivated to find the best solutions to tasks. They create new ideas, are open to new information, and operate from multiple perspectives. By contrast, adolescents who are not mindful are entrapped in old ideas, engage in automatic behavior, and operate from a single perspective.

Recently, Robert Roeser and Philip Zelazo (2012) have emphasized that mindfulness is an important mental process that children and adolescents can engage in to improve a number of cognitive and socioemotional skills, such as executive function, focused attention, emotion regulation, and empathy (Roeser & Zelazo, 2012). It has been proposed that mindfulness training could be implemented in schools, including the use of age-appropriate activities that increase children's and adolescents' reflection on moment-to-moment experiences and promote self-regulation (Zelazo & Lyons, 2012). A recent study of young adolescents found that a higher level of mindfulness attention awareness (assessed low identification with statements such as "I could be experiencing some emotion and not be conscious of it until sometime later" and "I snack without being aware of what I'm eating") was associated with cognitive inhibition (Oberle & others, 2012).

In addition to mindfulness, yoga, meditation, and tai chi have been recently proposed as candidates for enhancing children's and adolescents' cognitive and socioemotional development (Roeser & Pinela, 2014). Together these activities are being grouped under the topic of *contemplative science*, a cross-disciplinary term that involves the study of how various types of mental and physical training might enhance children's development (Roeser & Zelazo, 2012).

Developmental Changes   Adolescence is an important transitional period in the development of critical thinking (Keating, 1990). In one study of fifth-, eighth-, and eleventh-graders, critical thinking increased with age but still occurred only in 43 percent of eleventh-graders (Klaczynski & Narasimham, 1998). Many adolescents showed self-serving biases in their thinking.

Among the cognitive changes that allow improved critical thinking during adolescence are the following:

- Increased speed, automaticity, and capacity of information processing, which free cognitive resources for other purposes
- Greater breadth of content knowledge in a variety of domains
- Increased ability to construct new combinations of knowledge
- A greater range and more spontaneous use of strategies and procedures for obtaining and applying knowledge, such as planning, considering the alternatives, and cognitive monitoring

Although adolescence is an important period in the development of critical-thinking skills, if a solid base of fundamental skills (such as literacy and math skills) has not been developed during childhood, critical-thinking skills are unlikely to develop adequately in adolescence.

Schools   Considerable interest has been directed to teaching critical thinking in schools (Fairweather & Cramond, 2011). Cognitive psychologist Robert J. Sternberg (1985) concludes that most school programs that teach critical thinking are flawed. He thinks that schools focus too much on formal reasoning tasks and not enough on the critical-thinking skills needed in everyday life. Among the critical-thinking skills that Sternberg notes that adolescents need in everyday life are these: recognizing that problems exist, defining problems more clearly, handling problems with no single right answer or any clear criteria for the point at which the problem is solved (such as selecting a rewarding career), making decisions on issues of personal relevance (such as deciding to have a risky operation), obtaining information, thinking in groups, and developing long-term approaches for addressing long-term problems.

One way to encourage students to think critically is to present them with controversial topics or articles that present both sides of an issue to discuss (Kuhn & Franklin, 2006). Some teachers shy away from having students engage in these types of critical-thinking debates or discussions because it is not "polite" or "nice" (Winn, 2004). However, critical thinking is promoted when students encounter conflicting accounts of arguments and debates, which can motivate them to delve more deeply into a topic and attempt to resolve an issue (Kuhn, 2009; Kuhn & Franklin, 2006).

Getting students to think critically is not always an easy task. Many students come into a class with a history of passive learning, having been encouraged to recite the correct answer to a question rather than put forth the intellectual effort to think in more complex ways. By using more assignments that require students to focus on an issue, a question, or a problem, rather than just to recite facts, teachers stimulate students' ability to think critically.

To read about the work of one secondary school teacher who encourages students to think critically, see the *Connecting with Careers* profile.

developmental **connection**

Exercise

Recent research indicates that more physically fit adolescents have better thinking skills, including those involving executive function, than less physically fit adolescents. Connect to "Puberty, Health, and Biological Foundations."

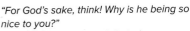

"*For God's sake, think! Why is he being so nice to you?*"
© Sam Gross/The New Yorker Collection/ www.cartoonbank.com.

Laura Bickford, Secondary School Teacher

Laura Bickford teaches English and journalism in grades 9 to 12, and she is chair of the English Department at Nordhoff High School in Ojai, California.

Bickford believes it is especially important to encourage students to think. Indeed, she says that "the call to teach is the call to teach students how to think." She believes that teachers need to show students the value of asking their own questions, having discussions, and engaging in stimulating intellectual conversations. Bickford says that she also encourages students to engage in metacognitive strategies (knowing about knowing). For example, she asks students to comment on their learning after particular pieces of projects have been completed. She requires students to maintain reading logs so they can observe their own thinking as it happens.

Laura Bickford, working with students writing papers.
Courtesy of Laura Johnson Bickford

For more information about the work that secondary school teachers do, see the Careers in Adolescent Development appendix.

Creative Thinking   **Creativity** is the ability to think in novel ways and discover unique solutions to problems. Thus, intelligence, which we discuss shortly, is not the same thing as creativity. J. P. Guilford (1967) first made this distinction by contrasting **convergent thinking,** which produces one correct answer and is characteristic of the kind of thinking required on a conventional intelligence test, and **divergent thinking,** which produces many answers to the same question and is more characteristic of creativity. For example, a typical item on a conventional intelligence test is "How many quarters will you get in return for 60 dimes?" This question has only one correct answer. In contrast, the following questions have many possible answers: "What image comes to mind when you hear the phrase *sitting alone in a dark room*?" or "Can you think of some unique uses for a paper clip?"

Are intelligence and creativity related? Although most creative adolescents are quite intelligent, the reverse is not necessarily true (Lubart, 2003). Many highly intelligent adolescents are not very creative.

A special concern is that adolescents' creative thinking appears to be declining. A study of approximately 300,000 U.S. children, adolescents, and adults found that creativity scores rose until 1990, but since then have been steadily declining (Kim, 2010). Among the likely causes of the creativity decline are the number of hours U.S. children and adolescents watch TV, play video games, connect on Facebook, and text message instead of engaging in creative activities, as well as the lack of emphasis on creative-thinking skills in schools (Gregorson, Kaufman, & Snyder, 2013; Kaufman & Sternberg, 2012, 2013). Some countries, though, are placing increased emphasis on creative thinking in schools. For example, historically, creative thinking has typically been discouraged in Chinese schools. However, Chinese educational administrators are now encouraging teachers to spend more classroom time on creative activities (Plucker, 2010).

An important teaching goal is to help students become more creative. Teachers need to recognize that students will show more creativity in some domains than in others (Kaufman & Sternberg, 2012, 2013). A student who shows creative-thinking skills in mathematics may not exhibit these skills in art, for example.

School environments that encourage independent work, are stimulating but not distracting, and make resources readily available are likely to encourage students' creativity. There is mounting concern that the U.S. government's No Child Left Behind legislation has harmed the development of students' creative thinking by focusing attention on memorization of materials to do well on standardized tests (Kaufman & Sternberg, 2012, 2013).

--- ➤

developmental connection

Schools

A number of criticisms of the government's No Child Left Behind legislation have been made. Connect to "Schools."

creativity The ability to think in novel and unusual ways and discover unique solutions to problems.

convergent thinking A pattern of thinking in which individuals produce one correct answer; characteristic of the items on conventional intelligence tests.

divergent thinking A pattern of thinking in which individuals produce many answers to the same question; more characteristic of creativity than convergent thinking.

Here are some good strategies for increasing adolescents' creative-thinking skills:

· *Have adolescents engage in brainstorming and come up with as many ideas as possible.* Brainstorming is a technique in which individuals are encouraged to come up with creative ideas in a group, play off each other's ideas, and say practically anything that comes to mind. However, recognize that some adolescents are more creative when they work alone. Indeed, one review of research on brainstorming concluded that for many individuals, working alone can generate more ideas and better ideas than working in groups (Rickards & deCock, 2003). One reason for this is that in groups, some individuals contribute only a few ideas, whereas others do most of the creative thinking. Nonetheless, there may be benefits to brainstorming, such as team building, that support its use.

· *Introduce adolescents to environments that stimulate creativity.* Some settings nourish creativity; others depress it (Baer & Kaufman, 2013). People who encourage creativity often rely on adolescents' natural curiosity. They provide exercises and activities that stimulate adolescents to find insightful solutions to problems, rather than asking a lot of questions that require rote answers. Adults also encourage creativity by taking adolescents to locations where creativity is valued.

· *Don't overcontrol.* Teresa Amabile (1993) says that telling individuals exactly how to do things leaves them feeling that any originality is a mistake and any exploration is a waste of time. Letting adolescents select their interests and supporting their inclinations are less likely to destroy their natural curiosity than dictating which activities they should engage in.

· *Build adolescents' confidence.* To expand adolescents' creativity, encourage them to believe in their own ability to create something innovative and worthwhile. Building adolescents' confidence in their creative skills aligns with Bandura's (2012) concept of self-efficacy, the belief that one can master a situation and produce positive outcomes.

· *Encourage internal motivation.* The excessive use of prizes such as gold stars or money can stifle creativity by undermining the intrinsic pleasure adolescents derive from creative activities. Creative adolescents' motivation is the satisfaction generated by the work itself. Competition for prizes and formal evaluations often undermine intrinsic motivation and creativity (Amabile & Hennessey, 1992; Hennessey, 2011).

· *Guide adolescents to be persistent and to delay gratification.* Most highly successful creative products take years to develop. Most creative individuals work on ideas and projects for months and years without being rewarded for their efforts (Sternberg & Williams, 1996). Adolescents don't become experts at sports, music, or art overnight. It usually takes many years of working at something to become an expert at it; the same is true for a creative thinker who produces a unique, worthwhile product.

· *Encourage adolescents to take intellectual risks.* Creative individuals take intellectual risks and seek to discover or invent something never before discovered or invented (Sternberg & Williams, 1996). They risk spending extensive time on an idea or project that may not work. Adolescents' creativity benefits when they are not afraid of failing or getting something wrong (Baer & Kaufman, 2013).

· *Introduce adolescents to creative people.* Think about some of the most creative people in your community. Teachers can invite these people to their classrooms and ask them to describe what helps them become creative or to demonstrate their creative skills. A writer, poet, musician, scientist, and many others can bring their props and productions to the class, turning it into a theater for stimulating students' creativity.

An adolescent boy painting in the streets of the African nation of Zanzibar. *If you were going to work with adolescents to encourage their creativity, what strategies would you adopt?*
© Gideon Mendel/Corbis

developmental **connection**

Achievement

Intrinsic motivation comes from a combination of factors such as self-determination and personal choice, optimal experiences, interest, and cognitive engagement. Connect to "Achievement, Work, and Careers."

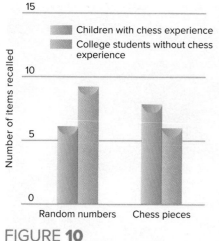

FIGURE **10**

MEMORY FOR NUMBERS AND CHESS PIECES

Chart legend:
- Children with chess experience
- College students without chess experience

Y-axis: Number of items recalled (0, 5, 10, 15)
X-axis categories: Random numbers, Chess pieces

Expertise   Recently psychologists have shown increased interest in exploring the differences between experts and novices in a specific knowledge domain (Guida & others, 2012). An expert is the opposite of a novice (someone who is just beginning to learn a content area). What is it, exactly, that experts do so well? They are better than novices at the following activities (National Research Council, 1999):

· Detecting features and meaningful patterns of information

· Accumulating more content knowledge and organizing it in a manner that shows an understanding of the topic

· Retrieving important aspects of knowledge with little effort

In areas where children and adolescents are experts, their memory is often extremely good. In fact, it often exceeds that of adults who are novices in that content area. This superiority was documented in a study of 10-year-old chess experts (Chi, 1978). These children were excellent chess players, but not especially brilliant in other ways. As with most 10-year-olds, their memory spans for digits were shorter than an adult's. However, when they were presented with chessboards, they remembered the configurations far better than did the adults who were novices at chess (see Figure 10).

Experts' knowledge is organized around important ideas or concepts more than novices' knowledge is (National Research Council, 1999). This ability provides experts with a much deeper understanding of knowledge than novices possess. Experts in a specific area usually have far more elaborate networks of information about that area than novices do. The information they represent in memory has more nodes, more interconnections, and better hierarchical organization.

What determines whether someone becomes an expert? Can motivation and practice elevate someone to expert status? Or does expertise also require a great deal of talent?

One perspective asserts that a specific kind of practice—deliberate practice—is required to become an expert. Deliberate practice involves practice that is at an appropriate level of difficulty for the individual, provides corrective feedback, and allows opportunities for repetition (Ericsson, 2014; Ericsson & others, 2006). In one study of violinists at a music academy, the extent to which children engaged in deliberate practice differed for novices and experts (Ericsson, Krampe, & Tesch-Römer, 1993). The top violinists averaged 7,500 hours of deliberate practice by age 18, the good violinists only 5,300 hours. Many individuals give up on becoming an expert because they won't put forth the effort it takes to engage in extensive deliberate practice over a number of years.

Such extensive practice requires considerable motivation. Students who are not motivated to practice long hours are unlikely to become experts in a specific area. Thus, a student who complains about all of the work involved, doesn't persevere, and doesn't extensively practice solving math problems over a number of years is not going to become an expert in math. However, talent is also usually required to become an expert (Plomin & others, 2014; Ruthsatz & others, 2008). Many individuals have attempted to become great musicians and athletes but have given up trying after only mediocre performances. Nonetheless, musicians such as Beethoven and athletes such as LeBron James would not have developed expertise in their fields without being highly motivated and engaging in extensive deliberate practice. Talent alone does not make someone an expert.

How are talent and deliberate practice involved in expertise?
© Rayman/Getty Images RF

Metacognition   You have studied some important ways in which adolescents process information. In this section, you will read about how adolescents monitor their information processing and think about thinking.

What Is Metacognition?   Earlier in this chapter, in discussing Piaget's theory, you learned that adolescents increase their thinking about thinking. Cognitive psychologists call this kind of thought **metacognition**—that is, cognition about cognition, or "knowing about knowing" (Flavell, 2004). Metacognition can take many forms. It includes thinking about and knowing when and where to use particular strategies for learning or for solving problems (Carretti & others, 2014; Destan & others, 2014). Conceptualization of metacognition includes several dimensions of

metacognition Cognition about cognition, or "knowing about knowing."

Rochelle Ballantyne, Chess Star

Rochelle Ballantyne, a Stanford University student who grew up in Brooklyn, New York, is close to becoming the first female African American to reach the level of chess master (Kastenbaum, 2012). Born in 1995, she grew up in a single-parent family in a lower-income context. Her grandmother taught her to play chess because she didn't want Rochelle's impoverished background to prevent her from reaching her full potential. Rochelle was fortunate to attend I.S. 318, an inner-city public middle school where the chess team is one of the best in the United States. Rochelle has won several national chess championships and she is a rising star in the world of chess. Rochelle's motivation and confidence are reflected in her comment: "When I push myself, then nothing can stop me."

Rochelle Ballantyne, chess champion from Brooklyn, New York, is a rising star in the world of chess. *How might her ability to process information about chess be different from that of a novice chess player?*
© First Run Features/Courtesy Everett Collection

executive function, such as planning (deciding on how much time to focus on the task, for example), evaluation (monitoring progress toward task completion, for example), and self-regulation (modifying strategies while working on the task, for example) (Dimmitt & McCormick, 2012).

Metacognition is increasingly recognized as a very important cognitive skill not only in adolescence but also in emerging adulthood (McCormick, Dimmitt, & Sullivan, 2013). In comparison with children, adolescents have an increased capacity to monitor and manage cognitive resources to effectively meet the demands of a learning task (Kuhn, 2009, 2013). This increased metacognitive ability results in improved cognitive functioning and learning. A longitudinal study revealed that from 12 to 14 years of age, adolescents increasingly used metacognitive skills and applied them more effectively in math and history classes (van der Stel & Veenman, 2010). For example, 14-year-olds monitored their own text comprehension more frequently and did so more effectively than did their younger counterparts. Another study documented the importance of metacognitive skills, such as planning, strategizing, and monitoring, in college students' ability to think critically (Magno, 2010).

Metacognitive skills have been taught to students to help them solve problems. In one study, for each of 30 daily lessons involving verbal math problems, a teacher guided low-achieving students in learning to recognize when they did not know the meaning of a word, did not have all the necessary information to solve a problem, did not know how to subdivide a problem into specific steps, or did not know how to carry out a computation (Cardelle-Elawar, 1992). After completing these lessons, the students who had received the metacognitive training had better math achievement and better attitudes toward math.

Strategies In addition to metamemory, metacognition includes knowledge about strategies. In the view of Michael Pressley (2003), the key to education is helping students learn a rich repertoire of strategies that produce solutions to problems. Good thinkers routinely use strategies and effective planning to solve problems (Fiorella & Mayer, 2015). Good thinkers also know when and where to use strategies. Understanding when and where to use strategies often results from monitoring the learning situation.

Pressley and his colleagues (Pressley & others, 2001, 2003, 2004, 2007) spent considerable time in recent years observing strategy instruction by teachers and strategy use by students in elementary and secondary school classrooms. They conclude that strategy instruction is far less complete and intense than what students need in order to learn how

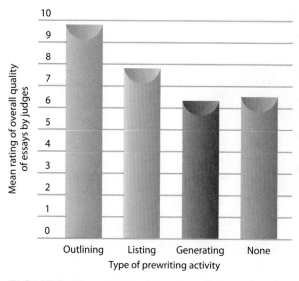

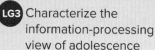

FIGURE 11

THE RELATION OF PREWRITING ACTIVITIES TO ESSAY QUALITY. The most effective prewriting activity for college students was outlining, which involved creating an outline with relevant ideas under multilevel headings. Judges rated the quality of each essay from 1 (lowest) to 10 (highest).

to use strategies effectively. They argue that education ought to be restructured so that students are provided with more opportunities to become competent strategic learners.

As an example of how important strategies are for adolescents, a recent meta-analysis revealed that strategy instruction was the most successful intervention for improving the writing quality of fourth- through twelfth-grade students (Graham & Perin, 2007).

Domain-Specific Thinking Skills Our coverage of metacognition mainly emphasized the importance of some general cognitive skills, such as strategies and self-regulation, in becoming a better thinker. Indeed, researchers have found that metacognitive skills can be taught. For example, adolescents have been effectively taught to become aware of their thinking processes and engage in self-regulation of their learning (Schunk, Meece, & Pintrich, 2014).

However, it also is very important to teach domain-specific thinking skills to adolescents (Mayer, 2012). In this regard, a review concluded that one of educational psychology's greatest accomplishments is the teaching of domain-specific thinking skills (Mayer & Wittrock, 2006). Thus, a rich tradition in quality education programs has been the teaching of thinking skills within specific subjects, such as writing, mathematics, science, and history (Allington, 2015; Chapin, 2015; Posamentier & Smith, 2015). Researchers have found that "it is possible to analyze and teach the underlying cognitive processes required in tasks such as comprehending a passage, writing an essay, solving an arithmetic word problem, answering a scientific question, or explaining an historical event . . ." (Mayer & Wittrock, 2006).

Planning is an important general cognitive skill for adolescents and emerging adults to use, but they also benefit when they apply this and other cognitive skills to specific subjects (Halonen & Santrock, 2013). For example, one study examined how prewriting activities can affect the quality of college students' writing (Kellogg, 1994). As indicated in Figure 11, the planning activity of outlining was the prewriting activity that helped writers the most.

Review Connect Reflect

LG3 Characterize the information-processing view of adolescence

Review

- What characterizes the development of cognitive resources?
- What developmental changes characterize attention and memory in adolescence?
- What is executive function?
- How can adolescent decision making be described?
- What characterizes critical thinking in adolescence?
- What distinguishes experts from novices, and how do individuals become experts?
- What is metacognition, and how does it change developmentally?
- What is self-regulatory learning?
- How important is domain-specific thinking?

Connect

- How does research on cognitive control shed light on adolescents' risk-taking behavior?

Reflect *Your Own Personal Journey of Life*

- What were your study skills like during adolescence? How have your study skills changed since adolescence? Has metacognition played a role in improving your study skills?

| Intelligence Tests | Multiple Intelligences | The Neuroscience of Intelligence | Heredity and Environment |

The two views of adolescent cognition that we have discussed so far—cognitive developmental and information processing—do not emphasize individual variations in intelligence. The **psychometric/intelligence view** does emphasize the importance of individual differences in intelligence; many advocates of this view favor the use of intelligence tests. An increasing issue in the field of intelligence involves pinning down what the components of intelligence really are.

How can intelligence be defined? **Intelligence** is the ability to solve problems and to adapt and learn from experiences. But even this broad definition doesn't satisfy everyone. As you will see shortly, Robert J. Sternberg (2014a, b; 2015a, b, c) proposes that practical know-how should be considered part of intelligence. In his view, intelligence involves weighing options carefully and acting judiciously, as well as developing strategies to improve shortcomings. Sternberg (2014b) also recently described intelligence as the ability to adapt to, shape, and select environments. In adapting to the environment, if individuals find the environment suboptimal, they can change it to make it more suitable for their skills and desires.

Interest in intelligence has often focused on individual differences and assessment (Kehle & Bray, 2014). *Individual differences* are the stable, consistent ways in which people differ from each other. We can talk about individual differences in personality or any other domain, but it is in the domain of intelligence that the most attention has been directed at individual differences. For example, an intelligence test purports to inform us about whether an adolescent can reason better than others who have taken the test.

Alfred Binet constructed the first intelligence test after being asked to create a measure to determine which children would benefit from instruction in France's schools.
© Bettmann/Corbis

INTELLIGENCE TESTS

Robert Sternberg recalls being terrified of taking IQ tests as a child. He literally froze, he says, when the time came to take such tests. Even as an adult, Sternberg is stung by humiliation when he recalls in the sixth grade being asked to take an IQ test with fifth-graders. Sternberg eventually overcame his anxieties about IQ tests. Not only did he begin to perform better on them, but at age 13 he devised his own IQ test and began using it to assess his classmates—that is, until the chief school-system psychologist found out and scolded him. Sternberg became so fascinated by intelligence that he made its study one of his lifelong pursuits. Later in this chapter we will discuss his theory of intelligence. To begin, though, let's step back in time to examine the first valid intelligence test.

The Binet Tests   In 1904, the French Ministry of Education asked psychologist Alfred Binet to devise a method of identifying children who were unable to learn in school. School officials wanted to reduce crowding by placing students who did not benefit from regular classroom teaching in special schools. Binet and his student Theophile Simon developed an intelligence test to meet this request. The test is called the 1905 Scale. It consisted of 30 questions on topics ranging from the ability to touch one's ear to the ability to draw designs from memory and to define abstract concepts.

Binet developed the concept of **mental age (MA),** an individual's level of mental development relative to others. Not much later, in 1912, William Stern created the concept of **intelligence quotient (IQ),** a person's mental age divided by chronological age (CA), multiplied by 100. That is: $IQ = MA/CA \times 100$. If mental age is the same as chronological age, then the person's IQ is 100. If mental age is above chronological age, then IQ is greater than 100. If mental age is below chronological age, then IQ is less than 100.

The Binet test has been revised many times to incorporate advances in the understanding of intelligence and intelligence tests. These revisions are called the *Stanford-Binet tests*

psychometric/intelligence view A view that emphasizes the importance of individual differences in intelligence; many advocates of this view also argue that intelligence should be assessed with intelligence tests.

intelligence The ability to solve problems and to adapt to and learn from everyday experiences; not everyone agrees on what constitutes intelligence.

mental age (MA) An individual's level of mental development relative to others; a concept developed by Binet.

intelligent quotient (IQ) A person's tested mental age divided by chronological age, multiplied by 100.

FIGURE 12

THE NORMAL CURVE AND STANFORD-BINET IQ SCORES. The distribution of IQ scores approximates a normal curve. Most of the population falls in the middle range of scores, between 84 and 116. Notice that extremely high and extremely low scores are rare. Only about 1 in 50 individuals has an IQ higher than 132 or lower than 68.

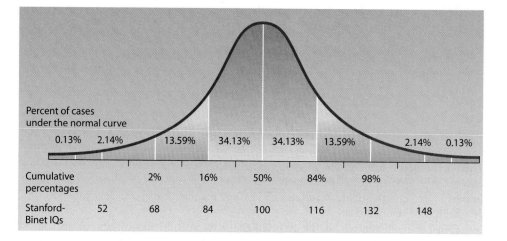

Verbal Subscales

Similarities

An individual must think logically and abstractly to answer a number of questions about how things might be similar.

Example: "In what way are a lion and a tiger alike?"

Comprehension

This subscale is designed to measure an individual's judgment and common sense.

Example: "What is the advantage of keeping money in a bank?"

Nonverbal Subscales

Block Design

An individual must assemble a set of multicolored blocks to match designs that the examiner shows.
Visual-motor coordination, perceptual organization, and the ability to visualize spatially are assessed.

Example: "Use the four blocks on the left to make the pattern on the right."

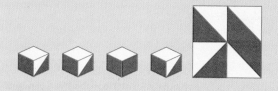

FIGURE 13

SAMPLE SUBSCALES OF THE WECHSLER ADULT INTELLIGENCE SCALE—THIRD EDITION (WAIS-III). The Wechsler includes 11 subscales, 6 verbal and 5 nonverbal. Three of the subscales are shown here. *Simulated items similar to those found in the Wechsler Adult Intelligence Scale—Third Edition (WAIS-III). Copyright © 1997 NCS Pearson, Inc. Reproduced with permission. All rights reserved. "Wechsler Adult Intelligence Scale" and "WAIS" are trademarks, in the USA and/or other countries, of Pearson Education, Inc. or its affiliates(s).*

normal distribution A symmetrical distribution of values or scores, with a majority of scores falling in the middle of the possible range of scores and few scores appearing toward the extremes of the range.

(Stanford University is where the revisions have been done). By administering the test to large numbers of people of different ages from different backgrounds, researchers have found that scores on the Stanford-Binet approximate a normal distribution (see Figure 12). A **normal distribution** is symmetrical, with a majority of the scores falling in the middle of the possible range of scores, and few scores appearing toward the extremes of the range.

In 2004, the test—now called the Stanford-Binet 5—was revised to analyze an individual's response in five content areas: fluid reasoning, knowledge, quantitative reasoning, visual-spatial reasoning, and working memory. A general composite score also is still obtained.

The Wechsler Scales Besides the Stanford-Binet, the other most widely used intelligence tests are the Wechsler scales. In 1939, David Wechsler introduced the first of his scales, designed for use with adults (Wechsler, 1939); the current edition is the Wechsler Adult Intelligence Scale—Fourth Edition (WAIS-IV). The Wechsler Intelligence Scale for Children—Fourth Edition (WISC-IV) is designed for children and adolescents between the ages of 6 and 16. The Wechsler Preschool and Primary Scale of Intelligence—Fourth Edition (WPPSI-IV) was published in 2012 and is appropriate for children from age 2 years 6 months to 7 years 7 months (Syeda & Climie, 2014).

Not only do the Wechsler scales provide an overall IQ, but they also yield a number of additional composite scores (for example, the Verbal Comprehension Index, the Working Memory Index, and the Processing Speed Index), allowing the examiner to quickly see patterns of strengths and weaknesses in different areas of the student's intelligence. Three of the Wechsler subscales are shown in Figure 13.

Using Intelligence Tests Psychological tests are tools. Like all tools, their effectiveness depends on the knowledge, skill, and integrity of the user. A hammer can be used to build a beautiful kitchen cabinet, or it can be used as a weapon of assault. Like a hammer, psychological tests can be used for positive purposes or they can be badly abused. Here are some cautions about IQ that can help you avoid the pitfalls of using information about an adolescent's intelligence in negative ways:

· *Avoid stereotyping and expectations.* A special concern is that the scores on an IQ test easily can lead to stereotypes and expectations about adolescents. Sweeping generalizations are too often made on the basis of an IQ score. An IQ test should always be considered a measure of current performance. It is not a measure of fixed potential. Maturational changes and enriched environmental experiences can advance an adolescent's intelligence.

- *Know that IQ is not a sole indicator of competence.* Another concern about IQ tests occurs when they are used as the main or sole assessment of competence. A high IQ is not the ultimate human value. It is important to consider not only students' competence in such areas as verbal skills but also their practical skills, their relationship skills, and their moral values (Mayer & others, 2011).

MULTIPLE INTELLIGENCES

Is it more appropriate to think of an adolescent's intelligence as a general ability or as a number of specific abilities? Robert Sternberg and Howard Gardner have proposed influential theories that describe specific types of intelligence. The concept of emotional intelligence also has been proposed as a type of intelligence that differs from what is measured by traditional intelligence tests.

Sternberg's Triarchic Theory   Robert J. Sternberg (1986, 2004, 2010, 2012, 2013, 2014a, b, 2015a, b, c) developed the **triarchic theory of intelligence,** which states that intelligence comes in three forms: (1) *analytical intelligence*, which refers to the ability to analyze, judge, evaluate, compare, and contrast; (2) *creative intelligence*, which consists of the ability to create, design, invent, originate, and imagine; and (3) *practical intelligence*, which involves the ability to use, apply, implement, and put ideas into practice.

Sternberg (2014a, b, 2015a, b, c) says that students with different triarchic patterns perform differently in school. Students with high analytic ability tend to be favored in conventional schools. They often do well in classes in which the teacher lectures and gives objective tests. They often are considered smart students, typically get good grades, do well on traditional IQ tests and the SAT, and later gain admission to competitive colleges.

Students who are high in creative intelligence often are not in the top rung of their class. Creatively intelligent students might not conform to the expectations that teachers have about how assignments should be done. They give unique answers, for which they might get reprimanded or marked down.

Like students high in creative intelligence, students who are practically intelligent often do not relate well to the demands of school. However, these students frequently do well outside the classroom's walls. Their social skills and common sense may allow them to become successful managers, entrepreneurs, or politicians, despite undistinguished school records.

Robert J. Sternberg, who developed the triarchic theory of intelligence.
Courtesy of Dr. Robert Sternberg

Sternberg (2014a, b, 2015) argues that it is important for classroom instruction to give students opportunities to learn by exercising all three types of intelligence.

Gardner's Eight Frames of Mind   Howard Gardner (1983, 1993, 2002, 2014) suggests there are eight types of intelligence, or "frames of mind." These are described here, with examples of the types of vocations in which they are reflected as strengths (Campbell, Campbell, & Dickinson, 2004):

- *Verbal.* The ability to think in words and use language to express meaning (occupations: authors, journalists, speakers)
- *Mathematical.* The ability to carry out mathematical operations (occupations: scientists, engineers, accountants)
- *Spatial.* The ability to think three-dimensionally (occupations: architects, artists, sailors)
- *Bodily-kinesthetic.* The ability to manipulate objects and be physically adept (occupations: surgeons, craftspeople, dancers, athletes)
- *Musical.* A sensitivity to pitch, melody, rhythm, and tone (occupations: composers, musicians).
- *Interpersonal.* The ability to understand and effectively interact with others (occupations: successful teachers, mental health professionals)
- *Intrapersonal.* The ability to understand oneself (occupations: theologians, psychologists)
- *Naturalist*: The ability to observe patterns in nature and understand natural and human-made systems (occupations: farmers, botanists, ecologists, landscapers)

"You're wise, but you lack tree smarts."
© Donald Reilly/The New Yorker Collection/
www.cartoonbank.com.

triarchic theory of intelligence Sternberg's view that intelligence comes in three main forms: analytical, creative, and practical.

Which of Gardner's eight intelligences are adolescent girls using in this situation?
© Tom Stewart/Corbis

According to Gardner, everyone has all of these intelligences but to varying degrees. As a result, we prefer to learn and process information in different ways. People learn best when they can apply their strong intelligences to the task.

Both Gardner's and Sternberg's theories include one or more categories related to social intelligence. In Gardner's theory, the categories are interpersonal intelligence and intrapersonal intelligence; in Sternberg's theory, practical intelligence. Another theory that emphasizes interpersonal, intrapersonal, and practical aspects of intelligence is called **emotional intelligence,** which has been popularized by Daniel Goleman (1995) in his book *Emotional Intelligence.* The concept of emotional intelligence was initially developed by Peter Salovey and John Mayer (1990), who define it as the ability to perceive and express emotion accurately and adaptively (such as taking the perspective of others), to understand emotion and emotional knowledge (such as understanding the roles that emotions play in friendship and marriage), to use feelings to facilitate thought (such as being in a positive mood, which is linked to creative thinking), and to manage emotions in oneself and others (such as being able to control one's anger). In one study, assessment of emotional intelligence predicted high school students' final grades in their courses (Gil-Olarte Marquez, Palomera Martin, & Brackett, 2006).

There continues to be considerable interest in the concept of emotional intelligence (Brouzos, Misailidi, & Hadjimattheou, 2014; Fiori & others, 2014). A recent study of college students revealed that both a general mental abilities test and an emotional intelligence assessment were linked to academic performance, although the general mental abilities test was a better predictor of success (Song & others, 2010). In this study, emotional intelligence was related to the quality of peer relations. And a recent study revealed that emotional intelligence abilities were linked to academic achievement above and beyond cognitive and personality factors (Lanciano & Curci, 2014). However, critics argue that too often emotional intelligence broadens the concept of intelligence too far and that its accuracy has not been adequately assessed and researched (Matthews, Zeidner, & Roberts, 2006, 2011).

Do People Have One or Many Intelligences? Figure 14 provides a comparison of Sternberg's, Gardner's, and Mayer/Salovey/Goleman's views of intelligence. Notice that Sternberg's view is unique in emphasizing creative intelligence and that Gardner's includes a number of types of intelligence that are not addressed by the other views. These theories of multiple intelligences have much to offer. They have stimulated us to think more broadly about what makes up people's intelligence and competence (Sternberg, 2014a, b, 2015a, b, c). And they have motivated educators to develop programs that instruct students in different domains (Campbell, 2008).

Theories of multiple intelligences have their critics (Jensen, 2008). Some critics argue that the research base to support these theories has not yet developed. In particular, some critics say that Gardner's classification seems arbitrary. For example, if musical skills represent a type of intelligence, why don't we also refer to chess intelligence, prize-fighter intelligence, and so on?

A number of psychologists still support the concept of *g* (general intelligence) (Irwin & others, 2012; Lynn, 2012). For example, one expert on intelligence, Nathan Brody (2007) argues that people who excel at one type of intellectual task are likely to excel in other intellectual tasks. Thus, individuals who do well at memorizing lists of digits are also likely to be good at solving verbal problems and spatial layout problems. This general intelligence includes abstract reasoning or thinking, the capacity to acquire knowledge, and problem-solving ability (Brody, 2007; Carroll, 1993).

Some experts who argue for the existence of general intelligence conclude that individuals also have specific intellectual abilities (Brody, 2007; Chiappe & MacDonald, 2005; Hunt, 2011). In one study, John Carroll (1993) conducted an extensive examination of intellectual abilities and concluded that all intellectual abilities are related to each other, a view that supports the concept of general intelligence, but he also pointed out that there are many specialized abilities as well. Some of these specialized abilities, such as spatial abilities and mechanical abilities, are not adequately reflected in the curriculum of most schools. In sum, controversy still surrounds the question of whether it is more accurate to conceptualize intelligence as a general ability, as specific abilities, or as both (Gardner, 2014; Haier & others, 2014). Sternberg (2014a, b, 2015a, b, c) actually accepts that there is a *g* in the kinds of analytical tasks that traditional IQ tests assess but thinks that the range of intellectual tasks those tests measure is too narrow.

Sternberg	Gardner	Mayer/Salovey/Goleman
Analytical	Verbal Mathematical	
Creative	Spatial Movement Musical	
Practical	Interpersonal Intrapersonal	Emotional
	Naturalistic	

FIGURE 14

COMPARISON OF STERNBERG'S, GARDNER'S, AND MAYER/SALOVEY/GOLEMAN'S VIEWS

emotional intelligence The ability to perceive and express emotion accurately and adaptively, to understand emotion and emotional knowledge, to use feelings to facilitate thought, and to manage emotions in oneself and others.

THE NEUROSCIENCE OF INTELLIGENCE

In the current era of extensive research on the brain, interest in the neurological underpinnings of intelligence has increased (Deary, 2012). Among the questions about the brain's role in intelligence that are being explored are these: Is having a bigger brain linked to higher intelligence? Is intelligence located in certain brain regions? Is the speed at which the brain processes information linked to intelligence?

Are individuals with bigger brains more intelligent than those with smaller brains? Studies using MRI scans to assess total brain volume indicate a moderate correlation (about 1.3 to 1.4) between brain size and intelligence (Carey, 2007; Luders & others, 2009).

Might intelligence be linked to specific regions of the brain? Early consensus was that the frontal lobes are the likely location of intelligence. Today, some experts continue to emphasize that the highest level of thinking skills involved in intelligence are linked to the prefrontal cortex (Sternberg & Sternberg, 2013). However, other researchers recently have found that intelligence is distributed more widely across brain regions (Lee & others, 2012; Sepulcre & others, 2012). The most prominent finding from brain-imaging studies is that a distributed neural network involving the frontal and parietal lobes is related to higher intelligence (Margolis & others, 2013; Vakhtin & others, 2014) (see Figure 15). A recent study revealed that the fronto-parietal network is responsible for cognitive control and connectivity to brain regions outside the network (Cole & others, 2012). Albert Einstein's total brain size was average, but a region of his brain's parietal lobe that is very active in processing math and spatial information was 15 percent larger than average (Witelson, Kigar, & Harvey, 1999). Other brain regions that have been linked to higher intelligence (although at a lower level of significance than the frontal/parietal lobe network) include the temporal and occipital lobes, as well as the cerebellum (Luders & others, 2009).

Examining the neuroscience of intelligence has also led to study of the role that neurological speed might play in intelligence (Waiter & others, 2009). Research results have not been consistent for this possible link, although a recent study found that children who are gifted showed faster processing speed and more accurate processing of information than children who are not gifted (Duan, Dan, & Shi, 2014).

As technological advances allow closer study of the brain's functioning in coming decades, we are likely to see more specific conclusions about the brain's role in intelligence. As this research proceeds, keep in mind that both heredity and environment likely contribute to links between the brain and intelligence, including the connections we discussed between brain size and intelligence. Also, Robert Sternberg (2014b) recently concluded that research on the brain's role in intelligence has been more effective in answering some questions (such as "What aspects of the brain are involved in learning a list of words?" than it is has in answering others (such as "Why do some individuals consider shaking hands socially intelligent but others do not?").

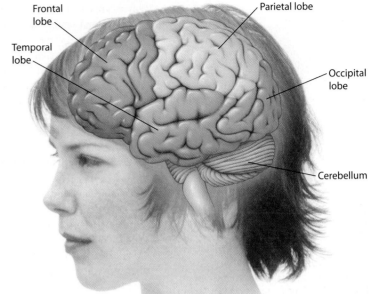

Frontal lobe • Parietal lobe • Temporal lobe • Occipital lobe • Cerebellum

FIGURE 15

INTELLIGENCE AND THE BRAIN. Researchers recently have found that a higher level of intelligence is linked to a distributed neural network in the frontal and parietal lobes. To a lesser extent than the frontal/parietal network, the temporal and occipital lobes, as well as the cerebellum, also have been found to have links to intelligence. The current consensus is that intelligence is likely to be distributed across brain regions rather than being localized in a specific region, such as the frontal lobes.

HEREDITY AND ENVIRONMENT

An ongoing issue involving intelligence is the extent to which it is due to heredity or to environment. It is difficult to tease apart these influences, but that has not kept psychologists from trying to untangle them.

Heredity Some psychologists argue that the effect of heredity on intelligence is strong (Plomin & Deary, 2015). However, most research on heredity and environment does not include

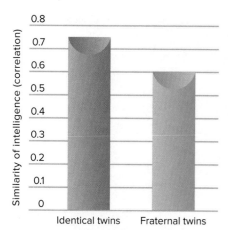

FIGURE **16**

CORRELATION BETWEEN INTELLIGENCE TEST SCORES AND TWIN STATUS. The graph represents a summary of research findings that have compared the intelligence test scores of identical and fraternal twins. An approximate 0.15 difference has been found, with a higher correlation for identical twins (0.75) and a lower correlation for fraternal twins (0.60).

developmental **connection**

Nature and Nurture

The epigenetic view emphasizes that development is an ongoing, bidirectional interchange between heredity and environment. Connect to "Puberty, Health, and Biological Foundations."

environments that differ radically. Thus, it is not surprising that many studies of heredity, environment, and intelligence show environment to be a fairly weak influence on intelligence.

One strategy for examining the role of heredity in intelligence is to compare the IQs of identical and fraternal twins. Identical twins have exactly the same genetic makeup, but fraternal twins do not. If intelligence is genetically determined, say some investigators, identical twins' IQs should be more similar than the intelligence of fraternal twins. Researchers have found that the IQs of identical twins are more similar than those of fraternal twins, but in some studies the difference is not very large (Grigorenko, 2000) (see Figure 16).

Have scientists been able to pinpoint specific genes that are linked to intelligence? A recent research review concluded that there may be more than 1,000 genes that affect intelligence, each possibly having a small influence on an individual's intelligence (Davies & others, 2011). However, researchers have not been able to identify the specific genes that contribute in significant ways to intelligence (Deary, 2012).

Environment   One of the ways that environmental influences on intelligence have been studied is to examine changes in IQ when certain groups of individuals experience improved conditions in their lives. For example, a recent research analysis found a 12- to 18-point increase when children are adopted from low-income families into middle- and upper-income families (Nisbett & others, 2012). Further, as African Americans have gained social, economic, and educational opportunities, the gap between African Americans and non-Latino Whites on standardized intelligence tests has begun to narrow. A recent research review concluded that the IQ gap between African Americans and non-Latino Whites has been reduced considerably in recent years (Nisbett & others, 2012). This gap especially narrows in college, where African American and non-Latino White students often experience more similar environments than in the elementary and high school years. Nonetheless, a recent analysis concluded that the underrepresentation of African Americans in STEM (science, technology, engineering, and math) subjects and careers is linked to practitioners' expectations that they have less innate talent than non-Latino Whites (Leslie & others, 2015).

Another way to study the environment's influence on intelligence is to compare adolescents who have experienced different amounts of schooling. Schooling does influence intelligence, with the largest effects occurring when adolescents have had no formal education for an extended period, which is linked to lower intelligence (Ceci & Gilstrap, 2000).

Another possible effect of education can be seen in rapidly increasing IQ test scores around the world (Flynn, 1999, 2007, 2011, 2013). IQ scores have been increasing so rapidly that a high percentage of people regarded as having average intelligence at the turn of the century would be considered below average in intelligence today (see Figure 17). If a representative sample of people today took the Stanford-Binet test used in 1932, about one-fourth would be defined as having very superior intelligence, a label usually accorded to fewer than 3 percent of the population. Because the increase has taken place in a relatively short time,

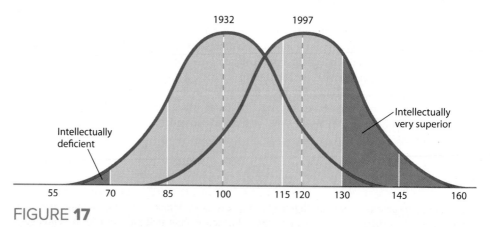

FIGURE **17**

THE INCREASE IN IQ SCORES FROM 1932 TO 1997. As measured by the Stanford-Binet intelligence test, American children seem to be getting smarter. Scores of a group tested in 1932 fell along a bell-shaped curve with half below 100 and half above. Studies show that if children took that same test today, half would score above 120 on the 1932 scale. Very few of them would score in the "intellectually deficient" end, on the left side, and about one-fourth would rank in the "very superior" range.

it can't be due to heredity, but rather may be due to increasing levels of education attained by a much greater percentage of the world's population or to other environmental factors such as the explosion of information to which people are exposed (Rönnlund & Nilsson, 2008). A recent meta-analysis of 53 studies since 1972 found that IQ scores have been rising about 3 points per decade since that year and that the increase in IQ scores does not seem to be diminishing (Trahan & others, 2014). The worldwide increase in intelligence test scores that has occurred over a short time frame has been called the *Flynn effect* after the researcher who discovered it—James Flynn (1999, 2007, 2011, 2013).

Heredity and Environment Interaction   Today, most researchers agree that genetics and environment interact to influence intelligence (Mandelman & Grigorenko, 2011; Sternberg, 2014a, b, 2015a, b, c). For many adolescents, this means that positive modifications in environment can change their IQ scores considerably. Although genetic endowment may always influence adolescents' intellectual ability, the environmental influences and opportunities provided to adolescents do make a difference.

Review Connect Reflect

LG4 Summarize the psychometric/intelligence view of adolescence

Review

- What is intelligence? What are the main individual tests of intelligence? What are some strategies for interpreting intelligence test scores?
- What theories of multiple intelligences have been developed? Do people have one intelligence or many intelligences?
- What are some links between the brain and intelligence?
- What roles do heredity and environment play in intelligence?

Connect

- Compare creative and critical thinking.

Reflect *Your Own Personal Journey of Life*

- Apply Gardner's, Sternberg's, and Mayer/Salovey/Goleman's categories of intelligence to yourself as an adolescent and emerging adult. Write a description of yourself based on each of these views.

5 Social Cognition   **LG5** Explain how social cognition is involved in adolescent development

Adolescent Egocentrism

Social Cognition in the Remainder of this Edition

Social cognition refers to the way individuals conceptualize and reason about their social worlds—the people they watch and interact with, their relationships with those people, the groups they participate in, and the way they reason about themselves and others. Our discussion will focus on adolescent egocentrism and on our coverage of social cognition in the remainder of this edition.

ADOLESCENT EGOCENTRISM

Adolescent egocentrism is the heightened self-consciousness of adolescents, which is reflected in their belief that others are as interested in them as they are in themselves, and in their sense of personal uniqueness and invulnerability. David Elkind (1976) argues that adolescent egocentrism can be dissected into two types of social thinking—imaginary audience and personal fable.

The *imaginary audience* refers to the aspect of adolescent egocentrism that involves attention-getting behavior—the attempt to be noticed, visible, and "onstage." An adolescent boy might think that others are as aware of a few hairs that are out of place as he is. An adolescent girl walks into her classroom and thinks that all eyes are riveted on her complexion. Adolescents

social cognition The way individuals conceptualize and reason about their social worlds—the people they watch and interact with, their relationships with those people, the groups they participate in, and the way they reason about themselves and others.

adolescent egocentrism The heightened self-consciousness of adolescents, which is reflected in their belief that others are as interested in them as they themselves are, and in their sense of personal uniqueness and invulnerability.

Are Social Media an Amplification Tool for Adolescent Egocentrism?

Are teens drawn to social media to express their imaginary audience and personal fable's sense of uniqueness? One analysis concluded that amassing a large number of friends (audience) may help to validate adolescents' perception that their life is a stage and everyone is watching them (Psychster Inc., 2010). Also, a recent study found that Facebook use does indeed increase self-interest (Chiou, Chen, & Liao, 2014).

A look at a teen's home Twitter comments may suggest to many adults that what teens are reporting is often rather mundane and uninteresting. Typical tweets might include updates like the following: "Studying heavy. Not happy tonight." or "At Starbucks with Jesse. Lattes are great." Possibly for adolescents, though, such tweets are not trivial but rather an expression of the personal fable's sense of uniqueness.

Might social media, such as Facebook, increase adolescent egocentrism?
© David J. Green-lifestyle themes/Alamy

What do you think? Are social media, such as Facebook and Twitter, amplifying the expression of adolescents' imaginary audience and their personal fable's sense of uniqueness? (Source: Psychster Inc., 2010)

What characterizes adolescent egocentrism?
© DreamPictures/Getty Images

especially sense that they are onstage in early adolescence, believing they are the main actors and all others are the audience. You may recall the story of my daughter, Tracy, from the beginning of the chapter. Tracy was exhibiting adolescent egocentrism when she perceived that every person in the restaurant was looking at her single out-of-place hair.

According to Elkind, the *personal fable* is the part of adolescent egocentrism that involves an adolescent's sense of personal uniqueness and invulnerability. Adolescents' sense of personal uniqueness makes them feel that no one can understand how they really feel. For example, an adolescent girl thinks that her mother cannot possibly sense the hurt she feels because her boyfriend has broken up with her. As part of their effort to retain a sense of personal uniqueness, adolescents might craft stories about themselves that are filled with fantasy, immersing themselves in a world that is far removed from reality. Personal fables frequently show up in adolescent diaries.

Elkind (1985) argued that the imaginary audience and personal fable reflect the cognitive egocentrism involved in the transition to formal operational thought. However, Daniel Lapsley and his colleagues (Hill, Duggan, & Lapsley, 2012; Hill & Lapsley, 2010; Lapsley & Hill, 2010; Lapsley & Stey, 2012) conclude that the distortions in the imaginary audience and personal fable involve the adolescent's ego. As they increasingly develop their own self and identity apart from their parents, their personal fable ideation likely reflects an adaptive narcissism that supports their ego. What role, then, does the personal fable play in adolescent adjustment? See the *Connecting with Health and Well-Being* interlude.

In early research, Elkind found that adolescent egocentrism peaked in early adolescence and then declined (Elkind & Bowen, 1979). However, a recent study of more than 2,300 adolescents and emerging adults from 11 to 21 years of age revealed that adolescent egocentrism was still prominent in the 18- to 21-year-olds (emerging adults) and the results varied by gender (Schwartz, Maynard, & Uzelac, 2008). For example, emerging adult males scored higher on the imaginary audience scale than did males in late adolescence (15- to 18-year-olds), but no age differences on this scale occurred for females.

What Role Does the Personal Fable Play in Adolescent Adjustment?

Some developmentalists conclude that the sense of uniqueness and invincibility that egocentrism generates is responsible for some of the seemingly reckless behavior of adolescents, including drag racing, drug use, failure to use contraceptives during intercourse, and suicide (Dolcini & others, 1989). For example, one study found that eleventh- and twelfth-grade females who were high in adolescent egocentrism were more likely to say they would not get pregnant from engaging in sex without contraception than were their counterparts who were low in adolescent egocentrism (Arnett, 1990).

A study of sixth- through twelfth-graders examined whether aspects of the personal fable were linked to various aspects of adolescent adjustment (Aalsma, Lapsley, & Flannery, 2006). A sense of invulnerability was linked to engaging in risky behaviors such as smoking cigarettes, drinking alcohol, and engaging in acts of delinquency, whereas a sense of personal uniqueness was related to depression and suicidal thoughts. A subsequent study confirmed the findings of the first in regard to the correlation between personal uniqueness, depression, and suicidal thoughts (Goossens & others, 2002).

These findings indicate that personal uniqueness fables should be treated as a risk factor for psychological problems, especially depression and suicidal tendencies in girls (Aalsma, Lapsley, & Flannery, 2006). Treating invulnerability as a risk factor for adjustment problems is less certain because in the earlier study just described (Aalsma, Lapsley, & Flannery, 2006), a sense of invulnerability was associated not only with risky behavior but also with some positive aspects of adjustment, such as coping and self-worth.

Further reason to question the accuracy of the invulnerability aspect of the personal fable is provided by other research that reveals many adolescents don't consider themselves invulnerable (de Bruin, Parker, & Fischhoff, 2007). Indeed, an increasing number of research studies suggest that, rather than perceiving themselves to be invulnerable, adolescents tend to portray themselves as vulnerable to experiencing a premature death (Jamieson & Romer, 2008; Reyna & Rivers, 2008). For example, in a recent study, 12- to 18-year-olds were asked about their chance of dying in the next year and prior to age 20 (Fischhoff & others, 2010). The adolescents greatly overestimated their chance of dying.

Some researchers have questioned the view that invulnerability is a unitary concept and have argued rather that it consists of two dimensions (Duggan, Lapsley, & Norman, 2000; Lapsley & Hill, 2010):

How are personal uniqueness and invulnerability linked to adolescent adjustment and problems?
© Car Culture/Getty Images

- Danger invulnerability, which describes adolescents' sense of indestructibility and tendency to take on physical risks (driving recklessly at high speeds, for example).
- Psychological invulnerability, which captures an adolescent's perceived invulnerability related to personal or psychological distress (getting one's feelings hurt, for example).

A recent study revealed that adolescents who scored high on a danger invulnerability scale were more likely to engage in juvenile delinquency and/or substance abuse, or to be depressed (Lapsley & Hill, 2010). In this study, adolescents who scored high on psychological invulnerability were less likely to be depressed, had higher self-esteem, and maintained better interpersonal relationships. In terms of psychological invulnerability, adolescents often benefit from the normal developmental challenges of exploring identity options, making new friends, asking someone to go out on a date, and learning a new skill. All of these important adolescent tasks include risk and failure as an option, but if successful result in enhanced self-image.

In the view of Daniel Lapsley and his colleagues (Hill, Duggan, & Lapsley, 2012; Lapsley & Stey, 2012), the separation-individuation process—which involves adolescents separating from their parents and developing independence and identity—is responsible for the findings just discussed, rather than attributing these characteristics to cognitive developmental changes. With respect to personal fables, they argue that invulnerability and personal uniqueness are forms of adolescent narcissism.

Do these findings about the two dimensions of perceived invulnerability have practical applications? For instance, could they help identify adolescents at risk for engaging in self-destructive behavior such as delinquency and substance abuse?

SOCIAL COGNITION IN THE REMAINDER OF THIS EDITION

developmental **connection**

Identity

Major changes in self-understanding take place in the adolescent years. Connect to "The Self, Identity, Emotion, and Personality."

Interest in social cognition has blossomed, and the approach has infiltrated many aspects of the study of adolescent development. In our overview of the self and identity in this edition, we explore social cognition's role in understanding the self and identity. In our evaluation of moral development, considerable time is devoted to discussing Kohlberg's theory, which is a prominent aspect of the study of social cognition in adolescence. Further, in our discussion of families, the emerging cognitive abilities of the adolescent are evaluated in concert with parent-adolescent conflict and parenting strategies. Also, our description of peer relations highlights the importance of social knowledge and social information processing in peer relations.

In chapter on "The Self, Identity, Emotion, and Personality," you will read extensively about the changes that occur in self-understanding during adolescence. As described in this chapter, the development of the brain coupled with advances in information processing provides a foundation for adolescent self-understanding, which gradually becomes more conscious and reflective.

Review Connect Reflect

LG5 Explain how social cognition is involved in adolescent development

Review

- What characterizes adolescent egocentrism?
- How is social cognition related to other topics discussed in this text?

Connect

- Compare and contrast the concepts of the imaginary audience and the personal fable.

Reflect *Your Own Personal Journey of Life*

- Think about your friends in early adolescence, late adolescence, and emerging adulthood. Did adolescent egocentrism decline for all of them as they moved through late adolescence and emerging adulthood? Explain how it might especially be maladaptive if adolescent egocentrism continues to strongly characterize the outlook of individuals in the emerging adult years.

reach your **learning goals**

The Brain and Cognitive Development

1 The Brain

LG1 Describe the developmental changes in the brain during adolescence

The Neuroconstructivist View

- This increasingly popular view states that biological processes and environmental conditions influence the brain's development; the brain has plasticity; and cognitive development is closely linked with brain development.

Neurons

- Neurons, the basic units of the nervous system, are made up of a cell body, dendrites, and an axon. Myelination is the process by which the axon portion of the neuron becomes covered and insulated with a layer of fat cells, which increases the speed and efficiency of information processing in the nervous system. Myelination continues to increase during adolescence. Synaptogenesis in the prefrontal cortex, where reasoning and self-regulation occur, also continues through adolescence.

Brain Structure, Cognition, and Emotion

- The corpus callosum, a large bundle of axon fibers that connects the brain's left and right hemispheres, thickens in adolescence, and this thickening improves the adolescent's ability to process information. The prefrontal cortex, the highest level of the frontal lobes that is involved in reasoning, decision making, and self-control, matures much later (continuing to develop in emerging adulthood) than the amygdala, the part of the limbic system that is the seat of emotions such as anger. The later development of the prefrontal cortex combined with the earlier maturity of the amygdala may explain the difficulty adolescents have in putting the brakes on their emotional intensity.

Experience and Plasticity

- Experience plays an important role in development of the brain in childhood and adolescence. Although early experiences are very important influences on brain development, the brain retains considerable plasticity in adolescence. New brain cells may be generated during adolescence. The earlier brain injury occurs, the more successful recovery is likely to be.

2 The Cognitive Developmental View   LG2   Discuss the cognitive developmental view of adolescence

Piaget's Theory

- Piaget's widely acclaimed theory stresses the concepts of adaptation, schemas, assimilation, accommodation, and equilibration. Piaget said that individuals develop through four cognitive stages: sensorimotor, preoperational, concrete operational, and formal operational. Formal operational thought, which Piaget expected to appear from 11 to 15 years of age, is characterized by abstract, idealistic, and hypothetical-deductive thinking. Some experts argue that formal operational thought has two phases: early and late. Individual variation in adolescent cognition is extensive. Many young adolescents are still consolidating their concrete operational thought or are early formal operational thinkers rather than full-fledged ones. Piaget's ideas have been applied to education. In terms of Piaget's contributions, we owe to him the entire field of cognitive development and a masterful list of concepts. He also was a genius at observing children. Criticisms of Piaget's theory focus on estimates of competence, stages, training to reason at higher stages, and the role of culture and education. Neo-Piagetians have proposed some substantial changes in Piaget's theory. Some experts argue that the idealism of Piaget's formal operational stage declines in young adults, being replaced by more realistic, pragmatic thinking. Perry said that adolescents often engage in dualistic, absolutist thinking, whereas young adults are more likely to think reflectively and relativistically. Postformal thought is reflective, relativistic, and contextual; provisional; realistic; and open to emotions and subjective.

  Wisdom is expert knowledge about the practical aspects of life that permits excellent judgment about important matters. Baltes and his colleagues have found that high levels of wisdom are rare, the time frame of late adolescence and early adulthood is the main age window for wisdom to emerge, factors other than age are critical for a high level of wisdom to develop, and personality-related factors are better predictors of wisdom than cognitive factors such as intelligence. Sternberg argues that wisdom involves both academic and practical aspects of intelligence. His balance theory emphasizes making competent decisions that take into account self-interest, the interests of others, and contexts to produce a common good. Sternberg argues that wisdom should be taught in schools.

Vygotsky's Theory

- Vygotsky's view stimulated considerable interest in the idea that knowledge is situated and collaborative. One of his important concepts is the zone of proximal development, which involves guidance by more skilled peers and adults. Vygotsky argued that learning the skills of the culture is a key aspect of development. Piaget's and Vygotsky's views are both constructivist, although Vygotsky's view is a stronger social constructivist view than Piaget's. In both views, teachers should be facilitators, not directors, of learning. Criticisms of Vygotsky's view focus on facilitators possibly being too helpful and adolescents expecting others to do things for them.

3 The Information-Processing View   LG3   Characterize the information-processing view of adolescence

Cognitive Resources

- Capacity and speed of processing, often referred to as cognitive resources, increase across childhood and adolescence. Changes in the brain serve as biological foundations for developmental changes in cognitive resources. In terms of capacity, the increase is reflected in older children and adolescents being able to hold in mind simultaneously several dimensions of a topic. A reaction-time task has often been used to assess speed of processing. Processing speed continues to improve in adolescence.

Attention and Memory

· Attention is the focusing of mental resources. Adolescents typically have better attentional skills than children do, although there are wide individual differences in how effectively adolescents deploy their attention. Four ways that adolescents can allocate their attention are selective attention, divided attention, sustained attention, and executive attention. Multitasking is an example of divided attention, and it can harm adolescents' attention when they are engaging in a challenging task. Adolescents have better short-term memory, working memory, and long-term memory than children do.

Executive Function

· Higher-order cognitive processes such as exercising cognitive control, making decisions, reasoning, thinking critically, thinking creatively, and metacognition are often called executive function. Adolescence is characterized by a number of advances in executive function. Cognitive control involves aspects such as focusing attention, reducing interfering thoughts, and being cognitively flexible. Across childhood and adolescence, cognitive control (inhibition) increases with age, and this increase is likely due to the maturation of the prefrontal cortex. Older adolescents make better decisions than younger adolescents, who in turn are better at this than children are. Being able to make competent decisions, however, does not mean adolescents will make such decisions in everyday life, where breadth of experience comes into play. Adolescents often make better decisions when they are calm than when they are emotionally aroused. Social contexts, especially the presence of peers, influence adolescent decision making. Critical thinking involves thinking reflectively and productively and evaluating the evidence. Mindfulness is an important aspect of thinking critically. Cognitive and physical training, such as mindfulness and yoga, are increasingly being recommended to improve adolescents' functioning. Adolescence is an important transitional period in critical thinking because of such cognitive changes as increased speed, automaticity, and capacity of information processing; more breadth of content knowledge; increased ability to construct new combinations of knowledge; and a greater range and spontaneous use of strategies. Thinking creatively is the ability to think in novel and unusual ways and discover unique solutions to problems. Guilford distinguished between convergent and divergent thinking. A number of strategies, including brainstorming, not overcontrolling, encouraging internal control, and introducing adolescents to creative people, can be used to stimulate creative thinking. An expert is the opposite of a novice (someone who is just beginning to learn a content area). Experts are better than novices at detecting features and meaningful patterns of information, accumulating more content knowledge and organizing it effectively, and retrieving important aspects of knowledge with little effort. Becoming an expert usually involves talent, deliberate practice, and motivation. Metacognition is cognition about cognition, or knowing about knowing. In Pressley's view, the key to education is helping students learn a rich repertoire of strategies that can be applied in solving problems. Adolescents' thinking skills benefit when they are taught general metacognitive skills and domain-specific thinking skills.

4 The Psychometric/Intelligence View

LG4 Summarize the psychometric/intelligence view of adolescence

Intelligence Tests

· Intelligence is the ability to solve problems and to adapt and learn from everyday experiences. A key aspect of intelligence focuses on its individual variations. Traditionally, intelligence has been measured by tests designed to compare people's performance on cognitive tasks. Alfred Binet developed the first intelligence test and created the concept of mental age. William Stern developed the concept of IQ for use with the Binet test. Revisions of the Binet test are called the Stanford-Binet. The test scores on the Stanford-Binet approximate a normal distribution. The Wechsler scales, created by David Wechsler, are the other main intelligence assessment tool. These tests provide an overall IQ and other composite scores, including the Working Memory Index and the Information Processing Speed Index. The single number provided by many IQ tests can lead to false expectations, and IQ test scores should be only one type of information used to evaluate an adolescent.

Multiple Intelligences

· Sternberg's triarchic theory states that there are three main types of intelligence: analytical, creative, and practical. Gardner has proposed that there are eight types of intelligence: verbal, mathematical, spatial, bodily-kinesthetic, musical, interpersonal, intrapersonal, and naturalist. Emotional intelligence is the ability to perceive and express emotion accurately and adaptively, to understand emotion and emotional knowledge, to use feelings to facilitate thought, and to manage emotions in oneself and others. The multiple intelligences approaches have broadened the definition of intelligence and motivated educators to develop programs that instruct students in different domains. Critics maintain that the multiple intelligence theories have classifications that seem arbitrary and factors that really aren't part of intelligence, such as musical skills and creativity.

The Neuroscience of Intelligence

- Interest in discovering links between the brain and intelligence have been stimulated by advances in brain imaging. A moderate correlation has been found between brain size and intelligence. Some experts emphasize that the highest level of intelligence that involves reasoning is linked to the prefrontal cortex. However, other researchers recently have found a link between a distributed neural network in the frontal and parietal lobes and intelligence. The search for a connection between neural processing speed and intelligence has produced mixed results.

Heredity and Environment

- Many studies show that by late adolescence intelligence is strongly influenced by heredity, but many of these studies do not reflect environments that are radically different. A well-documented environmental influence on intelligence is schooling. Also, probably because of increased education, intelligence test scores have risen considerably around the world in recent decades—an increase called the Flynn effect—and this supports the role of environment in intelligence. In sum, intelligence is influenced by both heredity and environment.

5 Social Cognition

LG5 Explain how social cognition is involved in adolescent development

Adolescent Egocentrism

- Social cognition refers to how people conceptualize and reason about their social world, including the relation of the self to others. Adolescent egocentrism is adolescents' heightened self-consciousness, mirrored in their belief that others are as interested in them as they are. According to Elkind, adolescent egocentrism consists of an imaginary audience and a personal fable. Researchers have recently found that adolescents actually overestimate their chance of experiencing a premature death, indicating that they perceive themselves to be far less invulnerable than Elkind's personal fable indicates. An alternative to Elkind's cognitive egocentrism concept is the view that the imaginary audience and personal fable are mainly the result of changes in perspective taking and the adolescent's ego. Also, recently invulnerability has been described as having two dimensions—danger invulnerability and psychological invulnerability—which have different outcomes for adolescence.

Social Cognition in the Remainder of This Edition

- We study social cognition throughout this text, especially in chapters on the self and identity, moral development, peers, and families.

key terms

accommodation	emotional intelligence	mental age (MA)	selective attention
adolescent egocentrism	equilibration	metacognition	sensorimotor stage
amygdala	executive attention	myelination	social cognition
assimilation	executive function	neo-Piagetians	social constructivist approach
attention	formal operational stage	neuroconstructivist view	sustained attention
cognitive control	fuzzy-trace theory dual-process	neurons	synapses
concrete operational stage	model	normal distribution	triarchic theory of intelligence
convergent thinking	hypothetical-deductive reasoning	postformal thought	wisdom
corpus callosum	intelligence	prefrontal cortex	zone of proximal development
creativity	intelligence quotient (IQ)	preoperational stage	(ZPD)
critical thinking	limbic system	psychometric/intelligence view	
divergent thinking	memory	schema	

key people

Paul Baltes
Alfred Binet
Nathan Brody
Robbie Case
David Elkind
Howard Gardner
Jay Giedd
Daniel Goleman

J. P. Guilford
Mark Johnson
Deanna Kuhn
Gisela Labouvie-Vief
Ellen Langer
Daniel Lapsley
John Mayer
Charles Nelson

William Perry
Jean Piaget
Michael Pressley
Valerie Reyna
Robert Roeser
Peter Salovey
Elizabeth Sowell
Laurence Steinberg

William Stern
Robert Sternberg
Lev Vygotsky
David Wechsler
Philip Zelazo

resources for improving the lives of adolescents

The Neuroscience of Decision Making
Edited by Valerie Reyna and Vivian Zayas (2014)
Washington, DC: American Psychological Association

> Leading experts in such diverse areas as neuroscience, psychology, and behavioral economics explore research and social implications of risky decisions, with many applications to adolescent development.

Adolescent Thinking
Deanna Kuhn
In R. M. Lerner and L. Steinberg (Eds.), *Handbook of Adolescent Psychology* (2009, 3rd ed.)
New York: Wiley

> An in-depth examination of the important changes in executive function and other aspects of cognitive development in adolescence.

Child Development Perspectives (2012, Vol. 6, Issue 2, 105–173)
> A number of articles address the recent interest in executive function in adolescence and the use of cognitive and physical training activities, such as mindfulness and yoga, to improve adolescents' functioning.

chapter 4

THE SELF, IDENTITY, EMOTION, AND PERSONALITY

chapter **outline**

How do adolescents describe themselves? How would you have described yourself when you were 15 years old? What features would you have emphasized? The following is a self-portrait of one 15-year-old girl:

> What am I like as a person? Complicated! I'm sensitive, friendly, outgoing, popular, and tolerant, though I can also be shy, self-conscious, and even obnoxious. Obnoxious! I'd like to be friendly and tolerant all of the time. That's the kind of person I want to be, and I'm disappointed when I'm not. I'm responsible, even studious now and then, but on the other hand, I'm a goof-off, too, because if you're too studious, you won't be popular. I don't usually do that well at school. I'm a pretty cheerful person, especially with my friends, where I can even get rowdy. At home I'm more likely to be anxious around my parents. They expect me to get all A's. It's not fair! I worry about how I probably should get better grades. But I'd be mortified in the eyes of my friends. So I'm usually pretty stressed out at home, or sarcastic, since my parents are always on my case. But I really don't understand how I can switch so fast. I mean, how can I be cheerful one minute, anxious the next, and then be sarcastic? Which one is the real me? Sometimes I feel phony, especially around boys. Say I think some guy might be interested in asking me out. I try to act different, like Madonna. I'll be flirtatious and fun-loving. And then everybody, I mean everybody else is looking at me like they think I'm totally weird. Then I get self-conscious and embarrassed and become radically introverted, and I don't know who I really am! Am I just trying to impress them or what? But I don't really care what they think anyway. I don't want to care, that is. I just want to know what my close friends think. I can be my true self with my close friends. I can't be my real self with my parents. They don't understand me. What do they know about what it's like to be a teenager? They still treat me like I'm still a kid. At least at school people treat you more like you're an adult. That gets confusing, though. I mean, which am I, a kid or an adult? It's scary, too, because I don't have any idea what I want to be when I grow up. I mean, I have lots of ideas. My friend Sheryl and I talk about whether we'll be flight attendants, or teachers, or nurses, veterinarians, maybe—mothers, or actresses. I know I don't want to be a waitress or a secretary. But how do you decide all of this? I really don't know. I mean, I think about it a lot, but I can't resolve it. There are days when I wish I could just become immune to myself. (Harter, 1990b, pp. 352–353)

preview

This teenage girl's self-portrait illustrates the increased self-reflection, identity exploration, and emotional changes that are among the hallmarks of adolescent development. Far more than children, adolescents seek to know who they are, what they are all about, and where they are going in life. In the first sections of this chapter, you will read about the self and identity, which are often considered to be central aspects of personality development in adolescence. Next, you will study emotional development in adolescence. Finally, you will explore the personality traits and temperament of adolescents.

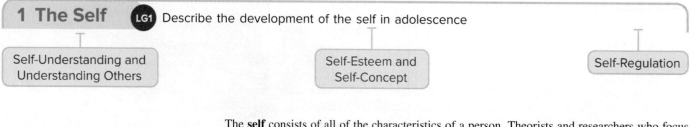

1 The Self **LG1** Describe the development of the self in adolescence

| Self-Understanding and Understanding Others | Self-Esteem and Self-Concept | Self-Regulation |

The **self** consists of all of the characteristics of a person. Theorists and researchers who focus on the self usually argue that the self is the central aspect of the individual's personality and that the self lends an integrative dimension to our understanding of different personality

self All of the characteristics of a person.

characteristics (Harter, 2013; Spencer, Swanson, & Harpalani, 2015). Several aspects of the self have been studied more than others. These include self-understanding and understanding others, self-esteem and self-concept, and self-regulation.

More so than children, adolescents carry with them a sense of who they are and what makes them different from everyone else. Consider one adolescent boy's self-description: "I am male, bright, an athlete, a political liberal, an extravert, and a compassionate individual." He takes comfort in his uniqueness: "No one else is quite like me. I am 5 feet 11 inches tall and weigh 160 pounds. I live in a suburb and plan to attend the state university. I want to be a sports journalist. I am an expert at building canoes. When I am not going to school and studying, I write short stories about sports figures, which I hope to publish someday." Real or imagined, an adolescent's developing sense of self and uniqueness is a motivating force in life. Our exploration of the self begins with information about adolescents' self-understanding and understanding others, then turns to their self-esteem and self-concept.

SELF-UNDERSTANDING AND UNDERSTANDING OTHERS

Although individuals become more introspective in adolescence and even more so in emerging adulthood, this self-understanding is not completely internal; rather, self-understanding is a social cognitive construction (Harter, 2006, 2012, 2013). That is, adolescents' and emerging adults' developing cognitive capacities interact with their sociocultural experiences to influence their self-understanding. These are among the questions you will explore in this section: What is self-understanding? What are some important dimensions of adolescents' and emerging adults' self-understanding? What developmental changes characterize understanding others?

What Is Self-Understanding?   **Self-understanding** is the individual's cognitive representation of the self—the substance and content of self-conceptions. For example, a 12-year-old boy understands that he is a student, a football player, a family member, and a video game lover. A 14-year-old girl understands that she is a soccer player, a student council member, a movie lover, and a rock music fan. An adolescent's self-understanding is based, in part, on the various roles and membership categories that define who adolescents are (Harter, 2006, 2012, 2013). Although self-understanding provides the rational underpinnings, it is not the whole of personal identity.

Self-Understanding in Adolescence   The development of self-understanding in adolescence is complex and involves a number of aspects of the self (Harter, 2006, 2012, 2013). Let's examine how the adolescent's self-understanding differs from the child's, then describe how self-understanding changes during emerging adulthood.

Abstraction and Idealism   Remember from our discussion of Piaget's theory of cognitive development that many adolescents begin to think in more abstract and idealistic ways. When asked to describe themselves, adolescents are more likely than children to use abstract and idealistic terms. Consider 14-year-old Laurie's abstract description of herself: "I am a human being. I am indecisive. I don't know who I am." Also consider her idealistic description of herself: "I am a naturally sensitive person who really cares about people's feelings. I think I'm pretty good-looking." Not all adolescents describe themselves in idealistic ways, but most adolescents distinguish between the real self and the ideal self.

Differentiation   Over time, an adolescent's self-understanding becomes increasingly *differentiated* (Harter, 2006, 2012, 2013). Adolescents are more likely than children to note contextual or situational variations when describing themselves (Harter, Waters, & Whitesell, 1996). For example, a 15-year-old girl might describe herself by using one set of characteristics in connection with her family and another set of characteristics in connection with her peers and friends. Yet another set of characteristics might appear in her self-description of her romantic relationship. In sum, adolescents are more likely than children to understand that they possess several different selves, each one to some degree reflecting a specific role or context.

Know thyself, for once we know ourselves, we may learn how to care for ourselves, but otherwise we never shall.

—SOCRATES
Greek philosopher, 5th century B.C.

developmental **connection**

Cognitive Theory

In Piaget's fourth stage of cognitive development, thought becomes more abstract, idealistic, and logical. Connect to "The Brain and Cognitive Development."

self-understanding The individual's cognitive representation of the self; the substance and content of self-conceptions.

What are some characteristics of self-understanding in adolescence?
© Jupiterimages/Getty Images RF

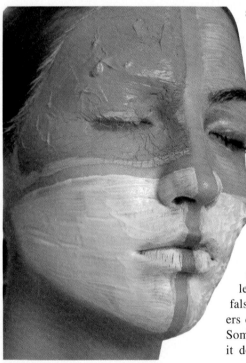

What characterizes adolescents' possible selves?
© Hugh Arnold/The Image Bank/Getty Images

possible self What individuals might become, what they would like to become, and what they are afraid of becoming.

The Fluctuating Self   Given the contradictory nature of the self in adolescence, it is not surprising that the self fluctuates across situations and across time (Harter, 1990b). The 15-year-old girl who was quoted at the beginning of this chapter remarked that she could not understand how she could switch from being cheerful one moment to being anxious the next, and then sarcastic a short time later. One researcher has referred to the fluctuating adolescent's self as "the barometric self" (Rosenberg, 1979). In most cases, the self continues to be characterized by instability until late adolescence or even early adulthood, when a more unified theory of self is constructed. You will learn more about fluctuations in adolescents' emotions later in the chapter.

Contradictions Within the Self   As adolescents begin to differentiate their concept of the self into multiple roles in different relationship contexts, they sense potential contradictions between their differentiated selves. In one study, Susan Harter (1986) asked seventh-, ninth-, and eleventh-graders to describe themselves. She found that the number of contradictory self-descriptions they mentioned (moody and understanding, ugly and attractive, bored and inquisitive, caring and uncaring, introverted and fun-loving) increased dramatically between the seventh and ninth grades. Though the number of contradictory self-descriptions students mentioned declined in the eleventh grade, they still outnumbered those noted in the seventh grade. Adolescents develop the cognitive ability to detect these inconsistencies as they strive to construct a general theory of the self (Harter & Monsour, 1992).

Real Versus Ideal, True Versus False Selves   Adolescents' emerging ability to construct ideal selves can be perplexing to them. Although the capacity to recognize a discrepancy between the *real* and *ideal* selves represents a cognitive advance, the humanistic theorist Carl Rogers (1950) argued that a strong discrepancy between the real and ideal selves is a sign of maladjustment. Too great a discrepancy between one's actual self and one's ideal self—the person one wants to be—can produce a sense of failure and self-criticism and can even trigger depression.

Although some theorists consider a strong discrepancy between the ideal and real selves maladaptive, others argue that it need not always be so, especially in adolescence. In one view, an important aspect of the ideal or imagined self is the **possible self**: what individuals might become, what they would like to become, and what they are afraid of becoming (Markus & Nurius, 1986). Thus, adolescents' possible selves include both what they hope to be as well as what they fear they could become (Oyserman & James, 2011). In this view, the presence of both hoped-for and feared ideal selves is psychologically healthy, lending balance to an adolescent's perspective and motivation. That is, the attributes of the future positive self—getting into a good college, being admired, having a successful career—can direct an adolescent's positive actions, whereas the attributes of the future negative self—being unemployed, feeling lonely, not getting into a good college—can identify behaviors to be avoided. A recent study of Hong Kong secondary school students found that the main content of hoped-for possible selves focused on school and career (Zhu & others, 2014). In this study, girls had more strategies to attain their positive selves than did boys.

Can adolescents distinguish between their *true* and *false* selves? In one research study, they could (Harter & Lee, 1989). Adolescents are most likely to show their false selves with classmates and in romantic or dating situations; they are least likely to show their false selves with close friends. Adolescents may display a false self to impress others or to try out new behaviors or roles. They may feel that others do not understand their true selves or that others force them to behave in false ways. Some adolescents report that they do not like their false-self behavior, but others say that it does not bother them. One study found that experienced authenticity of the self is highest among adolescents who say they receive support from their parents (Harter, Stocker, & Robinson, 1996).

Social Comparison   Young adolescents are more likely than children to compare themselves with others and to understand that others are making comparisons about them (Ruble & others, 1980; Sebastian, Burnett, & Blakemore, 2010). An individual's beliefs about how

How does self-consciousness change as individuals go through adolescence?
(left): © Regine Mahaux/Getty Images; (right): © Randy Faris/Corbis

he or she is viewed by others are referred to as the *looking glass* self. However, most adolescents are unwilling to *admit* that they engage in social comparison because they view social comparison as socially undesirable. That is, they think that acknowledging their social comparison motives will endanger their popularity. Relying on social comparison information can be confusing to adolescents because of the large number of reference groups available to them. Should adolescents compare themselves to classmates in general? To friends of their own gender? To popular adolescents, good-looking adolescents, athletic adolescents? Considering all of these social comparison groups simultaneously can be perplexing for adolescents.

Self-Consciousness   Adolescents are more likely than children to be *self-conscious* about, and preoccupied with, their self-understanding (Harter, 2006). Although adolescents become more introspective, they do not always develop their self-understanding in social isolation. Adolescents turn to their friends for support and self-clarification, seeking out their friends' opinions in shaping their emerging self-definitions. As one researcher on self-development commented, adolescents' friends are often the main source of reflected self-appraisals, the social mirror into which adolescents anxiously stare (Rosenberg, 1979).

Self-Protection   In adolescence, the sense of confusion and conflict that is stimulated by efforts to understand oneself is accompanied by a need to *protect the self*. In an attempt to protect the self, adolescents are prone to deny their negative characteristics. For example, in Harter's investigation of self-understanding, adolescents were more likely than not to see positive self-descriptions such as *attractive, fun-loving, sensitive, affectionate*, and *inquisitive* as central, important aspects of the self, and to see negative self-descriptions such as *ugly, mediocre, depressed, selfish*, and *nervous* as peripheral, less important aspects of the self (Harter, 1986). This tendency is consistent with adolescents' tendency to describe the self in idealistic ways.

The Unconscious Self   In adolescence, self-understanding involves greater recognition that the self includes unconscious as well as conscious components. This recognition is not likely to occur until late adolescence, however. That is, older adolescents are more likely than younger adolescents to believe that certain aspects of their mental experience are beyond their awareness or control.

Not Quite Yet a Coherent, Integrated Self   Because of the proliferation of selves and unrealistic self-portraits during adolescence, the task of integrating these varying self-conceptions becomes problematic (Harter, 2006, 2012). Only later, usually in emerging adulthood, do individuals successfully integrate the many aspects of the self.

How does self-understanding change in emerging adulthood?
© ML Harris/Getty Images

Self-Understanding in Emerging Adulthood and Early Adulthood   In emerging adulthood, self-understanding becomes more integrative, with the disparate parts of the self pieced together more systematically. Emerging adults may detect inconsistencies in their earlier self-descriptions as they attempt to construct a general theory of self, an integrated sense of identity.

Gisela Labouvie-Vief (2006) concludes that considerable restructuring of the self can take place in emerging adulthood. She emphasizes that key aspects of self-development in emerging adulthood involve an increase in self-reflection and a decision about a specific worldview.

However, Labouvie-Vief (2006) argues that although emerging adults engage in more complex and critical thinking than they did when they were adolescents, many still have difficulty integrating their complex view of the world. She says this difficulty occurs because emerging adults are still easily influenced by their emotions, which can distort their thinking and cause them to be too self-serving and self-protective. In her research, it is not until 30 to 39 years of age that adults effectively develop a coherent, integrated worldview.

developmental **connection**

Cognitive Theory

Understanding cognitive changes in emerging adulthood and early adulthood requires consideration of how emotional maturity might affect cognitive development. Connect to "The Brain and Cognitive Development."

Self-Awareness   An aspect of self-understanding that becomes especially important in emerging and early adulthood is *self-awareness*—that is, how much an emerging adult is aware of his or her psychological makeup, including strengths and weaknesses. Many individuals do not have very good awareness of their psychological makeup and skills, as well as the causes of their weaknesses (Hull, 2012). For example, how aware is the person that she or he is a good or bad listener, uses the best strategies to solve personal problems, and is assertive rather than aggressive or passive in resolving conflicts? Awareness of strengths and weaknesses in these and many other aspects of life is an important dimension of self-understanding throughout the adult years, and emerging adulthood is a time when individuals can benefit considerably from addressing some of their weaknesses.

Possible Selves   Another aspect of self-understanding in emerging adulthood that is important involves *possible selves* (Markus & Kitayama, 2012; Zhu & others, 2014). Recall that possible selves are what individuals might become, what they would like to become, and what they are afraid of becoming (Frazier & others, 2012). Emerging adults mention many possible selves that they would like to become and might become. Some of these are unrealistic, such as being happy all of the time and being very rich. As individuals get older, they often describe fewer possible selves and portray them in more concrete and realistic ways. By middle age, individuals frequently describe their possible selves in terms of areas of their life in which they already have performed well, such as "being good at my work" or "having a good marriage" (Cross & Markus, 1991).

Self-Understanding and Social Contexts   You have learned that the adolescent's self-understanding can vary across relationships and social roles. Researchers have found that adolescents' portraits of themselves can differ depending on whether they are describing themselves when they are with their mother, father, close friend, romantic partner, or peer. They also can differ depending on whether they describe themselves in the role of student, athlete, or employee. Similarly, adolescents might create different selves depending on their ethnic and cultural background and experiences (Chandler & Dunlop, 2015; Lalonde & Chandler, 2004).

The multiple selves of ethnically diverse youth reflect their experiences in navigating their multiple worlds of family, peers, school, and community (Cooper, 2011; Halfond, Corona, & Moon, 2013; Schwartz & others, 2012). As U.S. youth from different ethnic backgrounds move from one culture to another, they can encounter barriers related to language, racism, gender, immigration, and poverty. In each of their different worlds, however, they also can find resources—in institutions, in other people, and in themselves. Youth who have difficulty moving between worlds can experience alienation from their school, family, or peers. This in turn can lead to other problems. However, youth who can navigate effectively between different worlds can develop bicultural or multicultural selves and become "culture brokers" for others.

> The contemporary perspective on the self emphasizes the construction of multiple self-representations across different relational contexts.
>
> —SUSAN HARTER
> *Contemporary developmental psychologist, University of Denver*

How are the multiple selves of a U.S. adolescent different from those of Japanese adolescents?
(left): © Jose Luis Pelaez Inc./Getty Images RF; (right): © Charles Gupton/Getty Images

Hazel Markus and her colleagues (Markus & Kitayama, 2010; Markus, Mullally, & Kitayama, 1999) stress the importance of understanding how multiple selves emerge through participation in cultural practices. They argue that all selves are culture-specific, emerging as individuals adapt to their cultural environments. In North American contexts, especially middle-socioeconomic-status (SES) contexts, the culture promotes and maintains individuality. When given the opportunity to describe themselves, North Americans often provide not only current portraits but notions of their future selves as well. They frequently show a need for multiple selves that are stable and consistent. In Japan, multiple selves are often described in terms of relatedness to others (Sedikdes & Brewer, 2001). For many Japanese, self-improvement is also an important aspect of these multiple selves. Markus and her colleagues (2006) recognize that cultural groups are characterized by diversity, but they believe that considering the dominant aspects of multiple selves in a culture (relatedness to others in Japan, for example) is helpful in understanding culture's influence.

- - - - - - - - - - →
developmental **connection**
Culture
One way to study cultures is to categorize them as individualist or collectivist. Connect to "Culture."

Understanding Others   Of course, becoming a competent adolescent involves not only understanding one's self but also understanding others (Carpendale & Lewis, 2015). Among the aspects of understanding others that are important in adolescent development are perceiving others' traits and understanding multiple perspectives.

Perceiving Others' Traits   One way to study how adolescents perceive others' traits is to ask them to assess the extent to which others' self-reports are accurate. In one comparison of 6- and 10-year-olds, the 10-year-olds were much more skeptical about others' self-reports of their intelligence and social skills than the 6-year-olds were (Heyman & Legare, 2005). In this study, the 10-year-olds understood that other people at times may distort the truth about their own traits to make a better impression on others.

As adolescence proceeds, teenagers develop a more sophisticated understanding of others. They come to understand that other people are complex and have public and private faces (Harter, 2006, 2012, 2013).

What are some important aspects of social understanding in adolescence?
© Jim Craigmyle/Corbis

Perspective Taking   **Perspective taking** is the ability to assume another person's perspective and understand his or her thoughts and feelings. Robert Selman (1980) proposed a developmental theory of changes in perspective taking that occur between 3 years and 15 years of age. These developmental changes begin with the egocentric viewpoint in early childhood and end with in-depth perspective taking in adolescence.

perspective taking The ability to assume another person's perspective and understand his or her thoughts and feelings.

Only recently has research on perspective taking in adolescence taken hold. Following are the results of several recent research investigations on this topic:

· In sixth through eighth grades, girls engaged in more social perspective taking than did boys (Smith, 2009; Smith & Rose, 2011) but they also experienced more empathic distress by taking on their friend's distress as their own than did boys.

· A lower level of perspective taking was linked to increased relational aggression (intentionally harming someone through strategies such as spreading vicious rumors) one year later in middle school students (Batanova & Loukas, 2011).

Social Cognitive Monitoring An important aspect of metacognition is cognitive monitoring, which can also be very helpful in social situations. As part of their increased awareness of themselves and others, adolescents monitor their social world more extensively than they did when they were children. Adolescents engage in a number of social cognitive monitoring activities on virtually a daily basis. An adolescent might think, "I would like to get to know this guy better but he is not very open. Maybe I can talk to some other students about what he is like." Another adolescent might check incoming information about a club or a clique to determine if it is consistent with her impressions of the club or clique. Yet another adolescent might question someone or paraphrase what the person has just said about her feelings to make sure that he has accurately understood them. Adolescents' ability to monitor their social cognition may be an important aspect of their social maturity (Flavell, 1979).

At this point, we have discussed many aspects of self-understanding and social understanding. Recall, however, that the self involves not only self-understanding but also self-esteem and self-concept. That is, not only do adolescents try to define and describe attributes of the self (self-understanding), but they also evaluate those attributes (self-concept and self-esteem).

SELF-ESTEEM AND SELF-CONCEPT

What are self-esteem and self-concept? How are they measured? Are some domains more salient to the adolescent's self-esteem than others? How do relationships with parents and peers influence adolescents' self-esteem? What are the consequences of low self-esteem in adolescents and emerging adults, and how can their self-esteem be raised?

What Are Self-Esteem and Self-Concept? In the field of developmental psychology, leading expert Susan Harter (2006, 2012) distinguishes between self-esteem and self-concept. In her view, **self-esteem**, also referred to as *self-worth* or *self-image*, is the global evaluative dimension of the self. For example, an adolescent or emerging adult might perceive that she is not merely a person but a good person. Of course, not all adolescents and emerging adults have an overall positive image of themselves. An adolescent with low self-esteem may describe himself as a bad person.

In Harter's view, **self-concept** refers to domain-specific evaluations of the self. Adolescents and emerging adults make self-evaluations in many domains—academic, athletic, physical appearance, and so on. For example, an adolescent may have a negative academic self-concept because he is getting poor grades but have a positive athletic self-concept because he is a star swimmer. In sum, self-esteem refers to global self-evaluations, self-concept to domain-specific evaluations.

Investigators have not always made a clear distinction between self-esteem and self-concept, sometimes using the terms interchangeably or not precisely defining them (Donnellan & Robins, 2009). As you read the remaining discussion of self-esteem and self-concept, recalling the distinction between self-esteem as global self-evaluation and self-concept as domain-specific self-evaluation can help you to keep the terms straight.

Measuring Self-Esteem and Self-Concept Measuring self-esteem and self-concept hasn't always been easy, especially in assessing adolescents. For many years, such measures were designed primarily for children or for adults, with little attention paid to adolescents. Then Susan Harter (1989) developed a separate measure for adolescents: the Self-Perception Profile for Adolescents. It assesses eight domains—scholastic competence, athletic competence, social acceptance, physical appearance, behavioral conduct, close friendship, romantic appeal, and job competence—plus global self-worth. The adolescent measure

self-esteem The global evaluative dimension of the self; also referred to as self-worth or self-image.

self-concept Domain-specific evaluations of the self.

has three skill domains not present in the measure she developed for children: job competence, romantic appeal, and close friendship.

Some assessment experts argue that a combination of several methods should be used in measuring self-esteem. In addition to self-reporting, rating of an adolescent's self-esteem by others and observations of the adolescent's behavior in various settings could provide a more complete and accurate self-esteem picture. Peers, teachers, parents, and even others who do not know the adolescent could be asked to rate the adolescent's self-esteem.

Adolescents' facial expressions and the extent to which they congratulate or condemn themselves are also good indicators of how they view themselves. For example, adolescents who rarely smile or rarely act happy are revealing something about their self-esteem.

One investigation that used behavioral observations in assessing self-esteem shows some of the positive as well as the negative behaviors that can provide clues to the adolescent's self-esteem (see Figure 1) (Savin-Williams & Demo, 1983). By using a variety of methods (such as self-report and behavioral observations) and obtaining information from various sources (such as the adolescent, parents, friends, and teachers), investigators are likely to construct a more accurate picture of the adolescent's self-esteem than they could get by relying on only one assessment method.

Self-Esteem: Perception and Reality
Self-esteem reflects perceptions that do not always match reality (Jordan & Zeigler-Hill, 2013; Krueger, Vohs, & Baumeister, 2008). An adolescent's or emerging adult's self-esteem might indicate a perception about whether he or she is intelligent and attractive, for example, but that perception may not be accurate. Thus, high self-esteem may refer to accurate, justified perceptions of one's worth as a person and one's successes and accomplishments, but it can also indicate an arrogant, grandiose, unwarranted sense of superiority over others. In the same manner, low self-esteem may suggest either an accurate perception of one's shortcomings or a distorted, even pathological sense of insecurity and inferiority.

Narcissism refers to a self-centered and self-concerned approach toward others. Typically, narcissists are unaware of their actual self and how others perceive them. This lack of awareness contributes to their adjustment problems (Grijalva & others, 2015; Lapsley & Stey, 2012). Narcissists are excessively self-centered and self-congratulatory, viewing their own needs and desires as paramount. As a result, narcissists rarely show any empathy toward others. In fact, narcissists often devalue people around them to protect their own precarious self-esteem, yet they often respond with rage and shame when others do not admire them or treat them in accordance with their grandiose fantasies about themselves. Narcissists are at their most grandiose when their self-esteem is threatened. Narcissists may fly into a frenzy if they have given an unsatisfactory performance.

One study revealed that narcissistic adolescents were more aggressive than other adolescents but only when they were shamed (Thomaes & others, 2008). Low self-esteem was not linked to aggression, but narcissism combined with high self-esteem was related to exceptionally high aggression. And a recent longitudinal study found that narcissistic adolescents and emerging adults were more impulsive, histrionic (behaving dramatically), active, and self-focused as young children than were others (Carlson & Gjerde, 2010). In this study, narcissism increased from 14 to 18 years of age, then slightly declined from 18 to 23.

So far, narcissism has been portrayed as a negative aspect of adolescent and emerging adult development. However, Daniel Lapsley and Matthew Aalsma (2006) found that college students' adjustment varied according to the type of narcissism. In their research, moderate narcissists showed healthy adjustment, whereas covert and overt narcissists were characterized by poor adjustment. Covert narcissists were described as reflecting "narcissistic grandiosity and entitlement lurking behind a façade of personal inadequacy, inferiority, and vulnerability" (p. 68). Overt narcissists openly displayed their grandiosity and exploitativeness at a high level.

Positive indicators

1. Gives others directives or commands
2. Uses voice quality appropriate for situation
3. Expresses opinions
4. Sits with others during social activities
5. Works cooperatively in a group
6. Faces others when speaking or being spoken to
7. Maintains eye contact during conversation
8. Initiates friendly contact with others
9. Maintains comfortable space between self and others
10. Has little hesitation in speech, speaks fluently

Negative indicators

1. Puts down others by teasing, name-calling, or gossiping
2. Uses gestures that are dramatic or out of context
3. Engages in inappropriate touching or avoids physical contact
4. Gives excuses for failures
5. Brags excessively about achievements, skills, appearance
6. Verbally puts self down; self-deprecation
7. Speaks too loudly, abruptly, or in a dogmatic tone

FIGURE 1
BEHAVIORAL INDICATORS OF SELF–ESTEEM

developmental **connection**

Social Cognition

Adolescent egocentrism increases in early adolescence, especially the imaginary audience dimension. Connect to "The Brain and Cognitive Development."

narcissism A self-centered and self-concerned approach toward others.

What characterizes narcissistic individuals?
© Klawitter Productions/Corbis

Are today's adolescents and emerging adults more self-centered and narcissistic than their counterparts in earlier generations? Research by Jean Twenge and her colleagues (2008a, b) indicated that compared with baby boomers who were surveyed in 1975, twelfth-graders surveyed in 2006 were more self-satisfied overall and far more confident that they would be very good employees, mates, and parents. Today's adolescents are sometimes labeled "Generation Me." However, other recent large-scale analyses have revealed no increase in high school and college students' narcissism from 1976 through 2006 (Trzesniewski & Donnellan, 2010; Trzesniewski, Donnellan, & Robins, 2008a, b). In sum, the extent to which recent generations of adolescents have higher self-esteem and are more narcissistic than earlier generations is controversial (Arnett, 2010; Donnellan & Trzesniewski, 2010; Eckersley, 2010; Roberts, Edmonds, & Grijaiva, 2010; Twenge & Campbell, 2010).

In one study, age changes in narcissism were much stronger than generational changes (Roberts, Edmonds, & Grijaiva, 2010). In this study, across three generations, college students were the most narcissistic, followed by their parents, and then students' grandparents were the least narcissistic. These researchers say that it is more accurate to label today's adolescents and emerging adults "Developmental Me" than "Generation Me."

Does Self-Esteem Change During Adolescence and Emerging Adulthood?
Researchers have found that self-esteem often decreases when children make the transition from elementary school to middle or junior high school (Twenge & Campbell, 2001). Indeed, during and just after many life transitions, individuals' self-esteem often decreases.

A recent study found that preexisting gender differences in self-esteem (higher in males) narrowed between the ninth and twelfth grades (Falci, 2012). In this study, adolescents from higher-SES backgrounds had higher self-esteem than did their lower-SES counterparts.

Self-esteem fluctuates across the life span (Trzesniewski, Donnellan, & Robins, 2013; Zeigler-Hill, 2013). One cross-sectional study assessed the self-esteem of a very large, diverse sample of 326,641 individuals from 9 to 90 years of age (Robins & others, 2002). About two-thirds of the participants were from the United States. The individuals were asked to respond to the statement, "I have high self-esteem" on a 5-point scale in which 5 stood for "strongly agree" and 1 stood for "strongly disagree." Self-esteem decreased in adolescence, increased in the twenties, leveled off in the thirties, rose in the forties through the mid-sixties, and then dropped in the seventies and eighties (see Figure 2). At most ages, males reported higher self-esteem than females did.

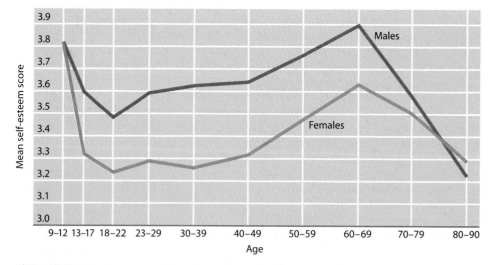

FIGURE **2**

SELF-ESTEEM ACROSS THE LIFE SPAN. One large-scale study asked more than 300,000 individuals to rate the extent to which they have high self-esteem on a 5-point scale, with 5 being "strongly agree" and 1 being "strongly disagree." Self-esteem dropped in adolescence and late adulthood. Self-esteem of females was lower than self-esteem of males through most of the life span.

Another study also found that the gender gap (lower for females) in self-esteem decreased as individuals went through emerging adulthood from 18 to 25 years of age (Galambos, Barker, & Krahn, 2006). In this study, social support and marriage were linked with an increase in self-esteem, whereas unemployment was related to a decrease in self-esteem.

Some researchers argue that although there may be a decrease in self-esteem during adolescence, the drop is actually very slight and not nearly as pronounced as it is presented in the media (Harter, 2013; Hyde, 2005; Hyde & Else-Quest, 2013; Kling & others, 1999). Also note in Figure 2 that, despite the drop in self-esteem among adolescent girls, their average score (3.3) was still slightly higher than the neutral point on the scale (3.0).

One explanation for the decline in self-esteem among females during early adolescence focuses on girls' more negative body images during pubertal change compared with boys (Harter, 2006). Another explanation involves the greater interest young adolescent girls take in social relationships and society's failure to reward that interest.

A current concern is that too many of today's college students grew up receiving empty praise and as a consequence have inflated self-esteem (Graham, 2005; Stipek, 2005). Too often they were given praise for performance that was mediocre or even poor. Now that they are in college, they may have difficulty handling competition and criticism. The title of a book, *Dumbing Down Our Kids: Why American Children Feel Good About Themselves But Can't Read, Write, or Add* (Sykes, 1995), vividly captured the theme that many U.S. students' academic problems may stem at least in part from unmerited praise that was provided in an effort to prop up their self-esteem. In a series of studies, researchers found that inflated praise, although well intended, may cause children with low self-esteem to avoid important learning experiences such as tackling challenging tasks (Brummelman & others, 2014).

Is Self-Esteem Linked to Academic Success or Initiative?

School performance and self-esteem are only moderately correlated, and these correlations do not suggest that high self-esteem produces better school performance (Baumeister & others, 2003). Efforts to increase students' self-esteem have not always led to improved school performance (Davies & Brember, 1999). Adolescents with high self-esteem have greater initiative, but this can produce positive or negative outcomes (Baumeister & others, 2003). Adolescents with high self-esteem are prone to take both prosocial and antisocial actions.

Are Some Domains More Closely Linked to Self-Esteem Than Others?

Many adolescents are preoccupied with their body image (Markey, 2010). Physical appearance is an especially powerful contributor to self-esteem in adolescence (Harter, 2006, 2012). In Harter's (1999) research, for example, global self-esteem was correlated most strongly with physical appearance, a link that has been found in both the United States and other countries (see Figure 3). In another study, adolescents' concept of their physical attractiveness was the strongest predictor of their overall self-esteem (Lord & Eccles, 1994). This strong association between perceived appearance and general self-worth is not confined to adolescence but holds across most of the life span, from early childhood through middle age (Harter, 1999).

Social Contexts and Self-Esteem

Social contexts such as the family, peers, and schools contribute to the development of an adolescent's self-esteem (McLoyd, Purtell, & Hardaway, 2015; Murry & others, 2015). One study found that as family cohesiveness increased, adolescents' self-esteem increased over time (Baldwin & Hoffman, 2002). In this study, family cohesion was based on the amount of time the family spent together, the quality of their communication, and the extent to which the adolescent was involved in family decision making. In another investigation, the following parenting attributes were associated with boys' high self-esteem: expression of affection; concern about the boys' problems; harmony in the home; participation in joint family activities; availability to give competent, organized help when the boys needed it; setting clear and fair rules; abiding by the rules; and allowing the boys freedom within well-prescribed limits (Coopersmith, 1967).

Peer judgments gain increasing importance in adolescence (Villanti, Boulay, & Juon, 2011). The link between peer approval and self-worth increases during adolescence (Harter, 1990b). The transition from elementary school to middle

developmental **connection**

Gender

Gender differences characterize adolescents' body images, with adolescent girls having a more negative body image than boys do, especially in early adolescence. Connect to "Puberty, Health, and Biological Foundations."

Domain	Harter's U.S. samples	Other countries
Physical Appearance	.65	.62
Scholastic Competence	.48	.41
Social Acceptance	.46	.40
Behavioral Conduct	.45	.45
Athletic Competence	.33	.30

FIGURE 3

CORRELATIONS BETWEEN GLOBAL SELF-ESTEEM AND DOMAINS OF COMPETENCE. *Note:* The correlations shown are the average correlations computed across a number of studies. The other countries in this evaluation were England, Ireland, Australia, Canada, Germany, Italy, Greece, the Netherlands, and Japan. Recall that correlation coefficients can range from −1.00 to +1.00. The correlations between physical appearance and global self-esteem (.65 and .62) are moderately high.

developmental **connection**

School

The transition to middle or junior high school is stressful for many individuals because it coincides with a number of physical, cognitive, and socioemotional changes. Connect to "Schools."

or junior high school is associated with a drop in self-esteem (Harter, 2012). Self-esteem is higher in the last year of elementary school than in middle or junior high school, especially in the first year after the transition (Simmons & Blyth, 1987).

Consequences of Low Self-Esteem   For most adolescents and emerging adults, the emotional discomfort of low self-esteem is only temporary, but for some, low self-esteem can develop into other problems. Low self-esteem has been implicated in overweight and obesity, anxiety, depression, suicide, and delinquency (Blanco & others, 2014; O'Brien, Bartoletti, & Leitzel, 2013; Zeigler-Hill, 2013). A recent study revealed that youth with low self-esteem had lower life satisfaction at 30 years of age (Birkeland & others, 2012). Another recent study found that low and decreasing self-esteem in adolescence was linked to adult depression two decades later (Steiger & others, 2014).

Also keep in mind that the seriousness of the problem depends not only on the nature of the adolescent's or emerging adult's low self-esteem but on other conditions as well. When low self-esteem is compounded by difficult school transitions, a troubled family life, or other stressful events, an individual's problems can intensify.

Does self-esteem in adolescence foreshadow adjustment and competence in adulthood? A New Zealand longitudinal study assessed self-esteem at 11, 13, and 15 years of age and adjustment and competence of the same individuals when they were 26 years old (Trzesniewski & others, 2006). The results revealed that adults characterized by poorer mental and physical health, worse economic prospects, and higher levels of criminal behavior were more likely to have low self-esteem in adolescence than their better adjusted, more competent adult counterparts.

An important point needs to be made about much of the research on self-esteem: It is correlational rather than experimental. Remember that correlation does not equal causation. Thus, if a correlational study finds an association between self-esteem and depression, it could be equally likely that depression causes low self-esteem or that low self-esteem causes depression. A recent longitudinal study explored whether self-esteem is a cause or consequence of social support in youth (Marshall & others, 2014). In this study, self-esteem predicted subsequent changes in social support, but social support did not predict subsequent changes in self-esteem.

Given the potential consequences of low self-esteem, how can the self-esteem of adolescents and emerging adults be increased? To explore possible answers to this question, see the *Connecting with Health and Well-Being* interlude.

SELF-REGULATION

Self-regulation involves the ability to control one's behavior without having to rely on others' help. Self-regulation includes the self-generation and cognitive monitoring of thoughts, feelings, and behaviors in order to reach a goal. Throughout most of the life span, individuals who engage in self-regulation are higher achievers, enjoy better health, and are more satisfied with their lives than their counterparts who let external factors dominate their lives (Eisenberg & others, 2014; McClelland & others, 2015). For example, researchers have found that, compared with low-achieving students, high-achieving students engage in greater self-regulation. They do this by setting more specific learning goals, using more strategies to learn and adapt, self-monitoring more, and more systematically evaluating their progress toward a goal (Schunk, Meece, & Pintrich, 2014).

A key component of self-regulation is engaging in *effortful control*, which involves inhibiting impulses and not engaging in destructive behavior, focusing and maintaining attention despite distractions, and initiating and completing tasks that have long-term value, even if they may seem unpleasant (Rothbart & Bates, 1998). A recent study found that effortful control at 17 years of age predicted academic persistence and educational attainment at 23 to 25 years of age (Veronneau & others, 2014). In this study, effortful control was just as strong a predictor of educational attainment as were parents' education and past grade point average.

The increased capacity for self-regulation is linked to developmental advances in the brain's prefrontal cortex and increasing cognitive control in adolescence and emerging adulthood (Botvinick & Braver, 2015; Casey, 2015). Few studies of self-regulation, though, have focused on adolescents. On the one hand, advances in cognitive skills (logical thinking and executive function, for example), increased introspection, and the greater independence of

developmental **connection**

Achievement

Self-regulation and delay of gratification are key processes in the development of achievement and academic success in adolescence. Connect to "Achievement, Work, and Careers."

self-regulation The ability to control one's behavior without having to rely on others for help.

How Can Adolescents' Self-Esteem Be Increased?

Four ways to improve adolescents' and emerging adults' self-esteem are to (1) identify the causes of low self-esteem and the domains of competence important to the self, (2) provide emotional support and social approval, (3) foster achievement, and (4) help adolescents to cope with challenges.

Identifying an adolescent's and emerging adult's sources of self-esteem—that is, the domains that are important to the self—is critical to improving self-esteem. Self-esteem theorist and researcher Susan Harter (1990b) points out that the self-esteem enhancement programs of the 1960s, in which self-esteem itself was the target and individuals were encouraged to simply feel good about themselves, were ineffective. Rather, Harter (1998) concludes that intervention must occur at the level of the causes of self-esteem if self-esteem is to improve significantly. Adolescents and emerging adults have the highest self-esteem when they perform competently in domains important to the self. Therefore, adolescents and emerging adults should be encouraged to identify and value their domains of competence. For example, some adolescents and emerging adults might have artistic strengths, others academic strengths, and yet others might excel in sports.

Emotional support and social approval in the form of confirmation from others can also powerfully influence self-esteem (Harter, 1990a, b). Some youth with low self-esteem come from conflicted families or conditions in which they experienced abuse or neglect—situations in which support is unavailable. In some cases, alternative sources of support can be implemented, either informally through the encouragement of a teacher, a coach, or another significant adult, or

What are some strategies for increasing self-esteem?
© Anthony Redpath/Corbis

more formally through programs such as Big Brothers and Big Sisters. Although peer approval becomes increasingly important during adolescence, both adult and peer support are important influences on the adolescent's self-esteem. In one study, both parental and peer support were related to the adolescent's general self-worth (Robinson, 1995).

Achievement can also improve adolescents' and emerging adults' self-esteem (Bednar, Wells, & Peterson, 1995; Mruk & O'Brien, 2013). For example, the straightforward teaching of real skills to adolescents and emerging adults often results in increased achievement and thus in enhanced self-esteem. Adolescents and emerging adults develop higher self-esteem when they know what tasks are important for achieving goals and they have experienced success in performing them or similar behaviors. This emphasis on the importance of achievement in improving self-esteem has much in common with Albert Bandura's (2010) social cognitive concept of self-efficacy, which refers to individuals' beliefs that they can master a situation and produce positive outcomes.

Self-esteem often increases when adolescents face a problem and try to cope with it rather than avoid it (Dyson & Renk, 2006). Facing problems realistically, honestly, and nondefensively produces favorable self-evaluative thoughts, which lead to the self-generated approval that raises self-esteem.

Can individuals have too much self-esteem? How can research address this question?

adolescence might lead to increased self-control (Muller & Kerns, 2015). Also, advances in cognitive abilities provide adolescents with a better understanding of the importance of delaying gratification in exchange for something desirable (such as a good grade in a class) rather than seeking immediate gratification (listening to music rather than studying) (Fino & others, 2014). On the other hand, an increased motivation for risk taking might produce less self-control (Monahan & others, 2015; Steinberg 2014, 2015a, b).

Some researchers emphasize the early development of self-regulation in childhood and adolescence as a key contributor to adult health and even longevity (Drake, Belsky, & Fearon, 2014; Reiss, Eccles, & Nielsen, 2014; Wigfield & others, 2015). For example, Nancy Eisenberg and her colleagues (2014) concluded that research indicates self-regulation fosters conscientiousness later in life, both directly and through its link to academic motivation/success and internalized compliance with norms.

Review

- What is self-understanding? What are the key dimensions of self-understanding in adolescence? What are some important aspects of understanding others in adolescence?
- What are self-esteem and self-concept? How can they be measured? Are some domains more salient than others to adolescents' self-esteem? How are social contexts linked with adolescents' self-esteem? What are the consequences of low self-esteem? How can adolescents' self-esteem be increased?
- What characterizes self-regulation in adolescence?

Connect

- Contrast self-esteem, self-concept, and narcissism.

Reflect *Your Own Personal Journey of Life*

- Think about what your future selves might be. What do you envision will make you the happiest about the future selves you aspire to become? What prospective selves hold negative possibilities?

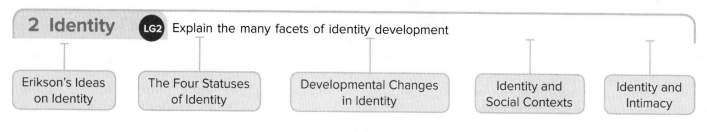

2 Identity   **LG2** Explain the many facets of identity development

| Erikson's Ideas on Identity | The Four Statuses of Identity | Developmental Changes in Identity | Identity and Social Contexts | Identity and Intimacy |

"Who are you?" said the Caterpillar. Alice replied, rather shyly, "I—I hardly know, Sir, just at present—at least I know who I was when I got up this morning, but I must have changed several times since then."

—Lewis Carroll
English writer, 19th century

developmental **connection**

Theories

Erikson suggested that individuals go through eight stages in the course of human development. Connect to "Introduction."

identity Who a person believes he or she is, representing a synthesis and integration of self-understanding.

identity versus identity confusion Erikson's fifth developmental stage, which occurs during adolescence. At this time, individuals are faced with deciding who they are, what they are all about, and where they are going in life.

psychosocial moratorium Erikson's term for the gap between childhood security and adult autonomy that adolescents experience as part of their identity exploration.

Identity is who a person believes she or he is, representing a synthesis and integration of self-understanding. By far the most comprehensive and provocative theory of identity development is that of Erik Erikson. In fact, some experts on adolescence consider Erikson's ideas to be the single most influential theory of adolescent development. Let's look further at his theory, beginning with an analysis of his ideas on identity.

ERIKSON'S IDEAS ON IDENTITY

Who am I? What am I all about? What am I going to do with my life? What is different about me? How can I make it on my own? These questions, not usually considered in childhood, surface as a common, virtually universal concern during adolescence. Adolescents clamor for solutions to questions of identity. Erik Erikson (1950, 1968) was the first to realize how central such questions are to understanding adolescent development. Today's emphasis on identity as a key concept in adolescent development results directly from Erikson's masterful thinking and analysis.

Identity Versus Identity Confusion   In Erikson's theory, **identity versus identity confusion** is the fifth developmental stage (or crisis) in the human life span and it occurs during the adolescent years. At this time, adolescents are faced with deciding who they are, what they are all about, and where they are going in life. They confront many new roles, from vocational to romantic. As part of their identity exploration, adolescents experience a **psychosocial moratorium**, Erikson's term for the gap between childhood security and adult autonomy. In the course of exploring and searching their culture's identity files, they often experiment with different roles. Youth who successfully cope with these conflicting roles and identities emerge with a new sense of self that is both refreshing and acceptable. But adolescents who do not successfully resolve the identity crisis suffer what Erikson calls *identity confusion*. Either they withdraw, isolating themselves from peers and family, or they immerse themselves in the world of peers and lose their identity in the crowd.

Role Experimentation A core ingredient of Erikson's theory of identity development is role experimentation. As we have seen, Erikson stressed that adolescents face an overwhelming number of choices and at some point during their youth enter a period of psychosocial moratorium. During this moratorium and before they reach a stable sense of self, they try out different roles and behaviors. They might be argumentative one moment, cooperative the next. They might dress neatly one day and sloppily the next day. One week they might like a particular friend, and the next week they might despise the friend. This identity experimentation is a deliberate effort on the part of adolescents to find their place in the world.

As adolescents gradually come to realize that they will soon be responsible for themselves and their lives, they try to determine what those lives are going to be. Many parents and other adults, accustomed to having children go along with what they say, may be bewildered or incensed by the wisecracks, rebelliousness, and rapid mood changes that accompany adolescence. But it is important for these adults to give adolescents the time and opportunity to explore different roles and personalities. In turn, most adolescents eventually discard undesirable roles.

There are literally hundreds of roles for adolescents to try out and probably just as many ways to pursue each role. Erikson argued that by late adolescence, vocational roles become central to identity development, especially in a highly technological society like that of the United States. Youth who have been well trained to enter a workforce that offers the potential of reasonably high self-esteem will experience the least stress during this phase of identity development. Some youth may reject jobs offering good pay and traditionally high social status, choosing instead work that allows them to be more genuinely helpful to others, perhaps in the Peace Corps, a mental health clinic, or a school for children in a low-income neighborhood. Some youth may prefer unemployment to the prospect of work that they feel they could not perform well or that would make them feel useless. To Erikson, such choices reflect the desire to achieve a meaningful identity by being true to oneself rather than by burying one's identity within the larger society.

Identity is a self-portrait that is composed of many pieces:

- The career and work path a person wants to follow (vocational/career identity)
- Whether a person is politically conservative, liberal, or middle of the road (political identity)
- A person's spiritual beliefs (religious identity)
- Whether a person is single, married, divorced, or cohabiting (relationship identity)
- The extent to which a person is motivated to achieve and is intellectually oriented (achievement, intellectual identity)
- Whether a person is heterosexual, homosexual, or bisexual (sexual identity)
- Which part of the world or country a person is from and how intensely the person identifies with his or her cultural heritage (cultural/ethnic identity)
- The things a person likes to do, including sports, music, and hobbies (interests)
- An individual's personality characteristics—being introverted or extraverted, anxious or calm, friendly or hostile, and so on (personality)
- A person's body image (physical identity)

Some Contemporary Thoughts on Identity Contemporary views of identity development suggest that it is a lengthy process, in many instances more gradual and less cataclysmic than Erikson's term *crisis* implies (Azmitia, Syed, & Radmacher, 2013; Coté, 2015; Waterman, 2015). Today's theorists note that this extraordinarily complex process neither begins nor ends with adolescence. It begins in infancy with the appearance of attachment, the development of a sense of self, and the emergence of independence. It ends with a life review and integration in old age. What is important about identity development in adolescence and emerging adulthood is that this is the first time when physical, cognitive, and socioemotional development advance to the point at which the individual can sort through and synthesize childhood identities and identifications to construct a viable path toward adult maturity (Marcia & Carpendale, 2004). Resolution of the identity issue during adolescence and emerging adulthood does not mean that identity will be stable through the remainder of

Erik Erikson.
© Bettmann/Corbis

As long as one keeps searching, the answers come.

—JOAN BAEZ
American folk singer, 20th century

One of Erik Erikson's strategies for explaining the nature of identity development was to analyze the lives of famous individuals. One such individual was Mahatma Gandhi (*center*), the spiritual leader of India in the mid-twentieth century, about whom Erikson (1969) wrote in *Gandhi's Truth*.
© Bettmann/Corbis

What are some contemporary thoughts about identity formation and development?
© Somos/Veer/Getty Images RF

one's life. An individual who develops a healthy identity is flexible and adaptive, open to changes in society, in relationships, and in careers. This openness assures numerous reorganizations of identity throughout the individual's life.

Just as researchers increasingly describe adolescents' and emerging adults' self-understanding in terms of multiple selves, there also is a trend toward characterizing adolescents' and emerging adults' identity in terms of multiple identities, such as ethnicity, spirituality, sexuality, and so on (Schwartz & others, 2013). Although adolescent and emerging adult identities are preceded by childhood identities, central questions such as "Who am I?" come up more frequently during the adolescent and emerging adult years. During adolescence and emerging adulthood, identities are characterized more strongly by the search for balance between the needs for autonomy and for connectedness.

Identity formation seldom happens neatly nor is it usually cataclysmic (McLean & Syed, 2015; Rivas-Drake & others, 2014a, b; Schwartz & others, 2013, 2014, 2015a, b). At the bare minimum, it involves commitment to a vocational direction, an ideological stance, and a sexual orientation. Synthesizing the components of identity can be a long, drawn-out process, with many negations and affirmations of various roles. Identity development takes place in bits and pieces (Duriez & others, 2012). Decisions are not made once and for all but must be made again and again (Schwartz & others, 2013, 2014). Although the decisions might seem trivial at the time—whom to date, whether or not to have sex, whether to break up; whether to take drugs; whether to go to college or get a job, to study or play; whether to be politically active or not—over the years, they begin to form the core of what an individual is all about.

A current concern about the development of identity in adolescence and emerging adulthood was voiced in William Damon's (2008) book, *The Path to Purpose*. Damon acknowledges that successful identity development is a long-term process of extended exploration and reflection, and in some instances it can involve postponing decisions for a number of years. However, what concerns Damon is that too many of today's youth aren't moving toward any identity resolution. In Damon's (2008, pp. 5, 7) words,

> Their delay is characterized more by indecision than by motivated reflection, more by confusion than by pursuit of clear goals, more by ambivalence than by determination. Directionless shift is not a constructive moratorium in either a developmental or a societal sense. Without a sense of direction, opportunities are lost, and doubt and self-absorption can set in. Maladaptive habits are established and adaptive ones not built. . . . What is too often missing is . . . the kind of wholehearted dedication to an activity or interest that stems from serious purpose, a purpose that can give meaning and direction to life.

In Damon's (2008, p. 47) view, too many youth are left to their own devices in dealing with some of life's biggest questions: "What is my calling?" "What do I have to contribute to the world?" "What am I here for?" Damon acknowledges that adults can't make youths' decisions for them, but he emphasizes that it is very important for parents, teachers, mentors, and other adults to provide guidance, feedback, and contexts that will improve the likelihood that youth will develop a positive identity. Youth need a cultural climate that inspires rather than demoralizes them and supports their chances of reaching their aspirations.

- - - - - - - - →

developmental **connection**

Achievement

In interviews with 12- to 22-year-olds, Damon found that only about 20 percent had a clear vision of where they wanted to go in life, what they wanted to achieve, and why. Connect to "Achievement, Work, and Careers."

THE FOUR STATUSES OF IDENTITY

James Marcia (1980, 1994, 2002) analyzed Erikson's theory of identity development and concluded that it involves four identity statuses, or ways of resolving the identity crisis: identity diffusion, identity foreclosure, identity moratorium, and identity achievement. That is, Marcia uses the extent of an adolescent's crisis and commitment to classify individuals according to these four identity statuses. He defines the term **crisis** as a period of identity development during which the adolescent is choosing among meaningful alternatives. (Most researchers use the term *exploration*.) By **commitment,** he means a personal investment in what an individual is going to do.

crisis A period of identity development during which the adolescent is choosing among meaningful alternatives.

commitment The part of identity development in which adolescents show a personal investment in what they are going to do.

Position on Occupation and Ideology	Identity Status			
	Identity Diffusion	**Identity Foreclosure**	**Identity Moratorium**	**Identity Achievement**
Crisis	Absent	Absent	Present	Present
Commitment	Absent	Present	Absent	Present

FIGURE 4
MARCIA'S FOUR STATUSES OF IDENTITY

Let's examine each of Marcia's four identity statuses:

- **Identity diffusion** is Marcia's term for the state adolescents are in when they have not yet experienced an identity crisis (that is, have not yet explored meaningful alternatives) and have not made any commitments. Not only are adolescents in this status undecided about occupational and ideological choices, but they usually show little interest in such matters.
- **Identity foreclosure** is Marcia's term for the state adolescents are in when they have made a commitment but have not experienced an identity crisis. This status occurs most often when parents hand down commitments to their adolescents, usually in an authoritarian way. Thus, adolescents with this status have not had adequate opportunities to explore different approaches, ideologies, and vocations on their own.
- **Identity moratorium** is Marcia's term for the state of adolescents who are in the midst of an identity crisis, but who have not made a clear commitment to an identity.
- **Identity achievement** is Marcia's term for the status of adolescents who have undergone an identity crisis and made a commitment.

Figure 4 summarizes Marcia's four identity statuses.

Let's explore some specific examples of Marcia's identity statuses. A 13-year-old adolescent has neither begun to explore her identity in a meaningful way nor made an identity commitment; she is *identity diffused*. An 18-year-old boy's parents want him to be a doctor, so he is planning on majoring in premedicine in college and has not adequately explored any other options; he is *identity foreclosed*. Nineteen-year-old Sasha is not quite sure what life path she wants to follow, but she recently went to the counseling center at her college to find out about different careers; she is in an *identity moratorium*. Twenty-one-year-old Marcelo extensively explored a number of different career options in college, eventually got his degree in science education, and is looking forward to his first year of teaching high school; he is *identity achieved*. Although these examples of identity statuses focus on careers, remember that the whole of identity has multiple dimensions.

Earlier in this chapter we described various dimensions of identity. To explore your identity status on a number of identity's dimensions, see Figure 5.

Marcia's approach has been sharply criticized by some researchers who conclude that it distorts and overly simplifies Erikson's concepts of crisis and commitment (Coté, 2009, 2015; Luyckx, Schwartz, Goossens, & others, 2008). Erikson emphasized that youth question the perceptions and expectations of their culture and the development of an autonomous position with regard to one's society. In Marcia's approach, these complex questions are reduced to whether a youth has thought about certain issues and considered the alternatives. Similarly, in Marcia's approach, Erikson's idea of commitment loses its meaning of investing oneself in certain lifelong projects and is interpreted simply as having made a firm decision. Other researchers still maintain that Marcia's approach is a valuable contribution to understanding identity (Crocetti & Meeus, 2015; Kroger, 2012, 2015; Kunnen & Metz, 2015).

Recently, Belgian psychologists Luc Goossens, Koen Luyckx, and their colleagues (Goossens & Luyckx, 2007; Luyckx, Schwartz, Berzonsky, & others, 2008; Luyckx & others, 2010, 2013, 2014) have proposed an extension of Marcia's concepts of exploration and commitment. The revisionist theorizing stresses that effective identity development involves evaluating identity commitments on a continuing basis. Two processes that have been devised to

identity diffusion Marcia's term for the state adolescents are in when they have not yet experienced an identity crisis or made any commitments.

identity foreclosure Marcia's term for the state adolescents are in when they have made a commitment but have not experienced an identity crisis.

identity moratorium Marcia's term for the state of adolescents who are in the midst of an identity crisis but who have not made a clear commitment to an identity.

identity achievement Marcia's term for an adolescent who has undergone an identity crisis and made a commitment.

FIGURE 5

EXPLORING YOUR IDENTITY. If you checked diffused or foreclosed for any areas, take some time to think about what you need to do to move into a moratorium identity status in those areas.

Think deeply about your exploration and commitment in the areas listed here. For each area, check whether your identity status is diffused, foreclosed, moratorium, or achieved.

Identity Component	Identity Status			
	Diffused	Foreclosed	Moratorium	Achieved
Vocational (career)				
Political				
Religious				
Relationships				
Achievement				
Sexual				
Gender				
Ethnic/Cultural				
Interests				
Personality				
Physical				

capture this ongoing identity examination are (1) exploration in depth, which involves "gathering information and talking to others about current commitments"; and (2) identification with commitment, which consists of "the degree of security and certainty one experiences with regard to current commitments" (Luyckx, 2006, p. i).

For example, consider a first-year college student who makes a commitment to become a lawyer. Exploring this commitment in depth might include finding out as much as possible about what is involved in being a lawyer, such as educational requirements, the work conducted by lawyers in different areas, what types of college classes might be beneficial for this career, and so on. It might also include talking with several lawyers about their profession. As a result of this in-depth exploration, the college student may become more confident that being a lawyer is the career that best suits her, which reflects identification with commitment (Goossens, 2006). As she goes through the remainder of her college years, she will continue to evaluate the commitment she has made to becoming a lawyer and may change her commitment as she continues to gather new information and reflect on the life path she wants to take. In a recent study, planfulness was a consistent predictor of engagement in identity exploration and commitment (Luyckx & Robitschek, 2014).

One way that researchers are examining identity changes in depth is to use a *narrative approach*. This involves asking individuals to tell their life stories and evaluate the extent to which their stories are meaningful and integrated (Habermas & Kober, 2015; McAdams, 2012; McAdams & McLean, 2013; McAdams & Zapata-Gietl, 2015; McLean & Pasupathi, 2010; Pasupathi, 2015; Singer & Kasmark, 2015; Syed, 2013). The term *narrative identity* "refers to the stories people construct and tell about themselves to define who they are for themselves and others. Beginning in adolescence and young adulthood, our narrative identities are the stories we live by" (McAdams, Josselson, & Lieblich, 2006, p. 4). A recent study using the narrative identity approach revealed that from age 11 to 18, boys increasingly engaged in thinking about the meaningfulness of their lives, especially meaning related to the self as changing (McLean, Breen, & Fournier, 2010). In other research, relationship, autonomy, and mortality events were important contributors to searching for a meaningful identity in late adolescence and emerging adulthood (McLean & Pratt, 2006; McLean & Thorne, 2006). There also is increasing evidence that the effective management of difficult life events and circumstances contributes to the development of a meaningful identity in emerging adulthood (Pals, 2006).

A recent study used both identity status and narrative approaches to examine college students' identity domains. In both approaches, the interpersonal domain was most frequently described (McLean & others, 2015). In the interpersonal domain, dating and friendships were frequently mentioned, although there was no mention of gender roles. In the narrative domain, family stories were common.

DEVELOPMENTAL CHANGES IN IDENTITY

During early adolescence, most youth are primarily in the identity statuses of *diffusion*, *foreclosure*, or *moratorium*. According to Marcia (1987, 1996), at least three aspects of the young adolescent's development are important to identity formation. Young adolescents must be confident that they have parental support, must have an established sense of industry (positive orientation toward work), and must be able to take a self-reflective stance toward the future.

How does identity change in emerging adulthood?
© lev dolgachov/age fotostock RF

A recent study found that as individuals aged from early adolescence to emerging adulthood, they increasingly pursued in-depth exploration of their identity (Klimstra & others, 2010). Also, a study of 1,200 Dutch 12- to 20-year-olds revealed that the majority did not often experience identity conflicts and that their identity development proceeded more smoothly than is commonly thought (Meeus & others, 2010). In this study, though, approximately one in eight adolescents struggled with identity conflicts throughout adolescence. And in a recent study, the number of individuals who were identity achieved was higher in the late teens than early teens (Meeus & others, 2012). In this study, girls had more advanced identity trajectories than did boys.

Researchers have developed a consensus that many of the key changes in identity are most likely to take place in emerging adulthood, the period from about 18 to 25 years of age, not in adolescence (Arnett, 2015; Kroger, 2012, 2015; Syed, 2013). For example, Alan Waterman (1985, 1992) has found that from the years preceding high school through the last few years of college, the number of individuals who are identity achieved increases, whereas the number of individuals who are identity diffused decreases. Many young adolescents are identity diffused. College upperclassmen are more likely than high school students or college freshmen to be identity achieved.

Why might college produce some key changes in identity? Increased complexity in the reasoning skills of college students combined with a wide range of new experiences that highlight contrasts between home and college and between themselves and others stimulate them to reach a higher level of integrating various dimensions of their identity (Phinney, 2008). College contexts serve as a virtual "laboratory" for identity development through such experiences as diverse coursework and exposure to peers from diverse backgrounds. Also, one of emerging adulthood's key themes is not having many social commitments, which gives individuals considerable independence in developing a life path (Arnett, 2014; Arnett & Fischel, 2013).

James Coté (2006, 2009, 2015) argues that, because of this freedom, developing a positive identity in emerging adulthood requires considerable self-discipline and planning. Without this self-discipline and planning, emerging adults are likely to drift and not follow any particular direction. Coté also stresses that emerging adults who obtain a higher education are more likely to be on a positive identity path. Those who don't obtain a higher education, he says, tend to experience frequent job changes, not because they are searching for an identity but rather because they are just trying to eke out a living in a society that rewards higher education.

A meta-analysis of 124 studies by Jane Kroger and her colleagues (2010) revealed that during adolescence and emerging adulthood, identity moratorium status rose steadily to age 19 and then declined; identity achievement rose across late adolescence and emerging adulthood; and foreclosure and diffusion statuses declined across the high school years but fluctuated during the late teens and emerging adulthood. The studies also found that a large portion of individuals were not identity achieved by the time they reached their twenties. This important finding—that so few older adolescents and emerging adults had reached an identity achieved status—suggests that mastering identity development by the end of adolescence is more elusive for most individuals than Erikson (1968) envisioned.

A study of more than 9,000 emerging adult students at 30 U.S. universities examined various identity statuses and their links to psychological adjustment (Schwartz & others, 2011).

developmental **connection**

Emerging Adulthood

Emerging adults have few social obligations, which allows them considerable autonomy in running their lives (Arnett, 2010, 2014). Connect to "Introduction."

The clusters of identity status that emerged included all four of Marcia's identity statuses (diffusion, foreclosure, moratorium, and achievement), although in some cases multiple variations of a given status were extracted that provided more specific dimensions. For example, two types of diffusion appeared: diffused diffusion (low commitment but high ruminative exploration and exploration in depth) and carefree diffusion (low commitment, low exploration, low synthesis, and high confusion). The diffused-status emerging adults had the lowest self-esteem, internal control, and psychological well-being. The carefree diffused cluster had the highest level of externalizing problems (antisocial, alienated) and health-compromising behaviors (dangerous drug use, for example) of all identity clusters. More males than females were categorized as carefree diffused. The achievement cluster was high on exploration and commitment, and the identity-achieved emerging adults had the highest scores on all of the positive aspects of psychological functioning (self-esteem, internal locus of control, psychological well-being, satisfaction with life, and self-realization, for example). A recent research review also concluded that adolescents who have a mature identity show high levels of adjustment and a positive personality profile (Meeus, 2011). For example, adolescents who are highly committed in their identity development are characterized by higher levels of conscientiousness and emotional stability (Meeus, 2011).

In the research review just described, identity was found to be more stable in adulthood than in adolescence (Meeus, 2011). However, resolution of identity during adolescence and emerging adulthood does not mean that identity will be stable through the remainder of life (Kroger, 2015; McAdams & Zapata-Gietl, 2015). Many individuals who develop positive identities follow what are called "MAMA" cycles; that is, their identity status changes from *moratorium* to *achievement* to *moratorium* to *achievement* (Marcia, 1994). These cycles may be repeated throughout life (Francis, Fraser, & Marcia, 1989). Marcia (2002) points out that the first identity is just that—it is not, and should not be expected to be, the final product.

Researchers have shown that identity consolidation—the process of refining and enhancing the identity choices that are made in emerging adulthood—continues well into early adulthood and possibly the early part of middle adulthood (Kroger, 2007, 2012, 2015). One research study found that women and men continued to show identity development from 27 through 36 years of age, with the main changes in the direction of greater commitment (Pulkkinen & Kokko, 2000). In this study, adults more often moved into achieved and foreclosed identities than into moratorium or diffused identities. Further, as individuals move from early to middle adulthood, they become more certain about their identity. For example, a longitudinal study of Smith College women found that identity certainty increased from the thirties through the fifties (Stewart, Ostrove, & Helson, 2001).

IDENTITY AND SOCIAL CONTEXTS

Social contexts influence an adolescent's identity development (Azmitia, 2015; Cooper, Gonzales, & Wilson, 2015). Questions we will explore in this regard are: Do family and peer relationships influence identity development? How are culture and ethnicity linked to identity development? Is the identity development of females and males different?

Family Influences on Identity Parents are important figures in the adolescent's development of identity (Cooper, 2011). For example, one study found that poor communication between mothers and adolescents, as well as persistent conflicts with friends, was linked to less positive identity development (Reis & Youniss, 2004). Catherine Cooper and her colleagues (Cooper, 2011; Cooper, Behrens, & Trinh, 2009; Cooper & Grotevant, 1989) have found that a family atmosphere that promotes both individuality and connectedness is important in the adolescent's identity development:

- **Individuality** consists of two dimensions: self-assertion, which is the ability to have and communicate a point of view; and separateness, which is the use of communication patterns to express how one is different from others.
- **Connectedness** also consists of two dimensions: mutuality, which involves sensitivity to and respect for others' views; and permeability, which involves openness to others' views.

developmental **connection**

Attachment

Even while adolescents seek autonomy, attachment to parents is important; secure attachment in adolescence is linked to a number of positive outcomes. Connect to "Families."

individuality An important element in adolescent identity development. It consists of two dimensions: self-assertion, the ability to have and communicate a point of view; and separateness, the use of communication patterns to express how one is different from others.

connectedness An important element in adolescent identity development. It consists of two dimensions: mutuality, which is sensitivity to and respect for others' views; and permeability, which is openness to others' views.

Increasing research interest also has focused on the role that attachment to parents might play in identity development. A meta-analysis found weak to moderate correlations between attachment to parents in adolescence and identity development (Arseth & others, 2009). In this meta-analysis, though, securely attached adolescents were far more likely to be identity achieved than their counterparts who were identity diffused or identity foreclosed. And a recent study found that attachment-avoidant adolescents were less likely to engage in identity exploration related to dating (Pittman & others, 2012).

Identity and Peer/Romantic Relationships Researchers have recently found that the capacity to explore one's identity during adolescence and emerging adulthood is linked to the quality of friendships and romantic relationships (Galliher & Kerpelman, 2012). For example, a recent study found that an open, active exploration of identity when adolescents are comfortable with close friends contributes to the positive quality of the friendship (Doumen & others, 2012). In another study, friends were often a safe context for exploring identity-related experiences, providing a testing ground for how self-disclosing comments are viewed by others (McLean & Jennings, 2012).

In terms of links between identity and romantic relationships in adolescence and emerging adulthood, two individuals in a romantic relationship are both in the process of constructing their own identities and each person provides the other with a context for identity exploration (Pittman & others, 2011). The extent of their secure attachment to each other can influence how each partner constructs his or her own identity.

Cultural and Ethnic Identity Most research on identity development has historically been based on data obtained from adolescents and emerging adults in the United States and Canada, especially those who are non-Latino Whites (Schwartz & others, 2012). Many of these individuals have grown up in cultural contexts that value individual autonomy. However, in many countries around the world, adolescents and emerging adults have grown up influenced by a collectivist emphasis on fitting in with the group and connecting with others. The collectivist emphasis is especially prevalent in East Asian countries such as China. Researchers have found that self-oriented identity exploration may not be the main process through which identity achievement is attained in East Asian countries (Schwartz & others, 2012). Rather, East Asian adolescents and emerging adults may develop their identity through identification with and imitation of others in the cultural group (Bosma & Kunnen, 2001). This emphasis on interdependence in East Asian cultures includes an emphasis on adolescents and emerging adults accepting and embracing social and family roles (Berman & others, 2011). Thus, some patterns of identity development, such as the foreclosed status,

How might parents influence the adolescent's identity development?
© moodboard/Corbis RF

What role might romantic relationships play in identity development?
© Mike Kemp/Rubberball/Corbis RF

developmental **connection**

Culture and Ethnicity

Historical, economic, and social experiences produce differences between various ethnic groups and the majority non-Latino White group in the United States. Connect to "Culture."

What are some cross-cultural variations in identity in countries such as China and Italy?
(left): © Liu Dongyue/Xinhua Press/Corbis; *(right):* © Christian Goupi/age fotostock

One adolescent girl, 16-year-old Michelle Chinn, made these comments about ethnic identity development: "My parents do not understand that teenagers need to find out who they are, which means a lot of experimenting, a lot of mood swings, a lot of emotions and awkwardness. Like any teenager, I am facing an identity crisis. I am still trying to figure out whether I am a Chinese American or an American with Asian eyes." *What are some other aspects of developing an ethnic identity in adolescence?*
© Red Chopsticks/Getty Images RF

Many ethnic minority youth must bridge "multiple worlds" in constructing their identities.

—CATHERINE COOPER

Contemporary developmental psychologist, University of California–Santa Cruz

ethnic identity An enduring, basic aspect of the self that includes a sense of membership in an ethnic group and the attitudes and feelings related to that membership.

bicultural identity Identity formation that occurs when adolescents identify in some ways with their ethnic group and in other ways with the majority culture.

may be more adaptive in East Asian countries than in North American countries (Chen & Berman, 2012).

Identity development may take longer in some countries than in others (Schwartz & others, 2012). For example, research indicates that Italian youth may postpone significant identity exploration beyond adolescence and emerging adulthood, not settling on an identity until their mid- to late-twenties (Crocetti, Rabaglietti, & Sica, 2012). This delayed identity development is strongly influenced by many Italian youth living at home with their parents until 30 years of age and older.

Seth Schwartz and his colleagues (2012) recently pointed out that while everyone identifies with a particular "culture," many individuals in cultural majority groups take their cultural identity for granted. Thus, many adolescents and emerging adults in the cultural majority of non-Latino Whites in the United States likely don't spend much time thinking of themselves as "White American." However, for many adolescents and emerging adults who have grown up as a member of an ethnic minority group in the United States or emigrated from another country, cultural dimensions likely are an important aspect of their identity. Researchers recently have found that at both the high school and college level, Latino students were more likely than non-Latino White students to indicate that their cultural identity was an important dimension of their overall self-concept (Urdan, 2012).

Throughout the world, ethnic minority groups have struggled to maintain their ethnic identities while blending in with the dominant culture (Erikson, 1968). **Ethnic identity** is an enduring aspect of the self that includes a sense of membership in an ethnic group, along with the attitudes and feelings related to that membership (Phinney, 2006; Vedder & Phinney, 2014). Thus, for adolescents from ethnic minority groups, the process of identity formation has an added dimension: the choice between two or more sources of identification—their own ethnic group and the mainstream, or dominant, culture (Benet-Martinez & Hong, 2014; Berry & Sam, 2014). Many adolescents resolve this choice by developing a **bicultural identity.** That is, they identify in some ways with their ethnic group and in other ways with the majority culture (Cooper, 2011; Cooper, Gonzales, & Wilson, 2015). A study of Mexican American and Asian American college students found that they identified both with the American mainstream culture and with their culture of origin (Devos, 2006).

A recent study explored bicultural identity in 14- to 21-year-olds (Marks, Patton, & Garcia Coll, 2011). Younger bicultural adolescents primarily responded to the label "White" with an inhibited response, suggesting hesitation in determining whether the label was "like me" or "not like me."

With their advancing cognitive skills of abstract thinking and self-reflection, adolescents (especially older adolescents) increasingly consider the meaning of their ethnicity and also have more ethnic-related experiences (O'Hara & others, 2012; Syed, 2013). Because adolescents are more mobile and independent from their parents, they are more likely to experience ethnic stereotyping and discrimination as they interact with diverse individuals in school contexts and other public settings (Potochnick, Perreira, & Fuligni, 2012). Researchers have found that many ethnic minority groups experience stereotyping and discrimination, including African American, Latino, and Asian American adolescents (Hughes, Way, & Rivas-Drake, 2011). Further, African American and Latino adolescents living in impoverished conditions may not go to college even if they have the academic skills to succeed in college, which may preclude identity pursuits that are stimulated by a college education and experiences (Oyserman & Destin, 2010). In some cases, some ethnic minority adolescents may need to go to work to help their parents meet their family's expenses, which also may make their pursuit of a college education more difficult (Schwartz & others, 2012).

Time is another aspect of the context that influences ethnic identity. The indicators of identity often differ for each succeeding generation of immigrants (Phinney, 2006; Phinney & Baldelomar, 2011; Phinney & Vedder, 2013). The degree to which first-generation immigrants begin to feel "American" appears to be related to whether or not they learn English, develop social networks beyond their ethnic group, and become culturally competent in their new country. For second-generation immigrants, ethnic identity is likely to be linked to retention of their ethnic language and social networks. In the third and later generations, the issues become more complex. Broad social factors may affect the extent to which members of this generation retain their ethnic identities. For example, media images may either discourage or encourage members of an ethnic group to identify with their group or retain parts of its culture. Discrimination may force people to see themselves as cut off from the majority group and encourage them to seek the support of their own ethnic culture (Marks & others, 2015).

As indicated in the following studies, researchers are also increasingly finding that a positive ethnic identity is related to positive outcomes for ethnic minority adolescents:

- Asian American adolescents' ethnic identity was associated with high self-esteem, positive relationships, academic motivation, and lower levels of depression over time (Kiang, Witkow, & Champagne, 2013).
- Having a positive ethnic identity helped to buffer some of the negative effects of discrimination experienced by Mexican American adolescents (Umana-Taylor & others, 2012).
- Navajo adolescents' positive ethnic heritage was linked to higher self-esteem, school connectedness, and social functioning (Jones & Galliher, 2007).
- Exploration was an important aspect of establishing a secure sense of one's ethnic identity, which in turn was linked to a positive attitude toward one's own group and other groups (Whitehead & others, 2009).
- Cultural socialization (measured by items such as, "How often have your parents said it was important to follow the traditions of your racial or ethnic group?") was linked to higher self-esteem through a pathway of ethnic centrality (assessed by items such as the importance of ethnicity in "how I see myself") in Latino college students (Rivas-Drake, 2011).
- Ethnic identity was linked to adjustment in adolescents primarily by fostering a positive sense of meaning (Kiang & Fuligni, 2010). In this study, Asian American adolescents reported engaging in a search for meaning in life more than did non-Latino White and Latino adolescents.

The Contexts of Ethnic Identity Development The contexts in which ethnic minority youth live influence their identity development (Cooper, Gonzales, & Wilson, 2015; Murry & others, 2015; Spencer, Swanson, & Harpalani, 2015). In the United States, many ethnic minority youth live in low-SES urban settings where there is little support for developing a positive identity. Many of these youth live in pockets of poverty; are exposed to drugs, gangs, and criminal activities; and interact with youth and adults who have dropped out of school or are unemployed. In such settings, supportive organizations and programs for youth can make an important contribution to their identity development.

Might there be aspects of the social contexts in which adolescents live that increase the likelihood they will develop a positive ethnic identity? One study analyzed 60 youth organizations that served 24,000 adolescents over a period of five years and found that these organizations were especially good at building a sense of ethnic pride in inner-city youth (Heath & McLaughlin, 1993). Many inner-city youth have too much time on their hands, too little to do, and too few places to go. Organizations that nurture youth and respond positively to their needs and interests can enhance their identity development. And organizations that perceive youth as capable, worthy, and eager to have a healthy and productive life contribute in positive ways to the identity development of ethnic minority youth.

Ethnic Identity in Emerging Adulthood Jean Phinney (2006) described how ethnic identity may change in emerging adulthood, especially highlighting how certain experiences may shorten or lengthen the duration of emerging adulthood among ethnic minority individuals. For ethnic minority individuals who have to take on family responsibilities and do not go to college, identity commitments may occur earlier. By contrast, especially for ethnic minority individuals who go to college, identity formation may take longer because of the complexity of exploring and understanding a bicultural identity. The cognitive challenges of higher education likely stimulate ethnic minority individuals to reflect on their identity and examine changes in the way they want to identify themselves. This increased reflection may focus on integrating parts of one's ethnic minority culture and the mainstream non-Latino White culture. For example, some emerging adults have to come to grips with resolving a conflict between family loyalty and interdependence

How do social contexts influence adolescents' ethnic identity?
© Patrick Sheandell/Photo Alto RF

emphasized in their ethnic minority culture and the values of independence and self-assertion emphasized by the mainstream non-Latino White culture (Arnett, 2014).

Moin Syed and Margarita Azmitia (Azmitia, 2015; Syed, 2013; Syed & Azmitia, 2008, 2009) have recently examined ethnic identity in emerging adulthood. In one study, they found that ethnic identity exploration and commitment increased from the beginning to the end of college (Syed & Azmitia, 2009). Exploration especially began to increase in the second year of college and continued to increase into the senior year. In another study, Syed and Azmitia (2008) found that the narrative stories told by emerging adults who held identity-moratorium and identity-achieved status involved more personally meaningful experiences that linked to their sense of identity and self-integration. Identity-achieved emerging adults told about more experiences involving prejudice and cultural connections than did their counterparts in an unexamined identity status.

Gender and Identity   Girls and women are more likely to report having a more advanced level of identity formation (moratorium or achievement statuses) than are boys and men (Galliher & Kerpelman, 2012). Further, girls and women are more likely to have more elaborate self-representations in their identity narratives (Fivush & others, 2003; Fivush & Zaman, 2015). And a recent study revealed that female adolescents were more likely to engage in identity exploration related to dating (Pittman & others, 2012).

Erikson's (1968) classic presentation of identity development reflected the traditional division of labor between the sexes that was common at the time. Erikson wrote that males were mainly oriented toward career and ideological commitments, whereas females were mainly oriented toward marriage and childbearing. In the 1960s and 1970s, researchers found support for this assertion of gender differences in identity. For example, they found that vocational concerns were more central to male identity, whereas affiliative concerns were more central to female identity (LaVoie, 1976). In the last several decades, however, as females have developed stronger vocational interests, these gender differences have begun to disappear (Hyde & Else-Quest, 2013; Sharp & others, 2007).

Recent research on emerging adults indicated that the lowest level of intimacy in short-term friendships was reported by males who were identity foreclosed and females who were identity achieved (Johnson, 2012). In this research, the highest levels of intimacy were reported by males who were in an identity moratorium and females who were identity achieved and in longer-term friendships.

IDENTITY AND INTIMACY

Erikson (1968) argued that intimacy should develop after individuals are well on their way to establishing a stable and successful identity. **Intimacy versus isolation** is Erikson's sixth developmental stage, which individuals experience during early adulthood. At this time, individuals face the task of forming intimate relationships with others. Erikson describes intimacy as finding oneself, yet merging oneself with another. If young adults form healthy friendships and an intimate relationship with another individual, intimacy will be achieved; if not, isolation will result.

In one study of unmarried college students 18 to 23 years of age, a strong sense of self, expressed through identity achievement and an instrumental orientation, was an important factor in forming intimate connections, for both males and females (Madison & Foster-Clark, 1996). However, insecurity and a defensive posture in relationships were expressed differently in males' and females' relationships, with males displaying greater superficiality and females more dependency. Another study also found that a higher level of intimacy was linked to a stronger identity for both male and female college students, although the intimacy scores of the college females were higher than for the males (Montgomery, 2005). A recent study confirmed Erikson's theory that identity development in adolescence is a precursor to intimacy in romantic relationships during emerging adulthood (Beyers & Seiffge-Krenke, 2011). And a meta-analysis revealed a positive link between identity development and intimacy, with the connection being stronger for men than for women (Arseth & others, 2009).

What characterizes ethnic identity development in emerging adulthood?
© Mark Edward Atkinson/Getty Images RF

What are some gender differences in identity development?
© Donna Day/Imagestate RF

developmental **connection**

Gender

Debate continues about gender similarities and differences in adolescents and possible reasons for the differences. Connect to "Gender."

intimacy versus isolation Erikson's sixth developmental stage, which individuals experience during early adulthood. At this time, individuals face the developmental task of forming intimate relationships with others.

Review Connect Reflect

LG2 Explain the many facets of identity development

Review
- What is Erikson's view of identity development?
- What are the four statuses of identity development?
- What developmental changes characterize identity?
- How do social contexts influence identity development?
- What is Erikson's view on identity and intimacy?

Connect
- Compare the influence of family and of ethnicity/culture on identity development.

Reflect *Your Own Personal Journey of Life*
- How would you describe your identity in adolescence? How has your identity changed since adolescence?

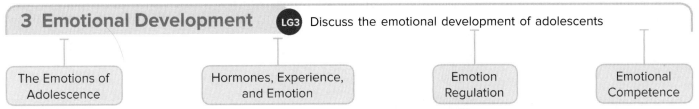

3 Emotional Development

LG3 Discuss the emotional development of adolescents

| The Emotions of Adolescence | Hormones, Experience, and Emotion | Emotion Regulation | Emotional Competence |

Defining emotion is difficult because it is not easy to tell when an adolescent is in an emotional state. For our purposes, we will define **emotion** as feeling, or affect, that occurs when a person is in a state or an interaction that is important to the individual, especially to his or her well-being. Emotion is characterized by behavior that reflects (expresses) the pleasantness or unpleasantness of the state the individual is in, or the transactions he or she is experiencing.

How are emotions linked to the two main concepts we have discussed so far in this chapter—the self and identity? Emotion is closely connected to self-esteem. Negative emotions, such as sadness, are associated with low self-esteem, whereas positive emotions, such as joy, are linked to high self-esteem. The emotional experiences involved in events such as emerging sexual experiences, dating and romantic encounters, and driving a car contribute to the adolescent's developing identity (Rosenblum & Lewis, 2003).

THE EMOTIONS OF ADOLESCENCE

Adolescence has long been described as a time of emotional turmoil (Hall, 1904). In its extreme form, this view is too stereotypical because adolescents are not constantly in a state of "storm and stress." Nonetheless, early adolescence is a time when emotional highs and lows occur more frequently (Rosenblum & Lewis, 2003). Young adolescents can be on top of the world one moment and down in the dumps the next. In many instances, the intensity of their emotions seems out of proportion to the events that elicit them (Steinberg, 2011). Young adolescents may sulk a lot, not knowing how to express their feelings adequately. With little or no provocation, they may blow up at their parents or siblings, projecting their unpleasant feelings onto another person.

In research conducted with families, adolescents reported more extreme emotions and more fleeting emotions than did their parents (Larson & Richards, 1994). For example, adolescents were five times more likely than their parents to report being "very happy" and three times more likely to report being "very sad." These findings lend support to the perception that adolescents are moody and changeable (Rosenblum & Lewis, 2003). Researchers have also found that from the fifth through the ninth grades, both boys and girls experience a 50 percent decrease in the state of being "very happy" (Larson & Lampman-Petraitis, 1989). In this study, adolescents were more likely than preadolescents to report mildly negative mood states.

What characterizes adolescents' emotions?
© C. Devan/Corbis

emotion Feeling, or affect, that occurs when a person is in a state or an interaction that is important to the individual, especially to his or her well-being.

It is important for adults to recognize that moodiness is a *normal* aspect of early adolescence and that most adolescents eventually emerge from these moody times and become competent adults. Nonetheless, for some adolescents, intensely negative emotions can reflect serious problems. For example, rates of depressed moods become more frequent in girls during adolescence (Nolen-Hoeksema, 2011). We will have much more to say about adolescent depression later in this edition.

Gender expectations for expressing emotions can differ across cultures. In one study, emerging adult U.S. males expressed less positive and negative emotions than their female counterparts did (Brody, 1997). In this study, there was no difference in the emotional expression of Asian American or Asian male and female emerging adults, except that Asian males expressed more shame than Asian females. In the United States, males are more likely to suppress emotions than are females (Flynn, Hollenstein, & Mackey, 2010).

HORMONES, EXPERIENCE, AND EMOTIONS

Significant hormonal changes occur during puberty, and the emotional fluctuations of early adolescence may be related to variability in hormone levels during this period. As adolescents move into adulthood, their moods become less extreme, perhaps because of their adaptation to hormone levels over time or to maturation of the prefrontal cortex (Casey, 2015; Rosenblum & Lewis, 2003).

Researchers have discovered that pubertal change is associated with an increase in negative emotions (Dorn & others, 2006). However, most researchers conclude that such hormonal influences are small and are usually associated with other factors, such as stress, eating patterns, sexual activity, and social relationships (Susman & Dorn, 2013). Indeed, environmental experiences may contribute more to the emotions of adolescence than do hormonal changes. In one study, social factors accounted for two to four times as much variance as hormonal factors in young adolescent girls' depression and anger (Brooks-Gunn & Warren, 1989).

Among the stressful experiences that might contribute to changes in emotion during adolescence are the transition to middle or junior high school and the onset of sexual experiences and romantic relationships (Furman & Rose, 2015). In one study, real and fantasized sexual/romantic relationships were responsible for more than one-third of ninth- to twelfth-graders' strong emotions (Wilson-Shockley, 1995).

In sum, both hormonal changes and environmental experiences are involved in the changing emotions of adolescence. So is the young person's ability to manage emotions, as we explore next.

What characterizes emotion regulation in adolescence?
© funstock/Getty Images RF

EMOTION REGULATION

The ability to effectively manage and control one's emotions is a key dimension of positive outcomes in adolescent development (Lantrip & others, 2015; Raver & others, 2013; Sheppes & Gross, 2015). Emotion regulation consists of effectively managing arousal in order to adapt and reach a goal (Lewis, 2013; Thompson, 2015). Arousal involves a state of alertness or activation, which can reach levels that are too high for effective functioning in adolescence. Anger, for example, often requires regulation.

With increasing age, adolescents are more likely to improve their use of cognitive strategies for regulating emotion, to modulate their emotional arousal, to become more adept at managing situations to minimize negative emotion, and to choose effective ways to cope with stress. Of course, there are wide variations in individuals' ability to modulate their emotions (Casey, 2015; Thompson, 2015). Indeed, a prominent feature of adolescents with problems is that they often have difficulty managing their emotions.

A recent study found that young adolescents in Taiwan who used a cognitive reappraisal strategy rather than a suppression strategy were more likely to have a positive self-concept, which in turn was associated with having fewer internalizing problems such as depression (Hsieh & Stright, 2012). Cognitive reappraisal is a coping strategy that actively involves changing how one thinks about a situation to regulate the emotional impact. Another recent study of young adolescents revealed that depression often preceded the use of suppression (Larsen & others, 2013). Suppressing or avoiding the emotional circumstance typically does not lead to an adaptive, positive outcome. Later in this edition, you will read more extensively about different coping strategies for dealing with emotional difficulties and problems, including depression.

developmental **connection**

Problems

In many circumstances, a problem-focused coping strategy is better than an emotion-focused strategy. Connect to "Problems in Adolescence and Emerging Adulthood."

EMOTIONAL COMPETENCE

In adolescence, individuals are more likely to become aware of their emotional cycles, such as feeling guilty about being angry. This new awareness may improve their ability to cope with their emotions. Adolescents also become more skillful at presenting their emotions to others. For example, they become aware of the importance of covering up their anger in social relationships. And they are more likely to understand the importance of being able to communicate their emotions constructively to improve the quality of a relationship (Saarni & others, 2006).

Although the increased cognitive abilities and awareness of adolescents prepare them to cope more effectively with stress and emotional fluctuations, as we indicated earlier in our discussion of emotion regulation, many adolescents do not effectively manage their emotions (Steinberg, 2014, 2015a, b). As a result, they may become prone to depression, anger, and poor emotion regulation, which in turn can trigger problems such as academic difficulties, drug abuse, juvenile delinquency, or eating disorders. For example, one study illustrated the importance of emotion regulation and mood in academic success (Gumora & Arsenio, 2002). Even when their level of cognitive ability was controlled for, young adolescents who said they experienced more negative emotion regarding academic routines had lower grade-point averages.

The emotional competencies that are important for adolescents to develop include the following (Saarni, 1999):

What are some characteristics of emotional competence in adolescence and emerging adulthood?
© Izabela Habur/Getty Images RF

developmental **connection**

Intelligence

Emotional intelligence includes managing one's emotions effectively. Connect to "The Brain and Cognitive Development."

Emotional Competence	**Example**
· Being aware that the expression of emotions plays a major role in relationships.	· Knowing that expressing anger toward a friend on a regular basis can harm the friendship.
· Adaptively coping with negative emotions by using self-regulatory strategies that reduce the intensity and duration of such emotional states.	· Reducing anger by walking away from a negative situation and engaging in an activity that takes one's mind off it.
· Understanding that inner emotional states do not have to correspond to outer expressions. (As adolescents become more mature, they begin to understand how their emotionally expressive behavior may impact others and to take that understanding into account in the way they present themselves.)	· Recognizing that one can feel anger yet manage one's emotional expression so that it appears neutral.
· Being aware of one's emotional states without becoming overwhelmed by them.	· Differentiating between sadness and anxiety, and focusing on coping rather than being overwhelmed by these feelings.
· Being able to discern others' emotions.	· Perceiving that another person is sad rather than afraid.

Review *Connect* Reflect

LG3 Discuss the emotional development of adolescents

Review

- How would you characterize adolescents' emotions?
- How extensively are adolescents' emotions linked to their hormones and experiences?
- What characterizes emotion regulation in adolescence?
- What does it take to be emotionally competent in adolescence?

Connect

- Connect the development of emotional competence to the development of self-esteem, as described in the preceding section of this chapter.

Reflect *Your Own Personal Journey of Life*

- How would you describe your emotions in early adolescence? Did you experience more extremes of emotion when you were in middle or junior high school than you do today? Have you learned how to control your emotions better now than you did in early adolescence? Explain.

4 Personality Development

LG4 Characterize the personality development of adolescents

Personality   Temperament

So far in this chapter, we have discussed the development of the self, identity, and emotion in adolescence and emerging adulthood. In this section, we explore the nature of personality and temperament in adolescence and emerging adulthood.

PERSONALITY

How can personality be defined? **Personality** refers to the enduring personal characteristics of individuals. How is personality linked to the self, identity, and emotion? Personality is usually viewed as encompassing the self and identity. The description of an individual's personality traits sometimes involves emotions. For example, an adolescent may be described in terms of emotional stability/instability and positive/negative affectivity. How are such traits manifested in adolescence? Which traits are most important?

personality The enduring personal characteristics of individuals.

Big Five factors of personality Five core traits of personality: openness to experience, conscientiousness, extraversion, agreeableness, and neuroticism (emotional stability).

Big Five Factors of Personality   One trait theory that has received considerable attention involves the **Big Five factors of personality**—the view that personality is made up of *o*penness to experience, *c*onscientiousness, *e*xtraversion, *a*greeableness, and *n*euroticism (see Figure 6). (Notice that if you create an acronym from these trait names, you will get the

FIGURE 6

THE BIG FIVE FACTORS OF PERSONALITY. Each of the broad super traits encompasses more narrow traits and characteristics. Use the acronym OCEAN to remember the Big Five personality factors (openness, conscientiousness, extraversion, agreeableness, neuroticism).

word *OCEAN.*) A number of research studies point toward these five factors as important dimensions of personality (Costa & McCrae, 1998, 2013; Costa & others, 2014; McCrae & Costa, 2006; McCrae, Gaines, & Wellington, 2013).

Evidence for the importance of the Big Five factors indicates that they are related to such important aspects of a person's life as health, intelligence and cognitive functioning, achievement and work, and relationships (English & Carstensen, 2014; Hill & others, 2014). The following research supports these links:

- *Openness to experience.* Individuals high on openness to experience are more likely to engage in identity exploration (Luyckx & others, 2014), to be tolerant (McCrae & Sutin, 2009), and to have superior cognitive functioning, achievement, and IQ across the life span (Briley, Domiteaux, & Tucker-Drob, 2014; Sharp & others, 2010).

- *Conscientiousness.* The major finding in the study of the Big Five factors in adolescence is the emergence of conscientiousness as a key predictor of adjustment and competence (Roberts & others, 2009). Individuals high in conscientious often do well in a variety of life domains. For example, they have better health and less stress (Gartland & others, 2014), achieve higher grade point averages in college (McAbee & Oswald, 2013), and engage in less substance abuse (Walton & Roberts, 2004). In one study, conscientiousness was linked to better interpersonal relationships among fifth- to eighth-graders: higher-quality friendships, greater acceptance by peers, and less victimization by peers (Jenson-Campbell & Malcolm, 2007). And in a study of emerging adults, conscientiousness was linked to fewer delays in studying (Klimstra & others, 2012). Further, a longitudinal study of more than 1,200 individuals across seven decades revealed that conscientious individuals lived longer from childhood through late adulthood (Martin, Friedman, & Schwartz, 2007).

- *Extraversion.* Individuals high in *extraversion* are more likely than others to engage in social activities (Emmons & Diener, 1986), have fewer sleep problems (Hintsanen & others, 2014), and have a more positive sense of well-being in the future (Soto, 2015).

- *Agreeableness.* People who are high in agreeableness are more likely to be generous and altruistic (Caprara & others, 2010), have more satisfying romantic relationships (Donnellan, Larsen-Rife, & Conger, 2005), view other people positively (Wood, Harms, & Vazire, 2010), and lie less about themselves in online dating profiles (Hall & others, 2010). One study found that adolescents who were high on agreeableness and conscientiousness engaged in fewer counterproductive workplace behaviors (absenteeism, substance abuse on the job, and theft, for example) (Le & others, 2014).

- *Neuroticism.* People high in neuroticism are more likely to feel negative emotion than positive emotion in daily life and to experiencing more lingering negative states (Widiger, 2009), have more health complaints (Carver & Connor-Smith, 2010), be more drug dependent (Valero & others, 2014), and have a lower sense of well-being 40 years later (Gale & others, 2013). One study of more than 2,000 college students found that being emotionally stable and extraverted were related to identity achievement (Lounsbury & others, 2007).

How do the Big Five factors change during adolescence? A recent large-scale cross-sectional study found that several of the Big Five factors show negative trends in early adolescence (Soto & others, 2011). In this study, young adolescents showed a decrease in conscientiousness, extraversion, and agreeableness. However, conscientiousness and agreeableness increased in late adolescence and the beginning of emerging adulthood.

Debate continues about whether the Big Five theory is the best way to conceptualize the personality traits of people (Veselka, Schermer, & Vernon, 2011). One analysis proposed a model of six traits—the Big Five plus an honesty-humility dimension (Lee & Ashton, 2008). And some cross-cultural researchers conclude that only three of the Big Five factors (extraversion, agreeableness, and conscientiousness) consistently portray people's personality traits in different cultures (De Raad & others, 2010).

An adolescent with a high level of conscientiousness organizes her daily schedule and plans how to use her time effectively. *What are some characteristics of conscientiousness? How is it linked to adolescents' competence?*
© Alejandro Rivera/Getty Images RF

Optimism   Another important personality characteristic is **optimism**, which involves having a positive outlook on the future and minimizing problems. Optimism is often referred to as a style of thinking.

optimism Involves having a positive outlook on the future and minimizing problems.

Somewhat surprisingly, little research has been conducted recently on optimism in children and adolescents. One recent study did find that from 5 to 10 years of age children increasingly understood that thinking positively improves emotions and that thinking negatively makes them worse (Bamford & Lagattuta, 2012). In *The Optimistic Child,* Martin Seligman (2007) described how parents, teachers, and coaches can instill optimism in children, which he argues helps to make them more resilient and less likely to develop depression.

In adolescence, one study found that having an optimistic style of thinking predicted a reduction in suicidal ideation for individuals who had experienced negative and potentially traumatic life events (Hirsch & others, 2009). Another study revealed that adolescents with an optimistic thinking style had a lower risk of developing depressive symptoms than their pessimistic counterparts (Patton & others, 2011). And in the study of more than 2,000 college students discussed earlier, the personality trait of optimism was more strongly linked to identity achievement than were any of the Big Five factors (Lounsbury & others, 2007).

Traits and Situations   Many psychologists argue that it is better to view personality not only in terms of traits but also in terms of contexts and situations (Steyer & others, 2015). They conclude that the trait approach ignores environmental factors and places too much emphasis on stability and lack of change. This criticism was first leveled by social cognitive theorist Walter Mischel (1968), who argued that personality varies according to the situation. Thus, adolescents who are in a library might behave quite differently from the way they would act at a party.

Today, most psychologists are interactionists, arguing that both traits and situations need to be taken into account in understanding personality (Engler, 2014). Let's again consider the situations of being in a library or at a party and consider the preferences of two adolescents: Jenna, who is an introvert, and Stacey, who is an extravert. Jenna, the introvert, is more likely to enjoy being in the library, whereas Stacey, the extravert, is more likely to have a good time at the party.

TEMPERAMENT

Although the study of personality has focused mainly on adults, the study of temperament has been limited primarily to infants and children (Bates, 2013; Chen & Schmidt, 2015; Kagan, 2013). However, both personality and temperament are important in understanding adolescent development. **Temperament** can be defined as an individual's behavioral style and characteristic way of responding. Many psychologists emphasize that temperament forms the foundation of personality. Through increasing capacities and interactions with the environment, temperament evolves or becomes elaborated across childhood and adolescence into a set of personality traits.

The close link between temperament and personality is supported by research that connects some of the Big Five personality factors to temperament categories (Shiner & DeYoung, 2013). For example, the temperament category of positive emotionality is related to the personality trait of extraversion, negative emotionality maps onto neuroticism (emotional instability), and effortful control is linked to conscientiousness (Putnam, Sanson, & Rothbart, 2002).

Temperament Categories   Just as with personality, researchers are interested in discovering what the key dimensions of temperament are (Chen & Schmidt, 2015; Rothbart, 2011). Psychiatrists Alexander Chess and Stella Thomas (Chess & Thomas, 1977; Thomas & Chess, 1991) followed a group of infants into adulthood and concluded that there are three basic types, or clusters, of temperament:

- An **easy child** is generally in a positive mood, quickly establishes regular routines, and adapts readily to new experiences.
- A **difficult child** reacts negatively to many situations and is slow to accept new experiences.
- A **slow-to-warm-up child** has a low activity level, is somewhat negative, and displays a low intensity of mood.

New classifications of temperament continue to be forged (Bates, 2012a, b; Rothbart, 2011). In a review of temperament research, Mary Rothbart and John Bates (1998) concluded that the best framework for classifying temperament involves a revision of Chess and Thomas'

temperament An individual's behavioral style and characteristic way of responding.

easy child A child who generally is in a positive mood, quickly establishes regular routines, and adapts easily to new experiences.

difficult child A child who reacts negatively to many situations and is slow to accept new experiences.

slow-to-warm-up child A child who has a low activity level, is somewhat negative, and displays a low intensity of mood.

What temperament categories have been used to describe adolescents?
© Paul/age fotostock

categories of easy, difficult, and slow to warm up. The general classification of temperament now focuses more on the following aspects:

- *Positive affect and approach.* This category is much like the personality trait of extra-version/introversion.
- *Negative affectivity.* This involves being easily distressed. Children with a temperament that involves negative affectivity may fret and cry often. Negative affectivity is closely related to the personality traits of introversion and neuroticism (emotional instability).
- *Effortful control (self-regulation).* This involves the ability to control one's emotions. Thus, adolescents who are high on effortful control show an ability to keep their arousal from getting too high and have strategies for soothing themselves. By contrast, adolescents who are low on effortful control often show an inability to control their arousal, and they become easily agitated and intensely emotional (Eisenberg & others, 2002). Earlier in the chapter, we described the importance of effortful control in academic persistence and educational attainment (Veronneau & others, 2014).

One study revealed that adolescents characterized by high positive affectivity, low negative affectivity, and high effortful control had lower levels of depressive symptoms (Verstraeten & others, 2009).

Developmental Connections and Contexts   How stable is temperament from childhood to adulthood? Do young adults show the same behavioral style and characteristic emotional responses that they did when they were infants or young children? For instance, activity level is an important dimension of temperament. Are children's activity levels linked to their personality in emerging and early adulthood? In one longitudinal study, children who were highly active at age 4 were likely to be very outgoing at age 23, a finding that reflects continuity (Franz, 1996, p. 337). Yet, in other ways, temperament may change. From adolescence into early adulthood, most individuals show fewer mood swings, greater responsibility, and less risk-taking behavior, characteristics reflecting discontinuity of temperament (Caspi, 1998).

Is temperament in childhood linked to adjustment in adolescence and adulthood? Here is what is known based on the few longitudinal studies that have been conducted on this topic (Caspi, 1998). A longitudinal study using Chess and Thomas' categories found a link between temperament assessed at 1 year of age and adjustment at 17 years of age (Guerin & others, 2003). Those with easier temperaments as infants showed more optimal development across behavioral and intellectual domains in late adolescence. The individuals with easier temperaments experienced a family environment that was more stimulating and cohesive and had more positive relationships with their parents during adolescence than did their counterparts with more difficult temperaments. When the participants were characterized by a difficult temperament in combination with a family environment that was high in conflict, an increase in externalizing behavior problems (conduct problems, delinquency) occurred.

In regard to a link between temperament in childhood and adjustment in adulthood, in one longitudinal study children who had an easy temperament at 3 to 5 years of age were likely to be well adjusted as young adults (Chess & Thomas, 1977). In contrast, many children who had a difficult temperament at 3 to 5 years of age were not well adjusted as young adults. Other researchers have found that boys who have a difficult temperament in childhood are less likely than others to continue their formal education as adults; girls with a difficult temperament in childhood are more likely to experience marital conflict as adults (Wachs, 2000).

In sum, across a number of longitudinal studies, an easy temperament in childhood is linked with more optimal development and adjustment in adolescence and adulthood. When the contexts in which individuals live are problematic, such as a family environment high in conflict, the long-term outcomes of having a difficult temperament are exacerbated.

Inhibition is another temperament characteristic that has been studied extensively (Kagan, 2013). Researchers have found that individuals with an inhibited temperament in childhood are less likely to be assertive or to experience social support as adolescents and emerging adults, and more likely to delay entering a stable job track (Wachs, 2000).

Yet another aspect of temperament is emotionality and the ability to control one's emotions (Rothbart, 2011). In one longitudinal study, individuals who as 3-year-old children showed good control of their emotions and were resilient in the face of stress were likely to continue to handle their emotions effectively as adults (Block, 1993). In contrast, individuals who as 3-year-olds had low emotional control and were not very resilient were likely to show those same problems as young adults.

In sum, these studies reveal some continuity between certain aspects of temperament in childhood and adjustment in early adulthood (Shiner & DeYoung, 2013; Wachs & Kohnstamm, 2013). Keep in mind, however, that these connections between childhood temperament and adult adjustment are based on only a small number of studies; more research is needed to verify the links. Indeed, Theodore Wachs (1994, 2000) has proposed ways that the links between childhood temperament and adult personality might vary, depending on the intervening contexts an individual experiences (see Figure 7).

goodness of fit The match between an individual's temperament style and the environmental demands faced by the individual.

The match between an individual's temperament and the environmental demands the individual must cope with, called **goodness of fit,** can be important to an adolescent's

Initial Temperament Trait: Inhibition

	Child A	Child B
Intervening Context		
Caregivers	Caregivers (parents) who are sensitive and accepting, and let child set his or her own pace.	Caregivers who use inappropriate "low-level control" and attempt to force the child into new situations.
Physical Environment	Presence of "stimulus shelters" or "defensible spaces" that the children can retreat to when there is too much stimulation.	Child continually encounters noisy, chaotic environments that allow no escape from stimulation.
Peers	Peer groups with other inhibited children with common interests, so the child feels accepted.	Peer groups consist of athletic extraverts, so the child feels rejected.
Schools	School is "undermanned," so inhibited children are more likely to be tolerated and feel they can make a contribution.	School is "overmanned," so inhibited children are less likely to be tolerated and more likely to feel undervalued.
Personality Outcomes		
	As an adult, individual is closer to extraversion (outgoing, sociable) and is emotionally stable.	As an adult, individual is closer to introversion and has more emotional problems.

FIGURE 7

TEMPERAMENT IN CHILDHOOD, PERSONALITY IN ADULTHOOD, AND INTERVENING CONTEXTS. Varying experiences with caregivers, the physical environment, peers, and schools may modify links between temperament in childhood and personality in adulthood. The example given here is for inhibition.

adjustment (Rothbart, 2011). In general, the temperament characteristics of effortful control, manageability, and agreeableness reduce the effects of adverse environments, whereas negative emotionality increases their effects (Rothbart, 2011).

In this chapter, we examined many aspects of the self, identity, emotions, and personality. In our discussion of identity and emotion, we evaluated the role of gender, a topic that is discussed in more detail in another chapter of this edition.

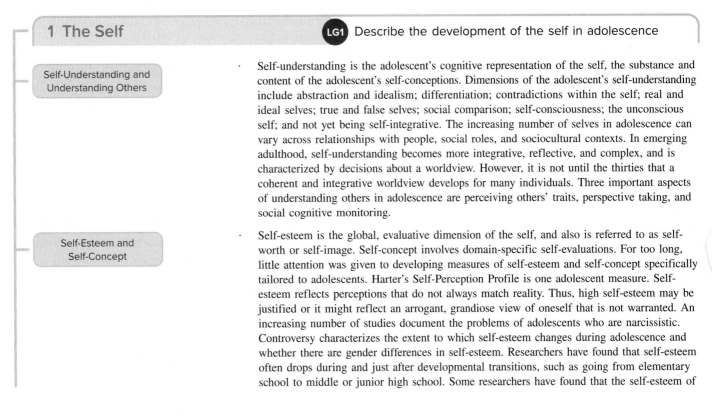

Review Connect Reflect

LG4 Characterize the personality development of adolescents

Review

- What are some key personality traits in adolescence? Is personality influenced by situations?
- What is temperament, and how is it linked to personality? What are some key temperament categories? What developmental connections and contexts characterize temperament?

Connect

- How might the Big Five factors of personality be linked to the concept of risk taking?

Reflect *Your Own Personal Journey of Life*

- Consider your own temperament. We described a number of different temperament categories. Which one best describes your temperament? Has your temperament changed as you have grown older, or is it about the same as it was when you were a child or an adolescent? If your temperament has changed, what factors contributed to the changes?

reach your **learning goals**

The Self, Identity, Emotion, and Personality

1 The Self

LG1 Describe the development of the self in adolescence

Self-Understanding and Understanding Others

- Self-understanding is the adolescent's cognitive representation of the self, the substance and content of the adolescent's self-conceptions. Dimensions of the adolescent's self-understanding include abstraction and idealism; differentiation; contradictions within the self; real and ideal selves; true and false selves; social comparison; self-consciousness; the unconscious self; and not yet being self-integrative. The increasing number of selves in adolescence can vary across relationships with people, social roles, and sociocultural contexts. In emerging adulthood, self-understanding becomes more integrative, reflective, and complex, and is characterized by decisions about a worldview. However, it is not until the thirties that a coherent and integrative worldview develops for many individuals. Three important aspects of understanding others in adolescence are perceiving others' traits, perspective taking, and social cognitive monitoring.

Self-Esteem and Self-Concept

- Self-esteem is the global, evaluative dimension of the self, and also is referred to as self-worth or self-image. Self-concept involves domain-specific self-evaluations. For too long, little attention was given to developing measures of self-esteem and self-concept specifically tailored to adolescents. Harter's Self-Perception Profile is one adolescent measure. Self-esteem reflects perceptions that do not always match reality. Thus, high self-esteem may be justified or it might reflect an arrogant, grandiose view of oneself that is not warranted. An increasing number of studies document the problems of adolescents who are narcissistic. Controversy characterizes the extent to which self-esteem changes during adolescence and whether there are gender differences in self-esteem. Researchers have found that self-esteem often drops during and just after developmental transitions, such as going from elementary school to middle or junior high school. Some researchers have found that the self-esteem of girls declines in adolescence, especially during early adolescence, although other researchers argue that this decline has been exaggerated and actually is only modest in nature. Self-esteem is only moderately linked to school success. Adolescents with high self-esteem have greater initiative, but this can produce positive or negative outcomes. Perceived physical appearance is an especially strong contributor to global self-esteem. Peer acceptance also is linked to global self-esteem in adolescence. In Coopersmith's study, children's self-esteem was associated with such parenting practices as showing affection and allowing children freedom within well-prescribed limits. Peer and friendship relations also are linked with self-esteem. Self-esteem is higher in elementary school than in middle or junior high school. For most adolescents, low self-esteem results in only temporary emotional discomfort. However, for others, especially when low self-esteem persists, it is linked with depression, delinquency, and even suicide. Four ways to increase adolescents' self-esteem are to (1) identify the causes of low self-esteem and determine which domains of competence are important to the adolescent, (2) provide emotional support and social approval, (3) help the adolescent to achieve success, and (4) improve the adolescent's coping skills.

Self-Regulation

- Self-regulation involves the ability to control one's behavior without having to rely on others' help. Self-regulation includes the self-generation and cognitive monitoring of thoughts, feelings, and behavior in order to reach a goal. Self-regulation plays a key role in many aspects of adolescent development, especially achievement and academic success. Various factors might enhance or inhibit an adolescent's ability to engage in self-regulation.

2 Identity

LG2 Explain the many facets of identity development

Erikson's Ideas on Identity

- Identity versus identity confusion is Erikson's fifth developmental stage, which individuals experience during adolescence. As adolescents are confronted with new roles, they enter a psychosocial moratorium. Role experimentation is a key ingredient of Erikson's view of identity development. In technological societies like that of the United States, the vocational role is especially important. Identity development is extraordinarily complex and takes place in bits and pieces. A current concern voiced by William Damon is the difficulty too many youth today encounter in developing a purposeful identity.

The Four Statuses of Identity

- Marcia proposed four identity statuses: diffused, foreclosed, moratorium, and achieved. A combination of crisis (exploration) and commitment yields each of the statuses. Some critics argue that Marcia's four identity statuses oversimplify identity development. Recently, emphasis has been given to expanding Marcia's concepts of exploration and commitment to focus more on in-depth exploration and ongoing evaluation of one's commitment.

Developmental Changes in Identity

- Some experts argue that the main identity changes take place in late adolescence rather than in early adolescence. College upperclassmen are more likely to be identity achieved than are freshmen or high school students, although many college students are still wrestling with ideological commitments. Individuals often follow MAMA ("moratorium–achievement–moratorium–achievement") cycles.

Identity and Social Contexts

- Parents are important figures in adolescents' identity development. Researchers have found that democratic parenting, individuality, connectedness, and enabling behaviors are linked with positive aspects of identity. Erikson was especially sensitive to the role of culture in identity development, underscoring the fact that throughout the world ethnic minority groups have struggled to maintain their cultural identities while blending into majority culture. Adolescence is often a special juncture in the identity development of ethnic minority individuals because for the first time they consciously confront their ethnic identity. Many ethnic minority adolescents have a bicultural identity. Ethnic identity increases with age during adolescence and emerging adulthood, and higher levels of ethnic identity are linked to more positive attitudes. The contexts in which ethnic minority youth live influence their identity development. The cognitive challenges of higher education likely stimulate ethnic minority individuals to reflect on their identity. Erikson noted that adolescent males have a stronger vocational identity, female adolescents a stronger social identity. However, researchers are finding that these gender differences are disappearing.

Identity and Intimacy

- Intimacy versus isolation is Erikson's sixth stage of development, which individuals experience during early adulthood. Erikson argued that an optimal sequence is to develop a positive identity before negotiating the intimacy versus isolation stage.

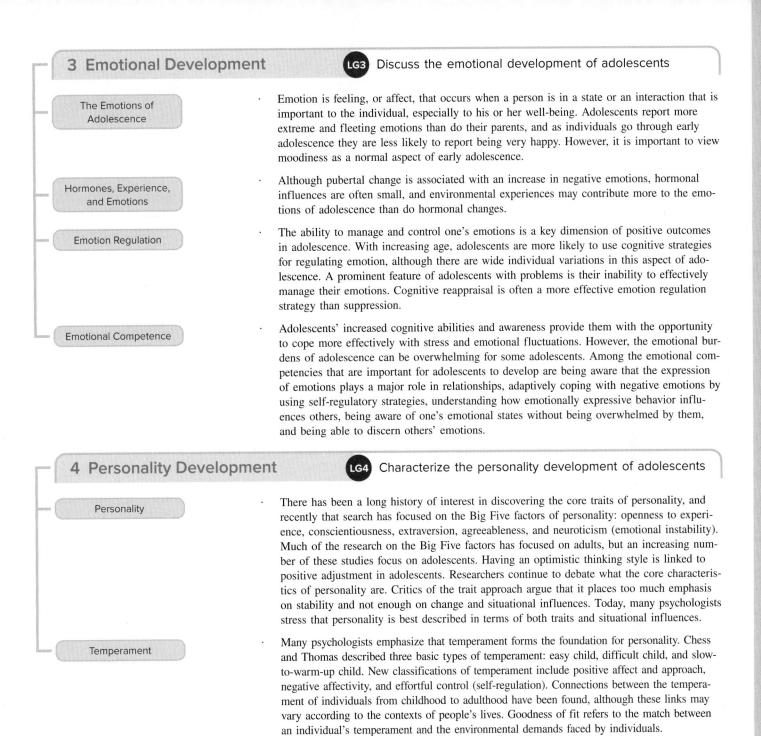

3 Emotional Development

LG3 Discuss the emotional development of adolescents

The Emotions of Adolescence

- Emotion is feeling, or affect, that occurs when a person is in a state or an interaction that is important to the individual, especially to his or her well-being. Adolescents report more extreme and fleeting emotions than do their parents, and as individuals go through early adolescence they are less likely to report being very happy. However, it is important to view moodiness as a normal aspect of early adolescence.

Hormones, Experience, and Emotions

- Although pubertal change is associated with an increase in negative emotions, hormonal influences are often small, and environmental experiences may contribute more to the emotions of adolescence than do hormonal changes.

Emotion Regulation

- The ability to manage and control one's emotions is a key dimension of positive outcomes in adolescence. With increasing age, adolescents are more likely to use cognitive strategies for regulating emotion, although there are wide individual variations in this aspect of adolescence. A prominent feature of adolescents with problems is their inability to effectively manage their emotions. Cognitive reappraisal is often a more effective emotion regulation strategy than suppression.

Emotional Competence

- Adolescents' increased cognitive abilities and awareness provide them with the opportunity to cope more effectively with stress and emotional fluctuations. However, the emotional burdens of adolescence can be overwhelming for some adolescents. Among the emotional competencies that are important for adolescents to develop are being aware that the expression of emotions plays a major role in relationships, adaptively coping with negative emotions by using self-regulatory strategies, understanding how emotionally expressive behavior influences others, being aware of one's emotional states without being overwhelmed by them, and being able to discern others' emotions.

4 Personality Development

LG4 Characterize the personality development of adolescents

Personality

- There has been a long history of interest in discovering the core traits of personality, and recently that search has focused on the Big Five factors of personality: openness to experience, conscientiousness, extraversion, agreeableness, and neuroticism (emotional instability). Much of the research on the Big Five factors has focused on adults, but an increasing number of these studies focus on adolescents. Having an optimistic thinking style is linked to positive adjustment in adolescents. Researchers continue to debate what the core characteristics of personality are. Critics of the trait approach argue that it places too much emphasis on stability and not enough on change and situational influences. Today, many psychologists stress that personality is best described in terms of both traits and situational influences.

Temperament

- Many psychologists emphasize that temperament forms the foundation for personality. Chess and Thomas described three basic types of temperament: easy child, difficult child, and slow-to-warm-up child. New classifications of temperament include positive affect and approach, negative affectivity, and effortful control (self-regulation). Connections between the temperament of individuals from childhood to adulthood have been found, although these links may vary according to the contexts of people's lives. Goodness of fit refers to the match between an individual's temperament and the environmental demands faced by individuals.

key **terms**

bicultural identity
Big Five factors of personality
commitment
connectedness
crisis
difficult child
easy child
emotion

ethnic identity
goodness of fit
identity
identity achievement
identity diffusion
identity foreclosure
identity moratorium
identity versus identity confusion

individuality
intimacy versus isolation
narcissism
optimism
personality
perspective taking
possible self
psychosocial moratorium

self
self-concept
self-esteem
self-regulation
self-understanding
slow-to-warm-up child
temperament

key people

Matthew Aalsma

Margarita Azmitia

Alexander Chess

Catherine Cooper

James Coté

William Damon

Nancy Eisenberg

Erik Erikson

Luc Goossens

Susan Harter

Jane Kroger

Gisela Labouvie-Vief

Daniel Lapsley

Koen Luyckx

James Marcia

Walter Mischel

Jean Phinney

Seth Schwartz

Moin Syed

Stella Thomas

Alan Waterman

resources for improving the lives of adolescents

The Construction of the Self
Susan Harter (2nd ed.) (2012)
New York: Guilford Press
> Leading self theorist and researcher Susan Harter provides an in-depth analysis of how the self develops in childhood and adolescence.

Oxford Handbook of Identity Development
Kate McLean and Moin Syed (Editors) (2015)
New York: Oxford University Press
> Leading experts provide contemporary and important reviews of research and theory on identity development in adolescence and emerging adulthood.

Gandhi's Truth
Erik Erikson (1969)
New York: Norton
> This Pulitzer Prize–winning book by Erik Erikson, who developed the concept of identity as a central aspect of adolescent development, analyzes the life of Mahatma Gandhi, the spiritual leader of India in the middle of the twentieth century.

Bridging Multiple Worlds
Catherine Cooper (2011)
New York: Oxford University Press
> This excellent book by a leading expert explores the development of cultural identities and describes ways to improve the educational opportunities of immigrant, minority, and low-income youth as they develop through adolescence and emerging adulthood.

The Structure of Temperament and Personality Traits
Rebecca Shiner and Colin DeYoung
In P. D. Zelazo (Ed.) (2013). *Oxford Handbook of Developmental Psychology*. New York: Oxford University Press.
> Leading experts describe recent research on how temperament and personality are structured and how they develop.

chapter 5

GENDER

chapter **outline**

"You know, it seems like girls are more emotionally sensitive than guys, especially teenage guys.** We don't know all the reasons, but we have some ideas about why this might be true. Once a girl reaches 12 or so and begins to mature physically, it seems as though nature is preparing her to be sensitive to others the way a mother might be to her baby, to feel what others feel so she can provide love and support to her children. Our culture tells boys different things. They are expected to be 'tough' and not get carried away with their feelings . . . In spite of this, don't think that girls cannot be assertive and boys cannot be sensitive. In fact, boys do feel emotions but many of them simply don't know how to express their feelings or fear that they will be teased." (Zager & Rubenstein, 2002, pp. 21–22)

—ZOE, AGE 13

"With all the feminist ideas in the country and the equality, I think guys sometimes get put on the spot. Guys might do something that I think or they think might not be wrong at all, but they still get shot down for it. If you're not nice to a girl, she thinks you don't care. But if you are nice, she thinks you are treating her too much like a lady. Girls don't understand guys, and guys don't understand girls very well." (Pollack, 1999, p. 164)

—TOBY, AGE 17

The comments of these two adolescents—one female, one male—reflect the confusion that many adolescents feel about how to act as a female or a male. Nowhere in adolescents' socioemotional development have more sweeping changes occurred in recent years than in the area of gender, and these changes have led to confusion about gender behavior.

preview

What exactly is meant by gender? **Gender** refers to the characteristics of people as males and females. Few aspects of adolescents' lives are more central to their identity and to their social relationships than gender. One aspect of gender bears special mention: a **gender role** is a set of expectations that prescribes how females and males should think, act, and feel. For example, should males be more assertive than females, and should females be more sensitive than males to others' feelings? Though individuals become aware of gender early in childhood, a new dimension is added to gender with the onset of puberty and the sexual maturation it brings. This chapter begins with a discussion of the biological as well as the social and cognitive influences on gender. We will distinguish gender stereotypes from actual differences between the sexes and examine the range of gender roles that adolescents can adopt. The chapter closes by exploring the developmental changes in gender that characterize adolescence.

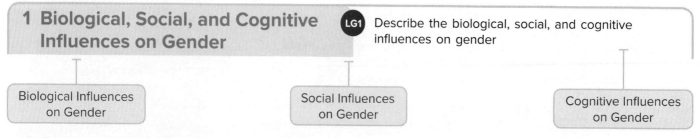

1 Biological, Social, and Cognitive Influences on Gender

LG1 Describe the biological, social, and cognitive influences on gender

Biological Influences on Gender

Social Influences on Gender

Cognitive Influences on Gender

gender The characteristics of people as males or females.

gender role A set of expectations that prescribes how females and males should think, act, and feel.

Gender development is influenced by biological, social, and cognitive factors. Our discussion of these influences focuses on questions like these: How strong is biology's influence on gender? How extensively does experience shape children's and adolescents' gender development? To what extent do cognitive factors influence gender development?

BIOLOGICAL INFLUENCES ON GENDER

Pubertal change is a biological influence on gendered behavior in adolescence (Hines, 2013, 2015). Both Freud and Erikson argued that the physical characteristics of males and females influence their behavior. And evolutionary psychologists emphasize the role of gender in the survival of the fittest.

Pubertal Change and Sexuality   Puberty intensifies the sexual aspects of adolescents' gender attitudes and behavior (Galambos, Berenbaum, & McHale, 2009). As their bodies flood with hormones, young adolescent boys and girls incorporate sexuality into their gender attitudes and behaviors, especially when they interact with the other sex or with a same-sex individual to whom they are sexually attracted. Thus, adolescent girls might behave in a sensitive, charming, and soft-spoken manner with a boy to whom they are sexually attracted, whereas boys might behave in an assertive, cocky, and forceful way when they are around girls, perceiving that such behaviors enhance their sexuality.

Few attempts have been made to relate puberty's sexual changes to gender behavior. Researchers have found, however, that sexual behavior is related to hormonal changes during puberty, at least for boys. For example, in one study, rising androgen levels were related to boys' increased sexual activity (Udry, 1990). For adolescent girls, androgen levels and sexual activity were associated, but girls' sexual activity was more strongly influenced by the type of friends they had than by their hormone levels. The same study also evaluated whether hormone increases in puberty were related to gender behaviors, such as being affectionate, charming, assertive, or cynical, but a significant link was not found.

In sum, pubertal changes may result in masculinity and femininity being renegotiated during adolescence, and much of the renegotiation likely involves sexuality. Toward the end of this chapter, we will return to the role that puberty plays in gender attitudes and behavior.

developmental **connection**

Biological Processes

Hormones are powerful chemical substances secreted by the endocrine glands and carried through the body by the bloodstream. Connect to "Puberty, Health, and Biological Foundations."

Freud and Erikson—Anatomy Is Destiny   Both Sigmund Freud and Erik Erikson argued that an individual's genitals influence his or her gender behavior and, therefore, that anatomy is destiny. One of Freud's basic assumptions was that human behavior is directly related to reproductive processes. From this assumption arose his belief that gender and sexual behavior are essentially unlearned and instinctual. Erikson (1968) extended Freud's argument, claiming that the psychological differences between males and females stem from their anatomical differences. Erikson argued that, because of genital structure, males are more intrusive and aggressive, females more inclusive and passive. Critics of the anatomy-is-destiny view stress that experience is not given enough credit. The critics say that females and males have more freedom to choose their gender roles than Freud and Erikson envisioned. In response to the critics, Erikson modified his view, saying that females in today's world are transcending their biological heritage and correcting society's overemphasis on male intrusiveness.

Evolutionary Psychology and Gender   Evolutionary psychology emphasizes that adaptation during the evolution of humans produced psychological differences between males and females (Buss, 2008, 2012, 2015; Buss & Penke, 2014). Evolutionary psychologists argue that primarily because of their differing roles in reproduction, males and females faced different pressures in primeval environments when the human species was evolving (Geary, 2010). In particular, because having multiple sexual liaisons improves the likelihood that males will pass on their genes, natural selection favored males who adopted short-term mating strategies. These males competed with other males to acquire more resources in order to access females. Therefore, say evolutionary psychologists, males evolved dispositions that favor violence, competition, and risk taking.

In contrast, according to evolutionary psychologists, females' contributions to the gene pool were improved by securing resources for their offspring, which was promoted by obtaining long-term mates who could support a family. As a consequence, natural selection favored females who devoted effort to parenting and chose mates who could provide their offspring

"It's a guy thing."
© Donald Reilly/The New Yorker Collection/
www.cartoonbank.com

developmental **connection**

Theories

Evolutionary psychology emphasizes the importance of adaptation, reproduction, and "survival of the fittest" in shaping behavior. Connect to "Puberty, Health, and Biological Foundations."

As the man beholds the woman,
As the woman sees the man,
Curiously they note each other,
As each other only can.

—**Bryan Procter**
English poet, 19th century

with resources and protection (Bjorklund, 2006). Females developed preferences for successful, ambitious men who could provide these resources (Geary, 2010).

This evolutionary unfolding, according to some evolutionary psychologists, explains key gender differences in sexual attitudes and sexual behavior (Shackelford & Goetz, 2012). For example, in one study, men said that ideally they would like to have more than 18 sexual partners in their lifetime, whereas women stated that ideally they would like to have only 4 or 5 (Buss & Schmitt, 1993). In another study, 75 percent of the men but none of the women approached by an attractive stranger of the opposite sex consented to a request for sex (Clark & Hatfield, 1989).

Such gender differences, says David Buss (2008, 2012, 2015), are exactly the type predicted by evolutionary psychology. Buss argues that men and women differ psychologically in those domains in which they have faced different adaptive problems during evolutionary history. In all other domains, predicts Buss, the sexes will be psychologically similar.

Critics of evolutionary psychology argue that its hypotheses are backed by speculations about prehistory, not evidence, and that in any event people are not locked into behavior that was adaptive in the evolutionary past. Critics also claim that the evolutionary view pays too much attention to biology and too little attention to environmental experiences in explaining gender differences (Hyde & Else-Quest, 2013; Matlin, 2012).

SOCIAL INFLUENCES ON GENDER

Many social scientists do not locate the cause of psychological gender differences in biological dispositions. Rather, they argue that these differences are due mainly to social experiences. Alice Eagly (2001, 2010, 2012, 2013) proposed **social role theory,** which states that gender differences mainly result from the contrasting roles of females and males. In most cultures around the world, females have less power and status than males have, and they control fewer resources (UNICEF, 2015). Compared with men, women perform more domestic work, spend fewer hours in paid employment, receive lower pay, and are more thinly represented in the highest levels of organizations. In Eagly's view, as women adapted to roles with less power and less status in society, they showed more cooperative, less dominant profiles than men. Thus, the social hierarchy and division of labor are important causes of gender differences in power, assertiveness, and nurturing behavior (Eagly & Antonakis, 2014; Eagly, Gartzia, & Carli, 2014).

Parental Influences   Parents, by action and example, influence their children's and adolescents' gender development (Hilliard & Liben, 2012; Leaper, 2015). During the transition from childhood to adolescence, parents give boys more independence than they allow for girls, and concern about girls' sexual vulnerability may cause parents to monitor their behavior more closely and ensure that they are chaperoned. Families with young adolescent daughters indicate that they experience more intense conflict about sex, choice of friends, and curfews than do families with young adolescent sons (Papini & Sebby, 1988).

Parents may also have different achievement expectations for their adolescent sons and daughters, especially in academic areas such as math and science (Leaper & Friedman, 2007;

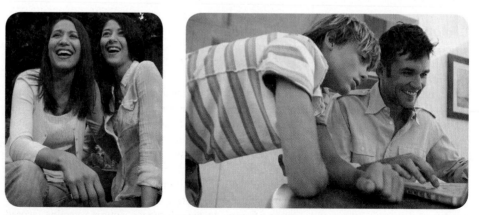

How do mothers and fathers interact differently with their daughters and sons?
(left): © Charles Gullung/Corbis; (right): © Dylan Ellis/Corbis RF

social role theory Theory stating that gender differences mainly result from the contrasting roles of females and males, with females having less power and status and controlling fewer resources than males.

Petersen & Hyde, 2014; Wigfield & others, 2015). For example, many parents believe that math is more important to their sons' futures than to their daughters'. These beliefs influence the value that adolescents place on math achievement (Eccles, 1987a, b). We will discuss gender and achievement in more detail later in this chapter.

Mothers and fathers often interact differently with their adolescents. Mothers are more involved with their children and adolescents than are fathers, although fathers increase the time they spend in parenting when they have sons and are less likely to become divorced when they have sons (Diekman & Schmidheiny, 2004). Mothers' interactions with their adolescents often center on caregiving and teaching activities, whereas fathers' interactions often involve leisure activities (Galambos & others, 2009).

Mothers and fathers also often interact differently with their sons and daughters. In a research review, the following conclusions were reached (Bronstein, 2006):

· *Mothers' socialization strategies.* In many cultures, mothers socialize their daughters to be more obedient and responsible than their sons. They also place more restrictions on daughters' autonomy.

· *Fathers' socialization strategies.* Fathers show more attention to sons than daughters, engage in more activities with sons, and put forth more effort to promote sons' intellectual development.

Thus, despite a trend toward more egalitarian gender roles in many aspects of society, many mothers and fathers showed marked differences in the way they interacted with their sons and daughters, and these differences persisted through adolescence (Bronstein, 2006; Galambos & others, 2009).

Recent research provided further support for the belief that some aspects of gender roles are still not egalitarian (Eagly, 2013; Mann, Legewie, & DiPrete, 2015). In one study, college students were interviewed about their future selves in the near future (1 year) and the distant future (10–15 years) (Brown & Diekman, 2010). Stronger gender patterns were found for distant than near selves. For distant selves, females were more likely to list "family" while men were more likely to list "career." In terms of "family" selves in the future, males were more likely to list their role as "economic provider" while females were more likely to list their role as "caregiver."

Social cognitive theory has been especially important in understanding social influences on gender (Bussey & Bandura, 1999; Leaper, 2015). The **social cognitive theory of gender** emphasizes that children's and adolescents' gender development is influenced by their observation and imitation of others' gender behavior, as well as by the rewards and punishments they experience for gender-appropriate and gender-inappropriate behavior. By observing parents and other adults, as well as peers, at home, at school, in the neighborhood, and in the media, adolescents are exposed to a myriad of models that display masculine and feminine behavior. And parents often use verbal reinforcement to teach their daughters to be feminine ("Karen, that dress you are wearing makes you look so beautiful") and their sons to be masculine ("Bobby, you were so aggressive in that game. Way to go!").

Siblings Siblings also play a role in gender socialization (Galambos & others, 2009). One study revealed that over a two-year time frame in early adolescence, younger siblings became more similar to their older siblings in terms of gender-role and leisure activity (McHale & others, 2001). For example, if a younger sibling had an older sibling who was masculine and engaged in masculine leisure activities, over the two years the younger sibling became more masculine and participated in more masculine leisure activities. In contrast, older siblings became less like their younger siblings over the two-year period.

Peers Parents provide the first models of gender behavior, but before long peers also are responding to and modeling masculine and feminine behavior (Leaper, 2013, 2015; Rubin, Bukowski, & Bowker, 2015). In middle and late childhood, children show a clear preference for being with and liking same-sex peers (Maccoby, 1998, 2002). After extensive observations of elementary school playgrounds, two researchers characterized the play settings as "gender school," pointing out that boys teach one another the required masculine behavior and reinforce it, and that girls also teach one another the required feminine behavior and reinforce it (Luria & Herzog, 1985).

developmental **connection**

Achievement

Parents' and teachers' expectations are important influences on adolescents' achievement. Connect to "Achievement, Work, and Careers."

developmental **connection**

Social Cognitive Theory

Social cognitive theory holds that behavior, environment, and person/cognitive factors are the key aspects of development. Connect to "Introduction."

social cognitive theory of gender Theory emphasizing that children's and adolescents' gender development occurs through observation and imitation of gender behavior, and through rewards and punishments they experience for gender-appropriate and gender-inappropriate behavior.

What role does gender play in adolescent peer relations?
© Corbis RF

Adolescents spend increasing amounts of time with peers (Brown & others, 2008; Furman & Rose, 2015). In adolescence, peer approval or disapproval is a powerful influence on gender attitudes and behavior (Prinstein & Dodge, 2008). Peer groups in adolescence are more likely to be a mix of boys and girls than they were in childhood. However, a recent study of 15- to 17-year-olds indicated that gender segregation characterizes some aspects of adolescents' social life (Mehta & Strough, 2010). In this study, 72 percent of peers said they were most likely to "hang out" with adolescents of the same gender as themselves.

Peers can socialize gender behavior partly by accepting or rejecting others on the basis of their gender-related attributes (Rubin, Bukowski, & Bowker, 2015). From adolescence through late adulthood, friendships mainly involve same-sex peers (Mehta & Strough, 2009, 2010).

Peers extensively reward and punish gender behavior (Leaper, 2013, 2015; Leaper & Bigler, 2011). For example, when children and adolescents behave in ways that the culture says are sex-appropriate, they tend to be rewarded by their peers. Those who engage in activities that are considered sex-inappropriate tend to be criticized or abandoned by their peers. It is generally more accepted for girls to act like boys than it is for boys to act like girls; thus, use of the term *tomboy* to describe masculine girls is often thought of as less derogatory than the term *sissy* to describe feminine boys (Pasterski, Golombok, & Hines, 2011).

Schools and Teachers Some observers have expressed concern that schools and teachers have biases against both boys and girls (Leaper & Brown, 2015). What evidence exists that the classroom setting is biased against boys? Here are some factors to consider (DeZolt & Hull, 2001):

- Compliance, following rules, and being neat and orderly are valued and reinforced in many classrooms. These are behaviors that usually characterize girls more than boys.
- A large majority of teachers are females, especially at the elementary school level. This trend may make it more difficult for boys than for girls to identify with their teachers and model their teachers' behavior. A recent study revealed that male teachers perceived boys more positively and viewed them as more educationally competent than did female teachers (Mullola & others, 2012).
- Boys are more likely than girls to have a learning disability, ADHD, and to drop out of school.
- Boys are more likely than girls to be criticized by their teachers.
- School personnel tend to ignore clear evidence that many boys are having academic problems, especially in the language arts.
- School personnel tend to stereotype boys' behavior as problematic.

What evidence is there that the classroom setting is biased against girls? Consider the views of Myra and David Sadker (2012):

- In a typical classroom, girls are more compliant and boys are more rambunctious. Boys demand more attention, and girls are more likely to quietly wait their turn. Teachers are more likely to scold and reprimand boys, as well as send boys to school authorities for disciplinary action. Educators worry that girls' tendency to be compliant and quiet comes at a cost: diminished assertiveness.
- In many classrooms, teachers spend more time watching and interacting with boys, whereas girls work and play quietly on their own. Most teachers don't intentionally favor boys by spending more time with them, yet somehow the classroom frequently ends up with this type of gendered profile.
- Boys get more instruction than girls and more help when they have trouble with a question. Teachers often give boys more time to answer a question, more hints at the correct answer, and further tries if they give the wrong answer.

- Boys are more likely than girls to get lower grades and to be grade repeaters, yet girls are less likely to believe that they will be successful in college work.
- Girls and boys enter first grade with roughly equal levels of self-esteem. Yet by the middle school years, girls' self-esteem is lower than boys'.
- When elementary school children are asked to list what they want to do when they grow up, boys describe more career options than girls do.

Thus, there is evidence of gender bias against both males and females in schools (Leaper & Brown, 2015). Many school personnel are not aware of their gender-biased attitudes. These attitudes are deeply entrenched in and supported by the general culture. Increasing awareness of gender bias in schools is clearly an important strategy in reducing such bias.

Might single-sex education be better for children than coed education? The argument for single-sex education is that it eliminates distraction from the other sex and reduces sexual harassment. Single-sex public education has increased dramatically in recent years. In 2002, only 12 public schools in the United States provided single-sex education; during the 2011–2012 school year, 116 public schools were single-sex and an additional 390 provided such experiences (NASSPE, 2012).

How does gender affect school experiences during adolescence?
© Dann Tardif/LWA/Corbis

The increase in single-sex education has especially been fueled by its inclusion in the No Child Left Behind legislation as a means of improving the educational experiences and academic achievement of low-income students of color. It appears that many of the public schools offering single-sex education have a high percentage of such youth (Klein, 2012). However, three recent research reviews concluded that there have been no documented benefits of single-sex education, especially in the highest-quality studies (Goodkind, 2013; Halpern & others, 2011; Pahlke, Hyde, & Allison, 2014). One review, titled "The Pseudoscience of Single-Sex Schooling," by Diane Halpern and her colleagues (2011) concluded that single-sex education is highly misguided, misconstrued, and unsupported by any valid scientific evidence. They emphasize that among the many arguments against single-sex education, the strongest is its reduction in the opportunities for boys and girls to work together in a supervised, purposeful environment. Other leading experts on gender also have recently argued that the factors that benefit students' education and development are more likely to be found in coeducational rather than single-sex schools (Bigler, Hayes, & Liben, 2014; Huston, 2015; Liben, 2015).

There has been a special call for single-sex public education for one group of adolescents— African American boys—because of their historically poor academic achievement and high dropout rate from school (Mitchell & Stewart, 2013). In 2010, Urban Prep Academy for Young Men became the first all-male, all African American public charter school. One hundred percent of its first graduates enrolled in college, despite the school's location in a section of Chicago where poverty, gangs, and crime predominate. Because so few public schools focus solely on educating African American boys, it is too early to tell whether this type of single-sex education can be effective across a wide range of participants (Barbarin, Chinn, & Wright, 2014).

Mass Media Influences As already described, adolescents encounter gender roles in their everyday interactions with parents, peers, and teachers. The messages about gender roles carried by the mass media also are important influences on adolescents' gender development (Senden, Sikstrom, & Lindholm, 2015; Silverman, 2012). Television shows directed at adolescents are highly stereotyped in their portrayal of the sexes, especially teenage girls (Adams, 2012; Starr, 2015). One study found that teenage girls were portrayed as being concerned primarily with dating, shopping, and their appearance (Campbell, 1988). They rarely were shown as being interested in school or career plans. Attractive girls were often stereotyped as "airheads" and intelligent girls as unattractive.

Another highly stereotyped form of programming that specifically targets teenage viewers is music videos (Roberts & Foehr, 2008). What

What are some recent changes in single-sex education in the United States? What does research say about whether same-sex education is beneficial?
© Jim Weber/The Commercial Appeal/Landov

Females are often portrayed in sexually provocative ways in entertainment and music videos.
© Joeri DE ROCKER/Alamy

developmental **connection**

Identity

Girls have more negative body images than do boys during adolescence. Connect to "Puberty, Health, and Biological Foundations."

adolescents see on MTV and some other TV networks is highly stereotyped and slanted toward a male audience. MTV has been described as a teenage boy's "dream world," filled with beautiful, aroused women who outnumber men, seek out and even assault them to have sex, and always mean yes, even when they say no (Jhally, 1990). One study found that MTV videos reinforced stereotypical notions of women as sexual objects and females as subordinate to males (Wallis, 2011).

Early adolescence may be a period of heightened sensitivity to televised messages about gender roles. Increasingly, young adolescents view programs designed for adults that include messages about gender-appropriate behavior, especially in heterosexual relationships. Cognitively, adolescents engage in more idealistic thoughts than children do, and the media offers many idealized images that adolescents can identify with and imitate—highly appealing actors and models who are young, thin, and glamorous, for example.

The world of television is highly gender-stereotyped and conveys clear messages about the relative power and importance of women and men (Bazzini & others, 2015; Kosut, 2012). Men are portrayed as more powerful than women on many TV shows. On music videos, male characters are portrayed more often than female characters as aggressive, dominant, competent, autonomous, and active, whereas female characters are more often portrayed as passive. In one study of prime-time commercials, women were underrepresented as primary characters except in commercials for health and beauty products (Ganahl, Prinsen, & Netzley, 2003).

The media influence adolescents' body images, and some studies reveal gender differences in this area (Frechette, 2012; Hyde & Else-Quest, 2013; Pecot-Hebert, 2012). For example, one study of 10- to 17-year-olds found that girls were more likely than boys to perceive that the media influenced their body images (Polce-Lynch & others, 2001). Another study revealed that the more time adolescent girls and boys spent watching television for entertainment, the more negative their body images were (Anderson & others, 2001). Adolescent boys are exposed to a highly muscular body ideal for males in media outlets, especially in advertisements that include professional athletes and in video games (Near, 2013). A recent analysis of men's magazines found that more than half of their advertisements reflected hyper-masculine beliefs (toughness as emotional control, violence as manly, danger as exciting, and callous attitudes toward women and sex) (Vokey, Tefft, & Tysiaczny, 2013). Some of the magazines included at least one hyper-masculine belief in more than 90 percent of their ads.

In the last decade, adolescents have spent huge amounts of time on social media, yet few researchers have examined social media effects on adolescents' body images (Prieler & Choi, 2014). A recent review proposed that the interactive format and content features of social media, such as strong peer pressure and exchange of various visual images, might have a strong influence on adolescents' body images, especially adolescent girls' body satisfaction/dissatisfaction and eating disorders (Perloff, 2014).

COGNITIVE INFLUENCES ON GENDER

Observation, imitation, rewards and punishment—these are the mechanisms by which gender develops, according to social cognitive theory. Interactions between the child/adolescent and the social environment are the most influential mechanisms for gender development in this view. Some critics who adopt a cognitive approach argue that social cognitive explanations pay too little attention to the child's own mind and understanding, portraying children as passively accepting gender roles (Martin, Ruble, & Szkrybalo, 2002).

One influential cognitive theory is **gender schema theory,** which states that gender-typing emerges as children and adolescents gradually develop gender schemas of what is gender-appropriate and gender-inappropriate in their culture (Martin, Fabes, & Hanish, 2014; Martin & Ruble, 2010; Miller & others, 2013). A schema is a cognitive structure, a network of associations that guide an individual's perceptions. A gender schema organizes the world in terms of female and male. Children and adolescents are internally motivated to perceive the world and to act in accordance with their developing schemas. Bit by bit, children and adolescents pick up what is gender-appropriate and gender-inappropriate in their culture, developing gender schemas that shape how they perceive the world and what they remember (Conry-Murray, Kim, & Turiel, 2012). Children and adolescents are motivated to act in ways that conform to these gender schemas.

gender schema theory Theory stating that an individual's attention and behavior are guided by an internal motivation to conform to gender-based sociocultural standards and stereotypes.

In sum, cognitive factors contribute to the way adolescents think and act as males and females (Blakemore, Berenbaum, & Liben, 2009). Through biological, social, and cognitive processes, children and adolescents develop their gender attitudes and behaviors (Leaper, 2013, 2015).

Regardless of the factors that influence gender behavior, the consequences of gender have become the subject of intense focus and research over the last several decades. Next, we explore the myths and realities of how females and males do or do not differ.

Review Connect Reflect

LG1 Describe the biological, social, and cognitive influences on gender

Review
- How can gender and gender roles be defined? What are some important biological influences on gender?
- What are some important social influences on gender?
- What are some important cognitive influences on gender?

Connect
- How might the characteristics of Piaget's stage of formal operational thought be linked to the way adolescents think about gender?

Reflect *Your Own Personal Journey of Life*
- Which theory do you think best explains your gender development through adolescence? What might an eclectic view of gender development be like?

2 Gender Stereotypes, Similarities, and Differences

LG2 Discuss gender stereotypes, similarities, and differences

Gender Stereotyping

Gender Similarities and Differences

Gender Controversy

Gender in Context

How pervasive is gender stereotyping? What are the real differences between boys and girls, and why is this issue such a controversial one? In this section, our goal is not just to answer these questions but also to discuss controversy regarding gender and to place gender behavior in context.

GENDER STEREOTYPING

Gender stereotypes are general impressions and beliefs about females and males. For example, men are powerful; women are weak. Men make good mechanics; women make good nurses. Men are good with numbers; women are good with words. Women are emotional; men are not. All of these are stereotypes. They are generalizations about a group that reflect widely held beliefs. Recent research has found that gender stereotypes are, to a great extent, still present in today's world, in the lives of both children and adults (Kaatz & Carnes, 2014; Leaper & Brown, 2015; Liben, Bigler, & Hilliard, 2014). Researchers also have found that boys' gender stereotypes are more rigid than girls' (Blakemore & others, 2009).

A classic study in the early 1970s assessed which traits and behaviors college students believed were characteristic of females and which they believed were characteristic of males (Broverman & others, 1972). The traits associated with males were labeled *instrumental:* They included characteristics such as being independent, aggressive, and power-oriented. The traits associated with females were labeled *expressive:* They included characteristics such as being warm and sensitive.

Thus, the instrumental traits associated with males suited them for the traditional masculine role of going out into the world as the breadwinner. The expressive traits associated

gender stereotypes Broad categories that reflect our impressions and beliefs about females and males.

with females paralleled the traditional feminine role of being the sensitive, nurturing caregiver in the home. These roles and traits, however, are not just different; they also are unequal in terms of social status and power. The traditional feminine characteristics are childlike, suitable for someone who is dependent on others and subordinate to them. The traditional masculine characteristics suit one to deal competently with the wider world and to wield authority.

Researchers continue to find that gender stereotyping is pervasive (Leaper, 2013, 2015; Silverman, 2012). For example, one study found extensive differences in the stereotyping of females' and males' emotions (Durik & others, 2006). Females were stereotyped as expressing more fear, guilt, love, sadness, shame, surprise, and sympathy than their male counterparts. Males were stereotyped as expressing more anger and pride than their female counterparts.

GENDER SIMILARITIES AND DIFFERENCES

What is the reality behind gender stereotypes? Let's now examine some of the differences between the sexes, keeping the following in mind:

· The differences are based on averages and do not apply to all females or all males.
· Even when gender differences occur, there often is considerable overlap between males and females, especially in aspects of cognitive and socioemotional development.
· The differences may be due primarily to biological factors, to sociocultural factors, or to both.

First, we examine physical similarities and differences, and then we turn to cognitive and socioemotional similarities and differences.

Physical Similarities and Differences   We could devote many pages to describing physical differences between the average man and woman. For example, women have about twice the body fat of men, most of it concentrated around breasts and hips. In males, fat is more likely to go to the abdomen. On average, males grow to be 10 percent taller than females. Males have greater physical strength than females.

Many physical differences between men and women are tied to health. From conception on, females have a longer life expectancy than males do, and females are less likely than males to develop physical or mental disorders. Females are more resistant to infection, and their blood vessels are more elastic than males'. Males have higher levels of stress hormones, which cause faster clotting and higher blood pressure. For example, a study of emerging adults found that the hypothalamic-pituitary-adrenal (HPA) axis responses in males were greater than in females following a psychological stress test (Uhart & others, 2006). This greater response of the HPA axis in males was reflected in elevated levels of such stress-related hormones as cortisol.

Much of the research on gender similarities and differences in the brain has been conducted with adults rather than children or adolescents (Giedd & others, 2012). Among the differences that have been discovered in studies with adults are the following:

· One part of the hypothalamus involved in sexual behavior tends to be larger in men than in women (Swaab & others, 2001).
· An area of the parietal lobe that functions in visuospatial skills tends to be larger in males than in females (Frederikse & others, 2000).
· Female brains are approximately 10 percent smaller than male brains (Giedd, 2012; Giedd & others, 2012).
· Female brains have more folds, and the larger folds (called convolutions) allow more surface brain tissue within the skulls of females than of males (Luders & others, 2004).

Although some gender differences in brain structure and function have been found, many of these differences are either small or research is inconsistent regarding the differences (Eliot, 2013; Halpern, 2012; Hyde, 2014; Hyde & Else-Quest, 2013). Also, when gender differences in the brain have been revealed, in many cases they have not been directly linked to psychological differences (Blakemore & others, 2009; Eliot, 2013). Although research on gender differences in the brain is still in its infancy, it is likely that there are far more similarities than differences in the brains of females and males (Eliot, 2013; Halpern, 2012; Hyde, 2014; Hyde & Else-Quest, 2013). Similarities and differences in the brains of males and females could be due to evolution and heredity, as well as to experiences.

Cognitive Similarities and Differences

No gender differences occur in overall intellectual ability—but in some cognitive areas, gender differences do appear (Blakemore & others, 2009; Ganley, Vasilyeva, & Dulaney, 2014; Halpern, 2012).

Research indicates that girls show better self-control (controlling impulses and focusing attention, for example) than do boys (Else-Quest & others, 2006; Hyde & Else-Quest, 2013).

Many years ago, Eleanor Maccoby and Carol Jacklin (1974) concluded that males have better math and visuospatial skills (the kinds of skills an architect needs to design a building's angles and dimensions) than do females, whereas females have better verbal abilities than do males. Subsequently, Maccoby (1987) concluded that the verbal differences between females and males had virtually disappeared but that the math and visuospatial differences persisted.

Are there gender differences in mathematical abilities? A very large-scale study of more than 7 million U.S. students in grades 2 through 11 revealed no differences in math scores for boys and girls (Hyde & others, 2008). And a recent meta-analysis found no gender differences in math scores for adolescents (Lindberg & others, 2010). A recent research review concluded that girls have more negative math attitudes and that parents' and teachers' expectations for children's math competence are often gender-biased in favor of boys (Gunderson & others, 2012). And a recent study of 6- to 12-year-olds reported that the majority of the participants stated that math is mainly for boys (Cvencek, Meltzoff, & Greenwald, 2011). In the most recent National Assessment of Educational Progress (2012) reports, girls scored significantly higher than boys in reading and writing but there were virtually no gender differences in math scores at the fourth- and eighth-grade levels.

One area of math that has been examined for possible gender differences is visuospatial skills, which include being able to rotate objects mentally and determine what they would look like when rotated. These types of skills are important in courses such as plane and solid geometry and geography. Recent research reviews have revealed that boys have better visuospatial skills than girls do (Halpern, 2012; Halpern & others, 2007). For example, despite equal participation in the National Geography Bee, in most years all 10 finalists have been boys (Liben, 1995). A recent research review found that having a stronger masculine gender role was linked to better spatial ability in males and females (Reilly & Neumann, 2013).

However, some experts in gender, such as Janet Shibley Hyde (2005, 2007, 2014; Hyde & Else-Quest, 2013), conclude that the cognitive differences between females and males have been exaggerated. For example, Hyde points out that there is considerable overlap in the distributions of female and male scores on math and visuospatial tasks (see Figure 1).

Debate continues about how extensive cognitive gender differences are and the extent to which there are stereotypes about the differences (Halpern, 2012; Hyde, 2014; Hyde & Else-Quest, 2013). In a recent study, highly educated adults gave estimates of male and female success for 12 cognitive tasks (Halpern, Straight, & Stephenson, 2011). Their estimates were compared with published research on the tasks. The adults were generally accurate about the direction of the differences but underestimated the size of the differences.

Are there gender differences in reading and writing skills? There is strong evidence that females outperform males in reading and writing. In the 2014 report from the National Assessment of Educational Progress (NAEP), girls had higher scores in reading than boys in both fourth- and eighth-grade assessments (National Assessment of Educational Progress, 2014). Girls also have consistently outperformed boys in writing skills in NAEP's fourth-, eighth-, and twelfth-grade assessments.

Keep in mind that measures of achievement in school or scores on standardized tests may reflect many factors besides cognitive ability. For example, performance in school may in part reflect attempts to conform to gender roles or differences in motivation, self-regulation, or other socioemotional characteristics (Eccles, 2014; Watt, 2008; Watt & Eccles, 2008).

Let's further explore gender differences related to schooling and achievement. Gender differences characterize U.S. dropout rates, with males more likely to drop out than females (7.3 versus 5.9 percent) (data for 2012) (National Center for Education Statistics, 2014). Boys predominate in the academic bottom half of high school classes. That is, although many boys perform at the average or advanced level, the bottom 50 percent academically is made up mainly of boys. Half a century ago, in 1961, less than 40 percent of females who graduated from high school went on to attend college. Beginning in 1996, females were more likely to enroll in college than were males. In 2012, 76 percent of females attended college after high school, compared with 62 percent of males (Pew Research Center, 2014; Women in Academia, 2011). In 1994, 63 percent of females and 61 percent of males enrolled in college;

"So according to the stereotype, you can put two and two together, but I can read the handwriting on the wall."
© 1994 Joel Pett. Reprinted with permission.

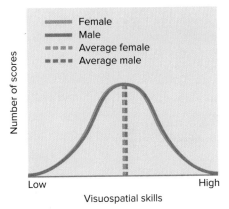

FIGURE 1

VISUOSPATIAL SKILLS OF MALES AND FEMALES. Notice that although an average male's visuospatial skills are higher than an average female's, scores for the two sexes almost entirely overlap. Not all males have better visuospatial skills than all females do—the overlap indicates that, although the average male score is higher, many females outperform most males on such tasks.

thus, women's college enrollment gains have left males behind. Also, in 2012, the gender gap in college attendance was significant for African Americans (69 percent of women versus 57 percent of men) and Latinos (76 percent of women versus 62 percent of men), but college attendance was similar for Asian Americans (86 percent of women, 83 percent of men) (Pew Research Center, 2014).

Piecing together the information about school dropout rates, the percentage of males in the bottom half of high school classes, and the percentage of males enrolled in college classes, we can conclude that currently females show greater overall academic interest and achievement than do males in the United States. Females are more likely to be engaged with academic material, be attentive in class, put forth more academic effort, and participate more in class than boys are (DeZolt & Hull, 2001). A recent large-scale study revealed that girls had more positive attitudes about school than boys did (Orr, 2011). Also in this study, girls' positive attitudes about school were linked to their higher grades; boys' negative attitudes about school were related to their lower grades.

Despite these positive academic characteristics of girls, the increasing evidence that there is similarity in the math and science skills of girls and boys, and the legislative efforts to attain gender equality in recent years, gender differences in science, technology, and math careers continue to favor males (Eccles, 2014; Liben & Coyle, 2014; Meece & Askew, 2012; Watt & Eccles, 2008; Wigfield & others, 2015). Toward the end of high school, girls are less likely to be taking high-level math courses and less likely to plan to enter the so-called "STEM" fields of science, technology, engineering, and math (Eccles, 2014; Liben & Coyle, 2014; Rosser, 2012; Wigfield & others, 2015). We will have more to say about the topic of gender disparity in career development in the chapter on "Achievement, Work, and Careers."

A recent study assessed an intervention that provided parents with information about the value of math and science courses for enhancing future career success (Harackiewicz & others, 2012). Adolescents whose parents who were given these materials were more likely than other adolescents to take math and science courses in high school, especially daughters of mothers with a college education.

Socioemotional Similarities and Differences

Are "men from Mars" and "women from Venus," as John Gray (1992) suggested in the title of his highly popular book on gender differences in relationships? The answer to the question is no. Males and females are not so different that they should be thought of as being from different planets (Hyde & Else-Quest, 2013; Perry & Pauletti, 2011). For just about every imaginable socioemotional characteristic, researchers have examined whether there are differences between males and females. Here we examine four of these characteristics: aggression, communication in relationships, prosocial behavior (behavior that is intended to benefit other people), and emotion.

Aggression   One of the most consistent gender differences is that boys are more physically aggressive than girls. The difference occurs in all cultures and appears very early in children's development (Kistner & others, 2010). The difference in physical aggression is especially pronounced when children are provoked. Although boys are consistently more physically aggressive than girls, might girls show as much verbal aggression, such as yelling, as boys do? When verbal aggression is examined, gender differences typically either disappear or the behavior is more pronounced in girls than in boys (Eagly & Steffen, 1986).

Recently, increased interest has been shown in *relational aggression*, which involves harming someone by manipulating a relationship (Busching & Krahe, 2015; Kawabata, Tseng, & Crick, 2014; Mathieson, Klimes-Dougan, & Crick, 2014; Orpinas, McNicholas, & Nahapetyan, 2015). Relational aggression includes such behaviors as trying to make others dislike a certain individual by spreading malicious rumors about the person or ostracizing him or her (Underwood, 2011). Relational aggression increases in

What have researchers found about gender similarities and differences in relational aggression in children and adolescents?
© SW Productions/Getty Images RF

What are little boys made of?
Frogs and snails
and puppy dogs' tails.
What are little girls made of?
Sugar and spice
And all that's nice.

—J. O. Halliwell
English author, 19th century

middle and late childhood (Dishion & Piehler, 2009). Mixed findings have characterized research on whether girls show more relational aggression than boys, but one consistent finding is that relational aggression comprises a greater percentage of girls' overall aggression than it does for boys (Putallaz & others, 2007). And a research review revealed that girls engage in more relational aggression than boys in adolescence but not in childhood (Smith, Rose, & Schwartz-Mette, 2010). Further, in a longitudinal study, preschool relational aggression predicted adolescent relational aggression for girls, but not for boys (Nelson & others, 2014).

What have researchers found about gender similarities and differences in communication in relationships?
© Ariel Skelly/Blend Images/Corbis RF

Communication in Relationships   In comparing communication styles of males and females, sociolinguist Deborah Tannen (1990) distinguishes between rapport talk and report talk:

- **Rapport talk** is the language of conversation and a way of establishing connections and negotiating relationships. Females enjoy rapport talk and conversation that is relationship-oriented more than boys do.

- **Report talk** is talk that gives information. Public speaking is an example of report talk. Males hold center stage through report talk with such verbal performances as storytelling, joking, and lecturing with information.

Tannen says that boys and girls grow up in different worlds of talk—parents, siblings, peers, teachers, and others talk differently to boys and girls. The play of boys and girls is also different. Boys tend to play in large groups that are hierarchically structured, and their groups usually have a leader who tells the others what to do and how to do it. Boys' games have winners and losers and often are the subject of arguments. And boys often boast of their skills and argue about who is best at what. In contrast, girls are more likely to play in small groups or pairs, and at the center of a girl's world is often a best friend. In girls' friendships and peer groups, intimacy is pervasive. Turn-taking is more characteristic of girls' games than of boys' games. And, much of the time, girls simply like to sit and talk with each other, concerned more about being liked by others than jockeying for status in some obvious way.

Researchers have found that girls are more "people oriented" and adolescent boys are more "things oriented" (Galambos & others, 2009; Su, Rounds, & Armstrong, 2009). In a recent research review, this conclusion was supported by findings that girls spend more time in relationships, while boys spend more time alone, playing video games, and playing sports; that girls work at part-time jobs that are people-oriented such as waitressing and baby-sitting, while boys are more likely to take part-time jobs that involve manual labor and using tools; and that girls are interested in careers that are more people-oriented, such as teaching and social work, while boys are more likely to be interested in object-oriented careers, such as mechanics and engineering (Perry & Pauletti, 2011). Also, in support of Tannen's view, researchers have found that adolescent girls engage in more self-disclosure (communication of intimate details about themselves) in close relationships, are better at actively listening in a conversation than are boys, and emphasize affiliation or collaboration (Hall, 2011; Leaper, 2013, 2015). Adolescent girls, in particular, are more likely to engage in self-disclosure and to provide emotional support in friendship than are boys (Leaper, 2013, 2015). By contrast, boys are more likely to value self-assertion and dominance than are girls in their interactions with friends and peers (Leaper, 2013, 2015; Rose & Rudolph, 2006).

However, Tannen's view has been criticized on the grounds that it is overly simplistic and that communication between males and females is more complex than Tannen suggests (Edwards & Hamilton, 2004). Further, some researchers have found similarities in males' and females' relationship communication strategies (Hyde, 2014; Hyde & Else-Quest, 2013). In one study, men and women talked about and responded to relationship problems in ways that were more similar than different (MacGeorge, 2004).

Prosocial Behavior   Are there gender differences in prosocial behavior? Not only do girls view themselves as more prosocial and empathic than boys (Eisenberg, Spinrad, & Knafo, 2015; Eisenberg, Spinrad, & Morris, 2013), across childhood and adolescence, but they also engage in more prosocial behavior and show more empathy than boys do (Christov-Moore &

developmental **connection**

Identity

Researchers have found that female adolescents are more likely than male adolescents to engage in identity exploration related to dating. Connect to "The Self, Identity, Emotion, and Personality."

developmental **connection**

Moral Development

Prosocial behavior is behavior intended to benefit other people. Connect to "Moral Development, Values, and Religion."

rapport talk The language of conversation, establishing connections and negotiating relationships.

report talk Talk that gives information, such as public speaking.

others, 2014; Eisenberg, Spinrad, & Knafo, 2015). A recent meta-analysis concluded that females are better than males at recognizing nonverbal displays of emotion (Thompson & Voyer, 2014). The biggest gender difference occurred for kind and considerate behavior, with a smaller difference for sharing.

Emotion and Its Regulation   Gender differences occur in some aspects of emotion (Leaper, 2015). Females express emotion more readily than do males, are better than males at decoding emotions, smile more, cry more, and are happier (Gross, Fredrickson, & Levenson, 1994; LaFrance, Hecht, & Paluck, 2003). Males report experiencing and expressing more anger than do females (Kring, 2000). A recent meta-analysis found that overall gender differences in children's emotional expression were small, with girls showing more positive emotions (sympathy, for example) and more internalized emotions (sadness and anxiety, for example) (Chaplin & Aldao, 2013). In this analysis, the gender difference in positive emotions became more pronounced with age as girls more strongly expressed positive emotions than boys in middle and late childhood and in adolescence.

An important skill is the capacity to regulate and control one's emotions and behavior (Thompson, 2015). Boys usually show less self-regulation of their emotions than girls do, and this low self-control can translate into behavior problems (Pascual & others, 2012). In one study, children's low self-regulation was linked with greater aggression, teasing of others, overreaction to frustration, low cooperation, and inability to delay gratification (Block & Block, 1980).

GENDER CONTROVERSY

Controversy continues about the extent of gender differences and what might cause them (Leaper, 2013, 2015). As we saw earlier, evolutionary psychologists such as David Buss (2012, 2015) argue that gender differences are extensive and caused by the adaptive problems the genders have faced across evolutionary history. Alice Eagly (2012, 2013) also concludes that gender differences are substantial but reaches a very different conclusion about their cause. She emphasizes that gender differences are due to social conditions that have resulted in women having less power and controlling fewer resources than men do.

By contrast, Janet Shibley Hyde (2005, 2007, 2014) concludes that gender differences have been greatly exaggerated, particularly after the publication of popular books such as John Gray's (1992) *Men Are from Mars, Women Are from Venus* and Deborah Tannen's (1990) *You Just Don't Understand.* She argues that the research shows that females and males are similar on most psychological factors. In one research review, Hyde (2005) summarized the results of 44 meta-analyses of gender differences and similarities. Gender differences either were nonexistent or small, in most areas, including math ability and communication. The largest difference occurred on motor skills (favoring males), followed by sexuality (males masturbate more and are more likely to endorse sex in a casual, uncommitted relationship), and physical aggression (males are more physically aggressive than females). A research review also concluded that gender differences in adolescence are quite small (Perry & Pauletti, 2011).

Hyde's summary of meta-analyses and the research review by Perry and Pauletti are not likely to quiet the controversy about gender differences and similarities anytime soon, but further research should continue to provide a basis for more accurate conclusions about this topic.

GENDER IN CONTEXT

In thinking about gender, it is important to consider the context of behavior, as gender behavior often varies across contexts (Leaper, 2013, 2015). Consider helping behavior. Males are more likely to help in contexts in which a perceived danger is present and they feel competent to help (Eagly & Crowley, 1986). For example, males are more likely than females to help a person who is stranded by the roadside with a flat tire; automobile problems are an area in which many males feel competent. In contrast, when the context involves volunteering time to help a child with a personal problem, females are more likely to help than males are because there is little danger present and females feel more competent at nurturing. In many cultures, girls show more caregiving behavior than boys do. However, in the few cultures where they both care for younger siblings on a regular basis, girls and boys are similar in their tendencies to nurture (Whiting, 1989).

There is more difference within the sexes than between them.

—Ivy Compton-Burnett
English novelist, 20th century

developmental **connection**

Theories

Bronfenbrenner's ecological theory emphasizes the importance of contexts; in his theory, the macrosystem includes cross-cultural comparisons. Connect to "Introduction."

Context is also relevant to gender differences in the display of emotions. Consider anger. Males are more likely to show anger toward strangers, especially other males, when they think they have been challenged. Males also are more likely than females to turn their anger into aggressive action, especially when their culture endorses such action (Tavris & Wade, 1984).

Contextual variations regarding gender in specific situations occur not only within a particular culture but also across cultures (Matsumoto & Juang, 2013). Although in recent decades roles assumed by males and females in the United States have become increasingly similar, in many countries gender roles have remained more gender-specific. For example, in a number of Middle Eastern countries, the division of labor between males and females is dramatic: males are socialized to work in the public sphere, females in the private world of home and child rearing; a man's duty is to provide for his family, the woman's to care for her family and household. Any deviations from this traditional division of gender roles encounter severe disapproval.

How might gender-role socialization for these adolescent girls in Iran compare with that in the United States?
© Reuters/Corbis

Review Connect Reflect

LG2 Discuss gender stereotypes, similarities, and differences

Review

- How extensive is gender stereotyping?
- How similar or different are adolescent males and females in their physical, cognitive, and socioemotional development?
- What is the controversy about the cause of gender differences?
- How extensively is gender development influenced by contexts?

Connect

- How do socioemotional similarities and differences between girls and boys relate to the development of self-esteem?

Reflect *Your Own Personal Journey of Life*

- Some decades ago, the word *dependency* was used to describe the relational orientation of femininity. Dependency took on a negative connotation for females—for instance, the perception that females can't take care of themselves whereas males can. Today, the term *dependency* is being replaced by the term *relational abilities,* which has more positive connotations (Caplan & Caplan, 1999). Rather than being thought of as dependent, women are now more often described as skilled in forming and maintaining relationships. Make up a list of words that you associate with masculinity and femininity. Do these words have any negative connotations for males and females? For the words that do have negative connotations, can you think of words with positive connotations that could be used instead?

3 Gender-Role Classification   **LG3** Characterize the variations in gender-role classification

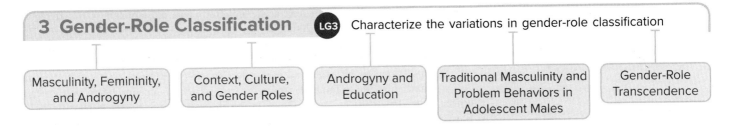

| Masculinity, Femininity, and Androgyny | Context, Culture, and Gender Roles | Androgyny and Education | Traditional Masculinity and Problem Behaviors in Adolescent Males | Gender-Role Transcendence |

Not long ago, it was accepted that boys should grow up to be masculine and girls to be feminine, that boys are made of "frogs and snails" and girls are made of "sugar and spice and all that's nice." Let's further explore gender classifications of boys and girls as "masculine" and "feminine."

Examples of masculine items

Defends own beliefs
Forceful
Willing to take risks
Dominant
Aggressive

Examples of feminine items

Does not use harsh language
Affectionate
Loves children
Understanding
Gentle

FIGURE 2

THE BEM SEX-ROLE INVENTORY (BSRI).
These items are from the Bem Sex-Role Inventory. When taking the BSRI, a person is asked to indicate on a 7-point scale how well each of the 60 characteristics describes herself or himself. The scale ranges from 1 (never or almost never true) to 7 (always or almost always true). The items are scored on independent dimensions of masculinity and femininity as well as androgyny and undifferentiated classifications.

Reproduced by special permission of the Publisher, Mind Garden, Inc., www.mindgarden.com from the Bem Sex Role Inventory by Sandra Bem. Copyright 1978, 1981 by Consulting Psychologists Press, Inc. Further reproduction is prohibited without the Publisher's written consent.

MASCULINITY, FEMININITY, AND ANDROGYNY

In the past, a well-adjusted boy was supposed to be independent, aggressive, and powerful. A well-adjusted girl was supposed to be dependent, nurturing, and uninterested in power. The masculine characteristics were considered to be healthy and good by society; the feminine characteristics were considered weak.

In the 1970s, as both males and females became dissatisfied with the burdens imposed by their stereotyped roles, alternatives to "masculinity" and "femininity" were explored. Instead of thinking of masculinity and femininity as a continuum, with more of one characteristic meaning less of the other, it was proposed that individuals could show both expressive and instrumental traits. This thinking led to the development of the concept of **androgyny,** the presence of a high degree of masculine and feminine characteristics in the same individual (Bem, 1977; Spence & Helmreich, 1978). The androgynous individual might be a male who is both assertive (masculine) and sensitive to others' feelings (feminine), or a female who is both dominant (masculine) and caring (feminine).

Measures have been developed to assess androgyny. One of the most widely used gender measures, the *Bem Sex-Role Inventory*, was constructed by a leading early proponent of androgyny, Sandra Bem (1977). Figure 2 shows examples of masculine and feminine items on the Bem Sex-Role Inventory. Based on their responses to the items in this inventory, individuals are classified as having one of four gender-role orientations—masculine, feminine, androgynous, or undifferentiated (see Figure 3):

- The androgynous individual is simply a female or a male who has a high degree of both feminine and masculine traits. No new characteristics are used to describe the androgynous individual.

- A feminine individual is high on expressive traits and low on instrumental traits.

- A masculine individual is high on instrumental traits and low on expressive traits.

- An undifferentiated person is low on both feminine and masculine traits.

Androgynous women and men, according to Bem, are more flexible and more mentally healthy than either masculine or feminine individuals; undifferentiated individuals are the least competent. One study found that androgyny was linked to well-being and lower levels of stress (Stake, 2000). Another study conducted with emerging adults revealed that androgynous individuals reported better health practices (such as safety belt use, less smoking) than masculine, feminine, or undifferentiated individuals (Shifren, Furnham, & Bauserman, 2003).

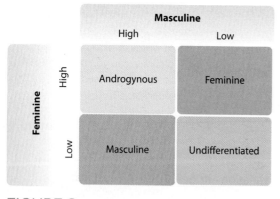

FIGURE 3

GENDER-ROLE CLASSIFICATION

androgyny The presence of a high degree of desirable feminine and masculine characteristics in the same individual.

CONTEXT, CULTURE, AND GENDER ROLES

The concept of gender-role classification involves a personality-trait-like categorization of a person. However, it is important to think of personality in terms of both traits and contexts rather than traits alone (Engler, 2014; Steyer & others, 2015). In close relationships, a feminine or androgynous gender role may be more desirable because of the expressive nature of close relationships. However, a masculine or androgynous gender role may be more desirable in academic and work settings that require action and assertiveness. For example, one study found that masculine and androgynous individuals had higher expectations for being able to control the outcomes of their academic efforts than did feminine or undifferentiated individuals (Choi, 2004).

The importance of considering gender in context is nowhere more apparent than when examining what is culturally prescribed behavior for females and males in different countries around the world (Matsumoto & Juang, 2013). However, it may be helpful to think of gender in terms of person-situation interaction instead of gender traits alone (Engler, 2014). Thus, in our discussion of gender-role classification, we have described how some gender roles might be more appropriate for some cultural contexts than others,

Increasing numbers of children and adolescents in the United States and other modernized countries such as Sweden are being raised to behave in androgynous ways. In the last 30 to 40 years in the United States, a decline in the adoption of traditional gender roles has occurred. For example, in recent years U.S. female college students have shown a propensity

for pursuing careers outside the home. In 1967, more than 40 percent of college females and more than 60 percent of college males agreed with the statement, "The activities of married women are best confined to home and family." In 2005, those percentages had dropped to 15 percent for college females and 26 percent for college males (Pryor & others, 2005). As shown in Figure 4, the greatest change in these attitudes occurred in the late 1960s and early 1970s.

But traditional gender roles continue to dominate the cultures of many countries around the world today. As we indicated earlier in this chapter, in such cultures the man's duty is to provide for his family; the woman's duty to care for her family and household. Any deviations from this traditional gender-role orientation meet with severe disapproval. In the United States, the cultural backgrounds of adolescents influence how boys and girls will be socialized. In one study, Latino and Latina adolescents were socialized differently as they were growing up (Raffaelli & Ontai, 2004). Latinas experienced far greater restrictions than Latinos in curfews, interaction with members of the other sex, acquisition of a driver's license, exploration of job possibilities, and involvement in after-school activities. To read about the work of one individual who is interested in expanding the horizons of Latinas, see the *Connecting with Careers* profile.

Access to education for girls has improved somewhat around the world, but girls' educational opportunities still lag behind those available to boys (UNICEF, 2015). For example, according to a UNICEF (2003) analysis of education around the world, by age 18, girls have received, on average, 4.4 years less education than boys have. This lack of education reduces their chances of reaching their full potential. Exceptions to lower participation and completion rates in education for girls occur in Western nations, Japan, and the Philippines (Brown & Larson, 2002). Opportunities to receive advanced training or advanced degrees are higher in most countries for males than for females (Fussell & Greene, 2002).

Despite these gender gaps, evidence of increasing gender equality is appearing. For example, "among upper income

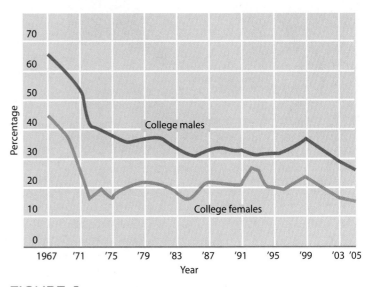

FIGURE 4

CHANGING ATTITUDES ABOUT GENDER ROLES. *Note:* Data show the percentage of first-year U.S. college students agreeing with the statement, "The activities of married women are best confined to home and family" from 1967 through 2005.

families in India and Japan, fathers are assuming more child-rearing responsibilities. Rates of employment and career opportunities for women are expanding in many parts of the globe. Control over adolescent girls' social relationships, especially romantic and sexual relationships, is easing in some nations" (Brown & Larson, 2002, p. 16).

ANDROGYNY AND EDUCATION

Can and should androgyny be taught to students? In general, it is easier to teach androgyny to girls than to boys and easier to teach it before the middle school grades. For example, in one study, a gender curriculum was put in place for one year in the kindergarten, fifth, and ninth grades (Guttentag & Bray, 1976). It involved books, discussion materials, and classroom exercises with an androgynous bent. The program was most successful with the fifth-graders, least successful with the ninth-graders. The ninth-graders, especially the boys, showed a boomerang effect, in which they had more traditional gender-role attitudes after the year of androgynous instruction than before it.

Despite such mixed findings, the advocates of androgyny programs argue that traditional sex-typing is harmful for all students and especially has prevented many girls from experiencing equal opportunity. The detractors respond that androgynous educational programs are too value-laden and ignore the diversity of gender roles in our society.

TRADITIONAL MASCULINITY AND PROBLEM BEHAVIORS IN ADOLESCENT MALES

In our discussion of masculinity so far, we have considered how the masculine role has been accorded a prominent status in the United States and in most other cultures. However, might there be a negative side to traditional masculinity, especially in adolescence? An increasing number of gender theorists and researchers conclude that there is (Levant, 2001).

What are some concerns about boys who adopt a strong masculine role?
© image100/Corbis RF

Concern about the effects of bringing up boys in traditional ways has brought attention to what has been called a "national crisis of boyhood" by William Pollack (1999) in his book *Real Boys*. He says that although there has been considerable talk about the "sensitive male," little has been done to change what he calls the "boy code."

Pollack argues that this code tells boys they should show little if any emotion as they are growing up. Too often boys are socialized to not show their feelings and to act tough, says Pollack. Boys learn the boy code in many different contexts—sandboxes, playgrounds, schoolrooms, camps, hangouts—and are taught the code by parents, peers, coaches, teachers, and other adults. Pollack, as well as many others, notes that boys would benefit from being socialized to express their anxieties and concerns rather than keeping them bottled up, as well as being taught how to better regulate their aggression.

There also is a special concern about boys who adopt a strong masculine role in adolescence, because this is increasingly being found to be associated with problem behaviors. Joseph Pleck (1983, 1995) concludes that what defines traditional masculinity in many Western cultures includes behaviors that do not have social approval but nonetheless validate the adolescent boy's masculinity. That is, in the male adolescent culture, male adolescents perceive that they will be thought of as more masculine if they engage in premarital sex, drink alcohol and take drugs, and participate in illegal delinquent activities. A recent study revealed that both boys and girls who engaged in extreme gender-typed (hyper-gender) behaviors had lower levels of school engagement and school attachment (Ueno & McWilliams, 2010).

GENDER-ROLE TRANSCENDENCE

gender-role transcendence The belief that, when an individual's competence is at issue, it should be conceptualized not on the basis of masculinity, femininity, or androgyny but on an individual basis.

Some critics of androgyny say enough is enough and that there is too much talk about gender. They stress that androgyny is less of a panacea than was originally envisioned (Paludi, 2002). An alternative is **gender-role transcendence,** the view that when an individual's competence is at issue, it should be conceptualized on a person-by-person basis rather than on the basis of masculinity, femininity, or androgyny (Pleck, 1983). That is, we should think of ourselves as people first, not as masculine, feminine, or androgynous. Parents should rear their children to be competent persons, not masculine, feminine, or androgynous, say the gender-role critics. They argue that such gender-role classification encourages stereotyping.

Review Connect Reflect

(LG3) Characterize the variations in gender-role classification

Review

- How can traditional gender roles be described? What is androgyny? How is androgyny related to social competence?
- How do context and culture influence gender roles?
- How effectively can androgyny be taught in schools?
- How is traditional masculinity linked with the behavior of adolescent males?
- What is gender-role transcendence?

Connect

- Compare and contrast the concepts of androgyny and gender-role transcendence.

Reflect *Your Own Personal Journey of Life*

- How would you describe your gender-role classification today? How satisfied are you with your gender-role classification? What factors contributed to your classification?

4 Developmental Changes and Junctures

(LG4) Summarize developmental changes in gender

Early Adolescence and Gender Intensification

Is Early Adolescence a Critical Juncture for Females?

What changes take place during early adolescence that might affect gender roles? Is early adolescence a critical juncture in girls' development?

EARLY ADOLESCENCE AND GENDER INTENSIFICATION

Toward the beginning of this chapter, we considered how pubertal changes might be linked to gendered behavior. Here we expand on the earlier discussion. During early adolescence, individuals develop the adult, physical attributes of their sex. Some theorists and researchers have proposed that with the onset of puberty, girls and boys experience an intensification in gender-related expectations (Basow, 2006). The **gender intensification hypothesis** states that psychological and behavioral differences between boys and girls become greater during early adolescence because of increased socialization pressures to conform to traditional masculine and feminine gender roles (Hill & Lynch, 1983; Lynch, 1991). Puberty may signal to socializing others—parents, peers, and teachers—that an adolescent is approaching adulthood and should begin to act in stereotypical male or female ways. Some researchers have reported evidence of gender intensification in early adolescence (Hill & Lynch, 1983). However, a longitudinal study of individuals from 7 to 19 years of age revealed stable gender differences in activity interests but a decline in both male- and female-typed activity interests across the age range (McHale & others, 2009). And another recent study found no evidence for intensification in masculinity or femininity in young adolescents (Priess, Lindberg, & Hyde, 2009). The jury is still out on the validity of the gender intensification hypothesis, but recent research has raised questions about its accuracy (Galambos & others, 2009).

gender intensification hypothesis
Hypothesis stating that psychological and behavioral differences between boys and girls become greater during early adolescence because of increased socialization pressure to conform to masculine and feminine gender roles.

As adolescent boys and girls grow older, they tend to show less stereotypic gender behavior. In one study of eighth- and eleventh-graders, the eleventh-graders were more similar to each other on both masculine and feminine traits than were the eighth-graders (Karniol & others, 1998). Irrespective of gender, the eleventh-graders showed less masculinity than the eighth-graders did. The eleventh-grade girls were also lower on femininity than the eighth-grade girls, and the eleventh-grade boys higher on femininity than the eighth-grade boys. Indeed, no eighth-grade boys fell into the low-masculinity/high-femininity category.

What is the gender intensification hypothesis? How strong is the evidence for this hypothesis?
© Tony Freeman/PhotoEdit

IS EARLY ADOLESCENCE A CRITICAL JUNCTURE FOR FEMALES?

Carol Gilligan has conducted extensive interviews with girls from 6 to 18 years of age (Gilligan, 1982, 1996; Gilligan, Brown, & Rogers, 1990). She and her colleagues have reported that girls consistently reveal detailed knowledge of human relationships that is based on their experiences with others. According to Gilligan, girls are sensitive to different rhythms and emotions in relationships. Gilligan argues that girls experience life differently from boys; in her words, girls have a "different voice."

Gilligan also stresses that adolescence is a critical juncture in girls' development. In early adolescence (usually around 11 to 12 years of age), she says, girls become aware that the male-dominated culture does not value their intense interest in intimacy, even though society values women's caring and altruism. The dilemma, says Gilligan, is that girls are presented with a choice that makes them appear either selfish (if they become independent and self-sufficient) or selfless (if they remain responsive to others). As young adolescent girls struggle with this dilemma, Gilligan states, they begin to "silence" their "different voice," becoming less confident and more tentative in offering their opinions. This reticence often persists into adulthood. Some researchers note that the self-doubt and ambivalence girls experience in early adolescence translate into depression and eating disorders.

- - - - - - - - - →

developmental **connection**

Moral Development

Gilligan argues that the care perspective, which emphasizes the importance of connectedness to others, is especially important in adolescent girls' moral development. Connect to "Moral Development, Values, and Religion."

Contextual variations influence the degree to which adolescent girls silence their "voice" (Ryan, 2003). In one study, Susan Harter and her colleagues (Harter, Waters, & Whitesell, 1996) found that feminine girls reported lower levels of voice in public contexts (at school with teachers and classmates) but not in more private interpersonal relationships (with close friends and parents). However, androgynous girls reported a strong voice in all contexts. Harter and her colleagues found that adolescent girls who buy into societal messages that females should be seen and not heard are at the greatest risk in their development. The greatest liabilities occurred for females who not only lacked a "voice" but who emphasized the importance of appearance. In focusing on their outer selves, these girls faced formidable challenges in meeting the punishing cultural standards of attractiveness.

Some critics argue that Gilligan and her colleagues overemphasize differences in gender (Dindia, 2006; Hyde, 2014). One of those critics is developmentalist Eleanor Maccoby (2007), who says that Gilligan exaggerates the differences in intimacy and connectedness between males and females. Other critics fault Gilligan's research strategy, which rarely includes a comparison group of boys or statistical analysis. Instead, Gilligan conducts extensive interviews with girls and then provides excerpts from the girls' narratives to buttress her ideas. Other critics fear that Gilligan's findings reinforce stereotypes—females as nurturing and self-sacrificing, for example—that might undermine females' struggle for equality. These critics say that Gilligan's "different voice" perhaps should be called "the voice of the victim." What we should be stressing, say these critics, is the need to provide more opportunities for females to reach higher levels of achievement and self-determination.

Carol Gilligan. *What is Gilligan's view of moral development?*
Courtesy of Dr. Carol Gilligan

Whether you accept the connectionist arguments of Gilligan or the achievement/self-determination arguments of her critics, there is increasing evidence that early adolescence is a critical juncture in the psychological development of females (Basow, 2006). A large-scale national study revealed a decrease in the self-esteem of boys and girls during

How Can We Best Guide Adolescents' Gender Development?

Boys

- Encourage boys to be more sensitive in relationships and to engage in more prosocial behavior. An important socialization task is to help boys become more interested in having positive close relationships and become more caring. Fathers can play an especially important role for boys in this regard by being a model of a male who is sensitive and caring.
- Encourage boys to be less physically aggressive. Too often, boys are encouraged to be tough, virile, and aggressive. A positive strategy is to encourage them to be self-assertive but not overly physically aggressive.
- Encourage boys to handle their emotions more effectively. This guideline involves not only helping boys to regulate their emotions, as in controlling their anger, but also helping them learn to express their anxieties and concerns rather than to keep them bottled up.
- Work with boys to improve their school performance. Girls get better grades, put forth more academic effort, and are less likely than boys to be assigned to special/remedial classes. Parents and teachers can help boys by emphasizing the importance of school and expecting better academic effort from them.

Girls

- Encourage girls to be proud of their relationship skills and caring. The strong interest that girls show in relationships and caring should be rewarded by parents and teachers.
- Encourage girls to develop their self-competencies. While guiding girls to retain their relationship strengths, adults can help girls to develop their ambition and achievement.
- Encourage girls to be more self-assertive. Girls tend to be more passive than boys and can benefit from being encouraged to be more self-assertive.
- Encourage girls' achievement. Girls should be encouraged to have higher academic expectations and they should be introduced to a wide range of career options.

Boys and Girls

- Help adolescents to reduce gender stereotyping and discrimination. Don't engage in gender stereotyping and discrimination yourself—otherwise, you will be providing a model of gender stereotyping and discrimination for adolescents.

How can adopting one set of suggestions for girls and another for boys ensure that we do not "assign one set of values and behaviors to one sex and a different set to the other"?

adolescence, but a more substantial decrease for adolescent girls than boys (Robins & others, 2002). In another national survey that was conducted by the American Association of University Women (1992), girls experienced a significantly greater drop in self-esteem during adolescence than boys did. In yet another study, the self-esteem of girls declined during adolescence (Rosner & Rierdan, 1994). At ages 8 and 9, 60 percent of the girls were confident and assertive and felt positive about themselves, compared with 67 percent of the boys. However, over the next eight years, the girls' self-esteem fell 31 percentage points—only 29 percent of high school girls felt positive about themselves. Across the same age range, boys' self-esteem dropped 21 points—leaving 46 percent of the high school boys with high self-esteem, which makes for a gender gap of 17 percentage points. Another study found that the self-esteem of high school girls was lower than the self-esteem of elementary school girls and college women (Frost & McKelvie, 2004). Keep in mind, though, that some psychologists conclude that gender differences in self-esteem during adolescence are quite small (Hyde, 2007).

We should also recognize that many experts emphasize the need for adolescent girls and emerging adult women to maintain their competency in relationships and also to be self-motivated (Brabeck & Brabeck, 2006). In Phyllis Bronstein's (2006, p. 269) view, "It is beneficial neither to individuals nor to society as a whole to assign one set of values and behaviors to one sex and a different set to the other." How might we put this view into practice? The *Connecting with Health and Well-Being* interlude provides some recommendations for improving the gendered lives of adolescents.

In this chapter, you have read about many aspects of gender. You learned that sexuality influences gender in adolescence more than in childhood. We'll discuss adolescent sexuality more extensively later in this edition.

developmental **connection**

Identity

Self-esteem, also referred to as self-worth or self-image, is the global evaluative dimension of the self. Connect to "The Self, Identity, Emotion, and Personality."

Summarize
developmental changes
in gender

Review
- How might early adolescence
  influence gender development?
- Is early adolescence a critical juncture
  for females?

Connect
- How might gender intensification be
  linked to media influences?

Reflect *Your Own Personal
Journey of Life*
- Did your gender behavior change as
  you went through early adolescence?
  Explain.

reach your **learning goals**

Gender

1 Biological, Social, and Cognitive Influences on Gender

LG1 Describe the biological, social, and cognitive influences on gender

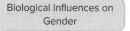

Biological Influences on
Gender

- Gender refers to the characteristics of people as females and males. A gender role is a set of expectations that prescribes how females and males should think, act, and feel. Because of pubertal change, sexuality plays a more important role in gender development for adolescents than for children. Freud's and Erikson's theories promote the idea that anatomy is destiny. Today's developmentalists are interactionists when biological and environmental influences on gender are at issue. In the evolutionary psychology view, evolutionary adaptations produced psychological sex differences, especially in the area of mate selection. However, criticisms of the evolutionary psychology view have been made, such as gender differences being influenced more strongly by environmental experiences. Gender differences have been found in the developmental trajectories of the brain in adolescence, but overall there are more similarities than differences in the brains of males and females.

Social Influences on
Gender

- In the social role view, women have less power and status than men do and control fewer resources. In this view, gender hierarchy and sexual division of labor are important causes of sex-differentiated behavior. The social cognitive theory of gender emphasizes that adolescents' gender development is influenced by their observation and imitation of others' gender behavior, as well as by rewards and punishments for gender-appropriate and gender-inappropriate behavior. Parents and siblings influence adolescents' gender roles. Mothers and fathers often interact with their adolescents differently and also interact differently with sons and daughters. Peers are especially adept at rewarding gender-appropriate behavior. There is still concern about gender inequity in education. Despite improvements, TV continues to portray males as more competent than females.

Cognitive Influences on
Gender

- Gender schema theory states that gender-typing emerges as individuals develop schemas for what is gender-appropriate and gender-inappropriate in their culture.

2 Gender Stereotypes, Similarities, and Differences

LG2 Discuss gender stereotypes, similarities, and differences

Gender Stereotyping

- Gender stereotypes are general impressions and beliefs about males and females. Gender stereotypes are widespread.

Gender Similarities and Differences

· There are a number of physical differences in males and females. In the cognitive domain, gender differences in math ability are either small or nonexistent. However, girls significantly outperform boys in reading and writing skills, get better grades in school, and are less likely to drop out of school. Socioemotional differences include the following: males are more physically aggressive and active; females show a stronger interest in relationships, are better at self-regulation of behavior and emotion, and engage in more prosocial behavior.

Gender Controversy

· There continues to be controversy about the extent of gender differences and what causes them. Buss argues that gender differences are extensive and attributable to evolutionary history. Eagly also concludes that gender differences are extensive but believes that they are caused by social conditions. Hyde states that gender differences have been exaggerated and that females and males are similar on most psychological factors.

Gender in Context

· Gender in context is an important concept. Gender roles can vary according to the culture in which adolescents develop and the immediate contexts in which they behave.

3 Gender-Role Classification

LG3 Characterize the variations in gender-role classification

Masculinity, Femininity, and Androgyny

· In the past, the well-adjusted male was supposed to show instrumental traits, the well-adjusted female expressive traits. In the 1970s, alternatives to traditional gender roles were introduced. It was proposed that competent individuals could show both masculine and feminine traits. This thinking led to the development of the concept of androgyny, the presence of masculine and feminine traits in one individual. Gender-role measures often categorize individuals as masculine, feminine, androgynous, or undifferentiated. Most androgynous individuals are flexible and mentally healthy, although the specific context and the individual's culture also determine how adaptive a gender-role orientation is.

Context, Culture, and Gender Roles

· In thinking about gender, it is important to keep in mind the context in which gendered behavior is displayed. In many countries around the world, traditional gender roles are still dominant.

Androgyny and Education

· Androgyny education programs have been more successful with females than with males and more successful with children than with adolescents.

Traditional Masculinity and Problem Behaviors in Adolescent Males

· A special concern is that boys raised in a traditional manner are socialized to conceal their emotions. Researchers have found that problem behaviors often characterize highly masculine adolescents.

Gender-Role Transcendence

· One alternative to androgyny states that there has been too much emphasis on gender and that a better strategy is to emphasize becoming competent persons.

4 Developmental Changes and Junctures

LG4 Summarize developmental changes in gender

Early Adolescence and Gender Intensification

· The gender intensification hypothesis states that psychological and behavioral differences between boys and girls become greater during adolescence because of increased socialization pressures to conform to traditional gender roles. The jury is still out on the validity of the gender intensification hypothesis, although an increasing number of studies do not support this hypothesis.

Is Early Adolescence a Critical Juncture for Females?

· Gilligan argues that girls reach a critical juncture in their development during early adolescence. Girls become aware that their intense interest in intimacy is not prized by the male-dominated society. Some critics say that Gilligan exaggerates gender differences in intimacy.

key terms

androgyny	gender role	gender stereotypes	social cognitive theory
gender	gender-role transcendence	rapport talk	of gender
gender intensification hypothesis	gender schema theory	report talk	social role theory

key people

Sandra Bem	Erik Erikson	Diane Halpern	Eleanor Maccoby
David Buss	Sigmund Freud	Janet Shibley Hyde	Joseph Pleck
Alice Eagly	Carol Gilligan	Carol Jacklin	Deborah Tannen

resources for improving the lives of adolescents

Gender Development in Adolescence
Nancy Galambos, Sheri Berenbaum, and Susan McHale
In R. Lerner and L. Steinberg (Eds.), *Handbook of Adolescence* (2009, 3rd ed.)
New York: Wiley
> Discusses many different research areas exploring gender development in adolescence.

Gender Similarities and Differences
Janet Shibley-Hyde (2014)
Annual Review of Psychology (Vol.65). Palo Alto, CA: Annual Reviews
> An up-to-date overview of research findings on many topics related to gender similarities and differences.

Analysis and Evaluation of the Rationales of Single-Sex Schooling
Rebecca Bigler, Amy Hayes, and Lynn Liben (2014)
Advances in Child Development and Behavior, 47, 225–260.
> Leading experts provide a number of arguments for why they think coeducational schools are more beneficial for adolescents than are single-sex schools.

The Inside Story on Teen Girls
Karen Zager and Alice Rubenstein (2002)
Washington, DC: American Psychological Association

> Provides insight into the lives of adolescent girls and offers many excellent recommendations for areas such as identity, puberty, sex, dating, school, peers, and relationships with parents.

Real Boys
William Pollack (1999)
New York: Owl Books
> Pollack examines the ways boys have been reared and concludes that there needs to be a major change in this rearing.

YMCA (www.ymca.net)
> The YMCA provides a number of programs for teenage boys. A number of personal health and sports programs are available. The Web site provides information about the YMCA closest to your location.

YWCA (www.ywca.org)
> The YWCA promotes health, sports participation, and fitness for women and girls. Its programs include instruction in health, teen pregnancy prevention, family life education, self-esteem enhancement, parenting, and nutrition. The Web site provides information about the YWCA closest to your location.

chapter 6

SEXUALITY

chapter outline

" I guess when you give a girl a sexy kiss you're supposed to open your lips and put your tongue in her mouth. That doesn't seem very sexy to me. I can't imagine how a girl would like that. What if she has braces on her teeth and your tongue gets scratched? And how are you supposed to breathe? Sometimes I wish I had an older brother I could ask stuff like this."

—FRANK, AGE 12

"I can't believe I'm so much in love! I just met him last week but I know this is the real thing. He is much more mature than the boys who have liked me before. He's a senior and has his own car. When he brought me home last night, we got so hot I thought we were going to have sex. I'm sure it will happen the next time we go out. It goes against everything I've been taught—but I can't see how it can be wrong when I'm so much in love and he makes me feel so fantastic!"

—AMY, AGE 15

"Ken and I went on a camping trip last weekend and now I'm sure that I'm gay. For a long time I've known I've been attracted to other guys, like in the locker room at school it would sometimes be embarrassing. Ken and I are great friends and lots of times we would mess around wrestling or whatever. I guessed that he felt the way I did. Now I know. Sooner or later, I'll have to come out, as they say, but I know that is going to cause a lot of tension with my parents and for me."

—TOM, AGE 15

"I'm lucky because I have a good figure and I'm popular. I've had boyfriends since middle school and I know how to take care of myself. It's fun when you're out with a guy and you can be intimate. The only thing is, Dan and I had sex a few weeks ago and I'm wondering if I'm pregnant. He used a contraceptive, but maybe it didn't work. Or maybe I'm just late. Anyway, if I have a baby, I could deal with it. My aunt wasn't married when she got pregnant with my cousin, and it turned out okay."

—CLAIRE, AGE 16

"About a month ago my mom's friend's daughter tested positive for HIV. Until then my mom and stepfather never talked about sex with me, but now they're taking turns lecturing me on the theme of "don't have sex until you're married." Give me a break! Nicole and I have been together for a year and a half. What do they think we do when we go out, just talk? Besides, my real father never remarried and has girlfriends all the time. All my life I've been seeing movies and TV shows where unmarried people sleep together and the worst that happens is maybe a broken heart. I don't know that woman's daughter, but she must have been mixed up with some pretty bad characters. Me, I always use a condom."

—SEAN, AGE 17

preview

During adolescence and emerging adulthood, the lives of adolescents are wrapped in sexuality. Adolescence and emerging adulthood are time frames when individuals engage in sexual exploration and incorporate sexuality into their identity. We have studied the biological basis of sexual maturation, including the timing of these changes and the hormones that are involved. This chapter focuses on the sexual experiences, attitudes, and behaviors of adolescents and emerging adults. We begin with an overview of sexuality in adolescence and emerging adulthood and then examine some problems involving sexual activity, such as adolescent pregnancy, sexually transmitted infections, and forcible sex. Finally, we explore the ways in which adolescents learn about sex.

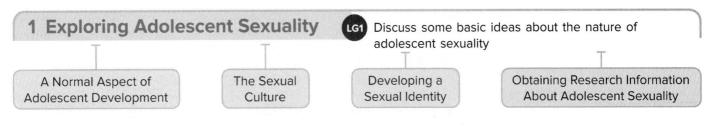

1 Exploring Adolescent Sexuality

LG1 Discuss some basic ideas about the nature of adolescent sexuality

| A Normal Aspect of Adolescent Development | The Sexual Culture | Developing a Sexual Identity | Obtaining Research Information About Adolescent Sexuality |

Adolescents have an almost insatiable curiosity about the mysteries of sex. They wonder whether they are sexually attractive, how to behave sexually, and what the future holds for their sexual lives. Most adolescents eventually manage to develop a mature sexual identity, even though, as adults can attest, there are always times of vulnerability and confusion along life's sexual journey.

A NORMAL ASPECT OF ADOLESCENT DEVELOPMENT

Much of what we hear about adolescent sexuality involves problems, such as adolescent pregnancy and sexually transmitted infections. Although these are significant concerns, it is important not to lose sight of the fact that sexuality is a normal part of adolescence (Lefkowitz & Vasilenko, 2014; Maas & Lefkowitz, 2015; Tolman & McClelland, 2011).

An important theme of adolescence that is underscored in this book is that too often adolescents are negatively stereotyped (Lewin-Bizan, Bowers, & Lerner, 2010). The themes of negative stereotyping and adolescent problems also apply to the topic of adolescent sexuality (Diamond & Savin-Williams, 2015). Although we will discuss a number of problems that can occur in the area of adolescent sexuality, it is important to keep in mind that the majority of adolescents have healthy sexual attitudes and engage in sexual behaviors that will not compromise their journey to adulthood.

Every society pays some attention to adolescent sexuality. In some societies, adults chaperone adolescent females to protect them from males; others promote very early marriage. Still other societies, such as the United States, allow some sexual experimentation, although there is a wide range of opinions about just how far this experimentation should be allowed to go.

In other chapters we have introduced topics that provide a backdrop for understanding sexual attitudes and behavior in adolescence. We saw that an important aspect of pubertal change involves sexual maturation and a dramatic increase in androgens in males and estrogens in females. We also discussed how puberty is coming earlier today than in previous generations, which can lead to early dating and early sexual activity.

We have noted that the prefrontal cortex (where the highest level of cognitive functioning occurs in processes such as self-control, reasoning, and decision making) develops later than the limbic system (a lower, subcortical system that is the seat of emotions and experience of rewards). Thus, the prefrontal cortex may not have developed to the point at which it can adequately control the adolescent's sexual feelings and passions.

We have considered sexual identity as one of the dimensions of personal identity. Intimacy with another is an important aspect of the dyadic nature of adolescent sexuality.

We have examined the physical and biological differences between females and males. We also saw that, according to the gender intensification hypothesis, pubertal changes can lead boys and girls to conform to traditional masculine and feminine behavior, respectively. Further, when college students are asked to rate the strength of their sex drive, men report higher levels of sexual desire than women. The adolescent developmental transition, then, may be seen as a bridge between the asexuality of childhood and the fully developed sexual identity of adulthood.

Subsequent chapters also include discussions that are important for understanding adolescent sexuality. We will learn that intense, prolonged conflict with parents is associated with adolescent sexual problems, as is a lack of parental monitoring. Better relationships with parents are correlated with the postponement of sexual intercourse, less frequent intercourse, and fewer partners in adolescence. Later in this chapter, we see that adolescents receive very little sex education from parents and that parents and adolescents rarely discuss sex.

We will read about how same-sex siblings, peers, and friends often discuss sexuality. We also learn that early dating is associated with a number of adolescent problems and that romantic love is important (especially for girls) in adolescence.

Sexual arousal emerges as a new phenomenon in adolescence, and it is important to view sexuality as a normal aspect of adolescent development.

—**SHIRLEY FELDMAN**
Contemporary psychologist, Stanford University

developmental **connection**
Biological Processes

Early maturation in girls is linked with earlier sexual experiences. Connect to "Puberty, Health, and Biological Foundations."

developmental **connection**
Peers

Early dating and "going with" someone are linked with adolescent pregnancy. Connect to "Peers, Romantic Relationships, and Lifestyles."

We will study how schools are playing an increasingly important role in adolescent sexuality. And later in this chapter, we will see that most parents now recognize that sex education in schools is an important aspect of education.

We will explore the vast cultural variations in sexuality. In some cultures sexuality is highly repressed, while other cultures have far more liberal standards for sexuality.

As you can see, sexuality is tied to virtually all areas of adolescent development that we discuss in this edition. Let's now explore the sexual culture to which American adolescents are exposed.

THE SEXUAL CULTURE

It is important to put adolescent sexuality into the broader context of sexuality in the American culture (Herdt & Polen-Petit, 2014). Whereas 50 years ago sex was reserved for married couples, today adult sex is openly acknowledged among both married and single adults. Sex among unmarried teenagers is an extension of this general trend toward greater sexual permissiveness in the adult culture. In the United States, society sends mixed messages about sex to youth—on the one hand, adolescents (especially girls) are told not to have sex—but on the other hand, they see sex portrayed in the media as positive (especially for boys). Thus, it is no wonder that adolescents find sexual development and choices so confusing. Consider the portrayal of sex in the media:

The messages conveyed about sexuality (in the media) are not always ideal . . . and they are often limited, unrealistic, and stereotypical. Dominating is a recreational orientation to sexuality in which courtship is treated as a competition, a battle of the sexes, characterized by dishonesty, game playing, and manipulation. . . . Also prominent are stereotypical sexual roles featuring women as sexual objects, whose value is based solely on their physical appearance, and men as sex-driven players looking to "score" at all costs. . . . (Ward, Day, & Epstein, 2006, p. 57)

Sex is explicitly portrayed in movies, TV shows, videos, lyrics of popular music, MTV, and Web sites (Doornwaard & others, 2015; Ybarra, Strasburger, & Mitchell, 2014). A study of 1,762 12- to 17-year-olds found that those who watched more sexually explicit TV shows were more likely than their counterparts who watched fewer of these shows to initiate sexual intercourse in the next 12 months (Collins & others, 2004). Adolescents in the highest 10 percent of viewing sexually explicit TV shows were twice as likely to engage in sexual intercourse as those in the lowest 10 percent. The results held regardless of whether the exposure to explicit sex involved sexual behavior or just talk about sex. In another study, U.S. high school students who frequently viewed talk shows and "sexy" prime-time programs were more likely to endorse sexual stereotypes than their counterparts who viewed these shows infrequently (Ward & Friedman, 2006). Also in this study, more frequent viewing and stronger identification with popular TV characters were linked with higher levels of sexual experience in adolescents. And a research review concluded that adolescents who view more sexual content on TV are likely to initiate sexual intercourse earlier than their peers who view less sexual content on TV (Brown & Strasburger, 2007). Further, a study of adolescents across a three-year period revealed a link between watching sex on TV and subsequent higher risk of pregnancy (Chandra & others, 2009). And a recent study revealed that adolescents' music video viewing was linked to asking someone for a sexting message and having received a sexting message (Van Ouytsel, Ponnet, & Walrave, 2014).

Adolescents are exposed to sex virtually everywhere in the American culture, and sex is used to sell just about everything.
© The McGraw-Hill Companies, Inc./John Flournoy, photographer

Adolescents increasingly have had access to sexually explicit Web sites (Doornwaard & others, 2015). One study revealed that adolescents who reported ever visiting a sexually explicit Web site were more sexually permissive and were more likely to have multiple lifetime sexual partners, to have had more than one sexual partner in the last three months, to have used alcohol or other substances at their last sexual encounter, and to engage in anal sex more than their counterparts who reported that they had never visited a sexually explicit Web site (Braun-Courville & Rojas, 2009). A recent study of Korean boys found that a higher risk of Internet addiction was linked to sexual intercourse experience (Sung & others, 2013).

Adolescents and emerging adults also increasingly use the Internet as a resource for information about sexuality. A recent study of 177 sexual health Web sites found that inaccuracies were few but that the quality of the information (such as display of authorship and authors' credentials, and clear information about sources, for example) was low (Buhi & others, 2010). The topic category with the lowest-rated quality was sexual assault.

A special concern is *sexting,* which involves sending sexually explicit images, videos, or text messages via electronic communication. A recent national study of 13- to 18-year-olds found that 7 percent reported sending or showing someone sexual pictures of themselves (Ybarra & Mitchell, 2014). In this study, sharing sexual photos was linked to a wide range of sexual behaviors including oral sex and vaginal sex.

The American Academy of Pediatrics (2010) recently issued a policy statement on sexuality, contraception, and the media. They pointed out that television, films, music, and the Internet are all becoming increasingly explicit, yet information about abstinence, sexual responsibility, and birth control rarely is included in these media outlets.

Adolescents are exposed to sex in many contexts, including TV and the Internet. *Is it surprising, then, that adolescents are so curious about sex and tempted to experiment with sex?*
© The CW/Courtesy Everett Collection

DEVELOPING A SEXUAL IDENTITY

Dealing with emerging sexual feelings and forming a sense of sexual identity is a multifaceted process (Diamond & Savin-Williams, 2015). This lengthy process involves learning to manage sexual feelings such as sexual arousal and attraction, developing new forms of intimacy, and learning the skills required to regulate sexual behavior so as to avoid undesirable consequences. Developing a sexual identity also involves more than just sexual behavior. Sexual identities emerge in the context of physical factors, social factors, and cultural factors, with most societies placing constraints on the sexual behavior of adolescents. An adolescent's sexual identity is strongly influenced by social norms related to sex—the extent to which adolescents perceive that their peers are having sex, using protection, and so on. These social norms have important influences on adolescents' sexual behavior. For example, one study revealed that when adolescents perceived that their peers were sexually permissive, the adolescents had a higher rate of initiating sexual intercourse and engaging in risky sexual practices (Potard, Courtois, & Rusch, 2008).

An adolescent's sexual identity involves an indication of sexual orientation (whether an individual has same-sex or other-sex attractions), and it also involves activities, interests, and styles of behavior. A study of 470 tenth- to twelfth-grade Australian youth found considerable variation in their sexual attitudes and practices (Buzwell & Rosenthal, 1996). Some were virgins and sexually naive. Some had high anxiety about sex and perceived their bodies as underdeveloped and unappealing, whereas others had low anxiety about sex and an interest in exploring sexual options. Yet others felt sexually attractive, were sexually experienced, and had confidence in their ability to manage sexual situations.

We are born twice over, the first time for existence, the second for life; Once as human beings and later as men and as women.

—JEAN-JACQUES ROUSSEAU
Swiss-born French philosopher, 18th century

OBTAINING RESEARCH INFORMATION ABOUT ADOLESCENT SEXUALITY

Assessing sexual attitudes and behavior is not always a straightforward matter (Saewyc, 2011). Consider how you would respond if someone asked you, "How often do you have intercourse?" or "How many different sexual partners have you had?" The individuals most likely to respond to sexual surveys are those with liberal sexual attitudes who engage in liberal sexual behaviors. Thus, research is limited by the reluctance of some individuals to provide candid answers to questions about extremely personal matters, and by researchers' inability to get any answer, candid or otherwise, from individuals who simply refuse to talk to strangers about sex. In addition, when asked about their sexual activity, individuals may respond

developmental **connection**
Research Methods
One drawback of surveys and interviews is the tendency of some participants to answer questions in a socially desirable way. Connect to "Introduction."

truthfully or they may give socially desirable answers. For example, a ninth-grade boy might report that he has had sexual intercourse even if he has not, because he is afraid someone will find out that he is sexually inexperienced. One study of high school students revealed that 8 percent of the girls understated their sexual experience, while 14 percent of the boys overstated their sexual experience (Siegel, Aten, & Roghmann, 1998). Thus, boys tend to exaggerate their sexual experiences to increase perceptions of their sexual prowess, while girls tend to downplay their sexual experience so they won't be perceived as irresponsible or promiscuous (Diamond & Savin-Williams, 2015).

Review Connect Reflect

LG1 Discuss some basic ideas about the nature of adolescent sexuality

Review

- How can sexuality be explained as a normal aspect of adolescent development?
- What kind of sexual culture are adolescents exposed to in the United States?
- What is involved in developing a sexual identity in adolescence?
- What are some difficulties involved in obtaining research information about adolescent sexuality?

Connect

- How does the sexual culture you learned about in this section contribute to gender stereotypes?

Reflect *Your Own Personal Journey of Life*

- How would you describe your sexual identity as an adolescent and emerging adult? What contributed to this identity?

2 Sexual Attitudes and Behavior

LG2 Summarize sexual attitudes and behavior in adolescence

| Heterosexual Attitudes and Behavior | Sexual Minority Youths' Attitudes and Behavior | Self-Stimulation | Contraceptive Use |

How is it that, in the human body, reproduction is the only function to be performed by an organ of which an individual carries only one half so that he has to spend an enormous amount of time and energy to find another half?

—FRANÇOIS JACOB
French biologist, 20th century

Let's now explore adolescents' sexual attitudes and behavior. First, we study heterosexual attitudes and behavior, and then sexual minority attitudes and behavior.

HETEROSEXUAL ATTITUDES AND BEHAVIOR

How early do adolescents engage in various sexual activities? What sexual scripts do adolescents follow? Are some adolescents more vulnerable than others to irresponsible sexual behavior? We will examine each of these questions in this section.

Development of Sexual Activities in Adolescents What is the current profile of sexual activity of adolescents? In a U.S. national survey conducted in 2013, 64 percent of twelfth-graders reported having experienced sexual intercourse, compared with 30 percent of ninth-graders (Kann & others, 2014). By age 20, 77 percent of U.S. youth report having engaged in sexual intercourse (Dworkin & Santelli, 2007). Nationally, in 2013, 49 percent of twelfth-graders, 40 percent of eleventh-graders, 29 percent of tenth-graders, and 20 percent of ninth-graders recently reported that they were currently sexually active (Kann & others, 2014). A recent analysis of more than 12,000 adolescents in the Longitudinal Study of Adolescent Health found a predominant overall pattern of vaginal sex first, average age of sexual initiation of 16 years, and spacing of more than 1 year between initiation of first and second sexual behaviors (Haydon & others, 2012). In this study, about a third of the adolescents initiated sex slightly later but initiated oral-genital and vaginal sex within the same year.

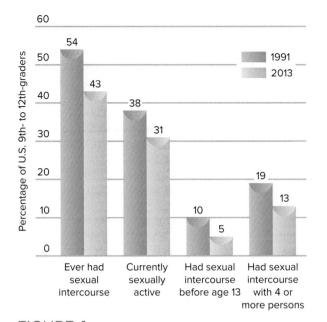

FIGURE 1

SEXUAL ACTIVITY OF U.S. ADOLESCENTS FROM 1991 TO 2013

Sexual timetable	Non-Latino White	African American	Latino	Asian American
Kiss	14.3	13.9	14.5	15.7
French kiss	15.0	14.0	15.3	16.2
Touch breast	15.6	14.5	15.5	16.9
Touch penis	16.1	15.0	16.2	17.8
Touch vagina	16.1	14.6	15.9	17.1
Sexual intercourse	16.9	15.5	16.5	18.0
Oral sex	17.1	16.9	17.1	18.3

FIGURE 2

SEXUAL TIMETABLES OF NON-LATINO WHITE, AFRICAN AMERICAN, LATINO, AND ASIAN AMERICAN ADOLESCENTS. *Note:* These data were reported in 1999. In the twenty-first century, adolescents are reporting that they engage in oral sex earlier in the sexual timetable. The numbers reflect the age at which adolescents reported having first engaged in the sexual activity.

Further, compared with non-Latino adolescents, African American adolescents were more likely to engage in vaginal sex first. Also, adolescents from low-SES backgrounds were characterized by earlier sexual initiation.

What trends in adolescent sexual activity have occurred in recent decades? From 1991 to 2013, fewer adolescents reported any of the following: ever having had sexual intercourse, currently being sexually active, having had sexual intercourse before the age of 13, and having had sexual intercourse with four or more persons during their lifetime (Kann & others, 2014) (see Figure 1).

Sexual initiation varies by ethnic group in the United States (Kann & others, 2014). African Americans are likely to engage in sexual behaviors earlier than other ethnic groups, whereas Asian Americans are likely to engage in them later (Feldman, Turner, & Araujo, 1999) (see Figure 2). In a more recent national U.S. survey (2014) of ninth- to twelfth-graders, 61 percent of African Americans, 49 percent of Latinos, and 44 percent of non-Latino Whites said they had experienced sexual intercourse (Kann & others, 2014). In this study, 14 percent of African Americans (compared with 6 percent of Latinos and 3 percent of non-Latino Whites) said they had their first sexual experience before 13 years of age.

Oral Sex Recent research indicates that oral sex is now a common occurrence for U.S. adolescents (Fava & Bay-Cheng, 2012; Halpern & Haydon, 2012). In a national survey, 55 percent of U.S. 15- to 19-year-old boys and 54 percent of girls of the same age said they had engaged in oral sex (National Center for Health Statistics, 2002). Figure 3 shows the developmental trends in oral sex. Noteworthy is that in this survey, a slightly higher percentage of 15- to 19-year-olds (55 percent of boys, 54 percent of girls) said they had engaged in oral sex than had engaged in sexual intercourse (49 percent of girls, 53 percent of boys). Also in the survey, more than 20 percent of the adolescents who had not had sexual intercourse had engaged in oral sex.

In an editorial in the *Journal of Adolescent Health*, Bonnie Halpern-Felsher (2008) discussed the pluses and minuses of oral

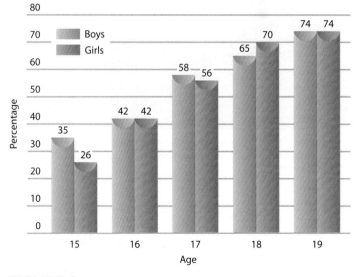

FIGURE 3

PERCENTAGE OF U.S. 15- TO 19-YEAR-OLD BOYS AND GIRLS WHO REPORT ENGAGING IN ORAL SEX

versus vaginal sex. Oral sex negates the risk of pregnancy and is linked to fewer negative outcomes than is vaginal sex. However, oral sex is not risk-free, being related to such negative health outcomes as sexually transmitted infections (herpes, chlamydia, and gonorrhea, for example). In recent research, Halpern-Felsher and her colleagues have examined the merits of engaging in oral versus vaginal sex (Brady & Halpern-Felsher, 2007; Song & Halpern-Felsher, 2010).

In one study, the temporal order between oral and vaginal sex in sexually active adolescents was examined (Song & Halpern-Felsher, 2010). In this study, most of the adolescents initiated vaginal sex after or within the same 6-month period of starting to have oral sex. Those who initiated oral sex at the end of the ninth grade had a 50 percent chance of having vaginal sex by the end of the eleventh grade, but those who delayed having oral sex until the end of the eleventh grade had less than a 20 percent chance of initiating vaginal sex by the end of the eleventh grade.

In another study, the consequences of having oral sex versus vaginal sex were explored (Brady & Halpern-Felsher, 2007). Compared with adolescents who engaged in oral sex and/or vaginal sex, adolescents who engaged only in oral sex were less likely to become pregnant or incur a sexually transmitted infection, feel guilty or used, have their relationship deteriorate, and get into trouble with their parents about sex. Adolescents who engaged only in oral sex also were more likely to report experiencing pleasure, feeling good about themselves, and having their relationship improve as a result of the sexual experience than did their counterparts who engaged only in vaginal sex or in both oral and vaginal sex.

A recent study also found that among female adolescents who reported having vaginal sex first, 31 percent reported having a teen pregnancy, whereas among those who initiated oral-genital sex first, only 8 percent reported having a teen pregnancy (Reese & others, 2013). Thus, how adolescents initiate their sex lives may have positive or negative consequences for their sexual health.

Cross-Cultural Comparisons   The timing of teenage sexual initiation varies widely by culture and gender, and in most instances is linked to the culture's values and customs (Carroll, 2016). In one study, among females, the proportion having first intercourse by age 17 ranged from 72 percent in Mali to 47 percent in the United States and 45 percent in Tanzania (Singh & others, 2000). The proportion of males who had their first intercourse by age 17 ranged from 76 percent in Jamaica to 64 percent in the United States and 63 percent in Brazil. Not all countries were represented in this study, and it is generally agreed that in some Asian countries, such as China and Japan, first intercourse occurs much later than in the United States.

Sexual activity patterns for 15- to 19-year-olds differ greatly for males and females in almost every geographic region of the world (Singh & others, 2000). In developing countries, the vast majority of sexually experienced males in this age group are unmarried, whereas two-thirds or more of the sexually experienced females at these ages are married. However, in the United States and in other developed nations such as the Netherlands, Sweden, and Australia, the overwhelming majority of 15- to 19-year-old females are unmarried.

What are some trends in the sexual behavior of adolescents? What characterizes adolescents' sexual scripts?
© Photomorgana/Corbis

Sexual Scripts   As adolescents and emerging adults explore their sexual identities, they are guided by sexual scripts (Lefkowitz & others, 2014). A **sexual script** is a stereotyped pattern of role prescriptions for how individuals should behave sexually (Morrison & others, 2015). By the time individuals reach adolescence, girls and boys have been socialized to follow different sexual scripts. Differences in female and male sexual scripting can cause problems and confusion for adolescents as they work out their sexual identities. Female adolescents learn to link sexual intercourse with love (Michael & others, 1994). They often rationalize their sexual behavior by telling themselves that they were swept away by the passion of the moment. A number of studies have found that adolescent girls are more likely than their male counterparts to report being in love as the main reason they are sexually active (Crooks & Baur, 2014; Hyde & DeLamater, 2014). Other reasons that girls give for being sexually active include giving in to male pressure, gambling that sex is a way to get a boyfriend, curiosity, and sexual desire unrelated to loving and caring.

sexual script A stereotyped pattern of role prescriptions for how individuals should behave in sexual contexts. Females and males have been socialized to follow different sexual scripts.

Struggling with a Sexual Decision

Elizabeth is an adolescent girl who is reflecting on her struggle with whether to have sex with a guy she is in love with. She says it is not a question of whether she loves him or not. She does love him, but she still doesn't know if it is right or wrong to have sex with him. He wants her to have sex, but she knows her parents would disapprove. Among her friends, some say yes, others say no. So Elizabeth is confused. After a few days of contemplation, in a moment of honesty, she admits that she is not his special love. This finally tilts the answer to not having sex with him. She realizes that if the relationship falls through, she will look back and regret it if she does have sex. In the end, Elizabeth decides not to have sex with him.

Elizabeth's reflections reveal her struggle to understand what is right and what is wrong, whether to have sex or not. In her circumstance, the fact that in a moment of honesty she admitted that she was not his special love made a big difference in her decision.

What sexual script probably lies behind Elizabeth's decision?

The majority of adolescent sexual experiences involve the male making sexual advances and the female setting limits on the male's sexual overtures. Adolescent boys experience considerable peer pressure to have sexual intercourse. As one adolescent remarked, "I feel a lot of pressure from my buddies to go for the score."

Deborah Tolman (2002) interviewed a number of girls about their sexuality and was struck by how extensively a double standard still restricts girls from experiencing and talking about sexuality but allows boys more free rein with their sexuality. In movies, magazines, and music, girls are often depicted as the object of someone else's desire but rarely as someone who has acceptable sexual feelings of her own. Tolman says that girls face a difficult challenge related to their sexual selves: to be the perfect sexual object, they are supposed to be sexy but control their desire. A recent study indicated that adolescent girls often recognized the existence of a sexual double standard on a societal or school level, but support or acceptance in their close friend network served as a buffer against the double standard (Lyons & others, 2010).

A recent study explored heterosexual sexual scripts in focus groups with 18- to 26-year-old males and females (Sakaluk & others, 2014). The following sexual scripts were supported:

· *Sex Drive.* Men are always ready for sex; women inhibit their sexual expression.
· *Physical and Emotional Sex.* Men have a physical approach to sex; women have an emotional/relational approach to sex.
· *Sexual Performance.* Men and women should both be sexually skilled and knowledgeable. One new aspect of this sexual script for women was agreement that women should especially have oral sex skills.
· *Initiation and Gateway Scripts.* Men initiate sex (most men and some women agreed with this script); women are gatekeepers (most men and women agreed that women set the sexual limits)
· *Sexual Evaluation.* Single women who appear sexual are judged negatively; men are rewarded for being sexual. However, there was negative judgment of men who come across as too sexual and too often engage in casual sex, especially with different women.

Another recent study of young adult men found two main sexual scripts: (1) A traditional male "player" script, and (2) a script that emphasized mutual sexual pleasure (Morrison & others, 2014).

Risk Factors in Adolescent Sexuality   Many adolescents are not emotionally prepared to handle sexual experiences, especially in early adolescence. Early sexual activity is linked with risky behaviors such as drug use, delinquency, and school-related problems (Chan & others, 2015; Coley & others, 2013; Skinner & others, 2015). A recent study confirmed that early engagement in sexual intercourse (prior to 14 years of age) is associated with high-risk

What are some risks for early initiation of sexual intercourse?
© Stockbyte/PunchStock RF

sexual factors (forced sex using drugs/alcohol at last sex, not using a condom at last sex, having multiple partners in last month, and becoming pregnant or causing a pregnancy), as well as experiencing dating violence (Kaplan & others, 2013). Also, a recent study of more than 3,000 Swedish adolescents revealed that sexual intercourse before age 14 was linked to risky behaviors such as an increased number of sexual partners, experience of oral and anal sex, negative health behaviors (smoking, drug and alcohol use), and antisocial behavior (being violent, stealing, running away from home) at 18 years of age (Kastbom & others, 2015). And a study of adolescents in five countries, including the United States, found that substance use was related to early sexual intercourse (Madkour & others, 2010).

In addition to having sex in early adolescence, other risk factors for sexual problems in adolescence include contextual factors such as socioeconomic status (SES) and poverty, immigration/ethnic minority status, family/parenting and peer factors, and school-related influences (Van Ryzin & others, 2011). The percentage of sexually active young adolescents is higher in low-income areas of inner cities (Morrison-Beedy & others, 2013). A recent study revealed that neighborhood poverty concentrations predicted 15- to 17-year-old girls' and boys' sexual initiation (Cubbin & others, 2010). And a recent study in low-income neighborhoods found that caregiver hostility was linked to early sexual activity and sex with multiple partners while caregiver warmth was related to later sexual initiation and a lower incidence of sex with multiple partners (Gardner, Martin, & Brooks-Gunn, 2012). Also, a recent national survey of 15- to 20-year-olds found that Spanish-speaking immigrant youth were more likely to have a sexual partner age difference of 6 or more years and less likely to use contraception at first sexual intercourse than their native Latino, non-Latino White, and English-speaking Latino immigrant counterparts (Haderxhanaj & others, 2014).

A number of family factors are associated with sexual risk-taking (de Looze & others, 2015; Widman & others, 2014). A recent study found that family strengths (family closeness, support, and responsiveness to health needs, for example) in childhood were protective against early initiation of sexual activity and adolescent pregnancy (Hillis & others, 2010). Another recent study revealed that sexual risk-taking behavior was more likely to occur in girls living in single-parent homes (Hipwell & others, 2011). Further, a recent study found that difficulties and disagreements between Latino adolescents and their parents were linked to the adolescents' early sex initiation (Cordova & others, 2014). Also, having older sexually active siblings or pregnant/parenting teenage sisters placed adolescent girls at higher risk for pregnancy (Miller, Benson, & Galbraith, 2001).

Peer, school, and sports contexts provide further information about sexual risk taking in adolescents (Choukas-Bradley & others, 2014; Coley & others, 2013; Young & Vazsonyi, 2011). A recent study found that adolescents who associated with more deviant peers in early adolescence were likely to have more sexual partners at age 16 (Lansford & others, 2010). And a recent research review found that school connectedness was linked to positive sexuality outcomes (Markham & others, 2010). Also, a study of middle school students revealed that better academic achievement was a protective factor in keeping boys and girls from engaging in early initiation of sexual intercourse (Laflin, Wang, & Barry, 2008). Further, in a recent study adolescent females who skipped school or failed a test were more likely to frequently have sexual intercourse and less likely to use contraceptives (Hensel & Sorge, 2014). Also, a recent study found that adolescent males who play sports engage in a higher level of sexual risk taking, while adolescent females who play sports engage in a lower level of sexual risk taking (Lipowski & others, 2015).

Cognitive and personality factors are increasingly implicated in sexual risk taking in adolescence (Fantasia, 2008). Two such factors are attention problems and weak self-regulation (difficulty controlling one's emotions and behavior). A longitudinal study revealed that attention problems and high rates of aggressive disruptive behavior at school entry increased the risk of multiple problem behaviors (school maladjustment, antisocial behavior, and substance use) in middle school, which in turn was linked to early initiation of sexual activity (Schofield & others, 2008). Another longitudinal study found that weak self-regulation at 8 to 9 years of age and risk proneness (tendency to seek sensation and make poor decisions) at 12 to 13 years of age set the stage for sexual risk taking at 16 to 17 years of age (Crockett, Raffaelli, & Shen, 2006). And a recent study also found that a high level of impulsiveness was linked to early adolescent sexual risk taking (Khurana & others, 2012).

- - - - - - - - ->
developmental **connection**

Religious Development

Certain aspects of being religious are linked to lower sexual risk taking. Connect to "Moral Development, Values, and Religion."

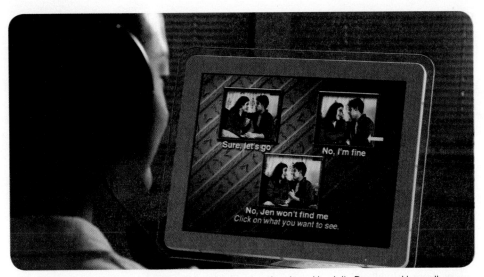

An adolescent participates in an interactive video session developed by Julie Downs and her colleagues at the department of Social and Decision Sciences at Carnegie Mellon University. The videos help adolescents evaluate their responses and decisions in high-risk sexual contexts.
© Michael Ray

Also, a recent meta-analysis indicated that the link between impulsivity and risky sexual behavior was likely to be more characteristic of adolescent females than males (Dir, Coskunpinar, & Cyders, 2014).

Might adolescents' character traits and spirituality protect them from negative sexual outcomes? A research review concluded that *prosocial norms* (providing youth with information about norms of risk behaviors; having youth make public commitments to behave in a prosocial manner, such as avoiding risk behaviors; and having peers and older youth communicate positive aspects of prosocial behavior) and *spirituality* (being spiritual, religious, or believing in a higher power, for example) were linked to positive sexual outcomes for adolescents: being less likely to intend to have sex, not likely to engage in early sex, having sex less frequently, and not becoming pregnant (House & others, 2010). A recent study also found that parents' religiosity was linked to a lower level of adolescents' risky sexual behavior, in part resulting from adolescents hanging out with less sexually permissive peers (Landor & others, 2011).

A recent effort to develop a strategy to reduce negative outcomes for adolescent sexuality focuses on positive youth development (PYD) (Lerner & others, 2015). PYD programs seek to strengthen adolescents' relationships and skills and help them develop a more positive future outlook by enhancing academic, economic, and volunteer activities. An increasing number of efforts utilizing a PYD focus to improve sexual outcomes in adolescence are being implemented (Catalano, Gavin, & Markham, 2010; Gavin & others, 2010; House & others, 2010; Markham & others, 2010).

A recent intervention study with adolescent girls (mean age of 16.5 years) living in a high-risk, low-income area was successful in increasing the number of girls who were sexually abstinent over a one-year time frame compared with a control group of girls who did not experience the intervention (Morrison-Beedy & others, 2013). Among girls who were sexually active, the girls in the intervention group also showed decreases in the number of times they had vaginal sex, the number of times they had unprotected sex, and a 50 percent reduction in positive pregnancy texts. The intervention consisted of four weekly two-hour group sessions (six to nine girls in a group) and two 90-minute booster sessions at 3 and 6 months post-intervention. The intervention included (1) HIV information, (2) motivation to reduce sexually risky behaviors, and (3) instruction in practicing interpersonal and self-management skills in risky sexual situations, including effective use of condoms.

Further Exploration of Sexuality in Emerging Adults

We already have covered some aspects of heterosexual attitudes and behavior in emerging adults. For example, recall in our discussion of sexual scripts that a number of sexual scripts continue to characterize emerging adult females and males (Lefkowitz & others, 2014; Sakaluk & others, 2014).

developmental **connection**

Positive Youth Development

The "Five Cs" of PYD are competence, confidence, connection, character, and caring/compassion. Connect to "Introduction."

What are some characteristics of sexual patterns in emerging adulthood?
© Image Source/Getty Images RF

Here we consider further analysis and integration of information about patterns of heterosexual behavior in emerging adults.

Surveys indicate that at the beginning of emerging adulthood (age 18), a little more than half of individuals have experienced sexual intercourse—but by the end of emerging adulthood (age 25), most individuals have had sexual intercourse (Lefkowitz & Gillen, 2006; Regenerus & Uecker, 2011). Also, the average age of marriage in the United States is currently 29 for males and 27 for females (U.S. Census Bureau, 2014). Thus, emerging adulthood is a time frame during which most individuals are "both sexually active and unmarried" (Lefkowitz & Gillen, 2006, p. 235).

Patterns of heterosexual behavior for males and females in emerging adulthood include the following (Lefkowitz & Gillen, 2006):

- Males have more casual sexual partners, and females report being more selective about their choice of a sexual partner.

- Approximately 60 percent of emerging adults have had sexual intercourse with only one individual in the past year, but compared with young adults in their late twenties and thirties, emerging adults are more likely to have had sexual intercourse with two or more individuals.

- Although emerging adults have sexual intercourse with more individuals than do young adults, they have sex less frequently. Approximately 25 percent of emerging adults report having sexual intercourse only a couple of times a year or not at all (Michael & others, 1994).

- Uncertainty characterizes many emerging adults' sexual relationships. Consider a recent study of emerging adult daters and cohabitors that found nearly half reported a reconciliation (a breakup followed by a reunion) (Halpern-Meekin & others, 2013).

- A recent study found that sexual risk factors increase in emerging adulthood, with males engaging in more of these risk factors than females (Mahalik & others, 2013).

Casual sex is more common in emerging adulthood than it is during the late twenties (Fielder & others, 2013). A recent trend has involved "hooking up" to have non-relationship sex (from kissing to intercourse) (Olmstead & others, 2015; Robertson, Olmstead, & Fincham, 2015; Vrangalova, 2015a, b). One study revealed that 20 percent of first-year college women on one large university campus had engaged in at least one hookup over the course of the school year (Fielder & others, 2013). In this study, impulsivity, sensation seeking, and alcohol use were among the predictors of a higher likelihood of hooking up. In addition to hooking up, another type of casual sex that has recently increased among emerging adults is "friends with benefits," which involves a relationship formed by the integration of friendship and sexual intimacy without an explicit commitment characteristic of an exclusive romantic relationship (Owen, Fincham, & Manthos, 2013). Further, another recent study indicated that 40 percent of 22-year-olds reporting having had a recent casual sexual partner (Lyons & others, 2015). And a recent study of more than 3,900 18- to 25-year-olds revealed that having casual sex was negatively linked to well-being and positively related to psychological distress (Bersamin & others, 2014).

What are some predictors of risky heterosexual behavior in emerging adults, such as engaging in casual and unprotected sexual intercourse? Some research findings indicate that individuals who become sexually active in adolescence engage in more risky sexual behaviors in emerging adulthood than do their counterparts who delay their sexual debuts until emerging adulthood (Capaldi & others, 2002; Pflieger & others, 2013; Scott & others, 2011). One study indicated that college students who practiced unsafe sexual behavior were likely to have also done so in high school (Wetherill, Neal, & Fromme, 2010). Another recent study revealed that emerging adults who were enrolled in college or who had graduated from college reported having fewer casual sex partners than those without a high school diploma (Lyons & others, 2013). More religious emerging adults have had fewer sexual partners and engage in less risky sexual behaviors than their less religious counterparts (Lefkowitz, Boone, & Shearer, 2004). And when emerging adults drink alcohol, they are more likely to have casual sex and less likely to discuss possible risks (Johnson & Chen, 2015). Also, a recent study revealed that parent-child closeness was linked to lower-risk sexual factors in emerging adult African American males, including less permissive sexual attitudes, more consistent condom use, and fewer sexual partners (Harris, Sutherland, & Hutchinson, 2013). Further, in a recent study of

Christine's Thoughts About Sexual Relationships

As a college freshman, Christine tried to suppress the sexual feelings she had in her romantic relationship and later decided it was best to lose her virginity to a friend rather than a boyfriend:

> I think the first time you have sex should be with a friend, not necessarily with a boyfriend, because there's too many emotions involved. And with a friend, there's that closeness there but there's not those deep-running feelings that could really (mess) you up if the relationship doesn't work out.

Christine also made these comments:

> I won't really enjoy (sex) until after college . . . because in college, everything's so helter-skelter. You don't know what you're going to do

the next day or the day after that. And after college, you're probably going to get into a routine of going to work, coming back home, feeding your dog, feeding your boyfriend, you know? It's going to feel like you have more of a stable life with this person, and think that they're going to be more intimate. And with that, you're probably going to have better sex.

(Source: Gilmartin, 2006, pp. 444, 447)

Do Christine's efforts to be selective about her sexual partners mirror an observed pattern of behavior among people her age?

almost 8,000 emerging adults, males had more permissive sexual attitudes, especially regarding sexual encounters, than did females (Sprecher, Treger, & Sakaluk, 2013). Another recent study found that more frequent viewing of pornography by college students was associated with a higher incidence of hooking up and a higher number of different hookup partners (Braithwaite & others, 2015).

How extensive are gender differences in sexuality? A meta-analysis revealed that men said they engaged more often in masturbation, pornography use, and casual sex, and they expressed more permissive attitudes about casual sex than did their female counterparts (Petersen & Hyde, 2010).

In a recent provocative book, *Premarital Sex in America: How Young Americans Meet, Mate, and Think About Marrying,* sociologists Mark Regenerus and Jeremy Uecker (2011) described the free, temporary, and self-rewarding sexual "benefits" of emerging adulthood as superficial and incompatible with long-term, secure relationships such as marriage. They conclude that the sexual life of emerging adults is often characterized by serial monogamy: one partner at a time. Regenerus and Uecker also state that these patterns of emerging adults' sexual behavior are more likely to produce sexual regrets and diminished emotional well-being in emerging adult women than men because the emotional connection of a relationship is so important to women. They further argue that many emerging adult women are not aware of how damaging such short-term, serial monogamous relationships can be to their emotional health. Critics have asserted that Regenerus and Uecker's analysis is male-biased and devalues women (Katz & Smith, 2012).

SEXUAL MINORITY YOUTHS' ATTITUDES AND BEHAVIOR

The majority of sexual minority individuals experience their first same-sex attraction, sexual behavior, and self-labeling as a gay or lesbian during adolescence (Diamond & Savin-Williams, 2015; Savin-Williams, 2015). However, some sexual minority individuals have these experiences for the first time during emerging adulthood. Also, while most gays and lesbians have their first same-sex experience in adolescence, they often have their first extended same-sex relationship in emerging adulthood.

Preference for a sexual partner of the same or other sex is not always a fixed decision, made once in life and adhered to forever. For example, it is not unusual for an individual, especially a male, to engage in same-sex experimentation in adolescence but not to engage in same-sex behavior as an adult. For others, the opposite progression applies.

Until the middle of the twentieth century, it was generally thought that people were either heterosexual or homosexual. However, there has been a move away from using the term "homosexual" because the term has negative historical connotations (Crooks & Baur, 2014).

What are some characteristics of sexual minority adolescents?
© Nati Harnik/AP Images

Also, the use of the term "homosexual" as a clear-cut sexual type is often oversimplified. For example, many more individuals report having same-sex attractions and behavior than ever identify themselves as members of a **sexual minority**—individuals who self-identify as lesbian, gay, or bisexual. The term **bisexual** refers to someone who is attracted to people of both sexes. Researchers have gravitated toward more descriptive and limited terms than "homosexual," preferring such terms as "individuals with same-sex attractions," or "individuals who have engaged in same-sex behavior."

National surveys reveal that 2.3 to 2.7 percent of U.S. individuals identify with being a gay male, and 1.1 to 1.3 percent identify with being a lesbian (Alan Guttmacher Institute, 1995; Michael & others, 1994). Although some estimates of same-sex sexual activity (intercourse or oral sex) are in the 2 to 3 percent range for adults (Remafedi & others, 1992), others are higher (Mosher, Chandra, & Jones, 2005).

Factors Associated with Sexual Minority Behavior   Researchers have explored the possible biological basis of sexual minority behavior. In this regard, we next evaluate hormone, brain, and twin studies regarding same-sex attraction. The results of hormone studies have been inconsistent. Indeed, if sexual minority males are given male sexual hormones (androgens), their sexual orientation does not change; their sexual desire merely increases.

A very early critical period might influence sexual orientation (Hines, 2013, 2015). In the second to fifth months after conception, exposure of the fetus to hormone levels characteristic of females might cause the individual (female or male) to become attracted to males (Ellis & Ames, 1987). If this critical-period hypothesis turns out to be correct, it would explain why clinicians have found that sexual orientation is difficult, if not impossible, to modify (Meyer-Bahlburg & others, 1995).

Researchers have also examined genetic influences on sexual orientation by studying twins. A recent Swedish study of almost 4,000 twins found that only about 35 percent of the variation in homosexual behavior in men and 19 percent in women were explained by genetic differences (Langstrom & others, 2010). This result suggests that although genes likely play a role in sexual orientation, they are not the only factor (King, 2014).

An individual's sexual orientation—same-sex, heterosexual, or bisexual—is most likely determined by a combination of genetic, hormonal, cognitive, and environmental factors (Carroll, 2016; King, 2014). Most experts on same-sex relations believe that no one factor alone causes sexual orientation, and that the relative weight of each factor can vary from one individual to the next.

developmental **connection**

Research Methods

A twin study compares the behavioral similarities between identical twins with those between fraternal twins. Connect to "Puberty, Health, and Biological Foundations."

sexual minority Someone who self-identifies as lesbian, gay, or bisexual.

bisexual A person who is attracted to people of both sexes.

Developmental Pathways   It is commonly perceived that most gays and lesbians quietly struggle with same-sex attractions in childhood, do not engage in heterosexual dating, and gradually recognize that they are gay or lesbian in mid- to late adolescence (Diamond & Savin-Williams, 2015). However, there is much more fluidity in sexual orientation than this developmental milestone approach suggests (Saewyc, 2011). Many youth do follow this developmental pathway, but others do not. For example, many youth have no recollection of same-sex attractions and experience a more abrupt sense of their same-sex attraction in late adolescence (Savin-Williams & Cohen, 2015). Researchers also have found that the majority of adolescents with same-sex attractions also experience some degree of other-sex attractions (Garofalo & others, 1999). And, although some adolescents who are attracted to same-sex individuals fall in love with these individuals, others claim that their same-sex attractions are purely physical (Savin-Williams, 2015).

In sum, sexual minority youth have diverse patterns of initial attraction, often have bisexual attractions, and may have physical or emotional attraction to same-sex individuals but do not always fall in love with them (Savin-Williams & Cohen, 2015).

Gay or Lesbian Identity and Disclosure   Establishing a gay or lesbian identity is often referred to as the coming-out process (Savin-Williams & Cohen, 2015). In one study of gay adolescents, the majority said that as children they felt different from other boys (Newman & Muzzonigro, 1993). The average age at which they had their first crush on another boy was 12.7 years, and the average age when they realized they were gay was 12.5 years. Most of the boys said they felt confused when they first became aware that they were gay. About half the boys said they initially tried to deny their identity as a gay male.

Similarities and Differences with Heterosexual Youth   A large-scale study found similarities and differences in the lives of adolescents who are heterosexual, those who have same-sex attractions, and those who are bisexual (Bosséri & others, 2006). Similarities across sexual orientations occurred for friendship quality, academic orientation, and perception of school climate. Bisexual adolescents reported the most negative results, including areas of their lives such as relationships with parents, psychological functioning, and victimization. Adolescents with same-sex attractions reported less positive experiences than did exclusively heterosexual adolescents in relationships with parents, psychological functioning, and victimization. These results confirm findings in other studies that suggest that non-heterosexual adolescents face certain risks and challenges in their lives. However, the findings also indicate that adolescents with same-sex attractions have a number of positive aspects to their lives, including intrapersonal strengths (academic orientation) and interpersonal resources (friendship quality) (Bosséri & others, 2006).

Discrimination, Bias, and Violence   Having irrational negative feelings against individuals who have same-sex attractions is called **homophobia.** In its more extreme forms, homophobia can lead individuals to ridicule, physically assault, or even murder people they believe to have same-sex attractions. More typically, homophobia is associated with avoidance of individuals who have same-sex attractions, faulty beliefs about sexual minority lifestyles (such as falsely thinking that most child molesters have same-sex attractions), and subtle or overt discrimination in housing, employment, and other areas of life (Meyer, 2003).

One of the harmful aspects of the stigmatization of same-sex attraction is the self-devaluation engaged in by sexual minority individuals (Diamond & Savin-Williams, 2015). One common form of self-devaluation is called passing, the process of hiding one's real social identity. Without adequate support, and with fear of stigmatization, many gay and lesbian youth retreat to the closet and then emerge at a safer time later, often in college.

Sexual minority youth are more likely to be targeted for violence than heterosexual youth in a number of contexts, including forced sex and dating violence, and verbal and physical harassment at school and in the community (Coker, Austin, & Schuster, 2010; Ryan & others, 2009). Many sexual minority adolescents also experience discrimination and rejection in interactions with their families, peers, schools, and communities (Diamond & Savin-Williams, 2015; Savin-Williams, 2015). Sexual minority youths' exposure to stigma and discrimination has been cited as the main reason they are more likely to develop problems (Saewyc, 2011).

> In the last decade, an increasing number of youths have disclosed their gay, lesbian, or bisexual attraction to their parents.
>
> **—RICHARD SAVIN-WILLIAMS**
> *Contemporary psychologist, Cornell University*

homophobia Irrational negative feelings against individuals who have same-sex attractions.

For example, one study found that family rejection of coming out by sexual minority adolescents was linked to their higher rates of depression, substance use, and unprotected sex (Ryan & others, 2009). A recent study of 15-year-olds found that sexual minority status was linked to depression mainly via peer harassment (Martin-Storey & Crosnoe, 2012). Despite these negative circumstances, many sexual minority adolescents successfully cope with the challenges they face and develop levels of health and well-being that are similar to those of their heterosexual peers (Saewyc, 2011).

Health   Concern has been voiced about the possible sexual health risks for sexual minority youth. A recent national survey revealed that the prevalence of health-risk behaviors was higher for sexual minority youth than for heterosexual youth in 7 of 10 risk-behavior categories: behaviors that contribute to violence, behaviors related to attempted suicide, tobacco use, alcohol use, other drug use, sexual behaviors, and weight management (Kann & others, 2011). However, a research review concluded that there are mixed results as to whether sexual minority adolescents are more likely to attempt suicide (Saewyc, 2011). A recent research review of more than 300 studies concluded that bisexual youth had a higher rate of suicide ideation and attempts than their gay, lesbian, and heterosexual counterparts (Pompili & others, 2014). And a recent study of more than 72,000 adolescents, more than 6,200 of whom were sexuality minority adolescents, revealed that the sexual minority adolescents had a higher incidence of suicide ideation, planning, and attempts than the heterosexual adolescents (Bostwick & others, 2014). A recent study also found that family support was linked to a decreased risk of suicide attempts in sexual minority youth (Reisner & others, 2014).

Recent research also indicates that sexual minority adolescents are more likely to develop substance abuse problems and engage in sexual risk taking (Rosario & others, 2014; Saewyc, 2011). A longitudinal study revealed that sexual minority adolescents were more likely to begin drinking earlier than their heterosexual counterparts and that most sexual minority groups had higher levels of drinking, including binge drinking in late adolescence (Coker, Austin, & Schuster, 2010). Another recent study also found a higher rate of substance use and suicide ideation and attempts in sexual minority youth, especially when they lacked connections with adults at their school (Seil, Desai, & Smith, 2014).

Sexual minority adolescents are more likely to have an early sexual debut (before age 13 in some studies, prior to age 14 in others), report a higher number of lifetime or recent sexual partners, and have more sexually transmitted infections than do heterosexual adolescents, although mixed findings have been found for condom use across these groups (Parkes & others, 2011; Saewyc, 2011).

A special concern is the higher rate of sexually transmitted infections, especially HIV, in males who have sex with males (Morgan, 2014). Also, researchers recently found a higher incidence of sexually transmitted infections in adolescent girls with same-sex partners (especially when they have sexual relations with male partners as well) (Morgan, 2014). Further, a recent national study of 15- to 20-year-olds found that bisexual and lesbian young women experienced a younger sexual debut and had more male and female sexual partners than did their heterosexual counterparts (Tornello, Riskind, & Patterson, 2014). In this study, bisexual women reported the earliest sexual debut, highest numbers of sexual partners, greatest usage of emergency contraception, and highest frequency of pregnancy termination. Other research has found more extensive sexual health risks for bisexual adolescent females and males than for members of other groups (Morgan, 2014).

SELF-STIMULATION

Regardless of whether adolescents have a heterosexual or same-sex attraction, they will experience increasing feelings of sexual arousal. One way in which many youths who are not dating or who consciously choose not to engage in sexual intercourse or sexual explorations deal with these insistent feelings of sexual arousal is through self-stimulation, or masturbation.

As indicated earlier, a heterosexual continuum of kissing, petting, and intercourse or oral sex characterizes many adolescents' sexual experiences. Substantial numbers of adolescents, though, have sexual experience outside this heterosexual continuum through masturbation or same-sex behavior. Most boys have an ejaculation for the first time at about 12 to 13 years of age. Masturbation, genital contact with a same-sex or other-sex partner, or a wet dream during sleep are common circumstances for ejaculation.

Masturbation is the most frequent sexual outlet for many adolescents, especially male adolescents. A recent study of 14- to 17-year-olds found that 74 percent of the males and 48 percent of the females reported that they had masturbated at some point (Robbins & others, 2012).

Adolescents today do not feel as guilty about masturbation as members of previous generations did, although they still may feel embarrassed or defensive about it. In past eras, masturbation was denounced as causing everything from warts to insanity. Today, as few as 15 percent of adolescents attach any stigma to masturbation (Hyde & DeLamater, 2014).

In one study, the masturbation practices of female and male college students were studied (Leitenberg, Detzer, & Srebnik, 1993). Almost twice as many males as females said they had masturbated (81 percent versus 45 percent), and the males who masturbated did so three times more frequently during early adolescence and early adulthood than did the females who masturbated during the same age periods. No association was found between the quality of sexual adjustment in adulthood and a history of engaging in masturbation during preadolescence and/or early adolescence.

Much of the existing data on masturbation are difficult to interpret because they are based on self-reports in which many adolescents may not be responding accurately. Most experts on adolescent sexuality likely would agree that boys masturbate more than girls—but masturbation is more stigmatized behavior for girls, so they may actually masturbate more than they indicate in self-reports.

CONTRACEPTIVE USE

Sexual activity is a normal behavior that is necessary for procreation, but if appropriate safeguards are not taken it brings the risk of unintended, unwanted pregnancy and sexually transmitted infections (Crooks & Baur, 2014; Jaccard & Levitz, 2013). Both of these risks can be reduced significantly by using barrier methods of contraception, such as condoms.

Are adolescents increasingly using condoms? A recent national study revealed a substantial increase in the use of a contraceptive (59 percent in 2013 compared with 46 percent in 1991) by U.S. high school students the last time they had sexual intercourse (Kann & others, 2014). Also, a recent study in 20 European countries found that condom use increased from 2002 to 2010 (Ramiro & others, 2015).

Many sexually active adolescents do not use contraceptives, or they use them inconsistently (Amialchuk & Gerhardinger, 2015; Finer & Philbin, 2013; Tschann & others, 2010; Yen & Martin, 2013; Vasilenko, Kreager, & Lefkowitz, 2015). In 2013, 34 percent of sexually active adolescents had not used a condom the last time they had sexual intercourse (Kann & others, 2014). In the recent national U.S. survey (2014), among sexually active adolescents, ninth-graders (63 percent), tenth-graders (62 percent), and eleventh graders (62 percent) reported that they had used a condom during their last sexual intercourse more than did twelfth-graders (53 percent) (Kann & others, 2014). A recent study also found that 50 percent of U.S. 15- to 19-year-old girls with unintended pregnancies ending in live births were not using any birth control method when they got pregnant, and 34 percent believed they could not get pregnant at the time (Centers for Disease Control and Prevention, 2015a). Also, a recent study found that a greater age difference between sexual partners in adolescence is associated with less consistent condom use (Volpe & others, 2013).

Researchers also have found that U.S. adolescents use condoms less than their counterparts in Europe (Jorgensen & others, 2015). Studies of 15-year-olds revealed that in Europe 72 percent of the girls and 81 percent of the boys had used condoms during their last intercourse (Currie & others, 2008). Use of birth control pills also continues to be higher in European countries (Santelli, Sandfort, & Orr, 2009). Such comparisons provide insight into why adolescent pregnancy rates are much higher in the United States than in European countries.

© Patrick Steel/Alamy

Review

- How would you describe adolescent heterosexual attitudes and behaviors?
- How would you characterize adolescent sexual minority behavior and attitudes?
- What is known about sexual self-stimulation in adolescence?
- How extensively do U.S. adolescents use contraceptives?

Connect

- Connect what you have learned about identity with this section's discussion of gay or lesbian identity and disclosure.

Reflect *Your Own Personal Journey of Life*

- Think about your sexual experiences or lack of sexual experiences in adolescence. If you could go back to that period in your life, what would you change?

3 Problematic Sexual Outcomes in Adolescence

LG3 Describe the main problematic sexual outcomes that can emerge in adolescence

| Adolescent Pregnancy | Sexually Transmitted Infections | Forcible Sexual Behavior and Sexual Harassment |

Problematic sexual outcomes in adolescence include adolescent pregnancy, sexually transmitted infections, forcible sexual behavior, and sexual harassment. Let's begin by exploring adolescent pregnancy and its prevalence in the United States and around the world.

ADOLESCENT PREGNANCY

Angela is 15 years old. She reflects, "I'm three months pregnant. This could ruin my whole life. I've made all of these plans for the future, and now they are down the drain. I don't have anybody to talk with about my problem. I can't talk to my parents. There is no way they can understand." Pregnant adolescents were once virtually invisible and unmentionable, shuttled off to homes for unwed mothers where relinquishment of the baby for adoption was their only option, or subjected to unsafe and illegal abortions. But yesterday's secret has become today's dilemma. Our exploration of adolescent pregnancy focuses on its incidence and nature, its consequences, cognitive factors that may be involved, adolescents as parents, and ways in which adolescent pregnancy rates can be reduced.

Incidence of Adolescent Pregnancy Adolescent girls who become pregnant are from different ethnic groups and from different places, but their circumstances have the same stressfulness. To many adults, adolescent pregnancy represents a flaw in America's social fabric. Each year more than 200,000 females in the United States have a child before their eighteenth birthday. Like Angela, far too many become pregnant in their early or middle adolescent years. As one 17-year-old Los Angeles mother of a 1-year-old son said, "We are children having children."

In cross-cultural comparisons, the United States continues to have one of the highest adolescent pregnancy and childbearing rates in the industrialized world, despite a considerable decline since the 1980s (Cooksey, 2009). The adolescent pregnancy rate is six times as high in the United States as it is in the Netherlands. This dramatic difference exists in spite of the fact that U.S. adolescents are no more sexually active than their counterparts in the Netherlands. A recent cross-cultural comparison found that among 21 countries, the United States had the highest adolescent pregnancy rate among 15- to 19-year-olds and Switzerland the lowest (Sedgh & others, 2015).

Why are adolescent pregnancy rates in other countries lower than they are in the United States? Three reasons identified in cross-cultural studies are described below (Boonstra, 2002, pp. 9–10):

· *"Childbearing regarded as adult activity."* European countries and Canada share a strong consensus that childbearing belongs in adulthood "when young people have completed their education, have become employed and independent from their parents and are living in stable relationships. . . . In the United States, this attitude is much less strong and much more variable across groups and areas of the country."

· *"Clear messages about sexual behavior."* Although adults in other countries strongly encourage teens to wait until they have established themselves before having children, they are generally more accepting than American adults of teens having sex. In France and Sweden, in particular, teen sexual expression is seen as normal and positive, but there is also widespread expectation that sexual intercourse will take place within committed relationships. (In fact, relationships among U.S. teens tend to be more sporadic and of shorter duration.) Equally strong is the expectation that young people who are having sex will take precautions to protect themselves and their partners from pregnancy and sexually transmitted infections, an expectation that is much stronger in Europe than in the United States. "In keeping with this view, . . . schools in Great Britain, France, Sweden, and most of Canada" have sex education programs that provide more comprehensive information about prevention than do U.S. schools. In addition, these countries use the media more often in "government-sponsored campaigns for promoting responsible sexual behavior."

· *"Access to family planning services."* In countries that are more accepting of teenage sexual relationships, teenagers also have easier access to reproductive health services. "In Canada, France, Great Britain, and Sweden, contraceptive services are integrated into other types of primary health care and are available free or at low cost for all teenagers. Generally, teens (in these countries) know where to obtain information and services and receive confidential and nonjudgmental care. . . . In the United States, where attitudes about teenage sexual relationships are more conflicted, teens have a harder time obtaining contraceptive services. Many do not have health insurance or cannot get birth control as part of their basic health care."

Trends in U.S. Adolescent Pregnancy Rates   Despite the negative comparisons of the United States with many other developed countries, there have been some encouraging trends in U.S. adolescent pregnancy rates. In 2013, the U.S. birth rate for 15- to 19-year-olds was 26.5 births per 1,000 females, the lowest rate ever recorded, which represents a dramatic decrease from the 61.8 births for the same age range in 1991 (Martin & others, 2015) (see Figure 4). As can be seen in Figure 4, the 2013 figures reflect a substantial decrease in adolescent pregnancies across ethnic groups. Reasons for the decline include school/community health classes, increased contraceptive use, and fear of sexually transmitted infections such as AIDS.

Ethnic variations characterize adolescent pregnancy (Bartlett & others, 2014; Centers for Disease Control and Prevention, 2015a; Kappeler & Farb, 2014) (see Figure 5). Latina adolescents are more likely than African American and non-Latina White adolescents to become pregnant (Martin & others, 2015). For 15- to 19-year-old U.S. females in 2013, per 1,000 females the birth rate for Latinas was 41.7, for African Americans 39.0, and for non-Latina Whites 18.6 (Martin & others, 2015). Latina and African American adolescent girls who have a child are also more likely to have a second child than are non-Latina White adolescent girls (Rosengard, 2009). And daughters of teenage mothers are at risk for teenage childbearing, thus perpetuating an intergenerational cycle. A study using data from the National Longitudinal Survey of Youth revealed that daughters of teenage mothers were 66 percent more

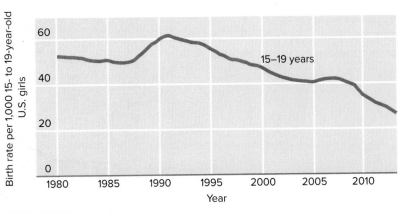

FIGURE 4

BIRTH RATES FOR U.S. 15- TO 19-YEAR-OLD GIRLS FROM 1980 TO 2013.
Source: Martin & others (2015)

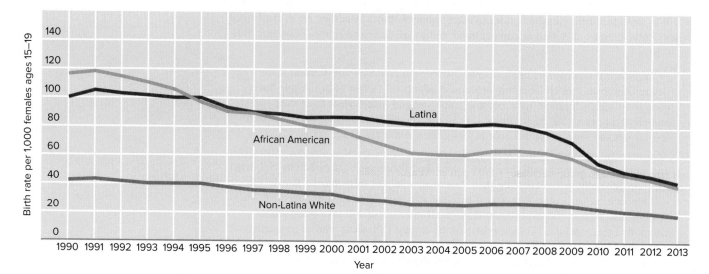

FIGURE 5

ADOLESCENTS WHO GAVE BIRTH, 1990 TO 2013, BY ETHNICITY. *Source: Martin & others (2015)*

likely to become teenage mothers themselves (Meade, Kershaw, & Ickovics, 2008). In this study, risks that increased the likelihood that daughters of the teenage mothers would become pregnant included low parental monitoring and poverty.

Even though adolescent childbearing overall has declined steeply over the last half century, the proportion of adolescent births that are nonmarital has increased in an equally dramatic fashion, from 13 percent in 1950 to 89 percent in 2013 (Martin & others, 2015) (see Figure 6). Two factors are responsible for this trend. First, marriage in adolescence has now become quite rare (the average age of first marriage in the United States is now 26.5 for women and 28.7 for men). Second, pregnancy is no longer seen as a reason for marriage. In contrast with the days of the "shotgun marriage" (when youth were forced to marry if a girl became pregnant), very few adolescents who become pregnant now marry before their baby is born.

Abortion   Impassioned debate surrounds the topic of abortion in the United States today, and this debate is likely to continue in the foreseeable future (Coleman & Rosoff, 2013). The experiences of U.S. adolescents who want to have an abortion vary by state and region. Thirty-eight states prohibit abortions after a specified point in pregnancy, most often fetal

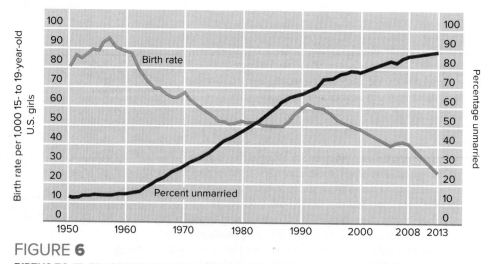

FIGURE 6

BIRTHS TO 15- TO 19-YEAR-OLD GIRLS AND THE PERCENTAGE UNMARRIED, 1950 TO 2013.
Source: Martin & others (2015).

viability (Alan Guttmacher Institute, 2010). Thirty-four states require some form of parental involvement in a minor's decision to have an abortion.

Abortion is easier to obtain in some countries, most notably the Scandinavian countries, than in the United States, where abortion and adolescent sexual activity are more stigmatized. In many developing countries, such as Nigeria, abortion is far more unsafe than in the United States. A recent cross-cultural comparison of 21 countries found the highest abortion rate for 15- to 19-year-olds in England and Sweden, the lowest in Switzerland (Sedgh & others, 2015).

In 2006, 27 percent of teen pregnancies ended in abortion (Alan Guttmacher Institute, 2010). A recent analysis found that the percentage of abortions that were performed on 15- to 19-year-olds in the United States decreased 21 percent between 2002 and 2011 and the abortion rate for this age group decreased by 34 percent (Pazol & others, 2014). Adolescent girls are more likely than older women to delay having an abortion until after 15 weeks of pregnancy, when medical risks associated with abortion increase significantly.

Legislation mandating parental consent for an adolescent girl's abortion has been justified by several assumptions, including high risk of harm from abortion, adolescents' inability to make an adequately informed decision, and benefits of parental involvement (Adler, Ozer, & Tschann, 2003).

Legal abortion in the United States itself carries few medical risks if performed in the first trimester of pregnancy, especially compared with the risks of childbearing for adolescent girls. And, in terms of psychological risks, a recent study revealed that abortion did not lead to mental health problems for adolescent girls (Warren & others, 2010). Other studies have found that adolescents are not psychologically harmed by their abortion experience (Pope, Adler, & Tschann, 2001; Quinton, Major, & Richards, 2001).

Regardless of research outcomes, pro-life and pro-choice advocates are convinced of the rightness of their positions (Hyde & DeLamater, 2014). Their viewpoints are rooted in religious beliefs, political convictions, and morality. This conflict has no easy solutions.

Consequences of Adolescent Pregnancy   The consequences of America's high adolescent pregnancy rate are cause for great concern (Lau, Lin, & Flores, 2015; Siegel & Brandon, 2014). Adolescent pregnancy creates health risks for both the baby and the mother (Bartlett & others, 2014; Kappeler & Farb, 2014). Infants born to adolescent mothers are more likely to be born preterm and have low birth weights—a prominent factor in infant mortality—as well as neurological problems and childhood illness (Khashan, Baker, & Kenny, 2010). Adolescent mothers often drop out of school (Siegel & Brandon, 2014). Although many adolescent mothers resume their education later in life, they generally do not catch up economically with women who postpone childbearing until their twenties. A longitudinal study revealed that several characteristics of adolescent mothers were related to their likelihood of having problems as emerging adults: a history of school problems, delinquency, hard substance use, and mental health problems (Oxford & others, 2006). Also, a recent study of African American urban youth found that at 32 years of age, women who had been teenage mothers were more likely than women who had not been teenage mothers to be unemployed, live in poverty, depend on welfare, and not have completed college (Assini-Meytin & Green, 2015). In this study, at 32 years of age, men who had been teenage fathers were more likely to be unemployed than were men who had not been teenage fathers.

Researchers have found that adolescent mothers interact less effectively with their infants than do adult mothers. A recent study revealed that adolescent mothers spent more time negatively interacting and less time in play and positive interactions with their infants than did adult mothers (Riva Crugnola & others, 2014). A recent intervention, "My Baby and Me," that involved frequent (55), intensive home visitation coaching sessions with adolescent mothers across three years resulted in improved maternal behavior and child outcomes (Guttentag & others, 2014).

Although the consequences of America's high adolescent pregnancy rate are cause for great concern, it often is not pregnancy alone that leads to negative outcomes for an adolescent mother and her offspring. Adolescent mothers are more likely to come from low-SES backgrounds (Molina & others, 2010). Many adolescent mothers also were not good students before

What are some consequences of adolescent pregnancy?
© Geoff Manasse/Getty Images RF

Sixteen-Year-Old Alberto: Wanting a Different Kind of Life

Sixteen-year-old Alberto's maternal grandmother was a heroin addict who died of cancer at the age of 40. His father, who was only 17 when Alberto was born, has been in prison most of Alberto's life. His mother and stepfather are not married but have lived together for a dozen years and have four other children. Alberto's stepbrother dropped out of school when he was 17, fathered a child, and is now unemployed. But Alberto, who lives in the Bronx in New York City, has different plans for his own future. He wants to be a dentist, he said, "like the kind of woman who fixed his teeth at Bronx-Lebanon Hospital Center clinic when he was a child" (Bernstein, 2004, p. A22). And Alberto, along with his girlfriend, Jasmine, wants to remain a virgin until he is married.

What cultural influences, negative and positive, might be helping Alberto plan his future?

Alberto with his girlfriend.
© Suzanne DeChillo/The New York Times/Redux Pictures

they became pregnant (Malamitsi-Puchner & Boutsikou, 2006). However, not every adolescent girl who bears a child lives a life of poverty and low achievement. Thus, although adolescent pregnancy is a high-risk circumstance, and adolescents who do not become pregnant generally fare better than those who do, some adolescent mothers do well in school and have positive outcomes (Schaffer & others, 2012).

Adolescents as Parents Children of adolescent parents face problems even before they are born (Jeha & others, 2015). Only one of every five pregnant adolescent girls receives any prenatal care at all during the important first three months of pregnancy. Pregnant adolescents are more likely to have anemia and complications related to preterm delivery than are mothers aged 20 to 24. The problems of adolescent pregnancy double the normal risk of delivering a low birth weight baby (one that weighs under 5.5 pounds), a category that places the infant at risk for physical and mental deficits (Dryfoos & Barkin, 2006). In some cases, infant problems may be due to poverty rather than the mother's age.

What are adolescents like as parents?
© Erproductions Ltd/Getty Images RF

Infants who escape the medical hazards of having an adolescent mother might not escape the psychological and social perils. Adolescent mothers are less competent at child rearing and have less realistic expectations for their infants' development than do older mothers (Osofsky, 1990). Children born to adolescent mothers do not perform as well on intelligence tests and have more behavioral problems than children born to mothers in their twenties (Silver, 1988). One longitudinal study found that the children of women who had their first birth during their teens had lower achievement test scores and more behavioral problems than did children whose mothers had their first birth as adults (Hofferth & Reid, 2002). And a recent study assessed the reading and math achievement trajectories of children born to adolescent and non-adolescent mothers with different levels of education (Tang & others, 2015). In this study, higher levels of maternal education were linked to growth in achievement through the eighth grade. Nonetheless, the achievement of children born to adolescent mothers never reached the levels of children born to adult mothers.

So far, we have talked exclusively about adolescent mothers. Although some adolescent fathers are involved with their children, the majority are not. In one study, only one-fourth of adolescent mothers with a 3-year-old child said the father had a close relationship with them (Leadbeater, Way, & Raden, 1994).

Adolescent fathers have lower incomes, less education, and more children than do men who delay having children until their twenties. One reason for these difficulties is that the adolescent father often compounds the problem of becoming a parent at a young age by dropping out of school (Resnick, Wattenberg, & Brewer, 1992).

Lynn Blankinship, Family and Consumer Science Educator

Lynn Blankinship is a family and consumer science educator. She has an undergraduate degree in her specialty from the University of Arizona and has taught for more than 20 years, the last 14 at Tucson High Magnet School.

Blankinship was awarded the Tucson Federation of Teachers Educator of the Year Award for 1999–2000 and was honored in 1999 as the Arizona Association of Family and Consumer Science Teacher of the Year.

Blankinship especially enjoys teaching life skills to adolescents. One of her favorite activities is having students care for an automated baby that imitates the needs of real babies. Blankinship says that this program has a profound impact on students because the baby must be cared for around the clock for the duration of the assignment. Blankinship also coordinates real-world work experiences and training for students in several child-care facilities in the Tucson area.

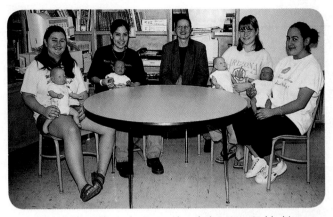

Lynn Blankinship, with students carrying their automated babies.
Courtesy of Lynn Blankinship

For more information about what a family and consumer science educator does, see the Careers in Adolescent Development appendix.

Reducing Adolescent Pregnancy Serious, extensive efforts are needed to reduce adolescent pregnancy and to help pregnant adolescents and young mothers enhance their educational and occupational opportunities (Dobkin, Perrucci, & Dehlendorf, 2013; Glassman & others, 2015; Graves & others, 2011; Gruber, 2012). John Conger (1988) offered the following four recommendations for reducing the high rate of adolescent pregnancy: (1) sex education and family planning, (2) access to contraceptive methods, (3) the life options approach, and (4) broad community involvement and support. We will consider each of these recommendations in turn.

Age-appropriate family-life education benefits adolescents (Asheer & others, 2014). One strategy that is used in some family-life education programs is the Baby Think It Over doll, a life-size computer-driven baby doll that engages in realistic responses and gives adolescents the opportunity to experience the responsibilities of being a parent. A study of primarily Latino ninth-grade students who took care of the Baby Think It

Students in a teen pregnancy and parenting class at Independence School in Brentwood, California. *What are some strategies that you think should be taught to the students in such a class?*
© *Zuma Press, Inc./Alamy*

Over doll found that the experience increased the age at which they wanted to have their first child, produced a greater interest in career and educational planning, and raised their awareness of how having a baby might interfere with those plans (de Anda, 2006). To read about the work of one individual who incorporates the Baby Think It Over automated doll in her effort to educate adolescents about the reality of having a baby, see the *Connecting with Careers* profile.

In addition to age-appropriate family-life and sex education, sexually active adolescents need access to contraceptive methods (Crooks & Baur, 2014). These needs often can be fulfilled through adolescent clinics that provide comprehensive, high-quality health services.

Better sex education, family planning, and access to contraceptive methods alone will not remedy the adolescent pregnancy crisis, especially for high-risk adolescents. Adolescents have to become motivated to reduce their pregnancy risk. This motivation will come only when adolescents look to the future and see that they have an opportunity to become self-

What are some strategies for reducing adolescent pregnancy?
© iStockphoto.com/Rosemarie Gearhart

sufficient and successful. To achieve this goal, adolescents need opportunities to improve their academic and career-related skills, job prospects, life-planning consultation, and extensive mental health services.

Finally, for adolescent pregnancy prevention to ultimately succeed, high-risk adolescents must receive broad community involvement and support. This support is a major reason for the success of pregnancy prevention efforts in other developed nations where rates of adolescent pregnancy, abortion, and childbearing are much lower than in the United States despite similar levels of sexual activity. In the Netherlands as well as other European countries such as Sweden, sex does not carry the mystery and controversy it does in American society. The Netherlands does not have a mandated sex education program, but adolescents can obtain contraceptive counseling at government-sponsored clinics for a small fee. The Dutch media also have played an important role in educating the public about sex through frequent broadcasts focused on birth control, abortion, and related matters. Perhaps as a result, Dutch adolescents are unlikely to have sex without contraception.

In the United States. an organization called Girls Inc. offers four programs that are intended to increase adolescent girls' motivation to avoid pregnancy until they are mature enough to make responsible decisions about motherhood (Roth & others, 1998). "Growing Together," a series of five two-hour workshops for mothers and adolescents, and "Will Power/Won't Power," a series of six two-hour sessions that focus on assertiveness training, are for 12- to 14-year-old girls. For older adolescent girls, "Taking Care of Business" provides nine sessions that emphasize career planning as well as information about sexuality, reproduction, and contraception. "Health Bridge" coordinates health and education services—girls can participate in this program as one of their club activities. Research on girls' participation in these programs revealed a significant drop in their likelihood of getting pregnant compared with girls who had not participated (Girls Inc., 1991).

So far, we have discussed four ways to reduce adolescent pregnancy: sex education and family planning, access to contraceptive methods, enhanced life options, and broad community involvement and support. A fifth consideration, which is especially important for young adolescents, is abstinence. Abstinence is increasingly being included as a theme in sex education classes, as discussed later in this chapter; however, criticisms of abstinence-only sex education programs have recently been made (Constantine, 2008; Schalet, 2011).

Also, in 2010, the U.S. government launched the Teen Pregnancy Prevention (TPP) Program under the direction of the newly created Office of Adolescent Health (Koh, 2014). Currently, a number of studies are being funded by the program as part of a national effort to find ways to reduce the rate of adolescent pregnancy.

SEXUALLY TRANSMITTED INFECTIONS

Tammy, age 15, has just finished listening to an expert lecture in her health class. We overhear her talking to one of her girlfriends as she walks down the school corridor: "That was a disgusting lecture. I can't believe all the infections you can get by having sex. I think she was probably trying to scare us. She spent a lot of time talking about AIDS, which I have heard that normal people do not get. Right? I've heard that only homosexuals and drug addicts get AIDS. And I've also heard that gonorrhea and most other sexual infections can be cured, so what is the big deal if you get something like that?" Tammy's views on sexually transmitted infections—that they always happen to someone else, that they can be easily cured without any harm done, that they are too disgusting for a nice young person to hear about, let alone get—are common among adolescents. Tammy's views are wrong. Adolescents who are having sex run the risk of getting sexually transmitted infections.

Sexually transmitted infections (STIs) are infections that are contracted primarily through sexual contact. This contact is not limited to vaginal intercourse but includes oral-genital and anal-genital contact as well. STIs are an increasing health problem. Every year more than 3 million American adolescents (about one-fourth of those who are sexually experienced) acquire an STI (Centers for Disease Control and Prevention, 2015b). Recent estimates indicate that while 15- to 24-year-olds represent only 25 percent of the sexually experienced U.S. population, they acquire nearly 50 percent of all new STIs (Centers for Disease Control and Prevention, 2015b).

Among the main STIs adolescents can get are three STIs caused by viruses—acquired immune deficiency syndrome (AIDS), genital herpes, and genital warts—and three STIs caused by bacteria—gonorrhea, syphilis, and chlamydia.

A youth group presents a play in the local marketplace in Morogoro, Tanzania. The play is designed to educate the community about HIV and AIDS.
© Wendy Stone/Corbis

A 13-year-old boy pushes his friends around in his barrow during his break from his work as a barrow boy in a community in sub-Saharan Africa. He became the breadwinner in the family after both of his parents died of AIDS.
© Louise Gubb/Corbis SABA

HIV and AIDS   No single STI has caused more deaths, had a greater impact on sexual behavior, or created more public fear in recent decades than HIV (Carroll, 2016). We explore here its nature and incidence, how it is transmitted, and how to prevent it from spreading.

AIDS stands for acquired immune deficiency syndrome, a sexually transmitted infection that is caused by the human immunodeficiency virus (HIV), which destroys the body's immune system. Following exposure to HIV, an individual is vulnerable to germs that a normal immune system could destroy.

Through December 2012, there were 62,400 cumulative cases of AIDS among 13- to 24-year-olds in the United States (Centers for Disease Control and Prevention, 2015b). Of these youth, 32,000 were living with an undiagnosed HIV infection. Worldwide, the greatest concern about AIDS is in sub-Saharan Africa, where it has reached epidemic proportions (UNICEF, 2015). Adolescent girls in many African countries are especially vulnerable to becoming infected with the HIV virus through sexual contact with adult men (Cherutich & others, 2008). Approximately six times as many adolescent girls as boys have AIDS in these countries. In Kenya, 25 percent of 15- to 19-year-old girls are HIV-positive, compared with only 4 percent of boys in the same age group. In Botswana, more than 30 percent of the adolescent girls who are pregnant are infected with HIV. In some sub-Saharan countries, less than 20 percent of women and 40 percent of 15- to 19-year-olds reported having used a condom the last time they had sexual intercourse (Bankole & others, 2004).

AIDS also has resulted in a dramatic increase in the number of African children and adolescents who are orphaned and left to care for themselves because their parents acquired the disease. In 2006, 12 million children and adolescents had become orphans because of the deaths of their parents due to AIDS (UNICEF, 2006). This figure is expected to increase to 16 million by the end of the second decade of the twenty-first century, when AIDS orphans could represent 15 to 20 percent of the population in some sub-Saharan countries. As a result of the dramatic increase in AIDS orphans, more of these children and adolescents are being cared for by their grandmothers or by no one, in which case all too often they turn to a lifestyle of crime or prostitution.

There continues to be great concern about AIDS in many parts of the world, not just sub-Saharan Africa (UNICEF, 2015). In the United States, prevention is especially targeted at groups that show the highest incidence of AIDS. These include drug users, individuals with other STIs, young gay males, individuals living in low-income circumstances, Latinos, and African Americans (Centers for Disease Control and Prevention, 2015b). Also, in recent years, there has been increased heterosexual transmission of HIV in the United States.

AIDS Stands for acquired immune deficiency syndrome, a sexually transmitted infection caused by the human immunodeficiency virus (HIV), which destroys the body's immune system.

There are some differences in AIDS cases in U.S. adolescents, compared with AIDS cases in U.S. adults:

· A higher percentage of adolescent AIDS cases are acquired by heterosexual transmission.

· A higher percentage of adolescents are asymptomatic individuals (but will become symptomatic in adulthood—that is, they are HIV-positive, but do not yet have AIDS).

· A higher percentage of African American and Latino AIDS cases occur among adolescents.

· A special set of ethical and legal issues is involved in testing and informing partners and parents of adolescents.

· Adolescents have less access to contraceptives and are less likely to use them than are adults.

Experts say that HIV can be transmitted only by sexual contact, the sharing of needles, or blood transfusion (which in recent years has been tightly monitored) (Carroll, 2016). Approximately 90 percent of AIDS cases in the United States continue to occur among men who have sex with other men and intravenous drug users. Penile-anal sex involves a higher risk of microscopic tearing and therefore blood-semen contact. A disproportionate increase among females who are heterosexual partners of bisexual males or of intravenous drug users has recently been noted (Centers for Disease Control and Prevention, 2015b). This increase suggests that the risk of AIDS may be increasing among heterosexual individuals who have multiple sex partners. Figure 7 describes which activities are risky and which ones are not, regarding the spread of AIDS and HIV.

Merely asking a date about his or her sexual behavior, of course, does not guarantee protection from HIV or other STIs. For example, in one investigation, 655 college students were asked to answer questions about lying and sexual behavior (Cochran & Mays, 1990). Of the 422 respondents who said they were sexually active, 34 percent of the men and 10 percent of the women said they had lied so their partner would have sex with them. Much higher percentages—47 percent of the men and 60 percent of the women—said they had been lied to by a potential sexual partner. When asked what aspects of their past they would be most likely to lie about, more than 40 percent of the men and women said they would understate the number of their sexual partners. Twenty percent of the men, but only 4 percent of the women, said they would lie about their results from an HIV blood test. A recent study revealed that 40 percent of sexually active adolescents who were HIV-positive had not disclosed their status to their partners (Michaud & others, 2009).

Because it is possible, and even probable, among high-risk groups to have more than one STI at a time, efforts to prevent one infection help reduce the prevalence of other infections. Efforts to prevent AIDS can also help prevent adolescent pregnancy and other sexually related problems. An extensive recent research review revealed that behavioral interventions can succeed in reducing HIV through such methods as increasing condom use, reducing or delaying penetrative sex, and increasing partner communication skills involving safe sex (Johnson & others, 2011). Further, a recent research review of 150 studies from 2001 to 2013 concluded that the following interventions were effective in reducing the risk of adolescent girls acquiring HIV: (1) an enabling environment, which includes keeping girls in school, promoting gender equality, and reducing gender-based violence; (2) information and service provision, including age-appropriate comprehensive sex education and knowledge about how to access information and services; and (3) social support, including promotion of caring relationships with adults and providing support for female orphans and vulnerable children (Hardee & others, 2014).

Genital Herpes   **Genital herpes** is a sexually transmitted infection caused by a large family of viruses with many different strains, some of which produce nonsexually transmitted diseases such as cold sores, chicken pox, and mononucleosis. Three to five days after contact, itching and tingling can occur, followed by an eruption of painful sores and blisters. The attacks can last up to three weeks and can recur as frequently as every few weeks or as infrequently as every few years. The virus can also pass through nonlatex condoms as well as contraceptive foams and creams. It is estimated that approximately 20 percent of adolescents have genital herpes (Centers for Disease Control and Prevention, 2015b). It also is estimated that more than 600,000 new genital herpes infections are appearing in the 15- to 24-year-old age group in the United States each year.

genital herpes A sexually transmitted infection caused by a large family of viruses of different strains. These strains also produce nonsexually transmitted diseases such as chicken pox and mononucleosis.

The HIV virus is not transmitted like colds or the flu, but by an exchange of infected blood, semen, or vaginal fluids. This usually occurs during sexual intercourse, in sharing drug needles, or to babies infected before or during birth.

You won't get the HIV virus from:	Everyday contact with individuals around you in school or the workplace, at parties, child-care centers, or stores Swimming in a pool, even if someone in the pool has the AIDS virus A mosquito bite, or from bedbugs, lice, flies, or other insects Saliva, sweat, tears, urine, or feces A kiss Clothes, telephones, or toilet seats Using a glass or eating utensils that someone else has used Being on a bus, train, or crowded elevator with an individual who is infected with the virus or who has AIDS
Risky behavior:	Your chances of coming into contact with the virus increase if you: Have more than one sex partner Share drug needles and syringes Engage in anal, vaginal, or oral sex without a condom Perform vaginal or oral sex with someone who shoots drugs Engage in sex with someone you don't know well or with someone who has several sex partners Engage in unprotected sex (without a condom) with an infected individual
Blood donations and transfusions:	You will not come into contact with the HIV virus by donating blood at a blood bank. The risk of getting AIDS from a blood transfusion has been greatly reduced. Donors are screened for risk factors, and donated blood is tested for HIV antibodies.
Safe behavior:	Not having sex Having sex that does not involve fluid exchange (rubbing, holding, massage) Sex with one mutually faithful, uninfected partner Sex with proper protection Not shooting drugs Source: *America Responds to AIDS*. U.S. Government educational pamphlet, 1988.

FIGURE 7
UNDERSTANDING AIDS: WHAT'S RISKY, WHAT'S NOT

Although drugs such as acyclovir can alleviate symptoms, there is no known cure for herpes. Thus, individuals infected with herpes often experience severe emotional distress in addition to the considerable physical discomfort. They may feel conflicted or reluctant about sex, angry about the unpredictability of the infection, and fearful that they won't be able to cope with the pain of the next attack. For these reasons, many communities have established support groups for victims of herpes.

Genital Warts **Genital warts** are caused by the human papillomavirus (HPV), which is difficult to test for and does not always produce symptoms but is very contagious nonetheless. Genital warts usually appear as small, hard, painless bumps on the penis, in the vaginal area, or around the anus. More than 9 million individuals in the United States in the 15- to 24-year-old age group are estimated to have an HPV infection, making HPV the most commonly acquired STI in this age group. Treatment involves the use of a topical drug, freezing, or surgery. Unfortunately, genital warts may return despite treatment, and in some cases they are linked to cervical cancer and other genital cancers. Condoms afford some protection against

genital warts An STI caused by the human papillomavirus; genital warts are very contagious and are the most commonly acquired STI in the United States in the 15- to 24-year-old age group.

HPV infection. In 2010, the Centers for Disease Control and Prevention recommended that all 11- and 12-year-old girls as well as females 13 to 26 years of age be given a three-dose HPV vaccine, which helps to fight off HPV and cervical cancer (Friedman & others, 2011). Females as young as 9 years of age can be given the HPV vaccine.

We now turn to three STIs—gonorrhea, syphilis, and chlamydia—caused by bacteria.

Gonorrhea **Gonorrhea** is an STI that is commonly called the "drip" or the "clap." It is caused by a bacterium called *Neisseria gonorrhoeae*, which thrives in the moist mucous membranes lining the mouth, throat, vagina, cervix, urethra, and anal tract. The bacterium is spread by contact between the infected moist membranes of one individual and the membranes of another. Although the incidence of gonorrhea has declined, it is estimated that more than 400,000 new cases appear each year in the 15- to 24-year-old age group (Weinstock, Berman, & Cates, 2004). A recent large-scale study revealed that adolescents who were most likely to screen positive for gonorrhea were female, African American, and 16 years of age or older (Han & others, 2011).

Early symptoms of gonorrhea are more likely to appear in males, who are likely to have a discharge from the penis and burning during urination. The early sign of gonorrhea in females, often undetectable, is a mild, sometimes irritating vaginal discharge. Complications of gonorrhea in males include prostate, bladder, and kidney problems, as well as sterility. In females, gonorrhea may lead to infertility due to the abdominal adhesions or pelvic inflammatory disease (PID) that it can cause (Crooks & Baur, 2014). Gonorrhea can be successfully treated in its early stages with penicillin or other antibiotics.

Syphilis **Syphilis** is an STI caused by the bacterium *Treponema pallidum*, a member of the spirochaeta family. The spirochete needs a warm, moist environment to survive, and it is transmitted by penile-vaginal, oral-genital, or anal contact. It can also be transmitted from a pregnant woman to her fetus after the fourth month of pregnancy; if she is treated before this time with penicillin, the syphilis will not be transmitted to the fetus.

If left untreated, syphilis may progress through four phases: primary (chancre sores appear), secondary (general skin rash occurs), latent (a period that can last for several years during which no overt symptoms are present), and tertiary (cardiovascular disease, blindness, paralysis, skin ulcers, liver damage, mental problems, and even death may occur) (Crooks & Baur, 2014). In its early phases, syphilis can be effectively treated with penicillin.

Chlamydia **Chlamydia**, one of the most common of all STIs, is named for *Chlamydia trachomatis*, an organism that spreads by sexual contact and infects the genital organs of both sexes. Although fewer individuals have heard of chlamydia than have heard of gonorrhea and syphilis, its incidence is much higher. Many of the new cases of chlamydia reported each year are in 15- to 25-year-old females. A recent large-scale survey found that adolescents who screened positive for chlamydia were more likely to be female, African American, and 16 years of age and older (Han & others, 2011). About 10 percent of all college students have chlamydia. This STI is highly infectious; women run a 70 percent risk of contracting it in a single sexual encounter with an infected partner. The male risk is estimated at between 25 and 50 percent. The estimated annual incidence of chlamydia in the 15- to 24-year-old age group is 1 million individuals (Weinstock, Berman, & Cates, 2004).

Many females with chlamydia have few or no symptoms. When symptoms do appear, they include disrupted menstrual periods, pelvic pain, elevated temperature, nausea, vomiting, and headache. Possible symptoms of chlamydia in males are a discharge from the penis and burning during urination.

Because many females with chlamydia are asymptomatic, the infection often goes untreated and the chlamydia spreads to the upper reproductive tract, where it can cause pelvic inflammatory disease (PID). The resultant scarring of tissue in the fallopian tubes can produce infertility or ectopic pregnancies (tubal pregnancies)—that is, a pregnancy in which the fertilized egg is implanted outside the uterus. One-quarter of females who have PID become infertile; multiple cases of PID increase the rate of infertility to half. Some researchers suggest that chlamydia is the number one preventable cause of female infertility.

Although they can occur without sexual contact and are therefore not classified as STIs, urinary tract or bladder infections and vaginal yeast infections (also called *thrush*)

gonorrhea A sexually transmitted infection caused by the bacterium *Neisseria gonorrhoeae*, which thrives in the moist mucous membranes lining the mouth, throat, vagina, cervix, urethra, and anal tract. This STI is commonly called the "drip" or the "clap."

syphilis A sexually transmitted infection caused by the bacterium *Treponema pallidum*, a spirochete.

chlamydia One of the most common sexually transmitted infections, named for *Chlamydia trachomatis*, an organism that spreads by sexual contact and infects the genital organs of both sexes.

are common in sexually active females, especially those who have an intense "honey-moon" lovemaking experience. Both of these infections clear up quickly with medication, but their symptoms (urinary urgency and burning in urinary tract infections; itching, irritation, and whitish vaginal discharge in yeast infections) may be frightening, especially to adolescents who may already have considerable anxiety about sex. We discuss them because one of the non-STIs may be what brings an adolescent girl to a doctor, nurse practitioner, or family-planning clinic, providing an opportunity for her to receive sex education and contraception.

So far we have discussed the problems of adolescent pregnancy and sexually transmitted infections. Next, we explore two additional problems involving sexuality: forcible sexual behavior and sexual harassment.

FORCIBLE SEXUAL BEHAVIOR AND SEXUAL HARASSMENT

Most people choose whether they will engage in sexual intercourse or other sexual activities—but, unfortunately, some people force others to engage in sex. Too many adolescent girls and young women report that they believe they don't have adequate sexual rights (East & Adams, 2002). These include the right not to have sexual intercourse when they don't wish to, the right to tell a partner that he is being too rough, or the right to use any form of birth control during intercourse. One study found that almost 20 percent of sexually active 14- to 26-year-old females believed that they never have the right to make decisions about contraception; to tell their partner that they don't want to have intercourse without birth control, that they want to make love differently, or that their partner is being too rough; or to stop foreplay at any time, including at the point of intercourse (Rickert, Sanghvi, & Wiemann, 2002). In this study, poor grades in school and sexual inexperience were linked to a lack of sexual assertiveness in females.

Forcible Sexual Behavior **Rape** is forcible sexual intercourse with a person who does not give consent. Legal definitions of rape vary from state to state. In some states, for example, the law allows husbands to force their wives to have sex. Because of the difficulties involved in reporting rape, the actual incidence is not easily determined (Krebs, 2014; Walfield, 2015). A recent national study found that 8 percent of U.S. ninth- to twelfth-grade students reported that they had been physically forced to have intercourse against their will (Eaton & others, 2012). In this study, 11.8 percent of the female students and 4.5 percent of the male students reported they had been forced to have sexual intercourse. A recent meta-analysis found that 60 percent of rape victims do not acknowledge that they have been raped, with the percentage of unacknowledged rape especially high in college students (Wilson & Miller, 2015).

Why is rape so pervasive in the American culture? Feminist writers assert that males are socialized to be sexually aggressive, to regard females as inferior beings, and to view their own pleasure as the most important objective (Davies, Gilston, & Rogers, 2012). Researchers have found that the following characteristics are common among rapists: aggression enhances their sense of power or masculinity; they are angry at females generally; and they want to hurt their victims (Yarber, Sayad, & Strong, 2013). Research indicates that rape is more likely to occur when alcohol and marijuana are being used (Fair & Vanyur, 2011). A recent study revealed that regardless of whether or not the victim was using substances, sexual assault was more likely to occur when the offender was using substances (Brecklin & Ullman, 2010).

A form of rape that went unacknowledged until recent decades is **date rape,** or **acquaintance rape,** which is coercive sexual activity directed at someone whom the perpetrator knows. Acquaintance rape is an increasing problem in high schools and on college campuses (Angelone, Mitchell, & Grossi, 2015; Sabina & Ho, 2014; Turchik & Hassija, 2014).

What are some characteristics of date or acquaintance rape?
© Creasource/Corbis

rape Forcible sexual intercourse with a person who does not give consent.

date rape, or **acquaintance rape** Coercive sexual activity directed at someone whom the perpetrator knows.

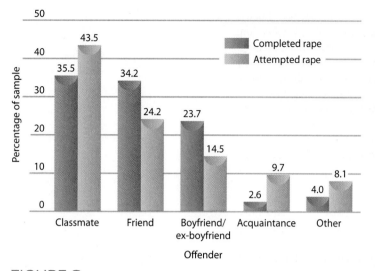

FIGURE 8

COMPLETED RAPE AND ATTEMPTED RAPE OF COLLEGE WOMEN ACCORDING TO VICTIM-OFFENDER RELATIONSHIP

- - - - - - - - ➤

developmental **connection**

Peers

Romantic relationships in adolescence often trigger positive and negative aspects of adjustment. Connect to "Peers, Romantic Relationships, and Lifestyles."

A recent national survey indicated that 10 percent of high school students reported being hurt by a boyfriend or a girlfriend in the past year (Centers for Disease Control and Prevention, 2012). When dating violence occurs in adolescence, the participants are at risk for escalating partner violence in adulthood. More than 20 percent of women and 15 percent of men who become rape victims or experience physical assault by an intimate partner during adulthood initially experienced dating violence in adolescence (Black & others, 2011). In a recent study, an intervention program called "Shifting Boundaries" that emphasizes laws/consequences of dating violence and sexual harassment, establishing boundaries, and creating safe relationships was effective in reducing the frequency of sexual dating violence victimization in young adolescents (Taylor, Mumford, & Stein, 2015).

A major study that focused on campus sexual assault involved a phone survey of 4,446 women attending two- or four-year colleges (Fisher, Cullen, & Turner, 2000). In this study, slightly less than 3 percent said that they had experienced either rape or an attempted rape during the academic year. About one of ten college women said that they had experienced rape in their lifetime. Unwanted or uninvited sexual contacts were widespread, with more than one-third of the college women reporting such incidents. As shown in Figure 8, in this study most women (about nine of ten) knew the person who sexually victimized them. Most of the women attempted to take protective actions against their assailants but were then reluctant to report the victimization to the police. Several factors were associated with sexual victimization: living on campus, being unmarried, getting drunk frequently, and having been sexually victimized on a prior occasion.

A number of colleges and universities have identified a "red zone"— a period of time early in the first year of college when women are at especially high risk for unwanted sexual experiences (Cranney, 2015). A recent study revealed that first-year college women were more at risk for unwanted sexual experiences, especially early in the fall term, than were second-year women (Kimble & others, 2008).

In another study, about two-thirds of the sexual victimization incidents were perpetrated by a romantic acquaintance (Flanagan, 1996). In yet another study, approximately 2,000 ninth-through twelfth-grade girls were asked about the extent to which they had experienced physical and sexual violence (Silverman & others, 2001). About 20 percent of the girls said they had been physically or sexually abused by a dating partner. Further, the physical and sexual abuse was linked with substance use.

Might an older adolescent's engagement in dating violence be linked to the adolescent's family history and aggressive behavior earlier in development? A longitudinal study found that elevated rates of aggressive-disruptive behavior at home at age 6 and aggression at home and school at age 12 were associated with the emergence of dating violence at 18 years of age (Makin-Byrd, Bierman, & The Conduct Problems Prevention Research Group, 2013).

A recent coach-delivered intervention study with more than 2,000 male high school athletes focused on recognition of abusive behavior, gender-equity attitudes, and intention to intervene when witnessing abusive behavior (Miller & others, 2012). The study found that the intervention was successful in increasing the participants' intention to try to stop incidents of dating violence if they were to see such incidents occurring (Miller & others, 2012).

Rape is a traumatic experience for the victim and those close to her or him (Jozkowsi & Sanders, 2012; Padmanabhanunni & Edwards, 2015; Rosenthal, 2013). The rape victim initially feels shock and numbness and often is acutely disorganized. Some women show their distress through words and tears, while others experience more internalized suffering. As victims strive to get their lives back to normal, they might experience depression, fear, and anxiety for months or years (Iverson & others, 2015; Zinzow & others, 2010). Sexual dysfunctions, such as reduced sexual desire and the inability to reach orgasm, occur in 50 percent of rape victims. Many rape victims make lifestyle changes, moving to a new apartment or refusing to go out at night. About one-fifth of rape victims have made a suicide attempt—a rate eight times higher than that of women who have not been raped.

A girl's or woman's recovery from rape depends on both her coping abilities and her psychological adjustment prior to the assault. Social support from parents, her partner, and others close to her are also important factors in recovery, as is the availability of professional counseling, sometimes obtained through a rape crisis center (Ahrens & Aldana, 2012; Resick & others, 2012). Many rape victims become empowered by reporting their rape to the police and assisting in prosecution if the rapist is caught. However, women who take a legal approach are especially encouraged to use supportive counselors to aid them throughout the legal ordeal. Each female must be allowed to make her own, individual decision about whether to report the rape.

Although most victims of rape are girls and women, rape of boys and men does occur. Men in prisons are especially vulnerable to rape, usually by heterosexuals who are using homosexual rape to establish their domination and power within the prison (Barth, 2012).

Sexual Harassment Girls and women encounter sexual harassment in many different forms—ranging from sexist remarks and covert physical contact (patting, brushing against bodies) to blatant propositions and sexual assaults. Literally millions of girls and women experience such sexual harassment each year in educational and work settings (Cantalupo, 2014). One study of adolescent girls indicated that most (90 percent) of the girls said they had experienced sexual harassment at least once (Leaper & Brown, 2008). In this study, 52 percent of the girls reported that they had experienced academic sexism (involving science, math, and computer technology) and 76 percent said that they had encountered athletic sexism.

Further, a recent national survey on adolescent relationships found the following percentages of adolescents who were involved in various types of relationship abuse (perpetration and victimization) (Taylor & Mumford, 2015):

· Relationship abuse: 68 percent reported ever experiencing any relationship victimization and 62 percent indicated they has ever perpetrated any abuse
· Psychological abuse: 64 percent said they had been the victims of psychological abuse (name-calling and excessive stalking, for example)
· Sexual abuse: 18 percent reported being the victims of sexual abuse and 12 percent said they had perpetrated such abuse
· Sexual harassment: 31 percent indicated they had been the victims of sexual harassment and 11 percent reported that they had perpetrated such abuse; 13 percent said they had been the victims of online sexual harassment and 4 percent indicated they had perpetrated such abuse

Also, in this study, girls perpetrated serious threats or physical violence more than boys did at 12 to 14 years of age, but boys were more likely to engage in these behaviors at 15 to 18 years of age.

In a survey of 2,000 college women by the American Association of University Women (2006), 62 percent of the respondents reported that they had experienced sexual harassment while attending college. Most of the college women said that the sexual harassment involved noncontact forms such as crude jokes, remarks, and gestures. However, almost one-third said that the sexual harassment was physical in nature. A recent study of almost 1,500 college women revealed that when they had been sexually harassed they reported an increase in psychological distress, greater physical illness, and an increase in disordered eating (Huerta & others, 2006).

The Office for Civil Rights in the U.S. Department of Education published a 40-page policy guide on sexual harassment. In this guide, a distinction is made between quid pro quo and hostile environment sexual harassment (Chmielewski, 1997):

· **Quid pro quo sexual harassment** occurs when a school employee (such as a teacher) threatens to base an educational decision (such as a grade) on a student's submission to unwelcome sexual conduct. For example, a teacher gives a student an A for allowing the teacher's sexual advances, or the teacher gives the student an F for resisting the teacher's approaches.
· **Hostile environment sexual harassment** occurs when students are subjected to unwelcome sexual conduct that is so severe, persistent, or pervasive that it limits the students' ability to benefit from their education. Such a hostile environment is usually created by a series of incidents, such as repeated sexual overtures.

quid pro quo sexual harassment Sexual harassment in which a school employee threatens to base an educational decision (such as a grade) on a student's submission to unwelcome sexual conduct.

hostile environment sexual harassment Sexual harassment in which students are subjected to unwelcome sexual conduct that is so severe, persistent, or pervasive that it limits the students' ability to benefit from their education.

Quid pro quo and hostile environment sexual harassment are illegal in the workplace as well as in educational settings, but potential victims are often not given access to a clear reporting and investigation mechanism where they can make a complaint.

Sexual harassment involves one person asserting power and dominance over another, which can result in harmful consequences for the victim. Sexual harassment can be especially damaging when the perpetrators are teachers, employers, and other adults who have considerable power and authority over students. As a society, we need to be less tolerant of sexual harassment (Nielsen & Einarsen, 2012).

Review Connect Reflect

LG3 Describe the main problematic sexual outcomes that can emerge in adolescence

Review

- How would you characterize adolescent pregnancy?
- What are the main sexually transmitted infections in adolescence?
- What is the nature of forcible sexual behavior and sexual harassment in adolescence?

Connect

- Connect what you learned about sexually transmitted infections in this chapter to earlier discussions of adolescent health and well-being.

Reflect *Your Own Personal Journey of Life*

- Have you experienced any of the negative sexual outcomes in adolescence and emerging adulthood that have just been described—adolescent pregnancy, sexually transmitted infections, forcible sexual behavior, or sexual harassment? If so, is there anything you could have done differently to avoid the negative outcome(s)? If you didn't experience these negative outcomes, what factors likely contributed to your prevention of these outcomes?

---

4 Sexual Literacy and Sex Education

LG4 Characterize the sexual literacy of adolescents and sex education

| Sexual Literacy | Sources of Sex Information | Cognitive Factors | Sex Education in Schools |

Given the high rate of STIs in the United States, a special concern is the knowledge that both adolescents and adults have about these infections and about other aspects of sexuality. How sexually literate are Americans? What are adolescents' sources of sex education? What cognitive factors might be involved in whether sex education is effective? What is the role of schools in sex education?

SEXUAL LITERACY

According to June Reinisch (1990), director of the Kinsey Institute for Sex, Gender, and Reproduction, U.S. citizens know more about how their automobiles function than about how their bodies function sexually. American adolescents and adults are not sheltered from sexual messages; indeed, Reinisch says, adolescents too often are inundated with sexual messages, but not sexual facts. Sexual information is abundant, but much of it is misinformation. In some cases, even sex education teachers display sexual ignorance. One high school sex education teacher referred to erogenous zones as "erroneous zones," causing students to wonder if their sexually sensitive zones were in error!

A recent study assessed sixth-grade students' knowledge and curiosity about sex-related topics (Charmaraman, Lee, & Erkut, 2012). The questions most frequently asked by the sixth-graders involved sexual activity, female anatomy, reproduction, and puberty, while questions about sexually transmitted infections, sexual violence, and drug/alcohol use were less frequent. Questions asked in lower-risk schools tended to avoid sexual topics, whereas those asked in higher-risk schools focused more on sexual topics such as sexual initiation, contraception, and vaginal and anal sex. Following are several of the questions asked by the sixth-graders that reflect a lack of sexual knowledge:

· If you have had sex the night before your period you're not going to get pregnant, right?

· If a guy puts his penis in a girl's mouth, will she get pregnant?

· If you have anal sex, is it still considered sex?

· If you are trying to have abstinence and you have sex more than once, is that abstinence?

SOURCES OF SEX INFORMATION

Adolescents can get information about sex from many sources, including parents, siblings, other relatives, schools, peers, magazines, television, and the Internet. A special concern is the accuracy of sexual information adolescents can view on the Internet. One study revealed that adolescents' most frequently consulted sources of information about sexuality were friends, teachers, mothers, and the media (Bleakley & others, 2009). In this study, learning about sex from parents, grandparents, and religious leaders was linked with adolescent beliefs that were likely to delay having sexual intercourse, whereas learning about sex from friends, cousins, and the media was related to beliefs that were likely to increase the likelihood of having sexual intercourse earlier.

Many parents feel uncomfortable talking about sex with adolescents, and many adolescents feel uncomfortable with such conversations as well (Guilamo-Ramos & others, 2008; Tanton & others, 2015). One study revealed that 94 percent of fathers and 76 percent of mothers had never discussed sexual desire with their daughters (Feldman & Rosenthal, 1999).

Many adolescents say that they cannot talk freely with their parents about sexual matters, but those who can talk with their parents openly and freely about sex are less likely to be sexually active (Chia-Chen & Thompson, 2007). Contraceptive use by female adolescents also increases when adolescents report that they can communicate about sex with their parents (Fisher, 1987). Also, a recent study found that first-semester college women who felt more comfortable talking openly about sex with their mothers were more likely to have positive beliefs about condoms and confidence in using them (Lefkowitz & Espinosa-Hernandez, 2006).

Adolescents are far more likely to have conversations about sex with their mothers than with their fathers (Kirkman, Rosenthal, & Feldman, 2002). This tendency is true for both female and male adolescents, although female adolescents report having more frequent conversations about sex with their mothers than their male counterparts do (Feldman & Rosenthal, 2002).

COGNITIVE FACTORS

Cognitive changes have intriguing implications for adolescents' sex education (Lipsitz, 1980). With their developing idealism and ability to think in more abstract and hypothetical ways, some young adolescents may become immersed in a mental world far removed from reality. They may see themselves as omnipotent and indestructible and believe that bad things cannot or will not happen to them, characteristics of adolescent egocentrism. Consider the personal fable aspect of adolescent egocentrism reflected in this 14-year-old's words: "Hey, it won't happen to me." However, increasingly it is recognized that a majority of adolescents see themselves as more vulnerable than invulnerable (Fischhoff & others, 2010).

Informing adolescents about contraceptives is not enough—what seems to predict whether or not they will use contraceptives is their acceptance of themselves and their sexuality. This acceptance requires not only emotional maturity but cognitive maturity.

Most discussions of adolescent pregnancy and its prevention assume that adolescents have the ability to anticipate consequences, to weigh the probable outcome of behavior, and to project into the future what will happen if they engage in certain acts, such as sexual intercourse. That is, prevention is based on the belief that adolescents have the cognitive

The AIDS epidemic has led to an increased awareness of the importance of sex education in adolescence.
© James D. Wilson/Woodfin Camp & Associates

ability to approach problem solving in a planned, organized, and analytical manner. However, although many adolescents 16 years of age and older have these capacities, it does not mean they will use them, especially in emotionally charged situations such as when they are sexually aroused or are being pressured by a partner.

Indeed, young adolescents (10 to 15 years of age) seem to experience sex in a depersonalized way that is filled with anxiety and denial. This depersonalized orientation toward sex is not likely to lead to preventive behavior. Middle adolescents (15 to 17 years of age) often romanticize sexuality. Late adolescents (18 to 19 years of age) are to some degree realistic and future-oriented about sexual experiences, just as they are about careers and marriage.

SEX EDUCATION IN SCHOOLS

A survey revealed that 89 percent of parents in Minnesota recommended teaching adolescents about abstinence and also providing them with comprehensive sex education that includes contraception information (Eisenberg & others, 2008, 2013). The parents said that most sex education topics should first be introduced in middle schools. Other surveys also indicate that a large percentage of U.S. parents want schools to provide adolescents with comprehensive sex education (Constantine, Jerman, & Juang, 2007; Ito & others, 2006). One study indicated that parents think adolescents too often get their information about sex from friends and the media (Lagus & others, 2011).

A recent study in Minnesota of what more than 350 middle and high school sex educators can or cannot teach found that almost two-thirds faced structural barriers, one-half were concerned about parent, student, or administrators' responses, and one-fourth reported having restrictions on what they could teach (Eisenberg & others, 2013). Structural barriers were reported related to teaching about communication, teen parenting, and abortion; concerns about responses were linked to teaching about sexual violence; and restrictive policies were associated with teaching about abortion and sexual orientation.

One survey found that 93 percent of Americans support the teaching of sex education in high schools, and 84 percent support its teaching in middle/junior high schools (SIECUS, 1999). The dramatic increase in HIV/AIDS and other STIs is the main reason that Americans have increasingly supported sex education in schools in recent years. This survey also found

In many countries, contraceptive knowledge is included in sex education. Here students in a sex education class in Beijing, China, learn about condoms.
© China Features/Sygma/Corbis

What Is the Most Effective Sex Education?

Currently, a major controversy in sex education is whether schools should have an abstinence-only program or a program that provides information about contraceptive methods (Kraft & others, 2012; Markham & others, 2012). Two research reviews found that abstinence-only programs do not delay the initiation of sexual intercourse and do not reduce HIV risk behaviors (Kirby, Laris, & Rolleri, 2007; Underhill, Montgomery, & Operario, 2007). Further, a recent study revealed that adolescents who experienced comprehensive sex education were less likely to report adolescent pregnancies than those who were given abstinence-only sex education or no sex education (Kohler, Manhart, & Lafferty, 2008). A number of leading experts on adolescent sexuality now conclude that sex education programs that emphasize contraceptive knowledge do not increase the incidence of sexual intercourse and are more likely to reduce the risk of adolescent pregnancy and sexually transmitted infections than are abstinence-only programs (Constantine, 2008; Eisenberg & others, 2008; Hampton, 2008; Hyde & DeLamater, 2014).

Some sex education programs are starting to adopt an abstinence-plus sexuality approach that promotes abstinence while providing information on contraceptive use (Realini & others, 2010). A recent study found that sex education about abstinence and birth control was associated with healthier sexual behaviors, such as using some form of contraception at first sex, than no instruction at all (Lindberg & Maddow-Zimet, 2012). For girls whose behavior was tracked in this study, condom use at first sex was more likely among those who received instruction about both abstinence and birth control.

U.S. sex education typically has focused on the hazards of sex and the need to protect adolescent females from male predators. The contrast between the United States and other Western nations is remarkable (Hampton, 2008). For example, the Swedish State Commission on Sex Education recommends that students gain knowledge to help them to experience sexual life as a source of happiness and fellowship with others. Swedish adolescents are sexually active at an earlier age than are American adolescents, and they are exposed to even more explicit sex on television. However, the Swedish National Board of Education has developed a curriculum to give every child, beginning at age 7, a thorough grounding in reproductive biology and, by the age of 10 or 12, information about various forms of contraception. Teachers handle the subject of sex whenever it becomes relevant, regardless of the subject they are teaching. The idea is to demystify sex so that familiarity will make students less vulnerable to unwanted pregnancy and STIs. Despite a relatively early onset of sexual activity, the adolescent pregnancy rate in Sweden is one of the lowest in the world.

Why do you suppose that, despite the evidence, sex education in U.S. schools today increasingly focuses on abstinence?

How is sex education in Sweden different from sex education in the United States?
© Steve Raymer/Corbis

that more than eight in ten Americans think that adolescents should be given information to protect themselves from unwanted pregnancies and STIs, as well as about abstinence. In a recent national survey, 85 percent of ninth- to twelfth-grade students said that they had been taught in school about AIDS or HIV (Kann & others, 2014).

The question of what information should be provided in sex education courses in U.S. schools today is a controversial topic (Barr & others, 2014; Erkut & others, 2012). Three ways this controversial topic is dealt with are to focus on: (1) abstinence; (2) sex education that includes information about contraceptive use; and (3) abstinence-plus programs that promote abstinence as well as contraceptive use. To read further about sex education in the United States and around the world, see the *Connecting with Health and Well-Being* interlude.

LG4 Characterize the sexual literacy of adolescents and sex education

Review

- How sexually literate are U.S. adolescents?
- What are adolescents' sources of sexual information?
- What cognitive factors might be involved in the effectiveness of sex education?
- How would you describe sex education in schools?

Connect

- Recall what you have learned about adolescent attention and memory. How does that information support this section's discussion of adolescents and sexual literacy?

Reflect *Your Own Personal Journey of Life*

- Think about how you learned the "facts of life." Did most of your information come from well-informed sources? Were you able to talk freely and openly with your parents about what to expect sexually? Did you acquire some false beliefs through trial-and-error efforts? As you grew older, did you discover that some of what you thought you knew about sex was inaccurate? Think also about the sex education you received in school. How adequate was it? What do you wish the schools you attended would have done differently in regard to sex education?

reach your **learning goals**

Sexuality

1 Exploring Adolescent Sexuality

LG1 Discuss some basic ideas about the nature of adolescent sexuality

A Normal Aspect of Adolescent Development

- Too often the problems adolescents encounter with sexuality are emphasized rather than the fact that sexuality is a normal aspect of adolescent development. Adolescence is a bridge between the asexual child and the sexual adult. Adolescent sexuality is related to many other aspects of adolescent development, including physical development and puberty, cognitive development, the self and identity, gender, families, peers, schools, and culture.

The Sexual Culture

- Increased permissiveness in adolescent sexuality is linked to increased permissiveness in the larger culture. Adolescent initiation of sexual intercourse is related to exposure to explicit sex on TV.

Developing a Sexual Identity

- Developing a sexual identity is multifaceted. An adolescent's sexual identity involves an indication of sexual orientation, interests, and styles of behavior.

Obtaining Research Information About Adolescent Sexuality

- Obtaining valid information about adolescent sexuality is not easy. Much of the data are based on interviews and questionnaires, which can involve untruthful or socially desirable responses.

2 Sexual Attitudes and Behavior

LG2 Summarize sexual attitudes and behavior in adolescence

Heterosexual Attitudes and Behavior

- The progression of sexual behaviors is typically kissing, petting, sexual intercourse, and oral sex. The number of adolescents who reported having had sexual intercourse increased significantly in the twentieth century. The proportion of females engaging in intercourse increased more rapidly than that of males. National data indicate that slightly more than half of all adolescents today have had sexual intercourse by age 17, although the percentage varies by sex, ethnicity, and context. Male, African American, and inner-city adolescents report the highest rates of sexual activity. The percentage of 15- to 17-year-olds who have had sexual intercourse declined between 1991 and 2001. A common adolescent sexual script involves the male making sexual advances, and it is left up to the female to set limits on the male's sexual overtures. Adolescent females' sexual scripts link sex with love more than adolescent males' sexual scripts do. Risk factors for sexual problems include early sexual activity, having a number of sexual partners, not using contraception, engaging in other at-risk behaviors such as drinking and delinquency, living in a low-SES neighborhood, and ethnicity, as well as cognitive factors such as attentional problems and low self-regulation. Heterosexual behavior patterns change in emerging adulthood.

Sexual Minority Youths' Attitudes and Behavior

An individual's sexual attraction—whether heterosexual or sexual minority—is likely caused by a mix of genetic, hormonal, cognitive, and environmental factors. Terms such as "sexual minority individuals" (who identify themselves as gay, lesbian, or bisexual) and "same-sex attraction" are increasingly used, whereas the term "homosexual" is used less frequently. Developmental pathways for sexual minority youth are often diverse, may involve bisexual attractions, and do not always involve falling in love with a same-sex individual. Recent research has focused on adolescents' disclosure of same-sex attractions and the struggle they often go through in doing this. The peer relations of sexual minority youth differ from those of heterosexual youth. Sexual minority youth are more likely to engage in substance abuse, show sexual risk-taking behavior, and be the target of violence in a number of contexts. Discrimination and bias produce considerable stress for adolescents with a same-sex attraction. The stigma, discrimination, and rejection experienced by sexual minority youth are thought to explain why they may develop problems. Despite such negative experiences, many sexual minority youth successfully cope with the challenges they face and have health and well-being outcomes that are similar to those of their heterosexual counterparts.

Self-Stimulation

Self-stimulation, or masturbation, is part of the sexual activity of virtually all adolescents and one of their most frequent sexual outlets.

Contraceptive Use

Adolescents are increasing their use of contraceptives, but large numbers of sexually active adolescents still do not use them. Adolescents from low-SES backgrounds are less likely to use contraceptives than are their middle-SES counterparts.

3 Problematic Sexual Outcomes in Adolescence

LG3 Describe the main problematic sexual outcomes that can emerge in adolescence

Adolescent Pregnancy

The U.S. adolescent pregnancy rate is one of the highest in the Western world, but it also has declined in the last two decades. A complex, impassioned issue involving an unintended pregnancy is the decision of whether to have an abortion. Adolescent pregnancy increases health risks for the mother and the offspring. Adolescent mothers are more likely to drop out of school and have lower-paying jobs than their adolescent counterparts who do not bear children. It is important to remember, though, that it often is not pregnancy alone that places adolescents at risk. Adolescent mothers frequently come from low-income families and were not doing well in school prior to their pregnancy. The infants of adolescent parents are at risk both medically and psychologically. Adolescent parents are less effective in rearing their children than older parents are. Many adolescent fathers do not have a close relationship with their baby and the adolescent mother. Recommendations for reducing adolescent pregnancy include education about sex and family planning, access to contraception, life options, community involvement and support, and abstinence. In one study, volunteer community service was linked with a lower incidence of adolescent pregnancy.

Sexually Transmitted Infections

Sexually transmitted infections (STIs) are contracted primarily through sexual contact with an infected partner. The contact is not limited to vaginal intercourse but includes oral-genital and anal-genital contact as well. AIDS stands for acquired immune deficiency syndrome, a sexually transmitted infection that is caused by the human immunodeficiency virus (HIV), which destroys the body's immune system. Currently, the rate of AIDS in U.S. adolescents is relatively low, but it has reached epidemic proportions in sub-Saharan Africa, especially among adolescent girls. AIDS can be transmitted through sexual contact, sharing needles, and blood transfusions. A number of intervention projects are focusing on AIDS prevention. Genital herpes is caused by a family of viruses with different strains. Genital warts, caused by a virus, is the most common STI in the 15- to 24-year-old age group. Commonly called the "drip" or "clap," gonorrhea is another common STI. Syphilis is caused by the bacterium *Treponema pallidum,* a spirochete. Chlamydia is one of the most common STIs.

Forcible Sexual Behavior and Sexual Harassment

Some individuals force others to have sex with them. Rape is forcible sexual intercourse with a person who does not give consent. About 95 percent of rapes are committed by males. An increasing concern is date, or acquaintance, rape. Sexual harassment is a form of power asserted by one person over another. Sexual harassment of adolescents is widespread. Two forms are quid pro quo and hostile environment sexual harassment.

4 Sexual Literacy and Sex Education

 LG4 Characterize the sexual literacy of adolescents and sex education

- Sexual Literacy
- Sources of Sex Information
- Cognitive Factors
- Sex Education in Schools

- American adolescents and adults are not very knowledgeable about sex. Sex information is abundant, but too often it is inaccurate.

- Adolescents get their information about sex from many sources, including parents, siblings, schools, peers, magazines, TV, and the Internet.

- Cognitive factors, such as idealism and the personal fable, can make it difficult for sex education to be effective, especially with young adolescents.

- A majority of Americans support teaching sex education in schools, and this support has increased in concert with increases in STIs, especially AIDS. Currently, a major controversy is whether sex education should emphasize abstinence only or provide instruction on the use of contraceptive methods.

key **terms**

AIDS
bisexual
chlamydia
date rape, or acquaintance rape

genital herpes
genital warts
gonorrhea
homophobia

hostile environment sexual
   harassment
quid pro quo sexual harassment
rape

sexual minority
sexual script
sexually transmitted infections (STIs)
syphilis

key **people**

Bonnie Halpern-Felsher

June Reinisch

Ritch Savin-Williams

Deborah Tolman

resources for **improving the lives of adolescents**

Alan Guttmacher Institute (www.guttmacher.org)

The Alan Guttmacher Institute is an especially good resource for information about adolescent sexuality. The Institute publishes a well-respected journal, *Perspectives on Sexual and Reproductive Health* (renamed in 2003, formerly *Family Planning Perspectives*), which includes articles on many dimensions of sexuality, such as adolescent pregnancy, statistics on sexual behavior and attitudes, and sexually transmitted infections.

Positive and Negative Outcomes of Sexual Behaviors

Eva Lefkowtiz and Sara Vasilenko (Eds.) (2014, Summer), *New Directions in Child and Adolescent Development, 144,* 1–98.

Contemporary coverage of a wide range of important aspects of adolescent and emerging adult sexuality are examined, including healthy adolescent sex, sexual minority youth, online sexual activities, and dating and sexual relationships.

Adolescent Sexuality

Lisa Diamond and Ritch Savin-Williams (2009)

In R.M. Lerner & L. Steinberg (Eds.), *Handbook of Adolescent Psychology* New York: Wiley

Leading researchers on adolescent gay males and lesbians, Lisa Diamond and Ritch Savin-Williams, explore many aspects of

sexual minority adolescents' development and relationships, as well as sexual behavior in heterosexual adolescents.

National Sexually Transmitted Diseases Hotline

800-227-8922

This hotline provides information about a wide variety of sexually transmitted infections.

AIDS Hotline

National AIDS Information Clearinghouse

800-342-AIDS

800-344-SIDA (Spanish)

800-AIDS-TTY (Deaf)

The people answering the hotline will respond to any questions children, youth, or adults have about HIV infection or AIDS. Pamphlets and other materials on AIDS are available.

Sex Information and Education Council of the United States (SIECUS) (www.siecus.org)

This organization serves as an information clearinghouse for sex education. The group's objective is to promote the concept of human sexuality as an integration of physical, intellectual, emotional, and social dimensions.

chapter 7

MORAL DEVELOPMENT, VALUES, AND RELIGION

chapter **outline**

© Tim Pannell/Corbis

Jewel Cash, seated next to her mother, participates in a crime watch meeting at a community center. She is an exemplar of positive teenage community involvement.
© Matthew J. Lee/The Boston Globe/Getty Images

T he mayor of the city says that she is "everywhere." She persuaded the city's school committee to consider ending the practice of locking tardy students out of their classrooms. She also swayed a neighborhood group to support her proposal for a winter jobs program. According to one city councilman, "People are just impressed with the power of her arguments and the sophistication of the argument" (Silva, 2005, pp. B1, B4). She is Jewel E. Cash.

Jewel was raised in one of Boston's housing projects by her mother, a single parent. As a high school student at Boston Latin Academy, she was a member of the Boston Student Advisory Council, mentored children, volunteered at a women's shelter, managed and danced in two troupes, and was a member of a neighborhood watch group—among other activities. Jewel told an interviewer from the *Boston Globe*, "I see a problem and I say, 'How can I make a difference?' . . . I can't take on the world, even though I can try. . . . I'm moving forward but I want to make sure I'm bringing people with me" (Silva, 2005, pp. B1, B4). As an emerging adult, Jewel now works with a public consulting group and has continued working to help others as a mentor and community organizer.

preview

Jewel Cash's caring for people in her community reflects the positive side of moral development, a major focus of this chapter. Moral development involves the distinction between what is right and wrong, what matters to people, and what people should do in their interactions with others. We begin by discussing the three main traditional domains of moral development—moral thoughts, behavior, and feeling—and the recent emphasis on moral personality. Next, we explore the contexts in which moral development takes place, focusing on families and schools. We conclude with an examination of adolescent values, religion, and spirituality.

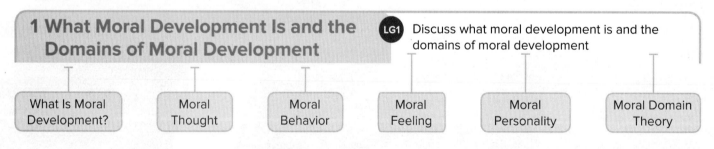

1 What Moral Development Is and the Domains of Moral Development

LG1 Discuss what moral development is and the domains of moral development

| What Is Moral Development? | Moral Thought | Moral Behavior | Moral Feeling | Moral Personality | Moral Domain Theory |

Moral development has been a topic of great concern to societies, communities, and families. It is also one of the oldest topics of interest to those who are curious about human nature. Philosophers and theologians have talked about it and written about it for many centuries. In the twentieth century, psychologists began theorizing about and studying moral development.

WHAT IS MORAL DEVELOPMENT?

moral development Thoughts, feelings, and behaviors regarding standards of right and wrong.

Moral development involves changes in thoughts, feelings, and behaviors regarding standards of right and wrong. Moral development has an *intrapersonal* dimension, which regulates a person's activities when she or he is not engaged in social interaction, and an *interpersonal* dimension, which regulates social interactions and arbitrates conflict. To understand moral development, we need to consider five basic questions:

First, how do adolescents reason, *or think, about rules for ethical conduct?* For example, we might present an adolescent with a story in which someone has a conflict about whether or not to cheat in a specific situation, such as taking an exam in school. The adolescent is asked to decide what is appropriate for the person to do and why. The focus is placed on the reasoning adolescents use to justify their moral decisions.

Second, how do adolescents actually behave *in moral circumstances?* For example, with regard to cheating, we might observe adolescents' cheating and the environmental circumstances that produced and maintain the cheating. We could conduct our study through a one-way mirror as adolescents are taking an exam. We might note whether they take out "cheat" notes, look at another student's answers, and so on.

Third, how do adolescents feel *about moral matters?* In the example of cheating, do the adolescents feel enough guilt to resist temptation? If adolescents do cheat, do feelings of guilt after the transgression keep them from cheating the next time they face temptation?

Fourth, what comprises an adolescent's moral personality? Continuing with the example of cheating, does the adolescent have a moral identity and moral character that are so strong the adolescent resists the temptation to cheat?

Fifth, how is the adolescent's moral domain *different from the adolescent's* social conventional and personal domains? In domain theory, cheating resides in the moral domain, along with lying, stealing, and harming another person. Behaviors such as cutting in a line or speaking out of turn are in the social conventional domain rather than the moral domain, and choosing friends is in the personal domain and not the moral domain.

Keep in mind that although we have separated moral development into different domains, the components often are interrelated. For example, if the focus is on the adolescent's behavior, it is still important to evaluate the adolescent's intentions (moral thought). Similarly, emotions accompany, and can distort, moral reasoning.

Let's now discuss the various domains of moral development. We begin with the cognitive domain.

MORAL THOUGHT

How do adolescents think about standards of right and wrong? Piaget had some thoughts about this, but they applied to children's moral development. It was Lawrence Kohlberg (1958, 1976, 1986) who crafted a major theory of how adolescents think about right and wrong. He proposed that moral development is based primarily on moral reasoning and unfolds in a series of stages.

Kohlberg's Stages   Central to Kohlberg's work on moral development were interviews with individuals of different ages. In the interviews, individuals were presented with a series of stories in which characters face moral dilemmas. The following is the most cited of the Kohlberg dilemmas:

> In Europe, a woman was near death from a special kind of cancer. There was one drug that the doctors thought might save her. It was a form of radium that a druggist in the same town had recently discovered. The drug was expensive to make, but the druggist was charging ten times what the drug cost him to make. He paid $200 for the radium and charged $2,000 for a small dose of the drug. The sick woman's husband, Heinz, went to everyone he knew to borrow the money, but he could only get together $1,000, which is half of what it cost. He told the druggist that his wife was dying and asked him to sell it cheaper or let him pay later. But the druggist said, "No, I discovered the drug, and I am going to make money from it." So Heinz got desperate and broke into the man's store to steal the drug for his wife. (Kohlberg, 1969, p. 379)

This story is one of eleven that Kohlberg devised to investigate the nature of moral thought. After reading the story, interviewees are asked a series of questions about the moral dilemma: Should Heinz have stolen the drug? Was stealing it right or wrong? Why? Is it a husband's duty to steal the drug for his wife if he can get it no other way? Would a good husband steal it? Did the druggist have the right to charge that much when there was no law setting a limit on the price? Why or why not?

Lawrence Kohlberg.
UAV 605. 295. 8, Box 7, Harvard University Archives

LEVEL 1	LEVEL 2	LEVEL 3
Preconventional Level **No Internalization**	**Conventional Level** **Intermediate Internalization**	**Postconventional Level** **Full Internalization**
Stage 1 Punishment and Obedience Orientation *Children obey because adults tell them to obey. People base their moral decisions on fear of punishment.*	**Stage 3** Mutual Interpersonal Expectations, Relationships, and Interpersonal Conformity *Individuals value trust, caring, and loyalty to others as a basis for moral judgments.*	**Stage 5** Social Contract or Utility and Individual Rights *Individuals reason that values, rights, and principles undergird or transcend the law.*
Stage 2 Individualism, Instrumental Purpose, and Exchange *Individuals pursue their own interests but let others do the same. What is right involves an equal exchange.*	**Stage 4** Social System Morality *Moral judgments are based on understanding and the social order, law, justice, and duty.*	**Stage 6** Universal Ethical Principles *The person has developed moral judgments that are based on universal human rights. When faced with a dilemma between law and conscience, a personal, individualized conscience is followed.*

FIGURE 1

KOHLBERG'S THREE LEVELS AND SIX STAGES OF MORAL DEVELOPMENT

From the answers interviewees gave for this and other moral dilemmas, Kohlberg hypothesized three levels of moral development, each of which is characterized by two stages (see Figure 1). A key concept in understanding progression through the levels and stages is that people's morality becomes more internal or mature. That is, their judgments of whether given behaviors are morally right or wrong begin to go beyond the external or superficial reasons they gave when they were younger to encompass more complex coordinations of multiple perspectives. Each stage integrates previous stages into a qualitatively different type of thought. Let's further examine Kohlberg's stages.

Kohlberg's Level 1: Preconventional Reasoning

Preconventional reasoning is the lowest level in Kohlberg's theory of moral development. Its two stages are (1) punishment and obedience orientation; and (2) individualism, instrumental purpose, and exchange.

- Stage 1. *Punishment and obedience orientation* is the first Kohlberg stage of moral development. At this stage, moral thinking is often tied to punishment. For example, children and adolescents obey adults because adults tell them to obey.
- Stage 2. *Individualism, instrumental purpose, and exchange* is the second stage in Kohlberg's model. At this stage, individuals pursue their own interests but also let others do the same. Thus, what is right involves an equal exchange. People are nice to others so that others will be nice to them in return. This stage has been described as reflecting an attitude of "What's in it for me?"

Kohlberg's Level 2: Conventional Reasoning

Conventional reasoning is the second, or intermediate, level in Kohlberg's theory of moral development. Individuals abide by certain standards (internal), but they are the standards of others (external), such as parents or the laws of society. In conventional reasoning, individuals develop expectations about social roles. The conventional reasoning level consists of two stages: (3) mutual interpersonal expectations, relationships, and interpersonal conformity; and (4) social systems morality.

- Stage 3. *Mutual interpersonal expectations, relationships, and interpersonal conformity* is Kohlberg's third stage of moral development. At this stage, individuals value trust, caring, and loyalty to others as a basis of moral judgments. Children and adolescents often adopt their parents' moral standards at this stage, seeking to be thought of by their parents as a "good girl" or a "good boy."
- Stage 4. *Social systems morality* is the fourth stage in Kohlberg's theory of moral development. At this stage, moral judgments are based on understanding the social order, law, justice, and duty. For example, adolescents may say that, for a community

preconventional reasoning The lowest level in Kohlberg's theory of moral development. At this level, morality is often focused on reward and punishment. The two stages in preconventional reasoning are punishment and obedience orientation (stage 1) and individualism, instrumental purpose, and exchange (stage 2).

conventional reasoning The second, or intermediate, level in Kohlberg's theory. Individuals abide by certain standards (internal), but they are the standards of others (external), such as parents or the laws of society. The conventional level consists of two stages: mutual interpersonal expectations, relationships, and interpersonal conformity (stage 3) and social systems morality (stage 4).

Stage Description	Examples of Moral Reasoning that Support Heinz's Theft of the Drug	Examples of Moral Reasoning that Indicate that Heinz Should Not Steal the Drug
	Preconventional Reasoning	
Stage 1: Punishment and obedience orientation	Heinz should not let his wife die; if he does, he will be in big trouble.	Heinz might get caught and sent to jail.
Stage 2: Individualism, instrumental purpose, and exchange	If Heinz gets caught, he could give the drug back and maybe they would not give him a long jail sentence.	The druggist is a businessman and needs to make money.
	Conventional Reasoning	
Stage 3: Mutual interpersonal expectations, relationships, and interpersonal conformity	Heinz was only doing something that a good husband would do; it shows how much he loves his wife.	If his wife dies, he can't be blamed for it; it is the druggist's fault. The druggist is the selfish one.
Stage 4: Social systems morality	It isn't morally wrong for Heinz to steal the drug in this case because the law is not designed to take into account every particular case or anticipate every circumstance.	Heinz should obey the law because laws serve to protect the productive and orderly functioning of society.
	Postconventional Reasoning	
Stage 5: Social contract or utility and individual rights	Heinz was justified in stealing the drug because a human life was at stake and that transcends any right the druggist had to the drug.	It is important to obey the law because laws represent a necessary structure of common agreement if individuals are to live together in society.
Stage 6: Universal ethical principles	Human life is sacred because of the universal principle of respect for the individual and it takes precedence over other values.	Heinz needs to decide whether or not to consider the other people who need the drug as badly as his wife does. He ought not to act based on his particular feelings for his wife, but consider the value of all the lives involved.

FIGURE 2

MORAL REASONING AT KOHLBERG'S STAGES IN RESPONSE TO THE "HEINZ AND THE DRUGGIST" STORY

to work effectively, it needs to be protected by laws that are adhered to by its members. Thus, in Stage 4 reasoning, individuals engage in social perspective taking that goes beyond intimate acquaintances to encompass the importance of being a good citizen.

Kohlberg's Level 3: Postconventional Reasoning **Postconventional reasoning** is the highest level in Kohlberg's theory of moral development. At this level, morality is more internal. The individual recognizes alternative moral courses, explores the options, and then decides on a moral code. In postconventional reasoning, individuals engage in deliberate checks on their reasoning to ensure that it meets high ethical standards. The postconventional level of morality consists of two stages: (5) social contract or utility and individual rights, and (6) universal ethical principles.

· Stage 5. *Social contract or utility and individual rights* is the fifth Kohlberg stage. At this stage, individuals reason that values, rights, and principles undergird or transcend the law. A person evaluates the validity of actual laws and examines social systems in terms of the degree to which they preserve and protect fundamental human rights and values.

· Stage 6. *Universal ethical principles* is the sixth and highest stage in Kohlberg's theory of moral development. At this stage, the person has developed a moral standard based on universal human rights. When faced with a conflict between law and conscience, the person will follow conscience, even though the decision might involve personal risk.

How might individuals at each of the six Kohlberg stages respond to the "Heinz and the druggist" moral dilemma described earlier? Figure 2 provides some examples of possible responses.

postconventional reasoning The third and highest level in Kohlberg's theory. At this level, morality is more internal. The postconventional level consists of two stages: social contract or utility and individual rights (stage 5) and universal ethical principles (stage 6).

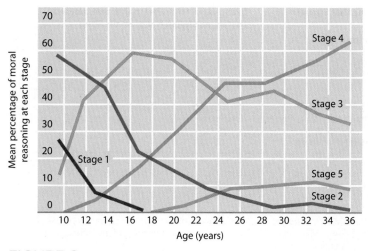

FIGURE **3**

AGE AND THE PERCENTAGE OF INDIVIDUALS AT EACH KOHLBERG STAGE. In one longitudinal study of males from 10 to 36 years of age, at age 10 most moral reasoning was at stage 2 (Colby & others, 1983). At 16 to 18 years of age, stage 3 became the most frequent type of moral reasoning and it was not until the mid-twenties that stage 4 became the most frequent. Stage 5 did not appear until 20 to 22 years of age and it never characterized more than 10 percent of the individuals. In this study, the moral stages appeared somewhat later than Kohlberg envisioned and stage 6 was absent.

Kohlberg argued that these levels and stages occur in a sequence and are age-related: Before age 9, most children reason about moral dilemmas in a preconventional way; by early adolescence, they reason in more conventional ways. Most adolescents reason at stage 3, with some signs of stages 2 and 4. By early adulthood, a small number of individuals reason in postconventional ways. In a 20-year longitudinal investigation, the uses of stages 1 and 2 decreased (Colby & others, 1983) (see Figure 3). Stage 4, which did not appear at all in the moral reasoning of 10-year-olds, was reflected in the moral thinking of 62 percent of 36-year-olds. Stage 5 did not appear until age 20 to 22 and never characterized more than 10 percent of the individuals. Thus, the moral stages appeared somewhat later than Kohlberg initially envisioned, and the higher stages, especially stage 6, were extremely elusive. Recently, stage 6 was removed from the Kohlberg moral judgment scoring manual, but it still is considered to be theoretically important in the Kohlberg scheme of moral development. A review of data from 45 studies in 27 diverse world cultures provided support for the universality of Kohlberg's first four stages but suggested that stages 5 and 6 tend to vary across cultures (Snarey, 1987).

Any change in moral reasoning between late adolescence and early adulthood appears to be relatively gradual (Eisenberg & others, 2009). One study found that when 16- to 19-year-olds and 18- to 25-year-olds were asked to reason about real-life moral dilemmas and their responses were coded using Kohlberg stages, there was no significant difference in the moral reasoning of the two age groups (Walker & others, 1995).

Influences on the Kohlberg Stages Kohlberg theorized that the individual's moral orientation unfolds as a consequence of cognitive development and exposure to appropriate social experiences. Children and adolescents construct their moral thoughts as they pass from one stage to the next, rather than passively accepting a cultural norm of morality. Investigators have sought to understand factors that influence movement through the moral stages, among them modeling, cognitive conflict, peer relations, and role-taking opportunities.

Several investigators have attempted to advance individuals' levels of moral development by having a model present arguments that reflect moral thinking one stage above the individuals' established levels. These studies are based on the cognitive developmental concepts of equilibrium and conflict (Walker & Taylor, 1991). By presenting moral information slightly beyond the individual's cognitive level, a disequilibrium is created that motivates a restructuring of moral thought. The resolution of the disequilibrium and conflict should be toward increased competence. In one study, participants preferred stages higher than their own more than stages lower than their own (Walker, de Vries, & Bichard, 1984). In sum, an adolescent's moral thought can be moved to a higher level through exposure to models or discussion that is more advanced than the adolescent's level.

Like Piaget, Kohlberg emphasized that peer interaction is a critical part of the social stimulation that challenges individuals to change their moral orientation. Whereas adults characteristically impose rules and regulations on children, the mutual give-and-take in peer interaction provides the child with an opportunity to take the role of another person and to generate rules democratically (Rubin, Bukowski, & Parker, 2006). Kohlberg stressed that role-taking opportunities can, in principle, be engendered by any peer group encounter. Researchers have found that more advanced moral reasoning takes place when peers engage in challenging, even moderately conflicting, conversation (Berkowitz & Gibbs, 1983; Walker, Hennig, & Krettenauer, 2000).

Kohlberg did note that certain types of parent-child experiences can induce the child and adolescent to think at more advanced levels of moral reasoning. In particular, parents who allow or encourage conversation about value-laden issues promote more advanced moral thought in their children and adolescents. Unfortunately, many parents do not systematically provide their children and adolescents with such role-taking opportunities. Nonetheless, in

Why did Kohlberg think peer relations are so important in moral development?
© Randy Faris/Corbis

one study, children's moral development was related to their parents' discussion style, which involved questioning and supportive interaction (Walker & Taylor, 1991). In recent years, there has been increasing emphasis on the role of parenting in moral development (Thompson & Newton, 2010).

Why Is Kohlberg's Theory Important for Understanding Moral Development in Adolescence? Kohlberg's theory is essentially a description of the progressive conceptions people use to understand social cooperation. In short, it tells the developmental story of people trying to understand things like society, rules and roles, and institutions and relationships. Such basic conceptions are fundamental to adolescents, for whom ideology becomes important in guiding their lives and helping them to make life decisions.

Kohlberg's Critics Kohlberg's theory has provoked debate, research, and criticism (Gibbs, 2014; Killen & Smetana, 2015; Narváez, 2014, 2015, 2016; Turiel, 2014, 2015; Walker, 2014a, b). Key criticisms involve the link between moral thought and moral behavior, whether moral reasoning is conscious/deliberative or unconscious/automatic, inadequate attention given to emotion, the roles of culture and the family in moral development, the significance of concern for others, and how moral development is assessed.

Moral Thought and Moral Behavior Kohlberg's theory has been criticized for placing too much emphasis on moral thought and not enough emphasis on moral behavior. Moral reasons can always be used as a shelter for immoral behavior. Some presidents, business executives, and religious figures endorse the loftiest of moral virtues when commenting about moral dilemmas, yet their own behavior may be immoral. No one wants a nation of cheaters and liars who can reason at the postconventional level. The cheaters and liars may know what is right and wrong yet still do what is wrong.

In evaluating the relationship between moral thought and moral behavior, consider the corrupting power of rationalizations and other defenses that disengage us from self-blame; these include interpreting a situation in our favor and attributing blame to authorities, circumstances, or victims (Bandura, 1991). One area in which a link between moral judgment and behavior has been found involves antisocial behavior and delinquency. Researchers have found that less advanced moral reasoning in adolescence is related to antisocial behavior and delinquency (Gibbs, 2014; Taylor & Walker, 1997). One study also revealed that moral reasoning was related to self-reported altruism (Maclean, Walker, & Matsuba, 2004).

How does Bandura describe the way terrorists justify their actions?
© Sean Adair/Reuters/Corbis

Given the terrorist attacks of September 11, 2001, and the continuing war on terrorism, it is intriguing to explore how heinous actions can be cloaked in a mantle of moral virtue and to consider why that is especially dangerous. Social cognitive theorist Albert Bandura (1999, 2002) argues that people usually don't engage in harmful conduct until they have justified the morality of their actions to themselves. In this process of moral justification, immoral conduct is made personally and socially acceptable by portraying it as serving socially worthy or moral purposes. In many instances throughout history, perpetrators of violence have twisted theology so that they see themselves as doing God's will. Bandura provides the example of Islamic extremists who perceive their actions as self-defense against tyrannical, decadent people whom they see as seeking to enslave the Islamic world.

Moral Thinking: Conscious/Deliberative Versus Unconscious/Automatic Social psychologist Jonathan Haidt (2010, 2013) argues that a major flaw in Kohlberg's theory is his view that moral thinking is deliberative and that individuals go around all the time contemplating and reasoning about morality. Haidt believes that most moral thinking is more of an intuitive gut reaction and the deliberative moral reasoning is often an after-the-fact justification. Thus, in his view, much of morality begins by making rapid evaluative judgments of others, not initially strategically reasoning about moral circumstances.

The Role of Emotion Kohlberg argued that emotion has negative effects on moral reasoning. However, increasing evidence indicates that emotions play an important role in moral thinking. Researchers have found that individuals who have received damage in a particular region in the brain's prefrontal cortex lose the ability to integrate emotions into their moral judgments (Damasio & Carvalho, 2013). Losing their intuitive feelings of what is right, they can't adequately decide which actions to take or end up making more choices about moral issues.

Research with healthy individuals also has shown that the moral decisions individuals make are linked to the intensity and activation of emotion in the same region of the prefrontal cortex mentioned as well as the amygdala (Thomas, Croft, & Tranel, 2011). Later in the chapter, we will further explore the importance of emotion in moral development.

Culture and Moral Development Kohlberg emphasized that his stages of moral reasoning are universal, but some critics claim his theory is culturally biased (Miller & Bland, 2014; Mrkva & Narváez, 2015; Wainryb & Recchia, 2014). Both Kohlberg and his critics may be partially correct. One review of 45 studies in 27 cultures around the world, mostly non-European, provided support for the universality of Kohlberg's first four stages (Snarey, 1987). Individuals in diverse cultures developed through these four stages in sequence as Kohlberg predicted. A more recent research review revealed support for the qualitative shift from stage 2 to stage 3 across cultures (Gibbs & others, 2007). Stages 5 and 6, however, have not been found in all cultures (Gibbs & others, 2007; Snarey, 1987). Furthermore, Kohlberg's scoring system does not recognize the higher-level moral reasoning of certain cultures and thus underestimates the influence of culture (Snarey, 1987).

In the view of John Gibbs (2010), most young adolescents around the world use the moral judgment of mutuality (stage 3) that makes intimate friendships possible. And by late adolescence, many individuals also are beginning to grasp the importance of agreed-upon standards and institutions for the common good (stage 4). A main exception, though, is the delayed moral judgment of adolescents who regularly engage in delinquency.

In sum, Kohlberg's approach captures much—but not all—of the moral reasoning voiced in various cultures around the world. As we have just seen, there are some important moral concepts in specific cultures that his approach misses or misconstrues (Miller, 2007).

One study explored links between culture, mindset, and moral judgment (Narváez & Hill, 2010). In this study, higher levels of multicultural experience were linked to open-mindedness (being cognitively flexible), a growth mindset (perceiving that one's qualities can change and improve through effort), and higher moral judgment.

Darcia Narváez and Tracy Gleason (2013) recently described cohort effects regarding moral reasoning. In recent years, postconventional moral reasoning has been declining in college students, not down to the next level (conventional), but to the lowest level (personal interests) (Thoma & Bebeau, 2008). Narváez and Gleason (2013) also argue that declines in prosocial behavior have occurred in recent years and that humans, especially those living in Western cultures, are "on a fast train to demise." They propose that the solution to improving

developmental connection

Research Methods

Cross-cultural studies provide information about the degree to which children's development is universal, or similar, across cultures or is culture-specific. Connect to "Introduction" and "Culture."

people's moral lives lies in better child-rearing strategies and social supports for families and children.

Families and Moral Development Kohlberg argued that family processes are essentially unimportant in children's and adolescents' moral development. As noted earlier, he argued that parent-child relationships usually provide children with little opportunity for give-and-take or perspective taking. Rather, Kohlberg said that such opportunities are more likely to be provided by children's and adolescents' peer relations. Did Kohlberg underestimate the contribution of family relationships to moral development? Most developmentalists emphasize that parents play more important roles in children's and adolescents' moral development than Kohlberg envisioned (Dunn, 2014; Eisenberg, Spinrad, & Knafo, 2015; Grusec & others, 2014; Thompson, 2014). They stress that parents' communication with children and adolescents, their discipline techniques, and many other aspects of parent-child relationships influence children's and adolescents' moral development—we will have more to discuss about this topic later in the chapter. Nonetheless, most developmentalists agree with Kohlberg and Piaget that peers play an important role in moral development.

Gender and the Care Perspective The most publicized criticism of Kohlberg's theory has come from Carol Gilligan (1982, 1992, 1996), who argues that Kohlberg's theory reflects a gender bias. According to Gilligan, Kohlberg's theory is based on a male norm that puts abstract principles above relationships and concern for others and sees the individual as standing alone and independently making moral decisions. It puts justice at the heart of morality. In contrast with Kohlberg's **justice perspective**, Gilligan argues for a **care perspective**, which is a moral perspective that views people in terms of their connectedness with others and emphasizes interpersonal communication, relationships with others, and concern for others. According to Gilligan, Kohlberg greatly underplayed the care perspective, perhaps because he was a male, because most of his research was with males rather than females, and because he used male responses as a model for his theory.

This 14-year-old boy in Nepal is thought to be the sixth holiest Buddhist in the world. In one study of 20 adolescent male Buddhist monks in Nepal, the issue of justice, a basic theme in Kohlberg's theory, was not a central focus in the monks' moral views (Huebner & Garrod, 1993). Also, the monks' concerns about prevention of suffering and the importance of compassion are not captured in Kohlberg's theory.
© Raghu-Rai/Magnum Photos

In extensive interviews with girls from 6 to 18 years of age, Gilligan and her colleagues found that girls consistently interpret moral dilemmas in terms of human relationships and base these interpretations on listening and watching other people (Gilligan, 1992; Gilligan & others, 2003). However, a meta-analysis (a statistical analysis that combines the results of many different studies) casts doubt on Gilligan's claim of substantial gender differences in moral judgment (Jaffee & Hyde, 2000). And a recent analysis concluded that girls' moral orientations are "somewhat more likely to focus on care for others than on abstract principles of justice, but they can use both moral orientations when needed (as can boys . . .)" (Blakemore, Berenbaum, & Liben, 2009, p. 132).

developmental **connection**

Gender

Janet Shibley Hyde concluded that many views and studies of gender exaggerate differences. Connect to "Gender."

Assessment of Moral Reasoning Some developmentalists fault the quality of Kohlberg's research and stress that more attention should be paid to the way moral development is assessed. For example, James Rest (1986; Rest & others, 1999) argued that alternative methods should be used to collect information about moral thinking instead of relying on a single method that requires individuals to reason about hypothetical moral dilemmas. Rest also said that responses to Kohlberg's stories are extremely difficult to score. To help remedy this problem, Rest developed his own measure of moral development, called the Defining Issues Test (DIT).

Unlike Kohlberg's procedure, the DIT attempts to determine which moral issues individuals feel are crucial in a given situation by presenting a series of dilemmas and a list of potential considerations in making a decision. In the dilemma of Heinz and the druggist, individuals are asked to rate such matters as whether a community's laws should be upheld or whether Heinz should be willing to risk being injured or caught as a burglar. They might also be asked to list the most important values that govern human interaction. They are given six stories and asked to rate the importance of each issue involved in deciding what ought to be done. Then they are asked to list what they believe are the four most important issues. Rest argued that this method provides a more valid and reliable way to assess moral thinking than does Kohlberg's method (Rest & others, 1999).

justice perspective A moral perspective that focuses on the rights of the individual. Individuals are viewed as making moral decisions independently.

care perspective The moral perspective of Carol Gilligan, which views people in terms of their connectedness with others and emphasizes interpersonal communication, relationships with others, and concern for others.

Story subject	Grade		
	7	9	12
		Percentage	
Alcohol	2	0	5
Civil rights	0	6	7
Drugs	7	10	5
Interpersonal relations	38	24	35
Physical safety	22	8	3
Sexual relations	2	20	10
Smoking	7	2	0
Stealing	9	2	0
Working	2	2	15
Other	1	26	20

FIGURE 4

ACTUAL MORAL DILEMMAS GENERATED BY ADOLESCENTS

DIT researchers recently have described their theory as neo-Kohlbergian, reflecting a connection to Kohlberg's theory but an important shift away from his theory (Rest & others, 1999; Thoma, 2006). The departure from Kohlberg's theory includes replacement of his clear-cut stage model with a continuum involving a gradual shift from lower-level to more complex moral thinking.

Researchers also have found that the hypothetical moral dilemmas posed in Kohlberg's stories do not match the moral dilemmas many children and adults face in their everyday lives (Walker, de Vries, & Trevethan, 1987; Yussen, 1977). Most of Kohlberg's stories focus on the family and authority. However, when one researcher invited adolescents to write stories about their own moral dilemmas, the adolescents generated dilemmas that were broader in scope, focusing on friends, acquaintances, and other issues, as well as family and authority (Yussen, 1977). The adolescents' moral dilemmas also were analyzed in terms of their content. As shown in Figure 4, the moral issue that concerned adolescents more than any other was interpersonal relationships.

In sum, Kohlberg's theory was a very important pioneering effort in describing and understanding the development of moral reasoning. As indicated in the criticisms of the theory, although still relevant in understanding the development of moral reasoning, the theory is no longer as influential as it once was. Let's now explore some alternative views of moral development.

MORAL BEHAVIOR

We saw that one of the criticisms of Kohlberg's theory is that it does not give adequate attention to the link between moral thought and moral behavior. In our exploration of moral behavior, we focus on these questions: What are the basic processes that behaviorists argue are responsible for adolescents' moral behavior? How do social cognitive theorists view adolescents' moral development? What is the nature of prosocial behavior?

Basic Processes Behavioral views emphasize the moral behavior of adolescents. The familiar processes of reinforcement, punishment, and imitation have been invoked to explain how and why adolescents learn certain moral behaviors and why their behaviors differ from those of one another (Grusec, 2006). The general conclusions to be drawn are the same as those for other domains of social behavior. When adolescents are positively reinforced for behavior that is consistent with laws and social conventions, they are likely to repeat that behavior. When models who behave morally are provided, adolescents are likely to adopt similar behavior. And, when adolescents are punished for immoral or unacceptable behavior, those behaviors can be eliminated, but at the expense of sanctioning punishment by its very use and of causing emotional side effects for the adolescent. For example, when adolescent drivers act responsibly and are praised by their parents for doing so, they are more likely to continue driving safely. If adolescents see their parents driving responsibly, they are more likely to follow the same patterns. If driving privileges are revoked from adolescents who do not drive responsibly, the behavior is eliminated but the adolescent may feel humiliated by the punishment.

To these general conclusions, we can add several qualifiers. The effectiveness of reinforcement and punishment depends on how consistently they are administered and the schedule that is adopted. The effectiveness of modeling depends on the characteristics of the model (power, warmth, uniqueness, and so on) and the presence of cognitive processes, such as symbolic codes and imagery, that enhance retention of the modeled behavior.

What kind of adult moral models are adolescents being exposed to in American society? Do such models usually do what they say? Adolescents are especially alert to adult hypocrisy, and evidence indicates that they are right to believe that many adults display a double standard—that is, their moral actions do not always correspond to their moral thoughts or pronouncements (Bandura, 1991).

In addition to emphasizing the role of environmental determinants and the gap between moral thought and moral action, behaviorists also emphasize that moral behavior is situationally dependent. That is, they say that adolescents are not likely to display consistent moral behavior in diverse social settings (Eisenberg & others, 2009). In a classic investigation of moral behavior—one of the most extensive ever conducted—Hugh Hartshorne and Mark May

(1928–1930) observed the moral responses of 11,000 children and adolescents who were given the opportunity to lie, cheat, and steal in a variety of circumstances—at home, at school, at social events, and in athletics. A completely honest or a completely dishonest child or adolescent was difficult to find. Situation-specific moral behavior was the rule. Adolescents were more likely to cheat when their friends pressured them to do so and when the chance of being caught was slim. Other analyses suggest that some adolescents are more likely to lie, cheat, and steal than others, an indication of greater consistency of moral behavior in some adolescents than in others (Burton, 1984).

In further support of the situational determinants of morality, a recent study found that very few 7-year-olds were willing to donate any money after watching a UNICEF film on children suffering from poverty (van IJzendoorn & others, 2010). However, after gentle prompting by an adult, most children were willing to donate some of their money.

Social Cognitive Theory of Moral Development

The **social cognitive theory of moral development** emphasizes a distinction between adolescents' moral competence—the ability to produce moral behaviors—and moral performance—the enactment of those behaviors in specific situations (Mischel & Mischel, 1975). Competence, or acquisition, is primarily the outgrowth of cognitive-sensory processes. Competencies include what adolescents are capable of doing, what they know, their skills, their awareness of moral rules and regulations, and their cognitive ability to construct behaviors. In contrast, adolescents' moral performance, or behavior, is determined by their motivation and the rewards and incentives to act in a specific moral way.

Albert Bandura (1991, 2002) also concludes that moral development is best understood by considering a combination of social and cognitive factors, especially those involving self-control. He proposes that in developing a "moral self, individuals adopt standards of right and wrong that serve as guides and deterrents for conduct. In this self-regulatory process, people monitor their conduct and the conditions under which it occurs, judge it in relation to moral standards, and regulate their actions by the consequences they apply to themselves. They do things that provide them with satisfaction and a sense of self-worth. They refrain from behaving in ways that violate their moral standards because such conduct will bring self-condemnation. Self-sanctions keep conduct in line with internal standards" (Bandura, 2002, p. 102). Thus, in Bandura's view, self-regulation rather than abstract reasoning is the key to positive moral development.

Overall, the findings are mixed with regard to the association of moral thought and behavior, although in one investigation with college students, individuals with both highly principled moral reasoning and high ego strength were less likely to cheat in a resistance-to-temptation situation than were their low-principled and low-ego-strength counterparts (Hess, Lonky, & Roodin, 1985).

Moral behavior includes both negative aspects of behavior—cheating, lying, and stealing, for example—and positive aspects of behavior—such as being considerate to others and giving to a worthy cause. Let's now explore the positive side of moral behavior—prosocial behavior.

Prosocial Behavior

Many prosocial acts involve **altruism,** an unselfish interest in helping another person. Altruism is found throughout the human world and is a guiding principle in Christianity, Buddhism, Hinduism, Islam, and Judaism. Although adolescents have often been described as egocentric and selfish, adolescent acts of altruism are, nevertheless, plentiful (Carlo, 2014; Eisenberg, Spinrad, & Knafo, 2015). We see examples daily in the hardworking adolescent who places a five-dollar bill in the church offering plate each week; the adolescent-sponsored car washes, bake sales, and concerts organized to make money to feed the hungry and help children with a disability; and the adolescent who takes in and cares for a wounded cat. How do psychologists account for such altruistic acts?

The circumstances most likely to involve altruism by adolescents are empathetic or sympathetic emotion for an individual in need or a close relationship between the benefactor and the recipient (Clark & others, 1987). Prosocial behavior occurs more often in adolescence than in childhood, although examples of caring for others and comforting someone in distress occur even during the preschool years (Eisenberg, Spinrad, & Knafo, 2015; Eisenberg, Spinrad, & Morris, 2013).

developmental **connection**

Social Cognitive Theory

What are the main themes of Bandura's social cognitive theory? Connect to "Introduction."

It is one of the most beautiful compensations of this life that no one can sincerely try to help another without helping himself.

—CHARLES DUDLEY WARNER
American essayist, 19th century

social cognitive theory of moral development The theory that distinguishes between moral competence (the ability to produce moral behaviors) and moral performance (enacting those behaviors in specific situations).

altruism Unselfish interest in helping another person.

What are some characteristics of prosocial behavior in adolescence?
© Angela Hampton Picture Library/Alamy

Why might prosocial behavior increase in adolescence? Cognitive changes involving advances in abstract, idealistic, and logical reasoning as well as increased empathy and emotional understanding likely are involved. With such newfound cognitive abilities, young adolescents increasingly sympathize with members of abstract groups with whom they have little experience, such as people living in poverty in other countries (Eisenberg, Spinrad, & Knafo, 2015; Eisenberg, Spinrad, & Morris, 2013). The increase in volunteer opportunities in adolescence also contributes to more frequent prosocial behavior.

Are there gender differences in prosocial behavior during adolescence? Adolescent females view themselves as more prosocial and empathic, and also engage in more prosocial behavior than do males (Eisenberg, Spinrad, & Morris, 2013). For example, a review of research found that across childhood and adolescence, females engaged in more prosocial behavior (Eisenberg & Fabes, 1998). The biggest gender difference occurred in kind and considerate behavior, with a smaller difference in sharing.

Are there different types of prosocial behavior? In a recent study, Gustavo Carlo and his colleagues (2010, pp. 340–341) investigated this question and confirmed the presence of six types of prosocial behavior in young adolescents:

· altruism ("One of the best things about doing charity work is that it looks good.")
· public ("Helping others while I'm being watched is when I work best.")
· emotional ("I usually help others when they are very upset.")
· dire ("I tend to help people who are hurt badly.")
· anonymous ("I prefer to donate money without anyone knowing.")
· compliant ("I never wait to help others when they ask for it.")

In this study, adolescent girls reported more emotional, dire, compliant, and altruistic behavior than did boys, while boys engaged in more public prosocial behavior. Parental monitoring was positively related to emotional, dire, and compliant behavior but not to the other types of behavior. Compliant, anonymous, and altruistic prosocial behavior were positively related to religiosity.

Most research on prosocial behavior conceptualizes the concept in a global and unidimensional manner. The study by Carlo and colleagues (2010) illustrates the important point that in thinking about and studying prosocial behavior, it is essential to consider its dimensions.

What role do parents play in adolescents' prosocial behavior? A recent study found that authoritative parenting by mothers, but not by fathers, contributed to adolescents' engagement in prosocial behavior one year later (Padilla-Walker & others, 2012). Other research also has found that mothers are more likely to influence adolescents' prosocial behavior than are fathers (Carlo & others, 2011). In the study just discussed (Padilla-Walker & others, 2012), a bidirectional connection between parenting and prosocial behavior was found. Mothers' authoritative parenting increased one year after adolescents engaged in prosocial behavior and this direction—adolescent prosocial behavior preceding authoritative parenting—was stronger than the other direction—authoritative parenting preceding adolescent prosocial behavior.

Forgiveness is an aspect of prosocial behavior that occurs when the injured person releases the injurer from possible behavioral retaliation (Flanagan & others, 2012; Klatt & Enright, 2009). In one investigation, individuals from the fourth grade through college and adulthood were asked questions about forgiveness (Enright, Santos, & Al-Mabuk, 1989). The adolescents were especially swayed by peer pressure in their willingness to forgive others. Also, a recent study revealed that when adolescents encountered hurtful experiences in school settings, if they disliked the transgressor they had more hostile thoughts, feelings of anger, and avoidance/revenge tendencies than they did when they liked the transgressing peer (Peets, Hodges, & Salmivalli, 2013).

Gratitude is a feeling of thankfulness and appreciation, especially in response to someone doing something kind or helpful (Grant & Gino, 2010). Interest in studying adolescents' gratitude or lack thereof is increasing. Consider the following recent studies:

· Gratitude was linked to a number of positive aspects of development in young adolescents, including satisfaction with one's family, optimism, and prosocial behavior (Froh, Yurkewicz, & Kashdan, 2009).
· Adolescents' expression of gratitude was linked to having fewer depressive symptoms (Lambert, Fincham, & Stillman, 2012).

forgiveness An aspect of prosocial behavior that occurs when an injured person releases the injurer from possible behavioral retaliation.

gratitude A feeling of thankfulness and appreciation, especially in response to someone doing something kind or helpful.

- Chinese adolescents who had a higher level of gratitude were less likely to engage in suicidal ideation and attempts (Li & others, 2012).
- A longitudinal study assessed the gratitude of adolescents at 10 to 14 years of age (Bono, 2012). Four years later, the most grateful adolescents (top 20 percent) had a stronger sense of the meaning of life, were more satisfied with their life, were happier and more hopeful, and had a lower level of negative emotions and were less depressed than the least grateful students (bottom 20 percent).

Compared with antisocial behavior such as juvenile delinquency, less attention has been given to prosocial behavior in adolescence. We still do not have adequate research information about such topics as how youth perceive prosocial norms and how school policies and peers influence prosocial behavior (Siu, Shek, & Law, 2012).

So far we have examined two of the three main domains of moral development: thought and behavior. Next, we explore the third main domain: moral feeling.

MORAL FEELING

Among the ideas formulated about the development of moral feeling are concepts central to psychoanalytic theory, the nature of empathy, and the role of emotions in moral development.

Psychoanalytic Theory Sigmund Freud's psychoanalytic theory describes the superego as one of the three main structures of personality (the id and the ego being the other two). In Freud's classical psychoanalytic theory, an individual's *superego*—the moral branch of personality—develops in early childhood when the child resolves the Oedipus conflict and identifies with the same-sex parent. According to Freud, one reason why children resolve the Oedipus conflict is to alleviate the fear of losing their parents' love and of being punished for their unacceptable sexual wishes toward the opposite-sex parent. To reduce anxiety, avoid punishment, and maintain parental affection, children form a superego by identifying with the same-sex parent. In Freud's view, through this identification, children internalize the parents' standards of right and wrong that reflect societal prohibitions. At the same time, children turn inward the hostility that was previously aimed at the same-sex parent. This inwardly directed hostility is then experienced self-punitively (and unconsciously) as guilt. In the psychoanalytic account of moral development, self-punitiveness of guilt keeps children and, later on, adolescents from committing transgressions. That is, children and adolescents conform to societal standards to avoid guilt.

In Freud's view, the superego consists of two main components—the ego ideal and the conscience—which promote children's and adolescents' development of moral feelings. The **ego ideal** is the component of the superego that involves ideal standards approved by parents, whereas the **conscience** is the component of the superego that involves behaviors not approved of by parents. An individual's ego ideal rewards the individual by conveying a sense of pride and personal value when the individual acts according to moral standards. The conscience punishes the individual for acting immorally by making the individual feel guilty and worthless. In this way, self-control replaces parental control.

Freud's claims regarding the formation of the ego ideal and conscience cannot be verified. However, researchers can examine the extent to which children feel guilty when they misbehave. Contemporary views of conscience emphasize that conscience is rooted in close relationships, constructed from advances in children's self-understanding and understanding of others, and linked to their emotional makeup (Thompson, 2009, 2014). Contemporary views also stress that the development of conscience goes well beyond discipline encounters with parents to include communication about emotion and conversations with parents about relationships (Thompson, 2009, 2014).

Erik Erikson (1970) outlined three stages of moral development: specific moral learning in childhood, ideological concerns in adolescence, and ethical consolidation in adulthood. According to Erikson, during adolescence individuals search for an identity. If adolescents become disillusioned with the moral and religious beliefs they acquired during childhood, they are likely to lose, at least temporarily, their sense of purpose and feel that their lives are empty. This loss may lead adolescents to search for an ideology that will give some purpose to their lives. For the ideology to be acceptable, it must both fit the evidence and mesh with adolescents' logical reasoning abilities. If others share this ideology, a sense of community

developmental **connection**

Psychoanalytic Theory

Freud theorized that individuals go through five main stages of psychosexual development. Connect to "Introduction."

ego ideal The component of the superego that involves ideal standards approved by parents.

conscience The component of the superego that discourages behaviors disapproved of by parents.

What characterizes empathy in adolescence?
© ThinkStock/Corbis RF

is felt. For Erikson, ideology surfaces as the guardian of identity during adolescence because it provides a sense of purpose, assists in tying the present to the future, and contributes meaning to the behavior (Hoffman, 1988).

Empathy   Positive feelings, such as empathy, contribute to adolescents' moral development (Grusec & others, 2014; Malti & Ongley 2014). Feeling **empathy** means reacting to another's feelings with an emotional response that is similar to that person's feelings. Although empathy is experienced as an emotional state, it often has a cognitive component— the ability to discern another's inner psychological states, or what we have previously called *perspective taking*.

At about 10 to 12 years of age, individuals develop empathy for people who live in unfortunate circumstances (Damon, 1988). Children's concerns are no longer limited to the feelings of specific persons in situations they directly observe. Instead, 10- to 12-year-olds expand their concerns to the general problems of people in unfortunate circumstances—the poor, those with disabilities, social outcasts, and so forth. This newfound sensitivity may lead older children to behave altruistically, and later may give a humanitarian flavor to adolescents' development of ideological and political views.

Although every adolescent may be capable of responding with empathy, not all do so. Adolescents' empathic behavior varies considerably. For example, in older children and adolescents, empathic dysfunctions can contribute to antisocial behavior. Some delinquents convicted of violent crimes show a lack of feeling for their victims' distress. A 13-year-old boy convicted of violently mugging a number of older adults, when asked about the pain he had caused one blind woman, said, "What do I care? I'm not her" (Damon, 1988).

A recent study found that empathy increased from 12 to 16 years of age (Allemand, Steiger, & Fend, 2015). Also in this study, girls showed more empathy than did boys. Further, adolescent empathy predicted a number of social competencies (adult empathy, communication skills, and relationship satisfaction, for example) two decades later.

The Contemporary Perspective   You have learned that classical psychoanalytic theory emphasizes the power of unconscious guilt in moral development but that other theories, such as that of Damon, emphasize the role of empathy. Today, many developmentalists note that both positive feelings, such as empathy, sympathy, admiration, and self-esteem, and negative feelings, such as anger, outrage, shame, and guilt, contribute to adolescents' moral development (Eisenberg, Spinrad, & Morris, 2013; Lapsley & Carlo, 2014; Malti & Ongley, 2014). When strongly experienced, these emotions influence adolescents to act in accord with standards of right and wrong. Such emotions as empathy, shame, guilt, and anxiety over other people's violations of standards are present early in development and undergo developmental change throughout childhood and adolescence.

*Sympath*y—an other-oriented emotional response in which the observer experiences emotions that are the same as or similar to what the other person is feeling—often motivates prosocial behavior (Eisenberg, Spinrad, & Knafo, 2015; Eisenberg, Spinrad, & Morris, 2013, 2014). A recent study found that sympathy in childhood predicted increases in moral reasoning and social justice values in early adolescence (Daniel & others, 2014).

These emotions provide a natural base for adolescents' acquisition of moral values, both orienting adolescents toward moral events and motivating them to pay close attention to such events (Thompson, 2009, 2014). However, moral emotions do not operate in a vacuum to build adolescents' moral awareness, and they are not sufficient in themselves to generate moral responsivity. They do not give the "substance" of moral regulation—the rules, values, and standards of behavior that adolescents need to understand and act on. Moral emotions are inextricably interwoven with the cognitive and social aspects of adolescents' development.

MORAL PERSONALITY

So far we have examined three key dimensions of moral development: thoughts, behavior, and feelings. Recently there has been a surge of interest in a fourth dimension: personality (Frimer & others, 2011; Hardy & others, 2014a, b; Walker & Frimer, 2011). Thoughts, behavior, and feelings can all be involved in an individual's moral personality (Walker, 2014a, b).

empathy Reaction to another's feelings with an emotional response that is similar to the other's feelings.

In this view, behaving in a manner that violates this moral commitment places the integrity of the self at risk (Lapsley & Stey, 2014).

For many years, skepticism greeted the assertion that a set of moral characteristics or traits could be discovered that would constitute a core of moral personality. Much of this skepticism stemmed from the results of Hartshorne and May's (1928–1930) classic study, and Walter Mischel's (1968) social learning theory and research, which argued that situations trump traits when attempts are made to predict moral behavior. Mischel's (2004) subsequent research and theory and Bandura's (2010a, b) social cognitive theory have emphasized the importance of "person" factors while still recognizing situational variation. Until recently, though, there has been little interest in studying what might comprise a moral personality. Three aspects of moral personality that have recently been emphasized are (1) moral identity, (2) moral character, and (3) moral exemplars.

developmental connection

Personality

The contemporary view of personality emphasizes the interaction of traits and situations. Connect to "The Self, Identity, Emotion, and Personality."

Moral Identity   A central aspect of the recent interest in the role of personality in moral development focuses on **moral identity.** Individuals have a moral identity when moral notions and commitments are central to their life. In this view, behaving in a manner that violates this moral commitment places the integrity of the self at risk (Hardy & others, 2014a, b; Walker & Frimer, 2011).

Recently, Darcia Narváez (2010b) concluded that a mature moral individual cares about morality and being a moral person. For these individuals, moral responsibility is central to their identity. Mature moral individuals engage in moral metacognition, including moral self-monitoring and moral self-reflection. Moral self-monitoring involves monitoring one's thoughts and actions related to moral situations, and engaging in self-control when it is needed. Moral self-reflection encompasses critical evaluations of one's self-judgments and efforts to minimize bias and self-deception.

Sam Hardy and his colleagues (Hardy & others, 2013, 2014) also emphasize that identity is a way of caring about morality. Thus, when morality becomes an important aspect of one's identity, then the person has a greater sense of obligation. If you do something immoral, you are not just violating an abstract principle (as in Kohlberg's moral reasoning theory), you are violating who you are.

What are some outcomes of having a moral identity? A recent study of 9,500 college students revealed that moral identity predicted all five health outcomes assessed (anxiety, depression, hazardous alcohol use, sexual risk taking, and self-esteem) (Hardy & others, 2013). A recent study of 15- to 18-year-olds found that a higher level of moral identity could possibly reduce the negative effects of moral disengagement and low self-regulation (Hardy, Bean, & Olsen, 2014).

developmental connection

Identity

According to James Marcia, what are the four statuses of identity development? Connect to "The Self, Identity, Emotion, and Personality."

Daniel Hart and his colleagues (Hart, 2005; Hart & Matsuba, 2010; Hart, Matsuba, & Atkins, 2008, 2014; Hart & others, 2011; Hart, Richardson, & Wilkenfeld, 2011; Matsuba, Murzyn, & Hart, 2014) argue that poor urban neighborhoods provide contexts that work against the formation of moral identity and commitment to moral projects. Living in high-poverty contexts often undermines moral attitudes and reduces tolerance for divergent viewpoints. And high-poverty neighborhoods offer fewer opportunities for effective engagement in the community because they lack an extensive network of organizations that support projects connected to moral goals. There are fewer opportunities for volunteering in such contexts. Hart and his colleagues advocate providing more service learning and community opportunities as a way of improving youths' moral attitudes and identity.

Moral Character   James Rest (1995) argued that moral character has not been adequately emphasized in moral development. In Rest's view, *moral character* involves having the strength of your convictions, persisting, and overcoming distractions and obstacles. If individuals don't have moral character, they may wilt under pressure or fatigue, fail to follow through, or become distracted and discouraged and fail to behave morally. Moral character presupposes that the person has set moral goals and that achieving those goals involves the commitment to act in accord with those goals. Rest (1995) also concluded that motivation has not been adequately emphasized in moral development. In Rest's view, *moral motivation* involves prioritizing moral values over other personal values.

Lawrence Walker (2002) has studied moral character by examining people's conceptions of moral excellence. Among the moral virtues people emphasize are "honesty, truthfulness, and trustworthiness, as well as those of care, compassion, thoughtfulness, and considerateness.

moral identity An aspect of personality that is present when individuals have moral notions and commitments that are central to their lives.

Rosa Parks (*left photo*, sitting in the front of a bus after the U.S. Supreme Court ruled that segregation was illegal on her city's bus system) and Andrei Sakharov (*right photo*) are moral exemplars. Parks (1913–2005), an African American seamstress in Montgomery, Alabama, became famous for her quiet, revolutionary act of not giving up her bus seat to a non-Latino White man in 1955. Her heroic act is cited by many historians as the beginning of the modern civil rights movement in the United States. Across the next four decades, Parks continued to work for progress in civil rights. Sakharov (1921–1989) was a Soviet physicist who spent several decades designing nuclear weapons for the Soviet Union and came to be known as the father of the Soviet hydrogen bomb. However, later in his life he became one of the Soviet Union's most outspoken critics and worked relentlessly to promote human rights and democracy.
(left): © Bettmann/Corbis; (right): © Alain Nogues/Sygma/Corbis

developmental **connection**

Personality

Conscientiousness is linked to a number of positive outcomes in adolescence. Connect to "The Self, Identity, Emotion, and Personality."

moral exemplars People who have led exemplary lives.

social domain theory Theory that identifies different domains of social knowledge and reasoning, including moral, social conventional, and personal domains. These domains arise from children's and adolescents' attempts to understand and deal with different forms of social experience.

Other salient traits revolve around virtues of dependability, loyalty, and conscientiousness" (Walker, 2002, p. 74). In Walker's perspective, these aspects of moral character provide a foundation for positive social relationships and functioning.

Moral Exemplars   **Moral exemplars** are people who have lived exemplary lives. Moral exemplars, such as Jewel Cash who was portrayed at the beginning of the chapter, have a moral personality, identity, character, and set of virtues that reflect moral excellence and commitment (Frimer & others, 2011; 2014a, b; Walker & Frimer, 2011). The point of studying and conducting research on moral exemplars is to be able to characterize the ideal endpoint of moral development and how people got there.

In one study, three different exemplars of morality were examined—brave, caring, and just (Walker & Hennig, 2004). Different personality profiles emerged for the three exemplars. The brave exemplar was characterized by being dominant and extraverted, the caring exemplar by being nurturant and agreeable, and the just exemplar by being conscientious and open to experience. However, a number of traits characterized all three moral exemplars, considered by the researchers to reflect a possible core of moral functioning. This core included being honest and dependable.

Another study examined the personalities of exemplary young adults to determine what characterized their moral excellence (Matsuba & Walker, 2004). Forty young adults were nominated by executive directors of a variety of social organizations (such as Big Brothers, AIDS Society, and Ronald McDonald House) as moral exemplars based on their extraordinary moral commitment to these social organizations. They were compared with 40 young adults matched in age, education, and other variables who were attending a university. The moral exemplars were more advanced in moral reasoning, further along in developing an identity, and more likely to be in close relationships.

SOCIAL DOMAIN THEORY

Social domain theory states that there are different domains of social knowledge and reasoning, including moral, social conventional, and personal domains. In social domain theory, children's and adolescents' moral, social conventional, and personal knowledge and reasoning emerge from their attempts to understand and deal with different forms of social experience

(Killen & Smetana, 2015; Smetana, 2011a, b, 2013; Turiel, 2014, 2015). In the view of leading experts Judith Smetana (2013) and Eliot Turiel (2014, 2015), social domain theory emphasizes that the key aspects of morality involve judgments about welfare, justice, and rights and struggles individuals have with moral issues in their social lives. Social domain theory stresses that children, even very young ones, are motivated to evaluate and make sense of their social world (Smetana, Jambon, & Ball, 2014).

Social conventional reasoning focuses on conventional rules that have been established by social consensus in order to control behavior and maintain the social system. The rules themselves are arbitrary, such as raising your hand in class before speaking, using one staircase at school to go up and the other to go down, not cutting in front of someone standing in line to buy movie tickets, and stopping at a stop sign when driving. There are sanctions if we violate these conventions, although the rules can be changed by consensus.

In contrast, moral reasoning focuses on ethical issues and rules of morality. Unlike conventional rules, moral rules are not arbitrary. They are obligatory, widely accepted, and somewhat impersonal (Turiel, 2015). Rules pertaining to lying, cheating, stealing, and physically harming another person are moral rules because violation of these rules affronts ethical standards that exist apart from social consensus and convention. Moral judgments involve concepts of justice, whereas social conventional judgments are concepts of social organization. Violating moral rules is usually more serious than violating conventional rules.

The social conventional approach is a serious challenge to Kohlberg's approach because Kohlberg argued that social conventions are a stop-over on the road to higher moral sophistication. For social conventional reasoning advocates, social conventional reasoning is not lower than postconventional reasoning but rather something that needs to be disentangled from the moral thread (Killen & Smetana, 2015; Smetana, Jambon, & Ball, 2014; Turiel, 2014, 2015).

Recently, a distinction also has been made between moral and conventional issues, which are viewed as legitimately subject to adult social regulation, and personal issues, which are more likely subject to the child's or adolescent's independent decision making and personal discretion (Killen & Smetana, 2015). Personal issues include control over one's body, privacy, and choice of friends and activities. Thus, some actions belong to a *personal* domain not governed by moral strictures or social norms.

social conventional reasoning Thoughts about social consensus and convention, as opposed to moral reasoning that stresses ethical issues.

Review Connect Reflect

LG1 Discuss what moral development is and the domains of moral development

Review

- What is moral development?
- What are the main points of Kohlberg's theory of moral development? What aspects of Kohlberg's theory have been criticized?
- What are some basic processes in the behavioral view of moral development? What is the social cognitive view of moral development? What is the nature of prosocial behavior?
- What is the psychoanalytic view of moral development? What role does empathy play in moral development? What is the contemporary perspective on moral feeling?
- What is the moral personality approach to moral development?
- What characterizes the social domain theory of moral development?

Connect

- Considering what you have learned about gender similarities and differences, were you surprised by findings cited in this section about gender's role in moral development?

Reflect *Your Own Personal Journey of Life*

- Which of the five approaches we have discussed—cognitive, psychoanalytic, behavioral/social cognitive, personality, and domain theory—do you think best describes the way you have developed morally? Explain.

2 Contforments of Moral Development Describe how the contexts of parenting and schools can influence moral development

Parenting   Schools

Earlier in the chapter, you learned that both Piaget and Kohlberg maintain that peer relations are an important context for moral development. Adolescents' experiences in families and schools also are important contexts for moral development.

PARENTING

Both Piaget and Kohlberg held that parents do not provide any unique or essential inputs to children's moral development. They do believe that parents are responsible for providing general role-taking opportunities and cognitive conflict, but they attribute the primary role in moral development to peers. Researchers have revealed how both parents and peers contribute to the development of moral maturity (Dunn, 2014; Grusec & others, 2014; Yoo, Feng, & Day, 2013). In general, higher-level moral reasoning in adolescence is linked with parenting that is supportive and encourages adolescents to question and expand on their moral reasoning (Eisenberg, Spinrad, & Morris, 2014; Eisenberg & others, 2009).

Culture plays a role in links between families and adolescents' moral development. A recent study revealed that Mexican American adolescents who valued traditional familism had stronger prosocial tendencies (Calderon-Tena, Knight, & Carlo, 2011). Asian children and adolescents also are more likely to engage in prosocial behavior than North American children and adolescents (Eisenberg, Spinrad, & Morris, 2013). Next, we focus on parental discipline and its role in moral development and then draw some conclusions about parenting and moral development.

In Freud's psychoanalytic theory, the aspects of child rearing that encourage moral development are practices that instill the fears of punishment and of losing parental love. Developmentalists who have studied child-rearing techniques and moral development have focused on parents' discipline techniques (Grusec, 2006). These include love withdrawal, power assertion, and induction (Hoffman, 1970):

- **Love withdrawal** comes closest to the psychoanalytic emphasis on fear of punishment and of losing parental love. It is a discipline technique in which a parent withholds attention or love from the adolescent, as when the parent refuses to talk to the adolescent or states a dislike for the adolescent.
- **Power assertion** is a discipline technique in which a parent attempts to gain control over the adolescent or the adolescent's resources. Examples include spanking, threatening, or removing privileges.
- **Induction** is the discipline technique in which a parent uses reason and explanation of the consequences for others of the adolescent's actions. Examples of induction include, "Don't hit him. He was only trying to help" and "Why are you yelling at her? She didn't mean to hurt your feelings."

Moral development theorist and researcher Martin Hoffman (1970) argues that any discipline produces emotional arousal on the adolescent's part. Love withdrawal and power assertion are likely to evoke a very high level of arousal, with love withdrawal generating considerable anxiety and power assertion considerable hostility. Induction is more likely to produce a moderate level of arousal in adolescents, a level that permits them to attend to the cognitive rationales parents offer.

When a parent uses power assertion or love withdrawal, the adolescent may be so aroused emotionally that, even if the parent gives accompanying explanations about the consequences for others of the adolescent's actions, the adolescent might not attend to them. Power assertion presents parents as weak models of self-control—as individuals who cannot control how they express their own feelings. Accordingly, adolescents may imitate this model of poor self-control when they face stressful circumstances. The use of induction, however, focuses the adolescent's attention on the action's consequences for others, not on the adolescent's own

love withdrawal A discipline technique in which a parent withholds attention or love from the adolescent.

power assertion A discipline technique in which a parent attempts to gain control over the adolescent or the adolescent's resources.

induction A discipline technique in which a parent uses reason and explains how the adolescent's actions affect others.

shortcomings. For these reasons, Hoffman (1988) notes that parents should use induction to encourage adolescents' moral development.

Research on parental discipline techniques has found that induction is more positively related to moral development than is love withdrawal or power assertion, although the findings vary according to developmental level and socioeconomic status. For example, induction works better with adolescents and older children than with preschool children (Brody & Schaffer, 1982) and better with middle-SES than with lower-SES children (Hoffman, 1970). Older children and adolescents are generally better able to understand the reasons given to them and better at perspective taking than younger children are. Some theorists believe the reason that internalization of society's moral standards is more likely among middle-SES than among lower-SES individuals is that internalization is more rewarding in the middle-SES culture (Kohn, 1977).

A recent study explored the role of inductive discipline in the moral development of adolescents (Patrick & Gibbs, 2012). In this study, adolescents considered parental induction and expression of disappointed expectations to be more appropriate than power assertion and love withdrawal and responded with more positive emotion, as well as guilt, to parental induction than to the other discipline techniques. Further, parental induction was linked to a higher moral identity in this study.

How can parents apply such findings to strategies for raising a moral child and adolescent? For some suggestions, see the *Connecting with Health and Well-Being* interlude.

SCHOOLS

Schools are an important context for moral development (Narváez, 2014; Nucci, Krettenauer, & Narváez, 2014). Moral education is a hotly debated topic in educational circles. We first study one of the earliest analyses of moral education and then turn to some contemporary views on moral education.

The Hidden Curriculum   Eight decades ago, educator John Dewey (1933) recognized that even when schools do not have specific programs in moral education, they provide moral education through a "hidden curriculum." The **hidden curriculum** is conveyed by the moral atmosphere that is a part of every school.

The moral atmosphere is created by school and classroom rules, the moral orientation of teachers and school administrators, and text materials. Teachers serve as models of ethical or unethical behavior. Classroom rules and peer relations at school transmit attitudes about cheating, lying, stealing, and consideration for others. And, by enforcing rules and regulations, the school administration infuses the school with a value system.

Recently, increased attention has been directed to the influence of classroom and school climate as part of the hidden curriculum. Darcia Narváez (2010a, 2014) argues that attention should be given to the concept of "sustaining climates." In her view, a sustaining classroom climate is more than a positive learning environment and more than a caring context. Sustaining climates involve focusing on students' sense of purpose, social engagement, community connections, and ethics. In sustaining classroom and school climates, students learn skills for flourishing and reaching their potential and help others to do so as well.

Character Education   Considerable interest has recently been shown in **character education,** a direct education approach that involves teaching students a basic moral literacy to prevent them from engaging in immoral behavior and doing harm to themselves or others (Arthur, 2014; Narváez, 2014). Currently 40 of 50 states have mandates regarding character education (Nucci & Narváez, 2008). The argument is that such behaviors as lying, stealing, and cheating are wrong and that students should be taught this throughout their education (Berkowitz, 2012; Berkowitz, Battistich, & Bier, 2008; Davidson, Lickona, & Khmelkov, 2008).

Every school should have an explicit moral code that is clearly communicated to students. According to traditional views of character education, any violations of the code should be met with sanctions; however, recent approaches advocate a more democratic solution. Instruction in specified moral concepts, such as cheating, can take the form of example and definition, class discussions and role playing, or rewarding students for proper behavior. More recently, encouraging students to develop a care perspective has been accepted as a relevant aspect of character education (Noddings, 2008, 2014). Rather than just instructing adolescents

hidden curriculum The pervasive moral atmosphere that characterizes every school.

character education A direct moral education approach that involves teaching students a basic moral literacy to prevent them from engaging in immoral behavior or doing harm to themselves or others.

How Can We Raise Moral Children and Adolescents?

Parental discipline contributes to children's moral development, but other aspects of parenting also play an important role, including providing opportunities for perspective taking and modeling moral behavior and thinking. Nancy Eisenberg and her colleagues (Eisenberg, Spinrad, & Knafo, 2015; Eisenberg, Spinrad, & Morris, 2014; Eisenberg & Valiente, 2002) suggest that when parents adopt the following strategies they are more likely to have children and adolescents who behave morally:

- Are warm and supportive, use inductive reasoning, and engage in authoritative parenting
- Are not punitive and do not use love withdrawal as a disciplinary strategy
- Use inductive discipline
- Provide opportunities for the children and youth to learn about others' perspectives and feelings
- Involve children and youth in family decision making and in the process of thinking about moral decisions
- Model moral behaviors and thinking themselves, and provide opportunities for their children and youth to do so
- Provide information about what behaviors are expected and why
- Foster an internal rather than an external sense of morality
- Help children and youth to understand and regulate negative emotion rather than becoming overaroused

Parents who show this configuration of behaviors likely foster concern and caring about others in their children and youth, and create a positive parent-child relationship. A recent study found that adolescents' moral motivation was positively linked to the quality of their relationship with their parents (Malti & Buchmann, 2010). Another recent study revealed that dimensions of authoritative parenting (such as a combination of responsiveness, autonomy-granting, and demandingness) predicted a strengthening of adolescents' moral identity (Hardy & others, 2010).

In terms of relationship quality, secure attachment may play an important role in children's and adolescents' moral development. A secure attachment can place children on a positive path for internalizing parents' socializing goals and family values. In a recent study, early secure attachment defused a maladaptive trajectory toward antisocial outcomes (Kochanska & others, 2010a). In another recent

What are some parenting characteristics and practices that are linked with children's and adolescents' moral development?
© Digital Vision/Getty Images RF

study, securely attached children's willing, cooperative stance was linked to positive future socialization outcomes such as a lower incidence of externalizing problems (high levels of aggression, for example) (Kochanska & others, 2010b).

Recently, an interest has developed in determining which parenting strategies work best when children and adolescents are confronted with situations in which they are exposed to values outside the home that conflict with parental values (Grusec, 2006). Two strategies that parents often use in this regard are cocooning and pre-arming (Bugental & Goodnow, 2006). Cocooning occurs when parents protect children and adolescents from exposure to deviant behavior and thus eliminate the temptation to engage in negative moral behavior. In adolescence, cocooning involves monitoring the contexts in which adolescents spend time and restricting their interaction with deviant peers. Pre-arming involves anticipating conflicting values and preparing adolescents to handle them in their lives outside their home. In using pre-arming, parents discuss strategies with adolescents to help them deal with harmful situations.

What type of studies do you think researchers might design to compare the relative effectiveness of cocooning and pre-arming?

to refrain from morally deviant behavior, advocates of a care perspective encourage students to engage in prosocial behaviors such as considering others' feelings, being sensitive to others, and helping others (Frank, 2013).

Lawrence Walker (2002) argues that it is important for character education to involve more than a listing of moral virtues on a classroom wall. Instead, he emphasizes that children and adolescents need to participate in critical discussions of values; they need to discuss and reflect on how to incorporate virtues into their daily lives. Walker also advocates exposing children to moral exemplars worthy of emulating and getting children to participate in community service. The character education approach reflects the moral personality domain of moral development discussed earlier in the chapter (Walker, Frimer, & Dunlop, 2011).

Values Clarification   A second approach to providing moral education is **values clarification,** which involves helping individuals to clarify what their lives are for and what is worth working for. Unlike character education, which tells students what their values should be, values clarification encourages students to define their own values and to understand the values of others.

Advocates of values clarification say it is value-free. However, critics argue that the content of these programs offends community standards and that the values-clarification exercises fail to stress right behavior.

Cognitive Moral Education   A third approach to moral education, **cognitive moral education,** is based on the belief that students should learn to value such things as democracy and justice as their moral reasoning develops. Kohlberg's theory has served as the foundation for a number of cognitive moral education programs (Snarey & Samuelson, 2008). In a typical program, high school students meet in a semester-long course to discuss a number of moral issues. The instructor acts as a facilitator rather than as a director of the class. The hope is that students will develop more advanced notions of such concepts as cooperation, trust, responsibility, and community (Power & Higgins-D'Alessandro, 2008).

Service Learning   Over the last several decades, there has been a growing understanding that the quality of a society can be considerably enhanced when citizens become proactive in providing service to the community and the nation. The initial call to serve came in John F. Kennedy's inaugural address after he was sworn in as president on January 20, 1961. In his words, "Ask not what your country can do for you—ask what you can do for your country." This idea helped to increase the government's commitment to develop programs that emphasize service. Over time, this commitment has produced the Peace Corps, Americorps, Senior Corps, VISTA, and Learn and Serve America. The latter initiative provides grants to schools, universities, and communities to engage students in service to communities. Much of this effort is orchestrated through the Corporation for National and Community Service. For program descriptions and opportunities to volunteer, go to www.nationalservice.gov.

At the beginning of the chapter you read about Jewel Cash, who is strongly motivated to make a positive difference in her community. Jewel Cash has a sense of social responsibility that an increasing number of educational programs seek to promote in students through **service learning,** a form of education in which students provide service to the community. In service learning, adolescents engage in activities such as tutoring, helping older adults, working in a hospital, assisting at a child-care center, or cleaning up a vacant lot to make a play area. An important goal of service learning is that adolescents become less self-centered and more strongly motivated to help others (Hart, Matsuba, & Atkins, 2014; Schmidt, Shumow, & Kackar, 2012). Service learning is often more effective when two conditions are met (Nucci, 2006): (1) students are given some degree of choice in the service activities in which they participate, and (2) students are provided opportunities to reflect about their participation.

What are some positive outcomes of service learning?
© Tony Freeman/PhotoEdit

Service learning takes education out into the community (Flanagan, Beyers, & Zukauskiene, 2012; Rosenkranz, 2012). Adolescent volunteers tend to be extraverted, to feel committed to others, and to have a high level of self-understanding (Eisenberg & Morris, 2004). Also, one study revealed that adolescent girls participated in service learning more than adolescent boys do (Webster & Worrell, 2008).

Researchers have found that service learning benefits adolescents in a number of ways (Zaff & others, 2010). Improvements in adolescent development related to service learning include higher grades in school, increased goal setting, higher self-esteem, an improved sense of being able to make a difference for others, identity achievement, exploration of moral issues, and an increased likelihood that they will serve as volunteers in the future. In one study, 74 percent of African American and 70 percent of Latino adolescents said that service-learning programs could have a "fairly or very big effect" on keeping students from dropping out of school (Bridgeland, Dilulio, & Wulsin, 2008).

Recently, interest has been shown in the role that civic engagement might play in adolescents' identity and moral development (Flanagan, Beyers, & Zukauskiene, 2012). A recent study

values clarification An educational approach that focuses on helping people clarify what is important to them, what is worth working for, and what is their purpose in life. Students are encouraged to define their own values and understand others' values.

cognitive moral education An approach based on the belief that students should learn to value things like democracy and justice as their moral reasoning develops; Kohlberg's theory has been the basis for many of the cognitive moral education approaches.

service learning A form of education that promotes social responsibility and service to the community.

Finding a Way to Get a Playground

Twelve-year-old Katie Bell more than just about anything else wanted a playground in her New Jersey town. She knew that other kids also wanted one too, so she put together a group that generated fund-raising ideas for the playground. They presented their ideas to the town council. Her group got more youth involved. They helped raise money by selling candy and sandwiches door-to-door. Katie says, "We learned to work as a community. This will be an important place for people to go and have picnics and make new friends." Katie's advice: "You won't get anywhere if you don't try."

What moral lessons from her family or school do you think Katie Bell had already learned when she undertook the playground project?

Katie Bell *(front)* and some of her volunteers.
© Ronald Cortes

found that compared with adolescents who had a diffused identity status, those who were identity achieved were more involved in volunteering in their community (Crocetti, Jahromi, & Meeus, 2012). In this study, adolescents' volunteer activity also was linked to their values, such as social responsibility, and the view that they, along with others, could make an impact on their community. Another recent study revealed that adolescents' volunteer activities provided opportunities to explore and reason about moral issues (van Goethem & others, 2012).

An analysis revealed that 26 percent of U.S. public high schools require students to participate in service learning (Metz & Youniss, 2005). The benefits of service learning, both for the volunteers and for the recipients, suggest that more adolescents should be required to participate in such programs (Enfield & Collins, 2008; Zaff & others, 2010).

Cheating A moral education concern is how extensive cheating is and how to handle the cheating if it is detected (Anderman & Anderman, 2010). Academic cheating can take many forms including plagiarism, using "cheat sheets" during an exam, copying from a neighbor during a test, purchasing papers, and falsifying lab results. A 2006 survey revealed that 60 percent of secondary school students said they had cheated on a test in school during the past year, and one-third of the students reported that they had plagiarized information from the Internet in the past year (Josephson Institute of Ethics, 2006). A recent study with 8- to 12-year-olds found that a majority of them cheated in a game that required them to report the accuracy of their success in the game, and older children cheated less than the younger ones (Ding & others, 2014). Also in this study, children with better working memory and inhibitory control cheated less.

Why do students cheat? Among the reasons students give for cheating include pressure to get high grades, time constraints, poor teaching, and lack of interest (Stephens, 2008). In terms of poor teaching, "students are more likely to cheat when they perceive their teacher to be incompetent, unfair, and uncaring" (Stephens, 2008, p. 140).

A long history of research also implicates the power of the situation in determining whether students cheat (Hartshorne & May, 1928–1930; Vandehey, Diekhoff, & LaBeff, 2007). For example, students are more likely

What are some factors that influence whether adolescents engage in cheating?
© Rubberball/Nicole Hill/Getty Images RF

to cheat when they are not being closely monitored during a test; when they know their peers are cheating; when they know whether or not another student has been caught cheating; and when student scores are made public (Anderman & Murdock, 2007; Harmon, Lambrinos, & Kennedy, 2008). A recent study revealed that college students who engaged in academic cheating were characterized by the personality traits of low conscientiousness and low agreeableness (Williams, Nathanson, & Paulhus, 2010).

Among the strategies for decreasing academic cheating are preventive measures such as making sure students are aware of what constitutes cheating, making clear the consequences if they do cheat, closely monitoring students' behavior while they are taking tests, and emphasizing the importance of being a moral, responsible individual who engages in academic integrity. In promoting academic integrity, many colleges have instituted an honor code policy that emphasizes self-responsibility, fairness, trust, and scholarship. However, few secondary schools have developed honor code policies. The Center for Academic Integrity (www.academicintegrity.org) has extensive materials available to help schools develop academic integrity policies.

An Integrative Approach Darcia Narváez (2006, 2008, 2010a, b, 2014) emphasizes an *integrative approach* to moral education that encompasses both the reflective moral thinking and commitment to justice advocated in Kohlberg's approach, and the development of a particular moral character advocated in the character education approach. She highlights the Child Development Project as an excellent example of an integrative moral education approach. In the Child Development Project, students are given multiple opportunities to discuss other students' experiences, which inspire empathy and perspective taking, and they participate in exercises that encourage them to reflect on their own behaviors in terms of values such as fairness and social responsibility (Battistich, 2008). Adults coach students in ethical decision making and guide them in becoming more caring individuals. Students experience a caring community, not only in the classroom, but also in after-school activities and through parental involvement in the program. Research evaluations of the Child Development Project indicate that it is related to an improved sense of community, an increase in prosocial behavior, better interpersonal understanding, and an increase in social problem solving (Battistich, 2008; Solomon & others, 1990).

Another integrative moral education program that is being implemented is called *integrative ethical education* (Narváez, 2006, 2008, 2010a, b, 2014; Narváez & others, 2004). This program builds on the concept of expertise development within a supportive community. The goal is to turn moral novices into moral experts by educating students about four ethical skills that moral experts possess: ethical sensitivity, ethical judgment, ethical focus, and ethical action (Narváez, 2010b). Figure 5 further describes components of these four ethical skills.

Ethical Sensitivity	Understanding emotional expression
	Taking the perspective of others
	Connecting to others
	Responding to diversity
	Controlling social bias
	Interpreting situations
	Communicating effectively
Ethical Judgment	Understanding ethical problems
	Using codes and identifying judgment criteria
	Reasoning generally
	Reasoning ethically
	Understanding consequences
	Reflecting on the process and outcome
	Coping and being resilient
Ethical Focus	Respecting others
	Cultivating conscience
	Acting responsibly
	Helping others
	Finding meaning in life
	Valuing traditions and institutions
	Developing ethical identity and integrity
Ethical Action	Resolving conflicts and problems
	Asserting respectfully
	Taking initiative as a leader
	Implementing decisions
	Cultivating courage
	Persevering
	Working hard

FIGURE 5

ETHICAL SKILLS IN INTEGRATIVE ETHICAL EDUCATION
Narváez, D., *Handbook of Moral Development*. Copyright © 2006 by Taylor & Francis Group LLC-Books. Reproduced with permission of Taylor & Francis Group LLC Books in the format Books and Other book via Copyright Clearance Center.

Review Connect Reflect

LG2 Describe how the contexts of parenting and schools can influence moral development

Review
- How does parental discipline affect moral development? What are some effective parenting strategies for advancing children's and adolescents' moral development?
- What is the hidden curriculum? What are some contemporary approaches to moral education used in schools? How does service learning affect adolescents?

Connect
- How might cultural and ethnic identity influence parents' approaches to their children's moral development?

Reflect *Your Own Personal Journey of Life*
- What type of discipline did your parents use with you? What effect do you think this has had on your moral development?

3 Values, Religion, and Spirituality

LG3 Explain the roles of values, religion, and spirituality in adolescents' and emerging adults' lives.

| Values |

| Religion and Spirituality |

What are adolescents' and emerging adults' values like today? How powerful are religion and spirituality in adolescents' and emerging adults' lives?

VALUES

Values are beliefs and attitudes about the way things should be. They involve what is important to us. We attach values to all sorts of things: politics, religion, money, sex, education, helping others, family, friends, career, cheating, self-respect, and so on. Values reflect the intrapersonal dimension of morality introduced at the beginning of the chapter.

One way of measuring what people value is to ask them what their goals are. Over the past three decades, traditional-aged college students have shown an increased concern for personal well-being and a decreased concern for the well-being of others, especially for the disadvantaged (Eagan & others, 2014). As shown in Figure 6, today's college freshmen are more strongly motivated to be well-off financially and less motivated to develop a meaningful philosophy of life than were their counterparts of 40 years ago. In 2014, 82 percent of students (the highest percent ever in this survey) viewed becoming well-off financially as an "essential" or a "very important" objective compared with only 42 percent in 1971.

There are, however, some signs that U.S. college students are shifting toward a stronger interest in the welfare of society. In the survey just described, interest in developing a meaningful philosophy of life increased from 39 percent to 45 percent of U.S. college freshmen from 2001 through 2014 (Eagan & others, 2014) (see Figure 6). Also in this survey, the percentage of college freshmen who said the chances are very good that they will participate in volunteer activities or community service programs increased from 18 percent in 1990 to 34 percent in 2014 (Eagan & others, 2014).

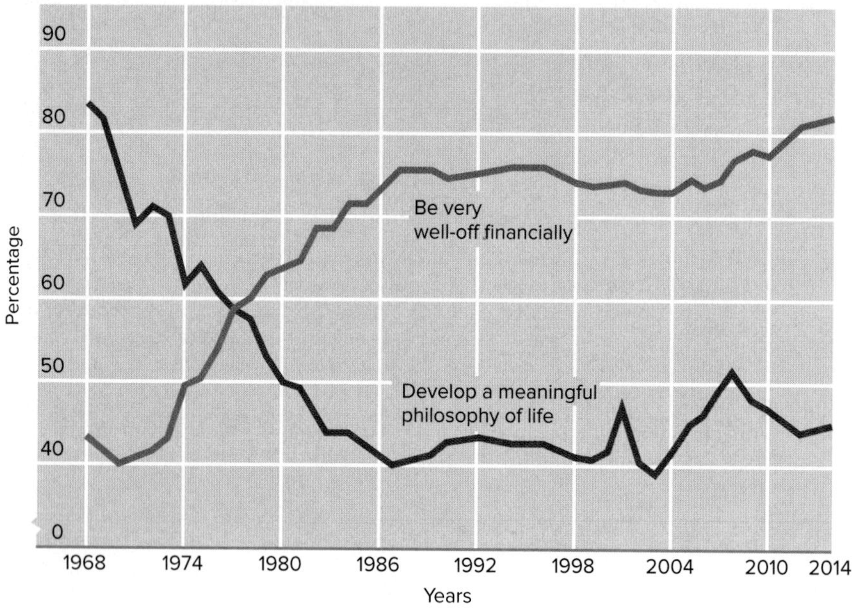

Other research on values has found that adolescents who are involved in groups that connect them to others in school, their communities, or faith-based institutions report higher levels of social trust, altruism, commitments to the common good of people, and endorsements of the rights of immigrants for full inclusion in society (Flanagan & Faison, 2001). In this research, adolescents who were uninvolved in such groups were more likely to endorse self-interested and materialistic values.

The research we have just discussed was conducted by Constance Flanagan and her colleagues. To read further about her work, see the *Connecting with Careers* profile.

Our discussion of values relates to the view William Damon (2008) proposed in *The Path to Purpose*. Damon concluded that a major difficulty confronting today's youth is their lack of a clear sense of what they want to do with their lives—that too many youth are essentially "rudderless." Damon (2008, p. 8) found that only about 20 percent of 12- to 22-year-olds in the United States expressed "a clear vision of where they want to go, what they want to accomplish in life, and why." He argues that their goals and values too often focus on the short term, such as getting a good

FIGURE 6

CHANGING FRESHMAN LIFE GOALS, 1968 TO 2014. In the last four decades, a significant change has occurred in freshman students' life goals. A far greater percentage of today's college freshmen state that an "essential" or "very important" life goal is to be well-off financially, and far fewer state that developing a meaningful philosophy of life is an "essential" or a "very important" life goal.

values Beliefs and attitudes about the way things should be.

Constance Flanagan, Professor of Youth Civic Development

Constance (Connie) Flanagan is a professor of youth civic development in the College of Agricultural Sciences at Pennsylvania State University. Her research focuses on youths' views about justice and the factors in families, schools, and communities that promote civic values, connections, and skills in youth (Flanagan, 2004).

Flanagan obtained her undergraduate degree in psychology from Duquesne University, her master's degree in education from the University of Iowa, and her Ph.D. from the University of Michigan. She has a special interest in improving the U.S. social policy for adolescents and serves as co-chair of the Committee on Child Development. In addition to teaching undergraduate and graduate classes, conducting research, and serving on various committees, Flanagan evaluates research for potential publication as a member of the editorial board of *Journal of Adolescent Research* and *Journal of Research on Adolescence*. She also presents her ideas and research at numerous national and international meetings.

Connie Flanagan with adolescents.
Courtesy of Dr. Connie Flanagan

Nina Vasan, Superstar Volunteer and Author

Nina Vasan's leadership began at home in Vienna, West Virginia, where she grew up watching her family and community champion a shared value: social responsibility. At age 16, she observed that fellow adolescents had passion and promising ideas for addressing social problems, but there was no system to engage their efforts. Inspired to help create this opportunity, she worked with the American Cancer Society to launch ACS Teens. Through an online network, ACS Teens served as an incubator for social change: it trained, mobilized, mentored, and united adolescent volunteers, empowering them to recognize their potential as leaders and work together to find creative solutions for improving health in their communities.

Motivated by the sense of purpose she felt when ACS Teens helped change tobacco-related legislation in West Virginia, Nina decided to study Government at Harvard University. As an MD student at Harvard Medical School, she felt compelled to apply the methods she learned in fighting cancer to mental health. She is currently a Resident Physician in Psychiatry at Stanford University Hospital.

In 2013, Nina published her first book with co-author Jennifer Przybylo, another superstar volunteer whom she met in high school. Their book, Do Good Well, reflects Nina and Jennifer's motivation to get others involved in leadership and encourage them to take action in improving people's lives. Do Good Well became a #1 Amazon Best Seller and is being used in schools around the world.

Nina Vasan (left) with Jennifer Przybylo
Courtesy of Nina Vasan

What values are likely to motivate Nina Vasan?

grade on a test this week and finding a date for a dance, rather than developing a plan for the future based on positive values. The types of questions that adults can pose to youth to guide them in the direction of developing more purposeful values include "What's most important in your life? Why do you care about those things? . . . What does it mean to be a good person?" (Damon, 2008, p. 135).

> **developmental connection**
>
> **Work and Achievement**
>
> Purpose is an important aspect of many aspects of adolescents' lives, including their identity, values, achievement, and careers. Connect to "Introduction" and "Achievement, Work, and Careers."

RELIGION AND SPIRITUALITY

In Damon's (2008) view, one long-standing source for discovering purpose in life is religion. Can religion be distinguished from spirituality? A recent analysis by Pamela King and her colleagues (King, Ramos, & Clardy, 2013) makes the following distinctions:

- **Religion** is an organized set of beliefs, practices, rituals, and symbols that increases an individual's connection to a sacred or transcendent other (God, higher power, or ultimate truth).
- **Religiousness** refers to the degree of affiliation with an organized religion, participation in its prescribed rituals and practices, connection with its beliefs, and involvement in a community of believers.
- **Spirituality** involves experiencing something beyond oneself in a transcendent manner and living in a way that benefits others and society.

Religious issues are important to many adolescents and emerging adults (King & Boyatzis, 2015). However, in the twenty-first century, a downturn in religious interest among college students has occurred. In a 2012 national study of American college freshmen, 73 percent said they had attended religious services frequently or occasionally during their senior year in high school, down from a high of 85 percent in 1997 (Pryor & others, 2012). Further, in 2012, three times as many first-year students (24 percent) reported having no religious preference as did first-year students in 1978 (8 percent). And in one study, across the first three semesters of college, students were less likely to attend religious services or engage in religious activities (Stoppa & Lefkowitz, 2010).

A developmental study revealed that religiousness declined from 14 to 20 years of age in the United States (Koenig, McGue, & Iacono, 2008) (see Figure 7). In this study, religiousness was assessed with items such as frequency of prayer, frequency of discussing religious teachings, frequency of deciding moral actions for religious reasons, and the overall importance of religion in everyday life. As indicated in Figure 7, more change in religiousness occurred from 14 to 18 years of age than from 20 to 24 years of age. Also, attending religious services was highest at 14 years of age, declining from 14 to 18 years of age and increasing at 20 years of age. More change occurred in attending religious services than in religiousness.

Also, a recent national survey found that 20 percent of the American public do not have a religious affiliation and that one-third of individuals under 30 years of age are religiously unaffiliated—the highest percentages with no religious affiliation ever identified in the Pew Research Center (2012) poll, which has been taken every year from 2007 to 2012.

Analysis of the World Values Survey of 18- to 24-year-olds revealed that emerging adults in less-developed countries were more likely to be religious than their counterparts in more-developed countries (Lippman & Keith, 2006). For example, emerging adults' reports that religion is very important in their lives ranged from a low of 0 in Japan to 93 percent in Nigeria, and belief in God ranged from a low of 40 percent in Sweden to a high of 100 percent in Pakistan.

Researchers have found that adolescent girls are more religious than are adolescent boys (King & Boyatzis, 2015; King & Roeser, 2009). One study of 13- to 17-year-olds revealed that girls are more likely to frequently attend religious services, perceive that religion shapes their daily lives, participate in religious youth groups, pray more alone, and feel closer to God (Smith & Denton, 2005).

The Positive Role of Religion and Spirituality in Adolescents' and Emerging Adults' Lives
Researchers have found that various aspects of religion are linked with positive outcomes for adolescents (Harakeh & others, 2012; King & Boyatzis, 2015). A recent study revealed that a higher level of church engagement (based on years of attendance, choice in attending, and participation in activities) was related to higher grades for male adolescents (Kang & Romo, 2011). Churchgoing may benefit students because religious communities encourage socially acceptable behavior, which includes doing well in school. Churchgoing also may benefit students because churches often offer positive role models for students.

One study found that youth generally thought about spirituality in positive ways (James, Fine, & Turner, 2012). In this study, 10- to 18-year-olds' self-ratings of spirituality were positively linked to the 5 Cs of Positive Youth Development (competence, confidence,

---

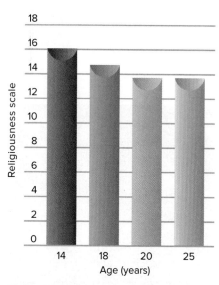

FIGURE 7

DEVELOPMENTAL CHANGES IN RELIGIOUSNESS FROM 14 TO 25 YEARS OF AGE. *Note:* The religiousness scale ranged from 0 to 32, with higher scores indicating stronger religiousness.

religion An organized set of beliefs, practices, rituals, and symbols that increases an individual's connection to a sacred or transcendent other (God, higher power, or higher truth).

religiousness The degree of affiliation with an organized religion, participation in prescribed rituals and practices, connection with its beliefs, and involvement in a community of believers.

spirituality Experiencing something beyond oneself in a transcendent manner and living in a way that benefits others and society.

character, connection, and caring/compassion). In the longitudinal aspect of the study, the youths' self-ratings of spirituality predicted their character ratings one year later.

Religion also plays a role in adolescents' health and whether they engage in problem behaviors (Salas-Wright & others, 2012). A recent meta-analysis found that spirituality/religiosity was positively related to well-being, self-esteem, and three of the Big Five factors of personality (conscientiousness, agreeableness, openness) (Yonker, Schnabelrauch, & DeHaan, 2012). In this meta-analysis, spirituality/religion was negatively associated with risk behavior and depression. In a national random sample of more than 2,000 11- to 18-year-olds, those who were higher in religiosity were less likely to smoke, drink alcohol, use marijuana, be truant from school, engage in delinquent activities, and be depressed than were their low-religiosity counterparts (Sinha, Cnaan, & Gelles, 2007). A study of ninth- to twelfth-graders revealed that more frequent religious attendance in one grade predicted lower levels of substance abuse in the next grade (Good & Willoughby, 2010).

Many religious adolescents also internalize their religion's message about caring and concern for people (Lerner & others, 2013; Saroglou, 2013). For example, in one survey, religious youth were almost three times as likely to engage in community service as were nonreligious youth (Youniss, McLellan, & Yates, 1999).

Adolescents participating in a church youth group. *What are some positive aspects of religion in adolescents' lives?*
© Digital Vision/Getty Images RF

Developmental Changes Adolescence and emerging adulthood can be especially important junctures in religious development (Day, 2010; King & Roeser, 2009). Even if children have been indoctrinated into a religion by their parents, because of advances in their cognitive development adolescents and emerging adults may question what their own religious beliefs truly are.

Cognitive Changes Many of the cognitive changes thought to influence religious development involve Piaget's cognitive developmental theory. More so than in childhood, adolescents think abstractly, idealistically, and logically. The increase in abstract thinking lets adolescents consider various ideas about religious and spiritual concepts. For example, an adolescent might ask how a loving God can possibly exist given the extensive suffering of many people in the world (Good & Willoughby, 2008). Adolescents' increased idealism provides a foundation for thinking about whether religion is the best route to creating a better, more ideal world. And adolescents' increased logical reasoning gives them the ability to develop hypotheses and systematically sort through different answers to spiritual questions (Good & Willoughby, 2008).

How does religious thinking change in adolescence? How is religion linked to adolescents' health?
© Christopher Futcher/Getty Images RF

Identity During adolescence and emerging adulthood, especially emerging adulthood, identity development becomes a central focus (Erikson, 1968; Kroger, 2015). Adolescents and emerging adults search for answers to questions like these: "Who am I?" "What am I all about as a person?" "What kind of life do I want to lead?" As part of their search for identity, adolescents and emerging adults begin to grapple in more sophisticated, logical ways with such questions as "Why am I on this planet?" "Is there really a God or higher spiritual being, or have I just been believing what my parents and the church imprinted in my mind?" "What really are my religious views?" One study found that college students' identity integration, defined as "the extent to which one's moral values have become integrated into identity," was related to intrinsic religious orientation, defined as "one's motivation for engaging in religious practice," and self-reported altruism (Maclean, Walker, & Matsuba, 2004, p. 429). In one analysis, it was proposed that the link between identity and spirituality in adolescence and emerging adulthood can serve as a gateway for developing a spiritual identity that "transcends, but not necessarily excludes, the assigned religious identity in childhood" (Templeton & Eccles, 2006, p. 261).

A recent study of Latino, African American, Asian, and non-Latino White adolescents revealed that their religious identity remained stable across high school grades but that religious participation declined (Lopez, Huynh, & Fuligni, 2011). In this study, Latino and Asian adolescents had the highest levels of religious identity, while Latino adolescents had the highest level of religious participation.

Religious Socialization and Parenting   Religious institutions created by adults are designed to introduce certain beliefs to children and thereby ensure that they will carry on a religious tradition. Various societies utilize Sunday schools, parochial education, tribal transmission of religious traditions, and parental teaching of children at home to further this aim.

Does this religious socialization work? In many cases it does (Oser, Scarlett, & Bucher, 2006). In general, children and adolescents tend to adopt the religious teachings of their upbringing. If a religious change or reawakening occurs, it is most likely to take place during adolescence or emerging adulthood. A recent study revealed that parents' religiousness assessed during youths' adolescence was positively related to youths' own religiousness during adolescence, which in turn was linked to their religiousness following the transition to adulthood (Spilman & others, 2013). Another recent study found that when youth attend religious services with parents, this activity increases the positive influence of parenting on their psychological well-being (Petts, 2014).

Many children and adolescents show an interest in religion, and many religious institutions created by adults (such as this Muslim school in Malaysia) are designed to introduce them to religious beliefs and ensure that they will carry on a religious tradition.
© Paul Chesley/Getty Images

However, it is important to consider the quality of the parent-adolescent relationship and whether mothers or fathers are more influential (Granqvist & Dickie, 2006; King, Ramos, & Clardy, 2013; Ream & Savin-Williams, 2003). Adolescents who have a positive relationship with their parents or are securely attached to them are likely to adopt their parents' religious affiliation. But, when conflict or insecure attachment characterizes parent-adolescent relationships, adolescents may seek a religious affiliation that is different from their parents' (Streib, 1999). A number of studies also have documented that mothers are more influential in their children's and adolescents' religious development than fathers are (King & Roeser, 2009). Mothers probably are more influential because they are more likely than fathers to go to church, lead family prayer, and converse with their children and youth about religion.

Peers also play a role in adolescents' religious interest. A recent study of Indonesian adolescents found that adolescents were similar to their friends in religiosity, and the religiosity of friends and others in the peer network increased adolescents' self-religiosity in predicting whether they engaged in antisocial behavior (French, Purwono, & Rodkin, 2012).

Religiousness and Sexuality in Adolescence and Emerging Adulthood   One area of religion's influence on adolescent and emerging adult development involves sexual activity. Although variability and change in church teachings make it difficult to generalize about religious doctrines, most churches discourage premarital sex. Thus, the degree of adolescent and emerging adult participation in religious organizations may be more important than affiliation with a specific religion as a determinant of premarital sexual attitudes and behavior. Adolescents and emerging adults who frequently attend religious services are likely to hear messages about abstaining from sex. Involvement of adolescents and emerging adults in religious organizations also enhances the probability that they will become friends with adolescents who have restrictive attitudes toward premarital sex. A recent study revealed that adolescents with high religiosity were less likely to have had sexual intercourse (Gold & others, 2010).

One study found that parents' religiosity was linked to a lower level of adolescents' risky sexual behavior, in part by adolescents hanging out with less sexually permissive peers (Landor & others, 2011). A research review concluded that spirituality was linked to the following positive adolescent outcomes: being less likely to intend to have sex, not engaging in early sex, having sex less frequently, and not becoming pregnant (House & others, 2010).

developmental **connection**

Sexuality

An increasing number of positive youth development (PYD) programs include a focus on improving sexual outcomes in adolescence. Connect to "Sexuality."

Review *Connect* Reflect

 Explain the roles of values, religion, and spirituality in adolescents' and emerging adults' lives

Review

• What are values? What are some of the values of today's college students, and how have they changed over the last three decades?

• How important are religion and spirituality in adolescents' and emerging adults' lives? What characterizes religious and spiritual development in adolescents and emerging adults?

Connect

• How might spirituality influence adolescents' identity development?

Reflect *Your Own Personal Journey of Life*

• What were your values, religious involvement, and spiritual interests in middle school and high school? Have they changed since then? If so, how?

reach your **learning goals**

Moral Development, Values, and Religion

1 What Moral Development Is and the Domains of Moral Development

 Discuss what moral development is and the domains of moral development

What Is Moral Development?

Moral Thought

Moral Behavior

Moral Feeling

· Moral development involves changes in thoughts, feelings, and behaviors regarding right and wrong. Moral development has intrapersonal and interpersonal dimensions.

· Kohlberg developed a provocative theory of moral reasoning. He argued that moral development consists of three levels—preconventional, conventional, and postconventional—and six stages (two at each level). Increased internalization characterizes movement to levels 2 and 3. Influences on progress through the stages include modeling, cognitive conflict, peer relations, and role-taking opportunities. Kohlberg's critics say that he gave inadequate attention to moral behavior, did not adequately assess moral development, underestimated cultural and family influences, and underestimated the care perspective (Gilligan's theory).

· Behaviorists argue that moral behavior is determined by the processes of reinforcement, punishment, and imitation. Situational variability in moral behavior is stressed by behaviorists. Hartshorne and May's classic study found considerable variation in moral behavior across situations. The social cognitive theory of moral development emphasizes a distinction between moral competence (the ability to produce moral behaviors) and moral performance (performing those behaviors in specific situations). Social cognitive theorists note that Kohlberg gave inadequate attention to moral behavior and situational variations. Prosocial behavior has especially been studied in the realm of altruism. Adolescents engage in more prosocial behavior than children do, and adolescent girls engage in more prosocial behavior than adolescent boys do. Forgiveness and gratitude are important aspects of prosocial behavior.

· In Freud's theory, the superego—the moral branch of personality—is one of personality's three main structures. Freud also argued that through identification children internalize a parent's standards of right and wrong. In the Freudian view, children may conform to moral standards in order to avoid guilt. The two main components of the superego are the ego ideal and conscience. Feeling empathy means reacting to another's feelings with an emotional response that is similar to that person's feelings. Empathy involves perspective taking as a cognitive component. Empathy changes developmentally. The contemporary perspective on emotions and moral development is that both positive feelings (such as empathy) and negative feelings (such as guilt) contribute to adolescents' moral development. Emotions are interwoven with the cognitive and social dimensions of moral development.

| Moral Personality | Recently, there has been a surge of interest in studying moral personality. This interest has focused on moral identity, moral character, and moral exemplars. Moral character involves having the strength of your convictions, persisting, and overcoming distractions and obstacles. Moral character consists of having certain virtues, such as honesty, care, and conscientiousness. Moral exemplars are people who have lived exemplary lives. |

| Social Domain Theory | Social domain theory states that there are different domains of social knowledge and reasoning, including moral, social conventional, and personal domains. |

2 Contexts of Moral Development

LG2 Describe how the contexts of parenting and schools can influence moral development

Parenting

· Parental discipline can involve love withdrawal, power assertion, or induction. Induction has proven to be the most effective technique, especially with middle-SES children. Children's moral development is advanced when parents are supportive, create opportunities for their children to learn about others' perspectives, include children in family decision making, model moral behavior and thinking, state the behaviors that are expected and why, and encourage an internal moral orientation.

Schools

· The hidden curriculum, initially described by Dewey, is the moral atmosphere of every school. Contemporary approaches to moral education include character education, values clarification, cognitive moral education, service learning, and integrative ethical education. Cheating is a moral education concern and can take many forms. Various aspects of the situation influence whether students will cheat.

3 Values, Religion, and Spirituality

LG3 Explain the roles of values, religion, and spirituality in adolescents' and emerging adults' lives

Values

· Values are beliefs and attitudes about the way things should be. Over the last two decades, adolescents have shown an increased concern for personal well-being and a decreased interest in the welfare of others. Recently, adolescents have shown an increased interest in community values and societal issues.

Religion and Spirituality

· Distinctions have been made between the concepts of religion, religiousness, and spirituality. Many children, adolescents, and emerging adults show an interest in religion, and religious institutions are designed to introduce them to religious beliefs. Adolescence and emerging adulthood may be special junctures in religious and spiritual development for many individuals. Various aspects of religion and spirituality are linked with positive outcomes in adolescent development. Cognitive changes—such as increases in abstract, idealistic, and logical thinking—influence adolescents' religious and spiritual development. Erikson's ideas on identity can be applied to understanding the increased interest in religion during adolescence and emerging adulthood. When adolescents have a positive relationship with parents or are securely attached to them, they often adopt their parents' religious beliefs. Links have been found between adolescent/emerging adult sexuality and religiousness.

key terms

altruism
care perspective
character education
cognitive moral education
conscience
conventional reasoning
ego ideal
empathy

forgiveness
gratitude
hidden curriculum
induction
justice perspective
love withdrawal
moral development
moral exemplars

moral identity
postconventional reasoning
power assertion
preconventional reasoning
religion
religiousness
service learning

social cognitive theory of moral
    development
social conventional reasoning
social domain theory
spirituality
values
values clarification

key **people**

Albert Bandura
Gustavo Carlo
William Damon
John Dewey
Nancy Eisenberg
Erik Erikson

Sigmund Freud
John Gibbs
Carol Gilligan
Jonathan Haidt
Sam Hardy
Daniel Hart

Hugh Hartshorne
Pamela King
Lawrence Kohlberg
Walter Mischel
Darcia Narváez

Mark May
James Rest
Judith Smetana
Eliot Turiel
Lawrence Walker

resources for **improving the lives of adolescents**

Moral Development and Reality
John C. Gibbs (2014, 3rd ed.)
New York: Oxford University Press
> Leading researcher and theorist John Gibbs provides an insightful, contemporary examination of many aspects of moral development, including treatment programs for antisocial youth.

Handbook of Character Education
Edited by Larry Nucci and Darcia Narváez (2008)
New York: Routledge
> A number of leading experts describe their views of many aspects of moral education.

Handbook of Moral Development (2nd ed.)
Edited by Melanie Killen and Judith Smetana (2014)
New York: Psychology Press
> A number of leading experts discuss recent trends in theory and research on many aspects of moral development.

Prosocial Development
Nancy Eisenberg, Tracy Spinrad, and Ariel Knafo (2015)
In R.M. Lerner (Ed.), *Handbook of Child Psychology and Developmental Science* (7th ed.).
New York: Wiley
> Provides a thorough, detailed exploration of many aspects of prosocial development in adolescents.

The Nature and Functions of Religious and Spiritual Development in Childhood and Adolescence
Pamela King and Chris Boyatzis (2015)
In R.M. Lerner (Ed.), *Handbook of Child Psychology and Developmental Science* (7th ed.).
New York: Wiley
> An up-to-date, contemporary examination of theory and research on religious and spiritual development in adolescence.

chapter 8

FAMILIES

chapter **outline**

"My mother and I depend on each other. However, if something separated us, I think I could still get along OK. I know that my mother continues to have an important influence on me. Sometimes she gets on my nerves, but I still basically like her, and respect her, a lot. We have our arguments, and I don't always get my way, but she is willing to listen to me."

—AMY, AGE 16

"You go from a point at which your parents are responsible for you to a point at which you want a lot more independence. Finally, you are more independent, and you feel like you have to be more responsible for yourself; otherwise you are not going to do very well in this world. It's important for parents to still be there to support you, but at some point, you've got to look in the mirror and say, 'I can do it myself.'"

—JOHN, AGE 18

"I don't get along very well with my parents. They try to dictate how I dress, who I date, how much I study, what I do on weekends, and how much time I spend on Facebook or texting. They are big intruders in my life. Why won't they let me make my own decisions? I'm mature enough to handle these things. When they jump down my throat at every little thing I do, it makes me mad and I say things to them I probably shouldn't. They just don't understand me very well."

—ED, AGE 17

"My father never seems to have any time to spend with me. He is gone a lot on business, and when he comes home, he is either too tired to do anything or plops down and watches TV and doesn't want to be bothered. He thinks I don't work hard enough and don't have values that are as solid as his generation. It is a very distant relationship. I actually spend more time talking to my mom than to him. I guess I should work a little harder in school than I do, but I still don't think he has the right to say such negative things to me. I like my mom a lot better because I think she is a much nicer person."

—TOM, AGE 14

"We have our arguments and our differences, and there are moments when I get very angry with my parents, but most of the time they are like heated discussions. I have to say what I think because I don't think they are always right. Most of the time when there is an argument, we can discuss the problem and eventually find a course that we all can live with. Not every time, though, because there are some occasions when things just remain unresolved. Even when we have an unresolved conflict, I still would have to say that I get along pretty good with my parents."

—ANN, AGE 16

preview

Although parent-adolescent relationships can vary considerably, researchers are finding that for the most part, the relationships are both (1) very important aspects of development, and (2) more positive than was once thought. This chapter examines families as a context for adolescent development. We begin by exploring family processes and then discuss parent-adolescent relationships, followed by relationships with siblings. Next, we consider the substantial changes that are taking place in families within a changing society. The chapter concludes by focusing on social policy recommendations for the well-being of adolescents and their families.

Reciprocal Socialization and
the Family as a System

Maturation

It is not enough for parents to understand children. They must accord children the privilege of understanding them.

—MILTON SAPERSTEIN
American author, 20th century

As we examine the adolescent's family relationships, think back to Urie Bronfenbrenner's (1986, 2004; Bronfenbrenner & Morris, 2006) ecological theory, which we discussed in the "Introduction" chapter. Recall that Bronfenbrenner analyzes the social contexts of development in terms of five environmental systems:

· The *microsystem*, or the setting in which the individual lives, such as the family, the world of peers, schools, work, and so on

· The *mesosystem*, which consists of links between microsystems, such as the connection between family processes and peer relations

· The *exosystem*, which consists of influences from another setting (such as parents' work) that the adolescent does not experience directly

· The *macrosystem*, or the culture in which the adolescent lives, such as an ethnic group or a nation

· The *chronosystem*, or sociohistorical circumstances, such as the increased numbers of working mothers, divorced parents, stepparent families, gay and lesbian parents, and multiethnic families in the United States in recent decades

RECIPROCAL SOCIALIZATION AND THE FAMILY AS A SYSTEM

For many years, socialization between parents and their children or adolescents was considered to be a one-way process: Children and adolescents were seen as the products of their parents' socialization techniques. However, today parent-adolescent relationships are viewed as reciprocal (Bornstein, 2015; Deater-Deckard, 2013; Maccoby, 2015; Qin & Pomerantz, 2013). **Reciprocal socialization** is the process by which children and adolescents socialize parents, just as parents socialize them.

Increasingly, genetic and epigenetic factors are being studied to discover not only parental influences on adolescents but also adolescents' influence on parents (Avinun & Knafo-Noam, 2015; Bornstein & Leventhal, 2015; Brody & others, 2013; Deater-Deckard, 2013; Hartman & Belsky, 2015). The *epigenetic view* emphasizes that development is the result of an ongoing, bidirectional interchange between heredity and the environment (Gottlieb, 2007; Lickliter, 2013; Lickliter & Honeycutt, 2015; Moore, 2013, 2015). For example, harsh, hostile parenting is associated with negative outcomes for adolescents, such as being defiant and oppositional (Deater-Deckard, 2013). This likely reflects bidirectional influences rather than a unidirectional parenting effect. That is, the parents' harsh, hostile parenting and the adolescent's defiant, oppositional behavior may mutually influence each other. In this bidirectional influence, the parents' and adolescents' behavior may have genetic linkages as well as experiential connections.

As a social system, the family can be thought of as a constellation of subsystems defined in terms of generation, gender, and role. Divisions of labor among family members define specific subunits, and attachments define others. Each family member participates in several subsystems—some dyadic (involving two people) and some polyadic (involving more than two people) (Gavazzi, 2013). The father and the adolescent represent one dyadic subsystem, the mother and the father another; the mother-father-adolescent represent one polyadic subsystem, the mother and two siblings another. Thus, when the behavior of one family member changes, it can influence the behavior of other family members (Clarke-Stewart & Parke, 2014).

An organizational scheme that highlights the reciprocal influences of family members and family subsystems is illustrated in Figure 1 (Belsky, 1981). As the arrows in the figure show, marital relations, parenting, and adolescent behavior can have both direct and indirect

developmental **connection**

Genetic Influences

Genotype-environment correlations, shared and nonshared environments, and gene × environment interactions (G × E) reflect ways that the genetic heritage of adolescents can be conceptualized and possibly influence parent-adolescent relationships. Connect to "Puberty, Health, and Biological Foundations."

reciprocal socialization The process by which children and adolescents socialize parents, just as parents socialize them.

FIGURE **1**

INTERACTION BETWEEN ADOLESCENTS AND THEIR PARENTS: DIRECT AND INDIRECT EFFECTS

© LJM Photo/Design Pics/Design Pics/Corbis RF

effects on each other. An example of a direct effect is the influence of the parent's behavior on the adolescent. An example of an indirect effect is how the relationship between the spouses mediates the way a parent acts toward the adolescent. For example, marital conflict might reduce the efficiency of parenting, in which case marital conflict would have an indirect effect on the adolescent's behavior.

As researchers have broadened their focus in families beyond just studying the parent-adolescent relationship, an increasingly studied aspect of the family system involves the link between marital relationships and parenting (Bernier, Jarry-Boileau, & Lacharite, 2014; Liu & Wang, 2015). The most consistent findings are that happily married parents are more sensitive, responsive, warm, and affectionate toward their children and adolescents (Fosco & Grych, 2010). Researchers have also found that marital satisfaction is often related to good parenting. The marital relationship is an important support for parenting (Kouros & others, 2014; Liu & Wang, 2015). When parents report more intimacy and better communication in their marriage, they are more affectionate to their children and adolescents (Grych, 2002). Therefore, an important, if unintended, benefit of marriage enhancement programs is the improvement of parenting—and consequently healthier children and adolescents. Programs that focus on parenting skills might also benefit from including attention to the participants' marriages.

Thus, a positive family climate for adolescents involves not only effective parenting but also a positive relationship between the parents, whether they are married or divorced. A longitudinal study found that a positive family climate (based on positive interaction between spouses and between parents and a seventh-grader) was linked to the degree of positive engagement the adolescents showed toward their own spouses almost 20 years later during early adulthood (Ackerman & others, 2013).

MATURATION

American author Mark Twain once remarked that when he was 14 his father was so ignorant he could hardly stand to have the man around him, but when Twain got to be 21, he was astonished at how much his father had learned in those seven years! Mark Twain's comments suggest that maturation is an important theme of parent-adolescent relationships. Adolescents change as they make the transition from childhood to adulthood, but their parents also change during their adult years.

Adolescent Changes   Among the changes in the adolescent that can influence parent-adolescent relationships are puberty, expanded logical reasoning, increasingly idealistic thinking, violated expectations, changes in schooling, peers, friendships, dating, and movement toward independence. Several investigations have shown that conflict between parents and adolescents, especially between mothers and sons, is the most stressful during the apex of pubertal growth (Steinberg, 1988). Also, early-maturing adolescents experience more conflict with their parents than do adolescents who mature late or on time (Collins & Steinberg, 2006).

What are some of the cognitive and socioemotional changes in adolescents that might influence parent-adolescent relationships?
© Creatas/Punchstock RF

developmental **connection**

Cognitive Theory

In Piaget's formal operational stage, adolescents' thought becomes more abstract, idealistic, and logical. Connect to "The Brain and Cognitive Development."

developmental **connection**

Peers

The transition to middle or junior high school can be stressful because it takes place when significant biological, cognitive, and socioemotional changes are occurring. Connect to "Schools."

multiple developmental trajectories Concept that adults follow one trajectory and children and adolescents another one; how these trajectories mesh is important.

In terms of cognitive changes, the adolescent can now reason in more logical ways with parents than in childhood. During childhood, parents may be able to get by with saying, "Okay. That is it. We do it my way or else," and the child conforms. But with increased cognitive skills adolescents no longer are likely to accept such a statement as a reason for conforming to parental dictates. Adolescents want to know, often in fine detail, why they are being disciplined. Even when parents give what seem to be logical reasons for discipline, adolescents' cognitive sophistication may call attention to deficiencies in the reasoning.

In addition, the adolescent's increasing idealistic thought comes into play in parent-adolescent relationships. Parents are now evaluated vis-à-vis what an ideal parent might be. The very real interactions with parents, which inevitably involve some negative interchanges and flaws, are placed next to the adolescent's schema of an ideal parent. And, as part of their egocentrism, adolescents' concerns with how others view them are likely to produce over-reactions to parents' comments. A mother may comment to her adolescent daughter that she needs a new blouse. The daughter might respond, "What's the matter? You don't think I have good taste? You think I look gross, don't you? Well, you are the one who is gross!" The same comment made to the daughter several years earlier, during late childhood, probably would have elicited a less intense response.

Another effect of the adolescent's cognitive development on parent-adolescent relations involves the expectations parents and adolescents have for each other. Preadolescent children are often compliant and easy to manage. As they enter puberty, children begin to question or seek rationales for parental demands. Parents might perceive this behavior as resistant and oppositional because it departs from the child's previously compliant behavior. Parents often respond to the lack of compliance with increased pressure for compliance. In this situation, expectations that were stabilized during a period of relatively slow developmental change are lagging behind the behavior of the adolescent in the period of rapid pubertal change.

What dimensions of the adolescent's socioemotional world influence parent-adolescent relationships? Adolescence brings with it new definitions of socially appropriate behavior. In most societies, these definitions are associated with changes in schooling. As they make the transition to middle or junior high school, adolescents are required to function in a more anonymous, larger environment with multiple and varying teachers. More work is required, and students must show more initiative and responsibility to adapt successfully. Adolescents spend more time with peers than they did when they were children, and they develop more sophisticated friendships than in childhood (Furman & Rose, 2015). Adolescents also begin to push more strongly for independence. In sum, parents are called on to adapt to the changing world created by the adolescent's school environment, peer relations, and push for autonomy (Wigfield & others, 2015).

Parental Changes   Parental changes that affect parent-adolescent relationships involve marital satisfaction, economic burdens, career reevaluation and time constraints, and health and body concerns. For most parents, marital satisfaction increases after adolescents or emerging adults leave home (Gorchoff, John, & Helson, 2008). In addition, parents feel a greater economic burden when their children are in adolescence and emerging adulthood. During this time, parents may reevaluate their occupational achievement, deciding whether they have met their youthful aspirations of success. They may look to the future and think about how much time they have remaining to accomplish their life goals. Many adolescents, meanwhile, look to the future with unbounded optimism, feeling that they have an unlimited amount of time to accomplish what they desire. Parents of adolescents may become preoccupied with concerns about their own health, body integrity, and sexual attractiveness (Almeida, 2011). Even when their body and sexual attractiveness are not deteriorating, many parents of adolescents perceive that they are. By contrast, many adolescents have reached or are beginning to reach the peak of their physical attractiveness, strength, and health. Although both adolescents and their parents show a heightened preoccupation with their bodies, adolescents' outlook probably is more positive.

Multiple Developmental Trajectories   The concept of **multiple developmental trajectories** refers to the fact that adults follow one trajectory and children and adolescents another one (Clarke-Stewart & Parke, 2014; Parke & Buriel, 2006). How adult and child/

adolescent developmental trajectories mesh affects the timing of entry into various family tasks. Adult developmental trajectories include timing of entry into marriage, cohabitation, or parenthood; child developmental trajectories include timing of child care and entry into middle school. The timing of some family tasks and changes can be planned, such as reentry into the workforce or delaying parenthood, whereas other changes may occur unexpectedly, such as job loss or divorce (Parke & Buriel, 2006).

The changes in adolescents' parents that we considered earlier are typical of development in middle adulthood (Fingerman & others, 2014). Most adolescents' parents either are in middle adulthood or are rapidly approaching this period of life. However, in the last two decades, the timing of parenthood in the United States has undergone some dramatic shifts. Parenthood is taking place earlier for some, and later for others, than in previous decades. First, the number of adolescent pregnancies in the United States increased considerably during the 1970s and 1980s. Although the adolescent pregnancy rate has decreased since then, the U.S. adolescent pregnancy rate remains one of the highest in the developed world. Second, the number of women who postpone childbearing until their thirties and early forties simultaneously increased (Welch, 2014). We discussed adolescents as parents in the chapter on "Sexuality." Here we focus on sociohistorical changes related to postponement of childbearing until the thirties or forties.

There are many contrasts between becoming a parent in adolescence and becoming a parent 15 to 30 years later. Delayed childbearing allows for considerable progress in occupational and educational domains. For both males and females, education usually has been completed and career development is well established.

The marital relationship varies with the timing of parenthood onset. In one investigation, couples who began childbearing in their early twenties were compared with those who began in their early thirties (Walter, 1986). The later-starting couples had more egalitarian relationships, with men more often participating in child care and household tasks.

Is parent-child interaction different for families in which parents delay having children until their thirties or forties? Investigators have found that older fathers are warmer, communicate better, encourage more achievement, place fewer demands on their children, are more lax in enforcing rules, and show less rejection with their children than younger fathers. However, older fathers also are less likely to engage in physical play or sports with their children (MacDonald, 1987). These findings suggest that sociohistorical changes are resulting in different developmental trajectories for many families, trajectories that involve changes in the ways that marital partners and parents and adolescents interact.

What are some maturational changes in parents that might influence parent-adolescent relationships?
© Jack Hollingsworth/Corbis RF

The generations of living things pass in a short time and like runners hand on the torch of life.

—LUCRETIUS
Roman poet, 1st century B.C.

Review Connect Reflect

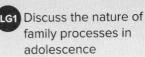

LG1 Discuss the nature of family processes in adolescence

Review
- What is reciprocal socialization? How can the family be described as a system?
- What roles do maturation of the adolescent and maturation of parents play in understanding parent-adolescent relationships?

Connect
- What has the historical perspective on adolescence contributed to our view of the family as a system?

Reflect *Your Own Personal Journey of Life*
- Think about your family as a system as you developed through adolescence. How might your parents' marital relationship have influenced your development?

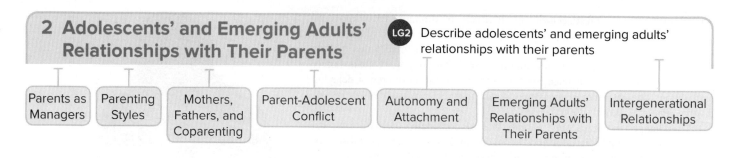

2 Adolescents' and Emerging Adults' Relationships with Their Parents

LG2 Describe adolescents' and emerging adults' relationships with their parents

| Parents as Managers | Parenting Styles | Mothers, Fathers, and Coparenting | Parent-Adolescent Conflict | Autonomy and Attachment | Emerging Adults' Relationships with Their Parents | Intergenerational Relationships |

We have seen how the expectations of adolescents and their parents often seem to be violated as adolescents change dramatically during the course of puberty. Many parents see their child changing from a compliant being into someone who is noncompliant, oppositional, and resistant to parental standards. Parents often respond by clamping down and putting more pressure on the adolescent to conform to parental standards. Many parents often deal with the young adolescent as if they expect him or her to become a mature being within the next 10 to 15 minutes. But the transition from childhood to adulthood is a long journey with many hills and valleys. Adolescents are not going to conform to adult standards immediately. Parents who recognize that adolescents take a long time "to get it right" usually deal more competently and calmly with adolescent transgressions than do parents who demand immediate conformity to parental standards. Yet other parents, rather than placing heavy demands on their adolescents for compliance, do virtually the opposite, letting them do as they please in a very permissive manner.

Our discussion of parent-adolescent relationships will indicate that neither high-intensity demands for compliance nor an unwillingness to monitor and be involved in the adolescent's development is likely to be a wise parenting strategy. Further, we will explore another misperception that parents of adolescents sometimes entertain. Parents may perceive that virtually all conflict with their adolescent is bad. We will discover that a moderate degree of conflict with parents in adolescence is not only inevitable but may also serve a positive developmental function. We also will explore relationships between emerging adults and their parents, and we will examine strategies that emerging adults and their parents can use to get along better. And, to conclude this section, we will discuss how adolescent development is influenced by intergenerational relationships.

PARENTS AS MANAGERS

Parents can play important roles as managers of adolescents' opportunities, as monitors of adolescents' social relationships, and as social initiators and arrangers (Chu & others, 2015; Clark & others, 2015; Lowe & Dotterer, 2013; Williams, Burton, & Warzinski, 2014). An important developmental task in adolescence is learning to make competent decisions in an increasingly independent manner. To help adolescents reach their full potential, parents can assume an important role as effective managers who find information, make contacts, help structure choices, and provide guidance (Gauvain & Perez, 2007). Parents who fulfill this important managerial role help adolescents to avoid pitfalls and to work their way through a myriad of choices and decisions they face (Mounts, 2007, 2011).

Parents can serve as regulators of opportunities for their adolescents' social contact with peers, friends, and adults (Lippold & others, 2014; Seedall & Anthony, 2015). Mothers are more likely than fathers to have a managerial role in parenting. In adolescence, it could involve participating in a parent-teacher conference and subsequently managing the adolescent's homework activity.

Researchers have found that family-management practices are positively related to students' grades and self-responsibility, and negatively to school-related problems (Eccles, 2007; Lowe & Dotterer, 2013). One of the most important family-management practices in this regard is maintaining a structured and organized family environment, such as establishing routines for homework, chores, bedtime, and so on. One study focused on African American families, examining links between mothers' reports of family-management practices, including routine, and adolescents' school-related behavior (Taylor & Lopez, 2005). Family routine (well managed and organized) was positively related to adolescents' grades, attentiveness in class, and school attendance, and negatively linked to their school-related problems.

Needing Parents as Guides

Stacey Christensen, age 16: "I am lucky enough to have open communication with my parents. Whenever I am in need or just need to talk, my parents are there for me. My advice to parents is to let your teens grow at their own pace, be open with them so that you can be there for them. We need guidance; our parents need to help but not be too overwhelming."

Parental Monitoring A key aspect of the managerial role of parenting is effective monitoring, which is especially important as children move into the adolescent years (Lowe & Dotterer, 2013). Monitoring includes supervising an adolescent's choice of social settings, activities, and friends. Consider the following studies of parental monitoring and adolescent development:

· In a study of more than 36,000 eighth- and tenth-grade students revealed that a higher level of parental monitoring was associated with lower rates of alcohol and marijuana use, with the effects strongest for girls and adolescents with the highest risk-taking profiles (Dever & others, 2012).

· A higher level of parental monitoring in the last year of high school was linked to a lower probability of alcohol dependence in the first year of college (Kaynak & others, 2013).

· A high level of parental monitoring within the context of parental warmth was linked to positive academic outcomes for ethnic minority youth (Lowe & Dotterer, 2013).

· A low level of parental monitoring was linked to sexual risk taking in Iranian high school students (Ahmadi & others, 2013).

· A meta-analysis concluded that low parental monitoring was associated with adolescent depression (Yap & others, 2014).

· Low parental monitoring was a key factor in predicting a developmental trajectory of delinquency and substance use in adolescence (Wang & others, 2014).

Adolescents' Information Management A current interest involving effective parenting of adolescents focuses on adolescents' management of their parents' access to information, especially the extent to which adolescents disclose or conceal details about their activities (Amsel & Smetana, 2011; Keijsers & Laird, 2014; Metzger & others, 2013; Smetana, Robinson, & Rote, 2015; Tilton-Weaver & others, 2013). Researchers have found that adolescents' disclosure to parents about their whereabouts, activities, and friends is linked to positive adolescent adjustment (Smetana, 2011a, b; Smetana & others, 2015). A recent study of 10- to 18-year-olds found that lower adolescent disclosure to parents was linked to antisocial behavior (Criss & others, 2015). Also, a recent study revealed that adolescents in three countries—Costa Rica, Thailand, and South Africa—who engaged in a higher level of self-disclosure to parents were more competent (Hunter & others, 2011). And a recent study of U.S. and Chinese young adolescents found that adolescents' disclosure to parents was linked with a higher level of academic competence (better learning strategies, autonomous motivation, and better grades) over time (Cheung, Pomerantz, & Dong, 2012).

What characterizes adolescents' management of their parents' access to information?
© Ryan McVay/Getty Images RF

Adolescents' willingness to disclose information to parents also is related to responsive parenting and a higher level of parental behavioral control, which are components of a positive parenting style, *authoritative parenting*, which we discuss in the next section. For example, a recent study revealed that authoritative parenting predicted increased youth disclosure and a lower incidence of problem behavior (Low, Snyder, & Shortt, 2012).

PARENTING STYLES

Parents want their adolescents to grow into socially mature individuals, and they often feel a great deal of frustration in their role as parents. Psychologists have long searched for parenting methods that promote competent social development in adolescents (Baumrind, 1971; Bornstein, 2015; Maccoby, 2015; Sears, Maccoby, & Levin, 1957). For example, behaviorist John Watson (1930) urged parents not to be too affectionate with their children. Early research focused on a distinction between physical and psychological discipline, or between controlling and permissive parenting. More recently, there has been greater precision in unraveling the dimensions of competent parenting (Grusec & Davidov, 2015; Grusec & others, 2014).

Especially widespread is the view of Diana Baumrind (1971, 1991, 2012), who notes that parents should be neither punitive nor aloof from their adolescents, but rather should develop rules and show affection. She describes four styles of parenting—authoritarian, authoritative, neglectful, and indulgent—that are associated with different aspects of the adolescent's social behavior:

authoritarian parenting A restrictive, punitive style in which the parent exhorts the adolescent to follow the parent's directions and to respect work and effort. Firm limits and controls are placed on the adolescent, and little verbal exchange is allowed. This style is associated with adolescents' socially incompetent behavior.

authoritative parenting A style encouraging adolescents to be independent but still placing limits and controls on their actions. Extensive verbal give-and-take is allowed, and parents are warm and nurturant toward the adolescent. This style is associated with adolescents' socially competent behavior.

neglectful parenting A style in which the parent is very uninvolved in the adolescent's life. It is associated with adolescents' social incompetence, especially a lack of self-control.

- **Authoritarian parenting** is a restrictive, punitive style in which the parent exhorts the adolescent to follow directions and to respect work and effort. The authoritarian parent places firm limits and controls on the adolescent and allows little verbal exchange. For example, an authoritarian parent might say, "You do it my way or else. There will be no discussion!" Authoritarian parenting is associated with adolescents' socially incompetent behavior. Adolescents of authoritarian parents often are anxious about social comparison, fail to initiate activity, and have poor communication skills.

- **Authoritative parenting** encourages adolescents to be independent but still places limits and controls on their actions. Extensive verbal give-and-take is allowed, and parents are warm and nurturant toward the adolescent. An authoritative father, for example, might put his arm around the adolescent in a comforting way and say, "You know you should not have done that. Let's talk about how you can handle the situation better next time." Authoritative parenting is associated with adolescents' socially competent behavior. The adolescents of authoritative parents are self-reliant and socially responsible.

- **Neglectful parenting** is a style in which the parent is uninvolved in the adolescent's life. The neglectful parent cannot answer the question, "It is 10:00 p.m. Do you know where your adolescent is?" Neglectful parenting is associated with adolescents' socially incompetent behavior, especially a lack of self-control. Adolescents have a

CHEEVERWOOD   by Michael Fry strong need for their parents to care about them; adolescents whose parents are neglectful develop the sense that other aspects of their parents' lives are more important than they are. Adolescents whose parents are neglectful are socially incompetent: they show poor self-control and do not handle independence well. Closely related to the concept of neglectful parenting is a lack of parental monitoring which, as we discussed earlier, is linked to a number of negative outcomes for adolescents.

· **Indulgent parenting** is a style in which parents are highly involved with their adolescents but place few demands or controls on them. Indulgent parents allow their adolescents to do whatever they want, and the result is that the adolescents never learn to control their own behavior and always expect to get their way. Some parents deliberately rear their adolescents in this way because they mistakenly believe that combining warm involvement with few restraints will produce a creative, confident adolescent. However, indulgent parenting is associated with adolescents' social incompetence, especially a lack of self-control.

In our discussion of parenting styles, we have talked about parents who vary along the dimensions of acceptance, responsiveness, demand, and control. As shown in Figure 2, the four parenting styles—authoritarian, authoritative, neglectful, and indulgent—can be described in terms of these dimensions (Maccoby & Martin, 1983).

In general, researchers have found authoritative parenting to be related to positive aspects of development (Cai & others, 2013; Morris, Cui, & Steinberg, 2012; Steinberg, 2014). For example, a recent study revealed that delinquency was lowest in families with at least one authoritative parent and highest in families with two neglectful parents (Hoeve & others, 2011). Also, a recent study of Chinese adolescents revealed that authoritative parenting positively predicted parent-adolescent attachment, which in turn was associated with a higher level of adolescent self-esteem and positive attachment to peers (Cai & others, 2013). Why is authoritative parenting likely to be the most effective style? The following reasons have been offered (Steinberg & Silk, 2002):

· Authoritative parents establish an appropriate balance between control and autonomy, giving adolescents opportunities to develop independence while providing the standards, limits, and guidance that children and adolescents need.

· Authoritative parents are more likely to engage adolescents in verbal give-and-take and to allow adolescents to express their views. This type of family discussion is likely to help adolescents to understand social relationships and the requirements for being a socially competent person.

· The warmth and parental involvement provided by authoritative parents make the adolescent more receptive to parental influence.

Parenting Styles and Ethnicity Do the benefits of authoritative parenting transcend the boundaries of ethnicity, socioeconomic status, and household composition? Although some exceptions have been found, evidence linking authoritative parenting with competence on the part of the adolescent occurs in research across a wide range of ethnic groups, social strata, cultures, and family structures (Morris, Cui, & Steinberg, 2012; Steinberg, 2014).

Other research with ethnic groups suggests that some aspects of the authoritarian style may be associated with positive child outcomes (Clarke-Stewart & Parke, 2014). Elements of the authoritarian style may take on different meanings and have different effects depending on the context. For example, Asian American parents often continue aspects of traditional Asian child-rearing practices that have sometimes been described as authoritarian. The parents exert considerable control over their children's lives. However, Ruth Chao (2005, 2007; Chao & Otsuki-Clutter, 2011) argues that the style of parenting used by many Asian American parents is distinct from the domineering control of the authoritarian style. Instead, Chao argues that the control reflects concern and involvement in their children's lives and is best

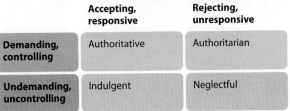

FIGURE **2**

FOURFOLD SCHEME OF PARENTING STYLES
© *Photolibrary RF*

indulgent parenting A style in which parents are highly involved with their adolescents but place few demands or controls on them. This is associated with adolescents' social incompetence, especially a lack of self-control.

conceptualized as a type of training. The high academic achievement of Asian American children may be a consequence of their "training" parents (Stevenson & Zusho, 2002). In recent research involving Chinese American adolescents and their parents, parental control was endorsed as were the Confucian parental goals of perseverance, hard work in school, obedience, and sensitivity to parents' wishes (Russell, Crockett, & Chao, 2010).

Further Thoughts on Parenting Styles Several caveats about parenting styles are in order. First, the parenting styles do not capture the important themes of reciprocal socialization and synchrony (Clarke-Stewart & Parke, 2014). Keep in mind that adolescents socialize parents, just as parents socialize adolescents (Bush & Peterson, 2013). Second, many parents use a combination of techniques rather than a single technique, although one technique may be dominant. Although consistent parenting is usually recommended, the wise parent may sense the importance of being more permissive in certain situations, more authoritarian in others, and more authoritative in others. Also, some critics argue that the concept of parenting style is too broad and that more research needs to be conducted to "unpack" parenting styles by studying various components that comprise the styles (Grusec & Davidov, 2015). For example, is parental monitoring more important than warmth in predicting adolescent outcomes?

MOTHERS, FATHERS, AND COPARENTING

The vast majority of research on parenting adolescents has focused on mothers rather than fathers. In this section, we explore the importance of mothers and fathers in adolescents' lives and then examine coparenting and adolescent development.

Mothers, Fathers, and Adolescents What roles do mothers and fathers play in their adolescents' development? Historically, mothers have usually been assigned the main parenting responsibility for raising infants, children, and adolescents. However, in recent decades, many fathers have taken a more active parenting role.

Mothers and fathers often interact differently with their adolescents. Mothers are more involved with their children and adolescents than are fathers, although fathers increase the time they spend in parenting when they have sons and are less likely to become divorced when they have sons (Diekman & Schmidheiny, 2004). Mothers' interactions with their adolescents often center on caregiving and teaching activities, whereas fathers' interactions often involve leisure activities (Galambos, Berenbaum, & McHale, 2009).

Mothers and fathers also often interact differently with their sons and daughters (Bronstein, 2006). In many cultures, mothers socialize their daughters to be more obedient and responsible than their sons. They also place more restrictions on daughters' autonomy. Fathers show more attention to sons than daughters, engage in more activities with sons, and put forth more effort to promote sons' intellectual development.

Much of the research we describe in this chapter on families is based on interviews and observations of mothers. Let's look at several recent studies that have included fathers and their adolescents.

A recent study of non-Latino White two-parent families examined the amount of time mothers and fathers spent with their children from 8 to 18 years of age and how such time use was linked to their children's and adolescents' development (Lam, McHale, & Crouter, 2012). The amount of time that adolescents spent with their parents declined from early to late adolescence. Most of that time was labeled "social time," which involved time shared with friends and other relatives. However, private one-on-one time between a parent and his/her adolescent increased from age 8 to 12 or 13, leveled off in middle adolescence, and then began declining at about 15 to 18 years of age. For both boys and girls, adolescents spent the most time with the same-sex parent. Further, an important finding in the study was that more private one-on-one time spent with the father was linked to a higher level of adolescent self-worth and social skills. This study is important is calling attention to different types of time—social and private—and different developmental trajectories in adolescence for those two types of time adolescents spend with parents.

Another recent study focused on two-parent African American families with adolescents (Stanik, Riina, & McHale, 2013). Mothers reported having a warmer relationship with their adolescents than did fathers, and both parents indicated they had a warmer relationship with

What parenting style do many Asian Americans practice?
© JGI/Tom Grill/Blend Images/Corbis RF

- - - - - - - - - - ➤

developmental **connection**

Families

Recent research on adolescents in Chinese American families has also focused on whether a "tiger parenting" style is common and whether it is associated with positive or negative outcomes for adolescents. Connect to "Achievement, Work, and Careers."

developmental **connection**

Parenting

A bidirectional association was found between the prosocial behavior of adolescents and their mothers' authoritative parenting (Padilla-Walker & others, 2012). Connect to "Moral Development, Values, and Religion."

◄ - - - - - - - - - - -

younger than older adolescents. A higher level of maternal warmth was linked to a lower level of depressive symptoms and less risky behavior in sons, while a higher level of paternal warmth and shared time with fathers was associated with less risky adolescent behavior.

The two studies just described involved two-parent families. Of course, there is concern about the large number of adolescents who grow up in a single-parent family, especially when the father is completely absent or spends little time with his adolescent (Raeburn, 2014; Raymo & others, 2014). A recent research review concluded that the negative effects of father absence are especially evident in these outcomes: lower rates of high school graduation, problems with socioemotional adjustment during adolescence, and adult mental health problems (McLanahan, Tach, & Schneider, 2013). Later in this chapter, we will further explore the father's role in divorced families and stepfamilies.

Coparenting   The organizing theme of coparenting is that poor coordination, active undermining and disparagement of the other parent, lack of cooperation and warmth, and disconnection by one parenting partner—either alone or in combination with overinvolvement by the other—are conditions that place children and adolescents at developmental risk (Garneu & Adler-Baeder, 2015; Goldberg & Carlson, 2015; Gonzales, Jones, & Parent, 2014; Lewin & others, 2015; Solmeyer & others, 2011). By contrast, parental solidarity, cooperation, and warmth show clear ties to children's and adolescents' prosocial behavior and competence in peer relations. When parents show cooperation, mutual respect, balanced communication, and attunement to each other's needs, these attributes help children and adolescents to develop positive attitudes toward both males and females (Tamis-LeMonda & Cabrera, 2002). A recent study found that parents' joint involvement predicted that adolescents would engage in fewer risky behaviors (Riina & McHale, 2014). In this study, there was a bidirectional influence in which adolescents' engagement in a lower level of risky behaviors predicted higher levels of joint parental involvement.

PARENT-ADOLESCENT CONFLICT

It is commonly believed that a huge gulf separates parent and adolescents in the form of a so-called generation gap between the values and attitudes of adolescents and those of their parents. For the most part, the generation gap is an inaccurate stereotype. For example, most adolescents and their parents share similar beliefs about the value of hard work, achievement, and career aspirations (Gecas & Seff, 1990). They also tend to hold similar religious and political beliefs. As you will see in our discussion of research on parent-adolescent conflict, a minority of adolescents (perhaps 20 to 25 percent) have a high degree of conflict with their parents, but for a substantial majority the conflict levels are moderate or low.

That said, the fact remains that early adolescence is a time when parent-adolescent conflict escalates beyond levels experienced during childhood (Juang & Umana-Taylor, 2012). This increase may be due to a number of factors already discussed involving the maturation of the adolescent and the maturation of parents: the biological changes of puberty; cognitive changes involving increased idealism and logical reasoning; social changes focused on independence and identity; violated expectations; and physical, cognitive, and social changes in parents associated with middle adulthood. A research review concluded that parent-adolescent conflict decreases from early adolescence through late adolescence (Laursen, Coy, & Collins, 1998).

Although conflict with parents does increase in early adolescence, it does not reach the tumultuous proportions envisioned by G. Stanley Hall at the beginning of the twentieth century (Laursen & Collins, 2009). Rather, much of the conflict involves everyday aspects of family life, such as keeping a bedroom clean, dressing neatly, getting home by a certain time, not talking on the phone forever, and so on. The conflicts rarely involve major dilemmas like drugs and delinquency. In a study of middle-socioeconomic-status African American families, parent-adolescent conflict was common but low in intensity and focused on everyday living issues such as the adolescent's room, chores, choice of activities, and homework (Smetana & Gaines, 1999). Nearly all conflicts were resolved by adolescents' giving in to parents, but adolescent concession declined with age.

Conflict with parents increases in early adolescence. *What is the nature of this conflict in a majority of American families?*
© BananaStock/PunchStock RF

Martha Chan, Marriage and Family Therapist

Martha Chan is a marriage and family therapist who works for Adolescent Counseling Services in Palo Alto, California. She has been the program director of Adolescent Counseling Services for more than a decade.

Among her activities, Chan counsels parents and adolescents about family issues, conducts workshops for parents at middle schools, and writes a monthly column that addresses topics such as "I'm a single mom; how do I talk with my son about sex?" "My daughter wants to dye her hair purple," and "My son is being bullied."

For more information about what a marriage and family therapist does, see the Careers in Adolescent Development appendix.

In one study of conflict in a number of social relationships, adolescents reported having more disagreements with their mothers than with anyone else—followed in order by friends, romantic partners, siblings, fathers, other adults, and peers (Laursen, 1995). In another study of 64 high school sophomores, interviews were conducted in their homes on three randomly selected evenings during a three-week period (Montemayor, 1982). The adolescents were asked to tell about the events of the previous day, including any conflicts they had experienced with their parents. During a period of 192 days of tracking the 64 adolescents, an average of 68 arguments with parents was reported. This represents a rate of 0.35 argument with parents per day or about one argument every three days. The average length of the arguments was 11 minutes. Most conflicts were with mothers, and the majority were between mothers and daughters.

Still, a high degree of conflict characterizes some parent-adolescent relationships (Fuligni, 2012; Juang & Umana-Taylor, 2012; Moed & others, 2015; Rengasamy & others, 2013). It has been estimated that in about 20 to 25 percent of families, parents and adolescents engage in prolonged, intense, repeated, unhealthy conflict (Montemayor, 1982). Although this figure represents a minority of adolescents, it indicates that 4 to 5 million American families encounter serious, highly stressful parent-adolescent conflict.

This prolonged, intense conflict is associated with a number of adolescent problems—moving away from home, juvenile delinquency, school dropout, pregnancy and early marriage, membership in religious cults, and drug abuse (Brook & others, 1990). For example, a recent study found that a higher level of parent-adolescent conflict was associated with higher adolescent anxiety, depression, and aggression, and lower self-esteem (Smokowski & others, 2015). Also, a recent study found that high parent-adolescent conflict was associated with a lower level of empathy in adolescents throughout the six years of the study from 13 to 18 years of age (Van Lissa & others, 2015). Further, a recent study revealed that a higher level of parent-adolescent conflict was related to peer-reported aggression and delinquency (Ehrlich, Dykas, & Cassidy, 2012).

To read about the career of one individual who counsels families with high levels of parent-adolescent conflict, see the *Connecting with Careers* profile.

Although in some cases adolescent problems may be caused by intense, prolonged parent-adolescent conflict, in others the problems might have originated before the onset of adolescence (Darling, 2008). Simply because children are physically much smaller than parents, parents might be able to suppress oppositional behavior. But, by adolescence, increased size and strength—especially in boys—can result in an indifference to or confrontation with parental dictates. At the same time, some psychologists have argued that conflict is a normal part of adolescent development.

Cross-cultural studies reveal that parent-adolescent conflict is lower in some countries than in the United States. Two countries where parent-adolescent conflict is lower than in the United States are Japan and India (Larson, 1999; Rothbaum & others, 2000).

When families emigrate to another country, adolescents typically acculturate more quickly to the norms and values of their new country than do their parents (Fuligni, 2012; Fuligni & Tsai, 2015). This likely occurs because of immigrant adolescents' exposure in school to the language and culture of the host country. The norms and values immigrant adolescents experience are especially likely to diverge from those of their parents in areas such as autonomy and romantic relationships. Such divergences are likely to increase parent-adolescent conflict in immigrant families. Andrew Fuligni (2012) argues that these conflicts aren't always expressed openly but are often present in underlying, internal feelings. For example, immigrant adolescents may feel that their parents want them to give up their personal interests for the sake of the family, but the adolescents don't think this is fair. Such acculturation-based conflict focuses on issues related to core cultural values and is likely to occur in immigrant families, such as Latino and Asian American families, who come to the United States to live (Fuligni & Tsai, 2015; Juang & Umana-Taylor, 2012).

AUTONOMY AND ATTACHMENT

It has been said that there are only two lasting bequests that parents can leave their children—one is roots, the other wings. These words reflect the importance of attachment and autonomy in the adolescent's successful adaptation to the world. Historically, developmentalists have shown far more interest in autonomy than in attachment during the adolescent period. Recently, however, increasing attention has been paid to attachment's role in healthy development of adolescents and emerging adults (Jones & Cassidy, 2014; Zack & others, 2015). Adolescents and their parents live in a coordinated social world that requires both autonomy and attachment. In keeping with the historical interest in these processes, we discuss autonomy first.

What are strategies that parents can use to guide adolescents in effectively handling their increased motivation for autonomy?
© BananaStock/PunchStock RF

Autonomy   The increased independence that typifies adolescence is interpreted as rebellion by some parents, but in many instances adolescents' push for autonomy has little to do with their feelings toward their parents. Psychologically healthy families adjust to adolescents' push for independence by treating the adolescents in more adult ways and including them more often in family decision making. Psychologically unhealthy families often remain locked into power-oriented parental control, and parents move even more heavily toward an authoritarian posture in their relationships with their adolescents.

The adolescent's quest for autonomy and sense of responsibility create puzzlement and conflict for many parents. Parents begin to see their teenagers slipping away from their grasp. As we have discussed, they often feel an urge to take stronger control as the adolescent seeks autonomy and personal responsibility. Heated, emotional exchanges might ensue, with either side calling names, making threats, and doing whatever seems necessary to gain control. Parents can become frustrated because they expected their teenager to heed their advice, to want to spend time with the family, and to grow up to do what is right. To be sure, they anticipated that their teenager would have some difficulty adjusting to the changes adolescence brings, but few parents are able to imagine and predict the strength of adolescents' determination to spend time with their peers and to show that it is they, not the parents, who are responsible for their success or failure.

The Complexity of Adolescent Autonomy   Defining adolescent autonomy is a more complex and elusive task than it might at first seem (Fuligni & Tsai, 2015; Van Petegem, Vansteenkiste, & Beyers, 2013). The term *autonomy* generally connotes self-direction and independence. But what does it really mean? Is it an internal personality trait that consistently characterizes the adolescent's immunity from parental influence? Is it the ability to make responsible decisions for oneself? Does autonomy imply consistent behavior in all areas of adolescent life, including school, finances, dating, and peer relations? What are the relative contributions of peers and other adults to the development of an adolescent's autonomy? A longitudinal study of adolescents and emerging adults from 13 to 23 years of age revealed that adolescents' autonomy from peer influences predicted long-term success in avoiding problematic behavior but also more difficulty in establishing strong friendships in emerging adulthood (Allen, Chango, & Szwedo, 2014).

One aspect of autonomy that is especially important is **emotional autonomy,** the capacity to relinquish childlike dependencies on parents. In developing emotional autonomy, adolescents increasingly de-idealize their parents, perceive them as people rather than simply as parenting figures, and become less dependent on them for immediate emotional support.

Gender, Culture, and Ethnicity   Gender differences characterize autonomy granting in adolescence, with boys being given more independence than girls are allowed to have. In one study, this was especially true in U.S. families with a traditional gender-role orientation (Bumpus, Crouter, & McHale, 2001). Also, Latino families are more likely than non-Latino White families to protect and monitor their daughters more closely than their sons (Allen & others, 2008).

In contexts where adolescents experience a high level of risk, such as high-crime communities, and in cultural groups that place a high value on family solidarity and deference to parents, parental control either has not been linked to problem behaviors or has been shown to benefit adolescent outcomes (McElhaney & Allen, 2012). And expectations about the appropriate timing of adolescent autonomy often vary across cultures, parents, and adolescents (Fuligni, Hughes, & Way, 2009; McElhaney & Allen, 2012). For example, expectations for early autonomy on the part of adolescents are more prevalent in non-Latino Whites, single parents, and adolescents themselves than they are in Asian Americans or Latinos, married parents, and parents themselves (Feldman & Rosenthal, 1999). Nonetheless, although Latino cultures may place a stronger emphasis on parental authority and restrict adolescent autonomy, a recent study revealed that regardless of where they were born, Mexican-origin adolescent girls living in the United States expected autonomy at an earlier age than their mothers preferred (Bamaca-Colbert & others, 2012). Another recent study of Mexican immigrant mothers and their U.S-raised 13- to 14-year-old daughters explored future autonomy expectations when the daughters reached 15 years of age (Romo, Mireles-Rios, & Lopez-Tello, 2014). In this study, the daughters hoped for less strict rules regarding social activities while mothers reported that they still expected to exert control, although they were willing to allow more autonomy in personal matters such as physical appearance and to allow their daughter to group date.

In one study, adolescents in the United States sought autonomy from parents earlier than did adolescents in Japan (Rothbaum & others, 2000). Asian adolescents raised in the United States, however, usually do not seek autonomy as early as their Anglo-American peers do (Greenberger & Chu, 1996). Also, in the transition to adulthood, Japanese are less likely to live outside the family home than are Americans (Hendry, 1999).

Developmental Transitions in Autonomy and Going Away to College   Many emerging adults experience a transition in the development of autonomy when they leave home and go away to college (Kerig, Swanson, & Ward, 2012; Kloep & Hendry, 2010). The transition from high school to college involves increased autonomy for most individuals (Bucx & van Wel, 2008; Nelson & others, 2011). For some, homesickness sets in; for others, sampling the privileges of life without parents hovering around feels marvelous. For the growing number of students whose families have been torn by separation and divorce, though, moving away can be especially painful. Adolescents in such families may find themselves in the roles of comforter, confidant, and even caretaker of their parents as well as their siblings. In the words of one college freshman, "I feel responsible for my parents. I guess I shouldn't, but I can't help it. It makes my separation from them, my desire to be free of others' problems, my motivation to pursue my own identity more difficult." For yet other students, the independence of being a college freshman is somewhat stressful but not too difficult to manage. According to 18-year-old Brian, "Becoming an adult is kind of hard. I'm having to learn to balance my own checkbook, make my own plane reservations, do my own laundry, and the hardest thing of all is waking up in the morning. I don't have my mother there banging on the door."

How do relationships with parents change when individuals go to college?
© Tom Stewart/Corbis

emotional autonomy The capacity to relinquish childlike dependence on parents.

In one study, researchers evaluated the psychological separation and adjustment of 130 college freshmen and 123 college upperclassmen (Lapsley, Rice, & Shadid, 1989). As expected, freshmen showed more psychological dependency on their parents and poorer social and personal adjustment than did upperclassmen. Female students also showed more psychological dependency on their parents than male students did.

Adolescent Runaways/Homeless Youth   An estimated 1.6 million youth run away from home or are homeless each year in the United States (Walsh & Donaldson, 2010). Why do adolescents run away from their homes? Generally, runaways are desperately unhappy at home (Kidd, 2012). The reasons many of them leave seem legitimate by almost anyone's standards. When they run away, they usually do not leave a clue as to their whereabouts—they just disappear.

Many runaways and homeless youth are from families in which a parent or another adult beats them or sexually exploits them (Chen & others, 2004; Heerde, Scholes-Balog, & Hemphill, 2015; Tyler, Kort-Butler, & Swendener, 2014). Their lives may be in danger daily. Their parents may be drug addicts or alcoholics. In some cases, the family may be so impoverished that the parents are unable to feed and clothe their teenagers adequately. The parents may be so overburdened by their own emotional and/or material inadequacies that they fail to give their adolescents the attention and understanding they need. So teenagers hit the streets in search of the emotional and material rewards they are not getting at home.

But runaways and homeless youth are not all from our society's lower-SES tier. Teenage lovers, confronted by parental hostility toward their relationship, might decide to elope and try to make it on their own. Or a middle-SES teenager might decide that he has seen enough of his hypocritical parents—people who try to make him live by an unrealistically high set of moral standards, while they live by a loose, false set of ideals. Another teen might live with parents who constantly bicker. Any of these adolescents might decide that they would be happier away from home.

This adolescent has run away from home. *What kinds of family relationships might cause adolescents to run away from home? Are there ways society could better serve runaways?*
© Bill Aron/PhotoEdit

Peer relations also can contribute to adolescents making the decision to run away from home. A recent longitudinal study found that peer deviance was strongly linked to adolescents' decision to run away from home (Chen, Thrane, & Adams, 2012).

Running away often is a gradual process, as adolescents begin to spend less time at home and more time on the streets or with a peer group. The parents might be telling them that they really want to see them, to understand them; but runaways often feel that they are not understood at home and that their parents care much more about themselves. A recent study of homeless youth revealed that the longer they did not have stable housing, the more their resilience decreased and their mental health deteriorated (Cleverley & Kidd, 2011).

A recent longitudinal study of more than 4,000 youth from grade 9 to age 21 found that running away from home was linked to lack of parental support, school disengagement, depressive symptoms, and substance use in grade 9 (Tucker & others, 2011). Also, the runaways had higher levels of drug dependence and depressive symptoms at age 21. In another recent study of 18- to 24-year-old homeless youth in San Francisco and Chicago, a high rate of psychological disorders (especially mood disorders, antisocial personality disorder, and substance-related disorder) characterized the youth (Quimby & others, 2012). A large-scale study of 16- to 34-year-olds in England found that of those who had run away from home before 16 years of age, 45 percent reported being bullied, 25 percent experienced violence at home, and 9 percent said they had experienced unwanted sexual intercourse (Meltzer & others, 2012). Also, the runaways were three times more likely to have thought about or attempted suicide. Further, a U.S. study of more than 7,000 adolescents revealed that the odds of pregnancy in the next year were 1.7 times greater for runaways (Thrane & Chen, 2012). In this study, a history of sexual assault and romantic involvement increased the likelihood of pregnancy.

National Safe Place is a partnership of more than 360 agencies serving youth and more than 10,000 businesses and community organizations in the United States that provides runaways with immediate safety and access to food and shelter (Walsh & Donaldson, 2010). The Safe Place program educates youth about alternatives to running away and homelessness, and helps youth connect with service providers.

Conclusions About Adolescent Autonomy   In sum, the ability to attain autonomy and gain control over one's behavior in adolescence is acquired through appropriate adult reactions to the adolescent's desire for control. An individual at the onset of adolescence does not have the knowledge to make appropriate or mature decisions in all areas of life. As the adolescent pushes for greater autonomy, the wise adult relinquishes control in those areas in which the adolescent can make reasonable decisions and continues to guide the adolescent in areas where the adolescent's knowledge is more limited. Gradually, the adolescent acquires the ability to make mature decisions on his or her own (Harold, Colarossi, & Mercier, 2007). The discussion that follows reveals in greater detail how important it is to view the development of autonomy within the context of connectedness to parents.

Attachment and Connectedness Adolescents do not simply move away from parental influence into a decision-making world all on their own. As they become more autonomous, it is psychologically healthy for them to be attached to their parents. Let's first examine a general definition of secure attachment and then describe attachment in infancy, childhood, and adolescence.

Secure attachment involves a positive, enduring emotional bond between two people. In infancy, childhood, and adolescence, secure attachment usually involves an emotional bond between a child and a caregiver that benefits the child's exploration of the environment and further development. In adulthood, a secure attachment can take place not only between caregivers and children, but also between two people in a couple or marital relationship.

Infancy and Childhood Attachment theorists such as John Bowlby (1989) and Mary Ainsworth (1979) argue that secure attachment in infancy is central to the development of social competence. Secure attachment is theorized to be an important foundation for psychological development later in the life span. In **insecure attachment,** infants, children, and adolescents either avoid the caregiver or show considerable resistance or ambivalence toward the caregiver. Insecure attachment is theorized to be related to difficulties in relationships and problems in later development (Zeanah & Gleason, 2015). For example, a recent research review concluded that children who do not form secure attachments to their parents risk developing anxiety and other internalized problems (Kerns & Brumariu, 2014).

Adolescence One of the most widely discussed aspects of socioemotional development in infancy is secure attachment to caregivers (Thompson, 2015). In the past decade, researchers have explored whether secure attachment also might be an important concept in adolescents' relationships with their parents (Booth-LaForce & others, 2014; Dawson & others, 2014; de Vries & others, 2015; Glazebrook, Townsend, & Sayal, 2015; Kobak & Kerig, 2015; Lecompte & Moss, 2014; Steele & others, 2014; Zack & others, 2015). A recent study involving adolescents and emerging adults from 15 to 20 years of age found that insecure attachment to mothers was linked to becoming depressed and remaining depressed (Agerup & others 2015). Also, Joseph Allen and his colleagues (2009) found that adolescents who were securely attached at age 14 were more likely to report at age 21 that they were in an exclusive relationship, comfortable with intimacy in relationships, and were achieving increasing financial independence. A recent analysis concluded that the most consistent outcomes of secure attachment in adolescence involve positive peer relations and development of the adolescent's emotion regulation capacities (Allen & Miga, 2010). Recent research studies have found that adolescents who had attempted suicide were less securely attached to their mothers and fathers (Sheftall & others, 2013), and avoidant attachment predicted suicidal behavior in adolescents (Sheftall, Schoppe-Sullivan, & Bridge, 2014). Further, a recent study revealed that insecure attachment with mothers and fathers was linked to a lower level of parents' knowledge about adolescents' whereabouts (Jones & Cassidy, 2015).

Many studies that assess secure and insecure attachment in adolescence use the Adult Attachment Interview (AAI) (George, Main, & Kaplan, 1984). This measure examines an individual's memories of significant attachment relationships. Based on the responses to questions on the AAI, individuals are classified as secure/autonomous (which corresponds to secure attachment in infancy) or as being in one of three insecure categories:

· **Dismissing/avoidant attachment** is an insecure category in which individuals deemphasize the importance of attachment. This category is associated with consistent experiences of rejection of attachment needs by caregivers. One possible outcome of dismissing/avoidant attachment is that parents and adolescents mutually distance themselves from each other, a state that lessens parents' influence.

· **Preoccupied/ambivalent attachment** is an insecure category in which adolescents are hyperattuned to attachment experiences. This is thought to mainly occur because

secure attachment Involves a positive, enduring emotional bond between two people. In infancy, childhood, and adolescence, formation of a secure bond with a caregiver benefits the child's exploration of the environment and subsequent development. In adulthood, the bond can also be between two people in a couple or marital relationship.

insecure attachment Attachment pattern in which infants, children, and adolescents either avoid the caregiver or show considerable resistance or ambivalence toward the caregiver. This pattern is theorized to be related to difficulties in relationships and problems in later development.

dismissing/avoidant attachment An insecure attachment category in which individuals deemphasize the importance of attachment. This category is associated with consistent experiences of rejection of attachment needs by caregivers.

preoccupied/ambivalent attachment An insecure attachment category in which adolescents are hyperattuned to attachment experiences. This is thought mainly to occur because parents are inconsistently available to the adolescent.

Old Model		New Model
Autonomy, detachment from parents; parent and peer worlds are isolated Intense, stressful conflict throughout adolescence; parent-adolescent relationships are filled with storm and stress on virtually a daily basis		Attachment and autonomy; parents are important support systems and attachment figures; adolescent-parent and adolescent-peer worlds have some important connections Moderate parent-adolescent conflict is common and can serve a positive developmental function; conflict greater in early adolescence

FIGURE 3

OLD AND NEW MODELS OF PARENT-ADOLESCENT RELATIONSHIPS.
© UpperCut Images/Getty Images RF

parents are inconsistently available to the adolescent. This state can result in a high degree of attachment-seeking behavior, mixed with angry feelings. Conflict between parents and adolescents in this type of attachment classification can be too high for healthy development.

· **Unresolved/disorganized attachment** is an insecure category in which the adolescent has an unusually high level of fear and might be disoriented. This can result from traumatic experiences such as a parent's death or abuse by parents.

A recent study using the Important People Interview (IPI) assessed attachments of high school students (14 to 18 years of age) and emerging adult college students (18 to 23 years of age) to the four most important people in their lives, followed by their four most important peers (Rosenthal & Kobak, 2010). After identifying the important people in their lives, the students rank-ordered the people in terms of these contexts: attachment bond (closeness, separation distress, and an emergency situation), support seeking (comfort or support in daily contexts), and affiliative (enjoyable social contact). College students placed romantic partners in higher positions and fathers in lower positions than did high school students. Friends' placements in higher positions and fathers' exclusion from the most important people list or placement as the fourth most important person were linked to increased behavior problems (internalizing behaviors such as depression and externalizing behaviors such as rule-breaking).

Conclusions About Parent-Adolescent Conflict and Attachment in Adolescence   In sum, the old model of parent-adolescent relationships suggested that, as adolescents mature, they detach themselves from parents and move into a world of autonomy apart from parents. The old model also suggested that parent-adolescent conflict is intense and stressful throughout adolescence. The new model emphasizes that parents serve as important attachment figures, resources, and support systems as adolescents explore a wider, more complex social world. The new model also emphasizes that, in the majority of families, parent-adolescent conflict is moderate rather than severe and that everyday negotiations and minor disputes are normal, serving the positive developmental function of promoting independence and identity formation (see Figure 3).

Attachment in Emerging Adults   Although relationships with romantic partners differ from those with parents, romantic partners fulfill some of the same needs for adults as parents do for their children (Mikulincer & Shaver, 2014; Shaver & Mikulincer, 2007). *Securely attached* infants are defined as those who use the caregiver as a secure base from which to explore the environment. Similarly, emerging and young adults may count on their romantic partners to be a secure base to which they can return and obtain comfort and security in stressful times (Arnett, 2015).

unresolved/disorganized attachment An insecure category in which the adolescent has an unusually high level of fear and is disoriented. This can result from traumatic experiences such as a parent's death or abuse by parents.

What are some key dimensions of attachment in emerging adulthood, and how are they related to relationship patterns and well-being?
© Tom Grill/Corbis RF

Do adult attachment patterns with partners in emerging and early adulthood reflect childhood attachment patterns with parents? In a retrospective study, Cindy Hazan and Philip Shaver (1987) found that young adults who were securely attached in their romantic relationships were more likely to describe their early relationship with their parents as securely attached. In a longitudinal study, infants who were securely attached at 1 year of age were securely attached 20 years later in their adult romantic relationships (Steele & others, 1998). However, in another longitudinal study, links between early attachment styles and later attachment styles were lessened by stressful and disruptive experiences such as the death of a parent or instability of caregiving (Lewis, Feiring, & Rosenthal, 2000). In a recent meta-analysis of 127 research reports, the following conclusions were reached (Pinquart, Feubner, & Ahnert, 2013): (1) moderate stability of attachment security occurred from early infancy to adulthood; (2) no significant stability occurred for time intervals of more than 15 years; (3) attachment stability was greater when the time span was less than 2 years or more than 5 years.

Hazan and Shaver (1987, p. 515) measured attachment styles using the following brief assessment:

Read each paragraph and then place a check mark next to the description that best describes you:

1. I find it relatively easy to get close to others and I am comfortable depending on them and having them depend on me. I don't worry about being abandoned or about someone getting too close to me.
2. I am somewhat uncomfortable being close to others. I find it difficult to trust them completely and to allow myself to depend on them. I get nervous when anyone gets too close to me and it bothers me when someone tries to be more intimate with me than I feel comfortable with.
3. I find that others are reluctant to get as close as I would like. I often worry that my partner doesn't really love me or won't want to stay with me. I want to get very close to my partner, and this sometimes scares people away.

These items correspond to three attachment styles—secure attachment (option 1 above) and two insecure attachment styles (avoidant—option 2 above, and anxious—option 3 above):

- *Secure attachment style.* Securely attached adults have positive views of relationships, find it easy to get close to others, and are not overly concerned with or stressed out about their romantic relationships. These adults tend to enjoy sexuality in the context of a committed relationship and are less likely than others to have one-night stands.
- *Avoidant attachment style.* Avoidant individuals are hesitant about getting involved in romantic relationships and once in relationships tend to distance themselves from their partners.
- *Anxious attachment style.* These individuals demand closeness, are less trusting, and are more emotional, jealous, and possessive.

The majority of adults (about 60 to 80 percent) describe themselves as securely attached, and not surprisingly adults prefer having a securely attached partner (Zeifman & Hazan, 2008).

Researchers are studying links between adults' current attachment styles and many aspects of their lives (Craparo & others, 2014; Mikulincer & Shaver, 2014; Sheinbaum & others, 2015). For example, securely attached adults are more satisfied with their close relationships than insecurely attached adults, and the relationships of securely attached adults are more likely to be characterized by trust, commitment, and longevity. A recent meta-analysis of 94 samples of U.S. college students from 1988 to 2011 found the percentage of students with a secure attachment decreased in recent years while the percentage of students with insecure attachment styles increased (Konrath & others, 2014).

The following recent studies confirmed the importance of adult attachment styles in people's lives:

- Attachment security predicted more positive romantic relationships (Holland & Roisman, 2010).
- In newlywed marriages, spouses were more likely to engage in infidelity when either they or their partner had an anxious attachment style (Russell, Baker, & McNulty, 2013).
- A national survey indicated that insecure attachment in adults was associated with the development of disease and chronic illness, especially cardiovascular system problems such as high blood pressure, heart attack, and stroke (McWilliams & Bailey, 2010).

- Adults with avoidant and anxious attachment patterns had a lower level of sexual satisfaction than their counterparts with a secure attachment pattern (Brassard & others, 2012).
- Secure attachment in adults was linked to fewer sleep disruptions than insecure avoidant and anxious attachment (Adams & McWilliams, 2015).

If you have an insecure attachment style, are you stuck with it and does it doom you to have problematic relationships? Attachment categories are somewhat stable in adulthood, but adults do have the capacity to change their attachment thinking and behavior. Although attachment insecurities are linked to relationship problems, attachment style makes only a moderate-size contribution to relationship functioning, and additional factors influence relationship satisfaction and success (Mikulincer & Shaver, 2014).

EMERGING ADULTS' RELATIONSHIPS WITH THEIR PARENTS

For the most part, emerging adults' relationships with their parents improve when they leave home. They often grow closer psychologically to their parents and share more with them than they did before leaving home (Arnett, 2007; Arnett & Fishel, 2014). However, challenges in the parent–emerging adult relationship involve the emerging adult's increasing autonomy, as he or she has adult status in many areas yet still depends on parents in some manner (Kerig, Swanson, & Ward, 2012). Many emerging adults can make their own decisions about where to live, whether to stay in college, which lifestyle to adopt, whether to get married, and so on. At the same time, parents often provide support for their emerging adult children even after they leave home. This might be accomplished through loans and monetary gifts for education, purchase of a car, and financial contributions to living arrangements, as well as emotional support.

In successful emerging adulthood, individuals separate from their family of origin without cutting off ties completely or fleeing to some substitute emotional refuge. Complete cutoffs from parents rarely solve emotional problems. Emerging adulthood is a time for young people to sort out emotionally what they will take with them from their family of origin, what they will leave behind, and what they will create.

The vast majority of studies of parenting styles have focused on outcomes for children and adolescents and have involved mothers rather than fathers. A recent study revealed that parents act as "scaffolding" and "safety nets" to support their children's successful transition through emerging adulthood (Swartz & others, 2011). Another recent study examined mothers' and fathers' parenting styles with their emerging adult children (Nelson & others, 2011). An authoritative parenting style (defined in this study as high responsiveness, low control) by both mothers and fathers was linked with positive outcomes in emerging adult children (high self-worth and high social acceptance, and low depression, for example). The most negative outcomes for emerging adult children (low self-worth, high depression, and high anxiety, for example) were related to a controlling-indulgent style (low responsiveness, high control) on the part of both mothers and fathers. High control by parents may be especially detrimental to emerging adults who are moving toward more autonomy as they leave their parents' home. Negative outcomes for emerging adult children also resulted from an uninvolved parenting style (low responsiveness, low control) on the part of both mothers and fathers. The most positive outcomes for emerging adult children involved having fathers who used an authoritative style of parenting.

Recent research indicates that parents and their emerging adult/young adult children have more contact than in earlier generations, with the amount of contact especially increasing in the first decade of the twenty-first century (Fingerman, Cheng, & others, 2012). Aided by advances in technology, today's emerging and young adults frequently text their parents and become friends with their parents on Facebook. The recent research indicates that today's emerging adults and young adults appreciate their parents' emotional and financial support. Nonetheless, there is concern when this support becomes too intensive, in which case it can restrict emerging and young adults' development of autonomy (Fingerman, Cheng, & others, 2012; Fingerman, Pillemer, & others, 2012). The term "helicopter parents" has been applied to this type of support. A recent study of emerging adults found that helicopter parenting was positively linked to parental involvement and other aspects of positive parenting, such as

developmental **connection**

Emerging Adulthood

Residential changes peak during emerging adulthood, a time when there also is often instability in love, work, and education. Connect to "Introduction."

Can Emerging Adults and Their Parents Coexist?

When emerging adults ask to return home to live, parents and their emerging adult children should agree on the conditions and expectations beforehand. For example, they might discuss and agree on whether the emerging adults will pay rent, wash their own clothes, cook their own meals, do any household chores, pay their phone bills, come and go as they please, be sexually active or drink alcohol at home, and so on. If these conditions aren't negotiated at the beginning, conflict often results because the expectations of parents and young adult children will likely be violated. Parents need to treat emerging adult children more like adults than children and let go of much of their parenting role. Parents should interact with emerging adult children not as if they are dependent children who need to be closely monitored and protected but rather as if they are adults who are capable of responsible, mature behavior. Emerging adults have the right to choose how much they sleep and eat, how they dress, whom they choose as friends and lovers, what career they pursue, and how they spend their money. However, if the emerging adult children act in ways that interfere with their parents' lifestyles, parents need to say so. The discussion should focus not on emerging adults' choices but on why certain activities are unacceptable when both generations are living together in the same home.

Some parents don't let go of their emerging adult children when they should. They engage in "permaparenting," which can impede not only their emerging adult children's progress toward independence and responsibility but also postpone their own postparenting lives. As mentioned earlier, "helicopter parents" is another label used for parents who hover too closely in their effort to ensure that their children succeed in college and adult life (Paul, 2003). Although well intentioned, this intrusiveness by parents can slow the process by which their children become responsible adults.

When they move back home, emerging adults need to think about how they might need to modify their behavior to make the living arrangement work. Elina Furman (2005) provides some good recommendations in *Boomerang Nation: How to Survive Living with*

What are some strategies that can benefit the relationship between emerging adults and their parents?
© Tetra Images/Corbis RF

Your Parents . . . the Second Time Around. She recommends that when emerging adults move back home, they should expect to make adjustments. And, as recommended earlier, she urges emerging adults to sit down with their parents and negotiate the ground rules for living at home before they actually move back. Furman also recommends that emerging adults set a deadline for how long they will live at home and then stay focused on their goals (which might be to save enough money to pay off their debts, save enough to start a business or buy their own home, finish graduate school, and so on). Too often emerging adults spend the money they save by moving home on luxuries such as spending binges, nights on the town, expensive clothes, and unnecessary travel, which only delay their ability to move out of their parents' home.

How do you think emerging adults' relationship with their parents differs if they do not have to live at home?

guidance, disclosure, and emotional support, but negatively related to parental granting of autonomy and school engagement (Padilla-Walker & Nelson, 2012).

Many emerging adults, though, no longer feel compelled to comply with parental expectations and wishes. They shift to learning to deal with their parents on an adult-to-adult basis, which requires a mutually respectful form of relating—in which, by the end of emerging adulthood, individuals can appreciate and accept their parents as they are.

In today's uncertain economic times, many emerging adults continue to live at home or return to the family home after several years of college or after graduating from college, or while saving money after taking a full-time job (Furman, 2005). Emerging and young adults also may move back in with their parents after a job loss or a divorce. And some individuals don't leave home at all until their middle to late twenties because they cannot financially support themselves. Numerous labels have been applied to emerging and young adults who return to their parents' homes to live, including "boomerang kids" and "B2B" (or Back-to-Bedroom) (Furman, 2005).

As with most family living arrangements, there are both pluses and minuses when emerging adult children continue living at home or return to live at home. One of the most common complaints voiced by both emerging adults and their parents is a loss of privacy. Emerging adults complain that their parents restrict their independence, cramp their sex lives, reduce their music listening, and treat them as children rather than adults. Parents often complain that their quiet home has become noisy, that they stay up late worrying about when their emerging adult children will come home, that meals are difficult to plan because of conflicting schedules, that their relationship as a married couple has been invaded, and that they have to shoulder too much responsibility for their emerging adult children. In sum, when emerging adults return home to live, a disequilibrium in family life is created, which requires considerable adaptation on the part of parents and their emerging adult children.

How can emerging adults and their parents get along better? See the *Connecting with Health and Well-Being* interlude on the previous page for some ideas.

INTERGENERATIONAL RELATIONSHIPS

Connections between generations play important roles in development through the life span (Antonucci, Birditt, & Ajrouch, 2013; Antonucci, Birditt, & Akiyama, 2016; Fingerman, Sechrist, & Birditt, 2013; Fingerman & others, 2014). With each new generation, personality characteristics, attitudes, and values are replicated or changed. As older family members die, their biological, intellectual, emotional, and personal legacies are carried on in the next generation. Their children become the oldest generation and their grandchildren the second generation. A recent study revealed that emerging and young adults with children see their parents more frequently than do their counterparts who do not have children (Bucx, Raaijmakers, & van Wel, 2010).

Adults in midlife play important roles in the lives of the young and the old (Antonucci & others, 2016; Fingerman & others, 2014; Igarashi & others, 2013). Middle-aged adults share their experience and transmit values to the younger generation. They may be launching adolescents into adulthood, adjusting to having grown children return home, or becoming grandparents. They also may be giving or receiving financial assistance, or caring for a widowed or sick parent.

Middle-aged adults have been described as the "sandwich," "squeezed," or "overload" generation because of the responsibilities they have for their adolescent and young adult children on the one hand and their aging parents on the other (Etaugh & Bridges, 2010). However, an alternative view is that in the United States, a "sandwich" generation (in which the middle generation cares for both grown children and aging parents simultaneously) occurs less often than a "pivot" generation (in which the middle generation alternates attention between the demands of grown children and aging parents) (Fingerman, Sechrist, & Birditt, 2013; Luong, Rauers, & Fingerman, 2015). A recent study found that middle-aged adults positively supported family responsibility to emerging adult children but were more ambivalent about providing care for aging parents, viewing it as both a joy and a burden (Igarashi & others, 2013). A recent study, though, revealed that affection and support, reflecting solidarity, were more prevalent than ambivalence in intergenerational relationships (Hogerbrugge & Komter, 2012).

Gender differences also characterize intergenerational relationships (Etaugh & Bridges, 2010). Females play an especially important role in connecting family relationships across generations. Females' relationships across generations are thought to be closer than other family bonds (Antonucci, Birditt, & Ajrouch, 2013).

Culture and ethnicity also are important aspects of intergenerational relationships. For example, cultural brokering has increasingly occurred in the United States as children and adolescents serve as mediators (cultural and linguistic translators) for their immigrant parents (Villanueva & Buriel, 2010).

The following studies provide evidence of the importance of intergenerational relationships in the development of adolescents and emerging adults:

· In a longitudinal study, hostility and positive engagement by parents and adolescents during family interaction at age 14 were related to levels of hostility and positive engagement expressed by offspring and their spouses during marital

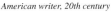

How do intergenerational relationships influence adolescents' development?
© Digital Vision RF

interactions 17 years later (Whitton & others, 2008). A higher level of family-of-origin hostility during adolescence showed an especially strong link to a higher level of marital hostility and a lower level of positive engagement 17 years later.

- Supportive family environments and parenting in childhood (assessed when the children were 3 to 15 years of age) were linked with more positive relationships (in terms of contact, closeness, conflict, and reciprocal assistance) between the children and their middle-aged parents when the children were 26 years of age (Belsky & others, 2001).

- Adult children of divorce who were classified as securely attached were less likely to divorce in the early years of their marriage than were their insecurely attached counterparts (Crowell, Treboux, & Brockmeyer, 2009).

- Children of divorce were disproportionately likely to end their own marriage as compared with children from intact, never-divorced families, although the transmission of divorce across generations has declined in recent years (Wolfinger, 2011).

- Middle-aged parents are more likely to provide support to their grown children than to their parents (Fingerman & others, 2011).

So far in this chapter we have examined the nature of family processes, adolescent/emerging adult relationships with parents, and intergenerational relationships. In addition, there is another aspect to the family worlds of most adolescents and emerging adults—sibling relationships—that we will discuss next.

Review Connect Reflect

LG2 Describe adolescents' and emerging adults' relationships with their parents

Review
- How can parents be effective managers of adolescents?
- What are four important parenting styles, and how are they linked with adolescent development?
- What roles do mothers and fathers play in adolescent development? How effective is coparenting?
- How can parent-adolescent conflict be accurately described?
- What roles do autonomy and attachment play in the development of adolescents and emerging adults?
- What are some issues involved in relationships between emerging adults and their parents?

- How do intergenerational relationships influence adolescent development?

Connect
- Connect the earlier discussion of emotional development to this section's discussion of autonomy and attachment.

Reflect Your Own Personal Journey of Life
- What has characterized your own development of attachment and autonomy up to this point in your life?

---

3 Sibling Relationships

LG3 Characterize sibling relationships in adolescence

Sibling Roles   Birth Order

What characterizes sibling roles? As we examine the roles siblings play in social development, you will discover that conflict is a common dimension of sibling relationships but that siblings also play many other roles in social development (Buist, Dekovic, & Prinzie, 2013; Feinberg & others, 2013; McHale, Updegraff, & Whiteman, 2013). And how influential is birth order in the adolescent's development?

SIBLING ROLES

Approximately 80 percent of American adolescents have one or more siblings—that is, sisters and brothers (Dunn, 2007, 2015). As anyone who has had a sibling knows, conflict is a common interaction style of siblings. However, conflict is only one of the many dimensions of sibling relations (Conger & Kramer, 2010; Dunn, 2015; Feinberg & others, 2013; Whiteman, McHale, & Soli, 2011). Adolescent sibling relations include helping, sharing, teaching, fighting, and playing—and adolescent siblings can act as emotional supports, rivals, and communication partners (Buist, Dekovic, & Prinzie, 2013; East, 2009).

How much time do adolescent siblings spend with each other? One study found that adolescent siblings spent an average of 10 hours a week together, with an average of 12 percent of it spent in constructive time (creative activities such as art, music, and hobbies; sports; religious activities; and games) and 25 percent in nonconstructive time (watching TV and hanging out) (Tucker, McHale, & Crouter, 2001). In Mexican American families, adolescent siblings spend even more time together—more than 17 hours a week (Updegraff & others, 2005). However, a research review concluded that sibling relationships are less close, less intense, and more egalitarian in adolescence than in childhood (East, 2009). Indeed, beginning in adolescence, sibling companionship begins to decline in many cultures as boys and girls become increasingly involved in the world beyond their family (McHale, Updegraff, & Whiteman, 2013).

What do adolescent siblings talk about when they are together? One study revealed that siblings most often talked about extracurricular activities, media, and school (Tucker & Winzeler, 2007). Less than 10 percent of their time together was spent discussing friends, family, eating, and body image.

Judy Dunn (2007, 2015), a leading expert on sibling relationships, recently described three important characteristics of these relationships:

· *Emotional quality of the relationship*. Both intensely positive and intensely negative emotions are often expressed by siblings toward each other. Many children and adolescents have mixed feelings toward their siblings.

· *Familiarity and intimacy of the relationship*. Siblings typically know each other very well, and this intimacy suggests that they can either provide support or tease and undermine each other, depending on the situation.

· *Variation in sibling relationships*. Some siblings describe their relationships more positively than do others. Thus, there is considerable variation in sibling relationships. We've seen that many siblings have mixed feelings about each other, but some adolescents mainly describe their sibling in warm, affectionate ways, whereas others primarily talk about how irritating and mean a sibling is.

Do parents usually favor one sibling over others, and does such favoritism make a difference in an adolescent's development? One study of 384 adolescent sibling pairs revealed that 65 percent of their mothers and 70 percent of their fathers showed favoritism toward one sibling (Shebloski, Conger, & Widaman, 2005). When favoritism toward one sibling occurred, it was linked to lower self-esteem and sadness in the less-favored sibling. Indeed, equality and fairness are major concerns of siblings' relationships with each other and affect how they are treated by their parents (Campione-Barr, Greer, & Kruse, 2013).

In some instances, siblings can be stronger socializing influences on the adolescent than parents or peers are (Dunn, 2007). Someone close in age to the adolescent—such as a sibling—might be able to understand the adolescent's problems and communicate more effectively than parents can. In dealing with peers, coping with difficult teachers, and discussing taboo subjects (such as sex), siblings can be more influential in socializing adolescents than parents are. In one study, both younger and older adolescent siblings viewed older siblings as sources of support for social and scholastic activities (Tucker, McHale, & Crouter, 2001).

Having an older sibling who engages in problematic behaviors is a risk factor for young siblings. In a recent study, having an older sibling who engaged in externalizing problem behavior increased the likelihood that a younger sibling would also engage in that type of problem behavior (Defoe & others, 2013).

About 80 percent of us have one or more siblings. *What are some characteristics of sibling relationships in adolescence?*
© Alain Shroder/Getty Images RF

What role might sibling conflict play in adolescent development? High levels of sibling conflict and low levels of sibling warmth can be detrimental to adolescent development. A recent meta-analysis found that less sibling conflict and higher sibling warmth were associated with fewer internalizing and externalizing problems (Buist, Dekovic, & Prinzie, 2013). And a longitudinal study found that increased sibling conflict was linked to increased depression and that increased sibling intimacy was related to increased peer competence and, for girls, decreased depression (Kim & others, 2007).

Sibling conflict may be especially damaging when combined with ineffective parenting (Kramer, 2010; Milevsky, 2011). A longitudinal study revealed that a combination of ineffective parenting (poor problem-solving skills, weak supervision skills, parent-adolescent conflict) and sibling conflict (hitting, fighting, stealing, cheating) at 10 to 12 years of age was linked to antisocial behavior and poor peer relations from 12 to 16 years of age (Bank, Burraston, & Snyder, 2004).

As just indicated, negative aspects of sibling relationships, such as high conflict, are linked to negative outcomes for adolescents. The negative outcomes can develop not only through conflict but also through direct modeling of a sibling's behavior, as when a young adolescent has an older sibling who has poor study habits and engages in delinquent behavior. By contrast, close and supportive sibling relationships can buffer the negative effects of stressful circumstances in an adolescent's life (East, 2009).

What are sibling relationships like in emerging adulthood? Most siblings spend far less time with each other in emerging adulthood than they did in adolescence. Mixed feelings about siblings are still common in emerging adulthood. However, as siblings move out of the family home and sibling contact becomes more optional, conflicted sibling relationships in adolescence often become less emotionally intense (Hetherington & Kelly, 2002).

BIRTH ORDER

Some reports have indicated that whether an adolescent has older or younger siblings is linked to development of certain personality characteristics. For example, a recent review concluded that "firstborns are the most intelligent, achieving, and conscientious, while later-borns are the most rebellious, liberal, and agreeable" (Paulhus, 2008, p. 210). Compared with later-born children, firstborn children have also been described as more adult-oriented, helpful, conforming, and self-controlled. However, when such birth order differences are measured, they often are small.

Birth order also plays a role in siblings' relationships with each other (Vandell, Minnett, & Santrock, 1987). Older siblings invariably take on the dominant role in sibling interaction, and older siblings report feeling resentful that parents give preferential treatment to younger siblings.

The one-child family is becoming much more common in China because of the strong motivation to limit the population growth in the People's Republic of China. The effects of this policy have not been fully examined. *In general, what have researchers found the only child to be like?*
© Jason Hosking/Getty Images

What are later-borns like? Characterizing later-borns is difficult because they can occupy so many different sibling positions. For example, a later-born might be the second-born male in a family of two siblings or a third-born female in a family of four siblings. In two-child families, the profile of the later-born child is related to the sex of his or her sibling. For example, a boy with an older sister is more likely to develop "feminine" interests than is a boy with an older brother. Overall, later-borns usually enjoy better relations with peers than firstborns. Last-borns, who are often described as the "baby" in the family even after they have outgrown infancy, run the risk of becoming overly dependent. Middle-borns tend to be more diplomatic, often performing the role of negotiator in times of dispute (Sutton-Smith, 1982).

The popular conception of the only child is that of a "spoiled brat" with undesirable characteristics such as dependency, lack of self-control, and self-centered behavior. But research presents a more positive portrayal of the only child, who often is achievement-oriented and displays a desirable personality, especially in comparison with later-borns and children from large families (Thomas, Coffman, & Kipp, 1993).

So far our consideration of birth-order effects suggests that birth order might be a strong predictor of adolescent behavior. However, family researchers have found that the influence of birth order has often been overemphasized. The critics argue that, when all of the factors that influence adolescent behavior are considered, birth order by itself shows limited ability to predict adolescent behavior. Consider sibling relationships alone. They are influenced not only by birth order but also by the number of siblings, age of siblings, age spacing of siblings, and sex of siblings. In one study, male sibling pairs had a less positive relationship (less caring, less intimate, and lower conflict resolution) than male/female or female/female sibling pairs (Cole & Kerns, 2001). Consider also the temperament of siblings. Researchers have found that siblings' temperamental traits (such as "easy" and "difficult"), as well as differential treatment of siblings by parents, influence how siblings get along (Brody, Stoneman, & Burke, 1987). Siblings with "easy" temperaments who are treated in relatively equal ways by parents tend to get along with each other the best, whereas siblings with "difficult" temperaments, or siblings whose parents gave one sibling preferential treatment, get along the worst.

In addition to gender, temperament, and differential treatment of siblings by parents, think about some of the other important factors in adolescents' lives that influence their behavior beyond birth order. They include heredity, models of competency or incompetency that parents present to adolescents on a daily basis, peer influences, school influences, socioeconomic factors, sociohistorical factors, cultural variations, and so on. Although birth order by itself may not be a good predictor of adolescent behavior, sibling relationships and interaction are important dimensions of family processes in adolescence (Dunn, 2005).

Review Connect Reflect

LG3 Characterize sibling relationships in adolescence

Review
- What is the nature of sibling roles?
- How strongly is birth order linked to adolescent development?

Connect
- Compare a family with multiple children to a family with a single child in terms of the family-as-a-system perspective.

Reflect *Your Own Personal Journey of Life*
- If you grew up with one or more siblings, what was your relationship with your sibling(s) like? If you could have changed anything in your relationship with your sibling(s) in adolescence, what would that have been? If you are an only child, how do you think this sibling status influenced your development?

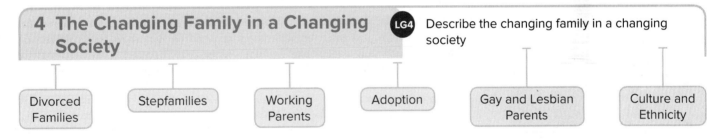

4 The Changing Family in a Changing Society

LG4 Describe the changing family in a changing society

Divorced Families | Stepfamilies | Working Parents | Adoption | Gay and Lesbian Parents | Culture and Ethnicity

More U.S. adolescents are growing up in a wider variety of family structures than ever before in history. Many mothers spend the greater part of their day away from their children. More than one of every two mothers with a child under the age of 5, and more than two of every three with a child from 6 to 17 years of age, is in the labor force. The number of adolescents growing up in single-parent families is staggering. The United States has a higher percentage of single-parent families than most other countries (see Figure 4). And, by age 18, approximately one-fourth of all American children will have spent part of their lives in a stepfamily.

DIVORCED FAMILIES

The U.S. divorce rate increased dramatically in the 1960s and 1970s but has declined overall since the 1980s (Amato & Dorius, 2010; Braver & Lamb, 2013). However, a recent analysis of divorce trends in the United States concluded that U.S. divorce rates increased from 1990 to 2008 (Kennedy & Ruggles, 2014). Divorce rates doubled in the last two decades for individuals over 35 years of age, but among the youngest couples, divorce rates have recently

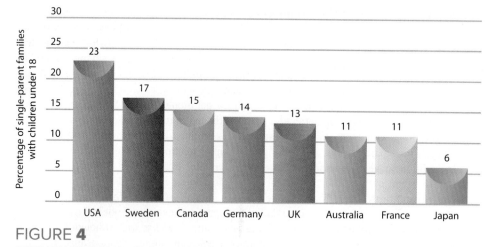

FIGURE 4

SINGLE-PARENT FAMILIES IN DIFFERENT COUNTRIES

been stable or are declining. If current trends continue, U.S. divorce rates overall could level off or even decline in the next several decades.

Many other countries around the world have also experienced significant changes in their divorce rate. For example, Japan experienced an increase in its divorce rate in the 1990s and the first decade of the twenty-first century. However, the divorce rate in the United States is still much higher than that in Japan and higher than that in most other countries as well. Also, the divorce rate increased 7 percent in Norway from 1997 to 2009 (Reiter & others, 2013). It is estimated that 40 percent of U.S. children born to married parents will experience their parents' divorce (Hetherington & Stanley-Hagan, 2002).

We will explore a number of questions regarding the effects of divorce: Is the adjustment of adolescents and emerging adults better in intact, never-divorced families than in divorced families? Should parents stay together for the sake of their children and adolescents? How much do parenting skills matter in divorced families? What factors affect the adolescent's individual risk and vulnerability in a divorced family? What role does socioeconomic status play in the lives of adolescents in divorced families? (Hetherington, 2005, 2006; Hetherington & Kelly, 2002; Hetherington & Stanley-Hagan, 2002).

Adolescents' Adjustment in Divorced Families Most researchers agree that children, adolescents, and emerging adults from divorced families show poorer adjustment than their counterparts in nondivorced families (Arkes, 2015; Braver & Lamb, 2013; Hetherington, 2005, 2006; Lansford, 2009, 2012, 2013; Wallerstein, 2008; Weaver & Schofield, 2015) (see Figure 5). In the longitudinal study conducted by E. Mavis Hetherington and her colleagues (Hetherington, 2005, 2006; Hetherington, Cox, & Cox, 1982; Hetherington & Kelly, 2002), 25 percent of children from divorced families had emotional problems, but that figure decreased to 20 percent in emerging adulthood. In this study, 10 percent of children and emerging adults from nondivorced families had emotional problems.

In Hetherington's research, the 20 percent of emerging adults from divorced families who continued to have emotional problems were characterized by impulsive, irresponsible, antisocial behavior, or were depressed. Toward the end of emerging adulthood, this troubled group was having problems at work and difficulties in romantic relationships. The 10 percent of emerging adults from nondivorced families who had emotional problems mainly came from homes where family conflict was high and authoritative parenting was rare. As in childhood, emerging adults who had gone from a highly conflicted intact family to a more harmonious divorced family context with a caring, competent parent had fewer emotional problems. In another longitudinal study, parental divorce in childhood and adolescence was linked to poor relationships with fathers, unstable romantic or marital relationships, and low levels of education in adulthood (Amato, 2006).

Those who have experienced multiple divorces are at greater risk. Adolescents and emerging adults in divorced families are more likely than adolescents from nondivorced families to have academic problems, to show externalized problems (such as acting out and delinquency) and internalized problems (such as anxiety and depression), to be less socially

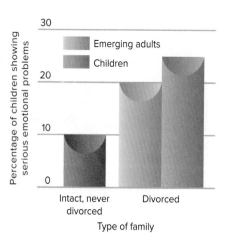

FIGURE 5

EMOTIONAL PROBLEMS IN CHILDREN AND EMERGING ADULTS FROM DIVORCED FAMILIES. In Hetherington's research, 25 percent of children from divorced families had emotional problems, but that figure decreased to 20 percent in emerging adulthood. Ten percent of children and emerging adults from nondivorced families had emotional problems.

responsible, to have less competent intimate relationships, to drop out of school, to become sexually active at an earlier age, to take drugs, to associate with antisocial peers, and to have lower self-esteem (Conger & Chao, 1996; Hetherington, 2005, 2006; Hetherington & Kelly, 2002). A recent study found that adolescent girls from divorced families displayed lower levels of romantic competence (Shulman & others, 2012). However, mothers' ability to provide their daughters with a coherent account of their own adolescent romantic experiences alleviated the negative link of divorce to daughters' romantic behavior. And in another recent study, individuals who had experienced their parents' divorce were at a higher lifetime risk for engaging in a suicide attempt (Alonzo & others, 2015).

One study found that 20 years after their parents had divorced when they were children, approximately 80 percent of adults concluded that their parents' decision to divorce had been a wise one (Ahrons, 2004). However, a recent study concluded that parental divorce during childhood was linked to an increased number of cohabiting/marital partnerships and negative partner relationships at 16 to 30 years of age (Fergusson, McLeod, & Horwood, 2014). An important point is that the outcomes just described for the life event of parental divorce during childhood were explained by a variety of other factors and social contexts—parental history of illicit drug use, experience of childhood sexual abuse, lower SES status at the child's birth, and parental history of criminality.

Note that marital conflict may have negative consequences for children in the context of marriage or divorce (Bergman, Cummings, & Davies, 2014; Cummings, Koss, & Davies, 2014). A longitudinal study revealed that conflict in nondivorced families was associated with emotional problems in children (Amato, 2006). A recent study of 14- to 17-year-olds in Spain found that those living in nondivorced, intact families who perceived the existence of high marital conflict between their parents engaged in more frequent and higher-risk sexual activity than their counterparts living in divorced families (Orgiles, Carratala, & Espada, 2015).

Indeed, many of the problems that children from divorced homes experience begin during the predivorce period, a time when parents are often in active conflict with each other. Thus, when children from divorced homes show problems, the problems may be due not only to the divorce but to the marital conflict that led to it (Thompson, 2008).

E. Mark Cummings and his colleagues (Cummings & Davies, 2010; Cummings, El-Sheikh, & Kouros, 2009; Cummings, Koss, & Davies, 2015; Cummings & Kouros, 2008; Cummings & Miller, 2015; Cummings & others, 2012; Cummings & Valentino, 2015; Koss & others, 2013, 2014; Yan, Cheung, & Cummings, 2015) have proposed *emotional security theory,* which has its roots in attachment theory and states that children appraise marital conflict in terms of their sense of security and safety in the family. These researchers make a distinction between marital conflict that is negative for children (such as hostile emotional displays and destructive conflict tactics) and marital conflict that can be positive for children (such as a marital disagreement that involves calmly discussing each person's perspective and working together to reach a solution). In a recent study, Cummings and his colleagues (2012) found that parental conflict in their children's kindergarten year was linked to children's emotional insecurity later in childhood, which in turn was associated with adolescent adjustment difficulties, including higher levels of depression and anxiety.

Despite the emotional problems that some adolescents and emerging adults from divorced families have, the weight of the research evidence underscores that most adolescents and emerging adults cope successfully with their parents' divorce and that a majority of adolescents and emerging adults in divorced families do not have significant adjustment problems (Ahrons, 2007; Barber & Demo, 2006).

Should Parents Stay Together for the Sake of Their Children and Adolescents? Whether parents should stay in an unhappy or conflicted marriage for the sake of their children and adolescents is one of the most commonly asked questions about divorce (Hetherington, 2005, 2006). If the stresses and disruptions in family relationships associated with an unhappy, conflicted marriage that erode the well-being of the children and adolescents are reduced by the move to a divorced, single-parent family, divorce might be advantageous (Yu & others, 2010). However, if the diminished resources and increased risks associated with divorce also are accompanied by inept parenting and sustained or increased conflict, not only between the divorced couple but also between parents, children, and siblings, the best choice for the children would be for an unhappy marriage to be retained (Hetherington &

What concerns are involved in whether parents should stay together for the sake of the children or become divorced?
© BananaStock/PunchStock RF

As marriage has become a more optional, less permanent institution in contemporary America, children and adolescents are encountering stresses and adaptive challenges associated with their parents' marital transitions.

—E. MAVIS HETHERINGTON
Contemporary psychologist, University of Virginia

developmental **connection**

Personality

Easy, difficult, and slow to warm up represent one classification of temperament styles. Connect to "The Self, Identity, Emotion, and Personality."

Stanley-Hagan, 2002). These are "ifs," and it is difficult to determine how these will play out when parents either remain together in an acrimonious marriage or become divorced.

How Much Do Family Processes Matter in Divorced Families?

In divorced families, family processes matter a great deal (Braver & Lamb, 2013; Hetherington, 2006; Lansford, 2009, 2012, 2013; Sigal & others, 2011; Warshak, 2014). When the divorced parents have a harmonious relationship and use authoritative parenting, the adjustment of adolescents is improved (Hetherington, 2006). When the divorced parents can agree on child-rearing strategies and can maintain a cordial relationship with each other, frequent visits by the noncustodial parent usually benefit the child (Fabricus & others, 2010). In a recent study, children were more likely to have behavior problems if their post-divorce home environment was less supportive and stimulating, their mother was less sensitive and more depressed, and if their household income was lower (Weaver & Schofield, 2015).

However, two longitudinal studies revealed that conflict (especially when it is intense and prolonged) between divorced parents was linked to emotional problems, insecure social relationships, and antisocial behavior in adolescents (Hetherington, 2006). A secure attachment also matters. Researchers have shown that a disequilibrium, including diminished parenting skills, occurs in the year following the divorce, but that by two years after the divorce restabilization has occurred and parenting skills have improved (Hetherington, 1989). Father involvement with children drops off more than mother involvement, especially for fathers of girls. About one-fourth to one-third of adolescents in divorced families, compared with 10 percent in nondivorced families, become disengaged from their families, spending as little time as possible at home and in interaction with family members (Hetherington & Kelly, 2002). This disengagement is higher for boys than for girls in divorced families. However, if the adolescent interacts with a caring adult outside the home, such as a mentor, the disengagement can be a positive solution to a disrupted, conflicted family circumstance. Also, a recent study of divorced families revealed that an intervention focused on improving the mother-child relationship was linked to improvements in relationship quality that increased children's and adolescents' coping skills over the short term (6 months) and long term (6 years) (Velez & others, 2011).

What Factors Are Involved in the Adolescent's Risk and Vulnerability in a Divorced Family?

Among the factors involved in the adolescent's risk and vulnerability are the adolescent's adjustment prior to the divorce, personality and temperament, developmental status, gender, and custody. Children and adolescents whose parents later divorce show poorer adjustment before the breakup (Amato & Dorius, 2010).

Personality, temperament, and intelligence also play a role in adolescent adjustment in divorced families. Adolescents who are socially mature and responsible, who show few behavioral problems, and who have an easy temperament are better able to cope with their parents' divorce. Children and adolescents with a difficult temperament often have problems coping with their parents' divorce (Hetherington & Stanley-Hagan, 2002). In a recent study, a higher level of predivorce maternal sensitivity and child IQ served as protective factors in reducing child problems after the divorce (Weaver & Schofield, 2015).

Focusing on the developmental status of the child or adolescent involves taking into account the age at onset of the divorce and the time when the child's or adolescent's adjustment is assessed. In most studies, these factors are confounded with length of time since the divorce occurred. Some researchers have found that preschool children whose parents divorce are at greater risk for long-term problems than are older children (Zill, Morrison, & Coiro, 1993). The explanation for this increased vulnerability focuses on their inability to realistically appraise the causes and consequences of divorce, their anxiety

A College Student Reflects on Growing Up in a Divorced Family

"It has always been painful knowing that I have a father who is alive and perfectly capable of acting like a parent, but who does not care about me. As a child, I was often depressed and acted out. As I grew older I had very low self-esteem. In junior high school, although I was successful, I felt like I belonged to the 'loser crowd.' . . . After I graduated from high school, I decided I still needed to fill the emptiness in my life by finding out at least a little bit about my father. I was seventeen when I found his number and called to see if he would be willing to talk. After a long hesitation, he agreed. We met and spent the day together. He has called me regularly ever since. Today I am better able to understand what I was feeling all those years. Now I am able to say without guilt that the absence of my father caused me much pain. I no longer feel abandoned, but many of the scars still remain. I still haven't been able to bring myself to call him 'Dad.'

There were two positive consequences of my parents' divorce for me: I discovered my own strength by living through this most difficult experience and surviving the loss of my father, and I developed this close bond with my mother from sharing the experience. She and I have become best friends.

Fortunately I had my friends, my teachers, my grandparents, and my brother to help me through the whole crazy-making time after my parents' divorce. The most important people were my brother and a teacher I had in the sixth and seventh grades. My brother was important because he was the only constant in my life; we shared every experience. My teacher was important because she took an interest in me and showed compassion. My grandparents offered consistent support. They gave my mother money for rent and food and paid for private schools for my brother and me; they were like second parents to us."

about the possibility of abandonment, their self-blame for the divorce, and their inability to use extrafamilial protective resources. However, problems in adjustment can emerge or increase during adolescence, even if the divorce occurred much earlier. As we discussed earlier, whether a divorce occurs earlier or later in children's or adolescents' development is linked to the types of problems the children and adolescents are likely to develop (Lansford & others, 2006).

In recent decades, an increasing number of children and adolescents have lived in father-custody and joint-custody families (Gunsberg & Hymowitz, 2013; Laftman & others, 2014; Sodermans & Matthijs, 2014; Wulach & Shapiro, 2013). What is their adjustment like, compared with the adjustment of children and adolescents in mother-custody families? Although there have been few thorough studies of the topic, a review of studies concluded that children benefit from joint custody because it facilitates ongoing positive involvement with both parents (Bauserman, 2003). Joint custody works best for children when the parents can get along with each other (Clarke-Stewart & Parke, 2014; Solnit & Nordhaus, 2013; Warshak, 2014).

Some studies have shown that boys adjust better in father-custody families and that girls adjust better in mother-custody families, but other studies have not shown these results. In one study, adolescents in father-custody families had higher rates of delinquency, believed to be due to less-competent monitoring by the fathers (Buchanan, Maccoby, & Dornsbusch, 1992).

Another factor involved in an adolescent's adjustment in a divorced family is relocation. One study found that when children and adolescents whose parents have divorced experience a move away by either of their parents, they show less effective adjustment (Braver, Ellman, & Fabricus, 2003).

What Role Does Socioeconomic Status Play in the Lives of Adolescents in Divorced Families? On average, custodial mothers' income decreases about 25 to 50 percent from their predivorce income, in comparison to a decrease of only 10 percent for custodial fathers (Emery, 1999). This income decrease for divorced mothers is typically accompanied by increased workloads, high rates of job instability, and residential moves to less desirable neighborhoods with inferior schools (Braver & Lamb, 2013). A recent study found that children from families that had higher incomes before the separation/divorce had fewer internalizing problems (Weaver & Schofield, 2015).

STEPFAMILIES

Not only are parents divorcing more, they are also getting remarried more (Ganong, Coleman, & Russell, 2015; Hetherington, 2006; Marsiglio & Hinojosa, 2010; van Eeden-Moorefield & Pasley, 2013). It takes time for couples to marry, have children, get divorced, and then remarry. Consequently, there are far more elementary and secondary school children than infant or preschool children in stepfamilies.

The number of remarriages involving children has grown steadily in recent years. As a result of their parents' successive marital transitions, about half of all children whose parents divorce will have a stepfather within four years of parental separation. Furthermore, divorces occur at a 10 percent higher rate in remarriages than in first marriages (Cherlin & Furstenberg, 1994).

Types of Stepfamilies   There are different types of stepfamilies. Some types are based on family structure, others on relationships. The stepfamily may have been preceded by a circumstance in which a spouse died. However, a large majority of stepfamilies are preceded by a divorce rather than a death.

Three common types of stepfamily structure are (1) stepfather, (2) stepmother, and (3) blended or complex. In stepfather families, the mother typically had custody of the children and became remarried, introducing a stepfather into her children's lives. In stepmother families, the father usually had custody and became remarried, introducing a stepmother into his children's lives. And, in a blended or complex stepfamily, both parents bring children from previous marriages to live in the newly formed stepfamily.

Adjustment   As in divorced families, adolescents in stepfamilies have more adjustment problems than do their counterparts in nondivorced families (Ganong, Coleman, & Russell, 2015; Hetherington, 2006; Hetherington & Kelly, 2002). The adjustment problems of adolescents in stepfamilies are much like those of adolescents in divorced families: academic problems, externalizing and internalizing problems, lower self-esteem, early sexual activity, delinquency, and so on (Hetherington, 2006). Adjustment for parents and children may take longer in stepfamilies (up to five years or more) than in divorced families, in which a restabilization is more likely to occur within two years (Anderson & others, 1999; Hetherington, 2006). One aspect of a stepfamily that makes adjustment difficult is **boundary ambiguity,** the uncertainty in stepfamilies about who is in or out of the family and who is performing or responsible for certain tasks in the family system.

Researchers have found that children's relationships with custodial parents (mother in stepfather families, father in stepmother families) are often better than with stepparents (Santrock, Sitterle, & Warshak, 1988). However, when adolescents have a positive relationship with their stepfather, it is related to fewer adolescent problems (Flouri, 2004). Also, adolescents in simple stepfamilies (stepfather, stepmother) often show better adjustment than their counterparts in complex (blended) families (Anderson & others, 1999; Hetherington, 2006).

There is an increase in adjustment problems of adolescents in newly remarried families (Hetherington, 2006; Hetherington & Clingempeel, 1992). In research conducted by James Bray and his colleagues (Bray, Berger, & Boethel, 1999; Bray & Kelly, 1998), the formation of a stepfamily often meant that adolescents had to move, and the move involved changing schools and friends. It took time for the stepparent to get to know the stepchildren. The new spouses had to learn how to cope with the challenges of their relationship and parenting together. In Bray's view, the formation of a stepfamily was like merging two cultures.

Bray and his colleagues also found that when the stepparent tried to discipline the stepchild, it often did not work well. Most experts recommend that in the early period of a

How does living in a stepfamily influence children's and adolescents' development?
© Todd Wright/Blend Images/Getty Images RF

boundary ambiguity Uncertainty in stepfamilies about who is in or out of the family and who is performing or responsible for certain tasks in the family system.

stepfamily the biological parent should be the parent doing any disciplining of the child that is needed. The stepparent-stepchild relationship develops best when the stepparent spends time with the stepchild in activities that the child enjoys.

In Hetherington's (2006) most recent analysis, adolescents who had been in a simple stepfamily for a number of years were adjusting better than in the early years of the remarried family and were functioning well in comparison with adolescents in conflicted nondivorced families and adolescents in complex stepfamilies. More than 75 percent of the adolescents in long-established simple stepfamilies described their relationships with their stepparents as "close" or "very close." Hetherington (2006) concludes that in long-established simple step-families adolescents seem eventually to benefit from the presence of a stepparent and the resources provided by the stepparent.

In terms of the age of the child, researchers have found that early adolescence is an especially difficult time for the formation of a stepfamily (Bray & Kelly, 1998; Hetherington & others, 1999). Problems may occur because the stepfamily circumstances exacerbate normal adolescent concerns about identity, sexuality, and autonomy.

Now that we have considered the changing social worlds of adolescents when their parents divorce and remarry, we turn our attention to another aspect of the changing family worlds of adolescents—the situation when both parents work outside the home.

WORKING PARENTS

Interest in the effects of parental work on the development of children and adolescents has increased in recent years. Our examination of parental work focuses on the following issues: the role of working parents in adolescents' development and the adjustment of latchkey adolescents.

Working Parents and Adolescent Adjustment   More than one of every two U.S. mothers with a child under the age of 5 is in the labor force; more than two of every three with a child from 6 to 17 years of age is employed. Maternal employment is a part of modern life, but its effects are still debated.

Most of the research on parental work has focused on young children and on the mother's employment (Brooks-Gunn, Han, & Waldfogel, 2010). However, the effects of working parents involve the father as well when such matters as work schedules, work-family stress, and unemployment are considered (O'Brien & Moss, 2010; Clarke-Stewart & Parke, 2014). For example, a recent study of almost 3,000 adolescents found a negative association of the father's, but not the mother's, unemployment on the adolescents' health (Bacikova-Sleskova, Benka, & Orosova, 2014).

Until recently, little attention has been given to the role of parents' work on adolescents (Crouter, 2006). Recent research indicates that what matters for adolescent development is the nature of parents' work rather than whether one parent works outside the home (Goodman & others, 2011; Han, 2009; Parke & Clarke-Stewart, 2011). Ann Crouter (2006) described how parents bring their experiences at work into their homes. She concluded that parents who have poor working conditions, such as long hours, overtime work, stressful work, and lack of autonomy at work, are likely to be more irritable at home and engage in less effective parenting than their counterparts who have better working conditions in their jobs. The negative working conditions of parents are linked to more behavior problems and lower grades in their adolescents. One study found that, when fathers worked more than 60 hours per week and perceived that their work overload gave them too little time to do what they wanted, their relationship with their adolescents was more conflicted (Crouter & others, 2001). Also, a recent study revealed that mothers' positive mood after work was linked with adolescents' reports of more positive affect, better sleep quality, and longer sleep duration (Lawson & others, 2014). Further in this study, mothers with more positive work experiences had adolescents who reported less negative affect and fewer physical health

How might parents' work schedules and work stress influence adolescents' development?
© The Photo Works/Alamy

problems. A consistent finding is that the children (especially girls) of working mothers engage in less gender stereotyping and have more egalitarian views of gender (Goldberg & Lucas-Thompson, 2008).

Latchkey Adolescents   Although the mother's employment is not necessarily associated with negative outcomes for adolescents, a certain set of adolescents from working-mother families bears further scrutiny—those called *latchkey adolescents*. Latchkey adolescents typically do not see their parents from the time they leave for school in the morning until about 6:00 or 7:00 p.m. They are called "latchkey" children or adolescents because they carry a key to their home and let themselves into the home while their parents are still at work. Many latchkey adolescents are largely unsupervised for two to four hours a day during each school week, or for entire days, five days a week, during the summer months. A recent survey found that 15.1 million children and adolescents in the United States are alone and unsupervised after school (Afterschool Alliance, 2009).

Some latchkey children may grow up too quickly, hurried by the responsibilities placed on them. How do latchkey children handle the lack of limits and structure during the latchkey hours? Without limits and parental supervision, latchkey children find their way into trouble more easily, possibly stealing, vandalizing, or abusing a sibling. Joan Lipsitz (1983), in testifying before the Select Committee on Children, Youth, and Families, called the lack of adult supervision of children in the after-school hours a major problem. Lipsitz called it the "three-to-six o'clock problem" because it was during this time that the Center for Early Adolescence in North Carolina, when Lipsitz was director, experienced a peak of referrals for clinical help.

Although latchkey adolescents can be vulnerable to problems, keep in mind that the experiences of latchkey adolescents vary enormously, just as do the experiences of all adolescents with working mothers. Parents need to give special attention to the ways they can monitor their latchkey adolescents' lives effectively. Variations in latchkey experiences suggest that parental monitoring and authoritative parenting help the adolescent to cope more effectively with latchkey experiences, especially in resisting peer pressure (Galambos & Maggs, 1991; Steinberg, 1986). The degree to which latchkey adolescents are at developmental risk remains undetermined. A positive sign is that researchers are beginning to conduct more precise analyses of adolescents' latchkey experiences in an effort to determine which aspects of latchkey circumstances are the most detrimental and which aspects foster better adaptation. One study that focused on the after-school hours found that unsupervised peer contact, lack of neighborhood safety, and low monitoring were linked with externalizing problems (such as acting out and delinquency) in young adolescents (Pettit & others, 1999).

ADOPTION

Another variation in the type of family in which children live involves adoption, the social and legal process by which a parent-child relationship is established between persons unrelated at birth. As we see next, an increase in diversity has characterized the adoption of children in the United States in recent years.

The Increased Diversity of Adopted Children and Adoptive Parents   A number of changes have characterized adoptive children and adoptive parents in the last three to four decades (Brodzinsky & Pinderhughes, 2002; Kim, Reichwald, & Lee, 2013). In the first half of the twentieth century, most U.S. adopted children were healthy, non-Latino White infants who were adopted at birth or soon after; however, in recent decades as abortion became legal and contraception increased, fewer of these infants became available for adoption. Increasingly, U.S. couples have adopted a much wider diversity of children—from other countries, from other ethnic groups, children with physical and/or mental problems, and children who had been neglected or abused (Kim, Reichwald, & Lee, 2013).

Changes also have characterized adoptive parents in the last three to four decades (Brodzinsky & Pinderhughes, 2002). In the first half of the twentieth century, most adoptive parents were people from non-Latino White middle or upper socioeconomic status backgrounds who were married and did not have any type of disability. However, in recent decades, increased diversity has characterized adoptive parents. Many adoption agencies today have no income requirements for adoptive parents and now allow adults from a wide range of backgrounds

developmental **connection**

Schools

Adolescents who participate in high-quality extracurricular activities have positive developmental outcomes. Connect to "Schools."

to adopt children, including single adults, gay and lesbian adults, and older adults. Further, many adoptions involve other family members (such as aunts, uncles, or grandparents); currently, 30 percent of U.S. adoptive placements are with relatives (Ledesma, 2012). And slightly more than 50 percent of U.S. adoptions occur through the foster care system; recently, more than 100,000 children in the U.S. foster care system were waiting for someone to adopt them (Ledesma, 2012).

Three pathways to adoption are: (1) domestic adoption from the public welfare system, (2) domestic infant adoption through private agencies and intermediaries, and (3) international adoption (Grotevant & McDermott, 2014). In the next decade, the mix of U.S. adoptions is likely to include fewer domestic infant and international adoptions and more adoptions via the child welfare system (Grotevant & McDermott, 2014).

The changes in adoption practice over the last several decades make it difficult to generalize about the average adopted child or average adoptive parent (Woolgar & Scott, 2013). As we see next, though, some researchers have provided useful comparisons between adopted children and nonadopted children and their families.

Developmental Outcomes for Adopted and Nonadopted Children How do adopted children fare after they are adopted? A recent research review concluded that adopted children are at higher risk for externalizing (aggression and conduct problems, for example), internalizing (anxiety and depression, for example), and attention problems (ADHD, for example) (Grotevant & McDermott, 2014). However, a majority of adopted children and adolescents (including those adopted at older ages, transracially, and across national borders) adjust effectively, and their parents report considerable satisfaction with their decision to adopt (Brodzinsky & Pinderhughes, 2002; Castle & others, 2010).

An ongoing issue in adopting children is whether there should be any connection with children's biological parents. Open adoption involves sharing identifying information and having contact with the biological parents, versus closed adoption, which consists of not having such sharing and contact. Most adoption agencies today offer adoptive parents the opportunity to have either an open or a closed adoption. A longitudinal study found that when their adopted children reached adulthood, adoptive parents described open adoption positively and saw it as serving the child's best interests (Siegel, 2013). Another longitudinal study found that birth mothers, adoptive parents, and birth children who had contact were more satisfied with their arrangements than those who did not have contact (Grotevant & others, 2013). Also, in this study, contact was linked to more optimal adjustment for adolescents and emerging adults (Grotevant & others, 2013). Further, birth mothers who were more satisfied with their contact arrangements had less unresolved grief 12 to 20 years after placement.

Parenting Adopted Children Many of the keys to effectively parenting adopted children are no different from those for effectively parenting biological children: be supportive and caring; be involved and monitor the child's behavior and whereabouts; be a good communicator; and help the child learn to develop self-control. However, parents of adopted children face some unique circumstances. They need to recognize the differences involved in adoptive family life, communicate about these differences, show respect for the birth family, and support the child's search for self and identity.

Because many children begin to ask where they came from when they are about 4 to 6 years old, this is a natural time for parents to begin talking in simple ways to children about their adoption status (Warshak, 2008). Some parents (although not as many as in the past) decide not to tell their children about the adoption. This secrecy may create psychological risks for the child if he or she later finds out about the adoption.

GAY AND LESBIAN PARENTS

Increasingly, gay and lesbian couples are creating families that include children (Golombok & Tasker, 2015; Patterson, 2013, 2014; Patterson & D'Augelli, 2013) (see Figure 6). Approximately 33 percent of lesbian couples and 23 percent of gay couples are parents (Patterson, 2004). There may be more than 1 million gay and lesbian parents in the United States today.

What are some changes in adoption practice in recent decades in the United States?
© Xinhua/ZUMApress/Newscom

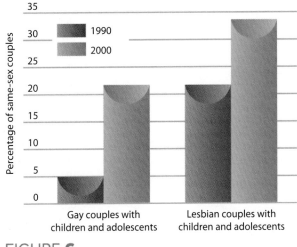

FIGURE 6

PERCENTAGE OF GAY AND LESBIAN COUPLES WITH CHILDREN: 1990 AND 2000. *Why do you think more lesbian couples have children than gay couples?*

An important aspect of gay and lesbian families with children is the sexual identity of parents at the time of a child's birth or adoption (Patterson, 2013, 2014). The largest group of children with gay and lesbian parents are likely those who were born in the context of heterosexual relationships, with one or both parents only later identifying themselves as gay or lesbian. Gay and lesbian parents may be single or they may have same-gender partners. In addition, gays and lesbians are increasingly choosing parenthood through donor insemination or adoption. Researchers have found that the children created through new reproductive technologies—such as in vitro fertilization—are as well adjusted as their counterparts conceived by natural means (Golombok, 2011a, b; Golombok & Tasker, 2015).

Earlier in the chapter, we describe the positive outcomes of coparenting for children. A recent study compared the incidence of coparenting in adoptive heterosexual, lesbian, and gay couples with preschool-aged children (Farr & Patterson, 2013). Both self-reports and observations found that lesbian and gay couples shared child care more than heterosexual couples, with lesbian couples being the most supportive. Further, a recent study revealed more positive parenting in adoptive gay father families and fewer child externalizing problems in these families than in heterosexual families (Golombok & others, 2014).

Another issue focuses on custody arrangements for adolescents. Many gays and lesbians have lost custody of their adolescents to heterosexual spouses following divorce. For this reason, many gay fathers and lesbian mothers are noncustodial parents.

Researchers have found few differences between children growing up with gay fathers and lesbian mothers and children growing up with heterosexual parents (Patterson, 2013, 2014; Patterson, Farr, & Hastings, 2015). For example, children growing up in gay or lesbian families are just as popular with their peers, and there are no differences between the adjustment and mental health of children living in these families and children living in heterosexual families (Hyde & DeLamater, 2014). Also, the overwhelming majority of children growing up in a gay or lesbian family have a heterosexual orientation (Golombok & Tasker, 2015).

CULTURE AND ETHNICITY

What are some variations in families across different cultures? How do families vary across different ethnic groups?

Cross-Cultural Comparisons   Cultures vary on a number of issues involving families, such as what the father's role in the family should be, the extent to which support systems are available to families, and how children and adolescents should be disciplined (Fuligni & Tsai, 2015; Mistry & Dutta, 2015). Although there are cross-cultural variations in parenting, in one study of parenting behavior in 186 cultures around the world, the most common pattern was a warm and controlling style, one that was neither permissive nor restrictive (Rohner & Rohner, 1981). The investigators commented that the majority of cultures have discovered, over many centuries, a "truth" that has only recently emerged in the Western world—namely, that children's and adolescents' healthy social development is most effectively promoted by love and at least some moderate parental control.

Nonetheless, in some countries, authoritarian parenting continues to be widely practiced (Rothbaum & Trommsdorff, 2007). In the Arab world, families today are still very authoritarian and dominated by the father's rule (Booth, 2002). In Arab countries, adolescents are taught strict codes of conduct and family loyalty.

Cultural change is coming to many families around the world (Fuligni & Tsai, 2015). There are trends toward greater family mobility, migration to urban areas, family members working in distant cities or countries, smaller families, fewer extended-family households, and increases in the mothers' employment (Brown & Larson, 2002). These trends can change the resources that are available to adolescents. For example, many families have fewer extended family members nearby, resulting in decreased support and guidance for adolescents. Also, smaller families may produce more openness and communication between parents and adolescents.

Ethnicity and Parenting   Ethnic minority families differ from non-Latino White American families in their size, structure and composition, reliance on kinship networks, and levels of income and education (Duncan, Magnuson, & Votruba-Drzal, 2015; Murry & others, 2015). Large and extended families are more common among ethnic minority groups than

The family reunion of the Limon family in Austin, Texas. Mexican American children and adolescents often grow up in families with a network of relatives that encompasses scores of individuals.
© Ariel Skelly/Blend Images LLC RF

A 14-year-old adolescent, his 6-year-old sister, and their grandmother. The African American cultural tradition of an extended-family household has helped many African American parents cope with adverse social conditions.
© Erika Stone

among non-Latino White Americans. For example, more than 30 percent of Latino families consist of five or more individuals. African American and Latino children interact more with grandparents, aunts, uncles, cousins, and more distant relatives than do non-Latino White American children (McAdoo, 2006).

Ethnic minority adolescents are more likely to come from low-income families than non-Latino White American adolescents are (Leventhal, Dupere, & Shuey, 2015; McLoyd, Purtell, & Hardaway, 2015). Single-parent families are more common among African Americans and Latinos than among non-Latino White Americans (Harris & Graham, 2007). In comparison with two-parent households, single-parent households often have more limited resources of time, money, and energy. This shortage of resources can prompt parents to encourage autonomy among their adolescents prematurely. Ethnic minority parents, on average, are less well educated and engage in less joint decision making than non-Latino White American parents. Although impoverished families often raise competent youth, poor parents can have a diminished capacity for supportive and involved parenting (McLoyd & others, 2009).

Some aspects of home life can help to protect ethnic minority youth from social patterns of injustice. The community and family can filter out destructive racist messages, parents can provide alternate frames of reference to counteract those presented by the majority, and parents can also provide competent role models and encouragement. And the extended-family system in many ethnic minority families constitutes an important buffer to stress (Gonzales & others, 2007).

A sense of family duty and obligation also varies across ethnic groups (Fuligni & Tsai, 2015). Asian American and Latino families place a greater emphasis on family duty and obligation than do non-Latino White families (Perez-Brena, Updegraff, & Umana-Taylor, 2015). In a study of 18- to 25-year-olds, more Asian Americans said family interdependence was important to them than did non-Latino Whites (Tseng, 2004). Researchers have found that more Asian American and Latino adolescents believe that they should spend time taking care of their siblings, helping around the house, assisting their parents at work, and being with their family than do adolescents with a European heritage (Fuligni, Tseng, & Lamb, 1999). A recent study of Asian American adolescents found that family obligation was linked to their adjustment and helped to buffer the negative influence of financial stress in lower-income families during the later high school years (Kiang & others, 2013). Another recent study of Mexican American adolescents revealed that having family obligation values was linked to lower substance use, which was due in part to less association with deviant peers and a higher level of adolescent disclosure to parents (Telzer, Gonzales, & Fuligni, 2014).

developmental **connection**

Culture and Ethnicity

Many families that have immigrated to the United States in recent decades, such as Mexican American and Asian American families, come from collectivist cultures in which family obligation is strong. Connect to "Culture."

Of course, individual families vary, and how ethnic minority families deal with stress depends on many factors (Fuligni & Tsai, 2015; Xia, Kieu, & Xie, 2013). Whether the parents are native-born or immigrants, how long the family has been in the United States, their socioeconomic status, and their specific national origin all make a difference (Hayashino & Chopra, 2009). The characteristics of the family's social context also influence its adaptation. What are the attitudes toward the family's ethnic group within its neighborhood or city? Can the family's children attend good schools? Are there community groups that welcome people from the family's ethnic group? Do members of the family's ethnic group form community groups of their own?

Review Connect Reflect

 LG4 Describe the changing family in a changing society

Review

- What are the effects of divorce on adolescents?
- How does growing up in a stepfamily influence adolescents' development?
- How do working parents influence adolescent development?
- How does being adopted affect adolescent development?
- What are the effects on adolescents of having gay or lesbian parents?
- What roles do culture and ethnicity play in families with adolescents?

Connect

- What did you learn about siblings earlier in this chapter that might inform your understanding of stepfamilies and the issues they face?

Reflect *Your Own Personal Journey of Life*

- You have studied many aspects of families and adolescents in this chapter. Imagine that you have decided to write a book describing life in your family when you were an adolescent. What would the title of the book be? What would be the main theme of the book?

5 Social Policy, Adolescents, and Families

LG5 Explain what is needed for improved social policy involving adolescents and their families

We have seen in this chapter that parents play very important roles in adolescent development. Although adolescents are moving toward independence, they are still connected with their families, which are far more important to them than is commonly believed (Kerig & others, 2012; Kobak & Kerig, 2015; Kobak & others, 2015). We know that competent adolescent development is most likely to happen when adolescents have parents who do the following things:

- Show them support, warmth, and respect
- Demonstrate sustained interest in their lives
- Recognize and adapt to their changing cognitive and socioemotional development
- Communicate expectations for high standards of conduct and achievement
- Display authoritative, constructive ways of dealing with problems and conflict

However, compared with families who have young children, families with adolescents have been neglected in community programs and public policies. The Carnegie Council on Adolescent Development (1995) identified some key opportunities for improving social policy regarding families with adolescents. Even now, in the middle of the second decade of the twenty-first century, the recommendations made by the council in 1995 still need to be followed:

- Schools, cultural arts centers, religious and youth organizations, and health-care agencies should examine the extent to which they involve parents in activities with adolescents and should develop ways to engage parents and adolescents in activities that both generations enjoy.

- Professionals such as teachers, psychologists, nurses, physicians, youth specialists, and others who have contact with adolescents need not only to work with the individual adolescent but also to increase the time they spend interacting with the adolescent's family.
- Employers should extend to the parents of young adolescents the workplace policies now reserved only for the parents of young children. These policies include flexible work schedules, job sharing, telecommuting, and part-time work with benefits. This change in work/family policy would free parents to spend more time with their teenagers.
- Community institutions such as businesses, schools, and youth organizations should become more involved in providing after-school programs. After-school programs for elementary school children are increasing, but such programs for adolescents are rare. More high-quality, community-based programs for adolescents are needed in the after-school, weekend, and vacation time periods.

Community programs such as this one in East Orange, New Jersey, can provide a monitored, structured context for adolescents to study in during the after-school hours. *In addition to improving after-school options for adolescents, what are some other ways that U.S. social policy could be improved to support families with adolescents?*
© Tim Farrell/Star Ledger/Corbis

Several national organizations develop and advocate supportive family policies at the federal, state, and local levels. Four of the best organizations in this regard are listed below:

- The Annie E. Casey Foundation (www.aecf.org)
- First Focus, a Washington, D.C.-based policy center whose mission is to make children and families a major priority (www.firstfocus.net)
- The Institute for Youth, Education, and Families at the National League of Cities (www.nlc.org)
- The National Collaboration for Youth (www.collab4youth.org)

Review Connect Reflect

LG5 Explain what is needed for improved social policy involving adolescents and their families

Review
- What is needed for improved social policy involving adolescents and their families?

Connect
- Do current social policies appear to view the family as a system?

Reflect *Your Own Personal Journey of Life*
- If you were a U.S. senator, what would you seek to do to improve social policy involving the families of adolescents? What would be your number one priority?

reach your **learning goals**

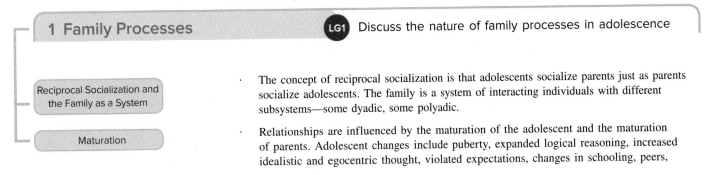

Families

1 Family Processes

LG1 Discuss the nature of family processes in adolescence

Reciprocal Socialization and the Family as a System

Maturation

- The concept of reciprocal socialization is that adolescents socialize parents just as parents socialize adolescents. The family is a system of interacting individuals with different subsystems—some dyadic, some polyadic.

- Relationships are influenced by the maturation of the adolescent and the maturation of parents. Adolescent changes include puberty, expanded logical reasoning, increased idealistic and egocentric thought, violated expectations, changes in schooling, peers, friendships, dating, and movement toward independence. Changes in parents might include decreased marital satisfaction, economic burdens, career reevaluation, time perspective, and health/body concerns. Adults follow one developmental trajectory and children and adolescents another one. How these trajectories mesh affects timing of entry into various family tasks.

2 Adolescents' and Emerging Adults' Relationships with Their Parents

LG2 Describe adolescents' and emerging adults' relationships with their parents

Parents as Managers

· An increasing trend is to conceptualize parents as managers of adolescents' lives. This involves being a parent who finds information, makes contacts, helps structure choices, and provides guidance. Parents can serve as regulators of their adolescents' social contacts with peers, friends, and adults. A key aspect of the managerial role involves parental monitoring. A current interest focuses on adolescents' management of their parents' access to information.

Parenting Styles

· Authoritarian, authoritative, neglectful, and indulgent are four main parenting styles. Authoritative parenting, which encourages independence but places limits and controls on adolescents, is associated with socially competent adolescent behavior more than the other styles. Some ethnic variations in parenting have been found, such as the positive relation between training by Asian American parents and the achievement of their adolescents. Recent research indicates that an authoritative parenting style also benefits emerging adults but a controlling-indulgent style is related to negative outcomes for emerging adults.

Mothers, Fathers, and Coparenting

· Both mothers and fathers play important, but sometimes different, roles in adolescents' development. Coparenting, father-mother cooperation, and mutual respect enhance the adolescent's development.

Parent-Adolescent Conflict

· Conflict with parents increases in early adolescence, but such conflict is usually moderate and can serve a positive developmental function related to increased independence and identity exploration. The magnitude of the generation gap has been exaggerated, although in as many as 20 percent of families parent-adolescent conflict is too high and is linked with adolescent problems.

Autonomy and Attachment

· Many parents have a difficult time handling the adolescent's push for autonomy. Autonomy is a complex concept with many referents. Developmental transitions in autonomy include the onset of early adolescence and the time when individuals leave home and go to college. A special concern about autonomy involves runaways. The wise parent relinquishes control in areas where the adolescent makes mature decisions and retains more control in areas where the adolescent makes immature decisions. Adolescents do not simply move away into a world isolated from parents. Attachment to parents in adolescence increases the probability that an adolescent will be socially competent and explore a widening social world in a healthy way. Increasingly, researchers classify attachment in adolescence into one secure category (secure/autonomous) and three insecure categories (dismissing/avoidant, preoccupied/ambivalent, and unresolved/disorganized). Increased interest in attachment during emerging adulthood is revealing that securely attached emerging adults have better social relationships than do insecurely attached emerging adults.

Emerging Adults' Relationships with Their Parents

· An increasing number of emerging adults are returning to live at home with their parents, often for economic reasons. Both emerging adults and their parents need to adapt when emerging adults return home to live.

Intergenerational Relationships

· Connections between parents play important roles in development through the life span. An increasing number of studies indicate that intergenerational relationships influence the development of adolescents. Marital interaction, a supportive family environment, divorce, and conduct disorder in the adolescent's family of origin are among the factors that are linked to later characteristics and relationships when the adolescent moves into adulthood.

3 Sibling Relationships

LG3 Characterize sibling relationships in adolescence

Sibling Roles

· Sibling relationships often involve more conflict than do relationships with other individuals. However, adolescents also share many positive moments with siblings by providing emotional support and social communication.

| Birth Order | • | The influence of birth order has been of special interest to researchers, and differences between firstborns and later-borns have been reported. The only child often is more socially competent than the "spoiled brat" stereotype suggests. An increasing number of family researchers believe that birth-order effects have been exaggerated and that other factors are more important in predicting the adolescent's behavior. |

4 The Changing Family in a Changing Society

LG4 Describe the changing family in a changing society

- Adolescents in divorced families have more adjustment problems than their counterparts in nondivorced families, although the size of the effects is debated. Whether parents should stay together for the sake of the adolescent is difficult to determine, although conflict has a negative effect on the adolescent. Adolescents are better adjusted in divorced families when their parents have a harmonious relationship with each other and use authoritative parenting. Among other factors to be considered in adolescent adjustment are adjustment prior to the divorce, personality and temperament, and developmental status, gender, and custody. Income loss for divorced mothers is linked to a number of other stresses that can affect adolescent adjustment.

Divorced Families

- An increasing number of adolescents are growing up in stepfamilies. Stepfamilies involve different structures (stepfather, stepmother, blended). Adolescents in stepfamilies have more adjustment problems than do children in nondivorced homes. Adjustment is especially difficult during the first several years of a stepfamily's existence and is challenging for young adolescents.

Stepfamilies

- It is the nature of parents' work, not whether one parent works outside the home or does not, that is linked to adolescents' development. Latchkey experiences do not have a uniformly negative effect on adolescents. Parental monitoring and structured activities during the after-school hours benefit latchkey adolescents.

Working Parents

- Although adopted adolescents have more problems than their nonadopted counterparts do, the majority of adopted adolescents function effectively. When adoption occurs very early in development, the outcomes for the adolescent are better than when adoption occurs later. Because of the dramatic changes that have occurred in adoption in recent decades, it is difficult to generalize about the average adopted adolescent or average adoptive family.

Adoption

- There is considerable diversity among lesbian mothers, gay fathers, and their adolescents. Researchers have found few differences between adolescents growing up in gay or lesbian families and adolescents growing up in heterosexual families.

Gay and Lesbian Parents

- Authoritative parenting is the most common form of parenting around the world. Ethnic minority families differ from non-Latino White families in their size, structure, and composition, their reliance on kinship networks, and their levels of income and education.

Culture and Ethnicity

5 Social Policy, Adolescents, and Families

LG5 Explain what is needed for improved social policy involving adolescents and their families

- Families with adolescents have been neglected in social policy. A number of recommendations for improving social policy for families target the extent to which parents are involved in schools, youth organizations, and health-care agencies; the degree to which teachers and other professionals invite and encourage parents to be involved in schools and other settings that adolescents frequent; the extent to which policies are developed to allow employers to provide more flexible scheduling for parents; and the provision of greater funding by institutions such as businesses, schools, and youth organizations for high-quality programs for adolescents in after-school, weekend, and vacation time periods.

key **terms**

authoritarian parenting
authoritative parenting
boundary ambiguity
dismissing/avoidant attachment
emotional autonomy

indulgent parenting
insecure attachment
multiple developmental
  trajectories

neglectful parenting
preoccupied/ambivalent
  attachment
reciprocal socialization

secure attachment
unresolved/disorganized
  attachment

key **people**

Mary Ainsworth
Joseph Allen
Diana Baumrind

John Bowlby
Urie Bronfenbrenner
Ann Crouter

E. Mark Cummings
Judy Dunn

Andrew Fuligni
E. Mavis Hetherington

resources for **improving the lives of adolescents**

101 Insights and Strategies for Parenting Teenagers
Sheryl Feinstein (2010)
Monterey, CA: Healthy Learning
> An excellent, easy-to-read book for parents that provides valuable
> strategies for guiding adolescents through the transition from
> childhood to emerging adulthood.

You and Your Adolescent
Laurence Steinberg (2011)
New York: Simon and Schuster
> Leading adolescence expert Laurence Steinberg provides a broad,
> developmental overview of adolescence, with good advice for
> parents along the way.

Building a Brighter Future
National Collaboration for Youth (2011) (www.collab4youth.org)
> The National Collaboration for Youth is one of the most
> important national organizations involved in advocating positive
> social policy for youth and their families. This up-to-date report
> provides an essential agenda for America's youth.

Getting to 30: A Parent's Guide to the 20-Something Years
Jeffrey Arnett and Elizabeth Fishel (2014)
New York: Workman
> A parent's guide to emerging adulthood and the late twenties with
> many helpful strategies

Big Brothers Big Sisters of America (www.bbbsa.org)
> Single mothers and single fathers who are having problems with a
> son or daughter might want to get a responsible adult to spend at
> least one afternoon every other week with the son or daughter.

*Divorce Lessons: Real-Life Stories and What You Can Learn from
  Them*
Alison Clarke-Stewart and Cornelia Brentano (2006)
Charleston, SC: BookSurge
> An outstanding book that gives special attention to emerging adults'
> experiences and development while growing up in divorced families.

National Stepfamily Resource Center (www.stepfamilies.info)
This organization serves as a clearinghouse of information, resources,
and support for stepfamilies.

chapter 9

PEERS, ROMANTIC RELATIONSHIPS, AND LIFESTYLES

chapter outline

© omgimages/Getty Images RF

ynn Brown and Carol Gilligan (1992) conducted in-depth interviews of one hundred 10- to 13-year-old girls who were making the transition to adolescence. They listened to what these girls were saying about how important friends were to them. The girls were very curious about the human world they lived in and kept track of what was happening to their peers and friends. The girls spoke about the pleasure they derived from the intimacy and fun of human connection, and about the potential for hurt in relationships. They especially highlighted the importance of clique formation in their lives.

One girl, Noura, said that she learned about what it feels like to be the person that everyone doesn't like and that it was very painful. A number of the girls talked about how many girls say nice and kind things to be polite but often don't really mean them. They know the benefits of being perceived as the perfect, happy girl, at least on the surface. Suspecting that people prefer the "perfect girl," they experiment with her image and the happiness she might bring. Cliques can provide emotional support for girls who are striving to be perfect but know they are not. One girl, Victoria, commented that she and three other girls who are like her and who weren't very popular decided to form a "club." She now felt that when she was sad or depressed she could count on the "club" for support. Though they were "leftovers" and did not get into the most popular cliques, these four girls said they knew they were liked.

Another girl, Judy, at age 13, spoke about her interest in romantic relationships. She said that although she and her girlfriends were only 13 they wanted to be romantic, and she talked about her lengthy private conversations about boys with her girlfriends.

preview

In this chapter we consider peers, romantic relationships, and lifestyles. When you think back to your adolescent years, you may recall that many of your most enjoyable moments were spent with peers—on the telephone, in school activities, in the neighborhood, on dates, at dances, or just hanging out. Adolescents typically have a larger number of acquaintances than children do. Beginning in early adolescence, teenagers also typically prefer a smaller number of friendships that are more intense and intimate than those of children. Cliques and crowds take on more importance as adolescents "hang out" together. Dating and romantic relationships become part of most adolescents' and emerging adults' lives, and deciding on a specific lifestyle becomes particularly important in emerging adulthood.

1 Exploring Peer Relations and Friendship	**LG1** Discuss the roles of peer relations, friendship, and loneliness in adolescent development

Peer Relations	Friendship	Loneliness

Peers and friends play powerful roles in the lives of adolescents. Let's explore what these roles are.

PEER RELATIONS

What functions do peer groups serve? How are family and peer relations linked? How extensively do adolescents strive for conformity? What kinds of statuses do peers have? How do social cognition and emotions influence peer relations? What are some strategies for improving social skills? We will consider these and other questions in this section.

Peer Group Functions Adolescents have strong needs to be liked and accepted by friends and the larger peer group, which can result in pleasurable feelings when they are accepted or extreme stress and anxiety when they are excluded and disparaged by peers. To many adolescents, how they are seen by peers is the most important aspect of their lives.

Peers are individuals who are about the same age or maturity level. Same-age peer interaction serves a unique role in U.S. culture. Age grading would occur even if schools were not age graded and adolescents were left alone to determine the composition of their own societies. One of the most important functions of the peer group is to provide a source of information about the world outside the family. From the peer group, adolescents receive feedback about their abilities. Adolescents learn whether what they do is better than, as good as, or worse than what other adolescents do. Learning this at home is difficult because siblings are usually older or younger, and sibling rivalry can cloud the accuracy of comparison.

What functions do peers serve?
© Eric Audras/PhotoAlto/Getty Images RF

As you read about peers, also keep in mind that, although peer experiences have important influences on adolescents' development, those influences vary according to the way peer experience is measured, the outcomes specified, and the developmental trajectories traversed (Brown & Larson, 2009; Choukas-Bradley & Prinstein, 2013; Hartup, 2005; Prinstein & Giletta, 2015). "Peers" and "peer group" are global concepts that can be beneficial in understanding peer influences as long as their variations are considered. For example, the term *peers* can be used to describe acquaintances, members of a clique, neighborhood associates, friends, and participants in an activity group such as a sports team.

Peer Contexts Peer interaction is influenced by contexts, which can include the type of peer the adolescent interacts with (such as an acquaintance, a crowd, a clique, a friend, a romantic partner) and the situation or location where they are, such as school, neighborhood, community center, dance, religious setting, sporting event, and so on, as well as the culture in which the adolescent lives (Brown & others, 2008; Bukowski & others, 2015; Choukas-Bradley & Prinstein, 2013; Foshee & others, 2013; Prinstein & Giletta, 2015; Rubin, Bukowski, & Bowker, 2015). As they interact with peers in these various contexts, adolescents are likely to encounter different messages and different opportunities to engage in adaptive and maladaptive behavior that can influence their development (Brechwald & Prinstein, 2011). These peer contexts also are influenced by factors such as how effectively parents manage adolescents' peer interactions and whether adults are present (Caruthers, Van Ryzin, & Dishion, 2013; Mounts, 2011; Prinstein & Giletta, 2015). For example, one study revealed that when

developmental **connection**

Theory

Bronfenbrenner's ecological theory emphasizes the contexts of adolescent development. Connect to "Introduction."

peers Individuals who are about the same age or maturity level.

What are some examples of how social contexts and individual difference factors influence adolescents' peer relations'?
© Creatas/Punchstock RF

parents failed to monitor young adolescents adequately, the young adolescents were more susceptible to peer pressure (Steinberg, 1986).

Individual Difference Factors Individual differences among peers also are important influences on peer relations (Brechwald & Prinstein, 2011; Brown & others, 2008; Choukas-Bradley & Prinstein, 2013; Prinstein & Giletta, 2015). Among the wide range of individual differences that can affect peer relations are personality traits, such as how shy or outgoing an adolescent is. For example, a very shy adolescent is more likely than a gregarious adolescent to be neglected by peers and to feel anxious about introducing himself or herself to new peers. One individual difference factor that has been found to impair peer relations is the trait of negative emotionality, which involves a relatively low threshold for experiencing anger, fear, anxiety, and irritation. For example, one study revealed that adolescents who were characterized by negative emotionality tended to engage in negative interpersonal behavior when interacting with a friend or a romantic partner (Hatton & others, 2008). Other individual differences include the adolescent's openness to peer influence and the status/power of the adolescent versus the status/power of the other adolescent or adolescent peer group (Brown & Larson, 2009). Being in a subordinate social position in a dyad or group can decrease the likelihood that the adolescent can influence other peers but increases the probability that the adolescent will be open to peer influence.

developmental **connection**

Personality

Personality traits and temperament styles influence adolescent development. Connect to "The Self, Identity, Emotion, and Personality."

Developmental Changes in Time Spent with Peers Boys and girls spend an increasing amount of time in peer interaction during middle and late childhood and adolescence. In one investigation, children interacted with peers 10 percent of their day at age 2, 20 percent at age 4, and more than 40 percent between the ages of 7 and 11 (Barker & Wright, 1951). In a typical school day, there were 299 episodes with peers per day. By adolescence, peer relations occupy large chunks of an individual's life. In one investigation, over the course of one weekend, young adolescent boys and girls spent more than twice as much time with peers as with parents (Condry, Simon, & Bronfenbrenner, 1968).

Are Peers Necessary for Development? Good peer relations might be necessary for normal social development in adolescence. Social isolation, or the inability to "plug into" a social network, is linked with many different forms of problems and disorders, ranging from delinquency and problem drinking to depression and academic difficulties (Benner, 2011; Van Ryzin & Dishion, 2013).

Positive and Negative Peer Relations Peer influences can be both positive and negative (Bukowski & others, 2015; Rubin & others, 2013, 2015; Wentzel, 2013, 2015). A recent study found that children who associated with peers who engaged in prosocial behavior at age 9 had a higher level of self-control at age 10 and that those who associated with peers who engaged in deviant behavior at age 9 had a lower level of self-control at age 10 (Meldrum & Hay, 2012).

Adolescents explore the principles of fairness and justice by working through disagreements with peers. They also learn to be keen observers of peers' interests and perspectives in order to smoothly integrate themselves into ongoing peer activities. And adolescents learn to be skilled and sensitive partners in intimate relationships by forging close friendships with selected peers. They carry these intimacy skills forward to help form the foundation of later dating and marital relationships.

Of course, peer influences can be negative as well as positive (Chen, Drabick, & Burgers, 2015; Rubin & others, 2015; Rulison, Kreager, & Osgood, 2014). For example, a longitudinal study of adolescents and emerging adults from 13 to 23 years of age revealed adolescents' autonomy from peer influences predicted long-term success in avoiding problematic behavior but also more difficulty in establishing strong friendships in emerging adulthood (Allen, Chango, & Swedo, 2014). Further, peer relations are linked to adolescents' patterns of drug use, delinquency, depression, sexual activity, and self-injury (Barrocas & others, 2015; Choukas-Bradley & others, 2014; Giletta & others, 2015). A recent study

What are some of the positive and negative aspects of peer relations?
(left): © Tom Grill/Corbis RF; (right): © Creasource/Corbis

revealed that of the various types of negative interpersonal events encountered by adolescents, including those involving parents (such as being yelled at by a parent), teacher (such as getting into trouble with a teacher), and peers, negative peer events (such as getting into a fight with or arguing with another kid, for example) were most likely to account for maintaining depressive symptoms across a two-year period in early adolescence (Herres & Kobak, 2015). Another recent study found that college students with risky social networks (friends who drink, for example) were ten times more likely to engage in heavy drinking (Mason, Zaharakis, & Benotsch, 2014). One study also revealed that having friends who engage in delinquent behavior is associated with early onset and more persistent delinquency (Evans, Simons, & Simons, 2015). Next, we will further explore various connections between parents and peers in adolescence.

Family-Peer Linkages   Parents may influence their children's peer relations in many ways, both direct and indirect (Chan, Brown, & Von Bank, 2015; Ninio, 2015; Pallini & others, 2014). Parents affect their adolescents' peer relations through their interactions with them, how they manage their lives, and the opportunities they provide them.

Some researchers have found that parents and adolescents perceive that parents have little authority over adolescents' choices in some areas but more authority over their choices in other areas. For example, Judith Smetana's (2008, 2011a, b) research has revealed that both parents and adolescents view peer relations as an arena in which parents have little authority to dictate adolescents' choices, in contrast with moral, religious, and educational arenas, in which parents are perceived as having more authority.

Adolescents do show a strong motivation to be with their peers and become independent. However, it is not accurate to assume that movement toward peer involvement and autonomy is unrelated to parent-adolescent relationships. Researchers have provided persuasive evidence that adolescents live in a connected world with parents and peers, not one in which parents and peers are disconnected from each other (Tilton-Weaver & others, 2013).

What are some of the ways that the worlds of parents and peers are connected? Parents' choices of neighborhoods, churches, schools, and their own friends influence the pool from which their adolescents select possible friends (Cooper & Ayers-Lopez, 1985). For example, parents can choose to live in a neighborhood with playgrounds, parks, and youth organizations or in a neighborhood where houses are far apart, few adolescents live, and youth organizations are not well developed.

Parents can model or coach their adolescents in ways of relating to peers (Mounts, 2011). In one study, parents acknowledged that they recommended specific strategies to their adolescents to help them develop more positive peer relations (Rubin & Slomon, 1994). For example, parents discussed with their adolescents how disputes could be mediated and how to become less shy. They also encouraged them to be tolerant and to resist peer pressure.

developmental **connection**

Problems and Disorders

The types of friends adolescents have are linked to whether adolescents engage in substance abuse and delinquency. Connect to "Problems in Adolescence and Emerging Adulthood."

developmental **connection**

Family

Parents play an important role in adolescents' peer relations. Connect to "Families."

One of the most consistent outcomes of attachment research in adolescence is the finding that secure attachment to parents is linked to positive peer relations (Allen & Miga, 2010; Cai & others, 2013). A recent meta-analysis found that the link between mother attachment and peer attachment was much stronger than the relationship between father attachment and peer attachment (Gorrese & Ruggieri, 2012).

Although adolescent-parent attachments are correlated with adolescent outcomes, the correlations are moderate, an indication that the success or failure of parent-adolescent attachments does not necessarily guarantee success or failure in peer relationships. Clearly, secure attachment with parents can be an asset for the adolescent, fostering the trust to engage in close relationships with others and providing a foundation for developing interpersonal skills. Nonetheless, a significant minority of adolescents from strong, supportive families struggle with peer relations for a variety of reasons, such as being physically unattractive, maturing late, and experiencing cultural and socioeconomic-status (SES) discrepancies. On the other hand, some adolescents from troubled families find a positive, fresh start with peer relations that can compensate for their problematic family backgrounds.

Peer Pressure   Young adolescents conform more to peer standards than children do. Around the eighth and ninth grades, conformity to peers—especially to their antisocial standards—peaks (Berndt, 1979; Brechwald & Prinstein, 2011; Prinstein & Giletta, 2015). At this point, adolescents are most likely to go along with a peer to steal hubcaps off a car, draw graffiti on a wall, or steal cosmetics from a store counter. Another study found that U.S. adolescents are more likely than Japanese adolescents to put pressure on their peers to resist parental influence (Rothbaum & others, 2000). A recent study of young adolescent Latinas revealed that a peer resistance skill-building game involving avatar-based reality technology was effective in strengthening the girls' peer-resistance skills and tendencies to be pressured into risky behavior (Norris & others, 2013).

Which adolescents are most likely to conform to peers? Mitchell Prinstein and his colleagues (Brechwald & Prinstein, 2011; Prinstein, 2007; Prinstein & Dodge, 2008; Prinstein & others, 2009) have conducted research and analysis addressing this question. They conclude that adolescents who are uncertain about their social identity, which can appear in the form of low self-esteem and high social anxiety, are most likely to conform to peers. This uncertainty often increases during times of transition at school or at home. Also, adolescents are more likely to conform when they are in the presence of someone they perceive to have higher status than they do.

Peer Statuses   The term **sociometric status** is used to describe the extent to which children and adolescents are liked or disliked by their peer group. Sociometric status is typically assessed by asking children to rate how much they like or dislike each of their classmates (Rubin

What characterizes peer pressure in adolescence?
© Corbis RF

& others, 2015; van den Berg & Cillessen, 2014). Alternatively, it may be assessed by asking children and adolescents to nominate the peers they like the most and those they like the least. Most adolescents conform to the mainstream standards of their peers. However, the rebellious or anticonformist adolescent reacts counter to the mainstream peer group's expectations, deliberately moving away from the actions or beliefs this group advocates. A recent study revealed that low peer status in childhood was associated with an increased probability of being unemployed and having mental health problems in adulthood (Almquist & Brannstrom, 2014).

Developmentalists have distinguished five types of peer statuses (Wentzel & Asher, 1995):

· **Popular children** are frequently nominated as a best friend and are rarely disliked by their peers.
· **Average children** receive an average number of both positive and negative nominations from their peers.
· **Neglected children** are infrequently nominated as a best friend but are not disliked by their peers.
· **Rejected children** are infrequently nominated as someone's best friend and are actively disliked by their peers.
· **Controversial children** are frequently nominated both as someone's best friend and as being disliked.

Popular children have a number of social skills that contribute to their being well liked (Cillessen & van den Berg, 2012). Researchers have found that popular children give out reinforcements, listen carefully, maintain open lines of communication with peers, are happy, control their negative emotions, show enthusiasm and concern for others, and are self-confident without being conceited (Hartup, 1983; Rubin, Bukowski, & Parker, 1998). A recent study revealed that the importance of being popular in comparison with other priorities (such as friendship, achievement, and romantic interests) peaked in early adolescence (LaFontana & Cillessen, 2010). Another study found that adolescents who had the worst social outcomes at age 14 had been rated as unpopular by their peers at age 13 (McElhaney, Antonishak, & Allen, 2008). And in a recent study, how popular adolescents were with their peers was associated with their dating popularity (Houser, Mayeux, & Cross, 2015). Also, a recent study of 13- to 23-year-olds revealed that early adolescent pseudomature behavior (trying to appear mature or be "cool" among peers, such as engaging in minor delinquency or precocious romantic involvement) was associated with a desire to be popular with peers (Allen & others, 2014). In

What are some peer statuses that characterize adolescents?
© image100/Corbis RF

this study, early adolescent pseudomature behavior was linked to long-term problems in close relationships, substance abuse, and a higher level of criminal behavior.

Neglected children engage in low rates of interaction with their peers and are often described as shy by peers. Rejected children often have more serious adjustment problems than those who are neglected (Dishion, Piehler, & Myers, 2008). A recent study revealed a link between peer rejection and depression in adolescence (Platt, Kadosh, & Lau, 2013). In one study, fifth-grade boys were evaluated over a period of seven years until the end of high school (Kupersmidt & Coie, 1990). The best predictor of whether rejected children would engage in delinquent behavior or drop out of school later during adolescence was aggression toward peers in elementary school. Peer rejection is consistently linked to the development and maintenance of conduct problems (Chen & others, 2015). An analysis by John Coie (2004, pp. 252–253) provided three reasons why aggressive peer-rejected boys have problems in social relationships:

· First, the rejected, aggressive boys are more impulsive and have problems sustaining attention. As a result, they are more likely to be disruptive of ongoing activities in the classroom and in focused group play.
· Second, rejected, aggressive boys are more emotionally reactive. They are aroused to anger more easily and probably have more difficulty calming down once aroused. Because of this they are more prone to become angry at peers and attack them verbally and physically. . . .
· Third, rejected children have fewer social skills in making friends and maintaining positive relationships with peers.

sociometric status The extent to which children and adolescents are liked or disliked by their peer group.

popular children Children who are frequently nominated as a best friend and are rarely disliked by their peers.

average children Children who receive an average number of both positive and negative nominations from their peers.

neglected children Children who are infrequently nominated as a best friend but are not disliked by their peers.

rejected children Children who are infrequently nominated as a best friend and are actively disliked by their peers.

controversial children Children who are frequently nominated both as a best friend and as being disliked.

developmental **connection**

Relationships

Bullying is an increasing concern in adolescence. Connect to "Schools."

developmental **connection**

Theory

In Bandura's social cognitive theory, adolescent development is influenced by reciprocal interaction between person/cognitive, environmental, and behavioral factors. Connect to "Introduction."

developmental **connection**

Social Cognition

One aspect of social cognition in adolescence is adolescent egocentrism. Connect to "The Brain and Cognitive Development."

Not all rejected children are aggressive (Hymel & others, 2011; Rubin & others, 2015). Although aggression and its related characteristics of impulsiveness and disruptiveness underlie rejection about half the time, approximately 10 to 20 percent of rejected children are shy. In a later section, "Strategies for Improving Social Skills," we discuss ways to help rejected and neglected children and adolescents improve their social skills.

A final comment about peer statuses in adolescence is in order (Wentzel, 2004). Much of the peer status research involves samples from middle and late childhood, and in some cases early adolescence, but not late adolescence. One reason for this focus is that to assess peer status, a fairly well-defined group of classmates who know each other well and interact on a regular basis is needed (Bellmore, Jiang, & Juvonen, 2010). In contrast with elementary school and middle school, where students stay with the same group most of the day (more prevalent in elementary school than in middle school), it is difficult to assess peer status in high school contexts where students are in contact with large numbers of peers and are not likely to know all of their classmates.

Social Cognition and Emotion The social cognitive skills and social knowledge of adolescents are important aspects of successful peer relations. So is the ability to manage and regulate one's emotions.

Social Cognition *Social cognition* involves thoughts about social matters. A distinction can be made between knowledge and process in social cognition. Learning about the social knowledge adolescents bring with them to peer relations is important, as is studying how adolescents process information during peer interaction (Carpendale & Lewis, 2015; Laible, Murphy, & Augustine, 2014; Vetter & others, 2013).

As children move into adolescence, they acquire more social knowledge (also sometimes referred to as social intelligence), and there is considerable individual variation in how much each adolescent knows about what it takes to make friends, to get peers to like him or her, and so forth. For example, does the adolescent know that to have a high status with peers it is beneficial to understand others' needs, goals, and intentions, and to act accordingly? Does the adolescent know that giving out reinforcements will increase the likelihood that she will be popular? That is, does Teriana consciously know that, by telling Sierra such things as "I really like that sweater you have on today" and "You sure are popular with the guys," she will enhance the likelihood Sierra will want her to be her friend? Does the adolescent know that friendship involves sharing intimate conversations and that a friendship usually improves when the adolescent shares private, confidential information with another adolescent? And, to what extent does the adolescent know that comforting and listening skills will improve friendship relations?

A recent study of 14- and 15-year-olds examined links between social intelligence and peer popularity (Meijs & others, 2010). In this study, social intelligence was related to peer popularity but not to academic achievement.

From a social cognitive perspective, children and adolescents may have difficulty with peer relations because they lack appropriate social cognitive skills (Dodge, 2011b; Laible, Murphy, & Augustine, 2014; Rubin & others, 2015). One investigation explored the possibility that social cognitive skill deficits characterize children who have peer-related difficulties (Asarnow & Callan, 1985). Boys with and without peer adjustment difficulties were identified, and then a number of social cognitive processes or skills were assessed. These included the boys' ability to generate alternative solutions to hypothetical problems, to evaluate these solutions in terms of their effectiveness, and to describe self-statements. It was found that boys without peer adjustment problems generated more alternative solutions, proposed more assertive and mature solutions, gave less intense aggressive solutions, showed more adaptive planning, and evaluated physically aggressive responses less positively than did the boys with peer adjustment problems. For example, as shown in Figure 1, negative-peer-status sixth-grade boys were much less likely to adaptively plan ahead and slightly less likely to generate alternative solutions than were their positive-peer-status counterparts.

Social information processing influences peer relations (Dodge, 2011a, b). For example, consider the situation when a peer accidentally trips and knocks a boy's soft drink out of his hand. The boy misinterprets the encounter

What are some aspects of social cognition that are involved in getting along with peers?
© SW Productions/Getty Images RF

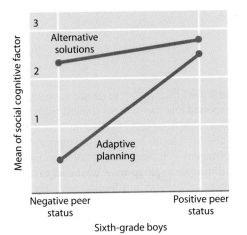

FIGURE **1**

GENERATION OF ALTERNATIVE SOLUTIONS AND ADAPTIVE PLANNING BY NEGATIVE- AND POSITIVE-PEER-STATUS BOYS. Notice that negative-peer-status boys were less likely to generate alternative solutions and plan ahead than were their positive-peer-status counterparts. © Tony Freeman/PhotoEdit

as a hostile one, which leads him to retaliate aggressively against the peer. Through repeated encounters of this kind, peers come to perceive the boy as having a habit of acting inappropriately. Kenneth Dodge (1993) argues that adolescents go through five steps in processing information about their social world: decoding of social cues, interpretation, response search, selection of an optimal response, and enactment. Dodge has found that aggressive boys are more likely to perceive another child's actions as hostile when the peer's intention is ambiguous. And, when aggressive boys search for cues to determine a peer's intention, they respond more rapidly, less efficiently, and less reflectively than do nonaggressive children. These are among the social cognitive factors believed to be involved in adolescents' conflicts with one another.

Do adults show more advanced social cognition than adolescents? A recent study found that adolescents performed more poorly than adults in two social cognitive areas: (1) theory of mind (thoughts about how one's mental processes work and the mental processes of others), and (2) emotion recognition (Vetter & others, 2013).

Emotion   Not only does cognition play an important role in peer relations, so does emotion (Baker, Hudson, & Taylor, 2014; Bukowski, Buhrmester, & Underwood, 2011; Rowsell & others, 2014). For example, the ability to regulate emotion is linked to successful peer relations. Moody and emotionally negative individuals experience greater rejection by peers, whereas emotionally positive individuals are more popular (Saarni & others, 2006). A recent study of young adolescents found that anger displays and depression were linked to being unpopular with peers (Martinez & others, 2014). Adolescents who have effective self-regulatory skills can modulate their emotional expressiveness in contexts that evoke intense emotions, as when a peer says something negative (Denham & others, 2011).

One study focused on the emotional aspects of social information processing in aggressive boys (Orobio de Castro & others, 2005). Highly aggressive boys and a control group of less-aggressive boys listened to vignettes involving provocations with peers. The highly aggressive boys expressed less guilt, attributed more hostile intent, and generated less adaptive emotion regulation strategies than did the comparison group of boys.

developmental **connection**

Emotion

Emotional swings and intensity of emotion characterize adolescent development. Connect to "The Self, Identity, Emotion, and Personality."

Strategies for Improving Social Skills   A number of strategies have been proposed for improving social skills to achieve better peer relations (Ladd, Kochenderfer-Ladd, & Rydell, 2011). **Conglomerate strategies,** also referred to as coaching, use a combination of techniques, rather than a single approach, to improve adolescents' social skills. A conglomerate strategy might consist of demonstration or modeling of appropriate social skills, discussion, and reasoning about the social skills, as well as the use of reinforcement for their enactment in actual social situations.

In one study using a conglomerate strategy, middle school adolescents were instructed in ways to improve their self-control, stress management, and social problem solving (Weissberg & Caplan, 1989). For example, as problem situations arose, teachers modeled and students practiced six sequential steps:

1. Stop, calm down, and think before you act.
2. Go over the problem and state how you feel.

conglomerate strategies The use of a combination of techniques, rather than a single approach, to improve adolescents' social skills; also called coaching.

3. Set a positive goal.

4. Think of lots of solutions.

5. Plan ahead for the consequences.

6. Go ahead and try the best plan.

The adolescents who participated in the program improved their ability to devise cooperative solutions to problem situations, and their teachers reported that the students showed improved social relations in the classroom following the program.

More specifically, how can neglected children and adolescents be trained to interact more effectively with their peers? The goal of training programs with neglected children and adolescents is often to help them attract attention from their peers in positive ways and to hold their peers' attention by asking questions, by listening in a warm and friendly way, and by saying things about themselves that relate to the peers' interests. They also are taught to enter groups more effectively. The goal of training programs with rejected children and adolescents is often to help them listen to peers and "hear what they say" instead of trying to dominate peer interactions. Rejected children and adolescents are trained to join peers without trying to change what is taking place in the peer group.

Despite the positive outcomes of some programs that attempt to improve the social skills of adolescents, researchers have often found it difficult to improve the social skills of adolescents who are actively disliked and rejected. Many of these adolescents are rejected because they are aggressive or impulsive and lack the self-control to keep these behaviors in check. Still, some intervention programs have been successful in reducing the aggressive and impulsive behaviors of these adolescents (Ladd, Kochenderfer-Ladd, & Rydell, 2011).

Social-skills training programs have generally been more successful with children 10 years of age or younger than with adolescents (Malik & Furman, 1993). Peer reputations become more fixed as cliques and peer groups take on more significance in adolescence. Once an adolescent gains a negative reputation among peers as being "mean," "weird," or a "loner," the peer group's attitude is often slow to change, even after the adolescent's problem behavior has been corrected. Thus, researchers have found that skills interventions may need to be supplemented by efforts to change the minds of peers. One such intervention strategy involves cooperative group training (Slavin, 2015). In this approach, children or adolescents work toward a common goal that holds promise for changing reputations. Most cooperative group programs have been conducted in academic settings, but other contexts might be used. For example, participation in cooperative games and sports increases sharing and feelings of happiness. And some video games require cooperative efforts by the players.

FRIENDSHIP

Earlier we noted that peers are individuals who are about the same age or maturity level. **Friends** are a subset of peers who engage in mutual companionship, support, and intimacy. Thus, relationships with friends are much closer and more involved than are relationships with the peer group. Some adolescents have several close friends, others one, and yet others none.

The Importance of Friendship   The functions that adolescents' friendships serve can be categorized in six ways (Gottman & Parker, 1987) (see Figure 2):

1. *Companionship.* Friendship provides adolescents with a familiar partner, someone who is willing to spend time with them and join in collaborative activities.

2. *Stimulation.* Friendship provides adolescents with interesting information, excitement, and amusement.

3. *Physical support.* Friendship provides resources and assistance.

4. *Ego support.* Friendship provides the expectation of support, encouragement, and feedback that helps adolescents to maintain an impression of themselves as competent, attractive, and worthwhile individuals.

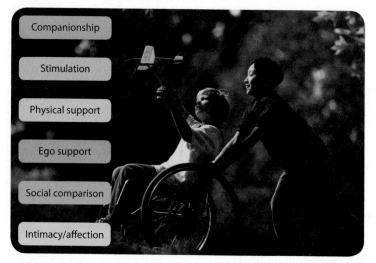

FIGURE **2**

THE FUNCTIONS OF FRIENDSHIP
© Michael Pole/Corbis

Companionship

Stimulation

Physical support

Ego support

Social comparison

Intimacy/affection

friends A subset of peers who engage in mutual companionship, support, and intimacy.

We Defined Each Other with Adjectives

"I was funky. Dana was sophisticated. Liz was crazy. We walked to school together, went for bike rides, cut school, got stoned, talked on the phone, smoked cigarettes, slept over, discussed boys and sex, went to church together, and got angry at each other. We defined each other with adjectives and each other's presence. As high school friends, we simultaneously resisted and anticipated adulthood and womanhood. . . .

"What was possible when I was 15 and 16? We still had to tell our parents where we were going! We wanted to do excitedly forbidden activities like going out to dance clubs and drinking whiskey sours. Liz, Dana, and I wanted to do these forbidden things in order to feel: to have intense emotional and sensual experiences that removed us from the suburban sameness we shared with each other and everyone else

we knew. We were tired of the repetitive experiences that our town, our siblings, our parents, and our school offered to us. . . .

"The friendship between Dana, Liz, and myself was born out of another emotional need: the need for trust. The three of us had reached a point in our lives when we realized how unstable relationships can be, and we all craved safety and acceptance. Friendships all around us were often uncertain. We wanted and needed to be able to like and trust each other."

(Source: Garrod, A., Adolescent Portraits: Identity, Relationships, and Challenges, 1st, © 1992. Printed and Electronically reproduced by permission of Pearson Education, Inc., New York, New York.)

5. *Social comparison.* Friendship provides information about where adolescents stand vis-à-vis others and whether adolescents are doing okay.

6. *Intimacy/affection.* Friendship provides adolescents with a warm, close, trusting relationship with another individual, a relationship that involves self-disclosure.

The importance of friendship was underscored in a two-year longitudinal study (Wentzel, Barry, & Caldwell, 2004). Sixth-grade students who did not have a friend engaged in less prosocial behavior (cooperation, sharing, helping others), had lower grades, and were more emotionally distressed (depression, low well-being) than their counterparts who had one or more friends. Two years later, in the eighth grade, the students who had not had a friend in the sixth grade remained more emotionally distressed than their counterparts with one or more friends.

Friendship in Adolescence   For most children, being popular with their peers is a strong motivator. The focus of their peer relations is on being liked by classmates and being included in games or lunchroom conversations. Beginning in early adolescence, however, teenagers typically prefer to have a smaller number of friendships that are more intense and intimate than those of young children.

Harry Stack Sullivan (1953) has been the most influential theorist in the study of adolescent friendships. Sullivan argued that friends are important in shaping the development of children and adolescents. Everyone, said Sullivan, has basic social needs, such as the need for secure attachment, playful companionship, social acceptance, intimacy, and sexual relations. Whether or not these needs are fulfilled largely determines our emotional well-being. For example, if the need for playful companionship goes unmet, then we become bored and depressed; if the need for social acceptance is not met, we suffer a diminished sense of self-worth.

During adolescence, said Sullivan, friends become increasingly important in meeting social needs. In particular, Sullivan argued that the need for intimacy intensifies during early adolescence, motivating teenagers to seek out close friends. If adolescents fail to forge such close friendships, they experience loneliness and a reduced sense of self-worth.

Many of Sullivan's ideas have withstood the test of time. For example, adolescents report disclosing intimate and personal information to their friends more often than do younger children (Buhrmester, 1998) (see Figure 3). Adolescents also say they depend more on friends than on parents to satisfy their needs for companionship, reassurance of worth, and intimacy. The ups and downs of experiences with friends shape adolescents' well-being (Mason & others, 2014; Sirard & others, 2013).

A man's growth is seen in the successive choirs of his friends.

—**RALPH WALDO EMERSON**
American poet and essayist, 19th century

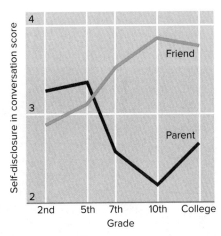

FIGURE 3

DEVELOPMENTAL CHANGES IN SELF-DISCLOSING CONVERSATIONS. Self-disclosing conversations with friends increased dramatically in adolescence while declining in an equally dramatic fashion with parents. However, self-disclosing conversations with parents began to pick up somewhat during the college years. The measure of self-disclosure involved a 5-point rating scale completed by the children and youth, with a higher score representing greater self-disclosure. The data shown represent the means for each age group.

How do the characteristics of an adolescent's friends influence whether the friends have a positive or negative influence on the adolescent?

© Walter Hodges/Jetta Productions/Getty Images RF

developmental **connection**

Exercise

Peers and friends play an important role in adolescents' physical activity. Connect to "Puberty, Health, and Biological Foundations."

Describe the nature of intimacy and similarity in friendship.

© Don Mason/Getty Images RF

intimacy in friendship In most research studies, this concept is defined narrowly as self-disclosure, or sharing of private thoughts.

Willard Hartup (1996), who has studied peer relations across four decades, concluded that children and adolescents use friends as cognitive and social resources on a regular basis. Hartup also commented that normative transitions, such as moving from elementary to middle school, are negotiated more competently by children who have friends than by those who don't.

Although having friends can be a developmental advantage, not all friendships are alike and the quality of friendship is also important to consider (Deutsch & others, 2015; Furman & Rose, 2015; Rubin & others, 2015; Wentzel, 2013). People differ in the company they keep—that is, who their friends are (Van Ryzin & Dishion, 2013). Positive friendship relationships in adolescence are associated with a host of positive outcomes, including lower rates of delinquency, substance abuse, risky sexual behavior, and bullying victimization, and a higher level of academic achievement and exercise (Chow, Tan, & Buhrmester, 2015; Lopes, Gabbard, & Rodriques, 2013; Rubin & others, 2015; Wentzel, 2013). Not having a close relationship with a best friend, having less contact with friends, having friends who are depressed, and experiencing peer rejection all increase depressive tendencies in adolescents (Harris, Qualter, & Robinson, 2013; Waller & Rose, 2013). Researchers have found that interacting with delinquent peers and friends greatly increases the risk of becoming delinquent (Deutsch & others, 2012).

Let's examine two studies that document how having friends with positive characteristics can influence the adolescent's development. In one study, friends' grade-point average was a consistent predictor of positive school achievement and also was linked to less drug abuse and acting out (Cook, Deng, & Morgano, 2007). And a recent study found that adolescents who had more in-school friends—compared with out-of-school friends—had higher grade point averages (Witkow & Fuligni, 2010).

Friendship in Emerging Adulthood Many aspects of friendship are the same in adolescence and in emerging adulthood. One difference between close relationships in adolescence and emerging adulthood was found in a longitudinal study (Collins & van Dulmen, 2006). Close relationships—between friends, family members, and romantic partners—were more integrated and similar in emerging adulthood than in adolescence. Also in this study, the number of friendships declined from the end of adolescence through emerging adulthood.

Another research study indicated that best friendships often decline in satisfaction and commitment in the first year of college (Oswald & Clark, 2003). In this study, maintaining communication with high school friends and keeping the same best friends across the transition to college lessened the decline.

Intimacy and Similarity Two important characteristics of friendship are intimacy and similarity.

Intimacy In the context of friendship, *intimacy* has been defined in different ways. For example, it has been defined broadly to include everything in a relationship that makes the relationship seem close or intense. In most research studies, though, **intimacy in friendship** is defined narrowly as self-disclosure, or sharing of private thoughts. Private or personal knowledge about a friend also has been used as an index of intimacy.

The most consistent finding in the last two decades of research on adolescent friendships is that intimacy is an important feature of friendship (Berndt & Perry, 1990). When young adolescents are asked what they want from a friend, or how they can tell if someone is their best friend, they frequently say that a best friend will share problems with them, understand them, and listen when they talk about their own thoughts or feelings. When young children talk about their friendships, comments about intimate self-disclosure or mutual understanding are rare. In one investigation, friendship intimacy was more prominent in 13- to 16-year-olds than in 10- to 13-year-olds (Buhrmester, 1990).

Similarity Another predominant characteristic of friendship is that, throughout the childhood and adolescent years, friends are generally similar—in terms of age, sex, ethnicity, and many other factors. Similarity is referred to as *homophily*, the tendency to associate with similar others (Brechwald & Prinstein, 2011; Daw, Margolis, & Verdery, 2015). Friends often have similar attitudes toward school, similar educational aspirations, and closely aligned achievement orientations.

Mixed-Age Friendships   Although most adolescents develop friendships with individuals who are close to their own age, some adolescents become best friends with younger or older individuals. Do older friends encourage adolescents to engage in delinquent behavior or early sexual behavior? Adolescents who interact with older youth do engage in these behaviors more frequently, but it is not known whether the older youth guide younger adolescents toward deviant behavior or whether the younger adolescents were already prone to deviant behavior before they developed the friendship with the older youth. A study also revealed that over time from the sixth through tenth grades girls were more likely to have older male friends, which places some girls on a developmental trajectory for engaging in problem behavior (Poulin & Pedersen, 2007). However, a recent study of young adolescents found that mixed-grade friends may protect same-grade friendless girls from feelings of loneliness and same-grade friendless and anxious-withdrawn boys from victimization (Bowker & Spencer, 2010).

What are some characteristics of other-sex friendships?
© Ocean/Corbis RF

Other-Sex Friendships   Although adolescents are more likely to have same-sex friends, associations with other-sex friends are more common than is often thought (Brown, 2004). The number of other-sex friendships increases in early adolescence, with girls reporting more other-sex friends than boys, and these other-sex friendships increase as adolescence proceeds (Poulin & Pedersen, 2007). Other-sex friendships and participation in mixed-sex groups provide a context that can help adolescents learn how to communicate with the other sex and reduce their anxiety in social and dating heterosexual interactions. Later in this chapter, you will read further about how these other-sex relationships are linked to romantic experiences.

Despite these potential benefits, researchers have found that some other-sex friendships are linked to negative behaviors such as earlier sexual intercourse, as well as increases in alcohol use and delinquency (Mrug, Borch, & Cillessen, 2012). Parents likely monitor their daughters' other-sex friendships more closely than those of their sons because they perceive boys to have a more negative influence, especially in initiating problem behavior (Poulin & Denault, 2012). A recent study revealed that a higher level of parental monitoring of young adolescent girls led to the girls having fewer friendships with boys, which in turn was associated with a lower level of subsequent alcohol use by the girls in late adolescence (Poulin & Denault, 2012).

Are there strategies that can help adolescents develop friendships? See the *Connecting with Health and Well-Being* interlude.

LONELINESS

In some cases individuals who don't have friends are vulnerable to loneliness, and loneliness can set in when individuals leave a close relationship (Harris, Qualter, & Robinson, 2013; Kaur & others, 2014; Rubin & others, 2015; Zhang & others, 2014). Each of us has times in our lives when we feel lonely, but for some individuals loneliness is a chronic condition. More than just an unwelcome social situation, chronic loneliness is linked with impaired physical and mental health (Karnick, 2005). For example, a recent study of Malaysian adolescents revealed that feeling lonely was associated with depressive symptoms (Kaur & others, 2014). A recent study also found that increasing and chronic loneliness of Latino high school students was associated with academic difficulties (Benner, 2011). In this study, support from friends buffered the negative relation of loneliness to academic difficulties.

What factors contribute to loneliness in adolescence? A recent study revealed that individual characteristics (low self-esteem and shyness) and peer experiences (low social acceptance, victimization, having fewer friends, and having poor-quality friendships) were linked to higher levels of loneliness in adolescence (Vanhalst, Luyckx, & Goossens, 2014).

It is important to distinguish loneliness from the desire for solitude. Some individuals value solitary time. Loneliness is often interwoven with the passage through life transitions, such as a move to a different part of the country, a divorce, or the death of a close friend or family member. Another situation that often creates loneliness is the first year of college, especially if students leave the familiar world of their hometown and family to enter college. Freshmen rarely bring their popularity and social standing from high school into the college environment. There may be a dozen high school basketball stars, National Merit scholars, and

Loneliness can develop when individuals go through life transitions. *What are some strategies for reducing loneliness?*
© PunchStock/Image Source RF

What Are Effective and Ineffective Strategies for Making Friends?

Here are some strategies that adults can recommend to adolescents for making friends (Wentzel, 1997):

- *Initiate interaction.* Learn about a friend—ask for his or her name, age, favorite activities. Use these prosocial overtures: introduce yourself, start a conversation, and invite him or her to do things.
- *Be nice.* Show kindness, be considerate, and compliment the other person.
- *Engage in prosocial behavior.* Be honest and trustworthy: tell the truth, keep promises. Be generous, share, and be cooperative.
- *Show respect for yourself and others.* Have good manners, be polite and courteous, and listen to what others have to say. Have a positive attitude and personality.
- *Provide social support.* Show you care.

And here are some inappropriate strategies for making friends that adults can recommend that adolescents avoid using (Wentzel, 1997):

- *Be psychologically aggressive.* Show disrespect and have bad manners. Use others, be uncooperative, don't share, ignore others, gossip, and spread rumors.
- *Present yourself negatively.* Be self-centered, snobby, conceited, and jealous; show off; care only about yourself. Be mean, have a bad attitude, be angry, throw temper tantrums, and start trouble.
- *Behave antisocially.* Be physically aggressive, yell at others, pick on them, make fun of them, be dishonest, tell secrets, and break promises.

What are some effective and ineffective strategies for making friends?
© Tim Pannell/Corbis

Which of the positive strategies have been successful for you? Has someone developed a friendship with you using one of the recommended approaches?

former student council presidents in a single dormitory wing. Especially if students attend college away from home, they face the task of forming completely new social relationships.

In one study of more than 2,600 undergraduates, lonely individuals were less likely to actively cope with stress than were individuals who were able to make friends (Cacioppo & others, 2000). Also in this study, lonely college students had higher levels of stress-related hormones and poorer sleep patterns than did students who had positive relationships with others.

Review Connect Reflect

LG1 Discuss the roles of peer relations, friendship, and loneliness in adolescent development

Review

- What roles do peers play in adolescent development?
- How does friendship contribute to adolescent development?
- How would you distinguish between loneliness and the desire to be alone?

Connect

- Relate emotional competence to the topic of social cognition that was described in this section.

Reflect *Your Own Personal Journey of Life*

- As an adolescent, how much time did you spend with friends, and what activities did you engage in? What were your friends like? Were they similar to you or different? Has the nature of your friendships changed since adolescence? Explain.

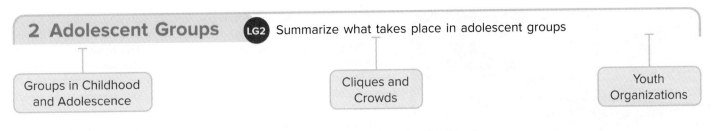

2 Adolescent Groups **LG2** Summarize what takes place in adolescent groups

Groups in Childhood and Adolescence

Cliques and Crowds

Youth Organizations

During your adolescent years, you probably were a member of both formal and informal groups. Examples of formal groups include the basketball team or drill team, Girl Scouts or Boy Scouts, the student council, and so on. A more informal group could be a group of peers, such as a clique. Our study of adolescent groups focuses on differences between childhood groups and adolescent groups, cliques and crowds, and youth organizations.

GROUPS IN CHILDHOOD AND ADOLESCENCE

Childhood groups differ from adolescent groups in several important ways. The members of childhood groups often are friends or neighborhood acquaintances, and the groups usually are not as formalized as many adolescent groups. During the adolescent years, groups tend to include a broader array of members; in other words, adolescents other than friends or neighborhood acquaintances often are members of adolescent groups. Try to recall the student council, honor society, art club, football team, or another organized group at your junior high school. If you were a member of any of these organizations, you probably remember that they were made up of many individuals you had not met before and that they were a more heterogeneous group than were your childhood peer groups. Rules and regulations were probably well defined, and captains or leaders were formally elected or appointed in the adolescent groups.

A classic observational study by Dexter Dunphy (1963) indicates that opposite-sex participation in social groups increases during adolescence. In late childhood, boys and girls tend to form small, same-sex groups. As they move into the early adolescent years, the same-sex groups begin to interact with each other. Gradually, the leaders and high-status members form further groups based on mixed-sex relationships. Eventually, the newly created mixed-sex groups replace the same-sex groups. The mixed-sex groups interact with each other in large crowd activities, too—at dances and athletic events, for example. In late adolescence, the crowd begins to dissolve as couples develop more serious relationships and make long-range plans that may include engagement and marriage. A summary of Dunphy's ideas is presented in Figure 4.

CLIQUES AND CROWDS

In our discussion of Dunphy's work, the importance of heterosexual relationships in the evolution of adolescent crowds was noted. Let's now examine adolescent cliques and crowds in greater detail.

Cliques and crowds assume more important roles during adolescence than during childhood (Brown, 2011; Doornwaard & others, 2012; Rubin & others, 2013). **Cliques** are small groups that range from 2 to about 12 individuals and average about 5 to 6 individuals. The clique members are usually of the same sex and about the same age.

Cliques can form because adolescents engage in similar activities, such as being in a club or on a sports team (Brown, 2011; Brown & Dietz, 2009). Several adolescents may form a clique because they have spent time with each other and enjoy each other's company. Not necessarily friends, they often develop a friendship if they stay in the clique.

What do adolescents do in cliques? They share ideas and hang out together. Often they develop an in-group identity and believe that their clique is better than other cliques.

Crowds are larger than cliques and less personal. Adolescents are usually members of a crowd based on reputation, and they may or may not spend much time together. Many crowds are defined by the activities adolescents engage in (such as "jocks," who are good at sports, or "druggies," who take drugs) (Brown, 2011; Brown & others, 2008). Reputation-based crowds often appear for the first time in early adolescence and usually become

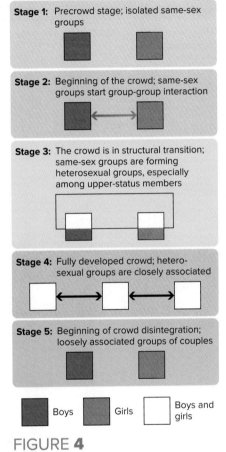

Stage 1: Precrowd stage; isolated same-sex groups

Stage 2: Beginning of the crowd; same-sex groups start group-group interaction

Stage 3: The crowd is in structural transition; same-sex groups are forming heterosexual groups, especially among upper-status members

Stage 4: Fully developed crowd; heterosexual groups are closely associated

Stage 5: Beginning of crowd disintegration; loosely associated groups of couples

Boys   Girls   Boys and girls

FIGURE 4
DUNPHY'S PROGRESSION OF PEER GROUP RELATIONS IN ADOLESCENCE

cliques Small groups that range from 2 to about 12 individuals and average about 5 to 6 individuals. Members are usually of the same sex and are similar in age; cliques can form because of similar interests, such as sports, and also can form purely from friendship.

crowds A larger group structure than cliques. Adolescents are usually members of a crowd based on reputation and may or may not spend much time together.

What characterizes adolescent cliques? How are they different from crowds?
© PunchStock/Brand X Pictures RF

less prominent in late adolescence (Collins & Steinberg, 2006). A recent study indicated that adolescents who identify with some crowds ("populars," for example) have fewer externalizing problem behaviors than their counterparts who identify with other crowds ("metal heads," for example) (Doornwaard & others, 2012). In this study, some crowds had a higher level of internalizing problems ("nonconformists," for example) than others ("jocks," for example).

In one study, crowd membership was associated with adolescent self-esteem (Brown & Lohr, 1987). The crowds included jocks (athletically oriented), populars (well-known students who led social activities), normals (middle-of-the-road students who made up the masses), druggies or toughs (known for illicit drug use or other delinquent activities), and nobodies (those who were low in social skills or intellectual abilities). The self-esteem of the jocks and the populars was highest, while that of the nobodies was lowest. One group of adolescents not in a crowd had self-esteem equivalent to that of the jocks and the populars; this group was the independents, who indicated that crowd membership was not important to them. Keep in mind that these data are correlational; self-esteem could increase an adolescent's probability of becoming a crowd member, just as crowd membership could increase the adolescent's self-esteem.

YOUTH ORGANIZATIONS

The positive youth movement includes youth development programs and organized youth activities (Lerner & others, 2010, 2015). Youth organizations can have an important influence on the adolescent's development (Agans & others, 2014; Larson & Angus, 2011; Larson & Tran, 2014; Vandell & others, 2015). Currently there are more than 400 national youth organizations in the United States. These organizations include career groups such as Junior Achievement; groups aimed at building character such as Girl Scouts and Boy Scouts; political groups such as Young Republicans and Young Democrats; and ethnic groups such as Indian Youth of America. They serve approximately 30 million young people each year. The largest youth organization is 4-H, with nearly 5 million participants. Among the smallest organizations are ASPIRA, a Latino youth organization that provides intensive educational enrichment programs for about 13,000 adolescents each year, and WAVE, a dropout-prevention program that serves about 8,000 adolescents each year.

Adolescents who join such groups are more likely to participate in community activities in adulthood and have higher self-esteem, and they tend to be better educated and to come from families with higher incomes than their counterparts who do not participate in youth groups (Erickson, 1982). Participation in youth groups can help adolescents practice the interpersonal and organizational skills that are important for success in adult roles.

The Search Institute (1995) conducted a study that sheds light on both the potential for and barriers to participation in youth programs. The study focused on Minneapolis, which faces many of the same challenges regarding youth as other major U.S. cities. After-school hours and summer vacations are important time slots during which adolescents could form positive relationships with adults and peers. Yet this study found that more than 50 percent of the youth said they did not participate in any type of after-school youth program in a typical week. More than 40 percent reported no participation in youth programs during the summer months.

About 350 youth programs were identified in Minneapolis, about one program for every 87 adolescents. However, about one-half of the youth and their parents agreed that there were not enough youth programs. Parents with the lowest incomes were the least satisfied with program availability. Some of the reasons given by middle school adolescents for not participating in youth programs were a lack of interest in available activities, a lack of transportation, and lack of awareness about what is available.

According to Reed Larson and his colleagues (Larson, 2000; Larson & Walker, 2010; Larson & others, 2011), structured voluntary youth activities are especially well suited for the development of initiative. One study of structured youth activities that led to increased

These adolescents are participating in Boys & Girls Club activities. *What effects do youth organizations have on adolescents?*
(left): © Jason DeCrow/AP Images; (right): © Jonathan Fickies/AP Images

initiative involved adolescents in low-income areas who began participating in art and drama groups, sports teams, Boys & Girls Clubs, YMCA gang intervention programs, and other community organizations (Heath, 1999; Heath & McLaughlin, 1993). When the adolescents first joined these organizations, they seemed bored. Within three to four weeks, though, they reported greater confidence in their ability to affect their world and adjusted their behavior in pursuit of a goal. A recent study examined how high school students come to see themselves as more responsible by participating in youth programs (Wood, Larson, & Brown, 2009). The study revealed that participation in three of the programs increased the responsibility of half of the students in the programs. In these three programs, it was not the fun and games involved in the programs that increased the students' responsibility but rather showing persistence in completing demanding tasks.

Further research demonstrated that successful youth programs had stable characteristics such as positive relationships, trust, and commitment to youth (Larson & Angus, 2011). Successful programs also included learning experiences that were challenging, required reaching a demanding goal, and provided feedback to youth.

In sum, youth activities and organizations provide excellent developmental contexts in which adolescents can develop many positive qualities (Flanagan, 2004; Vandell & others, 2015). Participation in these contexts can help to increase achievement and decrease delinquency (Larson, 2000). For example, a study of vulnerable youth revealed that those who participated in positive extracurricular activities in high school were more likely to subsequently enroll in college (Peck & others, 2008).

Review Connect Reflect

LG2 Summarize what takes place in adolescent groups

Review
- How are childhood groups different from adolescent groups?
- What are cliques and crowds? What roles do they play in adolescent development?
- How can youth organizations be characterized?

Connect
- Contrast membership in a clique with the experience of loneliness

discussed in the preceding section. What influence does each have on adolescent development?

Reflect *Your Own Personal Journey of Life*
- What would have been the ideal youth organization to support your needs when you were an adolescent?

developmental **connection**

Gender

Recent research indicates that relational aggression occurs more often in girls than boys in adolescence but not in childhood. Connect to "Gender."

The social worlds of adolescent peer groups and friendships are linked to gender and culture (Rubin & others, 2013, 2015). During the elementary school years children spend a large majority of their free time interacting with children of their own sex. Preadolescents spend an hour or less a week interacting with the other sex (Furman & Shaffer, 2003, 2013). With puberty, though, more time is spent in mixed-sex peer groups, which was reflected in Dunphy's developmental view that was just discussed (Buhrmester & Chong, 2009). And, by the twelfth grade, boys spend an average of five hours a week with the other sex, girls ten hours a week (Furman, 2002). Nonetheless, there are some significant differences between adolescent peer groups made up of males and those made up of females.

GENDER

There is increasing evidence that gender plays an important role in peer groups and friendships (Kenney, Dooley, & Fitzgerald, 2013; Leaper, 2015; Rancourt & others, 2013; Rose & others, 2012; Rubin & others, 2015). The evidence related to the peer group focuses on peer attachment, group size, and interaction in same-sex groups (Maccoby, 2002):

· *Peer attachment.* A recent meta-analysis concluded that adolescent girls show higher peer attachment, especially related to trust and communication, than do adolescent boys (Gorrese & Ruggieri, 2012).

· *Group size.* From about 5 years of age onward, boys are more likely than girls to associate in larger clusters. Boys are more likely to participate in organized games and sports than girls are.

· *Interaction in same-sex groups.* Boys are more likely than girls to engage in competition, conflict, ego displays, and risk taking and to seek dominance. By contrast, girls are more likely to engage in "collaborative discourse" in which they talk and act in a more reciprocal manner.

Are the friendships of adolescent girls more intimate than the friendships of adolescent boys? A recent meta-analysis concluded that research indicates girls' friendships are more intimate (Gorrese & Ruggieri, 2012). In this meta-analysis, girls' friendships were deeper and more interdependent, and female friends showed more empathy, revealed a greater need for nurturance, and had a greater desire to sustain intimate relationships. In contrast, boys gave more importance to having a congenial friend with whom they could share their interests in activities such as hobbies and sports, and boys showed more cooperativeness than girls in their friendships. Another analysis concluded that boys' friendships tend to emphasize power and excitement in contrast with girls' interest in intimacy and self-disclosure (Buhrmester & Chong, 2009). Boys may discourage one another from openly disclosing their problems because they perceive that self-disclosure is not masculine (Maccoby, 2002). And a recent study revealed that girls' friendships were more positive than were those of boys (Kenney, Dooley, & Fitzgerald, 2013).

Recently, researchers have found that some aspects of girls' friendships may be linked to adolescent problems (Schwartz-Mette & Rose, 2012; Tompkins & others, 2011; Waller & Rose, 2013). For example, a study of third- through ninth-graders revealed that girls' co-rumination (as reflected in excessively discussing problems) predicted not only an increase in positive

What are some gender differences in peer relations and friendships in adolescence?

(top): © Kevin Dodge/Corbis; (bottom): © Michael A. Keller/Corbis

friendship quality but also an increase in further co-rumination as well as an increase in depressive and anxiety symptoms (Rose, Carlson, & Waller, 2007). One implication of the research is that some girls who are vulnerable to developing internalized problems may go undetected because they have supportive friendships.

SOCIOECONOMIC STATUS AND ETHNICITY

In many schools, peer groups are strongly segregated according to socioeconomic status and ethnicity (Way & Silverman, 2012). In schools with large numbers of middle- and lower-SES students, middle-SES students often assume the leadership roles in formal organizations, such as student council, the honor society, fraternity-sorority groups, and so on. Athletic teams are one type of adolescent group in which African American adolescents and adolescents from low-income families have been able to gain parity or even surpass adolescents from middle- and upper-SES families in achieving status.

For many ethnic minority youth, especially immigrants, peers from their own ethnic group provide a crucial sense of brotherhood or sisterhood within the majority culture. Peer groups may form to oppose those of the majority peer groups and to provide adaptive supports that reduce feelings of isolation.

CULTURE

So far, we have considered adolescents' peer relations in regard to gender, socioeconomic status, and ethnicity. Are there also some foreign cultures in which the peer group plays a role different from that in the United States?

In some countries, adults restrict adolescents' access to peers. For example, in many areas of rural India and in Arab countries, opportunities for peer relations in adolescence are severely restricted, especially for girls (Brown & Larson, 2002). If girls attend school in these regions of the world, it is usually in sex-segregated schools. In these countries, interaction with the other sex and opportunities for romantic relationships are restricted if not totally prohibited (Booth, 2002).

Researchers have found that Japanese adolescents seek autonomy from their parents later and have less conflict with them than American adolescents do. In a cross-cultural analysis, the peer group was more important to U.S. adolescents than to Japanese adolescents (Rothbaum & others, 2000). Japanese adolescents spend less time outside the home, have less recreational leisure time, and engage in fewer extracurricular activities with peers than U.S. adolescents do (White, 1993). Also, U.S. adolescents are more likely to put pressure on their peers to resist parental influence than Japanese adolescents are (Rothbaum & others, 2000).

A trend, though, is that in societies in which adolescents' access to peers has been restricted, adolescents are engaging in more peer interaction during school and in shared leisure activities, especially in middle-SES contexts (Brown & Larson, 2002). For example, in Southeast Asia and some Arab regions, adolescents are starting to rely more on peers for advice and to share interests with them (Booth, 2002; Santa Maria, 2002).

In many countries and regions, though, peers play more prominent roles in adolescents' lives (Brown & Larson, 2002; Way & Silverman, 2012). For example, in sub-Saharan Africa, the peer group is a pervasive aspect of adolescents' lives (Nsamenang, 2002); similar social dynamics have been observed throughout Europe and North America (Arnett, 2004).

In some cultures, children are placed in peer groups for much greater lengths of time at an earlier age than they are in the United States. For example, in the Murian culture of eastern India, both male and female children live in a dormitory from the age of 6 until they get married (Barnouw, 1975). The dormitory is a religious haven where members are devoted to work and spiritual harmony. Children work for their parents, and the parents arrange the children's marriages. The children continue to live in the dormitory through adolescence, until they

developmental **connection**

Culture

Cross-cultural variations not only characterize peer relationships but also parent-adolescent relationships. Connect to "Introduction" and "Culture."

What are some cross-cultural variations in peer relations? How are American and Japanese adolescents socialized differently in regard to peer relations?
© Eri Morita/Getty Images

marry. In some cultural settings, peers even assume responsibilities usually assumed by parents. For example, street youth in South America rely on networks of peers to help them negotiate survival in urban environments (Welti, 2002).

Might acceptance by peers be more important for adolescents' life satisfaction in some cultures than in others? A recent study found that in countries where family values are more important (India, for example), peer acceptance was less important for adolescents' life satisfaction than in countries that place more importance on independence from the family (the United States and Germany, for example) (Schwarz & others, 2012).

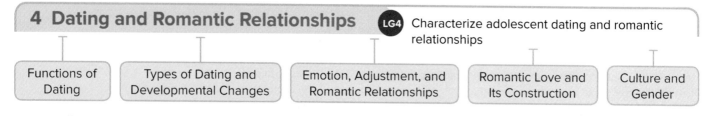

Review Connect Reflect

LG3 Describe the roles of gender and culture in adolescent peer groups and friendships.

Review
- What role does gender play in adolescent peer groups and friendships?
- How are socioeconomic status and ethnicity linked to adolescent peer relations?
- How is culture involved in adolescent peer relations?

Connect
- Compare the influence of families to that of socioeconomic status in the

development of adolescent peer relations.

Reflect *Your Own Personal Journey of Life*
- How did your peer relations and friendships during adolescence likely differ depending on whether you are a female or a male?

4 Dating and Romantic Relationships

LG4 Characterize adolescent dating and romantic relationships

| Functions of Dating | Types of Dating and Developmental Changes | Emotion, Adjustment, and Romantic Relationships | Romantic Love and Its Construction | Culture and Gender |

Although many adolescent boys and girls have social interchanges through formal and informal peer groups, it is through dating that more serious contacts between the sexes occur (Florsheim, 2003, 2013; Furman & Rose, 2015; Furman & Shaffer, 2003, 2013; Ogolsky, Lloyd, & Cate, 2013; Suleiman & Deardorff, 2015; Young, Furman, & Laursen, 2014). Let's explore the functions of dating.

FUNCTIONS OF DATING

In the first half of the twentieth century, dating served mainly as a courtship for marriage.
© Bob Barrett/FPG/Hulton Archive/Getty Images

Dating is a relatively recent phenomenon. It wasn't until the 1920s that dating as we know it became a reality, and even then, its primary role was to select and win a mate. Prior to this period, mate selection was the sole purpose of dating, and "dates" were carefully monitored by parents, who completely controlled the nature of any heterosexual companionship. Often, parents bargained with each other about the merits of their adolescents as potential marriage partners and even chose mates for their children. In recent times, of course, adolescents have gained much more control over the dating process and whom they go out with. Furthermore, dating has evolved into something far more than just courtship for marriage (Collins, Welsh, & Furman, 2009; Furman & Rose, 2015).

Dating today can serve at least eight functions (Paul & White, 1990):

1. Dating can be a form of recreation. Adolescents who date seem to have fun and see dating as a source of enjoyment and recreation.

2. Dating is a source of status and achievement. Part of the social comparison process in adolescence involves evaluating the status of the people one dates: Are they the best looking, the most popular, and so forth?

3. Dating is part of the socialization process in adolescence: It helps adolescents learn how to get along with others and assists them in learning manners and sociable behavior.

4. Dating involves learning about intimacy and serves as an opportunity to establish a unique, meaningful relationship with a person of the opposite sex.

5. Dating can be a context for sexual experimentation and exploration.

6. Dating can provide companionship through interaction and shared activities in an opposite-sex relationship.

7. Dating experiences contribute to identity formation and development; dating helps adolescents to clarify their identity and to separate from their families of origin.

8. Dating can be a means of mate sorting and selection, thereby retaining its original courtship function.

Today the functions of dating include courtship but also many others. *What are some of these other functions of dating?*
© Photodisc/Getty Images RF

TYPES OF DATING AND DEVELOPMENTAL CHANGES

A number of dating variations and developmental changes characterize dating and romantic relationships. First, we examine heterosexual romantic relationships and then turn to romantic relationships among sexual minority youth (gay and lesbian adolescents).

Heterosexual Romantic Relationships   Three stages characterize the development of romantic relationships in adolescence (Connolly & McIsaac, 2009):

1. *Entry into romantic attractions and affiliations at about 11 to 13 years of age.* This initial stage is triggered by puberty. From 11 to 13 years old, adolescents become intensely interested in romance, and it dominates many conversations with same-sex friends. Developing a crush on someone is common, and the crush often is shared with a same-sex friend. Young adolescents may or may not interact with the individual who is the object of their infatuation. When dating occurs, it usually takes place in a group setting.

2. *Exploring romantic relationships at approximately 14 to 16 years of age.* At this point in adolescence, casual dating and dating in groups—two types of romantic involvement—occur. *Casual dating* emerges between individuals who are mutually attracted. These dating experiences are often short-lived, last a few months at best, and usually endure for only a few weeks. *Dating in groups* is common and reflects embeddedness in the peer context. A friend often acts as a third-party facilitator of a potential dating relationship by communicating their friend's romantic interest and determining whether this attraction is reciprocated.

What are dating relationships like in adolescence?
© Image Source/PictureQuest RF

FIGURE **5**

AGE AT ONSET OF ROMANTIC ACTIVITY.
In this study, announcing that "I like someone" occurred earliest, followed by going out with the same person three or more times, having a sustained romantic relationship that lasted longer than two months, and finally planning an engagement or marriage (which characterized only a very small percentage of participants by the twelfth grade) (Buhrmester, 2001).

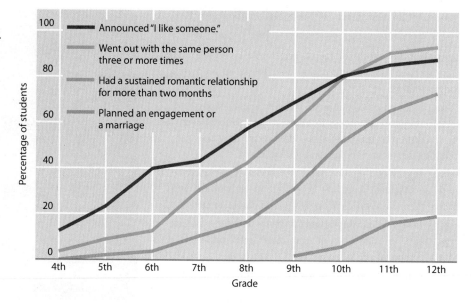

3. *Consolidating dyadic romantic bonds at about 17 to 19 years of age.* At the end of the high school years, more serious romantic relationships develop. This stage is characterized by strong emotional bonds more closely resembling those in adult romantic relationships. These bonds often are more stable and enduring than earlier bonds, typically lasting one year or more.

Two variations on these stages in the development of romantic relationships in adolescence involve early starters and late bloomers (Connolly & McIsaac, 2009). *Early starters* include 15 to 20 percent of 11- to 13-year-olds who say that they currently are in a romantic relationship and 35 percent who indicate that they have had some prior experience in romantic relationships. *Late bloomers* comprise approximately 10 percent of 17- to 19-year-olds who say that they have had no experience with romantic relationships and another 15 percent who report that they have not engaged in any romantic relationships that lasted more than four months. A recent study by Jennifer Connolly and her colleagues (2013) found support for the series of three stages described above (described as on-time) and also the presence of the two off-time groups—early starters and late bloomers. In this study, the early starters had more externalizing symptoms (aggressive and delinquent behaviors) while late bloomers and the on-time sequence group did not show any indications of maladjustment.

In one study, announcing that "I like someone" occurred by the sixth grade for about 40 percent of the individuals sampled (Buhrmester, 2001) (see Figure 5). However, it was not until the tenth grade that 50 percent of the adolescents had a sustained romantic relationship that lasted two months or longer. By their senior year, 25 percent still had not engaged in this type of sustained romantic relationship. In another study, a rather large portion of adolescents in a steady dating relationship said that their steady relationship had persisted 11 months or longer: 20 percent of adolescents 14 or younger, 35 percent of 15- to 16-year-olds, and almost 60 percent of 17- and 18-year-olds (Carver, Joyner, & Udry, 2003).

Adolescents often find comfort in numbers in their early exploration of romantic relationships (Connolly & McIsaac, 2009). They may begin hanging out together in heterosexual groups. Sometimes they just hang out at someone's house or get organized enough to ask an adult to drive them to a mall or a movie. A special concern in early dating and "going with" someone is the associated risk for adolescent pregnancy and problems at home and school.

developmental connection

Sexuality

Sexual minority youth have diverse patterns of initial attraction. Connect to "Sexuality."

Romantic Relationships in Sexual Minority Youth   Most research on romantic relationships in adolescence has focused on heterosexual relationships. Recently, researchers have begun to study romantic relationships in gay, lesbian, and bisexual youth (Diamond, Bonner, & Dickenson, 2015; Diamond & Savin-Williams, 2015; Savin-Williams, 2015).

The average age of the initial same-sex activity for females ranges from 14 to 18 years of age and for males from 13 to 15 (Savin-Williams, 2015). The most common initial same-sex partner is a close friend. Lesbian adolescents are more likely to have sexual encounters with boys before same-sex activity, whereas gay adolescents show the opposite sequence (Diamond & Savin-Williams, 2015).

Most sexual minority youth have same-sex sexual experience, but relatively few have same-sex romantic relationships because of limited opportunities and the social disapproval such relationships may generate from families or heterosexual peers (Savin-Williams & Cohen, 2015). The importance of romance to sexual minority youth was underscored in a study that found that they rated the breakup of a current romance as their second most stressful problem, second only to disclosure of their sexual orientation to their parents (D'Augelli, 1991). The romantic possibilities of sexual minority youth are complex (Diamond, Bonner, & Dickenson, 2015; Diamond & Savin-Williams, 2015). To adequately address the relational interests of sexual minority youth, we can't generalize from heterosexual youth and simply switch the labels. Instead, we need to consider the full range of variation in sexual minority youths' sexual desires and romantic relationships for same- and other-sex partners.

EMOTION, ADJUSTMENT, AND ROMANTIC RELATIONSHIPS

Romantic emotions can envelop adolescents' and emerging adults' lives (Furman & Rose, 2015). In some cases, these emotions are positive, in others negative. A concern is that in some cases the negative emotions are so intense and prolonged that they can lead to adjustment problems.

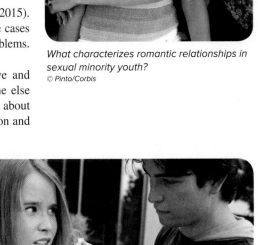

What characterizes romantic relationships in sexual minority youth?
© Pinto/Corbis

Emotions in Romantic Relationships A 14-year-old reports being in love and feeling unable to think about anything else. A 15-year-old is distressed that "everyone else has a boyfriend but me." As we just saw, adolescents spend a lot of time thinking about romantic involvement. Some of this thought can involve positive emotions of compassion and joy, but it also can include negative emotions such as worry, disappointment, and jealousy. And the breakup of a romantic relationship can result in depression or other problems.

Romantic relationships often are involved in an adolescent's emotional experiences. In one study of ninth- to twelfth-graders, girls gave real and fantasized heterosexual relationships as the explanation for more than one-third of their strong emotions, and boys gave this reason for 25 percent of their strong emotions (Wilson-Shockley, 1995). Strong emotions were attached far less to school (13 percent), family (9 percent), and same-sex peer relations (8 percent). The majority of the emotions were reported as positive, but a substantial minority (42 percent), were reported as negative, including feelings of anxiety, anger, jealousy, and depression.

Adolescents who had a boyfriend or girlfriend reported wider daily emotional swings than their counterparts who did not (Richards & Larson, 1990). In a period of three days, one eleventh-grade girl went from feeling "happy because I'm with Dan" to upset, because they had a "huge fight" and "he won't listen to me and keeps hanging up on me" to feeling "suicidal because of the fight" to feeling "happy because everything between me and Dan is fine."

How is emotion involved in adolescent romantic relationships? How are romantic relationships linked to adolescent adjustment?
© Pascal Broze/SuperStock RF

Dating and Adjustment Researchers have linked dating and romantic relationships with various measures of how well-adjusted adolescents are (Connolly & McIsaac, 2009; Furman & Rose, 2015; Soller, 2014). Consider the following studies:

· The more romantic experiences tenth-graders had, the more they reported higher levels of social acceptance, friendship competence, and romantic competence; however, having more romantic experience also was linked to a higher level of substance use, delinquency, and sexual behavior (Furman, Low, & Ho, 2009).

· Adolescent girls' higher frequency of dating was linked to having depressive symptoms and emotionally unavailable parents (Steinberg & Davila, 2008).

· Adolescent girls who engaged in co-rumination (excessive discussion of problems with friends) were more likely to be involved in a romantic relationship, and together co-rumination and romantic involvement predicted an increase in depressive symptoms (Starr & Davila, 2009).

developmental **connection**

Relationships

Dating violence and acquaintance rape are increasing concerns in adolescence and emerging adulthood. Connect to "Sexuality."

- Among adolescent girls but not adolescent males, having an older romantic partner was linked to an increase in depressive symptoms, largely influenced by an increase in substance use (Haydon & Halpern, 2010).
- Adolescents with a stronger romantic involvement were more likely to engage in delinquency than their counterparts with a lower level of romantic involvement (Cui & others, 2012).

Dating and romantic relationships at an early age can be especially problematic (Connolly & others, 2013; Furman & Rose, 2015). Researchers have found that early dating and "going with" someone are linked with adolescent pregnancy and problems at home and school (Florsheim, Moore, & Edgington, 2003).

Dissolution of a Romantic Relationship   When things don't go well in a romantic relationship, adolescents and emerging adults need to consider dissolving the relationship. In particular, falling out of love may be wise if you are obsessed with a person who repeatedly betrays your trust; if you are involved with someone who is draining you emotionally or financially; or if you are desperately in love with someone who does not return your feelings.

Being in love when love is not returned can lead to depression, obsessive thoughts, sexual dysfunction, inability to work effectively, difficulty in making new friends, and self-condemnation. Thinking clearly in such relationships is often difficult, because they are so often linked to arousing emotions.

Some individuals get taken advantage of in relationships. For example, without either person realizing it, a relationship can evolve in a way that creates dominant and submissive roles. Detecting this pattern is an important step toward learning either to reconstruct the relationship or to end it if the problems cannot be worked out.

Studies of romantic breakups have mainly focused on their negative aspects (Kato, 2005). For example, a recent study of 18- to 20-year-olds revealed that heavy drinking, marijuana use, and cigarette smoking increased following the dissolution of a romantic relationship (Fleming & others, 2010). Few studies, however, have examined the possibility that a romantic breakup might lead to positive changes (Sbarra & Ferrer, 2006). One study of college students assessed the personal growth that can follow the breakup of a romantic relationship (Tashiro & Frazier, 2003). The participants were 92 undergraduate students who had experienced a relationship breakup in the past nine months. They were asked to describe "what positive changes, if any, have happened as a result of your breakup that might serve to improve your future romantic relationships" (p. 118). Self-reported positive growth was common following the romantic breakups. The most commonly reported types of growth were feeling stronger emotionally and being more self-confident, being more independent, and developing new friendships. Women reported more positive growth than did men.

ROMANTIC LOVE AND ITS CONSTRUCTION

developmental **connection**

Sexuality

Sexual interest plays an important role in adolescents' romantic relationships. Connect to "Sexuality."

romantic love Love that has strong sexual and infatuation components; also called passionate love or *eros*. It often predominates in the early part of a love relationship.

affectionate love Love in which an individual desires to have another person near and has a deep, caring affection for that person; also called companionate love.

Romantic love, also called passionate love or *eros,* has strong sexual and infatuation components, and it often predominates in the early part of a love relationship. Romantic love characterizes most adolescent love, and romantic love is also extremely important among college students. In one investigation, unmarried college males and females were asked to identify their closest relationship (Berscheid, Snyder, & Omoto, 1989). More than half named a romantic partner, rather than a parent, sibling, or friend.

Romantic love includes a complex intermingling of emotions—fear, anger, sexual desire, joy, and jealousy, for example. Obviously, some of these emotions are a source of anguish. One study found that romantic lovers were more likely than friends to be the cause of depression (Berscheid & Fei, 1977). A recent study revealed that a heightened state of romantic love in young adults was linked to stronger depression and anxiety symptoms but better sleep quality (Bajoghli & others, 2014).

Another type of love is **affectionate love,** also called companionate love, which occurs when individuals desire to have another person near and have a deep, caring affection for that person. There is evidence that affectionate love is more characteristic of adult love than adolescent love and that the early stages of love have more romantic ingredients than the later stages (Berscheid, 2010; Sternberg & Sternberg, 2013).

Physical attractiveness and similarity are important aspects of romantic relationships. A recent study revealed that physically attractive adolescents were more satisfied with their romantic life (Furman & Winkles, 2010). In another study, girls and boys who were dating each other tended to be from the same ethnic group, come from similar socioeconomic backgrounds, and have similar academic success as measured by their grade point averages (Furman & Simon, 2008). In yet another study, there were substantial pre-relationship similarities between adolescents and their future romantic partners on peer popularity, attractiveness, body appeal, and depressive symptoms (Simon, Aikins, & Prinstein, 2008). Also in this study, the influence of a dating partner on the adolescent was examined over time. Especially important was the positive influence of a high-functioning dating partner on a low-functioning dating partner as the relationship endured. For example, an adolescent who initially reported having a high level of depression but dated an adolescent who reported having a low level of depression indicated that she or he had a lower level of depression 11 months later.

Recently, romantic attraction has not only taken place in person but also over the Internet (Paul, 2014). In 2006, approximately million individuals in the United States had tried online matchmaking, but by 2014 that figure had skyrocketed to more than 41 million individuals in the United States (Masters, 2008; statisticbrain, 2014). In 2014, match.com alone had more than 21 million members. Some critics argue that online romantic relationships lose the interpersonal connection, whereas others suggest that the Internet may benefit shy or anxious individuals who find it difficult to meet potential partners in person (Holmes, Little, & Welsh, 2009). One problem with online matchmaking is that many individuals misrepresent their characteristics, such as how old they are, how attractive they are, and their occupation. Despite such dishonesty, researchers have found that romantic relationships initiated on the Internet are more likely than relationships established in person to last for more than two years (Bargh & McKenna, 2004). And in a recent large-scale study of more than 19,000 individuals it was discovered that more than one-third of marriages now begin with online contact and that these marriages are slightly less likely to break up and are characterized by slightly higher marital satisfaction than marriages than begin in offline contexts (Cacioppo & others, 2013).

To fully understand romantic relationships in adolescence and emerging adulthood, we also need to know how experiences with family members and peers contribute to the way adolescents and emerging adults construct their romantic relationships (Furman & Shaffer, 2003, 2013; Furman & Rose, 2015; Ivanova, Mills, & Veenstra, 2012; Rauer & others, 2013). A recent study revealed that young adolescent girls who had negative relationships with their parents turned to romantic relationships for intimacy and support, which in turn provided the opportunity for early sexual initiation (de Graaf & others, 2012).

A longitudinal study examined how youths' personality traits and beliefs about marriage are related to romantic relationships in early adulthood (Masarik & others, 2013). In this study, a higher level of neuroticism in the ninth grade was linked with the belief in late adolescence/early adulthood that marriage is not likely to lead to fulfillment in life and happiness as an adult. And less endorsement of the marriage/fulfillment belief, in turn, predicted fewer observed positive interactions with a romantic partner and lower perceived relationship quality in early adulthood.

Attachment history also is linked to couple relationships in adolescence and emerging adulthood (Sroufe & others, 2005; Sroufe, Coffino, & Carlson, 2010). A recent study found that greater attachment insecurity with parents and peers at age 14 was linked to having a more anxious attachment style at age 22 (Pascuzzo, Cyr, & Moss, 2013). Another recent study found that a positive relationship with parents during adolescence was linked to better-quality romantic relationships in emerging adulthood (Madsen & Collins, 2011). In this study, better adolescent dating quality was related to a smoother romantic relationship process and less negative affect in emerging adult romantic relationships.

Wyndol Furman and Elizabeth Wehner (1998) discussed how specific insecure attachment styles might be related to adolescents' romantic relationships. Adolescents with a secure attachment to parents are likely to approach romantic relationships expecting closeness, warmth, and intimacy. Thus, they are likely to feel comfortable developing close, intimate romantic relationships. Adolescents with a dismissing/avoidant attachment to parents are likely to expect romantic partners to be unresponsive and unavailable. Thus, they might tend to behave in ways that distance themselves from romantic relationships. Adolescents with a preoccupied/ambivalent attachment to parents are likely to be disappointed and frustrated with intimacy and closeness in romantic relationships.

Love is a canvas furnished by nature and embroidered by imagination.

—VOLTAIRE
French philosopher, 18th century

developmental **connection**

Attachment

Researchers are discovering numerous links between attachment styles and romantic relationships in emerging adulthood. Connect to "Families."

Is Online Dating a Good Idea?

Is looking for love online likely to work out? It didn't work out so well in 2012 for Notre Dame linebacker Manti Te'o, whose online girlfriend turned out to be a "catfish," someone who fakes an identity online. However, online dating sites claim that their sites often have positive outcomes. A poll commissioned by match.com in 2009 reported that twice as many marriages occurred between individuals who met through an online dating site as between people who met in bars or clubs or at other social events.

Connecting online for love turned out positively for two Columbia graduate students, Michelle Przbyksi and Andy Lalinde (Steinberg, 2011). They lived only a few blocks away from each other, so soon after they communicated online through Datemyschool.com, an online dating site exclusively for college students, they met in person, hit it off, applied for a marriage license 10 days later, and eventually got married.

However, a recent editorial by Samantha Nickalls (2012) in *The Tower*, the student newspaper at Arcadia University in Philadelphia,

argued that online dating sites might be okay for people in their thirties and older but not for college students. She commented:

> The dating pool of our age is huge. Huge. After all, marriage is not on most people's minds when they're in college, but dating (or perhaps just hooking up) most certainly is. A college campus, in fact, is like living a dating service because the majority of people are looking for the same thing you are. As long as you put yourself out there, flirt a bit, and be friendly, chances are that people will notice.
>
> If this doesn't work for you right away, why should it really matter? As a college student, you have so many other huge things going on in your life—your career choice, your transition from kid to adult, your crazy social life. Unless you are looking to get married at age 20 (which is a whole other issue that I could debate for hours), dating shouldn't be the primary thing on your mind anyway. Besides, as the old saying goes, the best things come when you least expect them. Oftentimes, you find the best dates by accident—not by hunting them down.

(Left) Manti Te'o; *(Right)* Michelle Przbyksi and Andy Lalinde.
(left): © John Biever/Sports Illustrated/Getty Images; (right): Courtesy of Michelle and Andres Lalinde

What do you think? Is searching online for romantic relationships a good idea? What are some precautions that need to be taken if you pursue an online romantic relationship?

Adolescents' observations of their parents' marital relationship also contribute to their own construction of dating relationships. A recent study of 17-year-old Israeli girls and their mothers revealed that mothers who reported a higher level of marital satisfaction had daughters who were more romantically competent (based on multiple dimensions, such as maturity, coherence, and realistic perception of the romantic relationship) (Shulman, Davila, & Shachar-

How might experiences with family members influence the way adolescents construct their dating relationships?
© Ronnie Kaufman/Corbis

Shapira, 2011). Another study revealed that parents' marital conflict was linked to increased conflict in an emerging adult's romantic relationships (Cui, Fincham, & Pasley, 2008). In addition, adolescent girls from divorced families had lower levels of romantic competence in dating relationships (Shulman, Scharf, & Shachar-Shapira, 2012). However, mothers' effective communication of their own adolescent romantic experiences alleviated the negative influence of divorce on adolescent girls.

In a classic study, E. Mavis Hetherington (1972, 1977) found that divorce was associated with a stronger interest in boys on the part of adolescent daughters than was the death of a parent or living in an intact family. Further, the daughters of divorced parents had a more negative opinion of males than did the girls from other family structures. And girls from divorced and widowed families were more likely to marry images of their fathers than were girls from intact families. Hetherington stresses that females from intact families likely have had a greater opportunity to work through relationships with their fathers and therefore are more psychologically free to date and marry someone different from their fathers.

Recent research confirms that the divorce of parents influences adolescents' romantic relationships. For example, one study revealed that an adolescent's first romantic relationship occurred earlier in divorced than never-divorced intact families but only when the divorce occurred in early adolescence (Ivanova, Mills, & Veenstra, 2011). One explanation for this timing of divorce impact is heightened sensitivity during transition periods, such as early adolescence.

Parents are likely to be more involved or interested in their daughters' dating patterns and relationships than their sons'. For example, in one investigation, college females were much more likely than their male counterparts to say that their parents tried to influence whom they dated during adolescence (Knox & Wilson, 1981). They also indicated that it was not unusual for their parents to try to interfere with their dating choices and relationships.

Peer relations and friendships provide the opportunity to learn modes of relating that are carried over into romantic relationships (Collins, Welsh, & Furman, 2009; Furman & Rose, 2015; Furman & Winkles, 2010; Rauer & others, 2013). A longitudinal study revealed that friendship in middle childhood was linked with security in dating, as well as intimacy in dating, at age 16 (Collins, Hennighausen, & Sroufe, 1998; Collins & van Dulmen, 2006).

Research by Jennifer Connolly and her colleagues (Connolly, Furman, & Konarski, 2000; Connolly & Stevens, 1999; Connolly & others, 2004) documents the role of peers in the emergence of romantic involvement in adolescence. In one study, adolescents who were part of mixed-sex peer groups moved more readily into romantic relationships than their counterparts whose experience with mixed-sex peer groups was more limited (Connolly, Furman, & Konarski, 2000). Another study also found that young adolescents increase their participation

developmental connection

Gender

Gender differences have been found in sexual scripts. Connect to "Sexuality."

What characterizes dating scripts in adolescence?
© moodboard/Corbis RF

in mixed-gender peer groups (Connolly & others, 2004). This participation was "not explicitly focused on dating but rather brought boys and girls together in settings in which heterosocial interaction might occur but is not obligatory. . . . We speculate that mixed-gender groups are important because they are easily available to young adolescents who can take part at their own comfort level" (p. 201).

GENDER AND CULTURE

Dating and romantic relationships may vary according to gender and culture. Think back to your middle school/junior high and high school years and consider how gender likely influenced your romantic relationships.

Gender Do male and female adolescents bring different motivations to the dating experience? Candice Feiring (1996) found that they did. Fifteen-year-old girls were more likely to describe romance in terms of interpersonal qualities; boys described it in terms of physical attraction. For young adolescents, the affiliative qualities of companionship, intimacy, and support were frequently mentioned as positive dimensions of romantic relationships, but love and security were not. Also, the young adolescents described physical attraction more in terms of being cute, pretty, or handsome than in terms of sexuality (such as being a good kisser). Possibly, however, the failure to discuss sexual interests was due to the adolescents' discomfort in talking about such personal feelings with an unfamiliar adult.

Dating scripts are the cognitive models that adolescents and adults use to guide and evaluate dating interactions. In one study, first dates were highly scripted along gender lines (Rose & Frieze, 1993). Males followed a proactive dating script, females a reactive one. The male's script involved initiating the date (asking for and planning it), controlling the public domain (driving and opening doors), and initiating sexual interaction (making physical contact, making out, and kissing). The female's script focused on the private domain (concern about appearance, enjoying the date), participating in the structure of the date provided by the male (being picked up, having doors opened), and responding to his sexual gestures. These gender differences give males more power in the initial stage of a relationship.

What are some ethnic variations in dating during adolescence?
© Jenny Acheson/Getty Images

dating scripts The cognitive models that adolescents and adults use to guide and evaluate dating interactions.

Ethnicity and Culture The sociocultural context exerts a powerful influence on adolescent dating patterns and on mate selection. Values and religious beliefs of people in various cultures often dictate the age at which dating begins, how much freedom in dating is allowed, the extent to which dates are chaperoned by parents or other adults, and the respective roles of males and females in dating. In the Arab world, Asian countries, and South America, adults are typically highly restrictive of adolescent girls' romantic relationships.

Immigrants to the United States have brought these restrictive standards with them. For example, in the United States, Latino and Asian American families typically have more conservative standards regarding adolescent dating than does the Anglo-American culture. Especially when an immigrant adolescent wants to date outside his or her ethnic group, dating can be a source of cultural conflict for families who come from cultures in which dating begins at a late age, little freedom in dating is allowed, dates are chaperoned, and adolescent girls' dating is especially restricted (Romo, Mireles-Rios, & Lopez-Tello, 2013).

In one study, Latino young adults living in the midwestern region of the United States reflected on their socialization for dating and sexuality (Raffaelli & Ontai, 2001). Because most of their parents viewed U.S.-style dating as a violation of traditional courtship styles, strict boundaries were imposed on youths' romantic involvements. As a result, many of the Latinos described their adolescent dating experiences as filled with tension and conflict. The average age at which the girls began dating was 15.7 years, with early dating experiences usually occurring without parental knowledge or permission. Over half of the girls engaged in "sneak dating."

Review

- What functions does dating serve?
- What are some different types of dating? How does dating change developmentally during adolescence?
- How are romantic relationships linked to emotion and adjustment?
- What is romantic love, and how is it constructed?
- How are gender and culture involved in dating and romantic relationships?

Connect

- How do U.S. adolescents' dating patterns and the purpose of dating differ from those of adolescents in other parts of the world?

Reflect *Your Own Personal Journey of Life*

- Think back to your middle school/ junior high and high school years. How much time did you spend thinking about dating? If you dated, what were your dating experiences like? What would you do over again the same way? What would you do differently? What characteristics did you seek in the people you wanted to date? Were you too idealistic? What advice would you give today's adolescents about dating and romantic relationships?

5 Emerging Adult Lifestyles

LG5 Explain the diversity of emerging adult lifestyles

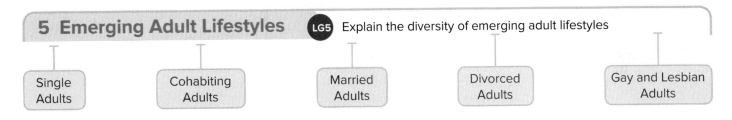

Single Adults | Cohabiting Adults | Married Adults | Divorced Adults | Gay and Lesbian Adults

Emerging adulthood not only is a time when changes often take place in romantic relationships; it also is a time characterized by residential and lifestyle changes. In 2000, approximately one-half of U.S. 18- to 24-year-olds were living with their parents or other relatives, whereas about one-fourth of the 18- to 24-year-olds had formed their own households and another one-fourth were living with nonrelatives, such as roommates or an unmarried partner (Jekielek & Brown, 2005). A 2011 poll found that 53 percent of U.S. 18- to 24-year-olds were living at home with their parents (Parker, 2011). Among the questions that many emerging adults pose to themselves as they consider their lifestyle options are: Should I get married? If so, when? If I wait too long, will I be left out? Should I stay single or is it too lonely a life? Do I want to have children?

A striking social change in recent decades is the decreased stigma attached to individuals who do not maintain what were long considered conventional families. Emerging adults today choose many lifestyles and form many types of families (Arnett, 2014; Benokraitis, 2015). They live alone, cohabit, marry, divorce, or live with someone of the same sex.

In a recent book, *The Marriage-Go-Round*, sociologist Andrew Cherlin (2009) concluded that the United States has more marriages and remarriages, more divorces, and more short-term cohabiting (living together) relationships than most countries. Combine these lifestyles and it's apparent that there is more turnover and movement in and out of relationships in the United States than in virtually any other country. Let's explore these varying relationship lifestyles.

SINGLE ADULTS

Recent decades have seen a dramatic rise in the percentage of single adults. In 2009, for the first time in history the proportion of individuals 25 to 34 years of age who had never been married (46 percent) exceeded those who were married (45 percent) (U.S. Census Bureau, 2010). The increasing number of single adults is the result of rising rates of cohabitation and postponement of marriage.

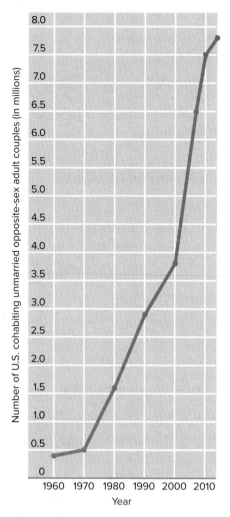

FIGURE 6

THE INCREASE IN COHABITATION IN THE UNITED STATES. Since 1970, there has been a dramatic increase in the number of unmarried adults living together in the United States.

cohabitation Living together in a sexual relationship without being married.

Even when singles enjoy their lifestyles and are highly competent individuals, they often are stereotyped (Schwartz & Scott, 2012). Stereotypes associated with being single range from the "swinging single" to the "desperately lonely, suicidal single." Of course, most single adults are somewhere between these extremes. Common problems of single adults may include forming intimate relationships with other adults, confronting loneliness, and finding a niche in a society that is marriage-oriented. Bella DePaulo (2007, 2011) argues that society holds a widespread bias against unmarried adults that is seen in everything from missed perks in jobs to deep social and financial prejudices.

Advantages of being single include having time to make decisions about one's life course, time to develop personal resources to meet goals, freedom to make autonomous decisions and pursue one's own schedule and interests, opportunities to explore new places and try out new things, and privacy.

A recent nationally representative U.S. survey of more than 5,000 single adults 21 years of age and older who were not in a committed relationship revealed that men are more interested in love, marriage, and children than their counterparts were in earlier generations (Match.com, 2011). In this study, today's women desire more independence in their relationships than their mothers did. Across every age group, more women than men reported wanting to pursue their own interests, have personal space, have their own bank account, have regular nights out with friends, and take vacations on their own. In a second nationally representative survey, many single adults reported that they were looking for love, but not marriage (Match.com, 2012). In this survey, 39 percent of the single adults were uncertain about whether they wanted to get married, 34 percent said they did want to marry, and 27 percent said they didn't want to get married.

COHABITING ADULTS

Cohabitation refers to living together in a sexual relationship without being married. Cohabitation has undergone considerable changes in recent years (Benokraitis, 2015; Copen, Daniels, & Mosher, 2013; Rose-Greenland & Smock, 2013; Smock & Gupta, 2013; Tach & Eads, 2015). There has been a dramatic increase in the number of cohabiting U.S. couples since 1970, with approximately 75 percent now cohabiting prior to getting married, compared with about 10 percent in 1970 (National Marriage Project, 2011). And as shown in Figure 6, the upward trend shows no sign of letting up—from 3.8 million cohabiting couples in 2000 to 7.8 million cohabiting couples in 2012 (Vespa, Lewis, & Kreider, 2013). Cohabiting rates are even higher in some countries—in Sweden, for example, cohabitation before marriage is virtually universal (Kiernan, 2013).

Some couples view their cohabitation not as a precursor to marriage but as an ongoing lifestyle (Rose-Greenland & Smock, 2013). These couples do not want the official aspects of marriage. In the United States, cohabiting arrangements tend to be short-lived, with one-third lasting less than a year (Hyde & DeLamater, 2014). Fewer than 1 out of 10 lasts five years. Of course, it is easier to dissolve a cohabitation relationship than to divorce.

A recent study revealed that young adults' main reasons for cohabiting are to spend time together, share expenses, and evaluate compatibility (Huang & others, 2011). In this study, gender differences emerged regarding drawbacks in cohabiting: men were more concerned about their loss of freedom while women were more concerned about delays in getting married.

Couples who cohabit face certain problems (Rhoades, Stanley, & Markman, 2009). Disapproval by parents and other family members can place emotional strain on the cohabiting couple. Some cohabiting couples have difficulty owning property jointly. Legal rights on the dissolution of the relationship are less certain than in a divorce. A recent study also found that following the transition from dating to cohabitation, relationships were characterized by more commitment, lower satisfaction, more negative communication, and more physical aggression than when dating (noncohabiting) (Rhoades, Stanley, & Markham, 2012).

Cohabitation and Marital Stability/Happiness If a couple lives together before they marry, does cohabiting help or harm their chances of later having a stable and happy marriage? The majority of studies have found lower rates of marital satisfaction and higher rates of divorce in couples who lived together before getting married (Rose-Greenland & Smock, 2013). However, recent research indicates that the link between marital cohabitation and marital instability in first marriages has weakened in recent cohorts (Copen, Daniels, & Mosher, 2013; Manning & Cohen, 2012; Reinhold, 2010; Rose-Greenland & Smock, 2013; Smock & Gupta, 2013).

What might explain the finding that cohabiting is linked with divorce more than not cohabiting? The most frequently given explanation is that the less traditional lifestyle of cohabitation may attract less conventional individuals who are not great believers in marriage in the first place. An alternative explanation is that the experience of cohabiting changes people's attitudes and habits in ways that increase their likelihood of divorce.

Recent research has provided clarification of cohabitation outcomes. One meta-analysis found the negative link between cohabitation and marital instability did not hold up when only cohabitation with the eventual marital partner was examined, indicating that these cohabitors may attach more long-term positive meaning to living together (Jose, O'Leary, & Moyer, 2010). Another study also revealed that for first marriages, cohabiting with the spouse without first being engaged was linked to more negative interaction and a higher probability of divorce than cohabiting after engagement (Stanley & others, 2010). In contrast, premarital cohabitation prior to a second marriage placed couples at risk for divorce regardless of whether they were engaged. A recent study also found that the marriages of couples who were cohabiting but not engaged were less likely to survive to the 10- to 15-year mark than the marriages of their counterparts who were engaged when they cohabited (Copen, Daniels, & Mosher, 2013). Also, another analysis indicated that cohabiting does not have a negative effect on marriage if the couple did not have any previous live-in lovers and did not have children prior to the marriage (Cherlin, 2009). And a recent study concluded that the difference between the risk of marital dissolution for cohabitors and for those who married without previously cohabiting was much smaller when they had cohabited in their mid-twenties or later (Kuperberg, 2014).

What are some differences between cohabiting relationships and marriages? Does cohabiting help or harm a couple's chances of later having a successful marriage?
© Reed Kaestener/Corbis RF

MARRIED ADULTS

Until about 1930, stable marriage was widely accepted as the endpoint of adult development. In the last 70 to 80 years, however, personal fulfillment both inside and outside marriage has emerged as a goal that competes with marital stability. The changing norm of male-female equality in marriage and increasingly high expectations for what a marital relationship should be have produced marital relationships that are more fragile and intense than they were earlier in the twentieth century (Lavner & Bradbury, 2012). A recent study found that newlyweds who had a high level of general dispositional optimism were more satisfied with their marriages over the first year of the marriage while newlyweds who had a high level of relationship-specific optimism had more marital problems during this time frame (Neff & Geers, 2013). And another recent study revealed that the more relationships that individuals have before they get married, the less likely they are to report having a high-quality marriage (Rhoades & Stanley, 2014). Many young people think that the more serious relationships you have before you get married, the better your chances will be to know when the right person comes along for you. However, having a number of relationships with other partners provides a greater opportunity to engage in social comparison in such areas as physical attractiveness, sexual skills, communication skills, and personality traits, which may lead to more negative comparisons with a later marital partner. Further, having more relationship experiences prior to marriage means more experience in breaking up.

When two people are under the influence of the most violent, most insane, most delusive, and most transient of passions, they are required to swear that they will remain in that excited, abnormal, and exhausting condition continuously until death do them part.

—GEORGE BERNARD SHAW
Irish playwright, 20th century

Marital Trends In recent years, marriage rates in the United States have declined. In 2011 the marriage rate was 6.2 per 1,000 individuals, down from 8.2 in 2000 (National Center for Vital Statistics, 2013). In 2012, 48.6 percent of Americans were married, down from 72 percent in 1960 (U.S. Census Bureau, 2013).

Adults are remaining single longer today than in the past, with 27 percent of U.S. adults having never married (Pew Research Center, 2010). In 2011, the U.S. average age for a first marriage climbed to 28.7 years for men and 26.5 years for women, higher than at any other point in history (Pew Research Center, 2011). In 1980, the average age for a first marriage in the United States was 24 years for men and 21 years for women. In addition, the increase in cohabitation and a slight decline in the percentage of divorced individuals who remarry have contributed to declining marriage rates in the United States (Stokes & Raley, 2009). Also, men are more likely to never get married than are women (Wang, 2014).

© Stockdisc/PunchStock RF

A recent study explored what U.S. never-married men and women are looking for in a potential spouse (Wang, 2014). Following are the percentages who reported that various factors would be very important for them:

Factor	Men	Women
Similar ideas about having and raising children	62	70
A steady job	46	78
Same moral and religious beliefs	31	38
At least as much education	26	28
Same racial or ethnic background	7	10

Thus, in this study, never-married men said that the most important factor for a potential spouse was similar ideas about having and raising children, but never-married women placed greater importance on having a steady job.

Despite the decline in marriage rates, the United States is still a marrying society (Popenoe, 2009). Currently, about 70 percent of Americans have married at least once (U.S. Census Bureau, 2010). In a national poll, more than 40 percent of Americans under 30 said that marriage was headed for extinction yet only 5 percent of those young adults said they didn't want to get married (Pew Research Center, 2010). In one analysis, Andrew Cherlin (2009) explained these findings as reflecting marriage's impact as a way to show friends and family that you have a successful social life.

Is there a best age to get married? Marriages in adolescence are more likely to end in divorce than marriages in adulthood (Waite, 2009). One survey revealed that getting married in the United States between 23 and 27 years of age resulted in a lower likelihood of becoming divorced (Glenn, 2005). However, overall, researchers have not been able to pin down a specific age or age span of several years in adulthood when getting married is most likely to result in a successful marriage (Furstenberg, 2007).

An increasing number of children are growing up in families in which the parents have never married, a circumstance that is far more likely to occur when the parents have a low level of education (Pew Research Center, 2015). In a recent study, women with lower levels of education were more likely to have a birth in a cohabiting relationship established prior to conception (Gibson-Davis & Rackin, 2014). In this study, the probability that a less-educated mother would have a conventional married birth was only 11.5 percent compared with 78.4 percent for highly educated mothers.

(a)   (b)

(a) In Scandinavian countries, cohabitation is popular; only a small percentage of 20- to 24-year-olds are married.
(b) Japanese young adults live at home longer with their parents before marrying than young adults in most countries.
(a): © Mats Widen/Johner Images/Getty RF; (b): © David Hanover/The Image Bank/Getty Images

International comparisons of marriage also reveal that individuals in Scandinavian countries marry later than Americans, whereas their counterparts in many African, Asian, Latin American, and eastern European countries marry earlier (Waite, 2009). In Denmark, for example, almost 80 percent of the women and 90 percent of the men aged 20 to 24 have never been married. In Hungary, less than 40 percent of the women and 70 percent of the men aged 20 to 24 have never been married. In Scandinavian countries, cohabitation is popular among young adults; however, most Scandinavians eventually marry (Popenoe, 2008). In Sweden, on average women delay marriage until they are 31, men until they are 33. Some countries, such as Hungary, encourage early marriage and childbearing to offset declines in the population. Like Scandinavian countries, Japan has a high proportion of unmarried young people. However, rather than cohabiting as the Scandinavians do, unmarried Japanese young adults live at home longer with their parents before marrying.

The Benefits of a Good Marriage   Are there any benefits to having a good marriage? There are several (Benokratis, 2015; Seccombe, 2015). Individuals who are happily married live longer, healthier lives than either divorced individuals or those who are unhappily married (Proulx & Snyder-Rivas, 2013; Shor & others, 2012). A survey of U.S. adults 50 years of age and older also revealed that a lower portion of adult life spent in marriage was linked to an increased likelihood of dying at an earlier age (Henretta, 2010). And a recent large-scale analysis of data from a number of studies indicated a positive effect of marriage on life span, with being married benefitting the longevity of men more than women (Rendall & others, 2011). Further, an unhappy marriage can shorten a person's life by an average of four years (Gove, Style, & Hughes, 1990).

Premarital Education   Premarital education occurs in a group setting and focuses on relationship advice (Williamson & others, 2014). Might premarital education improve the quality of a marriage and possibly reduce the chances that the marriage will end in divorce? Researchers have found that it can (Owen & others, 2011). For example, a survey of more than 3,000 adults revealed that premarital education was linked to a higher level of marital satisfaction and commitment to a spouse, a lower level of destructive marital conflict, and a 31 percent lower likelihood of divorce (Stanley & others, 2006). The premarital education programs in the study ranged from several hours to 20 hours, with a median of 8 hours. Also, a recent study revealed that participating in premarital education predicted a higher quality of marriage (Rhoades & Stanley, 2014). A recent study also found that the effectiveness of a premarital education program was enhanced when the couples had a better level of communication prior to the intervention (Markman & others, 2013). It is recommended that premarital education begin approximately six months to a year before the wedding.

To improve their relationships, some couples seek counseling. To read about the work of couples counselor Susan Orenstein, see the *Connecting with Careers* profile.

DIVORCED ADULTS

Divorce has become an epidemic in the United States (Braver & Lamb, 2013; Hoelter, 2009). Until recently, it had been thought that the U.S. divorce rate had declined in the last three decades. However, the U.S. divorce rate overall actually increased from 1990 through 2008 due to the doubling of the divorce rate in individuals 35 and older while the rate remained stable or declined for the youngest couples (Kennedy & Ruggles, 2014). The world's highest divorce rate occurs in Russia (UNSTAT, 2011).

Individuals in some groups have a higher incidence of divorce (Amato, 2010). Youthful marriage, low educational level, low income, not having a religious affiliation, having parents who are divorced, and having a baby before marriage are factors that are associated with increased rates of divorce (Hoelter, 2009). And these characteristics of one's partner increase the likelihood of divorce: alcoholism, psychological problems, domestic violence, infidelity, and inadequate division of household labor (Hoelter, 2009).

Certain personality traits also have been found to predict divorce. In a recent study focused on the Big Five personality factors, low levels of agreeableness and conscientiousness, and high levels of neuroticism and openness to experience, were linked to daily

Susan Orenstein, Couples Counselor

Susan Orenstein provides counseling to emerging adults and young adults in Cary, North Carolina. She specializes in premarital and couples counseling to help couples increase their intimacy and mutual appreciation, and also works with couples to resolve long-standing conflicts, reduce destructive patterns of communication, and restore trust in the relationship. In addition to working privately with couples, she conducts workshops on relationships and gives numerous talks at colleges, businesses, and organizations.

Dr. Orenstein obtained an undergraduate degree in psychology from Brown University, a master's degree in counseling from Georgia Tech University, and a doctorate in counseling psychology from Temple University. Some couples therapists hold advanced degrees in clinical psychology or marriage and family therapy rather than counseling, and some practice with a master's degree. After earning a master's or doctoral degree in an appropriate program, before practicing couples therapy, individuals are required to do an internship and pass a state licensing examination.

At most colleges, the counseling or health center has a counselor or therapist who works with couples to improve their relationship.

experiences that over time negatively impacted relationship quality and eventually led to a marital breakup (Solomon & Jackson, 2014).

Earlier, we indicated that researchers have not been able to pin down a specific age that is the best time to marry so that the marriage will be unlikely to end in divorce. However, if a divorce is going to occur, it usually takes place between the fifth and tenth years of marriage (National Center for Health Statistics, 2000) (see Figure 7). For example, a recent study found that divorce peaked in Finland at approximately 5 to 7 years after a marriage, then the rate of divorce gradually declined (Kulu, 2014). This timing may reflect an effort by partners in troubled marriages to stay in the marriage and try to work things out. If after several years these efforts have not improved the relationship, the couple may then seek a divorce.

Even those adults who initiated their divorce undergo challenges after a marriage dissolves (Lee & others, 2011). Divorced adults have higher rates of depression, anxiety, physical illnesses, suicide, motor vehicle accidents, alcoholism, and mortality (Braver & Lamb, 2013). Both divorced women and divorced men complain of loneliness, diminished self-esteem, anxiety about the unknowns in their lives, and difficulty in forming satisfactory new intimate relationships.

Psychologically, one of the most common characteristics of divorced adults is difficulty trusting someone else in a romantic relationship. Following a divorce, though, people's lives can take diverse turns. For example, in one research study, 20 percent of the divorced group "grew more competent, well-adjusted, and self-fulfilled" following their divorce (Hetherington & Kelly, 2002, p. 98). They were competent in multiple areas of life and showed a

FIGURE **7**

THE DIVORCE RATE IN RELATION TO NUMBER OF YEARS MARRIED. Shown here is the percentage of divorces as a function of how long couples have been married. Notice that most divorces occur in the early years of marriage, peaking in the fifth to tenth years of marriage.
© *Digital Vision/Getty Images RF*

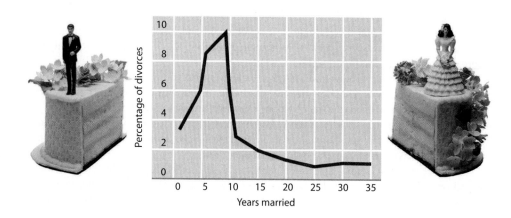

remarkable ability to bounce back from stressful circumstances and to create something meaningful out of problems.

There are gender differences in the process and outcomes of divorce (Braver & Lamb, 2013). Women are more likely to sense that something is wrong with the marriage and are more likely to seek a divorce than are men. Women also show better emotional adjustment and are more likely to perceive divorce as providing a "second chance" to increase their happiness, improve their social lives, and have better work opportunities. However, divorce typically has a more negative economic impact on women than it does on men.

GAY AND LESBIAN ADULTS

The legal and social context of marriage creates barriers to breaking up that do not usually exist for same-sex partners (Murphy, 2014). But in other ways, researchers have found that gay and lesbian relationships are similar—in their satisfactions, loves, joys, and conflicts—to heterosexual relationships (Crooks & Baur, 2014). For example, like heterosexual couples, gay and lesbian couples need to find a balance of romantic love, affection, autonomy, and equality that is acceptable to both partners (Fingerhut & Peplau, 2013; Hope, 2009). And an increasing number of gay and lesbian couples are creating families that include children.

Lesbian couples especially place a high priority on equality in their relationships (Fingerhut & Peplau, 2013). Indeed, some researchers have found that gay and lesbian couples are more flexible in their gender roles than heterosexual individuals are (Marecek, Finn, & Cardell, 1988). And a recent study of couples revealed that over the course of ten years of cohabitation, partners in gay and lesbian relationships showed a higher average level of relationship quality than did heterosexual couples (Kurdek, 2008).

There are a number of misconceptions about gay and lesbian couples (Cohler & Michaels, 2013; Diamond, Bonner, & Dickenson, 2015). Contrary to stereotypes, in only a small percentage of gay and lesbian couples is one partner masculine and the other feminine. Only a small segment of the gay population has a large number of sexual partners, and this is uncommon among lesbians. Furthermore, researchers have found that gay and lesbian couples prefer long-term, committed relationships (Fingerhut & Peplau, 2013). About half of committed gay couples do have an open relationship that allows the possibility of sex (but not affectionate love) outside of the relationship. Lesbian couples usually do not have this type of open relationship.

A special concern is the stigma, prejudice, and discrimination that lesbian, gay, and bisexual individuals experience because of widespread social devaluation of same-sex relationships (Cochran & others, 2013). However, a recent study indicated that many individuals in these relationships saw stigma as bringing them closer together and strengthening their relationship (Frost, 2011).

Review Connect Reflect

 LG5 Explain the diversity of emerging adult lifestyles

Review
- What characterizes single adults?
- What are the lives of cohabiting adults like?
- What are some key aspects of the lives of married adults?
- How does divorce affect adults?
- What characterizes the lifestyles of gay and lesbian adults?

Connect
- What are some similarities and differences between cohabiting relationships and marriages?

Reflect *Your Own Personal Journey of Life*
- Which type of lifestyle are you living today? What do you think are its advantages and disadvantages for you? If you could have a different lifestyle, which one would it be? Why?

reach your **learning goals**

Peers, Romantic Relationships, and Lifestyles

1 Exploring Peer Relations and Friendship

 Discuss the roles of peer relations, friendship, and loneliness in adolescent development

Peer Relations

· Peers are individuals who are about the same age or maturity level. Peers provide a means of social comparison and a source of information beyond the family. Contexts and individual difference factors influence peer relations. Good peer relations may be necessary for normal social development. The inability to "plug in" to a social network is associated with a number of problems. Peer relations can be negative or positive. Sullivan stressed that peer relations provide the context for learning the symmetrical reciprocity mode of relationships. Healthy family relations usually promote healthy peer relations. The pressure to conform to peers is strong during adolescence, especially around the eighth and ninth grades. Popular children are frequently nominated as a best friend and are rarely disliked by their peers. Average children receive an average number of both positive and negative nominations from their peers. Neglected children are infrequently nominated as a best friend but are not disliked by their peers. Rejected children are infrequently nominated as a best friend and are disliked by their peers. Controversial children are frequently nominated both as a best friend and as being disliked by peers. Social knowledge and social information-processing skills are associated with improved peer relations. Self-regulation of emotion is associated with positive peer relations. Conglomerate strategies, also referred to as coaching, involve the use of a combination of techniques, rather than a single strategy, to improve adolescents' social skills.

Friendship

· Friends are a subset of peers who engage in mutual companionship, support, and intimacy. The functions of friendship include companionship, stimulation, physical support, ego support, social comparison, and intimacy/affection. Sullivan argued that the psychological importance and intimacy of close friends increases dramatically in adolescence. Research supports this view. Children and adolescents who become close friends with older individuals engage in more deviant behaviors than do their counterparts with same-age friends. Early-maturing girls are more likely than late-maturing girls to have older friends, a characteristic that can contribute to problem behaviors. Some changes in friendship occur in emerging adulthood. Intimacy and similarity are two of the most important characteristics of friendships.

Loneliness

· Chronic loneliness is linked with impaired physical and mental health. Loneliness often emerges when people make life transitions, so it is not surprising that loneliness is common among college freshmen. Moderately or intensely lonely individuals never or rarely feel in tune with others and rarely or never find companionship when they want it, whereas other individuals may value solitary time.

2 Adolescent Groups

 Summarize what takes place in adolescent groups

Groups in Childhood and Adolescence

· Childhood groups are less formal, less heterogeneous, and less mixed-sex than adolescent groups. Dunphy's study found that adolescent group development proceeds through five stages.

Cliques and Crowds

· Cliques are small groups that range from two to about twelve individuals and average about five to six individuals. Clique members are similar in age, usually of the same sex, and often participate in similar activities, sharing ideas, hanging out, and developing an in-group identity. Crowds are a larger group structure than cliques and are less personal. Adolescents are members of crowds usually based on reputation and may or may not spend much time together. Many crowds are defined by adolescents' activities, such as jocks, druggies, populars, and independents.

- Youth organizations can have important influences on adolescent development. More than 400 national youth organizations currently exist in the United States. Boys & Girls Clubs are examples of youth organizations designed to increase membership in youth organizations in low-income neighborhoods. Participation in youth organizations may increase achievement and decrease delinquency. Youth activities and organizations also may provide opportunities for adolescents to develop initiative.

3 Gender and Culture

LG3 Describe the roles of gender and culture in adolescent peer groups and friendships

- The social world of adolescent peer groups varies according to gender, socioeconomic status, ethnicity, and culture. In terms of gender, boys are more likely to associate in larger clusters and organized sports than girls are. Boys also are more likely than girls to engage in competition, conflict, ego displays, and risk taking and to seek dominance. By contrast, girls are more likely to engage in collaborative discourse. Girls engage in more intimacy in their friendships than boys do.

- In many cases, peer groups are segregated according to socioeconomic status. In some cases, ethnic minority adolescents in the United States rely on peers more than non-Latino White adolescents do.

- In some countries, such as rural India, Arab countries, and Japan, adults restrict access to the peer group. In North America and Europe, the peer group is a pervasive aspect of adolescents' lives.

4 Dating and Romantic Relationships

LG4 Characterize adolescent dating and romantic relationships

- Dating can be a form of recreation, a source of social status and achievement, an aspect of socialization, a context for learning about intimacy and sexual experimentation, a source of companionship, and a means of mate sorting.

- Three stages characterize the development of romantic relationships in adolescence: (1) entry into romantic attractions and affiliations at about 11 to 13 years of age, (2) exploring romantic relationships at approximately 14 to 16 years of age, and (3) consolidating dyadic romantic bonds at about 17 to 19 years of age. Younger adolescents often begin to hang out together in mixed-sex groups. A special concern is early dating, which is associated with a number of problems. In early adolescence, individuals spend more time thinking about the opposite sex than actually being with them, but this trend tends to reverse in the high school years. Most sexual minority youth have same-sex sexual experience, but relatively few have same-sex romantic relationships.

- The emotions of romantic relationships can envelop adolescents' lives. Sometimes these emotions are positive, sometimes negative, and they can change very quickly. Adolescents who date have more problems, such as substance abuse, than those who do not date, but they also receive more acceptance from peers.

- Romantic love, also called passionate love, involves sexuality and infatuation more than affectionate love. Romantic love is especially prominent among adolescents and traditional-aged college students. Affectionate love is more common in middle and late adulthood, characterizing love that endures over time. Connolly's research revealed the importance of peers and friends in adolescent romantic relationships.

- Girls tend to view dating as an interpersonal experience; boys view dating more in terms of physical attraction. Culture can exert a powerful influence on dating. Many adolescents from immigrant families face conflicts with their parents about dating.

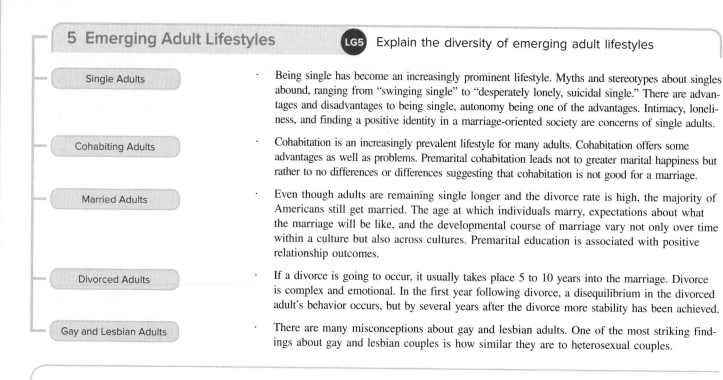

5 Emerging Adult Lifestyles

LG5 Explain the diversity of emerging adult lifestyles

Single Adults

Being single has become an increasingly prominent lifestyle. Myths and stereotypes about singles abound, ranging from "swinging single" to "desperately lonely, suicidal single." There are advantages and disadvantages to being single, autonomy being one of the advantages. Intimacy, loneliness, and finding a positive identity in a marriage-oriented society are concerns of single adults.

Cohabiting Adults

Cohabitation is an increasingly prevalent lifestyle for many adults. Cohabitation offers some advantages as well as problems. Premarital cohabitation leads not to greater marital happiness but rather to no differences or differences suggesting that cohabitation is not good for a marriage.

Married Adults

Even though adults are remaining single longer and the divorce rate is high, the majority of Americans still get married. The age at which individuals marry, expectations about what the marriage will be like, and the developmental course of marriage vary not only over time within a culture but also across cultures. Premarital education is associated with positive relationship outcomes.

Divorced Adults

If a divorce is going to occur, it usually takes place 5 to 10 years into the marriage. Divorce is complex and emotional. In the first year following divorce, a disequilibrium in the divorced adult's behavior occurs, but by several years after the divorce more stability has been achieved.

Gay and Lesbian Adults

There are many misconceptions about gay and lesbian adults. One of the most striking findings about gay and lesbian couples is how similar they are to heterosexual couples.

key terms

affectionate love	conglomerate strategies	friends	popular children
average children	controversial children	intimacy in friendship	rejected children
cliques	crowds	neglected children	romantic love
cohabitation	dating scripts	peers	sociometric status

key people

Andrew Cherlin	Dexter Dunphy	Willard Hartup	Judith Smetana
Jennifer Connolly	Candice Feiring	Reed Larson	Harry Stack Sullivan
Kenneth Dodge	Wyndol Furman	Mitchell Prinstein	Elizabeth Wehner

resources for improving the lives of adolescents

Friendships, Romantic Relationships, and Other Dyadic Peer Relationships in Child and Adolescence: A Unified Relational Perspective

Wyndol Furman and Amanda Rose (2015)

In R. M. Lerner (Ed.), *Handbook of Child Psychology and Developmental Science* (7th ed.). New York: Wiley.

> Leading experts provide an up-to-date review of research, theory, and applications involving the development of peer, friendship, and romantic relationships.

Just Friends

Lillian Rubin (1985)

New York: HarperCollins

> *Just Friends* explores the nature of friendship and intimacy, offering many recommendations for improving relationships with friends.

The Marriage-Go-Round

Andrew Cherlin (2009)

New York: Random House

> Leading sociologist Andrew Cherlin provides up-to-date information about trends in cohabitation, marriage, and divorce.

The Seven Principles for Making Marriages Work

John Gottman and Nan Silver (1999)

New York: Crown

> Leading relationship expert John Gottman provides valuable recommendations for what makes marriages work based on his extensive research.

chapter 10

SCHOOLS

chapter outline

To improve high school education in the United States, the National Research Council (2004) issued a strong recommendation that teachers find ways to engage students' motivation for learning. Here are some strategies that several award-winning teachers use to engage students in learning:

- A former at-risk student himself, Henry Brown, a recent Florida Teacher of the Year, teaches math. Half of the students enter the high school where Brown teaches with math skills below the fifth-grade level. Brown engages them by teaching real-world math skills. In one project, he devised a dummy corporation and had students play different roles in it, learning important math skills as they worked and made decisions in the corporation (*USA Today*, 2001).

- Peter Karpyk, a West Virginia high school chemistry teacher, uses an extensive range of activities to bring science alive for students. He has students give chemistry demonstrations at elementary schools and has discovered that some students who don't do well on tests excel when they teach younger children. He also adapts his teaching based on feedback from former students and incorporates questions from their college chemistry tests as bonus questions on his high school tests to challenge and motivate his current students (Wong Briggs, 2005).

- Peggy Schweiger, a physics teacher in Texas, makes science interesting by giving students opportunities to explore everyday science problems. Among the projects she has students do are wiring a doll house and making replicas of boats for a regatta. One of her former students, Alison Arnett, 19, said:

  > She taught us how to think and learn, not to succeed in physics class. We were encouraged to stand on desks, tape things to the ceiling, and even drop an egg on her head to illustrate physics—anything to make us discover that we live with physics every day (*USA Today*, 2001, p. 6).

Henry Brown teaches at-risk students real-world math skills to help them become more engaged in learning.
© Andrew Itkoff

Pete Karpyk shrink-wrapped himself to demonstrate the effects of air pressure in his high school chemistry class.
© Dale Sparks

Peggy Schweiger with a student who is learning how to think and discover how physics works in people's everyday lives.
© Patty Wood

Carmella Williams Scott has been successful in creating a learning atmosphere that stimulates students' critical thinking.
© Michael A. Schwarz Photography, Inc.

- Carmella Williams Scott, a middle school teacher in Georgia, created Juvenile Video Court TV, a student-run judicial system, so that students could experience how such systems function. She especially targeted gang leaders for inclusion in the system because they ran the school. Scott likes to use meaningful questions to stimulate students' critical thinking. She believes that mutual respect is a key factor in her success as a teacher and the absence of discipline problems in her classes (Wong Briggs, 1999).

preview

In youth, we learn. An important context for learning is school. Schools not only foster adolescents' academic learning but also provide a social arena where peers, friends, and crowds can have a powerful influence on their development. Our exploration of schools in this chapter focuses on approaches to educating students, transitions in schooling, the social contexts of schools, and strategies for educating adolescents who are exceptional.

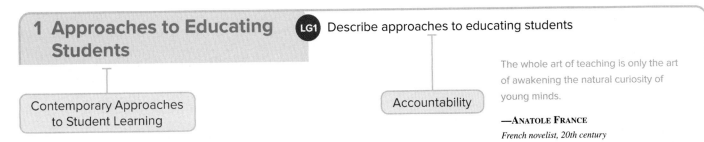

1 Approaches to Educating Students

LG1 Describe approaches to educating students

Contemporary Approaches to Student Learning

Accountability

> The whole art of teaching is only the art of awakening the natural curiosity of young minds.
>
> —**ANATOLE FRANCE**
> *French novelist, 20th century*

Because there are so many approaches for teaching students, controversy swirls about the best way to teach them (Burden & Byrd, 2013). There also is considerable interest in finding the best way to hold schools and teachers accountable for whether students are learning (McMillan, 2014; Popham, 2014).

CONTEMPORARY APPROACHES TO STUDENT LEARNING

There are two main contemporary approaches to student learning: constructivist and direct instruction. We examine both approaches and then consider whether effective teachers use both approaches.

The **constructivist approach** is learner centered and emphasizes the importance of individuals actively constructing their knowledge and understanding with guidance from the teacher. In the constructivist view, teachers should not attempt to simply pour information into students' minds. Rather, students should be encouraged to explore their world, discover knowledge, reflect, and think critically with careful monitoring and meaningful guidance from the teacher (Borich, 2014). Advocates of the constructivist approach believe that for too long in American education students have been required to sit still, be passive learners, and rotely memorize irrelevant as well as relevant information (Joyce, Weil, & Calhoun, 2015).

Today, constructivism may include an emphasis on collaboration—students working with each other in their efforts to know and understand (Lynch, 2015). A teacher with a constructivist instructional philosophy would not have students memorize information rotely but would give them opportunities to meaningfully construct their knowledge and understand the material while the teacher is guiding their learning.

By contrast, the **direct instruction approach** is structured and teacher centered. It is characterized by teacher direction and control, high teacher expectations for students' progress, maximum time spent by students on academic tasks, and efforts by the teacher to keep

© Tony Cordoza/Alamy RF

constructivist approach A learner-centered approach that emphasizes the adolescent's active, cognitive construction of knowledge and understanding with guidance from the teacher.

direct instruction approach A teacher-centered approach characterized by teacher direction and control, mastery of academic skills, high expectations for students, and maximum time spent on learning tasks.

In the History Alive! program of the Teachers' Curriculum Institute, students work in cooperative groups of four to prepare one student to be the actor in a lively panel debate. *Is the History Alive! program more characteristic of a constructivist or direct instruction approach?*
Courtesy of the Teacher's Curriculum Institute

No one can be given an education. All you can give is the opportunity to learn.

—CAROLYN WARNER
American author, 20th century

developmental **connection**

Intelligence

The intelligence quotient (IQ) gives students a specific number that indicates their intelligence. Connect to "The Brain and Cognitive Development."

negative affect to a minimum. An important goal in the direct instruction approach is maximizing student learning time (Kilbane & Milman, 2014; Parkay, 2016).

Advocates of the constructivist approach argue that the direct instruction approach turns students into passive learners and does not adequately challenge them to think in critical and creative ways (Armstrong, Henson, & Savage, 2015; Estes & Mintz, 2016). The direct instruction enthusiasts say that the constructivist approaches do not give enough attention to the content of a discipline, such as history or science. They also believe that the constructivist approaches are too relativistic and vague.

Some experts in educational psychology believe that many effective teachers use both a constructivist *and* a direct instruction approach rather than relying exclusively on one or the other (Bransford & others, 2006; Parkay, 2013). Further, some circumstances may call more for a constructivist approach, others for a direct instruction approach. For example, experts increasingly recommend an explicit, intellectually engaging direct instruction approach when teaching students with a reading or a writing disability (Berninger, 2006).

ACCOUNTABILITY

Since the 1990s, the U.S. public and governments at every level have demanded increased accountability from schools. One result has been the spread of state-mandated tests designed to measure what students have or have not learned (McMillan, 2014; Powell, 2015; Waugh & Gronlund, 2013). Many states have identified objectives for students in their state and created tests to measure whether students were meeting those objectives. This approach became national policy in 2002 when the No Child Left Behind (NCLB) legislation was signed into law.

Advocates argue that statewide standardized testing will have a number of positive effects. These include improved student performance; more time teaching the subjects that are tested; high expectations for all students; identification of poorly performing schools, teachers, and administrators; and improved confidence in schools as test scores rise.

Critics argue that the NCLB legislation is doing more harm than good (Sadker & Sadker, 2012). One criticism stresses that using a single test as the sole indicator of students' progress and competence presents a very narrow view of students' skills (Lewis, 2007). This criticism is similar to the one leveled at IQ tests. To assess student progress and achievement, many psychologists and educators emphasize that a number of measures should be used, including tests, quizzes, projects, portfolios, classroom observations, and so on. Also, the tests used as part of NCLB don't measure creativity, motivation, persistence, flexible thinking, or social skills (Brookhart & Nitko, 2015; Chappuis, 2015).

Critics point out that teachers end up spending far too much class time "teaching to the test" by drilling students and having them memorize isolated facts at the expense of teaching that focuses on thinking skills, which students need for success in life (Pressley, 2007). Also, some individuals are concerned that in the era of No Child Left Behind schools have been neglecting students who are gifted in the effort to raise the achievement level of students who are not doing well (Clark, 2008). And some critics stress that NCLB reflects social policy that focuses only on academic reforms and ignores the social aspects of schools (Crosnoe & Benner, 2015).

Consider also the following: Each state is allowed to have different criteria for what constitutes passing or failing grades on tests designated for NCLB inclusion. An analysis of NCLB data indicated that almost every fourth-grade student in Mississippi knows how to read, but only half of Massachusetts' students do (Birman & others, 2007). Clearly, Mississippi's standards for passing the reading test are far below those of Massachusetts. The state-by-state analysis suggests that many states have taken the safe route

What are some issues involved in the No Child Left Behind legislation?
© Jose Luis Pelaez, Inc./Corbis

and kept the standard for passing low. Thus, while one of NCLB's goals was to raise standards for achievement in U.S. schools, allowing states to set their own standards likely has lowered achievement standards.

Despite such criticisms, the U.S. Department of Education is committed to implementing No Child Left Behind, and schools are making accommodations to meet the requirements of this law. Indeed, most educators recognize the importance of high expectations and high standards of excellence for students and teachers. At issue, however, is whether the tests and procedures mandated by NCLB are the most effective ways to achieve these high standards (Darling-Hammond, 2011; Popham, 2014).

In 2009, the Common Core State Standards Initiative was endorsed by the National Governors Association in an effort to implement more rigorous state guidelines for educating students. The Common Core Standards specify what students should know and the skills they should develop at each grade level in various content areas (Common Core State Standards Initiative, 2014). A large majority of states have agreed to implement the Standards but they have generated considerable controversy, with some critics arguing that they are simply a further effort by the federal government to control education and that they emphasize a "one-size-fits-all" approach that pays little attention to individual variations in students. Supporters say that the Standards provide much-needed detailed guidelines and important milestones for students to achieve.

Review Connect Reflect

LG1 Describe approaches to educating students

Review
- What are the two main approaches to educating adolescents?
- What is involved in making schools more accountable?

Connect
- Relate the concept of multiple intelligences to this section's discussion of the constructivist and direct instruction approaches to student learning.

Reflect *Your Own Personal Journey of Life*
- When you were in secondary school, did your teachers take more of a direct instruction or constructivist approach? Which approach would you have liked your teachers to use more? Why?

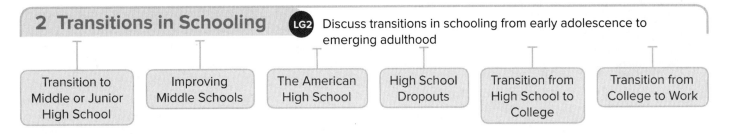

2 Transitions in Schooling

LG2 Discuss transitions in schooling from early adolescence to emerging adulthood

| Transition to Middle or Junior High School | Improving Middle Schools | The American High School | High School Dropouts | Transition from High School to College | Transition from College to Work |

As children become adolescents, and as adolescents become adults, they experience transitions in schooling: from elementary school to middle school or junior high school, from school to work for non-college youth, from high school to college, and from college to work.

TRANSITION TO MIDDLE OR JUNIOR HIGH SCHOOL

The transition to middle or junior high school can be difficult and stressful for many students (Anderman, 2012). Why? The transition takes place at a time when many changes—in the individual, in the family, and in school—are occurring simultaneously (Eccles & Roeser,

developmental **connection**

Cognitive Development

Formal operational thought is more abstract, idealistic, and logical than concrete operational thought. Connect to "The Brain and Cognitive Development."

The transition from elementary to middle or junior high school occurs at the same time as a number of other developmental changes. *What are some of these other developmental changes?*
© Will & Deni McIntyre/Corbis

‑ ‑ ‑ ‑ ‑ ‑ ‑ ‑ ‑ ➤

developmental **connection**

Achievement

Adolescence is a critical juncture in achievement that brings new social and academic pressures. Connect to "Achievement, Work, and Careers."

© Comstock/PictureQuest RF

top-dog phenomenon The circumstance of moving from the top position (in elementary school, the oldest, biggest, and most powerful students) to the lowest position (in middle or junior high school, the youngest, smallest, and least powerful students).

2013; Wigfield & others, 2015). These changes include puberty and related concerns about body image; the emergence of at least some aspects of formal operational thought, including accompanying changes in social cognition; advances in executive function; increased responsibility and decreased dependency on parents; change to a larger, more impersonal school structure; change from one teacher to many teachers and from a small, homogeneous set of peers to a larger, more heterogeneous set of peers; and an increased focus on achievement and performance and their assessment.

Also, when students make the transition to middle or junior high school, they experience the **top-dog phenomenon,** moving from being the oldest, biggest, and most powerful students in the elementary school to being the youngest, smallest, and least powerful students in the middle or junior high school. Researchers have found that students' self-esteem is higher in the last year of elementary school and that they like school better than in the first year of middle or junior high school (Hawkins & Berndt, 1985; Hirsch & Rapkin, 1987). A study in North Carolina schools revealed that sixth-grade students attending middle schools were far more likely to be cited for discipline problems than were their counterparts who were attending elementary schools (Cook & others, 2008). The transition to middle or junior high school is less stressful when students have positive relationships with friends and go through the transition in team-oriented schools in which 20 to 30 students take the same classes together (Hawkins & Berndt, 1985).

There can also be positive aspects to the transition to middle or junior high school (Bellmore, Villarreal, & Ho, 2011). Students are more likely to feel grown up, have more subjects from which to select, have more opportunities to spend time with peers and locate compatible friends, and enjoy increased independence from direct parental monitoring. They also may be more challenged intellectually by academic work.

IMPROVING MIDDLE SCHOOLS

In 1989 the Carnegie Council on Adolescent Development issued an extremely negative evaluation of U.S. middle schools. In the report—*Turning Points: Preparing American Youth for the Twenty-First Century*—the council concluded that most young adolescents attend massive, impersonal schools; learn from seemingly irrelevant curricula; trust few adults in school; and lack access to health care and counseling. The Carnegie report recommended the following changes (Carnegie Council on Adolescent Development, 1989):

· Develop smaller "communities" or "houses" to lessen the impersonal nature of large middle schools.

· Lower student-to-counselor ratios from hundreds-to-1 to 10-to-1.

· Involve parents and community leaders in schools.

· Develop curricula that produce students who are literate, understand the sciences, and have an awareness of health, ethics, and citizenship.

· Have teachers team-teach in more flexibly designed curriculum blocks that integrate several disciplines, instead of presenting students with disconnected, rigidly separated 50-minute segments.

· Boost students' health and fitness with more in-school programs and help students who need public health care to get it.

Turning Points 2000 continued to endorse the recommendations set forth in *Turning Points 1989* (Jackson & Davis, 2000). One new recommendation in the 2000 report stated that it is important to teach a curriculum grounded in rigorous academic standards for what students should know. A second new recommendation was to engage in instruction that encourages students to achieve higher standards and become lifelong learners. These new recommendations reflect the increasing emphasis on challenging students and setting higher academic expectations for them.

THE AMERICAN HIGH SCHOOL

I touch the future. I teach.

—CHRISTA McAULIFFE
American educator and astronaut, 20th century

Many high school graduates not only are poorly prepared for college, they also are poorly prepared for the demands of the modern, high-performance workplace (Crosnoe & Benner, 2015; Lauff, Ingels, & Christopher, 2014). A review of hiring practices at major companies concluded that many companies have identified sets of basic skills they want their employees to possess (Murnane & Levy, 1996). These include the ability to read at relatively high levels, do at least elementary algebra, use personal computers for straightforward tasks such as word processing, solve semistructured problems in which hypotheses must be formed and tested, communicate effectively (orally and in writing), and work effectively in groups with persons of various backgrounds.

Robert Crosnoe's (2011) book, *Fitting In, Standing Out,* highlighted another major problem with U.S. high schools: how the negative social aspects of adolescents' lives undermine their academic achievement. In his view, adolescents become immersed in complex peer group cultures that demand conformity. High school is supposed to be about getting an education, but for many youth it involves navigating the social worlds of peer relations that may or may not value education and academic achievement. Adolescents who fail to fit in, especially those who are obese or gay, become stigmatized.

The National Research Council (2004) made a number of recommendations for improving U.S. high schools. They especially emphasized the importance of finding ways to get students more engaged in learning. The council concluded that the best way to do so is to focus on the psychological factors involved in motivation. Increasing students' engagement in learning consists of promoting a sense of belonging "by personalizing instruction, showing an interest in students' lives, and creating a supportive, caring social environment" (National Research Council, 2004, p. 3). The council said that this description of engaging students applies to very few urban high schools, which too often are characterized by low expectations, alienation, and low achievement. By contrast, recall the chapter-opening vignette describing four teachers who created exciting, real-world opportunities for students to increase their motivation to become more engaged in learning.

HIGH SCHOOL DROPOUTS

Dropping out of high school has been viewed as a serious educational and societal problem for many decades. By leaving high school before graduating, adolescents approach adult life with educational deficiencies that severely curtail their economic and social well-being (Vaughn & others, 2011). For example, a recent study of more than 19,000 individuals from 18 to 25 years old revealed that those who had dropped out of high school were more likely than high school graduates to smoke cigarettes daily, to report having attempted suicide in the previous year, and to have been arrested for larceny, assault, and drug possession or drug sales (Maynard, Salas-Wright, & Vaughn, 2015).

High School Dropout Rates   In the last half of the twentieth century and the first decade of the twenty-first century, U.S. high school dropout rates declined (National Center for Education Statistics, 2014). In the 1940s, more than half of U.S. 16- to 24-year-olds had dropped out of school; by 2012, this figure had decreased to 6.6 percent. The dropout rate of Latino adolescents remains high, although it has been decreasing considerably in the twenty-first century (from 28 percent in 2000 to 15.1 percent in 2010 to 12.7 percent in 2012). In 2013, the lowest dropout rate occurred for Asian American adolescents (3.4 percent), followed by non-Latino White adolescents (5.1 percent), African American adolescents (7.9 percent), and Latino adolescents (11.7 percent) (Child Trends, 2014).

Gender differences characterize U.S. dropout rates, with males more likely to drop out than females in 2012 (7.3 percent versus 5.9 percent) (National Center for Education Statistics, 2014). The gender gap in dropout rates for Latino adolescents still favors females—11.3 percent for females, 12.7 percent for males—but that gender gap has narrowed considerably in recent years.

The average U.S. high school dropout rates just described mask some very high dropout rates in low-income areas of inner cities. For example, in cities such as Detroit, Cleveland, and Chicago, dropout rates are above 50 percent. Also, the percentages just cited are for 16- to 24-year-olds. When dropout rates are calculated in terms of students who do not

Students in the technology training center at Wellpinit Elementary/ High School, located on the Spokane Indian reservation in Washington State. An important educational goal is to increase the high school graduation rate of Native American adolescents.
© Ed Kashi/Corbis

graduate from high school in four years, the percentage of students who drop out is also much higher. Thus, in considering high school dropout rates, it is important to examine age, the number of years it takes to complete high school, and various contexts including ethnicity, gender, and school location.

The Causes of Dropping Out   Students drop out of school for school-related, economic, family-related, peer-related, and personal reasons. School-related problems are consistently associated with dropping out of school (Schoeneberger, 2012). In one investigation, almost 50 percent of the dropouts cited school-related reasons for leaving school, such as not liking school, being suspended, or being expelled (Rumberger, 1995). Twenty percent of the dropouts (but 40 percent of the Latino students) cited economic reasons for dropping out. Many of these students quit school and take jobs to help support their families. Students from low-income families are more likely to drop out than those from middle-income families. A recent study revealed that when children's parents were involved in their schools in middle and late childhood, and when parents and adolescents had good relationships in early adolescence, a positive trajectory toward academic success was the likely outcome (Englund, Egeland, & Collins, 2008). By contrast, those who had poor relationships with their parents were more likely to drop out of high school despite doing well academically and behaviorally. Many school dropouts have friends who also are school dropouts. Approximately one-third of the girls who drop out of school do so for personal reasons, such as pregnancy or marriage.

However, it is not just social reasons that explain student dropout rates. A recent study found that aspects of students' motivation—lower ability beliefs and lower educational expectations—were related to their dropping out of school (Fan & Wolters, 2014).

Reducing the Dropout Rate   A review of school-based dropout prevention programs found that the most effective ones encompassed early reading intervention, tutoring, counseling, and mentoring (Lehr & others, 2003). The reviewers also emphasized the importance of creating caring environments, building relationships, and offering community-service opportunities.

Clearly, then, early detection of children's school-related difficulties, and getting children and youth engaged with school in positive ways, are important strategies for reducing the dropout rate. One successful dropout prevention program is Talent Search, which provides low-income high school students mentoring, academic tutoring, and training on test-taking and study skills, as well as career development coaching, financial aid application assistance for college, and visits to college campuses (Constantine & others, 2006). Talent Search students had high school completion rates that were 9 percent higher than a control group of students who were not in the Talent Search program.

Also, recently the Bill and Melinda Gates Foundation (2006, 2008, 2012) has funded efforts to reduce the dropout rates in schools where rates are high. One strategy that is being emphasized in the Gates funding is keeping at-risk students with the same teachers throughout their high school years. The hope is that the teachers will get to know these students much better, their relationship with the students will improve, and they will be able to monitor and guide the students toward graduating from high school.

An initiative that has achieved impressive results is "I Have a Dream" (IHAD), an innovative, comprehensive, long-term dropout prevention program administered by the National "I Have a Dream" Foundation in New York. Since the National IHAD Foundation was created in 1986, it has grown to encompass more than 180 projects in 64 cities and 27 states, Washington, D.C., and New Zealand serving more than 15,000 children ("I Have a Dream" Foundation, 2015). Local IHAD projects around the country "adopt" entire grades (usually the third or fourth) from public elementary schools, or corresponding age cohorts from public housing developments.

These adolescents participate in the "I Have a Dream" (IHAD) program, a comprehensive, long-term dropout prevention program that has been very successful. What are some other strategies for reducing high school dropout rates?
Courtesy of "I Have a Dream" Foundation of Boulder County (www.ihadboulder.org)

These children—"Dreamers"—are then provided with a program of academic, social, cultural, and recreational activities throughout their elementary, middle school, and high school years. An important aspect of this program is that it is personal rather than institutional: IHAD sponsors and staff develop close, long-term relationships with the children. When participants complete high school, IHAD provides the tuition assistance necessary for them to attend a state or local college or vocational school.

The IHAD program was created when philanthropist Eugene Lang made an impromptu offer of college tuition to a class of graduating sixth-graders at P. S. 121 in East Harlem. Statistically, 75 percent of the students should have dropped out of school; instead, 90 percent graduated and 60 percent went on to college. Other evaluations of IHAD programs have found dramatic improvements in grades, test scores, and school attendance, as well as a reduction of behavioral problems of Dreamers. For example, in Portland, Oregon, twice as many Dreamers as control-group students had reached a math standard, and the Dreamers were less likely to be referred to the juvenile justice system (Davis, Hyatt, & Arrasmith, 1998). And in a recent analysis of the "I Have a Dream" program in Houston, 91 percent of the participants received passing grades in reading/English, 83 percent said they liked school, 98 percent said getting good grades was important to them, 100 percent said they planned to graduate from high school, and 94 percent reported that they planned to go to college ("I Have a Dream" Foundation, 2015).

TRANSITION FROM HIGH SCHOOL TO COLLEGE

Just as the transition from elementary school to middle or junior high school involves change and possible stress, so does the transition from high school to college. In many ways, the two transitions involve parallel changes. Going from being a senior in high school to being a freshman in college replays the top-dog phenomenon of going from the oldest and most powerful group of students to the youngest and least powerful group of students. The transition from high school to college involves a move to a larger, more impersonal school structure, interaction with peers from more diverse geographical and sometimes more diverse ethnic backgrounds, and an increased focus on achievement and performance and their assessment.

However, as with the transition from elementary school to middle or junior high school, the transition from high school to college can have positive aspects. Students are more likely to feel grown up, have more subjects from which to select, have more time to spend with peers, have more opportunities to explore different lifestyles and values, enjoy greater independence from parental monitoring, and may be more challenged intellectually by academic work (Halonen & Santrock, 2013).

Today's college students experience more stress and are more depressed than their counterparts in the past, according to a national study of more than 300,000 freshmen at more than 500 colleges and universities (Eagan & others, 2014). In 2014, 35 percent (up from 16 percent in 1985 and 27 percent in 2009) said they frequently "felt overwhelmed with what I have to do." College females in 2014 were more than twice as likely as their male counterparts to say that they felt overwhelmed with all they had to do. And college freshmen in 2014 indicated that they felt more depressed than their counterparts from the 1980s had indicated. The pressure to succeed in college, get a great job, and make lots of money are pervasive concerns of these students.

What makes college students happy? One study of 222 undergraduates compared the upper 10 percent of college students who were very happy with average and very unhappy college students (Diener & Seligman, 2002). The very happy college students were highly social, more extraverted, and had stronger romantic and social relationships than the less happy college students, who spent more time alone.

TRANSITION FROM COLLEGE TO WORK

Having a college degree is a strong asset. College graduates can enter careers that will earn them considerably more money in their lifetimes than those who do not go to college, and income differences between college graduates and high school graduates continue to grow (*Occupational Outlook Handbook, 2014–2015*). Recent media accounts have highlighted the dramatically rising costs of a college education and somewhat bleak job prospects for recent college graduates, raising questions about whether a college education is worth it. However,

The transition from high school to college often involves positive as well as negative features. In college, students are likely to feel grown up, be able to spend more time with peers, have more opportunities to explore different lifestyles and values, and enjoy greater freedom from parental monitoring. However, college involves a larger, more impersonal school structure and an increased focus on achievement and its assessment. *What was your transition to college like?*
© Stockbyte/PunchStock RF

What characterizes the transition from college to work?
© Wally McNamee/Corbis

developmental **connection**

Work

A diversity of school and work patterns characterize emerging adults. Connect to "Achievement, Work, and Careers."

recent data show that individuals with a bachelor's degree make over $20,000 a year more on average than those with only a high school diploma (Daly & Bengali, 2014). Recent data also indicated that in the United States a college graduate will make approximately $830,000 more on average than a high school graduate will earn (Daly & Bengali, 2014).

Nonetheless, in North American countries, the transition from college to work is often a difficult one. U.S. colleges train many students to develop general skills rather than vocationally specific skills, with the result that many college graduates are poorly prepared for specific jobs or occupations. After finishing college, many individuals have difficulty obtaining the type of job they desire, or any job at all. Bouncing from one job to another after college is also not unusual.

Accelerated technical and occupational change in the future may make it even more difficult for colleges to provide training that keeps up with a fluid and shifting job market. Thus, it is important for colleges and employers to become better connected with each other to provide improved training for changing job opportunities (Mortimer & Larson, 2002).

Review Connect Reflect

LG2 Discuss transitions in schooling from early adolescence to emerging adulthood

Review

- How can the transition to middle or junior high school be characterized?
- How can middle schools be improved?
- What is the American high school like? How can it be improved?
- What characterizes high school dropouts?
- How can the transition from high school to college be described?
- How can the transition from college to work be summarized?

Connect

- What impact might the concept of parents as "managers" have on reducing the high school dropout rate?

Reflect *Your Own Personal Journey of Life*

- What was your own middle or junior high school like? How did it measure up to the recommendations made by the Carnegie Council?

3 The Social Contexts of Schools

LG3 Explain how the social contexts of schools influence adolescent development

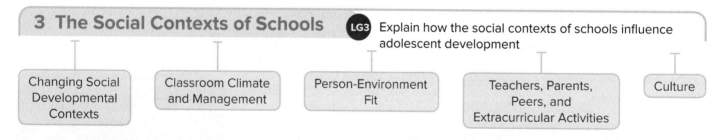

Changing Social Developmental Contexts

Classroom Climate and Management

Person-Environment Fit

Teachers, Parents, Peers, and Extracurricular Activities

Culture

Schools and classrooms vary along many dimensions, including the school or class social atmosphere. Adolescents' school life also involves thousands of hours of interactions with teachers. A special concern is parental involvement in the adolescent's schooling. Also, as we will see next, the social context of schools changes with the developmental level of students.

CHANGING SOCIAL DEVELOPMENTAL CONTEXTS

The social context differs at the preschool, elementary, and secondary levels. The preschool setting is a protected environment whose boundary is the classroom. The classroom is still the major context for the elementary school child, although it is more likely to be experienced as a social unit than at the preschool level. As children move into middle or junior high schools, the school environment increases in scope and complexity (Anderman, Gray, & Chang, 2003; Eccles & Roeser, 2013). The social field is the school as a whole rather than the classroom. Adolescents interact with many different teachers and peers from a range of social and ethnic backgrounds. Students are often exposed to a greater mix of male and female

What are some differences in the social contexts of elementary and secondary schools?
© Tim Pannell/Corbis

teachers. And social behavior is heavily weighted toward peers, extracurricular activities, clubs, and the community. The student in secondary school is usually aware of the school as a social system and may be motivated to conform and adapt to the system or to challenge it (Minuchin & Shapiro, 1983).

CLASSROOM CLIMATE AND MANAGEMENT

It is important for classrooms to present a positive environment for learning (Evertson & Emmer, 2013; Jones, 2015). One way to do this is to use an authoritative approach.

The idea of an authoritative classroom management strategy is derived from Diana Baumrind's (1971, 2012) typology of parenting styles, as discussed in the chapter on "Families." Like authoritative parents, authoritative teachers have students who tend to be self-reliant, delay gratification, get along well with their peers, and show high self-esteem. An **authoritative strategy of classroom management** encourages students to be independent thinkers and doers but still involves effective monitoring. Authoritative teachers engage students in considerable verbal give-and-take and show a caring attitude toward them. However, they still declare limits when necessary. Teachers clarify rules and regulations, establishing these standards with input from students.

The authoritative strategy contrasts with two ineffective strategies: authoritarian and permissive. The **authoritarian strategy of classroom management** is restrictive and punitive. The focus is mainly on keeping order in the classroom rather than on instruction and learning. Authoritarian teachers place firm limits and controls on students and have little verbal exchange with them. Students in authoritarian classrooms tend to be passive learners, fail to initiate activities, express anxiety about social comparison, and have poor communication skills.

The **permissive strategy of classroom management** offers students considerable autonomy but provides them with little support for developing learning skills or managing their behavior. Not surprisingly, students in permissive classrooms tend to have inadequate academic skills and low self-control.

Overall, an authoritative style benefits students more than do authoritarian or permissive styles. An authoritative style helps students become active, self-regulated learners. A study of ninth-grade English classrooms revealed that a combination of behavioral control and caring on the part of teachers was linked with positive student outcomes, such as students' engagement in learning, which is consistent with an authoritative style (Nie & Lau, 2009).

A well-managed classroom not only fosters meaningful learning but also helps prevent academic and emotional problems from developing. Well-managed classrooms keep students busy with active, appropriately challenging tasks. Well-managed classrooms have activities that encourage students to become absorbed and motivated and to learn clear rules and regulations. In such classrooms, students are less likely to develop academic and emotional problems. By contrast, in poorly managed classrooms, students' academic and emotional problems are more likely to fester. The academically unmotivated student becomes even less motivated. The shy student becomes more reclusive. The bully becomes meaner.

Secondary school students' problems can be more long-standing and more deeply ingrained, and therefore more difficult to modify, than those of elementary school students

MR. BROWN THIRD

"How come when you say we have a problem, I'm always the one who has the problem?" Copyright © by George Abbott. Used with permission.

authoritative strategy of classroom management A teaching strategy that encourages students to be independent thinkers and doers but still involves effective monitoring. Authoritative teachers engage students in considerable verbal give-and-take and show a caring attitude toward them. However, they still set and enforce limits when necessary.

authoritarian strategy of classroom management A teaching strategy that is restrictive and punitive. The focus is mainly on keeping order in the classroom rather than on instruction and learning.

permissive strategy of classroom management A teaching strategy that offers students considerable autonomy but provides them with little support for developing learning skills or managing their behavior.

What are some effective strategies teachers can use to manage the classroom? How is managing the classroom different in secondary school from managing it in elementary school?
© Bill Ross/Corbis

What is the concept of person-environment fit and how does it involve the mismatch between the needs of adolescents and the opportunities they have in middle/junior high schools?
© Dan Lassiter/The Janesville Gazette/AP Images

(Emmer & Evertson, 2013). Also in secondary schools, discipline problems are frequently more severe, as the students are potentially more unruly and even dangerous. Because most secondary school students have more advanced reasoning skills than do elementary school students, they might demand more elaborate and logical explanations of rules and discipline. And in secondary schools, hallway socializing can carry into the classroom. Every hour there is another "settling down" process.

PERSON-ENVIRONMENT FIT

Some of the negative psychological changes associated with adolescent development might result from a mismatch between the needs of developing adolescents and the opportunities afforded them by the schools they attend (Anderman & Dawson, 2011). Jacquelynne Eccles, Allan Wigfield, and their colleagues (Eccles, 2004, 2007; Eccles & Roeser, 2009, 2011, 2013; Wigfield & others, 2006, 2015) have described ways to create developmentally appropriate school environments that are better suited to adolescents' needs. Their recommendations are based on a large-scale study of 1,500 young adolescents in middle-income communities in Michigan. These adolescents were studied as they made the change from the sixth grade in an elementary school to the seventh grade in a junior high school.

Eccles (2004, 2007) argues that a lack of fit between the middle school/junior high environment and the needs of young adolescents produces increasingly negative self-evaluations and attitudes toward school. Her research has revealed that teachers become more controlling just at the time when adolescents are seeking greater autonomy, and the teacher-student relationship becomes more impersonal at a time when students are seeking more independence from their parents and need more support from other adults. At a time when adolescents are becoming more self-conscious, an increased emphasis on grades and other competitive comparisons only make things worse.

Although less research has been conducted on the transition from middle school to high school, the existing research suggests that, like the transition from elementary to middle school, it can produce similar problems (Eccles & Roeser, 2009, 2013). High schools often are even larger and more bureaucratic than middle schools. In such schools, a sense of community usually is undermined, with little opportunity for students and teachers to get to know each other. As a consequence, distrust between students and teachers develops easily and there is little communication about students' goals and values. Such contexts can especially harm the motivation of students who are not doing well academically.

What lessons can be drawn from this discussion? Perhaps the single most important lesson is that middle school and junior high school students benefit when teachers think of ways to make their school settings more personal, less formal, and more intrinsically challenging.

TEACHERS, PARENTS, PEERS, AND EXTRACURRICULAR ACTIVITIES

Adolescents' development is influenced by teachers. In addition, two increasingly important issues are parent involvement in schooling and the roles that peers and extracurricular activities play in schooling and academic achievement.

Teachers Competent teachers of adolescents have a good understanding of their development and know how to create instructional materials that are appropriate for the developmental levels of the adolescents in their classroom (Powell, 2015).

Psychologists and educators have tried to compile a profile of a good teacher's personality traits, but the complexity of personality, education, learning, and individuals makes this a difficult task. Nonetheless, some teacher traits and dimensions—enthusiasm, ability to plan, poise, adaptability, warmth, flexibility, and awareness of individual differences—are associated with positive student outcomes more than are other traits. And a recent analysis by leading experts in educational psychology concluded that the following teaching practices and strategies are linked with positive student outcomes (Roehrig & others, 2012):

· *Developing caring classroom communities* by monitoring behavior rather than punishing it and by establishing a democratic classroom
· *Enhancing students' motivation to learn* by providing informative feedback, focusing on improvement and effort, expressing high expectations, and fostering interest and engagement
· *Planning and delivering engaging, assessment-driven instruction* by organizing content and activities and individualizing instruction using assessment data
· *Supporting students' deep processing and self-regulation skills* by modeling thinking processes, balancing appropriate challenge level, and encouraging self-regulation.

Parents and Schools Parents play important roles in the adolescent's success in school. Among the ways that parents can positively contribute to adolescents' school success are effective family management practices and involvement in adolescents' schooling.

Family Management Researchers have found that family management practices are positively related to grades and self-responsibility, and negatively to school-related problems (Taylor, 1996). Among the family management practices important in this regard is maintaining a structured and organized family environment, such as establishing routines for homework, chores, bedtime, and so on. Creating a family environment in which high expectations for achievement are present also is important (Jeynes, 2003).

One study focusing on African American families examined links between mothers' reports of family management practices, including routine and achievement expectations, and adolescents' school-related behavior (Taylor & Lopez, 2005). Well-managed and organized family routines were positively related to adolescents' school achievement, paying attention in class, and attendance, and negatively linked to their school-related problems. Compared to mothers with low expectations for achievement, mothers with high expectations for achievement had adolescents who earned higher grades and had better school attendance.

Parental Involvement Even though parental involvement often is minimal in elementary school, it is even less evident in secondary school (Casas, 2011). In one study, teachers listed parental involvement as the number one priority in improving education (Chira, 1993). In an analysis of 16,000 students, students were more likely to get A's and less likely to repeat a grade or be expelled if both parents were highly involved in their schooling (National Center for Education Statistics, 1997).

Research by Eva Pomerantz and her colleagues (Pomerantz, Cheung, & Qin, 2012; Pomerantz & Kempner, 2013; Pomerantz, Kim, & Cheung, 2012;

developmental **connection**

Families

Key aspects of the managerial role of parenting are parental monitoring and adolescent management of information. Connect to "Families."

What are some important roles of parents in students' schooling?
© Photodisc/Getty Images RF

Qu & Pomerantz, 2015) indicates that the more involved parents are in their children's learning, the higher the level of achievement their children will attain. East Asian parents are far more involved in their children's and adolescents' learning than are U.S. parents. The greater East Asian parental involvement in children's learning is present as early as the preschool years and continues during the elementary school years (Cheung & Pomerantz, 2012). In East Asia, children's learning is considered to be a far greater responsibility of parents than in the United States (Pomerantz, Kim, & Cheung, 2012). However, a recent study revealed that when U.S. parents are more involved in their young adolescents' learning, achievement was higher (Cheung & Pomerantz, 2012). In this study, for both U.S. and Chinese young adolescents, the greater the amount of parental involvement, the more motivated the young adolescents were to achieve in school for parent-oriented reasons, and this was linked to enhanced self-regulated learning and higher grades. Also in recent research, Chinese mothers exerted more control (especially psychological control) over their young adolescents than U.S. mothers did (Ng, Pomerantz, & Deng, 2014). Further, Chinese mothers' self-worth was more contingent on their young adolescents' achievement than was the case for U.S. mothers. To reflect how important their children's and adolescents' achievement is to Chinese mothers, the authors titled their research article: "Why are Chinese parents more psychologically controlling than American parents? 'My child is my report card.'" And in a recent study, U.S. and Chinese young adolescents were assessed four times across the seventh and eighth grades (Qu & Pomerantz, 2015). In this study, the young adolescents' sense of responsibility to parents was linked with how much they valued school and were engaged in academic pursuits. The study showed a decline in U.S. students' responsibility to parents but not in Chinese students.

Eva Pomerantz (2014) recently offered these recommendations for parents who want their children and adolescents to do well in school:

- *Keep in mind that ability is not fixed and can change.* Although it is difficult and takes a lot of patience, understand that children's and adolescents' abilities can improve.
- *Be involved.* One of the most important things parents can do is to become involved in their children's and adolescents' academic life and talk often with them about what they are learning.
- *Support autonomy and self-initiative.* An important aspect of children's and adolescents' motivation to do well in school is being made to feel that they are responsible for their learning and must become self-motivated.
- *Be positive.* Too often school work and homework can be frustrating for children and adolescents. Interact with them in positive ways and let them know that life is often tough but that you know they can do well and overcome difficulties.
- *Understand that each child or adolescent is different.* Get to know your child or adolescent—don't let them be a psychological stranger to you. Be sensitive to their unique characteristics and know that sometimes you will need to adapt to such idiosyncrasies.

Peers You studied many aspects of adolescent peer relations in the chapter on "Peers, Romantic Relationships, and Lifestyles." Here you will explore peer relations in school contexts.

Structure of Middle Schools Middle schools are structured in a way that encourages students to interact with larger numbers of peers on a daily basis (Wentzel, 2013, 2015). The relative uncertainty and ambiguity of multiple classroom environments and more complex class schedules may result in middle school students turning to each other for information, social support, and strategies for coping.

Peer Statuses Peer statuses have been studied in relation to school success. Being popular or accepted by peers is usually associated with academic success, whereas being rejected by peers is related to more negative academic outcomes (Bellmore & others, 2011; Wentzel, 2013, 2015).

Bullying Significant numbers of students are victimized by bullies (Lereya & others, 2015; Perkins, Perkins, & Craig, 2014; Thornberg & Jungert, 2014; Tsitsika & others, 2014). In a national survey of more than 15,000 students in grades 6 through 10, nearly one of every three students said that they had experienced occasional or frequent involvement as a victim or perpetrator in bullying (Nansel & others, 2001). In this study, bullying was defined as

developmental **connection**

Peers

Peer statuses include popular, rejected, neglected, controversial, and average children. Connect to "Peers, Romantic Relationships, and Lifestyles."

verbal or physical behavior intended to disturb someone less powerful (see Figure 1). Boys are more likely to be bullies than girls, but gender differences regarding victims of bullying are less clear (Salmivalli & Peets, 2009).

Who is likely to be bullied? In the study just described, boys and younger middle school students were most likely to be affected (Nansel & others, 2001). Children who said they were bullied reported more loneliness and difficulty in making friends, while those who did the bullying were more likely to have low grades and to smoke cigarettes and drink alcohol.

Researchers have found that anxious, socially withdrawn, and aggressive children are often the victims of bullying (Hanish & Guerra, 2004). Anxious and socially withdrawn children may be victimized because they are nonthreatening and unlikely to retaliate if bullied, whereas aggressive children may be the targets of bullying because their behavior is irritating to bullies (Rubin, Bukowski, & Bowker, 2015). A recent study revealed that having supportive friends was linked to a lower level of bullying and victimization (Kendrick, Jutengren, & Stattin, 2012). Further, a recent meta-analysis indicated that positive parenting behavior (including having good communication, maintaining a warm relationship, being involved, and engaging in supervision of their children) was related to a lesser likelihood that a child would become either a bully/victim or a victim at school (Lereya, Samara, & Wolke, 2013).

The social context of the peer group also plays an important role in bullying (Hilliard & others, 2014; Troop-Gordon & Ladd, 2015). Recent research indicates that 70 to 80 percent of victims and their bullies are in the same school classroom (Salmivalli & Peets, 2009). Classmates are often aware of bullying incidents and in many cases witness bullying. Often bullies torment victims to gain higher status in the peer group, so bullies need others to witness their power displays. Many bullies are not rejected by the peer group. A recent longitudinal study explored the costs and benefits of bullying in the context of the peer group (Reijntjes & others, 2013). In this study children were initially assessed at 10 years of age and then followed into early adolescence. The results indicated that although young bullies may be on a developmental trajectory that over the long run is problematic, in the shorter term personal benefits of bullying often outweigh disadvantages. Frequent bullying was linked to high social status as indexed by perceived popularity in the peer group, and bullies also were characterized by self-perceived personal competence.

What are the outcomes of bullying? A recent study revealed that peer victimization in the fifth grade was associated with worse physical and mental health in the tenth grade (Bogart & others, 2014). Researchers have found that children who are bullied are more likely to experience depression, engage in suicidal ideation, and attempt suicide than their counterparts who have not been the victims of bullying (Undheim, 2013; Yen & others, 2014). A recent study revealed that peer victimization during the elementary school years was linked to stress and suicidal ideation (Kowalski & others, 2014). Another study indicated that peer victimization during the elementary school years was a leading indicator of internalizing problems (depression, for example) in adolescence (Schwartz & others, 2015). Also, a longitudinal study of more than 6,000 children found that children who were the victims of peer bullying from 4 to 10 years of age were more likely to engage in suicidal ideation at 11½ years of age (Winsper & others, 2012). And three meta-analyses concluded that engaging in bullying during middle school is linked to an increased likelihood of antisocial and criminal behavior later in adolescence and adulthood (Kim & others, 2011; Losel & Bender, 2011; Ttofi & others, 2011). Further, a recent analysis concluded that bullying can have long-term effects, including difficulty in forming lasting relationships and problems at work (Wolke & Lereya, 2015).

An increasing concern is peer bullying and harassment on the Internet (called *cyber bullying*) (Bonanno & Hymel, 2013). A recent study involving third- to sixth-graders revealed that engaging in cyber aggression was related to loneliness, lower self-esteem, fewer mutual friendships, and lower peer popularity (Schoffstall & Cohen, 2011). Further, recent research found that cyber bullying was more strongly associated with suicidal ideation than traditional bullying (van Geel, Vedder, & Tanilon, 2014). Also, a recent meta-analysis concluded that being the victim of cyber bullying was linked to stress and suicidal ideation (Kowalski & others, 2014). And another recent meta-analysis revealed that cyber bullying occurred twice as much as traditional bullying and that those who engaged in cyber bullying were often likely to also have engaged in traditional bullying (Modecki & others, 2014). Further, a longitudinal study found that adolescents who were experiencing social and emotional difficulties were more likely to be both cyber bullied and traditionally bullied than to be traditionally bullied only (Cross, Lester, & Brown, 2015). In this study, adolescents who were targeted in both ways

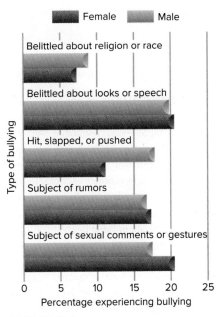

FIGURE 1

BULLYING BEHAVIORS AMONG U.S. YOUTH. This graph shows the types of bullying most often experienced by U.S. youth. The percentages reflect the extent to which bullied students said that they had experienced a particular type of bullying. In terms of gender, note that when they were bullied, boys were more likely to be hit, slapped, or pushed than girls were.

Bullying Prevention/Intervention

Extensive attention has been directed to finding ways to prevent and treat bullying and victimization (Low & others, 2014; Olweus, 2013; Saarento, Boulton, & Salmivalli, 2015; Salmivalli, Garandeau, & Veenstra, 2012). A research review revealed mixed results for school-based interventions (Vreeman & Carroll, 2007). School-based interventions vary greatly, ranging from involving the whole school in an antibullying campaign to providing individualized social skills training (Strohmeier & Noam, 2012). One of the most promising bullying intervention programs has been created by Dan Olweus (2003, 2013). This program focuses on 6- to 15-year-olds with the goal of decreasing opportunities and rewards for bullying. School staff are instructed in ways to improve peer relations and make schools safer. When properly implemented, the program reduces bullying by 30 to 70 percent (Olweus, 2003). A recent research review concluded that interventions focusing on the whole school, such as Olweus', are more effective than interventions involving classroom curricula or social skills training (Cantone & others, 2015).

To reduce bullying, schools can adopt these strategies (Cohn & Canter, 2003; Hyman & others, 2006; Limber, 2004):

- Get older peers to serve as monitors for bullying and to intervene when they see it taking place.
- Develop school-wide rules and sanctions against bullying and post them throughout the school.
- Form friendship groups for adolescents who are regularly bullied by peers.
- Incorporate the message of the antibullying program into places of worship, schools, and other community activity areas where adolescents are involved.

What are some strategies to reduce bullying?
© Photodisc/Getty Images RF

- Encourage parents to reinforce their adolescent's positive behaviors and model appropriate interpersonal interactions.
- Identify bullies and victims early and use social skills training to improve their behavior.
- Encourage parents to contact the school's psychologist, counselor, or social worker and ask for help with their adolescent's bullying or victimization concerns.

stayed away from school more than their counterparts who were traditionally bullied only. Information about preventing cyber bullying can be found at www.stopcyberbullying.org/.

To read about a number of strategies for reducing bullying, see the *Connecting with Health and Well-Being* interlude.

Friendship   Another aspect of peer relations that is linked with school success involves friendship (Wentzel, 2013). Having friends, especially friends who are academically oriented and earn good grades, is related to higher grades and test scores in adolescents (Ryan, 2011). One longitudinal study found that having at least one friend was related to academic success over a two-year period (Wentzel & Caldwell, 1997).

Extracurricular Activities   Adolescents in U.S. schools usually can choose from a wide array of extracurricular activities beyond their academic courses. These adult-sanctioned activities typically occur during after-school hours and can be sponsored by either the school or the community. They include such diverse activities as sports, honor societies, band, drama club, and various academic clubs (math and language, for example).

Researchers have found that participation in extracurricular activities is linked to higher grades, increased school engagement, reduced likelihood of dropping out of school, improved probability of going to college, higher self-esteem, and lower rates of depression, delinquency, and substance abuse (Eccles & Roeser, 2011, 2013; Fischer & Theis, 2014; Vandell & others, 2015).

A recent study revealed that immigrant adolescents who participated in extracurricular activities improved their academic achievement and increased their school engagement (Camacho & Fuligni, 2015). Also, a recent Australian study found that extracurricular participation in the eighth grade was linked to lower likelihood of binge drinking through the eleventh grade (Modecki & others, 2014).

Adolescents benefit from participating in a breadth of extracurricular activities more than they do from focusing on a single extracurricular activity (Morris & Kalil, 2006). Also, the more years adolescents spend in extracurricular activities, the stronger the likelihood of positive developmental outcomes (Fredricks & Eccles, 2006). For example, a longitudinal study revealed that youth who participated in organized school-sponsored activities (sports, cheerleading, music groups, plays, student government, honor societies, and service clubs, for example) and community-sponsored activities (religious activities, community youth groups, music/art/dance lessons, sports lessons, and community service, for example) for two years during adolescence had better educational and occupational outcomes in early adulthood than did those who participated for one year (Gardner, Roth, & Brooks-Gunn, 2008). In this study, more intensive participation was linked to more positive educational, occupational, and civic success in early adulthood. Further, a recent study revealed that intensive participation in after-school programs or extracurricular activities was linked to fewer internalized problems (depression, for example) in adolescents living in homes characterized by domestic violence (Gardner, Browning, & Brooks-Gunn, 2012). And another recent study also revealed that the more adolescents participated in organized out-of-school activities, the more likely they were to experience positive outcomes—educational attainment, civic engagement, and psychological flourishing—in emerging adulthood (Mahoney & Vest, 2012).

Of course, the quality of the extracurricular activities matters (Eccles & Roeser, 2013; Fischer & Theis, 2014). High-quality extracurricular activities that are likely to promote positive adolescent development have competent, supportive adult mentors, opportunities for increasing school connectedness, challenging and meaningful activities, and opportunities for improving skills (Fredricks & Eccles, 2006).

CULTURE

In some cultures—such as Arab countries and rural India—adults often restrict adolescents' access to peers, especially for girls. The peer restriction includes the social setting of schools, where girls are educated separately from boys. Let's now explore these aspects of culture and schools: socioeconomic status, ethnicity, and cross-cultural comparisons.

Socioeconomic Status and Ethnicity   Adolescents from low-income, ethnic minority backgrounds have more difficulties in school than do their middle-socioeconomic-status non-Latino White counterparts. Why? Critics argue that schools have not done a good job of educating low-income, ethnic minority adolescents and emerging adults to overcome the barriers to their achievement (Banks, 2014; Spring, 2013, 2014). Let's further explore the roles of socioeconomic status and ethnicity in schools.

The Education of Students from Low-Income Backgrounds   Many adolescents in poverty face problems that present barriers to their learning (Banks, 2014, 2015;

Forensics Teacher Tommie Lindsey's Students

Tommie Lindsey teaches competitive forensics (public speaking and debate) at Logan High School in Union City, California. In U.S. schools, forensics classes are mainly offered in affluent areas, but most of Lindsey's students come from impoverished or at-risk backgrounds. His students have won many public speaking honors.

The following comments by his students reflect Lindsey's outstanding teaching skills:

> He's one of the few teachers I know who cares so much. . . . He spends hours and hours, evenings, and weekends, working with us.
>
> —JUSTIN HINOJOZA, 17

> I was going through a tough time. . . . Mr. Lindsey helped me out. I asked how I could pay him back and he said, "Just help someone the way I helped you."
>
> —ROBERT HAWKINS, 21

> This amazing opportunity is here for us students and it wouldn't be if Mr. Lindsey didn't create it.
>
> —MICHAEL JOSHI, 17

As a ninth-grade student, Tommie Lindsey became a public speaker. He says that his English teacher doubted his ability, and he wanted to show her how good he could be at public speaking so he prepared a speech that received a standing ovation. Lindsey remembers, "She was expecting me to fail, and I turned the tables on her. . . . And we do that with our forensic program. When we

Tommie Lindsey works with his students on improving their public speaking and debate skills.
Courtesy of Tommie Lindsey

started a lot of people didn't believe our kids could do the things they do." For his outstanding teaching efforts, Tommie Lindsey was awarded a prestigious MacArthur Fellowship in 2005.

———

(*Source:* Seligson, 2005)

→

developmental connection

Socioeconomic Status

Socioeconomic differences are a proxy for material, human, and social capital beyond the family. Connect to "Culture."

Bennett, 2015; Duncan, Magnuson, & Votruba-Drzal, 2015; McLoyd, Mistry, & Hardaway, 2014; McLoyd, Purtell, & Hardaway, 2015). They might have parents who don't set high educational standards for them, who are incapable of reading to them, and who don't have enough money to pay for educational materials and experiences such as books and trips to zoos and museums. They might be malnourished and live in areas where crime and violence are a way of life.

Compared with schools in higher-income areas, schools in low-income areas are more likely to have higher percentages of students with low achievement test scores, lower graduation rates, and smaller percentages of students going to college. They are more likely to have young teachers with less experience, more noncredentialed or nonqualified teachers, and substitute teachers who regularly fill in to teach. Schools in low-income areas also tend to encourage rote learning, and are less likely to provide adequate support for English language learners. Too few schools in low-income neighborhoods provide students with environments that are conducive to learning (Bradley, 2015; Crosnoe & Benner, 2015). Many of the schools' buildings and classrooms are old and crumbling.

Living in economically disadvantaged families during adolescence may have more negative achievement outcomes than do corresponding circumstances in childhood (Cushner, McClelland, & Safford, 2015; Duncan & others, 2012; McLoyd & others, 2011). The possible timing difference in poverty effects might be due to the adolescents' greater awareness of barriers to their success and the difficulties they will encounter in becoming successful.

Some innovative programs indicate that improving certain characteristics of schools enhances the achievement of adolescents from economically disadvantaged backgrounds

(McLoyd & others, 2011). For example, the Center for Collaborative Education studied a series of pilot schools in Boston and found that the following changes were linked with higher levels of achievement in high school: smaller class sizes, longer class sessions, more advisory sessions, and allotment of more time for teachers to explore teaching methods (Tung & Ouimette, 2007).

Ethnicity in Schools   More than one-third of all African American and almost one-third of all Latino students attend schools in the 47 largest city school districts in the United States, compared with only 5 percent of all non-Latino White and 22 percent of all Asian American students. Many of these inner-city schools are still segregated, are grossly underfunded, and do not provide adequate opportunities for children to learn effectively (Banks, 2014, 2015; Cushner & others, 2015; Spring, 2014). Thus, the effects of SES and the effects of ethnicity are often intertwined (Duncan & others, 2015; Leventhal, Dupere, & Shuey, 2015; Murry & others, 2015).

In *The Shame of the Nation*, Jonathan Kozol (2005) described his visits to 60 U.S. schools in low-income areas of cities in 11 states. He saw many schools in which the minority population was 80 to 90 percent, concluding that school segregation is still present for many poor minority students. Kozol witnessed poorly kept classrooms, hallways, and restrooms; inadequate textbooks and supplies; and lack of resources. He also saw teachers mainly instructing students to rotely memorize material, especially as preparation for mandated tests, rather than encouraging students to engage in higher-level thinking. Kozol also frequently observed teachers using threatening disciplinary tactics to control the classroom.

Even outside inner-city schools, school segregation remains a factor in U.S. education (Bucher, 2015). Almost one-third of all African American and Latino students attend schools in which 90 percent or more of the students are from minority groups (Banks, 2008).

The school experiences of students from different ethnic groups vary considerably (Spring, 2014). African American and Latino students are much less likely than non-Latino White or Asian American students to be enrolled in academic, college preparatory programs and are much more likely to be enrolled in remedial and special education programs. Asian American students are far more likely than other ethnic minority groups to take advanced math and science courses in high school. African American students are twice as likely as Latinos, Native Americans, or non-Latino Whites to be suspended from school.

Latina (the term used for Latino females) adolescents are a special concern (Cooper, 2011). One study concluded that U.S. schools are doing an especially poor job of meeting the needs of America's fastest-growing minority population—Latinas (Ginorio & Huston, 2001). The study focused on how Latinas' futures—or "possible selves"—are influenced by their families, culture, peers, teachers, and media. The report indicates that many high school counselors view success as "going away to college," yet some Latinas, because of family responsibilities, believe it is important to stay close to home. The high school graduation rate for Latinas lags behind that for girls of any other ethnic minority group, except Native Americans. Latinas also are less likely to take the SAT exam than are non-Latino White and other ethnic-group females. Thus, stronger efforts should be made to support Latinas' academic success and to involve their families more fully in the process of college preparation (Suarez-Orozco & Suarez-Orozco, 2010).

Following are some strategies for improving relationships among ethnically diverse students:

· *Turn the class into a jigsaw classroom.* When Elliot Aronson was a professor at the University of Texas at Austin, the school system contacted him for ideas on how to reduce the increasing racial tension in classrooms. Aronson (1986) developed the concept of the **jigsaw classroom,** in which students from different cultural backgrounds are placed in a cooperative group in which they have to construct different parts of a project to reach a common goal. Aronson used the term *jigsaw* because he saw the technique as much like a group of students cooperating to put different pieces together to complete a jigsaw puzzle. How might this process work? Team sports, drama productions, and musical performances are examples of contexts in which students cooperatively participate to reach a common goal.

· *Encourage students to have positive personal contact with diverse other students.* Contact alone does not do the job of improving relationships with diverse others. For

developmental **connection**

Diversity

Asian American parents recently have been characterized as training parents because of their strong emphasis on rearing children to be academically successful. Connect to "Families."

Why is there a concern about the education of Latina adolescents?
© Vera Berger/Corbis RF

jigsaw classroom A classroom strategy in which students from different cultural backgrounds are placed in a cooperative group in which, together, they have to construct different parts of a project to reach a common goal.

Cover of an issue of *Teaching Tolerance* magazine, which includes numerous resources for improving interethnic relationships.
© James Ransome

example, busing ethnic minority students to predominantly non-Latino White schools, or vice versa, has not reduced prejudice or improved interethnic relations (Minuchin & Shapiro, 1983). What matters is what happens after children and adolescents get to school. Especially beneficial in improving interethnic relations is sharing one's worries, successes, failures, coping strategies, interests, and other personal information with people of other ethnicities. When such sharing takes place, people tend to view others as individuals rather than as members of a homogeneous group.

· *Encourage students to engage in perspective taking.* Exercises and activities that help students see others' perspectives can improve interethnic relations. These interactions help students "step into the shoes" of peers who are culturally different and feel what it is like to be treated in fair or unfair ways.

· *Help students to think critically and be emotionally intelligent about cultural issues.* Students who learn to think critically and deeply about interethnic relations are likely to decrease their prejudice. Becoming more emotionally intelligent includes understanding the causes of one's feelings, managing anger, listening to what others are saying, and being motivated to share and cooperate.

· *Reduce bias.* Teachers can reduce bias by displaying images of people from diverse ethnic and cultural groups, selecting classroom activities that encourage cultural understanding, helping students resist stereotyping, and working with parents.

· *View the school and community as a team.* James Comer (2004, 2006, 2010) emphasizes that a community, team approach is the best way to educate students. Three important aspects of the Comer Project for Change are (1) a governance and management team that develops a comprehensive school plan, assessment strategy, and staff development plan; (2) a mental health or school support team; and (3) a parents' program. Comer believes that the entire school community should have a cooperative rather than an adversarial attitude. The Comer program is currently operating in more than 600 schools in 26 states. To read further about James Comer's work, see the *Connecting with Careers* profile.

· *Be a competent cultural mediator.* Teachers can play a powerful role as cultural mediators by being sensitive to racist content in materials and classroom interactions, learning more about different ethnic groups, being sensitive to students' ethnic attitudes, viewing students of color positively, and thinking of positive ways to get parents of color more involved as partners with teachers in educating children (Kumar & Maehr, 2010).

Understanding the role of ethnicity in schooling also involves multicultural education. The hope is that multicultural education can contribute to making our nation more like what the late civil rights leader Martin Luther King, Jr., dreamed of: a nation where children and youth will be judged not by the color of their skin but by the quality of their character.

Multicultural education values diversity and includes the perspectives of a variety of cultural groups. Its proponents believe that children and youth of color should be empowered and that multicultural education benefits all students (Banks, 2014; Spring, 2014). An important goal of multicultural education is equal educational opportunity for all students. This includes closing the gap in academic achievement between mainstream students and students from underrepresented groups (Florence, 2010).

Multicultural education grew out of the civil rights movement of the 1960s and the call for equality and social justice for women and people of color (Spring, 2013, 2014). As a field, multicultural education addresses issues related to socioeconomic status, ethnicity, and gender. An increasing trend in multicultural education is not to make ethnicity a focal point but to also include socioeconomic status, gender, religion, disability, sexual orientation, and other forms of differences (Howe, 2010). Another important point about contemporary multicultural education is that many individuals think it is reserved for students of color. However, all students, including non-Latino White students, can benefit from multicultural education (Howe, 2010).

multicultural education Education that values diversity and includes the perspectives of a variety of cultural groups.

James Comer, Child Psychiatrist

James Comer grew up in a low-income neighborhood in East Chicago, Indiana, and credits his parents with leaving no doubt about the importance of education. He obtained a B.A. degree from Indiana University. He went on to obtain a medical degree from Howard University College of Medicine, a Master of Public Health degree from the University of Michigan School of Public Health, and psychiatry training at the Yale University School of Medicine's Child Study Center. He currently is the Maurice Falk Professor of Child Psychiatry at the Yale University Child Study Center and an associate dean at the Yale University Medical School. During his years at Yale, Comer has concentrated his career on promoting a focus on child development as a way of improving schools. His efforts in supporting healthy development of young people are known internationally.

In 1968 Dr. Comer founded the School Development program, which promotes the collaboration of parents, educators, and community members to improve social, emotional, and academic outcomes for children. His concept of teamwork is currently improving the educational environment in more than 600 schools throughout the United States.

James Comer (*left*) is shown with some of the inner-city African American students who attend a school that became a better learning environment because of Comer's intervention.
© *John S. Abbott*

Cross-Cultural Comparisons   Many countries recognize that quality, universal education of children and youth is critical for the success of any country. However, countries vary considerably in their ability to fulfill this mission. More than 100 million adolescents, mostly in sub-Saharan Africa, India, and southern Asia, don't even attend secondary schools (Paris & others, 2012). In developing countries, adolescent girls are less likely to be enrolled in school than are boys.

Secondary Schools   Secondary schools in various countries share a number of features but differ on others. Let's explore the similarities and differences in secondary schools in seven countries: Australia, Brazil, Germany, Japan, China, Russia, and the United States.

Most countries mandate that children begin school at 6 to 7 years of age and stay in school until they are 14 to 17 years of age. Brazil requires students to go to school only until they are 14 years old, whereas Russia mandates that students stay in school until they are 17. Germany, Japan, Australia, and the United States require school attendance until at least 15 to 16 years of age, with some states, such as California, recently raising the mandatory age to 18.

Most secondary schools around the world are divided into two or more levels, such as middle school (or junior high school) and high school. However, Germany's schools are divided according to three educational ability tracks: (1) the main school provides a basic level of education, (2) the middle school gives students a more advanced education, and (3) the academic school prepares students for entrance to a university. German schools, like most European schools, offer a classical education, which includes courses in Latin and Greek. Japanese secondary schools have an entrance exam, but secondary schools in the other four countries do not. Only Australia and Germany have comprehensive exit exams.

The United States and Australia are among the few countries in the world in which sports are an integral part of the public school system. Only a few private schools in other countries have their own sports teams, sports facilities, and highly organized sports events.

The juku, or "cramming school," is available to Japanese adolescents in the summertime and after school. It provides coaching to help them improve their grades and their entrance exam scores for high schools and universities. The Japanese practice of requiring an entrance exam for high school is a rarity among the nations of the world.
© Fujifotos/The Image Works

In Brazil, students are required to take Portuguese (the native language) and four foreign languages (Latin, French, English, and Spanish). Brazil requires these languages because of the country's international character and emphasis on trade and commerce. Seventh-grade students in Australia take courses in sheep husbandry and weaving, two areas of economic and cultural interest in the country. In Japan, students take a number of Western courses in addition to their basic Japanese courses; these courses include Western literature and languages (in addition to Japanese literature and language), Western physical education (in addition to Japanese martial arts classes), and Western sculpture and handicrafts (in addition to Japanese calligraphy). The Japanese school year is also much longer than that of other countries (225 days versus 180 days in the United States, for example).

I recently visited China and interviewed parents about their adolescents' education. Several aspects of education in China are noteworthy, especially in comparison with the United States. Being motivated to provide adolescents with the best possible education and ensuring that they work extremely hard in school and on homework were clearly evident in parents' comments. Also, when I asked parents if there are disciplinary problems in Chinese schools, they responded that if an adolescent acts up in school, the school immediately sends the adolescent home. In China, it is considered the parents' responsibility to orient their adolescents to behave in school and to focus on schoolwork. These observations coincide with our description of Asian American parents as training parents. When Chinese adolescents are sent home because of discipline problems, they are not allowed to return until parents work with the adolescents to ensure that the discipline problems don't recur. In China, classroom sizes are often large, in some cases having 50 to 70 students, yet observers describe such classes as orderly and disciplined (Cavanagh, 2007).

Colleges Which countries have the highest percentage of adults who have a college education? The Organisation for Economic Co-operation and Development (OECD, 2014) recently reported that the highest percentage of adults with a tertiary education (the term used in the report for a college education) were in order: (1) Russia (53.5 percent), (2) Canada (52.6 percent), (3) Japan (46.6 percent), (4) Israel (46.4 percent), and (5) the United States (43.1 percent). In 2012, 39 percent of young people were expected to graduate from college in the United States, a much lower rate than in Iceland (60 percent), New Zealand (57 percent), and Poland (53 percent) (OECD, 2014). In 1995, the United States was first among OECD countries (28 developed countries) in college graduation rates but has slipped considerably since then. Among the concerns about U.S. colleges are the soaring costs of attending college and low rate of students who graduate from college in four years, with many taking more than six years or never graduating.

learning disabilities Disabilities in which children experience difficulty in learning that involves understanding or using spoken or written language; the difficulty can appear in listening, thinking, reading, writing, and spelling. A learning disability also may involve difficulty in doing mathematics. To be classified as a learning disability, the learning problem is not primarily the result of visual, hearing, or motor disabilities; intellectual disability; emotional disorders; or environmental, cultural, or economic disadvantage.

4 Adolescents Who Are Exceptional

LG4 Characterize adolescents who are exceptional, and describe their education

| Who Are Adolescents with Disabilities? | Learning Disabilities | Attention Deficit Hyperactivity Disorder | Educational Issues Involving Students with Disabilities | Adolescents Who Are Gifted |

For many years, public schools did little to educate adolescents with disabilities. However, in the last several decades, federal legislation has mandated that all children and adolescents with disabilities receive a free, appropriate education. And increasingly, these students are being educated in the regular classroom.

WHO ARE ADOLESCENTS WITH DISABILITIES?

So far we have discussed schools that are experienced by the majority of U.S. students. Of all children in the United States, 13 percent from 3 to 21 years of age in the United States received special education or related services in 2011–2012, an increase of 3 percent since the 1980–1981 school year (Condition of Education, 2014). Figure 2 shows the five largest groups of students with a disability who were served by federal programs during the 2011–2012 school year (Condition of Education, 2014).

As indicated in Figure 2, students with a learning disability were by far the largest group of students with a disability to be given special education, followed by children with speech or language impairments, intellectual disability, autism, and emotional disturbance. Note that the U.S. Department of Education includes both students with a learning disability and students with ADHD in the category of learning disability.

LEARNING DISABILITIES

Adolescents with **learning disabilities** have difficulty in learning that involves understanding or using spoken or written language; the difficulty can appear in listening, thinking, reading, writing, or spelling. Learning disabilities also may involve difficulty in doing mathematics (Kucian & von Aster, 2015). To be classified as a learning disability, the learning problem is not primarily the result of visual, hearing, or motor disabilities; intellectual disability; emotional disorders; or environmental, cultural, or economic disadvantage (Swanson, 2014; Vaughn & Bos, 2015).

From the mid-1970s through the mid-1990s, there was a dramatic increase in the percentage of U.S. students receiving special education services for a learning disability

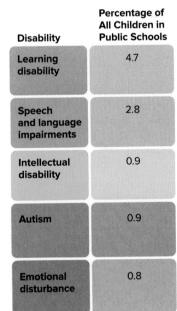

Disability	Percentage of All Children in Public Schools
Learning disability	4.7
Speech and language impairments	2.8
Intellectual disability	0.9
Autism	0.9
Emotional disturbance	0.8

FIGURE 2

U.S. CHILDREN WITH A DISABILITY WHO RECEIVE SPECIAL EDUCATION SERVICES. Figures are for the 2011–2012 school year and represent the five categories with the highest number and percentage of children. Both learning disability and attention deficit hyperactivity disorder are combined in the learning disabilities category (Condition of Education, 2014).

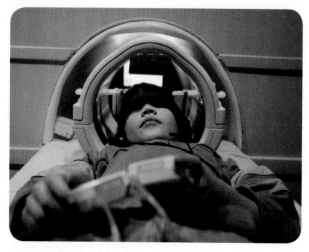

FIGURE 3

BRAIN SCANS AND LEARNING DISABILITIES. An increasing number of studies are using MRI brain scans to examine the brain pathways involved in learning disabilities. Shown here is Patrick Price, who has dyslexia. Patrick is going through an MRI scanner disguised by drapes to look like a child-friendly castle. Inside the scanner, children must lie virtually motionless as words and symbols flash on a screen, and they are asked to identify them by clicking different buttons.
© Manuel Balce Ceneta/AP Images

(from 1.8 percent in 1976–1977 to 5.8 percent in 1995–1996), although in the twenty-first century there has been a decrease in this percentage in recent years (from 6.1 percent in 2000 to 4.9 percent in 2010, for example) (Condition of Education, 2012). Some experts say that the dramatic increase reflected poor diagnostic practices and overidentification. They argue that teachers sometimes are too quick to label children with the slightest learning problem as having a learning disability, instead of recognizing that the problem may be caused by ineffective teaching. Other experts say the increase in the number of children being labeled with a learning disability is justified (Hallahan, Kauffman, & Pullen, 2015).

About three times as many boys as girls are classified as having a learning disability. Among the explanations for this gender difference are a greater biological vulnerability among boys and *referral bias*. That is, boys are more likely to be referred by teachers for treatment because of their behavior.

Approximately 80 percent of students with a learning disability have a reading problem (Shaywitz, Gruen, & Shaywitz, 2007). Three types of learning disabilities are dyslexia, dysgraphia, and dyscalculia:

· *Dyslexia* is a category reserved for individuals who have a severe impairment in their ability to read and spell (Ramus, 2014; Thompson & others, 2015).

· *Dysgraphia* is a learning disability that involves difficulty in handwriting (Berninger & others, 2015; Fischer-Baum & Rapp, 2014). Children with dysgraphia may write very slowly, their writing products may be virtually illegible, and they may make numerous spelling errors because of their inability to match up sounds and letters.

· *Dyscalculia*, also known as developmental arithmetic disorder, is a learning disability that involves difficulty in math computation (Cowan & Powell, 2014; Kucian & von Aster, 2015).

Researchers are using brain-imaging techniques in an effort to identify brain regions that might be involved in learning disabilities (Shaywitz & others, 2007) (see Figure 3). This research indicates that it is unlikely that learning disabilities reside in a single, specific brain location. More likely, learning disabilities are due to problems with integrating information from multiple brain regions or to subtle impairments in brain structures and functions.

Many interventions have focused on improving reading ability (Carlisle, Kenney, & Vereb, 2013). Intensive instruction over a period of time by a competent teacher can improve many students' reading ability (Berninger & Dunn, 2012; Del Campo & others, 2015).

ATTENTION DEFICIT HYPERACTIVITY DISORDER

Attention deficit hyperactivity disorder (ADHD) is a disability in which children or adolescents consistently show one or more of the following characteristics over a period of time: (1) inattention, (2) hyperactivity, and (3) impulsivity. For an ADHD diagnosis, onset of these characteristics early in childhood is required and the characteristics must be debilitating for the child. Children and adolescents who are inattentive have difficulty focusing on any one thing and may get bored with a task after only a few minutes. Children and adolescents who are hyperactive show high levels of physical activity and almost always seem to be in motion. They are impulsive, have difficulty curbing their reactions, and do not do a good job of thinking before they act. Depending on the characteristics that children and adolescents with ADHD display, they can be diagnosed as (1) ADHD with predominantly inattention, (2) ADHD with predominantly hyperactivity/impulsivity, or (3) ADHD with both inattention and hyperactivity/impulsivity.

The number of children and adolescents diagnosed and treated for ADHD has increased substantially, by some estimates doubling in the 1990s. The disorder occurs as much as four to nine times more often in boys than in girls. There is controversy, however, about the increased diagnosis of ADHD (Friend, 2014; Watson & others, 2014). Some experts attribute the increase mainly to heightened awareness of the disorder; others believe that many children and adolescents are being incorrectly diagnosed (Parens & Johnston, 2009).

developmental **connection**

Attention

Attention, which requires the focusing of mental resources, improves cognitive processing on many tasks. Connect to "The Brain and Cognitive Development."

attention deficit hyperactivity disorder (ADHD) A disability in which children or adolescents consistently show one or more of the following characteristics over a period of time: (1) inattention, (2) hyperactivity, and (3) impulsivity.

A recent study examined the possible misdiagnosis of ADHD (Bruchmiller, Margraf, & Schneider, 2012). In this study, child psychologists, psychiatrists, and social workers were given vignettes of children with ADHD (some vignettes matched the diagnostic criteria for the disorder, while others did not). Whether each child was male or female varied. The researchers assessed whether the mental health professionals gave a diagnosis of ADHD to the child described in the vignette. The professionals overdiagnosed ADHD almost 20 percent of the time, and regardless of the symptoms described, boys were twice as likely as girls to be given a diagnosis of ADHD.

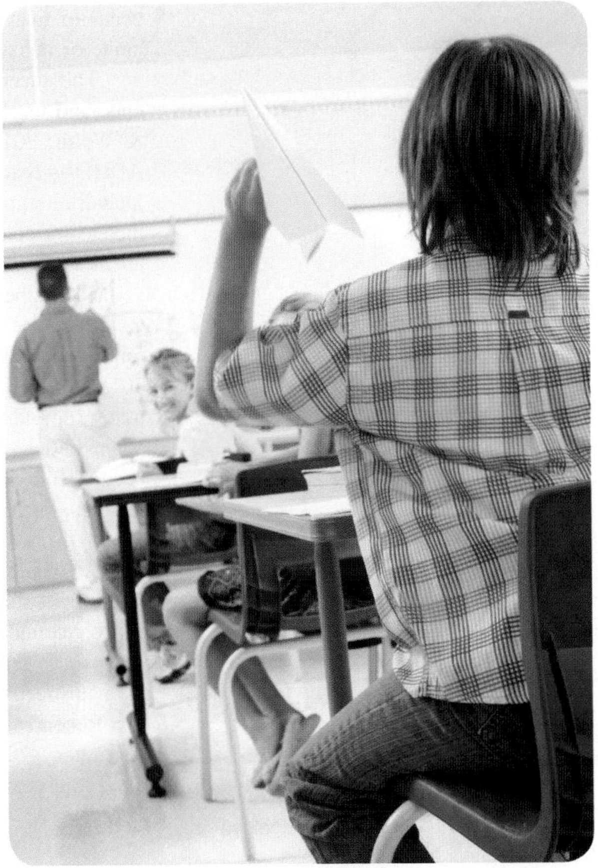

Many adolescents with ADHD show impulsive behavior, such as this student who is getting ready to hurl a paper airplane in the classroom. *How would you handle this situation if you were a teacher and this were to happen in your classroom?*
© Jupiterimages RF

Causes and Course of ADHD Definitive causes of ADHD have not been found; however, a number of causes have been proposed (American Academy of Pediatrics & Reiff, 2011). Some children and adolescents likely inherit a tendency to develop ADHD from their parents (Lee & Song, 2014). Others likely develop ADHD because of damage to their brain during prenatal or postnatal development (Strickland, 2014). Among early possible contributors to ADHD are cigarette and alcohol exposure, high levels of maternal stress during prenatal development, and low birth weight (Glover, 2014; Yochum & others, 2014). For example, a recent study revealed that cigarette smoking during pregnancy was linked to ADHD in elementary-school-age children (Sciberras, Ukoumunne, & Efron, 2011).

As with learning disabilities, the development of brain-imaging techniques is leading to a better understanding of the brain's role in ADHD (Berger & others, 2015; Chiang & others, 2015; Li & others, 2014). One study revealed that peak thickness of the cerebral cortex occurs three years later (10.5 years) in children with ADHD than in children without ADHD (peak at 7.5 years) (Shaw & others, 2007). The delay is more prominent in the prefrontal regions of the brain that especially are important in attention and planning (see Figure 4). Another recent study also found delayed development of the brain's frontal lobes in children with ADHD, likely due to delayed or decreased myelination (Nagel & others, 2011). Researchers also are exploring the roles that various neurotransmitters, such as serotonin and dopamine, might play in ADHD (Gold & others, 2014; Kollins & Adcock, 2014).

The delays in brain development just described are in areas linked to executive function. A focus of increasing interest in the study of children with ADHD is their difficulty on tasks involving executive function, such as behavioral inhibition when necessary, use of working memory, and effective planning (Dovis & others, 2015; Langberg, Dvorsky, & Evans, 2013; Saarinen & others, 2015).

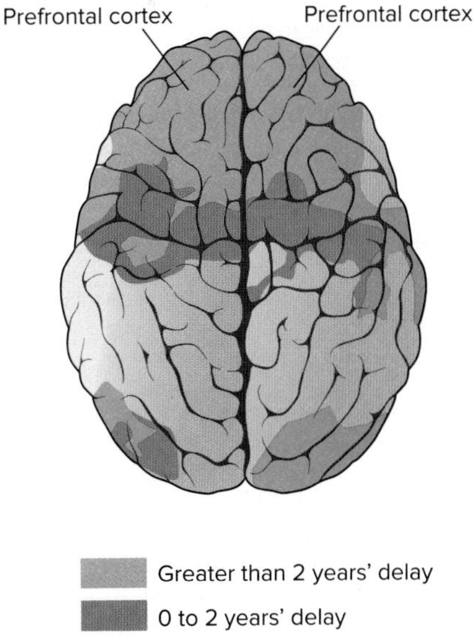

FIGURE **4**

REGIONS OF THE BRAIN IN WHICH CHILDREN WITH ADHD HAD A DELAYED PEAK IN THE THICKNESS OF THE CEREBRAL CORTEX. *Note:* The greatest delays occurred in the prefrontal cortex.

Adjustment and optimal development also are difficult for children who have ADHD, so it is important that the diagnosis be accurate (Bolea-Alamanac & others, 2014). Children diagnosed with ADHD have an increased risk of school dropout, adolescent pregnancy, substance use problems, and antisocial behavior (Brook & others, 2015; Molina & others, 2014).

The increased academic and social demands of formal schooling, as well as stricter standards for behavioral control, often intensify the problems of the child with ADHD. Elementary school teachers typically report that the child with ADHD has difficulty working independently, completing seatwork, and organizing work. Restlessness and distractibility also are often noted.

Experts previously thought that most children "grow out" of ADHD. However, recent evidence suggests that as many as 70 percent of adolescents (Sibley & others, 2012) and 66 percent of adults (Buitelaar, Karr, & Asherton, 2010) who were diagnosed as children continue to experience ADHD symptoms.

Treatment of ADHD Stimulant medication such as Ritalin or Adderall (which has fewer side effects than Ritalin) is effective in improving the attention of many children with ADHD, but it usually does not improve their attention to the same level as that of children without ADHD (Stray, Ellertsen, & Stray, 2010). A meta-analysis concluded that behavior management treatments are effective in reducing the effects of ADHD (Fabiano & others, 2009). Researchers have often found that a combination of medication (such as Ritalin) and behavior management improves the behavior of children with ADHD better than medication alone or behavior management alone, although not in all cases (Parens & Johnston, 2009).

The sheer number of ADHD diagnoses has prompted speculation that psychiatrists, parents, and teachers are in fact labeling normal childhood behavior as psychopathology (Mash & Wolfe, 2013; Molina & Pelham, 2014). One reason for concern about overdiagnosing ADHD is that the form of treatment in well over 80 percent of cases is psychoactive drugs, including stimulants such as Ritalin and Adderall (Garfield & others, 2012). Further, there is increasing concern that children who are given stimulant drugs such as Ritalin or Adderall are at a higher risk for developing substance abuse problems, although results on this concern so far have been mixed (Nogueira & others, 2014; Zulauf & others, 2014).

Recently, researchers have been exploring the possibility that neurofeedback might improve the attention of children with ADHD (Gevensleben & others, 2014; Marx & others, 2015; Steiner & others, 2014a, b; Zuberer, Brandeis, & Drechsler, 2015). Neurofeedback trains individuals to become more aware of their physiological responses so that they can attain better control over their brain's prefrontal cortex, where executive control primarily occurs. Individuals with ADHD have higher levels of electroencephalogram (EEG) abnormalities, such as lower beta waves that involve attention and memory, and lower sensorimotor rhythms (which involve control of movements). Neurofeedback produces audiovisual profiles of brain waves so that individuals can learn how to achieve normal EEG functioning. In a recent study, 7- to 14-year-olds with ADHD were randomly assigned either to take Ritalin or to undergo 40 sessions of a neurofeedback treatment (Meisel & others, 2013). Both groups showed a lower level of ADHD symptoms six months after the treatment, but only the neurofeedback group performed better academically.

Recently, mindfulness training also has been given to adolescents with ADHD (Anderson & Guthery, 2015; Cassone, 2014; Converse & others, 2014). In a recent study, 11- to 15-year-old adolescents with ADHD were given 8 weeks of mindfulness training (van de Weijer-Bergsma & others, 2012). Immediately after and 8 weeks following the training, the adolescents' attention improved and they exhibited fewer behavioral problems, although by 16 weeks post-training the effects had waned.

Exercise also is being investigated as a possible treatment for children with ADHD (Berwid & Halperin, 2012; Cassone, 2014; Huang & others, 2015; Pan & others, 2015). A recent study found that a single 20-minute bout of moderately intense aerobic exercise improved the neurocognitive function and inhibitory control of children with ADHD (Pontifex & others, 2013). Among the reasons given as to why exercise might reduce ADHD symptoms in children are (1) better allocation of attention resources, (2) positive influence on prefrontal cortex functioning, and (3) exercise-induced dopamine release (Chang & others, 2012).

Critics argue that many physicians are too quick to prescribe stimulants for children with milder forms of ADHD (Marcovitch, 2004). Also, in 2006, the U.S. government issued a warning about the cardiovascular risks of using stimulant medication to treat ADHD.

EDUCATIONAL ISSUES INVOLVING ADOLESCENTS WITH DISABILITIES

Until the 1970s most U.S. public schools either refused enrollment to children with disabilities or inadequately served them. This changed in 1975, when **Public Law 94-142,** the Education for All Handicapped Children Act, required that all students with disabilities be given a free, appropriate public education. In 1990, Public Law 94-142 was recast as the **Individuals with Disabilities Education Act (IDEA).** IDEA was amended in 1997 and then reauthorized in 2004 and renamed the Individuals with Disabilities Education Improvement Act.

IDEA spells out broad mandates for services to children with disabilities of all kinds (Deutsch Smith & Tyler, 2014; Kirk, Gallagher, & Coleman, 2015). These services include evaluation and eligibility determination, appropriate education and an individualized education plan (IEP), and education in the least restrictive environment (LRE).

An *individualized education plan (IEP)* is a written statement that spells out a program that is specifically tailored for a student with a disability. The **least restrictive environment (LRE)** is a setting that is as similar as possible to the one in which children who do not have a disability are educated. This provision of the IDEA has given a legal basis to efforts to

developmental connection

Cognitive Processes

Mindfulness training is being used to improve adolescents' executive function. Connect to "The Brain and Cognitive Development."

Public Law 94-142 The Education for All Handicapped Children Act, which requires all students with disabilities to be given a free, appropriate public education.

Individuals with Disabilities Education Act (IDEA) Federal legislation spelling out broad mandates for providing educational services to all children and adolescents with disabilities. These include evaluation and eligibility determination, appropriate education and an individualized education plan (IEP), and education in the least restrictive environment.

least restrictive environment (LRE) A setting that is as similar as possible to the one in which children or adolescents without a disability are educated; under the IDEA, efforts to educate the child or adolescent with a disability in this setting have been given a legal basis.

inclusion Educating a child or adolescent with special educational needs full-time in the regular classroom.

adolescents who are gifted Adolescents who have above-average intelligence (usually defined as an IQ of 130 or higher) and/or superior talent in some domain, such as art, music, or mathematics.

educate children with a disability in the regular classroom (Turnbull & others, 2016). The term **inclusion** describes educating a child with special educational needs full-time in the regular classroom (Deutsch Smith & Tyler, 2014; Salend, 2016; Vaughn, Bos, & Schumm, 2014). Recent analysis indicated that the percentage of time students with disabilities spend in the regular classroom had reached its highest level (61 percent) since it had first been assessed (Condition of Education, 2014).

Many legal changes regarding children with disabilities have been extremely positive (Friend, 2014; Smith & others, 2016; Turnbull & others, 2016). Compared with several decades ago, far more children today are receiving competent, specialized services. For many children, inclusion in the regular classroom, with modifications or supplemental services, is appropriate. However, some leading experts on special education argue that some children with disabilities may not benefit from inclusion in the regular classroom. James Kauffman and his colleagues, for example, advocate a more individualized approach that does not necessarily involve full inclusion but allows options such as special education outside the regular classroom with trained professionals and adapted curricula (Kauffman, McGee, & Brigham, 2004). They go on to say, "We sell students with disabilities short when we pretend that they are not different from typical students. We make the same error when we pretend that they must *not* be expected to put forth extra effort if they are to learn to do some things—or learn to do something in a different way" (p. 620). Like general education, special education should challenge students with disabilities "to become all they can be."

ADOLESCENTS WHO ARE GIFTED

The final type of exceptionality we discuss is quite different from the disabilities we have described so far. **Adolescents who are gifted** have above-average intelligence (usually defined as an IQ of 130 or higher) and/or superior talent in some domain, such as art, music, or mathematics. Programs for the gifted in most school systems select children who have intellectual superiority and academic aptitude. They tend to overlook children who are talented in the arts or athletics or who have other special aptitudes (Sternberg & Bridges, 2014; Winner, 2009). Estimates vary but indicate that approximately 3 to 5 percent of U.S. students are gifted (National Association for Gifted Children, 2009). This percentage is likely conservative because it focuses mainly on children and adolescents who are gifted intellectually and academically, often failing to include those who are gifted in creative thinking or the visual and performing arts (Ford, 2012; Gardner, 2012).

Eighteen-year-old Chandra "Peaches" Allen was born without arms. Despite this disability, she has learned to write, eat, type, paint, and draw with her feet. She can even put on earrings. She is well known for her artistic skills. She has won three grand-prize awards for her art in various shows. She is getting ready to enter college and plans to pursue a career in art and physical therapy. Chandra Allen's accomplishments reflect remarkable adaptation and coping. She is an excellent example of how adolescents can conquer a disability and pursue meaningful goals.
© The Dallas Morning News, Milton Hinnant

Characteristics of Children and Adolescents Who Are Gifted Aside from their abilities, do students who are gifted have distinctive characteristics? Lewis Terman (1925) conducted an extensive study of 1,500 children and youth whose Stanford-Binet IQs averaged 150. Contrary to the popular myth that children and youth who are gifted are maladjusted, Terman found that they were socially well adjusted.

Ellen Winner (1996) described three criteria that characterize adolescents who are gifted, whether in art, music, or academic domains:

1. *Precocity.* Children and adolescents who are gifted are precocious. They begin to master an area earlier than their peers. Learning in their domain is more effortless for them than for ordinary children. In most instances, these gifted children are precocious because they have an inborn high ability.

At 2 years of age, art prodigy Alexandra Nechita colored in coloring books for hours and also took up pen and ink. She had no interest in dolls or friends. By age 5 she was using watercolors. Once she started school, she would start painting as soon as she got home. At the age of 8, in 1994, she saw the first public exhibit of her work. In succeeding years, working quickly and impulsively on canvases as large as 5 feet by 9 feet, she has completed hundreds of paintings, some of which sell for close to $100,000 apiece. As a teenager (*left*), she continued to paint—relentlessly and passionately. It is, she said, what she loves to do. Today, as a young adult, Alexandra's passion for painting remains alive. *What are some characteristics of adolescents who are gifted?*
© Koichi Kamoshida/Newsmakers/Getty Images

2. *Marching to their own drummer.* Students who are gifted learn in a way that is qualitatively different from that of ordinary children. For one thing, they need minimal help from adults to learn. In many cases, they resist explicit instruction. They also often make discoveries on their own and solve problems in unique ways.

3. *A passion to master.* Students who are gifted are driven to understand the domain in which they have high ability. They display an intense, obsessive interest and an ability to focus. They do not need to be pushed by their parents. They motivate themselves, says Winner.

Nature/Nurture   Is giftedness a product of heredity or of environment? Likely both (Bouchard & Johnson, 2014; Ericsson, 2014; Winner, 2014). Individuals who are gifted recall that they had signs of high ability in a specific area at a very young age, prior to or at the beginning of formal training (Howe & others, 1995). This suggests the importance of innate ability in giftedness. However, researchers also have found that individuals with world-class status in the arts, mathematics, science, and sports all report strong family support and years of training and practice (Bloom, 1985). Deliberate practice is an important characteristic of individuals who become experts in a specific domain. For example, in one study, the best musicians engaged in twice as much deliberate practice over their lives as the least successful ones did (Ericsson, Krampe, & Tesch-Römer, 1993).

Domain-Specific Giftedness   Individuals who are highly gifted are typically not gifted in many domains, and research on giftedness is increasingly focused on domain-specific developmental trajectories (Sternberg & Bridges, 2014; Winner, 2009). During the childhood and adolescent years, the domains in which individuals are gifted usually emerge. Thus, at some point in childhood or adolescence, the individual who is to become a gifted artist or a gifted mathematician begins to show expertise in that domain. Regarding domain-specific giftedness, software genius Bill Gates (1998), the founder of Microsoft and one of the world's richest persons, commented that sometimes you have to be careful when you are good at something and resist the urge to think that you will be good at everything. Gates explains that because he has been so successful at software development, people expect him to be brilliant about other domains in which he is far from being a genius.

Identifying an individual's domain-specific talent and providing individually appropriate and optimal educational opportunities are tasks that need to be accomplished at the very latest by adolescence (Keating, 2009). During adolescence, individuals who are talented become less reliant on parental support and increasingly pursue their own interests.

Education of Children and Youth Who Are Gifted   An increasing number of experts argue that in the United States the education of students who are gifted requires a significant overhaul (Olszewski-Kubilius & Thompson, 2013; Sternberg & Bridges, 2014; Winner, 2014). This concern is reflected in the titles of these books: *Genius Denied: How to Stop Wasting Our Brightest Young Minds* (Davidson & Davidson, 2004) and *A Nation Deceived: How Schools Hold Back America's Brightest Students* (Colangelo, Assouline, & Gross, 2004).

Underchallenged students who are gifted can become disruptive, skip classes, and lose interest in achieving. Sometimes they just disappear into the woodwork, becoming passive and apathetic toward school. It is extremely important for teachers to challenge children and youth who are gifted to reach high expectations (Ambrose, Sternberg, & Sriraman, 2012).

A number of experts argue that too often students who are gifted are socially isolated and underchallenged in the classroom (Karnes & Stephens, 2008). It is not unusual for them to be ostracized and labeled "nerds" or "geeks." Ellen Winner (1996, 2006) concludes that a student who is truly gifted often is the only child in the room who does not have the opportunity to learn with students of like ability.

Many eminent adults report that school was a negative experience for them, that they were bored and sometimes knew more than their teachers (Bloom, 1985). Winner stresses that American education will benefit when standards are raised for all students. When some students are still underchallenged, she recommends that they be allowed to attend advanced classes in their domain of exceptional ability, such as allowing some especially precocious

A young Bill Gates, founder of Microsoft and now one of the world's richest persons. Like many highly gifted students, Gates was not especially fond of school. He hacked a computer security system when he was 13, and as a high school student, he was allowed to take some college math classes. He dropped out of Harvard University and began developing a plan for what was to become Microsoft Corporation. *What are some ways that schools can enrich the education of such highly talented students as Gates to make it a more challenging, interesting, and meaningful experience?*
© Doug Wilson/Corbis

middle school students to take college classes in their area of expertise. For example, Bill Gates, founder of Microsoft, took college math classes and hacked a computer security system at 13; Yo-Yo Ma, a famous cellist, graduated from high school at 15 and attended Juilliard School of Music in New York City.

A final concern is that African American, Latino, and Native American children are underrepresented in gifted programs (Ford, 2012). Much of the underrepresentation involves the lower test scores for these children compared with non-Latino White and Asian American children, which may be due to a number of factors such as test bias and fewer opportunities to develop language skills, such as vocabulary and comprehension (Ford, 2012).

In this chapter, you have read about many aspects of schools for adolescents. An important aspect of the education of adolescents involves achievement. Next we'll explore the development of achievement in adolescents.

Review Connect Reflect

LG4 Characterize adolescents who are exceptional, and describe their education

Review
- Who are adolescents with disabilities?
- How can learning disabilities be characterized?
- What is known about attention deficit hyperactivity disorder?
- What educational issues are involved in educating adolescents with disabilities?
- How can adolescents who are gifted be described?

Connect
- How does the concept of the family as a system support parents' efforts to seek the best outcomes for their children who are exceptional learners?

Reflect *Your Own Personal Journey of Life*
- Think back on your own schooling and how students with learning disabilities either were or were not diagnosed. Were you aware of such individuals in your classes? Were they helped by teachers and/or specialists? You might know one or more people with a learning disability. Interview them about their school experiences and what could have been done better to help them learn more effectively.

reach your **learning goals**

Schools

1 Approaches to Educating Students   **LG1** Describe approaches to educating students

Contemporary Approaches to Student Learning

- Two main contemporary approaches to student learning are constructivist and direct instruction. The constructivist approach is learner-centered and emphasizes the adolescent's active, cognitive construction of knowledge and understanding. The direct instruction approach is teacher-centered and characterized by teacher direction and control, emphasis on mastery of academic skills, high expectations for students, and maximum time spent on learning tasks. Many effective teachers use aspects of both approaches.

Accountability

- Accountability has become a major issue in U.S. education. Increased concern by the public and government in the United States has led to extensive state-mandated testing, which has both strengths and weaknesses and is controversial. The most visible example of the increased state-mandated testing is the No Child Left Behind federal legislation.

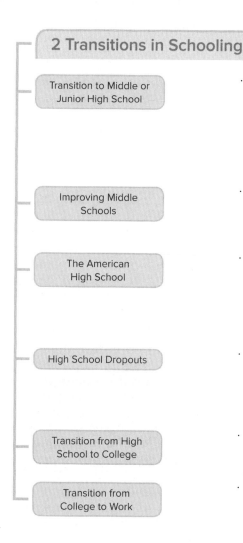

2 Transitions in Schooling

 LG2 Discuss transitions in schooling from early adolescence to emerging adulthood

Transition to Middle or Junior High School

· The emergence of junior high schools in the 1920s and 1930s was justified on the basis of the developmental changes occurring in early adolescence and an effort to meet the needs of a growing student population. Middle schools have become more popular, and their appearance has coincided with earlier pubertal development. The transition to middle/junior high school is often stressful because it occurs at the same time as a number of physical, cognitive, and socioemotional changes. This transition involves going from the "top-dog" to the "bottom-dog" position.

Improving Middle Schools

· *Turning Points 1989* provided a very negative evaluation of U.S. middle school education. *Turning Points 2000* continued to express serious concerns about middle school education and added new emphases on teaching a curriculum grounded in rigorous academic standards and engaging in instruction that prepares all students to achieve higher standards.

The American High School

· An increasing number of educators believe that U.S. high schools need a new mission for the twenty-first century, one that involves more support for graduating with the knowledge and skills to succeed in college and a career, higher expectations for achievement, less time spent working in low-level service jobs, and better coordination of the K–12 curriculum. The National Research Council provided a number of recommendations for improving U.S. high school education that focus on engaging students to learn.

High School Dropouts

· Many school dropouts have educational deficiencies that limit their economic and social well-being for much of their adult lives. Progress has been made in lowering the dropout rate for African American youth, but the dropout rate for Native American and Latino youth remains very high. Dropping out of school is associated with demographic, family-related, peer-related, school-related, economic, and personal factors.

Transition from High School to College

· In many ways, the transition to college parallels the transition from elementary to middle/junior high school. Reduced interaction with parents is usually involved in this transition. A special problem today is the discontinuity between high schools and colleges.

Transition from College to Work

· Having a college degree is highly beneficial for increasing one's income. However, the transition from college to work is often a difficult one. One reason is that colleges often train students to develop general skills rather than job-specific skills. Increasing concerns are the number of other countries who have a higher percentage of college graduates than the United States.

3 The Social Contexts of Schools

LG3 Explain how the social contexts of schools influence adolescent development

Changing Social Developmental Contexts

· The social context differs at the preschool, elementary school, and secondary school levels, increasing in complexity and scope for adolescents.

Classroom Climate and Management

· A positive classroom climate, which is promoted by an authoritative management strategy and effective management of group activities, improves student learning and achievement. An important teaching skill is managing the classroom to prevent problem behavior from developing and to maximize student learning. Some issues in classroom management in secondary schools are different from those in elementary schools.

Person-Environment Fit

· Person-environment fit involves the concept that some of the negative psychological changes associated with adolescent development might result from a mismatch between adolescents' developing needs and the lack of opportunities afforded by schools.

Teachers, Parents, Peers, and Extracurricular Activities

· Teacher characteristics involve many different dimensions, and compiling a profile of the competent teacher's characteristics has been difficult. Effective family management, especially an organized routine and high achievement expectations, is positively linked to adolescents' success in school. Parent involvement usually decreases as the child moves into adolescence. Epstein argues that greater collaboration among schools, families, and communities is needed. The way middle schools are structured encourages students to interact with larger numbers of peers on a daily basis. A popular or accepted peer status is linked with academic success; a rejected status is related to less academic success. An increasing concern in schools is bullying. Victims of bullying can experience both short-term and long-term negative effects. Friendship is also related to school success. Participation in extracurricular activities is associated with positive academic and psychological outcomes.

Culture

- At home, in their neighborhoods, and at school, adolescents in poverty face problems that present barriers to effective learning. In comparison with schools in higher-SES neighborhoods, schools in low-SES neighborhoods have fewer resources, have less experienced teachers, and encourage rote learning more than the development of thinking skills. The school experiences of students from different ethnic groups vary considerably. It is important for teachers to have positive expectations and to challenge students of color to achieve. Strategies that teachers can use to improve relations among ethnically diverse students include turning the classroom into a "jigsaw," encouraging positive personal contact, stimulating perspective taking, viewing the school and community as a team, and being a competent cultural mediator. Multicultural education values diversity and includes the perspectives of varying cultural groups. Schools vary across cultures. For example, U.S. schools have by far the strongest emphasis on athletics.

4 Adolescents Who Are Exceptional (LG4) Characterize adolescents who are exceptional, and describe their education

Who Are Adolescents with Disabilities?

- An estimated 13 percent of U.S. children and adolescents receive special education or related services. In the federal government classification, this category includes attention deficit hyperactivity disorder, or ADHD.

Learning Disabilities

- Learning disabilities are characterized by difficulties in learning that involve understanding or using spoken or written language; the difficulty can appear in listening, thinking, reading, writing, and spelling. A learning disability also may involve difficulty in doing mathematics. To be classified as a learning disability, the learning problem is not primarily the result of visual, hearing, or motor disabilities; intellectual disability; emotional disorders; or environmental, cultural, or economic disadvantage. Dyslexia is a category of learning disabilities that involves a severe impairment in the ability to read and spell. Dysgraphia and dyscalculia are two other categories of learning disabilities.

Attention Deficit Hyperactivity Disorder

- Attention deficit hyperactivity disorder (ADHD) involves problems in one or more of these areas: inattention, hyperactivity, and impulsivity. Most experts recommend a combination of interventions for ADHD—medical (stimulants such as Ritalin) and behavioral.

Educational Issues Involving Adolescents with Disabilities

- Public Law 94-142 requires that all students with disabilities be given a free, appropriate education. IDEA spells out broad mandates for services to all children and adolescents with disabilities. The concept of least restrictive environment (LRE) also has been set forth. Inclusion means educating students with disabilities in the regular classroom. Full inclusion has increasingly characterized U.S. schools, although some educators argue that this trend may not be best for some students with disabilities.

Adolescents Who Are Gifted

- Adolescents who are gifted have above-average intelligence (usually defined by an IQ of 130 or higher) and/or superior talent in some domain, such as art, music, or math. Characteristics of adolescents who are gifted include precocity, marching to their own drummer, a passion to master, and superior information-processing skills. Giftedness is likely a result of the interaction of heredity and environment, and for most individuals giftedness is domain-specific. Significant criticisms have been made of the way adolescents who are gifted have been educated in the United States.

key **terms**

adolescents who are gifted
attention deficit hyperactivity disorder (ADHD)
authoritarian strategy of classroom management

authoritative strategy of classroom management
constructivist approach
direct instruction approach
inclusion

Individuals with Disabilities Education Act (IDEA)
jigsaw classroom
learning disabilities
least restrictive environment (LRE)

multicultural education
permissive strategy of classroom management
Public Law 94-142
top-dog phenomenon

key people

Elliot Aronson

James Comer

Robert Crosnoe

Jacquelynne Eccles

James Kauffman

Jonathan Kozol

Eva Pomerantz

Allan Wigfield

Ellen Winner

resources for **improving the lives of adolescents**

APA Educational Psychology Handbook (Volumes 1–3)
Edited by Karen Harris and others (2012)
Washington, DC: American Psychological Association
> Leading experts in educational psychology provide an up-to-date account of a wide-ranging set of topics related to improving the education of children and adolescents.

Children at School
Robert Crosnoe and Aprile Benner (2015)
In R. M. Lerner (Ed.), *Handbook of Child Psychology and Developmental Science* (7th ed.). New York: Wiley.
> A contemporary view that especially emphasizes the importance of social aspects of schools and asserts that social policy focused solely on academic reforms is misguided.

Council for Exceptional Children (CEC) (www.cec.sped.org)
The CEC maintains an information center on the education of children and adolescents who are exceptional and publishes materials on a wide variety of topics.

Schools as Developmental Contexts During Adolescence
Jacquelynne Eccles and Robert Roeser (2013)
In I. B. Weiner & others (Eds.), *Handbook of Psychology* (2nd ed., Vol. 6). New York: Wiley.

> Leading experts provide up-to-date discussions of a wide range of topics, including academic expectations, teacher-student relationships, peer influences, and extracurricular activities.

National Dropout Prevention Center (www.dropoutprevention.org)
The center operates as a clearinghouse for information about dropout prevention and at-risk youth and publishes the *National Dropout Prevention Newsletter.*

Turning Points 2000: Educating Adolescents in the 21st Century
Anthony Jackson and Gayle Davis (2000)
New York: Teachers College Press
> This follow-up to earlier *Turning Points* recommendations includes a number of strategies for meeting the educational needs of adolescents.

Confronting Dogmatism in Gifted Education
Edited by Don Ambrose, Robert Sternberg, and Bharath Sriraman (2012)
New York: Routledge
> Leading experts discuss barriers that keep adolescents who are gifted from reaching their full potential.

chapter 11

ACHIEVEMENT, WORK, AND CAREERS

chapter outline

1 Achievement

Learning Goal 1 Discuss achievement in the lives of adolescents

The Importance of Achievement in Adolescence
Achievement Processes
Social Relationships and Contexts
Some Motivational Obstacles to Achievement

2 Work

Learning Goal 2 Describe the role of work in adolescence and in college

Work in Adolescence
Working During College
Work/Career-Based Learning
Work in Emerging Adulthood

3 Career Development

Learning Goal 3 Characterize career development in adolescence

Developmental Changes
Cognitive Factors
Identity Development
Social Contexts

© Laurence Mouton/Getty Images RF

Kim-Chi Trinh was only 9 years old in Vietnam when her father used his savings to buy passage for her on a fishing boat. It was a costly and risky sacrifice for the family, who placed Kim-Chi on the small boat, among strangers, in the hope that she eventually would reach the United States, where she would get a good education and enjoy a better life.

Kim made it to the United States and coped with a succession of three foster families. When she graduated from high school in San Diego in 1988, she had a straight-A average and a number of college scholarship offers. When asked why she excels in school, Kim-Chi says that she has to do well because she owes it to her parents, who are still in Vietnam.

Kim-Chi is one of a wave of bright, highly motivated Asians who are immigrating to America. Asian Americans are the fastest-growing ethnic minority group in the United States—two out of five immigrants are now Asian. Although Asian Americans make up only 5 percent of the U.S. population, they constitute 17 percent of the undergraduates at Harvard, 18 percent at MIT, 27 percent at the University of California at Berkeley, and a staggering 35 percent at the University of California at Irvine.

Not all Asian American youth do this well, however. Poorly educated Vietnamese, Cambodian, and Hmong refugee youth are especially at risk for school-related problems. Many refugee children's histories are replete with losses and trauma. Thuy, a 12-year-old Vietnamese girl, has been in the United States for two years and resides with her father in a small apartment with a cousin's family of five in the inner city of a West Coast metropolitan area (Huang, 1989). While trying to escape from Saigon, "the family became separated, and the wife and two younger children remained in Vietnam. . . . Thuy's father has had an especially difficult time adjusting to the United States. He struggles with English classes and has been unable to maintain several jobs as a waiter" (Huang, 1989, p. 307). When Thuy received a letter from her mother saying that her 5-year-old brother had died, Thuy's schoolwork began to deteriorate, and she showed marked signs of depression—lack of energy, loss of appetite, withdrawal from peer relations, and a general feeling of hopelessness. At the insistence of the school, she and her father went to the child and adolescent unit of a community mental health center. It took the therapist a long time to establish credibility with Thuy and her father, but eventually they began to trust the therapist, who was a good listener and gave them competent advice about how to handle different experiences in their new country. The therapist also contacted Thuy's teacher, who said that Thuy had been involved in several interethnic skirmishes at school. With the assistance of the mental health clinic, the school initiated interethnic student panels to address cultural differences and discuss reasons for ethnic hostility. Thuy was selected to participate in these panels. Her father became involved in the community mutual assistance association, and Thuy's academic performance began to improve.

preview

This chapter focuses on achievement, work, and careers. As adolescence and emerging adulthood unfold, achievement takes a more central role in development, work becomes a major aspect of life, and careers play an increasingly important role. The chapter begins by examining why adolescence is a key period in achievement. Next, we explore the roles of work in the lives of adolescents and emerging adults. The chapter concludes with an evaluation of the major theories of career development and the contexts that influence adolescents' career choices.

1 Achievement **LG1** Discuss achievement in the lives of adolescents

| The Importance of Achievement in Adolescence | Achievement Processes | Social Relationships and Contexts | Some Motivational Obstacles to Achievement |

Some developmentalists worry that the United States is rapidly becoming a nation of hurried, wired people who are raising their youth to become the same way—too uptight about success and failure, and far too preoccupied with how their personal accomplishments compare with those of others. However, an increasing number of experts argue that achievement expectations for youth are low, that adolescents are not adequately challenged to achieve, and that too many adolescents aren't being given adequate support and guidance to reach their achievement aspirations.

Life is a gift . . . Accept it.

Life is an adventure . . . Dare it.

Life is a mystery . . . Unfold it.

Life is a struggle . . . Face it.

Life is a puzzle . . . Solve it.

Life is an opportunity . . . Take it.

Life is a mission . . . Fulfill it.

Life is a goal . . . Achieve it.

—AUTHOR UNKNOWN

THE IMPORTANCE OF ACHIEVEMENT IN ADOLESCENCE

Adolescence is a critical juncture in achievement (Eccles & Roeser, 2013; Wigfield & others, 2015). New social and academic pressures force adolescents toward different roles. These new roles often involve more responsibility. Achievement becomes a more serious business in adolescence, and adolescents begin to sense that the game of life is now being played for real. They even may begin to perceive current successes and failures as predictors of future outcomes in the adult world. And, as demands on adolescents intensify, different areas of their lives may come into conflict. Adolescents' social interests may cut into the time they need to pursue academic matters, or ambitions in one area may undermine the attainment of goals in another, as when academic achievement leads to social disapproval (Schwartz, Kelly, & Duong, 2013).

How effectively adolescents adapt to these new academic and social pressures is determined, in part, by psychological, motivational, and contextual factors (Schunk & Zimmerman, 2013). Indeed, adolescents' achievement reflects much more than their intellectual ability. Students who are not as bright as others may show an adaptive motivational pattern—being persistent at tasks and confident about their ability to solve problems, for example—and turn out to be high achievers. In contrast, some of the brightest students may have maladaptive achievement patterns—giving up easily and not having confidence in their academic skills, for example—and turn out to be low achievers.

ACHIEVEMENT PROCESSES

Achievement involves a number of motivational processes. We explore these processes next, beginning with the distinction between intrinsic and extrinsic motivation.

Intrinsic and Extrinsic Motivation   **Intrinsic motivation** is based on internal factors such as self-determination, curiosity, challenge, and effort. **Extrinsic motivation** involves external incentives such as rewards and punishments. The humanistic and cognitive approaches

intrinsic motivation Internal motivational factors such as self-determination, curiosity, challenge, and effort.

extrinsic motivation External motivational factors such as rewards and punishments.

Meredith MacGregor, pictured here as a senior at Fairview High School in Boulder, Colorado, is an aspiring scientist and was one of Colorado's top high school long-distance runners. She maintained a 4.0 grade point average, participated in a number of school organizations, and cofounded the AfriAid Club. She was named a USA Today High School Academic All-Star and was awarded the Intel Foundation Young Scientist Award (Wong Briggs, 2007). *What are some factors that were likely involved in Meredith's motivation to achieve?*
© Kevin Moloney

stress the importance of intrinsic motivation in achievement. Some adolescents study hard because they are internally motivated to achieve high standards in their work (intrinsic motivation). Other adolescents study hard because they want to make good grades or avoid parental disapproval (extrinsic motivation).

Current evidence strongly favors establishing a classroom climate in which students are intrinsically motivated to learn (Gottfried & others, 2013; Weinstein, Deci, & Ryan, 2012). For example, a study of third- through eighth-grade students found that intrinsic motivation was positively linked with grades and standardized test scores, whereas extrinsic motivation was negatively related to achievement outcomes (Lepper, Corpus, & Iyengar, 2005). A recent study found that high school students' intrinsic motivation was linked to a higher level of academic achievement (Wormington, Corpus, & Anderson, 2012). And a study of fifth- and sixth-grade students revealed that framing goals extrinsically was related to a lower level of independent motivation and lower persistence on achievement tasks (Vansteenkiste & others, 2008). Parental intrinsic/extrinsic motivational practices are also linked to children's motivation. In one study, children and adolescents had higher intrinsic motivation in math and science from 9 to 17 years of age when their parents engaged in task-intrinsic practices (encouraging children's pleasure and engagement in learning) than when their parents engaged in task-extrinsic practices (providing external rewards and consequences contingent on children's performance) (Gottfried & others, 2009).

Students are more motivated to learn when they are given choices, become absorbed in challenges that match their skills, and receive rewards that have informational value but are not used for control. Praise also can enhance students' intrinsic motivation. To understand the importance of these aspects of achievement in adolescent development, let's first explore the following dimensions of intrinsic motivation: (1) self-determination and personal choice, (2) optimal experiences and flow, and (3) cognitive engagement and self-responsibility. Then we will offer some concluding thoughts about intrinsic and extrinsic motivation.

Self-Determination and Personal Choice   One view of intrinsic motivation emphasizes that students want to believe that they are doing something because of their own will, not because of external success or rewards (Deci, Koestner, & Ryan, 2001; Weinstein, Deci, & Ryan, 2012). Students' internal motivation and intrinsic interest in school tasks increase when they have opportunities to make choices and take responsibility for their learning (Stipek, 2002). In one study, students who were given some choice of activities and when to do them, and were encouraged to take personal responsibility for their behavior, had higher achievement gains and were more likely to graduate from high school than were the members of a control group (deCharms, 1984).

The architects of self-determination theory, Richard Ryan and Edward Deci (2009), refer to teachers who create circumstances that allow students to engage in self-determination as *autonomy-supportive teachers.* A recent study of 34 high school classrooms found that students who perceived their classrooms as allowing and encouraging autonomy in the first several weeks of the semester increased their engagement throughout the course (Hafen & others, 2012). Also, a recent study found that self-determined motivation and autonomy support were linked to how much adolescents engaged in physical activity (Christiana & others, 2014). And another recent study indicated that an emphasis on autonomy support in a supervised exercise program was related to an increase in obese adolescents' intrinsic motivation and habitual engagement in exercise one month after the program had ended (Gourlan, Sant, & Boiche, 2014).

Optimal Experiences and Flow   Mihaly Csikszentmihalyi (Abuhamdeh & Csikszentmihalyi, 2012; Csikszentmihalyi, 1990, 1993; Csikszentmihalyi & Csikszentmihalyi, 2006) has studied the optimal experiences of people for three decades. These optimal experiences occur when people report feelings of deep enjoyment and happiness. Csikszentmihalyi uses the term **flow** to describe optimal experiences in life. Flow occurs most often when people develop a sense of mastery and are absorbed in a state of concentration while they engage in an activity. He argues that flow occurs when individuals are engaged in challenges they find neither too difficult nor too easy.

Perceived levels of challenge and skill can result in different outcomes (see Figure 1). Flow is most likely to occur in areas in which adolescents are challenged and perceive themselves as having a high degree of skill

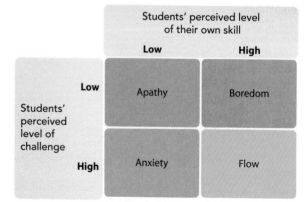

		Students' perceived level of their own skill	
		Low	High
Students' perceived level of challenge	Low	Apathy	Boredom
	High	Anxiety	Flow

FIGURE 1

OUTCOMES OF PERCEIVED LEVELS OF CHALLENGE AND SKILL

(Strati, Shernoff, & Kackar, 2012). When adolescents' skills are high but the activity provides little challenge, the result is boredom. When both challenge and skill levels are low, apathy occurs. And when adolescents perceive themselves as not having adequate skills to master a challenging task they face, they experience anxiety. In one study, students were less engaged in classrooms than in other contexts (Shernoff, 2009). In this study, students were more engaged when they participated in contexts they found challenging, relevant, and enjoyable. After-school programs, especially those involving organized sports, academic enrichment, and arts enrichment activities, elicited the highest level of engagement in the after-school hours (Shernoff, 2009).

Cognitive Engagement and Self-Responsibility   It is increasingly recognized that becoming cognitively engaged and developing self-responsibility are key aspects of achievement (Appleton, 2012; Wigfield & others, 2015). Phyllis Blumenfeld and her colleagues (Blumenfeld, Kempler, & Krajcik, 2006) have proposed another variation on intrinsic motivation that emphasizes the importance of creating learning environments that encourage students to become cognitively engaged and to take responsibility for their learning. The goal is to motivate students to expend the effort to persist and master ideas rather than simply to do enough work to just get by and make passing grades. Especially important in encouraging students to become cognitively engaged and responsible for their learning is embedding subject matter content and skills learning within meaningful contexts, especially real-world situations that mesh with students' interests (Wigfield & others, 2015). Award-winning teachers create meaningful real-world experiences that engage students in learning.

Some Final Thoughts About Intrinsic and Extrinsic Motivation   An overwhelming conclusion for parents and teachers involves the importance of encouraging students to become intrinsically motivated and creating learning environments that promote students' cognitive engagement and self-responsibility for learning (Sosic-Vasic & others, 2015; Townsend, 2011). That said, the real world is not just one of intrinsic motivation, and too often intrinsic and extrinsic motivation have been pitted against each other as polar opposites. In many aspects of students' lives, both intrinsic and extrinsic motivation are at work (Anderman, 2012; Cameron & Pierce, 2008; Schunk, 2012). Keep in mind, though, that many psychologists caution that extrinsic motivation by itself is not a good strategy.

Our discussion of extrinsic and intrinsic motivation sets the stage for consideration of other cognitive processes involved in motivating students to learn. As we explore these additional cognitive processes, notice how intrinsic and extrinsic motivation continue to be important. The processes are: (1) attribution; (2) mastery motivation and mindset; (3) self-efficacy; (4) expectations; (5) goal setting, planning, and self-monitoring; (6) sustained attention, effort, and task persistence; (7) delay of gratification; and (8) purpose.

Attribution   **Attribution theory** states that individuals are motivated to discover the underlying causes of their own performance and behavior. Attributions are perceived causes of outcomes (Graham & Weiner, 2012). In a way, attribution theorists say, adolescents are like intuitive scientists, seeking to explain the cause behind what happens (Weiner, 2005). For example, a secondary school student asks, "Why am I not doing well in this class?" or "Did I get a good grade because I studied hard or the teacher made up an easy test, or both?" The search for a cause or explanation is often initiated when unexpected and important events end in failure, as when a good student gets a low grade. Some of the most frequently inferred causes of success and failure are ability, effort, task ease or difficulty, luck, mood, and help or hindrance from others.

What are the best strategies for teachers to use in helping students who attribute their poor performance to factors such as lack of ability, bad luck, and hindrance from others? Educational psychologists recommend getting adolescents to attribute their poor performance to internal factors such as a lack of effort rather than to external factors such as bad luck or a test that was too difficult. They also emphasize getting adolescents to concentrate on the learning task at hand rather than worrying about failing; to retrace their steps to discover their mistake; and to analyze the problem to discover another approach.

Mastery Motivation and Mindset   Cognitive engagement and self-motivation to improve are reflected in adolescents with a mastery motivation. These adolescents also have a growth mindset and believe that they can produce positive outcomes if they put forth sufficient effort.

flow Csikszentmihalyi's concept of optimal life experiences, which he believes occur most often when people develop a sense of mastery and are absorbed in a state of concentration when they're engaged in an activity.

attribution theory The theory that in their effort to make sense of their own behavior or performance, individuals are motivated to discover its underlying causes.

The student:

- Says "I can't"
- Doesn't pay attention to teacher's instructions
- Doesn't ask for help, even when it is needed
- Does nothing (for example, stares out the window)
- Guesses or answers randomly without really trying
- Doesn't show pride in successes
- Appears bored, uninterested
- Is unresponsive to teacher's exhortations to try
- Is easily discouraged
- Doesn't volunteer answers to teacher's questions
- Maneuvers to get out of or to avoid work (for example, has to go to the nurse's office)

FIGURE 2

BEHAVIORS THAT SUGGEST HELPLESSNESS

developmental **connection**

Schools

A number of criticisms of No Child Left Behind have been made. Connect to "Schools."

mastery orientation An outlook in which individuals focus on the task rather than on their ability; they concentrate on learning strategies and the process of achievement instead of the outcome.

helpless orientation An outlook in which individuals seem trapped when experiencing difficulty and attribute their difficulty to a lack of ability. This orientation undermines performance.

performance orientation An outlook in which individuals are focused on winning rather than a specific achievement outcome. For performance-oriented students, winning results in happiness.

mindset The cognitive view, either fixed or growth, that individuals develop for themselves.

Mastery Motivation Developmental psychologists Valanne Henderson and Carol Dweck (1990) have found that adolescents often show two distinct responses to difficult or challenging circumstances. Adolescents who display a **mastery orientation** are task-oriented; instead of focusing on their ability or looking only at the desired outcome, they concentrate on learning strategies and engaging in the process of achievement. Those with a **helpless orientation** seem trapped by the experience of difficulty, and they attribute their difficulty to lack of ability. They frequently say such things as "I'm not very good at this," even though they might earlier have demonstrated their ability through many successes. And, once they view their behavior as failure, they often feel anxious and their performance worsens even further. Figure 2 describes some behaviors that might reflect feelings of helplessness (Stipek, 2002).

In contrast, mastery-oriented adolescents often instruct themselves to pay attention, to think carefully, and to remember strategies that have worked for them in previous situations. They frequently report feeling challenged and excited by difficult tasks, rather than being threatened by them (Anderman & Wolters, 2006). One study revealed that seventh- to eleventh-grade students' mastery goals were linked to how much effort they put forth in mathematics (Chouinard, Karsenti, & Roy, 2007).

Another issue in motivation involves whether to adopt a mastery orientation or a performance orientation. Adolescents with a **performance orientation** are focused on winning, rather than on achievement outcome, and believe that happiness results from winning. Does this mean that mastery-oriented adolescents do not like to win and that performance-oriented adolescents are not motivated to experience the self-efficacy that comes from being able to take credit for one's accomplishments? No. A matter of emphasis or degree is involved, though. For mastery-oriented individuals, winning isn't everything; for performance-oriented individuals, skill development and self-efficacy take a backseat to winning.

As described in the chapter on "Schools," the No Child Left Behind Act (NCLB) emphasizes testing and accountability. Although NCLB may motivate some teachers and students to work harder, motivation experts worry that it encourages a performance orientation rather than a mastery orientation on the part of students (Meece, Anderman, & Anderman, 2006).

A final point needs to be made about mastery and performance goals: They are not always mutually exclusive. Students can be both mastery- and performance-oriented, and researchers have found that mastery goals combined with performance goals often benefit students' success (Anderman & Anderman, 2010; Schunk, 2012).

Mindset Carol Dweck's (2006, 2007, 2012) most recent analysis of motivation for achievement stresses the importance of developing a specific **mindset,** which she defines as the cognitive view individuals develop for themselves. She concludes that individuals have one of two mindsets: (1) a fixed mindset, in which they believe that their qualities are carved in stone and cannot change; or (2) a growth mindset, in which they believe their qualities can change and improve through their effort. A fixed mindset is similar to a helpless orientation; a growth mindset is much like having mastery motivation.

In *Mindset,* Dweck (2006) argued that individuals' mindsets influence their outlook, whether optimistic or pessimistic; shape their goals and how hard they will strive to reach those goals; and affect many aspects of their lives, including achievement and success in school and sports. Dweck says that mindsets begin to be shaped when children and adolescents interact with parents, teachers, and coaches, who themselves have either a fixed mindset or a growth mindset.

Dweck and her colleagues (Blackwell & Dweck, 2008; Blackwell, Trzesniewski, & Dweck, 2007; Dweck, 2012; Dweck & Master, 2009) recently incorporated information about the brain's plasticity into their effort to improve students' motivation to achieve and succeed. In one study, they assigned two groups of students to eight sessions of either (1) study skills instruction or (2) study skills instruction plus information about the importance of developing a growth mindset (called incremental theory in the research) (Blackwell, Trzesniewski, & Dweck, 2007). One of the exercises in the growth mindset group was titled "You Can Grow Your Brain," which emphasized that the brain is like a muscle that can change and grow as it gets exercised and develops new connections. Students were informed that the more you challenge your brain to learn, the more your brain cells grow. Both groups had a pattern of declining math scores prior to the intervention. Following the intervention, the group who received only the study skills instruction continued to decline. The group who received study skills instruction plus the growth-mindset emphasis on how the brain develops when it is

Going into the virtual brain. A screen from Carol Dweck's "Brainology" program, which is designed to cultivate a growth mindset.

Courtesy of Dr. Carol S. Dweck

challenged were able to reverse the downward trend and improve their math achievement. In a recent study conducted by Dweck and her colleagues (Paunesku & others, 2015), underachieving high school students read online modules about how the brain changes when people learn and study hard. Following the online exposure about the brain and learning, the underachieving students improved their grade point averages.

In other work, Dweck has been creating a computer-based workshop called "Brainology" to teach students that their intelligence can change (Blackwell & Dweck, 2008). Students experience six modules about how the brain works and how to make their brain improve. After the program was tested in 20 New York City schools, students strongly endorsed the value of the computer-based brain modules. Said one student, "I will try harder because I know that the more you try the more your brain knows" (Dweck & Master, 2009, p. 137).

Dweck and her colleagues also recently have found that a growth mindset can prevent negative stereotypes from undermining achievement. For example, believing that math ability can be learned helped to protect women from negative gender stereotyping about math (Good, Rattan, & Dweck, 2012). And other research recently indicated that willpower is a virtually nonlimited mindset that predicts how long people will work and resist temptations during stressful circumstances (Dweck, 2012; Job, Dweck, & Walton, 2010; Miller & others, 2012). Also, in a longitudinal study of university students, a nonlimited mindset predicted better self-regulation (improvements in time management and less procrastination, unhealthy eating, and impulsive spending) (Job & others, 2015). In this study, among students taking a heavy courseload, those with a nonlimited mindset got higher grades.

Further, a recent meta-analysis found that having a malleable, growth-oriented mindset predicted whether individuals would have a higher level of self-regulation, which in turn was associated with goal attainment (Burnette & others, 2013). In this meta-analysis, having a malleable, growth-oriented mindset was linked to the extent to which individuals developed mastery-oriented strategies, whereas a fixed mindset was associated with developing helpless strategies.

Self-Efficacy Like having a growth mindset, **self-efficacy**—the belief that one can master a situation and produce favorable outcomes—is an important cognitive view for adolescents to develop. Albert Bandura (1997, 2004, 2010, 2012) argues that self-efficacy is a critical factor in whether adolescents achieve. Self-efficacy has much in common with mastery motivation. Self-efficacy is the belief that "I can"; helplessness is the belief that "I cannot" (Stipek, 2002). Adolescents with high self-efficacy endorse such statements as "I know that I will be able to learn the material in this class" and "I expect to be able to do well at this activity."

Dale Schunk (2008, 2012, 2016) has applied the concept of self-efficacy to many aspects of students' achievement. In his view, self-efficacy influences a student's choice of activities. Students with low self-efficacy for learning might avoid many learning tasks, especially those

developmental **connection**

Social Cognitive Theory

Social cognitive theory holds that behavior, environment, and person/cognitive factors are the key influences on development. Connect to "Introduction."

self-efficacy The belief that one can master a situation and produce positive outcomes.

that are challenging, whereas students with high self-efficacy eagerly approach these learning tasks. Students with high self-efficacy are more likely to persist with effort at a learning task than are students with low self-efficacy (Walsh, 2008). A study revealed that high-self-efficacy adolescents had higher academic aspirations, spent more time doing homework, and were more likely to associate learning activities with optimal experience than were their low self-efficacy counterparts (Bassi & others, 2007).

Expectations   Expectations play important roles in adolescents' achievement. These expectations involve not only the expectations of adolescents themselves but also those of their parents and teachers.

Adolescents   How hard students will work can depend on how much they expect to accomplish. If they expect to succeed, they are more likely to work hard to reach a goal than if they expect to fail. Jacquelynne Eccles (1987, 1993) defined expectations for students' success as beliefs about how well they will do on upcoming tasks, either in the immediate or long-term future. Three aspects of ability beliefs, according to Eccles, are students' beliefs about how good they are at a particular activity, how good they are in comparison with other individuals, and how good they are in relation to their performance in other activities.

How hard students work also depends on the *value* they place on the goal (Wigfield & Cambria, 2010). Indeed, the combination of expectancy and value has been the focus of a number of efforts to better understand students' achievement motivation. In Eccles' (1993, 2007) model, students' expectancies and values are assumed to directly influence their performance, persistence, and task choice.

Parents and Teachers   A student's motivation is often influenced by the expectations that parents, teachers, and other adults have for the person's achievement. Children and adolescents benefit when their parents and teachers have high expectations for them and provide the necessary support for them to meet those expectations (Anderman, Gray, & Chang, 2013). Special concerns have been voiced about the lower academic expectations parents and teachers have for African American adolescent boys compared with African American girls (Rowley & others, 2014).

Researchers have found that parents' expectations are linked with children's and adolescents' academic achievement (Burchinal & others, 2002). One longitudinal study revealed that children whose mothers had higher academic expectations for them in the first grade were more likely to reach a higher level of educational attainment in emerging adulthood (age 23) than children whose mothers had lower expectations for them in the first grade (Englund, Luckner, & Whaley, 2003). Also, a longitudinal study revealed that adolescents' achievement was higher when parents had higher expectations than adolescents did or when adolescents perceived that their parents' expectations were higher than theirs (Wang & Benner, 2014). Further, adolescents' achievement was lower when parents had lower expectations than adolescents did or when adolescents thought their parents' expectations were lower than their own. And a recent longitudinal study found that positive expectations of tenth-grade students, their parents, and their English and math teachers predicted their postsecondary status (highest level of education) four years later (Gregory & Huang, 2013). In this study, these expectations together were a better predictor of postsecondary status than student characteristics such as socioeconomic status and academic performance.

Too often parents attempt to protect children's and adolescents' self-esteem by setting low standards (Graham, 2005; Stipek, 2005). In reality, it is more beneficial to set standards that challenge children and adolescents and to expect students to perform at the highest levels they are capable of achieving. Those who are not challenged may develop low standards for themselves, and the fragile self-confidence they develop from reaching these low expectations can be shattered the first time they encounter more challenging work and are held to higher standards.

Teachers' expectations also are important influences on children's achievement (Rubie-Davies, 2011). In an observational study of 12 classrooms, teachers with high expectations spent more time providing a framework for students' learning, asked higher-level questions, and were more effective in managing students' behavior than were teachers with average and low expectations (Rubie-Davies, 2007).

To read about the work of one individual who had high expectations for his students, see the *Connecting with Careers* profile.

A student and teacher at Langston Hughes Elementary School in Chicago, a school whose teachers have high expectations for students. *How do teachers' expectations influence students' achievement?*
© Ralf-Finn Hestoft/Corbis

Jaime Escalante, Secondary School Math Teacher

An immigrant from Bolivia, Jaime Escalante became a math teacher at Garfield High School in East Los Angeles in the 1970s. When he began teaching at Garfield, many of the students had little confidence in their math abilities, and most of the teachers had low expectations for the students' success. Escalante took it as a special challenge to improve the students' math skills and even get them to the point where they could perform well on the Educational Testing Service Advanced Placement (AP) calculus exam.

Jaime Escalante in a classroom teaching math.
© AP Images

The first year was difficult. Escalante's calculus class began at 8 a.m. He told the students the doors would be open at 7 a.m. and that instruction would begin at 7:30 a.m. He also worked with them after school and on weekends. He put together lots of handouts, told the students to take extensive notes, and required them to keep a folder. He gave them a five-minute quiz each morning and a test every Friday. He started with 14 students but within two weeks only half remained. Only five students lasted through the spring. One of the boys who quit said, "I don't want to come at 7:00. Why should I?"

Subsequent years were better as increasing numbers of students surpassed their own expectations for math achievement. Because of Escalante's persistent, challenging, and inspiring teaching, Garfield High—a school plagued by poor funding, violence, and inferior working conditions—eventually ranked seventh in the United States in calculus. Escalante's commitment and motivation were transferred to his students, many of whom no one believed in before Escalante came along. Escalante's contributions were portrayed in the film *Stand and Deliver*. Escalante, his students, and celebrity guests also introduced basic math concepts for sixth- to twelfth-grade students on the *Futures with Jaime Escalante* PBS series during the 1990s. Now retired from teaching, Escalante continues to work in a consulting role to help improve students' motivation to do well in math and improve their math skills. Escalante's story is testimony to how one teacher can make a major difference in students' motivation and achievement.

For more information about the work of secondary school teachers, see the Careers in Adolescent Development appendix.

Goal Setting, Planning, and Self-Monitoring/Self-Regulation Self-efficacy and achievement improve when individuals set goals that are specific, proximal, and challenging (Anderman, Gray, & Chang, 2013; Schunk, 2012, 2016). A nonspecific, fuzzy goal is "I want to be successful." A more concrete, specific goal is "I want to make the honor roll by the end of the semester."

Students can set both long-term (distal) and short-term (proximal) goals. It is okay for individuals to set some long-term goals, such as "I want to graduate from high school" or "I want to go to college," but they also need to create short-term goals that will serve as steps along the way. "Getting an A on the next math test" is an example of a short-term, proximal goal. So is "Doing all of my homework by 4 p.m. Sunday."

Another good strategy is to set challenging goals (Anderman, 2012). A challenging goal is a commitment to self-improvement. Strong interest and involvement in activities are sparked by challenges. Goals that are easy to reach generate little interest or effort. However, goals should be optimally matched to the individual's skill level. If goals are unrealistically high, the result will be repeated failures that lower the individual's self-efficacy.

Yet another good strategy is to develop personal goals about desired and undesired future circumstances (Ford & Smith, 2007; Wigfield & Cambria, 2010). Personal goals can be a key aspect of an individual's motivation for coping and dealing with life's challenges and opportunities (Maehr & Zusho, 2009).

It is not enough just to set goals. In order to achieve, it also is important to plan how to reach those goals (Braver & others, 2014). Being a good planner means managing time effectively, setting priorities, and being organized.

Individuals should not only plan their next week's activities but also monitor how well they are sticking to their plan. Once engaged in a task, they need to monitor their progress,

An adolescent works with his daily planner.
How are goals, planning, and self-regulation involved in adolescent achievement?
© Martin Meyer/Corbis

developmental connection

Cognitive Development

Executive function is linked to the development of the brain's prefrontal cortex and involves managing one's thoughts to engage in goal-directed behavior and exercise self-control. Connect to "The Brain and Cognitive Development."

◀ — — — — — — — — — — — ◢

judge how well they are doing on the task, and evaluate the outcomes to regulate what they do in the future (Wigfield, Klauda, & Cambria, 2011). High-achieving youth are often self-regulatory learners (McClelland & others, 2015; Schunk & Zimmerman, 2013). For example, high-achieving youth monitor their learning and systematically evaluate their progress toward a goal more than low-achieving students do. Encouraging youth to monitor their learning conveys the message that they are responsible for their own behavior and that learning requires their active, dedicated participation.

One type of self-regulation is *intentional self-regulation,* which involves selecting goals or outcomes, optimizing the means to achieve desired outcomes, and compensating for setbacks along the path to goal achievement (Geldhof & others, 2015; Gestsdottir & others, 2009). One study found that intentional self-regulation was especially beneficial to young adolescents from low-income backgrounds (Urban, Lewin-Bizan, & Lerner, 2010). In this study, adolescents with high self-regulation were more likely to seek out extracurricular activities, which resulted in more positive developmental outcomes such as academic achievement. Selecting goals or outcomes was assessed by items such as "When I decide upon a goal, I stick to it"; optimizing the means to achieve desired outcomes was assessed by items such as "I think exactly about how I can best realize my plans"; and compensating for setbacks was assessed by items such as "When things don't work the way they used to, I look for other ways to achieve them."

Barry Zimmerman and his colleagues (Zimmerman, 2002, 2012; Zimmerman & Kitsantas, 1997; Zimmerman & Labuhn, 2012) have developed a model of self-regulation in achievement contexts that has three phrases:

· *Forethought.* Adolescents assess task demands, set goals, and estimate their ability to reach the goals.

· *Performance.* Adolescents create self-regulating strategies such as time management, attentional focusing, help seeking, and metacognition.

· *Self-Reflection.* Adolescents evaluate their performance, including attributions about factors that affected the outcome and how satisfied they are with their behavior.

Sustained Attention, Effort, and Task Persistence

Sustained attention, effort, and task persistence in school, work, and a career are important aspects of adolescents' ability to reach their goals (Padilla-Walker & others, 2013). *Sustained attention* is the ability to maintain attention to a selected stimulus for a prolonged period of time. Sustained attention requires effort, and as individuals develop through adolescence, school tasks, projects, and work become more complex and require longer periods of sustained attention, effort, and task persistence than in childhood. A recent study revealed that older adolescents who had spent a larger part of their life in poverty showed less persistence on a challenging task (Fuller-Roswell & others, 2015).

Might the effectiveness with which adolescents persist at tasks be linked to their career success in adulthood? A recent study revealed that task persistence at 13 years of age was related to occupational success in middle age (Andersson & Bergman, 2011).

Delay of Gratification

Delaying gratification also is an important aspect of reaching goals—especially long-term goals (Imuta, Hayne, & Scarf, 2014; Mischel, 2014; Schlam & others, 2013). *Delay of gratification* involves postponing immediate rewards in order to attain a larger, more valuable reward at a later point in time. While it may be more attractive to adolescents to hang out with friends today than to work on a project that is due for a class assignment later in the week, their decision not to delay gratification can have negative consequences for their academic achievement.

Walter Mischel and his colleagues (Mischel, Ebbesen, & Zeiss, 1972; Mischel & Moore, 1973; Zayas, Mischel, & Pandey, 2014) have conducted classic research on the delay of gratification with preschool children using the marshmallow task. In this research, young children were told the experimenter needed to leave the room to work on something and while s/he was gone they could choose to have one marshmallow immediately, or if they waited until the experimenter returned they could have two marshmallows. A majority of the children did wait a short while but only a subset of the young children waited the entire 15 minutes until the experimenter returned. On average, preschoolers succumbed to the temptation and ate the marshmallow within one minute.

In longitudinal research, Mischel and his colleagues have found that the preschool children who were able to delay gratification became more academically successful, had higher

What is the nature of the marshmallow task? How is delay of gratification linked to later development?
© Bill Aron/PhotoEdit

Hari Prabhakar, Student on a Path to Purpose

Hari Prabhakar's ambition is to become an international health expert. As he made the transition from high school to college, Hari created the Tribal India Health Foundation (www.tihf.org), which provides assistance in bringing low-cost health care to rural areas in India. Juggling his roles as a college student at Johns Hopkins University and as the foundation's director, Prabhakar spent about 15 hours a week leading Tribal India Health throughout his four undergraduate years.

Prabhakar also applied for, and received, $16,500 in research fellowships from different Johns Hopkins programs to advance his knowledge of public health care. He sought the expertise of health specialists on the Hopkins faculty to expand his understanding of international health care. Prabhakar worked an average of six hours each week conducting research on sickle-cell disease, which is prevalent among tribes in rural areas of India. He spent three months every summer during college in India working directly with the tribal people. In describing his work, Prabhakar said (Johns Hopkins University, 2006b):

> I have found it very challenging to coordinate the international operation. . . . It takes a lot of work, and there's not a lot of free time. But it's worth it when I visit our patients and see how they and the community are getting better.

Prabhakar graduated from Johns Hopkins University in 2006 with a 3.9 GPA and a double major in public health and writing. As a reward for his undergraduate accomplishments, in 2007 Prabhakar received a Marshall scholarship to study in Great Britain. He completed two master's degrees at Oxford University's Health Services Research Unit and the London School of Hygiene and Tropical

Hari Prabhakar (*in rear*) at a screening camp in India that he created as part of his Tribal India Health Foundation.
Courtesy of Hari Prabhakar

Medicine. Prabhakar seeks to combine clinical training with health systems management to improve the medical care of people in impoverished circumstances around the world. In 2010, Prabhakar began further education by entering Harvard Medical School. (Sources: Johns Hopkins University, 2006a, b; Lunday, 2006; Marshall Scholarships, 2007; Prabhakar, 2007.)

What kinds of goals did Prabhakar likely set for himself that strengthened his extraordinary sense of purpose?

SAT scores and higher grade point averages at the end of college, and coped better with stress as adolescents and emerging adults (Mischel, 2014; Mischel & others, 1989). And as adults, they made more money in their career, were more law-abiding, were more likely to have a lower body mass index, and were happier than individuals who had been unable to delay gratification as preschoolers (Mischel, 2014; Moffitt, 2012; Moffitt & others, 2011; Schlam & others, 2013). Although the ability to delay gratification in preschool was linked to academic success and coping in adolescence and competence in adulthood, Mischel (2014) emphasizes that adolescents and adults can improve their ability to delay gratification.

Purpose   Earlier in this edition we considered the view of purpose that William Damon (2008) proposed in his book *The Path to Purpose*. For example, we discussed the importance of purpose in identity development, and we saw that purpose is a key aspect of values. Here we expand on Damon's view and explore how purpose is a missing ingredient in many adolescents' and emerging adults' achievement.

For Damon, *purpose* is an intention to accomplish something meaningful to one's self and to contribute something to the world beyond the self. Finding purpose involves answering such questions as "*Why* am I doing this? *Why* does it matter? *Why* is it important for me and the world beyond me? *Why* do I strive to accomplish this end?" (Damon, 2008, pp. 33–34).

In interviews with 12- to 22-year-olds, Damon found that only about 20 percent had a clear vision of where they wanted to go in life, what they wanted to achieve, and why. The largest percentage—about 60 percent—had engaged in some potentially purposeful activities, such as service learning or fruitful discussions with a career counselor, but they did not yet have a real commitment or any reasonable plans for reaching their goals. Slightly more than

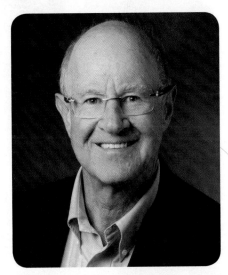

William Damon. In Damon's view, purpose is a missing ingredient in many adolescents' and emerging adults' achievement. *What are some strategies adults can adopt to guide adolescents and emerging adults to incorporate purpose into their paths to achievement?*
Courtesy William Damon, Stanford University

developmental connection

Identity

William Damon (2008) concludes that too many of today's youth aren't moving toward any identity resolution. Connect to "The Self, Identity, Emotion, and Personality."

20 percent expressed no aspirations, and some even said they didn't see any reason to have aspirations.

Damon concludes that most teachers and parents communicate the importance of goals such as studying hard and getting good grades, but rarely discuss what the goals might lead to—the purpose for studying hard and getting good grades. Damon emphasizes that too often students focus only on short-term goals and don't explore the big, long-term picture of what they want to do with their life. These interview questions that Damon (2008, p. 135) has used in his research are good springboards for getting students to reflect on their purpose:

- What's most important to you in your life?
- Why do you care about those things?
- Do you have any long-term goals?
- Why are these goals important to you?
- What does it mean to have a good life?
- What does it mean to be a good person?
- If you were looking back on your life now, how would you like to be remembered?

SOCIAL RELATIONSHIPS AND CONTEXTS

Adolescents' relationships with parents, peers, teachers, and mentors are important aspects of their achievement. And socioeconomic status, ethnicity, and culture are social contexts that influence adolescents' achievement.

Parents   Earlier we discovered that parents' expectations have an important influence on adolescents' achievement. A recent study revealed that adolescents whose parents were high in self-efficacy reported more competence in learning activities, fewer problems, and more daily opportunities for optimal experiences (Steca & others, 2011). Here are some additional positive parenting practices associated with improved achievement in adolescents (Wigfield & others, 2006):

- Knowing enough about the adolescent to provide the right amount of challenge and the right amount of support
  - Providing a positive emotional climate that motivates adolescents to internalize their parents' values and goals
  - Modeling motivated achievement behavior: working hard and persisting with effort at challenging tasks

What are some ways that peer relations can influence an adolescent's achievement?
© Comstock/PunchStock RF

Peers   Peers often play key roles in adolescents' achievement (Lynch, Lerner, & Leventhal, 2013; Rubin, Bukowski, & Bowker, 2015). The term *peers* is a multidimensional concept that ranges from acquaintances in the general peer group to cliques and close friends. Adolescents often do well academically if their friends also are doing well academically (Cook, Deng, & Morgano, 2007).

Peers can affect adolescents' achievement through social goals, social comparison, and peer status (Rodkin & Ryan, 2012; Wentzel, 2013). In considering adolescents' achievement, it is important to consider not only academic goals but social goals as well (Schwartz, Kelly, & Duong, 2013). One study revealed that young adolescents who were motivated to engage in social dominance over their peers had a low achievement level (Kiefer & Ryan, 2008). Popularity goals were not linked to adolescents' achievement.

Adolescents often compare themselves with their peers on where they stand academically and socially. Adolescents are more likely than younger children to engage in social comparison, although adolescents are prone to deny that they ever compare themselves with others (Harter, 2012). For example, in social comparison, one adolescent might learn that another adolescent did not do well on a test in school and think "I'm smarter than he is." Positive social comparisons usually result in higher self-esteem, and negative comparisons in lower self-esteem. Adolescents are most likely to compare themselves with others who are similar to them in age, ability, and interests.

Children and adolescents who are more accepted by their peers and who have good social skills often do better in school and have positive motivation for academic achievement (Rubin & others, 2013). In contrast, rejected adolescents, especially those who are highly aggressive, are at risk for a number of achievement problems, including getting low grades and dropping out of school (Wentzel, 2013). One study revealed that having aggressive-disruptive friends in adolescence was linked to a lower likelihood of graduating from high school (Veronneau & others, 2008).

Teachers Earlier we saw how important teachers' expectations for success are in adolescents' achievement. Here we further explore the key role that teachers play in adolescents' achievement. When researchers have observed classrooms, they have found that effective, engaging teachers provide support for adolescents to make good progress and they also encourage adolescents to become self-regulated achievers (Perry & Rahim, 2011). The encouragement takes place in a very positive environment, one in which adolescents are regularly being guided to become motivated to try hard and develop self-efficacy.

Nel Noddings (1992, 2001, 2006) stresses that students are most likely to develop into competent human beings when they feel cared for. This caring requires teachers to get to know students fairly well. She says that this is difficult in large schools with large numbers of adolescents in each class. She recommends that teachers remain with the same students for two to three years (voluntarily on the part of the teacher and the pupil) so that teachers are better positioned to attend to the interests and capacities of each student. This proposal is being examined in schools with high-risk adolescents, an effort that is being funded by the Bill and Melinda Gates Foundation (2008).

Mentors **Mentors** are usually older and more experienced individuals who are motivated to improve the competence and character of a younger person. Mentoring can involve demonstration, instruction, challenge, and encouragement over an extended period of time. As a positive mentoring experience proceeds, the mentor and the youth being mentored develop a bond of commitment, and the youth develops a sense of respect and identification with the mentor (Grossman & others, 2012; Hamilton & Hamilton, 2009; Keller & Pryce, 2012).

Mentoring may take place naturally or through a mentoring program (Chan & others, 2013; Hamilton & Hamilton, 2006; Hurd & Sellers, 2013; Hurd, Varner, & Rowley, 2013). Natural mentoring doesn't involve any formal program but rather emerges out of an individual's existing relationships. Natural mentors might be family members, friends, relatives, neighbors, coaches, extracurricular activity instructors, clergy, youth group leaders, bosses, or teachers. Mentoring programs, which are more formal arrangements than natural mentoring, involve matching an adult mentor with a young person. In many mentoring programs, a mentor assumes a quasi-parental role. A good mentor can help youth develop the sense of purpose William Damon (2008) describes as so critical for today's youth in their quest for achievement and success.

A recent study examined the influence of different types of mentors (kin, teacher, friend, community) and the age period in which they engaged in mentoring in predicting educational attainment (Fruiht & Wray-Lake, 2013). Having a teacher-mentor was a better predictor of educational attainment than having other types of mentors, and having a mentor after high school was linked to educational attainment. Kin and community mentors were more important to educational attainment during high school.

Mentoring programs are increasingly being advocated as a strategy for improving the achievement of secondary school and college students who are at risk for failure (Herrera & others, 2011). One of the largest mentoring programs is Big Brothers Big Sisters (BBBS), which pairs caring, volunteer mentors with at-risk youth (Rhodes & DuBois, 2008). In a large-scale study of BBBS's recently developed school-based mentoring program, significant improvements occurred in the at-risk students' academic achievement, school conduct, attendance, and perceived academic self-efficacy (Herrera & others, 2007). Of course, some mentoring relationships are more effective than

developmental connection

Peers

Adolescents with friends who are academically oriented have higher grades in school. Connect to "Peers, Romantic Relationships, and Lifestyles."

An effective mentoring program has been created at St. Luke's Methodist Church in Dallas to address the lack of ethnic minority role models for ethnic minority students. The program has signed up more than 200 men and 100 boys (ages 4 to 18). The mentoring program involves academic tutoring as well as trips to such activities as sporting and cultural events. The mentors also recently took the children and adolescents to the Johnson Space Center in Houston. Shown here is Dr. Leonard Berry, a mentor in the program, with Brandon Scarborough (age 13) in front, and his own son, Leonard (age 12). Brandon not only has benefited from Dr. Berry's mentoring but has become friends with his son.
© The Dallas Morning News, Irwin Thompson

mentors Individuals who are usually older and more experienced and are motivated to improve the competence and character of a younger person.

developmental connection

Diversity

Ethnicity refers to characteristics rooted in cultural heritage, including nationality, race, religion, and language. Connect to "Culture."

UCLA educational psychologist Sandra Graham is shown talking with adolescent boys about motivation. She has conducted a number of studies which reveal that middle-socioeconomic-status African American students—like their non-Latino White counterparts—have high achievement expectations and attribute success to internal factors such as effort rather than external factors such as luck.
Courtesy of Dr. Sandra Graham

Harold Stevenson and his colleagues have found that Asian schools embrace many of the ideals Americans have for their own schools, but are more successful in implementing them in interesting and productive ways that make learning more enjoyable for children and adolescents.
© Robert A. Isaacs/Science Source

others, and the matching of an adolescent with a mentor requires careful selection and monitoring (Rhodes & Lowe, 2009).

College students can play important roles as mentors for at-risk children and adolescents. One study indicated that mentoring at-risk fourth-grade students improved their understanding of children and the value of mentoring and community work (Schmidt, Marks, & Derrico, 2004).

Mentoring may be especially important for immigrant adolescents who live in neighborhoods with few college graduates. In some mentoring programs, such as AVID, immigrant adolescents are taken to local colleges where they meet mentors and guest speakers who are Latino college students or graduates (Urdan, 2012).

Sociocultural Contexts　How extensively do ethnicity and socioeconomic status affect adolescents' achievement? How does culture influence adolescents' achievement?

Ethnicity and Socioeconomic Status　The diversity that exists among ethnic minority adolescents is evident in their achievement (Marks, Godoy, & Garcia Coll, 2014; Murry & others, 2015). For example, many Asian American students have a strong academic achievement orientation, but some do not.

In addition to recognizing the diversity that exists within every cultural group in terms of adolescents' achievement, it also is important to distinguish between difference and deficiency. Too often the achievement of ethnic minority students—especially African American, Latino, and Native American students—has been interpreted as *deficits* by middle-socioeconomic-status non-Latino White standards, when these students simply are *culturally different and distinct*.

At the same time, many investigations overlook the socioeconomic status (SES) of ethnic minority students (Graham & Taylor, 2001). Many studies have found that socioeconomic status predicts achievement better than does ethnicity. Regardless of their ethnic background, students from middle- and upper-income families fare better than their counterparts from low-income backgrounds in a host of achievement situations—expectations for success, achievement aspirations, and recognition of the importance of effort, for example (Gibbs, 1989). An especially important factor in the lower achievement of students from low-income families is lack of adequate resources, such as an up-to-date computer, or even a computer at all, in the home to support students' learning (Schunk, Meece, & Pintrich, 2014). A recent longitudinal study revealed that African American children or children from low-income families benefited more than children from higher-income families when they did homework more frequently, had Internet access at home, and had a community library card (Xia, 2010).

Sandra Graham (1986, 1990) has conducted a number of studies that reveal not only differences in achievement that are more closely related to SES than to ethnicity, but also the importance of studying ethnic minority student motivation in the context of general motivational theory. Her inquiries focus on the causes African American students cite for their achievement orientation, such as why they succeed or fail. She has found that middle-SES African American students do not fit the stereotype of being unmotivated. Like their non-Latino White middle-SES counterparts, they have high achievement expectations and understand that failure is usually due to a lack of effort rather than bad luck.

Culture　Since the early 1990s, the poor performance of American children and adolescents in math and science has been well publicized. In a large-scale international comparison of 15-year-olds in 65 countries, the top five scores in reading, math, and science were held by Asian countries (China–Shanghai, South Korea, Singapore, China–Hong Kong, and Chinese Taipei), with the exception of 15-year-olds from Finland being third in reading and second in science (OECD, 2010).

China–Shanghai 15-year-olds held first place among the 65 countries in all three academic areas. In this study, U.S. 15-year-olds placed 17th in reading, 31st in math, and 23rd in science. Figure 3 shows international comparisons of reading and math scores in this study.

Critics of the cross-national comparisons argue that in many comparisons virtually all U.S. students are being compared with a "select" group of students from other countries, especially in the secondary school comparisons. Therefore, they conclude, it is no wonder that American students don't fare so well. That criticism holds for some international comparisons. However, when the top 25 percent of students in different countries were compared, U.S. students did not rank much better (Mullis & others, 1998).

Harold Stevenson (1995) explored possible reasons for the poor performance of American students. Stevenson and his colleagues (1990) compared the achievement of students in the United States, China, Taiwan, and Japan. Students in the three Asian countries consistently outperformed American students. And the longer the students were in school, the wider the gap became. The lowest difference between Asian and American students was in first grade; the highest was in the eleventh grade (the highest grade studied).

To learn more about the reasons for these large cross-cultural differences, Stevenson and his colleagues (1990) spent thousands of hours observing in classrooms, as well as interviewing and surveying teachers, students, and parents. They found that Asian teachers spent more of their time teaching math than American teachers did. For example, in Japan more than one-fourth of total classroom time in first grade was spent on math instruction, compared with only one-tenth of the time in U.S. first-grade classrooms. Also, Asian students were in school an average of 240 days a year compared with 178 days in the United States.

In addition to the substantially greater time spent on math instruction in Asian schools than in American schools, differences were found between Asian and American parents. American parents had much lower expectations for their children's education and achievement than the Asian parents did. Also, American parents were more likely to attribute their children's math achievement to innate ability, whereas Asian parents were more likely to say that their children's math achievement reflects effort and training (see Figure 4). Asian students were more likely than American students to do math homework, and Asian parents were far more likely to help their children with their math homework than American parents were (Chen & Stevenson, 1989).

Recently, a number of other studies have examined cross-cultural variations in adolescents' learning and achievement, focusing especially on comparisons of U.S. non-Latino White, Asian American, and East Asian families (Hsin & Xie, 2014; Qu & Pomerantz, 2015). In one recent study, factors that might account for the superior academic performance of Asian American children were examined (Hsin & Xie, 2014). In this study, the Asian American advantage was mainly due to children exerting greater academic effort and not to advantages in tested cognitive abilities or sociodemographic factors.

In the chapter on "Schools," we described a recent study that found Chinese mothers exerted more control (especially psychological control) over their children and adolescents than did U.S. mothers (Ng, Pomerantz, & Deng, 2014). Also in this study, Chinese mothers' self-worth was more contingent on their children's and adolescents' achievement than was the case for U.S. mothers. This research reflects the term "training parents," a variation of authoritarian parenting in which many Asian parents train their children to achieve high levels of academic success. In 2011, Amy Chua's book, *Battle Hymn of the Tiger Mom*, sparked considerable interest in the role of parenting in children's and adolescents' achievement. Chua uses the term "Tiger Mom" to mean a mother who engages in strict disciplinarian practices. In another recent book, *Tiger Babies Strike Back*, Kim Wong Keltner (2013) argues that the Tiger Mom parenting style can be so demanding and confining that being an Asian American child is like being in an "emotional jail." She says that the Tiger Mom authoritarian style does provide some advantages

	Reading		Mathematics	
1.	China: Shanghai	556	China: Shanghai	600
2.	Korea	539	Singapore	562
3.	Finland	536	China: Hong Kong	555
4.	China: Hong Kong	533	Korea	546
5.	Singapore	526	Chinese Taipei	543
6.	Canada	524	Finland	541
7.	New Zealand	521	Liechtenstein	536
8.	Japan	520	Switzerland	534
9.	Australia	515	Japan	529
10.	Netherlands	508	Canada	527
11.	Belgium	506	Netherlands	526
12.	Norway	503	China: Macao	525
13.	Estonia	501	New Zealand	519
14.	Switzerland	501	Belgium	515
15.	Iceland	500	Australia	514
16.	Poland	500	Germany	513
17.	**United States**	**500**	Estonia	512
18.	Liechtenstein	499	Iceland	507
19.	Germany	497	Denmark	503
20.	Sweden	497	Slovenia	501
21.	France	496	Norway	498
22.	Ireland	496	France	497
23.	Chinese Taipei	495	Slovak Republic	497
24.	Denmark	495	Austria	496
25.	Hungary	494	**OECD average**	**496**
26.	United Kingdom	494	Poland	495
	OECD average	**493**	Sweden	494
27.	Portugal	489	Czech Republic	493
28.	China: Macao	487	United Kingdom	492
29.	Italy	486	Hungary	490
30.	Latvia	484	Luxembourg	489
31.	Greece	483	**United States**	**487**

FIGURE 3

INTERNATIONAL COMPARISONS OF 15-YEAR-OLDS' READING AND MATH SCORES. Data from 2009 assessment of 65 countries by the Organization for Economic Cooperation and Development (OECD, 2010).

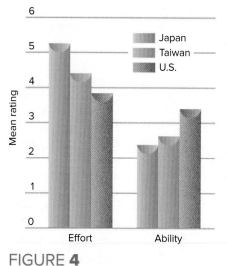

AND THEN AFTER HIGH SCHOOL, I SPENT TWELVE YEARS IN COLLEGE AND MAJORED IN PROCRASTINATION.
www.CartoonStock.com

www.CartoonStock.com.

FIGURE 4

MOTHERS' BELIEFS ABOUT THE FACTORS RESPONSIBLE FOR CHILDREN'S MATH ACHIEVEMENT IN THREE COUNTRIES. In one study, mothers in Japan and Taiwan were more likely to believe that their children's math achievement was due to effort rather than innate ability, whereas U.S. mothers were more likely to believe their children's math achievement was due to innate ability (Stevenson, Lee, & Stigler, 1986). If parents believe that their children's math achievement is due to innate ability and their children are not doing well in math, the implication is that they are less likely to think their children will benefit from putting forth more effort.

for children and youth, such as emphasizing the value of going for what you want and not taking no for an answer, but that too often the outcome is not worth the emotional costs that accompany it.

Recent research on Chinese-American immigrant families with first- and second-grade children has found that the children with authoritarian (highly controlling) parents are more aggressive, are more depressed, have a higher anxiety level, and show poorer social skills than children whose parents engaged in non-authoritarian styles (Zhou & others, 2012). Qing Zhou (2013), lead author on the study just described and the director of the University of California's Culture and Family Laboratory, is conducting workshops to teach Chinese mothers positive parenting strategies such as using listening skills, praising their children for good behavior, and spending more time with their children in fun activities.

In a longitudinal study that followed young Chinese Americans from early adolescence to emerging adulthood, Su Yeong Kim and her colleagues (2013) identified four distinct parenting profiles: supportive, tiger, easygoing, and harsh. The profiles reflect various combinations of positive parenting dimensions (warmth, inductive reasoning, monitoring, and democratic parenting) and negative dimensions (parental hostility, psychological control, shaming, and punitive parenting). Across adolescence, the percentage of tiger parenting (high on both the positive and negative dimensions) decreased for mothers and increased for fathers. In this study, the supportive parenting profile (high on positive dimensions, low on negative dimensions and the most common one) produced the best developmental outcomes, followed by easygoing (low on both positive and negative dimensions, tiger, and harsh (low on positive dimensions, high on negative dimensions) profiles.

Further in this study, the tiger parenting profile (in comparison with the supportive profile) was linked to a lower grade point average, lower sense of family obligation, more academic pressure, more depressive symptoms, and a greater feeling of alienation. Thus, this study indicates that tiger parenting is not the most common style in Chinese American families, nor is it associated with optimal adjustment in adolescents.

SOME MOTIVATIONAL OBSTACLES TO ACHIEVEMENT

Achievement problems can surface when individuals don't set goals, don't plan how to reach them, and don't monitor progress toward goals. They also can arise when individuals procrastinate, are too perfectionistic, become overwhelmed by anxiety, or try to protect their self-worth by avoiding failure. Many of these motivational obstacles to achievement have already surfaced during the secondary school years and then become more full-blown during college. We discuss a number of strategies that teachers, counselors, mentors, and parents can use to help adolescents overcome obstacles to their achievement. And many college students can benefit from adopting these strategies themselves.

Procrastination *Procrastination* is a common barrier to achievement for adolescents and emerging adults (Lakshminarayan, Potdar, & Reddy, 2013; Rice, Richardson, & Clark, 2012). A recent study revealed that low self-efficacy and low self-regulation increased the likelihood that college students would procrastinate (Strunk & Steele, 2011). Other reasons for procrastinating include the following (University of Buffalo Counseling Services, 2014): poor time management, difficulty in concentrating, fear and anxiety (feeling overwhelmed by the task and afraid of getting a bad grade, for example), negative beliefs ("I can never succeed at anything," for example), personal problems (financial difficulties, problems with a boyfriend or girlfriend, and so on), boredom, unrealistic expectations and perfectionism (believing you must read everything written on a subject before beginning to write a paper, for example), and fear of failure (thinking that if you don't get an A, you are a failure, for example).

Procrastination can take many forms, including the following behaviors (University of Illinois Counseling Center, 1984):

· Ignoring the task in the hope that it will go away.

· Underestimating the work involved in the task or overestimating your abilities and resources.

· Spending endless hours on computer games and surfing the Internet.

· Deceiving yourself that a mediocre or poor performance is acceptable.

Can You Tackle Procrastination?

Here are some good strategies for overcoming procrastination:

- *Acknowledge that procrastination is a problem.* Too often, procrastinators don't face up to their problem. When you admit that you are procrastinating, you can sometimes begin thinking about how to solve the problem.
- *Identify your values and goals.* Think about how procrastination can undermine your values and goals.
- *Work on your time management.* Make yearly (or term), monthly, weekly, and daily plans. Then monitor how you are using your time to discover ways to use it more wisely.
- *Divide the task into smaller parts.* Sometimes you might procrastinate because you view the task as so large and overwhelming that you will never be able to finish it. When this is the case, divide the task into smaller units and set subgoals for completing one unit at a time. This strategy can often make what seems to be a completely unmanageable task manageable.
- *Use behavioral strategies.* Identify the diversions that might be keeping you from focusing on the most important tasks and activities. Note when and where you engage in these diversions. Plan how to diminish and control their use. Another behavioral strategy is to make a contract with yourself or someone you see regularly related to your procrastination problem. And yet another behavioral strategy is to build in a reward for yourself, which gives you an incentive to complete all or part of the task. For example, if you complete all your math problems, treat yourself to a movie when you finish them.
- *Use cognitive strategies.* Watch for mental self-seductions that can lead to behavioral diversions, such as "I'll do it tomorrow," "What's the problem with watching an hour or so of TV now?" and "I can't do it." Dispute mental diversions (Watson & Tharp, 2014). For example, tell yourself "I really don't have much time left and other things are sure to come up later," "If I get this done, I'll be able to better enjoy my time," or "Maybe if I just go ahead and get going on this, it won't be so bad."

Do you think these strategies are more effective in creating intrinsic or extrinsic motivation, or both? Which strategies are likely to be most effective in enabling you to overcome procrastination?

- Substituting a worthy but lower-priority activity. For example, you might clean your room instead of studying for a test.
- Believing that repeated minor delays won't hurt you.
- Dramatizing a commitment to a task rather than doing it. For example, you might take your books along for a weekend trip but never open them.
- Persevering on only part of the task. For example, you might write and rewrite the first paragraph of a paper but never get to the body of it.

Can you become better at reducing or eliminating procrastination? For some proven strategies, see the *Connecting with Health and Well-Being* interlude.

Perfectionism Setting high standards for yourself and working hard to achieve them usually lead to positive outcomes. However, striving to be perfect and never to make a mistake can be maladaptive and highly stressful. Perfectionists tend to set excessively high, unrealistic goals that can't be reached (Herman & others, 2013; Rice & others, 2013). When perfectionists don't reach such lofty goals, they become very self-critical and perceive themselves as worthless. Such thoughts and feelings produce a high level of anxiety that can interfere with their ability to concentrate and think clearly in achievement contexts. A recent study found that college students with perfectionistic tendencies who engaged in high levels of self-criticism had lower self-esteem and showed more negative affect than those whose high standards for success were generated as personal standards (Dunkley, Berg, & Zuroff, 2012).

Perfectionism has been associated with suicidal ideation and attempts (Hassan & others, 2014; Kiamanesh & others, 2014; Wang, Wong, & Fu, 2013). A recent study found that perfectionism was linked to suicidal ideation and that perceiving oneself as a burden to others may be involved in this link (Rasmussen & others, 2012). Perfectionism also is linked to the development of obsessive-compulsive symptoms (Martinelli & others, 2014; Soreni & others, 2014). A recent study revealed that an intolerance of uncertainty was a key cognitive factor in the connection between perfectionism and the strength of obsessive-compulsive symptoms (Reuther & others, 2013).

Many adolescents and emerging adults who are perfectionists have parents who have had very high expectations for their success, in some cases expectations that go beyond the

What are some ways that perfectionism and anxiety can harm achievement?
© Iconica/Commercial Eye/Getty Images

adolescents' and emerging adults' abilities. A recent study of young adolescent male soccer players found that authoritative parenting on the part of both parents was linked to a healthier orientation to reaching high achievement goals in the sport than authoritarian parenting (Sapiela, Dunn, & Holt, 2011).

To break through an unhealthy obsession with being perfect, it is important for individuals to set realistic and attainable goals that they generate themselves, rather than strive to meet standards set by others (Counseling Center, University of Illinois, 2014). It also is important to recognize that everyone makes mistakes and that a key aspect of achievement is learning from your mistakes. Further, if you are a perfectionist, go to the counseling center at your college or university to talk with a professional about ways to reduce your perfectionistic tendencies.

Anxiety   **Anxiety** is a vague, highly unpleasant feeling of fear and apprehension. It is normal for students to feel concerned or worried when they face school challenges such as doing well on a test. Indeed, researchers have found that many successful students have moderate levels of anxiety (Bandura, 1997). However, some students have high levels of anxiety and worry constantly, characteristics that can significantly impair their ability to achieve (Affrunti & Woodruff-Borden, 2014).

Some adolescents' high anxiety levels are the result of parents' unrealistic achievement expectations and pressure. A recent study revealed that parents' perfectionism was linked to their children's and adolescents' higher anxiety level (Affrunti & Woodruff-Borden, 2014).

For many individuals, anxiety increases across the school years as they "face more frequent evaluation, social comparison, and (for some) experiences of failure" (Eccles, Wigfield, & Schiefele, 1998, p. 1043). When schools create such circumstances, they are likely to increase students' anxiety.

A number of intervention programs have been created to reduce high anxiety levels (Garcia-Lopez & others, 2014; Miltenberger, 2012; Wigfield & Eccles, 1989). Some intervention programs emphasize relaxation techniques. These programs often are effective at reducing anxiety but do not always lead to improved achievement. Anxiety intervention programs linked to worrying emphasize modifying the negative, self-damaging thoughts of anxious students by getting them to engage in more positive, task-focused thoughts (Meichenbaum & Butler, 1980; Watson & Tharp, 2014). These programs have been more effective than the relaxation programs in improving students' achievement.

Protecting Self-Worth by Avoiding Failure   Some individuals are so interested in protecting their self-worth and avoiding failure that they become distracted from pursuing goals and sabotage their own achievement.

These strategies include the following (Covington, 2002; Covington & Teel, 1996):

- *Nonperformance.* The most obvious strategy for avoiding failure is not to try at all. In the classroom, nonperformance tactics include appearing eager to answer a teacher's question but hoping the teacher will call on another student, sliding down in the seat to avoid being seen by the teacher, and avoiding eye contact. These can seem like minor deceptions, but they might portend other, more chronic forms of noninvolvement such as excessive absences or dropping out.

- *Procrastination.* Individuals who postpone studying for a test until the last minute can blame failure on poor time management, thus deflecting attention away from the possibility that they are incompetent (Steel, 2007).

- *Setting unreachable goals.* By setting goals so high that success is virtually impossible, individuals can avoid the implication that they are incompetent, because virtually anyone would fail to reach these goals.

Efforts to avoid failure often involve **self-handicapping** strategies (Akin & Akin, 2014; Callan, Kay, & Dawtry, 2014; Leondari & Gonida, 2007; Urdan & Midgley, 2001). That is,

developmental **connection**

Self-Esteem

A number of strategies can be implemented to improve students' self-esteem, also referred to as self-worth or self-image. Connect to "The Self, Identity, Emotion, and Personality."

anxiety A vague, highly unpleasant feeling of fear and apprehension.

self-handicapping Use of failure avoidance strategies such as not trying in school or putting off studying until the last minute so that circumstances, rather than a lack of ability, will be seen as the cause of low-level performance.

some individuals deliberately handicap themselves by not making an effort, by putting off a project until the last minute, by fooling around the night before a test, and so on, so that if their subsequent performance is at a low level, these circumstances, rather than lack of ability, will be seen as the cause. One study revealed that self-regulatory and in-depth learning strategies were negatively linked to students' use of self-handicapping strategies and that surface learning (staying on the surface instead of engaging in deep learning strategies) and test anxiety were positively linked to their use of self-handicapping behaviors (Thomas & Gadbois, 2007). Another study of college students discovered that self-handicapping was related to the use of superficial learning strategies, lower self-concept clarity, lower academic self-efficacy, greater test anxiety, and lower grades (Gadbois & Sturgeon, 2011). Yet another recent study of college students found that self-handicapping was associated with emotional exhaustion, reduced personal accomplishment, and depersonalization (Akin, 2012).

How do efforts to avoid failure often involve self-handicapping strategies?
© KidStock/age fotostock RF

Here are some strategies to reduce preoccupation with protecting self-worth and avoiding failure (Covington, 2002):

· Set challenging but realistic goals.
· Strengthen the link between your effort and self-worth. Take pride in your effort and minimize social comparison.
· Have positive beliefs about your abilities.

Review Connect Reflect

LG1 Discuss achievement in the lives of adolescents

Review

• Why is achievement so important in adolescence?
• What are some important achievement motivation processes?
• What are some key social relationships and contexts that influence adolescents' achievement?
• What are some motivational obstacles to achievement and ways to deal with them?

Connect

• Which aspects of achievement might benefit young adolescents as they

make the difficult transition through the first year of middle or junior high school?

Reflect *Your Own Personal Journey of Life*

• Would you consider yourself highly motivated to achieve? Or do you have trouble becoming motivated to achieve? Explain.

2 Work **LG2** Describe the role of work in adolescence and in college

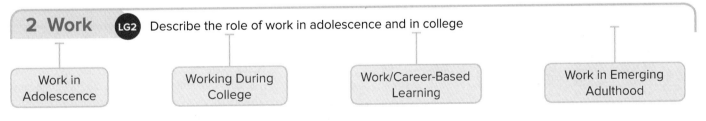

| Work in Adolescence | Working During College | Work/Career-Based Learning | Work in Emerging Adulthood |

Achievement and motivation show up not only in school but also in work. One of the greatest changes in adolescents' lives in recent years has been the increased likelihood that they will work in some part-time capacity and still attend school on a regular basis. Our discussion of work focuses on various aspects of work during adolescence and college, work/career-based learning, and work in emerging adulthood.

WORK IN ADOLESCENCE

What is the sociohistorical context of work in adolescents' lives? What characterizes part-time work in adolescence? What are the work profiles of adolescents around the world?

Sociohistorical Context of Work During Adolescence Even though education keeps many of today's youth from holding full-time jobs, it has not prevented them from working part-time while going to school. In 1940, only 1 of 25 tenth-grade males attended school and simultaneously worked part-time. In the 1970s, the number had increased to 1 in 4. Today, it is estimated that 80 to 90 percent of adolescents are employed at some point during high school (Staff, Messersmith, & Schulenberg, 2009). As shown in Figure 5, as adolescents go from the eighth to the twelfth grade, their likelihood of working and the average number of hours they work during the school year increases (Staff & others, 2009). As shown in Figure 5, in the eighth and tenth grades, the majority of students don't work in paid employment during the school year, but in the twelfth grade only one-fourth don't engage in paid employment during the school year. Almost 10 percent of employed twelfth-graders work more than 30 hours each week during the school year.

Part-Time Work in Adolescence What kinds of jobs are U.S. adolescents working at today? About 21 percent of U.S. twelfth-graders who work do so in restaurants, such as McDonald's and Burger King, waiting on customers and cleaning up (Staff & others, 2009). Other adolescents work in retail stores as cashiers or salespeople (23 percent), in offices as clerical assistants (7 percent), or as unskilled laborers (about 10 percent).

Overall, the weight of the evidence suggests that spending large amounts of time in paid labor has limited developmental benefits for youth, and for some it is associated with risky behavior and costs to physical health (Larson, Wilson, & Rickman, 2009). For example, one research study found that it was not just working that affected adolescents' grades—more important was how many hours they worked (Greenberger & Steinberg, 1986). Tenth-graders who worked more than 14 hours a week suffered a drop in grades. Eleventh-graders worked up to 20 hours a week before their grades dropped. When adolescents spend more than 20 hours per week working, there is little time to study for tests and to complete homework assignments. In addition, working adolescents felt less involved in school, were absent more, and said that they did not enjoy school as much as their nonworking counterparts did. Adolescents who worked also spent less time with their families—but just as much time with their peers—compared with their nonworking counterparts. Adolescents who worked long hours also were more frequent users of alcohol and marijuana.

A recent re-analysis of the data in the 1986 study (Monahan, Lee, & Steinberg, 2011) included a better matched control group of students who did not work. Even with the more careful matching of groups, adolescents in the tenth and eleventh grades who worked more than 20 hours a week were less engaged in school and showed increases in substance abuse and delinquency (Monahan & others, 2011). For adolescents who cut back their part-time work to 20 hours a week or less, negative outcomes disappeared. Also, a recent study found that high school students with paid part-time jobs were more likely to drink alcohol, binge drink, and use marijuana (Leeman & others, 2014).

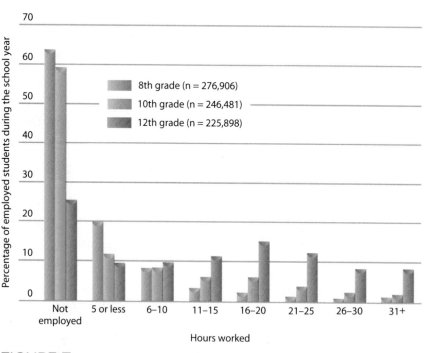

FIGURE 5

ADOLESCENT EMPLOYMENT. Percentage of employed students and number of hours worked per week during the school year by eighth, tenth, and twelfth grade (combined data for 1991 to 2006 Monitoring the Future, Institute of Social Research, cohorts).

Some youth, though, are engaged in challenging work activities, receive constructive supervision from adults, and experience favorable working conditions (Staff & others, 2009). In such cases, work may benefit adolescents in low-income, urban contexts by providing them with economic benefits and adult monitoring. This may increase school engagement and decrease delinquency.

Youth in high-poverty neighborhoods who often have difficulty finding work are a special concern. Joblessness is a common feature of such neighborhoods, as is poor-quality schooling and high crime rates. A recent study of African American youths, all of whom spent some years in high-poverty neighborhoods in Baltimore, found that before adolescents were legally old enough to work, boys were more likely than girls to participate in illegal, under-the-table work (Clampet-Lundquist, 2013).

Work Profiles of Adolescents Around the World

So far, our exploration of work during adolescence has primarily focused on U.S. adolescents. How does work in adolescence vary in different countries around the world?

In many developing countries, where it is common for adolescents not to attend school on a regular basis, boys often spend more time in income-generating labor than girls do, whereas girls spend more time in unpaid labor than boys do (Larson & Verma, 1999; Larson & others, 2009). Young adolescents work on average more than eight hours a day in many nonindustrial, unschooled populations. In the developed world, work averages less than one hour per day across childhood and adolescence except for U.S. adolescents. For example, U.S. adolescents are far more likely to participate in paid labor than European and East Asian adolescents. As we saw earlier, many U.S. high school students work 10 or even 20 hours or more per week. One study found that U.S. high school students spent an average of 50 minutes per day working at a job, whereas Northern European adolescents spent an average of only 15 minutes per day working at a job (Alsaker & Flammer, 1999). In this study, employment of adolescents was virtually nonexistent in France and Russia. In another study, 80 percent of Minneapolis eleventh-graders had part-time jobs compared with only 27 percent of Japanese eleventh-graders and 26 percent of Taiwanese eleventh-graders (Fuligni & Stevenson, 1995).

Overall, the weight of the evidence suggests that spending large amounts of time in paid labor has limited developmental benefits for youth, and for some it is associated with risky behavior and costs to physical health (Larson & Verma, 1999; Larson & others, 2009). Some youth, though, are engaged in challenging work activities, receive constructive supervision from adults, and experience favorable working conditions. However, in general, given the repetitive nature of most labor carried out by adolescents around the world, it is difficult to argue that working 15 to 25 hours per week in such labor provides developmental gains (Larson & Verma, 1999).

WORKING DURING COLLEGE

The percentage of full-time U.S. college students who also held jobs increased from 34 percent in 1970 to 47 percent in 2008, then declined to 41 percent in 2011 (down from a peak of 52 percent in 2000) (National Center for Education Statistics, 2013). In this recent survey, 74 percent of part-time U.S. college students were employed, down from 81 percent in 2008.

Working can pay for schooling or help offset some of the costs of attending college, but working can also restrict students' opportunities to learn and negatively influence their grades. One national study found that as the number of hours worked per week increased for those who identified themselves primarily as students, their grades suffered and the number of classes, class choice, and library access became more limited (National Center for Education Statistics, 2002) (see Figure 6).

Other research has found that the greater the number of hours college students work per week, the more likely they are to drop out of college (National Center for Education Statistics, 1998). Thus, college students need to carefully examine the number of hours they work and the extent to which

What are some advantages and disadvantages of part-time work during adolescence?
© Dennis MacDonald/PhotoEdit

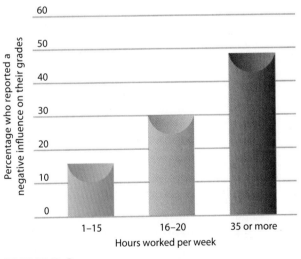

FIGURE 6

THE RELATION OF HOURS WORKED PER WEEK IN COLLEGE TO GRADES. Among students working to pay for school expenses, 16 percent of those working 1 to 15 hours per week reported that working negatively influenced their grades (National Center for Education Statistics, 2002). Thirty percent of college students who worked 16 to 20 hours a week said the same, as did 48 percent who worked 35 hours or more per week.

the work is having a negative impact on their college success. Although borrowing money to pay for education can leave students with considerable debt, working long hours reduces the amount of time students have for studying and can decrease the likelihood that these students will do well or even complete their college degree.

WORK/CAREER-BASED LEARNING

A number of experts note that a stronger connection between school and work needs to be forged. One way to improve this connection is through work/career-based learning experiences—especially for those adolescents going directly from high school into the workforce.

High School Work/career-based learning increasingly has become part of the effort to help youth make the transition from school to employment. Each year, approximately 500,000 high school students participate in cooperative education or other arrangements where learning objectives are met through part-time employment in office occupations, retailing, and other vocational fields. Vocational classes also involve large numbers of adolescents in school-based enterprises, through which they build houses, run restaurants, repair cars, operate retail stores, staff child-care centers, and provide other services.

Some important changes have recently taken place in vocational education. Today's high school diploma provides access to fewer and fewer stable, high-paying jobs. Thus, more of the training for specific occupations is occurring in two-year colleges and postsecondary technical institutes.

In high schools, new forms of career-related education are creating options for many students, ranging from students with disabilities to students who are gifted. Among the new models are career academies, technical preparation programs, early college high schools, and school-based enterprises (Perry & Wallace, 2012):

- *Career academies.* They function as either small schools within a more comprehensive high school or as separate schools, typically with 150 to 200 students beginning the program during ninth or tenth grade. The curriculum often focuses on a broad theme, such as health science or business, and students may participate in work-based learning.
- *Technical preparation programs.* Students combine the final two years of high school with two years in a community college and obtain a technical degree. They may or may not engage in work-based learning.
- *Early college high schools.* These are small high schools usually located on college campuses with the goal of giving students the opportunity to obtain a high school degree and an associate degree, or two years of college credit that can be transferred to a four-year college.
- *School-based enterprises.* Students explore community needs and participate in service-learning projects as part of their high school education.

College College students can participate in cooperative education programs or do part-time or summer jobs relevant to their field of study. This experience can be critical in helping students obtain the job they want when they graduate (Martinez, 2006). Many employers expect job candidates to have this type of experience. One survey found that almost 60 percent of employers said their entry-level college hires had co-op or internship experience (Collins, 1996).

More than 1,000 colleges offer co-op (cooperative education) programs. A co-op is a paid apprenticeship in a career that a college student is interested in pursuing. Many college students are not allowed to participate in co-op programs until their junior year.

WORK IN EMERGING ADULTHOOD

The work patterns of emerging adults have changed over the course of the last 100 years. As increasing numbers of emerging adults have participated in higher education, many leave home and begin their careers at later ages. Changing economic conditions have made the job

market more competitive for emerging adults and increased the demand for more skilled workers (Chen & others, 2012).

A diversity of school and work patterns characterize emerging adults (Arnett, 2014; Buchmann & Malti, 2012; Staff, Mont'Alvao, & Mortimer, 2015; Swanson, 2013). Some emerging adults are going to college full-time, others are working full-time. Some emerging adults work full-time immediately after high school, others after graduating from college. Many emerging adults who attend college drop out and enter the workforce before they complete their degree; some of these individuals return to college later. Some emerging adults are attending two-year colleges, others four-year colleges; some are working part-time while going to college, while others are not.

Special concerns are the unemployment rate of college graduates as well as the high percentage of recent college graduates who have had to take jobs that do not require a college degree. In 2013, the unemployment rate for college graduates dropped to 5.6 percent, down from 6.4 percent at the peak of the 2009 recession (Gabor, 2014). However, among 22-year-olds with a college degree who found jobs in 2013, more than 50 percent were in jobs that did not require a college degree (Center for Economic and Policy Research, 2014).

A trend in the U.S. workforce is the disappearing long-term career for an increasing number of adults, especially men in private-sector jobs. Among the reasons for this disappearance of many long-term jobs is the dramatic increase in technology and cheaper labor in other countries. Many young and older adults are working at a series of jobs, and many work in short-term jobs (Greenhaus & Callanan, 2013). Early careers are especially unstable as some young workers move from "survival jobs" to "career jobs" as they seek a job that matches their personal interests/goals (Mortimer, 2012; Staff & others, 2015). A study of more than 1,100 individuals from 18 to 31 years of age revealed that maintaining high aspirations and certainty over career goals better insulated individuals against unemployment during the severe economic recession that began in 2007 (Vuolo, Staff, & Mortimer, 2012).

As you explore the type of work you are likely to enjoy and in which you can succeed, it is important to become knowledgeable about different fields and companies. Occupations may have many job openings one year but few in another year as economic conditions change. Thus, it is critical to keep up with the occupational outlook in various fields. An excellent source for doing this is the U.S. government's *Occupational Outlook Handbook*, which is revised every two years.

According to the most recent *Handbook* (2014/2015), industrial/organizational psychologists, personal care aides, interpreters and translators, genetic counselors, physicians' assistants, information security analysts, and physical therapists are among the job categories that are projected to be the fastest growing through 2022. Projected job growth varies widely by educational requirements. Jobs that require a college degree are expected to grow the fastest. Most of the highest-paying occupations require a college degree.

These emerging adults are college graduates who started their own business. Emerging adults follow a diversity of work and educational pathways. *What are some of these variations in education and work that characterize emerging adults?*
© Jose Luis Pelaez, Inc./Corbis

Review Connect Reflect

LG2 Describe the role of work in adolescence and in college

Review

- What is the sociohistorical context of adolescent work? What are the advantages and disadvantages of part-time work in secondary school and college? What is the profile of adolescent work around the world?
- How does work during college influence students' academic success?
- What are some aspects of work/career-based learning?
- What characterizes work in emerging adulthood?

Connect

- How does this section's discussion of the recent sociohistorical context of adolescent work compare with the historical nature of adolescent work described in the "Introduction" chapter?

Reflect *Your Own Personal Journey of Life*

- Did you work during high school? What were some of the pluses and minuses of the experience if you did work? Are you working part-time or full-time now while you are going to college? If so, what effect does the work experience have on your academic success?

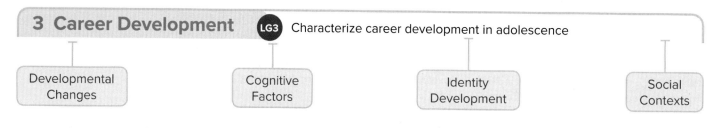

3 Career Development

LG3 Characterize career development in adolescence

| Developmental Changes | Cognitive Factors | Identity Development | Social Contexts |

What are some developmental changes that characterize adolescents' career choices? What are some cognitive factors that affect career development? How is career development related to identity development? How do sociocultural factors affect career development? We will explore the answers to these questions in this section.

DEVELOPMENTAL CHANGES

Many children have idealistic fantasies about what they want to be when they grow up. For example, many young children want to be superheroes, sports stars, or movie stars. In the high school years, they often begin to think about careers on a somewhat less idealistic basis. In their late teens and early twenties, their career decision making has usually turned more serious as they explore different career possibilities and zero in on the career they want to enter. In college, this path often means choosing a major or specialization that is designed to lead to work in a specific field. By their early and mid-twenties, many individuals have completed their education or training and embarked on a full-time occupation. From the mid-twenties through the remainder of early adulthood, individuals often seek to establish their emerging career in a certain field. They may work hard to move up the career ladder and improve their financial standing.

William Damon (2008) maintains that it is not only children who have idealistic fantasies about careers but that too many of today's adolescents also dream about fantasy careers that may have no connection to reality. Too often the adolescents have no idea about what it takes to become such a career star, and usually there is no one in their lives who can help them to reach this career pinnacle. Consider adolescents playing basketball who dream of becoming the next LeBron James and adolescents participating in theater who want to become the next Angelina Jolie, for example.

"Your son has made a career choice, Mildred. He's going to win the lottery and travel a lot."
Copyright © 2009 by Bunny Hoest. All rights reserved. Used with permission.

COGNITIVE FACTORS

Exploration, decision making, and planning play important roles in adolescents' career choices (Porfeli & Lee, 2012). In countries where equal employment opportunities have emerged—such as the United States, Canada, Great Britain, and France—exploration of various career paths is critical in adolescents' career development. Adolescents often approach career exploration and decision making with considerable ambiguity, uncertainty, and stress. Many of the career decisions made by youth involve floundering and unplanned changes. Many adolescents do not adequately explore careers on their own and also receive little direction from guidance counselors at their schools. On average, high school students spend less than three hours per year with guidance counselors, and in some schools the average is even less. In many schools, students not only do not know what information to seek about careers, they do not know how to seek it.

In *The Path to Purpose*, William Damon (2008) noted that most high school students aren't lacking in ambition when it comes to careers but rather don't have anything close to an adequate plan for reaching their career goals. Too many youth drift aimlessly through their high school years, Damon says, their behavior placing them at risk for not fulfilling their potential and not finding a life pursuit that energizes them.

In a large-scale longitudinal investigation, Mihaly Csikszentmihalyi and Barbara Schneider (2000) studied how U.S. adolescents develop attitudes and acquire skills to achieve their career goals and expectations. They assessed the progress of more than 1,000 students from 13 school districts across the United States. Students recorded at random moments their thoughts and feelings about what they did, and they filled out questionnaires regarding school, family, peers, and career aspirations. The researchers also interviewed the adolescents, as well as their friends, parents, and teachers. Among the findings of the study:

·   Girls anticipated the same lifestyles as boys in terms of education and income.

·   Lower-income minority students were more positive about school than more affluent students were.

·   Students who got the most out of school—and had the highest future expectations—were those who perceived school to be more play-like than work-like.

·   Clear vocational goals and good work experiences did not guarantee a smooth transition to adult work. Engaging activities—with intensive involvement regardless of content—were essential to building the optimism and resilience that are important for achieving a satisfying work life. This finding fits with Csikszentmihalyi's concept of flow, which we explored earlier in the chapter.

Especially in the recent economic downturn that is characterized by very high youth unemployment, the pathway to a satisfying career through early work experience has become less feasible than college or professional/vocational education for many individuals (Pew Research Center, 2012). More than 90 percent of today's high school seniors expect to attend college, and more than 70 percent anticipate working in professional jobs. Four decades ago, the picture was substantially different, with only 55 percent expecting to go to college and 42 percent anticipating working in professional jobs. Parents can help adolescents by becoming more knowledgeable about which courses their adolescents are taking in school, developing a better understanding of the college admissions process, providing adolescents with better information about various careers, and realistically evaluating their adolescents' abilities and interests in relation to these careers.

During college, students can benefit from the advice of college counselors, not only about careers but about many other aspects of life (Murphy & others, 2010). To read about the work of one college counselor, see the *Connecting with Careers* profile.

IDENTITY DEVELOPMENT

Career development is related to the adolescent's and emerging adult's identity development (Porfeli & Lee, 2012). Career decidedness and planning are positively related to identity achievement, whereas career planning and decidedness are negatively related to identity moratorium and identity diffusion statuses (Wallace-Broscious, Serafica, &

developmental connection

Cognitive Development

Adolescence is a time of increased decision making, and decision making appears to improve during early adulthood. Connect to "The Brain and Cognitive Development."

Grace Leaf, College/Career Counselor and College Administrator

Grace Leaf is a counselor at Spokane Community College in Washington. She has a master's degree in educational leadership and is working toward a doctoral degree in educational leadership at Gonzaga University in Washington. Her college counseling job has involved teaching, orientation for international students, conducting individual and group advising, and doing individual and group career planning. Leaf tries to connect students with their own goals and values and helps them design an educational program that fits their needs and visions. Following a long career as a college counselor, she is now vice-president of instruction at Lower Columbia College in Washington.

For more information about what career counselors do, see the Careers in Adolescent Development appendix.

Grace Leaf counsels college students at Spokane Community College about careers.
Courtesy of Grace Leaf

---

developmental connection

Identity

Emerging adulthood is characterized by identity exploration, especially in work and love, and by instability in work, love, and education. Connect to "Introduction."

Domain/ Identity Status	Grade		
	8	10	12
Vocational			
Moratorium	33.5	38.0	42.1
Achievement	13.5	13.5	19.6
General ideological			
Moratorium	25.5	27.8	36.4
Achievement	5.1	11.2	5.6
Religious			
Moratorium	14.6	15.6	20.0
Achievement	5.6	7.8	5.4
Lifestyle			
Moratorium	14.0	18.9	15.6
Achievement	3.6	6.5	4.6
Political			
Moratorium	11.3	13.8	11.2
Achievement	3.1	4.8	6.5

FIGURE 7

IDENTITY STATUS DEVELOPMENT IN DIFFERENT DOMAINS. *Note:* Numbers represent percentages.

Osipow, 1994). An individual's identity can be categorized as diffused, foreclosed, moratorium, and achieved. Identity moratorium describes individuals who have not yet made an identity commitment but are in the midst of exploring options, whereas identity diffusion identifies individuals who have neither made a commitment nor experienced a crisis (exploration of alternatives). Adolescents and emerging adults who are further along in the process of identity formation are better able to articulate their occupational choices and their next steps in attaining short-term and long-term goals. By contrast, adolescents and emerging adults in the moratorium and diffusion statuses of identity are more likely to struggle with making occupational plans and decisions.

One study focused on vocational identity development in relation to other identity domains (Skorikov & Vondracek, 1998). A cross-sectional study of 1,099 high school students in grades 7 through 12 revealed a developmental progression in adolescent vocational identity that was characterized by an increase in the proportion of students classified as identity diffused or foreclosed. Statuses in general ideological, religious, lifestyle, and political identity domains lagged behind identity status development in the domain of vocation (see Figure 7). Thus, in line with the developmental tasks outlined in Erikson's (1968) theory, vocational identity development plays a leading role in identity development.

SOCIAL CONTEXTS

Not every individual born into the world can grow up to become a nuclear physicist or a doctor—genetic limitations keep some adolescents from performing at the high intellectual levels necessary to enter such careers. Similarly, genetic limitations restrict some adolescents from becoming professional football players or professional dancers. But many careers are available to most of us, careers that provide a reasonable match with our abilities. Our sociocultural experiences exert strong influences on career choices from among the wide range available. Among the important social contexts that influence career development are culture, socioeconomic status, parents and peers, schools, gender, and ethnicity.

Culture A study of more than 11,000 adolescents from 18 countries who were living mainly in middle and upper socioeconomic families found that adolescents were experiencing considerable stress about their future (Seiffge-Krenke, 2012). In this study, adolescents in all 18 countries especially feared not being able to pursue the vocational training or academic studies required for entering the profession they desired. Many of them also had a fear of being unemployed at some point in the future.

In some countries, the work and career prospects for youth are worse than in other countries. For example, in southern European countries such as Italy and Spain, there is a mismatch for youth between the high number of university graduates and the relatively low demand for these graduates in the labor market (Tomasik & others, 2012).

Socioeconomic Status The channels of upward mobility that are open to lower-SES youth are largely educational in nature (Johnson & Reynolds, 2013; Vuolo, Mortimer, & Staff, 2014). The school hierarchy from grade school through high school, as well as through college and graduate school, is programmed to orient individuals toward some type of career. Less than 100 years ago, it was believed that only eight years of education were necessary for vocational competence, and anything beyond that qualified the individual for advanced placement in higher-status occupations. By the middle of the twentieth century, the high school diploma had already lost ground as a ticket to career success, and in today's workplace college is a prerequisite for entering a higher-status occupation.

Many of the ideas that have guided career development theory have been based on experiences in middle-income and well-educated contexts. Underlying this theory is the concept that individuals have a wide range of career choices from which they can select and pursue. However, many youth in low-income circumstances may have more limited career choices. The barriers that many low-income inner-city youth face, such as low-quality schools, violence, and lack of access to jobs, can restrict access to desirable careers (Ballentine & Roberts, 2009).

Parents and Peers Parents and peers also are strong influences on adolescents' career choices. Some experts argue that American parents have achievement expectations that are too low, whereas others maintain that some parents put too much pressure on adolescents to achieve beyond their capabilities.

Many factors influence parents' roles in adolescents' career development. For one, mothers who work regularly outside the home and show effort and pride in their work probably have strong influences on their adolescents' career choices. A reasonable conclusion is that when both parents work and enjoy their work, adolescents learn work values from both parents.

Parents can potentially influence adolescents' occupational choices through the way they present information about occupations and values, as well as through the experiences they provide adolescents. For example, parents can communicate to their children and adolescents that they believe in the value of going to college and achieving a professional degree as a means of attaining a career in medicine, law, or business. Other parents might communicate that college is not as important and place a higher value on being a champion athlete or movie star.

Peers also can influence adolescents' career development (Kiuru & others, 2011). Adolescents often choose peers from within the school setting at an achievement level similar to their own (Vondracek & Porfeli, 2003). In one investigation, when adolescents had friends and parents with high career standards, they were more likely to seek higher-status careers, even if they came from low-income families (Simpson, 1962).

Parents play an important role in the adolescent's achievement. It is important for parents to neither pressure the adolescent too much nor challenge the adolescent too little.
© SW Productions/Getty Images RF

School Influences Schools, teachers, and counselors can exert a powerful influence on adolescents' career development. School is the primary setting where individuals first encounter the world of work. School provides an atmosphere for continuing self-development in relation to achievement and work. And school is the only institution in society that is capable

Armando Ronquillo, High School Counselor/College Advisor

Armando Ronquillo has been a high school counselor and college advisor and currently is employed by the Tucson Unified School District. As a school counselor and college advisor, Ronquillo worked at Pueblo High School, which is in a low-socioeconomic-status area in Tucson, Arizona. More than 85 percent of the students have a Latino background. Armando was named top high school counselor in the state of Arizona for the year 2000. He has especially helped to increase the number of Pueblo High School students who go to college.

Ronquillo has an undergraduate degree in elementary and special education, and a master's degree in counseling. His work involves counseling students on the merits of staying in school and on the lifelong opportunities provided by a college education. Ronquillo guides students in obtaining the academic preparation that will enable them to go to college, and he shows them how to apply for financial aid and scholarships. He also works with parents to help them understand that sending their child to college is not only doable but also affordable.

Ronquillo works with students on setting goals and planning. He has students plan for the future in terms of one-year (short-term),

Armando Ronquillo counsels a Latina high school student about college.
Courtesy of Armando Ronquillo

five-year (midrange), and ten-plus-year (long-term) time periods. Ronquillo says he does this "to help students visualize how the educational plans and decisions they make today will affect them in the future." He also organizes a number of college campus visitations for students from Pueblo High School each year.

To read further about the work of school counselors, see the Careers in Adolescent Development appendix.

---

of providing the delivery systems necessary for career education—instruction, guidance, placement, and community connections.

School counseling has been criticized, both inside and outside the educational establishment (Heppner & Heppner, 2003). Insiders complain about the large number of students per school counselor and the weight of noncounseling administrative duties. One national survey found that 50 percent of U.S. high schools had student-to-counselor ratios of more than 250 to 1 (Radford & Ifil, 2009).

Outsiders complain that school counseling is ineffective, biased, and a waste of money. Short of creating a new profession, several options are possible (William T. Grant Foundation Commission on Work, Family, and Citizenship, 1988). First, twice the number of counselors are needed to meet all students' needs. Second, there could be a redefinition of teachers' roles, accompanied by retraining and reduction in teaching loads, so that classroom teachers could assume a greater role in handling the counseling needs of adolescents. The professional counselor's role in this plan would be to train and assist teachers in their counseling and to provide direct counseling in situations the teacher could not handle. Third, the whole idea of school counselors could be abandoned, and counselors would be located elsewhere—such as in neighborhood social service centers or labor offices. (Germany, for example, forbids teachers to give career counseling, reserving this task for officials in well-developed networks of labor offices.) To read about the work of one high school counselor, see the *Connecting with Careers* profile.

Gender Because females have been socialized to adopt nurturing roles rather than career or achieving roles more than males have, some females have not planned seriously for careers, have not explored career options extensively, and have restricted their career choices to careers that are gender stereotyped (Matlin, 2012). The motivation for work is the same for both sexes. However, females and males make different choices because of their socialization experiences and the ways that social forces structure the opportunities available to them

(Petersen & Hyde, 2014; Tracey, Robbins, & Hofsess, 2005). For example, many girls and women stop taking math courses in high school or college, which restricts their career options (Watt & Eccles, 2008; Watt, Eccles, & Durik, 2006).

As growing numbers of young women pursue careers, they are faced with questions involving career and family (Matlin, 2012; Richardson & Schaeffer, 2013). Should they delay marriage and childbearing and establish their career first? Or should they combine their career, marriage, and childbearing in their twenties? Some females in the last decade have embraced the domestic patterns of an earlier historical period. They have married, borne children, and committed themselves to full-time mothering. These stay-at-home mothers have worked outside the home only intermittently, if at all, and have subordinated the work role to the family role.

Increasingly, though, many other females have veered from this path and developed committed, permanent ties to the workplace that resemble the pattern once reserved only for males (Richardson & Schaeffer, 2013). When they have children, it has been after their careers are well established, and rather than leaving the workforce to raise children, they have made efforts to combine a career and motherhood. Although there have always been professional women who pursued work instead of marrying, today's women are more likely to try to "have it all."

Socioeconomic Status and Ethnicity   Many adolescents who have grown up in low-income or poverty conditions often face challenging circumstances in seeking upward mobility. These adolescents may have a difficult time deferring adult roles and may not be able to fully explore career opportunities.

Ethnic minority youth, especially those who grow up in low-income families, also may face barriers to preparing for successful careers (Banerjee, Harrell, & Johnson, 2011). A recent study of 18- to 20-year-old urban Latinos revealed that family obligation was a central theme in the decisions they made about their life and career after high school (Sanchez & others, 2010). In this study, financial circumstances were linked to whether they worked and/ or took college classes.

To intervene effectively in the career development of ethnic minority youth, counselors need to increase their knowledge of communication styles, values regarding the importance of the family, the impact of language fluency, and achievement expectations in various ethnic minority groups (Waller, 2006). Counselors need to be aware of and respect the cultural values of ethnic minority youth, but such values should be discussed within the context of the realities of the educational and occupational world (Ulloa & Herrera, 2006).

In this chapter, we have explored many aspects of achievement, careers, and work. One topic we examined was the influence of culture and ethnicity on achievement. Next we will focus entirely on culture and adolescent development.

Review Connect Reflect

(LG3) Characterize career development in adolescence

Review
- What are some developmental changes that characterize adolescents' career choices?
- How are cognitive factors involved in adolescents' career development?
- How is identity development linked with career development in adolescence?
- What roles do social contexts play in adolescents' career development?

Connect
- Are there aspects of executive function that might be applied to understanding the cognitive factors involved in adolescents' career development?

Reflect Your Own Personal Journey of Life
- What are your career goals? Write down some of the specific work, job, and career goals that you have for the next 20, 10, and 5 years. Be as concrete and specific as possible. In describing your career goals, start from the farthest point—20 years from now—and work backward. If you start from a near point, you run the risk of adopting goals that are not precisely and clearly connected to your long-term career goals.

Achievement, Work, and Careers

1 Achievement

 Discuss achievement in the lives of adolescents

The Importance of
Achievement in
Adolescence

· Social and academic pressures force adolescents to cope with achievement in new ways. Adolescents may perceive that their achievements are predictors of future, real-world outcomes in the adult world. Achievement expectations increase in secondary schools. Whether adolescents effectively adapt to these new pressures is determined in part by psychological, motivational, and contextual factors.

Achievement Processes

· Intrinsic motivation is based on internal factors such as self-determination, curiosity, challenge, and effort. Extrinsic motivation involves external incentives such as rewards and punishment. One view is that giving students some choice and providing opportunities for personal responsibility increase intrinsic motivation. It is important for teachers to create learning environments that encourage students to become cognitively engaged and to take responsibility for their learning. Overall, the overwhelming conclusion is that it is a wise strategy to create learning environments that encourage students to become intrinsically motivated. However, in many real-world situations, both intrinsic and extrinsic motivation are involved, and too often intrinsic and extrinsic motivation have been pitted against each other as polar opposites. Attribution theory states that individuals are motivated to discover the underlying causes of behavior in an effort to make sense of the behavior. In attribution, calling on internal factors, such as effort, to explain performance is more productive than calling on external factors, such as luck and blaming others. A mastery orientation is preferred over a helpless or a performance orientation in achievement situations. Mindset is the cognitive view, either fixed or growth, that individuals develop for themselves. Dweck argues that a key aspect of adolescents' development is to guide them in developing a growth mindset. Self-efficacy, the belief that one can master a situation and attain positive outcomes, helps to promote achievement. Students' expectations for success and the value they place on what they want to achieve influence their motivation. The combination of expectancy and value has been the focus of a number of efforts to understand students' achievement motivation. Adolescents benefit when their parents, teachers, and other adults have high expectations for their achievement. Goal setting, planning, and self-monitoring are important aspects of achievement. Adolescents' sustained attention, effort, and task persistence also are linked to their achievement. Delay of gratification plays a very important role in adolescents' and emerging adults' ability to reach their goals. Recently, Damon has proposed that purpose is an especially important aspect of achievement that has been missing from many adolescents' lives.

Social Relationships and
Contexts

· Social relationships and contexts play important roles in adolescents' achievement. In terms of social relationships, parents, peers, teachers, and mentors can be key influences on adolescents' achievement. In terms of social contexts, factors such as ethnicity, socioeconomic status, and culture influence adolescents' achievement.

Some Motivational
Obstacles to Achievement

· Some motivational obstacles to achievement include procrastinating, being too perfectionistic, being overwhelmed by anxiety, and protecting self-worth by avoiding failure. A special concern is adolescents having too much anxiety in achievement situations, which sometimes is linked to unrealistic parental expectations. The effort to avoid failure may involve self-handicapping strategies such as deliberately not trying in school or putting off studying until the last minute. Ways to deal with motivational obstacles include identifying values and goals, using better time management, and dividing an overwhelming task into smaller parts.

2 Work

Work in Adolescence

- Adolescents are not as likely to hold full-time jobs today as their counterparts from the nineteenth century were. The number of adolescents who work part-time, though, has increased dramatically. Advantages of part-time work in adolescence include learning how the business world works, how to get and keep a job, how to manage money, how to budget time, how to take pride in accomplishments, and how to evaluate goals. Disadvantages include reducing the amount of time available for extracurricular activities, socializing with peers, and sleep; as well as the difficulty of balancing the demands of school, family, peers, and work. Profiles of adolescent work vary around the world. In many developing countries, boys engage in considerably more paid labor than girls, who participate in more unpaid labor at home. U.S. adolescents engage in more work than their counterparts in many other developed countries. There appears to be little developmental advantage for most adolescents when they work 15 to 25 hours per week.

Working During College

- Working while going to college can help with schooling costs but can have a negative impact on students' grades and reduce the likelihood of graduation.

Work/Career-Based Learning

- Interest in work/career-based learning in high school is increasing. Many successful college students engage in cooperative learning or internship programs.

Work in Emerging Adulthood

- The work patterns of emerging adults have changed over the last 100 years, and a diversity of school and work patterns now characterize emerging adults. The nature of the transition from school to work is strongly influenced by the individual's educational level. Many emerging adults change jobs, which can either involve searching or floundering.

3 Career Development

Developmental Changes

- Many children have fantasies about what careers they want to enter when they grow up. In high school, these fantasies have lessened for many individuals, although too many adolescents have a fantasy career they want to enter but don't have an adequate plan for reaching their aspirations. In the late teens and early twenties, career decision making usually has turned more serious.

Cognitive Factors

- Exploration, decision making, and planning are important cognitive dimensions of career development in adolescence. Many adolescents have high aspirations but don't know how to reach these aspirations. Damon argues that adolescents and emerging adults need to incorporate thinking about purpose in their career decision making.

Identity Development

- Career development is linked to identity development in adolescence. Adolescents who are further along in the identity process are better able to articulate their career plans. In line with Erikson's theory, vocational identity plays a key role in overall identity development.

Social Contexts

- Among the most important social contexts that influence career development in adolescence are culture, socioeconomic status, parents and peers, schools, gender, and ethnicity.

key terms

anxiety	flow	mastery orientation	performance orientation
attribution theory	helpless orientation	mentors	self-efficacy
extrinsic motivation	intrinsic motivation	mindset	self-handicapping

key people

Albert Bandura

Amy Chua

Mihaly Csikszentmihalyi

William Damon

Edward Deci

Carol Dweck

Jacquelynne Eccles

Sandra Graham

Su Yeong Kim

Nel Noddings

Richard Ryan

Dale Schunk

Harold Stevenson

Kim Wong Keltner

Qing Zhou

Barry Zimmerman

resources for improving the lives of adolescents

Development of Achievement Motivation and Engagement

Allan Wigfield, Jacquelynne Eccles, Jennifer Fredricks, Sandra Simpkins, Robert Roeser, and Ulrich Schiefele (2015)

In R.M. Lerner (Ed.), *Handbook of Child Psychology and Developmental Science* (7th ed.).

New York: Wiley

> Leading experts provide recent updates on many aspects of theory, research, and applications focused on adolescent achievement.

Handbook of Self-Regulation of Learning and Performance

Edited by Barry Zimmerman and Dale Schunk (2011)

New York: Routledge

> A number of leading experts discuss many aspects of self-regulation, learning, and achievement processes.

Mindset

Carol Dweck (2006)

New York: Random House

> Extensive information and examples are provided to show how adolescents can develop a growth mindset that will improve their achievement.

The Marshmallow Test: Mastering Self-Control

Walter Mischel (2014)

Boston: Little Brown

> Well-know psychologist Walter Mischel extensively discusses the importance of delay of gratification and self-control in children's,

adolescents', and adults' lives, and he describes a number of strategies for improving delay of gratification and self-control.

Mentoring in Adolescence

Jean Rhodes and Sarah Lowe

In R.M. Lerner and L. Steinberg (Eds.), *Handbook of Adolescent Psychology* (2009, 3rd ed.)

New York: Wiley

> Leading experts describe research on mentoring and highlight the aspects of mentoring that are most successful in improving adolescents' achievement.

What Color Is Your Parachute?

Richard Bolles (2016)

Berkeley, CA: Ten Speed Press

> This is an extremely popular book on job hunting, first published in 1970 and updated each year. Additional resources are provided by the author at http://www.jobhuntersbible.com.

chapter 12

CULTURE

chapter **outline**

Sonya, a 16-year-old Japanese American girl, was upset over her family's reaction to her White American boyfriend. "Her parents refused to meet him and on several occasions threatened to disown her" (Sue & Morishima, 1982, p. 142). Her older brothers reacted angrily to Sonya's dating a White American, warning that they were going to beat him up. Her parents also were disturbed that Sonya's grades, above average in middle school, were beginning to drop.

Generational issues contributed to the conflict between Sonya and her family (Nagata, 1989). Her parents had experienced strong sanctions against dating Whites when they were growing up and were legally prevented from marrying anyone but a Japanese. As Sonya's older brothers were growing up, they valued ethnic pride and solidarity. The brothers saw her dating a White as "selling out" her own ethnic group. Sonya's and her family members' cultural values obviously differ.

Michael, a 17-year-old Chinese American high school student, was referred to a therapist by the school counselor because he was depressed and had suicidal tendencies (Huang & Ying, 1989). Michael was failing several classes and frequently was absent from school. Michael's parents were successful professionals who expected Michael to excel in school and go on to become a doctor. They were disappointed and angered by Michael's school failures, especially because he was the firstborn son, who in Chinese families is expected to achieve the highest standards of all siblings.

The therapist encouraged the parents to put less academic pressure on Michael and to have more realistic expectations for their son (who had no interest in becoming a doctor). Michael's school attendance improved and his parents noticed that his attitude toward school had become more positive. Michael's case illustrates how expectations that Asian American youth will be "whiz kids" can become destructive.

preview

Sonya's and Michael's circumstances underscore the influence of culture on adolescent development. Although we have much in common with all humans who inhabit the earth, we also vary according to our cultural and ethnic backgrounds. The sociocultural worlds of adolescents and emerging adults are a recurrent theme throughout this book. And, because culture is such a pervasive dimension of adolescence and emerging adulthood, in this chapter we explore it in greater depth. We will consider cross-cultural comparisons, study ethnicity and socioeconomic status as major aspects of culture, and examine ways in which the dramatic growth of mass media and technology affect the lives of adolescents.

The Relevance of Culture for the Study of Adolescence and Emerging Adulthood

Cross-Cultural Comparisons

Rites of Passage

We have defined **culture** as the behavior, patterns, beliefs, and all other products of a specific group of people that are passed on from generation to generation. The products result from the interaction between groups of people and their environment over many years. Here we examine the role of culture in adolescents' and emerging adults' development.

THE RELEVANCE OF CULTURE FOR THE STUDY OF ADOLESCENCE AND EMERGING ADULTHOOD

If the study of adolescence and emerging adulthood is to be a relevant discipline in the twenty-first century, increased attention must be paid to culture and ethnicity (Gauvain & Perez, 2015; Schwartz & others, 2015). Extensive contact between people from varied cultural and ethnic backgrounds is rapidly becoming the norm. Schools and neighborhoods are no longer the fortresses of a privileged group whose agenda is excluding people with a different skin color or different customs (Sernau, 2013). Immigrants, refugees, and ethnic minority individuals increasingly decline to become part of a homogeneous melting pot, instead requesting that schools, employers, and governments honor many of their cultural customs (Berry, 2015; Phinney & others, 2013a, b). Adult refugees and immigrants might find more opportunities and better-paying jobs in the United States than in their home countries, but some are concerned that their children and adolescents might learn attitudes in school that challenge traditional authority patterns at home.

During the twentieth century, the study of adolescents and emerging adults was primarily ethnocentric, emphasizing American values, especially middle-SES, non-Latino White, male values. Cross-cultural psychologists point out that many of the assumptions about contemporary ideas in fields like adolescence were developed in Western cultures (Triandis, 2007). One example of **ethnocentrism**—the tendency to favor one's own group over other groups—is the American emphasis on the individual or self. Many Eastern countries, such as Japan, China, and India, are group-oriented. So is the Mexican culture. The pendulum may have swung too far in the individualistic direction in many Western cultures.

People in all cultures have a tendency to behave in ways that favor their cultural group, to feel proud of their cultural group, and to feel less positive toward other cultural groups. Over the past few centuries, and at an increasing rate in recent decades, technological advances in transportation, communication, and commerce have made these ways of thinking obsolete. Global interdependence is no longer a matter of belief or choice. It is an inescapable reality. Adolescents and emerging adults are not just citizens of the United States or Canada. They are citizens of the world, a world that has become increasingly interactive. By understanding the behavior and values of cultures around the world, the hope is that we can learn to interact more effectively with each other and make this planet a more hospitable, peaceful place to live.

CROSS-CULTURAL COMPARISONS

Cross-cultural studies, which involve comparing a culture with one or more other cultures, provide information about other cultures and the role of culture in development. Such comparisons indicate the degree to which adolescents' and emerging adults' development is similar, or universal, across cultures, or the degree to which it is culture-specific (Goodnow & Lawrence, 2015; Mistry & Dutta, 2015). In terms of gender, for example, the experiences of male and female adolescents continue to be worlds apart in some cultures (Larson, Wilson,

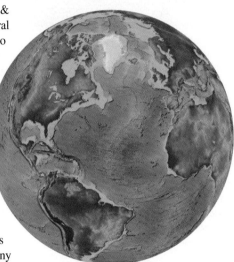

© Cartesia/Getty Images RF

culture The behavior, patterns, beliefs, and all other products of a particular group of people that are passed on from generation to generation.

ethnocentrism A tendency to favor one's own group over other groups.

cross-cultural studies Studies that compare a culture with one or more other cultures. Such studies provide information about the degree to which development in adolescents and emerging adults is similar, or universal, across cultures, or about the degree to which it is culture-specific.

Cross-cultural studies compare a culture with one or more other cultures. Shown here is a !Kung teenage girl. Delinquency and violence occur much less frequently in the African culture of the !Kung than in most cultures around the world.
© Images & Stories/Alamy

developmental **connection**

Education

Recent international comparisons indicate that the highest achievement test scores in math, science, and reading are held by students in Asian countries. Connect to "Achievement, Work, and Careers."

individualism Emphasizes values that serve the self and gives priority to personal goals rather than group goals.

collectivism Emphasizes values that serve the group by subordinating personal goals to preserve group integrity.

& Rickman, 2009). In many countries, males have far greater access to educational opportunities, more freedom to pursue a variety of careers, and fewer restrictions on sexual activity than do females (UNICEF, 2014).

We have discussed the higher math and science achievement of Asian adolescents in comparison with U.S. adolescents. One study revealed that from the beginning of the seventh grade through the end of the eighth grade, U.S. adolescents valued academics less and became less motivated to do well in school (Wang & Pomerantz, 2009). By contrast, the value placed on academics by Chinese adolescents did not change across this time frame and their academic motivation was sustained.

Individualism and Collectivism In cross-cultural research, the search for basic traits has often focused on the dichotomy between individualism and collectivism (Triandis, 2007):

· **Individualism** involves giving priority to personal goals rather than to group goals; it emphasizes values that serve the self, such as feeling good, personal distinction and achievement, and independence.

· **Collectivism** emphasizes values that serve the group by subordinating personal goals to preserve group integrity, interdependence of the members, and harmonious relationships.

Figure 1 summarizes some of the main characteristics of individualistic and collectivistic cultures. Many Western cultures, such as the United States, Canada, Great Britain, and

Individualistic	Collectivistic
Focuses on individual	Focuses on groups
Self is determined by personal traits independent of groups; self is stable across contexts	Self is defined by in-group terms; self can change with context
Private self is more important	Public self is most important
Personal achievement, competition, power are important	Achievement is for the benefit of the in-group; cooperation is stressed
Cognitive dissonance is frequent	Cognitive dissonance is infrequent
Emotions (such as anger) are self-focused	Emotions (such as anger) are often relationship based
People who are the most liked are self-assured	People who are the most liked are modest, self-effacing
Values: pleasure, achievement, competition, freedom	Values: security, obedience, in-group harmony, personalized relationships
Many casual relationships	Few, close relationships
Save own face	Save own and other's face
Independent behaviors: swimming, sleeping alone in room, privacy	Interdependent behaviors: co-bathing, co-sleeping
Relatively rare mother-child physical contact	Frequent mother-child physical contact (such as hugging, holding)

FIGURE **1**

CHARACTERISTICS OF INDIVIDUALISTIC AND COLLECTIVISTIC CULTURES

the Netherlands, are described as individualistic; many Eastern cultures, such as China, Japan, India, and Thailand, are described as collectivistic. The Mexican culture also is considered collectivistic. A recent study across 62 countries found that reported aggressive behavior among fourth- and eighth-graders was higher in individualistic cultures than in collectivistic cultures (Bergmuller, 2013). A study conducted from 1970 to 2008 found that although China still is characterized by collectivistic values, Chinese people are increasingly using words that index individualistic values (Zeng & Greenfield, 2015).

Researchers have found that self-conceptions are related to culture. In one study, American and Chinese college students completed 20 sentences beginning with "I am" (Trafimow, Triandis, & Goto, 1991). As indicated in Figure 2, the American college students were more likely than the Chinese students to describe themselves in terms of personal traits ("I am assertive"), whereas the Chinese students were more likely than the American students to identify themselves by their group affiliations ("I am a member of the math club"). However, a recent study found that from 1990 to 2007, Chinese 18- to 65-year-olds increasingly have included more individualistic characteristics in their descriptions of what constitutes happiness and well-being (Steele & Lynch, 2013).

Human beings have always lived in groups, whether large or small, and have always needed one another for survival. Critics of the Western notion of psychology argue that the Western emphasis on individualism may undermine our basic species need for relatedness (Kagitcibasi, 2007). Some social scientists argue that many problems in Western societies are intensified by the cultural emphasis on individualism. Compared with collectivistic cultures, individualistic cultures have higher rates of suicide, drug abuse, crime, teenage pregnancy, divorce, child abuse, and mental disorders.

One analysis proposed four values that reflect the beliefs of parents in individualistic cultures about what is required for children's and adolescents' effective development of autonomy: (1) *personal choice;* (2) *intrinsic motivation;* (3) *self-esteem;* and (4) *self-maximization,* which consists of achieving one's full potential (Tamis-LeMonda & others, 2008). The analysis also proposed that parents in collectivistic cultures emphasize three values that will help their children and adolescents become contributing members of society: (1) *connectedness to the family and other close relationships;* (2) *orientation to the larger group;* and (3) *respect and obedience.*

Critics of the dichotomy between individualistic and collectivistic cultures argue that these terms are too broad and simplistic, especially with the increase in globalization (Kagitcibasi, 2007). Regardless of their cultural background, people need both a positive sense of self and connectedness to others to develop fully as human beings. The analysis by Carolyn Tamis-LeMonda and her colleagues (2008) emphasizes that in many families children and adolescents are not reared in environments that uniformly endorse individualistic or collectivistic values, thoughts, and actions. Rather, in many families, children are "expected to be quiet, assertive, respectful, curious, humble, self-assured, independent, dependent, affectionate, or reserved depending on the situation, people present, children's age, and social-political and economic circles." Nonetheless, a number of studies continue to find differences between individualistic and collectivistic cultures in a number of areas (Boer & Fischer, 2013; Hitokoto & Tanaka-Matsumi, 2014; Strand, Pula, & Downs, 2015).

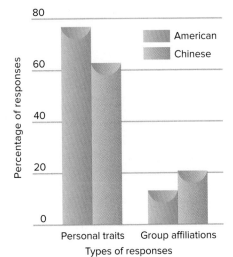

FIGURE 2

AMERICAN AND CHINESE SELF-CONCEPTIONS. College students from the United States and China completed 20 "I am _____" sentences. Both groups filled in personal traits more than group affiliations, but the Chinese students were more likely than the American students to identify themselves with group affiliations.

How Adolescents Around the World Spend Their Time Do adolescents around the world spend their time in ways similar to U.S. adolescents? There is considerable variation across different countries in the number of hours adolescents spend in paid work. For example, U.S. adolescents spend more time in paid work than do their counterparts in most developed countries. Adolescent males in developing countries often spend more time in paid work than do adolescent females, who spend more time in unpaid household labor.

Reed Larson and Suman Verma (Larson, 2001; Larson & Verma, 1999) examined how adolescents spend their time in work, play, and developmental activities such as school. Figure 3 summarizes the average daily time spent in various activities by adolescents in different regions of the world (Larson & Verma, 1999). Note that U.S. adolescents spend about 40 percent less time on schoolwork than East Asian adolescents do.

Activity	NonIndustrial, Unschooled Populations	POSTINDUSTRIAL, SCHOOLED POPULATIONS		
		United States	Europe	East Asia
Household labor	5 to 9 hours	20 to 40 minutes	20 to 40 minutes	10 to 20 minutes
Paid labor	0.5 to 8 hours	40 to 60 minutes	10 to 20 minutes	0 to 10 minutes
Schoolwork	—	3.0 to 4.5 hours	4.0 to 5.5 hours	5.5 to 7.5 hours
Total work time	6 to 9 hours	4 to 6 hours	4.5 to 6.5 hours	6 to 8 hours
TV viewing	*insufficient data*	1.5 to 2.5 hours	1.5 to 2.5 hours	1.5 to 2.5 hours
Talking	*insufficient data*	2 to 3 hours	*insufficient data*	45 to 60 minutes
Sports	*insufficient data*	30 to 60 minutes	20 to 80 minutes	0 to 20 minutes
Structured voluntary activities	*insufficient data*	10 to 20 minutes	10 to 20 minutes	0 to 10 minutes
Total free time	4 to 7 hours	6.5 to 8.0 hours	5.5 to 7.5 hours	4.0 to 5.5 hours

Note: The estimates in the table are averaged across a 7-day week, including weekdays and weekends. Time spent in maintenance activities like eating, personal care, and sleeping is not included. The data for nonindustrial, unschooled populations come primarily from rural peasant populations in developing countries.

FIGURE 3

AVERAGE DAILY TIME USE OF ADOLESCENTS IN DIFFERENT REGIONS OF THE WORLD

The researchers found that U.S. adolescents had more discretionary time (free time) than adolescents in other industrialized countries. In the Larson and Verma (1999) study, about 40 to 50 percent of U.S. adolescents' waking hours (not counting summer vacations) was spent in discretionary activities, compared with 25 to 35 percent in East Asia and 35 to 45 percent in Europe. Whether this additional discretionary time is a liability or an asset for U.S. adolescents, of course, depends on how they use it.

The largest amounts of U.S. adolescents' free time were spent using the media and engaging in unstructured leisure activities, often with friends. We further explore adolescents' media use later in this chapter. U.S. adolescents spent more time in voluntary structured activities—such as sports, hobbies, and organizations—than East Asian adolescents did.

According to Reed Larson and his colleagues (Larson, 2001, 2008, 2014; Larson & Walker, 2010; Larson & Dawes, 2015; Larson, Wilson, & Rickman, 2009), U.S. adolescents may have more unstructured time than is suitable for optimal development. When adolescents are allowed to choose what they do with their time, they typically engage in unchallenging activities such as hanging out and watching TV. Although relaxation and social interaction are important aspects of adolescence, it seems unlikely that spending large numbers of hours per week in unchallenging activities fosters development. Structured voluntary activities may provide more promise for adolescent development than does unstructured time, especially if adults give responsibility to adolescents, challenge them, and provide competent guidance in these activities (Larson, 2008, 2014; Larson & Dawes, 2015; Larson & Tran, 2014; Larson, Wilson, & Rickman, 2009).

How do U.S. adolescents spend their time differently from European and East Asian adolescents?
© Shine Pictures/Corbis

RITES OF PASSAGE

Rites of passage are ceremonies or rituals that mark an individual's transition from one status to another, such as the entry into adulthood. Some societies have elaborate rites of passage that signal the adolescent's transition to adulthood; others do not (Ember, Ember, & Peregrine, 2015; Kang, 2014; Kottak & Kozaitis, 2012). In many primitive cultures, rites of passage are the avenue through which adolescents gain access to sacred adult practices, responsibilities, knowledge, and sexuality (Skinner & others, 2013; Sommer, 1978). These rites often involve dramatic ceremonies intended to facilitate the adolescent's separation from the immediate family, especially boys from the mother. The transformation usually is characterized by some form of ritual death and rebirth, or by means of contact with the spiritual world. Bonds are forged between the adolescent and the adult instructors through shared rituals, hazards, and secrets to allow the adolescent to enter the adult world. This kind of ritual provides a forceful and discontinuous entry into the adult world at a time when the adolescent is perceived to be ready for the change.

Africa, especially sub-Saharan Africa, has been the location of many rites of passage for adolescents (Skinner & others, 2013). Under the influence of Western culture, many of these rites are disappearing today, although some vestiges remain. In locations where formal education is not readily available, rites of passage are still prevalent.

Carol Markstrom (2010) recently studied coming-of-age ceremonies among Native American girls. She observed that many Native American tribes consider the transition from childhood to adulthood as a pivotal and possibly vulnerable time and have created coming-of-age rituals to support traditional values. She emphasizes that these rituals are often a positive aspect of life in Native American tribes today as their youth face challenges of the modern world such as substance abuse, suicide, and dropping out of school (Markstrom, 2010).

Western industrialized countries are notable for their lack of formal rites of passage that mark the transition from adolescence to adulthood. Some religious and social groups, however, have initiation ceremonies that indicate an advance in maturity—the Jewish bat mitzvah and bar mitzvah, Catholic and Protestant confirmations, and social debuts, for example. School graduation ceremonies come the closest to being culture-wide rites of passage in the United States. The high school graduation ceremony has become nearly universal for middle-SES adolescents and increasing numbers of adolescents from low-income backgrounds (Fasick, 1994). Nonetheless, high school graduation does not result in universal changes—many high school graduates continue to live with their parents, to be economically dependent

rites of passage Ceremonies or rituals that mark an individual's transition from one status to another, such as the entry into adulthood.

These Congolese Kota boys painted their faces as part of a rite of passage to adulthood. *What rites of passage do American adolescents have?*
© Daniel Laine/Gamma-Rapho

The Apache Native Americans of the American Southwest celebrate a girl's entrance into puberty with a four-day ritual that includes special dress, day-long activities, and solemn spiritual ceremonies.
© RGB Ventures/SuperStock/Alamy

Maddie Miller, 13, sharing a prayer with her father, studied for a year to prepare for her bat mitzvah.
© Sylvia Plachy/Redux Pictures

on them, and to be undecided about questions of career and lifestyle. Another rite of passage for increasing numbers of American adolescents is sexual intercourse. By the end of adolescence, more than 70 percent of American adolescents have had sexual intercourse.

The absence of clear-cut rites of passage makes the attainment of adult status so ambiguous that many individuals are unsure whether they have reached it or not. In Texas, for example, the legal age for beginning employment is 15, but many younger adolescents and even children are employed, especially Mexican immigrants. The legal age for driving is 16, but when emergency need is demonstrated, a driver's license can be obtained at age 15, and some parents might not allow their son or daughter to obtain a driver's license even at age 16, believing that they are too young for this responsibility. The legal age for voting is 18, and the minimum age for drinking has been raised to 21. In sum, exactly when adolescents become adults in the United States has not been as clearly delineated as it has in primitive cultures where rites of passage are universal.

Review Connect Reflect

LG1 Discuss the role of culture in the development of adolescents and emerging adults

Review

- What is culture? What is the relevance of culture in the study of development in adolescence and emerging adulthood?
- What are cross-cultural comparisons? What characterizes individualistic and collectivistic cultures? How do cultures vary in the time adolescents spend in different activities?
- What are rites of passage? How do cultures vary in terms of rites of passage?

Connect

- In this section you learned that U.S. adolescents have far more discretionary time than do their European or Asian counterparts. Relate this fact to our earlier discussions of expectations.

Reflect Your Own Personal Journey of Life

- Have you experienced a rite of passage in your life? If so, what was it? Was it a positive or negative influence on your development? Is there a rite of passage you did not experience that you wished you had?

2 Socioeconomic Status and Poverty

LG2 Describe how socioeconomic status and poverty are related to adolescent development

What Is Socioeconomic Status?

Socioeconomic Variations in Families, Neighborhoods, and Schools

Poverty

Many subcultures exist within countries. For example, the values and attitudes of adolescents growing up in an urban ghetto or rural Appalachia may differ considerably from those of adolescents growing up in a wealthy suburb. A key difference between such subcultures is socioeconomic status.

WHAT IS SOCIOECONOMIC STATUS?

socioeconomic status (SES) Refers to a grouping of people with similar occupational, educational, and economic characteristics.

Socioeconomic status (SES) refers to a grouping of people with similar occupational, educational, and economic characteristics. Individuals with different SES have varying levels of power, influence, and prestige. In this chapter, for example, we evaluate what it is like for an adolescent to grow up in poverty.

Socioeconomic status carries with it certain inequalities. Generally, members of a society have (1) occupations that vary in prestige, with some individuals having more access than others to higher-status occupations; (2) different levels of educational attainment, with some individuals having more access than others to better education; (3) different economic resources; and (4) different levels of power to influence a community's institutions. These differences in the ability to control resources and to participate in society's rewards produce unequal opportunities for adolescents (Duncan, Magnuson, & Votruba-Drzal, 2015; McLoyd, Purtel, & Hardaway, 2015). Socioeconomic differences have been described as a "proxy for material, human, and social capital within and beyond the family" (Huston & Ripke, 2006, p. 425).

The number of visibly different socioeconomic statuses depends on the community's size and complexity. In most investigators' descriptions of SES, two categories, low and middle, are used, although as many as five categories have been delineated. Sometimes low SES is described as low-income, working class, or blue-collar; sometimes the middle category is described as middle-income, managerial, or white-collar. Examples of low-SES occupations are factory worker, manual laborer, welfare recipient, and maintenance worker. Examples of middle-SES occupations include salesperson, manager, and professional (doctor, lawyer, teacher, accountant, and so on). Professionals at the pinnacle of their field, high-level corporate executives, political leaders, and wealthy individuals are among those in the upper-SES category.

SOCIOECONOMIC VARIATIONS IN FAMILIES, NEIGHBORHOODS, AND SCHOOLS

The families, schools, and neighborhoods of adolescents have socioeconomic characteristics (Banks, 2014; Crosnoe & Benner, 2015; Murry & others, 2015). Some adolescents have parents who possess a great deal of money and who work in prestigious occupations. These adolescents live in attractive houses and neighborhoods, enjoy vacations abroad and at high-quality camps, and attend schools where the mix of students is primarily from middle- and upper-SES backgrounds. Other adolescents have parents who do not have very much money and who work in less prestigious occupations. These adolescents do not live in very attractive houses and neighborhoods, rarely go on vacations, and attend schools where the mix of students is mainly from lower-SES backgrounds. Such variations in neighborhood settings can influence adolescents' adjustment and achievement (McLoyd, Purtell, & Hardaway, 2015; Wigfield & others, 2015).

In the United States and most Western cultures, differences have been found in child rearing among different SES groups (Hoff, Laursen, & Tardif, 2002, p. 246):

· Lower-SES parents (1) "are more concerned that their children conform to society's expectations," (2) "create a home atmosphere in which it is clear that parents have authority over children," (3) use physical punishment more in disciplining their children, and (4) are more directive and less conversational with their children.

· Higher-SES parents (1) "are more concerned with developing children's initiative" and delay of gratification, (2) "create a home atmosphere in which children are more nearly equal participants and in which rules are discussed as opposed to being laid down" in an authoritarian manner, (3) are less likely to use physical punishment, and (4) "are less directive and more conversational" with their children.

Children and adolescents from low-SES backgrounds are at risk for experiencing low achievement and emotional problems, as well as lower occupational attainment in adulthood (Koppelman, 2014; McLoyd, Purtell, & Hardaway, 2015; Wigfield & others, 2015). Social maladaptation and psychological problems such as depression, low self-confidence, peer conflict, and juvenile delinquency are more prevalent among poor adolescents than among economically advantaged adolescents (Gibbs & Huang, 1989). Although psychological problems are more prevalent among adolescents from low-SES backgrounds, these adolescents vary considerably in intellectual and psychological functioning. For example, a sizable portion of adolescents from low-SES backgrounds perform well in school; in fact, some perform better than many middle-SES students. When adolescents from low-SES backgrounds are achieving well in school, it is not unusual to find a parent or parents

developmental **connection**

Education

Many adolescents in low-SES neighborhoods face problems that present barriers to their learning. Connect to "Schools."

making special sacrifices to provide the necessary living conditions and support to contribute to school success.

Schools in low-SES neighborhoods tend to have fewer resources than do schools in higher-SES neighborhoods. The schools in the low-SES areas also are likely to have more students with lower achievement test scores, lower rates of graduation, and fewer opportunities to attend college (Engle & Black, 2008). In some instances, however, federal aid to schools has provided a context for enhanced learning in low-income areas.

So far we have focused on the challenges that many adolescents from low-income families face. However, research by Suniya Luthar and her colleagues (Ansary & Luthar, 2009; Ansary, McMahon, & Luthar, 2012; Luthar, 2006; Luthar, Crossman, & Small, 2015; Luthar & Goldstein, 2008) has found that adolescents from affluent families also face challenges. Adolescents in the affluent families Luthar has studied are vulnerable to high rates of substance abuse. In addition, her research has found that adolescent males from such families have more adjustment difficulties than do females, with affluent female adolescents being more likely to attain superior levels of academic success. Luthar and her colleagues (Luthar, Barkin, & Crossman, 2013) also have found that youth in upwardly mobile, upper-middle SES families are more likely to engage in drug use and have more internalized and externalized problems than their counterparts in middle-SES families.

A recent study, though, found that it was neighborhood wealth rather than family affluence that was linked to adolescent problems (Lund & Dearing, 2013). In this study, boys in affluent neighborhoods had a higher rate of delinquency and girls in affluent neighborhoods had higher levels of anxiety and depression than youth in middle-class neighborhoods. Family affluence did not place these adolescents at risk in these domains.

POVERTY

The world is a dangerous and unwelcoming place for too many U.S. youth, especially those whose families, neighborhoods, and schools are low-income (Gershoff & Benner, 2014; Herberle & Carter, 2015; Leventhal, Dupere, & Shuey, 2015; McLoyd, Purtell, & Hardaway, 2015). Some adolescents are resilient and cope with the challenges of poverty without major setbacks, but many struggle unsuccessfully. Each adolescent who has grown up in poverty and reaches adulthood unhealthy, unskilled, or alienated keeps the United States from being as competent and productive as it could be.

What Is Poverty Like?   Poverty is defined by economic hardship, and its most common marker is the federal poverty threshold. The poverty threshold was originally based on the estimated cost of food (a basic diet) multiplied by 3. This federal poverty marker is adjusted annually for family size and inflation.

Children and youth who grow up in poverty represent a special concern (Duncan, Magnuson, & Votruba-Drzal, 2015; Leventhal, Dupere, & Shuey, 2015). In 2013, 19.9 percent of U.S. children and adolescents lived in families with incomes below the poverty threshold (De Navas-Walt & Proctor, 2014). The U.S. poverty rate for children and adolescents was an increase from 2001 (16.2 percent) but down from a peak of 22.7 percent in 1993 and also down from 21.8 percent in 2012. The U.S. figure of 19.9 percent of children and adolescents living in poverty is much higher than figures from other industrialized nations. For example, Canada has a child poverty rate of 9 percent and Sweden has a rate of 2 percent.

Poverty in the United States is demarcated along ethnic and family structure lines (De Navas-Walt & Proctor, 2014). In 2013, African American (27.2 percent) and Latino (23.5 percent) families with children and adolescents had especially high rates of poverty in comparison with a rate of 12.3 percent for their non-Latino White counterparts. And compared with non-Latino White children and adolescents, ethnic minority children and adolescents are more likely to experience persistent poverty over many years and to live in isolated poor neighborhoods where social supports are minimal and threats to positive development abundant (Jarrett, 1995) (see Figure 4).

In 2013, 39.6 percent of single-mother families lived in poverty, more than five times the poverty rate for married-couple families (7.6 percent). More than half (51.9 percent) of

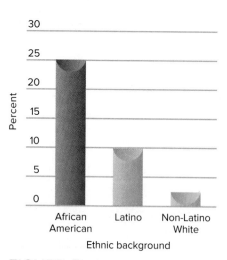

FIGURE **4**

LIVING IN DISTRESSED NEIGHBORHOODS.
Note: A distressed neighborhood is defined by high levels (at least one standard deviation above the mean) of (1) poverty, (2) female-headed families, (3) high school dropouts, (4) unemployment, and (5) reliance on welfare.

the single-mother families in poverty experienced extreme poverty, with incomes below half of the federal poverty level (about $9,900 for a family of three), which means a family budget of about $200 a week.

Living in poverty has many negative psychological effects on children and adolescents (Duncan, Magnuson, & Votruba-Drzal, 2015; McLoyd, Purtell, & Hardaway, 2015). First, the poor are often powerless. In the workplace, they rarely are the decision makers. Rules are handed down to them in an authoritarian manner. Second, the poor are often vulnerable to disaster. They are not likely to be given notice before they are laid off from work and usually do not have financial resources to fall back on when problems arise. Third, their range of alternatives is often restricted. Only a limited number of jobs are open to them. Even when alternatives are available, the poor might not know about them or be prepared to make a wise decision. Fourth, because of inadequate education and inability to read well, being poor means having less prestige.

One review concluded that compared with their economically more advantaged counterparts, poor children and adolescents experience widespread environmental inequities that include the following (Evans, 2004):

- They experience more conflict, violence, instability, and chaos in their homes (Emery & Laumann-Billings, 1998).
- They get less social support, and their parents are less responsive and more authoritarian (Bo, 1994).
- They watch more TV and have less access to books and computers (Bradley & others, 2001).
- Their schools and child-care facilities are inferior, and parents monitor their school activities less (Benveniste, Carnoy, & Rothstein, 2003).
- The air they breathe and the water they drink are more polluted, and their homes are more crowded and noisy (Myers, Baer, & Choi, 1996).
- They live in more dangerous and physically deteriorating neighborhoods with less adequate municipal services (Brody & others, 2001).

At a number of places in this edition, the negative aspects and outcomes of poverty for adolescents are highlighted: as a risk factor for sexual problems; running away from home; reduction of income for divorced mothers, which can lead to poverty and its negative consequences for adolescents; numerous school-related risks and problems, including inferior schools, increased risk of dropping out of school, and lower probability of going to college; lower achievement expectations, lower achievement, lack of access to jobs, and entry into less desirable careers; and higher rates of delinquency.

When poverty is persistent and long-standing, it can have especially damaging effects on children and adolescents (Duncan, Magnuson, & Votruba-Drzal, 2015; Evans, Li, & Sepanski Whipple, 2013). One study revealed that the more years 7- to 13-year-olds spent living in poverty, the higher were their physiological indices of stress (Evans & Kim, 2007). Also, a recent study of youth found that living in neighborhoods where poverty increased from the time they were 11 to 19 years of age was associated with high levels of *allostatic load,* which involves a wearing down of the body's physiological systems due to stressors (Brody & others, 2014). However, for youth who experienced high emotional support, allostatic load did not increase across this time frame even when poverty increased.

Because of advances in their cognitive growth, adolescents living in poverty conditions likely are more aware of their social disadvantage and the associated stigma than are children (McLoyd & others, 2009). Combined with the increased sensitivity to peers in adolescence, such awareness may cause them to try to hide their poverty status as much as possible from others.

A special concern is the high percentage of children and adolescents growing up in mother-headed households in poverty (De Navas-Walt & Proctor, 2014). Vonnie McLoyd (1998) concluded that because poor, single mothers are more distressed than their middle-SES counterparts are, they tend to show low support, nurturance, and involvement with their children. Among the reasons for the high poverty rate of single mothers are women's low pay, infrequent awarding of alimony payments, and poorly enforced child support from fathers (Schaefer, 2015).

developmental **connection**

Achievement

Many adolescents who have grown up in low-income or poverty conditions face challenging circumstances in seeking upward mobility in their careers. Connect to "Achievement, Work, and Careers."

The term **feminization of poverty** refers to the fact that far more women than men live in poverty (Ward & Edelstein, 2014). Women's low income, divorce, and the resolution of divorce cases by the judicial system, which leaves women with less money than they and their children need to adequately function, are the likely causes of the feminization of poverty.

Countering Negative Effects of Low Income and Poverty   One trend in antipoverty programs is to conduct two-generation interventions (McLoyd, Aikens, & Burton, 2006; Purtell & McLoyd, 2013). This involves providing services for children (such as educational child care, preschool education, or after-school programs for youth) as well as services for parents (such as adult education, literacy training, and job skills training). Evaluations of the two-generation programs suggest that they have more positive effects on parents than they do on children and adolescents (St. Pierre, Layzer, & Barnes, 1996).

Might intervention with families of children living in poverty improve children's school performance? In a recent experimental study, Aletha Huston and her colleagues (2006) evaluated the effects of New Hope, a program designed to increase parental employment and reduce family poverty, on adolescent development. They randomly assigned families with 6- to 10-year old children living in poverty to the New Hope program or a control group. To adults living in poverty who were employed 30 or more hours a week, New Hope offered benefits that were designed to increase family income (a wage supplement that ensured that net income increased as parents earned more) and to provide work supports through subsidized child care (for any child under age 13) and health insurance. Management services were provided to New Hope participants to assist them with job searches and other needs.

The New Hope program was available to the experimental group families for three years (until the children were 9 to 13 years old). Two years after the program had ended, researchers examined New Hope's effects on the children, who were now 11 to 16 years old. Compared with adolescents in the control group, New Hope adolescents were more competent at reading, had better school performance, were less likely to be in special-education classes, had more positive social skills, and were more likely to be in formal after-school arrangements. New Hope parents reported better psychological well-being and a greater sense of self-efficacy in managing their adolescents than control parents did. In a further assessment, the influence of the New Hope program on children 9 to 19 years after they left the program was evaluated (McLoyd & others, 2011). Positive outcomes especially occurred for African American boys, who were more optimistic about their future employment and career prospects. In the most recent assessment of the New Hope program, the intervention had positive effects on the youths' future orientation 5 years after the program had ended (Purtell & McLoyd, 2013). In this study, boys' positive educational expectations were linked to the intervention's influence on reducing the boys' pessimism about future employment.

Schools and school programs are the focus of some poverty interventions. A recent study assessed the effects of the Positive Action program in 14 urban, low-income Chicago schools across 6 years from grades 3 to 8 (Lewis & others, 2013). The Positive Action program is a K-12 curriculum that focuses on self-concept, self-control and responsibility, physical and mental health, honesty, getting along with others, and continually striving for self-improvement. The program includes teacher, counselor, family, and community training and activities to improve school-wide atmosphere. In comparison with control group schools that did not implement the Positive Action program, students in the program engaged in a lower rate of violence-related behavior and received fewer disciplinary referrals and suspensions from school.

In another recent study, more than 500 ninth- to twelfth-grade students living in low-income settings in Los Angeles were chosen through a random admissions lottery to attend high-performing public charter schools (Wong & others, 2014). Compared with a control group of students who did not get to attend the high-performing charter schools, the students attending the charter schools had better scores on math and English standardized tests and were less likely to drop out of school.

What other programs are benefiting adolescents living in poverty? See the *Connecting with Health and Well-Being* interlude.

developmental **connection**

Social Policy

Reducing the poverty level and improving the lives of children and adolescents living in poverty are important goals of U.S. social policy. Connect to "Introduction."

feminization of poverty Term reflecting the fact that far more women than men live in poverty. Likely causes include women's low income, divorce, and the resolution of divorce cases by the judicial system, which leaves women with less money than they and their children need to function adequately.

How Do the Quantum Opportunities and El Puente Programs Help Youth in Poverty?

One potential positive path for youth living in poverty is to become involved with a caring mentor. The Quantum Opportunities program, funded by the Ford Foundation, was a four-year, year-round mentoring effort (Carnegie Council on Adolescent Development, 1995). The students who participated were entering the ninth grade at a high school with high rates of poverty, were members of minority groups, and came from families that received public assistance. Each day for four years, mentors provided sustained support, guidance, and concrete assistance to the students.

The Quantum program required students to participate in (1) academic-related activities outside school hours, including reading, writing, math, science, and social studies, peer tutoring, and computer skills training; (2) community service projects, including tutoring elementary school students, cleaning up the neighborhood, and volunteering in hospitals, nursing homes, and libraries; and (3) cultural enrichment and personal development activities, including life skills training and college and job planning. In exchange for their commitment to the program, students were offered financial incentives that encouraged participation, completion, and long-range planning. A stipend of $1.33 was given to students for each hour they participated in these activities. For every 100 hours of education, service, or development activities, students received a bonus of $100. The average cost per participant was $10,600 for the four years, which is one-half the cost of one year in prison.

An evaluation of the Quantum project compared the mentored students with a nonmentored control group. Sixty-three percent of the mentored students graduated from high school, but only 42 percent of the control group did; 42 percent of the mentored students were enrolled in college at the time of the evaluation, but only 16 percent of the control group were. Furthermore, control-group students were twice as likely as the mentored students to receive food stamps or welfare, and they had more arrests. Such programs clearly have the potential to overcome the intergenerational transmission of poverty and its negative outcomes.

The original Quantum Opportunities program no longer exists, but the Eisenhower Corporation (2013) recently began replicating the Quantum program in Alabama, South Carolina, New Hampshire, Virginia, Mississippi, Oregon, Maryland, and Washington, D.C.

Another effort to improve the lives of adolescents living in poverty is the El Puente program, which is primarily aimed at Latino adolescents living in low-SES areas. El Puente ("the bridge") was opened in New York City in 1983 because of community dissatisfaction with the health, educational, and social services youth were receiving (Simons, Finlay, & Yang, 1991). El Puente emphasizes five areas of youth development: health, education, achievement, personal growth, and social growth.

Adolescent working on a computer at the Quantam Opportunities program in St. Petersburg, Florida.
© ZUMA Press, Inc./Alamy

El Puente is located in a former Roman Catholic church building on the south side of Williamsburg in Brooklyn, a neighborhood made up primarily of low-income Latino families, many of which are far below the poverty threshold. Sixty-five percent of the residents receive some form of public assistance. The neighborhood has the highest school dropout rate for Latinos in New York City and the highest felony rate for adolescents in Brooklyn.

When the youth (12 through 21 years of age) first enroll in El Puente, they meet with counselors and develop a four-month plan that includes the programs they are interested in joining. At the end of four months, youth and staff develop a plan for continued participation. Twenty-six bilingual classes are offered in such subjects as music, theater, photography, and dance. In addition, a medical and fitness center, a GED night school, and mental health and social services centers are also a part of El Puente.

How might the lessons learned from these successful programs be applied and studied in other cultural situations in which adolescents live in poverty?

Review Connect Reflect

LG2 Describe how socioeconomic status and poverty are related to adolescent development

Review
- What is socioeconomic status?
- What are some socioeconomic variations in families, neighborhoods, and schools?
- How is poverty related to adolescent development?

Connect
- How does the idea of the family as a system connect with the experience of adolescents living in poverty?

Reflect *Your Own Personal Journey of Life*
- What was the socioeconomic status of your family as you were growing up? How did it affect your development?

3 Ethnicity

LG3 Summarize how ethnicity is involved in the development of adolescents and emerging adults

| Immigration | Adolescence and Emerging Adulthood: A Special Juncture For Ethnic Minority Individuals | Ethnicity Issues |

developmental connection

Identity

Researchers are increasingly finding that a positive ethnic identity is linked to positive outcomes for ethnic minority adolescents. Connect to "The Self, Identity, Emotion, and Personality."

Adolescents and emerging adults live in a world that has been made smaller and more interactive by dramatic improvements in travel and communication. U.S. adolescents and emerging adults also live in a world that is far more diverse in its ethnic makeup than it was in past decades: Ninety-three languages are spoken in Los Angeles alone!

Ethnicity is based on cultural heritage, nationality characteristics, race, religion, and language. A striking feature of the United States today is the increasing ethnic diversity of America's adolescents and emerging adults (Schaefer, 2015). In this section, we study African American adolescents, Latino adolescents, Asian American adolescents, and Native American adolescents, and we explore the sociocultural issues involved in their development.

IMMIGRATION

Relatively high rates of immigration are contributing to the growing proportion of ethnic minority adolescents and emerging adults in the United States (Berry, 2015; Fuligni & Tsai, 2015; Marks, Godoy, & Garcia Coll, 2014; Phinney & others, 2013a, b). Immigrant families are those in which at least one of the parents is born outside the country of residence. Variations in immigrant families involve whether one or both parents are foreign-born, whether the child was born in the host country, and the ages at which immigration took place for both the parents and the children (Crosnoe & Fuligni, 2012; Kao & Huang, 2015; Schwartz & others, 2015).

Different models have been proposed as to whether children and adolescents in immigrant families are more vulnerable or more successful in relation to the general population of children and adolescents (Crosnoe & Fuligni, 2012). Historically, an *immigrant risk model* was emphasized, concluding that youth of immigrants had a lower level of well-being and were at risk for more problems. For example, one study found that the longer immigrant youth from the Dominican Republic lived in the United States, the higher their risk for suicide or suicide attempts (Pena & others, 2012).

More recently, an *immigrant paradox model* has been proposed, emphasizing that despite the many cultural, socioeconomic, language, and other obstacles that immigrant families face, their youth show a high level of well-being and fewer problems than native-born youth (Garcia Coll & others, 2012; Marks, Godoy, & Garcia Coll, 2014). Based on

ethnicity A dimension of culture based on cultural heritage, national characteristics, race, religion, and language.

current research, some support exists for each model. As was recently concluded by Robert Crosnoe and Andrew Fuligni (2012, p. 1473):

> Some children from immigrant families are doing quite well, some less so, depending on the characteristics of migration itself (including the nation of origin) and their families' circumstances in their new country (including their position in socioeconomic and race-ethnic stratification systems).

What are some of the circumstances immigrants face that challenge their adjustment? Immigrants often experience stressors uncommon to or less prominent among longtime residents, such as language barriers, dislocations and separations from support networks, the dual struggle to preserve identity and to acculturate, and changes in SES status (Fuligni & Tsai, 2015; Schaefer, 2015). Many individuals in immigrant families are dealing with the problem of being undocumented. Living in an undocumented family can affect children's and adolescents' developmental outcomes through parents being unwilling to sign up for services for which they are eligible, through conditions linked to low-wage work and lack of benefits, through stress, and through a lack of cognitive stimulation in the home (Nieto & Yoshikawa, 2014; Yoshikawa, 2012). Consequently, when working with adolescents and their immigrant families, counselors need to adapt intervention programs to optimize cultural sensitivity (Suárez-Orozco & Suárez-Orozco, 2010, 2013; Sue & others, 2013, 2014, 2015).

Latino immigrants in the Rio Grande Valley, Texas. *What are some of the adaptations immigrants make?*
© Alison Wright/Corbis

developmental **connection**

Diversity

Projections indicate that in 2100 there will be more Latino than non-Latino White adolescents in the United States and more Asian American than African American adolescents in the United States. Connect to "Introduction."

Parents and adolescents may be at different stages of *acculturation*, the process of adapting to the majority culture. The result may be conflict over cultural values (Berry, 2015; Fuligni & Tsai, 2015; Kim & others, 2012; Phinney & others, 2013a, b). One study examined values in immigrant families (Vietnamese, Armenian, and Mexican) and nonimmigrant families (African American and European American) (Phinney, 2006). In all groups, parents endorsed family obligations more than adolescents did, and the differences between generations generally increased with time spent in the United States.

Although many ethnic/immigrant families adopt a bicultural orientation, parenting in many ethnic minority families also focuses on issues associated with promoting children's ethnic pride, knowledge of their ethnic group, and awareness of discrimination (Ho & others, 2012; Simpkins & others, 2013).

Many of the families that have immigrated in recent decades to the United States, such as Mexican Americans and Asian Americans, come from collectivistic cultures in which family obligation and duty to one's family are strong (Fuligni & Telzer, 2012). Family obligation and duty may take the form of assisting parents in their occupations and contributing to the family's welfare (van Geel & Vedder, 2011). This often occurs in service and manual labor jobs, such as those in construction, gardening, cleaning, and restaurants. A recent study of immigrant families from Mexican backgrounds found that family obligation values were associated with lower substance use by adolescents, in part because of associating less with deviant peers and increased self-disclosure to parents (Telzer, Gonzales, & Fuligni, 2014). However, in this study, family assistance behaviors were linked to higher levels of substance use in families with high levels of parent-adolescent conflict.

It is important to remember that there are variations in immigrant families' experiences and the degree to which their children and adolescents change as they are exposed to American culture. A recent study found that following their immigration, Mexican American adolescents spent less time with their family and identified less with family values (Updegraff & others, 2012). However, in this study teens with stronger family values in early adolescence were less likely to engage in risky behavior in late adolescence.

The ways in which ethnic minority families deal with stress depend on many factors (Fuligni & Tsai, 2015; McLoyd, Purtell, & Hardaway, 2015; Murry & others, 2015). Whether the parents are native-born or immigrants, how long the family has been in the United States, its socioeconomic status, and its national origin all make a difference (Gonzales & others, 2012). A recent study revealed that parents' education before migrating was strongly linked to their children's academic achievement (Pong & Landale, 2012). Another recent study found

Carola Suárez-Orozco, Immigration Studies Researcher and Professor

Carola Suárez-Orozco currently is Professor of Education and Co-Director of the Institute for Immigration, Globalization, and Education at UCLA. She previously was chair and Professor of Applied Psychology and Co-Director of Immigration Studies at New York University. Earlier in her career, Dr. Suárez-Orozco was co-director of the Harvard University Immigration Projects. She obtained her undergraduate degree (in development studies) from UCLA and her doctoral degree from California School of Professional Psychology, San Diego.

Dr. Suárez-Orozco has worked in both clinical and public school settings in California and Massachusetts. While at Harvard, she conducted a five-year longitudinal study of adaptation to U.S. schools and society among immigrant adolescents from Central America, China, and the Dominican Republic. She especially advocates more research on cultural and psychological factors involved in the adaptation of immigrant and ethnic minority youth (Suárez-Orozco, 2007; Suárez-Orozco & Yoshikawa, 2013). Dr. Suárez-Orozco also was recently Chair of the American Psychological Association

Carola Suárez-Orozco, with her husband, Marcelo, who also studies the adaptation of immigrants.
Courtesy of Carola Suárez-Orozco and photographer Kris Snibbe, Harvard News Office

Presidential Task Force on Immigration. One of her important accomplishments was the creation of the APA video on undocumented immigrant children.

---

that first-generation immigrant adolescents had more internalizing problems (anxiety and depression, for example) than second-generation immigrants had (Katsiaficas & others, 2013).

The characteristics of the family's social context also influence its adaptation (Gershoff & Benner, 2014; Leventhal, Dupere, & Shuey, 2015). What are the attitudes toward the family's ethnic group within its neighborhood or city? Can the family's children attend good schools? Are there community groups that welcome people from the family's ethnic group? Do members of the family's ethnic group form community groups of their own?

To read about the work of one individual who studies immigrant adolescents, see the *Connecting with Careers* profile.

ADOLESCENCE AND EMERGING ADULTHOOD: A SPECIAL JUNCTURE FOR ETHNIC MINORITY INDIVIDUALS

For ethnic minority individuals, adolescence and emerging adulthood often represent a special juncture in their development (Schwartz & others, 2015; Spencer, Swanson, & Harpalani, 2015). Although children are aware of some ethnic and cultural differences, most ethnic minority individuals first consciously confront their ethnicity in adolescence. In contrast with children, adolescents and emerging adults have the ability to interpret ethnic and cultural information, to reflect on the past, and to speculate about the future. As they mature cognitively, ethnic minority adolescents and emerging adults become acutely aware of how the majority non-Latino White culture evaluates their ethnic group (Huynh & Fuligni, 2012). One researcher commented that the young African American child may learn that Black is beautiful but conclude as an adolescent that White is powerful (Semaj, 1985).

Ethnic minority youths' awareness of negative appraisals, conflicting values, and restricted occupational opportunities can influence their life choices and plans for the future (Huynh & Fuligni, 2012). As one ethnic minority youth stated, "The future seems shut off, closed. Why dream? You can't reach your dreams. Why set goals? At least if you don't set any goals, you don't fail."

For many ethnic minority youth, a special concern is the lack of successful ethnic minority role models. The problem is especially acute for inner-city youth. Because of the lack of adult ethnic minority role models, some ethnic minority youth may conform to middle-SES, non-Latino White values and identify with successful non-Latino White role models. However, for many ethnic minority adolescents, their ethnicity and skin color limit their acceptance within the non-Latino White culture. Thus, they face the difficult task of negotiating two value systems—that of their own ethnic group and that of the non-Latino White society (Verkuyten, 2012). Some adolescents reject the mainstream, forgoing the rewards controlled by non-Latino White Americans; others adopt the values and standards of the majority non-Latino White culture; and still others take the path of biculturality (Berry, 2015; Schwartz & others, 2012). Recent research indicates that many members of families that have recently immigrated to the United States adopt a bicultural orientation, selecting characteristics of the U.S. culture that help them to survive and advance, while still retaining aspects of their culture of origin (Marks, Godoy, & Garcia Coll, 2014; Marks, Patton, & Garcia Coll, 2011).

One study of Mexican American and Asian American college students revealed that both ethnic groups expressed a bicultural identity (Devos, 2006). Also, a recent study by Su Yeong Kim and her colleagues (2015) focused on how various dimensions of acculturation in Chinese American families were linked

Margaret Beale Spencer, shown here (on the right) talking with adolescents, believes that adolescence is a critical juncture in the identity development of ethnic minority individuals. Most ethnic minority individuals consciously confront their ethnicity for the first time in adolescence.
Courtesy of Margaret Beale Spencer

to adolescents' academic trajectories from the eighth to the twelfth grades. Adolescents with a Chinese-oriented father had a faster decline over time in their grade point average and Chinese-oriented adolescents had lower initial English language arts (ELA) scores. Also in this study, adolescents who were more Chinese-oriented than their parents had lower initial ELA scores and adolescents who were more American-oriented than their parents had the highest initial ELA scores. In another study of Chinese American families by Su Yeong Kim and her colleagues (2013), a discrepancy in parent-adolescent American orientation was linked to parents' use of unsupportive parenting techniques, which in turn was related to an increased sense of alienation between parents and adolescents, and that alienation was further associated with lower academic success and a higher level of depression in adolescents.

Immigration also involves cultural brokering, which has increasingly occurred in the United States as children and adolescents serve as mediators (cultural and linguistic) for their immigrant parents (Belhadj Kouider, Koglin, & Petermann, 2015; Kam & Lazarevic, 2014; Villanueva & Buriel, 2010). A recent study of Chinese American and Korean American adolescents revealed that they often serve as language brokers for their immigrant parents (Shen & others, 2014). In this study, language brokering for the mother was related to perceived maternal sacrifice, which in turn was associated with respect for the mother, and that respect was further linked to a lower level of externalizing problems in the adolescents.

In adopting characteristics of the U.S. culture, Latino families are increasingly embracing the importance of education (Garcia, 2012). Although their school dropout rates have remained higher than those of other ethnic groups, in the first decade of the twenty-first century they declined considerably (National Center for Education Statistics, 2012a, b).

In retaining positive aspects of their culture of origin, as research by Ross Parke and his colleagues (2011) indicates, Latino families continue to show a strong commitment to family after immigrating to the United States, even in the face of dealing with low-paying jobs and challenges in advancing economically. For example, divorce rates for Latino families are lower than for non-Latino White families of similar socioeconomic status.

ETHNICITY ISSUES

A number of ethnicity issues influence the development of adolescents and emerging adults. As we will see, however, it is important to consider factors related to SES when drawing conclusions about the role of ethnicity in the development of adolescents and emerging adults.

developmental **connection**

Families

Recent research on Chinese American families has focused on whether a "tiger parenting" style is common and whether it is associated with positive or negative developmental outcomes in adolescence. Connect to "Achievement, Work, and Careers."

Ethnicity and Socioeconomic Status A higher percentage of ethnic minority children and youth live in families characterized by poverty than do non-Latino children and youth (Schaefer, 2015). As indicated earlier in this chapter, in 2013, 27.2 percent of African American children and adolescents and 23.5 percent of Latino children and adolescents lived in poverty compared with 12.3 percent of non-Latino White children and adolescents (De Navas-Walt & Proctor, 2014).

Much of the research on ethnic minority adolescents and emerging adults has failed to distinguish between the dual influences of ethnicity and SES. Ethnicity and SES can interact in ways that exaggerate the influence of ethnicity because ethnic minority individuals are overrepresented in the lower socioeconomic levels of American society (Schaefer, 2015). Consequently, too often researchers have given ethnic explanations for aspects of adolescent and emerging adult development that were in reality based on SES rather than ethnicity.

A longitudinal study illustrated the importance of separating the influences of SES and ethnicity on the educational and occupational aspirations of individuals from 14 to 26 years of age (Mello, 2009). In this research, SES successfully predicted educational and occupational aspirations across ethnic groups. After controlling for SES, the researchers found that African American youth held the highest educational expectations, followed by Latino and Asian American/Pacific Islander, non-Latino White, and American Indian/Alaska Native youth.

Some ethnic minority youth are from middle-SES backgrounds, but economic advantage does not entirely enable them to escape the drawbacks of their ethnic minority status (Schaefer, 2015). Middle-SES ethnic minority youth are still subject to much of the prejudice, discrimination, and bias associated with being a member of an ethnic minority group. Despite being characterized as a "model minority" because of their strong achievement orientation and family cohesiveness, Japanese Americans still experience stress associated with ethnic minority status (Sue & others, 2015). Although middle-SES ethnic minority adolescents have more resources available to counter the destructive influences of prejudice and discrimination, they still cannot completely avoid the pervasive influences of negative stereotypes about ethnic minority groups.

That being said, the fact remains that many ethnic minority families are poor, and poverty contributes to the stressful life experiences of many ethnic minority adolescents (Harris & Graham, 2014; Koppelman, 2014). Vonnie McLoyd and her colleagues (McLoyd, Aikens, & Burton, 2006; McLoyd & others, 2009, 2011; McLoyd, Purtell, & Hardaway, 2015; Purtell & McLoyd, 2013) conclude that ethnic minority youth experience a disproportionate share of the adverse effects of poverty and unemployment in America today. Thus, many ethnic minority adolescents experience a double disadvantage: (1) prejudice, discrimination, and bias because of their ethnic minority status; and (2) the stressful effects of poverty.

Differences and Diversity   Historical, economic, and social experiences produce legitimate differences among various ethnic minority groups, and between ethnic minority groups and the majority non-Latino White group (Banks, 2014). Individuals belonging to a specific ethnic or cultural group share the values, attitudes, and stresses of that culture. Their behavior, while possibly different from that of the majority, nonetheless is often functional for them. Recognizing and respecting these differences is essential to getting along with others in a diverse, multicultural world. Every adolescent and adult needs to take the perspective of individuals from ethnic and cultural groups that are different from theirs and think, "If I were in their shoes, what kinds of experiences might I have had?" "How would I feel if I were a member of their ethnic or cultural group?" "How would I think and behave if I had grown up in their world?" Such perspective taking is a valuable way to increase one's empathy and understanding of individuals from other ethnic and cultural groups.

For most of the twentieth century, the ways ethnic minority groups differed from non-Latino Whites were conceptualized as *deficits,* or inferior characteristics on the part of the ethnic minority group. In recent years, there has been an effort to increasingly emphasize positive aspects of many ethnic groups, such as the family connectedness that characterizes many Latino families (Kopak & others, 2012).

Another important dimension of ethnic minority adolescents and emerging adults is their diversity (Schaefer, 2015; Trejos-Castillo, Bedore, & Trevino Schafer, 2013). Ethnic minority groups are not homogeneous; the individuals within them have different social, historical, and economic backgrounds. For example, Mexican, Cuban, and Puerto Rican immigrants are Latinos, but they had different reasons for migrating, came from varying socioeconomic backgrounds in their native countries, and experience different rates and types of employment in the United States. The U.S. federal government now recognizes the existence of 511 different Native American tribes, each having a unique ancestral background with differing values and characteristics. Asian Americans include Chinese, Japanese, Filipinos, Koreans, and Southeast Asians, each group having distinct ancestries and languages. The diversity of Asian Americans is reflected in their educational attainment: Some achieve a high level of education, whereas many others do not. For example, 95 percent of Taiwanese Americans and 92 percent of Korean Americans graduate from high school, but only 72 percent of Vietnamese Americans and 62 percent of Cambodian Americans do (Asian Pacific American Legal Center & Asian American Justice Center, 2011). Failure to recognize diversity and individual variations results in the stereotyping of an ethnic minority group.

Prejudice, Discrimination, and Bias   **Prejudice** is an unjustified negative attitude toward an individual because of the individual's membership in a group. These negative attitudes may be directed against people of a specific ethnic group, sex, age, religion, or other detectable characteristic. Our concern here is prejudice against ethnic minority groups.

Many ethnic minority individuals continue to experience persistent forms of prejudice, discrimination, and bias (Ajayi & Syed, 2014; Banks, 2014; Harris & Graham, 2014; Marks & others, 2015; Seaton & Douglass, 2014). Ethnic minority adolescents are taught in schools that often have a middle-SES, non-Latino White bias (Bucher, 2015; Spring, 2013). Discrimination and prejudice continue to be present in the media, interpersonal interactions, and daily conversations. Crimes, strangeness, poverty, mistakes, and deterioration can be mistakenly attributed to ethnic minority individuals or foreigners. One study revealed that adolescents' perceptions of racial discrimination were linked to negative views that the broader society holds about African Americans (Seaton, Yip, & Sellers, 2009).

Research studies provide insight into the discrimination experienced by ethnic minority adolescents (Benner & Graham, 2013; Cheng, Cohen, & Goodman, 2015; Smith-Bynum & others, 2014; Yip, 2015). Consider the following three studies:

· Discrimination against seventh- to tenth-grade African American students was related to their lower level of psychological functioning, including perceived stress,

prejudice An unjustified negative attitude toward an individual because of the individual's membership in a group.

Type of Racial Hassle	Percent of Adolescents Who Reported the Racial Hassle in the Past Year
Being accused of something or treated suspiciously	71.0
Being treated as if you were "stupid," being "talked down to"	70.7
Others reacting to you as if they were afraid or intimidated	70.1
Being observed or followed while in public places	68.1
Being treated rudely or disrespectfully	56.4
Being ignored, overlooked, not given service	56.4
Others expecting your work to be inferior	54.1
Being insulted, called a name, or harassed	52.2

FIGURE 5

AFRICAN AMERICAN ADOLESCENTS' REPORTS OF RACIAL HASSLES IN THE PAST YEAR

symptoms of depression, and lower perceived well-being; more positive attitudes toward African Americans were associated with more positive psychological functioning in adolescents (Sellers & others, 2006). Figure 5 shows the percentage of African American adolescents who reported experiencing different types of racial hassles in the past year.

- In a study of Dominican American, Chinese American, and African American sixth- to eighth-graders, Chinese Americans and boys perceived that they experienced more racial discrimination than did African Americans and girls (Niwa, Way, & Hughes, 2014).
- Latino adolescents encountered more discrimination than did Asian American adolescents, and the discrimination was linked to lower grade point averages and self-esteem and to more depressive symptoms and physical complaints (Huynh & Fuligni, 2010).
- African American adolescents' perceived personal experience of racial discrimination was linked to their higher level of delinquency (Martin & others, 2011).
- A research review concluded that mental health outcomes (depression and anxiety, for example) were the most commonly reported associations with racial discrimination in adolescence (Priest & others, 2013).
- In a study of perceptions of ethnic stigma by ethnic minority emerging adults across their transition to college, their perception that they were discriminated against decreased over time but their perception that their ethnic group is not valued and respected by society increased over time (Huynh & Fuligni, 2012).
- A recent study of more than 2,300 18- to 30-year-old African American and Latino college students found that perceived ethnic group discrimination was linked to depressive symptoms in both ethnic groups; however, having a positive ethnic identity lowered the depressive symptoms for Latino but not for African American students (Brittian & others, 2015).

Progress has been made in ethnic minority relations, but discrimination and prejudice still exist, and equality has not been achieved. Much remains to be accomplished (English, Lambert, & Ialongo, 2014; Grollman, 2012).

So far in this chapter, we have examined the effects of culture, socioeconomic status, and ethnicity on adolescent development. In the next section, you will see that there are substantial variations across countries, socioeconomic groups, and ethnic groups in the use of media and technology.

Review Connect Reflect

LG3 Summarize how ethnicity is involved in the development of adolescents and emerging adults

Review

- How has immigration affected ethnic minority adolescents and emerging adults?
- Why are adolescence and emerging adulthood a special juncture in the development of ethnic minority individuals?
- What are some important ethnicity issues that occur in adolescence and emerging adulthood?

Connect

- How can the concepts of individualism and collectivism,

described earlier in this chapter, help us understand the immigrant experiences of adolescents and emerging adults?

Reflect Your Own Personal Journey of Life

- Think for a few moments about your ethnic background. How did your ethnicity influence the way you experienced adolescence?

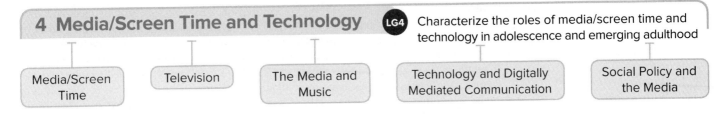

4 Media/Screen Time and Technology

LG4 Characterize the roles of media/screen time and technology in adolescence and emerging adulthood

Media/Screen Time

Television

The Media and Music

Technology and Digitally Mediated Communication

Social Policy and the Media

Few developments in society over the last 40 years have had a greater impact on adolescents than television, computers, and the Internet (Busschaert & others, 2015; Calvert, 2015; Maloy & others, 2014; Smaldino & others, 2015). The persuasive capabilities of television and the Internet are staggering.

MEDIA/SCREEN TIME

Many of today's adolescents have spent more time since infancy in front of a television set, and more recently in front of a computer and smart phones, than with their parents or in the classroom (Lever-Duffy & McDonald, 2015; Sterin, 2014). Television continues to have a strong influence on children's and adolescent's development, but children's use of other media and information/communication devices has led to the use of the term *screen time,* which includes how much time individuals spend watching television or DVDs, playing video games, and using computers or mobile media such as iPhones (Lloyd & others, 2014). Television is still the elephant in young children's media life, with 2- to 4-year-old children watching TV approximately 2 to 4 hours per day (Roberts & Foehr, 2008).

To better understand various aspects of U.S. adolescents' media use, the Kaiser Family Foundation funded three national surveys, in 1999, 2004, and 2009. The 2009 survey included more than 2,000 8- to 18-year-olds and documented that adolescent media use has increased dramatically in the last decade (Rideout, Foehr, & Roberts, 2010). Today's youth live in a world in which they are encapsulated by media, and media use increases dramatically in adolescence. According to the survey conducted in 2009, 8- to 11-year-olds used media 5 hours and 29 minutes a day, 11- to 14-year-olds an average of 8 hours and 40 minutes a day, and 15- to 18-year-olds an average of 7 hours and 58 minutes a day (see Figure 6). Thus, media use jumps more than 3 hours in early adolescence! The largest increases in media use in early adolescence are for TV and video games. TV use by youth increasingly has involved watching TV on the Internet, on an iPod/MP3 player, and on a cell phone. As indicated in Figure 6, time spent listening to music and using computers increases considerably among 11- to 14-year-old adolescents. And in the 2009 survey, adding up the daily media use figures to obtain weekly media use leads to the staggering levels of more than 60 hours a week of media use by 11- to 14-year-olds and almost 56 hours a week by 15- to 18-year-olds!

A major trend in the use of technology is the dramatic increase in media multitasking (Courage & others, 2015; Rothbart, & Posner, 2015; Smaldino & others, 2015). In the 2009 survey, when the amount of time spent multitasking was included in computing media use

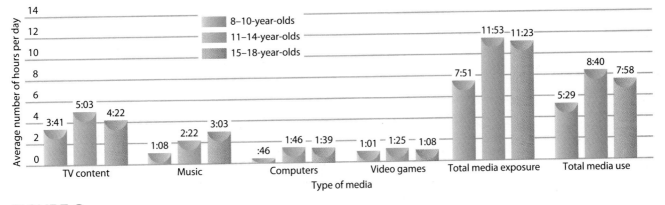

FIGURE 6

HOURS OF MEDIA USE BY U.S. 8- TO 18-YEAR-OLDS IN A TYPICAL DAY

(in other words, when each task was counted separately), 11- to 14-year-olds spent a total of nearly 12 hours a day exposed to media (the total is almost 9 hours a day when the effect of multitasking is not included) (Rideout, Foehr, & Roberts, 2010)! In this survey, 39 percent of seventh- to twelfth-graders said "most of the time" they use two or more media concurrently, such as surfing the Web while listening to music. In some cases, media multitasking—such as text messaging, listening to an iPod, and updating a YouTube site—is engaged in at the same time as doing homework. It is hard to imagine that this allows a student to do homework efficiently. Consider the following recent studies that involve media multitasking:

- A comparison of heavy and light media multitaskers revealed that heavy media multitaskers were more susceptible to interference from irrelevant information (Ophir, Nass, & Wagner, 2009).

- For 8- to 12-year-old girls, a higher level of media multitasking was linked to negative social well-being, while a higher level of face-to-face communication was associated with positive social-well-being indicators, such as greater social success, feeling more normal, and having fewer friends who parents thought were a bad influence (Pea & others, 2012).

- Heavy media multitaskers were more likely to be depressed and have social anxiety than their counterparts who engaged in a lower incidence of media multitasking (Becker, Alzahabi, & Hopwood, 2013).

- Individuals often engaged in media multitasking because they were less capable of blocking out distractions and focusing on a single task (Sanbonmatsu & others, 2013).

- A recent research review concluded that at a general level, digital technologies (surfing the Internet, texting someone) while engaging in a learning task (reading, listening to a lecture) distract learners and result in impaired performance on many tasks (Courage & others, 2015). Also in this research, it was concluded that when driving subtasks such as various perceptual-motor activities (steering control, changing lanes, maneuvering through traffic, braking, and acceleration) and ongoing cognitive tasks (planning, decision making, or maintaining a conversation with a passenger) are combined with interactive in-vehicle devices (phones, navigation aids, portable music devices), the task of driving becomes more complex and the potential for distraction high.

Mobile media, such as cell phones and iPods, are mainly driving the increased media use by adolescents. For example, in the 2004 survey, only 18 percent of youth owned an iPod or MP3 player; in 2009, 76 percent owned them. In 2004, 39 percent owned a cell phone; that figure jumped to 66 percent in 2009 (Rideout, Foehr, & Roberts, 2010).

Large individual differences characterize all forms of adolescent media use. In addition to the age differences described earlier, gender and ethnicity influence media use. Girls spend more time than boys on social networking sites and listening to music; boys spend more time than girls playing video games and computer games and going to video sites like YouTube (Rideout, Foehr, & Roberts, 2010).

In the recent national survey, African American and Latino youth used media daily more than did non-Latino White youth (Rideout, Foehr, & Roberts, 2010). The ethnic difference was especially pronounced in TV watching, with African American youth watching almost 6 hours a day, Latino youth more than 5 hours a day, and non-Latino White youth 3½ hours a day.

Screen time can have a negative influence on children and adolescents by making them passive learners, distracting them from doing homework, teaching them stereotypes, providing them with violent models of aggression, and presenting them with unrealistic views of the world. Among other concerns about children and adolescents having so much screen time are less time interacting with peers, decreased physical activity, increased rates of being overweight or obese, and poor sleep habits.

Consider the following recent research on links of screen time to obesity, changes in diet, sleep habits, physical activity, achievement, and anxiety and depression. A research review concluded that a higher level of screen time at 4 to 6 years of age was linked to increased obesity and lower physical activity from preschool through adolescence (te Velde & others, 2012). Another research review found that when their screen time exceeded two hours a day, children and adolescents were more likely to be overweight or obese (Atkin & others, 2014). Further, a recent study of 9- to 11-year-olds revealed that a higher number of screens in a child's bedroom was associated with higher obesity and lower sleep efficiency (Chaput & others, 2014). Also, a recent study found that greater screen time was associated with adolescent obesity (Mitchell & others, 2013). Another recent study of more than 10,000 9- to 16-year-olds found that each hour-per-day increase in television, electronic games, and DVDs/videos was linked with increased consumption of foods with low nutritional quality (Falbe & others, 2014). And a recent research review concluded that more extensive screen time was linked to more adverse sleep outcomes in children and adolescents, with the most negative associations involving computer use, video games, and mobile devices (Hale & Guan, 2015). A recent study also revealed that the higher the amount of screen time experienced by young adolescents, the lower their academic achievement (Syvaoja & others, 2013). Further, a recent study of Canadian youth found that duration of screen time was linked to anxiety and depression (Maras & others, 2015).

TELEVISION

Let's now look at a major aspect of screen time—television. Many children and adolescents spend more time in front of the television set than they do interacting with their parents. The persuasive capabilities of television are staggering. The 20,000 hours of television watched by the time the average American adolescent graduates from high school are greater than the number of hours spent in the classroom.

Television can have positive or negative effects on children's and adolescents' development. Television can have a positive influence by presenting motivating educational programs, increasing children's and adolescents' awareness of the world beyond their immediate environment, and providing models of prosocial behavior. However, television can have a negative influence on children and adolescents by making them passive learners, distracting them from doing homework, teaching them stereotypes, providing them with violent models of aggression, and presenting them with unrealistic views of the world (Murray & Murray, 2008). Further, researchers have found that a high level of TV viewing is linked to a greater incidence of obesity in youth (Escobar-Chaves & Anderson, 2008).

Television and Violence How strongly does televised violence influence a person's behavior? In one longitudinal study, the amount of violence viewed on television at age 8 was significantly related to the seriousness of criminal acts performed as an adult (Huesmann, 1986). In a second longitudinal study, childhood exposure to TV violence was linked with aggressive behavior on the part of young adult males and females (Huesmann & others, 2003).

These investigations are *correlational,* so we cannot conclude from them that television violence causes individuals to be more aggressive, only that watching television violence is *associated with* aggressive behavior. However, experimental research does provide evidence that viewing television violence can increase aggression. In one experiment, children were randomly assigned to one of two groups: One group watched shows taken directly from violent Saturday morning cartoon offerings on 11 different days; the second group watched cartoon shows with all of the violence removed (Steur, Applefield, & Smith, 1971). The children then were observed during play. The children who saw the TV cartoon violence kicked, choked, and pushed their playmates more than the children who watched nonviolent TV cartoon shows did. Because the children were assigned randomly to the two conditions (TV cartoons with violence versus TV cartoons with no violence), we can conclude that exposure to TV violence caused the increased aggression in this study.

A recent study revealed a link between media violence exposure and both physical aggression and relational aggression (Gentile, Mathieson, & Crick, 2010). In this study, the link with relational aggression was stronger for girls than for boys.

The television that young children watch may influence their behavior as adolescents. If so, then this conclusion supports the continuity view of adolescence. In a longitudinal study, girls who were more frequent preschool viewers of violent TV programs had lower grades than those who were infrequent viewers of such violence in preschool (Anderson & others, 2001). Also, viewing educational TV programs as

What are some positive and negative influences of television on adolescent development?
© Tom Stewart/Corbis

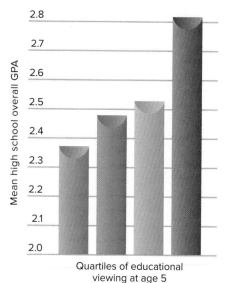

2.8
2.7
2.6
2.5
2.4
2.3
2.2
2.1
2.0

Mean high school overall GPA

Quartiles of educational
viewing at age 5

FIGURE 7

EDUCATIONAL TV VIEWING IN EARLY CHILDHOOD AND HIGH SCHOOL GRADE POINT AVERAGE FOR BOYS. When boys watched more educational television (especially Sesame Street) as preschoolers, they had higher grade point averages in high school. The graph displays the boys' early TV viewing patterns in quartiles and the means of their grade point averages. The bar on the left is for the lowest 25 percent of boys who viewed educational TV programs, the next bar the next 25 percent, and so on, with the bar on the right for the 25 percent of the boys who watched the most educational TV shows as preschoolers.

preschoolers was associated with higher grades, reading more books, and less aggression, especially for boys, in adolescence (see Figure 7).

Video Games   Violent video games, especially those that are highly realistic, also raise concerns about their effects on children and adolescents (DeWall, Anderson, & Bushman, 2013; Gentile & others, 2014a; Hollingdale & Greitemeyer, 2014). Correlational studies indicate that children and adolescents who extensively play violent electronic games are more aggressive and more likely to engage in delinquent acts than their counterparts who spend less time playing the games or do not play them at all (DeWall, Anderson, & Bushman, 2013; Gentile, 2011). A recent study found that playing violent video games was associated with higher degrees of desensitization to violence (Brockmyer, 2015). Also, a recent study of fifth-graders revealed that exposure to three types of media violence (television, video games, and music) was related to higher levels of aggressive behavior (Coker & others, 2015). And in a recent study of university students, violent video game playing by both males and females was linked to lower empathic concern (Fraser & others, 2012).

Are there any positive outcomes when adolescents play video games? Far more studies of video game use by adolescents have focused on possible negative outcomes than positive ones, but an increasing number of studies are examining possible positive outcomes (Adachi & Willoughby, 2013; Calvert, 2015). Researchers found that middle-school students who played prosocial video games subsequently behaved in more prosocial ways (Gentile & others, 2009). Research also indicates that playing video games can improve adolescents' visuospatial skills (Schmidt & Vandewater, 2008). And a recent study found that playing action video games improved attentional control (Chisholm & Kingstone, 2015).

Further, researchers such as Sandra Calvert and her colleagues (Bond, Richards, & Calvert, 2013; Calvert, 2015; Calvert, Bond, & Staiano, 2013; Calvert & Wartella, 2014) have revealed that video games requiring exercise are linked to weight loss in overweight adolescents. For example, a recent experimental study found that overweight adolescents lost more weight when they participated in a 10-week competitive exergame video condition (video games that require gross motor activity—in this study the Nintendo Wii EA Sports Active video game was used) than their overweight counterparts in a cooperative exergame condition or a no-video-game-play control condition (Staiano, Abraham, & Calvert, 2012). The weight loss in the competitive condition also was linked to improved executive function in this study.

A study of college students (average age 20 years old) found that a majority of the college men played games weekly or more frequently, while a majority of the college women had not played even one game in the past year (Padilla-Walker & others, 2010). In this study, video game use by college men was linked to a higher level of drug use and lower relationship quality with friends and parents. College women who played video games had a lower level of self-worth.

In sum, violence is pervasive in the media that adolescents use. Researchers have found that experiencing media violence is linked to adolescents' aggressive behavior (Brown & Bobkowski, 2011; Coker & others, 2015). Researchers also recently have found positive effects of video games that focus on prosocial behavior and exercise (Calvert, 2015).

Television, Video Games, and Sex   Adolescents, not unlike adults, like to watch television programs with sexual content (Hennessy & others, 2009). Watching television sex can influence adolescents' sexual attitudes and behavior. Researchers have shown that exposure to sexual content is related to more permissive attitudes about premarital and recreational sex (Ward, 2002). A research review concluded that adolescents who view more sexual content on TV are likely to initiate sexual intercourse earlier than their peers who view less sexual content on TV (Brown & Strasberger, 2007).

Further, a recent study revealed that video game consumption was linked to rape myth acceptance (shifting blame for sexual assault from the perpetrator to the victim) through connections with interpersonal aggression and hostile sexism (Fox & Potocki, 2015). Many recently developed video games have increased their sexualized portrayal of females to appeal to a male audience.

How might playing violent video games be linked to adolescent aggression?
© Bernhard Classen/age fotostock

A special concern about adolescents and television sex is that, although parents and teachers often feel comfortable discussing occupational and educational choices, independence, and consumer behavior with adolescents, they usually don't feel as comfortable discussing sex with them. The resulting absence of competing information (peers do talk about sex but often perpetuate misinformation) intensifies television's role in imparting information about sex. Nonetheless, as with television aggression, whether television sex influences the behavior of adolescents depends on a number of factors, including the adolescent's needs, interests, concerns, and maturity (Strasberger, Wilson, & Jordan, 2008).

Television and Achievement   The more time that children and adolescents spend watching TV, the lower their school achievement is (Comstock & Scharrer, 2006; Rideout, Foehr, & Roberts, 2010). Why might TV watching be negatively linked to achievement? Three possibilities involve interference, displacement, and self-defeating tastes/preferences (Comstock & Scharrer, 2006). In terms of interference, having a television on while doing homework can distract adolescents while they are doing cognitive tasks. In terms of displacement, television can take away time and attention from engaging in achievement-related tasks such as homework, reading, writing, and mathematics. Researchers have found that reading achievement is negatively linked with the amount of time spent watching TV (Comstock & Scharrer, 2006). In terms of self-defeating tastes and preferences, television attracts children to entertainment, sports, commercials, and other activities that capture their interest more than school achievement. Children who are heavy TV watchers tend to view books as boring (Comstock & Scharrer, 2006).

Are media use/screen time linked to changes in children's and adolescents' creativity? A recent research review concluded that there is a negative association between children's and adolescents' TV viewing and their creativity (Calvert & Valkenburg, 2011). An exception, though, is when they watch educational TV content that is designed to teach creativity through the use of imaginative characters (Calvert & Valkenburg, 2011).

Also, some types of television content—such as educational programming for young children—may enhance achievement. In one longitudinal study, viewing educational programs such as *Sesame Street* and *Mr. Rogers' Neighborhood* as preschoolers was related to a number of positive outcomes through high school, including higher grades, reading more books, and enhanced creativity (Anderson & others, 2001). Newer technologies, especially interactive television, hold promise for motivating children and adolescents to learn and become more exploratory in solving problems.

THE MEDIA AND MUSIC

Anyone who has been around adolescents very long knows that many of them spend huge amounts of time downloading MP3 files of their favorite music and watching music videos on television or on the Internet.

To date, no cause-and-effect studies exist to link either music or videos to an increased risk of early drug use in adolescence. For a small percentage of adolescents, though, certain music may provide a behavioral marker for psychological problems. For example, one study found that adolescents who spent more time listening to music with degrading sexual content were more likely to engage in sexual intercourse earlier than their peers who spent less time listening to this type of music (Martino & others, 2006). And another study revealed that higher use of music media was related to viewing the self as less physically attractive and having overall lower self-worth (Kistler & others, 2010). In this study, there were indications that adolescents may use music media as a source of social comparison against which they evaluate their own physical attractiveness and self-worth. Music media may also provide a context for modeling expectations about romantic relationships.

TECHNOLOGY AND DIGITALLY MEDIATED COMMUNICATION

Culture involves change, and nowhere is that change greater than in the technological revolution. Today's adolescents are experiencing this revolution with increased use of computers, the Internet, and cell phones (Lever-Duffy & McDonald, 2015; Smaldino & others, 2015).

developmental **connection**

Sexuality

Sex is explicitly portrayed in movies, TV shows, videos, lyrics of popular music, MTV, and Internet sites. Connect to "Sexuality."

They are using these and a variety of other digital devices to communicate, just as earlier generations used pens, postage stamps, and telephones to stay in touch with their friends. The new information society still relies on some basic non-technological competencies that adolescents need to develop: good communication skills, problem-solving ability, the capacity to think deeply, creativity, and positive attitudes. However, how young people pursue these competencies is being challenged and extended in ways and at a speed unknown to previous generations (Calvert, 2015).

The Internet   The **Internet** is the core of computer-mediated communication. The Internet combines thousands of interconnected computer networks worldwide to provide users with instant access to an incredible array of information—both positive and negative.

Internet Use by Adolescents   Youth throughout the world are increasingly using the Internet, despite substantial variation in usage rates in different countries around the world and in socioeconomic groups (Smaldino & others, 2015). Special concerns have emerged about children's and adolescents' access to information on the Internet, which has been largely unregulated. Youth can access adult sexual material, instructions for making bombs, and other information that is inappropriate for them (Straubhaar, LaRose, & Davenport, 2014). Concerns are being raised about the influence of excessive Internet use on adolescents' health. A recent study of Swiss eighth-graders found that excessive Internet users did not get adequate sleep (Suris & others, 2014). Another recent study of 14- to 17-year-olds revealed a link between high Internet use and elevated blood pressure (Cassidy-Bushrow & others, 2015).

A further concern is peer bullying and harassment on the Internet (called *cyberbullying*) (Bailin, Milanaik, & Adesman, 2014; Bayraktar & others, 2015; Bonanno & Hymel, 2013). One survey found that peer bullying offline and online were the most frequent threats that children and adolescents encountered (Palfrey & others, 2009). Another recent study revealed that victimization in both online and school settings were linked to lower self-esteem and higher stress and depression (Fredstrom, Adams, & Gilman, 2011). And yet another recent study found that offline relational aggression and having beliefs that support aggression predicted whether adolescents were likely to engage in Internet aggression (Werner, Bumpus, & Rock, 2010).

A recent study of college students found that when the Internet was used for shopping, entertainment, and pornography, negative outcomes resulted: higher levels of drinking and drug use, greater numbers of sexual partners, worse relationships with friends and parents, and lower self-worth; however, when college students used the Internet for schoolwork, positive outcomes resulted: lower levels of drug use and higher levels of self-worth (Padilla-Walker & others, 2010).

In one study, approximately half of parents reported that being online is more positive than watching TV for adolescents (Tarpley, 2001). However, a national survey indicated that 42 percent of U.S. 10- to 17-year-olds had been exposed to Internet pornography in the past year, with 66 percent of the exposure being unwanted (Wolak, Mitchell, & Finkelhor, 2007).

The Digitally Mediated Social Environment of Adolescents and Emerging Adults   The digitally mediated social environment of adolescents and emerging adults includes e-mail, instant messaging, social networking sites such as Facebook, chat rooms,

Internet The core of computer-mediated communication. The Internet system is worldwide and connects thousands of computer networks, providing an incredible array of information—both positive and negative—that adolescents can access.

videosharing and photosharing, multiplayer online computer games, and virtual worlds (Mesch, 2012; O'Keefe & others, 2011; Rideout, Foehr, & Roberts, 2010; Smaldone & others, 2015). The remarkable increase in the popularity of Facebook was reflected in its replacement of Google in 2010 as the most frequently visited Internet site. Most of these digitally mediated social interactions began on computers but more recently have also shifted to cell phones, especially smartphones (Underwood & others, 2012; Valkenburg & Peter, 2011).

What are some recent research results regarding adolescents' use of social media?
© Brendan O'Sullivan/Getty Images

Recent national surveys revealed dramatic increases in adolescents' use of social media and text messaging (Lenhart, Ling, & others, 2010; Lenhart, Purcell, & others, 2010; Rideout, Foehr, & Roberts, 2010). In 2009, nearly three-fourths of U.S. 12- to 17-year-olds reported using social networking sites (Lenhart, Purcell, & others, 2010). Eighty-one percent of 18- to 24-year-olds had created a profile on a social networking site and 31 percent of them visited a social networking site at least several times a day (Lenhart, Ling, & others, 2010). More emerging adult women were visiting a social networking site several times a day (33 percent) than were their male counterparts (24 percent).

In another report from the recent national survey, 75 percent of U.S. 12- to 17-year-olds had a cell phone (Lenhart, Ling, & others, 2010). In this survey and a further update (Lenhart, 2012), daily text messaging increased from 38 percent who texted friends daily in 2008 to 54 percent in 2009 to 60 percent in 2012. Also in the 2009 survey, half of the adolescents sent 50 or more text messages a day, with one-third sending 100 or more a day. Adolescent girls 14 to 17 years of age sent the most text messages, averaging more than 100 a day! The 12- to 13-year-old boys sent the fewest, approximately 20 a day. However, the 12- to 17-year-olds did not use Twitter to a great extent—just 8 percent of those who went online said they had tweeted. And fewer adolescents are blogging now: in 2006, 28 percent of adolescents said they blogged; by 2009 that percentage had dropped to 14 percent.

Text messaging has become the main way that adolescents connect with their friends, surpassing face-to-face contact, e-mail, instant messaging, and voice calling (Lenhart, Purcell, & others, 2010). In a recent update of how often adolescents send text messages, 12- to 17-year-olds sent an average of 60 text messages per day, an increase from 50 per day in 2009 (Lenhart, 2012). However, voice mail is the primary way that most adolescents prefer to connect with their parents.

In recent years, a special concern is the increase in sexualized text communication called *sexting*—that is, sending sexual word messages or sending sexually explicit/suggestive photographs via text messaging (Gordon-Messer & others, 2013; Klettke, Haliford, & Mellor, 2014; Temple & Choi, 2014). A recent study of emerging adults revealed that those who engaged in sexting were more likely to report recent substance use and high-risk sexual behaviors such as unprotected sex and sex with multiple partners (Benotsch & others, 2013).

One study examined the sequence of electronic communication technologies that college students in a Midwestern university used in managing their social networks (Yang & Brown, 2009). In this study, female college students followed a consistent sequence as their relationships developed, typically beginning by contacting new acquaintances on Facebook, then moving on to instant messaging, after which they might "exchange cell phone numbers, text each other, talk over their cell phone, and finally schedule a time to meet, if everything went well" (Yang & Brown, 2009, p. 2). Male college students were less likely to follow this sequence as consistently, although they did follow it more when communicating with females than males, suggesting that females may maintain more control over communication patterns.

A recent study of university students revealed that they expressed stronger interest in using Facebook to maintain social ties than to seek new relationships (Yang & Brown, 2013). In this study, the more the students were motivated to use Facebook to maintain existing relationships, the better their social adjustment was and the less lonely they said they were. By contrast, the more the students were motivated to pursue new relationships on Facebook, the poorer their social adjustment was and the more lonely they indicated they were. Another Facebook activity, status updating, was linked to poorer social adjustment and a higher level of loneliness.

developmental **connection**

Peers

Girls' friendships are more likely to focus on intimacy while boys' friendships tend to emphasize power and excitement. Connect to "Peers, Romantic Relationships, and Lifestyles."

What characterizes the online social environment of adolescents and emerging adults?
© L. Clarke/Corbis

Recent research has found that approximately one in three adolescents self-disclose better online than in person; in this research, boys report that they feel more comfortable self-disclosing online than do girls (Schouten, Valkenburg, & Peter, 2007; Valkenburg & Peter, 2009, 2011). In contrast, girls are more likely to feel comfortable self-disclosing in person than are boys. Thus, boys' self-disclosure may benefit from online communication with friends (Valkenburg & Peter, 2009, 2011). A recent study revealed that adolescents who were better adjusted at 13 to 14 years of age were more likely to use social networking sites at 20 to 22 years of age (Mikami & others, 2010). In this study, young adolescents' friendship quality and behavioral adjustment predicted similar qualities of interaction and problem behavior on social networking sites in emerging adulthood.

Facebook provides opportunities for adolescents and emerging adults to communicate with others who share their interests. Facebook is the most popular way that adolescents and emerging adults communicate on the Internet. Many adolescents and emerging adults who use Facebook apparently believe that the information they place on the site is private. However, social networking sites such as Facebook are not as secure in protecting private information as is often believed. Thus, if you are a Facebook user, you should never put your social security number, address, phone number, or date of birth on the site. Another good strategy is not to put information on Facebook that current or future employers might use against you in any way. And a final good strategy is to be aware that college administrators and personnel may be able to use the information you place on Facebook to evaluate whether you have violated college policies (such as college drug and language harassment policies).

Recently, concerns have been raised about links between online social networking and adolescents' mental health. For example, a recent research review concluded that prolonged use of social networking sites such as Facebook is related to having depressive symptoms, but researchers have not found a consistent link with self-esteem (Pantic, 2014).

Clearly, parents need to monitor and regulate adolescents' use of the Internet (Calvert & Wartella, 2014; Padilla-Walker & others, 2012). Consider Bonita Williams, who began to worry about how obsessed her 15-year-old daughter, Jade, had become with MySpace (Kornblum, 2006). She became even more concerned when she discovered that Jade was posting suggestive photos of herself and had given her cell phone number out to people in different parts of the United States. She grounded her daughter, blocked MySpace at home, and moved Jade's computer from her bedroom into the family room.

The following recent studies explored the role of parents in guiding adolescents' use of the Internet and media:

- A higher degree of parental monitoring of children's media use was linked to a number of positive outcomes (more sleep, better school performance, less aggressive behavior, and more prosocial behavior for third- through fifth-graders (Gentile & others, 2014b).

- Parents' high estimates of online dangers were not matched by their low rates of setting limits and monitoring their adolescents' online activities (Rosen, Cheever, & Carrier, 2008). Also in this study, adolescents who perceived that their parents had an indulgent parenting style (high in warmth and involvement but low in strictness and supervision) reported engaging in the most risky online behavior, such as meeting someone in person whom they had initially contacted on the Internet.

- Both maternal and paternal authoritative parenting predicted proactive monitoring of adolescent media use (Padilla-Walker & Coyne, 2011). As part of the authoritative parenting style, parental regulation included the use of active and restrictive mediation. Active mediation encourages parent/adolescent discussion of exposure to questionable media content; restrictive mediation involves parents' efforts to restrict certain media from adolescents' use.

- Problematic mother-adolescent (age 13) relationships that involved undermining attachment and autonomy predicted emerging adults' preference for online communication and greater probability of forming a relationship with someone met online, yet poorer quality in online relationships (Szwedo, Mikami, & Allen, 2011).

SOCIAL POLICY AND THE MEDIA

Adolescents are exposed to an expanding array of media that carry messages that shape adolescents' judgments and behavior (Roberts, Henriksen, & Foehr, 2009). The following social policy initiatives were recommended by the Carnegie Council on Adolescent Development (1995):

· *Encourage socially responsible programming.* There is good evidence of a link between media violence and adolescent aggression. The media also shape many other dimensions of adolescents' development—gender, ethnic, and occupational roles, as well as standards of beauty, family life, and sexuality. Writers, producers, and media executives need to recognize how powerful their messages are to adolescents and work with experts on adolescent development to provide more positive images to youth.

· *Support public efforts to make the media more adolescent-friendly.* Essentially, the U.S. media should better regulate themselves in regard to their influence on adolescents. All other Western nations have stronger regulations than the United States to foster appropriate educational programming.

· *Encourage media literacy programs as part of school curricula, youth and community organizations, and family life.* Many adolescents do not have the knowledge and skills to critically analyze media messages. Media literacy programs should focus not only on television, but also on the Internet, newspapers, magazines, radio, videos, music, and electronic games.

· *Increase media presentations of health promotions.* Community-wide campaigns using public service announcements in the media have been successful in reducing smoking and increasing physical fitness in adolescents. Use of the media to promote adolescent health and well-being should be increased.

· *Expand opportunities for adolescents' views to appear in the media.* The media should increase the number of adolescent voices in their presentations by featuring editorial opinions, news stories, and videos authored by adolescents. Some schools have found that this strategy of media inclusion of adolescents can be an effective dimension of education.

A review of social policy and the media by leading expert Amy Jordan (2008) acknowledged the difficulty of protecting the First Amendment right of free speech while still providing parents with adequate ways to protect their children and youth from unwanted content in their homes. Other experts argue that the government clearly can and should promote positive programming and provide more funding for media research (Brooks-Gunn & Donahue, 2008). For example, government can produce more public service media campaigns that focus on reducing risky behavior among adolescents.

---

developmental **connection**

Social Policy

The United States needs a developmentally attentive youth policy that applies to many areas of adolescents' lives. Connect to "Introduction."

Review *Connect* Reflect

 LG4 Characterize the roles of media/screen time and technology in adolescence and emerging adulthood

Review

- How extensively do adolescents use media and other electronic devices? How does their use vary across different types of devices?
- How is watching television related to adolescent development?
- What roles do music and the media play in adolescents' lives?
- How are technology, computers, the Internet, and cell phones linked to adolescent development?
- What are some social policy recommendations regarding media use by adolescents?

Connect

- What influence might heavy media use have on adolescents' goal setting?

Reflect *Your Own Personal Journey of Life*

- What was your use of various media in middle/junior and high school like? Did your use of the media in adolescence influence your development in positive or negative ways? Explain.

reach your **learning goals**

Culture

1 Culture, Adolescence, and Emerging Adulthood

 LG1 Discuss the role of culture in the development of adolescents and emerging adults

The Relevance of Culture for the Study of Adolescence and Emerging Adulthood

- Culture is the behavior, patterns, beliefs, and all other products of a specific group of people that are passed on from generation to generation. If the study of adolescence and emerging adulthood is to be a relevant discipline in the twenty-first century, increased attention will need to be focused on culture and ethnicity because there will be increased contact among people from varied cultural and ethnic backgrounds. For too long, the study of adolescence and emerging adulthood has been ethnocentric in the sense that the main participants in research studies have been middle-socioeconomic-status adolescents and emerging adults from the United States.

Cross-Cultural Comparisons

- Cross-cultural studies compare a culture with one or more other cultures, and they can provide information about the degree to which information about adolescent and emerging adult development is culture-specific. Cross-cultural comparisons reveal information such as variations in the time adolescents spend in different activities, in their levels of achievement, and in their attitudes about sexuality. Individualistic cultures focus on the individual—personal goals are more important than group goals, and values (feeling good, achievement, independence) are self-focused. Collectivistic cultures center on the group—the self is defined by in-group contexts, and personal goals are subordinated to preserve group integrity. U.S. adolescents have more discretionary time than do adolescents in other countries. In the United States, adolescents are more achievement-oriented than adolescents in many other countries, but East Asian adolescents spend more time on schoolwork.

Rites of Passage

- Rites of passage are ceremonies that mark an individual's transition from one status to another, especially into adult status. In many primitive cultures, rites of passage are well defined and provide an entry into the adult world. Western industrialized countries lack clearly delineated formal rites of passage that mark the transition to adulthood.

2 Socioeconomic Status and Poverty

LG2 Describe how socioeconomic status and poverty are related to adolescent development

What Is Socioeconomic Status?

- Socioeconomic status (SES) is the grouping of people with similar occupational, educational, and economic characteristics. Socioeconomic status often involves certain inequalities.

Socioeconomic Variation in Families, Neighborhoods, and Schools

- The families, neighborhoods, and schools of adolescents have socioeconomic characteristics that are related to the adolescent's development. Parents in low-SES families are more concerned that their children and adolescents conform to society's expectations; have an authoritarian parenting style; use physical punishment more in disciplining; and are more directive and less conversational with their children and adolescents than higher-SES parents are. Neighborhood variations such as housing quality and mix of high-, middle-, or low-SES residents can influence adolescents' adjustment and achievement. Schools in low-SES areas have fewer resources and are more likely to have students with lower achievement test scores and fewer students going on to college than schools in high-SES areas. Adolescents from affluent families also face adjustment challenges, especially high rates of substance use.

Poverty

- Poverty is defined by economic hardship, and its most common marker is the federal poverty threshold (based on the estimated cost of food multiplied by 3). Based on this threshold, the percentage of children under 18 years of age living in poverty increased from 17 percent in 2006 to 19 percent in 2008. The subculture of the poor often is characterized not only by economic hardship but also by social and psychological difficulties. When poverty is persistent and long-standing, it can have especially devastating effects on adolescent development.

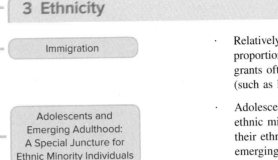

3 Ethnicity

LG3 Summarize how ethnicity is involved in the development of adolescents and emerging adults

Immigration

- Relatively high rates of immigration among minorities are contributing to the growth in the proportion of ethnic minority adolescents and emerging adults in the United States. Immigrants often experience stressors uncommon to or less prominent among longtime residents (such as language barriers, dislocations, and separation from support networks).

Adolescents and Emerging Adulthood: A Special Juncture for Ethnic Minority Individuals

- Adolescence and emerging adulthood are often a critical juncture in the development of ethnic minority individuals. Most ethnic minority individuals first consciously confront their ethnicity in adolescence. As they mature cognitively, ethnic minority adolescents and emerging adults become acutely aware of how the non-Latino White culture evaluates their ethnic group.

Ethnicity Issues

- Too often researchers do not adequately tease apart the influences of SES and ethnicity when they study ethnic minority groups, with the result that conclusions about ethnicity are sometimes made that are not warranted. Historical, economic, and social experiences produce many legitimate differences among ethnic minority groups and between ethnic minority groups and the White majority. Too often differences have been interpreted as deficits in ethnic minority groups. Failure to recognize the diversity within an ethnic minority group can lead to stereotyping. Many ethnic minority adolescents experience prejudice, discrimination, and bias.

4 Media/Screen Time and Technology

LG4 Characterize the roles of media/screen time and technology in adolescence and emerging adulthood

Media/Screen Time

- In terms of exposure, a significant increase in media/screen time has occurred recently, especially in 11- to 14-year-olds. Adolescents are increasing the amount of time they spend in media multitasking. The social environment of adolescents has increasingly become digitally mediated. Older adolescents reduce their TV viewing and video game playing and increase their music listening and computer use. There are large individual variations in adolescent media use.

Television

- Television can have a positive influence on adolescents by presenting motivating educational programs, increasing adolescents' information about the world beyond their immediate environment, and providing models of prosocial behavior. Negative aspects of television include promoting passive learning, being a distraction from homework, teaching stereotypes, providing violent models of aggression, presenting unrealistic views of the world, and increasing obesity. TV violence is not the only cause of adolescents' aggression, but most experts agree that it can induce aggression and antisocial behavior. There also is concern about adolescents' playing violent video games. However, some types of video games—such as those that focus on prosocial behavior or exercise—have positive effects on adolescent development. A special concern is the way sex is portrayed on television and the influence this can have on adolescents' sexual attitudes and behaviors. In general, TV viewing is negatively related to children's mental ability and achievement.

The Media and Music

- Adolescents are heavy consumers of music, spending huge amounts of time listening to music on their iPods or other electronic devices and watching music videos on television and the Internet.

Technology and Digitally Mediated Communication

- Today's adolescents are experiencing a technology revolution through the widespread availability of computers, the Internet, and sophisticated cell phones. The social environment of adolescents and emerging adults has increasingly become digitally mediated. The Internet continues to serve as the main focus of digitally mediated social interaction for adolescents and emerging adults but increasingly involves a variety of digital devices, including cell phones (especially smartphones). Adolescents' online time can have positive or negative outcomes. Large numbers of adolescents and college students engage in social networking on sites such as MySpace and Facebook.

Social Policy and the Media

- Social policy recommendations regarding the media include encouraging socially responsible programming, supporting public efforts to make the media more adolescent-friendly, and encouraging media literacy campaigns.

key terms

collectivism	ethnicity	individualism	rites of passage
cross-cultural studies	ethnocentrism	Internet	socioeconomic status (SES)
culture	feminization of poverty	prejudice	

key people

Sandra Calvert	Amy Jordan	Suniya Luthar	Carola Suárez-Orozco
Robert Crosnoe	Su Yeong Kim	Vonnie McLoyd	Carolyn Tamis-LeMonda
Andrew Fuligni	Reed Larson	Ross Parke	Suman Verma

resources for **improving the lives of adolescents**

Realizing the Potential of Immigrant Youth
Edited by Ann Masten and others (2012)
New York: Cambridge University Press
> Leading international researchers describe contemporary research on immigrant youth and the most promising strategies for their development.

Future Families: Diverse Forms, Rich Possibilities
Ross Parke (2013)
New York: Wiley
> Leading developmental psychologist Ross Parke explores the increasing diversity of families including immigrant families, and examines the cultural contexts of families.

The Eisenhower Foundation (www.eisenhowerfoundation.org)
> This foundation provides funds for a number of programs designed to improve the lives of children and adolescents living in low-income circumstances. The foundation is replicating in a number of states the successful Quantum Opportunities program developed by the Ford Foundation.

Children and Socioeconomic Status
Greg Duncan, Kathryn Magnuson, and Elizabeth Votruba-Drzal (2015)
> In M. H. Bornstein & T. Leventhal (Eds.), *Handbook of Child Psychology and Developmental Science* (7th ed., Vol. 4). New York: Wiley.

> An excellent, up-to-date chapter on poverty and the need for policies designed to improve the lives of children and adolescents who live in poverty conditions.

The African American Child (**2nd ed.**)
Yvette Harris and James Graham (2014)
New York: Springer
> Provides outstanding, up-to-date coverage of many aspects of the lives of African American children and adolescents, including a number of topics discussed in this chapter such as neighborhoods and communities, families, and media use.

Media and the Well-Being of Children and Adolescents
Amy Jordan and Daniel Romer (Eds.) (2014)
New York: Oxford University Press
> An excellent source for recent theory and research on many aspects of media influence on children and adolescents, with contributions from leading experts in the field.

chapter 13

PROBLEMS IN ADOLESCENCE AND EMERGING ADULTHOOD

chapter outline

1 Exploring Adolescent and Emerging Adult Problems

Learning Goal 1 Discuss the nature of problems in adolescence and emerging adulthood

The Biopsychosocial Approach

The Developmental Psychopathology Approach

Characteristics of Adolescent and Emerging Adult Problems

Stress and Coping

Resilience

2 Problems and Disorders

Learning Goal 2 Describe some problems and disorders that characterize adolescents and emerging adults

Drug Use

Juvenile Delinquency

Depression and Suicide

Eating Disorders

3 Interrelation of Problems and Prevention/Intervention

Learning Goal 3 Summarize the interrelation of problems and ways to prevent or intervene in problems

Adolescents with Multiple Problems

Prevention and Intervention

© BananaStock/PunchStock RF

Annie, a 15-year-old cheerleader, was tall, blonde, and attractive.

No one who sold liquor to her questioned her age. She got her money from babysitting and what her mother gave her to buy lunch. Annie was kicked off the cheerleading squad for missing practice so often, but that didn't stop her drinking. Soon she and several of her peers were drinking almost every day. Sometimes they skipped school and went to the woods to drink. Annie's whole life began to revolve around her drinking. After a while, her parents began to detect Annie's problem. But their attempts to get her to stop drinking by punishing her were unsuccessful. It went on for two years, and, during the last summer, anytime she saw anybody, she was drunk. Not long ago, Annie started dating a boy she really liked, and he refused to put up with her drinking. She agreed to go to Alcoholics Anonymous and has successfully stopped drinking for four consecutive months. Her goal is continued abstinence.

Arnie is 13 years old. He has a history of committing thefts and physical assaults. The first theft occurred when Arnie was 8—he stole an iPhone® from an Apple Retail Store. The first physical assault took place a year later, when he shoved his 7-year-old brother up against the wall, bloodied his face, and then threatened to kill him with a butcher knife. Recently, the thefts and physical assaults have increased. In just the past week, he stole a television set, struck his mother repeatedly and threatened to kill her, broke some neighborhood streetlights, and threatened youths with a wrench and a hammer. Arnie's father left home when Arnie was 3 years old. Until the father left, his parents argued extensively, and his father often beat up his mother. Arnie's mother indicates that, when Arnie was younger, she was able to control him, but in the last several years she has lost that control. Arnie's volatility and dangerous behavior have resulted in the recommendation that he be placed in a group home with other juvenile delinquents.

preview

At various points in other chapters, we have considered adolescent and emerging adult problems. For example, we have discussed sexual problems, school-related problems, and achievement-related problems. In this chapter we focus exclusively on adolescent and emerging adult problems, describing different approaches to understanding these problems, exploring some important problems we have not yet discussed, and outlining ways to prevent and intervene in problems.

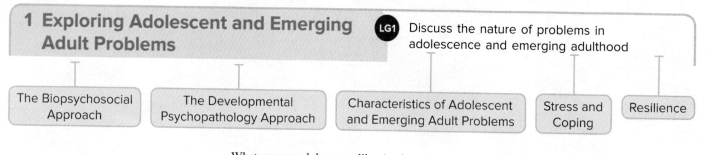

What causes adolescents like Annie and Arnie to have problems? What are some characteristics of the problems adolescents and emerging adults develop? How are stress and coping involved with these problems? What characterizes resilient adolescents?

THE BIOPSYCHOSOCIAL APPROACH

The **biopsychosocial approach** emphasizes that biological, psychological, and social factors interact to produce the problems experienced by adolescents, emerging adults, and people of other ages (see Figure 1). Thus, if an adolescent or emerging adult engages in substance abuse it may be due to a combination of biological factors (heredity and brain processes, for example), psychological factors (low conscientiousness and low self-control, for example), and social factors (relationship difficulties with parents and peers, for example). In other chapters we have explored biological, psychological, and social factors that can contribute to the development of problems in adolescence. In our further examination of the biopsychosocial approach, we will especially highlight biological, psychological, and social factors that adolescence uniquely contributes to these problems.

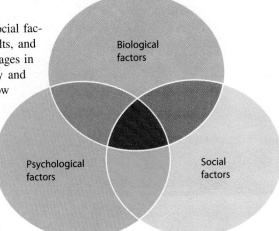

FIGURE 1

THE BIOPSYCHOSOCIAL APPROACH

Biological Factors Scientists who adopt a biological approach focus on factors such as genes, puberty, hormones, and the brain as causes of adolescent and emerging adult problems.

Early maturation is linked to a number of problems for adolescent girls, including drug abuse and delinquency (Susman & Dorn, 2013). Further, the hormonal changes associated with puberty have been proposed as a factor in the higher rate of depression in adolescent girls than adolescent boys (Conley & Rudolph, 2009). How adolescents handle their emerging sexual interest also is linked to whether or not they develop problems (Jeha & others, 2015; Ramiro & others, 2015). Early sexual intercourse is linked to other problems, including drug abuse and delinquency. The later development of the prefrontal cortex in concert with the earlier maturation of the amygdala may contribute to the increased incidence of risk taking and sensation seeking that emerges in adolescence (Casey, 2015; Steinberg, 2015a, b). The implication of these changes in the brain is that adolescents may not be mature enough in their thinking to control their behavior in risky situations—and thus may develop problems.

developmental **connection**

Brain Development

The emerging fields of developmental cognitive neuroscience and developmental social neuroscience emphasize the importance of studying connections across biological, cognitive, and socioemotional processes. Connect to "Introduction."

Psychological Factors Among the psychological factors that have been proposed as important influences on adolescent and emerging adult problems are identity, personality traits, decision making, and self-control. Developing a positive identity is central to healthy adjustment and academic success in adolescence and emerging adulthood (Cooper, Gonzales, & Wilson, 2015; McLean & Syed, 2015). The search for a coherent identity may lead to experimentation with different identities, one or more of which may involve problems. Wide emotional swings characterize adolescence, especially early adolescence. When such emotional swings become intensely negative, as in the emotion of sadness, depression may result (Consoli & others, 2015). Recall the Big Five personality traits (openness to experience, conscientiousness, extraversion, agreeableness, and neuroticism) and remember that adolescents who are low in conscientiousness are more likely to have substance abuse and conduct problems than their high-conscientiousness counterparts (Anderson & others, 2007). Adolescence is a time of increased decision making, and for many adolescents their emotions may overwhelm their decision-making ability and contribute to the development of problems (Steinberg, 2015a, b). Another psychological factor that is important in understanding adolescent problems is self-control. For example, adolescents who have not adequately developed self-control are more likely to develop substance-abuse problems and to engage in delinquent acts than those who have higher levels of self-control (Loeber & Burke, 2011).

developmental **connection**

Personality

Conscientiousness is increasingly recognized as a key trait in understanding adolescent problems. Connect to "The Self, Identity, Emotion, and Personality."

Social Factors The social factors that have especially been highlighted as contributors to adolescent problems are the social contexts of family, peers, schools, socioeconomic status, poverty, and neighborhoods. Many aspects of family processes can contribute to the development of problems in adolescence, including a persistent high level of parent-adolescent conflict, inadequate parental monitoring of adolescents, and insecure attachment (Kobak & Kerig, 2015; Smokowski & others, 2015).

In adolescence, individuals spend more time with peers than in childhood, and the increased time with peers can have positive or negative effects on adolescent development (Wentzel, 2013, 2015). Adolescents who don't become adequately connected to the world of peers may develop problems. Rejected adolescents may be especially prone to such problems.

biopsychosocial approach Approach that emphasizes that problems develop through an interaction of biological, psychological, and social factors.

What are some biological, psychological, and social factors that can contribute to the development of adolescent problems?
(top): © Adam Gault/Getty Images RF; (bottom): © Taxi/Getty Images RF

The term "developmental pathways" is central to discussions of developmental psychopathology as a way of conceptualizing the relations between early and later adaptation.

—Byron Egeland

Contemporary psychologist, University of Minnesota

developmental psychopathology approach
Approach that focuses on describing and exploring the developmental pathways of problems.

Hanging out with peers and friends who engage in delinquency or substance abuse contributes to the development of these problems in adolescence (Rubin, Bukowski, & Bowker, 2015). Also, some aspects of romantic relationships, which emerge in adolescence for the first time, are linked to adolescent problems (Cui & others, 2012). For example, early dating is related to substance abuse, and unwanted dissolution of a romantic relationship is associated with depression (Furman & Rose, 2015).

We have discussed how many middle schools are too impersonal to adequately meet the needs of young adolescents who are going through substantial biological, cognitive, and socioemotional changes (Wigfield & others, 2015). Most secondary schools don't offer adequate counseling services to help adolescents cope with these changes or to assist adolescents who have problems. Further, adolescents who are not adequately engaged with school drop out and often develop other problems such as substance abuse and delinquency.

Throughout this edition we have emphasized how socioeconomic status and poverty contribute to adolescent problems (McLoyd, Purtell, & Hardaway, 2015). Poverty makes adolescents vulnerable to many problems, especially delinquency (Duncan & others, 2015). However, recall that adolescents, especially boys, from affluent families are at risk for developing substance-abuse problems (Ansary, McMahon, & Luthar, 2012). Also, the quality of neighborhoods is linked to development of problems. For example, adolescents who grow up in neighborhoods with high crime rates and poor-quality schools are at increased risk for developing problems (Leventhal, Dupere, & Shuey, 2015).

THE DEVELOPMENTAL PSYCHOPATHOLOGY APPROACH

The **developmental psychopathology approach** focuses on describing and exploring the developmental pathways of problems. Many researchers in this field seek to establish links between early precursors of a problem (such as risk factors and early experiences) and outcomes (such as substance abuse, delinquency, and depression) (Cicchetti, 2016; Cicchetti & Toth, 2015; Fearon, 2015; Masten & others, 2015; Motti-Stefanidi, Masten, & Asendorph, 2015). A developmental pathway describes continuities and transformations in factors that influence outcomes. For example, Arnie's story (described at the beginning of the chapter) indicated a possible link between early negative parenting experiences, including his father's abuse of his mother, and Arnie's delinquency in adolescence.

The developmental psychopathology approach often involves the use of longitudinal studies to track the unfolding of problems over time (Fraley, Roisman, & Haltigan, 2013; Nigg, 2015). This approach also seeks to identify *risk factors* that might predispose children and adolescents to develop problems such as substance abuse, juvenile delinquency, and depression (Melchior & others, 2014; St. Clair & others, 2015; Steinberg & Drabick, 2015), as well as *protective factors* that might help to shield children from developing problems (Englund & others, 2011; Zeiders & others, 2015).

Recently considerable interest in the developmental psychopathology approach has focused on **developmental cascades,** which involve connections across domains over time that influence developmental pathways and outcomes (Cicchetti, 2016; Cicchetti & Toth, 2015; Masten, 2014a, b, c; Masten & others, 2015). Developmental cascades can encompass connections among a wide range of biological, cognitive, and social processes, including many social contexts such as families, peers, schools, and culture (Petersen & others, 2015; Zeiders & others, 2015). Further, links between domains that produce positive or negative outcomes may occur at various points in development, such as early childhood, later in adolescence or during emerging adulthood, and in intergenerational relationships. Gerald Patterson and his colleagues (Forgatch & Patterson, 2010; Forgatch & others, 2009; Patterson, Forgatch, & DeGarmo, 2010; Patterson, Reid, & Dishion, 1992) have conducted extensive research based on a developmental cascade approach. The theme of this approach is that high levels of coercive parenting and low levels of positive parenting lead to the development of antisocial behavior in children, which in turn connects children and adolescents to negative experiences in peer contexts (being rejected by nondeviant peers and becoming friends with deviant peers, for example) and school contexts (having academic difficulties, for example), which further intensifies the adolescent's antisocial behavior (Patterson & others, 2010).

The identification of risk factors might suggest avenues for both prevention and treatment (Cicchetti & Toth, 2015; Masten & others, 2015; Motti-Stefanidi, Masten, & Asendorpf, 2015). For example, researchers have identified parental psychopathology as a risk factor for childhood depression: Specifically, parents who suffer from depression, an anxiety disorder, or substance abuse are more likely to have children who experience depression (Wilson & others, 2014). One study revealed that maternal depressive symptoms during a child's infancy were linked to the development of depressive symptoms in childhood and adolescence (Bureau, Easterbrooks, & Lyons-Ruth, 2009). Further, a recent study revealed that fathers' and mothers' alcohol use predicted early alcohol use by their children (Kerr & others, 2012). And in a recent study, parental psychiatric status (depressive and anxiety disorders, substance use disorder, and others), offspring personality (negative emotionality) at 11 years of age, offspring internalizing and externalizing symptoms, poor parent-child relationships, early pubertal onset, and child maltreatment predicted the subsequent development of major depressive disorder (Wilson & others, 2014).

Adolescent and emerging adult problems can be categorized as internalizing or externalizing:

- **Internalizing problems** occur when individuals turn their problems inward. Examples of internalizing problems include anxiety and depression.
- **Externalizing problems** occur when individuals turn their problems outward. An example of an externalizing problem is juvenile delinquency.

Links have been established between patterns of problems in childhood and outcomes in adolescence and emerging adulthood (St. Clair & others, 2015). A longitudinal study found that internalizing problems at age 7 predicted a lower level of academic competence at age 12 and that academic competence at age 9 was associated with a lower incidence of internalizing and externalizing problems at age 12 (Englund & Siebenbruner, 2012). Also, in this study earlier externalizing problems were linked to increased alcohol use in adolescence. In another study, males with internalizing patterns (such as anxiety and depression) during the elementary school years were likely to have similar problems at age 21, but they did not have an increased risk of externalizing problems as young adults (Quinton, Rutter, & Gulliver, 1990). Similarly, the presence of an externalizing pattern (such as aggression or antisocial behavior) in childhood elevated the risk for antisocial problems at age 21. For females in the same study, both early internalizing and early externalizing patterns predicted internalizing problems at age 21.

What characterizes internalizing and externalizing problems?
(top): © Maria Taglienti-Molinari/Getty Images RF; (bottom): © SW Productions/Getty Images RF

Alan Sroufe and his colleagues (Sroufe, 2007; Sroufe & others, 2005; Sroufe, Coffino, & Carlson, 2010) have found that anxiety problems in adolescence are linked with insecure resistant attachment in infancy (sometimes the infant clings to the caregiver and at other times pushes away from closeness) and that conduct problems in adolescence are related to avoidant attachment in infancy (the infant avoids the caregiver). Sroufe concludes that a combination of early supportive care (attachment security) and early peer competence helps to buffer adolescents from developing problems. In another developmental psychopathology study, Ann Masten (2001; Masten & Reed, 2002; Masten & others, 2010) followed 205 children for ten years from childhood into adolescence and emerging adulthood. She found that good intellectual functioning and parenting served protective roles in keeping adolescents and emerging adults from engaging in antisocial behaviors. Later in this chapter, we further explore such factors in our discussion of resilient adolescents and emerging adults.

John Schulenberg and Nicole Zarrett (2006) described mental health, well-being, and problems during emerging adulthood and their continuity/discontinuity with adolescence. For the population in general, well-being tends to increase during emerging adulthood, and some problems, such as theft and property damage, decrease. For example, a recent study found that externalizing problems increased during adolescence and then decreased during emerging adulthood (Petersen & others, 2015). However, certain mental health disorders, such as major depression, increase for some individuals during emerging adulthood. One study revealed that

developmental cascades A developmental psychopathology approach that emphasizes connections across domains over time to influence developmental pathways and outcomes.

internalizing problems Emotional conditions that develop when individuals turn problems inward. Examples include anxiety and depression.

externalizing problems Behavior that occurs when individuals turn problems outward. An example is juvenile delinquency.

developmental **connection**

Family

In virtually every area of adolescent problems, family processes and parenting are thought to play important roles. Connect to "Sexuality" and "Families."

alcohol use, marijuana use, and sex with multiple partners increased, whereas driving after drinking, aggression, and property crimes decreased from the last three months of high school through the end of the first year of college (Fromme, Corbin, & Kruse, 2008).

Overall, though, there is continuity between the presence of mental health problems in adolescence and the presence of similar problems in emerging adulthood. As we consider various problems later in the chapter, such as drugs, delinquency, and depression, we will revisit the continuity and discontinuity of these problems from adolescence through emerging adulthood.

CHARACTERISTICS OF ADOLESCENT AND EMERGING ADULT PROBLEMS

The spectrum of adolescent and emerging adult problems is wide. The problems vary in their severity and in how common they are for females and males and for different socioeconomic groups. Some problems are short-lived; others can persist over many years. Some problems are more likely to appear at one developmental level than at another. In one study, depression, truancy, and drug abuse were more common among older adolescents, whereas arguing, fighting, and being too loud were more common among younger adolescents (Edelbrock, 1989).

In a large-scale investigation by Thomas Achenbach and Craig Edelbrock (1981), adolescents from a lower-SES background were more likely to have problems than those from a middle-SES background. Most of the problems reported for adolescents from a lower-SES background were undercontrolled, externalizing behaviors—destroying others' belongings and fighting, for example. These behaviors also were more characteristic of boys than of girls. The problems of middle-SES adolescents and girls were more likely to be overcontrolled and internalizing—anxiety or depression, for example.

The behavioral problems most likely to cause adolescents to be referred to a clinic for mental health treatment were feelings of unhappiness, sadness, or depression, and poor school performance (see Figure 2). Difficulties in school achievement, whether secondary to other kinds of problems or primary problems in themselves, account for many referrals of adolescents.

In another investigation, Achenbach and his colleagues (1991) compared the problems and competencies of 2,600 children and adolescents 4 to 16 years old who were assessed at intake into mental health services with those of 2,600 demographically matched nonreferred children and adolescents. Lower-SES children and adolescents had more problems and fewer competencies than did their higher-SES counterparts. Children and adolescents had more problems when they had fewer related adults in their homes, had biological parents who were

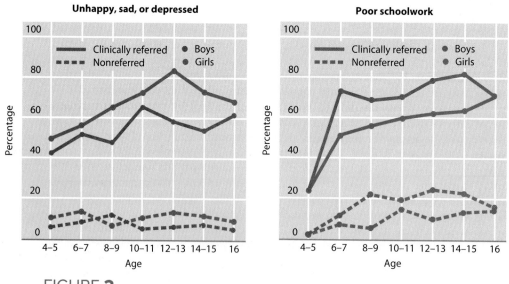

FIGURE **2**

THE TWO ITEMS MOST LIKELY TO DIFFERENTIATE CLINICALLY REFERRED AND NONREFERRED CHILDREN AND ADOLESCENTS

unmarried in their homes, had parents who were separated or divorced, lived in families who received public assistance, or lived in households in which family members had received mental health services. Children and adolescents who had more externalized problems came from families in which parents were unmarried, separated, or divorced, as well as from families who were receiving public assistance.

Many studies have shown that factors such as poverty, ineffective parenting, and mental disorders in parents predict adolescent problems (Cicchetti, 2016; Cicchetti & Toth, 2015; Duncan & others, 2015). Predictors of problems are called *risk factors*. A risk factor indicates an elevated probability of a problematic outcome in groups of people who have that factor. Children with many risk factors are said to have a "high risk" for problems in childhood and adolescence, but not every one of them will develop problems.

Some researchers think primarily in terms of risk factors when they study adolescent problems, whereas others argue that conceptualizing problems in terms of risk factors creates a perception that is too negative (Lerner & others, 2015). Instead, they highlight the developmental assets of youth (Lerner & others, 2015). For example, Peter Benson (2006; Benson & others, 2006; Benson & Scales, 2009, 2011), former director of the Search Institute in Minneapolis, has prescribed 40 developmental assets that adolescents need in order to achieve positive outcomes in their lives. Half of these assets are external, half internal. Each of the 40 assets has been shown scientifically to promote healthy adolescent development.

The 20 *external* assets include the following:

- *Support* (such as family and neighborhood)
- *Empowerment* (such as adults in the community valuing youth and giving them useful community roles)
- *Boundaries* and expectations (such as the family setting clear rules and consequences and monitoring the adolescent's whereabouts, as well as the presence of positive peer influence)
- *Constructive* use of time (such as engaging in creative activities three or more times a week and participating three or more hours a week in organized youth programs)

The 20 *internal* assets include the following:

- *Commitment* to learning (such as being motivated to achieve in school and doing at least one hour of homework on school days)
- *Positive values* (such as helping others and demonstrating integrity)
- *Social competencies* (such as knowing how to plan and make decisions and having interpersonal competencies like empathy and friendship skills)
- *Positive identity* (such as having a sense of control over life and high self-esteem)

developmental **connection**

Social Policy

An important social policy agenda is a strengths-based approach to adolescent problems. Connect to "Introduction."

In research conducted by the Search Institute, adolescents with more of the developmental assets reported engaging in fewer risk-taking behaviors, such as alcohol and tobacco use, sexual intercourse, and violence. For example, in one survey of more than 12,000 ninth- to twelfth-graders, 53 percent of the students with 0 to 10 assets reported using alcohol three or more times in the past month or getting drunk more than once in the past two weeks, compared with only 16 percent of the students with 21 to 30 assets or 4 percent of the students with 31 to 40 assets. On the other side of the coin, the assets not only prevent risky behaviors but also promote some behaviors that society values. For example, youth with 31 to 40 assets are far more likely to succeed in school and maintain good physical health than youth with 0 to 10 or 11 to 20 of the assets.

STRESS AND COPING

Seventeen-year-old Alan comments, "I never thought it would be so hard to grow up. I feel pressure all the time. My parents put tremendous pressure on me. I wish someone could help me cope better with all these pressures." Let's explore the nature of stress in individuals like Alan and ways they can cope effectively with the stress.

Stress Although G. Stanley Hall (1904) and others overdramatized the extent of storm and stress in adolescence, many adolescents and emerging adults today experience stressful circumstances that can affect their development. Just what is stress? **Stress** is the response of individuals to stressors, which are circumstances and events that threaten them and tax their coping abilities.

A car accident, a low grade on a test, a lost wallet, a conflict with a friend—all these might be stressors in your life. Some stressors are acute; in other words, they are sudden events or stimuli such as being cut by falling glass. Other stressors are chronic, or long-lasting, such as being malnourished or HIV-positive. These are physical stressors, but there also are emotional and psychosocial stressors such as the death of a loved one or being discriminated against.

Are there developmental changes in how much stress adolescents report that they experience? One study of 12- to 19-year-olds revealed that perceptions of having stress decreased in late adolescence and that the use of coping strategies that were active (such as seeking advice from parents or friends on emotional difficulties) and internal (such as reflecting about different solutions to a problem) increased as adolescents got older (Seiffge-Krenke, Aunola, & Nurmi, 2009).

Stress may come from many different sources for adolescents and emerging adults (Compas & Reeslund, 2009; Mash & Wolfe, 2015; Seiffge-Krenke, 2011). Sources of stress are life events, daily hassles, and sociocultural factors.

Life Events and Daily Hassles Think about your own life. What events have created the most stress for you? Some events are big problems and may occur in clusters, like the breakup of a long-standing relationship, the death of someone you loved, your parents' divorce, a life-threatening disease such as cancer, a personal injury, or the stress of a war or a disaster (Andreotti & others, 2015; Ganong, Coleman, & Russell, 2015; Howell & others, 2015; Masten & others, 2015; Schwarzer & Luszczynska, 2013). Other occurrences involve the everyday circumstances of your life, such as not having enough time to study, arguing with your girlfriend or boyfriend, or not getting enough credit for work you did at your job.

Individuals who have had major life changes (loss of a close relative, the divorce of parents) have a higher incidence of cardiovascular disease and early death than those who do not (Taylor, 2011b). Researchers have found that when several stressors are simultaneously experienced, the effects may be compounded (Rutter & Garmezy, 1983). For example, one study found that people who felt besieged by two chronic life stressors were four times more likely to eventually need psychological services than those who had to cope with only one chronic stressor (Rutter, 1979). One study revealed that adolescents who had positive relationships with their parents did not show an increase in externalizing problems after experiencing stressful life events (Oliva, Jimenez, & Parra, 2008). Another study found that adolescents with better emotion regulation skills who experienced negative life events were less likely to develop anxiety and depression than their counterparts with less effective emotion regulation skills (McLaughlin & Hatzenbuehler, 2009).

Some psychologists conclude that information about daily hassles and daily uplifts provides better clues about the effects of stressors than the examination of life events (Aldwin & others, 2014; Hamilton & Julian, 2014; Jacob & others, 2014). Enduring a boring but tense job or living in poverty does not show up on scales of major life events. Yet the everyday pounding from these conditions can add up to a highly stressful life and eventually contribute to psychological disorders or physical ailments.

Stress in relationships is especially common among adolescents (Persike & Seiffge-Krenke, 2015). Between 46 percent and 82 percent of the everyday stressful events reported by adolescents involve interpersonal relationships, especially conflicts with parents, peers, and romantic partners (Seiffge-Krenke & others, 2009). For example, recent studies across 21 countries revealed that adolescents' stress levels were highest with parents and at school, while the lowest stress occurred with peers and romantic partners (Persike & Seiffge-Krenke, 2012, 2014).

Adolescent girls are more sensitive to relationship stress; they report higher levels of relationship stress and are more likely to use coping strategies that maintain relationships (Seiffge-Krenke, 2011). When such relationships are destructive, staying in them too long can produce depressive symptoms (Brockie & others, 2015; Hamilton & others, 2015).

What are the biggest hassles for college students? One study showed that the most frequent daily hassles of college students were wasting time, being lonely, and worrying about

stress The response of individuals to stressors, which are circumstances and events that threaten and tax their coping abilities.

All Stressed Out

"Some of my friends are so messed up. My friend Abby is depressed all the time. She secretly told me that she thinks about killing herself. I want to tell someone, but she made me promise not to. I don't know what to do. I'm pretty sure my other friend Alexandra has an eating disorder. She's constantly talking about how many calories something has, and all she eats is lettuce! I try to be there for them, but I've got so much of my own stuff to deal with. I feel anxious and depressed all of the time. I don't know what to do."

—*LAUREN*

_____

(Source: Zager & Rubenstein, 2002, p. 141)

_____

What coping strategies might help an adolescent in Lauren's situation to better deal with the problems described here?

meeting high achievement standards (Kanner & others, 1981). In fact, the fear of failing in our success-oriented world often plays a role in college students' depression. College students also indicated that having fun, laughing, going to movies, getting along well with friends, and completing a task were their main sources of daily uplifts.

Critics of the daily-hassles approach argue that it suffers from some of the same weaknesses as life-events scales (Dohrenwend & Shrout, 1985). For example, knowing about a person's daily irritations and problems tells us nothing about her or his perceptions of stressors, physiological resilience to stress, or coping ability and strategies. Further, the daily-hassles and daily-uplifts scales have not been consistently linked to objective measures of health and illness.

Sociocultural Factors   Sociocultural factors help to determine which stressors individuals are likely to encounter, whether they are likely to perceive events as stressful or not, and how they believe stressors should be confronted (Gauvain & Perez, 2015; Nair & others, 2013). As examples of sociocultural factors involved in stress, let's examine gender, conflict between cultures, and poverty.

Do males and females respond to stressors in the same way? Shelley Taylor (2006, 2011a, b, c, 2015) proposed that females are less likely to respond to stressful and threatening situations with a fight-or-flight response than males are. Taylor argues that females are more likely to "tend and befriend." That is, females often respond to stressful situations by protecting themselves and others through nurturing behaviors (the *tend* part of the model) and forming alliances with a larger social group, especially one populated by other women (the *befriend* part of the model).

Do adolescent girls and boys experience stress and cope with it in similar or dissimilar ways? One study revealed no differences in the stress that adolescent girls and boys reported that they experience related to school (such as pressure to get good grades), parents (such as fighting with parents), self-related problems (such as not liking one's appearance), leisure (such as not having enough money), and their future (such as being unemployed) (Seiffge-Krencke & others, 2009). However, girls indicated that they experience more stress in peer relations (such as not having enough friends) and use more active strategies to cope with stress that include help from peers.

Acculturative stress refers to the negative consequences that result from contact between two distinctive cultural groups. Many individuals who have immigrated to the United States have experienced acculturative stress (Fuligni & Tsai, 2015). A recent study found that acculturative stress was linked to body image disturbance in Latino college students through an emphasis on the high status of a thin body (Menon & Harter, 2012).

What characterizes the acculturative stress of immigration for adolescents in the United States?
© Stephanie Maze/Corbis

acculturative stress The negative consequences that result from contact between two distinctive cultural groups.

Poverty can cause considerable stress for individuals and families (Duncan & others, 2015; Leventhal, Dupere, & Shuey, 2015). One expert on coping in youth, Bruce Compas (2004, p. 279), calls poverty "the single most important social problem facing young people in the United States." Chronic conditions such as inadequate housing, dangerous neighborhoods, burdensome responsibilities, and economic uncertainties are potent stressors in the lives of the poor (Bradley, 2015; Murry & others, 2015). Adolescents are more likely to experience threatening and uncontrollable life events if they live in low-income contexts than if they live in more economically robust contexts (McLoyd, Purtell, & Hardaway, 2015).

Coping   Adolescents and emerging adults respond to stress in different ways. Some youth give up quickly when the slightest thing goes wrong in their lives. Others are motivated to work hard to find solutions to personal problems, and some successfully adjust to even extremely taxing circumstances. A stressful circumstance can be rendered considerably less stressful if you know how to cope with it.

What Is Coping?   **Coping** involves managing taxing circumstances, expending effort to solve life's problems, and seeking to master or reduce stress. What makes the difference between effective and ineffective efforts to cope?

developmental **connection**

Attachment

Emerging adults with an avoidant or anxious insecure attachment are more likely to develop problems than are their counterparts who are securely attached. Connect to "Families."

Characteristics of the individual provide part of the answer. Success in coping has been linked with several characteristics, including a sense of personal control, positive emotions, and personal resources (Compas & others, 2014a, b; Folkman & Moskowitz, 2004; Howell & others, 2015; Xanthopoulos & Daniel, 2013). Success in coping, however, also depends on the strategies used and on the context (Kim & others, 2012). Adolescents and emerging adults have many ways of coping—some more successful than others (Seiffge-Krenke, 2011).

Adolescents have a wider range of coping strategies than do children, and the ability to choose among more coping options is likely adaptive (Aldwin & others, 2011). A recent research review concluded that two types of age trends occur from childhood through adolescence in coping: (1) an increase in coping *capacities* reflected in more self-reliance and less reliance on adults; greater use of planful problem solving; and greater reliance on cognitive strategies; and (2) an improvement in the *deployment* of different coping strategies depending on which ones are more effective in dealing with certain kinds of stressors (Zimmer-Gembeck & Skinner, 2011).

Problem-Focused and Emotion-Focused Coping   One way of classifying coping strategies has been especially influential among psychologists who study coping: distinguishing between problem-focused coping and emotion-focused coping, as proposed by Richard Lazarus (2000).

How can problem-focused and emotion-focused coping be distinguished?
© Gary Houlder/Corbis

Problem-focused coping is Lazarus' term for the strategy of squarely facing one's troubles and trying to solve them. For example, if you are having trouble with a class, you might go to the study-skills center at your college or university and enter a training program to learn how to study more effectively. Having done so, you have faced your problem and attempted to do something about it. A review of 39 research studies documented that problem-focused coping was associated with positive change following trauma and adversity (Linley & Joseph, 2004).

Emotion-focused coping is Lazarus' term for responding to stress in an emotional manner, especially by using defense mechanisms. Emotion-focused coping includes avoiding a problem, rationalizing what has happened, denying it is occurring, laughing it off, or calling on religious faith for support. If you use emotion-focused coping, you might avoid going to a class that you find difficult. You might say the class doesn't matter, deny that you are having a problem, or laugh and joke about it with your friends. This is not necessarily a good way to face a problem. For example, in one study, depressed individuals tried to avoid facing problems more than individuals who were not depressed (Ebata & Moos, 1989). In one study of inner-city youth, emotion-focused coping was linked to an increased risk for developing problems (Tolan & others, 2004).

Sometimes emotion-focused coping is adaptive. For example, denial is a protective mechanism for dealing with the flood of feelings that accompanies the realization that death is

coping Managing taxing circumstances, expending effort to solve life's problems, and seeking to master or reduce stress.

problem-focused coping Lazarus' term for the strategy of squarely facing one's troubles and trying to solve them.

emotion-focused coping Lazarus' term for responding to stress in an emotional manner, especially by using defense mechanisms.

imminent. Denial can protect against the destructive impact of shock by postponing the time when you will have to deal with stress. In other circumstances, however, emotion-focused coping is maladaptive. Denying that the person you were dating doesn't love you anymore when that person has become engaged to someone else keeps you from moving forward with your life.

Many individuals successfully use both problem-focused and emotion-focused coping to deal with a stressful circumstance (Romas & Sharma, 2010). Over the long term, though, problem-focused coping usually works better than emotion-focused coping (Heppner & Lee, 2001).

Another harmful coping strategy is *avoidant coping*, which involves ignoring a problem and hoping it will just go away (Wadsworth & others, 2011). A recent study found that adolescents who relied on avoidant coping and emotion-focused coping were more likely to be depressed and engage in suicidal ideation (Horwitz, Hill, & King, 2011).

Thinking Positively Thinking positively and avoiding negative thoughts are good strategies for coping with stress in just about any circumstance (Boyraz & Lightsey, 2012; Mavioglu, Boomsma, & Bartels, 2015). Why? A positive mood improves our ability to process information efficiently and enhances self-esteem. In most cases, an optimistic attitude is superior to a pessimistic one. It gives us a sense that we are controlling our environment, much like what Albert Bandura (2012) talks about when he describes the importance of self-efficacy in coping. Thinking positively reflects the positive psychology movement discussed in the introduction to this edition; recall that psychologists are calling for increased emphasis on positive individual traits, hope, and optimism (King, 2013, 2014, 2016). A prospective study of more than 5,000 young adolescents revealed that an optimistic thinking style predicted a lower level of depressive symptoms and a lower level of substance abuse and antisocial behavior (Patton & others, 2011b). And a recent study found that having a positive outlook was the most important cognitive factor associated with a decrease in depression severity in adolescents in the 36 weeks after they had been given antidepressant medication (Jacobs & others, 2014). Further, optimism was a key protective factor in lower depressive symptoms in Canadian Aboriginal youth (Ames & others, 2015).

Support Support from others is an important aspect of being able to cope with stress. Close, positive attachments to others—such as family members, friends, or a mentor—consistently show up as buffers to stress in adolescents' and emerging adults' lives (Schindler & Broning, 2015; Watson & others, 2014).

Individuals who provide support can recommend specific actions and plans to help an adolescent or emerging adult cope more effectively with stressful circumstances. For example, a mentor or counselor might notice that an adolescent is overloaded with schoolwork and this is causing considerable stress. The mentor or counselor might suggest ways for the adolescent or emerging adult to manage time better or to delegate tasks more efficiently. Friends and family members can reassure the adolescent or emerging adult under stress that he or she is a valuable person who is loved by others. Knowing that others care allows adolescents and emerging adults to cope with stress with greater assurance.

When adolescents experience severe stressors, such as the sudden death of a close friend or classmate, the event can be traumatic (Seiffge-Krenke, 2011). In these cases it is important for adolescents to reach out for support and share their feelings with others. One analysis found that online networking following a friend's death appears to help adolescents cope better (Williams & Merten, 2009).

Contexts and Coping Coping is not a stand-alone process; it is influenced by the demands and resources of the environment. Strategies for coping need to be evaluated in the specific context in which they occur (Mash & Wolfe, 2016). For example, a certain strategy may be effective in one situation but not another, depending on the extent to which the situation is controllable. Thus, it is adaptive to engage in problem-focused coping before an exam and in mental disengagement while waiting for the results. The contextual approach to coping points to the importance of *coping flexibility*, the ability to modify coping strategies to match the demands of the situation.

To read about one individual who helps adolescents cope with stress, see the *Connecting with Careers* interlude.

To read further about coping strategies, see the *Connecting with Health and Well-Being* interlude, which considers some of the strategies already discussed and introduces several others.

RESILIENCE

Despite being faced with challenges such as poverty, some adolescents and emerging adults triumph over adversity through *resilience* (Cotuli & others, 2013; Luthar, Crossman, & Small, 2015; Masten, 2013, 2014a, b, c; Masten & others, 2014, 2015). Think back to the story about Alice Walker at the beginning of the "Introduction" chapter. In spite of racism, poverty, low socioeconomic status, and a disfiguring eye injury, she became a successful author and champion for equality.

Are there certain characteristics that make adolescents resilient? Ann Masten and her colleagues (Masten, 2006, 2009, 2011, 2013, 2014a, b, c; Masten, Liebkind, & Hernandez, 2012; Masten & Monn, 2015; Masten & Narayan, 2012; Masten, Obradovic, & Burt, 2006; Masten & others, 2014, 2015; Masten & Tellegen 2012; Motti-Stefanidi, Masten, & Asendorpf, 2015) have discovered a number of factors, such as good intellectual functioning and effective parenting, that are often seen in children and adolescents who show resilience in the context of a wide range of stressful and even life-threatening circumstances. Figure 3 describes the individual, familial, and extrafamilial contexts that often have been found to characterize resilient children and adolescents (Masten & Coatsworth, 1998).

Masten and her colleagues (2006) concluded that being resilient in adolescence is linked to ongoing resilience in emerging adulthood, but that resilience also can develop in emerging adulthood. They also indicated that during emerging adulthood some individuals become motivated to better their lives and develop an improved ability to plan and make more effective decisions that place their lives on a more positive developmental course. In some instances, a specific person may influence an emerging adult in very positive ways, as was the case for Michael Maddaus, whose story was provided at the beginning of the "Introduction" chapter. You might recall that after a childhood and adolescence filled with stress, conflict, disappointment,

Source	Characteristic
Individual	Good intellectual functioning
	Appealing, sociable, easygoing disposition
	Self-confidence, high self-esteem
	Talents
	Faith
Family	Close relationship to caring parent figure
	Authoritative parenting: warmth, structure, high expectations
	Socioeconomic advantages
	Connections to extended supportive family networks
Extrafamilial Context	Bonds to caring adults outside the family
	Connections to positive organizations
	Attending effective schools

FIGURE 3

CHARACTERISTICS OF RESILIENT CHILDREN AND ADOLESCENTS

What Coping Strategies Work for Adolescents and Emerging Adults?

Here are some effective coping strategies that can benefit adolescents and emerging adults:

- **Think positively and optimistically.** Thinking positively and avoiding negative thoughts are good strategies when adolescents and emerging adults are trying to handle stress in just about any circumstance. Why? A positive mood improves your ability to process information efficiently and enhances self-esteem. In most cases, an optimistic attitude is superior to a pessimistic one. It provides a sense of controlling the environment, much like what Albert Bandura (2012) talks about when he describes the importance of self-efficacy in coping.

- **Increase self-control.** Developing better self-control is an effective coping strategy (Compas & others, 2014a). Coping successfully with a problem usually takes time—weeks, months, even years in some cases. Many adolescents and emerging adults who engage in problematic behavior have difficulty maintaining a plan for coping because their problematic behavior provides immediate gratification (such as eating, smoking, drinking, going to a party instead of studying for an exam). To maintain a self-control program over time, it is important to be able to forgo immediate satisfaction.

- **Seek social support.** Researchers consistently have found that social support helps adolescents and emerging adults cope with stress (Taylor, 2015). For example, depressed adolescents and emerging adults usually have fewer and less supportive relationships with family members, friends, and co-workers than do their counterparts who are not depressed (Neumann & others, 2015).

- **See a counselor or therapist.** If adolescents and emerging adults are not able to cope with the problem(s) they are encountering, it is very important for them to seek professional help from a counselor or therapist. Most colleges have a counseling service that provides unbiased, professional advice to students.

- **Use multiple coping strategies.** Adolescents and emerging adults who face stressful circumstances have many strategies from which to choose (Mash & Wolfe, 2016). Often it is wise to choose more than one because a single strategy may not work in a particular context. For example, an adolescent or emerging adult who has experienced a stressful life event or a cluster of such life events (such as the death of a parent or the breakup of a romantic relationship) might talk with a mental health professional, seek social support, exercise regularly, reduce drinking, and practice relaxation techniques.

When used alone, none of these strategies might be entirely adequate, but their combined effect may allow the adolescent or emerging adult to cope successfully with stress. Recall what you have learned from reading about research on peers, family, and ethnicity as you consider any other strategies that might be helpful.

and problems, his connection with a competent, caring mentor in emerging adulthood helped him to turn his life around, and he went on to become a successful surgeon. According to Masten and her colleagues (2006), a romantic relationship or the birth of a child also may stimulate change and motivate an emerging adult to develop a stronger commitment to a positive future.

Review *Connect* Reflect

 LG1 Discuss the nature of problems in adolescence and emerging adulthood

Review
- How can the biopsychosocial approach be characterized?
- What is the developmental psychopathology approach like?
- What are some general characteristics of adolescent and emerging adult problems?
- What is the nature of stress and coping in adolescence and emerging adulthood?
- How can the resilience of some adolescents and emerging adults be explained?

Connect
- How might friendships contribute to both stress and coping?

Reflect *Your Own Personal Journey of Life*
- What were the most significant stressors that you experienced as an adolescent? How effectively did you cope with them? Explain.

2 Problems and Disorders **LG2** Describe some problems and disorders that characterize adolescents and emerging adults

Drug Use

Juvenile Delinquency

Depression and Suicide

Eating Disorders

What are some of the major problems and disorders in adolescence and emerging adulthood? They include drugs and alcohol abuse, juvenile delinquency, school-related problems, high-risk sexual behavior, depression and suicide, and eating disorders. We discussed school-related and sexual problems in earlier chapters. Here we examine other problems, beginning with drugs.

DRUG USE

How pervasive is drug use among adolescents and emerging adults in the United States? What are the nature and effects of various drugs taken by adolescents and emerging adults? What factors contribute to adolescent and emerging adult drug use? Let's now explore these questions.

Trends in Overall Drug Use   The 1960s and 1970s were a time of marked increases in the use of illicit drugs. During the social and political unrest of those years, many youth turned to marijuana, stimulants, and hallucinogens. Increases in adolescent and emerging adult alcohol consumption during this period also were noted (Robinson & Greene, 1988). More precise data about drug use by adolescents and emerging adults have been collected in recent years. Each year since 1975, Lloyd Johnston and his colleagues at the Institute of Social Research at the University of Michigan have monitored the drug use of America's high school seniors in a wide range of public and private high schools. Since 1991, they also have surveyed drug use by eighth- and tenth-graders. In 2014, the study surveyed more than 41,000 secondary school students in more than 400 public and private schools (Johnston & others, 2015).

According to this study, the proportions of eighth-, tenth-, and twelfth-grade U.S. students who used any illicit drug declined in the late 1990s and the first decade of the twenty-first century (Johnston & others, 2015). The use of drugs among U.S. secondary school students declined in the 1980s but began to increase in the early 1990s (Johnston & others, 2015). In the late 1990s and the early part of the twenty-first century, the proportion of secondary school students reporting the use of any illicit drug has been declining. The overall decline in the use of illicit drugs by adolescents during this time frame is approximately one-third for eighth-graders, one-fourth for tenth-graders, and one-eighth for twelfth-graders. The most notable declines in drug use by U.S. adolescents in the twenty-first century have occurred for LSD, cocaine, cigarettes, sedatives, tranquilizers, and Ecstasy. Marijuana is the illicit drug most widely used in the United States and Europe (Hibell & others, 2004; Johnston & others, 2015). Even with the recent decline in use, the United States still has one of the highest rates of adolescent drug use of any industrialized nation.

As shown in Figure 4, in which marijuana is included, an increase in illicit drug use by U.S. adolescents occurred from 2008 to 2014. However, when marijuana use is subtracted from the illicit drug index, no increase in U.S. adolescent drug use occurred in this time frame (Johnston & others, 2015).

Johnston and his colleagues (2005) noted that "generational forgetting" contributed to the rise of adolescent drug use in the 1990s, as adolescents' beliefs about the dangers of drugs eroded considerably. The recent downturn in drug use by U.S. adolescents has been attributed to an increase in the perceived dangers of drug use among today's youth (Johnston & others, 2011).

Let's now consider separately a number of drugs that are abused by some adolescents and emerging adults.

Alcohol   To learn more about the role of alcohol in adolescents' and emerging adults' lives, we examine the use and abuse of alcohol by adolescents and emerging adults, and risk factors for alcohol abuse.

How extensive is alcohol use by U.S. adolescents? Sizable declines in adolescent alcohol use have occurred in recent years (Johnston & others, 2015). The percentage of U.S. eighth-graders who reported having had any alcohol to drink in the past 30 days fell from a high of

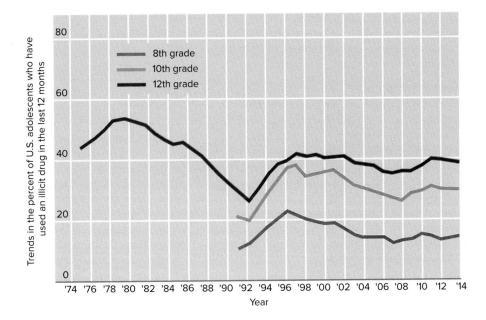

FIGURE 4

TRENDS IN DRUG USE BY U.S. EIGHTH-, TENTH-, AND TWELFTH-GRADE STUDENTS. This graph shows the percentage of U.S. eighth-, tenth-, and twelfth-grade students who reported having taken an illicit drug in the last 12 months from 1991 to 2014 (for eighth- and tenth-graders) and from 1975 to 2014 (for twelfth-graders) (Johnston & others, 2015).

26 percent in 1996 to 9 percent in 2014. The 30-day prevalence fell among tenth-graders from 39 percent in 2001 to 23.5 percent in 2014 and among high school seniors from 72 percent in 1980 to 37 percent in 2014. Binge drinking (defined in the University of Michigan surveys as having five or more drinks in a row in the last two weeks) by high school seniors declined from 41 percent in 1980 to 23.5 percent in 2014. Binge drinking by eighth- and tenth-graders also has dropped in recent years. A consistent gender difference occurs in binge drinking, with males engaging in this behavior more than females do (Johnston & others, 2015).

The transition from high school to college may be a critical transition in alcohol abuse (Johnston & others, 2012, 2013, 2014, 2015). The large majority of older adolescents and youth who drink recognize that drinking is common among people their age and is largely accepted or even expected by their peers. They also may perceive some social and coping benefits from alcohol use and even occasional heavy drinking.

In 2012, 37.4 percent of U.S. college students reported having had five or more drinks in a row at least once in the last two weeks (Johnston & others, 2013). The term *extreme binge drinking* describes individuals who had 10 or more drinks in a row. In 2010 approximately 13 percent of college students reported drinking this heavily (Johnston & others, 2011). While drinking rates among college students have remained high, drinking, including binge drinking, has declined in recent years. For example, binge drinking declined by 4 percent from 2007 to 2012 (Johnston & others, 2013).

The effects of heavy drinking take their toll on college students. In a national survey of drinking patterns on 140 campuses, almost half of the binge drinkers reported problems that included missing classes, physical injuries, trouble with police, and having unprotected sex (Wechsler & others, 1994). Also in this study, binge-drinking college students were 11 times more likely to drive after drinking, and twice as likely to have unprotected sex, than college students who did not binge drink.

Drinking alcohol before going out—called *pregaming*—has become common among college students (Ahmed & others, 2014). One study revealed that almost two-thirds of students on one campus had pregamed at least once during a two-week period (DeJong, DeRicco, & Schneider, 2010). Another recent study found that two-thirds of 18- to 24-year-old women on one college pregamed (Read, Merrill, & Bytschkow, 2010). Drinking games, in which the goal is to become intoxicated, also have become common on college campuses (LaBrie & others, 2011). Higher levels of alcohol use have been consistently linked to higher rates of sexual risk taking, such as engaging in casual sex, having sex without contraceptives, and being the perpetrator or victim of sexual assaults (Khan & others, 2012).

A special concern is the increase in binge drinking by females during emerging adulthood that occurred during the 1990s and the first part of the twenty-first

What kinds of problems are associated with binge drinking in college?

century (Bartoli & others, 2014; Wemm & others, 2013). However, a decline in binge drinking occurred among male and female college students from 2007 to 2011 (Johnston & others, 2012). For occurrences in the last 30 days, college men (45 percent) still were far more likely to engage in binge drinking than were college women (29 percent) (Johnston & others, 2012).

Risk Factors in Alcohol Abuse   Among the risk factors in adolescents' and emerging adults' abuse of alcohol are heredity, early alcohol consumption, family influences, peer relations, and education. There is evidence of a genetic predisposition to alcoholism, although it is important to remember that both genetic and environmental factors are involved (Neiderhiser, Marceau, & Reiss, 2013).

Parents play an important role in preventing adolescent drug abuse (Abar & others, 2015; Zehe & Colder, 2014). Positive relationships with parents and others can reduce adolescents' drug use (West & others, 2013). Researchers have found that parental monitoring is linked with a lower incidence of drug use (Hurt & others, 2013; Williams, Burton, & Warzinski, 2014). A research review concluded that the more frequently adolescents ate dinner with their families, the less likely they were to have substance abuse problems (Sen, 2010). And recent research revealed that authoritative parenting was linked to lower adolescent alcohol consumption (Piko & Balazs, 2012) while parent-adolescent conflict was related to higher adolescent alcohol consumption (Chaplin & others, 2012). Further, a recent study found that neighborhood disadvantage was linked a higher level of adolescent alcohol use two years later, mainly through a pathway that included exposure to delinquent peers (Trucco & others, 2014).

Peer relations also are linked to adolescent substance use (Shadur & Hussong, 2014; Valente & others, 2013). A recent study found that low parental knowledge of adolescents' peer relations and behavior, and friends' delinquency predicted adolescent substance use (McAdams & others, 2014). Another study indicated that of various risk factors the strongest predictors of adolescent substance use involved peer relations (Patrick & Schulenberg, 2010). A recent study found that drinking by peers increased adolescents' alcohol use (Cruz, Emery, & Turkheimer, 2012). Another study revealed that the drinking behavior of friends was linked to whether college students engaged in binge drinking (Jamison & Myers, 2008). In this study, the pressure to drink was stronger from male than female peers. And a recent study found that when the mother of an adolescent's friend engaged in authoritative parenting, the adolescent was less likely to binge drink, smoke cigarettes, or use marijuana than when the friend's mother engaged in neglectful parenting (Shakya, Christakis, & Fowler, 2012).

It is not just alcohol use by U.S. adolescents that is a major concern. There also is concern about adolescent use of other drugs. Next, we examine adolescent use of a number of other drugs, beginning with hallucinogens.

Hallucinogens   **Hallucinogens,** also called psychedelic (mind-altering) drugs, are drugs that modify an individual's perceptual experiences and produce hallucinations. First, we discuss LSD, which has powerful hallucinogenic properties, and then marijuana, a milder hallucinogen.

LSD   LSD (*lysergic acid diethylamide*) is a hallucinogen that—even in low doses—produces striking perceptual changes. Sometimes the images are pleasurable, sometimes unpleasant or frightening. LSD's popularity in the 1960s and 1970s was followed by a reduction in use by the mid-1970s as its unpredictable effects become publicized. However, adolescents' use of LSD increased in the 1990s (Johnston & others, 2013). In 1985, 1.8 percent of U.S. high school seniors reported LSD use in the last 30 days; in 1994, this increased to 4.0 percent. However, LSD use had declined to 2.3 percent in 2001 and dropped to 1 percent in 2014 (Johnston & others, 2015).

Marijuana   Marijuana, a milder hallucinogen than LSD, comes from the hemp plant *Cannabis sativa*. Because marijuana also can impair attention and memory, smoking marijuana is not conducive to optimal school performance. Marijuana use by adolescents decreased in the 1980s. For example, in 1979, 37 percent of high school seniors said they had used marijuana in the last month, but in 1992 that figure had dropped to 19 percent and then by 2006 to 18 percent. However, marijuana use by U.S. adolescents increased from 2008 to 2012, especially for twelfth-graders, but declined slightly in 2014 (Johnston & others, 2014). In 2013, 23 percent of U.S.

developmental **connection**

Families

Parental monitoring is a key aspect of parental management of adolescents' lives. Connect to "Families."

What are some factors that contribute to whether adolescents drink heavily?
© Daniel Allan/Taxi/Getty Images

hallucinogens Drugs that alter an individual's perceptual experiences and produce hallucinations; also called psychedelic (mind-altering) drugs.

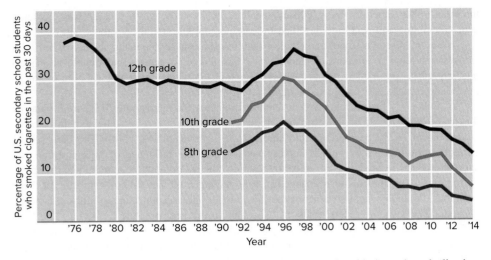

FIGURE 5

TRENDS IN CIGARETTE SMOKING BY U.S. SECONDARY SCHOOL STUDENTS
Note: Percentage smoking cigarettes in the last 30 days.

twelfth-graders reported that they had smoked marijuana in the last 30 days, then declined to 21 percent in 2014. One reason that marijuana use has recently increased is the trend that fewer adolescents today perceive much danger associated with its use.

There also is a concern about *synthetic marijuana (K-2, "Spice")* that is sold over the counter in many states, especially in gas stations, convenience stores, and head shops (Johnston & others, 2015). Synthetic marijuana has synthetic chemical components of marijuana sprayed onto plant material that is then smoked. This form of marijuana is unregulated and often imported from other countries. It can be very potent and has unpredictable effects. The percentage of twelfth-graders reporting use of synthetic marijuana annually fell from 11 percent in 2011 (the first time it was assessed in the study) to 6 percent in 2014 (Johnston & others, 2015).

Stimulants   **Stimulants** are drugs that increase the activity of the central nervous system. The most widely used stimulants are caffeine, nicotine, amphetamines, and cocaine.

Cigarette Smoking   Cigarette smoking (in which the active drug is nicotine) is one of the most serious yet preventable health problems. In the United States, smoking is likely to begin in grades 7 through 9, although sizable proportions of youth are still establishing regular smoking habits during high school and college. Since the national surveys by Johnston and others began in 1975, cigarettes have been the substance most frequently used on a daily basis by high school seniors (Johnston & others, 2015).

Cigarette smoking is decreasing among adolescents (see Figure 5). Cigarette smoking among U.S. adolescents peaked in 1996 and 1997 and has gradually declined since then (Johnston & others, 2015). Following peak use in 1996, smoking rates for U.S. eighth-graders have fallen by 50 percent. In 2014, the percentages of adolescents who said they had smoked cigarettes in the last 30 days were 14 percent (twelfth grade), 7 percent (tenth grade), and 4 percent (eighth grade). Since the mid-1990s an increasing percentage of adolescents have reported that they perceive cigarette smoking as dangerous, that they disapprove of it, that they are less accepting of being around smokers, and that they prefer to date nonsmokers (Johnston & others, 2015).

E-cigarettes are battery-powered devices that have a heating element and produce a vapor that users inhale. In most cases the vapor contains nicotine, but the specific contents are not regulated. In 2014, for the first time in the University of Michigan drug study, E-cigarette use was assessed (Johnston & others, 2015). E-cigarette use by U.S. adolescents in 2014 surpassed tobacco cigarette use—9 percent of eighth-graders, 16 percent of tenth-graders, and 17 percent of twelfth-graders reported using E-cigarettes in the last 30 days.

The devastating effects of early smoking were brought home in a research study that found that smoking in the adolescent years causes permanent genetic changes in the lungs and forever increases the risk of lung cancer, even if the smoker quits (Wiencke & others, 1999). The damage was much less likely among smokers in the study who started during their twenties. One of the remarkable findings in the study was that the early age of onset of smoking was more important in predicting genetic damage than how heavily the individuals smoked.

The peer group especially plays an important role in smoking (Valente & others, 2013). In one study, the risk of current smoking was linked with peer networks in which at least half of the members smoked, one or two best friends smoked, and smoking was common in

stimulants Drugs that increase the activity of the central nervous system.

"I'll tell you one thing. As soon as I'm thirteen I'm gonna stop!"
Wayne Stayskal © 1979 Tribune Media Services, Inc. All Rights Reserved. Reprinted with permission.

the school (Alexander & others, 2001). And in a recent study, early smoking was predicted better by sibling and peer smoking than by parental smoking (Kelly & others, 2011).

A recent research review concluded that in addition to acquiring a best friend who smokes, initiation of smoking in adolescence was linked to getting into trouble at school, poorer grades, and delinquency (Tucker & others, 2012). In this review, escalation of smoking in adolescence was predicted by depressive symptoms.

A number of researchers have developed strategies for interrupting behavioral patterns that lead to smoking. In one investigation, high school students were recruited to help seventh-grade students resist peer pressure to smoke (McAlister & others, 1980). The high school students encouraged the younger adolescents to resist the influence of high-powered ads suggesting that liberated women smoke by saying, "She is not really liberated if she is hooked on tobacco." The students also engaged in role-playing exercises called "chicken." In these situations, the high school students called the younger adolescents "chicken" for not trying a cigarette. The seventh-graders practiced resistance to the peer pressure by saying, "I'd be a real chicken if I smoked just to impress you." Following several sessions, the students in the smoking prevention group were 50 percent less likely to begin smoking compared with a group of seventh-grade students in a neighboring junior high school, even though the parents of both groups of students had the same smoking rate.

Cocaine   *Cocaine* is a stimulant that comes from the coca plant, native to Bolivia and Peru. Cocaine can have a number of seriously damaging effects on the body, including heart attacks, strokes, and brain seizures.

How many adolescents use cocaine? Use of cocaine in the last 30 days by high school seniors dropped from a peak of 6.7 percent in 1985 to 1.4 percent in 2014 (Johnston & others, 2015). A growing percentage of high school students are reaching the conclusion that cocaine use entails considerable unpredictable risk. Still, the percentage of adolescents who have used cocaine is precariously high. About 1 of every 13 high school seniors has tried cocaine at least once.

Amphetamines   Amphetamines, often called "pep pills" and "uppers," are widely prescribed stimulants, sometimes appearing in the form of diet pills. Amphetamine use among high school seniors has decreased significantly. Use of amphetamines in the last 30 days by high school seniors declined from 10.7 percent in 1982 to 3.8 percent in 2014 (Johnston & others, 2015). Although use of over-the-counter diet pills has decreased in recent years, 40 percent of today's females have tried using diet pills by the time they graduate from high school.

Ecstasy   *Ecstasy*, the street name for the synthetic drug MDMA, has both stimulant and hallucinogenic effects. Ecstasy produces euphoric feelings and heightened sensations (especially touch and sight). Ecstasy use can lead to dangerous increases in blood pressure, as well as an increased risk of stroke or heart attack.

Ecstasy use by U.S. adolescents began in the 1980s and then peaked in 2000 to 2001. Thirty-day prevalence of use in 2014 by eighth-, tenth-, and twelfth-graders was 0.4, 0.8, and 1.4 percent, respectively (down from 1.8, 2.6, and 2.8 percent in 2001) (Johnston & others, 2015). The downturn in reported use of Ecstasy coincides with adolescents' increasing knowledge that Ecstasy use can be dangerous.

Depressants   **Depressants** are drugs that slow down the central nervous system, bodily functions, and behavior. Medically, depressants have been used to reduce anxiety and to induce sleep. Among the most widely used depressants is alcohol, which we discussed earlier; others include barbiturates and tranquilizers. Though used less frequently than other depressants, the opiates are especially dangerous.

Barbiturates, such as Nembutal (pentobarbital) and Seconal (secobarbital), are depressant drugs that induce sleep or reduce anxiety. *Tranquilizers*, such as Valium (diazepam) and Xanax (alprazolam), are depressant drugs that reduce anxiety and induce relaxation. They can produce symptoms of withdrawal when an individual stops taking them. Since the initial surveys in 1975 of drug use by high school seniors, use of depressants has decreased. For example, use of barbiturates by high school seniors at least every 30 days in 1975 was 4.7 percent; in 2014, it was 2 percent (Johnston & others, 2015). Over the same time period, tranquilizer use also decreased from 4.1 percent to 2.1 percent for 30-day prevalence.

Opiates, which consist of opium and its derivatives, depress the activity of the central nervous system. They are commonly known as narcotics. Many drugs have been produced

depressants Drugs that slow down the central nervous system, bodily functions, and behavior.

from the opium poppy, among them morphine and heroin (which is converted to morphine when it enters the brain). For several hours after taking an opiate, an individual feels euphoria and pain relief; however, the opiates are among the most physically addictive drugs. The person soon craves more heroin and experiences very painful withdrawal unless he or she takes more.

The rates of heroin use among adolescents are quite low. In 2014, 0.4 percent of high school seniors said they had used heroin in the last 30 days (Johnston, 2015).

An alarming trend has recently emerged in adolescents' use of prescription painkillers. Many adolescents cite the medicine cabinets of their parents or of their friends' parents as the main source for their prescription painkillers. A 2004 survey revealed that 18 percent of U.S. adolescents had used Vicodin (acetaminophen and hydrocodone) at some point in their lifetime, whereas 10 percent had used OxyContin (oxycodone) (Partnership for a Drug-Free America, 2005). These drugs fall into the general class of drugs called narcotics, and they are highly addictive.

At this point, we have discussed a number of depressants, stimulants, and hallucinogens. Their medical uses, short-term effects, overdose symptoms, health risks, physical addiction risk, and psychological dependence risk are summarized in Figure 6.

Eighteen-year-old Paul Michaud began taking OxyContin in high school. Michaud says, "I was hooked." Now he is in drug treatment.
© Josh Reynolds

Drug Classification	Medical Uses	Short-term Effects	Overdose	Health Risks	Risk of Physical/ Psychological Dependence
DEPRESSANTS					
Alcohol	Pain relief	Relaxation, depressed brain activity, slowed behavior, reduced inhibitions	Disorientation, loss of consciousness, even death at high blood-alcohol levels	Accidents, brain damage, liver disease, heart disease, ulcers, birth defects	Physical: moderate; psychological: moderate
Barbiturates	Sleeping pill	Relaxation, sleep	Breathing difficulty, coma, possible death	Accidents, coma, possible death	Physical and psychological: moderate to high
Tranquilizers	Anxiety reduction	Relaxation, slowed behavior	Breathing difficulty, coma, possible death	Accidents, coma, possible death	Physical: low to moderate; psychological: moderate to high
Opiates (narcotics)	Pain relief	Euphoric feelings, drowsiness, nausea	Convulsions, coma, possible death	Accidents, infectious diseases such as AIDS (when the drug is injected)	Physical: high; psychological: moderate to high
STIMULANTS					
Amphetamines	Weight control	Increased alertness, excitability; decreased fatigue, irritability	Extreme irritability, feelings of persecution, convulsions	Insomnia, hypertension, malnutrition, possible death	Physical: possible; psychological: moderate to high
Cocaine	Local anesthetic	Increased alertness, excitability, euphoric feelings; decreased fatigue, irritability	Extreme irritability, feelings of persecution, convulsions, cardiac arrest, possible death	Insomnia, hypertension, malnutrition, possible death	Physical: possible; psychological: moderate (oral) to very high (injected or smoked)
HALLUCINOGENS					
LSD	None	Strong hallucinations, distorted time perception	Severe mental disturbance, loss of contact with reality	Accidents	Physical: none; psychological: low

FIGURE 6

PSYCHOACTIVE DRUGS: DEPRESSANTS, STIMULANTS, AND HALLUCINOGENS

What characterizes the use of inhalants by adolescents?
© BananaStock/JupiterImages/i2i/Alamy RF

Anabolic Steroids **Anabolic steroids** are drugs derived from the male sex hormone testosterone. They promote muscle growth and increase lean body mass. Nonmedical uses of these drugs carry a number of physical and psychological health risks (National Clearinghouse for Alcohol and Drug Information, 1999). Both males and females who take large doses of anabolic steroids usually experience changes in sexual characteristics. Psychological effects in both males and females can include irritability, uncontrollable bursts of anger, severe mood swings (which can lead to depression when individuals stop using the steroids), impaired judgment stemming from feelings of invincibility, and paranoid jealousy.

In the University of Michigan study, in 2014, 0.2 percent of eighth-graders, 0.4 percent of tenth-graders, and 0.9 percent of twelfth-graders said they had used anabolic steroids in the past 30 days (Johnston & others, 2015). The rate of steroid use by twelfth-graders has declined from 2004 (1.6 percent).

Inhalants Inhalants are ordinary household products that are inhaled or sniffed by children and adolescents to get high. Examples of inhalants include model airplane glue, nail polish remover, and cleaning fluids. Short-term use of inhalants can cause intoxicating effects that last for several minutes or even several hours if the inhalants are used repeatedly. Eventually the user can lose consciousness. Long-term use of inhalants can lead to heart failure and even death.

Use of inhalants is higher among younger than older adolescents. In the University of Michigan national survey, inhalant use by U.S. adolescents has decreased in the twenty-first century (Johnston & others, 2015). Use in the last 30 days by twelfth-graders was 0.7 percent in 2014, having peaked at 3.2 percent in 1995. The prevalence of inhalant use in the last 30 days by eighth-graders was 2.2 percent in 2014, down from a peak of 6.1 percent in 1995.

Factors in Adolescent and Emerging Adult Drug Abuse Earlier, we discussed the factors that place adolescents and emerging adults at risk for alcohol abuse. Researchers also have examined the factors that are related to drug use in general during adolescence and emerging adulthood, especially early substance use; parents, peers, and schools; and changes in substance use from adolescence through emerging and early adulthood.

Early Substance Use Most adolescents become drug users at some point in their development, whether their use is limited to alcohol, caffeine, and cigarettes or extended to marijuana, cocaine, and hard drugs. A special concern involves adolescents who begin to use drugs early in adolescence or even in childhood (Moss, Chen, & Yi, 2014; Trucco, Colder, & Wieczorek, 2011). One study revealed that individuals who began drinking alcohol before 14 years of age were more likely to become alcohol dependent than their counterparts who began drinking alcohol at 21 years of age or older (Hingson, Heeren, & Winter, 2006). A longitudinal study found that onset of alcohol use before 11 years of age was linked to increased adult alcohol dependence (Guttmannova & others, 2012). Also, a recent study found that early age of onset drinking and a quick progression to drinking to intoxication were linked to drinking problems in high school (Morean & others, 2014). And another recent study indicated that early- and rapid-onset trajectories of alcohol, marijuana, and substance use were associated with substance abuse in early adulthood (Nelson, Van Ryzin, & Dishion, 2015).

Parents, Siblings, Peers, and Schools Parents play an important role in preventing adolescent drug abuse (Abar & others, 2015; Broning & others, 2014; Hargreaves & others, 2013). Positive relationships with parents, siblings, peers and others can reduce adolescents' drug use (Hohman & others, 2014). Researchers have found that parental monitoring and positive relationships with parents are linked with a lower incidence of drug use (Abar & others, 2015). One study revealed that negative interactions with parents were linked to increased adolescent drinking and smoking, while positive identification with parents was related to declines in use of these substances (Gutman & others, 2011). Further, in a recent study, a higher level of parental monitoring during the last year of high school was linked to a lower risk of alcohol, but not marijuana, dependence in the first year of college (Kaynak & others, 2013).

What are ways that parents have been found to influence whether their adolescents take drugs?
© Charles Gullung/Corbis

anabolic steroids Drugs derived from the male sex hormone testosterone. They promote muscle growth and increase lean body mass.

A recent study revealed that older siblings' substance use was associated with their younger siblings' patterns of use (Whiteman, Jensen, & Maggs, 2013). Also, a recent study found that older siblings more strongly transmitted risk for substance abuse to their younger siblings than vice versa (Kendler & others, 2013).

A longitudinal study conducted by Kenneth Dodge and his colleagues (2006) examined the joint contributions of parents and peers to early substance use. The following sequence of factors was linked with the likelihood that an adolescent would take drugs by 12 years of age:

· Being born into a high-risk family (especially with a poor, single, or teenage mother)
· Experiencing an increase in harsh parenting in childhood
· Having conduct problems in school and getting rejected by peers in childhood
· Experiencing increased conflict with parents in early adolescence
· Having low parental monitoring
· Hanging out with deviant peers in early adolescence and engaging in increased substance use

Educational success is also a strong buffer for the emergence of drug problems in adolescence (Henry & others, 2009). An analysis by Jerald Bachman and his colleagues (2008) revealed that early educational achievement considerably reduced the likelihood that adolescents would develop drug problems, including those involving alcohol abuse, smoking, and abuse of various illicit drugs.

Emerging Adulthood and Early Adulthood   Fortunately, by the time individuals reach their mid-twenties, many have reduced their use of alcohol and drugs (Johnston & others, 2013). For example, in a longitudinal study of more than 38,000 individuals from the time they were high school seniors through their early thirties, Jerald Bachman and his colleagues (2002) found that binge drinking peaked at 21–22 years of age and then declined from 23–24 to 31–32 years of age (see Figure 7). Some of the main findings in the study are described below:

· College students drink more than youth who end their education after high school.
· Those who don't go to college smoke more.
· Singles use marijuana more than married individuals do.
· Drinking is heaviest among singles and divorced individuals. Becoming engaged, married, or even remarried quickly brings down alcohol use. Thus, living arrangements and marital status are key factors in alcohol and drug use rates during the twenties.
· Individuals who considered religion to be very important in their lives and who frequently attended religious services were less likely to take drugs than were their less-religious counterparts.

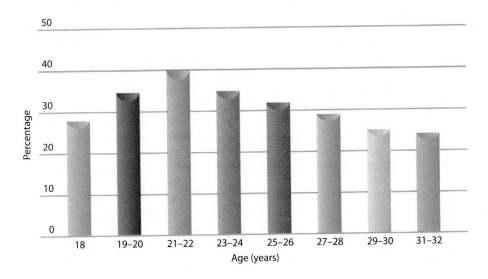

FIGURE 7

BINGE DRINKING IN THE TRANSITION FROM ADOLESCENCE TO ADULTHOOD. This figure shows the percentage of individuals from age 18 through 32 who said they had engaged in binge drinking (having five or more drinks on any one occasion) during the past two weeks. Notice the decline in binge drinking in the mid-twenties.

JUVENILE DELINQUENCY

© Comstock Images/Alamy RF

Thirteen-year-old Arnie, in the section that opened this chapter, is a juvenile delinquent with a history of thefts and physical assaults. What is a juvenile delinquent? What are the antecedents of delinquency? What types of interventions have been used to prevent or reduce delinquency?

What Is Juvenile Delinquency?   The term **juvenile delinquency** refers to a broad range of behaviors, from socially unacceptable behavior (such as acting out in school) to status offenses (such as running away from home) to criminal acts (such as burglary). For legal purposes, a distinction is made between index offenses and status offenses:

· **Index offenses** are criminal acts, whether they are committed by juveniles or adults. They include such acts as robbery, aggravated assault, rape, and homicide.
· **Status offenses,** such as running away, truancy, underage drinking, sexual promiscuity, and uncontrollability, are less serious acts. They are performed by youth under a specified age, which classifies them as juvenile offenses. One study found that status offenses increased through adolescence.

States often differ in the age used to classify an individual as a juvenile or an adult. Approximately three-fourths of the states have established age 18 as a maximum for defining juveniles. Two states use age 19 as the cutoff, seven states use age 17, and four states use age 16. Thus, running away from home at age 17 may be an offense in some states but not in others.

One issue in juvenile justice is whether an adolescent who commits a crime should be tried as an adult. Some psychologists have proposed that individuals 12 and under should not be evaluated under adult criminal laws and that those 17 and older should be (Cauffman & others, 2015). They also recommend that individuals 13 to 16 years of age be given some type of individualized assessment to determine whether they will be tried in a juvenile court or an adult criminal court. This framework argues strongly against court placement based solely on the nature of an offense and takes into account the offender's developmental maturity. The Society for Adolescent Medicine has argued that the death penalty should not be used with adolescents (Morreale, 2004).

In addition to the legal classifications of index offenses and status offenses, many of the behaviors considered delinquent are included in widely used classifications of abnormal behavior (Okado & Bierman, 2015). **Conduct disorder** is the psychiatric diagnostic category used when multiple behaviors occur over a six-month period. These behaviors include truancy, running away, fire setting, cruelty to animals, breaking and entering, excessive fighting, and others (Burke, 2011). When three or more of these behaviors co-occur before the age of 15 and the child or adolescent is considered unmanageable or out of control, the clinical diagnosis is conduct disorder. A recent study found that conduct disorder is a risk factor for substance abuse throughout adolescence (Hopfer & others, 2013).

Another recent study found that youth with conduct disorder characterized by its onset in childhood had higher rates of cognitive impairment (especially in executive function), psychiatric symptoms, and serious violent offenses than youth with conduct disorder characterized by the onset of antisocial behavior in adolescence (Johnson & others, 2015).

Conduct problems in children are best explained by a confluence of causes, or risk factors, operating over time (Conduct Problems Prevention Research Group, 2011, 2015). These include possible genetic inheritance of a difficult temperament, ineffective parenting, and living in a neighborhood where violence is the norm. In a recent study in 10 urban schools serving primarily African American children from low-income backgrounds, the children were randomly assigned to either a "pre-kindergarten as usual" control condition or an intervention that consisted of a family program (13 weeks of behavioral parenting strategies) and a professional development training program for early childhood teachers (Dawson-McClure & others, 2015). For boys, but not girls, the intervention led to lower rates of conduct problems two years later.

In sum, most children or adolescents at one time or another act out or do things that are destructive or troublesome for themselves or others. If these behaviors occur often in childhood or early adolescence, psychiatrists diagnose them as conduct disorders (Loeber & Burke, 2011). If these behaviors result in illegal acts by juveniles, society labels the offenders as *delinquents.*

What are some characteristics of conduct disorder?
© Stockdisc/PunchStock RF

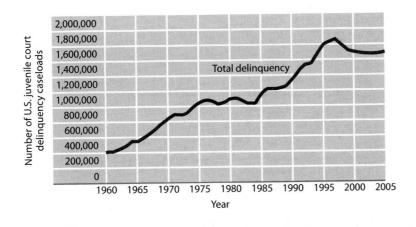

The number of juvenile court delinquency caseloads in the United States increased dramatically from 1960 to 1996 but has decreased slightly since 1996 (see Figure 8) (Puzzanchera & Sickmund, 2008). Note that this figure reflects only adolescents who have been arrested and assigned to juvenile court delinquency caseloads and does not include those who were arrested and not assigned to the delinquency caseloads, nor does the figure include youth who committed offenses but were not apprehended.

Males are more likely to engage in delinquency than are females (Colman & others, 2009). However, U.S. government statistics revealed that the percentage of delinquency caseloads involving females increased from 19 percent in 1985 to 27 percent in 2005 (Puzzanchera & Sickmund, 2008).

As adolescents become emerging adults, do their rates of delinquency and crime change? Analyses indicate that theft, property damage, and physical aggression decrease from 18 to 26 years of age (Schulenberg & Zarrett, 2006). The peak age for property damage is 16 to 18 for males and 15 to 17 for females. However, the peak age for violence is 18 to 19 for males and 19 to 21 for females (Farrington, 2004).

A distinction is made between early-onset (before age 11) and late-onset (after age 11) antisocial behavior. Early-onset antisocial behavior is associated with more negative developmental outcomes than late-onset antisocial behavior (Schulenberg & Zarrett, 2006). Early-onset antisocial behavior is more likely to persist into emerging adulthood and is associated with more mental health and relationship problems (Loeber & Burke, 2011; Loeber, Burke, & Pardini, 2009).

Antecedents of Juvenile Delinquency   Predictors of delinquency include conflict with authority, minor covert acts that are followed by property damage and other more serious acts, minor aggression followed by fighting and violence, identity (negative identity), self-control (low degree), cognitive distortions (egocentric bias), age (early initiation), sex (male), expectations for education (low expectations, little commitment), school achievement (low achievement in early grades), peer influence (heavy influence, low resistance), socioeconomic status (low), parental role (lack of monitoring, low support, and ineffective discipline), siblings (having an older sibling who is a delinquent), and neighborhood quality (urban, high crime, high mobility). A summary of these antecedents of delinquency is presented in Figure 9.

Let's look in more detail at several other factors that are related to delinquency. Erik Erikson (1968) notes that adolescents whose development has restricted their access to acceptable social roles or made them feel that they cannot measure up to the demands placed on them may choose a negative identity. Adolescents with a negative identity may find support for their delinquent image among peers, reinforcing the negative identity. For Erikson, delinquency is an attempt to establish an identity, although it is a negative identity.

Parenting factors play a key role in delinquency (Burke & Loeber, 2015; Hinnant, Erath, & El-Sheikh, 2015; Mann & others, 2015; Sobotkova & others, 2013). Recall from earlier in this chapter the description of the developmental cascade approach of Gerald Patterson and his colleagues (2010) and research indicating that high levels of coercive parenting and low levels of positive parenting lead to the development of antisocial behavior in children, which in turn connect children to negative experiences in peer and school contexts.

juvenile delinquency A broad range of behaviors, including socially unacceptable behavior, status offenses, and criminal acts.

index offenses Acts such as robbery, rape, and homicide that are crimes regardless of whether they are committed by juveniles or adults.

status offenses Juvenile offenses, performed by youth under a specified age, that are not as serious as index offenses. These offenses may include acts such as underage drinking, truancy, and sexual promiscuity.

conduct disorder The psychiatric diagnostic category for the occurrence of multiple delinquent activities over a six-month period. These behaviors include truancy, running away, fire setting, cruelty to animals, breaking and entering, and excessive fighting.

Antecedent	Association with Delinquency	Description
Authority conflict	High degree	Youth show stubbornness prior to age 12, then become defiant of authority.
Covert acts	Frequent	Minor covert acts, such as lying, are followed by property damage and moderately serious delinquency, then serious delinquency.
Overt acts of aggression	Frequent	Minor aggression is followed by fighting and violence.
Identity	Negative identity	Erikson argues that delinquency occurs because the adolescent fails to resolve a role identity.
Cognitive distortions	High degree	The thinking of delinquents is frequently characterized by a variety of cognitive distortions (such as egocentric bias, externalizing of blame, and mislabeling) that contribute to inappropriate behavior and lack of self-control.
Self-control	Low degree	Some children and adolescents fail to acquire the essential controls that others have acquired during the process of growing up.
Age	Early initiation	Early appearance of antisocial behavior is associated with serious offenses later in adolescence. However, not every child who acts out becomes a delinquent.
Sex	Male	Boys engage in more antisocial behavior than girls do, although girls are more likely to run away. Boys engage in more violent acts.
Expectations for education and school grades	Low expectations and low grades	Adolescents who become delinquents often have low educational expectations and low grades. Their verbal abilities are often weak.
Parental influences	Monitoring (low), support (low), discipline (ineffective)	Delinquents often come from families in which parents rarely monitor their adolescents, provide them with little support, and ineffectively discipline them.
Sibling relations	Older delinquent sibling	Individuals with an older delinquent sibling are more likely to become delinquent.
Peer influences	Heavy influence, low resistance	Having delinquent peers greatly increases the risk of becoming delinquent.
Socioeconomic status	Low	Serious offenses are committed more frequently by low-socioeconomic-status males.
Neighborhood quality	Urban, high crime, high mobility	Communities often breed crime. Living in a high-crime area, which also is characterized by poverty and dense living conditions, increases the probability that a child will become a delinquent. These communities often have grossly inadequate schools.

FIGURE 9

THE ANTECEDENTS OF JUVENILE DELINQUENCY

Let's further explore the role that family processes play in the development of delinquency. Parents of delinquents are less skilled in discouraging antisocial behavior and in encouraging skilled behavior than are parents of nondelinquents. Parental monitoring of adolescents is especially important in determining whether an adolescent becomes a delinquent (Fosco & others, 2012; Mann & others, 2015). For example, a recent study revealed that parental monitoring and youth disclosure in the fall of grade 6 were linked to a lower incidence of delinquency in grade 8 (Lippold & others, 2014). Also, a recent study found that parental monitoring in adolescence and ongoing parental support were linked to a lower incidence of criminal behavior in emerging adulthood (Johnson & others, 2011). Further, in a recent study, authoritative parenting increased adolescents' perception of the legitimacy of parents' authority, while authoritarian parenting reduced the perception of parental legitimacy of authority (Trinkner & others, 2012). In this study, youths' perception of parental legitimacy was linked to a lower level of future delinquency. And another study found that low rates of delinquency from 14 to 23 years of age were associated with an authoritative parenting style (Murphy & others, 2012).

Rare are the studies that actually demonstrate in an experimental design that changing parenting practices in childhood is related to a lower incidence of juvenile delinquency in adolescence. However, one recent study by Marion Forgatch and her colleagues (2009) randomly assigned divorced mothers with sons to an experimental group (mothers received extensive parenting training) and a control group (mothers received no parenting training) when their sons were in the first to third grades. The parenting training consisted of 14 parent group meetings that especially focused on improving parenting practices with their sons (skill encouragement, limit setting, monitoring, problem solving, and positive involvement). Best practices for emotion regulation, managing interparental conflict, and talking with children about divorce also were included in the sessions. Improved parenting practices and reduced contact with deviant peers were linked with lower rates of delinquency in the experimental group than in the control group at a nine-year follow-up assessment.

An increasing number of studies have found that siblings can have a strong influence on delinquency (Buist, 2010). In one study, high levels of hostile sibling relationships and older sibling delinquency were linked with younger sibling delinquency in both brother pairs and sister pairs (Slomkowski & others, 2001).

Having delinquent peers increases the risk of becoming delinquent (Loeber & Burke, 2011; Mann & others, 2015; Snyder & others, 2012). For example, one study revealed that peer rejection and having deviant friends at 7 to 13 years of age were linked with increased delinquency at 14 to 15 years of age (Vitaro, Pedersen, & Brendgen, 2007).

Although delinquency is less exclusively a phenomenon of lower socioeconomic status than it was in the past, some characteristics of the low-SES culture might promote delinquency (Dawson-McClure & others, 2015). Getting into and staying out of trouble are prominent features of life for some adolescents in low-income neighborhoods. Adolescents from low-income backgrounds may sense that they can gain attention and status by performing antisocial actions. Further, adolescents in communities with high crime rates observe many models who engage in criminal activities. Quality schooling, educational funding, and organized neighborhood activities may be lacking in these communities (Robinson & others, 2015). One study revealed that engaged parenting and the mothers' social network support were linked to a lower level of delinquency in low-income families (Ghazarian & Roche, 2010). And another study found that youth whose families had experienced repeated poverty were more than twice as likely to be delinquent at 14 and 21 years of age (Najman & others, 2010).

Lack of success in school also is associated with delinquency. A recent study found that poor academic performance and reduced attachment to school at age 15 predicted a higher level of criminal activity at 17 to 19 years of age (Savolainen & others, 2012).

Cognitive factors, such as low self-control, low intelligence, poor decision making, ineffective social information processing, and lack of sustained attention, also are implicated in delinquency (Dodge, Godwin, & Conduct Problems Prevention Research Group, 2013; Yun, Cheong, & Walsh, 2014). For example, one study revealed that low-IQ habitual delinquents were characterized by low self-control (Koolhof & others, 2007). And in one study, mothers' reports of their son's impulsiveness at 15 years of age predicted their arrest record up to 6 years in the future (Bechtold & others, 2014). Another study found that at age 16 nondelinquents were more likely to have a higher verbal IQ and engage in sustained attention than were delinquents (Loeber & others, 2007). Further, in a longitudinal study, one of the strongest predictive factors of reduced likelihood of engaging in serious theft and violence was high academic achievement (Loeber & others, 2008).

Effective Prevention and Intervention Programs In a research review of effective juvenile delinquency prevention and intervention programs, the most successful programs are those that prevent juvenile delinquency from

developmental **connection**

Research Methods

Experimental research designs, but not correlational research designs, allow researchers to determine cause-and-effect links. Connect to "Introduction."

What are some factors that are linked to whether adolescents engage in delinquent acts?
© Chuck Savage/Corbis

Rodney Hammond, Health Psychologist

Rodney Hammond described his college experiences: "When I started as an undergraduate at the University of Illinois, Champaign–Urbana, I hadn't decided on my major. But to help finance my education, I took a part-time job in a child development research program sponsored by the psychology department. There, I observed inner-city children in settings designed to enhance their learning. I saw first-hand the contribution psychology can make, and I knew I wanted to be a psychologist" (American Psychological Association, 2003, p. 26).

Rodney Hammond went on to obtain a doctorate in school and community psychology with a focus on children's development. For a number of years, he trained clinical psychologists at Wright State University in Ohio and directed a program to reduce violence in ethnic minority youth. There, he and his associates taught at-risk youth how to use social skills to effectively manage conflict and to recognize situations that could lead to violence. Today, Hammond is director of Violence Prevention at the Centers for Disease Control and Prevention in Atlanta. Hammond says that if you are interested in people and problem solving, psychology is a wonderful way to put these together.

Rodney Hammond talks with an adolescent about strategies for coping with stress and avoiding risk-taking behaviors.
Courtesy of Dr. Rodney Hammond

developmental **connection**

Research Methods

An important issue in the study of adolescent development is the role of early and later experiences. Connect to "Introduction."

occurring in the first place (Greenwood, 2008). Home visiting programs that provide services to pregnant adolescents and their at-risk infants have been found to reduce the risk of delinquency for both the adolescent mothers and their offspring. For example, in the Nurse Family Partnership program, nurses provide child-care recommendations and social-skills training for the mother in a sequence of 20 home visits beginning during prenatal development and continuing through the child's first two years of life (Olds & others, 2004, 2007). Quality preschool education that involves home visits and working with parents also reduces the likelihood that children will become delinquents. Later in the chapter, we will discuss one such program—the Perry Preschool program.

The most successful programs for adolescents who have engaged in delinquency focus on improving family interactions and providing skills to adults who supervise and train the adolescent (Baldwin & others, 2012). A recent meta-analysis found that of five program types (case management, individual treatment, youth court, restorative justice, and family treatment), family treatment was the only one that was linked to a reduction in recidivism for juvenile offenders (Schwalbe & others, 2012). Another recent research review revealed that prevention programs focused on improving the family context were more effective in reducing persistent delinquency than were individual and group-based programs (de Vries & others, 2015). Among the least effective programs for reducing juvenile delinquency are those that emphasize punishment or attempt to scare youth.

To read about the work of one individual who has made a commitment to reducing adolescent problems including delinquency, see the *Connecting with Careers* profile.

DEPRESSION AND SUICIDE

As we saw earlier in the chapter, one of the most frequent characteristics of adolescents referred for psychological treatment is sadness or depression, especially among girls. In this section, we discuss the nature of adolescent depression and adolescent suicide.

Depression   Adolescent depression is a concern not just in the United States but around the world (Bazrafshan & others, 2015; Chen & others, 2015; Gong & others, 2014; Lee &

Choi, 2015; Midgley, Ansaldo, & Target, 2014). An adolescent who says "I'm depressed" or "I'm so down" may be describing a mood that lasts only a few hours or a much longer-lasting mental disorder. In **major depressive disorder,** an individual experiences a major depressive episode and depressed characteristics, such as lethargy and hopelessness, for at least two weeks or longer and daily functioning becomes impaired. According to the *Diagnostic and Statistical Manual of Mental Disorders—Fifth Edition (DSM-V)* classification of mental disorders (American Psychiatric Association, 2013), nine symptoms define a major depressive episode, and to be classified as having major depressive disorder, at least five of these must be present during a two-week period:

1. Depressed mood most of the day
2. Reduced interest or pleasure in all or most activities
3. Significant weight loss or gain, or significant decrease or increase in appetite
4. Trouble sleeping or sleeping too much
5. Psychomotor agitation or retardation
6. Fatigue or loss of energy
7. Feeling worthless or guilty in an excessive or inappropriate manner
8. Problems in thinking, concentrating, or making decisions
9. Recurrent thoughts of death and suicide

In adolescence, pervasive depressive symptoms might be manifested in such ways as primarily wearing black clothes, writing poetry with morbid themes, or being preoccupied with music that has depressive themes. Sleep problems can appear as all-night television watching, difficulty in getting up for school, or sleeping during the day. Lack of interest in usually pleasurable activities may show up as withdrawal from friends or staying alone in the bedroom most of the time. A lack of motivation and energy level can show up in missed classes. Boredom might be a result of feeling depressed. Adolescent depression also can occur in conjunction with conduct disorder, substance abuse, or an eating disorder.

How serious a problem is depression in adolescence? Rates of ever experiencing major depressive disorder range from 1.5 to 2.5 percent in school-age children and 15 to 20 percent for adolescents (Graber & Sontag, 2009). By about age 15, adolescent females have a rate of depression that is twice that of adolescent males. Emerging adult females also have a higher rate of depression than their male counterparts (Morris & others, 2014). The following factors (among others) have been proposed to account for the gender difference in depression among adolescents and emerging adults:

· Females tend to ruminate in their depressed mood and amplify it.
· Females' self-images, especially their body images, are more negative than males'.
· Females experience more stress about weight-related concerns than do males.
· Females face more discrimination than males do.
· Hormonal changes alter vulnerability to depression in adolescence, especially among girls.
· Females may be more vulnerable to developing depression following the occurrence of relational victimization.

Do gender differences in adolescent depression hold for other cultures? In many cultures the gender difference of females experiencing more depression does hold, but a recent study of more than 17,000 Chinese 11- to 22-year-olds revealed that the male adolescents and emerging adults experienced more depression than did their female counterparts (Sun & others, 2010). Explanation of the higher rates of depression among males in China focused on stressful life events and a less positive coping style.

Mental health professionals note that depression often goes undiagnosed in adolescence (Hammen & Keenan-Miller, 2013). Why is this so? According to conventional wisdom, normal adolescents often show mood swings, ruminate in introspective ways, express boredom with life, and indicate a sense of hopelessness. Thus, parents, teachers, and other observers may see these behaviors as simply transitory and reflecting not a mental disorder but normal adolescent behaviors and thoughts.

Is adolescent depression linked to problems in emerging and early adulthood? A recent study initially assessed adolescents when they were 16 to 17 years of age and then again

major depressive disorder The diagnosis when an individual experiences a major depressive episode and depressed characteristics, such as lethargy and depression, for two weeks or longer and daily functioning becomes impaired.

every two years until they were 26 to 27 years of age (Naicker & others, 2013). In this study, significant effects that persisted after 10 years were depression recurrence, stronger depressive symptoms, migraine headaches, poor self-rated health, and low levels of social support. Adolescent depression was not associated with employment status, personal income, marital status, and educational attainment a decade later. In another longitudinal study from 14 to 24 years of age, mild to moderate levels of early adolescent depressive behaviors were linked to lower maternal relationship quality, less positive romantic relationships, and greater loneliness in emerging adulthood (Allen & others, 2014).

Family factors are involved in adolescent and emerging adult depression (Morris & others, 2014; Olino & others, 2015; Waller & Rose, 2013; Yap & others, 2014a, b). Reflecting the developmental cascade approach, Deborah Capaldi, Gerald Patterson, and their colleagues (Capaldi, 1992; Capaldi & Stoolmiller, 1999; Patterson, DeBaryshe, & Ramsey, 1989; Patterson & others, 1992) have proposed that behavior problems arising in the family in the early childhood years that are connected to inept parenting are carried forward into school contexts, producing problems in academics (poor grades, for example) and social competence (difficulty in peer relations, for example). This cascade of connecting relationships and contexts is expected to contribute to depressive symptoms.

Consider also the following research studies, which identify the roles that parents can have in the development of adolescent depression:

- Positive parenting characteristics (emotional support, parent-child future orientation, and education support) were associated with less depression in adolescents (Smokowski & others, 2015).
- Parent-adolescent conflict and low parental support were linked to adolescent depression (Sheeber & others, 2007).
- Mother-daughter co-rumination (extensively discussing, rehashing, and speculating about problems) was linked to an increase in anxiety and depression in adolescent daughters (Waller & Rose, 2010). A recent study also found that co-rumination increased internalizing symptoms in youths' friendships (Schwartz-Mette & Rose, 2012).
- Exposure to maternal depression by age 12 predicted risk processes during development (higher stress and difficulties in family relationships), which set the course for the development of the adolescent's depression (Garber & Cole, 2010).

Poor peer relationships also are associated with adolescent depression (Vanhalst & Lau, 2012). Not having a close relationship with a best friend, having less contact with friends, and being rejected by peers increase depressive tendencies in adolescents (Platt, Kadosh, & others, 2013; Vernberg, 1990). Problems in adolescent romantic relationships can also trigger depression (Furman & Rose, 2015; Sternberg & Davila, 2008).

Friendship often provides social support. One study found that friendship provided a protective effect to prevent an increase in depressive symptoms in adolescents who avoided peer relations or were excluded from them as children (Bukowski, Laursen, & Hoza, 2010). However, researchers have found that one aspect of social support—the tendency to co-ruminate by frequently discussing and rehashing problems—is a risk factor for the development of depression in adolescent girls (Rose, Carlson, & Waller, 2007; Rose & others, 2014). For example, a recent study revealed that adolescent girls who had a high level of co-rumination were more likely two years later to develop depressive symptoms more quickly, to have more severe symptoms, and to remain depressed for a longer period of time (Stone & others, 2011). One implication of this research is that some girls who are vulnerable to developing internalized problems may go undetected because they have supportive friendships.

A higher incidence of adolescent depression occurs in girls and boys, especially girls, when they are overweight or obese (Herpertz-Dahlmann & others, 2015). In a British study, obesity in adolescent girls, but not boys, was linked to depression in adulthood (Geoffrey, Li, & Power, 2014). Also, in a recent Chinese study, obesity was associated with depression in young adolescents (Wang & others, 2014). Being stressed about weight-related concerns is increasingly thought to contribute to the greater incidence of depression in adolescent girls than in adolescent boys (Marmorstein, Iacono, & Legrand, 2014). In one study a heightened tendency to perceive themselves as overweight and to diet was linked to adolescent girls' higher level of depressive symptoms (Vaughan & Halpern, 2010).

What type of treatment is most effective in reducing depression in adolescence? A recent research review concluded that treatment of adolescent depression needs to take into account the severity of the depression, suicidal tendencies, and social factors (Clark, Jansen, & Cloy, 2012). In this review, cognitive behavioral therapy and interpersonal therapy were recommended for adolescents with mild depression and in combination with drug therapy for adolescents experiencing moderate or severe depression. However, caution needs to be exercised when using antidepressants, such as Prozac, with adolescents (Morrison & Schwartz, 2014). In 2004, the U.S. Food and Drug Administration assigned warnings to such drugs, stating that they slightly increase the risk of suicidal behavior in adolescents. In the study just described, 15 percent of depressed adolescents who only took Prozac had suicidal thoughts or attempted suicide compared with 6 percent who only received cognitive behavioral therapy and 8 percent who received both Prozac and cognitive behavioral therapy. Nonetheless, a recent research review concluded that Prozac and other SSRIs (selective serotonin reuptake inhibitors) show clinical benefits for adolescents at risk for moderate and severe depression (Cousins & Goodyer, 2015).

Suicide Depression is linked to an increase in suicidal ideation and suicide attempts in adolescence (Clarke & others, 2014; Thompson & Light, 2011). Suicidal behavior is rare in childhood but escalates in adolescence and then increases further in emerging adulthood (Park & others, 2006). Suicide is the third leading cause of death in 10- to 19-year-olds today in the United States (National Center for Health Statistics, 2014).

What are some characteristics of adolescents who become depressed? What are some factors that are linked with suicide attempts by adolescents?
© BananaStock/PunchStock RF

Although a suicide threat should always be taken seriously, far more adolescents contemplate or attempt it unsuccessfully than actually commit it. After increasing to high levels in the 1990s, suicide rates in adolescents have declined in recent years. In 2013 in the United States, 17 percent of adolescents (22 percent of females, 12 percent of males) had considered attempting suicide in the previous 12 months (down from 29 percent in 1991) (Kann & others, 2014) (See Figure 10). In this survey, 8 percent of U.S. adolescents had actually attempted suicide in the previous 12 months (11 percent of females, 5 percent of males).

Approximately 4,600 adolescents commit suicide each year (Centers for Disease Control and Prevention, 2015). The rate of suicide among emerging adults is triple that of adolescents (Park & others, 2006). Although females are more likely to attempt suicide than males, males are more likely to succeed in committing suicide (Hamilton & Klimes-Dougan, 2015).

In emerging adulthood, males are six times as likely to commit suicide as females (National Center for Injury Prevention and Control, 2006). Males use more lethal means, such as guns, in their suicide attempts, whereas adolescent females are more likely to cut their wrists or take an overdose of sleeping pills—methods less likely to result in death.

Cultural contexts also are related to suicide attempts, and adolescent suicide attempts vary across ethnic groups in the United States (Kann & others, 2014; Sherman & others,

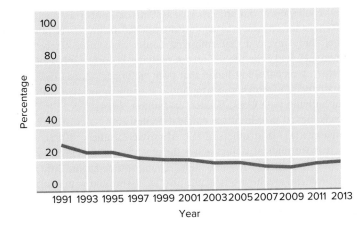

FIGURE **10**

PERCENTAGE OF U.S. NINTH- TO TWELFTH-GRADE STUDENTS WHO SERIOUSLY CONSIDERED ATTEMPTING SUICIDE IN THE PREVIOUS 12 MONTHS FROM 1991 TO 2013

FIGURE **11**

SUICIDE ATTEMPTS BY U.S. ADOLESCENTS FROM DIFFERENT ETHNIC GROUPS. *Note:* Data shown are for one-year rates of self-reported suicide attempts. NA/AN = Native American/Alaska Native; AA/PI = Asian American/Pacific Islander.

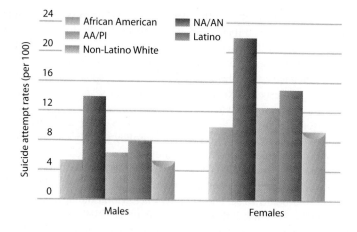

2014). As indicated in Figure 11, more than 20 percent of Native American/Alaska Native (NA/AN) female adolescents reported that they had attempted suicide in the previous year, and suicide accounts for almost 20 percent of NA/AN deaths in 15- to 19-year olds (Goldston & others, 2008). African American and non-Latino White males reported the lowest incidence of suicide attempts. A major risk factor in the high rate of suicide attempts by NA/AN adolescents is their elevated rate of alcohol abuse.

Both early and later experiences may be involved in suicide attempts (Brockie & others, 2015; Esposito-Smythers & others, 2014). The adolescent might have a long-standing history of family instability and unhappiness. Lack of affection and emotional support, high control, and pressure for achievement by parents during childhood are likely to show up as factors in suicide attempts. Adolescents who have experienced abuse also are at risk for suicidal ideation and attempts (Rhodes & others, 2012; Yen & others, 2013). And a recent study revealed that adolescents who engaged in suicidal ideation perceived their family functioning to be significantly worse than did their caregivers (Lipschitz & others, 2012). Another recent study found that family discord and negative relationships with parents were associated with increased suicide attempts by depressed adolescents (Consoli & others, 2013). And in recent study, authoritative parenting was linked to fewer adolescent suicide attempts; rejecting/neglecting parenting was associated with a greater likelihood of adolescent suicide attempts (Donath & others, 2014). Further, a recent study found that having an insecure avoidant attachment style was linked to a higher incidence of suicide attempts in adolescence (Sheftall, Schoppe-Sullivan, & Bridge, 2014). Recent and current stressful circumstances, such as getting poor grades in school or experiencing the breakup of a romantic relationship, may trigger suicide attempts (Antai-Otong, 2003; Soller, 2014).

Adolescents' peer relations also are linked to suicide attempts (Matlin, Molock, & Tebes, 2011). A research review concluded that prior suicide attempts by a member of an adolescent's social group increased the probability that the adolescent also would attempt suicide (de Leo & Heller, 2008). Another factor may be a lack of supportive friendships. For example, a recent study revealed that family support, peer support, and community connectedness were linked to a lower risk of suicidal tendencies in African American adolescents (Matlin & others, 2011). And adolescents who are involved in bullying, either as a victim or a perpetrator, are at higher risk for engaging in adolescent suicidal behavior (Hepburn & others, 2012). A longitudinal study revealed that emerging adults were more likely to engage in suicidal behavior when they had been the victims of bullying in early adolescence (Copeland & others, 2013). Further, a recent study found that peer victimization was linked to suicidal ideation and suicide attempts, with cyberbullying more strongly associated with suicidal ideation than traditional bullying (van Geel, Vedder, & Tanilon, 2014).

What is the psychological profile of the suicidal adolescent? Suicidal adolescents often have depressive symptoms (Fried & others, 2013; Mirkovic & others, 2015). Although not all depressed adolescents are suicidal, depression is the most frequently cited factor associated with adolescent suicide (Bethell & Rhoades, 2008; Thompson & Light, 2011). A sense of hopelessness, low self-esteem, and high self-blame also are associated with adolescent suicide (Asarnow & others, 2015; Kleiman, Law, & Anestis, 2014). A recent study found that college students with greater depression severity and a higher level of hopelessness were at risk for engaging in suicidal ideation (Farabaugh & others, 2012). In another recent study, both depression and hopelessness were predictors of adolescents who repeated a suicide attempt across a six-month period (Consoli & others, 2015). The following studies document a number of factors linked with adolescent suicide attempts:

· Overweight middle school students were more likely to think about, plan, and attempt suicide than their counterparts who were not overweight (Whetstone, Morrissey, & Cummings, 2007). Another study revealed that adolescent girls, but not boys, who perceived they were overweight were at risk for engaging in suicidal ideation (Seo & Lee, 2013).

· Playing sports predicted lower suicidal ideation in boys and venting by talking to others was associated with lower suicidal ideation in girls (Kim & others, 2014).

· More recent and frequent alcohol use among young adolescents increased the likelihood of suicidal ideation and attempts in African American youth (Tomek & others, 2015).

· Data from the National Longitudinal Study of Adolescent Health identified the following indicators of suicide risk: depressive symptoms, a sense of hopelessness, engaging in suicidal ideation, having a family background of suicidal behavior, and having friends with a history of suicidal behavior (Thompson, Kuruwita, & Foster, 2009).

· Frequent, escalating stress, especially at home, was linked with suicide attempts in young Latinas (Zayas & others, 2010). And in another study, Latina adolescents' suicidal ideation was associated with having a suicidal friend, as well as lower perceived parental and teacher support (De Luca, Wyman, & Warren, 2012).

· Sexual victimization was linked to a risk for suicide attempts in adolescence (Plener, Singer, & Goldbeck, 2011). Also, a recent study found that adolescent females who were the victims of dating violence were at a higher risk for planning and/or attempting suicide than were their counterparts who had not been victimized (Belshaw & others, 2012).

· No national studies have been conducted regarding suicide rates in gay, lesbian, and bisexual adolescents. However, a recent study in Boston found that sexual minority adolescents living in neighborhoods with higher rates of lesbian, gay, and bisexual crimes reported a higher rate of suicidal ideation and attempts (Duncan & Hatzenbuehler, 2014).

In some instances, suicides in adolescence occur in clusters (Haw & others, 2013). That is, when one adolescent commits suicide, other adolescents who find out about this also commit suicide. Such "copycat" suicides raise the issue of whether or not suicides should be reported in the media; a news report might plant the idea of committing suicide in other adolescents' minds.

Figure 12 provides valuable information about what to do and what not to do when you suspect someone is likely to attempt suicide.

What to do	What not to do
1. Ask direct, straightforward questions in a calm manner: "Are you thinking about hurting yourself?"	1. Do not ignore the warning signs.
2. Assess the seriousness of the suicidal intent by asking questions about feelings, important relationships, who else the person has talked with, and the amount of thought given to the means to be used. If a gun, pills, a rope, or other means have been obtained and a precise plan has been developed, clearly the situation is dangerous. Stay with the person until help arrives.	2. Do not refuse to talk about suicide if a person approaches you about it.
	3. Do not react with humor, disapproval, or repulsion.
	4. Do not give false reassurances by saying such things as "Everything is going to be OK." Also do not give out simple answers or platitudes, such as "You have everything to be thankful for."
3. Be a good listener and be very supportive without being falsely reassuring.	5. Do not abandon the individual after the crisis has passed or after professional help has commenced.
4. Try to persuade the person to obtain professional help and assist him or her in getting this help.	

FIGURE **12**

WHAT TO DO AND WHAT NOT TO DO WHEN YOU SUSPECT SOMEONE IS LIKELY TO ATTEMPT SUICIDE

EATING DISORDERS

Eating disorders have become increasingly common among adolescents (Schiff, 2015). Here are some research findings involving adolescent eating disorders:

- *Body image.* Body dissatisfaction and distorted body image play important roles in adolescent eating disorders (Kroon Van Diest & Perez, 2013). One study revealed that in general, adolescents were dissatisfied with their bodies, with males desiring to increase their upper body and females wanting to decrease the overall size of their body (Ata, Ludden, & Lally, 2007). In this study, low self-esteem and social support, weight-related teasing, and pressure to lose weight were linked to adolescents' negative body image. In another study, girls who felt negatively about their bodies in early adolescence were more likely to develop eating disorders two years later than were their counterparts who did not feel negatively about their bodies (Attie & Brooks-Gunn, 1989). And a recent study found that the key aspect of explaining depression in overweight adolescents involved body dissatisfaction (Mond & others, 2011).

- *Parenting.* Parents' attitudes, parenting styles, and behavior play important roles in adolescent eating disorders (Alia & others, 2013; Fuemmeler & others, 2012; Loth & others, 2013). Adolescents who reported observing more healthy eating patterns and exercise by their parents had more healthy eating patterns and exercised more themselves (Pakpreo & others, 2004). Negative parent-adolescent relationships were linked with increased dieting by girls over a one-year period (Archibald, Graber, & Brooks-Gunn, 1999).

- *Sexual activity.* Girls who were both sexually active with their boyfriends and in pubertal transition were the most likely to be dieting or engaging in disordered eating patterns (Cauffman, 1994).

- *Role models and the media.* Girls who were highly motivated to look like female celebrities were more likely than their peers to become very concerned about their weight (Field & others, 2001). Watching commercials with idealized thin female images increased adolescent girls' dissatisfaction with their bodies (Hargreaves & Tiggemann, 2004). Also, a study of adolescent girls revealed that frequently reading magazine articles about dieting and weight loss was linked with unhealthy weight-control behaviors such as fasting, skipping meals, and smoking more cigarettes five years later (van den Berg & others, 2007). And a recent study of female undergraduates revealed that they spent considerably more time viewing online appearance-oriented media than reading image-focused magazines (Bair & others, 2012). In this study, the college females' appearance-oriented Internet use was associated with eating pathology, especially internalization of the ideal of having a thin body.

Let's now examine different types of eating problems in adolescence, beginning with overweight and obesity.

© Jules Frazier/Getty Images RF

Overweight and Obese Adolescents Obesity is a serious and pervasive health problem for many adolescents and emerging adults (Donatelle, 2015; Lynch, Elmore, & Kotecki, 2015). The Centers for Disease Control and Prevention (2014) has a category of obesity for adults but does not have an obesity category for children and adolescents because of the stigma the label *obesity* may bring. Rather, they have categories for being overweight or at risk for being overweight in childhood and adolescence. These categories are determined by *body mass index (BMI)*, which is computed by a formula that takes into account height and weight. Only children and adolescents at or above the 95th percentile of BMI are included in the category of overweight, and those at or above the 85th percentile are included in the category of at risk for being overweight.

National data indicated that the percentage of overweight U.S. 12- to 19-year-olds increased from 11 percent in the early 1990s to nearly 21 percent in 2011–2012 (Ogden & others, 2014). In another recent study, 12.4 percent of U.S. kindergarten children were overweight but by 14 years of age, 20.8 percent were overweight (Cunningham, Kramer, & Narayan, 2014).

And more emerging adults are overweight or obese than are adolescents. A recent longitudinal study tracked more than 1,500 adolescents who were classified as not overweight, overweight, or obese when they were 14 years of age (Patton & others, 2011a). Across the 10-year period of the study, the percentage of overweight individuals increased from 20 percent at 14 years of age to 33 percent at 24 years of age. Obesity increased from 4 percent to 7 percent across the 10 years. Also, a recent study found that being overweight or obese increased from 25.6 percent for college freshman to 32 percent for college seniors (Nicoteri & Miskovsky, 2014).

Are there ethnic variations in being overweight during adolescence in the United States? A survey by the National Center for Health Statistics (2002) found that African American girls and Latino boys have especially high risks of being overweight during adolescence (see Figure 13). One study revealed that the higher obesity rate for African American females is linked with a diet higher in calories and fat, as well as sedentary behavior (Sanchez-Johnsen & others, 2004).

U.S. children and adolescents are more likely to be overweight or obese than their counterparts in most other countries (Lu & others, 2013; Spruijt-Metz, 2011). One comparison of 34 countries found that the United States had the second highest rate of childhood obesity (Janssen & others, 2005). In another study, U.S. children and adolescents (6 to 18 years of age) were four times more likely to be classified as obese than their counterparts in China and almost three times more likely to be classified as obese than their counterparts in Russia (Wang, 2000).

Eating patterns established in childhood and adolescence are strongly linked to obesity in adulthood. One study revealed that 62 percent of the male and 73 percent of the female adolescents in the 85th to 94th percentile of BMI became obese adults (Wang & others, 2008). In this study, of those at the 95th percentile and higher for BMI, 80 percent of the males and 92 percent of the females became obese adults. A study of more than 8,000 12- to 21-year-olds found that obese adolescents were more likely to develop severe obesity in emerging adulthood than were overweight or normal-weight adolescents (The & others, 2010).

Both heredity and environmental factors are involved in obesity. Some individuals inherit a tendency to be overweight (Tutone & others, 2014). Only 10 percent of children who do not have obese parents become obese themselves, whereas 40 percent of children who become obese have one obese parent, and 70 percent of children who become obese have two obese parents. Identical twins, even when they are reared apart, have similar weights.

Environmental factors play a role in obesity (Willett, 2013). Strong evidence of the environment's role in obesity is the doubling of the rate of obesity in the United States since 1900, as well as the significant increase in adolescent obesity since the 1960s, as described earlier. This dramatic increase in obesity likely is due to greater availability of food (especially food high in fat), energy-saving devices, and declining physical activity. A recent international study of adolescents in 56 countries found fast-food consumption is high in childhood but increases further in adolescence (Braithwaite & others, 2014). In this study, adolescents in the frequent and very frequent categories of eating fast food had higher body mass indices than adolescents in the lower frequency categories. Further, increases in screen time in adolescence are associated with adolescent overweight and obesity (Saunders, Chaput, & Tremblay, 2014).

Being overweight or obese has negative effects on adolescent health, in terms of both biological development and socioemotional development (Anspaugh & Ezell, 2013; Hampl & Campbell, 2015; Lobstein & others, 2015; Sypniewska, 2015). In terms of biological development, being overweight in adolescence is linked with high blood pressure, hip problems, pulmonary problems, and type 2 (adult-onset) diabetes. Researchers have found that adolescents' blood pressure has increased in the twenty-first century, and this increase is linked with the increase in being overweight in adolescence (Saunders & others, 2014; Sakou & others, 2015). In terms of socioemotional development, adolescents who are overweight are more likely than their normal-weight counterparts to have low self-esteem, to be depressed, and to have problems in relationships with peers (Sanders & others, 2015; Vaughan & Halpern, 2010). One study found that adolescent and young adult females who were overeaters or binge eaters were twice as likely as their peers to develop depressive symptoms across the next four years (Skinner & others, 2012). Also in this study, females who reported depressive symptoms were twice as likely as their peers to start overeating or binge eating in the next four years. One study also revealed that in most cases adolescent girls who were overweight were teased

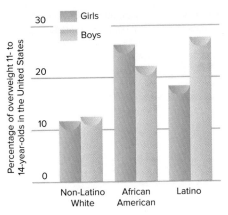

FIGURE 13

PERCENTAGE OF OVERWEIGHT U.S. ADOLESCENT BOYS AND GIRLS IN DIFFERENT ETHNIC GROUPS

developmental **connection**

Health

A special concern is the high amount of fat and low amount of vegetables in U.S. adolescents' diets. Connect to "Puberty, Health, and Biological Foundations."

about it more than boys who were overweight (Taylor, 2011). Another recent study found that adolescents who were often/sometimes bullied by their peer group were at greater risk for obesity at 21 years of age (Mamun & others, 2013).

What types of interventions and activities have been successful in reducing overweight in adolescents and emerging adults? Research indicates that dietary changes and regular exercise are key components of weight reduction in adolescence and emerging adulthood (Omorou & others, 2015; Ryan & others, 2014; Thompson & Manore, 2015). A recent three-month experimental study found that both aerobic exercise and resistance exercise without caloric restriction were effective in reducing abdominal fat and insulin sensitivity in overweight adolescent boys compared with a no-exercise control group (Lee & others, 2012). A recent study also revealed that playing on a sports team was an important factor in adolescents' weight. In this study, among a wide range of activities (other physical activity, physical education, screen time, and diet quality, for example), team sports participation was the strongest predictor of lower risk for being overweight or obese (Drake & others, 2012).

developmental connection

Health

Researchers have found that as boys and girls reach and progress through adolescence, they become less active. Connect to "Puberty, Health, and Biological Foundations."

One research review indicated that clinical approaches that focus on the individual adolescent and include a combination of caloric restriction, exercise (walking or biking to school, participating in a regular exercise program), reduction of sedentary activity (watching TV, playing video games), and behavioral therapy (such as keeping weight-loss diaries and receiving rewards for meeting goals) have been moderately effective in helping overweight adolescents lose weight (Fowler-Brown & Kahwati, 2004). A research review concluded that interventions targeted at changing family lifestyle were the most effective in helping children and adolescents lose weight (Oude Luttikhuis & others, 2009). A recent study revealed that family meals during adolescence protected against the development of being overweight or obese in adulthood (Berge & others, 2015). In general, school-based approaches (such as instituting a school-wide program to improve eating habits) have been less effective than clinically based individual approaches (Dobbins & others, 2009; Lytle, 2009). A research review concluded that school-based approaches for reducing adolescents' weight produce modest results, with TV watching the easiest behavior to change, followed by physical activity and then nutrition (Sharma, 2006).

A concern is that as schools are under increasing pressure to spend more time on academic topics, health-oriented programs are likely to be shortchanged. When this is an impediment, one possible solution is to include obesity prevention in after-school programs that conflict less with schools' academic mandates (Story, Kaphingst, & French, 2006). Another promising strategy is to provide students with more healthful foods to eat at school (Waters & others, 2011). In 2005, several states began enacting laws that require more healthful foods and less unhealthful foods be sold in vending machines at schools. Schools also can play an important role by implementing programs that increase the amount of time students exercise (Dumith & others, 2010).

Most parents with an overweight child or adolescent want to help them to lose weight but aren't sure how to accomplish this goal. Following are some recommendations for parents about helping their overweight children and adolescents to lose weight (DiLonardo, 2013; Matthiessen, 2013; Moninger, 2013):

·   *Work on a healthy project together and involve children and adolescents in the decision-making process.* Get involved in an activity that can help them lose weight such as purchasing pedometers for all family members and developing goals for how many steps to take each day. By involving children and adolescents in making decisions about the family's health, the hope is that they will begin to take responsibility for their own health.

·   *Be a healthy model for your children and adolescents.* In many aspects of life, what people do is more influential than what they say. So if parents are overweight and engaging in behaviors such as eating fast food and not exercising, but telling their overweight children and adolescents to lose weight, their words are unlikely to be effective. A recent study revealed that when adolescents' caregivers lost weight, the adolescents also lost weight (Xanthopoulos & others, 2013).

·   *Engage in physical activities with children and adolescents.* Parents and children can engage in activities like bicycling, jogging, hiking, and swimming together with their children and adolescents. Parents might say something like "Let's take a bike ride after dinner this evening. It would be fun and could help us both get in better shape."

·   *Give children and adolescents choices about what they want to do to lose weight.* Take them to the grocery store with you and let them select the fruits and vegetables they are willing to eat. Let them choose which sport or type of exercise they would like to do.

·   *Eat healthful family meals together on a regular basis.* Children and adolescents who eat meals together with their family are less likely to be overweight.

·   *Reduce screen time.* Children and adolescents who spend large numbers of hours per day in screen time are more likely to be overweight than their counterparts who are not overweight.

Anorexia Nervosa, Bulimia Nervosa, and Binge Eating Disorder   Three eating disorders that may appear in adolescence and emerging adulthood are anorexia nervosa, bulimia nervosa, and binge eating disorder.

Anorexia Nervosa   Although most U.S. girls have been on a diet at some point, slightly less than 1 percent ever develop anorexia nervosa. **Anorexia nervosa** is an eating disorder that involves the relentless pursuit of thinness through starvation. It is a serious disorder that can lead to death. Three main characteristics apply to people suffering from anorexia nervosa: (1) a clinically significant level of being underweight; (2) an intense fear of gaining weight that does not decrease with weight loss; (3) a distorted image of their body shape (Herpertz-Dahlmann, 2015; Hagman & others, 2015; Hartmann & others, 2015; Herpertz-Dahlmann & others, 2015). Obsessive thinking about weight and compulsive exercise also are linked to anorexia nervosa (Breithaupt, Payne, & Rose, 2014; Godier & Park, 2014). Even when they are extremely thin, they see themselves as too fat. They never think they are thin enough, especially in the abdomen, buttocks, and thighs. They usually weigh themselves frequently, often take their body measurements, and gaze critically at themselves in mirrors.

Anorexia nervosa typically begins in the early to middle adolescent years, often following an episode of dieting and some type of life stress (Bakalar & others, 2015; Fitzpatrick, 2012). It is about 10 times more likely to occur in females than males. When anorexia nervosa does occur in males, the symptoms and other characteristics (such as a distorted body image and family conflict) are usually similar to those reported by females who have the disorder (Ariceli & others, 2005).

Most individuals with anorexia are non-Latina White adolescent or young adult females from well-educated, middle- and upper-income families and are competitive and high achieving (Darcy, 2012). They set high standards, become stressed about not being able to reach the standards, and are intensely concerned about how others perceive them (Woelders & others, 2010). A recent study found that anorexics had an elevated level of perfectionism in

Anorexia nervosa has become an increasing problem for adolescent girls and emerging adult women. *What are some possible causes of anorexia nervosa?*
© Ian Thraves/Alamy

anorexia nervosa An eating disorder that involves the relentless pursuit of thinness through starvation.

comparison with non-anorexic individuals (Lloyd & others, 2014). Unable to meet their high expectations, they turn their focus to something they can control—their weight. Offspring of mothers with anorexia nervosa are at risk for becoming anorexic themselves (Striegel-Moore & Bulik, 2007). Problems in family functioning are increasingly being found to be linked to the appearance of anorexia nervosa in adolescent girls (Machado & others, 2014), and family therapy is often recommended as a treatment for adolescent girls with anorexia nervosa (Campbell & Peebles, 2014; Engman-Bredvik & others, 2015; Silber, 2013). A recent study revealed that family therapy was effective in helping adolescent girls with anorexia nervosa to gain weight over the course of one year (Gabel & others, 2014).

Biology and culture are involved in anorexia nervosa. Genes play an important role in the development of this disorder (Bakalar & others, 2015; Boraska & others, 2014). Also, the physical effects of dieting may change brain functioning and neural networks and thus sustain the disordered pattern (Fuglset & others, 2015). The fashion image in U.S. culture likely contributes to the incidence of anorexia nervosa (Benowitz-Fredericks & others, 2012). The media portray thin as beautiful in their choice of fashion models, whom many adolescent girls strive to emulate (Carr & Peebles, 2012). And many adolescent girls who strive to be thin hang out together.

Bulimia Nervosa   Although anorexics control their eating by restricting it, most bulimics cannot. **Bulimia nervosa** is an eating disorder in which the individual consistently follows a binge-and-purge eating pattern. The bulimic goes on an eating binge and then purges by self-induced vomiting or use of a laxative. Although some people binge and purge occasionally and some experiment with it, a person is considered to have a serious bulimic disorder only if the episodes occur at least twice a week for three months (Cuzzalaro, 2014).

As with anorexics, most bulimics are preoccupied with food, have a strong fear of becoming overweight, and are depressed or anxious. Like anorexics, bulimics are highly perfectionistic (Lampard & others, 2012). A recent study found that bulimics have difficulty controlling their emotions (Lavender & others, 2014). Unlike anorexics, people who binge and purge typically fall within a normal weight range, a characteristic that makes bulimia more difficult to detect.

Bulimia nervosa typically begins in late adolescence or early adulthood. About 90 percent of the cases are women. Approximately 1 to 2 percent of women are estimated to develop bulimia nervosa. Many women who develop bulimia nervosa were somewhat overweight before the onset of the disorder, and the binge eating often began during an episode of dieting. One study of adolescent girls found that increased dieting, pressure to be thin, exaggerated importance placed on appearance, body dissatisfaction, depression symptoms, low self-esteem, and low social support predicted binge eating two years later (Stice, Presnell, & Spangler, 2002). Another study of individuals with anorexia nervosa or bulimia nervosa revealed that attachment insecurity was linked with body dissatisfaction, which was a key aspect of predicting and perpetuating these eating disorders (Abbate-Daga & others, 2010). In this study, need for approval was an important predictor of bulimia nervosa. As with anorexia nervosa, about 70 percent of individuals who develop bulimia nervosa eventually recover from the disorder (Agras & others, 2004). Drug therapy and psychotherapy have been effective in treating anorexia nervosa and bulimia nervosa (Campbell & Peebles, 2014; Thompson-Brenner & others, 2014). Cognitive behavior therapy has especially been helpful in treating bulimia nervosa (Hay, 2013; Knott & others, 2015; Thompson-Brenner, 2015).

Binge Eating Disorder (BED)   **Binge eating disorder (BED)** involves frequent binge eating but without compensatory behavior like the purging that characterizes bulimics. Individuals with BED engage in recurrent episodes of eating large quantities of food during which they feel a lack of control over eating (Schag & others, 2013). Because they don't purge, individuals with BED are frequently overweight (Allen, Byrne, & Crosby, 2015; Field & others, 2012). For the first time, binge eating disorder was included by the American Psychiatric Association in the fifth edition of its classification of psychiatric disorders in 2013.

Researchers are examining the role of biological and psychological factors in BED (Degortes & others, 2014). Genes play a role, as does dopamine, the neurotransmitter related to reward pathways in the brain (Brownley & others, 2015; Hardaway & others, 2015). A recent fMRI study also found that the areas of the brain involved in self-regulation and impulse control, especially the prefrontal cortex, showed diminished activity in individuals with binge eating disorder (Balodis & others, 2013).

A recent research view indicated that the two best predictors that differentiated BED from other eating disorders were eating in secret and feeling disgust after the episode

bulimia nervosa An eating disorder in which the individual consistently follows a binge-and-purge eating pattern.

binge eating disorder (BED) Involves frequent binge eating without compensatory behavior like the purging that characterizes bulimics.

(White & Grilo, 2011). One study also found that individuals with BED showed a more negative pattern of everyday emotions, with anger being the emotion that was most often reported before a binging episode (Zeeck & others, 2010). And another recent study of adolescents and young adults revealed that dieters were two to three times more likely than nondieters to develop binge eating problems over a five-year period (Goldschmidt & others, 2012). In this study, at most points in time, depressive symptoms and low self-esteem predicted binge eating onset beyond the influence of dieting alone.

Adults in treatment for BED number approximately 1 to 2 million people, and they often say that their binging problems began in childhood or adolescence (New, 2008). Common health risks of BED are those related to being overweight or obese, such as high blood pressure, diabetes, and depression (Peterson & others, 2012).

Review Connect Reflect

LG2 Describe some problems and disorders that characterize adolescents and emerging adults

Review

- What are some trends in adolescent drug use? What are some characteristics of the use of alcohol, hallucinogens, stimulants, depressants, anabolic steroids, and inhalants by adolescents? What are the main factors that are related to adolescent and emerging adult drug use?
- What is juvenile delinquency? What are the antecedents of juvenile delinquency? What characterizes violence in youth?
- What characterizes adolescent depression? How common is suicide in adolescence and emerging adulthood? What are some possible causes of suicide in adolescence and emerging adulthood?
- What are some trends in eating disorders? What are the main eating disorders in adolescence and emerging adulthood? What are some of their characteristics?

Connect

- How might the development of values be related to an adolescent's or emerging adult's decision to engage in drug use or abstain?

Reflect Your Own Personal Journey of Life

- Imagine that you have just been appointed to head the U.S. President's Commission on Adolescent Drug Abuse. What would be the first program you would try to put in place? What would its components be?

3 Interrelation of Problems and Prevention/Intervention

LG3 Summarize the interrelation of problems and ways to prevent or intervene in problems

Adolescents with Multiple Problems

Prevention and Intervention

What problems affect the largest number of adolescents? What are the best strategies for preventing or intervening in adolescent problems?

ADOLESCENTS WITH MULTIPLE PROBLEMS

The four problems that affect the largest number of adolescents are (1) drug abuse, (2) juvenile delinquency, (3) sexual problems, and (4) school-related problems (Dryfoos, 1990; Dryfoos & Barkin, 2006a, b). The adolescents most at risk have more than one of these problems. Researchers are increasingly finding that problem behaviors in adolescence are interrelated (Nakawaki & Crano, 2015). For example, heavy substance abuse is related to early sexual

What characterizes the most at-risk adolescents?
© Peter Beavis/Getty Images RF

activity, lower grades, dropping out of school, and delinquency (Grigsby & others, 2014; Swartzendruber & others, 2015). Early initiation of sexual activity is associated with the use of cigarettes and alcohol, use of marijuana and other illicit drugs, lower grades, dropping out of school, and delinquency (Chan & others, 2015). Delinquency is related to early sexual activity, early pregnancy, substance abuse, and dropping out of school (Dudovitz, McCoy, & Chung, 2015; Pedersen & Mastekaasa, 2011). As much as 10 percent of the adolescent population in the United States have serious multiple-problem behaviors (adolescents who have dropped out of school, or are behind in their grade level, are users of heavy drugs, regularly use cigarettes and marijuana, and are sexually active but do not use contraception). Many, but not all, of these very high-risk youth "do it all." In 1990, it was estimated that another 15 percent of adolescents participate in many of these same behaviors but with slightly lower frequency and less deleterious consequences (Dryfoos, 1990). These high-risk youth often engage in two or three problem behaviors (Dryfoos, 1990). It was estimated that in 2005 the figure for high-risk youth had increased to 20 percent of all U.S. adolescents (Dryfoos & Barkin, 2006a, b).

PREVENTION AND INTERVENTION

In addition to understanding that many adolescents engage in multiple-problem behaviors, it also is important to develop programs that reduce adolescent problems (Friedberg & McClure, 2015; Mash & Wolfe, 2016). We considered a number of prevention and intervention strategies for specific adolescent problems, such as drug abuse and juvenile delinquency, earlier in the chapter. Here we focus on some general strategies for preventing and intervening in adolescent problems. In a review of the programs that have been successful in preventing or reducing adolescent problems, adolescent researcher Joy Dryfoos (1990, 1997; Dryfoos & Barkin, 2006a, b) described the common components of these successful programs. The common components include these:

1. *Intensive individualized attention.* In successful programs, high-risk youth are attached to a responsible adult who gives the youth attention and deals with the youth's specific needs (Glidden-Tracey, 2005; Nation & others, 2003). This theme occurred in a number of different programs. In a substance-abuse program, a student assistance counselor was available full-time for individual counseling and referral for treatment. Programs often require highly trained personnel, and they extend over a long period to remain successful (Dryfoos & Barkin, 2006a, b).

2. *Community-wide, multiagency collaborative approaches.* The basic philosophy of community-wide programs is that a number of different programs and services have to be in place. In one successful substance-abuse program, a community-wide health promotion campaign was implemented that used local media and community education in concert with a substance-abuse curriculum in the schools. Community programs that include policy changes and media campaigns are more effective when they are coordinated with family, peer, and school components (Wandersman & Florin, 2003).

3. *Early identification and intervention.* Reaching children and their families before children develop problems, or at the beginning of their problems, is a successful strategy (Cichetti & Toth, 2015).

Below are descriptions of three prevention programs/research studies that merit attention:

· *High Scope.* One preschool program serves as an excellent model for the prevention of delinquency, pregnancy, substance abuse, and dropping out of school. Operated by the High Scope Foundation in Ypsilanti, Michigan, the Perry Preschool approach has had a long-term positive impact on its students (Schweinhart & others, 2005; Weikert, 1993). The High Scope enrichment program, directed by David Weikert, services disadvantaged African American children. They attend a high-quality two-year preschool program and receive weekly home visits from program personnel.

Based on official police records, by age 19 individuals who had participated in the initial Perry Preschool Project program (1962–1967) were less likely to have been arrested and reported fewer adult offenses than a control group. The Perry Preschool students also were less likely to drop out of school, and teachers rated their social behavior as more competent than that of a control group who had not received the enriched preschool experience. In a more recent assessment, at age 40 those who had been in the Perry Preschool program were more likely to be in the workforce, to own their own homes, and to have had fewer arrests (Schweinhart & others, 2005).

What are some strategies for preventing and intervening in adolescent problems?
© Image Source/Getty Images RF

Fast Track. A program that attempts to lower the risk of juvenile delinquency and other problems is Fast Track (Conduct Problems Prevention Research Group, 2007, 2010a, b; 2011, 2013; Dodge, Godwin, & Conduct Problems Prevention Research Group, 2013; Dodge & McCourt, 2010; Dodge & others, 2015; Miller & others, 2010). Schools in four areas (Durham, North Carolina; Nashville, Tennessee; Seattle, Washington; and rural central Pennsylvania) were identified as high-risk based on neighborhood crime and poverty data. Researchers screened more than 9,000 kindergarten children in the four schools and randomly assigned 891 of the highest-risk and moderate-risk children to intervention or control conditions. The average age of the children when the intervention began was 6.5 years of age. The 10-year intervention consisted of behavior management training of parents, social cognitive skills training of children, reading tutoring, home visitations, mentoring, and a revised classroom curriculum that was designed to increase socioemotional competence and decrease aggression.

The extensive intervention was most successful for children and adolescents who were identified as the highest risk in kindergarten, lowering their incidence of conduct disorder, attention deficit hyperactivity disorder, any externalized disorder, and antisocial behavior. Positive outcomes for the intervention occurred as early as the third grade and continued through the ninth grade. For example, in the ninth grade the intervention reduced the likelihood that the highest-risk kindergarten children would develop conduct disorder by 75 percent, attention deficit hyperactivity disorder by 53 percent, and any externalized disorder by 43 percent. The comprehensive Fast Track early intervention was successful in reducing youth arrest rates through age 19 (Conduct Problems Prevention Research Group, 2011, 2013; Miller & others, 2010). And at age 25, the early intervention was effective in reducing violent and drug crimes, as well as risky sexual behavior (Dodge & others, 2015). Also, at age 25 those who were given the early intervention had higher well-being scores.

Also, a recent study found that the intervention's impact on adolescents' antisocial behavior was linked to three social cognitive processes: reducing hostile-attribution biases, improving responses to social problems, and devaluing aggression (Dodge, Godwin, & Conduct Problems Prevention Research Group, 2013).

National Longitudinal Study of Adolescent to Adult Health. This study initially was referred to as the National Longitudinal Study of Adolescent Health and was based on interviews with a nationally representative sample of adolescents in grades 7 to 12 in the United States, initially assessed during the 1994–1995 school year. Participants in the program (referred to also as Add Health) have been assessed in early adulthood, with the most recent interviews taking place with 24- to 32-year-olds in 2008 (National Longitudinal Study of Adolescent to Adult Health, 2015). The Add Health study has implications for the prevention of adolescent and emerging adult problems (Aronowitz & Morrison-Beedy, 2008; Allen & MacMillan, 2006; Beaver & others, 2009; Clark & others, 2015; Cubbin & others, 2005; Lynch & others, 2015; Richardson, Dietz, & Gordon-Larsen, 2014). Perceived adolescent connectedness to a parent and to a teacher were the main factors linked to preventing the following adolescent problems: emotional distress, suicidal thoughts and behavior, violence, use of cigarettes, use of alcohol, use of marijuana, and early sexual intercourse. This study also provides support for the first component of successful prevention/intervention programs as described in item 1 of the list at the beginning of this section. That is, intensive individualized attention is especially important when it comes from important people in the adolescent's life, such as parents and teachers (Greenberg & others, 2003; Kumpfer & Alvarado, 2003). Researchers are continuing to analyze data from the National Longitudinal Study on Adolescent Health to further understand how to prevent and intervene in adolescent problems (Abrutyn & Mueller, 2014; Chen & Jacobson, 2013; Hatzenbuehler, McLaughlin, & Xuan, 2015; Kane & Frisco, 2013; Lui & others, 2015; McQueen & others, 2015).

Review Connect Reflect

LG3 Summarize the interrelation of problems and ways to prevent or intervene in problems

Review

• Which four problems affect the largest numbers of adolescents? How are adolescent problems interrelated?
• What are the three main ways to prevent or intervene in adolescent problems?

Connect

• What role can parents play in preventing and intervening in adolescent problems?

Reflect *Your Own Personal Journey of Life*

• Did you have any of the problems in adolescence that were described in this chapter? If so, what factors do you think contributed to the development of the problem(s)? If you didn't experience any of the problems, what do you think protected you from developing the problems?

We have arrived at the end of this edition. I hope these chapters and course have been a window to improving your understanding of adolescence and emerging adulthood, including your own development in these key time frames in your life. I wish you all the best in the remaining years of your journey through the human life span.

reach your **learning goals**

Problems in Adolescence and Emerging Adulthood

1 Exploring Adolescent and Emerging Adult Problems

LG1 Discuss the nature of problems in adolescence and emerging adulthood

The Biopsychosocial Approach

The Developmental Psychopathology Approach

• Biological, psychological, and social factors have been proposed as causes of problems that adolescents, emerging adults, and others can develop. The biopsychosocial approach emphasizes that problems develop through an interaction of biological, psychological, and social factors.

• In the developmental psychopathology approach, the emphasis is on describing and exploring developmental pathways of problems. One way of classifying adolescent and emerging adult problems is as internalizing (for example, depression and anxiety) or externalizing (for example, juvenile delinquency).

| Characteristics of Adolescent and Emerging Adult Problems |

The spectrum of adolescent and emerging adult problems is wide, varying in severity, developmental level, sex, and socioeconomic status. Middle-SES adolescents and females have more internalizing problems; low-SES adolescents and males have more externalizing problems. Adolescents who have a number of external and internal assets have fewer problems and engage in fewer risk-taking behaviors than their counterparts with few external and internal assets.

| Stress and Coping |

Stress is the response of individuals to stressors, which are circumstances and events that threaten them and tax their coping abilities. Sources of stress include life events, daily hassles, and sociocultural factors (such as gender, acculturative stress, and poverty). Coping involves managing taxing circumstances, expending effort to solve life's problems, and seeking to master or reduce stress. Successful coping has been linked to a sense of personal control, positive emotions, personal resources, and strategies used. One way of classifying coping strategies focuses on problem-focused coping versus emotion-focused coping. In most situations, problem-focused coping is recommended over emotion-focused coping. Among the strategies for coping effectively are thinking positively and receiving support from others. Coping is influenced by the demands and resources of the environment, and individuals who face stressful circumstances often benefit from using more than one strategy.

| Resilience |

Three sets of characteristics are reflected in the lives of adolescents and emerging adults who show resilience in the face of adversity and disadvantage: (1) individual factors—such as good intellectual functioning; (2) family factors—such as a close relationship with a caring parent figure; and (3) extrafamilial factors—bonds to prosocial adults outside the family. Resilience in adolescence is linked to ongoing resilience in emerging adulthood, but resilience can also be developed during emerging adulthood.

2 Problems and Disorders

LG2 Describe some problems and disorders that characterize adolescents and emerging adults

| Drug Use |

The 1960s and 1970s were a time of marked increases in the use of illicit drugs. Drug use began to decline in the 1980s but increased again in the 1990s. Since the late 1990s, there has been a decline in the overall use of illicit drugs by U.S. adolescents. Understanding drug use requires an understanding of physical dependence and psychological dependence. Alcohol abuse is a major problem, although its occurence in adolescence has begun to decline. There is an increase in alcohol use and binge drinking during emerging adulthood. Binge drinking by college students is a continuing concern. Use of alcohol and drugs typically declines by the mid-twenties. Risk factors for alcohol use include heredity and negative family and peer influences. Other drugs that can be harmful to adolescents include hallucinogens (LSD and marijuana—their use increased in the 1990s), stimulants (such as nicotine, cocaine, and amphetamines), and depressants (such as barbiturates, tranquilizers, and alcohol). A special concern is cigarette use by adolescents, although the good news is that it has been declining in recent years. An alarming trend has recently occurred in the increased use of prescription painkillers by adolescents. Use of anabolic steroids has been linked with strength training, smoking, and heavy use of alcohol. Adolescents' use of inhalants has decreased in recent years. Drug use that begins in childhood and early adolescence has more negative long-term effects than when it first occurs in late adolescence. Parents and peers can provide important supportive roles in preventing adolescent drug use. Being born into a high-risk family, having conduct problems at school, and being rejected by peers are factors related to drug use by 12-year-olds. Early educational achievement by adolescents has a positive influence in reducing the likelihood of developing problems with drug and alcohol abuse. Substance use peaks in emerging adulthood but begins declining by the mid-twenties.

| Juvenile Delinquency |

Juvenile delinquency consists of a broad range of behaviors, from socially undesirable behavior to status offenses. For legal purposes, a distinction is made between index and status offenses. Conduct disorder is a psychiatric diagnostic category used to describe multiple delinquent-type behaviors occurring over a six-month period. Predictors of juvenile delinquency include authority conflict, minor covert acts such as lying, overt acts of aggression, a negative identity, cognitive distortions, low self-control, early initiation of delinquency, being a male, low expectations for education and school grades, low parental monitoring, low parental support and ineffective discipline, having an older delinquent sibling, heavy peer influence and low resistance to peers, low socioeconomic status, and living in a high-crime, urban area. Effective juvenile delinquency prevention and intervention programs have been identified.

Depression and Suicide

· Adolescents have a higher rate of depression than children do. Female adolescents are far more likely to develop depression than adolescent males are. Parent-adolescent conflict, low parental support, poor peer relationships, and problems in romantic relationships are factors associated with adolescent depression. Treatment of depression has involved both drug therapy and psychotherapy. Emerging adults have triple the rate of suicide compared with adolescents. The U.S. adolescent suicide rates increased in the 1990s but have fallen in recent years. Both early and later experiences may be involved in suicide. Family instability, lack of affection, poor grades in school, lack of supportive friendships, and romantic breakups may trigger suicide attempts.

Eating Disorders

· Eating disorders have become increasing problems in adolescence and emerging adulthood. The percentage of adolescents who are overweight increased dramatically in the 1980s and 1990s but began leveling off in the middle of the first decade of the twenty-first century. Being obese in adolescence is linked with being obese as an adult. An increase in obesity has also occurred in emerging adulthood. Both heredity and environmental factors are involved in obesity. Being overweight in adolescence has negative effects on physical health and socioemotional development. Clinical approaches that focus on the individual adolescent and involve a combination of caloric restriction, exercise, reduction of sedentary behavior, and behavioral therapy have been moderately effective in helping overweight adolescents lose weight. Anorexia nervosa is an eating disorder that involves the relentless pursuit of thinness through starvation. Anorexics weigh less than 85 percent of weight considered normal, intensely fear weight gain, and even when very thin see themselves as too fat. Bulimia nervosa is an eating disorder in which the individual consistently follows a binge-and-purge eating pattern. Most bulimics are depressed or anxious, preoccupied with their body weight and shape, and typically fall within a normal weight range. Binge eating disorder (BED) involves frequent binge eating but without compensatory behavior like the purging that characterizes bulimics.

3 Interrelation of Problems and Prevention/Intervention

LG3 Summarize the interrelation of problems and ways to prevent or intervene in problems

Adolescents with Multiple Problems

· The four problems that affect the most adolescents are (1) drug abuse, (2) juvenile delinquency, (3) sexual problems, and (4) school-related problems. Researchers are finding that adolescents who are the most at risk often have more than one problem and that the highest-risk adolescents often have all four of these problems.

Prevention and Intervention

· In Dryfoos' analysis, these were the common components of successful prevention/intervention programs: (1) extensive individual attention, (2) community-wide intervention, and (3) early identification and intervention.

key terms

acculturative stress	conduct disorder	emotion-focused coping	major depressive disorder
anabolic steroids	coping	externalizing problems	problem-focused coping
anorexia nervosa	depressants	hallucinogens	status offenses
binge eating disorder (BED)	developmental cascades	index offenses	stimulants
biopsychosocial approach	developmental psychopathology	internalizing problems	stress
bulimia nervosa	approach	juvenile delinquency	

key people

Thomas Achenbach	Kenneth Dodge	Richard Lazarus	Alan Sroufe
Jerald Bachman	Joy Dryfoos	Ann Masten	Shelley Taylor
Peter Benson	Craig Edelbrock	Gerald Patterson	Nicole Zarrett
Deborah Capaldi	Lloyd Johnston	John Schulenberg	

resources for **improving the lives of adolescents**

Adolescence

Joy Dryfoos and Carol Barkin (2006)

New York: Oxford University Press

> An outstanding book on adolescent problems and the programs and strategies that can successfully prevent and intervene in these problems.

Development and Psychopathology

(Vol. 22, Issues 3 and 4, 2010)

> These issues cover theory and research on the role of developmental cascades in predicting adolescent problems.

Ordinary Magic

Ann Masten (2014)

New York: Guilford Press

> Leading expert Ann Masten describes multiple pathways that children and adolescents can follow to become resilient in the face of numerous adversities, such as homelessness, child maltreatment, disease, wars, and disasters.

National Adolescent Suicide Hotline (800-621-4000)

> This hotline can be used 24 hours a day by teenagers contemplating suicide, as well as by their parents.

National Clearinghouse for Alcohol Information (www.health.org)

This site provides information about a wide variety of issues related to drinking problems, including adolescent drinking.

Help Your Teenager Beat an Eating Disorder (2nd ed.)

James Lock and Daniel Le Grange (2015)

New York: Guilford

> Leading experts provide excellent recommendations for parents to help them recognize characteristics of a number of eating disorders, including anorexia nervosa, bulimia disorder and others, and also address various treatment options.

National Longitudinal Study of Adolescent to Adult Health (2015)
(www.cpc.unc.edu/projects/addhealth)

> This national longitudinal study has involved data collection from adolescence into the adult years. A large number of studies have been conducted with the data that relate to the problems discussed in this chapter, such as substance use, delinquency, depression and suicide, and eating disorders. On this Web site, you can read about many of these studies in depth.

glossary

A

accommodation An adjustment of a schema in response to new information.

acculturative stress The negative consequences that result from contact between two distinctive cultural groups.

active (niche-picking) genotype-environment correlations Correlations that occur when children seek out environments that they find compatible and stimulating.

adaptive behavior A modification of behavior that promotes an organism's survival in the natural habitat.

adolescence The developmental period of transition from childhood to adulthood; it involves biological, cognitive, and socioemotional changes. Adolescence begins at approximately 10 to 13 years of age and ends in the late teens.

adolescent egocentrism The heightened self-consciousness of adolescents, which is reflected in their belief that others are as interested in them as they themselves are, and in their sense of personal uniqueness and invulnerability.

adolescent generalization gap Adelson's concept of generalizations being made about adolescents based on information regarding a limited, often highly visible group of adolescents.

adolescents who are gifted Adolescents who have above-average intelligence (usually defined as an IQ of 130 or higher) and/or superior talent in some domain, such as art, music, or mathematics.

adoption study A study in which investigators seek to discover whether the behavior and psychological characteristics of adopted children are more like their adoptive parents, who have provided a home environment, or more like those of their biological parents, who have contributed their heredity. Another form of adoption study involves comparing adopted and biological siblings.

adrenarche Puberty phase involving hormonal changes in the adrenal glands, which are located just above the kidneys. These changes occur from about 6 to 9 years of age in girls and about one year later in boys, before what is generally considered the beginning of puberty.

affectionate love Love in which an individual desires to have another person near and has a deep, caring affection for that person; also called companionate love.

AIDS Stands for acquired immune deficiency syndrome, a sexually transmitted infection caused by the human immunodeficiency virus (HIV), which destroys the body's immune system.

altruism Unselfish interest in helping another person.

amygdala A portion of the brain's limbic system that is the seat of emotions such as anger.

anabolic steroids Drugs derived from the male sex hormone testosterone. They promote muscle growth and increase lean body mass.

androgens The main class of male sex hormones.

androgyny The presence of a high degree of desirable feminine and masculine characteristics in the same individual.

anorexia nervosa An eating disorder that involves the relentless pursuit of thinness through starvation.

anxiety A vague, highly unpleasant feeling of fear and apprehension.

assimilation The incorporation of new information into existing knowledge.

attention Concentration and focusing of mental resources.

attention deficit hyperactivity disorder (ADHD) A disability in which children or adolescents consistently show one or more of the following characteristics over a period of time: (1) inattention, (2) hyperactivity, and (3) impulsivity.

attribution theory The theory that in their effort to make sense of their own behavior or performance, individuals are motivated to discover its underlying causes.

authoritarian parenting A restrictive, punitive style in which the parent exhorts the adolescent to follow the parent's directions and to respect work and effort. Firm limits and controls are placed on the adolescent, and little verbal exchange is allowed. This style is associated with adolescents' socially incompetent behavior.

authoritarian strategy of classroom management A teaching strategy that is restrictive and punitive. The focus is mainly on keeping order in the classroom rather than on instruction and learning.

authoritative parenting A style encouraging adolescents to be independent but still placing limits and controls on their actions. Extensive verbal give-and-take is allowed, and parents are warm and nurturant toward the adolescent. This style is associated with adolescents' socially competent behavior.

authoritative strategy of classroom management A teaching strategy that encourages students to be independent thinkers and doers but still involves effective monitoring. Authoritative teachers engage students in considerable verbal give-and-take and show a caring attitude toward them. However, they still set and enforce limits when necessary.

average children Children who receive an average number of both positive and negative nominations from their peers.

B

behavior genetics The field that seeks to discover the influence of heredity and environment on individual differences in human traits and development.

bicultural identity Identity formation that occurs when adolescents identify in some ways with their ethnic group and in other ways with the majority culture.

Big Five factors of personality Five core traits of personality: openness to experience, conscientiousness, extraversion, agreeableness, and neuroticism (emotional stability).

binge eating disorder (BED) Involves frequent binge eating without compensatory behavior like the purging that characterizes bulimics.

biological processes Physical changes in an individual's body.

biopsychosocial approach Approach that emphasizes that problems develop through an interaction of biological, psychological, and social factors.

bisexual A person who is attracted to people of both sexes.

boundary ambiguity Uncertainty in stepfamilies about who is in or out of the family and who is performing or responsible for certain tasks in the family system.

Bronfenbrenner's ecological theory A theory focusing on the influence of five environmental systems: microsystem, mesosystem, exosystem, macrosystem, and chronosystem.

bulimia nervosa An eating disorder in which the individual consistently follows a binge-and-purge eating pattern.

C

care perspective The moral perspective of Carol Gilligan, which views people in terms of their connectedness with others and emphasizes interpersonal communication, relationships with others, and concern for others.

case study An in-depth look at a single individual.

character education A direct moral education approach that involves teaching students a basic moral literacy to prevent them from engaging in immoral behavior or doing harm to themselves or others.

chlamydia One of the most common sexually transmitted infections, named for *Chlamydia trachomatis*, an organism that spreads by sexual contact and infects the genital organs of both sexes.

chromosomes Threadlike structures that contain deoxyribonucleic acid, or DNA.

cliques Small groups that range from 2 to about 12 individuals and average about 5 to 6 individuals. Members are usually of the same sex and are similar in age; cliques can form because of similar interests, such as sports, and also can form purely from friendship.

cognitive control The capacity to control attention, reduce interfering thoughts, and be cognitively flexible.

cognitive moral education An approach based on the belief that students should learn to value things like democracy and justice as their moral reasoning develops; Kohlberg's theory has been the basis for many of the cognitive moral education approaches.

cognitive processes Changes in an individual's thinking and intelligence.

cohabitation Living together in a sexual relationship without being married.

cohort effects Characteristics related to a person's year of birth, era, or generation rather than to his or her actual chronological age.

collectivism Emphasizes values that serve the group by subordinating personal goals to preserve group integrity.

commitment The part of identity development in which adolescents show a personal investment in what they are going to do.

concrete operational stage Piaget's third stage, which lasts approximately from 7 to 11 years of age. In this stage, children can perform operations. Logical reasoning replaces intuitive thought as long as the reasoning can be applied to specific or concrete examples.

conduct disorder The psychiatric diagnostic category for the occurrence of multiple delinquent activities over a six-month period. These behaviors include truancy, running away, fire setting, cruelty to animals, breaking and entering, and excessive fighting.

conglomerate strategies The use of a combination of techniques, rather than a single approach, to improve adolescents' social skills; also called coaching.

connectedness An important element in adolescent identity development. It consists of two dimensions: mutuality, which is sensitivity to and respect for others' views; and permeability, which is openness to others' views.

conscience The component of the superego that discourages behaviors disapproved of by parents.

constructivist approach A learner-centered approach that emphasizes the adolescent's active, cognitive construction of knowledge and understanding with guidance from the teacher.

contexts The settings in which development occurs. These settings are influenced by historical, economic, social, and cultural factors.

continuity-discontinuity issue Issue regarding whether development involves gradual, cumulative change (continuity) or distinct stages (discontinuity).

controversial children Children who are frequently nominated both as a best friend and as being disliked.

conventional reasoning The second, or intermediate, level in Kohlberg's theory. Individuals abide by certain standards (internal), but they are the standards of others (external), such as parents or the laws of society. The conventional level consists of two stages: mutual interpersonal expectations, relationships, and interpersonal conformity (stage 3) and social systems morality (stage 4).

convergent thinking A pattern of thinking in which individuals produce one correct answer; characteristic of the items on conventional intelligence tests.

coping Managing taxing circumstances, expending effort to solve life's problems, and seeking to master or reduce stress.

corpus callosum A large bundle of axon fibers that connect the brain's left and right hemispheres.

correlation coefficient A number based on a statistical analysis that is used to describe the degree of association between two variables.

correlational research Research whose goal is to describe the strength of the relationship between two or more events or characteristics.

creativity The ability to think in novel and unusual ways and discover unique solutions to problems.

crisis A period of identity development during which the adolescent is choosing among meaningful alternatives.

critical thinking Thinking reflectively and productively and evaluating the evidence.

cross-cultural studies Studies that compare a culture with one or more other cultures. Such studies provide information about the degree to which development in adolescents and emerging adults is similar, or universal, across cultures, or about the degree to which it is culture-specific.

cross-sectional research A research strategy that involves studying different people of varying ages all at one time.

crowds A larger group structure than cliques. Adolescents are usually members of a crowd based on reputation and may or may not spend much time together.

culture The behavior, patterns, beliefs, and all other products of a particular group of people that are passed on from generation to generation.

D

date rape, or **acquaintance rape** Coercive sexual activity directed at someone whom the perpetrator knows.

dating scripts The cognitive models that adolescents and adults use to guide and evaluate dating interactions.

dependent variable The factor that is measured in experimental research.

depressants Drugs that slow down the central nervous system, bodily functions, and behavior.

descriptive research Research that aims to observe and record behavior.

development The pattern of change that begins at conception and continues through the life span. Most development involves growth, although it also includes decay (as in death and dying).

developmental cascades A developmental psychopathology approach that emphasizes connections across domains over time to influence developmental pathways and outcomes.

developmental psychopathology approach Approach that focuses on describing and exploring the developmental pathways of problems.

difficult child A child who reacts negatively to many situations and is slow to accept new experiences.

direct instruction approach A teacher-centered approach characterized by teacher direction and control, mastery of academic skills, high expectations for students, and maximum time spent on learning tasks.

dismissing/avoidant attachment An insecure attachment category in which individuals deemphasize the importance of attachment. This category is associated with consistent experiences of rejection of attachment needs by caregivers.

divergent thinking A pattern of thinking in which individuals produce many answers to the same question; more characteristic of creativity than convergent thinking.

divided attention Concentrating on more than one activity at the same time.

DNA A complex molecule that contains genetic information.

E

early adolescence The developmental period that corresponds roughly to the middle school or junior high school years and includes most pubertal change.

early adulthood The developmental period beginning in the late teens or early twenties and lasting through the thirties.

early childhood The developmental period extending from the end of infancy to about 5 or 6 years of age; sometimes called the preschool years.

early-later experience issue Issue focusing on the degree to which early experiences (especially early in childhood) or later experiences are the key determinants of development.

easy child A child who generally is in a positive mood, quickly establishes regular routines, and adapts easily to new experiences.

eclectic theoretical orientation An orientation that does not follow any one theoretical approach but rather selects from each theory whatever is considered the best in it.

ego ideal The component of the superego that involves ideal standards approved by parents.

emerging adulthood The developmental period occurring from approximately 18 to 25 years of age; this transitional period between adolescence and adulthood is characterized by experimentation and exploration.

emotion Feeling, or affect, that occurs when a person is in a state or an interaction that is important to the individual, especially to his or her well-being.

emotion-focused coping Lazarus' term for responding to stress in an emotional manner, especially by using defense mechanisms.

emotional autonomy The capacity to relinquish childlike dependence on parents.

emotional intelligence The ability to perceive and express emotion accurately and adaptively, to understand emotion and emotional knowledge, to use feelings to facilitate thought, and to manage emotions in oneself and others.

empathy Reaction to another's feelings with an emotional response that is similar to the other's feelings.

epigenetic view Belief that development is the result of an ongoing bidirectional interchange between heredity and environment.

equilibration A mechanism in Piaget's theory that explains how individuals shift from one state of thought to the next. The shift occurs as individuals experience cognitive conflict or a disequilibrium in trying to understand the world. Eventually, the individual resolves the conflict and reaches a balance, or equilibrium, of thought.

Erikson's theory Theory that includes eight stages of human development. Each stage consists of a unique developmental task that confronts individuals with a crisis that must be faced.

estrogens The main class of female sex hormones.

ethnic gloss Use of an ethnic label such as African American or Latino in a superficial way that portrays an ethnic group as being more homogeneous than it really is.

ethnic identity An enduring, basic aspect of the self that includes a sense of membership in an ethnic group and the attitudes and feelings related to that membership.

ethnicity A dimension of culture based on cultural heritage, national characteristics, race, religion, and language.

ethnocentrism A tendency to favor one's own group over other groups.

evocative genotype-environment correlations Correlations that occur because an adolescent's genetically shaped characteristics elicit certain types of physical and social environments.

evolutionary psychology An approach that emphasizes the importance of adaptation, reproduction, and "survival of the fittest" in explaining behavior.

executive attention Type of attention that involves planning actions, allocating attention to goals, detecting and compensating for errors, monitoring progress on tasks, and dealing with novel or difficult circumstances.

executive function An umbrella-like concept that involves higher-order, complex cognitive processes that include exercising cognitive control, making decisions, reasoning, thinking critically, thinking creatively, and metacognition.

experience sampling method (ESM) Research method that involves providing participants with electronic pagers and then beeping them at random times, at which point they are asked to report on various aspects of their lives.

experimental research Research that involves an experiment, a carefully regulated procedure in which one or more of the factors believed to influence the behavior being studied are manipulated while all other factors are held constant.

externalizing problems Behavior that occurs when individuals turn problems outward. An example is juvenile delinquency.

extrinsic motivation External motivational factors such as rewards and punishments.

F

female athlete triad A combination of disordered eating, amenorrhea, and osteoporosis that may develop in female adolescents and college students.

feminization of poverty Term reflecting the fact that far more women than men live in poverty. Likely causes include women's low income, divorce, and the resolution of divorce cases by the judicial system, which leaves women with less money than they and their children need to function adequately.

flow Csikszentmihalyi's concept of optimal life experiences, which he believes occur most often when people develop a sense of mastery and are absorbed in a state of concentration when they're engaged in an activity.

forgiveness An aspect of prosocial behavior that occurs when an injured person releases the injurer from possible behavioral retaliation.

formal operational stage Piaget's fourth and final stage of cognitive development, which he argued emerges at 11 to 15 years of age. It is characterized by abstract, idealistic, and logical thought.

friends A subset of peers who engage in mutual companionship, support, and intimacy.

fuzzy-trace theory dual-process model States that decision making is influenced by two systems—"verbatim" analytical thinking (literal and precise) and gist-based intuition (simple, bottom-line meaning), which operate in parallel; in this model, it is the gist-based system that benefits adolescents' decision making most.

G

gender The characteristics of people as males or females.

gender bias A preconceived notion about the abilities of females and males that prevents individuals from pursuing their own interests and achieving their potential.

gender intensification hypothesis Hypothesis stating that psychological and behavioral differences between boys and girls become greater during early adolescence because of increased socialization pressure to conform to masculine and feminine gender roles.

gender role A set of expectations that prescribes how females and males should think, act, and feel.

gender schema theory Theory stating that an individual's attention and behavior are guided by an internal motivation to conform to gender-based sociocultural standards and stereotypes.

gender stereotypes Broad categories that reflect our impressions and beliefs about females and males.

gender-role transcendence The belief that, when an individual's competence is at issue, it should be conceptualized not on the basis of masculinity, femininity, or androgyny but on an individual basis.

genes The units of hereditary information, which are short segments composed of DNA.

gene × environment (G × E) interaction The interaction of a specific measured variation in DNA and a specific measured aspect of the environment.

genital herpes A sexually transmitted infection caused by a large family of viruses of different strains. These strains also produce nonsexually transmitted diseases such as chicken pox and mononucleosis.

genital warts An STI caused by the human papillomavirus; genital warts are very contagious and are the most commonly acquired STI in the United States in the 15- to 24-year-old age group.

genotype A person's genetic heritage; the actual genetic material.

gonadarche Puberty phase involving the maturation of primary sexual characteristics (ovaries in females, testes in males) and secondary sexual characteristics (pubic hair, breast and genital development). This period follows adrenarche by about two years and is what most people think of as puberty.

gonorrhea A sexually transmitted infection caused by the bacterium *Neisseria gonorrhoeae*, which thrives in the moist mucous membranes lining the mouth, throat, vagina, cervix, urethra, and anal tract. This STI is commonly called the "drip" or the "clap."

goodness of fit The match between an individual's temperament style and the environmental demands faced by the individual.

gratitude A feeling of thankfulness and appreciation, especially in response to someone doing something kind or helpful.

H

hallucinogens Drugs that alter an individual's perceptual experiences and produce hallucinations; also called psychedelic (mind-altering) drugs.

helpless orientation An outlook in which individuals seem trapped when experiencing difficulty and attribute their difficulty to a lack of ability. This orientation undermines performance.

hidden curriculum The pervasive moral atmosphere that characterizes every school.

homophobia Irrational negative feelings against individuals who have same-sex attractions.

hormones Powerful chemicals secreted by the endocrine glands and carried through the body by the bloodstream.

hostile environment sexual harassment Sexual harassment in which students are subjected to unwelcome sexual conduct that is so severe, persistent, or pervasive that it limits the students' ability to benefit from their education.

hypotheses Specific assertions and predictions that can be tested.

hypothetical-deductive reasoning Piaget's term for adolescents' ability, in the formal operational stage, to develop hypotheses, or best guesses, about ways to solve problems; they then systematically deduce, or conclude, the best path to follow in solving the problem.

I

identity Who a person believes he or she is, representing a synthesis and integration of self-understanding.

identity achievement Marcia's term for an adolescent who has undergone an identity crisis and made a commitment.

identity diffusion Marcia's term for the state adolescents are in when they have not yet experienced an identity crisis or made any commitments.

identity foreclosure Marcia's term for the state adolescents are in when they have made a commitment but have not experienced an identity crisis.

identity moratorium Marcia's term for the state of adolescents who are in the midst of an identity crisis but who have not made a clear commitment to an identity.

identity versus identity confusion Erikson's fifth developmental stage, which occurs during adolescence. At this time, individuals are faced with deciding who they are, what they are all about, and where they are going in life.

inclusion Educating a child or adolescent with special educational needs full-time in the regular classroom.

independent variable The factor that is manipulated in experimental research.

index offenses Acts such as robbery, rape, and homicide that are crimes regardless of whether they are committed by juveniles or adults.

individualism Emphasizes values that serve the self and gives priority to personal goals rather than group goals.

individuality An important element in adolescent identity development. It consists of two dimensions: self-assertion, the ability to have and communicate a point of view; and separateness, the use of communication patterns to express how one is different from others.

Individuals with Disabilities Education Act (IDEA) Federal legislation spelling out broad mandates for providing educational services to all children and adolescents with disabilities. These include evaluation and eligibility determination, appropriate education and an individualized education plan (IEP), and education in the least restrictive environment.

induction A discipline technique in which a parent uses reason and explains how the adolescent's actions affect others.

indulgent parenting A style in which parents are highly involved with their adolescents but place few demands or controls on them. This is associated with adolescents' social incompetence, especially a lack of self-control.

infancy The developmental period that extends from birth to 18 or 24 months of age.

information-processing theory A theory emphasizing that individuals manipulate information, monitor it, and strategize about it. Central to this approach are the processes of memory and thinking.

insecure attachment Attachment pattern in which infants, children, and adolescents either avoid the caregiver or show considerable resistance or ambivalence toward the caregiver. This pattern is theorized to be related to difficulties in relationships and problems in later development.

intelligence The ability to solve problems and to adapt to and learn from everyday experiences; not everyone agrees on what constitutes intelligence.

intelligent quotient (IQ) A person's tested mental age divided by chronological age, multiplied by 100.

internalizing problems Emotional conditions that develop when individuals turn problems inward. Examples include anxiety and depression.

Internet The core of computer-mediated communication. The Internet system is worldwide and connects thousands of computer networks, providing an incredible array of information—both positive and negative—that adolescents can access.

intimacy in friendship In most research studies, this concept is defined narrowly as self-disclosure, or sharing of private thoughts.

intimacy versus isolation Erikson's sixth developmental stage, which individuals experience during early adulthood. At this time, individuals face the developmental task of forming intimate relationships with others.

intrinsic motivation Internal motivational factors such as self-determination, curiosity, challenge, and effort.

inventionist view The view that adolescence is a sociohistorical creation. Especially important in this view are the sociohistorical circumstances at the beginning of the twentieth century, a time when legislation was enacted that ensured the dependency of youth and made their move into the economic sphere more manageable.

J

jigsaw classroom A classroom strategy in which students from different cultural backgrounds are placed in a cooperative group in which, together, they have to construct different parts of a project to reach a common goal.

justice perspective A moral perspective that focuses on the rights of the individual. Individuals are viewed as making moral decisions independently.

juvenile delinquency A broad range of behaviors, including socially unacceptable behavior, status offenses, and criminal acts.

L

laboratory A controlled setting in which many of the complex factors of the "real world" are removed.

late adolescence The developmental period that corresponds approximately to the latter half of the second decade of life. Career interests, dating, and identity exploration are often more pronounced in late adolescence than in early adolescence.

late adulthood The developmental period that lasts from about 60 to 70 years of age until death.

learning disabilities Disabilities in which children experience difficulty in learning that involves understanding or using spoken or written language; the difficulty can appear in listening, thinking, reading, writing, and spelling. A learning disability also may involve difficulty in doing mathematics. To be classified as a learning disability, the learning problem is not primarily the result of visual, hearing, or motor disabilities; intellectual disability; emotional disorders; or environmental, cultural, or economic disadvantage.

least restrictive environment (LRE) A setting that is as similar as possible to the one in which children or adolescents without a disability are educated; under the IDEA, efforts to educate the child or adolescent with a disability in this setting have been given a legal basis.

limbic system A lower, subcortical system in the brain that is the seat of emotions and experience of rewards.

longitudinal research A research strategy in which the same individuals are studied over a period of time, usually several years or more.

love withdrawal A discipline technique in which a parent withholds attention or love from the adolescent.

M

major depressive disorder The diagnosis when an individual experiences a major depressive episode and depressed characteristics, such as lethargy and depression, for two weeks or longer and daily functioning becomes impaired.

mastery orientation An outlook in which individuals focus on the task rather than on their ability; they concentrate on learning strategies and the process of achievement instead of the outcome.

memory The retention of information over time.

menarche A girl's first menstrual period.

mental age (MA) An individual's level of mental development relative to others; a concept developed by Binet.

mentors Individuals who are usually older and more experienced and are motivated to improve the competence and character of a younger person.

metacognition Cognition about cognition, or "knowing about knowing."

middle adulthood The developmental period that is entered at about 35 to 45 years of age and exited at about 55 to 65 years of age.

middle and late childhood The developmental period extending from about 6 to about 10 or 11 years of age; sometimes called the elementary school years.

Millennials The generation born after 1980, the first to come of age and enter emerging adulthood in the new millennium. Two characteristics of Millennials stand out: (1) their ethnic diversity, and (2) their connection to technology.

mindset The cognitive view, either fixed or growth, that individuals develop for themselves.

moral development Thoughts, feelings, and behaviors regarding standards of right and wrong.

moral exemplars People who have led exemplary lives.

moral identity An aspect of personality that is present when individuals have moral notions and commitments that are central to their lives.

multicultural education Education that values diversity and includes the perspectives of a variety of cultural groups.

multiple developmental trajectories Concept that adults follow one trajectory and children and adolescents another one; how these trajectories mesh is important.

myelination   The process by which the axon portion of the neuron becomes covered and insulated with a layer of fat cells, which increases the speed and efficiency of information processing in the nervous system.

N

narcissism   A self-centered and self-concerned approach toward others.

naturalistic observation   Observation of behavior in real-world settings.

nature-nurture issue   Issue involving the debate about whether development is primarily influenced by an organism's biological inheritance (nature) or by its environmental experiences (nurture).

neglected children   Children who are infrequently nominated as a best friend but are not disliked by their peers.

neglectful parenting   A style in which the parent is very uninvolved in the adolescent's life. It is associated with adolescents' social incompetence, especially a lack of self-control.

neo-Piagetians   Theorists who argue that Piaget got some things right but that his theory needs considerable revision. In their revision, they give more emphasis to information processing that involves attention, memory, and strategies; they also seek to provide more precise explanations of cognitive changes.

neuroconstructivist view   Developmental perspective in which biological processes and environmental conditions influence the brain's development; the brain has plasticity and is context dependent; and cognitive development is closely linked with brain development.

neurons   Nerve cells, which are the nervous system's basic units.

nonshared environmental experiences   The adolescent's own unique experiences, both within a family and outside the family, that are not shared by a sibling.

normal distribution   A symmetrical distribution of values or scores, with a majority of scores falling in the middle of the possible range of scores and few scores appearing toward the extremes of the range.

O

optimism   Involves having a positive outlook on the future and minimizing problems.

P

passive genotype-environment correlations   Correlations that occur because biological parents, who are genetically related to the child, provide a rearing environment for the child.

peers   Individuals who are about the same age or maturity level.

performance orientation   An outlook in which individuals are focused on winning rather than a specific achievement outcome. For performance-oriented students, winning results in happiness.

permissive strategy of classroom management   A teaching strategy that offers students considerable autonomy but provides them with little support for developing learning skills or managing their behavior.

personality   The enduring personal characteristics of individuals.

perspective taking   The ability to assume another person's perspective and understand his or her thoughts and feelings.

phenotype   The way an individual's genotype is expressed in observed and measurable characteristics.

Piaget's theory   A theory stating that children actively construct their understanding of the world and go through four stages of cognitive development.

popular children   Children who are frequently nominated as a best friend and are rarely disliked by their peers.

possible self   What individuals might become, what they would like to become, and what they are afraid of becoming.

postconventional reasoning   The third and highest level in Kohlberg's theory. At this level, morality is more internal. The postconventional level consists of two stages: social contract or utility and individual rights (stage 5) and universal ethical principles (stage 6).

postformal thought   Thought that is reflective, relativistic, and contextual; provisional; realistic; and open to emotions and subjective.

power assertion   A discipline technique in which a parent attempts to gain control over the adolescent or the adolescent's resources.

precocious puberty   The very early onset and rapid progression of puberty.

preconventional reasoning   The lowest level in Kohlberg's theory of moral development. At this level, morality is often focused on reward and punishment. The two stages in preconventional reasoning are punishment and obedience orientation (stage 1) and individualism, instrumental purpose, and exchange (stage 2).

prefrontal cortex   The highest level of the brain's frontal lobes that is involved in reasoning, decision making, and self-control.

prejudice   An unjustified negative attitude toward an individual because of the individual's membership in a group.

prenatal period   The time from conception to birth.

preoccupied/ambivalent attachment   An insecure attachment category in which adolescents are hyperattuned to attachment experiences. This is thought mainly to occur because parents are inconsistently available to the adolescent.

preoperational stage   Piaget's second stage, which lasts approximately from 2 to 7 years of age. In this stage, children begin to represent their world with words, images, and drawings.

problem-focused coping   Lazarus' term for the strategy of squarely facing one's troubles and trying to solve them.

psychoanalytic theories   Theories that describe development as primarily unconscious and heavily colored by emotion. Behavior is merely a surface characteristic, and the symbolic workings of the mind have to be analyzed to understand behavior. Early experiences with parents are emphasized.

psychometric/intelligence view   A view that emphasizes the importance of individual differences in intelligence; many advocates of this view also argue that intelligence should be assessed with intelligence tests.

psychosocial moratorium   Erikson's term for the gap between childhood security and adult autonomy that adolescents experience as part of their identity exploration.

puberty   A brain-neuroendocrine process occurring primarily in early adolescence that provides stimulation for the rapid physical changes that accompany this period of development.

Public Law 94-142   The Education for All Handicapped Children Act, which requires all students with disabilities to be given a free, appropriate public education.

Q

quid pro quo sexual harassment   Sexual harassment in which a school employee threatens to base an educational decision (such as a grade) on a student's submission to unwelcome sexual conduct.

R

rape   Forcible sexual intercourse with a person who does not give consent.

rapport talk   The language of conversation, establishing connections and negotiating relationships.

reciprocal socialization   The process by which children and adolescents socialize parents, just as parents socialize them.

rejected children   Children who are infrequently nominated as a best friend and are actively disliked by their peers.

religion   An organized set of beliefs, practices, rituals, and symbols that increases an individual's connection to a sacred or transcendent other (God, higher power, or higher truth).

religiousness   The degree of affiliation with an organized religion, participation in prescribed rituals and practices, connection with its beliefs, and involvement in a community of believers.

report talk   Talk that gives information, such as public speaking.

resilience   Adapting positively and achieving successful outcomes in the face of significant risks and adverse circumstances.

rites of passage   Ceremonies or rituals that mark an individual's transition from one status to another, such as the entry into adulthood.

romantic love   Love that has strong sexual and infatuation components; also called passionate love or *eros*. It often predominates in the early part of a love relationship.

S

schema   A mental concept or framework that is useful in organizing and interpreting information.

secular trends   Patterns of the onset of puberty over historical time, especially across generations.

secure attachment Involves a positive, enduring emotional bond between two people. In infancy, childhood, and adolescence, formation of a secure bond with a caregiver benefits the child's exploration of the environment and subsequent development. In adulthood, the bond can also be between two people in a couple or marital relationship.

selective attention Focusing on a specific aspect of experience that is relevant while ignoring others that are irrelevant.

self All of the characteristics of a person.

self-concept Domain-specific evaluations of the self.

self-efficacy The belief that one can master a situation and produce positive outcomes.

self-esteem The global evaluative dimension of the self; also referred to as self-worth or self-image.

self-handicapping Use of failure avoidance strategies such as not trying in school or putting off studying until the last minute so that circumstances, rather than a lack of ability, will be seen as the cause of low-level performance.

self-regulation The ability to control one's behavior without having to rely on others.

self-understanding The individual's cognitive representation of the self; the substance and content of self-conceptions.

sensorimotor stage Piaget's first stage of development, lasting from birth to about 2 years of age. In this stage, infants construct an understanding of the world by coordinating sensory experiences with physical, motoric actions.

service learning A form of education that promotes social responsibility and service to the community.

sexual minority Someone who self-identifies as lesbian, gay, or bisexual.

sexual script A stereotyped pattern of role prescriptions for how individuals should behave in sexual contexts. Females and males have been socialized to follow different sexual scripts.

sexually transmitted infections (STIs) Infections that are contracted primarily through sexual contact. This contact is not limited to vaginal intercourse but includes oral-genital contact and anal-genital contact as well.

shared environmental experiences Siblings' common experiences such as their parents' personalities and intellectual orientation, the family's socioeconomic status, and the neighborhood in which they live.

slow-to-warm-up child A child who has a low activity level, is somewhat negative, and displays a low intensity of mood.

social cognition The way individuals conceptualize and reason about their social worlds—the people they watch and interact with, their relationships with those people, the groups they participate in, and the way they reason about themselves and others.

social cognitive theory The view that behavior, environment, and person/cognition are the key factors in development.

social cognitive theory of gender Theory emphasizing that children's and adolescents' gender development occurs through observation and imitation of gender behavior, and through rewards and punishments they experience for gender-appropriate and gender-inappropriate behavior.

social cognitive theory of moral development The theory that distinguishes between moral competence (the ability to produce moral behaviors) and moral performance (enacting those behaviors in specific situations).

social constructivist approach Approach that emphasizes the social contexts of learning and the construction of knowledge through social interaction.

social conventional reasoning Thoughts about social consensus and convention, as opposed to moral reasoning that stresses ethical issues.

social domain theory Theory that identifies different domains of social knowledge and reasoning, including moral, social conventional, and personal domains. These domains arise from children's and adolescents' attempts to understand and deal with different forms of social experience.

social policy A national government's course of action designed to influence the welfare of its citizens.

social role theory Theory stating that gender differences mainly result from the contrasting roles of females and males, with females having less power and status and controlling fewer resources than males.

socioeconomic status (SES) Refers to a grouping of people with similar occupational, educational, and economic characteristics.

socioemotional processes Changes in an individual's personality, emotions, relationships with other people, and social contexts.

sociometric status The extent to which children and adolescents are liked or disliked by their peer group.

spermarche A boy's first ejaculation of semen.

spirituality Experiencing something beyond oneself in a transcendent manner and living in a way that benefits others and society.

standardized test A test with uniform procedures for administration and scoring. Many standardized tests allow a person's performance to be compared with the performance of other individuals.

status offenses Juvenile offenses, performed by youth under a specified age, that are not as serious as index offenses. These offenses may include acts such as underage drinking, truancy, and sexual promiscuity.

stereotype A generalization that reflects our impressions and beliefs about a broad group of people. All stereotypes refer to an image of what the typical member of a specific group is like.

stimulants Drugs that increase the activity of the central nervous system.

storm-and-stress view G. Stanley Hall's concept that adolescence is a turbulent time charged with conflict and mood swings.

stress The response of individuals to stressors, which are circumstances and events that threaten and tax their coping abilities.

sustained attention The ability to maintain attention to a selected stimulus for a prolonged period of time.

synapses Gaps between neurons, where connections between the axon and dendrites occur.

syphilis A sexually transmitted infection caused by the bacterium *Treponema pallidum,* a spirochete.

T

temperament An individual's behavioral style and characteristic way of responding.

theory An interrelated, coherent set of ideas that helps explain phenomena and make predictions.

top-dog phenomenon The circumstance of moving from the top position (in elementary school, the oldest, biggest, and most powerful students) to the lowest position (in middle or junior high school, the youngest, smallest, and least powerful students).

triarchic theory of intelligence Sternberg's view that intelligence comes in three main forms: analytical, creative, and practical.

twin study A study in which the behavioral similarity of identical twins is compared with the behavioral similarity of fraternal twins.

U

unresolved/disorganized attachment An insecure category in which the adolescent has an unusually high level of fear and is disoriented. This can result from traumatic experiences such as a parent's death or abuse by parents.

V

values Beliefs and attitudes about the way things should be.

values clarification An educational approach that focuses on helping people clarify what is important to them, what is worth working for, and what is their purpose in life. Students are encouraged to define their own values and understand others' values.

Vygotsky's theory A sociocultural cognitive theory that emphasizes how culture and social interaction guide cognitive development.

W

wisdom Expert knowledge about the practical aspects of life that permits excellent judgment about important matters.

Z

zone of proximal development (ZPD) Vygotsky's concept that refers to the range of tasks that are too difficult for an individual to master alone, but that can be mastered with the guidance or assistance of adults or more-skilled peers.

references

A

Aalsma, M.C., Lapsley, D.K., & Flannery, D.J. (2006). Personal fables, narcissism, and adolescent adjustment. *Psychology in the Schools, 43,* 481–491.

Abar, C.C., Jackson, K.M., Colby, S.M., & Barnett, N.P. (2015, in press). Parent-child discrepancies in reports of parental monitoring and their relationship to adolescent alcohol-related incidents. *Journal of Youth and Adolescence.*

Abbate-Daga, G., Gramaglia, C., Amianto, F., Marzola, E., & Fassino, S. (2010). Attachment insecurity, personality, and body dissatisfaction in eating disorders. *Journal of Nervous and Mental Disease, 198,* 520–524.

Abbott, B.D., & Barber, B.L. (2010). Embodied image: Gender differences in functional and aesthetic body image among Australian adolescents. *Body Image, 7,* 22–31.

Abrutyn, S., & Mueller, A.S. (2014). Are suicidal behaviors contagious in adolescence? *American Sociological Review, 79,* 227.

Abuhamdeh, S., & Csikszentmihalyi, M. (2012). The importance of challenge for the enjoyment of intrinsically motivated, goal-directed activities. *Personality and Social Psychology Bulletin, 38,* 317–330.

Abyzov, A., & others (2013). Analysis of variable retroduplications in human populations suggests coupling of retrotransposition to cell division. *Genome Research, 23,* 2042–2052.

Achenbach, T.M., & Edelbrock, C.S. (1981). Behavioral problems and competencies reported by parents of normal and disturbed children aged four through sixteen. *Monographs of the Society for Research in Child Development, 46*(1, Serial No. 188).

Achenbach, T.M., Howell, C.T., Quay, H.C., & Conners, C.K. (1991). National survey of problems and competencies among four- to sixteen-year-olds. *Monographs for the Society for Research in Child Development, 56*(3, Serial No. 225).

Ackerman, A., Thornton, J.C., Wang, J., Pierson, R.N., & Horlick, M. (2006). Sex differences in the effect of puberty on the relationship between fat mass and bone mass in 926 healthy subjects, 6 to 18 years old. *Obesity, 14,* 819–825.

Ackerman, R.A., & others (2013). The interpersonal legacy of a positive family climate in adolescence. *Psychological Science, 24*(3), 243–250.

Adachi, P.J.C., & Willoughby, T. (2013). Do video games promote positive youth development? *Journal of Adolescent Research, 28,* 55–66.

Adams, G.C., & McWilliams, L.A. (2015, in press). Relationships between adult attachment style ratings and sleep disturbances in a nationally representative sample. *Journal of Psychosomatic Research.*

Adams, M.A. (2012). Mass media. In M. Kosut (Ed.), *Encyclopedia of gender in media.* Thousand Oaks, CA: Sage.

Addo, O.Y., & others (2014). Age at hormonal onset of puberty based on luteinizing hormone, inhibin B, and body composition in preadolescent U.S. girls. *Pediatric Research, 76,* 564–570.

Adelson, J. (1979, January). Adolescence and the generalization gap. *Psychology Today, 13,* 33–37.

Adler, N.E., Ozer, E.J., & Tschann, J. (2003). Abortion among adolescents. *American Psychologist, 58,* 211–217.

Adolescent Sleep Working Group, AAP (2014). School start times for adolescents. *Pediatrics, 134,* 642–649.

Affrunti, N.W., & Woodruff-Borden, J. (2014). Perfectionism in pediatric anxiety and depression.

Clinical Child and Family Psychology Review, 17, 299–317.

Afterschool Alliance (2009). *America after 3 p.m.* Washington, DC: Author.

Agans, J.P., & others (2014). Activity involvement as an ecological asset: Profiles of participation and youth outcome. *Journal of Youth and Adolescence, 43,* 919–932.

Agerup, T., Lydersen, S., Wallander, J., & Sund, A.M. (2015, in press). Associations between parental attachment and course of depression between adolescence and young adulthood. *Child Psychiatry and Human Development.*

Agras, W.S., & others (2004). Report of the National Institutes of Health workshop on overcoming barriers to treatment research in anorexia nervosa. *International Journal of Eating Disorders, 35,* 509–521.

Ahmadi, K., & others (2013). The role of parental monitoring and affiliation with deviant peers in adolescents' sexual risk taking: Toward an interactional model. *International Journal of High-Risk Behaviors and Addiction, 2,* 22–27.

Ahmed, R., Hustad, J.T., Lasalle, L., & Bosari, B. (2014). Hospitalizations for students with an alcohol-related sanction: Gender and pregaming as risk factors. *Journal of American College Health, 62,* 293–300.

Ahrens, C.E., & Aldana, E. (2012). The ties that bind: Understanding the impact of sexual assault disclosure on survivors' relationships with friends, family, and partners. *Journal of Trauma & Dissociation, 13,* 226–243.

Ahrons, C.R. (2004). *We're still family.* New York: HarperCollins.

Ahrons, C.R. (2007). Family ties after divorce: Long-term implications for children. *Family Process, 46,* 53–65.

Ainsworth, M.D.S. (1979). Infant-mother attachment. *American Psychologist, 34,* 932–937.

Ajayi, A.A., & Syed, M. (2014). Links between patterns of racial socialization and discrimination experiences and psychological adjustment: A cluster analysis. *Journal of Adolescence, 37,* 1011–1020.

Akhter, N., & others (2014). Selective deletion of leptin receptors in gonadotropes reveals activin and GnRH-binding sites as leptin targets in support of fertility. *Endocrinology, 155,* 4027–4042.

Akin, A. (2012). Self-handicapping and burnout. *Psychological Reports, 110,* 187–196.

Akin, A., & Akin, U. (2014). Examining the relationship between authenticity and self-handicapping. *Psychology Reports, 115,* 795–804.

Alaimo, K., & others (2015, in press). The Michigan Healthy School Action Tools Process generates improvements in school nutrition policies and practices, and student dietary intake. *Health Promotion and Practice.*

Alan Guttmacher Institute (1995). *National survey of the American male's sexual habits.* New York: Author.

Alan Guttmacher Institute (2010, January 26). *U.S. teenage pregnancies, births, and abortions.* New York: Author.

Albert, D., & Steinberg, L. (2011a). Judgment and decision making in adolescence. *Journal of Research on Adolescence, 21,* 211–224.

Albert, D., & Steinberg, L. (2011b). Peer influences on adolescent risk behavior. In M. Bardo, D. Fishbein, & R. Milich (Eds.), *Inhibitory control and drug abuse prevention: From research to translation.* New York: Springer.

Aldwin, C.M., Jeong, Y.J., Igarashi, H., & Spiro, A. (2014). Do hassles and uplifts change with age? Longitudinal findings from the VA Normative Aging Study. *Psychology and Aging, 29,* 57–71.

Aldwin, C.M., Skinner, E.A., Zimmer-Gembeck, M.J., & Taylor, A. (2011). Coping and self-regulation across the life span. In K.L. Fingerman & others (Eds.), *Handbook of life-span development.* New York: Springer.

Alexander, C., Piazza, M., Mekos, D., & Valente, T. (2001). Peers, schools, and cigarette smoking. *Journal of Adolescent Health, 29,* 22–30.

Ali, F., & others (2015, in press). Energy drinks and their adverse health effects: A systematic review of the current evidence. *Postgraduate Medicine.*

Alia, K.A., & others (2013). Effects of parenting style and parent-related weight and diet on adolescent weight status. *Journal of Pediatric Psychology, 38,* 321–329.

Alikasifoglu, A., & others (2015, in press). Changing etiological trends in male precocious puberty: Evaluation of 100 cases with central precocious puberty over the last decade. *Hormone Research in Pediatrics.*

Allemand, M., Steiger, A.E., & Fend, H.A. (2015). Empathy development in adolescence predicts social competencies in adulthood. *Journal of Personality, 83,* 229–241.

Allen, G., & MacMillan, R. (2006). *Depression, suicidal behavior, and strain: Extending strain theory.* Paper presented at the meeting of the American Sociological Association, Montreal.

Allen, J., & Allen, C.W. (2009). *Escaping the endless adolescence.* New York: Ballantine.

Allen, J.P., Chango, J., & Szwedo, D. (2014). The adolescent relational dialectic and the peer roots of adult social functioning. *Child Development, 85,* 192–204.

Allen, J.P., Chango, J., Szwedo, D., & Schad, M. (2014). Long-term sequalae of subclinical depressive symptoms in early adolescence. *Development and Psychopathology, 26,* 171–180.

Allen, J.P., & Miga, E.M. (2010). Attachment in adolescence: A move to the level of emotion regulation. *Journal of Social and Personal Relationships, 27,* 181–190.

Allen, J.P., Schad, M.M., Oudekerk, B., & Chango, J. (2014). What ever happened to the "cool" kids? Long-term sequalae of early adolescent pseudomature behavior. *Child Development, 85,* 1866–1880.

Allen, J.P., & others (2009, April). *Portrait of the secure teen as an adult.* Paper presented at the meeting of the Society for Research in Child Development, Denver.

Allen, K.L., Byrne, S.M., & Crosby, R.D. (2015, in press). Distinguishing between risk factors for bulimia nervosa, binge eating disorder, and purging disorder. *Journal of Youth & Adolescence.*

Allen, M., Svetaz, M.V., Hardeman, R., & Resnick, M.D. (2008, February). *What research tells us about parenting practices and their relationship to youth sexual behavior.* Campaign to Prevent Teen and Unplanned Pregnancy. Retrieved December 2, 2008, from www.TheNationalCampaign.org

Allington, R.L. (2015). *What really matters for middle school readers.* Upper Saddle River, NJ: Pearson.

Almeida, D. (2011). Stress and aging. In K.W. Schaie & S.L. Willis (Eds.), *Handbook of the psychology of aging* (7th ed.). New York: Elsevier.

Almquist, Y.B., & Brannstrom, L. (2014). Childhood peer status and the clustering of social, economic, and health-related circumstances in adulthood. *Social Science & Medicine, 105,* 67–75.

Alonzo, D., Thompson, R.G., Stohl, M., & Hasin, D. (2014). The influence of parental divorce and alcohol abuse on adult offspring risk of lifetime suicide attempt in the United States. *American Journal of Orthopsychiatry, 84,* 316–320.

Alsaker, F.D., & Flammer, A. (1999). *The adolescent experience: European and American adolescents in the 1990s.* Mahwah, NJ: Erlbaum.

Amabile, T.M. (1993). (Commentary). In D. Goleman, P. Kaufman, & M. Ray (Eds.), *The creative spirit.* New York: Plume.

Amabile, T.M., & Hennessey, B.A. (1992). The motivation for creativity in children. In A.K. Boggiano & T.S. Pittman (Eds.), *Achievement and motivation.* New York: Cambridge University Press.

Amato, P.R. (2006). Marital discord, divorce, and children's well-being: Results from a 20-year longitudinal study of two generations. In A. Clarke-Stewart & J. Dunn (Eds.), *Families count.* New York: Cambridge University Press.

Amato, P.R. (2010). Research on divorce: Continuing trends and new developments. *Journal of Marriage and the Family, 72,* 650–666.

Amato, P.R., & Dorius, C. (2010). Fathers, children, and divorce. In M.E. Lamb (Ed.), *The role of the father in child development* (5th ed.). New York: Wiley.

Ambrose, D., Sternberg, R.J., & Sriraman, B. (Eds.). (2012). *Confronting dogmatism in gifted education.* New York: Routledge.

American Academy of Pediatrics (2010). Policy statement—sexuality, contraception, and the media. *Pediatrics, 126,* 576–582.

Academy of Pediatrics & Reiff, M.I. (2011). *ADHD: What every parent needs to know* (2nd ed.). Washington, DC: Author.

American Association of University Women (1992). *How schools shortchange girls: A study of major findings on girls and education.* Washington, DC: Author.

American Association of University Women (2006). *Drawing the line: Sexual harassment on campus.* Washington, DC: Author.

American Psychiatric Association (2013). *Diagnostic and statistical manual of mental disorders* (5th ed.). Washington, DC: Author.

American Psychological Association (2003). *Psychology: Scientific problem solvers.* Washington, DC: Author.

Ames, M.E., Rawana, J.S., Gentile, P., & Morgan, A.S. (2015). The protective role of optimism and self-esteem on depressive symptom pathways among Canadian Aboriginal youth. *Journal of Youth and Adolescence, 44,* 142–154.

Amialchuk, A., & Gerhardinger, L. (2015). Contraceptive use and pregnancies in adolescents' romantic relationships: Role of relationship activities and parental attitudes and communication. *Journal of Developmental and Behavioral Pediatrics, 36,* 86–97.

Amsel, E., & Smetana, J.G. (Eds.). (2011). *Adolescent vulnerabilities and opportunities: Constructivist and developmental perspectives.* New York: Cambridge University Press.

Amstalden, M., Cardoso, R.C., Alves, B.R., & Williams, G.L. (2014). Reproduction symposium: Hypothalamic peptides and the nutritional programming of puberty in heifers. *Journal of Animal Science, 92,* 3211–3222.

Anderman, E.M. (2012). Adolescence. In K. Harris, S. Graham, & T. Urdan (Eds.), *APA handbook of educational psychology.* Washington, DC: American Psychological Association.

Anderman, E.M., & Anderman, L.H. (2010). *Classroom motivation.* Upper Saddle River, NJ: Pearson.

Anderman, E.M., & Dawson, H. (2011). Learning and motivation. In P. Alexander & R. Mayer (Eds.), *Handbook of learning and instruction.* New York: Routledge.

Anderman, E.M., Gray, D.L., & Chang, Y. (2013). Motivation and classroom learning. In I.B. Weiner & others (Eds.), *Handbook of psychology* (2nd ed., Vol. 7). New York: Wiley.

Anderman, E.M., & Murdock, T.B. (Eds.). (2007). *Psychology of academic cheating.* San Diego: Academic Press.

Anderman, E.M., & Wolters, C.A. (2006). Goals, values, and affect: Influences on student motivation. In P.A. Alexander & P.H. Winne (Eds.), *Handbook of educational psychology* (2nd ed.). Mahwah, NJ: Erlbaum.

Anderson, D.R., Huston, A.C., Schmitt, K., Linebarger, D.L., & Wright, J.C. (2001). Early childhood viewing and adolescent behavior: The recontact study. *Monographs of the Society for Research in Child Development, 66*(1, Serial No. 264).

Anderson, E., Greene, S.M., Hetherington, E.M., & Clingempeel, W.G. (1999). The dynamics of parental remarriage. In E.M. Hetherington (Ed.), *Coping with divorce, single parenting, and remarriage.* Mahwah, NJ: Erlbaum.

Anderson, K.G., Tapert, S.F., Moadab, I., Crowley, T.J., & Brown, S.A. (2007). Personality risk profile for conduct disorder and substance use disorders in youth. *Addictive Behaviors, 32,* 2377–2382.

Anderson, M.L., & Finlay, B.L. (2014). Allocating structure to function: The strong links between neuroplasticity and natural selection. *Frontiers in Human Neuroscience, 7,* 918.

Anderson, S.B., & Guthery, A.M. (2015). Mindfulness-based psychoeducation for parents of children with attention-deficit/hyperactivity disorder: An applied clinical project. *Journal of Child and Adolescent Psychiatric Nursing, 28,* 43–49.

Andersson, H., & Bergman, L.R. (2011). The role of task persistence in young adolescence for successful educational and occupational attainment in middle adulthood. *Developmental Psychology, 47,* 950–960.

Andersson, U. (2010). The contribution of working memory capacity to foreign language comprehension in children. *Memory, 18,* 458–472.

Andreotti, C., Root, J.C., Ahles, T.A., McEwen, B.S., & Compas, B.E. (2015, in press). Cancer, coping, and cognition: A model for the role of stress reactivity in cancer-related cognitive decline. *Psycho-Oncology.*

Angelone, D.J., Mitchell, D., & Grossi, L. (2015, in press). Men's perceptions of an acquaintance rape: The role of relationship length, victim resistance, and gender role attitudes. *Journal of Interpersonal Violence.*

Ansary, N.S., & Luthar, S.S. (2009). Distress and academic achievement among adolescents of affluence: A study of externalizing and internalizing problem behaviors and school performance. *Development and Psychopathology, 21,* 319–341.

Ansary, N.S., McMahon, T.J., & Luthar, S.S. (2012). Socioeconomic context and emotional-behavioral achievement links: Concurrent and prospective associations among low- and high-income youth. *Journal of Research on Adolescence, 22,* 14–30.

Anspaugh, D., & Ezell, G. (2013). *Teaching today's health* (10th ed.). Upper Saddle River, NJ: Pearson.

Antai-Otong, D. (2003). Suicide: Life span considerations. *Nursing Clinics of North America, 38,* 137–150.

Antonucci, T.C., Ajrouch, K., & Birditt, K. (2014). The convoy model: Explaining social relations from a multidisciplinary perspective. *Gerontologist, 54,* 82–92.

Antonucci, T.C., Birditt, K., & Ajrouch, K. (2013). Social relationships and aging. In I.B. Weiner & others (Eds.), *Handbook of psychology* (2nd ed., Vol. 6). New York: Wiley.

Antonucci, T.C., Birditt, K., & Akiyama (2016, in press). Convoys of social relations: An interdisciplinary approach. In V. Bengtson & others (Eds.), *Handbook of theories of aging* (3rd ed.). New York: Springer.

Anyaegbu, E., & Dharnidharka, V.R. (2014). Hypertension in the teenagers. *Pediatric Clinics of North America, 61,* 131–151.

Appleton, J.J. (2012). Student engagement in school. In J.R. Levesque (Ed.), *Encyclopedia of adolescence.* New York: Springer.

Archibald, A.B., Graber, J.A., & Brooks-Gunn, J. (1999). Associations among parent-adolescent relationships, pubertal growth, dieting, and body image in young adolescent girls: A short-term longitudinal study. *Journal of Research on Adolescence, 9,* 395–415.

Ardelt, M. (2010). Are older adults wiser than college students? A comparison of two age cohorts. *Journal of Adult Development, 17,* 193–207.

Ariceli, G., Castro, J., Cesena, J., & Toro, J. (2005). Anorexia nervosa in male adolescents: Body image, eating attitudes, and psychological traits. *Journal of Adolescent Health, 36,* 221–226.

Arim, R.G., & others (2011). The family antecedents and the subsequent outcomes of early puberty. *Journal of Youth and Adolescence, 40,* 1423–1435.

Arkes, J. (2015). The temporal effects of divorces and separations on children's academic achievement and problem behavior. *Journal of Divorce and Remarriage, 56,* 25–42.

Armstrong, D.G., Henson, K.T., & Savage, T.V. (2015). *Teaching today* (9th ed.). Upper Saddle River, NJ: Pearson.

Armstrong, M.L. (1995). Adolescent tattoos: Educating and pontificating. *Pediatric Nursing, 21*(6), 561–564.

Armstrong, M.L., Roberts, A.E., Owen, D.C., & Koch, J.R. (2004). Contemporary college students and body piercing. *Journal of Adolescent Health, 35,* 58–61.

Arnett, J. (1990). Contraceptive use, sensation seeking, and adolescent egocentrism. *Journal of Youth and Adolescence, 19,* 171–180.

Arnett, J.J. (1995, March). *Are college students adults?* Paper presented at the meeting of the Society for Research in Child Development, Indianapolis.

Arnett, J.J. (2004). *Emerging adulthood.* New York: Oxford University Press.

Arnett, J.J. (2006). Emerging adulthood: Understanding the new way of coming of age. In J.J. Arnett & J.L. Tanner (Eds.), *Emerging adults in America.* Washington, DC: American Psychological Association.

Arnett, J.J. (2007). Socialization in emerging adulthood. In J.E. Grusec & P.D. Hastings (Eds.), *Handbook of socialization.* New York: Guilford.

Arnett, J.J. (2010). Oh, grow up! Generational grumbling and the new life stage of emerging adulthoods—Commentary on Trzesniewski & Donnellan (2010). *Perspectives on Psychological Science, 5,* 89–92.

Arnett, J.J. (Ed.) (2012). *Adolescent psychology around the world.* New York: Psychology Press.

Arnett, J.J. (2013). *Clark Poll: Parents of emerging adults.* Clark University: Worcester, MA.

Arnett, J.J. (2014). *Emerging adulthood* (2nd ed.). New York: Oxford University Press.

Arnett, J.J. (2015a). Identity development from adolescence to emerging adulthood: What we know and (especially) don't know. In K.C. McLean & M. Syed (Eds.), *Oxford handbook of identity development.* New York: Oxford University Press.

Arnett, J.J. (2015b). Socialization in emerging adulthood. In J.E. Grusec & P.D. Hastings (Eds.), *Handbook of socialization* (2nd ed.). New York: Guilford.

Arnett, J.J., & Brody, G.H. (2008). A fraught passage: The identity challenges of African American emerging adults. *Human Development, 51,* 291–293.

Arnett, J.J., & Fishel, E. (2013). *When will my grown-up kid grow up?* New York: Workman.

Arnett, J.J., & Fishel, E. (2014). *Getting to 30: A parent's guide to the 20-something years.* New York: Workman.

Aronowitz, T., & Morrison-Beedy, D. (2008). Comparison of the maternal role in resilience among impoverished and non-impoverished early adolescent African American girls. *Adolescent & Family Health, 3,* 155–163.

Aronson, E. (1986, August). *Teaching students things they think they know all about: The case of prejudice and desegregation.* Paper presented at the meeting of the American Psychological Association, Washington, DC.

Arseth, A., Kroger, J., Martinussen, M., & Marcia, J.E. (2009). Meta-analytic studies of identity status and the relational issues of attachment and intimacy. *Identity, 9,* 1–32.

Arthur, J. (2014). Traditional approaches to character education in Britain and America. In L. Nucci, T. Krettenauer, & D. Narváez (Eds.), *Handbook of moral and character education* (2nd ed.). New York: Routledge.

Asarnow, J.R., Berk, M., Hughes, J.L., & Anderson, N.L. (2015). The SAFETY program: A treatment-development trial of a cognitive-behavioral family treatment for adolescent suicide attempters. *Journal of Clinical Child and Adolescent Psychology, 44,* 194–203.

Asarnow, J.R., & Callan, J.W. (1985). Boys with peer adjustment problems: Social cognitive processes. *Journal of Consulting and Clinical Psychology, 53,* 80–87.

Asheer, S., Berger, A., Meckstroth, A., Kisker, E., & Keating, B. (2014). Engaging pregnant and parenting teens: Early challenges and lessons learned from the Evaluation of Adolescent Pregnancy Prevention Approaches. *Journal of Adolescent Health, 54*(Suppl. 3), S84–S91.

Asian Pacific American Legal Center & Asian American Justice Center (2011). *A community of contrasts.* Washington, DC: Asian American Center for Advancing Justice.

Assini-Meytin, L.C., & Green, K.M. (2015, in press). Long-term consequences of adolescent parenthood among African-American youth: A propensity score matching approach. *Journal of Adolescent Health.*

Ata, R.N., Ludden, A.B., & Lally, M.M. (2007). The effect of gender and family, friend, and media influences on eating behavior and body image during adolescence. *Journal of Youth and Adolescence, 36,* 1024–1037.

Atkin, A.J., & others (2014). Prevalence and correlates of screen time in youth: An international perspective. *American Journal of Preventive Medicine, 47,* 803–807.

Attie, I., & Brooks-Gunn, J. (1989). Development of eating problems in adolescent girls: A longitudinal study. *Developmental Psychology, 25,* 70–79.

Avinun, R., & Knafo-Noma, A. (2015). Socialization, genetics, and their interplay in development. In J.E. Grusec & P.D. Hastings (Eds.), *Handbook of socialization* (2nd ed.). New York: Guilford.

Azmitia, M. (2015). Reflections on the cultural lenses of identity development. In K.C. McLean & M. Syed (Eds.), *Oxford handbook of identity development.* New York: Oxford University Press.

Azmitia, M., Syed, M., & Radmacher, K.A. (2013). Finding your niche: Identity and emotional support in emerging adults' adjustment to the transition to college. *Journal of Research in Adolescence, 23,* 744–776.

B

Bachman, J.G., & others (2002). *The decline of substance abuse in young adulthood.* Mahwah, NJ: Erlbaum.

Bachman, J.G., & others (2008). *The education–drug use connection.* New York: Psychology Press.

Bacikova-Sleskova, M., Benka, J., & Orosova, O. (2014). Parental employment status and adolescents' health: The role of financial situation, parent-adolescent relationship, and adolescents' resilience. *Psychology and Health, 30,* 400–422.

Baddeley, A.D. (2008). What's new in working memory? *Psychology Review, 13,* 2–5.

Baddeley, A.D. (2010a). Long-term and working memory: How do they interact? In L. Bäckman & L. Nyberg (Eds.), *Memory, aging and the brain: A festschrift in honour of Lars-Göran Nilsson* (pp. 18–30). Hove, UK: Psychology Press.

Baddeley, A.D. (2010b). Working memory. *Current Biology, 20,* 136–140.

Baddeley, A.D. (2012). Working memory. *Annual Review of Psychology* (Vol. 63). Palo Alto, CA: Annual Reviews.

Baddeley, A.D. (2013). On applying cognitive psychology. *British Journal of Psychology, 104,* 443–456.

Baer, J., & Kaufman, J.C. (2013). *Being creative inside and outside the classroom.* The Netherlands: Sense Publishers.

Bailin, A., Milanaik, R., & Adesman, A. (2014). Health implications of new age technologies for adolescents: A review of the research. *Current Opinion in Pediatrics, 26,* 605–619.

Bair, C.E., Kelly, N.R., Serdar, K.L., & Mazzeo, S.E. (2012). Does the Internet function like magazines? An exploration of image-focused media, eating pathology, and body dissatisfaction. *Eating Behaviors, 13,* 398–401.

Bajoghli, H., & others (2014). "I love you more than I can stand!"—romantic love, symptoms of depression and anxiety, and sleep complaints among young adults. *International Journal of Psychiatry and Clinical Practice, 18,* 169–174.

Bakalar, J.L., & others (2015). Recent advances in developmental and risk factor research on eating disorders. *Current Psychiatry Reports, 17*(6), 585.

Baker, J.R., Hudson, J.L., & Taylor, A. (2014). An investigation into the lower peer liking of anxious than nonanxious children. *Journal of Anxiety Disorders, 28,* 599–611.

Baldwin, S.A., Christian, S., Berkeljon, A., & Shadish, W.R. (2012). The effects of family therapies for adolescent delinquency and substance abuse: A meta-analysis. *Journal of Marital and Family Therapy, 38,* 281–304.

Baldwin, S., & Hoffman, J.P. (2002). The dynamics of self-esteem: A growth curve analysis. *Journal of Youth and Adolescence, 31,* 101–113.

Ballentine, J.H., & Roberts, K.A. (2009). *Our social world* (2nd ed.). Thousand Oaks, CA: Sage.

Balodis, I.M., & others (2013). Divergent neural substrates of inhibitory control in binge eating disorder relative to other manifestations of obesity. *Obesity, 21*(2), 367–377.

Baltes, P.B., & Kunzmann, U. (2007). Wisdom and aging. In D.C. Park & N. Schwarz (Eds.), *Cognitive aging* (2nd ed.). Philadelphia: Psychology Press.

Baltes, P.B., Lindenberger, U., & Staudinger, U. (2006). Life-span theory in developmental psychology. In W. Damon & R. Lerner (Eds.), *Handbook of child psychology* (6th ed.). New York: Wiley.

Baltes, P.B., & Smith, J. (2008). The fascination of wisdom: Its nature, ontogeny, and function. *Perspectives on Psychological Science, 3,* 56–64.

Bamaca-Colbert, M., Umana-Taylor, A.J., Espinosa-Hernandez, G., & Brown, A.M. (2012). Behavioral autonomy expectations among Mexican-origin mother-daughter dyads: An examination of within-group variability. *Journal of Adolescence, 35,* 691–700.

Bamford, C., & Lagattuta, K.H. (2012). Looking on the bright side: Children's knowledge about the benefits of positive versus negative thinking. *Child Development, 83,* 667–682.

Bandura, A. (1986). *Social foundations of thought and action: A social cognitive theory.* Englewood Cliffs, NJ: Prentice Hall.

Bandura, A. (1991). Social cognitive theory of moral thought and action. In W.M. Kurtines & J. Gewirtz (Eds.), *Handbook of moral behavior and development* (Vol. 1). Hillsdale, NJ: Erlbaum.

Bandura, A. (1997). *Self-efficacy.* New York: W. H. Freeman.

Bandura, A. (1998, August). *Swimming against the mainstream: Accentuating the positive aspects of humanity.* Paper presented at the meeting of the American Psychological Association, San Francisco.

Bandura, A. (1999). Moral disengagement in the perpetuation of inhumanities. *Personality and Social Psychology Review, 3,* 193–209.

Bandura, A. (2001). Social cognitive theory. *Annual Review of Psychology* (Vol. 52). Palo Alto, CA: Annual Reviews.

Bandura, A. (2002). Selective moral disengagement in the exercise of moral agency. *Journal of Moral Education, 31,* 101–119.

Bandura, A. (2004, May). *Toward a psychology of human agency.* Paper presented at the meeting of the American Psychological Society, Chicago.

Bandura, A. (2009). Social and policy impact of social cognitive theory. In M. Mark, S. Donaldson, & B. Campbell (Eds.), *Social psychology and program/policy evaluation.* New York: Guilford.

Bandura, A. (2010a). Self-efficacy. In D. Matsumoto (Ed.), *Cambridge dictionary of psychology.* New York: Cambridge University Press.

Bandura, A. (2010b). Vicarious learning. In D. Matsumoto (Ed.), *Cambridge dictionary of psychology.* New York: Cambridge University Press.

Bandura, A. (2012). Social cognitive theory. *Annual Review of Clinical Psychology* (Vol. 8). Palo Alto, CA: Annual Reviews.

Banerjee, M., Harrell, Z.A.T., & Johnson, D.J. (2011). Racial/ethnic socialization and parental involvement in education as predictors of cognitive ability and achievement in African American children. *Journal of Youth and Adolescence, 40,* 595–605.

Bank, L., Burraston, B., & Snyder, J. (2004). Sibling conflict and ineffective parenting as predictors of boys' antisocial behavior and peer difficulties: Additive and international effects. *Journal of Research on Adolescence, 14,* 99–125.

Bankole, A., Singh, S., Woog, V., & Wulf, D. (2004). *Risk and protection: Youth and HIV/AIDS in sub-Saharan Africa.* New York: Alan Guttmacher Institute.

Banks, J.A. (2008). *Introduction to multicultural education* (4th ed.). Boston: Allyn & Bacon.

Banks, J.A. (2014). *Introduction to multicultural education* (5th ed.). Upper Saddle River, NJ: Pearson.

Banks, J.A. (2015). *Cultural diversity and education* (6th ed.). Upper Saddle River, NJ: Pearson.

Barbarin, O.A., Chinn, L., & Wright, Y.F. (2014). Creating developmentally auspicious school environments for African American boys. *Advances in Child Development and Behavior, 47,* 333–365.

Barber, B.L., & Demo, D. (2006). The kids are all right (at least most of them): Links to divorce and dissolution. In M.A. Fine & J.H. Harvey (Eds.), *Handbook of divorce and relationship dissolution.* Mahwah, NJ: Erlbaum.

Bargh, J.A., & McKenna, K.Y.A. (2004). The Internet and social life. *Annual Review of Psychology* (Vol. 55). Palo Alto, CA: Annual Reviews.

Barker, R., & Wright, H.F. (1951). *One boy's day.* New York: Harper.

Barnouw, V. (1975). *An introduction to anthropology, Vol. 2: Ethnology.* Homewood, IL: Dorsey Press.

Barr, E.M., & others (2014). New evidence: Data documenting parental support for earlier sexuality education. *Journal of School Health, 84,* 10–17.

Barrocas, A.L., & others (2015). Nonsuicidal self-injury in adolescence: Longitudinal course, trajectories, and intrapersonal predictors. *Journal of Abnormal Child Psychology, 43,* 369–380.

Barth, T. (2012). Relationships and sexuality of imprisoned men in the German penal system—a survey of inmates in a Berlin prison. *International Journal of Law and Psychiatry, 35,* 153–158.

Bartlett, J.D., & others (2014). An ecological analysis of infant neglect by adolescent mothers. *Child Abuse and Neglect, 38,* 723–734.

Bartoli, F., & others (2014). Prevalence and correlates of binge drinking among young adults using alcohol: A cross-sectional survey. *Biomed Research International, 2014,* 930795.

Basow, S.A. (2006). Gender role and gender identity development. In J. Worell & C.D. Goodheart (Eds.),

Handbook of girls' and women's psychological health. New York: Oxford University Press.

Bassett, D.R., & others (2015, in press). Trends in physical activity and sedentary behaviors in U.S. youth. *Journal of Physical Activity and Health.*

Bassi, M., Steca, P., Della Fave, A., & Caprara, G.V. (2007). Academic self-efficacy beliefs and quality of experience in learning. *Journal of Youth and Adolescence, 36,* 301–312.

Batanova, M.D., & Loukas, A. (2011). Social anxiety and aggression in early adolescents: Examining the moderating roles of empathic concern and perspective taking. *Journal of Youth and Adolescence, 40,* 1534–1543.

Bates, J.E. (2012a). Behavioral regulation as a product of temperament and environment. In S.L. Olson & A.J. Sameroff (Eds.), *Biopsychosocial regulatory processes in the development of childhood behavioral problems.* New York: Cambridge University Press.

Bates, J.E. (2012b). Temperament as a tool in promoting early childhood development. In S.L. Odom, E.P. Pungello, & N. Gardner-Neblett (Eds.), *Infants, toddlers, and families in poverty.* New York: Guilford University Press.

Bates, J.E. (2013). Adjustment style in childhood as a product of parenting and temperament. In T.D. Wachs & others (Eds.). *Temperament in context.* New York: Psychology Press.

Battistich, V.A. (2008). The Child Development Project: Creating caring school communities. In L. Nucci & D. Narváez (Eds.), *Handbook of moral and character education.* Clifton, NJ: Psychology Press.

Bauerlein, M. (2008). *The dumbest generation: How the digital age stupefies young Americans and jeopardizes our future (Or, don't trust anyone under 30).* New York: Tarcher.

Baumeister, R.F., Campbell, J.D., Krueger, J.I., & Vohs, K.D. (2003). Does high self-esteem cause better performance, interpersonal success, happiness, or healthier lifestyles? *Psychological Science in the Public Interest, 4*(1), 1–44.

Baumrind, D. (1971). Current patterns of parental authority. *Developmental Psychology Monographs, 4*(1, Pt. 2).

Baumrind, D. (1991). Effective parenting during the early adolescent transition. In P.A. Cowan & E.M. Hetherington (Eds.), *Advances in family research* (Vol. 2). Hillsdale, NJ: Erlbaum.

Baumrind, D. (2012). Authoritative parenting revisited: History and current status. In R.E. Larzelere, A.S. Morris, & A.W. Harrist (Eds.), *Authoritative parenting.* Washington, DC: American Psychological Association.

Bauserman, R. (2003). Child adjustment in joint-custody versus sole-custody arrangements: A meta-analytic review. *Journal of Family Psychology, 16,* 19–102.

Bayraktar, F., Machackova, H., Dedkova, L., & Cerna, A. (2015, in press). Cyberbullying: The discriminant factors among cyberbullies, cybervictims, and cyberbully-victims in a Czech adolescent sample. *Journal of Interpersonal Violence.*

Bazrafshan, M.R., Sharif, F., Molazem, Z., & Mani, A. (2015). Cultural concepts and themes of suicidal attempt among Iranian adolescents. *International Journal of High Risk Behaviors and Addiction, 4*(1), e22589.

Bazzini, D.G., Pepper, A., Swofford, R., & Cochran, K. (2015, in press). How healthy are health magazines? A comparative content analysis of cover captions and images of *Women's* and *Men's Health* magazines. *Sex Roles.*

Beaver, K.M., Wright, J.P., DeLisi, M., & Vaughn, M.G. (2009, March). Gene-environment interplay and delinquent involvement: Evidence of direct, indirect, and interactive effects. *Journal of Adolescent Research, 24,* 147–168.

Bechtold, J., Cavanagh, C., Shulman, E.P., & Caufmann, E. (2014). Does mother know best?

Adolescent and mother reports of impulsivity and subsequent delinquency. *Journal of Youth and Adolescence, 43,* 1903–1913.

Becker, M.W., Alzahabi, R., & Hopwood, C.J. (2013). Media multitasking is associated with symptoms of depression and social anxiety. *Cyberpsychology, Behavior, and Social Networking, 16,* 132–136.

Bednar, R.L., Wells, M.G., & Peterson, S.R. (1995). *Self-esteem* (2nd ed.). Washington, DC: American Psychological Association.

Beebe, D.W., Rose, D., & Amin, R. (2010). Attention, learning, and arousal of experimentally sleep-restricted adolescents in a simulated classroom. *Journal of Adolescent Health, 47,* 523–525.

Begley, S., & Interlandi, J. (2008, July 2). The dumbest generation? Don't be dumb. *Newsweek.* Retrieved July 15, 2008, from www.newsweek.com/id/138536

Behie, A.M., & O'Donnell, M.H. (2015). Prenatal smoking and age at menarche: Influence of the prenatal environment on the timing of puberty. *Human Reproduction, 30,* 957–962.

Belhadj Kouider, E., Koglin, U., & Petermann, F. (2015, in press). Emotional and behavioral problems in migrant children and adolescents in American countries: A systematic review. *Journal of Immigrant and Minority Health.*

Bellefontaine, N., & others (2014). Leptin-dependent neuronal NO signaling in the preoptic hypothalamus facilitates reproduction. *Journal of Clinical Investigation, 124,* 2550–2559.

Bellmore, A., Jiang, X.U., & Juvonen, J. (2010). Utilizing peer nominations in middle school: A longitudinal comparison between complete classroom-based and random list methods. *Journal of Research in Adolescence, 20,* 538–550.

Bellmore, A., Villarreal, V.M., & Ho, A.Y. (2011). Staying cool across the first year of middle school. *Journal of Youth and Adolescence, 40,* 776–785.

Belshaw, S.H., Siddique, J.A., Tanner, J., & Osho, G.S. (2012). The relationship between dating violence and suicidal behaviors in a national sample of adolescents. *Violence and Victims, 27,* 580–591.

Belsky, J. (1981). Early human experience: A family perspective. *Developmental Psychology, 17,* 3–23.

Belsky, J., & Beaver, K.M. (2011). Cumulative-genetic plasticity, parenting, and adolescent self-regulation. *Journal of Child Psychology and Psychiatry, 52,* 619–626.

Belsky, J., Jaffe, S., Hsieh, K., & Silva, P. (2001). Child-rearing antecedents of intergenerational relations in young adulthood: A prospective study. *Developmental Psychology, 37,* 801–813.

Belsky, J., Steinberg, L., Houts, R.M., Halpern-Felsher, B.L., & NICHD Child Care Research Network (2010). The development of reproductive strategy in females: Early maternal harshness → earlier menarche → increased sexual risk. *Developmental Psychology, 46,* 120–128.

Bem, S.L. (1977). On the utility of alternative procedures for assessing psychological androgyny. *Journal of Consulting and Clinical Psychology, 45,* 196–205.

Benet-Martinez, V., & Hong, Y. (Eds.) (2014). *Oxford handbook of cultural identity.* New York: Oxford University Press.

Benner, A.D. (2011). Latino adolescents' loneliness, academic performance, and the buffering nature of friendships. *Journal of Youth and Adolescence, 5,* 556–567.

Benner, A.D., & Graham, S. (2013). The antecedents and consequences of racial/ethnic discrimination during adolescence: Does the source of discrimination matter? *Developmental Psychology, 49,* 1602–1613.

Bennett, C.I. (2015). *Comprehensive multicultural education* (8th ed.). Upper Saddle River, NJ: Pearson.

Benokraitis, N. (2015). *Marriage and families* (8th ed.). Upper Saddle River, NJ: Pearson.

Benotsch, E.G., Snipes, D.J., Martin, A.M., & Bull, S.S. (2013). Sexting, substance use, and sexual risk in

young adults. *Journal of Adolescent Health, 52*(3), 307–313.

Benowitz-Fredericks, C.A., Garcia, K., Massey, M., Vassagar, B., & Borzekowski, D.L. (2012). Body image, eating disorders, and the relationship to adolescent media use. *Pediatric Clinics of North America, 59,* 693–704.

Benson, P.L. (2006). *All kids are our kids.* San Francisco: Jossey-Bass.

Benson, P.L. (2010). *Parent, teacher, mentor, friend: How every adult can change kids' lives.* Minneapolis: Search Institute Press.

Benson, P.L., & Scales, P.C. (2009). The definition and preliminary measurement of thriving in adolescence. *Journal of Positive Psychology, 4,* 85–104.

Benson, P.L., & Scales, P.C. (2011). Thriving and sparks: Development and emergence of new core concepts in positive youth development. In R.J.R. Levesque (Ed.), *Encyclopedia of adolescence.* Berlin: Springer.

Benson, P.L., Mannes, M., Pittman, K., & Ferber, T. (2004). Youth development, developmental assets, and public policy. In R. Lerner & L. Steinberg (Eds.), *Handbook of adolescent psychology* (2nd ed.). New York: Wiley.

Benson, P.L., Scales, P.C., Hamilton, S.F., & Sesma, A. (2006). Positive youth development. In W. Damon & R. Lerner (Eds.), *Handbook of child psychology* (6th ed.). New York: Wiley.

Benveniste, L., Carnoy, M., & Rothstein, R. (2003). *All else equal.* New York: Routledge-Farmer.

Berenbaum, S.A., Beltz, A.M., & Corley, R. (2015). The importance of puberty for adolescent development: Conceptualization and measurement. *Advances in Child Development and Behavior, 48,* 53–92.

Berge, J.M., & others (2013). Family functioning: Associations with weight status, eating behaviors, and physical activity in adolescents. *Journal of Adolescent Research, 52*(3), 351–357.

Berge, J.M., & others (2015). The protective role of family meals for youth obesity: 10-year longitudinal associations. *Journal of Pediatrics, 166,* 296–301.

Berger, I., Remington, A., Leitner, Y., & Leviton, A. (2015). Brain development and the attention spectrum. *Frontiers in Human Neuroscience, 9,* 23.

Bergman, K.N., Cummings, E.M., & Davies, P.T. (2014). Interparental aggression and adolescent adjustment: The role of emotional insecurity and adrenocortical activity. *Journal of Family Violence, 29,* 763–771.

Bergmuller, S. (2013). The relationship between cultural individualism-collectivism and student aggression across 62 countries. *Aggressive Behavior, 39,* 182–200.

Berkowitz, M.W. (2012). Moral and character education. In K.R. Harris, S. Graham, & T. Urdan (Eds.), *APA educational psychology handbook* (Vol. 2). New York: American Psychological Association.

Berkowitz, M.W., Battistich, V.A., & Bier, M. (2008). What works in character education: What is known and what needs to be known. In L. Nucci & D. Narváez (Eds.), *Handbook of moral and character education.* Clifton, NJ: Psychology Press.

Berkowitz, M.W., & Gibbs, J.C. (1983). Measuring the developmental features of moral discussion. *Merrill-Palmer Quarterly, 29,* 399–410.

Berman, S.L., You, Y., Schwartz, S., Teo, G., & Mochizuki, K. (2011). Identity exploration, commitment, and distress: A cross national investigation in China, Taiwan, Japan, and the United States. *Child Youth Care Forum, 40,* 65–75.

Berndt, T.J. (1979). Developmental changes in conformity to peers and parents. *Developmental Psychology, 15,* 608–616.

Berndt, T.J., & Perry, T.B. (1990). Distinctive features and effects of early adolescent friendships. In R. Montemayor (Ed.), *Advances in adolescent research.* Greenwich, CT: JAI Press.

Bernier, A., Jarry-Boileau, V., & Lacharite, C. (2014). Marital satisfaction and quality of father-child interactions: The moderating role of gender. *Journal of Genetic Psychology, 175,* 105–117.

Berninger, V.W. (2006). Learning disabilities. In W. Damon & R. Lerner (Eds.), *Handbook of child psychology* (6th ed.). New York: Wiley.

Berninger, V., & Dunn, M. (2012). Brain and behavioral response to intervention for specific reading, writing, and math disabilities: What works for whom? In B. Wong & D. Butler (Eds.), *Learning about LD* (4th ed.). New York: Elsevier.

Berninger, V.W., & others (2015). Computer instruction in handwriting, spelling, and composing for students with specific learning disabilities in grades 4 to 9. *Computers & Education, 81,* 154–168.

Bernstein, N. (2004, March 7). Young love, new caution. *The New York Times,* p. A22.

Berry, J.W. (2015). Acculturation. In J.E. Grusec & P.D. Hastings (Eds.), *Handbook of socialization* (2nd ed.). New York: Guilford.

Berry, J.W., & Sam, D. (2014). Multicultural societies. In V. Benet-Martinez & Y. Hong (Eds.), *Oxford handbook of multicultural identity.* New York: Oxford University Press.

Bersamin, M.M., & others (2014). Risky business: Is there an association between casual sex and mental health among emerging adults? *Journal of Sex Research, 51,* 43–51.

Berscheid, E. (2010). Love in the fourth dimension. *Annual Review of Psychology* (Vol. 61). Palo Alto, CA: Annual Reviews.

Berscheid, E., & Fei, J. (1977). Sexual jealousy and romantic love. In G. Clinton & G. Smith (Eds.), *Sexual jealousy.* Englewood Cliffs, NJ: Prentice-Hall.

Berscheid, E., Snyder, M., & Omoto, A.M. (1989). Issues in studying close relationships. In C. Hendrick (Ed.), *Close relationships.* Newbury Park, CA: Sage.

Berwid, O.G., & Halperin, J.M. (2012). Emerging support for a role of exercise in attention-deficit/hyperactivity disorder intervention planning. *Current Psychiatry Reports, 14,* 543–551.

Best, J.R. (2011). Effects of physical activity on children's executive function: Contributions of experimental research on aerobic exercise. *Developmental Review, 30,* 331–351.

Bethell, J., & Rhoades, A.E. (2008). Adolescent depression and emergency department use: The roles of suicidality and deliberate self-harm. *Current Psychiatry Reports, 10,* 53–59.

Beyers, E., & Seiffge-Krenke, I. (2011). Does identity precede intimacy? Testing Erikson's theory on romantic development in emerging adults of the 21st century. *Journal of Adolescent Research, 25*(3), 387–415.

Bigler, R.S., Hayes, A.R., & Liben, L.S. (2014). Analysis and evaluation of the rationales for single-sex schooling. *Advances in Child Development and Behavior, 47,* 225–260.

Bill and Melinda Gates Foundation (2006). *The silent epidemic: Perspectives on high school dropouts.* Seattle: Author.

Bill and Melinda Gates Foundation (2008). *Report gives voice to dropouts.* Retrieved August 31, 2008, from www.gatesfoundation.org/UnitedStates/Education/TransformingHighSchool/Related

Bill and Melinda Gates Foundation (2012). *College-ready education.* Retrieved November 21, 2012, from www.gatesfoundation.org/college-ready-education/Pages/default.aspx.

Birkeland, M.S., Melkevick, O., Holsen, I., & Wold, B. (2012). Trajectories of global self-esteem development during adolescence. *Journal of Adolescence, 35,* 43–54.

Birman, B.F., & others (2007). *State and local implementation of the "No Child Left Behind Act." Volume II—Teacher quality under "NCLB": Interim report.* Jessup, MD: U.S. Department of Education.

Biro, F.M., & others (2014). Hormone changes in peripubertal girls. *Journal of Clinical Endocrinology and Metabolism, 99,* 3829–3835.

Bjorklund, D.F. (2006). Mother knows best: Epigenetic inheritance, maternal effects, and the evolution of human intelligence. *Developmental Review, 26,* 213–242.

Bjorklund, D.F. (2012). *Children's thinking* (8th ed.). Boston: Cengage.

Bjorklund, D.F., & Pellegrini, A.D. (2002). *The origins of human nature.* New York: Oxford University Press.

Black, M.C., & others (2011). *The National Intimate Partner and Sexual Violence Survey (NISVS): 2010 Summary Report.* Atlanta: National Center for Injury Prevention and Control.

Blackwell, L.S., & Dweck, C.S. (2008). *The motivational impact of a computer-based program that teaches how the brain changes with learning.* Unpublished manuscript. Department of Psychology, Stanford University, Palo Alto, CA.

Blackwell, L.S., Trzesniewski, K.H., & Dweck, C.S. (2007). Implicit theories of intelligence predict achievement across an adolescent transition: A longitudinal study and an intervention. *Child Development, 78,* 246–263.

Blake, J.S. (2013). *Nutrition and you* (2nd ed.). Upper Saddle River, NJ: Pearson.

Blake, J.S. (2015). *Nutrition and you* (3rd ed.). Upper Saddle River, NJ: Pearson.

Blakemore, J.E.O., Berenbaum, S.A., & Liben, I.S. (2009). *Gender development.* New York: Psychology Press.

Blakemore, S.J., & Mills, K. (2014). The social brain in adolescence. *Annual Review of Psychology* (Vol. 65). Palo Alto, CA: Annual Reviews.

Blanco, C., & others (2014). Risk factors for anxiety disorders: Common and specific effects in a national sample. *Depression and Anxiety, 31,* 756–764.

Bleakley, A., Hennessy, M., Fishbein, M., & Jordan, A. (2009). How sources of sexual information relate to adolescents' beliefs about sex. *American Journal of Health Behavior, 33,* 37–48.

Block, J. (1993). Studying personality the long way. In D. Funder, R.D. Parke, C. Tomlinson-Keasey, & K. Widaman (Eds.), *Studying lives through time.* Washington, DC: American Psychological Association.

Block, J.H., & Block, J. (1980). The role of ego-control and ego-resiliency in the organization of behavior. In W.A. Collins (Ed.), *Minnesota symposium on child psychology* (Vol. 13). Minneapolis: University of Minnesota Press.

Blomeyer, D., & others (2008). Interaction between CRHRI gene and stressful life events predicts adolescent heavy alcohol use. *Biological Psychiatry, 63,* 146–151.

Bloom, B. (1985). *Developing talent in young people.* New York: Ballantine.

Blos, P. (1989). The inner world of the adolescent. In A.H. Esman (Ed.), *International annals of adolescent psychiatry* (Vol. 1). Chicago: University of Chicago Press.

Blumenfeld, P.C., Kempler, T.M., & Krajcik, J.S. (2006). Motivation and cognitive engagement in learning environments. In R.K. Sawyer (Ed.), *The Cambridge handbook of the learning sciences.* New York: Cambridge University Press.

Blumenthal, H., & others (2011). Elevated social anxiety among early maturing girls. *Developmental Psychology, 47,* 1133–1140.

Bo, I. (1994). The sociocultural environment as a source of support. In F. Nestmann & K. Hurrelmann (Eds.), *Social networks and social support in childhood and adolescence.* New York: Walter de Gruyter.

Boer, D., & Fischer, R. (2013). How and when do personal values guide our attitudes and sociality? Explaining cross-cultural variability in attitude-value linkages. *Psychological Bulletin, 139,* 1113–1147.

Bogart, L.M., & others (2014). Peer victimization in the fifth grade and health in the tenth grade. *Pediatrics, 133,* 440–447.

Bolea-Alamanac, B., & others (2014). Evidence-based guidelines for the pharmacological management of attention deficit hyperactivity disorder: Update on recommendations from the British Association of Psychopharmacology. *Journal of Psychopharmacology, 28,* 179–203.

Bonanno, R.A., & Hymel, S. (2013). Cyber bullying and internalizing difficulties: Above and beyond the impact of traditional forms of bullying. *Journal of Youth and Adolescence, 42,* 685–697.

Bond, B.J., Richards, M.N., & Calvert, S.L. (2013). Media and pediatric obesity. In D. Lemish (Ed.), *The handbook of children and the media.* New York: Routledge.

Bono, G. (2012, August 5). *Searching for the developmental role of gratitude: A 4-year longitudinal analysis.* Paper presented at the American Psychological Association, Orlando.

Boonstra, H. (2002, February). Teen pregnancy: Trends and lessons learned. *The Guttmacher Report on Public Policy,* pp. 7–10.

Booth, A., Johnson, D.R., Granger, D.A., Crouter, A.C., & McHale, S. (2003). Testosterone and child and adolescent adjustment: The moderating role of parent-child relationships. *Developmental Psychology, 39,* 85–98.

Booth, M. (2002). Arab adolescents facing the future: Enduring ideals and pressures to change. In B.B. Brown, R.W. Larson, & T.S. Saraswathi (Eds.), *The world's youth.* New York: Cambridge University Press.

Booth-LaForce, C., & others (2014). V. Caregiving and contextual sources of continuity and change in attachment security from infancy to late adolescence. *Monographs of the Society for Research in Child Development, 79*(3), 67–84.

Boraska, V., & others (2014). A genome-wide study of anorexia nervosa. *Molecular Psychiatry, 19,* 1085–1094.

Borich, G.D. (2014). *Effective teaching methods* (8th ed.). Upper Saddle River, NJ: Pearson.

Bornstein, M.H. (2015). Children and their parents. In R.M. Lerner (Ed.), *Handbook of child psychology and developmental science* (7th ed.). New York: Wiley.

Bornstein, M.H., & Leventhal, T. (2015). Children in bioecological landscapes of development. In R.M. Lerner (Ed.), *Handbook of child psychology and developmental science* (7th ed.). New York: Wiley.

Bosma, H.A., & Kunnen, E.S. (2001). Determinants and mechanisms in ego identity development: A review and synthesis. *Developmental Review, 21,* 39–66.

Bosselut, G., Heuze, J.P., Eys, M.A., Fontayne, P., & Sarrazin, P. (2012). Athletes' perceptions of role ambiguity and coaching competency in sports teams: A multilevel analysis. *Journal of Sport and Exercise Psychology, 34*(3), 345–364.

Bostwick, W.B., & others (2014). Mental health and suicidality among racially/ethnically diverse sexual minority youth. *American Journal of Public Health, 104,* 1129–1136.

Botvinick, M., & Braver, T. (2015). Motivation and cognitive control: From behavior to neural mechanism. *Annual Review of Psychology* (Vol. 66). Palo Alto, CA: Annual Reviews.

Bouchard, T.J., & Johnson, W. (2014). The genetics of intellectual and personality traits associated with genius. In D.K. Simonton (Ed.), *Wiley-Blackwell handbook of genius.* New York: Wiley-Blackwell.

Bowers, E.P., Geldhof, G.J., Johnson, S.K., Lerner, J.V., & Lerner, R.M. (2014). Special issue introduction. Thriving across the adolescent years: A view of the issues. *Journal of Youth and Adolescence, 43,* 859–868.

Bowker, J.C., & Spencer, S.V. (2010). Friendship and adjustment: A focus on mixed-grade friendships. *Journal of Youth and Adolescence, 39,* 1318–1329.

Bowlby, J. (1989). *Secure and insecure attachment.* New York: Basic Books.

Boynton-Jarrett, R., & others (2013). Childhood abuse and age at menarche. *Journal of Adolescent Health. 52*(2), 241–247.

Boyraz, G., & Lightsey, O.R. (2012). Can positive thinking help? Positive automatic thoughts as moderators of the stress-meaning relationship. *American Journal of Orthopsychiatry, 82,* 267–277.

Brabeck, M.M., & Brabeck, K.M. (2006). Women and relationships. In J. Worell & C.D. Goodheart (Eds.), *Handbook of girls' and women's psychological health.* New York: Oxford University Press.

Bradley, R.H. (2015). Children's housing and physical environments. In R.M. Lerner (Ed.), *Handbook of child psychology and developmental science* (7th ed.). New York: Wiley.

Bradley, R.H., Corwyn, R.F., McAdoo, H., & Coll, C. (2001). The home environments of children in the United States: Part I. Variations by age, ethnicity, and poverty status. *Child Development, 72,* 1844–1867.

Bradshaw, C.P., Goldweber, A., Fishbein, D., & Greenberg, M.T. (2012). Infusing developmental neuroscience into school-based preventive interventions: Implications and future directions. *Journal of Adolescent Health, 51,* S41–S47.

Brady, S.S., & Halpern-Felsher, B. (2007). Adolescents' reported consequences of having oral sex versus vaginal sex. *Pediatrics, 119,* 229–236.

Braithwaite, I., & others (2014). Fast-food consumption and body mass index in children and adolescents: An international cross-sectional study. *BMJ Open, 4*(12), e005813.

Braithwaite, S.R., Coulson, G., Keddington, K., & Fincham, F.D. (2015). The influence of pornography on sexual scripts and hooking up among emerging adults in college. *Archives of Sexual Behavior, 44,* 111–123.

Bralic, I., & others (2012). Association of early menarche age and overweight/obesity. *Journal of Pediatric Endocrinology and Metabolism, 25,* 57–62.

Bransford, J., & others (2006). Learning theories in education. In P.A. Alexander & P.H. Winne (Eds.), *Handbook of educational psychology* (2nd ed.). Mahwah, NJ: Erlbaum.

Brassard, A., & others (2012). Romantic attachment insecurity predicts sexual dissatisfaction in couples seeking marital therapy. *Journal of Sexual and Marital Therapy, 38,* 245–262.

Braun-Courville, D.K., & Rojas, M. (2009). Exposure to sexually explicit web sites and adolescent sexual attitudes and behaviors. *Journal of Adolescent Health, 45,* 156–162.

Braver, S.L., & Lamb, M.E. (2013). Marital dissolution. In G.W. Peterson & K.R. Bush (Eds.), *Handbook of marriage and the family* (3rd ed.). New York: Springer.

Braver, S.L., Ellman, I.M., & Fabricus, W.V. (2003). Relocation of children after divorce and children's best interests: New evidence and legal considerations. *Journal of Family Psychology, 17,* 206–219.

Braver, T.S., & others (2014). Mechanisms of motivation-cognition interaction: Challenges and opportunities. *Cognitive, Affective, and Behavioral Neuroscience, 14,* 443–472.

Bray, J.H., Berger, S.H., & Boethel, C.L. (1999). Marriage to remarriage and beyond. In E.M. Hetherington (Ed.), *Coping with divorce, single parenting, and remarriage.* Mahwah, NJ: Erlbaum.

Bray, J.H., & Kelly, J. (1998). *Stepfamilies.* New York: Broadway.

Brechwald, W.A., & Prinstein, M.J. (2011). Beyond homophily: A decade of advances in understanding peer influence processes. *Journal of Research on Adolescence, 21,* 166–179.

Brecklin, L.R., & Ullman, S.E. (2010). The roles of victim and offender substance use in sexual assault outcomes. *Journal of Interpersonal Violence, 25,* 1503–1522.

Breithaupt, L.E., Payne, H.A., & Rose, M. (2014). Body checking as a behavioral link: A preliminary study assessing inhibition and its association to idiosyncratic body checking in anorexia nervosa. *Eating Behavior, 15,* 591–594.

Bridgeland, J.M., Dilulio, J.J., & Wulsin, S.C. (2008). *Engaged for success.* Washington, DC: Civic Enterprises.

Briley, D.A., Domiteaux, M., & Tucker-Drob, E.M. (2014). Achievement-relevant personality: Relations with the big five and validation of an efficient instrument. *Learning and Individual Differences, 32,* 26–39.

Brittian, A.S., & others (2015, in press). Do dimensions of ethnic identity mediate the association between perceived ethnic group discrimination and depressive symptoms? *Cultural Diversity and Ethnic Minority Psychology.*

Brockie, T.N., & others (2015, in press). The relationship of adverse childhood experiences to PTSD, depression, poly-drug use, and suicide attempt in reservation-based Native American adolescents and young adults. *American Journal of Community Psychology.*

Brockmyer, J.F. (2015). Playing violent video games and desensitization to violence. *Child and Adolescent Psychiatric Clinics of North America, 24,* 65–77.

Broderick, R. (2003, July/August). A surgeon's saga. *Minnesota: The magazine of the University of Minnesota Alumni Association,* 26–31.

Brody, G.H., Lei, M.K., Chen, E., & Miller, G.E. (2014). Neighborhood poverty and allostatic load in African American youth. *Pediatrics, 134,* e1362–e1368.

Brody, G.H., & Schaffer, D.R. (1982). Contributions of parents and peers to children's moral socialization. *Developmental Review, 2,* 31–75.

Brody, G.H., Stoneman, Z., & Burke, M. (1987). Child temperaments, maternal differential behavior and sibling relationships. *Developmental Psychology, 23,* 354–362.

Brody, G.H., & others (2001). The influence of neighborhood disadvantage, collective socialization, and parenting on African American children's affiliation with deviant peers. *Child Development, 72,* 1231–1246.

Brody, G.H., & others (2013). Supportive family environments, genes that confer sensitivity, and allostatic load among rural African American emerging adults: A prospective analysis. *Journal of Family Psychology, 27,* 22–29.

Brody, L. (1997). Gender and emotion: Beyond stereotypes. *Journal of Social Issues, 53,* 369–374.

Brody, N. (2007). Does education influence intelligence? In P.C. Kyllonen, R.D. Roberts, & L. Stankov (Eds.), *Extending intelligence.* Mahwah, NJ: Erlbaum.

Brodzinsky, D.M., & Pinderhughes, E. (2002). Parenting and child development in adoptive families. In M.H. Bronstein (Ed.), *Handbook of parenting* (Vol. 1). Mahwah, NJ: Erlbaum.

Bronfenbrenner, U. (1986). Ecology of the family as a context for human development: Research perspectives. *Developmental Psychology, 22,* 723–742.

Bronfenbrenner, U. (2004). *Making human beings human.* Thousand Oaks, CA: Sage.

Bronfenbrenner, U., & Morris, P. (1998). The ecology of developmental processes. In W. Damon (Ed.), *Handbook of child psychology* (5th ed., Vol. 1). New York: Wiley.

Bronfenbrenner, U., & Morris, P. (2006). The ecology of developmental processes. In W. Damon & R. Lerner (Eds.), *Handbook of child psychology* (6th ed.). New York: Wiley.

Broning, S., & others (2014). Implementing and evaluating the German adaptation of the "Strengthening Families Program 10–14"—a randomized-controlled multicenter study. *BMC Public Health, 14,* 83.

Bronstein, P. (2006). The family environment: Where gender role socialization begins. In J. Worell & C.D. Goodheart (Eds.), *Handbook of girls' and women's psychological health.* New York: Oxford University Press.

Brook, J.S., Balka, E.B., Zhang, C., & Brook, D.W. (2015, in press). ADHD, conduct disorder, substance use disorder, and nonprescription stimulant use. *Journal of Attention Disorders.*

Brook, J.S., Brook, D.W., Gordon, A.S., Whiteman, M., & Cohen, P. (1990). The psychological etiology of adolescent drug use: A family interactional approach. *Genetic Psychology Monographs, 116*(2).

Brooker, R.J. (2015). *Genetics* (5th ed.). New York: McGraw-Hill.

Brooker, R.J. (2016, in press). *Concepts of genetics* (2nd ed.). New York: McGraw-Hill.

Brookhart, S.M., & Nitko, A.J. (2015). *Educational assessment of students* (7th ed.). Upper Saddle River, NJ: Pearson.

Brooks-Gunn, J., & Donahue, E.H. (2008). Introducing the issue. *The Future of Children, 18*(1), 3–10.

Brooks-Gunn, J., Han, W-J., & Waldfogel, J. (2010). First-year maternal employment and child development in the first seven years. *Monographs of the Society for Research in Child Development, 75*(2), 1–147.

Brooks-Gunn, J., & Warren, M.P. (1989). The psychological significance of secondary sexual characteristics in 9- to 11-year-old girls. *Child Development, 59,* 161–169.

Broughton, J. (1983). The cognitive developmental theory of adolescent self and identity. In B. Lee & G. Noam (Eds.), *Developmental approaches to self.* New York: Plenum.

Brouzos, Misailidi, P., & Hadjimattheou, A. (2014). Associations between emotional intelligences, socio-emotional adjustment, and academic achievement in childhood: The influence of age. *Canadian Journal of School Psychology, 29,* 83–99.

Broverman, L., Vogel, S., Broverman, D., Clarkson, F., & Rosenkranz, P. (1972). Sex-role stereotypes: A current appraisal. *Journal of Social Issues, 28,* 59–78.

Brown, B.B. (2004). Adolescents' relationships with peers. In R.M. Lerner & L. Steinberg (Eds.), *Handbook of adolescent psychology* (2nd ed.). New York: Wiley.

Brown, B.B. (2011). Popularity in peer group perspective: The role of status in adolescent peer systems. In A.H.N. Cillessen, D. Schwartz, & L. Mayeux (Eds.), *Popularity in the peer system.* New York: Guilford.

Brown, B.B., Bakken, J.P., Ameringer, S.W., & Mahon, S.D. (2008). A comprehensive conceptualization of the peer influence process in adolescence. In M.J. Prinstein & K.A. Dodge (Eds.), *Understanding peer influence in children and adolescents.* New York: Guilford.

Brown, B.B., & Dietz, E.L. (2009). Informal peer groups in middle childhood and adolescence. In K.H. Rubin, W.M. Bukowski, & B. Laursen (Eds.), *Handbook of peer interaction, relationships, and groups.* New York: Guilford.

Brown, B.B., & Larson, J. (2009). Peer relationships in adolescence. In R.L. Lerner & L. Steinberg (Eds.), *Handbook of adolescent psychology* (3rd ed.). New York: Wiley.

Brown, B.B., & Larson, R.W. (2002). The kaleidoscope of adolescence: Experiences of the world's youth at the beginning of the 21st century. In B.B. Brown, R.W. Larson, & T.S. Saraswathi (Eds.), *The world's youth.* New York: Cambridge University Press.

Brown, B.B., & Lohr, M.J. (1987). Peer-group affiliation and adolescent self-esteem: An integration of ego-identity and symbolic-interaction theories. *Journal of Personality and Social Psychology, 52,* 47–55.

Brown, E.R., & Diekman, A.B. (2010). What will I be? Exploring gender differences in near and distant possible selves. *Sex Roles, 63,* 568–579.

Brown, J.D., & Bobkowski, P.S. (2011). Older and newer media: Patterns of use and effects on adolescents' health and well-being. *Journal of Research on Adolescence, 21,* 95–113.

Brown, J.D., & Strasburger, V.C. (2007). From Calvin Klein to Paris Hilton and MySpace: Adolescents, sex, and the media. *Adolescent Medicine: State of the Art Reviews, 18,* 484–507.

Brown, K.N., Wengreen, H.J., & Beals, K.A. (2014). Knowledge of the female athlete triad, and prevalence of triad risk factors among female high school athletes and their coaches. *Journal of Pediatric and Adolescent Gynecology, 27,* 278–282.

Brown, L.K., & Gilligan, C. (1992). *Meeting at the crossroads.* Cambridge, MA: Harvard University Press.

Brownley, K.A., Peat, C.M., La Via, M., & Bulik, C.M. (2015). Pharmacological approaches to the management of binge eating disorder. *Drugs, 75,* 9–32.

Bruchmiller, K., Margraf, J., & Schneider, S. (2012). Is ADHD diagnosed in accord with diagnostic criteria? Overdiagnosis and influence of client gender on diagnosis. *Journal of Consulting and Clinical Psychology, 80,* 128–138.

Brummelman, J.E., Thomaes, S., Orbobio de Castro, B., Overbeek, G., & Bushman, B.J. (2014). "That's not just beautiful—that's incredibly beautiful!": The adverse impact of inflated praise on children with low self-esteem. *Psychological Science, 25,* 728–735.

Brune, M., & others (2012). The crisis of psychiatry—insights and prospects from evolutionary theory. *World Psychiatry, 11,* 55–57.

Bryant Ludden, A., & Wolfson, A.R. (2010). Understanding adolescent caffeine use: Connecting use patterns with expectancies, reasons, and sleep. *Health Education and Behavior, 37,* 330–337.

Buchanan, C.M., Maccoby, E.E., & Dornbusch, S. (1992). Adolescents and their families after divorce: Three residential arrangements compared. *Journal of Research on Adolescence, 2,* 261–291.

Bucher, R.D. (2015). *Diversity consciousness* (4th ed.). Upper Saddle River, NJ: Pearson.

Buchmann, M., & Malti, T. (2012). The future of young women's economic role in a globalized economy: New opportunities, persisting constraints. *New Directions in Youth Development, 135,* 77–86.

Bucx, F., Raaijmakers, Q., & van Wel, F. (2010). Life course stage in young adulthood and intergenerational congruence in family attitudes. *Journal of Marriage and the Family, 72,* 117–134.

Bucx, F., & van Wel, F. (2008). Parental bond and life course transitions from adolescence to young adulthood. *Adolescence, 43,* 71–88.

Budde, H., Voelcker-Rehage, C., Pietrabyk-Kendziorra, P., Ribeiro, P., & Tidow, G. (2008). Acute aerobic exercise improves attentional performance in adolescence. *Neuroscience Letters, 441,* 219–223.

Bugental, D.B., Corpuz, R., & Beaulieu, D.A. (2015). An evolutionary approach to socialization. In J.E. Grusec & P.D. Hastings (Eds.), *Handbook of socialization.* (2nd ed.). New York: Guilford.

Bugental, D.B., & Goodnow, J.J. (2006). Socialization processes. In W. Damon & R. Lerner (Eds.), *Handbook of child psychology* (6th ed.). New York: Wiley.

Buhi, E.R., & others (2010). Quality and accuracy of sexual health information web sites visited by young people. *Journal of Adolescent Health, 47,* 206–208.

Buhrmester, D. (1990). Friendship, interpersonal competence, and adjustment in preadolescence and adolescence. *Child Development, 61,* 1101–1111.

Buhrmester, D. (1998). Need fulfillment, interpersonal competence, and the developmental contexts of early adolescent friendship. In W.M. Bukowski & A.F. Newcomb (Eds.), *The company they keep: Friendship in childhood and adolescence.* New York: Cambridge University Press.

Buhrmester, D. (2001, April). *Does age at which romantic involvement starts matter?* Paper presented at the meeting of the Society for Research in Child Development, Minneapolis.

Buhrmester, D., & Chong, C.M. (2009). Friendship in adolescence. In H. Reis & S. Sprecher (Eds.), *Encyclopedia of human relationships.* Thousand Oaks, CA: Sage.

Buist, K.L. (2010). Sibling relationship quality and adolescent delinquency: A latent growth curve analysis. *Journal of Family Psychology, 24,* 400–410.

Buist, K.L., Dekovic, M., & Prinzie, P. (2013). Sibling relationship quality and psychopathology of children and adolescents: A meta-analysis. *Clinical Psychology Review, 33,* 97–106.

Buitelaar, J., Karr, C., & Asherton, P. (2010). *ADHD in adulthood.* New York: Cambridge University Press.

Bukowski, W.M., Buhrmester, D., & Underwood, M.K. (2011). Peer relations as a developmental context. In M.K. Underwood & L.H. Rosen (Eds.), *Social development.* New York: Guilford.

Bukowski, W.M., Castellanos, M., Vitaro, F., & Brendgen, M. (2015). Socialization and experience with peers. In J.E. Grusec & P.D. Hastings (Eds.), *Handbook of socialization* (2nd ed.). New York: Guilford.

Bukowski, W.M., Laursen, B., & Hoza, B. (2010). The snowball effect: Friendship moderates escalations in depressed affect among avoidant and excluded children. *Development and Psychopathology, 22,* 749–757.

Bumpus, M.F., Crouter, A.C., & McHale, S.M. (2001). Parental autonomy granting during adolescence: Gender differences in context. *Developmental Psychology, 37,* 163–173.

Burchinal, M.R., Peisner-Feinberg, E., Pianta, R., & Howes, C. (2002). Development of academic skills from preschool through second grade: Family and classroom predictors of developmental trajectories. *Journal of School Psychology, 40*(5), 415–436.

Burden, P.R., & Byrd, D.M. (2013). *Methods for effective teaching* (6th ed.). Upper Saddle River, NJ: Pearson.

Bureau, J-F., Easterbrooks, M.A., & Lyons-Ruth, K. (2009). Maternal depressive symptoms in infancy: Unique contribution to children's depressive symptoms in childhood and adolescence? *Development and Psychopathology, 21,* 519–537.

Burgess-Champoux, T.L., Larson, N., Neumark-Sztainer, D., Hannan, P.J., & Story, M. (2009). Are family meal patterns associated with overall diet quality during the transition from early to middle adolescence? *Journal of Nutrition Education and Behavior, 41,* 79–86.

Burke, J.D. (2011). The relationship between conduct disorder and oppositional defiant disorder and their continuity with antisocial behaviors. In D. Shaffer, E. Leibenluft, & L.A. Rohde (Eds.), *Externalizing disorders of childhood: Refining the research agenda for DSM-V.* Arlington, VA: American Psychiatric Association.

Burke, J.D., & Loeber, R. (2015). The effectiveness of the Stop Now and Plan (SNAP) program for boys at risk for violence and delinquency. *Prevention Science, 16,* 242–253.

Burnette, J.L., O'Boyle, E.H., Vanepps, E.M., Pollack, J.M., & Finkel, E.J. (2013). Mind-set matters: A meta-analytic review of implicit theories and self-regulation. *Psychological Bulletin, 139,* 655–701.

Burt, K.B., & Paysnick, A.A. (2012). Resilience in the transition to adulthood. *Development and Pyschopathology, 24,* 493–505.

Burt, S.A. (2014). Research review: The shared environment as a key source of variability in child and adolescent psychopathology. *Journal of Child Psychology and Psychiatry, 55,* 304–312.

Burton, R.V. (1984). A paradox in theories and research in moral development. In W.M. Kurtines & J.L. Gewirtz (Eds.), *Morality, moral behavior, and moral development.* New York: Wiley.

Busching, R., & Krahe, B. (2015, in press). The girls set the tone: Gendered classroom norms and the development of aggression in adolescence. *Personality and Social Psychology Bulletin.*

Bush, K.R., & Peterson, G.W. (2013). Parent-child relationships in diverse contexts. In G.W. Peterson & K.R. Bush (Eds.), *Handbook of marriage and the family* (3rd ed.). New York: Springer.

Buss, D. (2000). Evolutionary psychology. In A. Kazdin (Ed.), *Encyclopedia of psychology.* New York: Oxford University Press.

Buss, D.M. (2008). *Evolutionary psychology* (3rd ed.). Boston: Allyn & Bacon.

Buss, D.M. (2012). *Evolutionary psychology* (4th ed.). Boston: Allyn & Bacon.

Buss, D.M. (2015). *Evolutionary psychology* (5th ed.). Upper Saddle River, NJ: Pearson.

Buss, D.M., & Penke, L. (2014). Evolutionary personality psychology. In M. Mikulincer & P.R. Shaver (Eds.), *APA handbook of personality and social psychology.* Washington, DC: APA Books.

Buss, D.M., & Schmitt, D.P. (1993). Sexual strategies theory: An evolutionary perspective on human mating. *Psychological Review, 100,* 204–232.

Busschaert, C., & others (2015). Tracing and predictors of screen time from early adolescence to early adulthood: A 10-year follow-up study. *Journal of Adolescent Health, 56,* 440–448.

Busséri, M.A., Willoughby, T., Chalmers, H., & Bogaert, A.R. (2006). Same-sex attraction and successful adolescent development. *Journal of Youth and Adolescence, 35,* 563–575.

Bussey, K., & Bandura, A. (1999). Social cognitive theory of gender development and differentiation. *Psychological Review, 106,* 676–713.

Buttermore, E.D., Thaxton, C.L., & Bhat, M.A. (2013). Organization and maintenance of molecular domains in myelinated axons. *Journal of Neuroscience Research, 91*(5), 603–622.

Buzwell, S., & Rosenthal, D. (1996). Constructing a sexual self: Adolescents' sexual self-perceptions and sexual risk-taking. *Journal of Research on Adolescence, 6,* 489–513.

C

Cacioppo, J.T., & others (2000). Lonely traits and concomitant physiological processes: The MacArthur Social Neuroscience Studies. *International Journal of Psychophysiology, 35,* 143–154.

Cacioppo, J.T., Cacioppo, S., Gonzaga, G.C., Ogburn, E.L., & VanderWheele, T.J. (2013). Marital satisfaction and break-ups differ across on-line and off-line meeting venues. *Proceedings of the National Academy of Sciences, 110*(25), 10135–10140.

Cai, M., Hardy, S.A., Olsen, J.A., Nelson, D.A., & Yamawaki, N. (2013). Adolescent-parent attachment as a mediator of relationships between parenting and adolescent social behavior and wellbeing in China. *International Journal of Psychology, 48,* 1185–1190.

Cain, N., & Gradisar, M. (2010). Electronic media use and sleep in school-aged children and adolescents. *Sleep Medicine, 11,* 735–742.

Calamaro, C.J., Mason, T.B., & Ratcliffe, S.J. (2009). Adolescents living the 24/7 lifestyle: Effects of caffeine and technology on sleep duration and daytime functioning. *Pediatrics, 123,* e1005–e1010.

Calderon-Tena, C.O., Knight, G.P., & Carlo, G. (2011). The socialization of prosocial behavioral tendencies among Mexican American adolescents: The role of familism values. *Cultural Diversity and Ethnic Minority Psychology, 17,* 98–106.

Callan, M.J., Kay, A.C., & Dawtry, R.J. (2014). Making sense of misfortune: Deservingness, self-esteem, and patterns of self-defeat. *Journal of Personality and Social Psychology, 107,* 142–162.

Calvert, S.L. (2015). Children and digital media. In R.M. Lerner (Ed.), *Handbook of child psychology and developmental science* (7th ed.). New York: Wiley.

Calvert, S.L., Bond, B.J., & Staiano, A.E. (2013). Electronic game changers for the obesity crisis. In F. Blumberg (Ed.), *Learning by playing: Frontiers of video gaming in education.* New York: Oxford University Press.

Calvert, S.L., & Valkenburg, P.M. (2011). The influence of television, video games, and the Internet on children's creativity. In M. Taylor (Ed.), *Handbook of the development of imagination.* New York: Oxford University Press.

Calvert, S.L., & Wartella, E.A. (2014). Children and electronic media. In E.T. Gershoff, R.S. Mistry, & D.A. Crosby (Eds.), *Societal contexts of child development.* New York: Oxford University Press.

Camacho, D.E., & Fuligni, A.J. (2015, in press). Extracurricular participation among adolescents from immigrant families. *Journal of Youth and Adolescence.*

Cameron, J.L. (2004). Interrelationships between hormones, behavior, and affect during adolescence: Understanding hormonal, physical, and brain changes occurring in association with pubertal activation of the reproductive axis. Introduction to Part III. *Annals of the New York Academy of Sciences, 1021,* 110–123.

Cameron, J., & Pierce, D. (2008). Intrinsic versus extrinsic motivation. In N.J. Salkind (Ed.), *Encyclopedia of educational psychology.* Thousand Oaks, CA: Sage.

Campbell, B. (2008). *Handbook of differentiated instruction using the multiple intelligences.* Boston: Allyn & Bacon.

Campbell, C.Y. (1988, August 24). Group raps depiction of teenagers. *Boston Globe,* p. 44.

Campbell, I.G., Grimm, K.J., de Bie, E., & Feinberg, I. (2012). Sex, puberty, and the timing of sleep EEG measured in adolescent brain maturation. *Proceedings of the National Academy of Sciences U.S.A., 109,* 5740–5743.

Campbell, K., & Peebles, R. (2014). Eating disorders in children and adolescents: State of the art review. *Pediatrics, 134,* 582–592.

Campbell, L., Campbell, B., & Dickinson, D. (2004). *Teaching and learning through multiple intelligences* (3rd ed.). Boston: Allyn & Bacon.

Campione-Barr, N., Greer, K.B., & Kruse, A. (2013). Differential associations between domains of sibling conflict and adolescent emotional adjustment. *Child Development, 84*(3), 938–954.

Cantalupo. N.C. (2014). Institution-specific victimization surveys: Addressing legal and practical disincentives to gender-based violence reporting on college campuses. *Trauma, Violence, and Abuse, 15,* 227–241.

Cantone, E., & others (2015). Interventions on bullying and cyberbullying in schools: A systematic review. *Clinical Practice and Epidemiology in Mental Health, 11*(Suppl. 1), S58–S76.

Capaldi, D.M. (1992). Co-occurrence of conduct problems and depressive symptoms in early adolescent boys: II. A 2-year follow-up at grade 8. *Development and Psychopathology, 4,* 125–144.

Capaldi, D.M., & Stoolmiller, M. (1999). Co-occurrence of conduct problems and depressive symptoms in early adolescent boys: III. Prediction to young-adult adjustment. *Development and Psychopathology, 11,* 59–84.

Capaldi, D.M., Stoolmiller, M., Clark, S., & Owen, L.D. (2002). Heterosexual risk behaviors in at-risk young men from early adolescence to young adulthood: Prevalence, prediction, and association with STD contraction. *Developmental Psychology, 38,* 394–406.

Caplan, P.J., & Caplan, J.B. (1999). *Thinking critically about research on sex and gender* (2nd ed.). New York: Longman.

Caprara, G.V., & others (2010). The contributions of agreeableness and self-efficacy beliefs to prosociality. *European Journal of Personality, 24,* 36–55.

Cardelle-Elawar, M. (1992). Effects of teaching metacognitive skills to students with low mathematics ability. *Teaching & Teacher Education, 8,* 109–121.

Carey, D.P. (2007). Is bigger really better? The search for brain size and intelligence in the twenty-first century. In S. Della Sala (Ed.), *Tall tales about the mind and brain: Separating fact from fiction.* Oxford, UK: Oxford University Press.

Carlisle, J., Kenney, C., & Vereb, A. (2013). Vocabulary instruction for students with or at risk for learning disabilities: Promising approaches for learning words from text. In B.G. Cook & M.G. Tankersley (Eds.), *Research-based practices in special education.* Upper Saddle River, NJ: Pearson.

Carlo, G. (2014). The development and correlates of prosocial moral behaviors. In M. Killen & J.G. Smetana (Eds.), *Handbook of moral development* (2nd ed.). New York: Psychology Press.

Carlo, G., Knight, G.P., McGinley, M., Zamboanga, B.L., & Jarvis, L.H. (2010). The multidimensionality of prosocial behaviors and evidence of measurement equivalence in Mexican American and European American early adolescents. *Journal of Research on Adolescence, 20,* 334–358.

Carlo, G., Mestre, M.V., Samper, P., Tur, A., & Armenta, B.E. (2011). The longitudinal relations among dimensions of parenting styles, sympathy, prosocial moral reasoning, and prosocial behaviors. *International Journal of Behavioral Development, 35,* 116–124.

Carlson, K.S., & Gjerde, P.F. (2010). Preschool personality antecedents of narcissism in adolescence and emerging adulthood: A 20-year longitudinal study. *Journal of Research in Personality, 43,* 570–578.

Carlson, M.D., Mendle, J., & Harden, K.P. (2014). Early adverse environments and genetic influences on age at first sex: Evidence for gene x environment interaction. *Developmental Psychology, 50,* 1532–1542.

Carlson, S.M., Claxton, L.J., & Moses, L.J. (2015). The relation between executive function and theory of mind is more than skin deep. *Journal of Cognition and Development, 16*(1), 186–197.

Carnegie Council on Adolescent Development (1989). *Turning points: Preparing American youth for the twenty-first century.* New York: Carnegie Foundation.

Carnegie Council on Adolescent Development (1995). *Great transitions.* New York: Carnegie Foundation.

Carpendale, J.I.M., & Lewis, C. (2015). The development of social understanding. In R.M. Lerner (Ed.), *Handbook of child psychology and developmental science* (7th ed.). New York: Wiley.

Carpendale, J.I.M., & Lewis, C. (2015). The development of social understanding. In R.M. Lerner (Ed.), *Handbook of child psychology and developmental science* (7th ed.). New York: Wiley.

Carr, R., & Peebles, R. (2012). Developmental considerations of media exposure risk for eating disorders. In J. Lock (Ed.), *Oxford handbook of child and adolescent eating disorders: Developmental perspectives.* New York: Oxford University Press.

Carretti, B., Caldarola, N., Tencati, C., & Cornoldi, C. (2014). Improving reading comprehension in reading and listening settings: The effect of two training programs focusing on metacognition and working memory. *British Journal of Educational Psychology, 84*(Pt. 2), 194–210.

Carroll, J. (1993). *Human cognitive abilities.* Cambridge, UK: Cambridge University Press.

Carroll, J.L. (2016, in press). *Sexuality now* (5th ed.). Boston: Cengage.

Carskadon, M.A. (Ed.) (2002). *Adolescent sleep patterns.* New York: Cambridge University Press.

Carskadon, M.A. (2004). Sleep difficulties in young people. *Archives of Pediatric and Adolescent Medicine, 158,* 597–598.

Carskadon, M.A. (2006, March). *Too little, too late: Sleep bioregulatory processes across adolescence.* Paper presented at the meeting of the Society for Research on Adolescence, San Francisco.

Carskadon, M.A. (2011). Sleep in adolescents: The perfect storm. *Pediatric Clinics of North America, 58,* 637–647.

Carskadon, M.A., & Tarokh, L. (2014). Developmental changes in sleep biology and potential effects on adolescent behavior and caffeine use. *Nutrition Reviews, 72* (Suppl. 1), S60–S64.

Cartwright, K.B., Galupo, M.P., Tyree, S.D., & Jennings, J.G. (2009). Reliability and validity of the Complex Postformal Thought questionnaire: Assessing adults' cognitive development. *Journal of Adult Development, 16,* 183–189.

Caruthers, A.S., Van Ryzin, M.J., & Dishion, T.J. (2013). Preventing high-risk sexual behavior in early adulthood with family interventions in adolescence: Outcomes and developmental processes. *Prevention Science, 15*(Suppl. 1), S59–S69.

Carver, C.S., & Connor-Smith, J. (2010). Personality and coping. *Annual Review of Psychology* (Vol. 61). Palo Alto, CA: Annual Reviews.

Carver, K., Joyner, K., & Udry, J.R. (2003). National estimates of romantic relationships. In P. Florsheim (Ed.), *Adolescent romantic relations and sexual behavior.* Mahwah, NJ: Erlbaum.

Casas, M. (2011). *Enhancing student learning in middle school.* New York: Routledge.

Case, R. (Ed.) (1992). *The mind's staircase: Exploring the conceptual underpinnings of children's thought and knowledge.* Hillsdale, NJ: Erlbaum.

Case, R. (2000). Conceptual development. In M. Bennett (Ed.), *Developmental psychology.* Philadelphia: Psychology Press.

Casey, B.J. (2015). The adolescent brain and self-control. *Annual Review of Psychology* (Vol. 66). Palo Alto, CA: Annual Reviews.

Caspi, A. (1998). Personality development across the life course. In W. Damon (Series Ed.) & N. Eisenberg (Ed.), *Handbook of child psychology: Vol. 3. Social, emotional, and personality development* (5th ed.). New York: Wiley.

Caspi, A., & others (2003). Influence of life stress on depression: Moderation by a polymorphism in the 5-HTT gene. *Science, 301,* 386–389.

Cassidy, J., Woodhouse, S.S., Sherman, L.J., Stupica, B., & Lejuez, C.W. (2011). Enhancing infant attachment security: An examination of treatment efficacy and differential susceptibility. *Development and Psychopathology, 23,* 131–148.

Cassidy-Bushrow, A.E., & others (2015, in press). Time spent on the Internet and adolescent blood pressure. *Journal of School Nursing.*

Cassoff, J., Knauper, B., Michaelsen, S., & Gruber, R. (2013). School-based sleep promotion programs: Effectiveness, feasibility, and insights for future research. *Sleep Medicine Reviews, 17*(3), 207–214.

Cassone, A.R. (2014). Mindfulness training as an adjunct to evidence-based treatment for ADHD within families. *Journal of Attention Disorders, 19,* 147–157.

Castle, J., & others (2010). Parents' evaluation of adoption success: A follow-up study of intercountry and domestic adoptions. *American Journal of Orthopsychiatry, 79,* 522–531.

Catalano, R.F., Gavin, L.E., & Markham, C.M. (2010). Future directions for positive youth development as a strategy to promote adolescent sexual and reproductive health. *Journal of Adolescent Health, 46* (Suppl. 1), S92–S96.

Cauffman, B.E. (1994, February). *The effects of puberty, dating, and sexual involvement on dieting and disordered eating in young adolescent girls.* Paper presented at the meeting of the Society for Research on Adolescence, San Diego.

Cauffman, E., Shulman, E., Bechtold, J., & Steinberg, L. (2015). Children and the law. In R. Lerner (Ed.), *Handbook of child psychology and developmental science* (7th ed.). New York: Wiley.

Cavanagh, S. (2007, October 3). U.S.-Chinese exchanges nurture ties between principals. *Education Week.* Retrieved July 15, 2008, from www.edweek.org

Cavanagh, S.E. (2009). Puberty. In D. Carr (Ed.), *Encyclopedia of the life course and human development.* Boston: Gale Cengage.

Ceci, S.J., & Gilstrap, L.L. (2000). Determinants of intelligence: Schooling and intelligence. In A. Kazdin (Ed.), *Encyclopedia of psychology.* New York: Oxford University Press.

Center for Economic and Policy Research (2014, May). *A college degree is no guarantee.* Washington, DC: Author.

Centers for Disease Control and Prevention (2012). Understanding teen dating violence factsheet. Retrieved November 14, 2012, from www.cdc.gov/ncipc/pubres/DatingAbuseFactSheet-a.pdf

Centers for Disease Control and Prevention (2014). *Body mass index for children and teens.* Atlanta: Centers for Disease Control and Prevention.

Centers for Disease Control and Prevention (2015). *Injury prevention and control: Division of Violence Prevention.* Retrieved April 21, 2015, from www.cdcgov/violenceprevention/pub/youth_suicide.html

Centers for Disease Control and Prevention (2015a). *Adolescent pregnancy.* Atlanta, GA: U.S. Department of Health and Human Services.

Centers for Disease Control and Prevention (2015b). *Sexually transmitted disease surveillance.* Atlanta, GA: U.S. Department of Health and Human Services.

Chan, C.H., & others (2015). Sexual initiation and emotional/behavioral problems in Taiwanese adolescents: A multivariate response profile analysis. *Archives of Sexual Behavior, 44,* 717–727.

Chan, C.S., & others (2013). Pathways of influence in school-based mentoring: The mediating role of parent and teacher relationships. *Journal of School Psychology, 51,* 129–142.

Chan, H.Y., Brown, B.B., & Von Bank, H. (2015). Adolescent disclosure of information about peers: The mediating role of perceptions of parents' right to know. *Journal of Youth and Adolescence, 44,* 1048–1065.

Chance, P. (2014). *Learning and behavior* (7th ed.). Boston: Cengage.

Chandler, M.J., & Dunlop, W.L. (2015). Personal and cultural identities: Conceptual and methodological issues. In R.M. Lerner (Ed.), *Handbook of child psychology and developmental science* (7th ed.). New York: Wiley.

Chandra, A., & others (2009). Does watching sex on television predict teen pregnancy? Findings from a national longitudinal study of youth. *Pediatrics, 122,* 1047–1054.

Chang, Y.K., Liu, S., Yu, H.H., & Lee, Y.H. (2012). Effects of acute exercise on executive function in children with attention deficit hyperactivity disorder. *Archives of Clinical Neuropsychology, 27,* 225–237.

Chao, R.K. (2005, April). *The importance of Guan in describing control of immigrant Chinese.* Paper presented at the meeting of the Society for Research in Child Development, Atlanta.

Chao, R.K. (2007, March). *Research with Asian Americans: Looking back and moving forward.* Paper presented at the meeting of the Society for Research in Child Development, Boston.

Chao, R.K., & Otsuki-Clutter, M. (2011). Racial and ethnic differences: Sociocultural and contextual explanations. *Journal of Research on Adolescence, 21,* 47–60.

Chapin, J.R. (2015). *Practical guide to middle and secondary school social sciences* (4th ed.). Upper Saddle River, NJ: Pearson.

Chaplin, T.M., & Aldao, A. (2013). Gender differences in emotion in children: A meta-analytic review. *Psychological Bulletin.* doi:10.1037/a0030737

Chaplin, T.M., & others (2012). Parent-adolescent conflict interactions and adolescent alcohol use. *Addictive Behaviors, 37,* 605–612.

Chappuis, J. (2015). *Seven strategies of assessment for learning* (2nd ed.). Upper Saddle River, NJ: Pearson.

Chaput, J.P., & others (2014). Electronic screens in children's bedroooms and adiposity, physical activity, and sleep: Do the number and types of electronic devices matter? *Canadian Journal of Public Health, 105,* e273–e279.

Charmaraman, L., Lee, A.J., & Erkut, S. (2012). "What if you already know everything about sex?" Content analysis of questions from early adolescents in a middle school sex education program. *Journal of Adolescent Health, 50,* 527–530.

Chehab, F.F. (2014). 20 years of leptin: Leptin and reproduction: Past milestones, present undertakings, and future endeavors. *Journal of Endocrinology, 223,* T37–T48.

Chen, C., & Stevenson, H.W. (1989). Homework: A cross-cultural examination. *Child Development, 60,* 551–561.

Chen, D., Drabick, D.A., & Burgers, D.E. (2015, in press). A developmental perspective on peer rejection, deviant peer affiliation, and conduct problems among youth. *Child Psychiatry and Human Development.*

Chen, L.J., Fox, K.R., Ku, P.W., & Taun, C.Y. (2013). Fitness change and subsequent academic performance in adolescents. *Journal of School Health, 83,* 631–638.

Chen, M., & Berman, S.L. (2012). Globalization and identity development: A Chinese perspective. *New Directions in Child and Adolescent Development, 2012*(138), 103–121.

Chen, M.J., Grube, J.W., Nygaard, P., & Miller, B.A. (2008). Identifying social mechanisms for the prevention of adolescent drinking and driving. *Accident Analysis and Prevention, 40,* 576–585.

Chen, P., & Jacobson, K.C. (2013). Longitudinal relationships between college education and patterns of heavy drinking: A comparison between Caucasians and African-Americans. *Journal of Adolescent Health, 53,* 356–362.

Chen, T.Y., & others (2015). Effects of a selective educational system on fatigue, sleep problems, daytime sleepiness, and depression among senior high school adolescents in Taiwan. *Neuropsychiatric Disease and Treatment, 11,* 741–750.

Chen, X., Christmas-Best, V., Titzmann, P.F., & Weichold, K. (2012). Youth success and adaptation in times of globalization and economic change. *New Directions for Youth Development, 135,* 1–10.

Chen, X., & Schmidt, L.A. (2015). Temperament and personality. In R.M. Lerner (Ed.), *Handbook of child psychology and developmental science* (7th ed.). New York: Wiley.

Chen, X., Thrane, L., & Adams, M. (2012). Precursors of running away during adolescence: Do peers matter? *Journal of Research on Adolescence, 22,* 487–497.

Chen, X., Tyler, K.A., Whitbeck, L.B., & Hoyt, D.R. (2004). Early sexual abuse, street adversity, and drug use among female homeless and runaway adolescents in the Midwest. *Journal of Drug Issues, 34,* 1–20.

Cheng, E.R., Cohen, A., & Goodman, E. (2015). The role of perceived discrimination during childhood and adolescence in understanding racial and socioeconomic influences on depression in young adulthood. *Journal of Pediatrics, 166,* 370–377.

Cheng, Y.Y., Shein, P.P., & Chiou, W.B. (2012). Escaping the impulse to immediate gratification: The prospect concept promotes a future-oriented mindset, prompting an inclination towards delayed gratification. *British Journal of Psychology, 103,* 129–141.

Cherlin, A.J. (2009). *The marriage-go-round.* New York: Random House.

Cherlin, A.J., & Furstenberg, F.F. (1994). Stepfamilies in the United States: A reconsideration. In J. Blake & J. Hagen (Eds.), *Annual Review of Sociology* (Vol. 20). Palo Alto, CA: Annual Reviews.

Cherutich, P., & others (2008). Condom use among sexually active Kenyan female adolescents at risk for HIV-1 infection. *AIDS Behavior, 12,* 923–929.

Chess, S., & Thomas, A. (1977). Temperamental individuality from childhood to adolescence. *Journal of Child Psychiatry, 16,* 218–226.

Cheung, C., & Pomerantz, E.M. (2012). Why does parents' involvement in children's learning enhance children's achievement? The role of parent-oriented motivation. *Journal of Educational Psychology, 104,* 820–832.

Cheung, C.S., Pomerantz, E.M., & Dong, W. (2012). Does adolescents' disclosure to their parents matter for their academic adjustment? *Child Development, 84*(2), 693–710.

Chi, M.T.H. (1978). Knowledge structures and memory development. In R.S. Siegler (Ed.), *Children's thinking: What develops?* Hillsdale, NJ: Erlbaum.

Chia-Chen, C.A., & Thompson, E.A. (2007). Preventing adolescent risky behavior: Parents matter! *Journal for Specialists in Pediatric Nursing, 12,* 119–122.

Chiang, H.L., & others (2015). Altered white matter tract property related to impaired focused attention, sustained attention, cognitive impulsivity, and vigilance in attention-deficit/hyperactivity disorder. *Journal of Psychiatry and Neuroscience, 40,* 140106.

Chiappe, D., & MacDonald, K. (2005). The evolution of domain-general mechanisms in intelligence and learning. *Journal of General Psychology, 132,* 5–40.

Chick, C.F., & Reyna, V.F. (2012). A fuzzy trace theory of adolescent risk taking: Beyond self-control and sensation seeking. In V. Reyna & others (Eds.), *The adolescent brain.* Washington, DC: American Psychological Association.

Child Trends (2014, October). *High school dropout rates.* Bethesda, MD: Child Trends.

Chiou, W.B., Chen, S.W., & Liao, D.C. (2014). Does Facebook promote self-interest? Enactment of indiscriminate one-to-many communication on online social networking sites decreases prosocial behavior. *Cyberpsychology, Behavior, and Social Networking, 17,* 68–73.

Chira, S. (1993, June 23). What do teachers want most? Help from parents. *The New York Times,* p. 17.

Chisholm, J.D., & Kingstone, A. (2015, in press). Action video games and improved attentional control: Disentangling selection- and response-based processes. *Psychonomic Bulletin and Review.*

Chmielewski, C. (1997, September). Sexual harassment, meet Title IX. *NEA Today, 16*(2), 24–25.

Choi, N. (2004). Sex role group differences in specific, academic, and general self-efficacy. *Journal of Psychology, 138,* 149–159.

Chouinard, R., Karsenti, T., & Roy, N. (2007). Relations among competence beliefs, utility value, achievement goals, and effort in mathematics. *British Journal of Educational Psychology, 77,* 501–517.

Choukas-Bradley, S., Giletta, M., Widman, L., Cohen, G.L., & Prinstein, M.J. (2014). Experimentally measured susceptibility to peer influence and adolescent sexual behavior trajectories: A preliminary study. *Developmental Psychology, 50,* 2221–2227.

Choukas-Bradley, S., & Prinstein, M.J. (2013). Peer relationships and the development of psychopathology. In M. Lewis & K.D. Rudolph (Eds.), *Handbook of developmental psychopathology* (3rd ed.). New York: Springer.

Chow, C.M., Tan, C.C., & Buhrmester, D. (2015). Interdependence of depressive symptoms, school involvement, and academic performance between adolescent friends: A dyadic analysis. *British Journal of Educational Psychology.*

Christakou, A. (2014). Present simple and continuous: Emergence of self-regulation and contextual sophistication in adolescent decision-making. *Neuropsychologia, 65,* 302–312.

Christensen, L.B., Johnson, R.B., & Turner, L.A. (2015). *Research methods* (12th ed.). Upper Saddle River, NJ: Pearson.

Christiana, R.W., & others (2014). Factors related to rural young adolescents' participation in outdoor, noncompetitive physical activity. *Research Quarterly for Exercise and Sport, 85,* 509–518.

Christov-Moore, L., & others (2014). Empathy: Gender effects in brain and behavior. *Neuroscience and Biobehavioral Reviews, 46,* 604–627.

Chu, J.T., & others (2015). Parent and adolescent effects of a universal group program for the parenting of adolescents. *Prevention Science, 16,* 609–620.

Chua, A. (2011). *Battle hymn of the tiger mom.* New York: Penguin.

Cicchetti, D. (2016, in press). Multilevel developmental perspectives on child maltreatment: Current research and future perspectives. *Development and Psychopathology.*

Cicchetti, D., & Toth, S.L. (2015). A multilevel perspective on child maltreatment. In M. Lamb & C. Garcia Coll (Eds.), *Handbook of child psychology and developmental science* (7th ed., Vol. 3). New York: Wiley.

Cillessen, A.H.N., & van den Berg, Y.H.M. (2012). Popularity and school adjustment. In A.M. Ryan & G.W. Ladd (Eds.), *Peer relationships and adjustment at school.* Charlotte, NC: Information Age Publishing.

Clampet-Lundquist, S. (2013). Baltimore teens and work: Gender opportunities in disadvantaged neighborhoods. *Journal of Adolescent Research, 28*(1), 122–149.

Clark, B. (2008). *Growing up gifted* (7th ed.). Upper Saddle River, NJ: Prentice Hall.

Clark, C.J., & others (2015). Disparities in long-term cardiovascular disease risk by sexual identity: The National Longitudinal Study of Adolescent to Adult Health. *Preventive Medicine, 76,* 26–30.

Clark, D.A., Donnellan, M.B., Robins, R.W., & Conger, R.D. (2015). Early adolescent temperament, parental monitoring, and substance use in Mexican-origin adolescents. *Journal of Adolescence, 41,* 121–130.

Clark, M.S., Jansen, K.L., & Cloy, J.A. (2012). Treatment of childhood and adolescent depression. *American Family Physician, 86,* 442–446.

Clark, M.S., Powell, M.C., Ovellette, R., & Milberg, S. (1987). Recipient's mood, relationship type, and helping. *Journal of Personality and Social Psychology, 43,* 94–103.

Clark, R.D., & Hatfield, E. (1989). Gender differences in receptivity to sexual offers. *Journal of Psychology and Human Sexuality, 2,* 39–55.

Clarke, M.C., & others (2014). The impact of adolescent cannabis use, mood disorder, and lack of education on attempted suicide in young adulthood. *World Psychiatry, 13,* 322–323.

Clarke-Stewart, A., & Brentano, C. (2006). *Divorce: Causes and consequences.* New Haven, CT: Yale University Press.

Clarke-Stewart, A.K., & Parke, R.D. (2014). *Social development* (2nd ed.). New York: Wiley.

Clausen, M.B., & others (2014). High injury incidence in adolescent female soccer. *American Journal of Sports Medicine, 42,* 2487–2494.

Cleverley, K., & Kidd, S.A. (2011). Resilience and suicidality among homeless youth. *Journal of Adolescence, 34,* 1049–1054.

Clinkinbeard, S.S., Simi, P., Evans, M.K., & Anderson, A.L. (2011). Sleep and delinquency: Does amount of sleep matter? *Journal of Youth and Adolescence, 40*(7), 916–930.

Cochran, B.N., & others (2013). Mental health characteristics of sexual minority veterans. *Journal of Homosexuality, 60,* 419–435.

Cochran, S.D., & Mays, V.M. (1990). Sex, lies, and HIV. *New England Journal of Medicine, 322*(11), 774–775.

Cohen, P., Kasen, S., Chen, H., Hartmark, C., & Gordon, K. (2003). Variations in patterns of developmental transitions in the emerging adulthood period. *Developmental Psychology, 39,* 657–669.

Cohler, B., & Michaels, S. (2013). Emergent adulthood in lesbian and gay lives. In G.W. Peterson & K.R. Bush (Eds.), *Handbook of marriage and the family* (3rd ed.). New York: Springer.

Cohn, A., & Canter, A. (2003). *Bullying: Facts for schools and parents.* Washington, DC: National Association of School Psychologists Center.

Coie, J. (2004). The impact of negative social experiences on the development of antisocial behavior.

In J.B. Kupersmidt & K.A. Dodge (Eds.), *Children's peer relations: From development to intervention.* Washington, DC: American Psychological Association.

Coker, T.R., Austin, S.B., & Schuster, M.A. (2010). The health and health care of lesbian, gay, and bisexual adolescents. *Annual Review of Public Health, 31,* 457–477.

Coker, T.R., & others (2015). Media violence exposure and physical aggression in fifth-grade children. *Academic Pediatrics, 15,* 82–88.

Colangelo, N.C., Assouline, S.G., & Gross, M.U.M. (2004). *A nation deceived: How schools hold back America's brightest students.* Retrieved March 6, 2005, from http://nationdeceived.org/

Colby, A., Kohlberg, L., Gibbs, J., & Lieberman, M. (1983). A longitudinal study of moral judgment. *Monographs of the Society for Research in Child Development, 48*(21, Serial No. 201).

Cole, A.K., & Kerns, K.A. (2001). Perceptions of sibling qualities and activities of early adolescents. *Journal of Early Adolescence, 21,* 204–226.

Cole, M. (2006). Culture and cognitive development in phylogenetic, historical, and ontogenetic perspective. In W. Damon & R. Lerner (Eds.), *Handbook of child psychology* (6th ed.). New York: Wiley.

Cole, M.W., Yarkoni, T., Repovs, G., Anticevic, A., & Braver, T.S. (2012). Global connectivity of prefrontal cortex predicts cognitive control and intelligence. *Journal of Neuroscience, 32,* 8988–8999.

Coleman, D.L., & Rosoff, P.M. (2013). The legal authority of mature minors to consent to general medical treatment. *Pediatrics, 131,* 786–793.

Coley, R.L., & others (2013). Sexual partner accumulation from adolescence through early adulthood: The role of family, peer, and school norms. *Journal of Adolescent Health, 53,* 91–97.

Collins, M. (1996, Winter). The job outlook for '96 grads. *Journal of Career Planning, 23,* 51–54.

Collins, R.L., & others (2004). Watching sex on television predicts adolescent initiation of sexual behavior. *Pediatrics, 114,* e280–e289.

Collins, W.A., Hennighausen, K.H., & Sroufe, L.A. (1998, June). *Developmental precursors of intimacy in romantic relationships: A longitudinal analysis.* Paper presented at the International Conference on Personal Relationships, Saratoga Springs, NY.

Collins, W.A., & Steinberg, L. (2006). Adolescent development in interpersonal context. In W. Damon & R. Lerner (Eds.), *Handbook of child psychology* (6th ed.). New York: Wiley.

Collins, W.A., & van Dulmen, M. (2006). Friendship and romance in emerging adulthood. In J.J. Arnett & J.L. Tanner (Eds.), *Emerging adults in America.* Washington, DC: American Psychological Association.

Collins, W.A., Welsh, D.P., & Furman, W. (2009). Adolescent romantic relationships. *Annual Review of Psychology* (Vol. 60). Palo Alto, CA: Annual Reviews.

Colman, R.A., Kim, D.H., Mitchell-Herzfeld, S., & Shady, T.A. (2009). Delinquent girls grown up: Young adult offending patterns and their relation to early legal, individual, and family risk. *Journal of Youth and Adolescence, 38,* 355–366.

Colrain, I.M., & Baker, F.C. (2011). Changes in sleep as a function of adolescent development. *Neuropsychology Review, 21,* 5–21.

Comer, J.P. (2004). *Leave no child behind.* New Haven, CT: Yale University Press.

Comer, J.P. (2006). Child development: The underweighted aspect of intelligence. In P.C. Kyllonen, R.D. Roberts, & L. Stankov (Eds.), *Extending intelligence.* Mahwah, NJ: Erlbaum.

Comer, J.P. (2010). Comer School Development Program. In J. Meece & J. Eccles (Eds.), *Handbook of research on schools, schooling, and human development.* New York: Routledge.

Common Core State Standards Initiative (2014). *Common Core.* Retrieved June 1, 2014, from www.core standards.org/

Commoner, B. (2002). Unraveling the DNA myth: The spurious foundation of genetic engineering. *Harper's Magazine, 304,* 39–47.

Commons, M.L., & Richards, F.A. (2003). Four postformal stages. In J. Demick & C. Andreoletti (Eds.), *Handbook of adult development.* New York: Kluwer.

Compas, B.E. (2004). Processes of risk and resilience during adolescence: Linking contexts and individuals. In R. Lerner & L. Steinberg (Eds.), *Handbook of adolescent psychology* (2nd ed.). New York: Wiley.

Compas, B.E., & others (2014a). Coping and emotion regulation from childhood to early adulthood: Points of convergence and divergence. *Australian Journal of Psychology, 66,* 71–81.

Compas, B.E., & others (2014b). Children and adolescents coping with cancer: Self- and parent reports of coping and anxiety/depression. *Health Psychology, 33,* 853–861.

Compas, B.E., & Reeslund, K.L. (2009). Processes of risk and resilience during adolescence. In R.M. Lerner & L. Steinberg (Eds.), *Handbook of adolescent psychology* (3rd ed.). New York: Wiley.

Comstock, G., & Scharrer, E. (2006). Media and popular culture. In W. Damon & R. Lerner (Eds.), *Handbook of child psychology* (6th ed.). New York: Wiley.

Condition of Education (2012). *Participation in education,* Table A-9-1. Washington, DC: National Center for Education Statistics.

Condition of Education (2014). *Participation in education.* Washington, DC: U.S. Office of Education.

Condorelli, R.A., & others (2015, in press). The gonadal function in obese adolescents: Review. *Journal of Endocrinological Investigation.*

Condry, J.C., Simon, M.L., & Bronfenbrenner, U. (1968). *Characteristics of peer- and adult-oriented children.* Unpublished manuscript. Cornell University, Ithaca, NY.

Conduct Problems Prevention Research Group (2007). The Fast Track randomized controlled trial to prevent externalizing psychiatric disorders: Findings from grades 3 to 9. *Journal of the American Academy of Child and Adolescent Psychiatry, 46,* 1250–1262.

Conduct Problems Prevention Research Group (2010a). The difficulty of maintaining positive intervention effect: A look at disruptive behavior, deviant peer relations, and social skills during the middle school years. *Journal of Early Adolescence, 30,* 593–624.

Conduct Problems Prevention Research Group (2010b). Fast Track intervention effects on youth arrests and delinquency. *Journal of Experimental Criminology, 6,* 131–157.

Conduct Problems Prevention Research Group (2011). The effects of Fast Track preventive intervention on the development of conduct disorder across childhood. *Child Development, 82,* 331–345.

Conduct Problems Prevention Research Group (2013). Assessing findings from the Fast Track Study. *Journal of Experimental Criminology, 9,* 119–126.

Conduct Problems Prevention Research Group (2015). Impact of early intervention on psychopathology, crime, and well-being at age 25. *American Journal of Psychiatry, 172*(1), 59–70.

Conger, J.J. (1988). Hostages to the future: Youth, values, and the public interest. *American Psychologist, 43,* 291–300.

Conger, K.J., & Kramer, L. (2010). Introduction to the special section: Perspectives on sibling relationships: Advancing child development research. *Child Development Perspectives, 4,* 69–71.

Conger, R.D., & Chao, W. (1996). Adolescent depressed mood. In R.L. Simons (Ed.), *Understanding differences between divorced and intact families: Stress, interaction, and child outcome.* Thousand Oaks, CA: Sage.

Conley, C.S., & Rudolph, K.D. (2009). The emerging sex difference in adolescent depression: Interacting contributions of puberty and peer stress. *Developmental Psychopathology, 21,* 593–620.

Connolly, J., Furman, W., & Konarski, R. (2000). The role of peers in the emergence of heterosexual romantic relationships in adolescence. *Child Development, 71,* 1395–1408.

Connolly, J., Goldberg, A., Pepler, D., & Craig, W. (2004). Mixed-gender groups, dating, and romantic relationships in early adolescence. *Journal of Research on Adolescence, 14,* 185–207.

Connolly, J., & McIsaac, C. (2009). Romantic relationships in adolescence. In R.M. Lerner & L. Steinberg (Eds.), *Handbook of adolescent psychology* (3rd ed.). New York: Wiley.

Connolly, J., Nguyen, H.N., Pepler, D., Craig, W., & Jiang, D. (2013). Developmental trajectories of romantic stages and associations with problem behaviors during adolescence. *Journal of Adolescence, 36,* 1013–1024.

Connolly, J., & Stevens, V. (1999, April). *Best friends, cliques, and young adolescents' romantic involvement.* Paper presented at the meeting of the Society for Research in Child Development, Albuquerque.

Conry-Murray, C., Kim, J.M., & Turiel, E. (2012, April). *U.S. and Korean children's judgments of gender norm violations.* Paper presented at the Gender Development Research conference, San Francisco.

Consoli, A., & others (2013). Suicidal behaviors in depressed adolescents: Role of perceived relationships in the family. *Child and Adolescent Psychiatry and Mental Health, 7(1),* 8.

Consoli, A., & others (2015). Risk and protective factors for suicidality at 6-month follow-up in adolescent inpatients who attempted suicide: An exploratory model. *Canadian Journal of Psychology, 60*(Suppl. 2), S27–S36.

Constantine, J.M., Seftor, N.S., Martin, E.S., Silva, T., & Myers, D. (2006). *A study of the effect of the Talent Search program on secondary and postsecondary outcomes in Florida, Indiana, and Texas: Final report from phase II of the national evaluation.* Washington, DC: U.S. Department of Education.

Constantine, N.A. (2008). Editorial: Converging evidence leaves policy behind: Sex education in the United States. *Journal of Adolescent Health, 42,* 324–326.

Constantine, N.A., Jerman, P., & Juang, A. (2007). California parents' preferences and beliefs on school-based sexuality education policy. *Perspectives on Sexual and Reproductive Health, 39,* 167–175.

Converse, A.K., Ahlers, E.O., Travers, B.G., Davidson, R.J. (2014). Tai chi training reduces self-report of inattention in healthy young adults. *Frontiers in Human Neuroscience, 8,* 13.

Cook, P.J., MacCoun, R., Muschkin, C., & Vigdor, J. (2008). The negative impacts of starting middle school in the sixth grade. *Journal of Policy Analysis and Management, 27,* 104–121.

Cook, T.D., Deng, Y., & Morgano, E. (2007). Friendship influences during early adolescence: The special role of friends' grade point average. *Journal of Research on Adolescence, 17,* 325–356.

Cooksey, E.C. (2009). Sexual activity, adolescent. In D. Carr (Ed.), *Encyclopedia of the life course and human development.* Boston: Gale Cengage.

Cooper, C.R. (2011). *Bridging multiple worlds.* New York: Oxford University Press.

Cooper, C.R., & Ayers-Lopez, S. (1985). Family and peer systems in early adolescence: New models of the role of relationships in development. *Journal of Early Adolescence, 5,* 9–22.

Cooper, C.R., Behrens, R., & Trinh, N. (2009). Identity development. In R.A. Shweder, T.R. Dailey, S.D. Dixon, P.J. Miller, & J. Model (Eds.), *The Chicago companion to the child.* Chicago: University of Chicago Press.

Cooper, C.R., Gonzales, E., & Wilson, A.R. (2015). Identities, cultures, and schooling: How students navigate racial-ethnic, indigenous, immigrant, social class, and gender identities on their pathways through school. In K.C. McLean & M. Syed (Eds.), *Oxford handbook of identity development.* New York: Oxford University Press.

Cooper, C.R., & Grotevant, H.D. (1989, April). *Individuality and connectedness in the family and adolescent's self and relational competence.* Paper presented at the meeting of the Society for Research in Child Development, Kansas City.

Coopersmith, S. (1967). *The antecedents of self-esteem.* San Francisco: W.H. Freeman.

Copeland, W.E., Wolke, D., Angold, A., & Costello, A. (2013). Adult psychiatric outcomes of bullying and being bullied by peers in childhood and adolescence. *JAMA Psychiatry, 70,* 419–426.

Copeland, W., & others (2010). Outcomes of early pubertal timing in young women: A prospective population-based study. *American Journal of Psychiatry, 167,* 1218–1225.

Copen, C.E., Daniels, C.E., & Mosher, W.D. (2013, April 4). First premarital cohabitation in the United States: 2006–2010 National Survey of Family Growth. *National Health Statistics Reports, 64,* 1–16.

Cordova, D., Huang, S., Lally, M., Estrada, Y., & Prado, G. (2014). Do parent-adolescent discrepancies in family functioning increase the risk of Hispanic adolescent HIV risk behaviors? *Family Process, 53,* 348–363.

Costa, P.T., & McCrae, R.R. (1998). Personality assessment. In H.S. Friedman (Ed.), *Encyclopedia of mental health* (Vol. 3). San Diego: Academic Press.

Costa, P.T., & McCrae, R.R. (2013). A theoretical context for adult temperament. In T.D. Wachs & others (Eds.), *Temperament in context.* New York: Psychology Press.

Costa, P.T., & others (2014). Personality facets and all-causes mortality among Medicare patients aged 66 to 102 years: A follow-up study of Weiss and Costa (2005). *Psychosomatic Medicine, 76,* 370–378.

Costigan, S.A., Barnett, L., Plotnikoff, R.C., & Lubans, D.R. (2013). The health indicators associated with screen-based sedentary behavior among adolescent girls: A systematic review. *Journal of Adolescent Health, 52(4),* 382–392.

Coté, J.E. (2006). Emerging adulthood as an institutionalized moratorium: Risks and benefits to identity formation. In J.J. Arnett & J.L. Tanner (Eds.), *Emerging adults in America.* Washington, DC: American Psychological Association.

Coté, J.E. (2009). Identity formation and self-development. In R.M. Lerner & L. Steinberg (Eds.), *Handbook of adolescent psychology* (3rd ed.). New York: Wiley.

Coté, J.E. (2015). Identity-formation research from a critical perspective: Is a social science developing? In K.C. McLean & M. Syed (Eds.), *Oxford handbook of identity development.* New York: Oxford University Press.

Cotuli, J.J., & others (2013). Academic achievement trajectories of homeless and highly mobile students: Resilience in the context of chronic and acute risk. *Child Development, 84(3),* 841–857.

Counseling Center, University of Illinois (2014). *Perfectionism.* Retrieved November 3, 2014, from www.counselingcenter.illinois.edu?page_id=113

Courage, M.L., Bakhtiar, A., Fitzpatrick, C., Kenny, S., & Brandeau, K. (2015). Growing up multitasking: The costs and benefits for cognitive development. *Developmental Review, 35,* 5–41.

Cousins, L., & Goodyer, I.M. (2015, in press). Antidepressants and the adolescent brain. *Journal of Psychopharmacology.*

Covington, M.V. (2002). Patterns of adaptive learning study: Where do we go from here? In C. Midgley (Ed.), *Goals, goal structures, and patterns of adaptive learning.* Mahwah, NJ: Erlbaum.

Covington, M.V., & Teel, K.T. (1996). *Overcoming student failure.* Washington, DC: American Psychological Association.

Cowan, M.K. (2015). *Microbiology* (4th ed.). New York: McGraw-Hill.

Cowan, N. (2014). Short-term and working memory in childhood. In P. Bauer & R. Fivush (Eds.), *Wiley-Blackwell handbook of children's memory.* New York: Wiley.

Cowan, R., & Powell, D. (2014). The contributions of domain-general and numerical factors to third-grade arithmetic skills and mathematical learning disability. *Journal of Educational Psychology, 106,* 214–229.

Craft, C.S., & others (2014). The extracellular matrix protein MAGP1 supports thermogenesis and protects against obesity and diabetes through regulation of TGFB. *Diabetes, 63,* 1920–1932.

Cranney, S. (2015, in press). The relationship between sexual victimization and year in school in U.S. colleges: Investigating the parameters of the "red zone." *Journal of Interpersonal Violence.*

Craparo, G., Gori, A., Petruccelli, I., Cannella, V., & Simonelli, C. (2014). Intimate partner violence: Relationships between alexithymia, depression, attachment styles, and coping strategies of battered women. *Journal of Sexual Medicine, 11,* 1484–1494.

Cravo, R.M., & others (2013). Leptin signaling in Kiss1 neurons arises after pubertal development. *PLoS One, 8(3),* e58698.

Criss, M.M., & others (2015). Link between monitoring behavior and adolescent adjustment: An analysis of direct and indirect effects. *Journal of Child and Family Studies.*

Crocetti, E., Jahromi, P., & Meeus, W. (2012). Identity and civic engagement in adolescence. *Journal of Adolescence, 35,* 521–532.

Crocetti, E., & Meeus, W. (2015). The identity statuses: Strengths of a person-centered approach. In K.C. McLean & M. Syed (Eds.), *Oxford handbook of identity development.* New York: Oxford University Press.

Crocetti, E., Rabaglietti, E., & Sica, L.S. (2012). Personal identity in Italy. *New Directions in Child and Adolescent Development, 138,* 87–102.

Crockett, L.J., Raffaelli, M., & Shen, Y-L. (2006). Linking self-regulation and risk proneness to risky sexual behavior: Pathways through peer pressure and early substance use. *Journal of Research on Adolescence, 16,* 503–525.

Crooks, R.L., & Baur, K. (2014). *Our sexuality* (12th ed.). Boston: Cengage.

Crosnoe, R. (2011). *Fitting in, standing out.* New York: Cambridge University Press.

Crosnoe, R., & Benner, A.D. (2015). Children at school. In R.M. Lerner (Ed.), *Handbook of child psychology and developmental science* (7th ed.). New York: Wiley.

Crosnoe, R., & Fuligni, A.J. (2012). Children from immigrant families: Introduction to the special section. *Child Development, 83,* 1471–1476.

Cross, D., Lester, L., & Barnes, A. (2015). A longitudinal study of the social and emotional predictors and consequences of cyber and traditional bullying victimization. *International Journal of Public Health, 60,* 207–217.

Cross, S., & Markus, H. (1991). Possible selves across the lifespan. *Human Development, 34,* 230–255.

Crouter, A.C. (2006). Mothers and fathers at work. In A. Clarke-Stewart & J. Dunn (Eds.), *Families count.* New York: Cambridge University Press.

Crouter, A.C., Bumpus, M.F., Head, M.R., & McHale, S.M. (2001). Implications of overwork and overload for the quality of men's family relationships. *Journal of Marriage and Family, 63,* 404–416.

Crowell, J.A., Treboux, D., & Brockmeyer, S. (2009). Parental divorce and adult children's attachment representations and marital status. *Attachment and Human Development, 11*, 87–101.

Crowley, S.J., & Carskadon, M.A. (2010). Modifications to weekend recovery sleep delay circadian phase in older adolescents. *Chronobiology International, 27*, 1469–1492.

Cruz, J.E., Emery, R.E., & Turkheimer, E. (2012). Peer network drinking predicts increasing alcohol use from adolescence to early adulthood after controlling for genetic and shared environmental selection. *Developmental Psychology, 48*(5), 1390–1402.

Csikszentmihalyi, M. (1990). *Flow*. New York: HarperCollins.

Csikszentmihalyi, M. (1993). *The evolving self.* New York: Harper & Row.

Csikszentmihalyi, M., & Csikszentmihalyi, I.S. (Eds.). (2006). *A life worth living*. New York: Oxford University Press.

Csikszentmihalyi, M., & Schneider, B. (2000). *Becoming adult: How teenagers prepare for work.* New York: Basic Books.

Cubbin, C., Brindis, C.D., Jain, S., Santelli, J., & Braveman, P. (2010). Neighborhood poverty, aspirations and expectations, and initiation of sex. *Journal of Adolescent Health, 47*, 399–406.

Cubbin, C., Santelli, J., Brindis, C.D., & Braverman, P. (2005). Neighborhood context and sexual behaviors among adolescents: Findings from the National Longitudinal Study of Adolescent Health. *Perspectives on Sexual and Reproductive Health, 37*, 125–134.

Cui, M., Fincham, F.D., & Pasley, B.K. (2008). Young adult romantic relationships: The role of parents' marital problems and relationship efficiency. *Personality and Social Psychology Bulletin, 34*, 1226–1235.

Cui, M., Ueno, K., Fincham, F.D., Donnellan, M.B., & Wickrama, K.A. (2012). The association between romantic relationships and delinquency in adolescence and young adulthood. *Personal Relationships, 19*, 354–366.

Cummings, E.M., & Davies, P.T. (2010). *Marital conflict and children: An emotional security perspective*. New York: Guilford.

Cummings, E.M., El-Sheikh, M., & Kouros, C.D. (2009). Children and violence: The role of children's regulation in the marital aggression–child adjustment link. *Clinical Child and Family Psychology Review, 12*(1), 3–15.

Cummings, E.M., George, M.R.W., McCoy, K.P., & Davies, P.T. (2012). Interparental conflict in kindergarten and adolescent adjustment: Prospective investigation of emotion security as an explanatory mechanism. *Child Development, 83*, 1703–1715.

Cummings, E.M., Koss, K.J., & Davies, P.T. (2015). Prospective relations between family conflict and adolescent maladjustment: Security in the family system as a mediating process. *Journal of Abnormal Child Psychology, 43*, 503–515.

Cummings, E.M., & Kouros, C.D. (2008). Stress and coping. In M.M. Haith & J.B. Benson (Eds.), *Encyclopedia of infant and early childhood development* (Vol. 3, pp. 267–281). San Diego: Academic Press.

Cummings, E.M., & Miller, L.M. (2015, in press). Emotional security theory: An emerging theoretical model for youths' psychological and physiological responses across multiple developmental contexts. *Current Directions in Psychological Science.*

Cummings, E.M., & Valentino, K.V. (2015). Developmental psychopathology. In R.M. Lerner (Ed.), *Handbook of child psychology and developmental science* (7th ed.). New York: Wiley.

Cunningham, S.A., Kramer, M.R., & Narayan, K.M. (2014). Incidence of childhood obesity in the United States. *New England Journal of Medicine, 370*, 403–411.

Currie, C., & others (2008). *Inequalities in young people's health: HBSC international report from the 2005/2006 survey*. Geneva, Switzerland: World Health Organization.

Currie, C., & others (2012). Is obesity at individual and national level associated with lower age at menarche? Evidence from 34 countries in the Health Behavior and School-Aged Children Study. *Journal of Adolescent Health, 50*, 621–626.

Cushion, C., Ford, P.R., & Williams, A.M. (2012). Coach behaviours and practice structures in youth soccer: Implications for talent development. *Journal of Sports Science, 30*(15), 1631–1641.

Cushner, K.H., McClelland, A., & Safford, P. (2015). *Human diversity in education* (8th ed.). New York: McGraw-Hill.

Cuzzolaro, M. (2014). Eating and weight disorders: Studies on anorexia, bulimia, and obesity turns 19. *Eating and Weight Disorders, 19*, 1–2.

Cvencek, D., Meltzoff, A.N., & Greenwald, A.G. (2011). Math-gender stereotypes in elementary school children. *Child Development, 82*, 766–779.

Cvijetic, S., & others (2014). Influence of nutrition and lifestyle on bone mineral density of children from adoptive and biological families. *Journal of Epidemiology, 24*, 209–215.

D

D'Angelo, L.J., Halpern-Felsher, B.L., & Anisha, A. (2010). Adolescents and driving: Position paper of the Society for Adolescent Health and Medicine. *Journal of Adolescent Health, 47*, 212–214.

D'Augelli, A.R. (1991). Gay men in college: Identity processes and adaptations. *Journal of College Student Development, 32*, 140–146.

da Costa Souza, A., & Ribeiro, S. (2015, in press). Sleep deprivation and gene expression. *Current Topics in Behavioral Neurosciences.*

Dahl, R.E. (2004). Adolescent brain development: A period of vulnerabilities and opportunities. *Annals of the New York Academy of Sciences, 1021*, 1–22.

Daly, M.C., & Bengali, L. (2014, May 5). Is it still worth it to go to college? *FRBSF Economic Letter*, 1–6.

Damasio, A., & Carvalho, G.B. (2013). The nature of feelings: Evolutionary and biological origins. *Nature Reviews: Neuroscience, 14*, 143–152.

Damon, W. (1988). *The moral child*. New York: Free Press.

Damon, W. (2008). *The path to purpose: Helping our children find their purpose in life*. New York: Simon & Schuster.

Daniel, E., Dys, S.P., Buchmann, M., & Malti, T. (2014). Developmental relations between sympathy, moral emotion attributions, moral reasoning, and social justice values from childhood to early adolescence. *Journal of Adolescence, 37*, 1201–1214.

Daniels, H. (2011). Vygotsky and psychology. In U. Goswami (Ed.), *Wiley-Blackwell handbook of childhood cognitive development* (2nd ed.). New York: Wiley.

Darcy, E. (2012). Gender issues in child and adolescent eating disorders. In J. Lock (Ed.), *Oxford handbook of child and adolescent eating disorders: Developmental perspectives*. New York: Oxford University Press.

Darling, N. (2008). Commentary: Putting conflict in context. *Monographs of the Society for Research in Child Development, 73*(2), 169–175.

Darling-Hammond, N. (2011). Testing, No Child Left Behind, and educational equity. In L.M. Stulberg & S.L. Weinberg (Eds.), *Diversity in higher education*. New York: Routledge.

Darwin, C. (1859). *On the origin of species*. London: John Murray.

Davidson, J., & Davidson, B. (2004). *Genius denied: How to stop wasting our brightest young minds*. New York: Simon & Schuster.

Davidson, M., Lickona, T., & Khmelkov, V. (2008). A new paradigm for high school character education. In L. Nucci & D. Narváez (Eds.), *Handbook of moral and character education*. Clifton, NJ: Psychology Press.

Davies, G., & others (2011). Genome-wide association studies establish that human intelligence is highly heritable and polygenic. *Molecular Psychiatry, 16*, 996–1005.

Davies, J., & Brember, I. (1999). Reading and mathematics attainments and self-esteem in years 2 and 6—an eight-year cross sectional study. *Educational Studies, 25*, 145–157.

Davies, M., Gilston, J., & Rogers, P. (2012). Examining the relationship between male rape myth acceptance, female rape myth acceptance, victim blame, homophobia, gender roles, and ambivalent sexism. *Journal of Interpersonal Violence, 27*, 2807–2823.

Davies, P.T., & Cicchetti, D. (2014). How and why does the 5-HTTLPR gene moderate associations between maternal unresponsiveness and children's problems? *Child Development, 85*, 484–500.

Davis, A.E., Hyatt, G., & Arrasmith, D. (1998, February). "I Have a Dream" program. *Class One Evaluation Report*. Portland, OR: Northwest Regional Education Laboratory.

Davis, C.L., & others (2007). Effects of aerobic exercise on overweight children's cognitive functioning: A randomized controlled trial. *Research Quarterly for Exercise and Sport, 78*, 510–519.

Davis, C.L., & others (2011). Exercise improves executive function and alters neural activation in overweight children. *Health Psychology, 30*, 91–98.

Daw, J., Margolis, R., & Verdery, A.M. (2015). Siblings, friends, course-mates, club-mates: How adolescent health behavior homophily varies by race, class, gender, and health status. *Social Science and Medicine, 125*, 32–39.

Dawson, A.E., & others (2014). Adolescent insecure attachment as a predictor of maladaptive coping and externalizing behaviors in emerging adulthood. *Attachment and Human Development, 16*, 462–478.

Dawson-McClure, S., & others (2015). A population-level approach to promoting healthy child development and school success in low-income, urban neighborhoods: Impact on parenting and child conduct problems. *Prevention Science, 16*, 279–290.

Day, J.M. (2010). Religion, spirituality, and positive psychology in adulthood: A developmental view. *Journal of Adult Development, 17*, 215–229.

de Ànda, D. (2006). Baby Think It Over: Evaluation of an infant simulation intervention for adolescent pregnancy prevention. *Health and Social Work, 31*, 26–35.

de Bruin, W.B., Parker, A.M., & Fischhoff, B. (2007). Can adolescents predict significant life events? *Journal of Adolescent Health, 41*, 208–210.

de Graaf, H., van de Schoot, R., Woertman, L., Hawk, S.T., & Meeus, W. (2012). Family cohesion and romantic and sexual initiation: A three-wave longitudinal study. *Journal of Youth and Adolescence, 41*, 583–592.

de Guzman, N.S., & Nishina, A. (2014). A longitudinal study of body dissatisfaction and pubertal timing in an ethnically diverse adolescent sample. *Body Image, 11*, 68–71.

de Haan, M. (2015). Neuroscientific methods with children. In R.M. Lerner (Ed.), *Handbook of child psychology and developmental science* (7th ed.). New York: Wiley.

de Leo, D., & Heller, T. (2008). Social modeling in the transmission of suicide. *Crisis, 29*, 11–19.

de Looze, M., & others (2015). Parent-adolescent sexual communication and its association with adolescent sexual behaviors: A nationally representative analysis in the Netherlands. *Journal of Sex Research, 52*, 257–268.

De Luca, S.M., Wyman, P., & Warren, K. (2012). Latina adolescent suicide ideations and attempts:

Associations with connectedness to parents, peers, and teachers. *Suicide and Life-Threatening Behaviors, 42*(6), 672–683.

De Navas-Walt, C., & Proctor, B.D. (2014). *Income and poverty in the United States, 2013.* Washington, DC: U.S. Census Bureau.

De Raad, B., & others (2010). Only three factors of personality description are fully replicable across languages: A comparison of 14 trait taxonomies. *Journal of Personality and Social Psychology, 98,* 160–173.

de Vries, S.L., Hoeve, M., Assink, M., Stams, G.J., & Asscher, J.J. (2015). Practitioner review: Effective ingredients of prevention programs for youth at risk of persistent juvenile delinquency—recommendations for clinical practice. *Journal of Child Psychology and Psychiatry, 56,* 108–121.

de Vries, S.L., Hoeve, M., Stams, G.J., & Asscher, J.J. (2015, in press). Adolescent-parent attachment and externalizing behavior: The mediating role of individual and social factors. *Journal of Abnormal Child Psychology.*

Deardorff, J., & others (2011). Father absence, body mass index, and pubertal timing in girls: Differential effects by family income and ethnicity. *Journal of Adolescent Health, 48,* 441–447.

Deary, I.J. (2012). Intelligence. *Annual Review of Psychology* (Vol. 63). Palo Alto, CA: Annual Reviews.

Deater-Deckard, K. (2013). The social environment and the development of psychopathology. In P.D. Zelazo (Ed.), *Handbook of developmental psychology.* New York: Oxford University Press.

deCharms, R. (1984). Motivation enhancement in educational settings. In R. Ames & C. Ames (Eds.), *Research on motivation in education* (Vol. 1). Orlando, FL: Academic Press.

Deci, E.L., Koestner, R., & Ryan, R.M. (2001). Extrinsic rewards and intrinsic motivation in education: Reconsidered once again. *Review of Educational Research, 71,* 1–28.

Dedon, P.C., & Begley, T.H. (2014). A system of RNA modifications and biased codon use control cellular stress response at the level of transition. *Chemical Research in Toxicology, 27,* 330–337.

Defoe, I.N., & others (2013). Siblings versus parents and friends: Longitudinal linkages to adolescent externalizing problems. *Journal of Child Psychology and Psychiatry, 54,* 881–889.

Degortes, D., & others (2014). Stressful life events and binge eating disorder. *European Eating Disorders Review, 22,* 378–382.

Deimel, J.F., & Dunlap, B.J. (2012). The female athlete triad. *Clinical Sports Medicine, 31,* 247–254.

DeJong, W., DeRicco, B., & Schneider, S.K. (2010). Pregaming: An exploratory study of strategic drinking by college students in Pennsylvania. *Journal of American College Health, 58,* 307–316.

Del Campo, R., Buchanan, W.R., Abbott, R.D., & Berninger, V.W. (2015). Levels of phonology related to reading and writing in middle childhood. *Reading and Writing, 28,* 183–198.

Dempster, F.N. (1981). Memory span: Sources of individual and developmental differences. *Psychological Bulletin, 89,* 63–100.

Denham, S., & others (2011). Emotions and social development in childhood. In P.K. Smith & C.H. Hart (Eds.), *Wiley-Blackwell handbook of childhood social development* (2nd ed.). New York: Wiley.

Dennis, M., & others (2014). Functional plasticity in childhood brain disorders: When, what, how, and whom to assess. *Neuropsychology Review, 24,* 389–408.

DePaulo, B. (2007). *Singled out.* New York: St. Martin's Griffin.

DePaulo, B. (2011). Living single: Lightening up those dark, dopey myths. In W.R. Cupach & B.H. Spitzberg (Eds.), *The dark side of close relationships.* New York: Routledge.

DeRose, L., & Brooks-Gunn, J. (2008). Pubertal development in early adolescence: Implications for affective processes. In N.B. Allen & L. Sheeber (Eds.), *Adolescent emotional development and the emergence of depressive disorders.* New York: Cambridge University Press.

DeRose, L.M., Shiyko, M.P., Foster, H., & Brooks-Gunn, J. (2011). Associations between menarcheal timing and behavioral developmental trajectories for girls from age 6 to age 15. *Journal of Youth and Adolescence, 40,* 1329–1342.

Deschesnes, M., Fines, P., & Demers, S. (2006). Are tattooing and body piercing indicators of risk-taking behaviors among high school students? *Journal of Adolescence, 29,* 379–393.

Destan, N., Hembacher, E., Ghetti, S., & Roebers, C.M. (2014). Early metacognitive abilities: The interplay of monitoring and control processes in 5- to 7-year-old children. *Journal of Experimental Child Psychology, 126,* 213–228.

Deustch, A.R., Chernyavskiy, P., Steinley, D., & Slutscke, W.S. (2015). Measuring peer socialization for adolescent substance use: A comparison of perceived and actual friends' substance use effects. *Journal of Studies on Alcohol and Drugs, 76,* 267–277.

Deutsch, A.R., Crockett, L.J., Wolf, J.M., & Russell, S.T. (2012). Parent and peer pathways to adolescent delinquency: Variations by ethnicity and neighborhood context. *Journal of Youth and Adolescence, 41,* 1078–1094.

Deutsch Smith, D., & Tyler, N.C. (2014). *Introduction to contemporary special education.* Upper Saddle River, NJ: Pearson.

Dever, B.V., & others (2012). Predicting risk-taking with and without substance use: The effects of parental monitoring, school bonding, and sports participation. *Prevention Science, 13*(6), 605–615.

Devos, T. (2006). Implicit bicultural identity among Mexican American and Asian American college students. *Cultural Diversity and Ethnic Minority Psychology, 12,* 381–402.

DeWall, C.N., Anderson, C.A., & Bushman, B.J. (2013). Aggression. In I.B. Weiner & others (Eds.), *Handbook of psychology* (2nd ed., Vol. 5). New York: Wiley.

Dewey, J. (1933). *How we think.* Lexington, MA: D.C. Heath.

DeZolt, D.M., & Hull, S.H. (2001). Classroom and schools climate. In J. Worell (Ed.), *Encyclopedia of women and gender.* San Diego: Academic Press.

Diamond, L.M., Bonner, S.B., & Dickenson, J.A. (2015). The development of sexuality. In R.M. Lerner (Ed.), *Handbook of child psychology and developmental science* (7th ed.). New York: Wiley.

Diamond, L.M., & Savin-Williams, R.C. (2015). Same-sex activity in adolescence: Multiple meanings and implications. In R.F. Fassinger & S.L. Morrow (Eds.), *Sex in the margins.* Washington, DC: American Psychological Association.

Diekmann, A., & Schmidheiny, K. (2004). Do parents of girls have a higher risk of divorce? An eighteen-country study. *Journal of Marriage and the Family, 66,* 651–660.

Diener, E., & Seligman, M.E.P. (2002). Very happy people. *Psychological Science, 13,* 81–84.

DiLonardo, M.J. (2013). *Talking about weight with your child.* Retrieved February 21, 2013, from http://www.webmd.com/parenting/raising-fit-kids/weight/talk-child-obesity

Dimmitt, C., & McCormick, C.B. (2012). Metacognition in education. In K.R. Harris, S. Graham, & T. Urdan (Eds.), *Handbook of educational psychology.* Washington, DC: American Psychological Association.

Dindia, K. (2006). Men are from North Dakota, women are from South Dakota. In K. Dindia & D.J. Canary (Eds.), *Sex differences and similarities in communication.* Mahwah, NJ: Erlbaum.

Ding, X.P., & others (2014). Elementary school children's cheating behavior and its cognitive correlates. *Journal of Experimental Child Psychology, 121,* 85–95.

Dir, A.L., Coskunpinar, A., & Cyders, M.A. (2014). A meta-analytic review of the relationship between adolescent risky sexual behavior and impulsivity across gender, age, and race. *Clinical Psychology Review, 34,* 551–562.

Dishion, T.J., & Piehler, T.F. (2009). Deviant by design: Peer contagion in development, interventions, and schools. In K.H. Rubin, W.M. Bukowski, & B. Laursen (Eds.), *Handbook of peer interactions, relationships, and groups.* New York: Guilford.

Dishion, T.J., Piehler, T.F., & Myers, M.W. (2008). Dynamics and ecology of adolescent peer influence. In M.J. Prinstein & K.A. Dodge (Eds.), *Understanding peer influence in children and adolescents.* New York: Guilford.

Dobbins, M., & others (2009). School-based physical activity programs for promoting physical activity and fitness in children and adolescents 6–18. *Cochrane Database of Systematic Reviews (1),* CD007651.

Dobkin, L.M., Perrucci, A.C., & Dehlendorf, C. (2013). Pregnancy options counseling for adolescents: Overcoming barriers to care and preserving counseling. *Current Problems in Pediatric and Adolescent Health Care, 43,* 96–102.

Dodge, K.A. (1993). Social cognitive mechanisms in the development of conduct disorder and depression. *Annual Review of Psychology* (Vol. 44). Palo Alto, CA: Annual Reviews.

Dodge, K.A. (2011a). Context matters in child and family policy. *Child Development, 82,* 433–442.

Dodge, K.A. (2011b). Social information processing models of aggressive behavior. In M. Mikulincer & P.R. Shaver (Eds.), *Understanding and reducing aggression, violence, and their consequences.* Washington, DC: American Psychological Association.

Dodge, K.A., Godwin, J., & The Conduct Problems Prevention Research Group (2013). Social-information-processing patterns mediate the impact of preventive intervention on adolescent antisocial behavior. *Psychological Science, 24,* 456–465.

Dodge, K.A., & McCourt, S.N. (2010). Translating models of antisocial behavioral development into efficacious intervention policy to prevent adolescent violence. *Developmental Psychobiology, 52,* 277–285.

Dodge, K.A., & others (2006). Toward a dynamic developmental model of the role of parents and peers in early onset substance abuse. In A. Clarke-Stewart & J. Dunn (Eds.), *Families count.* New York: Cambridge University Press.

Dodge, K.A., & others (2015). Impact of early intervention on psychopathology, crime, and well-being at age 25. *American Journal of Psychiatry, 172,* 59–70.

Dohrenwend, B.S., & Shrout, P.E. (1985). "Hassles" in the conceptualization and measurement of life event stress variables. *American Psychologist, 40,* 780–785.

Dolcini, M.M., & others (1989). Adolescent egocentrism and feelings of invulnerability: Are they related? *Journal of Early Adolescence, 9,* 409–418.

Donatelle, R.J. (2015). *Access to health* (14th ed.). Upper Saddle River, NJ: Pearson.

Donatelle, R.J. (2016, in press). *My health* (2nd ed.). Upper Saddle River, NJ: Pearson.

Donath, C., Graessel, E., Baier, D., Bleich, S., & Hillemacher, T. (2014). Is parenting style a predictor of suicide attempts in a representative sample of adolescents? *BMC Pediatrics, 14*(1), 113.

Donnellan, M.B., Larsen-Rife, D., & Conger, R.D. (2005). Personality, family history, and competence in early adult romantic relationships. *Journal of Personality and Social Psychology, 88,* 562–576.

Donnellan, M.B., & Robins, R.W. (2009). The development of personality across the life span. In G. Matthews & P. Corr (Eds.), *Cambridge handbook of personality.* Cambridge, UK: Cambridge University Press.

Donnellan, M.B., & Trzesniewski, K.H. (2010). Groundhog Day versus Alice in Wonderland, red herrings versus Swedish fishes, and hopefully something constructive: A reply to comments. *Perspectives on Psychological Science, 5,* 103–108.

Donnelly, N., & Storchova, Z. (2015, in press). Causes and consequences of protein folding stress in aneuploidy cells. *Cell Cycle.*

Doornwaard, S.M., Branje, S., Meeus, W.H.J., & ter Bogt, T.F.M. (2012). Development of adolescents' peer crowd identification in relation to changes in problem behaviors. *Developmental Psychology, 48,* 1366–1380.

Doornwaard, S.M., van den Eijnden, R.J., Overbeek, G., & ter Bogt, T.F. (2015). Differential developmental profiles of adolescents using sexually explicit Internet material. *Journal of Sex Research, 52,* 269–281.

Dopp, P.R., Mooney, A.J., Armitage, R., & King, C. (2012). Exercise for adolescents with depressive disorders: A feasibility study. *Depression Research and Treatment.* doi:10.1155/2012/257472.

Dorn, L.D., & Biro, F.M. (2011). Puberty and its measurement: A decade in review. *Journal of Research on Adolescence, 21,* 180–195.

Dorn, L.D., Dahl, R.E., Woodward, H.R., & Biro, F. (2006). Defining the boundaries of early adolescence: A user's guide to assessing pubertal status and pubertal timing in research with adolescents. *Applied Developmental Science, 10,* 30–56.

Doumen, S., & others (2012). Identity and perceived peer relationship quality in emerging adulthood: The mediating role of attachment-related emotions. *Journal of Adolescence, 35,* 1417–1425.

Dovis, S., Van der Oord, S., Wiers, R.W., & Prins, P.J. (2015). Improving executive functioning in children with ADHD: Training multiple executive functions within the context of a computer game. A randomized double-blind placebo controlled trial. *PLoS One, 10*(4), e0121651.

Drake, K., Belsky, J., & Fearon, R.M.P. (2014). From early attachment to engagement with learning in school: The role of self-regulation and persistence. *Developmental Psychology, 50,* 1350–1361.

Drake, K.M., & others (2012). Influence of sports, physical education, and active commuting to school on adolescent weight status. *Pediatrics, 130,* e296–e304.

Dregan, A., & Armstrong, D. (2010). Adolescent sleep disturbances as predictors of adult sleep disturbances— A cohort study. *Journal of Adolescent Health, 46,* 482–487.

Dryfoos, J.G. (1990). *Adolescents at risk: Prevalence and prevention.* New York: Oxford University Press.

Dryfoos, J.G. (1997). The prevalence of problem behaviors: Implications for programs. In R.P. Weissberg, T.P. Gullotta, R.L. Hampton, B.A. Ryan, & G.R. Adams (Eds.), *Healthy children 2010: Enhancing children's wellness.* Thousand Oaks, CA: Sage.

Dryfoos, J.G., & Barkin, C. (2006a). *Adolescence.* New York: Oxford University Press.

Dryfoos, J.G., & Barkin, C. (2006b). *Growing up in America today.* New York: Oxford University Press.

Duan, X., Dan, Z., & Shi, J. (2014). The speed of information processing of 9- to 13-year-old intellectually gifted children. *Psychology Reports, 112,* 20–32.

Dudovitz, R.N., McCoy, K., & Chung, P.J. (2015). At-school substance use as a marker for serious health risks. *Academic Pediatrics, 15,* 41–56.

Duggan, P.M., Lapsley, D.K., & Norman, K. (2000, April). *Adolescent invulnerability and personal uniqueness: Scale development and initial construct validation.* Paper presented at the 8th Biennial Meeting of the Society for Research on Adolescence, Chicago.

Duke, S.A., Balzer, B.W., & Steinbeck, K.S. (2014). Testosterone and its effects on human male adolescent mood and behavior: A systematic review. *Journal of Adolescent Health, 55,* 315–322.

Dumith, S.C., & others (2010). Overweight/obesity and physical fitness among children and adolescents. *Journal of Physical Activity and Health, 7,* 641–648.

Duncan, D.T., & Hatzenbuehler, M.L. (2014). Lesbian, gay, bisexual, and transgender hate crimes and suicidality among a population-based sample of sexual-minority adolescents in Boston. *American Journal of Public Health, 104,* 272–278.

Duncan, G., Magnuson, K., Kalil, A., & Ziol-Guest, K. (2012). The importance of early childhood poverty. *Social Indicators, 108,* 87–98.

Duncan, G.J., Magnuson, K., & Votruba-Drzal, E. (2015). Children and socioeconomic status. In M.H. Bornstein & T. Leventhal (Eds.), *Handbook of child psychology and developmental science* (7th ed., Vol. 4). New York: Wiley.

Duncan, S.C., Duncan, T.E., Strycker, L.A., & Chaumeton, N.R. (2007). A cohort-sequential latent growth model of physical activity from 12 to 17 years. *Annals of Behavioral Medicine, 33,* 80–89.

Dunkley, D.M., Berg, J.L., & Zuroff, D.C. (2012). The role of perfectionism in daily self-esteem, attachment, and negative affect. *Journal of Personality, 80,* 633–663.

Dunlop, S.M., & Romer, D. (2010). Adolescent and young adult car crash risk: Sensation seeking, substance use propensity, and substance use behaviors. *Journal of Adolescent Health, 46,* 90–92.

Dunn, J. (2005). Commentary: Siblings in their families. *Journal of Family Psychology, 19,* 654–657.

Dunn, J. (2007). Siblings and socialization. In J.E. Grusec & P.D. Hastings (Eds.), *Handbook of socialization.* New York: Guilford.

Dunn, J. (2014). Moral development in early childhood and social interaction in the family. In M. Killen & J.G. Smetana (Eds.), *Handbook of moral development* (2nd ed.). New York: Psychology Press.

Dunn, J. (2015). Siblings. In J.E. Grusec & P.D. Hastings (Eds.), *Handbook of socialization* (2nd ed.). New York: Guilford.

Dunphy, D.C. (1963). The social structure of urban adolescent peer groups. *Society, 26,* 230–246.

Duriez, B., Luyckx, K., Soenens, B., & Berzonsky, M. (2012). A process-content approach to adolescent identity formation: Examining longitudinal associations between identity styles and goal pursuits. *Journal of Personality, 80,* 135–161.

Durik, A.M., & others (2006). Ethnicity and gender stereotypes of emotion. *Sex Roles, 54,* 429–445.

Durrant, R., & Ellis, B.J. (2013). Evolutionary psychology. In I.B. Weiner & others (Eds.), *Handbook of psychology* (2nd ed., Vol. 3). New York: Wiley.

Durston, S., & others (2006). A shift from diffuse to focal cortical activity with development. *Developmental Science, 9,* 1–8.

Dweck, C.S. (2006). *Mindset.* New York: Random House.

Dweck, C.S. (2007). Boosting achievement with messages that motivate. *Education Canada, 47,* 6–10.

Dweck, C.S. (2012). Mindsets and human nature: Promoting change in the Middle East, the school yard, the racial divide, and willpower. *American Psychologist, 67,* 614–622.

Dweck, C.S., & Master, A. (2009). Self-theories and motivation: Students' beliefs about intelligence. In K.R. Wentzel & A. Wigfield (Eds.), *Handbook of motivation at school.* New York: Routledge.

Dworkin, S.L., & Santelli, J. (2007). Do abstinence-plus interventions reduce sexual risk behavior among youth? *PLoS Medicine, 4,* 1437–1439.

Dwyer, D.B., & others (2014). Large-scale brain network dynamics supporting adolescent cognitive development. *Journal of Neuroscience, 34,* 14096–14107.

Dyson, R., & Renk, K. (2006). Freshman adaptation to university life: Depressive symptoms, stress, and coping. *Journal of Clinical Psychology, 62,* 1231–1244.

E

Eagan, K., & others (2014). *The American college freshman: National norms for fall 2014.* Los Angeles: Higher Education Research Institute, UCLA.

Eagly, A.H. (2001). Social role theory of sex differences and similarities. In J. Worell (Ed.), *Encyclopedia of women and gender.* San Diego: Academic Press.

Eagly, A.H. (2010). Gender roles. In J. Levine & M. Hogg (Eds.), *Encyclopedia of group processes and intergroup relations.* Thousand Oaks, CA: Sage.

Eagly, A.H. (2012). Women as leaders: Paths through the labyrinth. In M.C. Bligh & R. Riggio (Eds.), *When near is far and far is near: Exploring distance in leader-follower relationships.* New York: Wiley Blackwell.

Eagly, A.H. (2013). Science and politics: A reconsideration. In M.K. Ryan & N.R. Branscombe (Eds.), *Sage handbook of gender and psychology.* Thousand Oaks, CA: Sage.

Eagly, A.H., & Antonakis, J. (2014). Leadership. In G. Borgida & J. Bargh (Eds.), *APA handbook of personality and social psychology.* Washington, DC: APA Books.

Eagly, A.H., & Crowley, M. (1986). Gender and helping behavior: A meta-analytic review of the social psychological literature. *Psychological Bulletin, 100,* 283–308.

Eagly, A.H., Gartzia, L., & Carli, L.L. (2014). Female advantage: Revisited. In S. Kumra, R. Simpson, & R. Burke (Eds.), *Oxford handbook of gender in organizations.* New York: Oxford University Press.

Eagly, A.H., & Steffen, V.J. (1986). Gender and aggressive behavior: A meta-analytic review of the social psychological literature. *Psychological Bulletin, 100,* 309–330.

East, P. (2009). Adolescent relationships with siblings. In R.M. Lerner & L. Steinberg (Eds.), *Handbook of adolescent psychology* (3rd ed.). New York: Wiley.

East, P., & Adams, J. (2002). Sexual assertiveness and adolescents' sexual rights. *Perspectives on Sexual and Reproductive Health, 34,* 198–202.

Eaton, D.K., & others (2008). Youth risk behavior surveillance—United States, 2007. *MMWR, 57,* 1–131.

Eaton, D.K., & others (2012). Youth risk behavior surveillance—United States, 2011. *MMWR Surveillance Summary, 61,* 1–162.

Ebata, A.T., & Moos, R.H. (1989, April). *Coping and adjustment in four groups of adolescents.* Paper presented at the biennial meeting of the Society for Research in Child Development, Kansas City.

Eccles, J.S. (1987a). Gender roles and achievement patterns: An expectancy value perspective. In J.M. Reinisch, L.A. Rosenblum, & S.A. Sanders (Eds.), *Masculinity/femininity.* New York: Oxford University Press.

Eccles, J.S. (1987b). Gender roles and women's achievement-related decisions. *Psychology of Women Quarterly, 11,* 135–172.

Eccles, J.S. (1993). School and family effects on the ontogeny of children's interests, self-perceptions, and activity choice. In J. Jacobs (Ed.), *Nebraska Symposium on Motivation, 1992: Developmental perspectives on motivation.* Lincoln: University of Nebraska Press.

Eccles, J.S. (2004). Schools, academic motivation and stage-environment fit. In R. Lerner & L. Steinberg (Eds.), *Handbook of adolescent psychology.* New York: Wiley.

Eccles, J.S. (2007). Families, schools and developing achievement-related motivations and engagement. In J.E. Grusec & P.D. Hastings (Eds.), *Handbook of socialization.* New York: Guilford.

Eccles, J.S. (2014). Gender and achievement choices. In E.T. Gershoff, R.S. Mistry, & D.A. Crosby (Eds.), *Societal contexts of child development.* New York: Oxford University Press.

Eccles, J.S., Brown, B.V., & Templeton, J. (2008). A developmental framework for selecting indicators of well-being during the adolescent and young adult years. In B.V. Brown (Ed.), *Key indicators of child and youth well-being*. Clifton, NJ: Psychology Press.

Eccles, J.S., & Gootman, J. (2002). *Community programs to promote youth development*. Washington, DC: National Research Council Institute of Medicine, National Academy Press.

Eccles, J.S., & Roeser, R.W. (2009). Schools, academic motivation, and stage-environment fit. In R.M. Lerner & L. Steinberg (Eds.), *Handbook of adolescent psychology* (3rd ed.). New York: Wiley.

Eccles, J.S., & Roeser, R.W. (2011). Schools as developmental contexts during adolescence. *Journal of Research on Adolescence, 21*, 225–241.

Eccles, J.S., & Roeser, R.W. (2013). Schools as developmental contexts during adolescence. In I.B. Weiner & others (Eds.), *Handbook of psychology* (2nd ed., Vol. 6). New York: Wiley.

Eccles, J.S., Wigfield, A., & Schiefele, U. (1998). Motivation to succeed. In W. Damon (Ed.), *Handbook of child psychology* (5th ed., Vol. 3). New York: Wiley.

Echlin, P.S., & others (2014). The Sport Concussion Education Project: A brief report on an educational initiative: From concept to curriculum. *Journal of Neurosurgery, 121*, 1331–1336.

Eckerberg, B., Lowden, A., Nagai, R., & Akerstedt, T. (2012). Melatonin treatment effects on adolescent students' sleep timing and sleepiness in a placebo-controlled crossover study. *Chronobiology International, 29*, 1239–1248.

Eckersley, R. (2010). Commentary on Trzesniewski and Donnellan (2010): A transdisciplinary perspective on young people's well being. *Perspectives on Psychological Science, 5*, 76–80.

Edelbrock, C.S. (1989, April). *Self-reported internalizing and externalizing problems in a community sample of adolescents*. Paper presented at the meeting of the Society for Research in Child Development, Kansas City.

Edwards, R., & Hamilton, M.A. (2004). You need to understand my gender role: An empirical test of Tannen's model of gender and communication. *Sex Roles, 50*, 491–504.

Ehrlich, K.B., Dykas, M.J., & Cassidy, J. (2012). Tipping points in adolescent adjustment: Predicting social functioning from adolescents' conflict with parents and friends. *Journal of Family Psychology, 26*, 776–783.

Eisenberg, M.E., Bernat, D.H., Bearinger, L.H., & Resnick, M.D. (2008). Support for comprehensive sexuality education: Perspectives from parents of school-aged youth. *Journal of Adolescent Research, 42*, 352–359.

Eisenberg, M.E., Madsen, N., Oliphant, J.A., & Sieving, R.E. (2013). Barriers to providing sexuality education that teachers believe students need. *Journal of School Health, 83*, 335–342.

Eisenberg, M.E., & others (2004). Correlations between family meals and psychosocial well-being among adolescents. *Archives of Pediatric and Adolescent Medicine, 158*, 792–796.

Eisenberg, N., Duckworth, A., Spinrad, L., & Valiente, C. (2014). Conscientiousness and healthy aging. *Developmental Psychology, 50*, 1331–1349.

Eisenberg, N., & Fabes, R.A. (1998). Prosocial development. In N. Eisenberg (Ed.), *Handbook of child psychology* (5th ed., Vol. 3). New York: Wiley.

Eisenberg, N., Fabes, R.A., Guthrie, I.K., & Reiser, M. (2002). The role of emotionality and regulation in children's social competence and adjustment. In L. Pulkkinen & A. Caspi (Eds.), *Paths to successful development*. New York: Cambridge University Press.

Eisenberg, N., & Morris, A.S. (2004). Moral cognitions and prosocial responding in adolescence. In R. Lerner & L. Steinberg (Eds.), *Handbook of adolescent psychology* (2nd ed.). New York: Wiley.

Eisenberg, N., Morris, A.S., McDaniel, B., & Spinrad, T.L. (2009). Moral cognitions and prosocial responding in adolescence. In R.M. Lerner & L. Steinberg (Eds.), *Handbook of adolescent psychology* (3rd ed.). New York: Wiley.

Eisenberg, N., Spinrad, T.L., & Knafo, A. (2015). Prosocial development. In R.M. Lerner (Ed.), *Handbook of child psychology and developmental science* (7th ed.). New York: Wiley.

Eisenberg, N., Spinrad, T.L., & Morris, A.S. (2013). Prosocial development. In P.D. Zelazo (Ed.), *Oxford handbook of developmental psychology*. New York: Oxford University Press.

Eisenberg, N., Spinrad, T.L., & Morris, A.S. (2014). Empathy-related responding in children. In M. Killen & J.G. Smetana (Eds.), *Handbook of moral development* (2nd ed.). New York: Psychology Press.

Eisenberg, N., & Valiente, C. (2002). Parenting and children's prosocial and moral development. In M.H. Bornstein (Ed.), *Handbook of parenting* (2nd ed.). Mahwah, NJ: Erlbaum.

Eisenhower Corporation (2013). *Quantum Opportunities program*. Retrieved January 3, 2013 from http://www.eisenhowerfoundation.org/qop.php

El Ansari, W., Dibba, E., & Stock, C. (2014). Body image concerns: Levels, correlates, and gender differences among students in the United Kingdom. *Central European Journal of Public Health, 22*, 106–117.

Eliot, L. (2013). Single-sex education and the brain. *Sex Roles, 69*, 363–381.

Elkind, D. (1961). Quantity conceptions in junior and senior high school students. *Child Development, 32*, 531–560.

Elkind, D. (1976). *Child development and education: A Piagetian perspective*. New York: Oxford University Press.

Elkind, D. (1985). Egocentrism redux. *Developmental Review, 5*, 218–226.

Elkind, D., & Bowen, R. (1979). Imaginary audience behavior in children and adolescents. *Developmental Psychology, 15*, 38–44.

Elks, C.E., & Ong, K.K. (2011). Whole genome associated studies for age of menarche. *Briefings in Functional Genomics, 2*, 91–97.

Elliot, D.L., Cheong, J., Moe, E., & Goldberg, L. (2007). Cross-sectional study of female athletes reporting anabolic steroid use. *Archives of Pediatric and Adolescent Medicine, 161*, 572–577.

Ellis, B.J., Shirtcliff, E.A., Boyce, W.T., Deardorff, J., & Essex, M.J. (2011). Quality of early family relationships and the timing and tempo of puberty: Effects depend on biological sensitivity to context. *Development and Psychopathology, 23*, 85–99.

Ellis, L., & Ames, M.A. (1987). Neurohormonal functioning and sexual orientation: A theory of homosexuality-heterosexuality. *Psychological Bulletin, 101*, 233–258.

Ellison, A., & others (2014). Functional interaction between right parietal and bilateral frontal cortices during visual search tasks revealed using functional magnetic imaging and transcranial direct current stimulation. *PLoS One, 9*(4), e93767.

Ellwardt, L., & others (2015). Personal networks and mortality risk in older adults: A twenty-year longitudinal study. *PLoS One, 10*(3), e0116731.

Else-Quest, N., Hyde, J.S., Goldsmith, H., & Van Hulle, C. (2006). Gender differences in temperament: A meta-analysis. *Psychological Bulletin, 136*, 107–136.

Ember, M.R., Ember, C.R., & Peregrine, P.N. (2015). *Cultural anthropology* (14th ed.). Upper Saddle River, NJ: Pearson.

Emery, R.E. (1999). *Renegotiating family relationships* (2nd ed.). New York: Guilford.

Emery, R.E., & Laumann-Billings, L. (1998). An overview of the nature, causes, and consequences of abusive family relationships. *American Psychologist, 53*, 121–135.

Emes, R.D., & Grant, S.G.N. (2013). Evolution of synapse complexity and diversity. *Annual Review of Neuroscience* (Vol. 35). Palo Alto, CA: Annual Reviews.

Emmer, E.T., & Everston, C.M. (2013). *Classroom management for middle and high school teachers* (9th ed.). Upper Saddle River, NJ: Pearson.

Emmons, R.A., & Diener, E. (1986). Situation selection as a moderator of response consistency and stability. *Journal of Personality and Social Psychology, 51*, 1013–1019.

Enfield, A., & Collins, D. (2008). The relationship of service-learning, social justice, multicultural competence, and civic engagement. *Journal of College Student Development, 49*, 95–109.

Engle, P.L., & Black, M.M. (2008). The effect of poverty on child development and educational outcomes. *Annals of the New York Academy of Science, 1136*.

Engler, B. (2014). *Personality theories* (9th ed.). Boston: Cengage.

English, D., Lambert, S.F., & Ialongo, N.S. (2014). Longitudinal associations between experienced racial discrimination and depressive symptoms in African American adolescents. *Developmental Psychology, 50*, 1190–1196.

English, T., & Carstensen, L.L. (2014). Will interventions targeting conscientiousness improve aging outcomes? *Developmental Psychology, 50*, 1478–1481.

Englund, M.M., Egeland, B., & Collins, W.A. (2008). Exceptions to high school dropout predictions in a low-income sample: Do adults make a difference? *Journal of Social Issues, 64*(1), 77–93.

Englund, M., Kuo, S., Puig, J., & Collins, W.A. (2011). Early roots of adult competence: The significance of close relationships from infancy to adulthood. *International Journal of Behavioral Development, 35*(6), 490–496.

Englund, M.M., Luckner, A.E., & Whaley, G. (2003, April). *The importance of early parenting for children's long-term educational attainment*. Paper presented at the meeting of the Society for Research in Child Development, Tampa.

Englund, M., & Siebenbruner, J. (2012). Developmental pathways linking externalizing symptoms and academic competence to adolescent substance use. *Journal of Adolescence, 35*, 1123–1140.

Engman-Bredvik, S., Suarez, N.C., Levi, R., & Nilsson, K. (2015, in press). Multi-family therapy in anorexia nervosa—a qualitative study of parental experiences. *Eating Disorders*.

Enright, R.D., Santos, M.J.D., & Al-Mabuk, R. (1989). The adolescent as forgiver. *Journal of Adolescence, 12*, 95–110.

Ensembl Human (2008). *Explore the Homo sapiens genome*. Retrieved April 14, 2008, from www.ensembl.org/Homo_sapiens/index.html

Erickson, J.B. (1982). *A profile of community youth organization members, 1980*. Boys Town, NE: Boys Town Center for the Study of Youth Development.

Ericsson, K.A. (2014). Expertise and deliberate practice. In D.K. Simonton (Ed.), *Wiley-Blackwell handbook of genius*. New York: Wiley-Blackwell.

Ericsson, K.A. (2014). Expertise. *Current Biology, 24*, R508–R510.

Ericsson, K.A., Charness, N., Feltovich, P.J., & Hoffman, R.R. (2006). *The Cambridge handbook of expertise and expert performance*. New York: Cambridge University Press.

Ericsson, K.A., Krampe, R.T., & Tesch-Römer, C. (1993). The role of deliberate practice in the acquisition of expert performance. *Psychological Review, 100*, 363–406.

Erikson, E.H. (1950). *Childhood and society*. New York: Norton.

Erikson, E.H. (1968). *Identity: Youth and crisis*. New York: Norton.

Erikson, E.H. (1969). *Gandhi's truth.* New York: Norton.

Erikson, E.H. (1970). Reflections on the dissent of contemporary youth. *International Journal of Psychoanalysis, 51,* 11–22.

Erkut, S., & others (2012). Can sex education delay early sexual debut? *Journal of Early Adolescence, 33,* 482–497.

Ernst, M., & others (2015, in press). fMRI functional connectivity applied to adolescent neurodevelopment. *Annual Review of Clinical Psychology* (Vol. 11). Palo Alto, CA: Annual Reviews.

Ernst, M., & Spear, L.P. (2009). Reward systems. In M. de Haan & M.R. Gunnar (Eds.), *Handbook of developmental social neuroscience.* New York: Guilford.

Escobar-Chaves, S.L., & Anderson, C.A. (2008). Media and risky behavior. *Future of Children, 18*(1), 147–180.

Esposito-Smythers, C., & others (2014). Suicidal behaviors in children and adolescents. In M.K. Nock (Ed.), *Oxford handbook of suicide and self-injury.* New York: Oxford University Press.

Estes, T.H., & Mintz, S.L. (2016, in press). *Instruction: A models approach* (7th ed.). Upper Saddle River, NJ: Pearson.

Etaugh, C., & Bridges, J.S. (2010). *Women's lives* (2nd ed.). Boston: Allyn & Bacon.

Evans, G.W. (2004). The environment of childhood poverty. *American Psychologist, 59,* 77–92.

Evans, G.W., & Kim, P. (2007). Childhood poverty and health: Cumulative risk exposure and stress dysregulation. *Psychological Science, 18,* 953–957.

Evans, G.W., Li, D., & Sepanski Whipple, S. (2013). Cumulative risk and child development. *Psychological Bulletin, 139,* 1342–1396.

Evans, S.Z., Simons, L.G., & Simons, R.L. (2015, in press). Factors that influence trajectories of delinquency throughout adolescence. *Journal of Youth and Adolescence.*

Everton, C.M., & Emmer, E.T. (2013). *Classroom management for elementary teachers* (9th ed.). Upper Saddle River, NJ: Pearson.

Ezkurdia, L., & others (2014). The shrinking human protein coding complement: Are there fewer than 20,000 genes? *bioRxiv,* doi:10.1101/001909.

F

Fabiano, G.A., & others (2009). A meta-analysis of behavioral treatments for attention deficit/hyperactivity disorder. *Clinical Psychology Review, 29*(2), 129–140.

Fabricus, W.V., Braver, S.L., Diaz, P., & Schenck, C. (2010). Custody and parenting time: Links to family relationships and well-being after divorce. In M.E. Lamb (Ed.), *The role of the father in child development* (5th ed.). New York: Wiley.

Fair, C.D., & Vanyur, J. (2011). Sexual coercion, verbal aggression, and condom use consistency among college students. *Journal of American College Health, 59,* 273–280.

Fairweather, E., & Cramond, B. (2011). Infusing creative and critical thinking into the classroom. In R.A. Beghetto & J.C. Kaufman (Eds.), *Nurturing creativity in the classroom.* New York: Cambridge University Press.

Falbe, J., & others (2014). Longitudinal relations of television, electronic games, and digital versatile discs with changes in diet in adolescents. *American Journal of Clinical Nutrition, 100,* 1173–1181.

Falci, C.D. (2012). Self-esteem and mastery trajectories in high school by social class and gender. *Social Science Research, 40,* 586–601.

Fan, W., & Wolters, C.A. (2014). School motivation and high school dropout: The mediating role of educational expectation. *British Journal of Educational Psychology, 84,* 22–39.

Fantasia, H.C. (2008). Concept analysis: Sexual decision-making in adolescence. *Nursing Forum, 43,* 80–90.

Farabaugh, A., & others (2012). Depression and suicide ideation in college students. *Psychopathology, 45,* 228–234.

Farioli-Vecchioli, S., & others (2014). Running rescues defective adult neurogenesis by shortening the length of the cell cycle of neural stem and progenitor cells. *Stem Cells, 32,* 1968–1982.

Faroogi, I.S., & O'Rahilly, S. (2014). 20 years of leptin: Human disorders of leptin action. *Journal of Endocrinology, 223*(1), T63–T70.

Farr, R.H., & Patterson, C.J. (2013). Coparenting among lesbian, gay, and heterosexual couples: Associations with adopted children's outcomes. *Child Development, 84,* 226–240.

Farrington, D.P. (2004). Conduct disorder, aggression, and delinquency. In R.M. Lerner & L. Steinberg (Eds.), *Handbook of adolescent psychology* (2nd ed.). New York: Wiley.

Fasick, F.A. (1994). On the "invention" of adolescence. *Journal of Early Adolescence, 14,* 6–23.

Fatusi, A.O., & Hindin, M.J. (2010). Adolescents and youths in developing countries: Health and development issues in context. *Journal of Adolescence, 33,* 499–508.

Fava, N.M., & Bay-Cheng, L.Y. (2012). Young women's adolescent experiences of oral sex: Relation of age of initiation to sexual motivation, sexual coercion, and psychological functioning. *Journal of Adolescence, 35,* 1191–1201.

Fearon, P. (2015). Editorial: Capturing the dynamics of development and psychopathology: From neural circuits to global trends. *Journal of Child Psychology and Psychiatry, 56,* 203–205.

Fearon, P., Shmuell-Goetz, Y., Viding, E., Fongagy, P., & Plomin, R. (2014). Genetic and environmental influences on adolescent attachment. *Journal of Child Psychology and Psychiatry, 55,* 1043–1046.

Feinberg, M.E., Sakuma, K-L., Hostetler, M., & McHale, S.M. (2013). Enhancing sibling relationships to prevent adolescent problem behaviors: Theory, design, and feasibility of Siblings Are Special. *Evaluation and Program Planning, 36*(1), 97–106.

Feinstein, E.E., Richter, L., & Foster, S.E. (2012). Addressing the critical health problem of adolescent substance use through health care, research, and public policy. *Journal of Adolescent Health, 50,* 431–436.

Feiring, C. (1996). Concepts of romance in 15-year-old adolescents. *Journal of Research on Adolescence, 6,* 181–200.

Feldman, S.S., & Elliott, G.R. (1990). Progress and promise of research on normal adolescent development. In S.S. Feldman & G. Elliott (Eds.), *At the threshold: The developing adolescent.* Cambridge, MA: Harvard University Press.

Feldman, S.S., & Rosenthal, D.A. (1999). *Factors influencing parents' and adolescents' evaluations of parents as sex communicators.* Unpublished manuscript, Stanford Center on Adolescence, Stanford University.

Feldman, S.S., & Rosenthal, D.A. (Eds.) (2002). *Talking sexuality: Parent-adolescent communication.* San Francisco: Jossey-Bass.

Feldman, S.S., Turner, R., & Araujo, K. (1999). Interpersonal context as an influence on sexual timetables of youths: Gender and ethnic effects. *Journal of Research on Adolescence, 9,* 25–52.

Fenichel, P. (2012). Delayed puberty. *Endocrine Development, 22,* 138–139.

Fergusson, D.M., McLeod, G.F., & Horwood, L.J. (2014). Parental separation/divorce in childhood and partnership outcomes at age 30. *Journal of Child Psychology and Psychiatry, 55,* 352–360.

Field, A.E., & others (2001). Peer, parent, and media influences on the development of weight concerns and frequent dieting among preadolescent and adolescent girls and boys. *Pediatrics, 107,* 54–60.

Field, A.E., & others (2012). Prospective association of common eating disorders and adverse outcomes. *Pediatrics, 130,* e289–e295.

Field, T., Diego, M., & Sanders, C.E. (2001). Exercise is positively related to adolescents' relationships and academics. *Adolescence, 36,* 105–110.

Fielder, R.L., Walsh, J.L., Carey, K.B., & Carey, M.P. (2013). Predictors of sexual hookups: A theory-based, prospective study of first-year college women. *Archives of Sexual Behavior, 42,* 1425–1441.

Finer, L.B., & Philbin, J.M. (2013). Sexual initiation, contraceptive use, and pregnancy among young adolescents. *Pediatrics, 31,* 886–891.

Fingerhut, A.W., & Peplau, L.A. (2013). Same-sex romantic relationships. In C.J. Patterson & A.R. D'Augelli (Eds.), *Handbook of psychology and sexual orientation.* New York: Oxford University Press.

Fingerman, K.L., & others (2011). Who gets what and why: Help middle-aged adults provide to parents and grown children. *Journals of Gerontology B: Psychological Sciences and Social Sciences, 66,* 87–98.

Fingerman, K.L., & others (2012). Helicopter parents and landing pad kids: Intense parental support of grown children. *Journal of Marriage and the Family, 74*(4), 880–896.

Fingerman, K.L., Birditt, K.S., Nussbaum, J., & Schroeder, D. (2014). Generational juggling: Midlife. In A.L. Vangelisti (Ed.), *Handbook of family communication* (2nd ed.). New York: Elsevier.

Fingerman, K.L., Pillemer, K.A., Silverstein, M., & Suitor, J.J. (2012). The Baby Boomers' intergenerational relationships. *Gerontologist, 52,* 199–209.

Fingerman, K.L., Sechrist, J., & Birditt, K. (2013). Changing views of intergenerational ties. *Gerontology, 59,* 64–70.

Finistrella, V., & others (2015, in press). Eating disorders and psychopathological traits in obese preadolescents and adolescents. *Journal of the Amrerican College of Nutrition.*

Finn, A.S., Sheridan, M.A., Kam, C.L., Hinshaw, S., & D'Esposito, M. (2010). Longitudinal evidence for functional specialization of the neural circuit supporting working memory in the human brain. *Journal of Neuroscience, 18,* 11062–11067.

Fino, E., & others (2014). Executive functions, impulsivity, and inhibitory control in adolescents: A structural equation model. *Advances in Cognitive Psychology, 10,* 32–38.

Fino, E., & others (2014). Executive functions, impulsivity, and inhibitory control in adolescents: A structural equation model. *Advances in Cognitive Psychology, 10,* 32–38.

Fiorella, L., & Mayer, R.E. (2015). Learning as a generative activity: Eight learning strategies that promote understanding. New York: Cambridge University Press.

Fiori, M., & others (2014). What is the Ability Emotional Intelligence Test (MSCEIT) good for? An evaluation using item response theory. *PLoS One, 9*(6), e08827.

Fischer, K.W., & Immordino-Yang, M.H. (2008). The fundamental importance of the brain and learning for education. In *The Jossey-Bass reader on the brain and learning.* San Francisco: Jossey-Bass.

Fischer, N., & Theis, D. (2014). Extracurricular participation and the development of school attachment and learning goal orientation: The impact of school quality. *Developmental Psychology, 50,* 1788–1793.

Fischer-Baum, S., & Rapp, B. (2014). The analysis of perseverations in acquired dysgraphia reveals the internal structure of orthographic representations. *Cognitive Neuropsychology, 31,* 237–265.

Fischhoff, B., Bruine de Bruin, W., Parker, A.M., Millstein, S.G., & Halpern-Felsher, B.L. (2010). Adolescents' perceived risk of dying. *Journal of Adolescent Health, 46,* 265–269.

Fisher, B.S., Cullen, F.T., & Turner, M.G. (2000). *The sexual victimization of college women.* Washington, DC: National Institute of Justice.

Fisher, C.B., Busch-Rossnagel, N.A., Jopp, D.S., & Brown, J.L. (2013). Applied developmental science:

Contributions and challenges for the 21st century. In I.B. Weiner & others (Eds.), *Handbook of psychology* (2nd ed., Vol. 6). New York: Wiley.

Fisher, T.D. (1987). Family communication and the sexual behavior and attitudes of college students. *Journal of Youth and Adolescence, 16,* 481–495.

Fitzgerald, A., Fitzgerald, N., & Aherne, C. (2012). Do peers matter? A review of peer and/or friends' influence on physical activity among American adolescents. *Journal of Adolescence, 35,* 941–958.

Fitzpatrick, K.K. (2012). Developmental considerations when treating anorexia nervosa in adolescents and young adults. In J. Lock (Ed.), *Oxford handbook of child and adolescent eating disorders: Developmental perspectives.* New York: Oxford University Press.

Fivush, R., Berlin, L.J., Sales, J., Mennuti-Washburn, J., & Cassidy, J. (2003). Functions of parent-child reminiscing about emotionally negative events. *Memory, 11,* 179–192.

Fivush, R., & Zaman, W. (2015). Gendered narrative voices: Sociocultural and feminist approaches to emerging identity in childhood and adolescence. In K.C. McLean & M. Syed (Eds.), *Oxford handbook of identity development.* New York: Oxford University Press.

Flanagan, A.S. (1996, March). *Romantic behavior of sexually victimized and nonvictimized women.* Paper presented at the meeting of the Society for Research on Adolescence, Boston.

Flanagan, C.A. (2004). Volunteerism leadership, political socialization, and civic engagement. In R. Lerner & L. Steinberg (Eds.), *Handbook of adolescent psychology* (2nd ed.). New York: Wiley.

Flanagan, C.A., Beyers, W., & Zukauskiene, R. (2012). Editorial: Political and civic engagement development in adolescence. *Journal of Adolescence, 35,* 471–473.

Flanagan, C.A., & Faison, N. (2001). Youth civic development: Implications for social policy and programs. *SRCD Social Policy Report, XV*(1), 1–14.

Flanagan, K.S., Vanden Hoek, K.K., Ranter, J.M., & Reich, H.A. (2012). The potential of forgiveness as a response for coping with negative peer experiences. *Journal of Adolescence, 35,* 1215–1223.

Flannery, D.J., Rowe, D.C., & Gulley, B.L. (1993). Impact of pubertal status, timing, and age on adolescent sexual experience and delinquency. *Journal of Adolescent Research, 8,* 21–40.

Flavell, J.H. (1979). Metacognition and cognitive monitoring. A new area of psychological inquiry. *American Psychologist, 34,* 906–911.

Flavell, J.H. (2004). Theory-of-mind development: Retrospect and prospect. *Merrill-Palmer Quarterly, 50,* 274–290.

Fleming, C.B., White, H.R., Oesterie, S., Haggerty, K.P., & Catalano, R.F. (2010). Romantic relationship status changes and substance abuse among 18- to 20-year-olds. *Journal of Studies on Alcohol and Drugs, 71,* 847–856.

Flint, M.S., Baum, A., Chambers, W.H., & Jenkins, F.J. (2007). Induction of DNA damage, alteration of DNA repair, and transcriptional activation by stress hormones. *Psychoneuroendocrinology 32,* 470–479.

Florence, N. (2010). *Multiculturalism 101.* New York: McGraw-Hill.

Florsheim, P.C. (Ed.) (2003). *Adolescent romantic relations and sexual behavior.* Oxford, UK: Routledge.

Florsheim, P.C. (Ed.) (2013). *Adolescent romantic relations and sexual behavior* (reissued in paperback). Oxford, UK: Routledge.

Florsheim, P., Moore, D., & Edgington, C. (2003). Romantic relationships among adolescent parents. In P.C. Florsheim (Ed.), *Adolescent romantic relations and sexual behavior.* Oxford, UK: Routledge.

Flouri, E. (2004). Correlates of parents' involvement with their adolescent children in restructured and biological two-parent families: Role of child

characteristics. *International Journal of Behavioral Development, 28,* 148–156.

Flynn, J., Hollenstein, T., & Mackey, A. (2010). The effect of suppressing and not accepting emotions on depressive symptoms: Is suppression different for men and women? *Personality and Individual Differences, 49,* 582–586.

Flynn, J.R. (1999). Searching for justice: The discovery of IQ gains over time. *American Psychologist, 54,* 5–20.

Flynn, J.R. (2007). The history of the American mind in the 20th century: A scenario to explain gains over time and a case for the irrelevance of *g.* In P.C. Kyllonen, R.D. Roberts, & L. Stankov (Eds.), *Extending intelligence.* Mahwah, NJ: Erlbaum.

Flynn, J.R. (2011). Secular changes in intelligence. In R.J. Sternberg & S.B. Kaufman (Eds.), *Cambridge handbook of intelligence.* New York: Cambridge University Press.

Flynn, J.R. (2013). *Are we getting smarter?* New York: Cambridge University Press.

Folkman, S., & Moskowitz, J.T. (2004). Coping: Pitfalls and promises. *Annual Review of Psychology* (Vol. 55). Palo Alto, CA: Annual Reviews.

Ford, D.Y. (2012). Gifted and talented education: History, issues, and recommendations. In K.R. Harris, S. Graham, & T. Urdan (Eds.), *APA handbook of educational psychology.* Washington, DC: American Psychological Association.

Ford, M.E., & Smith, P.E. (2007). Thriving with social purpose: An integrative approach to the development of optimal human functioning. *Educational Psychologist, 42,* 153–171.

Forgatch, M.S., & Patterson, G.R. (2010). Parent Management Training—Oregon Model: An intervention for antisocial behavior in children and adolescents. In J.R. Weisz & A.E. Kazdin (Eds.), *Evidence-based psychotherapies for children and adolescents* (2nd ed.). New York: Guilford.

Forgatch, M.S., Patterson, G.R., DeGarmo, D.S., & Beldavs, Z.G. (2009). Testing the Oregon delinquency model with 9-year follow-up of the Oregon Divorce Study. *Development and Psychopathology, 21,* 637–660.

Fosco, G.M., & Grych, J.H. (2010). Adolescent triangulation into parental conflicts: Longitudinal implications for appraisals and adolescent-parent relations. *Journal of Marriage and the Family, 72,* 254–266.

Fosco, G.M., Stormshak, E.A., Dishion, T.J., & Winter, C. (2012). Family relationships and parental monitoring during middle school as predictors of early adolescent problem behavior. *Journal of Clinical Child and Adolescent Psychology, 41,* 202–213.

Foshee, V.A., & others (2013). The peer context and the development of the perpetration of adolescent dating violence. *Journal of Youth and Adolescence, 42,* 471–486.

Fowler-Brown, A., & Kahwati, L.C. (2004). Prevention and treatment of overweight in children and adolescents. *American Family Physician, 69,* 2591–2598.

Fox, J., & Potocki, B. (2015, in press). Lifetime videogame consumption, interpersonal aggression, hostile sexism, and rape myth acceptance: A cultivation perspective. *Journal of Interpersonal Violence.*

Fraley, R.C., Roisman, G.I., & Haltigan, J.D. (2013). The legacy of early experiences in development: Formalizing alternative models of how early experiences are carried forward over time. *Developmental Psychology, 49*(1), 109–126.

Francis, J., Fraser, G., & Marcia, J.E. (1989). *Cognitive and experimental factors in moratorium-achievement (MAMA) cycles.* Unpublished manuscript. Department of Psychology, Simon Fraser University, Burnaby, British Columbia.

Frank, L.S. (2013). *Journey toward the caring classroom* (2nd ed.). Bethany, OK: Wood & Barnes.

Franz, C.E. (1996). The implications of preschool tempo and motoric activity level for personality decades

later. Reported in A. Caspi (1998). Personality development across the life course. In W. Damon (Ed.), *Handbook of child psychology* (Vol. 3, p. 337). New York: Wiley.

Fraser, A.M., Padilla-Walker, L.M., Coyne, S.M., Nelson, L.J., & Stockdale, L.A. (2012). Association between violent video gaming, empathic concern, and prosocial behavior toward strangers, friends, and family members. *Journal of Youth and Adolescence, 41,* 636–649.

Frazier, L.D., Barreto, M.L., & Newman, F.L. (2012). Self-regulation and eudaimonic well-being across adulthood. *Experimental Aging Research, 38,* 394–410.

Frechette, J. (2012). Beauty and body image: Beauty myths. In M. Kosut (Ed.), *Encyclopedia of gender in media.* Thousand Oaks, CA: Sage.

Frederikse, M., & others (2000). Sex differences in inferior lobule volume in schizophrenia. *American Journal of Psychiatry, 157,* 422–427.

Fredricks, J.A., & Eccles, J.S. (2006). Is extracurricular participation associated with beneficial outcomes? Concurrent and longitudinal relations. *Developmental Psychology, 42,* 698–713.

Fredstrom, B.K., Adams, R.E., & Gilman, R. (2011). Electronic and school-based victimization: Unique contexts for adjustment difficulties during adolescence. *Journal of Youth and Adolescence, 40,* 405–415.

Freeman, D. (1983). *Margaret Mead and Samoa.* Cambridge, MA: Harvard University Press.

French, D.C., Purwono, U., & Rodkin, P.C. (2012). Religiosity of adolescents and their friends and network associates: Homophily and associations with antisocial behavior. *Journal of Research on Adolescence, 22,* 326–332.

Freud, A. (1966). Instinctual anxiety during puberty. In *The writings of Anna Freud: The ego and the mechanisms of defense.* New York: International Universities Press.

Freud, S. (1917). *A general introduction to psychoanalysis.* New York: Washington Square Press.

Frideres, J.E., Mottinger, S.G., & Palao, J.M. (2015, in press). Collegiate coaches' knowledge of the female athlete triad in relation to sport type. *Journal of Sports Medicine and Physical Fitness.*

Fried, L.E., Williams, S., Cabral, H., & Hacker, K. (2013). Differences in risk factors for suicide attempts among 9th and 11th grade youth: A longitudinal perspective. *Journal of School Nursing, 29,* 113–122.

Friedberg, R.D., & McClure, J.M. (2015). *Clinical practice of cognitive therapy with children and adolescents* (2nd ed.). New York: Guilford.

Friedman, J. (2013). Twin separation. Retrieved February 14, 2013, from http://christinabaglivitinglof.com/twin-pregnancy/six-twin-experts-tell-all/

Friedman, L., & others (2011). Human papillomavirus vaccine: An updated position of the Society for Adolescent Health and Medicine. *Journal of Adolescent Health, 48,* 215–216.

Friend, M. (2014). *Special education* (4th ed.). Upper Saddle River, NJ: Merrill.

Frimer, J.A., Walker, L.J., Dunlop, W.L., Lee, B., & Riches, A. (2011). The integration of agency and communion in moral personality: Evidence of enlightened self-interest. *Journal of Personality and Social Psychology, 101,* 149–163.

Frisen, A., & Holmqvist, K. (2010). What characterizes early adolescents with a positive body image? A qualitative investigation of Swedish boys and girls. *Body Image, 7,* 205–212.

Froh, J.J., Yurkewicz, C., & Kashdan, T.B. (2009). Gratitude and subjective well-being in early adolescence: Examining gender differences. *Journal of Adolescence, 32,* 633–650.

Fromme, K., Corbin, W.R., & Kruse, M.I. (2008). Behavioral risks during the transition from high school to college. *Developmental Psychology, 44,* 1497–1504.

Frost, D.M. (2011). Stigma and intimacy in same-sex relationships: A narrative approach. *Journal of Family Psychology, 25,* 1–10.

Frost, J., & McKelvie, S. (2004). Self-esteem and body satisfaction in male and female elementary school, high school, and university students. *Sex Roles, 51,* 45–54.

Fruiht, V.M., & Wray-Lake, L. (2013). The role of mentor type and timing in predicting educational attainment. *Journal of Youth and Adolescence, 42,* 1459–1472.

Fuemmeler, B.F., & others (2012). Parenting styles and body mass index trajectories from adolescence to adulthood. *Health Psychology, 31,* 441–449.

Fuglset, T.S., Endestad, T., Landro, N.I., & Ro, O. (2015). Brain structure alterations associated with weight changes in young females with anorexia nervosa: A case series. *Neurocase, 21,* 169–177.

Fuhs, M.W., Nesbitt, K.T., Farran, D.C., & Dong, N. (2014). Longitudinal associations between executive functioning and academic skills across content areas. *Developmental Psychology, 50,* 1698–1709.

Fuligni, A.J. (2012). Gaps, conflicts, and arguments between adolescents and their parents. *New Directions for Child and Adolescent Development, 135,* 105–110.

Fuligni, A., Hughes, D.L., & Way, N. (2009). Ethnicity and immigration. In R.M. Lerner & L. Steinberg (Eds.), *Handbook of adolescent psychology* (3rd ed.). New York: Wiley.

Fuligni, A., & Stevenson, H.W. (1995). Time use and mathematics achievement among American, Chinese, and Japanese high school students. *Child Development, 66,* 830–842.

Fuligni, A.J., & Telzer, E.H. (2012). The contributions of youth to immigrant families. In A.S. Masten & others (Eds.), *Realizing the potential of immigrant youth.* New York: Cambridge University Press.

Fuligni, A.J., & Tsai, K.M. (2015). Developmental flexibility in the age of globalization: Autonomy and identity development among immigrant adolescents. *Annual Review of Psychology* (Vol. 66). Palo Alto, CA: Annual Reviews.

Fuligni, A.J., Tseng, V., & Lamb, M. (1999). Attitudes toward family obligations among American adolescents from Asian, Latin American, and European backgrounds. *Child Development, 70,* 1030–1044.

Fuller-Roswell, T.E., Evans, G.W., Paul, E., & Curtis, D.S. (2015, in press). The role of poverty and chaos in the development of task persistence among adolescents. *Journal of Research on Adolescence.*

Fung, C., & others (2012). From "best practice" to "next practice": The effectiveness of school-based health promotion in improving healthy eating and physical activity and preventing childhood obesity. *International Journal of Behavioral Nutrition and Physical Activity, 9,* 27.

Furman, E. (2005). *Boomerang nation.* New York: Fireside.

Furman, W. (2002). The emerging field of adolescent romantic relationships. *Current Directions in Psychological Science, 11,* 177–180.

Furman, W., Low, S., & Ho, M.J. (2009). Romantic experience and psychosocial adjustment in middle adolescence. *Journal of Clinical Child and Adolescent Psychology, 38,* 75–90.

Furman, W., & Rose, A.J. (2015). Friendships, romantic relationships, and other dyadic peer relationships in childhood and adolescence: A unified relational perspective. In R.M. Lerner (Ed.), *Handbook of child psychology and developmental science* (7th ed.). New York: Wiley.

Furman, W., & Shaffer, L. (2003). The role of romantic relationships in adolescent development. In P. Florsheim (Ed.), *Adolescent romantic relations and sexual behavior.* Mahwah, NJ: Erlbaum.

Furman, W., & Shaffer, L. (2013). The role of romantic relationships in adolescent development. In P. Florsheim (Ed.), *Adolescent romantic relations and sexual behavior* (paperback edition). Mahwah, NJ: Erlbaum.

Furman, W., & Simon, V.A. (2008). Homophily in adolescent romantic relationships. In M.J. Prinstein & K.A. Dodge (Eds.), *Understanding peer influence in children and adolescents.* New York: Guilford.

Furman, W., & Wehner, E.A. (1998). Adolescent romantic relationships: A developmental perspective. In S. Shulman & W.A. Collins (Eds.), *New directions for child development: Adolescent romantic relationships.* San Francisco: Jossey-Bass.

Furman, W., & Winkles, J.K. (2010). Predicting romantic involvement, relationship cognitions, and relational styles regarding friends and parents. *Journal of Adolescence, 33,* 827–836.

Furstenberg, F.F. (2006). Growing up healthy: Are adolescents the right target group? *Journal of Adolescent Health, 39,* 303–304.

Furstenberg, F.F. (2007). The future of marriage. In A.S. Skolnick & J.H. Skolnick (Eds.), *Family in transition* (14th ed.). Boston: Allyn & Bacon.

Fussell, E., & Greene, M.E. (2002). Demographic trends affecting youth around the world. In B.B. Brown, R.W. Larson, & T.S. Saraswathi (Eds.), *The world's youth.* New York: Cambridge University Press.

G

Gabel, K., Pinhas, L., Eisler, I., Katzman, D., & Heinmaa, M. (2014). The effect of multiple family therapy on weight gain in adolescents with anorexia nervosa: Pilot data. *Journal of the Canadian Academy of Child and Adolescent Psychiatry, 23,* 196–199.

Gabor, M. (2014, March). New college degree in hand: Now what? *Monthly Labor Review.* Washington, DC: U.S. Department of Labor.

Gadbois, S.A., & Sturgeon, R.D. (2011). Academic self-handicapping: Relationships with learning-specific and general self-perceptions and academic performance over time. *British Journal of Educational Psychology, 81,* 207–222.

Galambos, N.L., Barker, E.T., & Krahn, H.J. (2006). Depression, self-esteem, and anger in emerging adulthood: Seven-year trajectories. *Developmental Psychology, 42,* 350–365.

Galambos, N.L., Berenbaum, S.A., & McHale, S.M. (2009). Gender development in adolescents. In R.M. Lerner & L. Steinberg (Eds.), *Handbook of adolescent psychology* (3rd ed.). New York: Wiley.

Galambos, N.L., Howard, A.L., & Maggs, J.L. (2011). Rise and fall of sleep quality with student experiences across the first year of the university. *Journal of Research on Adolescence, 21,* 342–349.

Galambos, N.L., & Maggs, J.L. (1991). Out-of-school care of young adolescents and self-reported behavior. *Developmental Psychology, 27,* 644–655.

Gale, C.R., Booth, T., Mottus, R., Kuh, D., & Deary, J.J. (2013). Neuroticism and extraversion in youth predict mental wellbeing and life satisfaction 40 years later. *Journal of Research in Personality, 47,* 687–697.

Galinsky, E. (2010). *Mind in the making.* New York: HarperCollins.

Galliher, R.V., & Kerpelman, J.L. (2012). The intersection of identity development and peer relationship processes in adolescence and young adulthood: Contributions of the special issue. *Journal of Adolescence, 35,* 1409–1415.

Galupo, M.P., Cartwright, K.B., & Savage, L.S. (2010). Cross-category friendships and postformal thought among college students. *Journal of Adult Development, 17,* 208–214.

Galvan, A., Hare, T., Voss, H., Glover, G., & Casey, B.J. (2007). Risk-taking and the adolescent brain: Who is at risk? *Developmental Science, 10,* F8–F14.

Ganahl, D.J., Prinsen, T.J., & Netzley, S.B. (2003). A content analysis of prime time commercials: A contextual framework of gender representation. *Sex Roles, 49,* 545–551.

Ganley, C.M., Vasilyeva, M., & Dulaney, A. (2014). Spatial ability mediates the gender difference in middle school students' science performance. *Child Development, 85,* 1419–1432.

Ganong, L., Coleman, M., & Russell, L. (2015). Children in diverse families. In R.M. Lerner (Ed.), *Handbook of child psychology and developmental science* (7th ed.). New York: Wiley.

Garber, J., & Cole, D.A. (2010). Intergenerational transmission of depression: A launch and grow model of change across adolescence. *Development and Psychopathology, 22,* 819–830.

Garcia Coll, C., & others (2012). Understanding the immigrant paradox in youth: Developmental and contextual considerations. In A.S. Masten & others (Eds.), *Realizing the potential of immigrant youth.* New York: Cambridge University Press.

Garcia, E.E. (2012). Latino education in the United States: Immigration, language, and achievement. In A.S. Masten & others (Eds.), *Realizing the potential of immigrant youth.* New York: Cambridge University Press.

Garcia-Lopez, L.J., Diaz-Castela, M.D., Muela-Martinez, J.A., & Espinosa-Fernandez, L. (2014). Can parent training for parents with high levels of expressed emotion have a positive effect on their child's social anxiety improvement? *Journal of Anxiety Disorders, 28,* 812–822.

Gardner, H. (1983). *Frames of mind.* New York: Basic Books.

Gardner, H. (1993). *Multiple intelligences.* New York: Basic Books.

Gardner, H. (2002). The pursuit of excellence through education. In M. Ferrari (Ed.), *Learning from extraordinary minds.* Mahwah, NJ: Erlbaum.

Gardner, H. (2012). Foreword. In D. Ambrose, R. Sternberg, & B. Sriraman (Eds.), *Confronting dogmatism in gifted education.* New York: Routledge.

Gardner, H. (2014). Theories of intelligence. In M.A. Bray & T.J. Kehle (Eds.), *Oxford handbook of school psychology.* New York: Oxford University Press.

Gardner, M., Browning, C., & Brooks-Gunn, J. (2012). Can organized youth activities protect against internalizing problems among adolescents living in violent homes? *Journal of Research in Adolescence, 22,* 662–677.

Gardner, M., Martin, A., & Brooks-Gunn, J. (2012). Exploring the link between caregiver affect and adolescent sexual behavior: Does neighborhood disadvantage matter? *Journal of Research on Adolescence, 22,* 135–149.

Gardner, M., Roth, J., & Brooks-Gunn, J. (2008). Adolescents' participation in organized activities and developmental success 2 and 8 years after high school: Do sponsorship, duration, and intensity matter? *Developmental Psychology, 44,* 814–830.

Gardner, M., & Steinberg, L. (2005). Peer influence on risk taking, risk preference, and risky decision making in adolescence and adulthood: An experimental study. *Developmental Psychology, 41,* 625–635.

Garfield, C.F., & others (2012). Trends in attention deficit hyperactivity disorder ambulatory diagnosis and medical treatment in the United States, 2000–2010. *Academic Pediatrics, 12,* 110–116.

Garneau, C.L., & Adler-Baeder, F. (2015, in press). Changes in stepparents' coparenting and parenting following participation in a community-based relationship education program. *Family Process.*

Garofalo, R., Wolf, R.C., Wissow, L.S., Woods, E.R., & Goodman, E. (1999). Sexual orientation and risk of suicide attempts among a representative sample of youth. *Archives of Pediatrics and Adolescent Medicine, 153,* 487–493.

Garrod, A., Smulyan, L., Powers, S.I., & Kilenny, R. (1992). *Adolescent portraits.* Boston: Allyn & Bacon.

Gartland, N., O'Connor, D.B., Lawton, R., & Ferguson, R. (2014). Investigating the effects of conscientiousness on daily stress, affect, and physical symptom processes: A daily diary study. *British Journal of Health Psychology, 19,* 311–328.

Gates, W. (1998, July 20). Charity begins when I'm ready (interview). *Fortune magazine.*

Gaudreau, P., Amiot, C.E., & Vallerand, R.J. (2009). Trajectories of affective states in adolescent hockey players: Turning point and motivational antecedents. *Developmental Psychology, 45,* 307–319.

Gauvain, M. (2013). Sociocultural contexts of development. In P.D. Zelazo (Ed.), *Oxford handbook of developmental psychology.* New York: Oxford University Press.

Gauvain, M., & Perez, S. (2015). Cognitive development in the context of culture. In R.M. Lerner (Ed.), *Handbook of child psychology and developmental science* (7th ed.). New York: Wiley.

Gauvain, M., & Perez, S.M. (2007). The socialization of cognition. In J.E. Grusec & P.D. Hastings (Eds.), *Handbook of socialization.* New York: Guilford.

Gavazzi, S. (2013). Theory and research pertaining to families with adolescents. In G.W. Peterson & K.R. Bush (Eds.), *Handbook of marriage and the family* (3rd ed.). New York: Springer.

Gavin, L.E., Catalano, R.F., David-Ferdon, C., Gloppen, K.M., & Markham, C.M. (2010). A review of positive youth development programs that promote adolescent sexual and reproductive health. *Journal of Adolescent Health, 46*(Suppl 1), S75–S91.

Geary, D.C. (2010). *Male, female: The evolution of sex differences.* Washington, DC: American Psychological Association.

Gecas, V., & Seff, M. (1990). Families and adolescents: A review of the 1980s. *Journal of Marriage and the Family, 52,* 941–958.

Geldhof, G.J., Bowers, E., Gestsdottir, S., Napolitano, C.M., & Lerner, R.M. (2015, in press). Self-regulation across adolescence: Exploring the structure of selection, optimization, and compensation. *Journal of Research on Adolescence.*

Gentile, D.A. (2011). The multiple dimensions of video game effects. *Child Development Perspectives, 5,* 75–81.

Gentile, D.A., Mathieson, L.C., & Crick, N.R. (2010). Media violence associations with the form and function of aggression among elementary school children. *Social Development, 20*(2), 213–232.

Gentile, D.A., & others (2009). The effects of prosocial video games on prosocial behaviors: International evidence from correlational, longitudinal, and experimental studies. *Personality and Social Psychology Bulletin, 35,* 752–763.

Gentile, D.A., & others (2014a). Mediators and moderators of long-term effects of violent video games on aggressive behavior: Practice, thinking, and action. *JAMA Pediatrics, 168,* 450–457.

Gentile, D.A., & others (2014b). Protective effects of parental monitoring of children's media use: A prospective study. *JAMA Pediatrics, 168,* 479–484.

Geoffrey, M.C., Li, L., & Power, C. (2014). Depressive symptoms and body mass index: Co-morbidity and directions of association in a British birth cohort followed over 50 years. *Psychology and Medicine, 44,* 2641–2652.

George, C., Main, M., & Kaplan, N. (1984). *Attachment interview with adults.* Unpublished manuscript, University of California, Berkeley.

Gerrard, M., Gibbons, F.X., Houlihan, A.E., Stock, M.L., & Pomery, E.A. (2008). A dual-process approach to health risk decision-making: The prototype willingness model. *Developmental Review, 28,* 29–61.

Gershoff, E.T., & Benner, A.D. (2014). Neighborhood and school contexts in the lives of children. In E.T. Gershoff, R.S. Mistry, & D.A. Crosby (Eds.), *Societal contexts of child development.* New York: Oxford University Press.

Gestsdottir, S., Lewin-Bizan, S., von Eye, A., Lerner, J.V., & Lerner, R.M. (2009). The structure and function of selection, optimization, and compensation in adolescence: Theoretical and applied implications. *Journal of Applied Developmental Psychology, 30*(5), 585–600.

Gevensleben, H., & others (2014). Neurofeedback in ADHD: Further pieces of the puzzle. *Brain Topography, 27,* 20–32.

Ghazarian, S.R., & Roche, K.M. (2010). Social support and low-income, urban mothers: Longitudinal associations with delinquency. *Journal of Youth and Adolescence, 39,* 1097–1108.

Gibbs, J.C. (2010). *Moral development and reality: Beyond the theories of Kohlberg and Hoffman* (2nd ed.). Boston: Allyn & Bacon.

Gibbs, J.C. (2014). *Moral development and reality* (3rd ed.). New York: Oxford University Press.

Gibbs, J.C., Basinger, K.S., Grime, R.L., & Snarey, J.R. (2007). Moral judgment across cultures: Revisiting Kohlberg's universality claims. *Developmental Review, 27,* 443–500.

Gibbs, J.T. (1989). Black American adolescents. In J.T. Gibbs & L.N. Huang (Eds.), *Children of color.* San Francisco: Jossey-Bass.

Gibbs, J.T., & Huang, L.N. (1989). A conceptual framework for assessing and treating minority youth. In J.T. Gibbs & L.N. Huang (Eds.), *Children of color.* San Francisco: Jossey-Bass.

Gibson-Davis, C., & Rackin, H. (2014). Marriage or carriage? Trends in union context and birth type by education. *Journal of Marriage and the Family, 76,* 506–519.

Giedd, J.N. (2007, September 27). Commentary in S. Jayson, "Teens driven to distraction." *USA Today,* pp. D1–D2.

Giedd, J.N. (2008). The teen brain: Insights from neuroimaging. *Journal of Adolescent Health, 42,* 335–343.

Giedd, J.N. (2012). The digital revolution and the adolescent brain. *Journal of Adolescent Health, 51,* 101–105.

Giedd, J.N., & others (2012). Anatomic magnetic resonance imaging of the developing child and adolescent brain. In V.F. Reyna & others (Eds.), *The adolescent brain.* Washington, DC: American Psychological Association.

Giletta, M., & others (2015). Trajectories of suicide ideation and nonsuicidal self-injury among adolescents in mainland China: Peer predictors, joint development, and risk for suicide attempts. *Journal of Consulting and Clinical Psychology, 83,* 265–279.

Gillen-O'Neel, C., Huynh, V.W., & Fuligni, A.J. (2013). To study or to sleep? The academic costs of extra studying at the expense of sleep. *Child Development, 84*(1), 133–142.

Gilligan, C. (1982). *In a different voice.* Cambridge, MA: Harvard University Press.

Gilligan, C. (1992, May). *Joining the resistance: Girls' development in adolescence.* Paper presented at the symposium on development and vulnerability in close relationships, Montreal.

Gilligan, C. (1996). The centrality of relationships in psychological development: A puzzle, some evidence, and a theory. In G.G. Noam & K.W. Fischer (Eds.), *Development and vulnerability in close relationships.* Hillside, NJ: Erlbaum.

Gilligan, C., Brown, L.M., & Rogers, A.G. (1990). Psyche embedded: A place for body, relationships, and culture in personality theory. In A.I. Rabin, R.A. Zuker, R.A. Emmons, & S. Frank (Eds.), *Studying persons and lives.* New York: Springer.

Gilligan, C., Spencer, R., Weinberg, M.K., & Bertsch, T. (2003). On the listening guide: A voice-centered relational model. In P.M. Carnie & J.E. Rhodes (Eds.), *Qualitative research in psychology.* Washington, DC: American Psychological Association.

Gilmartin, S.K. (2006). Changes in college women's attitudes toward sexual intimacy. *Journal of Research on Adolescence, 16,* 429–454.

Gil-Olarte Marquez, P., Palomera Martin, R., & Brackett, M. (2006). Relating emotional intelligence to social competence and academic achievement in high school students. *Psicothema, 18,* 118–123.

Ginorio, A.B., & Huston, M. (2001). *Si! Se puede! Yes, we can: Latinas in school.* Washington, DC: AAUW.

Girls Inc. (1991). *Truth, trusting, and technology: New research on preventing adolescent pregnancy.* Indianapolis, IN: Author.

Glassman, J.R., Potter, S.C., Baumier, E.R., & Coyle, K.K. (2015, in press). Estimates of intraclass correlation coefficients from longitudinal group-randomized trials of adolescent HIV/STI/pregnancy prevention programs. *Health Education and Behavior.*

Glazebrook, K., Townsend, E., & Sayal, K. (2015, in press). The role of attachment style in predicting repetition of adolescent self-harm: A longitudinal study. *Suicide and Life-Threatening Behavior.*

Glenn, N.D. (2005). *Fatherhood in America.* Report to the National Fatherhood Initiative, Washington, DC.

Glidden-Tracey, C. (2005). *Counseling and therapy with clients who abuse alcohol or other drugs.* Mahwah, NJ: Erlbaum.

Glover, V. (2014). Maternal depression, anxiety, and stress during pregnancy and child outcome: What needs to be done. *Best Practice and Research: Clinical Obstetrics and Gynecology, 28,* 25–35.

Godier, L.R., & Park, R.J. (2014). Compulsivity in anorexia nervosa: A transdiagnostic concept. *Frontiers in Psychology, 5,* 778.

Gogtay, N., & Thompson, P.M. (2010). Mapping grey matter development: Implications for typical development and vulnerability to psychopathology. *Brain and Cognition, 72,* 6–15.

Goji, K., & others (2009). Gonadotropin-independent precocious puberty associated with somatic activation mutation of the LH receptor gene. *Endocrine, 35,* 397–401.

Gold, M.A., & others (2010). Associations between religiosity and sexual and contraceptive behaviors. *Journal of Pediatric and Adolescent Gynecology, 23,* 290–297.

Gold, M.S., Blum, K., Oscar-Berman, M., & Braverman, E.R. (2014). Low dopamine function in attention deficit/hyperactivity disorder: Should genotyping signify early diagnosis in children? *Postgraduate Medicine, 126,* 153–177.

Goldberg, J.S., & Carlson, M.J. (2015, in press). Patterns and predictors of coparenting after unmarried parents part. *Journal of Family Psychology.*

Goldberg, W.A., & Lucas-Thompson, R. (2008). Maternal and paternal employment, effects of. In M.M. Haith & J.B. Benson (Eds.), *Encyclopedia of infant and early childhood development.* Oxford, UK: Elsevier.

Goldschmidt, A.B., & others (2012). Momentary affect surrounding loss of control and overeating in obese adults with and without binge eating disorder. *Obesity, 20,* 1206–1211.

Goldston, D.B., & others (2008). Cultural considerations in adolescent suicide prevention and psychosocial treatment. *American Psychologist, 63,* 14–31.

Goleman, D. (1995). *Emotional intelligence.* New York: Basic Books.

Golombok, S. (2011a). Children in new family forms. In R. Gross (Ed.), *Psychology* (6th ed.). London: Hodder.

Golombok, S. (2011b). Why I study lesbian families. In S. Ellis, V. Clarke, E. Peel, & D. Riggs (Eds.), *LGBTQ psychologies.* New York: Cambridge University Press.

Golombok, S., & Tasker, F. (2015). Socio-emotional development in changing family contexts. In R.M. Lerner (Ed.), *Handbook of child psychology and developmental science* (7th ed.). New York: Wiley.

Golombok, S., & others (2014). Adoptive gay father families: Parent-child relationships and children's psychological adjustment. *Child Development, 85,* 456–468.

Gong, Y., & others (2014). Case-control resting state fMRI study of brain functioning among adolescents with first-episode major depressive disorder. *Shanghai Archives of Psychiatry, 26,* 207–215.

Gonzales, M., Jones, D.J., Kincaid, C.Y., & Cuellar, J. (2012). Neighborhood context and adjustment in African American youths from single-mother homes: The intervening role of hopelessness. *Cultural Diversity and Ethnic Minority Psychology, 18,* 109–117.

Gonzales, M., Jones, D., & Parent, J. (2014). Coparenting experiences in African American families: An examination of single mothers and their nonmarital coparents. *Family Process, 53,* 33–54.

Gonzales, N.A., Dumka, L.E., Muaricio, A.M., & German, M. (2007). Building bridges: Strategies to promote academic and psychological resilience for adolescents of Mexican origin. In J.E. Lansford, K. Deater-Deckard, & M.H. Bornstein (Eds.), *Immigrant families in contemporary society.* New York: Guilford.

Good, C., Rattan, A., & Dweck, C.S. (2012). Why do women opt out? Sense of belonging and women's representation in mathematics. *Journal of Personality and Social Psychology, 102,* 700–717.

Good, M., & Willoughby, T. (2008). Adolescence as a sensitive period for spiritual development. *Child Development Perspectives, 2,* 32–37.

Good, M., & Willoughby, T. (2010). Evaluating the direction of effects in the relationship between religious versus non-religious activities, academic success, and substance use. *Journal of Youth and Adolescence, 40,* 680–693.

Goodkind, S. (2013). Single-sex public education for low-income youth of color: A critical theoretical review. *Sex Roles, 69,* 363–381.

Goodman, W.B., & others (2011). Parental work stress and latent profiles of father-infant parenting quality. *Journal of Marriage and the Family, 73,* 588–604.

Goodnow, J.J., & Lawrence, J.A. (2015). Children and cultural context. In R.M. Lerner (Ed.), *Handbook of child psychology and developmental science* (7th ed.). New York: Wiley.

Goossens, L. (2006, March). *Parenting, identity, and adjustment in adolescence.* Paper presented at the meeting of the Society for Research on Adolescence, San Francisco.

Goossens, L., Beyers, W., Emmen, M., & van Aken, M.A.G. (2002). The imaginary audience and personal fable. Factor analyses and concurrent validity of the "new look" measures. *Journal of Research on Adolescence, 12,* 193–215.

Goossens, L., & Luyckx, K. (2007). Identity development in college students: Variable-centered and person-centered analysis. In M. Watzlawik & A. Born (Eds.), *Capturing identity.* Lanham, MD: University of America Press.

Gorchoff, S.M., John, O.P., & Helson, R. (2008). Contextualizing change in marital satisfaction during middle age: An 18-year longitudinal study. *Psychological Science, 19,* 1194–2000.

Gordon-Messer, D., Bauermeister, J.A., Grodzinski, A., & Zimmerman, M. (2013). Sexting among young adults. *Journal of Adolescent Health, 52*(2), 301–306.

Gorrese, A., & Ruggieri, R. (2012). Peer attachment: A meta-analytic review of gender and age differences and associations with parent attachment. *Journal of Youth and Adolescence, 41,* 650–672.

Gottfried, A.E., Marcoulides, G.A., Gottfried, A.W., & Oliver, P.H. (2009). A latent curve model of motivational practices and developmental decline in math and science academic intrinsic motivation. *Journal of Educational Psychology, 101,* 729–739.

Gottfried, A.E., Marcoulides, G.A., Gottfried, A.W., & Oliver, P.H. (2013). Longitudinal pathways from math intrinsic motivation and achievement to math course accomplishments and educational attainment. *Journal of Research on Educational Effectiveness, 6,* 68–92.

Gottlieb, G. (2007). Probabilistic epigenesis. *Developmental Science, 10,* 1–11.

Gottman, J.M., & Parker, J.G. (Eds.). (1987). *Conversations of friends.* New York: Cambridge University Press.

Gould, S.J. (1981). *The mismeasure of man.* New York: W.W. Norton.

Gourlan, M., Sant, F., & Boiche, J. (2014). Impact of a supervised exercise program supporting autonomy on the adoption of an active lifestyle among obese adolescents: A self-determination theory perspective. *Journal of Sports Medicine and Physical Fitness, 54,* 793–801.

Gove, W.R., Style, C.B., & Hughes, M. (1990). The effect of marriage on the well-being of adults: A theoretical analysis. *Journal of Health and Social Behavior, 24,* 122–131.

Graber, J.A., Brooks-Gunn, J., & Warren, M.P. (2006). Pubertal effects on adjustment in girls: Moving from demonstrating effects to identifying pathways. *Journal of Youth and Adolescence, 35,* 391–401.

Graber, J.A., & Sontag, L.M. (2009). Internalizing problems during adolescence. In R.M. Lerner & L. Steinberg (Eds.), *Handbook of adolescent psychology* (3rd ed.). New York: Wiley.

Gradisar, M., Gardner, G., & Dohnt, H. (2011). Recent worldwide sleep patterns and problems during adolescence: A review and meta-analysis of age, region, and sleep. *Sleep Medicine, 12,* 110–118.

Graham, E.A. (2005). Economic, racial, and cultural influences on the growth and maturation of children. *Pediatrics in Review, 26,* 290–294.

Graham, S. (1986, August). *Can attribution theory tell us something about motivation in blacks?* Paper presented at the meeting of the American Psychological Association, Washington, DC.

Graham, S. (1990). Motivation in Afro-Americans. In G.L. Berry & J.K. Asamen (Eds.), *Black students: Psychosocial issues and academic achievement.* Newbury Park, CA: Sage.

Graham, S., & Perin, D. (2007). A meta-analysis of writing instruction for adolescent students. *Journal of Educational Psychology, 99,* 445–476.

Graham, S., & Taylor, A.Z. (2001). Ethnicity, gender, and the development of achievement values. In A. Wigfield & J.S. Eccles (Eds.), *Development of achievement motivation.* San Diego: Academic Press.

Graham, S., & Weiner, B. (2012). Motivation: Past, present, and future. In K.R. Harris & others (Eds.), *Handbook of educational psychology.* Washington, DC: American Psychological Association.

Granger, R.C., Tseng, V., & Wilcox, B.L. (2014). Connecting research and policy. In E.T. Gershoff, R.S. Mistry, & D.A. Crosby (Eds.), *Societal contexts of child development.* New York: Oxford University Press.

Granqvist, P., & Dickie, J.R. (2006). Attachment and spiritual development in childhood and adolescence. In E.C. Roehlkepartain, P.E. King, & L.M. Wegener (Eds.), *The handbook of spiritual development in childhood and adolescence.* Thousand Oaks, CA: Sage.

Grant, A.M., & Gino, F. (2010). A little thanks goes a long way: Explaining why gratitude expressions motivate prosocial behavior. *Journal of Personality and Social Psychology, 98,* 946–955.

Graves, K.N., Sentner, A., Workman, J., & Mackey, W. (2011). Building positive life skills the Smart Girls Way: Evaluation of a school-based sexual responsibility program for adolescent girls. *Health Promotion Practice, 12,* 463–471.

Gravetter, F.J., & Forzano, L.B. (2016, in press). *Research methods for the behavioral sciences* (5th ed.). Boston: Cengage.

Gray, J. (1992). *Men are from Mars, women are from Venus.* New York: HarperCollins.

Gray, W.N., Janicke, D.M., Ingerski, L.M., & Silverstein, J.H. (2008). The impact of peer victimization, parent distress, and child depression on barrier formation and physical activity in overweight youth. *Journal of Developmental Behavioral & Pediatrics, 29,* 26–33.

Greenberg, M.T., & others (2003). Enhancing school-based prevention and youth development through coordinated social, emotional, and academic learning. *American Psychologist, 58,* 466–474.

Greenberger, E., & Chu, C. (1996). Perceived family relationships and depressed mood in early adolescence: A comparison of European and Asian Americans. *Developmental Psychology, 32,* 707–716.

Greenberger, E., & Steinberg, L. (1986). *When teenagers work: The psychological and social costs of adolescent employment.* New York: Basic Books.

Greene, B. (1988, May). The children's hour. *Esquire,* pp. 47–49.

Greenhaus, J., & Callanan, G.A. (2013). Career dynamics. In I.B. Weiner & others (Eds.), *Handbook of psychology* (2nd ed.). New York: Wiley.

Greenwood, P. (2008). Prevention and intervention programs for juvenile offenders. *The Future of Children, 18*(2), 185–210.

Gregoire, C.A., & others (2014). Untangling the influence of voluntary running, environmental complexity, social housing, and stress on adult hippocampal neurogenesis. *PLoS One, 9*(1), e86237.

Gregorson, M., Kaufman, J.C., & Snyder, H. (Eds.). (2013). *Teaching creatively and teaching creativity.* New York: Springer.

Gregory, A., & Huang, F. (2013). It takes a village: The effects of 10th grade college-going expectations of students, parents, and teachers four years later. *American Journal of Community Psychology, 52,* 41–55.

Grigorenko, E. (2000). Heritability and intelligence. In R.J. Sternberg (Ed.), *Handbook of intelligence.* New York: Cambridge University Press.

Grigsby, T., & others (2014). Do adolescent drug use consequences predict externalizing and internalizing problems in emerging adulthood as well as traditional drug use measures in a Hispanic sample? *Addictive Behaviors, 39,* 644–651.

Grijalva, E., & others (2015). Gender differences in narcissism: A meta-analytic review. *Psychological Bulletin, 141,* 261–310.

Grollman, E.A. (2012). Multiple forms of perceived discrimination and health among adolescents and young adults. *Journal of Health and Social Behavior, 53,* 199–214.

Gross, J.J., Fredrickson, B.L., & Levenson, R.W. (1994). The psychophysiology of crying. *Psychophysiology, 31,* 460–468.

Grossman, J.B., Chan, J.S., Schwartz, S.E., & Rhoades, J.E. (2012). The test of time in school-based mentoring: The role of relationship duration and re-matching on educational outcomes. *American Journal of Community Psychology, 49,* 43–54.

Grotevant, H.D., & McDermott, J.M. (2014) Adoption: Biological and social processes linked to adaptation. *Annual Review of Psychology* (Vol. 65). Palo Alto, CA: Annual Reviews.

Grotevant, H.D., McRoy, R.G., Wrobel, G.M., & Ayers-Lopez, S. (2013). Contact between adoptive and birth families: Perspectives from the Minnesota/Texas Adoption Research Project. *Child Development Perspectives, 7,* 193–198.

Gruber, K.J. (2012). A comparative assessment of early adult life status of graduates of the North Carolina adolescent parenting program. *Journal of Child and Adolescent Psychiatric Nursing, 25,* 75–83.

Grusec, J.E. (2006). Development of moral behavior and a conscience from a socialization perspective. In M. Killen & J.G. Smetana (Eds.), *Handbook of moral development.* Mahwah, NJ: Erlbaum.

Grusec, J.E., Chaparro, M.P., Johnson, M., & Sherman, A. (2014). The development of moral behavior from a socialization perspective. In M. Killen & J.G. Smetana (Eds.), *Handbook of moral development* (2nd ed.). New York: Psychology Press.

Grusec, J.E., & Davidov, M. (2015). Analyzing socialization from a domain-specific perspective. In J.E. Grusec & P.D. Hastings (Eds.), *Handbook of socialization* (2nd ed.). New York: Guilford.

Grych, J.H. (2002). Marital relationships and parenting. In M.H. Bornstein (Ed.), *Handbook of parenting*. Mahwah, NJ: Erlbaum.

Guerin, D.W., Gottfried, A.W., Oliver, P.H., & Thomas, C.W. (2003). *Temperament: Infancy through adolescence*. New York: Kluwer.

Guida, A., Gobet, F., Tardieu, H., & Nicolas, S. (2012). How chunks, long-term memory and templates offer a cognitive explanation for neuroimaging data on expertise acquisition: A two-stage framework. *Brain and Cognition, 79,* 221–224.

Guilamo-Ramos, V., Jaccard, J., Dittus, P., & Collins, S. (2008). Parent-adolescent communication about sexual intercourse: An analysis of maternal reluctance to communicate. *Health Psychology, 27,* 760–769.

Guilford, J.P. (1967). *The structure of intellect*. New York: McGraw-Hill.

Gumora, G., & Arsenio, W. (2002). Emotionality, emotion regulation, and school performance in middle school children. *Journal of School Psychology, 40,* 395–413.

Gunderson, E.A., Ramirez, G., Beilock, S.L., & Levine, S.C. (2012). The role of parents and teachers in the development of gender-related attitudes. *Sex Roles, 66,* 153–166.

Gunnar, M.R., Doom, J.R., & Esposito, E.A. (2015). Psychoneuroendocrinology of stress: Normative development and individual differences. In R.M. Lerner (Ed.), *Handbook of child psychology and developmental science* (7th ed.). New York: Wiley.

Gunsberg, L., & Hymowitz, P. (2013). *A handbook of divorce and custody*. New York: Psychology Press.

Gutman, L.M., Eccles, J.S., Peck, S., & Malanchuk, O. (2011). The influence of early family relations on trajectories of cigarette and alcohol use from early to late adolescence. *Journal of Adolescence, 34,* 119–128.

Guttentag, C.L., & others (2014). "My Baby and Me": Effects of an early, comprehensive parenting intervention on at-risk mothers and their children. *Developmental Psychology, 50,* 482–496.

Guttentag, M., & Bray, H. (1976). *Undoing sex stereotypes: Research and resources for educators*. New York: McGraw-Hill.

Guttmannova, K., & others (2012). Examining explanatory mechanisms of the effects of early alcohol use on young adult alcohol competence. *Journal of Studies of Alcohol and Drugs, 73,* 379–390.

H

Habermas, T., & Kober, C. (2015). Autobiographical reasoning is constitutive for narrative identity: The role of the life story for personal continuity. In K.C. McLean & M. Syed (Eds.), *Oxford handbook of identity development*. New York: Oxford University Press.

Haderxhanaj, L.T., & others (2014). Acculturation, sexual behaviors, and health care access among Hispanic and non-Hispanic White adolescents and young adults in the United States, 2006–2010. *Journal of Adolescent Health, 55,* 716–719.

Hafen, C.A., & others (2012). The pivotal role of adolescent autonomy in secondary school classrooms. *Journal of Youth and Adolescence, 41,* 245–255.

Hagman, J., & others (2015, in press). Body size overestimation and its association with body mass index, body dissatisfaction, and drive for thinness in anorexia nervosa. *Eating and Weight Disorders.*

Haidt, J. (2010). Morality. In S. Fiske & D. Gilbert (Eds.), *Handbook of social psychology* (5th ed.). New York: Wiley.

Haidt, J. (2013). Moral psychology for the twenty-first century. *Journal of Moral Education, 42,* 281–297.

Haier, R.J., Karama, S., Colom, R., Jung, R., & Johnson, W. (2014). A comment on "fractionating intelligence" and the peer review process. *Intelligence, 46,* 323–332.

Hale, L., & Guan, S. (2015). Screen time and sleep among school-aged children and adolescents: A systematic review of the literature. *Sleep Medicine Reviews, 21,* 50–58.

Hale, S. (1990). A global developmental trend in cognitive processing speed. *Child Development, 61,* 653–663.

Halfond, R., Corona, R., & Moon, A. (2013). Latino parent and adolescent perceptions of hoped-for and feared possible selves for adolescents. *Journal of Adolescent Research, 28*(2), 209–240.

Halford, G.S., & Andrews, G. (2011). Information-processing models of cognitive development. In U. Goswami (Ed.), *Wiley-Blackwell handbook of childhood cognitive development* (2nd ed.). New York: Wiley.

Hall, G.S. (1904). *Adolescence* (Vols. 1 & 2). Englewood Cliffs, NJ: Prentice Hall.

Hall, J.A. (2011). Sex differences in friendship expectations: A meta-analysis. *Journal of Social and Personal Relationships, 28,* 723–747.

Hall, J.A., Park, N., Song, H., & Cody, M.J. (2010). Strategic misrepresentation in online dating: The effects of gender, self-monitoring, and personality traits. *Journal of Social and Personal Relationships, 27,* 117–135.

Hallahan, D.P., Kauffman, J.M., & Pullen, P.C. (2015). *Exceptional learners* (13th ed.). Boston: Allyn & Bacon.

Halonen, J.A., & Santrock, J.W. (2013). *Your guide to college success* (7th ed.). Boston: Cengage.

Halpern, C.T., & Haydon, A.A. (2012). Sexual timetables for oral-genital, vaginal, and anal intercourse: Sociodemographic comparisons in a nationally representative sample of adolescents. *American Journal of Public Health, 102,* 1221–1228.

Halpern, D.F. (2012). *Sex differences in cognitive abilities* (4th ed.). New York: Psychology Press.

Halpern, D.F., Benbow, C.P., Geary, D.C., Gur, R.C., & Hyde, J.S. (2007). The science of sex differences in science and mathematics. *Psychological Science in the Public Interest, 8,* 1–51.

Halpern, D.F., Straight, C.A., & Stephenson, C.L. (2011). Beliefs about cognitive gender differences: Accurate for direction, underestimated for size. *Sex Roles, 64,* 336–347.

Halpern, D.F., & others (2011). The pseudoscience of single-sex schooling. *Science, 333,* 1706–1717.

Halpern-Felsher, B. (2008). Editorial. Oral sexual behavior: Harm reduction or gateway behavior? *Journal of Adolescent Health, 43,* 207–208.

Halpern-Meekin, S., Manning, W., Giordano, P.C., & Longmore, M.A. (2013). Relationship churning in emerging adulthood: On/off relationships and sex with an ex. *Journal of Adolescent Research, 28,* 166–188.

Hamilton, E., & Klimes-Dougan, B. (2015). Gender differences in suicide prevention responses: Implications for adolescents based on an illustrative review of the literature. *International Journal of Environmental Research and Public Health, 12,* 2359–2372.

Hamilton, J.L., & others (2014). Pubertal timing and vulnerabilities to depression in early adolescence: Differential pathways to depressive symptoms by sex. *Journal of Adolescence, 37,* 165–174.

Hamilton, J.P., Farmer, M., Fogelman, P., & Gotlib, I.H. (2015, in press). Depressive rumination, the default-mode network, and the dark matter of clinical neuroscience. *Biological Psychiatry.*

Hamilton, L.D., & Julian, A.M. (2014). The relationship between daily hassles and sexual function in men and women. *Journal of Sex and Marital Therapy, 40,* 379–395.

Hamilton, S.F., & Hamilton, M.A. (2006). School, work, and emerging adulthood. In J.J. Arnett & J.L. Tanner (Eds.), *Emerging adults in America*. Washington, DC: American Psychological Association.

Hamilton, S.F., & Hamilton, M.A. (2009). The transition to adulthood: Challenges of poverty and structural lag. In R.M. Lerner & L. Steinberg (Eds.), *Handbook of adolescent psychology* (3rd ed.). New York: Wiley.

Hammen, C., & Keenan-Miller, D. (2013). Mood disorders. In I.B. Weiner & others (Eds.), *Handbook of psychology* (2nd ed., Vol. 8). New York: Wiley.

Hampl, S., & Campbell, A. (2015). Recognizing obesity and its complications: The story of Score 1 for Health. *NASN School Nurse, 30,* 46–52.

Hampton, J. (2008). Abstinence-only programs under fire. *Journal of the American Medical Association, 17,* 2013–2015.

Han, J.S., Rogers, M.E., Nurani, S., Rubin, S., & Blank, S. (2011). Patterns of chlamydia/gonorrhea positivity among voluntarily screened New York City public high school students. *Journal of Adolescent Health, 49,* 252–257.

Han, W-J. (2009). Maternal employment. In D. Carr (Ed.), *Encyclopedia of the life course and human development*. Boston: Gale Cengage.

Hanish, L.D., & Guerra, N.G. (2004). Aggressive victims, passive victims, and bullies: Developmental continuity or developmental change? *Merrill-Palmer Quarterly, 50,* 17–38.

Harackiewicz, J., Rozek, C.R., Hulleman, C.S., & Hyde, J.S. (2012). Helping parents to motivate adolescents in mathematics and science: An experimental test of utility-value intervention. *Psychological Science, 23,* 899–906.

Harakeh, Z., & others (2012). Individual and environmental predictors of health risk behaviors among Dutch adolescents: The HBSC study. *Public Health, 126*(7), 566–573.

Hardaway, J.A., Crowley, N.A., Bulik, C.M., & Kash, T.L. (2015). Integrated circuits and molecular compounds for stress and feeding: Implications for eating disorders. *Genes, Brain, and Behavior, 14,* 85–97.

Hardee, K., Gay, J., Croce-Galis, M., & Afari-Dwamena, N.A. (2014). What HIV programs work for adolescent girls? *Journal of Acquired Immune Deficiency Syndrome, 66*(Suppl. 2), S176–S185.

Hardy, S.A., Bean, D.S., & Olsen, J.A. (2015, in press). Moral identity and adolescent prosocial and antisocial behaviors: Interactions with moral disengagement and self-regulation. *Journal of Youth and Adolescence.*

Hardy, S.A., Bhattacharjee, A., Reed, A., & Aquino, K. (2010). Moral identity and psychological distance: The case of adolescent socialization. *Journal of Adolescence, 33,* 111–123.

Hardy, S.A., Walker, L.J., Olsen, J.A., Woodbury, R.D., & Hickman, J.R. (2014). Moral identity as moral ideal self: Links to adolescent outcomes. *Developmental Psychology, 50,* 45–57.

Hardy, S.A., & others (2014). The roles of identity formation and moral identity in college student mental health, health-risk behaviors, and psychological well-being. *Journal of Clinical Psychology, 69,* 364–382.

Hargreaves, D.A., & Tiggemann, M. (2004). Idealized body images and adolescent body image: "Comparing" boys and girls. *Body Image, 1,* 351–361.

Hargreaves, D.S., McVey, D., Nairn, A., & Viner, R.M. (2013). Relative importance of individual and social factors in improving adolescent health. *Perspectives on Public Health, 133,* 122–131.

Harmon, O.R., Lambrinos, J., & Kennedy, P. (2008). Are online exams an invitation to cheat? *Journal of Economic Education, 39,* 116–125.

Harold, R.D., Colarossi, L.G., & Mercier, L.R. (2007). *Smooth sailing or stormy waters: Family transitions through adolescence and their implications for practice and policy*. Mahwah, NJ: Erlbaum.

Harris, A.L., Sutherland, M.A., & Hutchinson, M.K. (2013). Parental influences of sexual risk among urban African American adolescent males. *Journal of Nursing Scholarship, 45,* 141–150.

Harris, R.A., Qualter, P., & Robinson, S.J. (2013). Loneliness trajectories from middle childhood to pre-adolescence: Impact on perceived health and sleep disturbance. *Journal of Adolescence, 6*(6), 1295–1304.

Harris, Y.R., & Graham, J.A. (2007). *The African American child.* New York: Springer.

Harris, Y.R., & Graham, J.A. (2014). *The African American child* (2nd ed.). New York: Springer.

Harrison, M.E., & others (2015). Systematic review of the effects of family meal frequency on psychosocial outcomes in youth. *Canadian Family Physician, 61,* e96–e106.

Hart, D. (2005). The development of moral identity. In G. Carlo & C.P. Edwards (Eds.), *Nebraska Symposium on Motivation* (Vol. 51). Lincoln: University of Nebraska Press.

Hart, D., & Matsuba, M.K. (2010). Urban neighborhoods as contexts for moral identity development. In D. Narváez & D.K. Lapsley (Eds.), *Moral personality, identity, and character.* New York: Cambridge University Press.

Hart, D., Matsuba, M.K., & Atkins, R. (2008). The moral and civic effects of learning to serve. In L. Nucci & D. Narváez (Eds.), *Handbook of moral and character education.* Clifton, NJ: Psychology Press.

Hart, D., Matsuba, M.K., & Atkins, R. (2014). The moral and civic effects of learning to serve. In L. Nucci, T. Krettenauer, & D. Narvaez (Eds.), *Handbook of moral and character education* (2nd ed.). New York: Routledge.

Hart, D., Richardson, C., & Wilkenfeld, B. (2011). Citizenship and civic identity. In S. Schwartz, K. Luyckx, & V. Fignoles (Eds.), *Handbook of identity theory and research.* New York: Springer.

Hart, D., Watson, N.C., Dr, A., & Atkins, R. (2011). Prosocial tendencies, antisocial behavior, and moral development in childhood. In A. Slater & G. Bremner (Eds.), *Introduction to developmental psychology* (2nd ed.). Oxford, UK: Blackwell.

Harter, S. (1986). Processes underlying the construction, maintenance, and enhancement of the self-concept of children. In J. Suls & A. Greenwald (Eds.), *Psychological perspective on the self* (Vol. 3). Hillsdale, NJ: Erlbaum.

Harter, S. (1989). *Self-perception profile for adolescents.* Denver: University of Denver, Department of Psychology.

Harter, S. (1990a). Processes underlying adolescent self-concept formation. In R. Montemayor, G.R. Adams, & T.P. Gullotta (Eds.), *From childhood to adolescence: A transitional period?* Newbury Park, CA: Sage.

Harter, S. (1990b). Self and identity development. In S.S. Feldman & G.R. Elliott (Eds.), *At the threshold: The developing adolescent.* Cambridge, MA: Harvard University Press.

Harter, S. (1998). The development of self-representations. In W. Damon (Ed.), *Handbook of child psychology* (5th ed., Vol. 3). New York: Wiley.

Harter, S. (1999). *The construction of the self.* New York: Guilford.

Harter, S. (2006). The development of self-representations in childhood and adolescence. In W. Damon & R. Lerner (Eds.), *Handbook of child psychology* (6th ed.). New York: Wiley.

Harter, S. (2012). *The construction of the self* (2nd ed.). New York: Wiley.

Harter, S. (2013). The development of self-esteem. In M.H. Kernis (Ed.), *Self-esteem issues and answers.* New York: Psychology Press.

Harter, S., & Lee, L. (1989). *Manifestations of true and false selves in adolescence.* Paper presented at the meeting of the Society for Research in Child Development, Kansas City.

Harter, S., & Monsour, A. (1992). Developmental analysis of conflict caused by opposing attributes in the adolescent self-portrait. *Developmental Psychology, 28,* 251–260.

Harter, S., Stocker, C., & Robinson, N.S. (1996). The perceived directionality of the link between approval and self-worth: The liabilities of a looking glass self orientation among young adolescents. *Journal of Research on Adolescence, 6,* 285–308.

Harter, S., Waters, P., & Whitesell, N. (1996, March). *False self behavior and lack of voice among adolescent males and females.* Paper presented at the meeting of the Society for Research on Adolescence, Boston.

Hartman, S., & Belsky, J. (2015). An evolutionary perspective on developmental plasticity: Differential susceptibility to environmental influences. In R.Scott & S. Kosslyn (Eds.), *Emerging trends in the social and behavioral sciences.* New York: Wiley.

Hartmann, A.S., & others (2015). Anorexia nervosa and body dysmorphic disorder: A comparison of body image concerns and explicit and implicit attractiveness beliefs. *Body Image, 14,* 77–84.

Hartshorne, H., & May, M.S. (1928–1930). *Moral studies in the nature of character: Studies in deceit* (Vol. 1); *Studies in self-control* (Vol. 2); *Studies in the organization of character* (Vol. 3). New York: Macmillan.

Hartup, W.W. (1983). The peer system. In P.H. Mussen (Ed.), *Handbook of child psychology* (4th ed., Vol. 4). New York: Wiley.

Hartup, W.W. (1996). The company they keep: Friendships and their developmental significance. *Child Development, 67,* 1–13.

Hartup, W.W. (2005). Peer interaction: What causes what? *Journal of Abnormal Child Psychology, 33,* 387–394.

Hashim, H.A., Freddy, G., & Rosmatunisah, A. (2012). Relationships between negative affect and academic achievement among secondary school students: The mediating effects of habituated exercise. *Journal of Physical Activity and Health, 9,* 1012–1019.

Hassan, S., Flett, G.L., Ganguili, R., & Hewitt, P.L. (2014). Perfectionistic self-presentation and suicide in a young woman with major depression and psychotic features. *Case Reports in Psychiatry, 2014,* 901981.

Hatton, H., & others (2008). Family and individual difference predictors of trait aspects of negative interpersonal behaviors during emerging adulthood. *Journal of Family Psychology, 22,* 448–455.

Hatzenbuehler, M.L., McLaughlin, K.A., & Xuan, Z. (2015). Social networks and sexual orientation disparities in tobacco and alcohol use. *Journal of Studies on Alcohal and Drugs, 76,* 117–126.

Haw, C., Hawton, K., Niedzwiedz, C., & Platt, S. (2013). Suicide clusters: A review of risk factors and mechanisms. *Suicide and Life-Threatening Behaviors, 43*(1), 97–108.

Hawkins, J.A., & Berndt, T.J. (1985, April). *Adjustment following the transition to junior high school.* Paper presented at the biennial meeting of the Society for Research in Child Development, Toronto.

Hay, P. (2013). A systematic review of evidence for psychological treatments in eating disorders: 2005–2012. *International Journal of Eating Disorders, 46,* 462–469.

Hayashino, D., & Chopra, S.B. (2009). Parenting and raising families. In N. Tewari & A. Alvarez (Eds.), *Asian American psychology.* Clifton, NJ: Psychology Press.

Haydon, A., & Halpern, G.T. (2010). Older romantic partners and depressive symptoms during adolescence. *Journal of Youth and Adolescence, 39,* 1240–1251.

Haydon, A.A., Herring, A., Prinstein, M.J., & Halpern, C.T. (2012). Beyond age at first sex: Patterns of emerging sexual behavior in adolescence and young adulthood. *Journal of Adolescent Health, 50,* 456–463.

Hazan, C., & Shaver, P.R. (1987). Romantic love conceptualized as an attachment process. *Journal of Personality and Social Psychology, 52,* 522–524.

Heath, S.B. (1999). Dimensions of language development: Lessons from older children. In A.S. Masten (Ed.), *Cultural processes in child development: The Minnesota symposium on child psychology* (Vol. 29). Mahwah, NJ: Erlbaum.

Heath, S.B., & McLaughlin, M.W. (Eds.) (1993). *Identity and inner-city youth: Beyond ethnicity and gender.* New York: Teachers College Press.

Heerde, J.A., Scholes-Balog, K.E., & Hemphill, S.A. (2015). Associations between youth homelessness, sexual offenses, sexual victimization, and sexual risk factors: A systematic literature review. *Archives of Sexual Behavior, 44,* 181–212.

Heiman, G.W. (2014). *Basic statistics for the behavioral sciences* (7th ed.). Boston: Cengage.

Heiman, G.W. (2015). *Behavioral sciences STAT* (2nd ed.). Boston: Cengage.

Heitzler, C.D., Martin, S., Duke, J., & Huhman, M. (2006). Correlates of physical activity in a national sample of children aged 9–13 years. *Preventive Medicine, 42,* 254–260.

Henderson, V.L., & Dweck, C.S. (1990). Motivation and achievement. In S.S. Feldman & G.R. Elliott (Eds.), *At the threshold: The developing adolescent.* Cambridge, MA: Harvard University Press.

Hendry, J. (1999). *Social anthropology.* New York: Macmillan.

Heneghan, A., & others (2015, in press). Health-risk behaviors in teens investigated by U.S. child welfare agencies. *Journal of Adolescent Health.*

Hennessey, B.A. (2011). Intrinsic motivation and creativity: Have we come full circle? In R.A. Beghetto & J.C. Kaufman (Eds.), *Nurturing creativity in the classroom.* New York: Cambridge University Press.

Hennessy, M., Bleakley, A., Fishbein, M., & Jordan, A. (2009). Estimating the longitudinal association between adolescent sexual behavior and exposure to sexual media content. *Journal of Sexual Research, 46,* 586–596.

Henretta, J.C. (2010). Lifetime marital history and mortality after age 50. *Journal of Aging and Health, 22,* 1198–1212.

Henry, K.L., Stanley, L.R., Edwards, R.W., Harkabus, L.C., & Chapin, L.A. (2009). Individual and contextual effects of school adjustment on adolescent alcohol use. *Prevention Science, 10,* 236–247.

Hensel, D.J., & Sorge, B.H. (2014). Adolescent women's daily academic behaviors, sexual behaviors, and sexually related emotions. *Journal of Adolescent Health, 55,* 845–847.

Hepburn, L., Azrael, D., Molnar, B., & Miller, M. (2012). Bullying and suicidal behaviors among urban high school youth. *Journal of Adolescent Health, 51,* 93–95.

Heppner, M.J., & Heppner, P.P. (2003). Identifying process variables in career counseling: A research agenda. *Journal of Vocational Behavior, 62,* 429–452.

Heppner, P., & Lee, D. (2001). Problem-solving appraisal and psychological adjustment. In C.R. Snyder & S.J. Lopez (Eds.), *Handbook of positive psychology.* New York: Oxford University Press.

Herberle, A.E., & Carter, A.S. (2015, in press). Cognitive aspects of young children's experience of economic disadvantage. *Psychological Bulletin.*

Herdt, G., & Polen-Petit, N. (2014). *Human sexuality.* New York: McGraw-Hill.

Herman, K.C., Wang, K., Trotter, R., Reinke, W.M., & Ialongo, N. (2013). Developmental trajectories of maladaptive perfectionism among African American adolescents. *Child Development, 84,* 1633–1650.

Herman-Giddens, M.E. (2007). The decline in the age of menarche in the United States: Should we be concerned? *Journal of Adolescent Health, 40,* 201–203.

Herman-Giddens, M.E., & others (2012). Secondary sex characteristics in boys: Data from the pediatric research in office settings network. *Pediatrics, 130,* e1058–e1068.

Herman-Giddens, M.E., Kaplowitz, P.B., & Wasserman, R. (2004). Navigating the recent articles on girls' puberty in *Pediatrics:* What do we know and where do we go from here? *Pediatrics, 113,* 911–917.

Herpertz-Dahlmann, B. (2015). Adolescent eating disorders: Update on definitions, symptomatology, epidemiology, and comorbidity. *Child and Adolescent Psychiatry Clinics of North America, 24,* 177–198.

Herpertz-Dahlmann, B., & others (2015). Eating disorder symptoms do not just disappear: The implications of adolescent eating-disordered behavior for body weight and mental health in young adulthood. *European Child and Adolescent Psychiatry, 24,* 177–196.

Herrera, C., Grossman, J.B., Kauh, T.J., Feldman, A.F., & McMaken, J. (2007). *Making a difference in schools: The Big Brothers Big Sisters school-based mentoring impact study.* Philadelphia, PA: Public/ Private Ventures.

Herrera, C., Grossman, J.B., Kauh, T.J., & McMaken, J. (2011). Mentoring in schools: An impact study of Big Brothers Big Sisters school-based mentoring. *Child Development, 82,* 346–361.

Herres, J., & Kobak, R. (2015). The role of parent, teacher, and peer events in maintaining depressive symptoms during early adolescence. *Journal of Abnormal Child Psychology, 43*(2), 325–337.

Herting, M.M., Colby, J.B., Sowell, E.R., & Nagel, B.J. (2014). White matter connectivity and aerobic fitness in male adolescents. *Developmental Cognitive Neuroscience, 7,* 65–75.

Hess, L., Lonky, E., & Roodin, P.A. (1985, April). *The relationship of moral reasoning and ego strength to cheating behavior.* Paper presented at the meeting of the Society for Research in Child Development, Toronto.

Hetherington, E.M. (1972). Effects of father-absence on personality development in adolescent daughters. *Developmental Psychology, 7,* 313–326.

Hetherington, E.M. (1977). *My heart belongs to daddy: A study of the remarriages of daughters of divorcees and widows.* Unpublished manuscript, University of Virginia.

Hetherington, E.M. (1989). Coping with family transitions: Winners, losers, and survivors. *Child Development, 60,* 1–14.

Hetherington, E.M. (2005). Divorce and the adjustment of children. *Pediatrics in Review, 26,* 163–169.

Hetherington, E.M. (2006). The influence of conflict, marital problem solving, and parenting on children's adjustment in nondivorced, divorced, and remarried families. In A. Clarke-Stewart & J. Dunn (Eds.), *Families count.* New York: Cambridge University Press.

Hetherington, E.M., & Clingempeel, W.G. (1992). Coping with marital transitions: A family systems perspective. *Monographs of the Society for Research in Child Development, 57*(2–3, Serial No. 227).

Hetherington, E.M., Cox, M., & Cox, R. (1982). Effects of divorce on parents and children. In M.E. Lamb (Ed.), *Nontraditional families: Parenting and child development.* Hillsdale, NJ: Erlbaum.

Hetherington, E.M., & Kelly, J. (2002). *For better or for worse: Divorce reconsidered.* New York: Norton.

Hetherington, E.M., & Stanley-Hagan, M. (2002). Parenting in divorced and remarried families. In M. Bornstein (Ed.), *Handbook of parenting* (2nd ed.). Mahwah, NJ: Erlbaum.

Heyman, G.D., & Legare, C.H. (2005). Children's evaluation of sources of information about traits. *Developmental Psychology, 41,* 636–647.

Hibell, B., & others (2004). *The ESPAD report 2003.* The Swedish Council for Information on Alcohol and Other Drugs (CAN) and Council of Europe Pompidou Group. Stockholm, Sweden: CAN.

Hill, J.P., & Lynch, M.E. (1983). The intensification of gender-related role expectations during early adolescence. In J. Brooks-Gunn & A.C. Petersen (Eds.), *Girls at puberty: Biological and psychosocial perspectives.* New York: Plenum.

Hill, P.L., Duggan, P.M., & Lapsley, D.K. (2012). Subjective invulnerability, risk behavior, and adjustment in early adolescence. *Journal of Early Adolescence, 32*(4), 498–501.

Hill, P.L., & Lapsley, D.K. (2010). Adaptive and maladaptive narcissism in adolescent development. In C.T. Barry, P. Kerig, K. Stellwagen, & T.D. Berry (Eds.), *Implications of narcissism and Machiavellianism for the development of prosocial and antisocial behavior in youth.* Washington, DC: American Psychological Association.

Hill, P.L., & others (2014). Perceived social support predicts increased conscientiousness during older adulthood. *Journals of Gerontology B: Psychological Sciences and Social Sciences, 69*(4), 543–547.

Hilliard, L., & Liben, L. (2012, April). *No boys in ballet: Response to gender bias in mother-child conversations.* Paper presented at the Gender Development Research conference, San Francisco.

Hilliard, L.J., & others (2014). Beyond the deficit model: Bullying and trajectories of character virtues in adolescence. *Journal of Youth and Adolescence, 43,* 991–1003.

Hillis, S.D., & others (2010). The protective effect of family strengths in childhood against adolescent pregnancy and its long-term psychological consequences. *The Permanente Journal, 4,* 18–27.

Hillman, C.H., & others (2009). The effect of acute treadmill walking on cognitive control and academic achievement in preadolescent children. *Neuroscience, 3,* 1044–1054.

Hines, M. (2013). Sex and sex differences. In P.D. Zelazo (Ed.), *Oxford handbook of developmental psychology.* New York: Oxford University Press.

Hines, M. (2015). Gendered development. In R.M. Lerner (Ed.), *Handbook of child psychology and developmental science* (7th ed.). New York: Wiley.

Hingson, R.W., Heeren, T., & Winter, M.R. (2006). Age at drinking onset and alcohol dependence: Age at onset, duration, and severity. *Archives of Pediatric and Adolescent Medicine, 160,* 739–746.

Hinkle, J.S., Tuckman, B.W., & Sampson, J.P. (1993). The psychology, physiology, and the creativity of middle school aerobic exercisers. *Elementary School Guidance & Counseling, 28,* 133–145.

Hinnant, J.B., Erath, S.A., & El-Sheikh, M. (2015). Harsh parenting, parasympathetic activity, and development of delinquency and substance use. *Journal of Abnormal Psychology, 124,* 137–151.

Hintsanen, M., & others (2014). Five-factor personality traits and sleep: Evidence from two population-based cohort studies. *Health Psychology, 33,* 1214–1223.

Hipwell, A.E., Stepp, S.D., Keenan, K., Chung, T., & Loeber, R. (2011). Brief report: Parsing the heterogeneity of adolescent girls' sexual behavior: Relationships to individual and interpersonal factors. *Journal of Adolescence, 34,* 589–592.

Hirsch, B.J., & Rapkin, B.D. (1987). The transition to junior high school: A longitudinal study of self-esteem, psychological symptomatology, school life, and social support. *Child Development, 58,* 1235–1243.

Hirsch, J.K., Wolford, K., Lalonde, S.M., Brunk, L., & Parker-Morris, A. (2009). Optimistic explanatory style as a moderator of the association between negative life events and suicide ideation. *Crisis, 30,* 48–53.

Hitokoto, H., & Tanaka-Matsumi, J. (2014). Living in the tide of change: Explaining Japanese subjective health from the socio-demographic change. *Frontiers in Psychology, 5,* 1221.

Ho, J., Yeh, M., McCabe, K., & Lau, A. (2012). Perceptions of the acceptability of parent training among Chinese immigrant parents: Contributions of cultural factors and clinical need. *Behavior Therapy, 43,* 436–449.

Hoare, E., & others (2014). Associations between obesogenic risk factors and depression among adolescents: A systematic review. *Obesity Reviews, 15,* 40–51.

Hoefnagels, M. (2015). *Biology* (3rd ed.). New York: McGraw-Hill.

Hoelter, L. (2009). Divorce and separation. In D. Carr (Ed.), *Encyclopedia of the life course and human development.* Boston: Gale Cengage.

Hoeve, M., Dubas, J.S., Gerris, J.R.M., van der Laan, P.H., & Smeenk, W. (2011). Maternal and paternal parenting styles: Unique and combined links to adolescent and early adulthood delinquency. *Journal of Adolescence, 34,* 813–827.

Hoff, E., Laursen, B., & Tardif, T. (2002). Socioeconomic status and parenting. In M.H. Bornstein (Ed.), *Handbook of parenting* (2nd ed.). Mahwah, NJ: Erlbaum.

Hofferth, S.L., & Reid, L. (2002). Early childbearing and children's achievement behavior over time. *Perspectives on Sexual and Reproductive Health, 34,* 41–49.

Hoffman, M.L. (1970). Moral development. In P.H. Mussen (Ed.), *Manual of child psychology* (3rd ed., Vol. 2). New York: Wiley.

Hoffman, M.L. (1988). Moral development. In M.H. Bornstein & E. Lamb (Eds.), *Developmental psychology: An advanced textbook* (2nd ed.). Hillsdale, NJ: Erlbaum.

Hogerbrugge, M.J., & Komter, A.E. (2012). Solidarity and ambivalence: Comparing two perspectives on intergenerational relations using longitudinal panel data. *Journals of Gerontology B: Psychological Sciences and Social Sciences, 67,* 372–383.

Hohman, Z.P., Crano, W.D., Siegel, J.T., & Alvaro, E.M. (2014). Attitude ambivalence, friend norms, and adolescent drug use. *Prevention Science, 15,* 165–174.

Holland, A.S., & Roisman, G.I. (2010). Adult attachment security and young adults' dating relationships over time: Self-reported, observational, and physiological evidence. *Developmental Psychology, 46,* 552–557.

Hollingdale, J., & Greitemeyer, T. (2014). The effect of online violent video games on levels of aggression. *PLoS One, 9,* e111790.

Holman, C., & de Villers-Sidani, E. (2014). Indestructible plastic: The neuroscience of the aging brain. *Frontiers in Human Neuroscience, 8,* 219.

Holmes, L.D. (1987). *Quest for the real Samoa: The Mead-Freeman controversy and beyond.* South Hadley, MA: Bergin & Garvey.

Holmes, R.M., Little, K.C., & Welsh, D. (2009). Dating and romantic relationships, adulthood. In D. Carr (Ed.), *Encyclopedia of the life course and human development.* Boston: Gale Cengage.

Holsen, I., Carlson Jones, D., & Skogbrott Birkeland, M. (2012). Body image satisfaction among Norwegian adolescents and young adults: A longitudinal study of interpersonal relationships and BMI. *Body Image, 9,* 201–208.

Hommel, B., Li, K.Z.H., & Li, S-C. (2004). Visual search across the life span. *Developmental Psychology, 40,* 545–558.

Hoover, K.W., Tao, G., Berman, S., & Kent, C.K. (2010). Utilization of health services in physician offices and outpatient clinics by adolescents and young women in the United States: Implications for improving access to reproductive services. *Journal of Adolescent Health, 46,* 324–330.

Hope, D.A. (2009). Contemporary perspectives on lesbian, gay, and bisexual identities: Introduction. *Nebraska Symposium on Motivation, 54,* 1–4.

Hopfer, C., & others (2013). Conduct disorder and initiation of substance use: A prospective longitudinal study. *Journal of the American Academy of Child and Adolescent Psychiatry, 52,* 511–518.

Horwitz, A.G., Hill, R.M., & King, C.A. (2011). Specific coping behaviors in relation to adolescent depression. *Journal of Adolescence, 34,* 1077–1085.

Hou, H., Wang, C., Jia, S., Hu, S., & Tian, M. (2014). Brain dopaminergic system changes in drug addiction: A review of positron emission tomography findings. *Neuroscience Bulletin, 30,* 765–776.

House, L.D., Mueller, T., Reininger, B., Brown, K., & Markham, C.M. (2010). Character as a predictor of reproductive health outcomes for youth: A systematic review. *Journal of Adolescent Health, 46*(Suppl 1), S59–S74.

Houser, J.J., Mayeux, L., & Cross, C. (2015). Peer status and aggression as predictors of dating popularity in adolescence. *Journal of Youth and Adolescence, 44*(3), 683–695.

Howe, M.J.A., Davidson, J.W., Moore, D.G., & Sloboda, J.A. (1995). Are there early childhood signs of musical ability? *Psychology of Music, 23,* 162–176.

Howe, M.L. (2015). An adaptive view of memory development. In R.M. Lerner (Ed.), *Handbook of child psychology and developmental science* (7th ed.). New York: Wiley.

Howe, W.A. (2010). Unpublished review of J.W. Santrock's *Educational psychology,* 5th ed. (New York: McGraw-Hill).

Howell, D.C. (2014). *Fundamental statistics for the behavioral sciences* (8th ed.). Boston: Cengage.

Howell, K.H., & others (2015). Predicting adolescent posttraumatic stress in the aftermath of war: Differential effects of coping strategies across trauma reminder, loss reminder, and family conflict domains. *Anxiety, Stress, & Coping, 28,* 88–104.

Hoyt, L.T., & Falconi, A.M. (2015). Puberty and perimenopause: Reproductive transitions and their implications for women's health. *Social Science and Medicine, 132,* 103–112.

Hsieh, M., & Stright, A.D. (2012). Adolescents' emotion regulation strategies, self-concept, and internalizing problems. *Journal of Early Adolescence, 32,* 876–901.

Hsin, A., & Xie, Y. (2014). Explaining Asian Americans' academic advantage over whites. *Proceedings of the National Academy of Sciences U.S.A., 111,* 8416–8421.

Hsu, H.C., Chang, W.C., Chong, Y.S., & An, J.S. (2015, in press). Happiness and social determinants across age cohorts in Taiwan. *Journal of Health Psychology.*

Hu, J.K., Wang, X., & Wang, P. (2014). Testing gene-gene interactions in genome-wide association studies. *Genetic Epidemiology, 38,* 123–134.

Huang, C.J., & others (2015, in press). A preliminary examination of aerobic exercise effects on resting EEG in children with ADHD. *Journal of Attention Disorders.*

Huang, L.N. (1989). Southeast Asian refugee children and adolescents. In J.T. Gibbs & L.N. Huang (Eds.), *Children of color.* San Francisco: Jossey-Bass.

Huang, L.N., & Ying, Y. (1989). Chinese American children and adolescents. In J.T. Gibbs & L.N. Huang (Eds.), *Children of color.* San Francisco: Jossey-Bass.

Huang, P.M., Smock, P.J., Manning, W.D., & Bergstrom-Lynch, C.A. (2011). He says, she says: Gender and cohabitation. *Journal of Family Issues, 32,* 876–905.

Huebner, A.M., & Garrod, A.C. (1993). Moral reasoning among Tibetan monks: A study of Buddhist adolescents and young adults in Nepal. *Journal of Cross-Cultural Psychology, 24,* 167–185.

Huerta, M., Cortina, L.M., Pang, J.S., Torges, C.M., & Magley, V.J. (2006). Sex and power in the academy: Modeling sexual harassment in the lives of college women. *Personality and Social Psychology Bulletin, 32,* 616–628.

Huesmann, L.R. (1986). Psychological processes promoting the relation between exposure to media violence and aggressive behavior by the viewer. *Journal of Social Issues, 42,* 125–139.

Huesmann, L.R., Moise-Titus, J., Podolski, C., & Eron, L.D. (2003). Longitudinal relations between children's exposure to TV violence and their aggressive and violent behavior in young adulthood: 1977–1992. *Developmental Psychology, 39,* 201–221.

Hughes, D., Way, N., & Rivas-Drake, D. (2011). Stability and change in private and public ethnic regard among African American, Puerto Rican, Dominican, and Chinese American early adolescents. *Journal of Research on Adolescence, 21,* 861–870.

Hull, J. (2012). A self-awareness model of the causes and effects of alcohol consumption. In K. Vohs & R.F. Baumeister (Eds.), *Self and identity.* Thousand Oaks, CA: Sage.

Hunt, E. (2011). Where are we? Where are we going? Reflections on the current and future state of research on intelligence. In R.J. Sternberg & S.B. Kaufman (Eds.), *Cambridge handbook of intelligence.* New York: Cambridge University Press.

Hunter, S.B., Barber, B.K., Olsen, J.A., McNeely, C.A., & Bose, K. (2011). Adolescents' self-disclosure across cultures: Who discloses and why. *Journal of Adolescent Research, 26,* 447–478.

Hurd, N.M., & Sellers, R.M. (2013). Black adolescents' relationships with natural mentors: Associations with academic engagement via social and emotional development. *Cultural Diversity and Ethnic Minority Psychology, 19,* 76–85.

Hurd, N.M., Varner, F.A., & Rowley, S.J. (2013). Involved-vigilant parenting and socio-emotional well-being among Black youth: The moderating influence of natural mentoring relationships. *Journal of Youth and Adolescence, 42,* 1583–1595.

Hurt, T.R., Brody, G.H., McBride, V., Berkel, C., & Chen, Y. (2013). Elucidating parenting processes that influence alcohol use: A qualitative inquiry. *Journal of Adolescent Research, 28,* 3–30.

Huston, A.C. (2015, in press). Thoughts on "Probability values and human values in evaluating single-sex education." *Sex Roles.*

Huston, A.C., & Ripke, N.N. (2006). Experiences in middle and late childhood and children's development. In A.C. Huston & M.N. Ripke (Eds.), *Developmental contexts in middle childhood.* New York: Cambridge University Press.

Huston, A.C., & others (2006). Effects of a family poverty intervention program lasting from middle childhood to adolescence. In A.C. Huston & M.N. Ripke (Eds.). *Developmental contexts of middle childhood.* New York: Cambridge University Press.

Huttenlocher, P.R., & Dabholkar, A.S. (1997). Regional differences in synaptogenesis in human cerebral cortex. *Journal of Comparative Neurology, 37,* 167–178.

Huynh, V.W., & Fuligni, A.J. (2010). Discrimination hurts: The academic, psychological, and physical well-being of adolescents. *Journal of Research on Adolescence, 20,* 916–941.

Huynh, V.W., & Fuligni, A.J. (2012). Perceived ethnic stigma across the transition to college. *Journal of Youth and Adolescence, 41,* 817–830.

Hyde, J.S. (2005). The gender similarities hypothesis. *American Psychologist, 60,* 581–592.

Hyde, J.S. (2007). New directions in the study of gender similarities and differences. *Current Directions in Psychological Science, 16,* 259–263.

Hyde, J.S. (2014). Gender similarities and differences. *Annual Review of Psychology* (Vol. 66). Palo Alto, CA: Annual Reviews.

Hyde, J.S., & DeLamater, J.D. (2014). *Understanding human sexuality* (12th ed.). New York: McGraw-Hill.

Hyde, J.S., & Else-Quest, N. (2013). *Half the human experience* (8th ed.). Boston: Cengage.

Hyde, J.S., Lindberg, S.M., Linn, M.C., Ellis, A.B., & Williams, C.C. (2008). Gender similarities characterize math performance. *Science, 321,* 494–495.

Hyman, I., & others (2006). Bullying: Theory, research, and interventions. In C.M. Evertson & C.S. Weinstein (Eds.), *Handbook of classroom management: Research, practice, and contemporary issues.* Mahwah, NJ: Erlbaum.

Hymel, S., Closson, L.M., Caravita, C.S., & Vaillancourt, T. (2011). Social status among peers: From sociometric attraction to peer acceptance to perceived popularity. In P.K. Smith & C.H. Hart (Eds.), *Wiley-Blackwell handbook of childhood social development* (2nd ed.). New York: Wiley.

I

"I Have a Dream" Foundation (2015). *About us.* Retrieved April 23, 2015, from www.ihad.org

Ibanez, L., & de Zegher, F. (2006). Puberty after prenatal growth restraint. *Hormone Research, 65*(Suppl. 3), 112–115.

Ibanez, L., Lopez-Bermejo, A., Diaz, M., & de Zegher, F. (2011). Catch-up growth in girls born small for gestational age precedes childhood progression to high adiposity. *Fertility and Sterility, 96,* 220–223.

Igarashi, H., Hooker, K., Coehlo, D.P., & Maoogian, M.M. (2013). "My nest is full": Intergenerational relationships at midlife. *Journal of Aging Studies, 27,* 102–112.

Imuta, K., Hayne, H., & Scarf, D. (2014). I want it all and I want it now: Delay of gratification in preschool children. *Developmental Psychobiology, 56,* 1541–1552.

Insel, P.N., & Roth, W.T. (2012). *Connect core concepts in health* (12th ed.). New York: McGraw-Hill.

Irwin, C.E. (2010). Young adults are worse off than adolescents. *Journal of Adolescent Health, 46,* 405–406.

Irwin, C.E., Adams, S.H., Park, M.J., & Newacheck, P.W. (2009). Preventive care for adolescents: Few get visits and fewer get services. *Pediatrics, 123,* e565–e572.

Irwin, P., Booth, T., Nyborg, H., & Rushton, J.P. (2012). Are *g* and the general factor of personality (GFP) correlated? *Intelligence, 40,* 296–305.

Ito, K.E., & others (2006). Parent opinion of sexuality education in a state with mandated abstinence education: Does policy match parental preference? *Journal of Adolescent Health, 39,* 634–641.

Ivanova, K., Mills, M., & Veenstra, R. (2012). The initiation of dating in adolescence: The effect of parental divorce. The TRAILS study. *Journal of Research on Adolescence, 37,* 340–363.

Iverson, K.M., King, M.W., Cunningham, K.C., & Resick, P.A. (2015). Rape survivors' trauma-related beliefs before and after cognitive processing therapy: Associations with PTSD and depression symptoms. *Behavior Research and Therapy, 66,* 49–55.

J

Jaccard, J., & Levitz, N. (2013). Counseling adolescents about contraception: Towards the development of an evidence-based protocol for contraceptive counselors. *Journal of Adolescent Health, 52* (Suppl. 4), S6–S13.

Jackson, A., & Davis, G. (2000). *Turning points 2000.* New York: Teachers College Press.

Jackson, S.L. (2016, in press). *Research methods* (5th ed.). Boston: Cengage.

Jacob, R., & others (2014). Daily hassles' role in health seeking behavior among low-income populations. *American Journal of Health Behavior, 38,* 297–306.

Jacobs, R.H., & others (2014). Increasing positive outlook partially mediates the effect of empirically supported treatments on depression symptoms among adolescents. *Journal of Cognitive Psychotherapy, 28,* 3–19.

Jacobson, L.A., & others (2011). Working memory influences processing speed and reading fluency in ADHD. *Child Neuropsychology, 17*(3), 209–224.

Jaffee, S., & Hyde, J.S. (2000). Gender differences in moral orientation: A meta-analysis. *Psychological Bulletin, 126,* 703–726.

James, A.G., Fine, M.A., & Turner, L.J. (2012). An empirical examination of youths' perceptions of spirituality as an internal developmental asset during adolescence. *Applied Developmental Science, 16,* 181–194.

James, J.E., Kristjansson, A.L., & Sigfusdottir, I.D. (2011). Adolescent substance use, sleep, and academic achievement: Evidence of harm due to caffeine. *Journal of Adolescence, 34,* 665–673.

Jamieson, P.E., & Romer, D. (2008). Unrealistic fatalism in U.S. youth ages 14 to 22: Prevalence and characteristics. *Journal of Adolescent Health, 42,* 154–160.

Jamison, J., & Myers, L.B. (2008). Peer-group and price influence students drinking along with planned behavior. *Alcohol and Alcoholism, 43,* 492–497.

Jamner, M.S., Spruit-Meitz, D., Bassin, S., & Cooper, D.M. (2004). A controlled evaluation of a school-based intervention to promote physical activity among sedentary adolescent females: Project FAB. *Journal of Adolescent Health, 34,* 279–289.

Jansen, A.G., & others (2015, in press). What twin studies tell us abuot the heritability of brain development, morphology, and function: A review. *Neuropsychology Review.*

Janssen, I., & others (2005). Comparison of overweight and obesity prevalence in school-aged youth from 34 countries and their relationships with physical activity and dietary patterns. *Obesity Research, 6,* 123–132.

Jarrett, R.L. (1995). Growing up poor: The family experience of socially mobile youth in low-income African-American neighborhoods. *Journal of Adolescent Research, 10,* 111–135.

Jayson, S. (2006, June 29). The "millennials" come of age. *USA Today,* pp. 1D–2D.

Jeha, D., Usta, I, Ghulmiyyah, L., & Nassar, A. (2015, in press). A review of the risks and consequences of adolescent pregnancy. *Journal of Neonatal and Perinatal Medicine.*

Jekielek, S., & Brown, B. (2005). *The transition to adulthood: Characteristics of young adults ages 18 to 24 in America.* Washington, DC: Child Trends and the Annie E. Casey Foundation.

Jenni, O.G., & Carskadon, M.A. (2007). Sleep behavior and sleep regulation from infancy through adolescence: Normative aspects. In O.G. Jenni & M.A. Carskadon (Eds.), *Sleep Medicine Clinics: Sleep in Children and Adolescents.* Philadelphia: W.B. Saunders.

Jensen, A.R. (2008). Book review. *Intelligence, 36,* 96–97.

Jenson-Campbell, L.A., & Malcolm, K.T. (2007). The importance of conscientiousness in adolescent interpersonal relationships. *Personality and Social Psychology Bulletin, 33,* 368–383.

Jeynes, W.H. (2003). A meta-analysis: The effects of parental involvement on minority children's academic achievement. *Education and Urban Society, 35,* 202–218.

Jhally, S. (1990). *Dreamworlds: Desire/sex/power in rock video* (Video). Amherst: University of Massachusetts at Amherst, Department of Communications.

Jin, D., & Lee, H. (2015). A computational approach to identifying gene-microRNA modules in cancer. *PLoS Computational Biology, 11*(1), e1004042.

Job, V., Dweck, C.S., & Walton, G.M. (2010). Ego-depletion—Is it all in your head? Implicit theories about willpower affect self-regulation. *Psychological Science, 21,* 1686–1693.

Job, V., Walton, G.M., Bernecker, K., & Dweck, C.S. (2015, in press). Implicit theories about willpower predict self-regulation and grades in everyday life. *Journal of Personality and Social Psychology.*

Johns Hopkins University (2006a). *Research: Tribal connections.* Retrieved January 31, 2008, from www.krieger.jhu.edu/research/spotlight/prabhakar.html

Johns Hopkins University (2006b, February 17). *Undergraduate honored for launching health programs in India.* Baltimore: Johns Hopkins University News Releases.

Johnson, B.T., Scott-Sheldon, L.A., Huedo-Medina, T.B., & Carey, M.P. (2011). Interventions to reduce sexual risk for human immunodeficiency virus in adolescents: A meta-analysis of trials, 1985–2008. *Archives of Pediatric and Adolescent Medicine, 165,* 177–184.

Johnson, G.B. (2015). *The living world* (8th ed.). New York: McGraw-Hill.

Johnson, H.D. (2012). Relationship duration moderation of identity status differences in emerging adults' same-sex friendship intimacy. *Journal of Adolescence, 35,* 1515–1525.

Johnson, L., Giordano, P.C., Manning, W.D., & Longmore, M.A. (2011). Parent-child relations and offending during young adulthood. *Journal of Youth and Adolescence, 40,* 286–299.

Johnson, M.B., & Chen, J. (2015, in press). Blame it on alcohol: The influence of alcohol consumption during adolescence, the transition to adulthood, and young adulthood on one-time sexual hookups. *Journal of Sex Research.*

Johnson, M.H., Grossmann, T., & Cohen-Kadosh, K. (2009). Mapping functional brain development: Building a social brain through interactive specialization. *Developmental Psychology, 45,* 151–159.

Johnson, M.H., Jones, E., & Gliga, T. (2015, in press). Brain adaptation and alternative developmental trajectories. *Development and Psychopathology.*

Johnson, M.K., & Reynolds, J.R. (2013). Educational expectation trajectories and attainment in the transition to adulthood. *Social Science Research, 42,* 818–835.

Johnson, S.B., Dariotis, J.K., & Wang, C. (2012). Adolescent risk taking under stressed and nonstressed conditions: Conservative, calculating, and impulsive types. *Journal of Adolescent Health, 51*(Suppl. 2), S34–S40.

Johnson, S.P., & Hannon, E.H. (2015). Perceptual development. In R.M. Lerner (Ed.), *Handbook of child psychology and developmental science* (7th ed.). New York: Wiley.

Johnson, V.A., Kemp, A.H., Heard, R., Lennings, C.J., & Hickie, I.B. (2015). Childhood- versus adolescent-onset antisocial youth with conduct disorder: Psychiatric illness, neuropsychological, and psychological function. *PLoS One, 10*(4), e0121627.

Johnston, L.D., O'Malley, P.M., & Bachman, J.G. (2004). *Monitoring the Future national survey results on drug use, 1975–2003: Volume II, College students and adults ages 19–45* (NIH Publication No. 04-5508). Bethesda, MD: National Institute on Drug Abuse.

Johnston, L.D., O'Malley, P.M., Bachman, J.G., & Schulenberg, J.E. (2005). *Monitoring the Future national results on adolescent drug use: Overview of key findings, 2004* (NIH Publication No. 05-5726). Bethesda, MD: National Institute on Drug Abuse.

Johnston, L.D., O'Malley, P.M., Bachman, J.G., & Schulenberg, J.E. (2009). *Monitoring the Future national results on adolescent drug use: Overview of key findings, 2008.* Bethesda, MD: National Institute on Drug Abuse.

Johnston, L.D., O'Malley, P.M., Bachman, J.G., & Schulenberg, J.E. (2011). *Monitoring the Future national results on adolescent drug use: Overview of key findings, 2010.* Institute for Social Research, University of Michigan, Ann Arbor.

Johnston, L.D., O'Malley, P.M., Bachman, J.G., & Schulenberg, J.E. (2012). *Monitoring the Future national survey results on drug use, 1975–2011* (Vol. II, College students and adults ages 19–50). Ann Arbor: Institute for Social Research, University of Michigan.

Johnston, L.D., O'Malley, P.M., Bachman, J.G., & Schulenberg, J.E. (2013). *Monitoring the Future national results on drug use: 2012 overview, key findings on adolescent drug use.* Ann Arbor: Institute of Social Research, University of Michigan.

Johnston, L.D., O'Malley, P.M., Bachman, J.G., & Schulenberg, J.E. (2014). *Monitoring the Future national results on drug use: 2013 overview, key findings on adolescent drug use.* Ann Arbor: Institute of Social Research, University of Michigan.

Johnston, L.D., O'Malley, P.M., Bachman, J.G., & Schulenberg, J.E. (2015). *Monitoring the Future national results on drug use: 2014 overview, key findings on adolescent drug use.* Ann Arbor: Institute of Social Research, University of Michigan.

Jones, J.D., & Cassidy, J. (2014). Parental attachment style: Examination of the links with parent secure base provision and adolescent secure base use. *Attachment and Human Development, 16,* 437–461.

Jones, J.M. (2005, October 7). *Gallup Poll: Most Americans approve of interracial dating.* Princeton, NJ: Gallup.

Jones, M.C. (1965). Psychological correlates of somatic development. *Child Development, 36,* 899–911.

Jones, M.D., & Galliher, R.V. (2007). Navajo ethnic identity: Predictors of psychosocial outcomes in Navajo adolescents. *Journal of Research on Adolescence, 17,* 683–696.

Jones, V. (2015). *Practical classroom management* (2nd ed.). Upper Saddle River, NJ: Pearson.

Jordan, A.B. (2008). Children's media policy. *The Future of Children, 18*(1), 235–253.

Jordan, C.H., & Zeigler-Hill, V. (2013). Secure and fragile forms of self-esteem. In V. Zeigler-Hill (Ed.), *Self-esteem.* New York: Psychology Press.

Jorgensen, M.J., & others (2015, in press). Sexual behavior among young Danes aged 15–29 years: A cross-sectional study of core indicators. *Sexually Transmitted Infections.*

Jose, A., O'Leary, K.D., & Moyer, A. (2010). Does premarital cohabitation predict subsequent marital stability and marital quality? A meta-analysis. *Journal of Marriage and the Family, 72,* 105–116.

Josephson Institute of Ethics (2006). *2006 Josephson Institute report card on the ethics of American youth. Part one—integrity.* Los Angeles: Josephson Institute.

Joyce, B.R., Weil, M., & Calhoun, E. (2015). *Models of teaching* (9th ed.). Upper Saddle River, NJ: Pearson.

Jozkowski, K.N., & Sanders, N.A. (2012). Health and sexual outcomes of women who have experienced forced or coercive sex. *Women's Health, 52,* 108–118.

Juang, L.P., & Umana-Taylor, A.J. (2012). Family conflict among Chinese- and Mexican-origin adolescents and their parents in the U.S.: An introduction. *New Directions in Child and Adolescent Development, 135,* 1–12.

K

Kaatz, A., & Carnes, M. (2014). Stuck in the out-group: Jennifer can't grow up, Jane's invisible, and Janet's over the hill. *Journal of Women's Health, 23,* 481–484.

Kadivar, H., & others (2014). Adolescent views on comprehensive health risk assessment and counseling: Assessing gender differences. *Journal of Adolescent Health, 55,* 24–32.

Kadlecova, P., & others (2015, in press). Alcohol consumption at midlife and risk of stroke during 43 years of follow-up: Cohort and twin analysis. *Stroke.*

Kagan, J. (1992). Yesterday's premises, tomorrow's premises. *Developmental Psychology, 28,* 990–997.

Kagan, J. (2000). Temperament. In A. Kazdin (Ed.), *Encyclopedia of psychology.* New York: Oxford University Press.

Kagan, J. (2010). Emotions and temperament. In M.H. Bornstein (Ed.), *Handbook of cultural developmental science.* New York: Psychology Press.

Kagan, J. (2013). Temperamental contributions to inhibited and uninhibited profiles. In P.D. Zelazo (Ed.), *Oxford handbook of developmental psychology.* New York: Oxford University Press.

Kagitcibasi, C. (2007). *Family, self, and human development across cultures.* Mahwah, NJ: Erlbaum.

Kahn, A., & Fraga, M.F. (2009). Epigenetics and aging: Status, challenges, and needs for the future. *Journals of Gerontology A: Biological Sciences and Medical Sciences, 64,* 195–198.

Kahn, J.A., & others (2008). Patterns and determinants of physical activity in U.S. adolescents. *Journal of Adolescent Health, 42,* 369–377.

Kail, R.V. (2007). Longitudinal evidence that increases in processing speed and working memory enhance children's reasoning. *Psychological Science, 18,* 312–313.

Kalak, N., & others (2012). Daily morning running for 3 weeks improved sleep and psychological functioning in healthy adolescents compared with controls. *Journal of Adolescent Health, 51*(6), 615–622.

Kam, J.A., & Lazarevic, V. (2014). The stressful (and not so stressful) nature of language brokering: Identifing when brokering functions as a cultural stressor for Latino immigrant children in early adolescence. *Journal of Youth and Adolescence, 43,* 1994–2011.

Kamp, C.F., Sperlich, B., & Holmberg, H.C. (2014). Exercise reduces the symptoms of attention-deficit/hyperactivity disorder and improves social behavior, motor skills, strength, and neuropsychological parameters. *Acta Pediatrica, 103,* 709–714.

Kane, J.B., & Frisco, M.L. (2013). Obesity, school obesity prevalence, and adolescent childbearing among U.S. young women. *Social Science and Medicine, 88,* 108–115.

Kang, J.Y., & others (2014). Puberty-related changes in cortisol, dihydroepiandrosterone, and estradiol-17*b* secretions within the first hour after waking in premenarcheal girls. *Neuroendocrinology, 99,* 168–177.

Kang, M.S. (2014). The health of "emerging adults" in Australia: Freedom, risk, and rites of passage. *Medical Journal of Australia, 201,* 562–563.

Kang, P.P., & Romo, L.F. (2011). The role of religious involvement on depression, risky behavior, and academic performance among Korean American adolescents. *Journal of Adolescence, 34,* 767–778.

Kann, L., & others (2011). Sexual identity, sex of sexual contacts, and health-risk behaviors among students in grades 9–12—youth risk behavior surveillance, selected sites, 2001–2009. *MMWR Surveillance Summary, 60,* 1–133.

Kann, L., & others (2014). Youth Risk Behavior Surveillance—United States, 2013. *MMWR Surevillance Summaries, 63*(4), 1–169.

Kanner, A.D., Coyne, J.C., Schaefer, C., & Lazarus, R.S. (1981). Comparisons of two modes of stress measurement: Daily hassles and uplifts versus major life events. *Journal of Behavioral Medicine, 4,* 1–39.

Kantowitz, B.H., Roediger, H.L., & Elmes, D.G. (2015). *Experimental psychology* (10th ed.). Boston: Cengage.

Kao, T.A., & Huang, B. (2015, in press). Bicultural standing among immigrant adolescents: A concept analysis. *Journal of Holistic Nursing.*

Kaplan, D.L., Jones, E.J., Olson, E.C., & Yunzal-Butler, C.B. (2013). Early age of first sex and health risk in an urban adolescent population. *Journal of School Health, 83,* 350–356.

Kaplowitz, P.B. (2009). Treatment of central precocious puberty. *Current Opinion in Endocrinology, Diabetes, and Obesity, 16,* 13–16.

Kappeler, E.M., & Farb, A.F. (2014). Historical context for the creation of the Office of Adolescent Health and the Teen Pregnancy Prevention Program, 54 (3 Suppl), S3–S9.

Karnes, F.A., & Stephens, K.R. (2008). *Achieving excellence: Educating the gifted and talented.* Upper Saddle River, NJ: Prentice Hall.

Karnick, P.M. (2005). Feeling lonely: Theoretical perspectives. *Nursing Science Quarterly, 18,* 7–12.

Karniol, R., Gabay, R., Ochioin, Y., & Harari, Y. (1998). *Sex Roles, 39,* 45–58.

Kastbom, A.A., Sydsjo, G., Bladh, M., Priee, G., & Svedin, C.G. (2015). Sexual debut before the age of 14 leads to poorer psychosocial health and risky behavior later in life. *Acta Pediatrica, 104,* 91–100.

Kastenbaum, S. (2012, October 26th). African-American blazing a trail through chess. Retrieved from http://cnnradio.cnn.com/2012/10/26/african-american-blazing-a-trail-. . .

Kato, T. (2005). The relationship between coping with stress due to romantic break-ups and mental health. *Japanese Journal of Social Psychology, 20,* 171–180.

Katsiaficas, D., Suarez-Orozco, C., Sirin, S.R., & Gupta, T. (2013). Mediators of the relationship between acculturative stress and internalizing symptoms for immigrant origin youth. *Cultural Diversity and Ethnic Minority Psychology, 19,* 27–37.

Katz, J., & Smith, J. (2012). Youth with benefits: Sex before the ball and chain. Book review. *Sex Roles, 66,* 807–809.

Kauffman, J.M., McGee, K., & Brigham, M. (2004). Enabling or disabling? Observations on changes in special education. *Phi Delta Kappan, 85,* 613–620.

Kaufman, J.C., & Sternberg, R.J. (2012). The creative mind. In C. Jones, M. Lorenzen, & J. Sapsed (Eds.), *Oxford handbook of creative industries.* New York: Oxford University Press.

Kaufman, J.C., & Sternberg, R.J. (2013). The creative mind. In C. Jones, M. Lorenzen, & R.F. Proctor (Eds.), *Handbook of psychology: Experimental psychology* (Vol. 4). New York: Wiley.

Kaur, J., & others (2014). Prevalence and correlates of depression among adolescents in Malaysia. *Asia Pacific Journal of Public Health, 26*(5 Suppl.), S53–S62.

Kawabata, Y., Tseng, W.L., & Crick, N.R. (2014). Adaptive, maladaptive, mediational, and bidirectional processes of relational and physical aggression, relational and physical victimization, and peer liking. *Aggressive Behavior, 40,* 273–287.

Kaynak, O., & others (2013). Relationships among parental monitoring and sensation seeking on the development of substance use disorder among college students. *Addictive Behaviors, 38,* 1457–1463.

Keating, D.P. (1990). Adolescent thinking. In S.S. Feldman & G.R. Elliott (Eds.), *At the threshold: The developing adolescent.* Cambridge, MA: Harvard University Press.

Keating, D.P. (2007). Understanding adolescent development: Implications for driving safety. *Journal of Safety Research, 38,* 147–157.

Keating, D.P. (2009). Developmental science and giftedness: An integrated life-span framework. In F.D. Horowitz, R.F. Subotnik, & D.J. Matthews (Eds.), *The development of giftedness and talent across the life span.* Washington, DC: American Psychological Association.

Keating, D.P., & Halpern-Felsher, B.L. (2008). Adolescent drivers: A developmental perspective on risk, proficiency, and safety. *American Journal of Preventive Medicine, 35,* S272–S277.

Kehle, T.J., & Bray, M.A. (2014). Individual differences. In M.A. Bray & T.J. Kehle (Eds.), *Oxford handbook of school psychology.* New York: Oxford University Press.

Keijsers, L., & Laird, R.D. (2014). Mother-adolescent monitoring dynamics and the legitimacy of parental authority. *Journal of Adolescence, 37,* 515–524.

Keller, T.E., & Pryce, J.M. (2012). Different roles and different results: How activity orientations correspond to relationship quality and student outcomes in school-based mentoring. *Journal of Primary Prevention, 33,* 47–64.

Kellogg, R.T. (1994). *The psychology of writing.* New York: Oxford University Press.

Kelly, A.B., & others (2011). The influence of parents, siblings, and peers on pre- and early-teen smoking: A multilevel model. *Drug and Alcohol Review, 30,* 381–387.

Keltner, K.W. (2013). *Tiger babies strike back.* New York: William Morrow.

Kendler, K.S., Ohlsson, H., Sundquist, K., & Sundquist, J. (2013). Within-family environmental transmission of drug abuse: A Swedish national study. *JAMA Psychiatry, 70,* 235–242.

Kendler, K.S., & others (2012). Genetic and familial environmental influences on the risk for drug abuse: A national Swedish adoption study. *Archives of General Psychiatry, 69*(7), 690–697.

Kendrick, K., Jutengren, G., & Stattin, H. (2012). The protective role of supportive friends against bullying perpetration and victimization. *Journal of Adolescence, 35*(4), 1069–1080.

Kennedy, K.M., & others (2015). Lifespan age trajectory differences in functional brain activation under conditions of low and high processing demands. *Neuroimage, 104,* 31–34.

Kennedy, S., & Ruggles, S. (2014). Breaking up is hard to count: The rise of divorce in the United States, 1980–2010. *Demography, 51,* 587–598.

Kenney, R., Dooley, B., & Fitzgerald, A. (2013). Interpersonal relationships and emotional distress in adolescence. *Journal of Adolescence, 36,* 351–360.

Kerig, P.K., Swanson, J.A., & Ward, R.M. (2012). Autonomy with connection: Influences of parental psychological control on mutuality in emerging adults' intimate relationships. In P.K. Kerig, M.S. Schulz, & S.T. Hauser (Eds.), *Adolescents and beyond: Family processes in development.* New York: Oxford University Press.

Kerns, K.A., & Brumariu, L.E. (2014). Is insecure parent-child attachment a risk factor for the development of anxiety in childhood or adolescence? *Child Development Perspectives, 8,* 12–17.

Kerr, D.R., Capaldi, D.M., Pears, K.C., & Owen, L.D. (2012). Intergenerational influences on early alcohol use: Independence from the problem behavior pathway. *Development and Psychopathology, 24,* 889–906.

Keyes, K.M., Maslowsky, J., Hamilton, A., & Schulenberg, J. (2015). The great sleep recession: Changes in sleep duration among U.S. adolescents, 1991–2012. *Pediatrics, 135,* 460–468.

Khairullah, A., & others (2014). Testosterone trajectories and reference ranges in a large longitudinal sample of adolescent males. *PLoS One, 9*(9), e108838.

Khan, M.R., Berger, A.T., Wells, B.E., & Cleland, C.M. (2012). Longitudinal associations between adolescent alcohol use and adult sexual risk behavior and sexually transmitted infection in the United States: Assessment of differences by race. *American Journal of Public Health, 102,* 867–876.

Khashan, A.S., Baker, P.N., & Kenny, L.C. (2010). Preterm birth and reduced birthweight in first and second teenage pregnancies: A register-based cohort study. *BMC Pregnancy and Childbirth, 10,* 36.

Khurana, A., & others (2012). Early adolescent sexual debut: The mediating role of working memory ability, sensation seeking, and impulsivity. *Developmental Psychology, 48,* 1416–1428.

Kiamanesh, P., Dyregrov, K., Haavind, H., & Dieserud, G. (2014). Suicide and perfectionism: A psychological autopsy study of non-clinical suicides. *Omega, 69,* 381–399.

Kiang, L. (2012). Deriving daily purpose through daily events and role fulfillment among Asian American youth. *Journal of Research on Adolescence, 22,* 185–198.

Kiang, L., & Fuligni, A.J. (2010). Meaning in life as a mediator of ethnic identity and adjustment among adolescents from Latin, Asian, and European American backgrounds. *Journal of Youth and Adolescence, 39,* 1253–1264.

Kiang, L., Andrews, K., Stein, G.L., Supple, A.J., & Gonzales, L.M. (2013). Socioeconomic stress and academic adjustment among Asian American adolescents: The protective role of family obligation. *Journal of Youth and Adolescence, 42*(6), 837–847.

Kiang, L., Witkow, M.R., & Champagne, M.C. (2013). Normative changes in ethnic and American identities and links with adjustment among Asian American adolescents. *Developmental Psychology, 49*, 1713–1722.

Kidd, S. (2012). Invited commentary: Seeking a coherent strategy in our response to homeless and street-involved youth: A historical review and suggested future directions. *Journal of Youth and Adolescence, 41*, 533–543.

Kiefer, S.M., & Ryan, A.M. (2008). Striving for social dominance over peers: The implications for academic adjustment during early adolescence. *Journal of Educational Psychology, 100*, 417–428.

Kiernan, K. (2013). Cohabitation in Western Europe: Trends, issues, and implications. In A. Booth, A.C. Crouter, & N.S. Landale (Eds.), *Just living together.* New York: Psychology Press.

Kilbane, C.R., & Milman, N.B. (2014). *Teaching models.* Upper Saddle River, NJ: Pearson.

Killen, M., & Smetana, J.G. (2015). Morality: Origins and development. In R.M. Lerner (Ed.), *Handbook of child psychology and developmental science* (7th ed.). New York: Wiley.

Kim, J., Suh, W., Kim, S., & Gopalan, H. (2012). Coping strategies to manage acculturative stress: Meaningful activity participation, social support, and positive emotion among Korean immigrant adolescents in the USA. *International Journal of Qualitative Studies on Health and Well-Being, 19*, 1–10.

Kim, J.-Y., McHale, S.M., Crouter, A.C., & Osgood, D.W. (2007). Longitudinal linkages between sibling relationships and adjustment from middle childhood through adolescence. *Developmental Psychology, 43*, 960–973.

Kim, K.H. (2010, July 10). Interview. In P. Bronson & A. Merryman. The creativity crisis. *Newsweek*, 42–48.

Kim, M.J., Catalano, R.F., Haggerty, K.P., & Abbott, R.D. (2011). Bullying at elementary school and problem behavior in young adulthood: A study of bullying, violence, and substance use from age 11 to age 21. *Criminal Behavior and Mental Health, 21*, 36–44.

Kim, O.M., Reichwald, R., & Lee, R. (2013). Cultural socialization in families with adopted Korean adolescents: A mixed-method, multi-informant study. *Journal of Adolescent Research, 28*, 69–95.

Kim, S.M., Han, D.H., Trksak, G.H., & Lee, Y.S. (2014). Gender differences in adolescent coping behaviors and suicidal ideation. *Anxiety, Stress, and Coping, 27*, 439–454.

Kim, S.Y., Chen, Q., Wang, Y., Shen, Y., & Orozco-Lapray, D. (2013). Longitudinal linkages among parent-child acculturation discrepancy, parenting, parent-child sense of alienation, and adolescent adjustment in Chinese American families. *Developmental Psychology, 49*, 900–912.

Kim, S.Y., Wang, Y., Chen, Q., Shen, Y., & Hou, Y. (2015, in press). Parent-child acculturation profiles as predictors of Chinese American adolescents' academic trajectories. *Journal of Youth and Adolescence.*

Kim, S.Y., Wang, Y., Orozco-Lapray, D., Shen, Y., & Murtuza, M. (2013). Does "tiger parenting" exist? Parenting profiles of Chinese Americans and adolescent developmental outcomes. *Asian American Journal of Psychology, 4*, 7–18.

Kimble, M., Neacsiu, A.D., Flack, W.F., & Horner, J. (2008). Risk of unwanted sex for college women: Evidence for a red zone. *Journal of American College Health, 57*, 331–338.

King, L. (2013). *Experience psychology* (2nd ed.). New York: McGraw-Hill.

King, L. (2014). *Psychology* (3rd ed.). New York: McGraw-Hill.

King, L. (2016, in press). *Experience psychology* (3rd ed.). New York: McGraw-Hill.

King, L.A. (2013). *Experience psychology* (2nd ed.). New York: McGraw-Hill.

King, L.A. (2014). *Psychology: An appreciative experience* (3rd ed.). New York: McGraw-Hill.

King, L.A. (2016, in press). *Experience psychology* (3rd ed.). New York: McGraw-Hill.

King, P.E., & Boyatzis, C.J. (2015). The nature and function of religious and spiritual development in childhood and adolescence. In R.M. Lerner (Ed.), *Handbook of child psychology and developmental science* (7th ed.). New York: Wiley.

King, P.E., Ramos, J.S., & Clardy, C.E. (2013). Searching for the sacred: Religious and spiritual development among adolescents. In K.I. Pargament, J. Exline, & J. Jones (Eds.), *APA handbook of psychology, religion, and spirituality.* Washington, DC: American Psychological Association.

King, P.E., & Roeser, R.W. (2009). Religion and spirituality in adolescent development. In R.M. Lerner & L. Steinberg (Eds.), *Handbook of adolescent psychology* (3rd ed.). New York: Wiley.

Kins, E., & Beyers, W. (2010). Failure to launch, failure to achieve criteria for adulthood? *Journal of Adolescent Research, 25*, 743–777.

Kirby, D.B., Laris, B.A., & Rolleri, L.A. (2007). Sex and HIV education programs: Their impact on sexual behavior of young people throughout the world. *Journal of Adolescent Health, 40*, 206–217.

Kirk, S.A., Gallagher, J.J., & Coleman, M.R. (2015). *Educating exceptional children* (14th ed.). Boston: Cengage.

Kirkman, M., Rosenthal, D.A., & Feldman, S.S. (2002). Talking to a tiger: Fathers reveal their difficulties in communicating about sexuality with adolescents. In S.S. Feldman & D.A. Rosenthal (Eds.), *Talking sexuality: Parent-adolescent communication.* San Francisco: Jossey-Bass.

Kistler, M., Rodgers, B., Power, T., Austin, E.W., & Hill, L.G. (2010). Adolescents and music media: Toward an involvement-mediational model of consumption and self-concept. *Journal of Research on Adolescence, 20*, 616–630.

Kistner, J., & others (2010). Sex differences in relational and overt aggression in the late elementary school years. *Aggressive Behavior, 36*, 282–291.

Kiuru, N., Kovisto, P., Mutanen, P., Vuori, J., & Nurmi, J-E. (2011). How do efforts to enhance career preparation influence peer groups? *Journal of Research on Adolescence, 21*, 677–690.

Klaczynski, P.A., Byrnes, J.P., & Jacobs, J.E. (2001). Introduction to the special issue: The development of decision making. *Applied Developmental Psychology, 22*, 225–236.

Klaczynski, P.A., & Narasimham, G. (1998). Development of scientific reasoning biases: Cognitive versus ego-protective explanations. *Developmental Psychology, 34*, 175–187.

Klahr, A.M., & Burt, S.A. (2014). Elucidating the etiology of individual differences in parenting: A meta-analysis of behavioral genetic research. *Psychological Bulletin, 140*, 544–586.

Klatt, J., & Enright, R. (2009). Investigating the place of forgiveness within the positive youth development paradigm. *Journal of Moral Education, 38*, 35–52.

Kleiman, E.M., Law, K.C., & Anestis, M.D. (2014). Do theories of suicide play well together? Integrating components of the hopelessness and interpersonal psychology theories of suicide. *Comprehensive Psychiatry, 55*, 431–438.

Klein, S. (2012). *State of public school segregation in the United States, 2007–2010.* Washington, DC: Feminist Majority Foundation.

Klettke, B., Haliford, D.J., & Mellor, D.J. (2014). Sexting prevalence and correlates: A systematic literature review. *Clinical Psychology Review, 34*, 44–53.

Klimstra, T.A., Hale, W.W., Raaijmakers, Q.A.W., Branje, S.J.T., & Meeus, W.H.H. (2010). Identity formation in adolescence: Change or stability? *Journal of Youth and Adolescence, 39*, 150–162.

Klimstra, T.A., Luyckx, K., Germeijs, V., Meeus, W.H., & Goossens, L. (2012). Personality traits and educational identity formation in late adolescents: Longitudinal associations and academic progress. *Journal of Youth and Adolescence, 41*, 346–361.

Kling, K.C., Hyde, J.S., Showers, C., & Buswell, B. (1999). Gender differences in self-esteem: A meta-analysis. *Psychological Bulletin, 125*, 470–500.

Kloep, M., & Hendry, L.B. (2010). Letting go or holding on? Parents' perceptions of their relationships with their children during emerging adulthood. *British Journal of Developmental Psychology, 28*, 817–834.

Kloss, J.D., Nash, C.O., Horsey, S.E., & Taylor, D.J. (2011). The delivery of sleep medicine to college students. *Journal of Adolescent Health, 48*, 553–561.

Kloss, J.D., & others (2015, in press). A "Sleep 101" program for college students improves sleep hygiene knowledge and reduces maladaptive beliefs about sleep. *Behavioral Medicine.*

Knott, S., Woodward, D., Hoefkens, A., Limbert, C. (2015, in press). Cognitive behavior therapy for bulimia nervosa and eating disorders not otherwise specified: Translation from randomized controlled trial to a clinical setting. *Behavioural and Cognitive Psychotherapy.*

Knox, D., & Wilson, K. (1981). Dating behaviors of university students. *Family Relations, 30*, 255–258.

Kobak, R.R., & Kerig, P.K. (2015). Introduction to the special issue: Attachment-based treatments for adolescents. *Attachment and Human Development, 17*, 111–118.

Kobak, R.R., & others (2015). Attachment-based treatments for adolescents: The secure cycle as a framework for assessment, treatment, and evaluation. *Attachment and Human Development, 17*, 220–239.

Kochanska, G., Barry, R.A., Stellern, S.A., & O'Bleness, J.J. (2010a). Early attachment organization moderates the parent-child mutually coercive pathway to children's antisocial conduct. *Child Development, 80*, 1288–1300.

Kochanska, G., Woodard, J., Iim, S., Koenig, J.L., Yoon, J.E., & Barry, R.A. (2010b). Positive socialization mechanisms in secure and insecure parent-child dyads: Two longitudinal studies. *Journal of Child Psychology and Psychiatry, 51*, 998–1009.

Koenig, L.B., McGue, M., & Iacono, W.G. (2008). Stability and change in religiousness during emerging adulthood. *Developmental Psychology, 44*, 523–543.

Koh, H. (2014). The Teen Pregnancy Prevention Program: An evidence-based public health program model. *Journal of Adolescent Health, 54*(Suppl. 1), S1–S2.

Kohlberg, L. (1958). *The development of modes of moral thinking and choice in the years 10 to 16.* Unpublished doctoral dissertation, University of Chicago.

Kohlberg, L. (1969). Stage and sequence: The cognitive-developmental approach to socialization. In D.A. Goslin (Ed.), *Handbook of socialization theory and research.* Chicago: Rand McNally.

Kohlberg, L. (1976). Moral stages and moralization: The cognitive developmental approach. In T. Lickona (Ed.), *Moral development and behavior.* New York: Holt, Rinehart, & Winston.

Kohlberg, L. (1986). A current statement on some theoretical issues. In S. Modgil & C. Modgil (Eds.), *Lawrence Kohlberg.* Philadelphia: Falmer.

Kohler, P.K., Manhart, L.E., &. Lafferty, W.E. (2008). Abstinence-only and comprehensive sex education and the initiation of sexual activity and teen pregnancy. *Journal of Adolescent Health, 42*, 344–351.

Kohn, M.L. (1977). *Class and conformity: A study in values* (2nd ed.). Chicago: University of Chicago Press.

Kollins, S.H., & Adcock, R.A. (2014). ADHD, altered dopamine neurotransmission, and disrupted reinforcement processes: Implications for smoking and nicotine dependence. *Progress in Neuro-Psychopharmacology and Biological Psychiatry, 52*, 70–78.

Konrath, S.H., Chopik, W.J., Hsing, C.K., & O'Brien, E. (2014). Changes in adult attachment styles in American college students over time: A meta-analysis. *Personality and Social Psychology Bulletin, 18,* 326–348.

Koolhof, R., Loeber, R., Wei, E.H., Pardini, D., & D'Escury, A.C. (2007). Inhibition deficits of serious delinquent boys with low intelligence. *Criminal Behavior and Mental Health, 17,* 274–292.

Koozehcian, M.S., & others (2014). The role of exercise training on lipoprotein profiles in adolescent males. *Lipids in Health and Disease, 13,* 95.

Kopak, A.M., Chen, A.C., Haas, S.A., & Gillmore, M.R. (2012). The importance of family factors to protect against substance use related problems among Mexican heritage and White youth. *Drug and Alcohol Dependence, 124,* 34–41.

Koppelman, K.L. (2014). *Understanding human differences* (4th ed.). Upper Saddle River, NJ: Pearson.

Kornblum, J. (2006, March 9). How to monitor the kids? *USA Today,* p. 1D.

Koss, K.J., & others (2013). Patterns of children's adrenocortical reactivity to interparental conflict and associations with child adjustment: A growth mixture modeling approach. *Developmental Psychology, 49*(2), 317–326.

Koss, K.J., & others (2014). Asymmetry in children's salivary cortisol and alpha-amylase in the context of marital conflict: Links to children's emotional security and adjustment. *Developmental Psychobiology, 56,* 836–849.

Kosut, M. (Ed.) (2012). *Encyclopedia of gender in media.* Thousand Oaks, CA: Sage.

Kottak, C., & Kozaitis, K. (2012). *On being different* (4th ed.). New York: McGraw-Hill.

Kouros, C.G., Papp, L.M., Goeke-Morey, M.C., & Cummings, E.M. (2014). Spillover between marital quality and parent-child relationship quality: Parental depressive symptoms as moderators. *Journal of Family Psychology, 28,* 315–325.

Kowalski, R.M., Giumetti, G.W., Schroeder, A.N., & Lattanner, M.R. (2014). Bullying in the digital age: A critical review and meta-analysis of cyberbullying research among youth. *Psychological Bulletin, 140,* 1073–1137.

Kozol, J. (2005). *The shame of a nation.* New York: Crown.

Kraft, J.M., & others (2012). Sex education and adolescent sexual behavior: Do community characteristics matter? *Contraception, 86,* 276–280.

Kramer, L. (2010). The essential ingredients of successful sibling relationships: An emerging framework for advancing theory and practice. *Child Development Perspectives, 4,* 80–86.

Krebs, C. (2014). Measuring sexual victimization: On what fronts is the jury still out and do we need it to come in? *Trauma, Violence, and Abuse, 15,* 170–180.

Kremer-Sadlik, T., & others (2015). Eating fruits and vegetables: An ethnographic study of American and French family dinners. *Appetite, 89,* 84–92.

Kring, A.M. (2000). Gender and anger. In A.H. Fischer (Ed.), *Gender and emotion: Social psychological perspectives.* New York: Cambridge University Press.

Kroger, J. (2007). *Identity development: Adolescence through adulthood* (2nd ed.). Thousand Oaks, CA: Sage.

Kroger, J. (2012). The status of identity developments in identity research. In P.K. Kerig, M.S. Schulz, & S.T. Hauser (Eds.), *Adolescence and beyond.* New York: Oxford University Press.

Kroger, J. (2015). Identity development through adulthood: The move toward "wholeness." In K.C. McLean & M. Syed (Eds.), *Oxford handbook of identity development.* New York: Oxford University Press.

Kroger, J., Martinussen, M., & Marcia, J.E. (2010). Identity change during adolescence and young adulthood: A meta-analysis. *Journal of Adolescence, 33,* 683–698.

Kroon Van Diest, A.M., & Perez, M. (2013). Exploring the integration of thin-ideal internalization and self-objectification in the prevention of eating disorders. *Body Image, 10,* 16–25.

Krueger, J.I., Vohs, K.D., & Baumeister, R.F. (2008). Is the allure of self-esteem a mirage after all? *American Psychologist, 63,* 64–65.

Krushkal, J., & others (2014). Epigenetic analysis of neurocognitive development at 1 year of age in a community-based pregnancy cohort. *Behavior Genetics, 44,* 113–125.

Kucian, K., & von Aster, M. (2015, in press). Developmental dyscalculia. *European Journal of Pediatrics.*

Kuhn, D. (2009). Adolescent thinking. In R.M. Lerner & L. Steinberg (Eds.), *Handbook of adolescent psychology* (3rd ed.). New York: Wiley.

Kuhn, D. (2013). Reasoning. In P.D. Zelazo (Ed.), *Oxford handbook of developmental psychology.* New York: Oxford University Press.

Kuhn, D., & Franklin, S. (2006). The second decade: What develops (and how)? In W. Damon & R. Lerner (Eds.), *Handbook of child psychology* (6th ed.). New York: Wiley.

Kulu, H. (2014). Marriage duration and divorce: The seven-year itch or a lifelong itch? *Demography, 51*(3), 881–893.

Kumar, R., & Maehr, M. (2010). Schooling, cultural diversity, and student motivation. In J.L. Meece & J.S. Eccles (Eds.), *Handbook of research on schools, schooling, and human development.* New York: Routledge.

Kumar, R., & others (2014). Interactions between the FTO and GNB3 genes contribute to varied phenotypes in hypertension. *PLoS One, 8*(5), e63934.

Kumpfer, K.L., & Alvarado, R. (2003). Family-strengthening approaches for the prevention of youth problem behaviors. *American Psychologist, 58,* 457–465.

Kunnen, S., & Metz, M. (2015). Commitment and exploration: The need for a developmental approach. In K.C. McLean & M. Syed (Eds.), *Oxford handbook of identity development.* New York: Oxford University Press.

Kunzweiler, C. (2007). Twin individuality. *Fresh Ink: Essays from Boston College's First-Year Writing Seminar, 9*(1), 2–3.

Kuperberg, A. (2014). Age at coresidence, premarital cohabitation, and marriage dissolution: 1985–2009. *Journal of Marriage and Family, 76,* 352–369.

Kupersmidt, J.B., & Coie J.D. (1990). Preadolescent peer status, aggression, and school adjustment as predictors of externalizing problems in adolescence. *Child Development, 61,* 1350–1363.

Kurdek, L.A. (2008). Change in relationship quality for partners from lesbian, gay male, and heterosexual couples. *Journal of Family Psychology, 22,* 701–711.

Kurth, S., & others (2010). Characteristics of sleep slow waves in children and adolescents. *Sleep, 33,* 475–480.

L

Labouvie-Vief, G. (1986, August). *Modes of knowing and life-span cognition.* Paper presented at the meeting of the American Psychological Association, Washington, DC.

Labouvie-Vief, G. (2006). Emerging structures of adult thought. In J.J. Arnett & J.L. Tanner (Eds.), *Emerging adults in America.* Washington, DC: American Psychological Association.

Labouvie-Vief, G. (2009). Cognition and equilibrium regulation in development and aging. In V. Bengtson & others (Eds.), *Handbook of theories of aging.* New York: Springer.

Labouvie-Vief, G., Gruhn, D., & Studer J. (2010). Dynamic integration of emotion and cognition: Equilibrium regulation in development and aging. In M.E. Lamb, A. Freund, & R.M. Lerner (Eds.), *Handbook of life-span development* (Vol. 2). New York: Wiley.

LaBrie, J.W., Hummer, J., Kenney, S., Lac, A., & Pedersen, E. (2011). Identifying factors that increase the likelihood for alcohol-induced blackouts in the prepartying context. *Substance Use and Misuse, 46,* 992–1002.

Ladd, G.W., Kochenderfer-Ladd, B., & Rydell, A-M. (2011). Children's interpersonal skills and school-based relationships. In P.K. Smith & C.H. Hart (Eds.), *Wiley-Blackwell handbook of social development* (2nd ed.). New York: Wiley.

Laflin, M.T., Wang, J., & Barry, M. (2008). A longitudinal study of adolescent transition from virgin to nonvirgin status. *Journal of Adolescent Health, 42,* 228–236.

LaFontana, K.M., & Cillessen, A.H.N. (2010). Developmental changes in the priority of perceived status in childhood and adolescence. *Social Development, 19,* 130–147.

LaFrance, M., Hecht, M.A., & Paluck, E.L. (2003). The contingent smile: A meta-analysis of sex differences in smiling. *Psychological Bulletin, 129,* 305–334.

Laftman, S.B., Bergstrom, M., Modin, G., & Ostberg, V. (2014). Joint physical custody, turning to parents for emotional support, and subjective health: A study of adolescents in Stockholm, Sweden. *Scandinavian Journal of Public Health, 42,* 456–462.

Lagus, K.A., Bernat, D.H., Bearinger, L.H., Resnick, M.D., & Eisenberg, M.E. (2011). Parental perspectives on sources of sex information for young people. *Journal of Adolescent Health, 49*(1), 87–89.

Laible, D.J., Murphy, T.P., & Augustine, M. (2014). Adolescents' aggressive and prosocial behaviors: Links with social information processing, negative emotionality, moral affect, and moral cognition. *Journal of Genetic Psychology, 175,* 270–286.

Lakshminarayan, N., Potdar, S., & Reddy, S.G. (2013). Relationship between procrastination and academic performance among a group of undergraduate dental students in India. *Journal of Dental Education, 77,* 524–528.

Lalonde, C., & Chandler, M. (2004). Culture, selves, and time. In C. Lightfoot, C. Lalonde, & M. Chandler (Eds.), *Changing conceptions of psychological life.* Mahwah, NJ: Erlbaum.

Lam, C.B., McHale, S.M., & Crouter, A.C. (2012). Parent-child shared time from middle childhood to adolescence: Developmental course and adjustment correlates. *Child Development, 83,* 2089–2103.

Lambert, N.M., Fincham, F.D., & Stillman, T.F. (2012). Gratitude and depressive symptoms: The role of positive reframing and positive emotion. *Cognition and Emotion, 26,* 615–633.

Lampard, A.M., Byrne, S.M., McLean, N., & Fursland, A. (2012). The Eating Disorder Inventory-2 perfectionism scale: Factor structure and associations with dietary restraint and weight and shape concern in eating disorders. *Eating Behaviors, 13,* 49–53.

Lanciano, T., & Curci, A. (2014). Incremental validity of emotional intelligence ability in predicting academic achievement. *American Journal of Psychology, 127,* 447–461.

Landor, A., Simons, L.G., Simons, R.L., Brody, G.H., & Gibbons, F.X. (2011). The role of religiosity in the relationship between parents, peers, and adolescent risky sexual behavior. *Journal of Youth and Adolescence, 40*(3), 296–309.

Langberg, J.M., Dvorsky, M.R., & Evans, S.W. (2013). What specific facets of executive function are associated with academic functioning in youth with attention-deficit/hyperactivity disorder? *Journal of Abnormal Child Psychology, 41,* 1145–1159.

Langer, E.J. (2005). *On becoming an artist.* New York: Ballantine.

Langsford, R., Bonell, C., Jones, H., & Campbell, R. (2015, in press). Obesity prevention and the health promoting schools framework: Essential components and barriers to success. *International Journal of Behavioral Nutrition and Physical Activity.*

Langstrom, N., Rahman, Q., Carlstrom, E., & Lichtenstein, P. (2010). Genetic and environmental effects on same-sex behavior: A population study of twins in Sweden. *Archives of Sexual Behavior, 39,* 75–80.

Lansford, J.E. (2009). Parental divorce and children's adjustment. *Perspectives on Psychological Science, 4,* 140–152.

Lansford, J.E. (2012). Divorce. In R.J.R. Levesque (Ed.), *Encyclopedia of adolescence.* New York: Springer.

Lansford, J.E. (2013). Single- and two-parent families. In J. Hattie & E. Anderman (Eds.), *International handbook of student achievement.* New York: Routledge.

Lansford, J.E., & others (2006). Trajectories of internalizing, externalizing, and grades for children who have and have not experienced their parents' divorce or separation. *Journal of Family Psychology, 20,* 292–301.

Lansford, J.E., & others (2010). Developmental precursors of number of sexual partners from ages 16 to 22. *Journal of Research on Adolescence, 20,* 651–677.

Lantrip, C., & others (2015, in press). Executive function and emotion regulation strategy use in adolescents. *Applied Neuropsychology: Child.*

Lapsley, D.K. (1990). Continuity and discontinuity in adolescent social cognitive development. In R. Montemayor, G. Adams, & T. Gulotta (Eds.), *From childhood to adolescence: A transitional period?* Newbury Park, CA: Sage.

Lapsley, D.K., & Aalsma, M.C. (2006). An empirical typology of narcissism and mental health in late adolescence. *Journal of Adolescence, 29,* 53–71.

Lapsley, D., & Carlo, G. (2014). Moral development at the crossroads: New trends and possible futures. *Developmental Psychology, 50,* 1–7.

Lapsley, D.K., Enright, R.D., & Serlin, R.C. (1985). Toward a theoretical perspective on the legislation of adolescence. *Journal of Early Adolescence, 5,* 441–466.

Lapsley, D.K., & Hill, P.L. (2010). Subjective invulnerability, optimism bias, and adjustment in emerging adulthood. *Journal of Youth and Adolescence, 39,* 847–857.

Lapsley, D.K., Rice, K.G., & Shadid, G.E. (1989). Psychological separation and adjustment to college. *Journal of Counseling Psychology, 36,* 286–294.

Lapsley, D.K., & Stey, P. (2012). Adolescent narcissism. In R. Levesque (Ed.), *Encyclopedia of adolescence.* New York: Springer.

Lapsley, D., & Stey, P.C. (2014). Moral self-identity as the aim of education. In L. Nucci, T. Krettenauer, & D. Narváez (Eds.), *Handbook of moral and character education* (2nd ed.). New York: Routledge.

Larsen, J.K., & others (2013). Emotion regulation in adolescence: A prospective study of expressive suppression and depressive symptoms. *Journal of Early Adolescence, 33*(2), 184–200.

Larson, N.I., & others (2008). Fast food intake: Longitudinal trends during the transition to young adulthood and correlates of intake. *Journal of Adolescent Health, 43,* 79–86.

Larson, R.W. (1999, September). Unpublished review of J.W. Santrock's *Adolescence,* 8th ed. (New York: McGraw-Hill).

Larson, R.W. (2000). Toward a psychology of positive youth development. *American Psychologist, 55,* 170–183.

Larson, R.W. (2001). How U.S. children and adolescents spend time: What it does (and doesn't) tell us about their development. *Current Directions in Psychological Science, 10,* 160–164.

Larson, R.W. (2008). Development of the capacity for teamwork in youth development. In R.K. Silbereisen & R.M. Lerner (Eds.), *Approaches to positive youth development.* Thousand Oaks, CA: Sage.

Larson, R.W. (2014). Studying experience: Pursuing the "something more." In R.W. Lerner & others (Eds.), *The developmental science of adolescence: History through autobiography.* New York: Springer.

Larson, R.W., & Angus, R.M. (2011). Pursuing paradox: The role of adults in creating empowering settings for youth. In M. Aber, K. Maton, & E. Seidman (Eds.), *Empowerment settings and voices for social change.* New York: Oxford University Press.

Larson, R.W., & Dawes, N.P. (2015). How to cultivate adolescents' motivation: Effective strategies employed by the professional staff of American youth programs. In S. Joseph (Ed.), *Positive psychology in practice.* New York: Wiley.

Larson, R.W., & Lampman-Petraitis, C. (1989). Daily emotional states as reported by children and adolescents. *Child Development, 60,* 1250–1260.

Larson, R.W., & Richards, M.H. (1994). *Divergent realities.* New York: Basic Books.

Larson, R.W., Rickman, A.N., Gibbons, C.M., & Walker, K.C. (2011). Practitioner expertise: Creating quality within the tumble of events in youth settings. *New Directions in Youth Development, 121,* 71–88.

Larson, R.W., & Tran, S.P. (2014). Invited commentary: Positive youth development and human complexity. *Journal of Youth and Adolescence, 43,* 1012–1017.

Larson, R.W., & Verma, S. (1999). How children and adolescents spend time across the world: Work, play, and developmental opportunities. *Psychological Bulletin, 125,* 701–736.

Larson, R.W., & Walker, K.C. (2010). Dilemmas of practice: Challenges to program quality encountered by youth program leaders. *American Journal of Community Psychology, 45,* 338–349.

Larson, R.W., Wilson, S., & Rickman, A. (2009). Globalization, societal change, and adolescence across the world. In R.M. Lerner & L. Steinberg (Eds.), *Handbook of adolescent psychology* (3rd ed.). New York: Wiley.

Latt, E., & others (2015, in press). Vigorous physical activity rather than sedentary behavior predicts overweight and obesity in pubertal boys: A 2-year follow-up study. *Scandinavian Journal of Public Health.*

Lau, J.S., Adams, S.H., Irwin, C.E., & Ozer, E.M. (2013). Receipt of preventive health services in young adults. *Journal of Adolescent Health, 52,* 42–49.

Lau, M., Lin, H., & Flores, G. (2015, in press). Clusters of factors identify a high prevalence of pregnancy involvement among U.S. adolescent males. *Maternal and Child Health Journal.*

Lauff, E., Ingels, S.J., & Christopher, E.M. (2014). *Educational longitudinal study of 2002 (ELS:2002): A first look at 2002 high school sophomores 10 years later.* NCES 2014-36. Washington, DC: U.S. Department of Education.

Laursen, B. (1995). Conflict and social interaction in adolescent relationships. *Journal of Research on Adolescence, 5,* 55–70.

Laursen, B., & Collins, W.A. (2009). Parent-child relationships during adolescence. In R.M. Lerner & L. Steinberg (Eds.), *Handbook of adolescent psychology* (3rd ed.). New York: Wiley.

Laursen, B., Coy, K.C., & Collins, W.A. (1998). Reconsidering changes in parent-child conflict across adolescence: A meta-analysis. *Child Development, 69,* 817–832.

Lavender, J.M., & others (2014). Dimensions of emotion dysregulation in bulimia nervosa. *European Eating Disorders Review, 22,* 212–216.

Lavner, J.A., & Bradbury, T.N. (2012). Why do even satisfied newlyweds eventually go on to divorce? *Journal of Family Psychology, 26,* 1–10.

LaVoie, J. (1976). Ego identity formation in middle adolescence. *Journal of Youth and Adolescence, 5,* 371–385.

Lazarus, R.S. (2000). Toward better research on stress and coping. *American Psychologist, 55*(6), 665–673.

Le, K., & others (2014). Workers behaving badly: Associations between adolescent reports of the Big Five and counterproductive work behaviors in adulthood. *Personality and Individual Differences, 61–62,* 7–12.

Leadbeater, B.J., Way, N., & Raden, A. (1994, February). *Barriers to involvement of father of the children of adolescent mothers.* Paper presented at the meeting of the Society for Research on Adolescence, San Diego.

Leaper, C. (2013). Gender development during childhood. In P.D. Zelazo (Ed.), *Oxford handbook of developmental psychology.* New York: Oxford University Press.

Leaper, C. (2015). Gender development from a social-cognitive perspective. In R.M. Lerner (Ed.), *Handbook of child psychology and developmental science* (7th ed.). New York: Wiley.

Leaper, C., & Bigler, R.H. (2011). Gender. In M.K. Underwood & L.H. Rosen (Eds.), *Social development.* New York: Guilford.

Leaper, C., & Brown, C.S. (2008). Perceived experience of sexism among adolescent girls. *Child Development, 79,* 685–704.

Leaper, C., & Brown, C.S. (2015). Sexism in schools. In L.S. Liben & R.S. Bigler (Eds.), *Advances in Child Development and Behavior.* San Diego: Elsevier.

Leaper, C., & Friedman, C.K. (2007). The socialization of gender. In J.E. Grusec & P.D. Hastings (Eds.), *Handbook of socialization.* New York: Guilford.

Lecompte, V., & Moss, E. (2014). Disorganized and controlling patterns of attachment, role reversal, and caregiving helplessness: Links to adolescents' externalizing problems. *American Journal of Orthopsychiatry, 84,* 581–589.

Ledesma, K. (2012). A place to call home. *Adoptive Families.* Retrieved August 8, 2012, from www.adoptivefamilies.com/articles.php?aid=2129

Lee, G.Y., & Choi, Y.J. (2015, in press). Association of school, family, and mental health characteristics with suicidal ideation among Korean adolescents. *Research in Nursing and Health.*

Lee, H., Hardy, J., & Zetterberg, H. (2015, in press). Neurological consequences of traumatic brain injuries in sports. *Molecular and Cellular Neurosciences.*

Lee, J.H., Jang, A.S., Park, S.W., Kim, D.J., & Park, C.S. (2014). Gene-gene interaction between CCR3 and Eotaxin genes: The relationship with blood eosinophilia in asthma. *Allergy, Asthma, and Immunology Research, 6,* 55–60.

Lee, K., & Ashton, M.C. (2008). The HEXACO personality factors in the indigenous personality lexicons and 11 other languages. *Journal of Personality, 76,* 1001–1054.

Lee, K.Y., & others (2011). Effects of combined radiofrequency radiation exposure on the cell cycle and its regulatory proteins. *Bioelectromagnetics, 32,* 169–178.

Lee, L.A., Sbarra, D.A., Mason, A.E., & Law, R.W. (2011). Attachment anxiety, verbal immediacy, and blood pressure: Results from a laboratory-analog study following marital separation. *Personal Relationships, 18,* 285–301.

Lee, S., & others (2012). Effects of aerobic versus resistance exercise without caloric restriction on abdominal fat, intrahepatic lipid, and insulin sensitivity in obese adolescent boys: A randomized, controlled trial. *Diabetes, 61,* 2787–2795.

Lee, T-W., Wu, Y-T., Yu, Y., Wu, H-C., & Chen, T-J. (2012). A smarter brain is associated with stronger neural interaction in healthy young females: A resting EEG coherence study. *Intelligence, 40,* 38–48.

Lee, Y.H., & Song, G.G. (2014). Genome-wide pathway analysis in attention-deficit/hyperactivity disorder. *Neurological Sciences, 35,* 1189–1196.

Leedy, P.D., & Ormrod, J.E. (2014). *Practical research* (11th ed.). Upper Saddle River, NJ: Pearson.

Leeman, R.F., & others (2014). Impulsivity, sensation-seeking, and part-time job status in relation to substance use and gambling in adolescents. *Journal of Adolescent Health, 54,* 460–466.

Lefkowitz, E.S., Boone, T.L., & Shearer, T.L. (2004). Communication with best friends about sex-related topics during emerging adulthood. *Journal of Youth and Adolescence, 33,* 339–351.

Lefkowitz, E.S., & Espinosa-Hernandez, G. (2006). *Sexual related communication with mothers and close friends during the transition to university.* Unpublished manuscript, Department of Human Development and Family Studies, Pennsylvania State University, University Park, PA.

Lefkowitz, E.S., & Gillen, M.M. (2006). "Sex is just a normal part of life": Sexuality in emerging adulthood. In J.J. Arnett & J.L. Tanner (Eds.), *Emerging adults in America.* Washington, DC: American Psychological Association.

Lefkowitz, E.S., Shearer, C.L., Gillen, M.M., & Espinosa-Hernandez, G. (2014). How gendered attitudes relate to women's and men's sexual behaviors and beliefs. *Sexuality and Culture, 18,* 833–846.

Lefkowitz, E.S., & Vasilenko, S.A. (2014). Healthy sex and sexual health: New directions for studying outcomes of sexual health. *New Directions in Child and Adolescent Development, 144,* 87–98.

Leger, D., Beck, F., Richard, J.B., & Godeau, E. (2012). Total sleep time severely drops in adolescence. *PLoS One, 7*(10), e45204.

Lehr, C.A., Hanson, A., Sinclair, M.F., & Christensen, S.I. (2003). Moving beyond dropout prevention towards school completion. *School Psychology Review, 32,* 342–364.

Leitenberg, H., Detzer, M.J., & Srebnik, D. (1993). Gender differences in masturbation and the relation of masturbation experience in preadolescence and/or early adolescence to sexual behavior and adjustment in young adulthood. *Archives of Sexual Behavior, 22,* 87–98.

Lenhart, A. (2012). Teens, smartphones, and texting: Texting volume is up while the frequency of voice calling is down. Retrieved May 2, 2013, from http://pewinternet.org/~/medai/Files/Reorts/2012/PIP_Teens_Smartphones_and-Texting.pdf

Lenhart, A., Ling, R., Campbell, S., & Purcell, K. (2010, April 20). *Teens and mobile phones.* Washington, DC: Pew Research Center.

Lenhart, A., Purcell, K., Smith, A., & Zickuhr, K. (2010, February 3). *Social media and young adults.* Washington, DC: Pew Research Center.

Leondari, A., & Gonida, E. (2007). Predicting academic self-handicapping in different age groups: The role of personal achievement goals and social goals. *British Journal of Educational Psychology, 77,* 595–611.

Leone, J.E., Mullin, E.M., Maurer-Starks, S.S., & Rovito, M.J. (2014). The Adolescent Body Image Satisfaction Scale (ABISS) for males: Exploratory factor analysis and implications for strength and conditioning professionals. *Journal of Strength and Conditioning Research, 28,* 2657–2668.

Lepper, M.R., Corpus, J.H., & Iyengar, S.S. (2005). Intrinsic and extrinsic orientations in the classroom: Age differences and academic correlates. *Journal of Educational Psychology, 97,* 184–196.

Lereya, S.T., Copeland, W.E., Zammit, S., & Wolke, D. (2015, in press). Bully/victims: A longitudinal, population-based cohort study of their mental health. *European Child and Adolescent Psychiatry.*

Lereya, S.T., Samara, M., & Wolke, D. (2013). Parenting behavior and the risk of becoming a victim and a bully/victim: A meta-analysis study. *Child Abuse and Neglect, 37,* 1091–1108.

Lerner, J.V., Phelps, E., Forman, Y., & Bowers, E.P. (2009). Positive youth development. In R.M. Lerner & L. Steinberg (Eds.), *Handbook of adolescent psychology* (3rd ed.). New York: Wiley.

Lerner, J.V., & others (2013). Positive youth development: Processes, philosophies, and programs. In I.B. Weiner & others (Eds.), *Handbook of psychology* (2nd ed., Vol. 6). New York: Wiley.

Lerner, R.M., Boyd, M., & Du, D. (2008). Adolescent development. In I.B. Weiner & C.B. Craighead (Eds.), *Encyclopedia of psychology* (4th ed.). Hoboken, NJ: Wiley.

Lerner, R.M., Lerner, J.V., Bowers, E., & Geldhof, J. (2015). Positive youth development: A relational developmental systems model. In R.M. Lerner (Ed.), *Handbook of child psychology and developmental science* (7th ed.). New York: Wiley.

Lerner, R.M., von Eye, A., Lerner, J.V., Lewin-Bizan, S., & Bowers, E.P. (2010). Special issue introduction: The meaning and measurement of thriving: A view of the issues. *Journal of Youth and Adolescence, 39,* 707–719.

Leslie, S.J., Cimpian, A., Meyer, M., & Freeland, E. (2015). Expectations of brilliance underlie gender distributions across academic disciplines. *Science, 347,* 262–265.

Levant, R.F. (2001). Men and masculinity. In J. Worell (Ed.), *Encyclopedia of women and gender.* San Diego: Academic Press.

Leventhal, T., Dupere, V., & Shuey, E. (2015). Children in neighborhoods. In R.M. Lerner (Ed.), *Handbook of child psychology and developmental science* (7th ed.). New York: Oxford University Press.

Lever-Duffy, J., & McDonald, J. (2015). *Teaching and learning with technology* (5th ed.). Upper Saddle River, NJ: Pearson.

Levin, J.A., Fox, J.A., & Forde, D.R. (2014). *Elementary statistics in social research* (12th ed.). Upper Saddle River, NJ: Pearson.

Lewin, A., & others (2015, in press). Strengthening positive coparenting in teen parents: A cultural adaptation of an evidence-based intervention. *Journal of Primary Prevention.*

Lewin-Bizan, S., Bowers, E., & Lerner, R.M. (2010). One good thing leads to another: Cascades of positive youth development among American adolescents. *Development and Psychopathology, 22,* 759–770.

Lewis, A.C. (2007). Looking beyond NCLB. *Phi Delta Kappan, 88,* 483–484.

Lewis, C.G. (1981). How adolescents approach decisions: Changes over grades seven to twelve and policy implications. *Child Development, 52,* 538–554.

Lewis, K.M., & others (2013). Problem behavior and urban, low-income youth: A randomized controlled trial of Positive Action in Chicago. *Amerian Journal of Prevention, 44,* 622–630.

Lewis, M., Feiring, C., & Rosenthal, S. (2000). Attachment over time. *Child Development, 71,* 707–720.

Lewis, M.D. (2013). The development of emotion regulation. In P.D. Zelazo (Ed.), *Handbook of developmental psychology.* New York: Oxford University Press.

Lewis, V.G., Money, J., & Bobrow, N.A. (1977). Idiopathic pubertal delay beyond the age of 15: Psychological study of 12 boys. *Adolescence, 12,* 1–11.

Li, D., Zhang, W., Li, X., Li, N., & Ye, B. (2012). Gratitude and suicidal ideation and suicide attempts among Chinese adolescents: Direct, mediated, and moderated effects. *Journal of Adolescence, 35,* 55–66.

Li, F., & others (2014). Intrinsic brain abnormalities in attention deficit hyperactivity disorder: A resting-state functional MR imaging study. *Radiology, 272,* 514–523.

Liben, L.S. (1995). Psychology meets geography: Exploring the gender gap on the national geography bee. *Psychological Science Agenda, 8,* 8–9.

Liben, L.S. (2015, in press). Probability values and human values in evaluating single-sex education. *Sex Roles.*

Liben, L.S., Bigler, R.S., & Hilliard, L.J. (2014). Gender development: From universality to individuality. In E.T. Gershoff, R.S. Mistry, & D.A. Crosby (Eds.), *Societal contexts of child development.* New York: Oxford University Press.

Liben, L.S., & Coyle, E.F. (2014). Developmental interventions to address the STEM gender gap: Exploring intended and unintended consequences. *Advances in Child Development and Behavior, 47,* 77–115.

Lickliter, R. (2013). Biological development: Theoretical approaches, techniques, and key findings. In P.D. Zelazo (Ed.), *Handbook of developmental psychology.* New York: Oxford University Press.

Lickliter, R., & Honeycutt, H. (2015). Biology development and human systems. In R.M. Lerner (Ed.), *Handbook of child psychology and developmental science* (7th ed.). New York: Wiley.

Limber, S.P. (2004). Implementation of the Olweus Bullying Prevention program in American schools: Lessons learned from the field. In D.L. Espelage & S.M. Swearer (Eds.), *Bullying in American schools.* Mahwah, NJ: Erlbaum.

Lindberg, L.D., & Maddow-Zimet, I. (2012). Consequences of sex education on teen and young adult sexual behaviors and outcomes. *Journal of Adolescent Health, 51,* 332–338.

Lindberg, S.M., Hyde, S.S., Petersen, J.L., & Lin, M.C. (2010). New trends in gender and mathematics performance: A meta-analysis. *Psychological Bulletin, 136,* 1123–1135.

Lindholm, M.E., & others (2014). An integrative analysis reveals coordinated reprogramming of the epigenome and the transcriptome in human skeletal muscle after training. *Epigenetics, 9,* 1557–1569.

Linley, P.A., & Joseph, S. (2004). Positive change following trauma and adversity: A review. *Journal of Traumatic Stress, 17,* 11–21.

Linver, M.R., Roth, J.L., & Brooks-Gunn, J. (2009). Patterns of adolescents' participation in organized activities: Are sports best when combined with other activities? *Developmental Psychology, 45,* 354–367.

Lipowski, M., Lipowska, M., Jochimek, M., & Krokosz, D. (2015, in press). Resilience as a factor protecting youths from risky behavior: Moderating effects of gender and sport. *European Journal of Sport Science.*

Lippman, L.A., & Keith, J.D. (2006). The demographics of spirituality among youth: International perspectives. In E. Roehlkepartain, P.E. King, L. Wagener, & P.L. Benson (Eds.), *The handbook of spirituality in childhood and adolescence.* Thousand Oaks, CA: Sage.

Lippold, M.A., Greenberg, M.T., Graham, J.W., & Feinberg, M.E. (2014). Unpacking the effect of parental monitoring on early adolescent problem behavior: Mediation by parental knowledge and moderation by parent-youth warmth. *Journal of Family Issues, 35,* 1800–1823.

Lipschitz, J.M., Yes, S., Weinstock, L.M., & Spirito, A. (2012). Adolescent and caregiver perception of family functioning: Relation to suicide ideation and attempts. *Psychiatry Research, 200,* 400–403.

Lipsitz, J. (1980, March). *Sexual development in young adolescents.* Invited speech given at the American Association of Sex Educators, Counselors, and Therapists, New York City.

Lipsitz, J. (1983, October). *Making it the hard way: Adolescents in the 1980s.* Testimony presented at the Crisis Intervention Task Force, House Select Committee on Children, Youth, and Families, Washington, DC.

Lisha, N.E., & others (2012). Evaluation of the psychometric properties of the Revised Inventory of the Dimensions of Emerging Adulthood (IDEA-R) in a sample of continuation high school students. *Evaluation & the Health Professions, 37,* 156–177.

Liu, L., & Wang, M. (2015, in press). Parenting stress and harsh discipline in China: The moderating roles of marital satisfaction and parent gender. *Child Abuse and Neglect.*

Lloyd, A.B., & others (2014). Maternal and paternal parenting practices and their influence on children's adiposity, screen-time, diet, and physical activity. *Appetite, 79*, 149–157.

Lloyd, S., Yiend, J., Schmidt, U., & Tchanturia, K. (2014). Perfectionism in anorexia nervosa: Novel performance-based evidence. *PLoS One, 9*(10), e111697.

Lobelo, F., Pate, R.R., Dowda, M., Liese, A.D., & Daniels, S.R. (2010). Cardiorespiratory fitness and clustered cardiovascular disease risk in U.S. adolescents. *Journal of Adolescent Health, 47*, 352–359.

Lobstein, T., & others (2015, in press). Child and adolescent obesity: Part of a bigger picture. *Lancet.*

Loeber, R., & Burke, J.D. (2011). Developmental pathways in juvenile externalizing and internalizing problems. *Journal of Research on Adolescence, 21*, 34–46.

Loeber, R., Burke, J., & Pardini, D. (2009). The etiology and development of antisocial and delinquent behavior. *Annual Review of Psychology* (Vol. 60). Palo Alto, CA: Annual Reviews.

Loeber, R., Farrington, D.P., Stouthamer-Loeber, M., & White, H.R. (2008). *Violence and serious theft: Development and prediction from childhood to adulthood.* New York: Routledge.

Loeber, R., Pardini, D.A., Stouthamer-Loeber, M., & Raine, A. (2007). Do cognitive, physiological, and psychosocial risk and promotive factors predict desistance from delinquency in males? *Development and Psychopathology, 19*, 867–887.

Lomniczi, A., Wright, H., & Ojeda, S.R. (2015). Epigenetic regulation of female puberty. *Frontiers in Neuroendocrinology, 36C*, 90–107.

Lopes, V.P., Gabbard, C., & Rodriques, L.P. (2013). Physical activity in adolescents: Examining influence of the best friend dyad. *Journal of Adolescent Health, 52*(6), 752–756.

Lopez, A.B., Huynh, V.W., & Fuligni, A.J. (2011). A longitudinal study of religious identity and participation during adolescence. *Child Development, 82*, 1297–1309.

Lord, S.E., & Eccles, J.S. (1994, February). *James revisited: The relationship of domain self-concepts and values to Black and White adolescents' self-esteem.* Paper presented at the meeting of the Society for Research on Adolescence, San Diego.

Losel, F., & Bender, D. (2011). Emotional and antisocial outcomes of bullying and victimization at school: A follow-up from childhood to adolescence. *Journal of Aggression, Conflict, and Peace Research, 3*, 89–96.

Loth, K.A., Maclehose, R.F., Fulkerson, J.A., Crow, S., & Neumark-Sztainer, D. (2013). Food-related parenting practices and adolescent weight status: A population-based study. *Pediatrics, 131*, e1443–e1450.

Louca, M., & Short, M.A. (2015). The effect of one night's sleep deprivation on adolescent neurobehavioral performance. *Sleep, 37*(11), 1799–1807.

Lounsbury, J.W., Levy, J.J., Leong, F.T., & Gibson, L.W. (2007). Identity and personality: The Big Five and narrow personality traits in relation to sense of identity. *Identity, 7*, 51–70.

Low, S., Snyder, J., & Shortt, J.W. (2012). The drift toward problem behavior during the transition to adolescence: The contributions of youth disclosure, parenting, and older siblings. *Journal of Research on Adolescence, 22*, 65–79.

Low, S., & others (2014). Engagement matters: Lessons from assessing classroom implementation of Steps to Respect: A bullying prevention program over a one-year period. *Prevention Science, 15*, 165–176.

Lowe, K., & Dotterer, A.M. (2013). Parental monitoring, parental warmth, and minority youths' academic outcomes: Exploring the integrative model of parenting. *Journal of Youth and Adolescence, 42*, 1413–1425.

Lowe, S.R., Dillon, C.O., Rhodes, J.E., & Zwiebach, L. (2012). Defining adult experiences: Perspectives of a diverse sample of young adults. *Journal of Adolescent Research, 28*, 31–68.

Lu, F.J., & others (2014). Adolescents' physical activities and peer norms: The mediating role of self-efficacy. *Perceptual and Motor Skills, 118*, 362–374.

Lu, X., & others (2013). Prevalence of hypertension in overweight and obese children from a large school-based population in Shanghai, China. *BMC Public Health, 13*, 24.

Lubart, T.I. (2003). In search of creative intelligence. In R.J. Sternberg, J. Lautrey, & T.I. Lubart (Eds.), *Models of intelligence: International perspectives.* Washington, DC: American Psychological Association.

Luders, E., Narr, K.L., Thompson, P.M., & Toga, A.W. (2009). Neuroanatomical correlates of intelligence. *Intelligence, 37*, 156–163.

Luders, E., & others (2004). Gender differences in cortical complexity. *Nature Neuroscience, 7*, 799–800.

Lui, C.K., & others (2015). Drinking behaviors and life course socioeconomic status during the transition to adulthood among Whites and Blacks. *Journal of Studies on Alcohol and Drugs, 76*, 68–79.

Lund, H.G., Reider, B.D., Whiting, A.B., & Prichard, J.R. (2010). Sleep patterns and predictors of disturbed sleep in a large population of college students. *Journal of Adolescent Health, 46*, 124–132.

Lund, T.J., & Dearing, E. (2013). Is growing up affluent risky for adolescents or is the problem growing up in an affluent neighborhood? *Journal of Research on Adolescence, 23*(2), 274–282.

Lunday, A. (2006, December 4). Two Homewood seniors collect Marshall, Mitchell scholarships. *The JHU Gazette, 36.*

Luo, Y., & Waite, L.J. (2014). Loneliness and mortality among older adults in China. *Journals of Gerontology B: Psychological Sciences and Social Sciences, 69*, 633–645.

Luong, G., Rauers, A., & Fingerman, K.L. (2015). The multi-faceted nature of late-life socialization: Older adults as agents and targets of socialization. In J.E. Grusec & P.D. Hastings (Eds.), *Handbook of socialization* (2nd ed.). New York: Guilford.

Luria, A., & Herzog, E. (1985, April). *Gender segregation across and within settings.* Paper presented at the biennial meeting of the Society for Research in Child Development, Toronto.

Luszcz, M. (2011). Executive functioning and cognitive aging. In K.W. Schaie & S.L. Willis (Eds.), *Handbook of the psychology of aging* (7th ed.). New York: Elsevier.

Luthar, S.S. (2006). Resilience in development: A synthesis of research across five decades. In D. Cicchetti & D.J. Cohen (Eds.), *Developmental psychopathology, Vol. 3: Risk, disorders, and adaptation* (2nd ed.). Hoboken, NJ: Wiley.

Luthar, S.S., Barkin, S.H., & Crossman, E.J. (2013). "I can, therefore I must": Fragility in the upper-middle classes. *Development and Psychopathology, 25*, 1529–1549.

Luthar, S.S., Crossman, E., & Small, P.J. (2015). Resilience in the face of adversities. In R.M. Lerner (Ed.), *Handbook of child psychology and developmental science* (7th ed.). New York: Wiley.

Luthar, S.S., & Goldstein, A.S. (2008). Substance use and related behaviors among suburban late adolescents: The importance of perceived parent containment. *Development and Psychopathology, 20*, 591–614.

Luyckx, K. (2006). *Identity formation in emerging adulthood: Developmental trajectories, antecedents, and consequences.* Doctoral dissertation, Katholieke Universiteit Leuven, Leuven, Belgium.

Luyckx, K., Klimstra, T., Schwartz, S., & Duriez, B. (2013). Personal identity in college and the work context: Developmental trajectories and psychosocial functioning. *European Journal of Personality, 27*(3), 222–237.

Luyckx, K., & Robitschek, C. (2014). Personal growth initiative and identity formation in adolescence through young adulthood: Mediating processes on the pathway to well-being. *Journal of Adolescence, 37*, 973–981.

Luyckx, K., Schwartz, S.J., Goossens, L., Soenens, B., & Beyers, W. (2008). Developmental typologies of identity formation and adjustment in female emerging adults: A latent class growth analysis approach. *Journal of Research on Adolescence, 18*, 595–619.

Luyckx, K., Schwartz, S.J., Soenens, B., Vansteenkiste, M., & Goossens, L. (2010). The path from identity commitments to adjustment: Motivational underpinnings and mediating mechanisms. *Journal of Counseling and Development, 88*, 52–60.

Luyckx, K., Teppers, E., Klimstra, T.A., & Rassart, J. (2014). Identity processes and personality traits and types in adolescence: Directionality of effects and developmental trajectories. *Developmental Psychology, 50*, 2144–2153.

Luyckx, K., & others (2008). Capturing ruminative exploration: Extending the four-dimensional model of identity formation in late adolescence. *Journal of Research in Personality, 42*, 58–62.

Lynch, A., Elmore, B., & Kotecki, J. (2015). *Choosing health* (2nd ed.). Upper Saddle River, NJ: Pearson.

Lynch, A.D., Lerner, R.M., & Leventhal, T. (2013). Adolescent academic achievement and school engagement: An examination of the role of school-wide peer culture. *Journal of Youth and Adolescence, 42*, 6–19.

Lynch, A.D., & others (2015, in press). Direct and interactive effects of parent, friend, and schoolmate drinking on alcohol use trajectories. *Psychology and Health.*

Lynch, M. (2015). *Call to teach.* Upper Saddle River, NJ: Pearson.

Lynch, M.E. (1991). Gender intensification. In R.M. Lerner, A.C. Petersen, & J. Brooks-Gunn (Eds.), *Encyclopedia of adolescence* (Vol. 1). New York: Garland.

Lynn, R. (2012). IQs predict differences in the technological development of nations from 1000 BC through 2000 AD. *Intelligence, 40*, 439–444.

Lynne-Landsman, S.D., Graber, J.A., Nichols, T.R., & Botvin, G.J. (2010). Is sensation seeking a stable trait or does it change over time? *Journal of Youth and Adolescence, 40*, 48–58.

Lyons, H., Giordano, P.C., Manning, W.D., & Longmore, M.A. (2010). Identity, peer relationships, and adolescent girls' sexual behavior: An exploration of the contemporary double standard. *Journal of Sex Research, 47*, 1–13.

Lyons, H., Manning, W., Giordano, P., & Longmore, M. (2013). Predictors of heterosexual casual sex among young adults. *Archives of Sexual Behavior, 42*, 585–593.

Lyons, H., Manning, W.D., Longmore, M.A., & Giordano, P.C. (2015, in press). Gender and casual sexual activity from adolescence to emerging adulthood: Social and life course correlates. *Journal of Sex Research.*

Lytle, L.A. (2009). School-based interventions: Where do we go from here? *Archives of Pediatric and Adolescent Medicine, 163*, 388–389.

M

Ma, Y., & others (2015). Genetic variants modify the effect of age on APOE methylation in the Genetics of Lipid Lowering Drugs and Diet Network Study, *14*, 49–59.

Maas, M.K., & Lefkowitz, E.S. (2015, in press). Sexual esteem in emerging adulthood: Associations with sexual behavior, contraception use, and romantic relationships. *Journal of Sex Research.*

Maccoby, E.E. (1987, November). Interview with Elizabeth Hall: All in the family. *Psychology Today*, 54–60.

Maccoby, E.E. (1998). *The two sexes.* Cambridge, MA: Harvard University Press.

Maccoby, E.E. (2002). Gender and group process: A developmental perspective. *Current Directions in Psychological Science, 11,* 54–57.

Maccoby, E.E. (2007). Historical overview of socialization theory and research. In J.E. Grusec & P.D. Hastings (Eds.), *Handbook of socialization.* New York: Guilford.

Maccoby, E.E. (2015). Historical overview of socialization theory and research. In J.E. Grusec & P.D. Hastings (Eds.), *Handbook of socialization* (2nd ed.). New York: Guilford.

Maccoby, E.E., & Jacklin, C.N. (1974). *The psychology of sex differences.* Palo Alto, CA: Stanford University Press.

Maccoby, E.E., & Martin, J.A. (1983). Socialization in the context of the family. In E.M. Hetherington (Ed.), *Handbook of Child Psychology, Vol. 4: Socialization, personality, and social development.* New York: Wiley.

MacDonald, K. (1987). Parent-child physical play with rejected, neglected, and popular boys. *Developmental Psychology, 23,* 705–711.

MacGeorge, E.L. (2004). The myth of gender cultures: Similarities outweigh differences in men's and women's provisions of and responses to supportive communication. *Sex Roles, 50,* 143–175.

Machado, B., & others (2014). Risk factors and antecedent life events in the development of anorexia nervosa: A Portuguese case-control study. *European Eating Disorders Review, 22,* 243–251.

Machielse, A. (2015, in press). The heterogeneity of socially isolated older adults: A social isolation typology. *Journal of Gerontological Social Work.*

MacKey, E.R., & La Greca, A.M. (2007). Adolescents' eating, exercise, and weight control behaviors: Does peer crowd affiliation play a role? *Journal of Pediatric Psychology, 32,* 13–23.

Maclean, A.M., Walker, L.J., & Matsuba, M.K. (2004). Transcendence and the moral self: Identity, integration, religion, and moral life. *Journal for the Scientific Study of Religion, 43,* 429–437.

Mader, S., & Windelspecht, M. (2016, in press). *Human biology* (14th ed.). New York: McGraw-Hill.

Madill, A. (2012). Interviews and interviewing techniques. In H. Cooper (Ed.), *APA handbook of research methods in psychology.* Washington, DC: American Psychological Association.

Madison, B.E., & Foster-Clark, F.S. (1996, March). *Pathways to identity and intimacy: Effects of gender and personality.* Paper presented at the meeting of the Society for Research on Adolescence, Boston.

Madkour, A.S., Farhat, T., Halpern, C.T., Godeu, E., & Gabhainn, S.N. (2010). Early adolescent sexual initiation as a problem behavior: A comparative study of five nations. *Journal of Adolescent Health, 47,* 389–398.

Madsen, S.D., & Collins, W.A. (2011). The salience of romantic experiences for romantic relationship qualities in young adulthood. *Journal of Research on Adolescence, 21,* 789–801.

Maehr, M.L., & Zusho, A. (2009). Goal-directed behavior in the classroom. In K. Wentzel & A. Wigfield (Eds.), *Handbook of motivation at school.* New York: Routledge.

Magno, C. (2010). The role of metacognitive skills in developing critical thinking. *Metacognition and Learning, 5,* 137–156.

Mahalik, J.R., & others (2013). Changes in health risk behaviors for males and females from early adolescence through early adulthood. *Health Psychology, 32,* 685–694.

Mahn, H., & John-Steiner, V. (2013). Vygotsky and sociocultural approaches to teaching and learning. In I.B. Weiner & others (Eds.), *Handbook of psychology* (2nd ed., Vol. 7). New York: Wiley.

Mahoney, J.L., & Vest, A.E. (2012). The overscheduling hypothesis revisited: Intensity of organized activity participation during adolescence and young adult outcomes. *Journal of Research on Adolescence, 22,* 409–418.

Makin-Byrd, K., Bierman, K.L., & The Conduct Problems Prevention Research Group (2013). Individual and family predictors of the perpetration of dating violence and victimization in late adolescence. *Journal of Youth and Adolescence, 42,* 536–550.

Malamitsi-Puchner, A., & Boutsikou, T. (2006). Adolescent pregnancy and perinatal outcome. *Pediatric Endocrinology Reviews, 3*(Suppl 1), 170–171.

Malik, N.M., & Furman, W. (1993). Practitioner review: Problems in children's peer relations: What can the clinician do? *Journal of Child Psychology and Psychiatry, 34,* 1303–1326.

Maloy, R.W., Verock, R-E., Edwards, S.A., & Woolf, B.P. (2014). *Transforming learning with new technologies* (2nd ed.). Upper Saddle River, NJ: Pearson.

Malti, T., & Buchmann, M. (2010). Socialization and individual antecedents of adolescents' and young adults' moral motivation. *Journal of Youth and Adolescence, 39,* 138–149.

Malti, T., & Ongley, S.F. (2014). The development of moral emotions and moral reasoning. In M. Killen & J.G. Smetana (Eds.), *Handbook of moral development* (2nd ed.). New York: Psychology Press.

Mamun, A.A., O'Callaghan, J.J., Williams, G.M., & Najman, J.M. (2013). Adolescent bullying and young adults' body mass index and obesity: A longitudinal study. *International Journal of Obesity, 37,* 1140–1146.

Mandal, S., Abebe, F., & Chaudhary, J. (2014). –174G/C polymorphism in the interleukin-6 promoter is differently associated with prostate cancer incidence depending on race. *Genetics and Molecular Research, 13,* 139–151.

Mandelman, S.D., & Grigorenko, E.L. (2011). Intelligence: Genes, environments, and their interactions. In R.J. Sternberg & S.B. Kaufman (Eds.), *Cambridge handbook of intelligence.* New York: Cambridge University Press.

Manis, F.R., Keating, D.P., & Morrison, F.J. (1980). Developmental differences in the allocation of processing capacity. *Journal of Experimental Child Psychology, 29,* 156–169.

Mann, A., Legewie, J., & DiPrete, T.A. (2015). The role of school performance in narrowing gender gaps in the formation of STEM aspirations: A cross-national study. *Frontiers in Psychology, 6,* 171.

Mann, F.D., & others (2015). Person x environment interactions on adolescent delinquency: Sensation seeking, peer deviance, and parental monitoring. *Personality and Individual Differences, 76,* 129–134.

Manning, W.D., & Cohen, J. (2012). Premarital cohabitation and marital dissolution: An examination of recent marriages. *Journal of Marriage and the Family, 74*(2), 377–387.

Manuck, S.B., & McCaffery, J.M. (2014). Gene-environment interaction. *Annual Review of Psychology* (Vol. 65). Palo Alto, CA: Annual Reviews.

Maras, D., & others (2015). Screen time is associated with depression and anxiety in Canadian youth. *Preventive Medicine, 73,* 133–138.

Marceau, K., Ram, N., Houts, R.M., Grimm, K.J., & Susman, E.J. (2011). Individual differences in boys' and girls' timing and tempo of puberty: Modeling development with nonlinear growth models. *Developmental Psychology, 47,* 1389–1409.

Marcell, A.V., & Halpern-Felsher, B.L. (2007). Adolescents' beliefs about preferred resources for help vary depending on the health issue. *Journal of Adolescent Health, 41,* 61–68.

Marcell, A.V., Klein, J.D., Fischer, I., Allan, M.J., & Kokotailo, P.K. (2002). Male adolescent use of health care services: Where are the boys? *Journal of Adolescent Health Care, 30,* 35–43.

Marcell, A.V., & Millstein, S.G. (2001, March). *Quality of adolescent preventive services: The role of physician attitudes and self-efficacy.* Paper presented at the meeting of the Society for Adolescent Medicine, San Diego.

Marcia, J.E. (1980). Ego identity development. In J. Adelson (Ed.), *Handbook of adolescent psychology.* New York: Wiley.

Marcia, J.E. (1987). The identity status approach to the study of ego identity development. In T. Honess & K. Yardley (Eds.), *Self and identity: Perspectives across the lifespan.* London: Routledge & Kegan Paul.

Marcia, J.E. (1994). The empirical study of ego identity. In H.A. Bosma, T.L.G. Graafsma, H.D. Grotevant, & D.J. De Levita (Eds.), *Identity and development.* Newbury Park, CA: Sage.

Marcia, J.E. (1996). Unpublished review of J.W. Santrock's *Adolescence,* 7th ed., for Brown & Benchmark, Dubuque, Iowa.

Marcia, J.E. (2002). Identity and psychosocial development in adulthood. *Identity: An International Journal of Theory and Research, 2,* 7–28.

Marcia, J.E., & Carpendale, J. (2004). Identity: Does thinking make it so? In C. Lightfoot, C. Lalonde, & M. Chandler (Eds.), *Changing conceptions of psychological life.* Mahwah, NJ: Erlbaum.

Marcovitch, H. (2004). Use of stimulants for attention deficit hyperactivity disorder: AGAINST. *British Medical Journal, 329,* 908–909.

Marecek, J., Finn, S.E., & Cardell, M. (1988). Gender roles in the relationships of lesbians and gay men. In J.P. De Cecco (Ed.), *Gay relationships.* New York: Harrington Park Press.

Margolis, A., & others (2013). Using IQ discrepancy scores to examine neural correlates of specific cognitive abilities. *Journal of Neuroscience, 33,* 14135–14145.

Markant, J.C., & Thomas, K.M. (2013). Postnatal brain development. In P.D. Zelazo (Ed.), *Handbook of developmental psychology.* New York: Wiley.

Markey, C.N. (2010). Invited commentary: Why body image is important to adolescent development. *Journal of Youth and Adolescence, 39,* 1387–1389.

Markham, C.M., & others (2010). Connectedness as a predictor of sexual and reproductive health outcomes for youth. *Journal of Adolescent Health, 46*(Suppl. 3), S23–S41.

Markham, C.M., & others (2012). Sexual risk avoidance and sexual risk reduction interventions for middle school youth: A randomized controlled trial. *Journal of Adolescent Health, 50,* 279–288.

Markman, H.J., Rhoades, G.K., Stanley, S.M., & Peterson, K.M. (2013). A randomized clinical trial of the effectiveness of premarital intervention: Moderators of divorce outcomes. *Journal of Family Psychology, 27,* 165–172.

Marks, A.K., Ejesi, K., McCullough, M.B., & Garcia Coll, C. (2015). The implications of discrimination for child and adolescent development. In R.M. Lerner (Ed.), *Handbook of child psychology and developmental science* (7th ed.). New York: Wiley.

Marks, A.K., Godoy, C., & Garcia Coll, C. (2014). An ecological approach to understanding immigrant child and adolescent developmental consequences. In E.T. Gershoff, R.S. Mistry, & D.A. Crosby (Eds.), *Societal contexts of child development.* New York: Oxford University Press.

Marks, A.K., Patton, F., & Garcia Coll, C. (2011). Being bicultural: A mixed-methods study of adolescents' implicitly and explicitly measured ethnic identities. *Developmental Psychology, 47,* 270–288.

Markstrom, C.A. (2010). *Empowerment of North American Indian girls.* Lincoln: University of Nebraska Press.

Markus, H.R., & Kitayama, S. (2010). Cultures and selves: A cycle of mutual constitution. *Perspectives on Psychological Science, 5,* 420–430.

Markus, H.R., & Kitayama, S. (2012). Culture and the self. In K. Vohs & R.F. Baumeister (Eds.), *Self and identity.* Thousand Oaks, CA: Sage.

Markus, H.R., Mullally, P.R., & Kitayama, S. (1999). *Selfways: Diversity in modes of cultural participation.* Unpublished manuscript, Department of Psychology, University of Michigan.

Markus, H.R., & Nurius, P. (1986). Possible selves. *American Psychologist, 41,* 954–969.

Markus, H.R., Uchida, Y., Omoregi, H., Townsend, S.S., & Kitayama, S. (2006). Going for the gold: Models of agency in Japanese and American contexts. *Psychological Science, 17,* 103–112.

Marmorstein, N.R., Iacono, W.G., & Legrand, L. (2014). Obesity and depression in adolescence and beyond: Reciprocal risks. *International Journal of Obesity, 38,* 906–911.

Marshall Scholarships (2007). Scholar profiles: 2007. Retrieved January 31, 2008, from www. marshallscholarship.org/profiles2007.html

Marshall, S.L., Parker, P.D., Ciarrochi, J., & Heaven, P.C.L. (2014). Is self-esteem a cause or consequence of social support? A 4-year longitudinal study. *Child Development, 85,* 1275–1291.

Marsiglio, W., & Hinojsoa, R. (2010). Stepfathers' lives: Exploring social context and interpersonal complexity. In M.E. Lamb (Ed.), *The role of the father in child development* (5th ed.). New York: Wiley.

Martin, C.L., Fabes, R.A., & Hanish, L.D. (2014). Gendered-peer relationships in educational contexts. *Advances in Child Development and Behavior, 47,* 151–187.

Martin, C.L., & Ruble, D.N. (2010). Patterns of gender development. *Annual Review of Psychology* (Vol. 61). Palo Alto, CA: Annual Reviews.

Martin, C.L., Ruble, D.N., & Szkrybalo, J. (2002). Cognitive theories of early gender development. *Psychological Bulletin, 128,* 903–933.

Martin, J.A., & others (2015). *Births: Final data for 2013.* Hyattsville, MD: National Center for Health Statistics.

Martin, L.R., Friedman, H.S., & Schwartz, J.E. (2007). Personality and mortality risk across the lifespan: The importance of conscientiousness as biopsychosocial attribute. *Health Psychology, 26,* 428–436.

Martin, M.J., & others (2011). The enduring significance of racism: Discrimination and delinquency among Black American youth. *Journal of Research on Adolescence, 21*(3), 662–676.

Martinelli, M., & others (2014). Perfectionism dimensions as predictors of symptom dimensions of obsessive-compulsive disorder. *Bulletin of the Menninger Clinic, 78,* 140–159.

Martinez, A. (2006). In the fast lane: Boosting your career through cooperative education and internships. *Careers and Colleges, 26,* 8–10.

Martinez, Y.A., Schneider, B.H., Zambrana, A., Batista, G.S., & Soca, Z.S. (2014, in press). Does comorbid anger exacerbate the rejection of children with depression by their school peers? *Child Psychiatry and Human Development.*

Martino, S.C., & others (2006). Exposure to degrading versus nondegrading music lyrics and sexual behavior among youth. *Pediatrics, 118,* e430–e431.

Martin-Storey, A., & Crosnoe, R. (2012). Sexual minority status, peer harassment, and adolescent depression. *Journal of Adolescence, 35,* 1001–1011.

Marx, A.M., & others (2015). Near-infrared spectroscopy (NIRS) neurofeedback as a treatment for children with attention deficit hyperactivity disorder (ADHD)—a pilot study. *Frontiers in Human Neuroscience, 8,* 1038.

Masarik, A.S., & others (2013). Romantic relationships in early adulthood: Influences of family, personality, and relationship cognitions. *Personal Relationships, 20*(2), 356–373.

Mascalo, M.F., & Fischer, K.W. (2010). The dynamic development of thinking, feeling, and acting over the life span. In W.F. Overton & R.M. Lerner (Eds.), *Handbook of life-span development* (Vol. 1). New York: Wiley.

Mash, E.J., & Wolfe, D.A. (2013). Disorders of childhood and adolescence. In I.B. Weiner & others (Eds.), *Handbook of psychology* (2nd ed., Vol. 8). New York: Wiley.

Mash, E.J., & Wolfe, D.A. (2016, in press). *Abnormal child psychology* (6th ed.). Boston: Cengage.

Mason, K.A., Johnson, G.B., Losos, J.B., & Singer, S. (2015). *Understanding biology.* New York: McGraw-Hill.

Mason, M.J., Mennis, J., Linker, J., Bares, C., & Zaharakis, N. (2014). Peer attitudes effects on adolescent substance use: The moderating role of race and gender. *Prevention Science, 15,* 56–64.

Mason, M.J., Zaharakis, N., & Benotsch, E.G. (2014). Social networks, substance use, and mental health in college students. *Journal of American College Health, 62,* 470–477.

Masten, A.S. (2001). Ordinary magic: Resilience processes in development. *American Psychologist, 56*(3), 227–238.

Masten, A.S. (2004). Regulatory processes, risk and resilience in adolescent development. *Annals of the New York Academy of Sciences, 1021,* 310–319.

Masten, A.S. (2006). Developmental psychopathology: Pathways to the future. *International Journal of Behavioral Development, 31,* 46–53.

Masten, A.S. (2009). Ordinary magic: Lessons from research on resilience in human development. Retrieved October 15, 2009, from http://www.cea-ace.ca/sites/cea-ace.ca/files/EdCan-2009-v49-n3-Masten.pdf

Masten, A.S. (2011). Resilience in children threatened by extreme adversity: Frameworks for research, practice, and translational synergy. *Development and Psychopathology, 23,* 493–506.

Masten, A.S. (2013). Risk and resilience in development. In P.D. Zelazo (Ed.), *Oxford handbook of developmental psychology.* New York: Oxford University Press.

Masten, A.S. (2014a). *Ordinary magic: Resilience in development.* New York: Guilford Press.

Masten, A.S. (2014b). Global perspectives on resilience in children and youth. *Child Development, 85,* 6–20.

Masten, A.S. (2014c). Invited commentary: Resilience and Positive Youth Development frameworks in developmental science. *Journal of Youth and Adolescence, 43,* 1018–1024.

Masten, A.S., & Coatsworth, J.D. (1998). The development of competence in favorable and unfavorable environments. *American Psychologist, 53,* 205–220.

Masten, A.S., Desjardins, C.D., McCormick, C.M., Kuo, S.I., & Long, J.D. (2010). The significance of childhood competence and problems for adult success in work: A developmental cascade analysis. *Developmental Psychopathology, 22,* 679–694.

Masten, A.S., Liebkind, K., & Hernandez, D.J. (Eds.). (2012). *Realizing the potential of immigrant youth.* New York: Cambridge University Press.

Masten, A.S., & Monn, A.R. (2015). Child and family resilience: Parallels and multilevel dynamics. *Family Relations, 64,* 5–21.

Masten, A.S., & Narayan, A.J. (2012). Child development in the context of disaster, war, and terrorism. *Annual Review of Psychology* (Vol. 63). Palo Alto, CA: Annual Reviews.

Masten, A.S., Narayan, A.J., Silverman, W.K., & Osofsky, J.D. (2015). Children in war and disaster. In R.M. Lerner (Ed.), *Handbook of child psychology and developmental science* (7th ed.). New York: Wiley.

Masten, A.S., Obradovic, J., & Burt, K.B. (2006). Resilience in emerging adulthood: Developmental perspectives on continuity and transformation. In J.J. Arnett & J.L. Tanner (Eds.), *Emerging adults in America.* Washington, DC: American Psychological Association.

Masten, A.S., & Reed, M.G. (2002). Resilience in development. In C.R. Snyder & S.J. Lopez (Eds.), *The handbook of positive psychology.* New York: Oxford University Press.

Masten, A.S., & Tellegen, A. (2012). Resilience in developmental psychology: Contributions of the Project Competence Study. *Development and Psychopathology, 24,* 345–361.

Masten, A.S., & others (2014). Academic risk and resilience in the context of homelessness. *Child Development Perspectives, 8,* 201–206.

Masters, C. (2008, January 17). We just clicked. *Time,* 84–89.

Match.com (2011). The Match.com Single in America Study. Retrieved February 7, 2011, from http://blog.match.com/singles-study

Match.com (2012). *Singles in America 2012.* Retrieved June 10, 2012, from http://blog.match.com/singles-in-america

Mathieson, L.C., Klimes-Dougan, B., & Crick, N.R. (2014). Dwelling on it may make it worse: The links between relational victimization, relational aggression, rumination, and depressive symptoms in adolescents. *Development and Psychopathology, 26,* 735–747.

Matlin, M.W. (2012). *The psychology of women* (7th ed.). Belmont, CA: Wadsworth.

Matlin, S.L., Molock, S.D., & Tebes, J.K. (2011). Suicidality and depression among African American adolescents: The role of family and peer support and community connectedness. *American Journal of Orthopsychiatry, 81,* 108–117.

Matsuba, M.K., Murzyn, T., & Hart, D. (2014). Moral identity development and community. In M. Killen & J.G. Smetana (Eds.), *Handbook of moral development* (2nd ed.). New York: Psychology Press.

Matsuba, M.K., & Walker, L.J. (2004). Extraordinary moral commitment: Young adults involved in social organizations. *Journal of Personality, 72,* 413–436.

Matsumoto, D., & Juang, L. (2013). *Culture and psychology* (5th ed.). Boston: Cengage.

Matthews, G., Zeidner, M., & Roberts, R.D. (2006). Models of personality and affect for education: A review and synthesis. In P.A. Alexander & P.H. Wynne (Eds.), *Handbook of educational psychology* (2nd ed.). Mahwah, NJ: Erlbaum.

Matthews, G., Zeidner, M., & Roberts, R.D. (2011). *Emotional intelligence 101.* New York: Springer.

Matthiessen, C. (2013). *Overweight children: Tips for parents.* Retrieved February 21, 2013, from www.webmd.com/parenting/raising-fit-kids/mood/talking-kids-about-weight

Mavioglu, R.N., Boomsma, D.I., & Bartels, M. (2015, in press). Causes of individual differences in adolescent optimism: A study in Dutch twins and their siblings. *European Journal of Child and Adolescent Psychiatry.*

Mayer, J.D., Salovey, P., Caruso, D.R., & Cherkasskiy, L. (2011). Emotional intelligence. In R.J. Sternberg & S.B. Kaufman (Eds.), *Cambridge handbook of intelligence.* New York: Cambridge University Press.

Mayer, R.E. (2012). Information processing. In K.R. Harris & others (Eds.), *APA educational psychology handbook.* Washington, DC: APA.

Mayer, R.E., & Wittrock, M.C. (2006). Problem solving. In P.A. Alexander & P.H. Winne (Eds.), *Handbook of educational psychology* (2nd ed.). Mahwah, NJ: Erlbaum.

Mayers, L.B., & Chiffriller, S.H. (2008). Body art (body piercing and tattooing) among undergraduate university students: "Then and now." *Journal of Adolescent Health, 42,* 201–203.

Maynard, B.R., Salas-Wright, C.P., & Vaughn, M.G. (2015). High school dropouts in emerging adulthood: Substance use, mental health problems, and crime. *Community Mental Health, 51,* 289–299.

McAbee, S.T., & Oswald, F.L. (2013). The criterion-related validity of personality measures for predicting GPA: A meta-analytic validity comparison. *Psychological Assessment, 25,* 532–544.

McAdams, D.P. (2012). Personality, modernity, and the storied self. In K. Vohs & R.F. Baumeister (Eds.), *Self and identity.* Thousand Oaks, CA: Sage.

McAdams, D.P., Josselson, R., & Lieblich, A. (Eds.). (2006). *Identity and story: Creating self in narrative.* Washington, DC: American Psychological Association Press.

McAdams, D.P., & McLean, K.C. (2013). Narrative identity. *Current Directions in Psychological Science, 22,* 233–238.

McAdams, D.P., & Zapata-Gietl, C. (2015). Three strands of identity development across the human life course: Reading Erik Erikson in full. In K.C. McLean & M. Syed (Eds.), *Oxford handbook of identity development.* New York: Oxford University Press.

McAdams, T.A., & others (2014). Co-occurrence of antisocial behavior and substance use: Testing for sex differences in the impact of older male friends, low parental knowledge, and friends' delinquency. *Journal of Adolescence, 37,* 247–256.

McAdoo, H.P. (2006). *Black families* (4th ed.). Thousand Oaks, CA: Sage.

McAlister, A., Perry, C., Killen, J., Slinkard, L.A., & Maccoby, N. (1980). Pilot study of smoking, alcohol, and drug abuse prevention. *American Journal of Public Health, 70,* 719–721.

McClelland, M.M., Geldhof, J., Cameron, C.E., & Wanless, S.B. (2015). Development and self-regulation. In R.M. Lerner (Ed.), *Handbook of child psychology and developmental science* (7th ed.). New York: Wiley.

McCormick, C.B., Dimmitt, C., & Sullivan, F.R. (2013). Metacognition, learning, and instruction. In I.B. Weiner & others (Eds.), *Handbook of psychology* (2nd ed., Vol. 7). New York: Wiley.

McCrae, R.R., & Costa, P.T. (2006). Cross-cultural perspectives on adult personality trait development. In D.K. Mroczek & T.D. Little (Eds.), *Handbook of personality development.* Mahwah, NJ: Erlbaum.

McCrae, R.R., & Sutin, A.R. (2009). Openness to experience. In M.R. Leary & R.H. Hoyle (Eds.), *Handbook of individual differences in social behavior.* New York: Guilford.

McCrae, R.R., Gaines, J.F., & Wellington, M.A. (2013). The five-factor personality model in fact and fiction. In I.B. Weiner & others, *Handbook of psychology* (2nd ed., Vol. 5). New York: Wiley.

McElhaney, K.B., & Allen, J.P. (2012). Sociocultural perspectives on adolescent autonomy. In P.K. Kerig, M.S. Schulz, & S.T. Hauser (Eds.), *Adolescence and beyond.* New York: Oxford University Press.

McElhaney, K.B., Antonishak, J., & Allen, J.P. (2008). "They like me, they like me not": Popularity and adolescents' perceptions of acceptance predicting social functioning over time. *Child Development, 79,* 720–731.

McEwen, B.S. (2013). Neuroscience. Hormones and the social brain. *Science, 339,* 279–280.

McHale, S.M., Kim, J.Y., Dotterer, A., Crouter, A.C., & Booth, A. (2009). The development of gendered interests and personality qualities from middle childhood through adolescence: A bio-social analysis. *Child Development, 80,* 482–495.

McHale, S.M., Updegraff, K.A., Helms-Erikson, H., & Crouter, A.C. (2001). Sibling influences on gender development in middle childhood and early adolescence: A longitudinal study. *Developmental Psychology, 37,* 115–125.

McHale, S.M., Updegraff, K.A., & Whiteman, S.D. (2013). Sibling relationships. In G.W. Peterson & K.R. Bush (Eds.), *Handbook of marriage and the family* (3rd ed.). New York: Springer.

McInnis, C.M., & others (2015, in press). Response and habituation of pro and anti inflammatory gene expression to repeated acute stress. *Brain, Behavior, and Immunity.*

McLanahan, S., Tach, L., & Schneider, D. (2013). The causal effects of father absence. *Annual Review of Sociology* (Vol. 39). Palo Alto, CA: Annual Reviews.

McLaughlin, K.A., & Hatzenbuehler, M.L. (2009). Mechanisms linking stressful life events and mental health problems in a prospective, community-based sample of adolescents. *Journal of Adolescent Health, 44,* 153–160.

McLean, K.C., Breen, A.V., & Fournier, M.A. (2010). Constructing the self in early, middle, and late adolescent boys: Narrative identity, individuation, and well-being. *Journal of Research on Adolescence, 20,* 166–187.

McLean, K.C., & Jennings, L.E. (2012). Teens telling tall tales: How maternal and peer audiences support narrative identity development. *Journal of Adolescence, 35,* 1455-1469.

McLean, K.C., & Pasupathi, M. (Eds.) (2010). *Narrative development in adolescence: Creating the storied self.* New York: Springer.

McLean, K.C., & Pratt, M.W. (2006). Life's little (and big) lessons: Identity statuses and meaning-making in the turning point narratives of emerging adults. *Developmental Psychology, 42,* 714–722.

McLean, K.C., & Syed, M. (2015). The field of identity development needs an identity: An introduction to the *Handbook of identity development.* In K.C. McLean & M. Syed (Eds.), *Oxford handbook of identity development.* New York: Oxford University Press.

McLean, K.C., Syed, M., Yoder, A., & Greenhoot, A.F. (2015, in press). The role of domain content in understanding identity developmental processes. *Journal of Research on Adolescence.*

McLean, K.C., & Thorne, A. (2006). Identity light: Entertainment stories as vehicle for self-development. In D.P. McAdams, R. Josselson, & A. Lieblich (Eds.), *Identity and story.* Washington, DC: American Psychological Association.

McLoyd, V.C. (1998). Children in poverty. In I.E. Siegel & K.A. Renninger (Eds.), *Handbook of child psychology* (5th ed., Vol. 4). New York: Wiley.

McLoyd, V.C., Aikens, N.L., & Burton, L.M. (2006). Childhood poverty, policy, and practice. In W. Damon & R. Lerner (Eds.), *Handbook of child psychology* (6th ed.). New York: Wiley.

McLoyd, V.C., Kaplan, R., Purtell, K.M., & Huston, A.C. (2011). Assessing the effects of a work-based antipoverty program for parents on youths' future orientation and employment experiences. *Child Development, 82,* 113–132.

McLoyd, V.C., Mistry, R.S., & Hardaway, C.R. (2014). Poverty and children's development: Familial processes and mediating influences. In E.T. Gershoff, R.S. Mistry, & D.A. Crosby (Eds.), *Societal contexts of child development.* New York: Oxford University Press.

McLoyd, V.C., Purtell, K.M., & Hardaway, C.R. (2015). Race, class, and ethnicity as they affect emerging adulthood. In R.M. Lerner (Ed.), *Handbook of child psychology and developmental science* (7th ed.). New York: Wiley.

McLoyd, V.C., & others (2009). Poverty and social disadvantage in adolescence. In R.M. Lerner & L. Steinberg (Eds.), *Handbook of adolescent psychology* (3rd ed.). New York: Wiley.

McMillan, J.H. (2014). *Classroom assessment* (6th ed.). Upper Saddle River, NJ: Pearson.

McMurray, R.G., Harrell, J.S., Creighton, D., Wang, Z., & Bangdiwala, S.I. (2008). Influence of physical activity on change in weight status as children become adolescents. *International Journal of Pediatric Obesity, 3,* 69–77.

McNeely, C.A., & Barber, B.K. (2010). How do parents make adolescents feel loved? Perspectives on supportive parenting from adolescents in 12 cultures. *Journal of Adolescent Research, 25,* 601–631.

McQueen, M.B., & others (2015). The National Longitudinal Study of Adolescent to Adult Health (Add Health) sibling pairs genome-wide data. *Behavior Genetics, 45,* 12–23.

McWilliams, L.A., & Bailey, S.J. (2010). Associations between adult attachment ratings and health conditions: Evidence from the National Comorbidity Survey replication. *Health Psychology, 29,* 446–453.

Mead, M. (1928). *Coming of age in Samoa.* New York: Morrow.

Meade, C.S., Kershaw, T.S., & Ickovics, J.R. (2008). The intergenerational cycle of teenage motherhood: An ecological approach. *Health Psychology, 27,* 419–429.

Meece, J.L., Anderman, E.M., & Anderman, L.H. (2006). Classroom goal structure, student motivation, and academic achievement. *Annual Review of Psychology* (Vol. 57). Palo Alto, CA: Annual Reviews.

Meece, J.L., & Askew, K.S. (2012). Gender, motivation, and educational achievement. In K.R. Harris & others (Eds.), *APA handbook of educational psychology.* Washington, DC: American Psychological Association.

Meeus, W. (2011). The study of adolescent identity formation 2000–2010: A review of longitudinal research. *Journal of Research in Adolescence, 21,* 75–84.

Meeus, W., van de Schoot, R., Keijser, L., & Branje, S. (2012). Identity statuses and developmental trajectories: A five-wave longitudinal study in early-to-middle and middle-to-late adolescents. *Journal of Youth and Adolescence, 41,* 1008–1021.

Meeus, W., van de Schoot, R., Keijser, L., Branje, S., & Schwartz, S.J. (2010). On the progression and stability of adolescent identity formation: A five-wave longitudinal study in early-to-middle and middle-to-late adolescence. *Child Development, 81,* 1565–1581.

Mehta, C.M., & Strough, J. (2009). Sex segregation in friendships and normative contexts across the life span. *Developmental Review, 29,* 201–220.

Mehta, C.M., & Strough, J. (2010). Gender segregation and gender-typing in adolescence. *Sex Roles, 63,* 251–263.

Meichenbaum, D., & Butler, L. (1980). Toward a conceptual model of the treatment of test anxiety: Implications for research and treatment. In I.G. Sarason (Ed.), *Test anxiety.* Mahwah, NJ: Erlbaum.

Meijs, N., Cillessen, A.H.N., Scholte, R.H.J., Segers, E., & Spijkerman, R. (2010). Social intelligence and academic achievement as predictors of adolescent popularity. *Journal of Youth and Adolescence, 39,* 62–72.

Meisel, V., Servera, M., Garcia-Banda, G., Cardo, E., & Moreno, I. (2013). Neurofeedback and standard pharmacological intervention in ADHD: A randomized controlled trial with six-month follow-up. *Biological Psychology, 94,* 12–21.

Melchior, M., & others (2014). Negative events in childhood predict trajectories of internalizing symptoms up to young adulthood: An 18-year longitudinal study. *PLoS One, 9*(12), 114526.

Meldrum, R.C., & Hay, C. (2012). Do peers matter in the development of self-control? Evidence from a longitudinal study of youth. *Journal of Youth and Adolescence, 41,* 691–703.

Mello, Z.R. (2009). Racial/ethnic group and socioeconomic status variation in educational and occupational expectations from adolescence to adulthood. *Journal of Applied Developmental Psychology, 30,* 494–504.

Meltzer, H., Ford, T., Bebbington, P., & Vostanis, P. (2012). Children who run away from home: Risks for suicidal behavior and substance misuse. *Journal of Adolescent Health, 51,* 415–421.

Mendelson, M., & others (2015, in press). Sleep quality, sleep duration, and physical activity in obese adolescents: Effects of exercise training. *Pediatric Obesity.*

Menon, C.V., & Harter, S.L. (2012). Examining the impact of acculturative stress on body image disturbance among Hispanic college students. *Cultural Diversity and Ethnic Minority Psychology, 18,* 239–246.

Mesch, G.S. (2012). Technology and youth. *New Directions in Youth Development, 135,* 97–105.

Metcalf, B.S., & others (2015, in press). Exploring the adolescent fall in physical activity: A 10-year cohort study (Early Bird 41). *Medicine and Science in Sports and Exercise.*

Metz, E.C., & Youniss, J. (2005). Longitudinal gains in civic development through school-based required service. *Political Psychology, 26,* 413–437.

Metzger, A., & others (2013). Information management strategies with conversations about cigarette smoking: Parenting correlates and longitudinal associations with teen smoking. *Developmental Psychology, 49,* 1565–1578.

Meyer, I.H. (2003). Prejudice, social stress, and mental health in gay, lesbian, and bisexual populations: Conceptual issues and research evidence. *Psychological Bulletin, 129,* 674–697.

Meyer-Bahlburg, H.F.L., & others (1995). Prenatal estrogens and the development of homosexual orientation. *Developmental Psychology, 31,* 12–21.

Michael, R.T., Gagnon, J.H., Laumann, E.O., & Kolata, G. (1994). *Sex in America.* Boston: Little, Brown.

Michaud, P-A., & others (2009). To say or not to say: A qualitative study on the disclosure of their condition by human immunodeficiency virus-positive adolescents. *Journal of Adolescent Health, 44,* 356–362.

Midgley, N., Ansaldo, F., & Target, M. (2014). The meaningful assessment of therapy outcomes: Incorporating a qualitative study into a randomized controlled trial evaluating the treatment of adolescent depression. *Psychotherapy, 51,* 128–137.

Mikami, A.Y., & others (2010). Adolescent peer relationships and behavior problems predict young adults' communication on social networking sites. *Developmental Psychology, 46,* 46–56.

Mikkelsson, L., & others (2006). School fitness tests as predictors of adult health-related fitness. *American Journal of Human Biology, 18,* 342–349.

Mikulincer, M., & Shaver, P.R. (2014). The role of attachment security in adolescent and adult close relationships. In J.A. Simpson & L. Campbell (Eds.), *Oxford handbook of close relationships.* NewYork: Oxford University Press.

Milevsky, A. (2011). *Sibling relations in childhood and adolescence.* New York: Columbia University Press.

Miller, B.C., Benson, B., & Galbraith, K.A. (2001). Family relationships and adolescent pregnancy risk: A research synthesis. *Developmental Review, 21,* 1–38.

Miller, C., Martin, C.L., Fabes, R., & Hanish, D. (2013). Bringing the cognitive and social together: How gender detectives and gender enforcers shape children's gender development. In M. Banaji & S. Gelman (Eds.), *Navigating the social world: A developmental perspective.* New York: Oxford University Press.

Miller, E., & others (2012). "Coaching boys into men": A cluster-randomized controlled trial of a dating violence prevention program. *Journal of Adolescent Health, 51,* 431–438.

Miller, E.M., & others (2012). Theories of willpower affect sustained learning. *PLoS One, 7*(6), e38680.

Miller, J.G. (2007). Insights into moral development from cultural psychology. In M. Killen & J.G. Smetana (Eds.), *Handbook of moral development.* Mahwah, NJ: Erlbaum.

Miller, J.G., & Bland, C.G. (2014). A cultural psychology perspective on moral development. In M. Killen & J.G. Smetana (Eds.), *Handbook of moral development* (2nd ed.). New York: Psychology Press.

Miller, P.H. (2011). Piaget's theory: Past, present, and future. In U. Goswami (Ed.), *Wiley-Blackwell handbook of childhood cognitive development* (2nd ed.). New York: Wiley-Blackwell.

Miller, R., Wankerl, M., Stalder, T., Kirschbaum, C., & Alexander, N. (2013). The serotonin transporter gene-linked polymorphic region (5-HTTLPR) and cortisol stress reactivity: A meta-analysis. *Molecular Psychiatry, 18,* 1018–1024.

Miller, S., Malone, P., Dodge, K.A., & The Conduct Problems Prevention Research Group (2010). Developmental trajectories of boys' and girls' delinquency: Sex differences and links to later adolescent outcomes. *Journal of Abnormal Child Psychology, 38,* 1021–1032.

Mills, K.L., Goddings, A.L., Clasen, L.S., Giedd, J.N., & Blakemore, S.J. (2014). The developmental mismatch in structural brain maturation during adolescence. *Developmental Neuroscience, 36,* 147–160.

Miltenberger, R.G. (2012). *Behavior modification* (5th ed.). Boston: Cengage.

Minuchin, P.P., & Shapiro, E.K. (1983). The school as a context for social development. In P.H. Mussen (Ed.), *Handbook of child psychology* (4th ed., Vol. 4). New York: Wiley.

Mirkovic, B., & others (2015). Coping skills among adolescent suicide attempters: Results of a multisite study. *Canadian Journal of Psychiatry, 60*(2, Suppl. 1), S37–S45.

Mirman, J.H., Albert, D., Jacobsohn, L.S., & Winston, F.K. (2012). Factors associated with adolescents' propensity to drive with multiple passengers and to engage in risky driving behaviors. *Journal of Adolescent Health, 50,* 634–640.

Mischel, W. (1968). *Personality and assessment.* New York: Wiley.

Mischel, W. (2004). Toward an integrative science of the person. *Annual Review of Psychology* (Vol. 55). Palo Alto, CA: Annual Reviews.

Mischel, W. (2014). *The marshmallow test: Mastering self-control.* Boston: Little Brown.

Mischel, W., Ebbesen, E.B., & Zeiss, A.R. (1972). Cognitive and attentional mechanisms in delay of gratification. *Journal of Personality and Social Psychology, 21,* 204–218.

Mischel, W., & Mischel, H. (1975, April). *A cognitive social-learning analysis of moral development.* Paper presented at the meeting of the Society for Research in Child Development, Denver.

Mischel, W., & Moore, B. (1973). Effects of attention to symbolically presented rewards on self control. *Journal of Personality and Social Psychology, 28,* 172–179.

Mischel, W., & others (1989). Delay of gratification in children. *Science, 244,* 933–938.

Mistry, J., & Dutta, R. (2015). Human development and culture: Conceptual and methodological issues in R.M. Lerner (Ed.), *Handbook of child psychology and developmental science* (7th ed.). New York: Wiley.

Mitchell, A.B., & Stewart, J.B. (2013). The efficacy of all-male academies: Insights from critical race theory (CRT). *Sex Roles, 69,* 382–392.

Mitchell, J.A., Pate, R.R., & Blair, S.N. (2012). Screen-based sedentary behavior and cardiorespiratory fitness from age 11 to 13. *Medical Science and Sports Exercise, 44,* 1302–1309.

Mitchell, J.A., Rodriquez, D., Schmitz, K.H., & Audrain-McGovern, J. (2013). Greater screen time is associated with adolescent obesity: A longitudinal study of the BMI distribution from ages 14 to 18. *Obesity.*

MMWR (2006, June 9). *Youth risk behavior surveillance—United States 2005* (Vol. 255). Atlanta, GA: Centers for Disease Control and Prevention.

Modecki, K.L., Barber, B.L., & Eccles, J.S. (2014). Binge drinking trajectories across adolescence: For early maturing youth, extra-curricular activities are protective. *Journal of Adolescent Health, 54,* 61–66.

Modecki, K.L., & others (2014). Bullying prevalence across contexts: A meta-analysis measuring cyber and traditional bullying. *Journal of Adolescent Health, 55,* 602–611.

Moed, A., & others (2015, in press). Parent-adolescent conflict as sequences of reciprocal negative emotion: Links with conflict resolution and adolescents' behavior problems. *Journal of Youth and Adolescence.*

Moffitt, T.E. (2012). *Childhood self-control predicts adult health, wealth, and crime.* Paper presented at the Symposium on Symptom Improvement in Well-Being, Copenhagen.

Moffitt, T.E., & others (2011). A gradient of childhood self-control predicts health, wealth, and public safety. *Proceedings of the National Academy of Sciences U.S.A., 108,* 2693–2698.

Molina, B.S., & Pelham, W.E. (2014). The attention deficit/hyperactivity disorder (ADHD) substance use connection. *Annual Review of Clinical Psychology* (Vol. 10). Palo Alto, CA: Annual Reviews.

Molina, R.C., Roca, C.G., Zamorano, J.S., & Araya, E.G. (2010). Family planning and adolescent pregnancy. *Best Practices and Research: Clinical Obstetrics and Gynecology, 24,* 209–222.

Monahan, C.J., & others (2012). Health-related quality of life among heavy-drinking college students. *American Journal of Health Behavior, 36,* 289–299.

Monahan, K., Guyer, A., Sil, J., Fitzwater, T., & Steinberg, L. (2015). Integration of developmental neuroscience and contextual approaches to the study of adolescent psychopathology. In D. Cicchetti (Ed.), *Handbook of developmental psychology* (3rd ed.). New York: Wiley.

Monahan, K.C., Lee, J.M., & Steinberg, L. (2011). Revisiting the impact of part-time work on adolescent adjustment: Distinguishing between selection and socialization using propensity score matching. *Child Development, 82,* 96–112.

Mond, J., van den Berg, P., Boutelle, K., Hannan, P., & Neumark-Sztainer, D. (2011). Obesity, body dissatisfaction, and emotional well-being in early and late adolescence: Findings from the Project EAT study. *Journal of Adolescent Health, 48,* 373–378.

Moninger, J. (2013). *How to talk with your child about losing weight.* Retrieved February 21, 2013, from http://www.parents.com/kids/teens/weight-loss/how-to-talk-to-your-child-about-losing-weight/

Montemayor, R. (1982). The relationship between parent-adolescent conflict and the amount of time adolescents spend with parents, peers, and alone. *Child Development, 53,* 1512–1519.

Montgomery, M. (2005). Psychosocial intimacy and identity: From early adolescence to emerging adulthood. *Journal of Adolescent Research, 20,* 346–374.

Monti, J.M., Hillman, C.H., & Cohen, N.J. (2012). Aerobic fitness enhances relational memory in preadolescent children: The FITKids randomized control trial. *Hippocampus, 22*(9), 1876–1882.

Moore, D. (2001). *The dependent gene.* New York: W.H. Freeman.

Moore, D. (2013). Behavioral genetics, genetics, and epigenetics. In P.D. Zelazo (Ed.), *Oxford handbook of developmental psychology.* New York: Oxford University Press.

Moore, D. (2015). *The developing genome.* New York: Oxford University Press.

Moore, S.R., Harden, K.P., & Mendle, J. (2014). Pubertal timing and adolescent sexual behavior in girls. *Developmental Psychology, 50,* 1734–1745.

Morean, M.E., & others (2014). First drink to first drunk: Age of onset and delay to intoxication are associated with adolescent alcohol use and binge drinking. *Alcoholism, Clinical and Experimental Research, 38,* 2615–2621.

Morgan, E.M. (2014). Outcomes of sexual behaviors among sexual minority youth. *New Directions for Child and Adolescent Development, 144,* 21–36.

Morreale, M.C. (2004). Executing juvenile offenders: A fundamental failure of society. *Journal of Adolescent Health, 35,* 341.

Morris, A.S., Cui, L., & Steinberg, L. (2012). Parenting research and themes: What we have learned and where to go next. In R.E. Larzelere, A.S. Morris, & A.W. Harrist (Eds.), *Authoritative parenting.* Washington, DC: American Psychological Association.

Morris, B.H., McGrath, A.C., Goldman, M.S., & Rottenberg, J. (2014). Parental depression confers greater prospective depression risk to females than males in emerging adulthood. *Child Psychiatry and Human Development, 45,* 78–89.

Morris, P., & Kalil, A. (2006). Out of school time use during middle childhood in a low-income sample: Do combinations of activities affect achievement and behavior? In A. Huston & M. Ripke (Eds.), *Middle childhood: Contexts of development.* New York: Cambridge University Press.

Morrison, D.M., & others (2015). "He enjoys giving her pleasure": Diversity and complexity in young men's sexual scripts. *Archives of Sexual Behavior, 44,* 655–688.

Morrison, J., & Schwartz, T.L. (2014). Adolescent angst or true intent? Suicidal behavior, risk, and neurobiological mechanisms in depressed children and teenagers taking antidepressants. *International Journal of Emergency Mental Health, 16,* 247–250.

Morrison-Beedy, D., & others (2013). Reducing sexual risk behavior in adolescent girls: Results from a randomized trial. *Journal of Adolescent Health, 52,* 314–322.

Mortimer, J.T. (2012). The evolution, contributions, and prospects of the Youth Development Study: An investigation in life course social psychology. *Social Psychology Quarterly, 75,* 5–27.

Mortimer, J.T., & Larson, R.W. (2002). Macrostructural trends and the reshaping of adolescence. In J.T. Mortimer & R.W. Larson (Eds.), *The changing adolescent experience.* New York: Cambridge University Press.

Mosher, W.D., Chandra, A., & Jones, J. (2005). *Sexual behavior and selected health measures: Men and women 15–44 years of age, United States, 2002.* Hyattsville, MD: National Center for Health Statistics.

Moss, H.B., Chen, C.M., & Yi, H.Y. (2014). Early adolescent patterns of alcohol, cigarettes, and marijuana polysubstance use and young adult substance use outcomes in a nationally representative sample. *Drugs and Alcohol Dependence, 136,* 51–62.

Motti-Stefanidi, F.M., Masten, A.S., & Asendorpf, J.B. (2015). School engagement trajectories of immigrant youth: Risks and longitudinal interplay with academic success. *International Journal of Behavioral Development, 39,* 32–42.

Mounts, N.S. (2007). Adolescents' and their mothers' perceptions of parental management of peer relationships. *Journal of Research on Adolescence, 17,* 169–178.

Mounts, N.S. (2011). Parental management of peer relationships and early adolescents' social skills. *Journal of Youth and Adolescence, 40,* 416–427.

Mouritsen, A., & others (2014). Longitudinal changes in circulating testosterone levels determined by LC-MS/MS and by a commercially available radioimmunoassay in healthy girls and boys during the pubertal transition. *Hormone Research in Pediatrics, 82,* 12–17.

Moutsiana, C., & others (2015, in press). Insecure attachment in infancy predicts greater amygdala volumes in early adulthood. *Journal of Child Psychology and Psychiatry.*

Mrkva, K., & Narváez, D. (2015, in press). Moral psychology and the "cultural other": Cultivating openness to experience and the new. In B. Zizek & A. Escher (Eds.), *Ways of approaching the strange.* Dornach, Switzerland: Steiner Verlag.

Mrug, S., Borch, C., & Cillessen, A.H.N. (2012). Other-sex friendships in late adolescence: Risky associations for substance abuse and sexual debut? *Journal of Youth and Adolescence, 40,* 875–888.

Mruk, C.J., & O'Brien, E.J. (2013). Changing self-esteem through competence and worthiness training: A positive therapy. In V. Zeigler-Hill (Ed.), *Self-esteem.* New York: Psychology Press.

Muller, U., & Kerns, K. (2015). Development of executive function. In R.M. Lerner (Ed.), *Handbook of child psychology and developmental science* (7th ed.). New York: Wiley.

Mullis, I.V.S., & others (1998). *Mathematics and science achievement in the final year of secondary school.* Chestnut Hill, MA: Boston College, TIMSS International Study Center.

Mullola, S., & others (2012). Gender differences in teachers' perceptions of students' temperament, educational competence, and teachability. *British Journal of Educational Psychology, 82*(2), 185–206.

Murnane, R.J., & Levy, F. (1996). *Teaching the new basic skills.* New York: Free Press.

Murphy, D.A., Brecht, M.L., Huang, D., & Herbeck, D.M. (2012). Trajectories of delinquency from age 14 to 23 in the National Longitudinal Survey of Youth sample. *International Journal of Adolescence and Youth, 17,* 47–62.

Murphy, K.A., Blustein, D.L., Bohlig, A.J., & Platt, M.G. (2010). The college-to-career transition: An exploration of emerging adulthood. *Journal of Counseling and Development, 88,* 174–181.

Murphy, T.F. (2014). Are gay and lesbian people fading into the history of bioethics? *Hastings Center Report, 44*(Suppl. 4), S6–S11.

Murray, J.P., & Murray, A.D. (2008). Television: Use and effects. In M.M. Haith & J.B. Benson (Eds.), *Encyclopedia of infant and early childhood development.* New York: Elsevier.

Murry, V.M., Hill, N.E., Witherspoon, D., Berkel, C., & Bartz, D. (2015). Children in diverse social contexts. In R.M. Lerner (Ed.), *Handbook of child psychology and developmental science* (7th ed.). New York: Wiley.

Musameh, M.D., & others (2015). Analysis of gene-gene interactions among common variants in candidate cardiovascular genes in coronary artery disease. *PLoS One, 10*(2), e117684.

Mussen, P.H., Honzik, M., & Eichorn, D. (1982). Early adult antecedents of life satisfaction at age 70. *Journal of Gerontology, 37,* 316–322.

Myers, D. (2008, June 2). Commentary in S. Begley & J. Interlandi, *The dumbest generation? Don't be dumb.* Retrieved July 22, 2008, from www.newsweek.com/id/138536/

Myers, D., Baer, W., & Choi, S. (1996). The changing problem of overcrowded housing. *Journal of the American Planning Association, 62,* 66–84.

Myers, D.G. (2010). *Psychology* (9th ed.). New York: Worth.

N

Nader, P.R., Bradley, R.H., Houts, R.M., McRitchie, S.L., & O'Brian, M. (2008). Moderate-to-vigorous physical activity from 9 to 15 years. *Journal of the American Medical Association, 300,* 295–305.

Nagata, P.K. (1989). Japanese American children and adolescents. In J.T. Gibbs & L.N. Huang (Eds.), *Children of color.* San Francisco: Jossey-Bass.

Nagel, B.J., & others (2011). Altered white matter microstructure in children with attention-deficit/hyperactivity disorder. *Journal of the American Academy of Child and Adolescent Psychiatry, 50,* 283–292.

Naicker, K., Galambos, N.L., Zeng, Y., Senthilselvan, A., & Colman, I. (2013). Social, demographic, and health outcomes in the 10 years following adolescent depression. *Journal of Adolescent Health, 52,* 533–538.

Nair, R.L., White, R.B., Roosa, M.W., & Zeiders, K.H. (2013). Cultural stressors and mental health symptoms among Mexican Americans: A prospective study examining the impact of the family and neighborhood context. *Journal of Youth and Adolescence, 42,* 1616–1623.

Najman, J.M., & others (2010). Timing and chronicity of family poverty and development of unhealthy behaviors in children: A longitudinal study. *Journal of Adolescent Health, 46,* 538–544.

Nakawaki, B., & Crano, W. (2015). Patterns of substance use, delinquency, and risk factors among adolescent inhalant users. *Substance Use and Misuse, 50,* 114–122.

Nansel, T.R., & others (2001). Bullying behaviors among U.S. youth. *Journal of the American Medical Association, 285,* 2094–2100.

Narváez, D. (2006). Integrative moral education. In M. Killen & J. Smetana (Eds.), *Handbook of moral development.* Mahwah, NJ: Erlbaum.

Narváez, D. (2008). Four component model. In F.C. Power, R.J. Nuzzi, D. Narváez, D.K. Lapsley, & T.C. Hunt (Eds.), *Moral education: A handbook.* Westport, CT: Greenwood.

Narváez, D. (2010a). The embodied dynamism of moral becoming. *Perspectives on Psychological Science, 5*(2), 185–186.

Narváez, D. (2010b). Moral complexity: The fatal attraction of truthiness and the importance of mature moral functioning. *Perspectives on Psychological Science, 5*(2), 163–181.

Narváez, D. (2014). *The neurobiology and development of human morality.* New York: Norton.

Narváez, D. (2015). The neurobiology of moral sensitivity: Evolution, epigenetics, and early experience. In D. Mowrer & P. Vanderberg (Eds.), *The art of morality.* New York: Routledge.

Narváez, D. (2016, in press). The ontogenesis of moral becoming. In A. Fuentes & A. Visala (Eds.), *Verbs, bones, and brains.* Notre Dame, IN: University of Notre Dame Press.

Narváez, D., Bock, T., Endicott, L., & Lies, J. (2004). Minnesota's Community Voices and Character Education Project. *Journal of Research in Character Education, 2,* 89–112.

Narváez, D., & Gleason, T.R. (2013). Developmental optimism. In D. Narváez & others, *Evolution, early experience, and human development.* New York: Oxford University Press.

Narváez, D., & Hill, P.L. (2010). The relation of multicultural experiences to moral judgment and mindsets. *Journal of Diversity in Higher Education, 3,* 43–55.

NASSPE (2012). *Single-sex schools/schools with single-sex classrooms/what's the difference.* Retrieved from www.singlesexschools.org/schools-schools.com

Nation, M., & others (2003). What works in prevention: Principles of effective prevention programs. *American Psychologist, 58,* 449–456.

National Assessment of Educational Progress (NAEP) (2012). *The nation's report card 2011.* Washington, DC: U.S. Department of Education.

National Assessment of Educational Progress (NAEP) (2014). *Reading 4th and 8th grades.* Washington, DC: National Center for Educational Statistics.

National Association for Gifted Children (2009). *State of the states in gifted education: 2008–2009.* Washington, DC: Author.

National Center for Education Statistics (1997). *School-family linkages.* Unpublished manuscript. Washington, DC: U.S. Department of Education.

National Center for Education Statistics (1998). *Postsecondary financing strategies: How undergraduates combine work, borrowing, and attendance.* Washington, DC: U.S. Department of Education.

National Center for Education Statistics (2002). *Contexts of postsecondary education: Earning opportunities.* Washington, DC: U.S. Department of Education.

National Center for Education Statistics (2012a). *The condition of education 2012.* Washington, DC: U.S. Department of Education.

National Center for Education Statistics (2012b). Indicator A-33-3: Status Dropout Rates. *Digest of Education Statistics.* Washington, DC: U.S. Department of Education.

National Center for Education Statistics (2013, May). *Characteristics of postsecondary students.* Washington: U.S. Department of Education.

National Center for Education Statistics (2014). *Condition of Education 2012.* Washington, DC: U.S. Department of Education.

National Center for Education Statistics (2014). *School dropouts.* Washington, DC: Author.

National Center for Health Statistics (2000). *Health United States, 1999.* Atlanta, GA: Centers for Disease Control and Prevention.

National Center for Health Statistics (2002). Prevalence of overweight among children and adolescents: United States 1999–2000 (Table 71). *Health United States, 2002.* Atlanta, GA: Centers for Disease Control and Prevention.

National Center for Health Statistics (2002). *Sexual behavior and selected health measures: Men and women 15–44 years of age, United States, 2002,* PHS 2003–1250. Atlanta, GA: Centers for Disease Control and Prevention.

National Center for Health Statistics (2014). *Death rates.* Atlanta: Centers for Disease Control and Prevention.

National Center for Injury Prevention and Control (2006). Fatal injury reports [online database]. Retrieved March 16, 2006, from www.cdc.gov/ncipc/wisqars/

National Center for Vital Statistics (2013). *Births, marriages, divorces, deaths: 2011.* Washington, DC: Author.

National Center on Addiction and Substance Abuse (CASA) (2011). *The importance of family dinners VII.* New York: Columbia University.

National Clearinghouse for Alcohol and Drug Information (1999). *Physical and psychological effects of anabolic steroids.* Washington, DC: Substance Abuse and Mental Health Services Administration.

National Longitudinal Study of Adolescent to Adult Health (2015). Retrieved May 2, 2015, from www.cpc.unc.edu/projects/addhealth

National Marriage Project (2011). *Unmarried cohabitation.* Retrieved June 9, 2012, from www.stateofourunions.org/2011/social_indicators.php

National Research Council (1999). *How people learn.* Washington, DC: National Academic Press.

National Research Council (2004). *Engaging schools: Fostering high school students' motivation to learn.* Washington, DC: National Academies Press.

National Sleep Foundation (2006). *2006 Sleep in America poll.* Washington, DC: National Sleep Foundation.

Nazem, T.G., & Ackerman, K.E. (2012). The female athlete triad. *Sports Health, 4,* 302–311.

Near, C.E. (2013). Selling gender: Associations of box art representation of female characters with sales for teen- and mature-rated video games. *Sex Roles, 68,* 252–269.

Neely, E.K., & Crossen, S.S. (2014). Precocious puberty. *Current Opinion in Obstetrics and Gynecology, 26,* 332–338.

Neff. L.A., & Geers, A.L. (2013). Optimistic expectations in early marriage: A resource or vulnerability for adaptive relationship functioning? *Journal of Personality and Social Psychology, 105,* 38–60.

Negriff, S., Susman, E.J., & Trickett, P.K. (2011). The development pathway from pubertal timing to delinquency and sexual activity from early to late adolescence. *Journal of Youth and Adolescence, 40,* 1343–1356.

Neiderhiser, J.M., Marceau, K., & Reiss, D. (2013). Four factors for the initiation of substance use by young adulthood: A 10-year follow-up twin and sibling study of marital conflict, monitoring, siblings, and peers. *Development and Psychopathology, 25,* 133–149.

Nelson, C. (2006). Unpublished review of J.W. Santrock's *Topical approach to life-span development,* 4th ed. (New York: McGraw-Hill).

Nelson, C.A. (2003). Neural development and lifelong plasticity. In R.M. Lerner, F. Jacobs, & D. Wertlieb (Eds.), *Handbook of applied developmental science* (Vol. 1). Thousand Oaks, CA: Sage.

Nelson, C.A. (2013). Brain development and behavior. In A.M. Rudolph, C. Rudolph, L. First, G. Lister, & A.A. Gershon (Eds.), *Rudolph's pediatrics* (22nd ed.). New York: McGraw-Hill.

Nelson, D.A., & others (2014). Parenting, relational aggression, and borderline personality features: Associations over time in a Russian longitudinal sample. *Development and Psychopathology, 26,* 773–787.

Nelson, L.J., & others (2007). "If you want me to treat you like an adult, start acting like one!" Comparing the criteria that emerging adults and their parents have for adulthood. *Journal of Family Psychology, 21,* 665–674.

Nelson, L.J., & others (2011). Parenting in emerging adulthood: An examination of parenting clusters and correlates. *Journal of Youth and Adolescence, 40,* 730–743.

Nelson, M.C., & Gordon-Larsen, P. (2006). Physical activity and sedentary behavior patterns are associated with selected adolescent health risk behaviors. *Pediatrics, 117,* 1281–1290.

Nelson, S.E., Van Ryzin, M.J., & Dishion, T.J. (2015). Alcohol, marijuana, and tobacco use trajectories from age 12 to 24 years: Demographic correlates and young adult substance use problems. *Development and Psychopathology, 27,* 253–277.

Neumann, E., & others (2015). Attachment in romantic relationships and somatization. *Journal of Nervous and Mental Disease, 203,* 101–106.

Neumark-Sztainer, D., Wall, M., Fulkerson, J.A., & Larson, N. (2013). Changes in the frequency of family meals from 1999 to 2010 in the homes of adolescents: Trends by sociodemographic characteristics. *Journal of Adolescent Health, 52,* 201–206.

New, M. (2008, October). *Binge eating disorder.* Retrieved February 27, 2011, from http://kidshealth.org/parent/emotions/behavior/binge_eating.html

Newman, B.S., & Muzzonigro, P.G. (1993). The effects of traditional family values on the coming out process of gay male adolescents. *Adolescence, 28,* 213–226.

Ng, F.F., Pomerantz, E.M., & Deng, C. (2014). Why are Chinese parents more psychologically controlling than American parents? "My child is my report card." iChild Development, 85, 355–369.

Nickalls, S. (2012, March 9). Why college students shouldn't online date. *The Tower,* Philadelphia: Arcadia University. Retrieved February 27, 2013, from http://tower.arcadia.edu/?p=754

Nicoteri, J.A., & Miskovsky, M.J. (2014). Revisiting the freshman "15": Assessing body mass index in the first college year and beyond. *Journal of the American Association of Nurse Practitioners, 26,* 220–224.

Nie, Y., & Lau, S. (2009). Complementary roles of care and behavioral control in classroom management: The self-determination theory perspective. *Contemporary Educational Psychology, 34,* 185–194.

Nielsen, M.B., & Einarsen, S. (2012). Prospective relationships between workplace sexual harassment and psychological distress. *Occupational Medicine, 62,* 226–228.

Nieto, A.M., & Yoshikawa, H. (2014). Beyond families and schools: Future directions in practice and policy for children in immigrant families. In E.T. Gershoff, R.S. Mistry, & D.A. Crosby (Eds.), *Societal contexts of child development.* New York: Oxford University Press.

Nigg, J.T. (2015). Editorial: The shape of the nosology to come in developmental psychopathology. *Journal of Child and Adolescent Psychiatry, 56,* 397–399.

Ninio, A. (2015, in press). Bids for joint attention by parent-child dyads and by dyads of young peers in interaction. *Journal of Child Language.*

Nisbett, R.E., & others (2012). Intelligence: New findings and theoretical developments. *American Psychologist, 67,* 130–159.

Niwa, E.Y., Way, N., & Hughes, D.L. (2014). Trajectories of ethnic-racial discrimination among ethnically diverse early adolescents: Associations with psychological and social adjustment. *Child Development, 85,* 2339–2354.

Noddings, N. (1992). *The challenge to care in the schools.* New York: Teachers College Press.

Noddings, N. (2001). The care tradition: Beyond "add women and stir." *Theory into Practice, 40,* 29–34.

Noddings, N. (2006). *Critical lessons: What our schools should teach.* New York: Cambridge University Press.

Noddings, N. (2008). Caring and moral education. In L. Nucci & D. Narváez (Eds.), *Handbook of moral and character education.* Clifton, NJ: Psychology Press.

Noddings, N. (2014). Caring and moral education. In L. Nucci, T. Krettenauer, & D. Narváez (Eds.), *Handbook of moral and character education* (2nd ed.). New York: Routledge.

Nogueira, M., & others (2014). Early-age clinical and developmental features associated with substance use disorders in attention-deficit/hyperactivity disorder in adults. *Comprehensive Psychiatry, 55,* 639–649.

Nolen-Hoeksema, S. (2011). *Abnormal psychology* (5th ed.). New York: McGraw-Hill.

Norris, A.E., Hughes, C., Hecht, M., Peragallo, N., & Nickerson, D. (2013). Randomized trial of a peer resistance skill-building game for Hispanic early adolescent girls. *Nursing Research, 62,* 25–35.

Nottelmann, E.D., & others (1987). Gonadal and adrenal hormone correlates of adjustment in early adolescence. In R.M. Lerner & T.T. Foch (Eds.), *Biological-psychological interactions in early adolescence.* Hillsdale, NJ: Erlbaum.

Nsamenang, A.B. (2002). Adolescence in Sub-Saharan Africa: An image constructed from Africa's triple inheritance. In B. Brown, R.W. Larson, & T.S. Saraswathi (Eds.), *The world's youth.* New York: Cambridge University Press.

Nucci, L. (2006). Education for moral development. In M. Killen & J. Smetana (Eds.), *Handbook of moral development.* Mahwah, NJ: Erlbaum.

Nucci, L., & Narváez, D. (2008). *Handbook of moral and character education.* New York: Psychology Press.

Nucci, L., Krettenauer, T., & Narváez, D. (Eds.) (2014). *Handbook of moral and character education* (2nd ed.). New York: Routledge.

Nudo, R.J., & McNeal, D. (2013). Plasticity of cerebral functions. *Handbook of clinical neurology, 110,* 13–21.

Nyberg, J., & others (2014). Cardiovascular and cognitive fitness at age 18 and risk of early-onset dementia. *Brain, 137,* 1514–1523.

O

O'Brien, E.J., Bartoletti, M., & Leitzel, J.D. (2013). Self-esteem, psychopathology, and psychotherapy. In M.H. Kernis (Ed.), *Self-esteem issues and answers.* New York: Psychology Press.

O'Brien, M., & Moss, P. (2010). Fathers, work, and family policies in Europe. In M.E. Lamb (Ed.), *The father's role in child development* (5th ed.). New York: Wiley.

O'Hara, R.E., Gibbons, F.X., Weng, C.Y., Gerrard, M., & Simons, R.L. (2012). Perceived racial discrimination as a barrier to college enrollment for African Americans. *Personality and Social Psychology Bulletin, 38,* 77–89.

O'Keefe, G.S., & others (2011). The impact of social media on children, adolescents, and families. *Pediatrics, 127,* 800–804.

Oberle, E., Schonert-Reichl, K.A., Lawlor, M.S., & Thomson, K.C. (2012). Mindfulness and inhibitory control in early adolescence. *Journal of Early Adolescence, 32,* 565–588.

Occupational outlook handbook (2014/2015). Washington, DC: U.S. Department of Labor, Bureau of Labor Statistics.

OECD (2010). *Strong performers and successful reformers in education: Lessons from PISA for the United States.* Paris, France: Author.

OECD (2014). *Education at a glance 2014: OECD indicators.* Paris, France: OECD.

Offer, D., Ostrov, E., Howard, K.I., & Atkinson, R. (1988). *The teenage world: Adolescents' self-image in ten countries.* New York: Plenum.

Ogden, C.L., Carroll, M.D., Kit, B.K., & Flegal, K.M. (2014). Prevalence of childhood obesity in the United States, 2011–2012. *Journal of the American Medical Association, 311,* 806–814.

Ogolsky, B.G., Lloyd, S.A., & Cate, R.M. (Eds.) (2013). *The developmental course of romantic relationships.* New York: Psychology Press.

Okado, Y., & Bierman, K.L. (2015). Differential risk for late adolescent conduct problems and mood dysregulation among children with early externalizing behavior problems. *Journal of Abnormal Child Psychology, 43,* 735–747.

Olds, D.L., & others (2004). Effects of home visits by paraprofessionals and nurses: Age four follow-up of a randomized trial. *Pediatrics, 114,* 1560–1568.

Olds, D.L., & others (2007). Effects of nurse home visiting on maternal and child functioning: Age 9 follow-up of a randomized trial. *Pediatrics, 120,* e832–e845.

Olino, T.M., & others (2015, in press). Maternal depression, parenting, and youth depressive symptoms: Mediation and moderation in short-term longitudinal study. *Journal of Clinical Child and Adolescent Psychology.*

Oliva, A., Jimenez, J.M., & Parra, A. (2008). Protective effect of supportive family relationships and the influence of stressful life events on adolescent adjustment. *Anxiety, Stress, and Coping, 12,* 1–15.

Olmstead, S.B., Roberson, P.N., Pasley, K., & Fincham, F.D. (2015). Hooking up and risk behaviors among first-semester college men: What is the role of precollege experience? *Journal of Sex Research, 52,* 186–198.

Olszewski-Kubilius, P., & Thompson, D. (2013). Gifted education programs and procedures. In I.B. Weiner & others (Eds.), *Handbook of psychology* (2nd ed., Vol. 7). New York: Wiley.

Olweus, D. (2003). Prevalence estimation of school bullying with the Olweus bully/victim questionnaire. *Aggressive Behavior, 29*(3), 239–269.

Olweus, D. (2013). School bullying: Development and some important changes. *Annual Review of Clinical Psychology* (Vol. 9). Palo Alto, CA: Annual Reviews.

Omorou, A.Y., & others (2015, in press). Adolescent physical activity and sedentary behavior: A pathway in reducing overweight and obesity. The PRALIMAP 2-year cluster randomized controlled trial. *Journal of Physical Activity and Health.*

Ong, K.K., Ahmed, M.L., & Dunger, D.B. (2006). Lesson from large population studies on timing and tempo of puberty (secular trends and relation to body size): The European trend. *Molecular and Cellular Endocrinology, 254–255,* 8–12.

Ophir, E., Nass, C., & Wagner, A.D. (2009). Cognitive control in media multitaskers. *Proceedings of the National Academy of Sciences USA, 106,* 15583–15587.

Oppenheimer, C.W., Hankin, B.L., Young, J.F., & Smolen, A. (2013). Youth genetic vulnerability to maternal depressive symptoms: 5-HTTLPR as moderator of intergenerational transmission effects in a multiwave prospective study. *Depression and Anxiety, 30*(3), 190–196.

Orbeta, R.L., Overpeck, M.D., Ramamcharran, D., Kogan, M.D., & Ledsky, R. (2006). High caffeine intake in adolescents: Associations with difficulty sleeping and feeling tired in the morning. *Adolescent Health, 38,* 451–453.

Orgiles, M., Carratala, E., & Espada, J.P. (2015). Perceived quality of the parental relationship and divorce effects on sexual behavior in Spanish adolescents. *Psychology, Health, and Medicine, 20,* 8–17.

Orobio de Castro, B., Merk, W., Koops, W., Veerman, J.W., & Bosch, J.D. (2005). Emotions in social information processing and their relations with reactive and proactive aggression in referred aggressive boys. *Journal of Clinical Child and Adolescent Psychology, 34,* 105–116.

Orpinas, P., McNicholas, C., & Nahapetyan, L. (2015, in press). Gender differences in trajectories of relational aggression perpetration and victimization from middle to high school. *Aggressive Behavior.*

Orr, A.J. (2011). Gendered capital: Childhood socialization and the "boy crisis" in education. *Sex Roles, 65,* 271–284.

Oser, F., Scarlett, W.G., & Bucher, A. (2006). Religious and spiritual development through the lifespan. In W. Damon & R. Lerner (Eds.), *Handbook of child psychology* (6th ed.). New York: Wiley.

Osofsky, J.D. (1990, Winter). Risk and protective factors for teenage mothers and their infants. *SRCD Newsletter,* pp. 1–2.

Oswald, D.L., & Clark, E.M. (2003). Best friends forever? High school best friendships and the transition to college. *Personal Relationships, 10,* 187–196.

Oude Luttikhuis, H., & others (2009). Interventions for treating obesity in children. *Cochrane Database of Systematic Reviews* (1), CD001872.

Owen, J., Fincham, F.D., & Manthos, M. (2013). Friendship after a friends with benefits relationship: Deception, psychological function, and social connectedness. *Archives of Sexual Behavior, 42,* 1443–1449.

Owen, J.J., Rhoades, G.K., Stanley, S.M., & Markman, H.J. (2011). The role of leaders' working alliance in premarital education. *Journal of Family Psychology, 25,* 49–57.

Owens, J.A. (2014). Insufficient sleep in adolescents and young adults: An update on causes and consequences. *Pediatrics, 134,* e921–e932.

Owens, J.A., Belon, K., & Moss, P. (2010). Impact of delaying school start time on adolescent sleep, mood, and behavior. *Archives of Pediatric and Adolescent Medicine, 164,* 608–614.

Oxford, M.L., Gilchrist, L.D., Gillmore, M.R., & Lohr, M.J. (2006). Predicting variation in the life course of adolescent mothers as they enter adulthood. *Journal of Adolescent Health, 39,* 20–36.

Oyserman, D., & Destin, M. (2010). Identity-based motivation: Implications for intervention. *Counseling Psychologist, 38,* 1001–1043.

Oyserman, D., & James, L. (2011). Possible identities. In S.J. Schwartz, K. Luyckx, & V.L. Vignoles (Eds.), *Handbook of identity theory and research.* New York: Springer.

P

Padilla-Walker, L.M., Carlo, G., Christensen, K.J., & Yorgason, J.B. (2012). Bidirectional relations between authoritative parenting and adolescents' prosocial behaviors. *Journal of Research on Adolescence, 22,* 400–408.

Padilla-Walker, L.M., & Coyne, S.M. (2011). "Turn that thing off!" Parent and adolescent predictors of proactive media monitoring. *Journal of Youth and Adolescence, 34,* 705–715.

Padilla-Walker, L.M., Coyne, S.M., Fraser, A.M., Dyer, W.J., & Yorgason, J.B. (2012). Parents and adolescents growing up in the digital age: Latent growth curve analysis of proactive media monitoring. *Journal of Adolescence, 35*(5), 1153–1165.

Padilla-Walker, L., Day, R.D., Dyer, W.J., & Black, B.C. (2013). "Keep on keeping on, even when it's hard!": Predictors of outcomes of adolescent persistence. *Journal of Early Adolescence, 33,* 433–457.

Padilla-Walker, L.M., & Nelson, L.J. (2012). Black hawk down?: Establishing helicopter parenting as distinct construct from other forms of parental control during emerging adulthood. *Journal of Adolescence, 35,* 1177–1190.

Padilla-Walker, L.M., Nelson, L.J., Carroll, J.S., & Jensen, A.C. (2010). More than just a game: Video game and Internet use during emerging adulthood. *Journal of Youth and Adolescence, 39,* 103–113.

Padmanabhanunni, A., & Edwards, D. (2015, in press). Rape survivors' experiences of the silent protest: Implications for promoting healing and resilience. *Qualitative Health Research.*

Pahlke, E., Hyde, J.S., & Allison, C.M. (2014). The effects of single-sex compared with coeducational schooling on students' performance and attitudes: A meta-analysis. *Psychological Bulletin, 140,* 1042–1072.

Pakpreo, P., Ryan, S., Auinger, P., & Aten, M. (2004). The association between parental lifestyle behaviors and adolescent knowledge, attitudes, intentions, and nutritional and physical activity behaviors. *Journal of Adolescent Health, 34,* 129–130.

Palfrey, J., Sacco, D., Boyd, D., & DeBonis, L. (2009). *Enhancing child safety and online technologies.* Cambridge, MA: Berkman Center for Internet & Society.

Pallini, S., & others (2014). Early child-parent attachment and peer relations: A meta-analysis of recent research. *Journal of Family Psychology, 28,* 118–123.

Pallotto, M., & Deprez, F. (2014). Regulation of adult neurogenesis by GABAergic transmission: Signaling beyond GABAA-receptors. *Frontiers in Cellular Neuroscience, 8,* 166.

Pals, J.L. (2006). Constructing the "springboard effect": Causal connections, self-making, and growth within the life story. In D.P. McAdams, R. Josselson, & A. Lieblich (Eds.), *Identity and story.* Washington, DC: American Psychological Association.

Paludi, M.A. (2002). *The psychology of women* (2nd ed.). Upper Saddle River, NJ: Prentice-Hall.

Pan, C.Y., & others (2015, in press). Effects of physical exercise intervention on motor skills and executive functions in children with ADHD: A pilot study. *Journal of Attention Disorders.*

Pantic, I. (2014). Online social networking and mental health. *Cyberpsychology, Behavior, and Social Networking, 17,* 652–657.

Papadimitriou, A., Nicolaidou, P., Fretzayas, A., & Chrousos, G.P. (2010). Clinical review: Constitutional advancement of growth, a.k.a., early growth acceleration, predicts early puberty and childhood obesity. *Journal of Clinical Endocrinology and Metabolism, 95,* 4535–4541.

Papini, D., & Sebby, R. (1988). Variations in conflictual family issues by adolescent pubertal status, gender, and family member. *Journal of Early Adolescence, 8,* 1–15.

Parens, E., & Johnston, J. (2009). Facts, values, and attention-deficit hyperactivity disorder (ADHD): An update on the controversies. *Child and Adolescent Psychiatry and Mental Health, 3,* 1.

Paris, S.G., Yeung, A.S., Wong, H.M., & Luo, S.W. (2012). Global perspectives on education during middle childhood. In K.R. Harris & others (Eds.), *APA handbook of educational psychology.* Washington, DC: American Psychological Association.

Park, D.C., & others (2014). The impact of sustained engagement on cognitive function in older adults: The Synapse Project. *Psychological Science, 25,* 103–112.

Park, M.J., Brindis, C.D., Chang, F., & Irwin, C.E. (2008). A midcourse review of the healthy people 2010: 21 critical health objectives for adolescents and young adults. *Journal of Adolescent Health, 42,* 329–334.

Park, M.J., Paul Mulye, T., Adams, S.H., Brindis, C.D., & Irwin, C.E. (2006). The health status of young adults in the United States. *Journal of Adolescent Health, 39,* 305–317.

Park, M.J., Scott, J.T., Adams, S.H., Brindis, C.D., & Irwin, C.E. (2014). Adolescent and young adult health in the United States in the past decade: Little improvement and young adults remain worse off than adolescents. *Journal of Adolescent Health, 55,* 3–16.

Parkay, F.W. (2013). *Becoming a teacher* (9th ed.). Upper Saddle River, NJ: Pearson.

Parkay, F.W. (2016, in press). *Becoming a teacher* (10th ed.). Upper Saddle River, NJ: Pearson.

Parke, R.D., & Buriel, R. (2006). Socialization in the family: Ethnic and ecological perspectives. In W. Damon & R. Lerner (Eds.), *Handbook of child psychology* (6th ed.). New York: Wiley.

Parke, R.D., & Clarke-Stewart, A.K. (2011). *Social development.* New York: Wiley.

Parke, R.D., Coltrane, S., & Schofield, T. (2011). The bicultural advantage. In J. Marsh, R. Mendoza-Denton, & J.A. Smith (Eds.), *Are we born racist?* Boston: Beacon Press.

Parker, K. (2011). The boomerang generation. *Pew Social & Demographic Trends,* 1–20.

Parkes, A., & others (2011). Comparison of teenagers' early same-sex and heterosexual behavior: UK data from the SHARE and RIPPLE studies. *Journal of Adolescent Health, 48,* 27–35.

Partnership for a Drug-Free America (2005). *Partnership Attitude Tracking Study.* New York: Author.

Pascual, A., Extebarria, I., Ortega, I., & Ripalda, A. (2012). Gender differences in adolescence in emotional variables relevant to eating disorders. *International Journal of Psychology and Psychological Therapy, 12,* 59–68.

Pascuzzo, K., Cyr, C., & Moss, E. (2013). Longitudinal association between adolescent attachment, adult romantic attachment, and emotion regulation strategies. *Attachment and Human Development, 15,* 83–103.

Pasterski, V., Golombok, S., & Hines, M. (2011). Sex differences in social behavior. In P.K. Smith & C.H. Hart (Eds.), *Wiley-Blackwell handbook of childhood social development* (2nd ed.). New York: Wiley.

Pasupathi, M. (2015). Autobiographical reasoning and my discontent: Alternative paths to narrative identity. In K.C. McLean & M. Syed (Eds.), *Oxford handbook of identity development.* New York: Oxford University Press.

Pate, R.R., & others (2009). Age-related change in physical activity in adolescent girls. *Journal of Adolescent Health, 44,* 275–282.

Patel, D.R., & Baker, R.J. (2006). Musculoskeletal injuries in sports. *Primary Care, 33,* 545–579.

Patrick, M.E., & Schulenberg, J.E. (2010). Alcohol use and heavy episodic drinking prevalence among national samples of American eighth- and tenth-grade students. *Journal of Studies on Alcohol and Drugs, 71,* 41–45.

Patrick, R.B., & Gibbs, J.C. (2012). Inductive discipline, parental expression of disappointed expectations, and moral identity in adolescence. *Journal of Youth and Adolescence, 41,* 973–983.

Patterson, C.J. (2004). What differences does a civil union make? Changing public policies and the experiences of same-sex couples: Comment on Solomon, Rothblum, and Balsam (2004). *Journal of Family Psychology, 18,* 287–289.

Patterson, C.J. (2013). Family lives of gay and lesbian adults. In G.W. Peterson & K.R. Bush (Eds.), *Handbook of marriage and the family* (3rd ed.). New York: Springer.

Patterson, C.J. (2014). Sexual minority youth and youth with sexual minority parents. In A. Ben Areah & others (Eds.), *Handbook of child research.* Thousand Oaks, CA: Sage.

Patterson, C.J., & D'Augelli, A.R. (Eds.) (2013). *The psychology of sexual orientation.* New York: Cambridge University Press.

Patterson, C.J., Farr, R.H., & Hastings, P.D. (2015). Socialization in the context of family diversity. In J.E. Grusec & P.D. Hastings (Eds.), *Handbook of socialization* (2nd ed.). New York: Guilford.

Patterson, G.R., DeBaryshe, B.D., & Ramsey, E. (1989). A developmental perspective on antisocial behavior. *American Psychologist, 44,* 329–335.

Patterson, G.R., Forgatch, M.S., & DeGarmo, D.S. (2010). Cascading effects following intervention. *Development and Psychopathology, 22,* 949–970.

Patterson, G.R., Reid, J.B., & Dishion, T.J. (1992). Antisocial boys (Vol. 4). Eugene, OR: Castalia.

Patton, G.C., & others (2011a). Overweight and obesity between adolescence and young adulthood: A 10-year prospective study. *Journal of Adolescent Health, 48,* 275–280.

Patton, G.C., & others (2011b). A prospective study of the effects of optimism on adolescent health risks. *Pediatrics, 127,* 308–316.

Paul, A. (2014). In online better than offline for meeting partners? Depends: Are you looking to marry or date? *Cyberpsychology, Behavior, and Social Networking, 17,* 664–667.

Paul, E.L., & White, K.M. (1990). The development of intimate relationships in late adolescence. *Adolescence, 25,* 375–400.

Paul, P. (2003, Sept./Oct.). The PermaParent trap. *Psychology Today, 36*(5), 40–53.

Paulhus, D.L. (2008). Birth order. In M.M. Haith & J.B. Benson (Eds.), *Encyclopedia of infant and early childhood development.* Oxford, UK: Elsevier.

Paunesku, D., & others (2015, in press). Mind-set interventions are a scaleable treatment for academic underachievement. *Psychological Science.*

Paus, T. (2010). Growth of white matter in the adolescent brain: Myelin or axon? *Brain and Cognition, 72,* 26–35.

Paus, T., & others (2007). Morphological properties of the action-observation cortical network in adolescents with low and high resistance to peer influence. *Social Neuroscience 3*(3), 303–316.

Pazol, K., Creange, A.A., Burley, K.D., & Jamieson, D.J. (2014). Abortion surveillance—United States, 2011. *MMWR Surveillance Summaries, 63,* 1–41.

Pea, R., & others (2012). Media use, face-to-face communication, media multitasking, and social well-being among 8- to 12-year-old girls. *Developmental Psychology, 48,* 327–336.

Pearlman, E. (2013). Twin psychological development. Retrieved February 14, 2013, from http://christinabaglivitinglof.com/twin-pregnancy/six-twin-experts-te...

Pearson, N., Biddle, S.J., & Gorely, T. (2009). Family correlates of breakfast consumption among children and adolescents: A systematic review. *Appetite, 52,* 1–7.

Peck, S.C., Roeser, R.W., Zarrett, N., & Eccles, J.S. (2008). Exploring the roles of extracurricular activity quantity and quality in the educational resilience of vulnerable adolescents: Variable- and pattern-centered approaches. *Journal of Social Issues, 64,* 135–155.

Pecot-Hebert, L. (2012). Beauty and body-image: Anorexia/eating disorders. In M. Kosut (Ed.), *Encyclopedia of gender in media.* Thousand Oaks, CA: Sage.

Pedersen, W., & Mastekaasa, A. (2011). Conduct disorder symptoms and subsequent pregnancy, childbirth, and abortion: A population-based longitudinal study of adolescents. *Journal of Adolescence, 34,* 1025–1033.

Peets, K., Hodges, E.V., & Salmivalli, C. (2013). Forgiveness and its determinants depending on the interpersonal context of hurt. *Journal of Experimental Child Psychology, 114*(1), 131–145.

Pena, J.B., Zayas, L.H., Cbrera-Hguyen, P., & Vega, W.A. (2012). U.S. cultural involvement and its association with suicidal behavior among youths in the Dominican Republic. *American Journal of Public Health, 102,* 664–671.

Peng, P., & Fuchs, D. (2015, in press). A meta-analysis of working memory deficits in children with learning difficulties: Is there a difference between the verbal doman and numerical domain? *Journal of Learning Disabilities.*

Peretto, P., & Bonafanti, L. (2014). Major unsolved points in adult neurogenesis: Doors open on a translational future? *Frontiers in Neuroscience, 8,* 154.

Perez-Brena, N.J., Updegraff, K.A., & Umana-Taylor, A.J. (2015, in press). Transmission of cultural values among Mexican American parents and their adolescent and emerging adult offspring. *Family Process.*

Perkins, H.W., Perkins, J.M., & Craig, D.W. (2014). No safe haven: Locations of harassment and bullying victimization in middle schools. *Journal of School Health, 84,* 810–818.

Perkinson-Gloor, N., Lemola, S., & Grob, A. (2013). Sleep duration, positive attitude toward life, and academic achievement: The role of daytime tiredness, behavioral persistence, and school start times. *Journal of Adolescence, 36,* 311–318.

Perlman, L. (2008, July 22). Am I an "I" or "We"? *Twins,* pp. 1–2.

Perloff, R.M. (2014). Social media effects on young women's body image concerns: Theoretical perspectives and an agenda for research. *Sex Roles, 71,* 363–377.

Perry, D.G., & Pauletti, R.E. (2011). Gender and adolescent development. *Journal of Research on Adolescence, 21,* 61–74.

Perry, J.C., & Wallace, E.W. (2012). What schools are doing around career development: Implications for policy and practice. *New Directions in Youth Development, 134,* 33–44.

Perry, N.E., & Rahim, A. (2011). Supporting self-regulated learning in classrooms. In B.J. Zimmerman & D.H. Schunk (Eds.), *Handbook of self-regulation of learning and performance.* New York: Routledge.

Perry, W.G. (1999). *Forms of ethical and intellectual development in the college years: A scheme.* San Francisco: Jossey-Bass.

Perry, W.G. (1970). *Forms of intellectual and ethical development in the college years.* New York: Holt, Rinehart & Winston.

Persike, M., & Seiffge-Krenke, I. (2012). Competence in coping with stress in adolescents from three regions of the world. *Journal of Youth and Adolescence, 41,* 863–879.

Persike, M., & Seiffge-Krenke, I. (2014). Is stress perceived differently in relationships with parents and peers? Inter- and intra-regional comparisons on adolescents from 21 nations. *Journal of Adolescence, 37,* 493–504.

Persike, M., & Seiffge-Krenke, I. (2015, in press). Stress with parents and peers: How adolescents from 18 nations cope with relationship stress. *Anxiety, Stress, and Coping.*

Pesce, C., Crova, L., Cereatti, L., Casella, R., & Bellucci, M. (2009). Physical activity and mental performance in preadolescents: Effects of acute exercise on free-recall memory. *Mental Health and Physical Activity, 2,* 16–22.

Peskin, H. (1967). Pubertal onset and ego functioning. *Journal of Abnormal Psychology, 72,* 1–15.

Petersen, A.C. (1987, September). Those gangly years. *Psychology Today, 21,* 28–34.

Petersen, A.C., & Crockett, L. (1985). Pubertal timing and grade effects on adjustment. *Journal of Youth and Adolescence, 14,* 191–206.

Petersen, I., Bates, J.E., Dodge, K.A., Lansford, J.E., & Pettit, G.S. (2015, in press). Describing and predicting developmental profiles of externalizing problems from childhood to adulthood. *Development and Psychopathology.*

Petersen, I.T., & others (2012). Interaction between serotonin transporter polymorphism (5-HTTLPR) and stressful life events in adolescents' trajectories of anxious/depressed symptoms. *Developmental Psychology, 48*(5), 1463–1475.

Petersen, J.L., & Hyde, J.S. (2010). A meta-analytic review of research on gender differences in sexuality, 1973–2007. *Psychological Bulletin, 136,* 21–38.

Petersen, J., & Hyde, J.S. (2014). Gender-related academic and occupational interests and goals. *Advances in Child Development and Behavior, 47,* 43–76.

Peterson, R.E., & others (2012). Binge eating disorder mediates links between symptoms of depression, anxiety, and caloric intake in overweight and obese women. *Journal of Obesity, 2012,* 40763.

Pettit, G.S., Bates, J.E., Dodge, K.A., & Meece, D.W. (1999). The impact of after-school peer contact on early adolescent externalizing problems is moderated by parental monitoring, perceived neighborhood safety, and prior adjustment. *Child Development, 70,* 768–778.

Petts, R.J. (2014). Family, religious attendance, and trajectories of psychological well-being among youth. *Journal of Family Psychology, 28,* 759–768.

Pew Research Center (2010). *Millennials: Confident, connected, open to change.* Washington, DC: Pew Research Center.

Pew Research Center (2010). *The decline of marriage and rise of new families.* Washington, DC: Pew Research Center.

Pew Research Center (2011, December). *Barely half of U.S. adults are married—a record low.* Washington, DC: Pew Research Center.

Pew Research Center (2012). *Young, underemployed, and optimistic.* Washington, DC: Pew Research Center.

Pew Research Center (2012, October 9). *Religion & Public Life Project: "Nones on the rise."* Washington, DC: Pew Research Center.

Pew Research Center (2014, March 6). *Women's college enrollment gains leave men behind.* Washington, DC: Pew Research Center.

Pew Research Center (2015). *For most highly educated women, motherhood doesn't start until the 30s.* Washington, DC: Pew Research Center.

Peykari, N., & others (2015, in press). Promoting physical activity participation among adolescents: The barriers and the suggestions. *International Journal of Preventive Medicine.*

Pflieger, J.C., Cook, E.C., Niccolai, L.M., & Connell, C.M. (2013). Racial/ethnic differences in patterns of sexual risk behavior and rates of sexually transmitted infections among female young adults. *American Journal of Public Health, 103,* 903–909.

Phinney, J.S. (2006). Ethnic identity exploration in emerging adulthood. In J.J. Arnett & J.L. Tanner (Eds.), *Emerging adults in America.* Washington, DC: American Psychological Association.

Phinney, J.S. (2008). Bridging identities and disciplines: Advances and challenges in understanding multiple identities. *New Directions for Child and Adolescent Development, 120,* 97–109.

Phinney, J.S., & Baldelomar, O.A. (2011). Identity development in multiple developmental contexts. In L. Jensen (Ed.), *Bridging cultural and developmental approaches to psychology.* New York: Oxford University Press.

Phinney, J.S., Berry, J.W., Sam, D.L., & Vedder, P. (2013a). Understanding immigrant youth: Conclusions and implications. In J.W. Berry & others (Eds.), *Immigrant youth in cultural transition.* New York: Psychology Press.

Phinney, J.S., Berry, J.W., Vedder, P., & Liebkind, K. (2013b). Acculturation experience: Attitudes, identities, and behaviors of immigrant youth. In J.W. Berry & others (Eds.), *Immigrant youth in cultural transition.* New York: Psychology Press.

Phinney, J.S., & Vedder, P. (2013). Family relationship values of adolescents and parents: Intergenerational discrepancies and adaptation. In J.W. Berry & others (Eds.), *Immigrant youth in cultural transition.* New York: Psychology Press.

Piaget, J. (1952). *The origins of intelligence in children.* (M. Cook, Trans.). New York: International Universities Press.

Piaget, J. (1954). *The construction of reality in the child.* New York: Basic Books.

Piaget, J. (1972). Intellectual evolution from adolescence to adulthood. *Human Development, 15,* 1–12.

Piko, B.F., & Balazs, M.A. (2012). Authoritative parenting style and adolescent smoking and drinking. *Addictive Behaviors, 37,* 353–356.

Pinquart, M., Feubner, C., & Ahnert, L. (2013). Meta-analytic evidence for stability in attachments from infancy to early adulthood. *Attachment and Human Development, 15,* 189–218.

Pittman, J.F., Keiley, M.H., Kerpelman, J.L., & Vaughn, B.E. (2011). Attachment, identity, and intimacy: Parallels between Bowlby's and Erikson's paradigms. *Journal of Family Theory and Review, 3,* 32–46.

Pittman, J.F., Kerpelman, J.L., Soto, J.B., & Adler-Baeder, F.M. (2012). Identity exploration in the dating domain: The role of attachment dimensions and parenting practices. *Journal of Adolescence, 35,* 1485–1499.

Platt, B., Kadosh, K.C., & Lau, J.Y. (2013). The role of peer rejection in adolescent depression. *Depression and Anxiety, 30*(9), 809–821.

Pleck, J.H. (1983). The theory of male sex role identity: Its rise and fall, 1936–present. In M. Levin (Ed.), *In the shadow of the past: Psychology portrays the sexes.* New York: Columbia University Press.

Pleck, J.H. (1995). The gender-role strain paradigm. In R.F. Levant & S. Pollack (Eds.), *A new psychology of men.* New York: Basic Books.

Plener, P.L., Singer, H., & Goldbeck, L. (2011). Traumatic events and suicidality in a German adolescent community sample. *Journal of Traumatic Stress, 24,* 121–124.

Plomin, R. (2004). Genetics and developmental psychology. *Merrill-Palmer Quarterly, 50,* 341–352.

Plomin, R. (2011). Commentary: Why are children in the same family so different? Nonshared environment three decades later. *International Journal of Epidemiology, 40,* 582–592.

Plomin, R., & Deary, I.J. (2015). Genetics and intelligence differences: Five special findings. *Molecular Psychiatry, 20,* 98–108.

Plomin, R., Shakeshaft, N.G., McMillan, A., & Trzaskowski, M. (2014). Nature, nurture, and expertise. *Intelligence, 45,* 46–59.

Plucker, J. (2010). Interview. In P. Bronson & A. Merryman. The creativity crisis. *Newsweek,* 42–48.

Pokhrel, P., & others (2013). Adolescent neurocognitive development, self-regulation, and school-based drug prevention. *Prevention Science, 14*(3), 218–228.

Polce-Lynch, M., Myers, B.J., Kliewer, W., & Kilmartin, C. (2001). Adolescent self-esteem and gender: Exploring relations to sexual harassment, body image, media influence, and emotional expression. *Journal of Youth and Adolescence, 30,* 225–244.

Pollack, W. (1999). *Real boys.* New York: Henry Holt.

Pomerantz, E.M. (2014). *Six principles to motivate your child to do well in school.* Retrieved November 20, 2014, from http://i-parents.illinois.edu/research/pomerantz.html

Pomerantz, E.M., Cheung, C.S., & Qin, L. (2012). Relatedness between children and parents: Implications for motivation. In R. Ryan (Ed.), *Oxford handbook of motivation.* New York: Oxford University Press.

Pomerantz, E.M., & Kempner, S.G. (2013). Mothers' daily person and process praise: Implications for children's intelligence and motivation. *Developmental Psychology, 49,* 2040–2046.

Pomerantz, E.M., Kim, E.M., & Cheung, C.S. (2012). Parents' involvement in children's learning. In K.R. Harris & others (Eds.), *APA educational psychology handbook.* Washington, DC: American Psychological Association.

Pompili, M., & others (2014). Bisexuality and suicide: A systematic review of the current literature. *Journal of Sexual Medicine, 11,* 1903–1913.

Pong, S., & Landale, N.S. (2012). Academic achievement of legal immigrants' children: The roles of parents' pre- and post-immigration characteristics in origin-group differences. *Child Development, 83,* 1543–1559.

Pontifex, M.B., Saliba, B.J., Raine, L.B., Picchietti, D.L., & Hillman, C.H. (2013). Exercise improves behavioral, neurocognitive, and scholastic performance in children with attention-deficit/hyperactivity disorder. *Journal of Pediatrics, 162,* 543–551.

Pope, L.M., Adler, N.E., & Tschann, J.M. (2001). Post-abortion psychological adjustment: Are minors at increased risk? *Journal of Adolescent Health, 29,* 2–11.

Popenoe, D. (2008). *Cohabitation, marriage, and child wellbeing: A cross-national perspective.* Piscataway, NJ: The National Marriage Project, Rutgers University.

Popenoe, D. (2009). *The state of our unions 2008. Updates of social indicators: Tables and charts.* Piscataway, NJ: The National Marriage Project.

Popham, W.J. (2014). *Classroom assessment* (7th ed.). Upper Saddle River, NJ: Pearson.

Porfeli, E.J., & Lee, B. (2012). Career development during childhood and adolescence. *New Directions for Youth Development, 134,* 11–22.

Posamentier, A.S., & Smith, B.S. (2015). *Teaching secondary mathematics* (9th ed.). Upper Saddle River, NJ: Pearson.

Potard, C., Courtois, R., & Rusch, E. (2008). The influence of peers on risky behavior during adolescence. *European Journal of Contraception and Reproductive Health Care, 13,* 264–270.

Potochnick, S., Perreira, K.M., & Fuligni, A. (2012). Fitting in: The roles of social acceptance and discrimination in shaping the daily psychological well-being of Latino youth. *Social Science Quarterly, 93,* 173–190.

Poulin, F., & Denault, A-S. (2012). Other-sex friendship as a mediator between parental monitoring and substance use in boys and girls. *Journal of Youth and Adolescence, 41,* 1488–1501.

Poulin, F., & Pedersen, S. (2007). Developmental changes in gender composition of friendship networks in adolescent girls and boys. *Developmental Psychology, 43,* 1484–1496.

Powell, S.D. (2015). *Your introduction to education* (3rd ed.). Upper Saddle River, NJ: Pearson.

Power, F.C., & Higgins-D'Alessandro, A. (2008). The Just Community Approach to moral education and moral atmosphere of the school. In L. Nucci & D. Narváez (Eds.), *Handbook of moral and character education.* New York: Psychology Press.

Prabhakar, H. (2007). Hopkins interactive guest blog: The public health experience at Johns Hopkins. Retrieved January 31, 2008, from http://hopkins.typepad.com/guest/2007/03/the_public_heal.html

Pressley, M. (2003). Psychology of literacy and literacy instruction. In I.B. Weiner & others (Eds.), *Handbook of psychology* (2nd ed., Vol. 7). New York: Wiley.

Pressley, M. (2007). An interview with Michael Pressley by Terri Flowerday and Michael Shaughnessy. *Educational Psychology Review, 19,* 1–12.

Pressley, M., Allington, R., Wharton-McDonald, R., Block, C.C., & Morrow, L.M. (2001). *Learning to read: Lessons from exemplary first grades.* New York: Guilford.

Pressley, M., & Hilden, K. (2006). Cognitive strategies. In W. Damon & R. Lerner (Eds.), *Handbook of child psychology* (6th ed.). New York: Wiley.

Pressley, M., Mohan, L., Reffitt, K., Raphael-Bogaert, L.R. (2007). Writing instruction in engaging and effective elementary settings. In S. Graham, C.A. MacArthur, & J. Fitzgerald (Eds.), *Best practices in writing instruction.* New York: Guilford.

Pressley, M., Raphael, L., Gallagher, D., & DiBella, J. (2004). Providence–St. Mel School: How a school that works for African-American students works. *Journal of Educational Psychology, 96,* 216–235.

Pressley, M., & others (2003). *Motivating primary-grades teachers.* New York: Guilford.

Prieler, M., & Choi, J. (2014). Broadening the scope of social media effect research on body image concerns. *Sex Roles, 71,* 378–388.

Priess, H.A., Lindberg, S.M., & Hyde, J.S. (2009). Adolescent gender-role identity and mental health: Gender intensification revisited. *Child Development, 80,* 1531–1544.

Priest, N., & others (2013). A systematic review of studies examining the relationship between reported racism and health and wellbeing for children and young people. *Social Science and Medicine, 95,* 115–127.

Prinstein, M.J. (2007). Moderators of peer contagion: A longitudinal examination of depression socialization between adolescents and their best friends. *Journal of Clinical Child and Adolescent Psychology, 36,* 159–170.

Prinstein, M.J., & Dodge, K.A. (2008). Current issues in peer influence research. In M.J. Prinstein & K.A. Dodge (Eds.), *Understanding peer influence in children and adolescents.* New York: Guilford.

Prinstein, M.J., & Giletta, M. (2015). Peer relations and developmental psychopathology. In D. Cicchetti (Ed.), *Developmental psychopathology* (3rd ed.). New York: Wiley.

Prinstein, M.J., Rancourt, D., Guerry, J.D., & Browne, C.B. (2009). Peer reputations and psychological adjustment. In K.H. Rubin, W.M. Bukowski, & B. Laursen (Eds.), *Handbook of peer interactions, relationships, and groups.* New York: Guilford.

Proulx, C.M., & Snyder-Rivas, L.A. (2013). *Journal of Family Psychology, 27,* 194–202.

Pryor, J.H., & others (2005). *The American freshman: National norms for fall 2005.* Los Angeles: Higher Education Research Institute, UCLA.

Psychster Inc. (2010). *Psychology of social media.* Retrieved February 21, 2013, from www.psychster.com

Pulkkinen, L., & Kokko, K. (2000). Identity development in adulthood: A longitudinal study. *Journal of Research in Personality, 34,* 445–470.

Purtell, K.M., & McLoyd, V.C. (2013). Parents' participation in a work-based anti-poverty program can enhance their children's future orientation: Understanding pathways of influence. *Journal of Youth and Adolescence, 42*(6), 777–791.

Putallaz, M., & others (2007). Overt and relational aggression and victimization: Multiple perspectives within the school setting. *Journal of School Psychology, 45,* 523–547.

Putnam, S.P., Sanson, A.V., & Rothbart, M.K. (2002). Child temperament and parenting. In M. Bornstein (Ed.), *Handbook of parenting* (2nd ed.). Mahwah, NJ: Erlbaum.

Puzzanchera, C., & Sickmund, M. (2008, July). *Juvenile court statistics 2005.* Pittsburgh: National Center for Juvenile Justice.

Q

Qin, L., & Pomerantz, E.M. (2013). Reciprocal pathways between American and Chinese early adolescents' sense of responsibility and disclosure to parents. *Child Development, 84,* 1887–1895.

Qu, Y., & Pomerantz, E.M. (2015, in press). Divergent school trajectories in early adolescence in the United States and China: An examination of underlying mechanisms. *Journal of Youth and Adolescence.*

Quimby, E.G., & others (2012). Psychiatric disorders and substance use in homeless youth: A preliminary comparison of San Francisco and Chicago. *Behavioral Sciences, 30,* 186–194.

Quinlan-Davidson, M., & others (2014). Suicide among young people in America. *Journal of Adolescent Health, 54,* 262–268.

Quinton, D., Rutter, M., & Gulliver, L. (1990). Continuities in psychiatric disorders from childhood to adulthood in the children of psychiatric patients. In L. Robins & M. Rutter (Eds.), *Straight and devious pathways from childhood to adulthood.* New York: Cambridge University Press.

Quinton, W., Major, B., & Richards, C. (2001). Adolescents and adjustment to abortion: Are minors at greater risk? *Psychology, Public Policy, and Law, 7,* 491–514.

R

Radford, A.W., & Ifil, N. (2009). *Preparing students for college.* Washington, DC: National Association of College Admission Counseling.

Raeburn, P. (2014). *Do fathers matter?* New York: Farrar, Straus, and Giroux.

Raffaelli, M., & Ontai, L. (2001). "She's sixteen years old and there's boys calling over to the house": An exploratory study of sexual socialization in Latino families. *Culture, Health, and Sexuality, 3,* 295–310.

Raffaelli, M., & Ontai, L.L. (2004). Gender socialization in Latino/a families: Results from two retrospective studies. *Sex Roles, 50,* 287–299.

Ramani, G.B., & Siegler, R.S. (2014). How informal learning activities can promote children's numerical knowledge. In R.C. Kadosh & A. Dowker (Eds.), *Oxford handbook of mathematical cognition.* New York: Oxford University Press.

Ramiro, L., & others (2015). Gendered trends in early and very early sex and condom use in 20 European countries from 2002 to 2010. *European Journal of Public Health, 25*(Suppl. 2), S65–S68.

Ramus, F. (2014). Neuroimaging sheds new light on the phonological deficit in dyslexia. *Trends in Cognitive Science, 18,* 274–275.

Rancourt, D., Conway, C.C., Burk, W.J., & Prinstein, M.J. (2013). Gender composition of preadolescents' friendship groups moderates peer socialization of body change behaviors. *Health Psychology, 32,* 283–292.

Rasmussen, K.A., & others (2012). Can perceived burdensomeness explain the relationship between suicide and perfectionism? *Suicide and Life-Threatening Behavior, 42,* 121–128.

Rathunde, K., & Csikszentmihalyi, M. (2006). The developing person: An experiential perspective. In W. Damon & R. Lerner (Eds.), *Handbook of child psychology* (6th ed.). New York: Wiley.

Rauer, A.J., Pettit, G.S., Lansford, J.E., Bates, J.E., & Dodge, K.A. (2013). Romantic relationship patterns in young adulthood and their developmental antecedents. *Developmental Psychology, 49,* 2159–2171.

Rauh, J.J., Barrack, M., & Nichols, J.F. (2014). Associations between the female athlete triad and injury among high school runners. *International Journal of Sports and Physical Therapy, 9,* 948–958.

Raven, P.H., Johnson, G.B., Mason, K.A., Losos, J., & Singer, S. (2014). *Biology* (10th ed.). New York: McGraw-Hill.

Raver, C.C., & others (2013). Predicting individual differences in low-income children's executive control from early to middle childhood. *Developmental Science, 16*(3), 394–408.

Raymo, J.M., Park, H., Iwasawa, M., & Zhou, Y. (2014). Single motherhood, living arrangements, and time with children in Japan. *Journal of Marriage and the Family, 76,* 843–861.

Raznahan, A., & others (2014). Longitudinal four-dimensional mapping of subcortical anatomy in human development. *Proceedings of the National Academy of Sciences USA, 111,* 1592–1597.

Read, J.P., Merrill, J.E., & Bytschkow, K. (2010). Before the party starts: Risk factors and reasons for "pregaming" in college students. *Journal of American College Health, 58,* 461–472.

Realini, J.P., Buzi, R.S., Smith, P. B., & Martinez, M. (2010). Evaluation of "big decisions": An abstinence-plus sexuality. *Journal of Sex and Marital Therapy, 36,* 313–326.

Ream, G.L., & Savin-Williams, R. (2003). Religious development in adolescence. In G. Adams & M. Berzonsky (Eds.), *Blackwell handbook of adolescence.* Malden, MA: Blackwell.

Reese, B.M., Haydon, A.A., Herring, A.H., & Halpern, C.T. (2013). The association between sequences of sexual initiation and the likelihood of teenage pregnancy. *Journal of Adolescent Health, 52,* 228–233.

Regenerus, M., & Uecker, J. (2011). *Premarital sex in America: How Americans meet, mate, and think about marrying.* New York: Oxford University Press.

Reid, P.T., & Zalk, S.R. (2001). Academic environments: Gender and ethnicity in U.S. higher education. In J. Worell (Ed.), *Encyclopedia of women and gender.* San Diego: Academic Press.

Reijmerink, N.E., & others (2011). Toll-like receptors and microbial exposure: Gene-gene and gene-environment interaction in the development of atopy. *European Respiratory Journal, 38,* 833–840.

Reijntjes, A., & others (2013). Costs and benefits of bullying in the context of the peer group: A three-wave longitudinal analysis. *Journal of Abnormal Psychology, 41,* 1217–1219.

Reilly, D., & Neumann, D.L. (2013). Gender-role differences in spatial ability: A meta-analytic review. *Sex Roles, 68,* 521–535.

Reinhold, S. (2010). Reassessing the link between premarital cohabitation and marital instability. *Demography, 47,* 719–733.

Reinisch, J.M. (1990). *The Kinsey Institute new report on sex: What you must know to be sexually literate.* New York: St. Martin's Press.

Reis, O., & Youniss, J. (2004). Patterns of identity change and development in relationships with mothers and friends. *Journal of Adolescent Research, 19,* 31–44.

Reisner, S.L., Biello, K., Perry, N.S., Gamarel, K.E., & Mimiage, M.J. (2014). A compensatory model of risk and resilience applied to adolescent sexual orientation disparities in nonsuicidal self-injury and suicide attempts. *American Journal of Orthopsychiatry, 84,* 545–556.

Reiss, D.E., Eccles, J.S., & Nielsen, L. (2014). Conscientiousness and public health: Synthesizing current research to promote healthy aging. *Developmental Psychology, 50,* 1303–1314.

Reiter, S.F., Hjorleifsson, S., Breidablik, H.J., & Meland, E. (2013). Impact of divorce and loss of parental contact on health complaints among adolescents. *Journal of Public Health, 35,* 278–285.

Remafedi, G., Resnick, M., Blum, R., & Harris, L. (1992). Demography of sexual orientation in adolescents. *Pediatrics, 89,* 714–721.

Rendall, M.S., Weden, M.M., Faveault, M.M., & Waldron, H. (2011). The protective effect of marriage for survival: A review and update. *Demography, 48,* 481–506.

Rengasamy, M., & others (2013). The bi-directional relationship between parent-adolescent conflict and treatment outcome for treatment-resistant adolescent depression. *Journal of the American Academy of Child and Adolescent Psychiatry, 52,* 370–377.

Renzetti, C.M., & Kennedy-Bergen, R.M. (2015). *Understanding diversity.* Upper Saddle River, NJ: Pearson.

Resick, P.A., & others (2012). Long-term consequences of cognitive-behavioral treatments for posttraumatic stress disorder among female rape survivors. *Journal of Consulting and Clinical Psychology, 80,* 201–210.

Resnick, M.D., Wattenberg, E., & Brewer, R. (1992, March). *Paternity avowal/disavowal among partners of low-income mothers.* Paper presented at the meeting of the Society for Research on Adolescence, Washington, DC.

Rest, J.R. (1986). *Moral development: Advances in theory and research.* New York: Praeger.

Rest, J.R. (1995). *Concerns for the social-psychological development of youth and educational strategies: Report for the Kaufmann Foundation.* Minneapolis: University of Minnesota, Department of Educational Psychology.

Rest, J.R., Narváez, D., Bebeau, M., & Thoma, S. (1999). *Postconventional moral thinking: A neo-Kohlbergian approach.* Hillsdale, NJ: Erlbaum.

Reuther, E.T., & others (2013). Intolerance of uncertainty as a mediator of the relationship between perfectionism and obsessive-compulsive symptom severity. *Depression and Anxiety, 30,* 773–777.

Reyna, V.F., & Brainerd, C.J. (2011). Dual processes in decision making and developmental neuroscience: A fuzzy-trace model. *Developmental Review, 31,* 180–206.

Reyna, V.F., & Farley, F. (2006). Risk and rationality in adolescent decision-making: Implications for theory, practice, and public policy. *Psychological Science in the Public Interest, 7,* 1–44.

Reyna, V.F., & Mills, B.A. (2014). Theoretically motivated interventions for reducing sexual risk taking in adolescence: A randomized controlled experiment applying fuzzy-trace theory. *Journal of Experimental Psychology: General, 143,* 1627–1648.

Reyna, V.F., & Rivers, S.E. (2008). Current theories of risk and rational decision making. *Developmental Review, 28,* 1–11.

Reyna, V.F., & Zayas, V. (Eds.). (2014). *The neuroscience of risky decision making.* Washington, DC: American Psychological Association.

Reyna, V.F., & others (2010). Gist-based conceptions of risk in adolescent alcohol consumption: A fuzzy trace theory approach. *Annals of Behavioral Medicine, 39,* s196.

Reyna, V.F., & others (2011). Neurobiological and memory models of risky decision making in adolescents versus young adults. *Journal of Experimental Psychology: Learning, Memory, and Cognition, 37,* 1125–1142.

Reynolds, E.H. (2014). The neurology of folic acid deficiency. *Handbook of Clinical Neurology, 120,* 927–943.

Reznick, J.S. (2013). Research designs and methods: Toward a cumulative developmental science. In P.D. Zelazo (Ed.), *Handbook of developmental psychology.* New York: Oxford University Press.

Reznick, J.S. (2014). Working memory in infancy. In P. Bauer & R. Fivush (Eds.), *Handbook on the development of children's memory.* New York: Wiley.

Rhoades, G.K., & Stanley, S.M. (2014). Before "I Do": What do premarital experiences have to do with marital quality among today's young adults? Charlottesville, VA: The National Marriage Project at the University of Virginia.

Rhoades, G.K., Stanley, S.M., & Markman, H.J. (2009). The pre-engagement cohabitation effect: A replication and extension of previous findings. *Journal of Family Psychology, 23,* 107–111.

Rhoades, G.K., Stanley, S.M., & Markman, H.J. (2012). The impact of transition to cohabitation on relationship functioning: Cross-sectional and longitudinal findings. *Journal of Family Psychology, 26,* 348–358.

Rhodes, A.E., & others (2012). Child maltreatment and onset of emergency department presentations for suicide-related behaviors. *Child Abuse and Neglect, 36,* 542–551.

Rhodes, J.E., & DuBois, D.L. (2008). Mentoring relationships and programs for youth. *Current Directions in Psychological Science, 17,* 254–258.

Rhodes, J.E., & Lowe, S.R. (2009). Mentoring in adolescence. In R.M. Lerner & L. Steinberg (Eds.), *Handbook of adolescent psychology* (3rd ed.). New York: Wiley.

Ricco, R.B. (2015). Reasoning. In R.M. Lerner (Ed.), *Handbook of child psychology and developmental science* (7th ed.). New York: Wiley.

Rice, K.G., Lopez, F.G., Richardson, C.M., & Stinson, J.M. (2013). Perfectionism moderates

stereotype threat effects on STEM majors' academic performance. *Journal of Counseling Psychology, 60,* 287–293.

Rice, K.G., Richardson, C.M., & Clark, D. (2012). Perfectionism, procrastination, and psychological distress. *Journal of Counseling Psychology, 59,* 288–302.

Richards, M.H., & Larson, R. (1990, July). *Romantic relations in early adolescence.* Paper presented at the Fifth International Conference on Personal Relations, Oxford University, England.

Richardson, A.S., Dietz, W.H., & Gordon-Larsen, P. (2014). The association between childhood sexual and physical abuse with incident adult severe obesity across 13 years of the National Study of Adolescent Health. *Pediatric Obesity, 9,* 351–361.

Richardson, M.S., & Schaeffer, C. (2013). From work and family to a dual model of working. In D.L. Blustein (Ed.), *Oxford handbook of the psychology of working.* New York: Oxford University Press.

Rickards, T., & deCock, C. (2003). Understanding organizational creativity: Toward a paradigmatic approach. In M.A. Runco (Ed.), *Creativity research handbook.* Cresskill, NJ: Hampton Press.

Rickert, V.I., Sanghvi, R., & Wiemann, C.M. (2002). Is lack of sexual assertiveness among adolescent women a cause for concern? *Perspectives on Sexual and Reproductive Health, 34,* 162–173.

Rideout, V., Foehr, U.G., & Roberts, D.P. (2010). *Generation M2: Media in the lives of 8- to 18-year-olds.* Menlo Park, CA: Kaiser Family Foundation.

Riina, E.M., & McHale, S.M. (2014). Bidirectional influences between dimensions of coparenting and adolescent adjustment. *Journal of Youth and Adolescence, 43,* 257–269.

Ristic, J., & Enns, J.T. (2015). Attentional development: The past, the present, and the future. In R.M. Lerner (Ed.), *Handbook of child psychology and developmental science.* New York: Wiley.

Rittenhouse, M.A., Salvy, S.J., & Barkley, J.E. (2011). The effect of peer influence on the amount of physical activity performed in 8- to 12-year-old boys. *Pediatric Exercise Science, 23*(1), 49–60.

Riva Crugnola, C., Ierardi, E., Gazzotti, S., & Albizzati, A. (2014). Motherhood in adolescent mothers: Maternal attachment, mother-infant styles of interaction, and emotion regulation at three months. *Infant Behavior and Development, 37,* 44–56.

Rivas-Drake, D. (2011). Ethnic-racial socialization and adjustment among Latino college students: The mediating roles of ethnic centrality, public regard, and perceived barriers to opportunity. *Journal of Youth and Adolescence, 40,* 606–619.

Rivas-Drake, D., & others (2014a). Ethnic and racial identity revisited: An integrated conceptualization. *Child Development, 85,* 21–39.

Rivas-Drake, D., & others (2014b). Feeling good, happy, and proud: A meta-analysis of positive ethnic-racial affect and adjustment. *Child Development, 85,* 77–102.

Rivers, S.E., Reyna, V.F., & Mills, B. (2008). Risk taking under the influence: A fuzzy-trace theory of emotion in adolescence. *Developmental Review, 28,* 107–144.

Roa, J., & Tena-Sempere, M. (2014). Connecting metabolism and reproduction: Roles of central energy sensors and key molecular mediators. *Molecular and Cellular Endocrinology, 397,* 4–14.

Robbins, C.L., & others (2012). Prevalence, frequency, and associations of masturbation with partnered sexual behaviors among U.S. adolescents. *Archives of Pediatric and Adolescent Medicine, 165,* 1087–1093.

Roberson, P.N., Olmstead, S.B., & Fincham, F.D. (2015). Hooking up during the college years: Is there a pattern? *Culture, Health, and Sexuality, 17,* 576–591.

Roberts, B.W., Edmonds, G., & Grijaiva, E. (2010). It is developmental me, not generation me:

Developmental changes are more important than generational changes in narcissism—Commentary on Trzesniewski & Donnellan (2010). *Perspectives on Psychological Science,* 97–102.

Roberts, B.W., Jackson, J.J., Fayard, J.V., Edmonds, G., & Meints, J. (2009). Conscientiousness. In M. Leary & R. Hoyle (Eds.), *Handbook of individual differences in social behavior.* New York: Guilford.

Roberts, D.F., & Foehr, U.G. (2008). Trends in media use. *The Future of Children, 18,* 11–38.

Roberts, D.F., Henriksen, L., & Foehr, U.G. (2009). Adolescence, adolescents, and the media. In R.M. Lerner & L. Steinberg (Eds.), *Handbook of adolescent psychology* (3rd ed.). New York: Wiley.

Roberts, G.C., Treasure, D.C., & Kavussanu, M. (1997). Motivation in physical activity contexts: An achievement goal perspective. *Advances in Motivation and Achievement, 10,* 413–447.

Robins, R.W., Trzesniewski, K.H., Tracey, J.L., Potter, J., & Gosling, S.D. (2002). Age differences in self-esteem from age 9 to 90. *Psychology and Aging, 17,* 423–434.

Robinson, B.A., & others (2015). Social context, parental monitoring, and multisystemic therapy. *Psychotherapy, 52,* 103–110.

Robinson, D.P., & Greene, J.W. (1988). The adolescent alcohol and drug problem: A practical approach. *Pediatric Nursing, 14,* 305–310.

Robinson, N.S. (1995). Evaluating the nature of perceived support and its relation to perceived self-worth in adolescents. *Journal of Research on Adolescence, 5,* 253–280.

Rodkin, P.C., & Ryan, A.M. (2012). Child and adolescent peer relations in educational context. In K.R. Harris & others (Eds.), *APA handbook of educational psychology.* Washington, DC: American Psychological Association.

Roehrig, A.D., & others (2012). Effective teachers and teaching: Characteristics and practices related to positive student outcomes. In K.R. Harris & others (Eds.), *APA handbook of educational psychology.* Washington, DC: American Psychological Association.

Roeser, R.W., & Pinela, C. (2014). Mindfulness and compassion training in adolescence: A developmental contemplative science perspective. *New Directions in Youth Development, 142,* 9–30.

Roeser, R.W., & Zelazo, P.D. (2012). Contemplative science, education and child development. *Child Development Perspectives, 6,* 143–145.

Rogers, C.R. (1950). The significance of the self regarding attitudes and perceptions. In M.L. Reymart (Ed.), *Feelings and emotions.* New York: McGraw-Hill.

Rogol, A.D., Roemmich, J.N., & Clark, P.A. (1998, September). *Growth at puberty.* Paper presented at a workshop, Physical Development, Health Futures of Youth II: Pathways to Adolescent Health, Maternal and Child Health Bureau, Annapolis, MD.

Rohner, R.P., & Rohner, E.C. (1981). Parental acceptance-rejection and parental control: Cross-cultural codes. *Ethnology, 20,* 245–260.

Romas, J.A., & Sharma, M. (2010). *Practical stress management* (5th ed.). Upper Saddle River, NJ: Pearson.

Romo, L.F., Mireles-Rios, R., & Lopez-Tello, G. (2014). Latina mothers' and daughters' expectations for autonomy at age 15 (La Quinceañera). *Journal of Adolescent Research, 29*(2), 279–294.

Rönnlund, M., & Nilsson, L.G. (2008). The magnitude, generality, and determinants of Flynn effects on forms of declarative memory and visuospatial ability: Time-sequential analyses of data from a Swedish cohort study. *Intelligence, 36,* 192–209.

Rosario, M., & others (2014). Sexual-orientation disparities in substance use in emerging adults: A function of stress and attachment paradigms. *Psychology of Addictive Behaviors, 28,* 790–804.

Rose, A.J., Carlson, W., & Waller, E.M. (2007). Prospective associations of co-rumination with friendship and emotional adjustment: Considering the socioemotional trade-offs of co-rumination. *Developmental Psychology, 43,* 1019–1031.

Rose, A.J., & Rudolph, K.D. (2006). A review of sex differences in peer relationship processes: Potential trade-offs for the emotional and behavioral development of girls and boys. *Psychological Bulletin, 132,* 98–132.

Rose, A.J., & others (2012). How girls and boys expect disclosure about problems will make them feel: Implications for friendship. *Child Development, 83,* 844–863.

Rose, A.J., & others (2014). An observational study of co-rumination in adolescent friendships. *Developmental Psychology, 50,* 2199–2209.

Rose, S., & Frieze, I.R. (1993). Young singles' contemporary dating scripts. *Sex Roles, 28,* 499–509.

Rose-Greenland, F., & Smock, P.J. (2013). Living together unmarried: What do we know about cohabiting families? In G.W. Peterson & K.R. Bush (Eds.), *Handbook of marriage and the family* (3rd ed.). New York: Springer.

Rosen, L., Cheever, N., & Carrier, L.M. (2008). The association of parenting style and child age with parental limit setting and adolescent MySpace behavior. *Journal of Applied Developmental Psychology, 29,* 459–471.

Rosenberg, M. (1979). *Conceiving the self.* New York: Basic Books.

Rosenblum, G.D., & Lewis, M. (2003). Emotional development in adolescence. In G. Adams & M. Berzonsky (Eds.), *Blackwell handbook of adolescence.* Malden, MA: Blackwell.

Rosengard, C. (2009). Confronting the intendedness of adolescent rapid repeat pregnancy. *Journal of Adolescent Health, 44,* 5–6.

Rosenkranz, R.R. (2012). Service-learning in higher education relevant to the promotion of physical activity, healthful eating, and prevention of obesity. *International Journal of Preventive Medicine, 3,* 672–681.

Rosenkranz, R.R., & others (2012). A cluster-randomized controlled trial of strategies to increase adolescents' physical activity and motivation during physical education lessons: The Motivating Active Learning in Physical Education (MALP) trial. *BMC Public Health, 12,* 834.

Rosenthal, M. (2013). *Human sexuality.* Boston: Cengage.

Rosenthal, N.L., & Kobak, R. (2010). Assessing adolescents' attachment hierarchies: Differences across developmental periods and associations with individual adaptation. *Journal of Research on Adolescence, 20,* 678–706.

Rosner, B.A., & Rierdan, J. (1994, February). *Adolescent girls' self-esteem: Variations in developmental trajectories.* Paper presented at the meeting of the Society for Research on Adolescence, San Diego.

Rosnow, R.L., & Rosenthal, R. (2013). *Beginning psychological research* (7th ed.). Boston: Cengage.

Rosser, S.V. (2012). *Breaking into the lab: Engineering progress for women in science.* New York: New York University Press.

Rossler, R., & others (2014). Exercise-based injury prevention in child and adolescent sport: A systematic review and meta-analysis. *Sports Medicine, 44,* 1733–1748.

Roth, J., Brooks-Gunn, J., Murray, L., & Foster, W. (1998). Promoting healthy adolescents: Synthesis of youth development program evaluations. *Journal of Research on Adolescence, 8,* 423–459.

Rothbart, M.K. (2011). *Becoming who we are.* New York: Guilford.

Rothbart, M.K., & Bates, J.E. (1998). Temperament. In W. Damon (Ed.), *Handbook of child psychology* (5th ed., Vol. 3). New York: Wiley.

Rothbart, M.K., & Posner, M.I. (2015). The developing brain in a multitasking world. *Developmental Review, 35,* 42–63.

Rothbaum, F., Poll, M., Azuma, H., Miyake, K., & Weisz, J. (2000). The development of close relationships in Japan and the United States: Paths of symbiotic harmony and generative tension. *Child Development, 71,* 1121–1142.

Rothbaum, F., & Trommsdorff, G. (2007). Do roots and wings complement or oppose one another?: The socialization of relatedness and autonomy in cultural context. In J.E. Grusec & P.D. Hastings (Eds.), *Handbook of socialization.* New York: Guilford.

Rowley, S.J., & others (2014). Framing Black boys: Parent, teacher, and student narratives of the academic lives of Black boys. *Advances in Child Development and Behavior, 47,* 301–332.

Rowsell, H.C., Ciarrochi, J., Heaven, P.C., & Deane, F.P. (2014). The role of emotion identification skill in the formation of male and female friendships: A longitudinal study. *Journal of Adolescence, 37,* 103–111.

Rubie-Davies, C.M. (2007). Classroom interactions: Exploring the practices of high- and low-expectation teachers. *British Journal of Educational Psychology, 77,* 289–306.

Rubie-Davies, C.M. (Ed.) (2011). *Educational psychology.* New York: Routledge.

Rubin, K.H., Bowker, J.C., McDonald, K.L., & Menzer, M. (2013). Peer relationships in childhood. In P.D. Zelazo (Ed.), *Oxford handbook of developmental psychology.* New York: Oxford University Press.

Rubin, K.H., Bukowski, W.M., & Bowker, J. (2015). Children in peer groups. In R.M. Lerner (Ed.), *Handbook of child psychology and developmental science* (7th ed.). New York: Wiley.

Rubin, K.H., Bukowski, W., & Parker, J.G. (1998). Peer interactions, relationships, and groups. In N. Eisenberg (Ed.), *Handbook of child psychology* (5th ed., Vol. 3). New York: Wiley.

Rubin, K.H., Bukowski, W., & Parker, J.G. (2006). Peer interactions, relationships, and groups. In W. Damon & R. Lerner (Eds.), *Handbook of child psychology* (6th ed.). New York: Wiley.

Rubin, Z., & Slomon, J. (1994). How parents influence their children's friendships. In M. Lewis (Ed.), *Beyond the dyad.* New York: Plenum.

Ruble, D.N., Boggiano, A.K., Feldman, N.S., & Loebl, J.H. (1980). Developmental analysis of the role of social comparison in self evaluation. *Developmental Psychology, 16,* 105–115.

Rudolph, K.D., & others (2014). Long-term consequences of pubertal timing for youth depression: Identifying personal and contextual pathways of risk. *Development and Psychopathology, 26,* 1423–1444.

Rueda, M.R., & Posner, M.I. (2013). Development of attentional networks. In P.D. Zelazo (Ed.), *Oxford handbook of developmental psychology.* New York: Oxford University Press.

Rulison, K.L., Kreager, D.A., & Osgood, D.W. (2014). Delinquency and peer acceptance in adolescence: A within-person test of Moffitt's hypotheses. *Developmental Psychology, 50,* 2437–2448.

Rumberger, R.W. (1995). Dropping out of middle school: A multilevel analysis of students and schools. *American Education Research Journal, 3,* 583–625.

Russell, S.T., Crockett, L.J., & Chao, R.K. (2010). *Asian American parenting and parent-adolescent relationships.* New York: Springer.

Russell, V.M., Baker, L.R., & McNulty, J.K. (2013). Attachment insecurity and infidelity in marriage: Do studies of dating relationships inform us about marriage? *Journal of Family Psychology, 27,* 242–251.

Ruthsatz, J., Detterman, D., Griscom, W.S., & Cirullo, B.A. (2008). Becoming an expert in the musical domain: It takes more than just practice. *Intelligence, 36,* 330–338.

Rutter, M. (1979). Protective factors in children's response to stress and disadvantage. In M.W. Kent & J.E. Rolf (Eds.), *Primary prevention in psychopathology* (Vol. 3). Hanover: University of New Hampshire Press.

Rutter, M., & Garmezy, N. (1983). Developmental psychopathology. In P.H. Mussen (Ed.), *Handbook of child psychology* (4th ed., Vol. 4). New York: Wiley.

Ryan, A.M. (2011). Peer relationships and academic adjustment during early adolescence. *Journal of Early Adolescence, 31,* 5–12.

Ryan, A.S., & others (2014). Aerobic exercise and weight loss reduce vascular markers of inflammation and improve insulin sensitivity in obese women. *Journal of the American Geriatrics Society, 62,* 607–614.

Ryan, C., Huebner, D., Diaz, R.M., & Sanchez, J. (2009). Family rejection as a predictor of negative health outcomes in white and Latino lesbian, gay, and bisexual young adults. *Pediatrics, 123,* 346–352.

Ryan, M.K. (2003). Gender differences in ways of knowing: The context dependence of the Attitudes Toward Thinking and Learning Survey. *Sex Roles, 49,* 11–12.

Ryan, R.M., & Deci, E.L. (2009). Promoting self-determined school engagement: Motivation, learning, and well-being. In K. Wentzel & A. Wigfield (Eds.), *Handbook of motivation at school.* New York: Routledge.

S

Saarento, S., Boulton, A.J., & Salmivalli, C. (2015). Reducing bullying and victimization: Student- and classroom-level mechanisms of change. *Journal of Abnormal Child Psychology, 43,* 61–76.

Saarinen, S., & others (2015). Visuospatial working memory in 7- to 12-year-old children with disruptive behavior disorders. *Child Psychiatry and Human Development, 46,* 34–43.

Saarni, C. (1999). *The development of emotional competence.* New York: Guilford.

Saarni, C., Campos, J.J., Camras, L., & Witherington, D. (2006). Emotional development. In W. Damon & R. Lerner (Eds.), *Handbook of child psychology* (6th ed.). New York: Wiley.

Sabina, C., & Ho, L.Y. (2014). Campus and college victim responses to sexual assault and dating violence: Disclosure, service utilization, and service provision. *Trauma, Violence, and Abuse, 15,* 201–226.

Sadker, M.P., & Sadker, D.M. (2012). *Teachers, schools, and society* (10th ed.). New York: McGraw-Hill.

Saewyc, E.M. (2011). Research on adolescent sexual orientation: Development, health disparities, stigma, and resilience. *Journal of Research on Adolescence, 21,* 256–272.

Sagan, C. (1977). *The dragons of Eden.* New York: Random House.

Sakaluk, J.K., & others (2014). Dominant heterosexual sexual scripts in emerging adulthood: Conceptualization and measurement. *Journal of Sex Research, 51,* 516–531.

Sakamaki, R., Toyama, K., Amamoto, R., Liu, C.J., & Shinfuku, N. (2005). Nutritional knowledge, food habits, and health attitude of Chinese university students—a cross-sectional study. *Nutrition Journal, 9,* 4.

Sakou, I., & others (2015). Insulin resistance and cardiometabolic risk factors in obese children and adolescents: A hierarchical approach. *Journal of Pediatric Endocrinology and Metabolism, 28,* 589–596.

Salas-Wright, C., Vaughn, M.G., Hodge, D.R., & Perron, B.E. (2012). Religiosity profiles of American youth in relation to substance use, violence, and delinquency. *Journal of Youth and Adolescence, 41,* 1560–1575.

Salend, S.J. (2016, in press). *Creating inclusive classrooms* (8th ed.). Upper Saddle River, NJ: Pearson.

Salgin, B., & others (2015, in press). Even transient rapid infancy weight gain is associated with higher BMI in young adults and early menarche. *International Journal of Obesity.*

Salmivalli, C., Garandeau, C.F., & Veenstra, R. (2012). KiVa Anti-Bullying Program: Implications for school adjustment. In A.M. Ryan & G.W. Ladd (Eds.),

Peer relationships and adjustment at school. Charlotte, NC: Information Age Publishing.

Salmivalli, C., & Peets, K. (2009). Bullies, victims, and bully-victim relationships in middle childhood and adolescence. In K.H. Rubin, W.M. Bukowski, & B. Laursen (Eds.), *Handbook of peer interactions, relationships, and groups.* New York: Guilford.

Salovey, P., & Mayer, J.D. (1990). Emotional intelligence. *Imagination, Cognition, and Personality, 9,* 185–211.

Sanbonmatsu, D.M., Strayer, D.L., Medeiros-Ward, N., & Watson, J.M. (2013). Who multi-tasks and why? Multi-tasking ability, perceived multi-tasking ability, impulsivity, and sensation seeking. *PLoS One, 8*(1), e54402.

Sanchez, B., Esparza, P., Colon, Y., & Davis, K.E. (2010). Tryin' to make it during the transition from high school: The role of family obligation attitudes and economic context for Latino emerging adults. *Journal of Adolescent Research, 25,* 858–884.

Sanchez-Garrido, M.A., & Tena-Sempere, M. (2013). Metabolic control of puberty: Roles of leptin and kissleptins. *Hormones and Behavior, 64,* 187–194.

Sanchez-Johnsen, L.A., & others (2004). Ethnic differences in correlates of obesity between Latin-American and black women. *Obesity Research, 12,* 652–660.

Sanders, R.H., Han, A., Baker, J.S., & Cobley, S. (2015, in press). Childhood obesity and its physical and psychological co-morbidities: A systematic review of Australian children and adolescents. *European Journal of Pediatrics.*

Santa Maria, M. (2002). Youth in Southeast Asia: Living within the continuity of tradition and the turbulence of change. In B.B. Brown, R.W. Larson, & T.S. Saraswathi (Eds.), *The world's youth.* New York: Cambridge University Press.

Santelli, J., Sandfort, T.G., & Orr, M. (2009). U.S./European differences in condom use. *Journal of Adolescent Health, 44,* 306.

Santrock, J.W., Sitterle, K.A., & Warshak, R.A. (1988). Parent-child relationships in stepfather families. In P. Bronstein & C.P. Cowan (Eds.), *Fatherhood today: Men's changing roles in the family.* New York: Wiley.

Sapiela, K.M., Dunn, J.G.H., & Holt, N.L. (2011). Perfectionism and parenting styles in male youth soccer. *Journal of Sport and Exercise Psychology, 33,* 20–39.

Sarchiapone, M., & others (2014). Hours of sleep in adolescents and its association with anxiety, emotional concerns, and suicidal ideation. *Sleep Medicine, 15,* 248–254.

Sarlos, P., & others (2014). Susceptibility to ulcerative colitis in Hungarian patients determined by gene-gene interaction. *World Journal of Gastroenterology, 20*(1), 219–227.

Saroglou, V. (2013). Religion, spirituality, and altruism. In K.I. Pargament, J. Exline, & J. Jones (Eds.), *Handbook of psychology, religion, and spirituality.* Washington, DC: American Psychological Association.

Saunders, T.J., Chaput, J.P., & Tremblay, M.S. (2014). Sedentary behavior as an emerging risk factor for cardiometabolic diseases in children and youth. *Canadian Journal of Diabetes, 38,* 53–61.

Savin-Williams, R.C. (2015). The new sexual-minority teenager. In D.A. Powell & J.S. Kaufman (Eds.), *The meaning of sexual identity in the 21st century.* New York: Cambridge.

Savin-Williams, R.C., & Cohen, K. (2015). Gay, lesbian, and bisexual youth. In J.D. Wright (Ed.), *International encyclopedia of the social and behavioral sciences* (2nd ed.). New York: Oxford University Press.

Savin-Williams, R.C., & Demo, D.H. (1983). Conceiving or misconceiving the self: Issues in adolescent self-esteem. *Journal of Early Adolescence, 3,* 121–140.

Savolainen, J., & others (2012). Antisocial personality, adolescent school outcomes, and the risk of criminal conviction. *Journal of Research on Adolescence, 22,* 54–64.

Sbarra, D.A., & Ferrer, E. (2006). The structure and process of emotional experience following nonmarital relationship dissolution: Dynamic factor analysis of love, anger, and sadness. *Emotion, 6,* 224–238.

Scarr, S. (1993). Biological and cultural diversity: The legacy of Darwin for development. *Child Development, 64,* 1333–1353.

Schaefer, R.T. (2015). *Racial and ethnic groups* (14th ed.). Upper Saddle River, NJ: Pearson.

Schaffer, M.A., Goodhue, A., Stennes, K., & Lanigan, C. (2012). Evaluation of a public health nurse visiting program for pregnant and parenting teens. *Public Health Nursing, 29,* 218–231.

Schag, K., & others (2013). Food-related impulsivity in obesity and binge eating disorder—a systematic review. *Obesity Reviews, 14*(6), 477–495.

Schaie, K.W. (2012). *Developmental influences on adult intellectual development: The Seattle Longitudinal Study.* New York: Oxford University Press.

Schalet, A.T. (2011). Beyond abstinence and risk: A new paradigm for adolescent sexual health. *Women's Health Issues, 21*(Suppl. 3), S5–S7.

Schiff, W.J. (2015). *Nutrition essentials.* New York: McGraw-Hill.

Schiff, W.J. (2015). *Nutrition for healthy living* (4th ed.). New York: McGraw-Hill.

Schindler, A., & Broning, S. (2015, in press). A review of attachment and substance abuse: Empirical evidence and implications for prevention and treatment. *Substance Abuse.*

Schlam, T.R., Wilson, N.L., Shoda, Y., Mischel, W., & Ayduk, O. (2013). Preschoolers' delay of gratification predicts their body mass 30 years later. *Journal of Pediatrics, 162*(1), 90–93.

Schmalz, D.L., Deane, G.D., Leann, L., Birch, L.L., & Krahnstoever Davison, K. (2007). A longitudinal assessment between physical activity and self-esteem in early adolescent non-Hispanic females. *Journal of Adolescent Health, 41,* 559–565.

Schmidt, J.A., Shumow, L., & Kackar, H.Z. (2012). Associations of participation in service activities with academic, behavioral, and civic outcomes of adolescents at varying risk levels. *Journal of Youth and Adolescence, 41,* 932–947.

Schmidt, M.E., Marks, J.L., & Derrico, L. (2004). What a difference mentoring makes: Service learning and engagement for college students. *Mentoring and Tutoring Partnership in Learning, 12,* 205–217.

Schmidt, M.E., & Vandewater, E.A. (2008). Media and attention, cognition, and school achievement. *Future of Children, 18*(1), 64–85.

Schneider, M., Dunton, G.F., & Cooper, D.M. (2008). Physical activity and physical self-concept among sedentary adolescent females: An intervention study. *Psychology of Sport and Exercise, 9,* 1–14.

Schoeneberger, J. (2012). Longitudinal attendance patterns: Developing high school dropouts. *Clearinghouse, 85,* 7–14.

Schoffstall, C.L., & Cohen, R. (2011). Cyber aggression: The relation between online offenders and offline social competence. *Social Development, 20*(3), 587–604.

Schofield, H.L., Bierman, K.L., Heinrichs, B., Nix, R.L., & The Conduct Problems Prevention Research Group (2008). Predicting early sexual activity with behavior problems exhibited at school entry and in early adolescence. *Journal of Abnormal Child Psychology, 36,* 1175–1188.

Schouten, A.P., Valkenburg, P.M., & Peter, J. (2007). Precursors and underlying processes of adolescents' online self-disclosure: Developing and testing an "Internet-attribute-perception" model. *Media Psychology, 10,* 292–314.

Schulenberg, J.E., & Zarrett, N.R. (2006). Mental health during emerging adulthood: Continuity and discontinuity in courses, causes, and functions. In J.J. Arnett & J.L. Tanner (Eds.), *Emerging adults in America.* Washington, DC: American Psychological Association.

Schunk, D.H. (2008). *Learning theories* (5th ed.). Upper Saddle River, NJ: Prentice Hall.

Schunk, D.H. (2012). *Learning theories: An educational perspective* (6th ed.). Upper Saddle River, NJ: Pearson.

Schunk, D.H. (2016, in press). *Learning theories: An educational perspective* (7th ed.). Upper Saddle River, NJ: Pearson.

Schunk, D.H., Meece, J.R., & Pintrich, P.R. (2014). *Motivation in education* (4th ed.). Upper Saddle River, NJ: Pearson.

Schunk, D.H., & Zimmerman, B.J. (2013). Self-regulation and learning. In I.B. Weiner & others (Eds.), *Handbook of psychology* (2nd ed., Vol. 7). New York: Wiley.

Schwalbe, C.S., Gearing, R.E., MacKenzie, M.J., Brewer, K.B., & Ibrahim, R. (2012). A meta-analysis of experimental studies of diversion programs for juvenile defenders. *Clinical Psychology Review, 32,* 26–33.

Schwartz, D., Kelly, B.M., & Duong, M.T. (2013). Do academically-engaged adolescents experience social sanctions from the peer group? *Journal of Youth and Adolescence, 42,* 1319–1330.

Schwartz, D., & others (2015). Peer victimization during middle childhood as a lead indicator of internalizing problems and diagnostic outcomes in late adolescence. *Journal of Clinical Child and Adolescent Psychology, 44,* 393–404.

Schwartz, M.A., & Scott, B.M. (2012). *Marriages and families, census update* (6th ed.). Upper Saddle River, NJ: Pearson.

Schwartz, P.D., Maynard, A.M., & Uzelac, S.M. (2008). Adolescent egocentrism: A contemporary view. *Adolescence, 43,* 441–448.

Schwartz, S.J., Donnellan, M.B., Ravert, R.D., Luyckx, K., & Zamboanga, B.L. (2013). Identity development, personality, and well-being in adolescence and emerging adulthood: Theory, research, and recent advances. In I.B. Weiner & others (Eds.), *Handbook of psychology* (2nd ed., Vol. 6). New York: Wiley.

Schwartz, S.J., Zamboanga, B.L., Meca, A., & Ritchie, R.A. (2012). Identity around the world: An overview. *New Directions in Child and Adolescent Development, 138,* 1–18.

Schwartz, S.J., & others (2011). Examining the light and dark sides of emerging adults' identity: A study of identity status differences in positive and negative psychosocial functioning. *Journal of Youth and Adolescence, 40,* 839–859.

Schwartz, S.J., & others (2014). The identity of acculturation and multiculturalism: Situational acculturation in context. In V. Benet-Martinez & Y.Y. Hong (Eds.), *Oxford handbook of multicultural identity.* New York: Oxford University Press.

Schwartz, S.J., & others (2015a). Identity. In J.J. Arnett (Ed.), *Oxford handbook of emerging adulthood.* New York: Oxford University Press.

Schwartz, S.J., & others (2015b). What have we learned since Schwartz (2001)? A reappraisal of the field In K. McLean & M. Syed (Eds.), *Oxford handbook of identity development.* New York: Oxford University Press.

Schwartz, S.J., & others (2015c). The identity of acculturation and multiculturalism: Situation acculturation in context. In V. Benet-Martinez & Y.Y. Hong (Eds.), *Oxford handbook of multicultural identity.* New York: Oxford University Press.

Schwartz-Mette, R.A., & Rose, A.J. (2012). Co-rumination mediates contagion of internalizing symptoms within youths' friendships. *Developmental Psychology, 58,* 1355–1365.

Schwarz, B., & others (2012). Does the importance of parent and peer relationships for adolescents' life satisfaction vary across cultures? *Journal of Early Adolescence, 32,* 55–80.

Schwarzer, R., & Luszczynska, A. (2013). Stressful life events. In I.B. Weiner & others (Eds.), *Handbook of psychology* (2nd ed., Vol. 9). New York: Wiley.

Schweinhart, L.J., & others (2005). *Lifetime effects: The High/Scope Perry Preschool Study through age 40.* Ypsilanti, MI: High/Scope Press.

Sciberras, E., Ukoumunne, O.C., & Efron, D. (2011). Predictors of parent-reported attention-deficit/ hyperactivity disorder in children aged 6–7 years: A national longitudinal study. *Journal of Abnormal Child Psychology, 39,* 1025–1034.

Scott, M.E., & others (2011). Risky adolescent behaviors and reproductive health in young adulthood. *Perspectives on Sexual and Reproductive Health, 43,* 110–118.

Scourfield, J., Van den Bree, M., Martin, N., & McGuffin, P. (2004). Conduct problems in children and adolescents: A twin study. *Archives of General Psychiatry, 61,* 489–496.

Search Institute (1995). *Barriers to participation in youth programs.* Unpublished manuscript, the Search Institute, Minneapolis.

Search Institute (2010). *Teens' relationships.* Minneapolis, MN: Author.

Sears, R.R., Maccoby, E.E., & Levin, H. (1957). *Patterns of child rearing.* Evanston, IL: Row, Peterson.

Seaton, E.K., & Douglass, S. (2014). School diversity and racial discrimination among African-American adolescents. *Cultural Diversity and Ethnic Minority Psychology, 20,* 156–165.

Seaton, E.K., Yip, T., & Sellers, R.M. (2009). A longitudinal examination of racial identity and racial discrimination among African American adolescents. *Child Development, 80,* 406–417.

Sebastian, C., Burnett, S., & Blakemore, S-J. (2010). Development of the self-concept in adolescence. *Trends in Cognitive Science, 12,* 441–446.

Seccombe, K. (2015). *Exploring marriages and families* (2nd ed.). Upper Saddle River, NJ: Pearson.

Sedgh, G., & others (2015). Adolescent pregnancy, birth, and abortion rates across countries: Levels and recent trends. *Journal of Adolescent Health, 56,* 223–230.

Sedikdes, C., & Brewer, M.B. (Eds.). (2001). *Individual self, relational self, and collective self.* Philadelphia: Psychology Press.

Seedall, R.B., & Anthony, J.C. (2015, in press). Monitoring by parents and hypothesized male-female differences in evidence from a nationally representative cohort re-sampled from age 12 to 17 years: An exploratory study using a "mutoscope" approach. *Prevention Science.*

Seib, D.R., & Martin-Villalba, A. (2015, in press). Neurogenesis in the normal aging hippocampus: A mini-review. *Gerontology.*

Seiffge-Krenke, I. (2011). Coping with relationship stressors: A decade review. *Journal of Research on Adolescence, 21,* 196–210.

Seiffge-Krenke, I. (2012). Competent youth in a "disorderly world": Findings from an eighteen-nation study. *New Directions for Youth Development, 135,* 107–117.

Seiffge-Krenke, I., Aunola, K., & Nurmi, J-E. (2009). Changes in stress perception and coping during adolescence: The role of situational and personal factors. *Child Development, 80,* 259–279.

Seil, K.S., Desai, M.M., & Smith, M.V. (2014). Sexual orientation, adult connectedness, substance use, and mental health outcomes among adolescents: Findings from the 2009 New York City Youth Risk Behavior Survey. *American Journal of Public Health, 104,* 1950–1956.

Seiter, L.N., & Nelson, L.J. (2011). An examination of emerging adulthood in college students and nonstudents in India. *Journal of Adolescent Research, 26*(4), 506–536.

Seligman, M.E.P (2007). *The optimistic child.* New York: Mariner.

Seligman, M.E.P., & Csikszentmihalyi, M. (2000). Positive psychology. *American Psychologist, 55,* 5–14.

Seligson, T. (2005, February 20). They speak for success. *Parade Magazine.*

Sellers, R.M., Copeland-Linder, N., Martin, P.P., & Lewis, R.L. (2006). Racial identity matters: The relationship between racial discrimination and psychological functioning in African American adolescents. *Journal of Research on Adolescence, 16,* 187–216.

Selman, R.L. (1980). *The growth of interpersonal understanding.* New York: Academic Press.

Semaj, L.T. (1985). Afrikanity, cognition, and extended self-identity. In M.B. Spencer, G.K. Brookins, & W.R. Allen (Eds.), *Beginnings: The social and affective development of black children.* Hillsdale, NJ: Erlbaum.

Sen, B. (2010). The relationship between frequency of family dinner and adolescent problem behaviors after adjusting for other characteristics. *Journal of Adolescence, 33,* 187–196.

Senden, M.G., Sikstrom, S., & Lindholm, T. (2015). "She" and "he" in news media messages: Pronoun use reflects gender biases in semantic contexts. *Sex Roles, 72,* 40–49.

Seo, D.C., & Lee, C.G. (2013). The effect of perceived body weight on suicide ideation among a representative sample of U.S. adolescents. *Journal of Behavioral Medicine, 36,* 498–507.

Sepulcre, J., & others (2012). Stepwise connectivity of the model cerebral cortex reveals the multimodal organization of the human brain. *Journal of Neuroscience, 32,* 10649–10661.

Sernau, S.R. (2013). *Global problems* (3rd ed.). Upper Saddle River, NJ: Pearson.

Shackelford, T.K., & Goetz, A.T. (Eds.) (2012). *Oxford handbook of sexual conflict in humans.* New York: Oxford University Press.

Shadur, J., & Hussong, A. (2014). Friendship intimacy, close friend drug use, and self-medication in adolescence. *Journal of Social and Personal Relationships, 31,* 997–1018.

Shakya, H.B., Christakis, N.A., & Fowler, J.H. (2012). Parental influence on substance use in adolescent social networks. *Archives of Pediatric and Adolescent Medicine, 166*(12), 1132–1139.

Sharma, M. (2006). School-based interventions for childhood and adolescent obesity. *Obesity Review, 7,* 261–269.

Sharp, E.H., Coatsworth, J.D., Darling, N., Cumsille, P., & Ranieri, S. (2007). Gender differences in the self-defining activities and identity experiences of adolescents and emerging adults. *Journal of Adolescence, 30,* 251–269.

Sharp, E.S., Reynolds, C.A., Pedersen, N.L., & Gatz, M. (2010). Cognitive engagement and cognitive aging: Is openness protective? *Psychology and Aging, 25,* 60–73.

Shaver, P.R., & Mikulincer, M. (2007). Attachment theory and research. In A.W. Kruglanski & E.T. Higgins (Eds.), *Social psychology* (2nd ed.). New York: Guilford.

Shaw, P., & others (2007). Attention-deficit/ hyperactivity disorder is characterized by a delay in cortical maturation. *Proceedings of the National Academy of Sciences, 104*(49), 19649–19654.

Shaywitz, S.E., Gruen, J.R., & Shaywitz, B.A. (2007). Management of dyslexia, its rationale and underlying neurobiology. *Pediatric Clinics of North America, 54,* 609–623.

Shebloski, B., Conger, K.J., & Widaman, K.F. (2005). Reciprocal links among differential parenting, perceived partiality, and self worth: A three-wave longitudinal study. *Journal of Family Psychology, 19,* 633–642.

Sheeber, L.B., Davis, B., Leve, C., Hops, H., & Tildesley, E. (2007). Adolescents' relationships with their mothers and fathers: Associations with depressive

disorder and subdiagnostic symptomatology. *Journal of Abnormal Psychology, 116,* 144–154.

Sheftall, A.H., Mathias, C.W., Furr, R.M., & Dougherty, D.M. (2013). Adolescent attachment security, family functioning, and suicide attempts. *Attachment and Human Development, 15*(4), 368–383.

Sheftall, A.H., Schoppe-Sullivan, S.J., & Bridge, J.A. (2014). Insecure attachment and suicidal behavior in adolescents. *Crisis, 35*(6), 426–430.

Sheinbaum, T., & others (2015). Attachment style predicts affect, cognitive appraisals, and social functioning in daily life. *Frontiers in Psychology, 6,* 296.

Shen, Y., Kim, S.Y., Wang, Y., & Chao, R.K. (2014). Language brokering and adjustment among Chinese and Korean American adolescents: A moderated mediation model of perceived maternal sacrifice, respect for the mother, and mother-child open communication. *Asian American Journal of Psychology, 5,* 86–95.

Sheppes, G., & Gross, J.J. (2015). Emotion regulation and psychopathology. *Annual Review of Clinical Psychology* (Vol. 11). Palo Alto, CA: Annual Reviews.

Sherman, R.M., D'Orio, B., Rhodes, M.N., Gantt, S., & Kaslow, N.J. (2014). Racial/ethnic, spiritual/religious, and sexual orientation influences on suicidal behaviors. In M.K. Nock (Ed.), *Oxford handbook of suicide and self-injury.* New York: Oxford University Press.

Shernoff, D.J. (2009, April). *Flow in educational contexts: Creating optimal learning environments.* Paper presented at the meeting of the Society for Research in Child Development, Denver.

Shifren, K., Furnham, A., & Bauserman, R.L. (2003). Emerging adulthood in American and British samples: Individuals' personality and health risk behaviors. *Journal of Adult Development, 10,* 75–88.

Shiner, R.L., & De Young, C.G. (2013). The structure of temperament and personality traits: A developmental perspective. In P.D. Zelazo (Ed.), *Handbook of developmental psychology.* New York: Oxford University Press.

Shor, E., Roelfs, D.J., Bugyi, P., & Schwartz, J.E. (2012). Meta-analysis of marital dissolution and mortality: Reevaluating the intersection of gender and age. *Social Science and Medicine, 75,* 46–59.

Shulman, S., Davila, J., & Shachar-Shapira, L. (2011). Assessing romantic competence among older adolescents. *Journal of Adolescence, 34,* 397–406.

Shulman, S., Scharf, M., & Shachar-Shapira, S. (2012). The intergenerational transmission of romantic relationships. In P.K. Kerig, M.S. Schulz, & S.T. Hauser (Eds.), *Adolescence and beyond.* New York: Oxford University Press.

Shulman, S., Zlotnik, A., Shachar-Shapira, L., Connolly, J., & Bohr, Y. (2012). Adolescent daughters' romantic competence: The role of divorce, quality of parenting, and maternal romantic history. *Journal of Youth and Adolescence, 41,* 593–606.

Sibley, M.H., & others (2012). Diagnosing ADHD in adolescence. *Journal of Consulting and Clinical Psychology, 80,* 139–150.

SIECUS (1999). *Public support for sex education.* Washington, DC: Author.

Siegel, D.H. (2013). Open adoption: Adoptive parents' reactions two decades later. *Social Work, 58,* 43–52.

Siegel, D.M., Aten, M.J., & Roghmann, K.J. (1998). Self-reported honesty among middle and high school students responding to a sexual behavior questionnaire. *Journal of Adolescent Health, 23,* 20–28.

Siegel, R.S., & Brandon, A.R. (2014). Adolescents, pregnancy, and mental health. *Journal of Pediatric and Adolescent Gynecology, 27,* 138–150.

Siegler, R.S. (2006). Microgenetic analysis of learning. In W. Damon & R. Lerner (Eds.), *Handbook of child psychology* (6th ed.). New York: Wiley.

Siegler, R.S. (2012). From theory to application and back: Following in the giant footsteps of David Klahr. In S.M. Carver & J. Shrager (Eds.), *The journey from* child to scientist: Integrating cognitive development and the education sciences. Thousand Oaks, CA: Sage.

Siegler, R.S. (2013). How do people become experts? In J. Staszewski (Ed.), *Experience and skill acquisition.* New York: Taylor & Francis.

Siegler, R.S. (2015, in press). Cognitive development in childhood. In E. Diener & R. Biswas-Diener (Eds.), *Noba textbook series: Psychology.* Champaign, IL: DEF Publishers.

Siegler, R.S., & Lortie-Forgues, H. (2015, in press). An integrative theory of numerical development. *Child Developmental Perspectives.*

Siegler, R.S., & Thompson, C.A. (2014). Numerical landmarks are useful—except when they're not. *Journal of Experimental Child Psychology, 120,* 39–58.

Siegler, R.S., & others (2015, in press). The Center for Improving Learning of Fractions: A progress report. In S. Chinn (Ed.), *Routledge international handbook of dyscalculia and mathematical learning difficulties.* New York: Routledge.

Sigal, A., Sandler, I., Wolchik, S., & Braver, S. (2011). Do parent education programs promote healthy post-divorce parenting? Critical directions and distinctions and a review of the evidence. *Family Court Review, 49,* 120–129.

Silber, T.J. (2013). Anorexia nervosa in children and adolescents: Diagnosis, treatment, and the role of the pediatrician. *Minerva Pediatrics, 65,* 1–18.

Silva, C. (2005, October 31). When teen dynamo talks, city listens. *Boston Globe,* pp. B1, B4.

Silver, S. (1988, August). *Behavior problems of children born into early-childbearing families.* Paper presented at the meeting of the American Psychological Association, Atlanta.

Silverman, J.G., Raj, A., Mucci, L.A., & Hathaway, J.E. (2001). Dating violence against adolescent girls and associated substance use, unhealthy weight control, sexual risk behavior, pregnancy, and suicidality. *Journal of the American Medical Association, 386,* 572–579.

Silverman, R. (2012). Stereotypes. In M. Kohut (Ed.), *Encyclopedia of gender in media.* Thousand Oaks, CA: Sage.

Simmons, R.G., & Blyth, D.A. (1987). *Moving into adolescence.* Hawthorne, NY: Aldine.

Simon, E.J. (2015). *Biology.* Upper Saddle River, NJ: Pearson.

Simon, V.A., Aikins, J.W., & Prinstein, M.J. (2008). *Homophily in adolescent romantic relationships.* Unpublished manuscript, College of Arts and Sciences, Wayne State University, Detroit.

Simons, J.M., Finlay, B., & Yang, A. (1991). *The adolescent and young adult fact book.* Washington, DC: Children's Defense Fund.

Simpkins, S.D., Delgado, M.Y., Price, C.D., Quach, A., & Starbuck, E. (2013). Socioeconomic status, ethnicity, culture, and immigration: Examining the potential mechanisms underlying Mexican-origin adolescents' organized activity participation. *Developmental Psychology, 49*(4), 706–721.

Simpson, R.L. (1962). Parental influence, anticipatory socialization, and social mobility. *American Sociological Review, 27,* 517–522.

Singer, J.A., & Kasmark, A.M. (2015). A translational approach to narrative identity in psychotherapy. In K.C. McLean & M. Syed (Eds.), *Oxford handbook of identity development.* New York: Oxford University Press.

Singh, S., Wulf, D., Samara, R., & Cuca, Y.P. (2000). Gender differences in the timing of first intercourse: Data from 14 countries. *International Family Planning Perspectives, 26,* 21–28, 43.

Sinha, J.W., Cnaan, R.A., & Gelles, R.J. (2007). Adolescent risk behaviors and religion: Findings from a national study. *Journal of Adolescence, 30,* 231–249.

Sinnott, J.D. (2003). Postformal thought and adult development: Living in balance. In J. Demick & C. Andreoletti (Eds.), *Handbook of adult development.* New York: Kluwer.

Sinnott, J.D., & Johnson, L. (1997). Brief report: Complex postformal thought in skilled research administrators. *Journal of Adult Development, 4*(1), 45–53.

Sirard, J.R., & others (2013). Physical activity and screen time in adolescents and their friends. *American Journal of Preventive Medicine, 44,* 48–55.

Sirsch, U., Dreher, E., Mayr, E., & Willinger, U. (2009). What does it take to be an adult in Austria? Views of adulthood in Austrian adolescents, emerging adults and adults. *Journal of Adolescent Research, 24,* 275–292.

Sisson, S.B., Broyles, S.T., Baker, B.L., & Katzmarzyk, P.T. (2010). Screen time, physical activity, and overweight in U.S. youth: National Survey of Children's Health 2003. *Journal of Adolescent Health, 47,* 309–311.

Siu, A.M., Shek, D.T., & Law, B. (2012). Prosocial norms as a positive youth development construct: A conceptual review. *Scientific World Journal,* #832026.

Skinner, B.F. (1938). *The behavior of organisms: An experimental analysis.* New York: Appleton-Century-Crofts.

Skinner, H.H., Haines, J., Austin, S.B., & Field, A.E. (2012). A prospective study of overeating, binge eating, and depressive symptoms among adolescent and young adult women. *Journal of Adolescent Health, 50,* 478–483.

Skinner, J., Underwood, C., Schwandt, H., & Magombo, A. (2013). Transitions to adulthood: Examining the influence of initiation rites on the HIV risk of adolescent girls in Mangochi and Thyolo districts of Malawi. *AIDS Care, 25,* 296–301.

Skinner, S.R., & others (2015). Childhood behavior problems and age at first sexual intercourse: A prospective birth cohort study. *Pediatrics, 135,* 255–263.

Skorikov, V., & Vondracek, F.W. (1998). Vocational identity development: Its relationship to other identity domains and to overall identity development. *Journal of Career Assessment, 6*(1), 13–35.

Skorupskaite, K., George, J.T., & Anderson, R.A. (2014). The kisspeptin-GnRH pathway in human reproductive health and disease. *Human Reproduction Update, 20,* 485–490.

Slavin, R.E. (2015). *Educational psychology* (12th ed.). Upper Saddle River, NJ: Pearson.

Slomkowski, C., Rende, R., Conger, K.J., Simons, R.L., & Conger, R.D. (2001). Sisters, brothers, and delinquency: Social influence during early and middle adolescence. *Child Development, 72,* 271–283.

Smaldino, S.E., Lowther, D.L., Mims, C.F., & Russell, J.D. (2015). *Instructional technology and media for learning* (11th ed.). Upper Saddle River, NJ: Pearson.

Smaldone, A., & others (2015). Adolescent and parent use of new technologies for health communication: A study in an urban Latino community. *Journal of Public Health Research, 4*(1), 376.

Smetana, J.G. (2008). "It's 10 o'clock: Do you know where your children are?" Recent advances in understanding parental monitoring and adolescents' information management. *Child Development Perspectives, 2,* 19–25.

Smetana, J.G. (2011a). *Adolescents, families, and social development: How adolescents construct their worlds.* New York: Wiley-Blackwell.

Smetana, J.G. (2011b). Adolescents' social reasoning and relationships with parents: Conflicts and coordinations within and across domains. In E. Amsel & J. Smetana (Eds.), *Adolescent vulnerabilities and opportunities: Constructivist and developmental perspectives.* New York: Cambridge University Press.

Smetana, J.G. (2013). Moral development: The social domain theory view. In P.D. Zelazo (Ed.), *Handbook of developmental psychology.* New York: Oxford University Press.

Smetana, J.G., & Gaines, C. (1999). Adolescent-parent conflict in middle-class African-American families. *Child Development, 70,* 1447–1463.

Smetana, J.G., Jambon, M., & Ball, C. (2014). The social domain approach to children's moral and social judgments. In M. Killen & J.G. Smetana (Eds.), *Handbook of moral development* (2nd ed.). New York: Psychology Press.

Smetana, J.G., Robinson, J., & Rote, W.M. (2015). Socialization in adolescence. In J.E. Grusec & P.D. Hastings (Eds.), *Handbook of socialization* (2nd ed.). New York: Guilford.

Smith, C., & Denton, M. (2005). *Soul searching: The religious and spiritual lives of American teenagers.* New York: Oxford University Press.

Smith, R.A., & Davis, S.F. (2013). *The psychologist as detective* (6th ed.). Upper Saddle River, NJ: Prentice Hall.

Smith, R.E., & Smoll, F.L. (1997). Coaching the coaches: Youth sports as a scientific and applied behavioral setting. *Current Directions in Psychological Science, 6,* 16–21.

Smith, R.L. (2009). *Social perspective-taking in the friendships of adolescents: Implications for friendship quality and emotional adjustment.* Thesis, University of Missouri—Columbia.

Smith, R.L., & Rose, A.J. (2011). The "cost of caring" in youths' friendships: Considering associations among social perspective taking, co-rumination, and empathetic distress. *Developmental Psychology, 47,* 1792–1803.

Smith, R.L., Rose, A.J., & Schwartz-Mette, R.A. (2010). Relational and overt aggression in childhood and adolescence: Clarifying mean-level gender differences and associations with peer acceptance. *Social Development, 19,* 243–269.

Smith, T.E., & others (2016, in press). *Teaching students with special needs in inclusive settings* (7th ed.). Upper Saddle River, NJ: Pearson.

Smith-Bynum, M.A., Lambert, S.F., English, D., & Ialongo, N.S. (2014). Associations between trajectories of perceived racial discrimination and psychological symptoms among African American adolescents. *Development and Psychopathology, 26,* 1049–1065.

Smock, P.J., & Gupta, S. (2013). Cohabitation in contemporary North America. In A. Booth, A.C. Crouter, & N.S. Landale (Eds.), *Just living together.* New York: Psychology Press.

Smokowski, P.R., Bacallao, M.L., Cotter, K.L., & Evans, C.B. (2015). The effects of positive and negative parenting practices on adolescent mental health outcomes in a multicultural sample of rural youth. *Child Psychiatry and Human Development, 46,* 333–345.

Smucny, M., Parikh, S.N., & Pandya, N.K. (2015). Consequences of single sport specialization in the pediatric and adolescent athlete. *Orthopedic Clinics of North America, 46*(2), 249–258.

Snarey, J. (1987, June). A question of morality. *Psychology Today, 21,* 6–8.

Snarey, J., & Samuelson, P. (2008). Moral education in the cognitive developmental tradition: Lawrence Kohlberg's revolutionary ideas. In L.P. Nucci & D. Narváez (Eds.), *Handbook of moral and character education.* New York: Routledge.

Snyder, J.J., Schrepferman, L.P., Bullard, L., McEachern, A.D., & Patterson, G.R. (2012). Covert antisocial behavior, peer deviancy training, parenting practices, and sex differences in the development of antisocial behavior in childhood. *Development and Psychopathology, 24,* 1117–1138.

Sobotkova, V., Blatny, M., Jelinek, M., & Hrdlicka, M. (2013). Antisocial behavior in adolescence: Typology and relation to family context. *Journal of Early Adolescence, 33,* 1091–1115.

Sodermans, A.K., & Matthijs, K. (2014). Joint physical custody and adolescents' subjective well-being: A personality x environment interaction. *Journal of Family Psychology, 28,* 346–356.

Soliman, A.T., & Sanctis, V.D. (2012). An approach to constitutional delay of growth and puberty. *Indian Journal of Endocrinology and Metabolism, 16,* 698–705.

Soller, B. (2014). Caught in a bad romance: Adolescent romantic relationships and mental health. *Journal of Health and Social Behavior, 55,* 56–72.

Solmeyer, A.R., McHale, S.M., Killoren, S.E., & Updegraff, K.A. (2011). Coparenting around siblings' differential treatment in Mexican-origin families. *Developmental Psychology, 25,* 251–260.

Solnit, A.J., & Nordhaus, B.F. (2013). Divorce and custody in a changing society. In L. Gunsberg & P. Hymowitz (Eds.), *A handbook of divorce and custody.* New York: Psychology Press.

Solomon, B.C., & Jackson, J.J. (2014). Why do personality traits predict divorce? Multiple pathways through satisfaction. *Journal of Personality and Social Psychology, 106,* 978–996.

Solomon, D., Watson, P., Schapes, E., Battistich, V., & Solomon, J. (1990). Cooperative learning as part of a comprehensive program designed to promote prosocial development. In S. Sharan (Ed.), *Cooperative learning.* New York: Praeger.

Sommer, B.B. (1978). *Puberty and adolescence.* New York: Oxford University Press.

Song, A.V., & Halpern-Felsher, B.L. (2010). Predictive relationship between adolescent oral and vaginal sex: Results from a prospective, longitudinal study. *Archives of Pediatric and Adolescent Medicine, 165,* 243–249.

Song, L.J., & others (2010). The differential effects of general mental ability and emotional intelligence on academic performance and social interactions. *Intelligence, 38,* 137–143.

Sontag, L.M., Graber, J., Brooks-Gunn, J., & Warren, M.P. (2008). Coping with social stress: Implications for psychopathology in young adolescent girls. *Journal of Abnormal Child Psychology, 36,* 1159–1174.

Sontag-Padilla, L.M., & others (2012). Executive functioning, cortisol reactivity, and symptoms of psychopathology in girls with premature adrenarche. *Development and Psychopathology, 24,* 211–223.

Soreni, N., & others (2014). Dimensions of perfectionism in children and adolescents with obsessive-compulsive disorder. *Journal of the Canadian Academy of Child and Adolescent Psychiatry, 23,* 136–143.

Sosic-Vasic, Z., & others (2015). The impact of motivation and teachers' autonomy support on children's executive functions. *Frontiers in Psychology, 6,* 146.

Soto, C.J. (2015). Is happiness good for your personality? Concurrent and prospective relations of the Big Five with subjective well-being. *Journal of Personality, 83*(1), 45–55.

Soto, C.J., John, O.P., Gosling, S.D., & Potter, J. (2011). Age differences in personality traits from 10 to 65: Big Five domains and facets in a large cross-cultural sample. *Journal of Personality and Social Psychology, 100,* 330–348.

Soto, C.J., John, O.P., Gosling, S.D., & Potter, J. (2011). Age differences in personality traits from 10 to 65: Big Five domains and facets in a large cross-cultural sample. *Journal of Personality and Social Psychology, 100,* 330–348.

Sowell, E. (2004, July). Commentary in M. Beckman, "Crime, culpability, and the adolescent brain." *Science Magazine, 305,* 599.

Spence, J.T., & Helmreich, R. (1978). *Masculinity and femininity: Their psychological dimensions.* Austin: University of Texas Press.

Spencer, M.B., Swanson, D.P., & Harpalani, V. (2015). Conceptualizing the self: Contributions of normative human processes, diverse social contexts, and opportunity. In R.M. Lerner (Ed.), *Handbook of child psychology and developmental science* (7th ed.). New York: Wiley.

Spencer, R.A., Bower, J., Kirk, S.F., & Hancock Friesen, C. (2014). Peer mentoring is associated with positive changes in physical activity and aerobic exercise fitness of grades 4, 5, and 6 students in the Heart Healthy Kids Program. *Health Promotion Practice, 15,* 803–811.

Spilman, S.K., Neppl, T.K., Donnellan, M.B., Schofield, T.J., & Conger, R.D. (2013). Incorporating religiosity into a developmental model of positive family functioning across generations. *Developmental Psychology, 49*(4), 762–774.

Sprecher, S., Treger, S., & Sakaluk, J.K. (2013). Premarital sexual standards and sociosexuality: Gender, ethnicity, and cohort differences. *Archives of Sexual Behavior, 42,* 1395–1405.

Spring, J. (2013). *Deculturalization and the struggle for equality* (7th ed.). New York: McGraw-Hill.

Spring, J. (2014). *American education* (16th ed.). New York: McGraw-Hill.

Spruijt-Metz, D. (2011). Etiology, treatment, and prevention of obesity in childhood and adolescence: A decade in review. *Journal of Research on Adolescence, 21,* 129–152.

Sroufe, L., Egeland, B., Carlson, E.A., & Collins, W.A. (2005). *The development of the person: The Minnesota Study of Risk and Adaptation from Birth to Adulthood.* New York: Guilford.

Sroufe, L.A. (2007). Commentary: The place of development in developmental psychology. In A.S. Masten (Ed.), *Multilevel dynamics in developmental psychology.* Mahwah, NJ: Erlbaum.

Sroufe, L.A., Coffino, B., & Carlson, E.A. (2010). Conceptualizing the role of early experience: Lessons from the Minnesota longitudinal study. *Developmental Review, 30,* 36–51.

St. Clair, M.C., & others (2015, in press). Childhood adversity subtypes and depressive symptoms in early and late adolescence. *Development and Psychopathology.*

St. Pierre, R., Layzer, J., & Barnes, H. (1996). *Regenerating two-generation programs.* Cambridge, MA: Abt Associates.

Staff, J., Messersmith, E.E., & Schulenberg, J.E. (2009). Adolescents and the world of work. In R.M. Lerner & L. Steinberg (Eds.), *Handbook of adolescent psychology* (3rd ed.). New York: Wiley.

Staff, J., Mont'Alvao, A., & Mortimer, J.T. (2015). Children at work. In R.M. Lerner (Ed.), *Handbook of child psychology and developmental psychology* (7th ed.). New York: Wiley.

Staiano, A.E., Abraham, A., & Calvert, S.L. (2012). Competitive versus cooperative exergame play for African American adolescents' executive functioning skills. *Developmental Psychology, 48,* 337–342.

Stake, J.E. (2000). When situations call for instrumentality and expressiveness: Resource appraisal, coping strategy choice, and adjustment. *Sex Roles, 42,* 865–885.

Stangor, C. (2015). *Research methods for the behavioral sciences* (5th ed.). Boston: Cengage.

Stanik, C.E., Riina, E.M., & McHale, S.M. (2013). Parent-adolescent relationship qualities and adolescent adjustment in two-parent African American families. *Family Relations 62,* 597–608.

Stanley, S.M., Amato, P.R., Johnson, C.A., & Markman, H.J. (2006). Premarital education, marital quality, and marital stability: Findings from a large, household survey. *Journal of Family Psychology, 20,* 117–126.

Stanley, S.M., Rhoades, G.K., Amato, P.R., Markman, H.J., & Johnson, C.A. (2010). The timing of cohabitation and engagement: Impact on first and second marriages. *Journal of Marriage and the Family, 72,* 906–918.

Starr, C. (2015). An objective look at early sexualization and the media. *Sex Roles, 72,* 85–87.

Starr, C., Evers, C., & Starr, L. (2015). *Biology* (9th ed.). Boston: Cengage.

Starr, C., Evers, C., & Starr, L. (2016, in press). *Biology today and tomorrow* (5th ed.). Boston: Cengage.

Starr, C., Taggart, R., Evers, C., & Starr, L. (2016, in press). *Biology: The unity and diversity of life* (14th ed.). Boston: Cengage.

Starr, L.R., & Davila, J. (2009). Clarifying co-rumination: Associations with internalizing symptoms and romantic involvement among adolescent girls. *Journal of Adolescence, 32,* 19–37.

statisticbrain (2014). *Online dating statistics.* Retrieved November 16, 2014, from www.statisticbrain.com/online-dating-statistics

Steca, P., Bassi, M., Caprara, G.V., & Fave, A.D. (2011). Parents' self-efficacy beliefs and their children's psychosocial adaptation during adolescence. *Journal of Youth and Adolescence, 40,* 320–331.

Steel, P. (2007). The nature of procrastination: A meta-analytic and theoretical review of quintessential self-regulatory failure. *Psychological Bulletin, 133,* 65–94.

Steele, J., Waters, E., Crowell, J., & Treboux, D. (1998, June). *Self-report measures of attachment: Secure bonds to other attachment measures and attachment theory.* Paper presented at the meeting of the International Society for the Study of Personal Relationships, Saratoga Springs, NY.

Steele, L.G., & Lynch, S.M. (2013). The pursuit of happiness in China: Individualism, collectivism, and subjective well-being during China's economic and social transformation. *Social Indicators Research, 114*(2), doi: 10.1007/s11205-012-0154-1.

Steele, R.D., & others (2014). Caregiving antecedents of secure base script knowledge: A comparative analysis of young adult attachment representations. *Developmental Psychology, 50,* 2526–2538.

Steiger, A.E., Allemand, M., Robins, R.W., & Fend, H.A. (2014). Low and decreasing self-esteem during adolescence predict adult depression two decades later. *Journal of Personality and Social Psychology, 106,* 325–338.

Steinberg, E.A., & Drabick, D.A. (2015, in press). A developmental psychopathology perspective on ADHD and comorbid conditions: The role of emotion regulation. *Child Psychiatry and Human Development.*

Steinberg, L. (2004). Risk taking in adolescence: What changes, and why? *Annals of the New York Academy of Sciences, 1021,* 51–58.

Steinberg, L. (2008). A neurobehavioral perspective on risk-taking. *Developmental Review, 28,* 78–106.

Steinberg, L. (2011). Adolescent risk-taking: A social neuroscience perspective. In E. Amsel & J. Smetana (Eds.), *Adolescent vulnerabilities and opportunities: Constructivist developmental perspectives.* New York: Cambridge University Press.

Steinberg, L. (2011). *You and your adolescent: The essential guide for ages 10 to 25.* New York: Simon & Schuster.

Steinberg, L. (2014). *Age of opportunity.* Boston: Houghn Mifflin Harcourt.

Steinberg, L. (2015a). How should the science of adolescent brain pathology inform legal policy? In J. Bhabba (Ed.), *Coming of age.* Philadelphia: University of Pennsylvania Press.

Steinberg, L. (2015b). The neural underpinnings of adolescent risk-taking: The roles of reward-seeking, impulse control, and peers. In G. Oettigen & P. Gollwitzer (Eds.), *Self-regulation in adolescence.* New York: Cambridge University Press.

Steinberg, L., & others (2008). Age differences in sensation-seeking and impulsivity as indexed by behavior and self-report: Evidence for a dual systems model. *Developmental Psychology, 44,* 1764–1778.

Steinberg, L., & others (2009). Age differences in future orientation and delay discounting. *Child Development, 80,* 28–44.

Steinberg, L.D. (1986). Latchkey children and susceptibility to peer pressure: An ecological analysis. *Developmental Psychology, 22,* 433–439.

Steinberg, L.D. (1988). Reciprocal relation between parent-child distance and pubertal maturation. *Developmental Psychology, 24,* 122–128.

Steinberg, L.D. (2014). *Age of opportunities.* Boston: Houghton Mifflin Harcourt.

Steinberg, L.D., & Silk, J.S. (2002). Parenting adolescents. In M. Bornstein (Ed.), *Handbook of parenting* (2nd ed., Vol. 1). Mahwah, NJ: Erlbaum.

Steinberg, S. (2011, June 11). New dating site helps college students find love. *CNN Living.* Retrieved February 27, 2013, from www.cnn.com/2011/LIVING/06/22date.my.school/index.html

Steinberg, S.J., & Davila, J. (2008). Romantic functioning and depressive symptoms among early adolescent girls: The moderating role of parental emotional availability. *Journal of Clinical Child and Adolescent Psychology, 37,* 350–362.

Steiner, N.J., & others (2014a). In-school neurofeedback traning for ADHD: Sustained improvements from a randomized controlled trial. *Pediatrics, 133,* 483–492.

Steiner, N.J., & others (2014b). Neurofeedback and cognitive attention training for children with attention deficit hyperactivity disorder in schools. *Journal of Developmental and Behavioral Pediatrics, 35,* 18–27.

Stephens, J.M. (2008). Cheating. In N. J. Salkind (Ed.), *Encyclopedia of educational psychology.* Thousand Oaks, CA: Sage.

Sterin, J.C. (2014). *Mass media revolution* (2nd ed.). Upper Saddle River, NJ: Pearson.

Sternberg, K., & Sternberg, R.J. (2013). Love. In H. Pashler (Ed.), *Encyclopedia of the mind.* Thousand Oaks, CA: Sage.

Sternberg, R.J. (1985, December). Teaching critical thinking, Part 2: Possible solutions. *Phi Delta Kappan,* 277–280.

Sternberg, R.J. (1986). *Intelligence applied.* Fort Worth: Harcourt Brace.

Sternberg, R.J. (2004). Individual differences in cognitive development. In P. Smith & C. Hart (Eds.), *Blackwell handbook of cognitive development.* Malden, MA: Blackwell.

Sternberg, R.J. (2010). The triarchic theory of successful intelligence. In B. Kerr (Ed.), *Encyclopedia of giftedness, creativity, and talent.* Thousand Oaks, CA: Sage.

Sternberg, R.J. (2012). Intelligence in its cultural context. In M. Gelfand, C-Y Chiu, & Y-Y Hong (Eds.), *Advances in cultures and psychology* (Vol. 2). New York: Oxford University Press.

Sternberg, R.J. (2013). Contemporary theories of intelligence. In I.B. Weiner & others (Eds.), *Handbook of psychology* (2nd ed., Vol. 7). New York: Wiley.

Sternberg, R.J. (2014a). Building wisdom and character. In S. Lynn (Ed.), *Health, happiness, and well-being.* Thousand Oaks, CA: Sage.

Sternberg, R.J. (2014b). Teaching about the nature of intelligence. *Intelligence, 42,* 176–179.

Sternberg, R.J. (2015a). Human intelligence: Historical and conceptual perspectives. In J. Wright (Ed.), *Encyclopedia of social and behavioral sciences* (2nd ed.). New York: Elsevier.

Sternberg, R.J. (2015b). Competence versus performance models of people and tests. *Applied Developmental Psychology.*

Sternberg, R.J. (2015c). Multiple intelligences in the new age of thinking. In S. Goldstein, D. Princiotta, & J. Naglieri (Eds.), *Handbook of intelligence.* New York: Springer.

Sternberg, R.J., & Bridges, S.L. (2014). Varieties of genius. In D.K. Simonton (Ed.), *The Wiley-Blackwell handbook of genius.* New York: Wiley-Blackwell.

Sternberg, R.J., & Sternberg, K. (2013). *Cognitive psychology* (7th ed.). Boston: Cengage.

Sternberg, R.J., & Williams, W.M. (1996). *How to develop student creativity.* Alexandria, VA: ASCD.

Steur, F.B., Applefield, J.M., & Smith, R. (1971). Televised aggression and the interpersonal aggression of preschool children. *Journal of Experimental Child Psychology, 11,* 442–447.

Stevenson, H.W. (1995). Mathematics achievement of American students: First in the world by the year 2000? In C.A. Nelson (Ed.), *Basic and applied perspectives on learning, cognition, and development.* Minneapolis: University of Minnesota Press.

Stevenson, H.W., & Zusho, A. (2002). Adolescence in China and Japan: Adapting to a changing environment. In B.B. Brown, R.W. Larson, & T.S. Saraswathi (Eds.), *The world's youth.* New York: Cambridge University Press.

Stevenson, H.W., & others (1990). Contexts of achievement. *Monograph of the Society for Research in Child Development, 55* (Serial No. 221).

Stevenson, H.W., Lee, S., & Stigler, J.W. (1986). Mathematics achievement of Chinese, Japanese, and American children. *Science, 231,* 693–699.

Stewart, A.J., Ostrove, J.M., & Helson, R. (2001). Middle aging in women: Patterns of personality change from the 30s to the 50s. *Journal of Adult Development, 8,* 23–37.

Steyer, R., Mayer, A., Geiser, C., & Cole, D.A. (2015). A theory of states and traits—revised. *Annual Review of Clinical Psychology* (Vol. 11). Palo Alto, CA: Annual Reviews.

Stice, F., Presnell, K., & Spangler, D. (2002). Risk factors for binge eating onset in adolescent girls: A 2-year prospective investigation. *Health Psychology, 21,* 131–138.

Stiles, J., Brown, T.T., Haist, F., & Jernigan, T.L. (2015). Brain and cognitive development. In R.M. Lerner (Ed.), *Handbook of child psychology and developmental science* (7th ed.). New York: Wiley.

Stipek, D.J. (2002). *Motivation to learn* (4th ed.). Boston: Allyn & Bacon.

Stipek, D.J. (2005, February 16). Commentary in *USA Today,* p. 1D.

Stokes, C.E., & Raley, R.K. (2009). Cohabitation. In D. Carr (Ed.), *Encyclopedia of the life course and human development.* Boston: Gale Cengage.

Stone, L.B., Hankin, B.L., Gibb, B.E., & Abela, J.R. (2011). Co-rumination predicts the onset of depressive disorders during adolescence. *Journal of Abnormal Psychology, 120*(3), 752–757.

Stoppa, T.M., & Lefkowitz, E.S. (2010). Longitudinal changes in religiosity among emerging adult college students. *Journal of Research on Adolescence, 20,* 23–38.

Story, M., Kaphingst, K.M., & French, S. (2006). The role of schools in obesity prevention. *Future of Children, 16*(1), 109–142.

Strahan, D.B. (1983). The emergence of formal operations in adolescence. *Transcendence, 11,* 7–14.

Strand, P.S., Pula, K., & Downs, A. (2015, in press). Social values and preschool behavioral adjustment: A comparative investigation of Latino and European American preschool children. *Cultural Diversity and Ethnic Minority Psychology.*

Strasberger, V.C., Wilson, B.J., & Jordan, A. (2008). *Children, adolescents, and the media.* Thousand Oaks, CA: Sage.

Strati, A.D., Shernoff, D., & Kackar, H.Z. (2012). Flow. In J.R. Levesque (Ed.), *Encyclopedia of adolescence.* New York: Springer.

Straubhaar, J., LaRose, R., & Davenport, L. (2014). *Media now* (8th ed.). Boston: Cengage.

Stray, L.L., Ellertsen, B., & Stray, T. (2010). Motor function and methylphenidate effect in children with attention deficit hyperactivity disorder. *Acta Pediatrica, 99,* 1199–1204.

Streib, H. (1999). Off-road religion? A narrative approach to fundamentalist and occult orientations of adolescents. *Journal of Adolescence, 22,* 255–267.

Strickland, A.D. (2014). Prevention of cerebral palsy, autism spectrum disorder, and attention deficit hyperactivity disorder. *Medical Hypotheses, 82,* 522–528.

Striegel-Moore, R.H., & Bulik, C.M. (2007). Risk factors for eating disorders. *American Psychologist, 62,* 181–198.

Strohmeier, D., & Noam, G.G. (2012). Bullying in schools: What is the problem and how can educators solve it? *New Directions in Youth Development, 133,* 7–13.

Stroth, S., & others (2009). Physical fitness, but not acute exercise modulates event-related potential indices for executive control in healthy adolescents. *Brain Research, 1269,* 114–124.

Stroud, L.R., Papandonatos, G.D., Williamson, D.E., & Dahl, R.E. (2011). Sex differences in cortisol response to corticotrophin releasing hormone challenge over puberty: Pittsburgh Pediatric Neurobehavioral Studies. *Psychoneuroimmunology, 36,* 1226–1238.

Strunk, K.K., & Steele, M.R. (2011). Relative contributions of self-efficacy, self-regulation, and self-handicapping in predicting student procrastination. *Psychological Reports, 109,* 983–989.

Su, R., Rounds, J., & Armstrong, P.I. (2009). Men and things, women and people: A meta-analysis of sex differences in interests. *Psychological Bulletin, 135,* 859–884.

Suárez-Orozco, C. (2007, March). *Immigrant family educational advantages and challenges.* Paper presented at the meeting of the Society for Research in Child Development, Boston.

Suárez-Orozco, C., & Yoshikawa, H. (2013). Undocumented status: Implications for child development, policy, and ethical research. *New Directions in Child and Adolescent Development, 141,* 61–78.

Suárez-Orozco, M.M., & Suárez-Orozco, C. (2010). Globalization, immigration, and schooling. In J.A. Banks (Ed.), *The Routledge international companion to multicultural education.* New York: Routledge.

Suárez-Orozco, M.M., & Suárez-Orozco, C. (2013). Taking perspective: Context, culture, and history. *New Directions in Child and Adolescent Development, 141,* 9–23.

Sue, D., Sue, D.W., Sue, D.M., & Sue, S. (2014). *Essentials of understanding abnormal psychology* (2nd ed.). Boston: Cengage.

Sue, D., Sue, D.W., Sue, S., & Sue, D.M. (2013). *Understanding abnormal behavior* (10th ed.). Boston: Cengage.

Sue, D., Sue, D.W., Sue, S., & Sue, D.M. (2015). *Understanding abnormal behavior* (11th ed.). Boston: Cengage.

Sue, S., & Morishima, J.K. (1982). *The mental health of Asian Americans: Contemporary issues in identifying and treating mental problems.* San Francisco: Jossey-Bass.

Sukys, S., Majauskiene, D., Cesnaitiene, V.J., & Karanauskiene, D. (2014). Do parents' exercise habits predict 13–18-year-old adolescents' involvement in sport? *Journal of Sports Science and Medicine, 13,* 522–528.

Suleiman, A.B., & Deardorff, J. (2015). Multiple dimensions of peer influence in adolescent romantic and sexual relationships: A descriptive, qualitative study. *Archives of Sexual Behavior, 44,* 765–775.

Sullivan, H.S. (1953). *The interpersonal theory of psychiatry.* New York: Norton.

Sun, Y., Tao, F., Hao, J., & Wan, Y. (2010). The mediating effects of stress and coping on depression among adolescents in China. *Journal of Child and Adolescent Psychiatric Nursing, 23,* 173–180.

Sun, Y., & others (2012). National estimates of the pubertal milestones among urban and rural Chinese girls. *Journal of Adolescent Health, 51,* 279–284.

Sung, J., Lee, J., Noh, H.M., Park, Y.S., & Ahn, E.J. (2013). Associations between the risk of Internet addiction and problem behaviors among Korean adolescents. *Korean Journal of Family Medicine, 34,* 115–132.

Suris, J.C., Jeannin, A., Chossis, I., & Michaud, P.A. (2007). Piercing among adolescents: Body art as a risk marker: A population-based approach. *Journal of Family Practice, 56,* 126–130.

Suris, J.C., & others (2014). Is Internet use unhealthy? A cross-sectional study of adolescent Internet overuse. *Swiss Medical Weekly, 144,* w14061.

Susman, E.J., & Dorn, L.D. (2009). Puberty: Its role in development. In R.M. Lerner & L. Steinberg (Eds.), *Handbook of adolescent psychology* (3rd ed.). New York: Wiley.

Susman, E.J., Dorn, L.D., & Schiefelbein, V.L. (2003). Puberty, sexuality, and health. In R.M. Lerner, M.A. Easterbrooks, & J. Mistry (Eds.), *Comprehensive handbook of psychology: Developmental psychology* (Vol. 6). New York: Wiley.

Susman, E.J., & others (2010). Longitudinal development of secondary sexual characteristics in girls and boys between ages 9½ and 15½ years. *Archives of Pediatric and Adolescent Medicine, 164,* 166–173.

Sutton-Smith, B. (1982). Birth order and sibling status effects. In M.E. Lamb & B. Sutton-Smith (Eds.), *Sibling relationships: Their nature and significance across the life span.* Hillsdale, NJ: Erlbaum.

Swaab, D.F., Chung, W.C., Kruijver, F.P., Hofman, M.A., & Ishunina, T.A. (2001). Structural and functional sex differences in the human hypothalamus. *Hormones and Behavior, 40,* 93–98.

Swanson, H.L. (1999). What develops in working memory? A life-span perspective. *Developmental Psychology, 35,* 986–1000.

Swanson, H.L. (2014). Learning disabilities. In M.A. Bray & T.J. Kehle (Eds.), *Oxford handbook of school psychology.* New York: Oxford University Press.

Swanson, J.L. (2013). Traditional and emerging career development theory and the psychology of working. In D.L. Blustein (Ed.), *Oxford handbook of the psychology of working.* New York: Oxford University Press.

Swartz, T.T., Kim, M., Uno, M., Mortimer, J., & O'Brien, K.B. (2011). Safety nets and scaffolds: Parental support in the transition to adulthood. *Journal of Marriage and the Family, 73,* 414–429.

Swartzendruber, A., & others (2015, in press). Comparison of substance use typologies as predictors of sexual risk outcomes in African American adolescent females. *Archives of Sexual Behavior.*

Syed, M. (2013). Assessment of ethnic identity and acculturation. In K. Geisinger (Ed.), *APA handbook of testing and assessment in psychology.* Washington, DC: American Psychological Association.

Syed, M., & Azmitia, M. (2008). A narrative approach to ethnic identity in emerging adulthood: Bringing life to the identity status model. *Developmental Psychology, 44,* 1012–1027.

Syed, M., & Azmitia, M. (2009). Longitudinal trajectories of ethnic identity during the college years. *Journal of Research on Adolescence, 19*(4), 601–624.

Syeda, M.M., & Climie, E.A. (2014). Test review: Wechsler Preschool and Primary Scale of Intelligence. *Journal of Psychoeducational Assessment, 32,* 265–272.

Sykes, C.J. (1995). *Dumbing down our kids: Why America's children feel good about themselves but can't read, write, or add.* New York: St. Martin's Press.

Sypniewska, G. (2015, in press). Laboratory assessment of cardiometabolic risk in overweight and obese children. *Clinical Biochemistry.*

Syvaoja, H.J., & others (2013). Physical activity, sedentary behavior, and academic performance in Finnish children. *Medicine and Science in Sports and Exercise, 45,* 2098–2104.

Szwedo, D.E., Mikami, A.Y., & Allen, J.P. (2011). Qualities of peer relations on social networking websites: Predictions from negative mother-teen interactions. *Journal of Research on Adolescence, 21,* 595–607.

T

Tach, L.M., & Eads, A. (2015). Trends in the economic consequences of marital and cohabitation dissolution in the United States. *Demography, 52,* 401–432.

Talpade, M. (2008). Hispanic versus African American girls: Body image, nutrition, and puberty. *Adolescence, 43,* 119–127.

Tam, H.M., Lam, C.L., Huang, H., Wang, B., & Lee, T.M. (2015). Age-related difference in relationships between cognitive processing speed and general cognitive status. *Applied Neuropsychology: Adult, 22,* 94–99.

Tamis-LeMonda, C.S., & Cabrera, N. (Eds.). (2002). *The handbook of father involvement.* Mahwah, NJ: Erlbaum.

Tamis-LeMonda, C.S., & others (2008). Parents' goals for children: The dynamic coexistence of individualism and collectivism in cultures and individuals. *Social Development, 17,* 183–209.

Tan, Q., Christiansen, L., Bornemann Hjelmborg, J., & Christiansen, K. (2015). Twin methodology in epigenetic studies. *Journal of Experimental Biology, 18,* 134–139.

Tang, S., Davis-Kean, P.E., Chen, M., & Sexton, H.R. (2015, in press). Adolescent pregnancy's intergenerational effects: Does an adolescent mother's education have consequences for her children's achievement? *Journal of Research on Adolescence.*

Tannen, D. (1990). *You just don't understand: Women and men in conversation.* New York: Ballantine.

Tanner, J.M. (1962). *Growth at adolescence* (2nd ed.). Oxford, UK: Blackwell.

Tanton, C., & others (2015). Patterns and trends in sources of information about sex among young people in Britain: Evidence from three national surveys of sexual attitudes and lifestyles. *BMJ Open, 5*(3), e007834.

Tarokh, L., & Carskadon, M.A. (2008). Sleep in adolescents. In L.R. Squire (Ed.), *New Encyclopedia of Neuroscience.* Oxford, UK: Elsevier.

Tarokh, L., & Carskadon, M.A. (2010). Developmental changes in the human sleep EEG during early adolescence. *Sleep, 33,* 801–809.

Tarokh, L., Carskadon, M.A., & Achermann, P. (2014). Early adolescent cognitive gains are marked by increased sleep EEG coherence. *PLoS One, 9*(9), e106847.

Tarpley, T. (2001). Children, the Internet, and other new technologies. In D. Singer & J. Singer (Eds.), *Handbook of children and the media.* Thousand Oaks, CA: Sage.

Tashiro, T., & Frazier, P. (2003). "I'll never be in a relationship like that again": Personal growth following romantic relationship breakups. *Personal Relationships, 10,* 113–128.

Tavris, C., & Wade, C. (1984). *The longest war: Sex differences in perspective* (2nd ed.). Fort Worth, TX: Harcourt Brace.

Taylor, B.G., & Mumford, E.A. (2015, in press). A national descriptive portrait of adolescent relationship abuse: Results from the National Survey on Teen Relationships and Intimate Violence. *Journal of Interpersonal Violence.*

Taylor, B.G., Mumford, E.A., & Stein, N.D. (2015). Effectiveness of "shifting boundaries" teen dating violence prevention program for subgroups of middle school students. *Journal of Adolescent Health.*

Taylor, E.M., Jones, A.D., & Henagan, T.M. (2014). A review of mitochondrial-derived fatty acids in epigenetic regulation of obesity and type 2 diabetes.

Journal of Nutrition, Health, and Food Sciences, 2(3), 1–4.

Taylor, J.H., & Walker, L.J. (1997). Moral climate and the development of moral reasoning: The effects of dyadic discussions between young offenders. *Journal of Moral Education, 26,* 21–43.

Taylor, L.M., & Fratto, J.M. (2012). *Transforming learning through 21st century skills.* Boston: Allyn & Bacon.

Taylor, N.L. (2011). "Guys, she's humongous!": Gender and weight-based teasing in adolescence. *Journal of Adolescent Research, 26,* 178–199.

Taylor, R.D. (1996). Kinship support, family management, and adolescent adjustment and competence in African American families. *Developmental Psychology, 32,* 687–695.

Taylor, R.D., & Lopez, E.I. (2005). Family management practice, school achievement, and problem behavior in African American adolescents: Mediating processes. *Applied Developmental Psychology, 26,* 39–49.

Taylor, S.E. (2006). Tend and befriend: Biobehavioral bases of affiliation under stress. *Current Directions in Psychological Science, 15,* 273–277.

Taylor, S.E. (2011a). Affiliation and stress. In S. Folkman (Ed.), *Oxford handbook of stress, health, and coping.* New York: Oxford University Press.

Taylor, S.E. (2011b). *Health psychology* (8th ed.). New York: McGraw-Hill.

Taylor, S.E. (2011c). Tend and befriend theory. In A.M. van Lange, A.W. Kruglanski, & E.T. Higgins (Eds.), *Handbook of theories of social psychology.* Thousand Oaks, CA: Sage.

Taylor, S.E. (2015). *Health psychology* (9th ed.). New York: McGraw-Hill.

te Velde, S.J., & others (2012). Energy balance-related behaviors associated with overweight and obesity in preschool children: A systematic review of prospective studies. *Obesity Reviews, 13*(Suppl. 1), S56–S74.

Teague, M.L., MacKenzie, S.L.C., & Rosenthal, D.M. (2015). *Your health today* (5th ed.). New York: McGraw-Hill.

Tebb, K.P., Sedlander, E., Bausch, S., & Brindis, C.D. (2015, in press). Opportunities and challenges for adolescent health under the Affordable Care Act. *Maternal and Child Health Journal.*

Teenage Research Unlimited (2004, November 10). *Diversity in word and deed: Most teens claim multicultural friends.* Northbrook, IL: Teenage Research Unlimited.

Teilmann, G., Juul, A., Skakkebaek, N.E., & Toppari, J. (2002). Putative effects of endocrine disruptors on pubertal development in the human. *Best Practices in Research and Clinical Endocrinology and Metabolism, 16,* 105–121.

Telzer, E.H., Fuligni, A.J., Lieberman, M.D., & Galvan, A. (2013). Meaningful family relationships: Neurocognitive buffers of adolescent risk taking. *Journal of Cognitive Neuroscience, 25,* 374–387.

Telzer, E.H., Fuligni, A.J., Lieberman, M.D., & Galvan, A. (2013). The effects of poor-quality sleep on brain function and risk taking in adolescence. *Neuroimage, 71,* 275–283.

Telzer, E.H., Gonzales, N., & Fuligni, A.J. (2014). Family obligation values and family assistance behaviors: Protective and risk factors for Mexican-American adolescents' substance use. *Journal of Youth and Adolescence, 43,* 270–283.

Telzer, E.H., Ichein, N.T., & Qu, Y. (2015, in press). Mother knows best: Redirecting adolescent reward sensitivity towards safe behavior during risk taking. *Social Cognitive and Affective Neuroscience.*

Temple, J.R., & Choi, H. (2014). Longitudinal association between teen sexting and sexual behavior. *Pediatrics, 134,* e1287–e1292.

Templeton, J.L., & Eccles, J.S. (2006). The relation between spiritual development and identity processes. In E. Roehlkepartain, P.E. King, L. Wagener, & P.L. Benson (Eds.), *The handbook of spirituality in childhood and adolescence*. Thousand Oaks, CA: Sage.

Ten Hoor, G.A., Plasqui, G., Schols, A.M., & Kok, G. (2014). Combating adolescent obesity: An integrated physiological and psychological perspective. *Current Opinion in Clinical Nutrition and Metabolic Care, 17,* 521–524.

Teplin, L.A., & others (2014). Firearm homicide and other causes of death in delinquents: A 16-year prospective study. *Pediatrics, 134,* 63–73.

Terman, L. (1925). *Genetic studies of genius: Vol. 1. Mental and physical traits of a thousand gifted children*. Stanford, CA: Stanford University Press.

Terry-McElrath, Y.M., O'Malley, P.M., & Johnston, L.D. (2011). Exercise and substance use among American youth, 1991–2009. *American Journal of Preventive Medicine, 40,* 530–540.

The, N.S., & others (2010). Association of adolescent obesity with risk of severe obesity in adulthood. *Journal of the American Medical Association, 304,* 2042–2047.

Thein-Nissenbaum, J.M., Rauh, M.J., Carr, K.E., Loud, K.J., & McGuine, T.A. (2012). Menstrual irregularity and musculoskeletal injury in female high school athletes. *Journal of Athletic Training, 47,* 74–82.

Thoma, S.J. (2006). Research on the Defining Issues Test. In M. Killen & J. Smetana (Eds.), *Handbook of moral development*. Mahwah, NJ: Erlbaum.

Thoma, S.J., & Bebeau, M. (2008). *Moral judgment competency is declining over time: Evidence from 20 years of defining issues test data*. Paper presented at the meeting of the American Educational Research Association, New York, NY.

Thomaes, S., Bushman, B.J., Stegge, H., & Olthof, T. (2008). Trumping shame by blasts of noise: Narcissism, self-esteem, shame, and aggression in young adolescents. *Child Development, 18,* 758–765.

Thomas, A., & Chess, S. (1991). Temperament in adolescence and its functional significance. In R.M. Lerner, A.C. Petersen, & J. Brooks-Gunn (Eds.), *Encyclopedia of adolescence* (Vol. 2). New York: Garland.

Thomas, A.G., Monahan, K.C., Lukowski, A.F., & Cauffman, E. (2014). Sleep problems across development: A pathway to adolescent risk taking through working memory. *Journal of Youth and Adolescence, 44,* 447–464.

Thomas, B.C., Croft, K.E., & Tranel, D. (2011). Harming kin to save strangers: Further evidence for abnormally utilitarian moral judgments after ventromedial prefrontal damage. *Journal of Cognitive Neuroscience, 23,* 2186–2196.

Thomas, C.R., & Gadbois, S.A. (2007). Academic self-handicapping: The role of self-concept clarity and students' learning strategies. *British Journal of Educational Psychology, 77,* 109–119.

Thomas, C.W., Coffman, J.K., & Kipp, K.L. (1993, March). *Are only children different from children with siblings? A longitudinal study of behavioral and social functioning*. Paper presented at the biennial meeting of the Society for Research in Child Development, New Orleans.

Thompson, A.E., & Voyer, D. (2014). Sex differences in the ability to recognize non-verbal displays of emotion: A meta-analysis. *Cognition and Emotion, 28,* 1164–1195.

Thompson, J., & Manore, M. (2015). *Nutrition* (4th ed.). Upper Saddle River, NJ: Pearson.

Thompson, M., Kuruwita, C., & Foster, E.M. (2009). Transitions in suicide risk in a nationally representative sample of adolescents. *Journal of Adolescent Health, 44,* 458–463.

Thompson, M.P., & Light, L.S. (2011). Examining gender differences in risk factors in suicide attempts made 1 and 7 years later in a nationally representative sample. *Journal of Adolescent Health, 48,* 391–397.

Thompson, P.A., & others (2015, in press). Developmental dyslexia: Predicting individual risk. *Journal of Child Psychology and Psychiatry.*

Thompson, R.A. (2008). Unpublished review of J.W. Santrock's *Life-span development*, 12th ed. (New York: McGraw-Hill).

Thompson, R.A. (2009). Early foundations: Conscience and the development of moral character. In D. Narváez & D. Lapsley (Eds.), *Personality, identity, and character: Explorations in moral psychology*. New York: Cambridge University Press.

Thompson, R.A. (2014). Conscience development in early childhood. In M. Killen & J.G. Smetana (Eds.), *Handbook of moral development* (2nd ed.). New York: Guilford.

Thompson, R.A. (2015). Relationships, regulation, and development. In R.M. Lerner (Ed.), *Handbook of child psychology and developmental science* (7th ed.). New York: Wiley.

Thompson, R.A., & Newton, E.K. (2010). Emotion in early conscience. In W. Arsenio & E. Lemerise (Eds.), *Emotions, aggression, and morality: Bridging development and psychopathology*. Washington, DC: American Psychological Association.

Thompson-Brenner, H. (2015). *Casebook of evidence-based therapy for eating disorders*. New York: Guilford.

Thompson-Brenner, H., & others (2014). Multiple measures of rapid response as predictors of remission in cognitive behavior therapy for bulimia nervosa. *Behavior Research and Therapy, 64C,* 9–14.

Thornberg, R., & Jungert, T. (2014). School bullying and mechanisms of moral disengagement. *Aggressive Behavior, 40,* 99–108.

Thrane, L.E., & Chen, X. (2012). Impact of running away on girls' pregnancy. *Journal of Adolescence, 35,* 443–449.

Tilton-Weaver, L.C., Burk, W.J., Kerr, M., & Stattin, H. (2013). Can parental monitoring and peer management reduce the selection or influence of delinquent peers? Testing the question using a dynamic social network approach. *Developmental Psychology, 49,* 2057–2070.

Tolan, P.H., Gorman-Smith, D., Henry, D., Chung, K., & Hunt, M. (2004). The relation of patterns of coping of inner-city youth to psychopathology symptoms. *Journal of Research on Adolescence, 12,* 423–449.

Tolman, D. (2002). *Dilemmas of desire: Teenage girls talk about sexuality*. Cambridge, MA: Harvard University Press.

Tolman, D.L., & McClelland, S.I. (2011). Normative sexuality development in adolescence: A decade in review, 2000–2009. *Journal of Research on Adolescence, 21,* 242–255.

Tomasik, M.J., Pavlova, M.K., Lechner, C.M., Blumenthal, A., & Korner, A. (2012). Changing contexts of youth development: An overview of recent social trends and a psychological model. *New Directions for Youth Development, 135,* 27–38.

Tomek, S., & others (2015, in press). Relations among suicidality, recent/frequent alcohol use, and gender in a Black American sample: A longitudinal investigation. *Journal of Clinical Psychology.*

Tomlinson-Keasey, C. (1972). Formal operations in females from 11 to 54 years of age. *Developmental Psychology, 6,* 364.

Tomova, A., Robeva, R., & Kumanov, P. (2015, in press). Influence of body weight on the onset and progression of puberty in boys. *Journal of Pediatric Endocrinology and Metabolism.*

Tompkins, T.L., Hockett, A.R., Abraibes, N., & Witt, J.L. (2011). A closer look at co-rumination: Gender, coping, peer functioning, and internalizing/externalizing problems. *Journal of Adolescence, 34,* 801–811.

Tornello, S.L., Riskind, R.G., & Patterson, C.J. (2014). Sexual orientation and sexual and reproductive health among adolescent young women in the United States. *Journal of Adolescent Health, 54,* 160–168.

Townsend, M. (2011). Motivation, learning, and instruction. In C.M. Rubie-Davies (Ed.), *Educational psychology*. New York: Routledge.

Tracey, T.J.G., Robbins, S.B., & Hofsess, C.D. (2005). Stability and change in interests: A longitudinal study of adolescents from grades 8 through 12. *Journal of Vocational Behavior, 66,* 1–25.

Trafimow, D., Triandis, H.C., & Goto, S.G. (1991). Some tests of the distinction between the private and collective self. *Journal of Personality and Social Psychology, 60,* 649–655.

Trahan, L.H., Stuebing, K.K., Fletcher, J.M., & Hiscock, M. (2014). The Flynn effect: A meta-analysis. *Psychological Bulletin, 140,* 1332–1360.

Trejos-Castillo, E., Bedore, S., & Trevino Schafer, N. (2013). Human capital development among immigrant youth. In E. Trejos-Castillo (Ed.), *Youth: Practices, perspectives, and challenges*. Hauppage, NY: Nova Science Publishers.

Triandis, H.C. (2007). Culture and psychology: A history of their relationship. In S. Kitayama & D. Cohen (Eds.), *Handbook of cultural psychology*. New York: Guilford.

Trinkner, R., Cohn, E.S., Rebellon, C.J., & Van Gundy, K. (2012). Don't trust anyone over 30: Parental legitimacy as a mediator between parenting style and changes in delinquent behavior over time. *Journal of Adolescence, 35,* 119–132.

Trochim, W., Donnelly, J.P., & Arora, K. (2016, in press). *Research methods: The essential knowledge base* (2nd ed.). Boston: Cengage.

Troop-Gordon, W., & Ladd, G.W. (2015). Teachers' victimization-related beliefs and strategies: Associations with students' aggressive behavior and peer victimization. *Journal of Abnormal Child Psychology, 43,* 1191–1202.

Trucco, E.M., Colder, C.R., & Wieczorek, W.F. (2011). Vulnerability to peer influence: A moderated mediation study of early adolescent alcohol initiation. *Addictive Behaviors, 36,* 729–736.

Trucco, E.M., & others (2014). Early adolescent alcohol use in context: How neighborhoods, parents, and peers impact youth. *Development and Psychopathology, 26,* 425–436.

Trzesniewski, K.H., & Donnellan, M.B. (2010). Rethinking "generation me": A study of cohort effects from 1976–2006. *Perspectives on Psychological Science, 5,* 58–75.

Trzesniewski, K.H., Donnellan, M.B., & Robins, R.W. (2008). Do today's young people really think they are so extraordinary? An examination of secular trends in narcissism and self-enhancement. *Psychological Science, 19,* 181–188.

Trzesniewski, K.H., & others (2006). Low self-esteem during adolescence predicts poor health, criminal behavior, and limited economic prospects during adulthood. *Developmental Psychology, 42,* 381–390.

Trzesniewski, M., Donnellan, M.B., & Robins, R.W. (2008). Is "Generation Me" really more narcissistic than previous generations? *Journal of Personality, 76,* 903–918.

Trzesniewski, M., Donnellan, M.B., & Robins, R.W. (2013). Development of self-esteem. In V. Zeigler-Hill (Ed.), *Self-esteem*. New York: Psychology Press.

Tschann, J.M., Flores, E., de Groat, C.L., Deardorff, J., & Wibbelsman, C.J. (2010). Condom negotiation strategies and actual condom use among Latino youth. *Journal of Adolescent Health, 47,* 254–262.

Tseng, V. (2004). Family interdependence and academic adjustment in college: Youth from immigrant and U.S. born families. *Child Development, 75,* 966–983.

Tsitsika, A.K., & others (2014). Bullying behaviors in children and adolescents: "An ongoing story." *Frontiers in Public Health, 2,* 7.

Ttofi, M.M., Farrington, D.P., Losel, F., & Loeber, R. (2011). The predictive efficiency of school bullying versus later offending: A systematic/meta-analytic review of longitudinal studies. *Criminal Behavior and Mental Health, 21,* 80–89.

Tu, W., & others (2015). Associations between menarche-related genetic variants and pubertal growth in male and female adolescents. *Journal of Adolescent Health, 56,* 66–72.

Tucker, C.J., McHale, S.M., & Crouter, A.C. (2001). Conditions of sibling support in adolescence. *Journal of Family Psychology, 15,* 254–271.

Tucker, C.J., & Winzeler, A. (2007). Adolescent siblings' daily discussions: Connections to perceived academic, athletic, and peer competency. *Journal of Research on Adolescence, 17,* 145–152.

Tucker, J.S., Edelen, M.O., Ellickson, P.L., & Klein, D.J. (2011). Running away from home: A longitudinal study of adolescent risk factors and adult outcomes. *Journal of Youth and Adolescence, 40,* 507–518.

Tucker, J.S., & others (2012). Resisting smoking when a best friend smokes: Do intrapersonal and contextual factors matter? *Journal of Research on Adolescence, 22,* 113–122.

Tung, R., & Ouimette, M. (2007). *Strong results, high demand: A four-year study of Boston's pilot high schools.* Boston: Center for Collaborative Education.

Turchik, J.A., & Hassija, C.M. (2014). Female sexual victimization among college students: Assault severity, health risk behaviors, and sexual functioning. *Journal of Interpersonal Violence, 29,* 2439–2457.

Turiel, E. (2014). Morality: Epistemology, development, and social opposition. In M. Killen & J.G. Smetana (Eds.), *Handbook of moral development* (2nd ed.). New York: Psychology Press.

Turiel, E. (2015). Moral development. In R.M. Lerner (Ed.), *Handbook of child psychology and developmental science* (7th ed.). New York: Wiley.

Turnbull, A., & others (2016, in press). *Exceptional lives* (8th ed.). Upper Saddle River, NJ: Pearson.

Tutone, M., Pantano, L., Lauria, A., & Almerico, A.M. (2014). Molecular dynamics, dynamic site mapping, and highthroughput virtual screening on leptin and the Ob receptor as anti-obesity target. *Journal of Molecular Medicine, 20*(5), 2247.

Twenge, J.M., & Campbell, W.K. (2001). Age and birth cohort differences in self-esteem: A cross-temporal meta-analysis. *Personality and Social Psychology Bulletin, 5,* 321–344.

Twenge, J.M., & Campbell, W.K. (2010). Birth cohort differences in the Monitoring the Future dataset and elsewhere: Further evidence for generation me—Commentary on Trzesniewski & Donnellan (2010). *Perspectives on Psychological Science, 5,* 81–88.

Twenge, J.M., Konrath, S., Foster, J.D., Campbell, W.K., & Bushman. B.J. (2008a). Egos inflating over time: A cross-temporal meta-analysis of the Narcissistic Personality Inventory. *Journal of Personality, 76,* 875–902.

Twenge, J.M., Konrath, S., Foster, J.D., Campbell, W.K., & Bushman, B.J. (2008b). Further evidence of an increase in narcissism among college students. *Journal of Personality, 76,* 919–928.

Tyler, K.A., Kort-Butler, L.A., & Swendener, A. (2014). The effect of victimization, mental health, and protective factors on crime and illicit drug use among homeless young adults. *Violence and Victims, 29,* 348–362.

U

U.S. Census Bureau (2010). *People.* Washington, DC: Author.

U.S. Census Bureau (2013). *Marriages, births, and deaths.* Washington, DC: U.S Department of Labor.

U.S. Census Bureau (2014). *Current population survey: Marriages and divorces.* Washington, DC: U.S. Department of Labor.

U.S. Department of Energy (2001). *The human genome project.* Washington, DC: Author.

Udry, J.R. (1990). Hormonal and social determinants of adolescent sexual initiation. In J. Bancroft & J.M. Reinisch (Eds.), *Adolescence and puberty.* New York: Oxford University Press.

Ueno, K., & McWilliams, S. (2010). Gender-typed behaviors and school adjustment. *Sex Roles, 63,* 580–591.

Uhart, M., Chong, R.Y., Oswald, L., Lin, P.I., & Wand, G.S. (2006). Gender differences in hypothalamic-pituitary-adrenal (HPA) axis reactivity. *Psychoneuroendocrinology, 31,* 642–652.

Ulloa, E.C., & Herrera, M. (2006). Strategies for multicultural student success: What about grad school? *Career Development Quarterly, 54,* 361–366.

Ulrich-French, S., & Smith, A.L. (2009). Social and motivational predictors of continued sports participation. *Psychology & Sports Exercise, 10,* 87–95.

Umana-Taylor, A.J., Wong, J.J., Gonzalez, N.A., & Dumka, L.E. (2012). Ethnic identity and gender as moderators of the association between discrimination and academic adjustment among Mexican-origin adolescents. *Journal of Adolescence, 35*(4), 773–786.

Underhill, K., Montgomery, P., & Operario, D. (2007). Sexual abstinence programs to prevent HIV infection in high-income countries. *British Medical Journal, 335,* 248.

Underwood, M.K. (2011). Aggression. In M.K. Underwood & L. Rosen (Eds.), *Social development.* New York: Guilford.

Underwood, M.K., & others (2012). The BlackBerry project: Capturing the content of adolescents' text messaging. *Developmental Psychology, 48,* 295–302.

Undheim, A.M. (2013). Involvement in bullying as predictor of suicidal ideation among 12- to 15-year-old Norwegian adolescents. *European Child and Adolescent Psychiatry, 22*(6), 357–365.

UNICEF (2003). *Annual report: 2002.* Geneva, Switzerland: Author.

UNICEF (2006). *The state of the world's children: 2006.* Geneva, Switzerland: Author.

UNICEF (2007). *The state of the world's children: 2007.* Geneva, Switzerland: Author.

UNICEF (2014). *The state of the world's children: 2014.* Geneva, Switzerland: Author.

UNICEF (2015). *The state of the world's children: 2015.* Geneva, Switzerland: Author.

University of Buffalo Counseling Services (2014). *Procrastination.* Retrieved November 20, 2014, from http://ub-counseling.buffalo.edu/stressprocrast.shtml

University of Illinois Counseling Center (1984). *Overcoming procrastination.* Urbana-Champaign, IL: Department of Student Affairs.

UNSTAT (2011). *Marriages and crude marriage rates.* Retrieved September 4, 2013, from http://unstats.un.org/unsd/demographic/products/dyb/dyb2011/Table23.pdf.

Updegraff, K.A., McHale, S., Whiteman, S.D., Thayer, S.M., & Delgado, M.Y. (2005). Adolescent sibling relationships in Mexican American families: Exploring the role of familism. *Journal of Family Psychology, 19,* 512–522.

Updegraff, K.A., & Umana-Taylor, A.J. (2015, in press). What can we learn from the study of Mexican-origin families in the United States? *Family Process.*

Updegraff, K.A., Umana-Taylor, A.J., McHale, S.M., Wheeler, L.A., & Perez-Brena, J. (2012). Mexican-origin youths' cultural orientations and adjustment: Changes from early to late adolescence. *Child Development, 83,* 1655–1671.

Urban, J.B., Lewin-Bizan, S., & Lerner, R.M. (2010). The role of intentional self-regulation, lower neighborhood ecological assets, and activity involvement in youth developmental outcomes. *Journal of Youth and Adolescence.*

Urdan, T. (2012). Factors affecting the motivation and achievement of immigrant students. In K.R. Harris, S. Graham, & T. Urdan (Eds.), *APA educational psychology handbook.* Washington, DC: American Psychological Association.

Urdan, T., & Midgley, C. (2001). Academic self-handicapping: What we know, what more there is to learn. *Educational Psychology Review, 13,* 115–138.

USA Today (2001, October 10). All-USA first teacher team. Retrieved November 20, 2004, from www.usatoday/com/news/education2001

V

Vakhtin, A.A., Ryman, S.G., Flores, R.A., & Jung, R.E. (2014). Functional brain networks contributing to the parieto-frontal integration theory of intelligence. *Neuroimage, 103C,* 349–354.

Valente, T.W., Fujimoto, K., Soto, D., Ritt-Olson, A., & Unger, J.B. (2013). A comparison of peer influence measures as predictors of smoking among predominately Hispanic/Latino high school adolescents. *Journal of Adolescent Health, 52*(3), 358–364.

Valero, S., & others (2014). Neuroticism and impulsivity: Their hierarchical organization in the personality characterization of drug-dependent patients from a decision tree learning perspective. *Comprehensive Psychiatry, 55,* 1227–1233.

Valkenburg, P.M., & Peter, J. (2009). Social consequences of the Internet for adolescents. *Current Directions in Psychological Science, 18,* 1–5.

Valkenburg, P.M., & Peter, J. (2011). Online communication among adolescents: An integrated model of its attraction, opportunities, and risks. *Journal of Adolescent Health, 48,* 121–127.

van de Weijer-Bergsma, E., Formsa, A.R., de Bruin, E.I., & Bogels, S.M. (2012). The effectiveness of mindfulness training on behavioral problems and attentional functioning in adolescents with ADHD. *Journal of Child and Family Studies, 21,* 775–787.

van den Berg, P., Neumark-Sztainer, D., Hannan, P.J., & Haines, J. (2007). Is dieting advice from magazines helpful or harmful? Five-year associations with weight control behaviors and psychological outcomes in adolescents. *Pediatrics, 119,* e30–e37.

van den Berg, Y.H., & Cillessen, A.H. (2014). Peer status and classroom seating arrangements: A social relations analysis. *Journal of Experimental Child Psychology, 130C,* 19–34.

van der Stel, M., & Veenman, M.V.J. (2010). Development of metacognitive skillfulness: A longitudinal study. *Learning and Individual Differences, 20,* 220–224.

Van Eeden-Moorefield, B., & Pasley, B.K. (2013). Remarriage and stepfamily life. In G.W. Peterson & K.R. Bush (Eds.), *Handbook of marriage and the family* (3rd ed.). New York: Springer.

van Geel, M., & Vedder, P. (2011). The role of family obligations and school adjustment in explaining the immigrant paradox. *Journal of Youth and Adolescence, 40*(2), 187–196.

van Geel, M., Vedder, P., & Tanilon, J. (2014). Relationship between peer victimization, cyberbullying, and suicide in children and adolescents: A meta-analysis. *JAMA Pediatrics, 168,* 435–442.

van Goethem, A.A.J., & others (2012). The role of adolescents' morality and identity in volunteering. Age and gender differences in the process model. *Journal of Adolescence, 35,* 509–520.

Van Goozen, S.H.M., Matthys, W., Cohen-Kettenis, P.T., Thisjssen, J.H.H., & van Engeland, H. (1998). Adrenal androgens and aggression in conduct disorder prepubertal boys and normal controls. *Biological Psychiatry, 43,* 156–158.

van IJzendoorn, M.H., Kranenburg, M.J., Pannebakker, F., & Out, D. (2010). In defense of situational morality: Genetic, dispositional, and situational determinants of children's donating to charity. *Journal of Moral Education, 39,* 1–20.

Van Lissa, C.J., & others (2015). Divergence between adolescent and parent perceptions of conflict in relationship to adolescent empathy development. *Journal of Youth and Adolescence, 44,* 48–51.

Van Ouytsel, J., Ponnet, K., & Walrave, M. (2014). The associations between adolescents' consumption of pornography and music videos and their sexting behavior. *Cyberpsychology, Behavior, and Social Networking, 17,* 772–778.

Van Petegem, S., Vansteenkiste, M., & Beyers, W. (2013). The jingle-jangle fallacy in adolescent autonomy in the family: In search of an underlying structure. *Journal of Youth and Adolescence, 42*(7), 992–1014.

Van Ryzin, M.J., & Dishion, T.J. (2013). From antisocial behavior to violence: A model for the amplifying role of coercive joining in adolescent friendships. *Journal of Child Psychology and Child Psychiatry, 54*(6), 661–669.

Van Ryzin, M.J., Johnson, A.B., Leve, L.D., & Kim, H.K. (2011). The number of sexual partners and health-risking sexual behavior: Prediction from high school entry to high school exit. *Archives of Sexual Behavior, 40,* 939–949.

Vandehey, M., Diekhoff, G., & LaBeff, E. (2007). College cheating: A 20-year follow-up and the addition of an honor code. *Journal of College Development, 48,* 468–480.

Vandell, D.L., Larson, R.W., Mahoney, J.L., & Watts, T. (2015). Children in organized activities. In R.M. Lerner (Ed.), *Handbook of child psychology and developmental science* (7th ed.). New York: Wiley.

Vandell, D.L., Minnett, A., & Santrock, J.W. (1987). Age differences in sibling relationships during middle childhood. *Applied Developmental Psychology, 8,* 247–257.

Vanhalst, J., Luyckx, K., & Goossens, L. (2014). Experiencing loneliness in adolescence: A matter of individual characteristics, negative peer experiences, or both? *Social Development, 23,* 100–118.

Vanhalst, J., Luyckx, K., Raes, F., & Goossens, L. (2012). Loneliness and depressive symptoms: The mediating and moderating role of uncontrollable ruminative thoughts. *Journal of Psychology, 146,* 259–276.

Vansteenkiste, M., Timmermans, T., Lens, W., Soenens, B., & Van den Broeck, A. (2008). Does extrinsic goal framing enhance extrinsic goal-oriented individuals' learning and performance? An experimental test of the match perspective versus self-determination theory. *Journal of Educational Psychology, 100,* 387–397.

Vasan, N. (2002). Commentary in "18-year-old inductees." Retrieved April 24, 2009, from http://thekidshalloffame.com/CustomPage19.html

Vasilenko, S.A., Kreager, D.A., & Lefkowitz, E.S. (2015). Gender, contraceptive attitudes, and condom use in adolescent romantic relationships: A dyadic approach. *Journal of Research on Adolescence, 25,* 51–62.

Vaughan, C.A., & Halpern, C.T. (2010). Gender differences in depressive symptoms during adolescence: The contributions of weight-related concerns and behaviors. *Journal of Research on Adolescence, 20,* 389–419.

Vaughn, M.G., Beaver, K.M., Wexler, J., DeLisi, M., & Roberts, G.J. (2011). The effect of school dropout on verbal ability in adulthood: A propensity score matching approach. *Journal of Youth and Adolescence, 40,* 197–206.

Vaughn, S.R., & Bos, C.S. (2015). *Strategies for teaching students with learning and behavior problems* (9th ed.). Upper Saddle River, NJ: Pearson.

Vaughn, S.R., Bos, C.S., & Schumm, J.S. (2014). *Teaching students who are exceptional, diverse, and at risk in the general education classroom* (6th ed.). Upper Saddle River, NJ: Pearson.

Vedder, P., & Phinney, J. (2014). Identity formation in bicultural youth. In V. Benet-Martinez & Y. Hong (Eds.), *Oxford handbook of multicultural identity.* New York: Oxford University Press.

Velez, C.E., Wolchik, S.A., Tein, J.Y., & Sandler, I. (2011). Protecting children from the consequences of divorce: A longitudinal study of the effects of parenting on children's coping responses. *Child Development, 82,* 244–257.

Verhaeghen, P. (2013). *The elements of cognitive aging: Meta-analyses of age-related differences in processing speed and their consequences.* New York: Oxford University Press.

Verhoef, M., van den Eijnden, R.J., Koning, I.M., & Vollebergh, W.A. (2014). Age at menarche and adolescent alcohol use. *Journal of Youth and Adolescence, 43,* 1333–1345.

Verkuyten, M. (2012). Understanding ethnic minority youth. In A.S. Masten & others (Eds.), *Realizing the potential of immigrant youth.* New York: Cambridge University Press.

Vermeersch, H., T'Sjoen, G., Kaufman, J.M., & Vincke, J. (2008). The role of testosterone in aggressive and non-aggressive risk-taking in boys. *Hormones and Behavior, 53,* 463–471.

Vernberg, E.M. (1990). Psychological adjustment and experience with peers during early adolescence: Reciprocal, incidental, or unidirectional relationships? *Journal of Abnormal Child Psychology, 18,* 187–198.

Veronneau, M.H., Racer, K.H., Fosco, G.M., & Dishion, T.J. (2014). The contribution of adolescent effortful control to early adult educational attainment. *Journal of Educational Psychology, 106,* 730–743.

Veronneau, M.H., Vitaro, F., Pedersen, S., & Tremblay, R.E. (2008). Do peers contribute to the likelihood of secondary graduation among disadvantaged boys? *Journal of Educational Psychology, 100,* 429–442.

Verstraeten, K., Vasey, M.W., Raes, F., & Bitjttebier, P. (2009). Temperament and risk for depressive symptoms in adolescence: Mediation by rumination and moderation by effortful control. *Journal of Abnormal Child Psychology, 37,* 349–361.

Veselka, L., Schermer, J.A., & Vernon, P.A. (2011). Beyond the big five: The Dark Triad and the supernumerary personality inventory. *Twin Research and Human Genetics, 14,* 158–168.

Vespa, J., Lewis, J.M., & Kreider, R.M. (2013, August). *America's families and living arrangements, 2012.* Washington, DC: U.S. Census Bureau.

Vetter, N.C., & others (2013). Ongoing development of social cognition in adolescence. *Child Neuropsychology, 19,* 615–629.

Villanti, A., Boulay, M., & Juon, H.S. (2011). Peer, parent, and media influences on adolescent smoking by developmental stage. *Addictive Behaviors, 36,* 133–136.

Villanueva, C.M., & Buriel, R. (2010). Speaking on behalf of others: A qualitative study of the perceptions and feelings of adolescent Latina language brokers. *Journal of Social Issues, 66,* 197–210.

Vitaro, F., Pedersen, S., & Brendgen, M. (2007). Children's disruptiveness, peer rejection, friends' deviancy, and delinquent behaviors: A process-oriented approach. *Development and Psychopathology, 19,* 433–453.

Vokey, M., Tefft, B., & Tysiaczny, C. (2013). An analysis of hyper-masculinity in magazine advertisements. *Sex Roles, 68,* 562–576.

Volpe, E.M., Hardie, T.L., Cerulli, C., Sommers, M.S., & Morrison-Beedy, D. (2013). What's age got to do with it? Partner age difference, power, intimate partner violence, and sexual risk in urban adolescents. *Journal of Interpersonal Violence, 28,* 2068–2087.

Vondracek, F.W., & Porfeli, E.J. (2003). The world of work and careers. In G. Adams & M. Berzonsky (Eds.), *Blackwell handbook of adolescence.* Malden, MA: Blackwell.

Vorona, R.D., & others (2014). Adolescent crash rates and school start times in two Central Virginia counties, 2009–2011: A follow-up study to a Southeastern Virginia study, 2007–2008. *Journal of Clinical Sleep Medicine, 10,* 1169–1177.

Vrangalova, Z. (2015a, in press). Does casual sex harm college students' well-being? A longitudinal investigation of the role of motivation. *Archives of Sexual Behavior.*

Vrangalova, Z. (2015b, in press). Hooking up and psychological well-being in college students: Short-term prospective links across different hookup definitions. *Journal of Sex Research.*

Vreeman, R.C., & Carroll, A.E. (2007). A systematic review of school-based interventions to prevent bullying. *Archives of Pediatric and Adolescent Medicine, 161,* 78–88.

Vuolo, M., Mortimer, J.T., & Staff, J. (2014). Adolescent precursors of pathways from school to work. *Journal of Research in Adolescence, 24,* 145–162.

Vuolo, M., Staff, J., & Mortimer, J.T. (2012). Weathering the great recession: Psychological and behavioral trajectories in the transition from school to work. *Developmental Psychology, 48,* 1759–1773.

Vygotsky, L.S. (1962). *Thought and language.* Cambridge, MA: MIT Press.

W

Wachs, T.D. (1994). Fit, context and the transition between temperament and personality. In C. Halverson, G. Kohnstamm, & R. Martin (Eds.), *The developing structure of personality from infancy to adulthood.* Hillsdale, NJ: Erlbaum.

Wachs, T.D. (2000). *Necessary but not sufficient.* Washington, DC: American Psychological Association.

Wachs, T.D., & Kohnstamm, G.A. (2013). The bidirectional nature of temperament-context links. In T.D. Wachs & others (Eds.), *Temperament in context.* New York: Psychology Press.

Wadsworth, M.E., Raviv, T., Santiago, C.D., & Etter, E.M. (2011). Testing the adaptation to poverty-related stress model: Predicting psychopathology symptoms in families facing economic hardship. *Journal of Clinical Child and Adolescent Psychology, 40,* 646–657.

Wainryb, C., & Recchia, H. (2014). Moral lives across cultures: Heterogeneity and conflict. In M. Killen & J.G. Smetana (Eds.), *Handbook of moral development* (2nd ed.). New York: Psychology Press.

Waite, L.J. (2009). Marriage. In D. Carr (Ed.), *Encyclopedia of the life course and human development.* Boston: Gale Cengage.

Waiter, G.D., & others (2009). Exploring possible neural mechanisms of intelligence differences using processing speed and working memory tasks. *Intelligence, 37,* 199–206.

Walfield, S.M. (2015, in press). When a cleared rape is not cleared: A multilevel study of arrest and exceptional clearance. *Journal of Interpersonal Violence.*

Walker, L.J. (2002). Moral exemplarity. In W. Damon (Ed.), *Bringing in a new era of character education.* Stanford, CA: Hoover Press.

Walker, L.J. (2014a). Moral personality, motivation, and identity. In M. Killen & J.G. Smetana (Eds.), *Handbook of moral development* (2nd ed.). New York: Routledge.

Walker, L.J. (2014b). Prosocial exemplarity in adolescence and adulthood. In L. Padilla-Walker & G. Carlos (Eds.), *The multidimensionality of prosocial behavior.* New York: Oxford University Press.

Walker, L.J., deVries, B., & Bichard, S.L. (1984). The hierarchical nature of stages of moral development. *Developmental Psychology, 20,* 960–966.

Walker, L.J., deVries, B., & Trevethan, S.D. (1987). Moral stages and moral orientation in real-life and hypothetical dilemmas. *Child Development, 58,* 842–858.

Walker, L.J., & Frimer, J.A. (2011). The science of moral development. In M.K. Underwood & L. Rosen (Eds.), *Social development.* New York: Guilford.

Walker, L.J., Frimer, J.A., & Dunlop, W.L. (2011). Varieties of moral personality: Beyond the banality of heroism. *Journal of Personality, 78(3),* 907–942.

Walker, L.J., & Hennig, K.H. (2004). Differing conceptions of moral exemplars: Just, brave, and caring. *Journal of Personality and Social Psychology, 86,* 629–647.

Walker, L.J., Hennig, K.H., & Krettenauer, R. (2000). Parent and peer contexts for children's moral reasoning development. *Child Development, 71,* 1033–1048.

Walker, L.J., Pitts, R.C., Hennig, K.H., & Matsuba, M.K. (1995). Reasoning about morality and real-life moral problems. In M. Killen & D. Hart (Eds.), *Morality in everyday life.* New York: Cambridge University Press.

Walker, L.J., & Taylor, J.H. (1991). Family interaction and the development of moral reasoning. *Child Development, 62,* 264–283.

Wallace-Broscious, A., Serafica, F.C., & Osipow, S.H. (1994). Adolescent career development: Relationships to self-concept and identity status. *Journal of Research on Adolescence, 4,* 127–150.

Waller, B. (2006). Math interest and choice intentions of non-traditional African-American college students. *Journal of Vocational Behavior, 68,* 538–547.

Waller, E.M., & Rose, A.J. (2010). Adjustment trade-offs of co-rumination in mother-adolescent relationships. *Journal of Adolescence, 33,* 487–497.

Waller, E.M., & Rose, A.J. (2013). Brief report: Adolescents' co-rumination with mothers, co-rumination with friends, and internalizing symptoms. *Journal of Adolescence, 36,* 429–433.

Wallerstein, J.S. (2008). Divorce. In M.M. Haith & J.B. Benson (Eds.), *Encyclopedia of infant and early childhood development.* Oxford, UK: Elsevier.

Wallis, C. (2011). Performing gender: A content analysis of gender display in music videos. *Sex Roles, 64,* 160–172.

Walsh, J. (2008). Self-efficacy. In N.J. Salkind (Ed.), *Encyclopedia of educational psychology.* Thousand Oaks, CA: Sage.

Walsh, R. (2011). Lifestyle and mental health. *American Psychologist, 666,* 579–592.

Walsh, S.M., & Donaldson, R.E. (2010). Invited commentary: National Safe Place: Meeting the immediate needs of runaways and homeless youth. *Journal of Youth and Adolescence, 39,* 437–445.

Walter, C.A. (1986). *The timing of motherhood.* Lexington, MA: D.C. Heath.

Walton, K.E., & Roberts, B.W. (2004). On the relationship between substance abuse and personality traits: Abstainers are not maladjusted. *Journal of Research in Personality, 38,* 515–535.

Walvoord, E.C. (2010). The timing of puberty: Is it changing? Does it matter? *Journal of Adolescent Health, 47,* 433–439.

Wandersman, A., & Florin, P. (2003). Community interventions and effective prevention. *American Psychologist, 58,* 441–448.

Wang, B., & others (2014). The impact of youth, family, peer, and neighborhood risk factors on developmental trajectories of risk involvement from early through middle adolescence. *Social Science Medicine, 106,* 43–52.

Wang, H., Fu, J., Lu, Q., Tao, F., & Hao, J. (2014). Physical activity, body mass index, and mental health in Chinese adolescents: A population based study. *Journal of Sports Medicine and Physical Fitness, 54,* 518–525.

Wang, J.Q. (2000, November). *A comparison of two international standards to assess child and adolescent obesity in three populations.* Paper presented at the meeting of the American Public Health Association, Boston.

Wang, K.T., Wong, Y.J., & Fu, C.C. (2013). Moderation effects of perfectionism and discrimination on interpersonal factors and suicide ideation. *Journal of Counseling Psychology, 60,* 367–378.

Wang, L.Y., Chyen, D., Lee, L., & Lowry, R. (2008). The association between body mass index in adolescence and obesity in adulthood. *Journal of Adolescent Health, 42,* 512–518.

Wang, M.C., & others (2010). Exposure to comprehensive school intervention increases vegetable consumption. *Journal of Adolescent Health, 47,* 74–82.

Wang, Q., & Pomerantz, E.M. (2009). The motivational landscape of early adolescence in the United States and China: A longitudinal study. *Child Development, 80,* 1272–1287.

Wang, W. (2014). *Record shares of Americans have never been married.* Washington, DC: Pew Research Center.

Wang, Y., & Benner, A.D. (2014). Parent-child discrepancies in educational expectations: Differential effects of actual versus perceived discrepancies. *Child Development, 85,* 891–900.

Ward, L.M. (2002). Does television exposure affect emerging adults' attitudes and assumptions about sexual relationships? Correlational and experimental confirmation. *Journal of Youth and Adolescence, 31,* 1–15.

Ward, L.M., Day, K.M., & Epstein, M. (2006). Uncommonly good: Exploring how mass media may be a positive influence on young women's sexual health and development. *New Directions for Child and Adolescent Development, 112,* 57–70.

Ward, L.M., & Friedman, K. (2006). Using TV as a guide: Associations between television viewing and adolescents' sexual attitudes and behavior. *Journal of Research on Adolescence, 16,* 133–156.

Ward, M.C., & Edelstein, M.D. (2014). *World full of women* (6th ed.). Upper Saddle River, NJ: Pearson.

Warren, J.T., & others (2010). Do depression and low self-esteem follow abortion among adolescents? Evidence from a national study. *Perspectives on Sexual and Reproductive Health, 42,* 230–235.

Warshak, R.A. (2008, January). Personal communication. Department of Psychology, University of Texas at Dallas, Richardson.

Warshak, R.A. (2014). Social science and parenting plans for young children: A consensus report. *Psychology, Public Policy, and the Law, 20,* 46–67.

Waszczuk, M.A., & others (2015, in press). A multivariate twin study of trait mindfulness, depressive symptoms, and anxiety sensitivity. *Depression and Anxiety.*

Waterman, A.S. (1985). Identity in the context of adolescent psychology. In A.S. Waterman (Ed.), *Identity in adolescence: Processes and contents.* San Francisco: Jossey-Bass.

Waterman, A.S. (1992). Identity as an aspect of optimal psychological functioning. In G.R. Adams, T.P. Gullotta, & R. Montemayor (Eds.), *Adolescent identity formation.* Newbury Park, CA: Sage.

Waterman, A.S. (2015). Identity as internal processes: How the "I" comes to define the "me." In K.C. McLean & M. Syed (Eds.), *Oxford handbook of identity development.* New York: Oxford University Press.

Waters, E., & others (2011). Interventions for preventing obesity in children. *Cochrane Database of Systematic Reviews, 7 (12),* CD001871.

Watson, D. (2012). Objective tests as instruments of psychological theory and research. In H. Cooper (Ed.), *APA handbook of research methods in psychology.* Washington, DC: American Psychological Association.

Watson, D.L., & Tharp, R.G. (2014). *Self-directed behavior* (10th ed.). Boston: Cengage.

Watson, G.L., Arcona, A.P., Antonuccio, D.O., & Healy, D. (2014). Shooting the messenger: The case of ADHD. *Journal of Contemporary Psychotherapy, 44,* 43–52.

Watson, J.B. (1930). *Behaviorism* (rev. ed.). Chicago: University of Chicago Press.

Watson, K.H., & others (2014). Observed parental responsiveness/warmth and children's coping: Cross-sectional and prospective relations in a family preventive intervention. *Journal of Family Psychology, 28,* 278–286.

Watt, H.M.G. (2008). Gender and occupational outcomes: An introduction. In H.M.G. Watt & J.S. Eccles (Eds.), *Gender and occupational outcomes.* Washington, DC: American Psychological Association.

Watt, H.M.G., & Eccles, J.S. (Eds.). (2008). *Gender and occupational outcomes.* Washington, DC: American Psychological Association.

Watt, H.M.G., Eccles, J.S., & Durik, A.M. (2006). The leaking mathematics pipeline for girls: A motivational analysis of high school enrollments in Australia and the United States. *Equal Opportunities International, 25,* 642–659.

Waugh, C.K., & Gronlund, N.E. (2013). *Assessment of student achievement* (10th ed.). Upper Saddle River, NJ: Pearson.

Way, N., & Silverman, L.R. (2012). The quality of friendships during adolescence: Patterns across context, culture, and age. In P.K. Kerig, M.S. Shulz, & S.T. Hauser (Eds.), *Adolescence and beyond.* New York: Oxford University Press.

Weaver. J.M., & Schofield, T.J. (2015). Mediation and moderation of divorce effects on children's behavior problems. *Journal of Family Psychology, 29,* 39–48.

Webster, N.S., & Worrell, F.C. (2008). Academically-talented adolescents' attitudes toward service in the community. *Gifted Child Quarterly, 52,* 170–179.

Wechsler, D. (1939). *The measurement of adult intelligence.* Baltimore: Williams & Wilkins.

Wechsler, H., Davenport, A., Sowdall, G., Moetykens, B., & Castillo, S. (1994). Health and behavioral consequences of binge drinking in college. *Journal of the American Medical Association, 272,* 1672–1677.

Weikert, D.P. (1993). *Long-term positive effects in the Perry Preschool Head Start program.* Unpublished data. High/Scope Foundation, Ypsilanti, MI.

Weiner, B. (2005). *Social motivation, justice, and the moral emotions.* Mahwah, NJ: Erlbaum.

Weinstein, N., Deci, E.L., & Ryan, R.M. (2012). Motivational determinants of integrating positive and negative past identities. *Journal of Personality and Social Psychology, 100,* 527–544.

Weinstock, H., Berman, S., & Cates, W. (2004). Sexually transmitted diseases among American youth: Incidence and prevalence estimates, 2000. *Perspectives on Sexual and Reproductive Health, 36,* 6–10.

Weissberg, R., & Caplan, M. (1989, April). *A follow-up study of a school-based social competence program for young adolescents.* Paper presented at the meeting of the Society for Research in Child Development, Kansas City.

Welch, K.J. (2014). *Family life now* (2nd ed.). Upper Saddle River, NJ: Pearson.

Welti, C. (2002). Adolescents in Latin America: Facing the future with skepticism. In B.B. Brown, R.W. Larson, & T.S. Saraswathi (Eds.), *The world's youth.* New York: Cambridge University Press.

Wemm, S., & others (2013). Problematic drinking and physiological responses among female college students. *Alcohol, 47,* 149–157.

Wentzel, K.R. (1997). Student motivation in middle school: The role of perceived pedagogical caring. *Journal of Educational Psychology, 89,* 411–419.

Wentzel, K.R. (2004). Unpublished review of J.W. Santrock's *Adolescence,* 11th ed. (New York: McGraw-Hill).

Wentzel, K.R. (2013). School adjustment. In I.B. Weiner & others (Eds.), *Handbook of psychology* (2nd ed., Vol. 7). New York: Wiley.

Wentzel, K.R. (2015). Socialization in school settings. In J.E. Grusec & P.D. Hastings (Eds.), *Handbook of socialization* (2nd ed.). New York: Guilford.

Wentzel, K.R., & Asher, S.R. (1995). The academic lives of neglected, rejected, popular, and controversial children. *Child Development, 66,* 754–763.

Wentzel, K.R., Barry, C.M., & Caldwell, K.A. (2004). Friendships in middle school: Influences on motivation and school adjustment. *Journal of Educational Psychology, 96,* 195–203.

Wentzel, K.R., & Caldwell, K. (1997). Close friend and group influence on adolescent cigarette smoking and alcohol use. *Child Development, 31,* 540–547.

Werner, N.E., Bumpus, M.F., & Rock, D. (2010). Involvement in Internet aggression during early adolescence. *Journal of Youth and Adolescence, 39,* 607–619.

Werner, R., & Holterhus, P.M. (2014). Androgen action. *Endocrine development, 27,* 28–40.

West, J.H., & others (2013). The role of parenting in alcohol and tobacco use among Latino adolescents. *Journal of Child and Adolescent Substance Abuse, 22,* 120–132.

Westermann, G., Thomas, M.S.C., & Karmiloff-Smith, A. (2011). Neuroconstructivism. In U. Goswami (Ed.), *Wiley-Blackwell handbook of childhood cognitive development* (2nd ed.). New York: Wiley.

Wetherill, R.R., Neal, D.J., & Fromme, K. (2010). Parents, peers, and sexual values influence sexual behavior during the transition to college. *Archives of Sexual Behavior, 39,* 682–694.

Whetstone, L.M., Morrissey, S.L., & Cummings, D.M. (2007). Children at risk: The association between weight status and suicidal thoughts and attempts in middle school youth. *Journal of School Health, 77,* 59–66.

White, E., Slane, J.D., Klump, K.L., Burt, S.A., & Pivarnik, J. (2014). Sex differences in genetic and environmental influences on percent body fatness and physical activity. *Journal of Physical Activity and Health, 11,* 1187–1193.

White, M. (1993). *The material child: Coming of age in Japan and America.* New York: Free Press.

White, M.A., & Grilo, C.M. (2011). Diagnostic efficiency of DSM-IV indicators for binge eating episodes. *Journal of Consulting and Clinical Psychology, 79,* 75–83.

Whitehead, K.A., Ainsworth, A.T., Wittig, M.A., & Gadino, B. (2009). Implications of ethnic identity exploration and ethnic identity affirmation and belonging for intergroup attitudes among adolescents. *Journal of Research on Adolescence, 19,* 123–135.

Whiteman, S.D., Jensen, A.C., & Maggs, J.L. (2013). Similarities in adolescent siblings' substance use: Testing competing pathways of influence. *Journal of Studies on Alcohol and Drugs, 74,* 104–113.

Whiteman, S.D., McHale, S.M., & Soli, A. (2011). Theoretical perspectives on sibling relationships. *Journal of Family Theory and Review, 3,* 124–139.

Whiting, B.B. (1989, April). *Culture and interpersonal behavior.* Paper presented at the meeting of the Society for Research in Child Development, Kansas City.

Whitton, S.W., & others (2008). Prospective associations from family-of-origin interactions to adult marital interactions and relationship adjustment. *Journal of Family Psychology, 22,* 274–286.

Widiger, T.A. (2009). Neuroticism. In M.R. Leary & R.H. Hoyle (Eds.), *Handbook of individual differences in social behavior.* New York: Guilford.

Widman, L., & others (2014). Sexual communication between early adolescents and their dating partners, parents, and best friends. *Journal of Sexual Research, 51,* 731–741.

Wiencke, J.K., & others (1999). Early age at smoking initiation and tobacco carcinogen DNA damage in the lung. *Journal of the National Cancer Institute, 91,* 614–619.

Wigfield, A., & Cambria, J. (2010). Students' achievement values, goal orientations, and interest: Definitions, development, and relations to achievement outcomes. *Developmental Review, 30,* 1–35.

Wigfield, A., & Eccles, J.S. (1989). Test anxiety in elementary and secondary school students. *Journal of Educational Psychology, 24,* 159–183.

Wigfield, A., Eccles, J.S., Schiefele, U., Roeser, R., & Davis-Kean, P. (2006). Development of achievement motivation. In W. Damon & R. Lerner (Eds.), *Handbook of child psychology* (6th ed.). New York: Wiley.

Wigfield, A., Klauda, S.L., & Cambria, J. (2011). Motivational sources and outcomes of self-regulated learning and performance. In B.J. Zimmerman & D.H. Schunk (Eds.), *Handbook of self-regulation of learning and performance.* New York: Routledge.

Wigfield, A., & others (2015). Development of achievement motivation and engagement. In R.M. Lerner (Ed.), *Handbook of child psychology and developmental science* (7th ed.). New York: Wiley.

Willett, W. (2013). The current evidence on healthy eating. *Annual Review of Public Health, 34,* 77–95.

William T. Grant Foundation Commission on Work, Family, and Citizenship (1988, February). *The forgotten half: Noncollege-bound youth in America.* New York: William T. Grant Foundation.

Williams, A.L., & Merten, M.J. (2009). Adolescents' online social networking following the death of a peer. *Journal of Adolescent Research, 24,* 67–90.

Williams, J.F., Burton, R.S., & Warzinski, S.S. (2014). The role of the parent in adolescent substance use. *Pediatric Annals, 43*(10), 410.

Williams, K.M., Nathanson, C., & Paulhus, D.L. (2010). Identifying and profiling academic cheaters: Their personality, cognitive ability, and motivation. *Journal of Experimental Psychology: Applied, 16,* 293–307.

Williamson, H.C., Trail, T.E., Bradbury, T.N., & Karney, B.R. (2014). Does premarital education decrease or increase couples' later help-seeking? *Journal of Family Psychology, 28,* 112–117.

Wilson, L.C., & Miller, K.E. (2015, in press). Meta-analysis of the prevalence of unacknowledged rape. *Trauma, Violence, and Abuse.*

Wilson, S., & others (2014). Premorbid risk factors for major depressive disorder: Are they associated with early onset and recurrent course? *Development and Psychopathology, 26,* 1477–1493.

Wilson-Shockley, S. (1995). *Gender differences in adolescent depression: The contribution of negative affect.* Unpublished master's thesis, University of Illinois at Urbana-Champaign.

Winerman, L. (2005). Leading the way. *Monitor on Psychology, 36,* 64–67.

Winn, I.J. (2004). The high cost of uncritical teaching. *Phi Delta Kappan, 85,* 496–497.

Winner, E. (1996). *Gifted children: Myths and realities.* New York: Basic Books.

Winner, E. (2006). Development in the arts. In W. Damon & R. Lerner (Eds.), *Handbook of child psychology* (6th ed.). New York: Wiley.

Winner, E. (2009). Toward broadening our understanding of giftedness: The spatial domain. In F.D. Horowitz, R.F. Subotnik, & D.J. Matthews (Eds.), *The development of giftedness and talent across the life span.* Washington, DC: American Psychological Association.

Winner, E. (2014). Child prodigies and adult genius. In D.K. Simonton (Ed.), *Wiley-Blackwell handbook of genius.* New York: Wiley-Blackwell.

Winsper, C., Lereya, T., Zanarini, M., & Wolke, D. (2012). Involvement in bullying and suicide-related behavior at 11 years: A prospective birth cohort study. *Journal of the Academy of Child and Adolescent Psychiatry, 51,* 271–282.

Witelson, S.F., Kigar, D.L., & Harvey, T. (1999). The exceptional brain of Albert Einstein. *The Lancet, 353,* 2149–2153.

Witkow, M.R., & Fuligni, A.J. (2010). In-school versus out-of-school friendships and academic achievement among an ethnically diverse sample of adolescents. *Journal of Research on Adolescence, 20,* 631–650.

Woelders, L.C.S., Larsen, J.K., Scholte, R., Cillessen, T., & Engles, R.C.M.E. (2010). Friendship group influences on body dissatisfaction and dieting among adolescent girls: A prospective study. *Journal of Adolescent Health, 47* (5), 456–462.

Wolak, J., Mitchell, K., & Finkelhor, D. (2007). Unwanted and wanted exposure to online pornography in a national sample of youth Internet users. *Pediatrics, 119,* 247–257.

Wolfinger, N.H. (2011). More evidence for trends in the intergenerational transmission of divorce: A completed cohort approach using data from the general social survey. *Demography, 48,* 581–592.

Wolfson, A.R. (2010). Adolescents' emerging adults' sleep patterns: New developments. *Journal of Adolescent Health, 46,* 97–99.

Wolke, D., & Lereya, S.T. (2015, in press). Long-term effects of bullying. *Archives of Disease in Childhood.*

Women in Academia (2011). *A historical summary of gender differences in college enrollment rates.* Retrieved June 12, 2011, from www.wiareport.com

Wong Briggs, T. (1999, October 14). Honorees find keys to unlocking kids' minds. Retrieved July 22, 2004, from www.usatoday.com/education/1999

Wong Briggs, T. (2005, October 13). USA Today's 2005 all-USA teacher team. *USA Today,* p. 6D.

Wong Briggs, T. (2007, February 14). *Academic skills meet the world.* Retrieved February 1, 2008, from www.usatoday.com/news/education/2007-02-14-all-starscover_x.htm

Wong, A.P., & others (2014). Estimating volume of the pituitary gland from T1-weighted magnetic-resonance images: Effects of age, puberty, testosterone, and estradiol. *Neuroimage, 94,* 216–221.

Wong, M.D., & others (2014). Successful schools and risky behaviors among low-income adolescents. *Pediatrics, 134,* e389–e396.

Wood, C., Angus, C., Pretty, J., Sandercock, G., & Barton, J. (2012). A randomized control trial of physical activity in a perceived environment on self-esteem and mood in UK adolescents. *International Journal of Environmental Health Research, 2012,* 1–10.

Wood, D., Harms, P., & Vazire, S. (2010). Perceiver effects as projective tests: What your perceptions of others say about you. *Journal of Personality and Social Psychology, 99,* 174–190.

Wood, D., Larson, R.W., & Brown, J.R. (2009). How adolescents come to see themselves as more responsible through participation in youth programs. *Child Development, 80,* 295–309.

Woodruff, S.J., Hanning, R.M., McGoldrick, K., & Brown, K.S. (2010). Healthy eating index-C is positively associated with family dinner frequency among students in grades 6–8 from Southern Ontario, Canada. *European Journal of Clinical Nutrition, 64,* 454–460.

Woolgar, M., & Scott, S. (2013). The negative consequences of over-diagnosing attachment disorders in adopted children: The importance of comprehensive formulations. *Clinical Child Psychology and Psychiatry, 19,* 355–366.

World Health Organization (2000). *The world health report.* Geneva: Author.

Wormington, S.V., Corpus, J.H., & Anderson, K.G. (2012). A person-centered investigation of academic motivation and its correlates in high school. *Learning and Individual Differences, 22,* 429–438.

Wu, X., Tao, S., Zhang, Y., Zhang, S., & Tao, F. (2015). Low physical activity and high screen time can increase the risks of mental health problems and poor sleep quality among Chinese college students. *PLoS One, 10,* e119607.

Wuest, D., & Fisette, J. (2015). *Foundations of physical education, exercise science, and sport* (18th ed.). New York: McGraw-Hill.

Wulach, J.S., & Shapiro, D.L. (2013). Ethical and legal considerations in child custody evaluations. In L. Gunsberg & P. Hymowitz (Eds.), *A handbook of divorce and custody.* New York: Psychology Press.

X

Xanthopoulos, M.S., & Daniel, L.C. (2013). Coping and social support. In I.B. Weiner & others (Eds.), *Handbook of psychology* (2nd ed., Vol. 9). New York: Wiley.

Xanthopoulos, M.S., & others (2013). The association between weight loss in caregivers and adolescents in a treatment trial of adolescents with obesity. *Journal of Pediatric Psychology, 38,* 766–774.

Xia, N. (2010). *Family factors and student outcomes.* Unpublished doctoral dissertation, RAND Corporation, Pardee RAND Graduate School, Pittsburgh.

Xia, Y.R., Kieu, A.D., & Xie, X. (2013). The adjustment of Asian American families in the U.S. context: The ecology of strengths and stresses. In G.W. Peterson & K.R. Bush (Eds.), *Handbook of marriage and the family* (3rd ed.). New York: Springer.

Y

Yan, L., Cheung, R., & Cummings, E.M. (2015, in press). Marital conflict and emotional insecurity among Chinese adolescents: Cultural value moderation. *Journal of Research on Adolescence.*

Yancey, A.K., Grant, D., Kurosky, S., Kravitz-Wirtz, N., & Mistry, R. (2011). Role modeling, risk, and resilience in California adolescents. *Journal of Adolescent Health, 48,* 36–43.

Yang, C., & Brown, B. (2009, April). *From Facebook to cell calls: Layers of electronic intimacy in college students' peer relations.* Paper presented at the meeting of the Society for Research in Child Development, Denver.

Yang, C., & Brown, B. (2013). Motives for using Facebook, patterns of Facebook activities, and late adolescents' social adjustment to college. *Journal of Youth and Adolescence, 42*(3), 403–416.

Yao, C.A., & Rhodes, R.E. (2015, in press). Parental correlates in child and adolescent physical activity: A meta-analysis. *International Journal of Behavioral Nutrition and Physical Activity.*

Yap, M.B., Pilkington, P.D., Ryan, S.M., & Jorm, A.F. (2014). Parental factors associated with depression and anxiety in young people: A systematic review and meta-analysis. *Journal of Affective Disorders, 156,* 8–23.

Yap, M.B., & others (2014a). Parenting strategies for reducing the risk of adolescent depression and anxiety disorders: A Delphi consensus study. *Journal of Affective Disorders, 156,* 67–75.

Yap, M.B., & others (2014b). Parental factors associated with depression and anxiety in young people: A systematic review and meta-analysis. *Journal of Affective Disorders, 156,* 8–23.

Yarber, W., Sayad, B., & Strong, B. (2013). *Human sexuality* (8th ed.). New York: McGraw-Hill.

Ybarra, M.L., & Mitchell, K.J. (2014). "Sexting" and its relation to sexual activity and sexual risk behavior in a national survey of adolescents. *Journal of Adolescent Health, 55,* 757–764.

Ybarra, M.L., Strasburger, V.C., & Mitchell, K.J. (2014). Sexual media exposure, sexual behavior, and sexual violence victimization in adolescence. *Clinical Pediatrics, 53,* 1239–1247.

Yen, C.F., & others (2014). Association between school bullying levels/types and mental health problems among Taiwanese adolescents. *Comprehensive Psychiatry, 55,* 405–413.

Yen, H.L., & Wong, J.T. (2007). Rehabilitation for traumatic brain injury to children and adolescents. *Annals of the Academy of Medicine Singapore, 36,* 62–66.

Yen, S., & Martin, S. (2013). Contraception for adolescents. *Pediatric Annals, 42,* 21–25.

Yen, S., & others (2013). Prospective predictors of adolescent suicidality: 6-month post-hospitalization follow-up. *Psychological Medicine, 43*(6), 983–993.

Yeung, L.F., & others (2014). Conclusions and future directions for periodic reporting on the use of selected clinical preventive services to improve the health of infants, children, and adolescents—United States. *MMWR Surveillance Summaries, 63,* 99–107.

Yin, R.K. (2012). Case study methods. In H. Cooper (Ed.), *APA handbook of research methods in psychology.* Washington, DC: American Psychological Association.

Yip, T. (2015). The effects of ethnic/racial discrimination and sleep quality on depressive symptoms and self-esteem trajectories among diverse adolescents. *Journal of Youth and Adolescence, 44,* 419–430.

Yochum, C., & others (2014). Prenatal cigarette smoke exposure causes hyperactivity and aggressive behavior: Role of catecholamines and BDNF. *Experimental Neurology, 254C,* 145–152.

Yokoyama, A., & others (2013). Trends in gastrectomy and ADH1B and ALDH2 genotypes in Japanese alcoholic men and their gene-gastrectomy, gene-gene, and gene-age interactions. *Alcohol and Alcoholism, 48,* 146–152.

Yonker, J.E., Schnabelrauch, C.A., & DeHaan, L.G. (2012). The relationship between spirituality and religiosity on psychological outcomes in adolescents and emerging adults: A meta-analytic review. *Journal of Adolescence, 35,* 299–314.

Yoo, H., Feng, X., & Day, R.D. (2013). Adolescents' empathy and prosocial behavior in the family context: A longitudinal study. *Journal of Youth and Adolescence, 42,* 1858–1872.

Yoshikawa, H. (2012). *Immigrants raising citizens: Undocumented parents and their young children.* New York: Russell Sage.

Young, B.J., Furman, W., & Laursen, B. (2014). Models of change and continuity in romantic experiences. In F.D. Fincham, & M. Cui (Eds.), *Romantic relationships in emerging adulthood.* New York: Cambridge University Press.

Young, M.A., & Vazsonyi, A.T. (2011). Parents, peers, and risky sexual behaviors in rural African American adolescents. *Journal of Genetic Psychology, 172,* 84–93.

Youngblade, L.M., & Curry, L.A. (2006). The people they know: Links between interpersonal contexts and adolescent risky and health-promoting behavior. *Developmental Science, 10,* 96–106.

Youngblade, L.M., Curry, L.A., Novak, M., Vogel, B., & Shenkman, E.A. (2006). The impact of community risks and resources on adolescent risky behavior and health care expenditures. *Journal of Adolescent Health, 38,* 486–494.

Youniss, J., McLellan, J.A., & Yates, M. (1999). Religion, community service, and identity in American youth. *Journal of Adolescence, 22,* 243–253.

Youniss, J., & Ruth, A.J. (2002). Approaching policy for adolescent development in the 21st century. In J.T. Mortimer & R.W. Larson (Eds.), *The changing adolescent experience.* New York: Cambridge University Press.

Yu, T., Pettit, G.S., Lansford, J.E., Dodge, K.A., & Bates, J.E. (2010). The interactive effects of marital conflict and divorce on parent-adult children's relationships. *Journal of Marriage and the Family, 72,* 282–292.

Yuan, A.S.V. (2010). Body perceptions, weight control behavior, and changes in adolescents' psychological well-being over time: A longitudinal examination of gender. *Journal of Youth and Adolescence, 39,* 927–939.

Yun, I., Cheong, J., & Walsh, A. (2014). The relationship between academic achievement and the likelihood of police arrest among delinquents. *International Journal of Offender Therapy and Comparative Criminology, 58,* 1107–1131.

Yussen, S.R. (1977). Characteristics of moral dilemmas written by adolescents. *Developmental Psychology, 13,* 162–163.

Z

Zack, S.E., & others (2015, in press). Attachment history as a moderator of the alliance outcome relationship in adolescents. *Psychotherapy.*

Zaff, J.F., Hart, D., Flanagan, C., Youniss, J., & Levine, P. (2010). Developing civic engagement within a civic context. In M.E. Lamb, A.M. Freund, & R.M. Lerner (Eds.), *Handbook of life-span development* (Vol. 2). New York: Wiley.

Zager, K., & Rubenstein, A. (2002). *The inside story on teen girls.* Washington, DC: American Psychological Association.

Zannas, A.S., & others (2012). Stressful life events, perceived stress, and 12-month course of geriatric depression: Direct effects and moderation by the 5-HTTLPR and COMT Val158Met polymorphisms. *Stress, 15*(4), 425–434.

Zarrett, N., & others (2009). More than child's play: Variable- and pattern-centered approaches for examining effects of sports participation on youth development. *Developmental Psychology, 45,* 368–382.

Zayas, L., Guibas, L.E., Fedoravicius, N., & Cabassa, L.J. (2010). Patterns of distress, precipitating events, and reflections on suicide attempts by young Latinas. *Social Science & Medicine, 70,* 1773–1779.

Zayas, V., Mischel, W., & Pandey, G. (2014). Mind and brain in delay of gratification. In V.F. Reyna & V. Zayas (Eds.), *The neuroscience of decision making.* Washington, DC: American Psychological Associaton.

Zeanah, C.H., & Gleason, M.M. (2015). Annual research review: Attachment disorders in early childhood—clinical presentation, causes, correlates, and treatments. *Journal of Child Psychology and Psychiatry, 57,* 207–222.

Zeeck, A., Stelzer, N., Linster, H.W., Joos, A., & Hartmann, A. (2010). Emotion and eating in binge eating disorder and obesity. *European Eating Disorders Review, 19,* 426–437.

Zehe, J.M., & Colder, C.R. (2014). A latent growth curve analysis of alcohol-use specific parenting and parent alcohol use. *Addictive Behaviors, 39,* 1701–1705.

Zeiders, K.H., Umana-Taylor, A.J., Updegraff, K.A., & Jahromi, L.B. (2015). Acculturative and enculturative stress, depressive symptoms, and maternal warmth: Examining within-person relations among Mexican-origin adolescent mothers. *Development and Psychopathology, 27,* 293–308.

Zeifman, D., & Hazan, C. (2008). Pair bonds as attachments: Reevaluating the evidence. In J. Cassidy & P.R. Shaver (Eds.), *Handbook of attachment* (2nd ed.). New York: Guilford.

Zeigler-Hill, V. (2013). The current state of research concerning self-esteem. In V. Zeigler-Hill (Ed.), *Self-esteem.* New York: Psychology Press.

Zelazo, P.D. (2013). Developmental psychology: A new synthesis. In P.D. Zelazo (Ed.), *Oxford handbook of developmental psychology.* New York: Oxford University Press.

Zelazo, P.D., & Lyons, K.E. (2012). The potential benefits of mindfulness training in early childhood: A developmental social cognitive perspective. *Child Development Perspectives, 6,* 154–160.

Zeng, R., & Greenfield, P.M. (2015). Cultural evolution over the last 40 years in China: Using the Google Ngram viewer to study implications of social and political change for cultural values. *International Journal of Psychology, 50,* 47–55.

Zhang, F., & others (2014). Friendship quality, social preference, proximity prestige, and self-perceived social competence: Interactive influences on children's loneliness. *Journal of School Psychology, 52,* 511–526.

Zhang, L-F., & Sternberg, R.J. (2012). Learning in cross-cultural perspective. In T. Husen & T.N. Postlethwaite (Eds.), *International encyclopedia of education* (3rd ed.). New York: Elsevier.

Zhou, Q. (2013). Commentary in S. Smith, "Children of 'tiger parents' develop more aggression and depression, research shows." Retrieved July 20, 2013, from http://www.cbsnews.com/news/children-of-tiger-parents-develop-more-aggression-and-depression-research-shows/

Zhou, Q., & others (2012). Asset and protective factors for Asian American children's mental health adjustment. *Child Development Perspectives, 6,* 312–319.

Zhu, S., Tse, S., Cheung, S.H., & Oyserman, D. (2014). Will I get there? Effects of parental support on children's possible selves. *British Journal of Educational Psychology, 84,* 435–453.

Zill, N., Morrison, D.R., & Coiro, M.J. (1993). Long-term effects of parental divorce on parent-child relationships, adjustment, and achievement in young adulthood. *Journal of Family Psychology, 7,* 91–103.

Zimmer-Gembeck, M.J., & Skinner, E.A. (2011). The development of coping across childhood and adolescence: An integrative review and critique of research. *International Journal of Behavioral Development, 35,* 1–17.

Zimmerman, B.J. (2002). Becoming a self-regulated learner: An overview. *Theory into Practice, 41,* 64–70.

Zimmerman, B.J. (2012). Motivational sources and outcomes of self-regulated learning and performance. In B.J. Zimmerman & D.H. Schunk (Eds.), *Handbook of self-regulation of learning and performance.* New York: Routledge.

Zimmerman, B.J., & Kitsantas, A. (1997). Developmental phases in self-regulation: Shifting from process goals to outcome goals. *Journal of Educational Psychology, 89,* 29–36.

Zimmerman, B.J., & Labuhn, A.S. (2012). Self-regulation of learning: Process approaches to personal development. In K.R. Harris & others (Eds.), *APA handbook of educational psychology.* Washington, DC: American Psychological Association.

Zinzow, H.M., & others (2010). Drug- or alcohol-facilitated, incapacitated, and forcible rape in relationship to mental health among a national sample of women. *Journal of Interpersonal Violence, 25,* 2217–2236.

Zittleman, K. (2006, April). *Being a girl and being a boy: The voices of middle schoolers.* Paper presented at the meeting of the American Educational Research Association, San Francisco.

Zuberer, A., Brandeis, D., & Drechsler, R. (2015). Are treatments for neurofeedback training in children with ADHD related to successful regulation of brain activity? A review on the learning of regulation of brain activity and a contribution to the discussion on specificity. *Frontiers in Human Neuroscience, 9,* 135.

Zulauf, C.A., Sprich, S.E., Safren, S.A., & Wilens, T.E. (2014). The complicated relationship between attention-deficit/hyperactivity disorder and substance use disorders. *Current Psychiatry Reports, 16*(3), 436.

Name Index

Subject Index

Obesity, 422–423, 460, 464–469
Observation, 32
Online dating, 323, 324
On the Origin of Species (Darwin), 74
Openness, 156, 157
Operant conditioning (Skinner), 30
Opiates, 450–451
Optimal experiences, 372–373
Optimism, 157–158
Oral sex, 195–196
Other-sex friendship, 311
Overweight and obese adolescents, 422–423, 460, 464–469. *See also* Obesity

Painkillers, prescription, 451
Parental monitoring, 265
Parenting styles
  authoritarian, 266, 292, 383–384, 457
  authoritative, 238, 266, 267, 286, 448, 457
  caveats on, 268
  culture and ethnicity and, 267–268
  differences between mothers and fathers, 268–269
  indulgent, 267
  moral development and, 244–245
  neglectful, 266–267
Parents/parenting. *See also* Families; Fathers; Mothers
  achievement and, 349–350, 380, 383–384
  adolescent autonomy and, 271–274
  adolescent depression and, 460
  adolescents as, 209, 210
  of adopted adolescents, 290–291
  attachment and connectedness to, 274–277
  career development and, 395
  changes in, 262
  conflict between, 285–286
  conflict with, 269–271
  coparents, 269, 292
  discipline techniques of, 245
  drug abuse and, 448, 452
  eating disorders and, 464, 467
  ethnicity and, 292–294
  exercise patterns and, 69
  expectations of, 376
  gender influences and, 168–169
  identity and, 148–149
  Internet use regulation by, 428
  juvenile delinquency and, 287, 455–457
  as managers, 264–266
  moral development and, 235, 244–246
  prosocial behavior and, 238
  relationship between adolescents and, 260–261
  relationship between emerging adults and, 277–279
  sexual minorities as, 291–292
  sibling favoritism and, 281
  working, 289–290
Part-time work, 388–389

Passive genotype-environment correlations, 79–80
The Path to Purpose (Damon), 6, 144, 379, 393
Peer attachment, 316
Peer groups
  in childhood and adolescence, 313
  cliques and crowds, 313–314
  culture and, 317–318, 353
  gender and, 169–170, 316–317, 325–326
  socioeconomic status and ethnicity and, 317
  youth organizations, 314–415
Peer pressure, 302, 304
Peers/peer relations. *See also* Friendship
  achievement and, 350–352, 380–381
  bullying and, 351, 352
  career development and, 395
  contexts and, 301–302
  depression and, 460
  emotional regulation and, 307
  exercise patterns and, 69
  explanation of, 301
  family influences and, 303–304
  gender socialization and, 169–170
  global perspectives on, 14
  identity and, 149
  individual difference factors and, 302
  influences of, 302–303
  peer statuses and, 304–306
  positive and negative, 302–303, 435–436
  runaways and, 273
  secure parental attachment and, 304
  sexual behavior and, 198
  social cognition and, 306–307
  social skills and, 307–308
  substance use and, 448–450
  suicide and, 462
  time spent with, 302
Peer statuses
  achievement and, 350
  explanation of, 304–305
  types of, 305–306
Perfectionism, 385–386, 467–468
Permissive strategy of classroom management, 347
Perry Preschool approach, 470–471
Personal choice, 372
Personal fable, 122, 123
Personality
  Big Five factors of, 156–157
  explanation of, 156
  Freud and, 26
  optimism and, 157–158
  romantic relationships and, 323
  temperament and, 158–161
  traits and situations and, 158
Person-environment fit, 348
Perspective taking, 135–136, 356
Phenotype, 78
Physical activity. *See* Exercise
Physical attractiveness, 323. *See also* Body image

Physiological measures, 33
Piaget's cognitive development theory
  cognitive processes and, 92–93
  evaluation of, 29, 95–96
  explanation of, 28
  stages of, 28–29, 93–95
  Vygotsky's theory vs., 100
Pituitary gland, 51, 52
Planning, 114
Plasticity, of brain, 91
Popular children, 305
Pornography, 201
Positive Action program, 412
Positive thinking, 443, 445
Positive youth development (PYD)
  adolescent sexuality and, 199
  explanation of, 8
  personal assets that facilitate, 20
Possible self, 132, 134
Postconventional reasoning (Kohlberg), 231–2232
Postformal thought, 97–98
Poverty. *See also* Socioeconomic status (SES)
  adolescent sexual activity and, 198, 199
  education of students living in, 353–355
  ethnic minorities and, 418–419
  feminization of, 412
  nature of, 410–411
  risks related to, 411, 436
  statistics for youth living in, 11–12, 410
  strategies to counter negative effects of, 412, 413
  stress and, 442
Power assertion, 244
Practical intelligence, 117, 118
Pragmatic thinking, 97
Praise, 372
Precocious puberty, 56
Preconventional reasoning (Kohlberg), 230
Prefrontal cortex, 63, 88–90, 191
Pregaming, 447
Pregnancy. *See* Adolescent pregnancy
Prejudice
  against ethnic minorities, 10
  explanation of, 419
Premarital education, 331
Prenatal period, 15
Preoccupied/ambivalent attachment, 274–275
Preoperational stage (Piaget), 28–29, 93
Prescription painkillers, 451
Problem-focused coping, 442
Problems. *See* Adolescent and emerging adult problems
Procrastination, 384–386
Professional journals, 36–38
Prosocial behavior
  explanation of, 237–238
  gender and, 177–178
  research on, 238–239
  types of, 238

Psychoanalytic theory
  Erikson's psychosocial, 27–28, 239–240
  evaluation of, 28
  explanation of, 25
  Freud's, 25–27, 244
  moral development and, 239–240
Psychological dimensions of puberty
  body image and, 57–58
  early and late maturation and, 59
  hormones and behavior and, 58–59
Psychological influences, on adolescent and emerging adult problems, 435
Psychometric/intelligence view of cognitive development
  explanation of, 115
  heredity and environment and, 119–121
  intelligence tests and, 115–117
  multiple intelligences and, 117–118
Psychosocial moratorium, 142
Psychosocial theory (Erikson), 27–28
Puberty
  determinants of, 50–54
  effects of, 59, 60
  explanation of, 49
  gender attitudes and, 167
  gender intensification hypothesis and, 183–184
  growth spurt in, 54
  hormones and, 50–52, 154
  precocious, 56
  psychological dimensions of, 57–59
  secular trends in, 56–57
  sexual maturation in, 54–56
Public Law 94-142, 362
Punishment, development and, 30
Purpose, achievement and, 379–380

Quantum Opportunities program, 413
Quid pro quo sexual harassment, 219, 220

Race. *See* Ethnicity/ethnic minorities
Random assignment, 36
Rape, 217–219
Rapport talk, 177
Real Boys (Pollack), 182
Realistic thinking, 97
Reasoning
  hypothetical-deductive, 95
  social conventional, 243
Reciprocal socialization, 260–261, 268
Referral bias, 360
Reflective thinking, 97
Rejected children, 305–306
Relational aggression, 176–177
Relationship stress, 440
Relativistic thinking, 97

Religion. *See also* Spirituality
  developmental changes and, 253–254
  explanation of, 252
  positive role of, 252–253
  rites of passage and, 407
  sexuality and, 200
Religiousness, 252
Religious socialization, 254
Report talk, 177
Repression, 26
Research
  bias in, 38–40
  data collection methods and, 32–36
  ethical, 38
  overview of, 31–32
  publication of, 36–38
  time span of, 36
Researchers, 61
Resilience, 21, 444–445
Responsibility
  in emerging adulthood, 20
  of latchkey adolescents, 290
Rewards, 30
Risk factors
  for adolescent problems, 436–439
  in adolescent sexuality, 197–199
  in alcohol abuse, 448
  divorced families and, 286–287
  identification of, 437
  pubertal onset and, 60
Risk taking
  creative thinking and, 111
  decision making and, 107
  health and, 62–63, 204
  hormones and, 59
Rites of passage, 407–408
Role experimentation, 143
Role models, 417, 464
Romantic relationships. *See also* Dating
  among sexual minorities, 320–321, 333
  attachment in, 276
  dating and adjustment in, 321–322
  dissolution of, 322
  emotions in, 321
  heterosexual, 319–320
  identity and, 149
  parental influences on, 323–325
  peer influences on, 325–326
  personality traits and, 323
  trust in, 332
Runaways, 273

Same-sex individuals. *See* Sexual minorities
Schema, 93
School-based enterprises, 390
School counselors, 393, 395, 396
Schools. *See also* Academic achievement; College/college students; Education; Learning
  accountability from, 340–341
  career development and, 390, 395–396
  character education in, 245–256
  cheating in, 248–249

classroom climate and
management and, 347–348
creative thinking in, 110
critical thinking in, 109
ethnicity and, 355–356
exercise patterns and, 69–70
extracurricular activities and,
352–353
gender bias in, 170–171
global access to, 14
hidden curriculum in, 245
high, 175, 176, 209, 272–273,
343–345, 357–358, 390
middle or junior high,
341–343, 350, 357–358, 436
moral education in, 245–249
nutritional intervention in, 66
person-environment fit
and, 348
poverty interventions in, 412
secondary, 357–358
sex education in, 220–223
socioeconomic status and,
353–355, 410
start times of, 73
School segregation, 355
School success. See Academic
achievement; Achievement
Scientific method, 25
Screen-based activity. See also
Internet; Media use; Social
media
diet and, 66
exercise patterns and, 70
Secondary schools. See also
High schools; Middle
schools
cross-cultural comparisons
of, 357–358
work/career-based learning
in, 390
Secondary school teachers,
110, 377
Secular trends, in puberty, 56–57
Secure attachment, 274, 276, 304
Segregation, school, 355
Selective attention, 102
Self
contradictions within, 132
explanation of, 130–131
fluctuation of, 132
possible, 132, 134
real vs. ideal, 132
true vs. false, 132
unconscious, 133
Self-awareness, 134
Self-concept, 136–137, 405
Self-consciousness, 133
Self-control, 445
Self-determination, 372
Self-devaluation, 203
Self-disclosure, online, 427
Self-efficacy, 106, 375–376
Self-esteem
academic success and, 139
from adolescence to
emerging adulthood,
138–140
body image and, 139
consequences of low, 140
explanation of, 136
gender differences in, 138–139,
184–185
in groups, 314
measurement of, 136–137

perception and reality and,
137–138
social contexts and, 139–140
strategies to increase, 141
Self-handicapping strategies,
386–387
Self-image. See Self-esteem
Self-monitoring, 377–378
Self-protection, 133
Self-regulation, 140–141, 378
Self-responsibility, 373
Self-stimulation, 204–205
Self-understanding
in adolescence, 131–133
in emerging and early
adulthood, 134
explanation of, 131
social contexts and, 134–135
Self-worth, 386–387
Semen, 52
Sensorimotor stage (Piaget), 28,
93, 94
Service learning, 247–248
SES. See Socioeconomic status
(SES)
Sex education
adolescent pregnancy
and, 211
cognitive factors and,
221–222
in schools, 220–223
Sex glands, 51
Sex hormones, 50–52
Sexting, 193, 427
Sexual activity
among sexual minorities,
201–204
cross-cultural comparisons
of, 196, 212
drug use and, 470
eating disorders and, 464
in emerging adults, 199–201
forcible, 217–220
oral, 195–196
risk factors related to, 197–199
sexual scripts and, 196–197
statistics related to
heterosexual, 194–195, 200
Sexual harassment, 219–220
Sexual identity, 193, 292
Sexuality
adolescent pregnancy and, 192
American culture and,
192–193
contraceptives and, 205, 211
early and late maturation
and, 60
gender differences in, 167,
197, 201
global perspectives on, 13
heterosexual attitudes and
behavior and, 194–201
information sources on, 221
as normal aspect of
development, 191–192
overview of, 190, 191
religiousness and, 254
research on, 193–194
self-stimulation and, 204–205
sexually transmitted infections
and, 212–218
in sexual minority
individuals, 201–204
television viewing and, 192
Sexual literacy, 220–221

Sexually transmitted infections
(STIs)
chlamydia as, 216–217
explanation of, 212
genital herpes as, 214–215
genital warts as, 215–216
gonorrhea as, 216
HIV/AIDS as, 13,
213–214, 222
oral sex and, 196
sex education and, 222–223
sexual minorities and, 204
syphilis as, 216
Sexual maturation, 54–56
Sexual minorities
dating among, 320–321
developmental pathways
and, 203
discrimination, bias and
violence against, 203–204
explanation of, 202
factors associated with, 202
health and, 204
identity and disclosure
and, 203
overview of, 201–202
as parents, 291–292
romantic relationships
among, 320–321, 333
similarities and differences
with heterosexuals, 203
statistics related to, 202
Sexual orientation
developmental pathways
of, 203
influences on, 202
sexual identity and, 193
Sexual scripts, 196–197
The Shame of the Nation
(Kozol), 355
Shared environmental
experiences, 80–81
Short-term memory, 104
Siblings. See also Families
birth order and, 282–283
gender socialization and, 169
juvenile delinquency and, 457
roles of, 281–282
substance use by, 453
Single adults, 327–328
Single-parent families, 269,
293, 410–411
Single-sex education, 171
Skinner's operant
conditioning, 30
Sleep, 71–73
Slow-to-warm-up child, 158
Social capital, 63
Social cognition
adolescent egocentrism and,
121–123
explanation of, 121
peer relations and, 306–307
role of, 124
Social cognitive monitoring, 136
Social cognitive theory
explanation of, 29–30
of moral development, 237
Social comparison, 132–133
Social constructivist
approach, 100
Social contexts
bullying and, 351–352
careers and, 394–397
coping and, 443

decision making and, 107
identity development and,
148–152
influence of, 10
peer interaction and, 301–302
of schools, 346–347
self-esteem and, 139–140
self-understanding and,
134–135
temperament and, 159–160
Social contract or utility and
individual rights stage
(Kohlberg), 231
Social conventional
reasoning, 243
Social domain theory, 242–243
Social influences
on adolescent and emerging
adult problems, 435–436
on gender, 168–172
Socialization. See also Parents/
parenting
reciprocal, 260–261, 268
religious, 254
Social media. See also Media
use; Technology
adolescent egocentrism and,
122
sexting and, 193, 427
social environment and,
426–428
trends in use of, 172, 427
Social policy
adolescent development and,
10–12
explanation of, 10
media and, 429
strength-based approach to,
10–11
Social role theory, 168
Social skill strategies, 307–308
Social support
coping and, 443, 445
depression and, 460
following rape, 219
self-esteem and, 139
suicide and, 462
Social systems morality stage
(Kohlberg), 230–231
Society for Adolescent Health
and Medicine (SAHM), 64
Sociocultural cognitive theory
(Vygotsky), 29, 99–100
Sociocultural factors
achievement and, 382–384
pubertal onset and, 53–54
stress and, 441–442
Sociocultural view of
adolescence (Mead), 4
Socioeconomic status (SES)
achievement and, 353–356,
382, 409
adolescent pregnancy and, 209
adolescent problems and,
436, 438
career development and,
395, 397
divorced families and,
287–288
education and, 353–355
ethnicity and, 353–355,
418–419
explanation of, 408–409
juvenile delinquency and, 457
peer groups and, 317

poverty and, 410–413 (See
also Poverty)
prejudice, discrimination and
bias and, 419–420
variations in families,
neighborhoods and schools
and, 409–410
Socioemotional development
in adolescence, 15, 17
gender and, 176–178
Spatial intelligence, 117
Spermarche, 52
Spirituality. See also Religion
developmental changes and,
253–254
explanation of, 252
positive role of, 252–253
rites of passage and, 407
sexual behavior and, 199
Sports, 70–71, 357
Sports injuries, 71
Standardized tests, 32–33,
340–341. See also
Tests/testing
Stanford-Binet tests, 115–116
Status offenses, 454, 455
Stepfamilies, 288–289. See also
Divorce; Divorced families
Stereotypes
of adolescents, 7, 191
explanation of, 7
gender, 173–174
generation gap as, 269
intelligence tests and, 116
of sexual minorities, 333
of single adults, 328
Sternberg's triarchic theory, 117
Stimulants, 449–451
STIs. See Sexually transmitted
infections (STIs)
Storm-and-stress view (Hall),
3–4, 8
Strengths-based approach, to
social policy, 10–11
Stress
acculturative, 441
adolescent problems and,
439–442
decision making and, 107–108
exercise and, 68
explanation of, 440
gender and, 440
immigrants and, 415–416
from life events and daily
hassles, 440–441
loneliness and, 312
poverty and, 11
relationship, 440
social support and, 443
sociocultural factors leading
to, 441–442
Substance abuse. See Drug use
Suicidal ideation, 204, 351,
461, 462
Suicide
bullying and, 351
cultural contexts of, 461–462
death due to, 64
factors related to, 462–463
sexual minorities and, 204
statistics related to, 461, 462
Superego, 26
Surveys, 32
Sustained attention, 102, 378
Sympathy, 240